THE ANTICHRIST
and a Cup of Tea
Charles, Prince of Wales, Foretold

Tim Cohen

PROPHECY HOUSE,® INC.
P.O. Box 461104 • Aurora, CO 80046-1104
www.prophecyhouse.com

For Tim Cohen's other items, and social media links, visit
www.prophecyhouse.com on the Internet.

THE ANTICHRIST AND A CUP OF TEA
Second edition

Copyright© 2024 by Timothy Cohen (TJMH)

May 2024, Prophecy House, Inc.

ISBN-13: 978-1-933689-01-2 / ISBN-10: 1-933689-01-3
Barcode "mark" intentionally omitted from cover.

Library of Congress Control Number: 2008942657

Printed in the United States of America.
09 / 12 11 10 9 8 7 6 5 4 3 2 1

Contents

Endorsements

The AntiChrist and a Cup of Tea was originally planned as an appendix to the author's upcoming and much more comprehensive work entitled *Messiah, History, and the Tribulation Period* (now a multiple-volume series). Due to significant delays in completing that overall work, however, demand grew from various reviewers of its early drafts, as well as others who heard of them, to publish the material that follows sooner rather than later. Since this material became quite voluminous, easily amounting to a work in its own right, it made sense not to publish it as a large appendix in the *Messiah, History, and the Tribulation Period* multi-volume series, but as an entirely separate book. Any endorsements or portions of endorsements cited for *Messiah, History, and the Tribulation Period* below, except where noted, also apply to this book, *The AntiChrist and a Cup of Tea,* inasmuch as they were given when it was still an appendix to the former. Also, all of these relate to the *first edition* of this book, published in 1998; they are just a sampling of literally hundreds of such endorsements and reviews. As you read through these, please know that the evidence offered in this *second edition* is more compelling than ever:[1]

> A lot of prophecy books cross my desk, but this one—this one you have to get, ... it's *The AntiChrist and a Cup of Tea*.... [The] premise is provocative and ... [the] book is historically fascinating, and it's far more illuminating than many.... It is the kind of book you really need for your library because it fills in all this background that you will run into.... It's one of the best-done historically documented works here.... [Moreover, it] exhaustively documents a possible identity of the coming world leader, and we find the book ... an absolute jewel...., especially for someone who's a student of history. I am profoundly impressed ... and it is ... an extremely interesting book.... And ... Tim [Cohen] may be right....
> — **Chuck Missler** • Founder, Koinonia House
> Author (with Mark Eastman), *Alien Encounters*

> I was highly skeptical that anyone could know the precise identity of Antichrist before he arose on the world scene. Thus, it was with great doubt that I began reading this well-documented 443 page book [(first edition)]. However, by the time I was two-thirds of the way through the book, I was convinced that Antichrist would come from the British Monarchy, from the House of Windsor. Tim Cohen, a Messianic Jew, provides overwhelming evidence, including heavy Antichrist symbolism, that proves his point beyond reasonable doubt. Once you read this book, you will be

---

1. It is this author's hope that what some others have said about this work will impress upon you, the reader, the importance of this work to your future, as well as the collective futures of every person you hold dear in your life. Like you, they too *need* to have this information, but above all, they need to know the *real* God and the *real* Christ Jesus. Please read the *Message of Salvation* at p. 647; the time get serious about God and Christ Jesus in your life is **now!**

checking out the travel itineraries of key world leaders when they travel to and from Washington, D.C.!!....

The only question is this: is the policy concerning Israel, Jerusalem, and the entire world generated in Washington and followed by London, or is the policy originated in London and followed by Washington? Whether you realize it or not, that IS one of the questions of the hour, and is fully answered by Tim Cohen in his monumentally important book, *Antichrist and A Cup of Tea!* Once you understand what Cohen has to teach you, you truly will look at the events of the day differently.

— **Dr. David Bay** • Founder and President, The Cutting Edge Ministry

The Antichrist's rise will be the product of a centuries-old plot to bring about a New World Order according to author Tim Cohen—[a plot] that was begun in the monarchy of Great Britain and that may even reveal the identity of the Antichrist *today*. [*The AntiChrist and a Cup of Tea* is] thought-provoking prophecy literature.

— **Dr. Jack Van Impe** / Jack Van Impe Ministries International

....I must say from the outset that the magnitude of your work staggers the mind, and at the same time challenges my thought processes, and presuppositions. You have done a great work and a tremendous service to the Body of Christ. It truly deserves to be read and studied by all of God's leaders.

At a time in church history when eschatological tradition has choked and blinded objective thought, your work, I believe, will prove to be the dynamite that breaks the log jam. We all need to have our Christian world view sharpened and clarified. Your work, *Messiah, History, and the Tribulation Period,* serves to bring us to the spiritual mountain top where we can see our times.

There are several concepts that were truly impressive to me. I particularly was transfixed by your analysis of <u>Passion Week</u> as a template for understanding the expanse of human history and Daniel's seventieth week. I will ponder your insight and watch as human history and the future unfold. Your book serves to help me understand contemporary times....

— **K. Klein**

Regardless of whether one agrees with all of Tim Cohen's conclusions, his masterpiece work *Messiah, History, and the Tribulation Period,* provides great food for thought. Articulately written, by a Messianic Jew with a deeply personal understanding of Scripture, this provocative book [series] is well researched and thoroughly documented. I commend Tim for the balance maintained in his research and for his non-sensational, scholarly approach....

At the very least, his presentation reaffirms our faith and hope in the risen Christ, while heightening our sense of urgency to share the good news with a lost and dying world. It also causes one to re-examine some popular views on eschatology by bringing together many intricate details and little known facts, and applying them to current world developments....

Challenging, informative, and timely, Tim Cohen's material is must reading!

— **Gary H. Kah**[1] • Founder, Hope for the World

Author, *En Route To Global Occupation*

....Bible prophecy has once again become an object of major attention on the part of the world and even the church....

....Provocatively titled, this book should become the object of the fascination of many and the even more careful attention of the thoughtful readers of our time. The reader will find many unique interpretations of Holy Scripture in the pages of this book. [Yet] ... unique interpretations become the first appearance of what may

---

1. Note that Kah gave this endorsement after reading an early draft of *The AntiChrist and a Cup of Tea,* when it was still an appendix to the large *Messiah, History, and the Tribulation Period* tome.

grow into standing theological positions in the church. ...[No doubt] every reader will be instantly fascinated....

It is a part of the providence of God that the Lord will bring new things to the attention of people.... This certainly will be the case with the reading of this book on the part of many....

....It takes no great capability to note developments *ex post facto* (which is so much the case in our time). Rather, it is of great value to know or even suspect the awful destiny of people and causes in advance. Tim Cohen may well be such a person [with such capability], valuable to the church, both now and in the increasingly provocative days to come. His book is surely destined to affect many an opinion both now and in the future. Prophetic developments are surely upon us and they will be examined with greater clarity by many as a consequence of *The AntiChrist and a Cup of Tea*.

— **Dr. David (Dave) Breese** • President, Christian Destiny, Inc.
Author, *Seven Men Who Rule the World from the Grave*

The AntiChrist and a Cup of Tea by Tim Cohen is the most comprehensive study of why ... Charles could be the AntiChrist. What [I say] is more important than the AntiChrist's identity, is the AntiChrist system that this book uncovers. For the first time, the average person can understand the organizations that are already in place that will allow one man to control the world. This book is must reading for those who desire to understand the real power brokers behind the New World Order.

— **Sid Roth** • Author and President, Messianic Vision

THE ANTICHRIST AND A CUP OF TEA by Tim Cohen is a fascinating book that connects the history of the royal family of England to end-time prophecy. The section dealing with the interpretation of the complicated and intricate designs in Prince Charles' Coat of Arms is especially intriguing. Tim was a guest on our ministry for a series of programs and received a tremendous response. History buffs and students of prophecy will enjoy this book.

— **Dr. Noah Hutchings** • President, Southwest Radio Church

Rarely has a book been so thoroughly researched! The uniqueness of Tim Cohen's work is the way he brings so many facts together that point to a possible candidate for the man the Bible describes as "[the] Antichrist." You may disagree with his conclusion, but you cannot argue with the thoroughness and details of his presentation. The historical "connections" are worth the price of the book alone. May this work prepare us all to be aware of how world events are coming together and fulfilling God's plan, and may it lead those who read it to a personal knowledge and commitment to the true Messiah as our only hope and salvation.

— **Dr. David Hocking** • Author and President, Hope for Today

Whenever someone points to a specific individual and suggests that this is indeed the anti-Christ, I start looking for the nearest exit. However, while I am still out with the jury on this one, I have to tell you that this book is one of the most captivating studies on the British Monarchy's leadership involvement with the occult, world wide Freemasonry and the New World Order that you could imagine.

— **Ed Decker** • Founder, Saints Alive in Jesus
Author, *The Dark Side of Freemasonry* and *The God Makers*

[We] have Tim Cohen's provocative [and excellent] new book..., *The AntiChrist and a Cup of Tea*.... [[It's] a great, thought-provoking book about the possible relationship between the Beast and the Royal Family.] Essentially, the entire book presents a fairly solid case for [Prince] Charles as a possible candidate for [the role of the] Antichrist. It is definitely worth a read! [Indeed,] there is creditable evidence ... for Charles being a candidate for the anti-Christ. Cohen ... gives an exhaustive list of reasons why he might be considered. This even goes down to Charles' "heraldic achievement" or coat of arms.... Many of the Biblical features of the Great Beast are present in the coat of arms, something which is strange, to say the least.... We normally do not get into "Let's identify the Anti-Christ" games, but right now he is more likely than any public figure. Note how Charles' popularity "magically" shot up after Diana's funeral.

— **William (Bill) Schnoebelen** • Founder, With One Accord Ministries
Author, *Wicca, Satan's Little White Lie* and *Masonry, Beyond The Light*

No matter how your eschatology is flavored, Tim Cohen's *The AntiChrist and a Cup of Tea* will rivet your attention. His book is no ordinary prophecy book; the massive documentation in it—that Prince Charles of [Wales] ... is the prophesied AntiChrist— will make you think of little else for a while. If you will provide your own cup of tea, Cohen will be sure to provide the AntiChrist!

— **Dave MacPherson** • President, P.O.S.T. Inc.
Author, *The Rapture Plot*

....*[Messiah, History, and the Tribulation Period]* is ... characterized by broad and vast Biblical knowledge.... I found myself fascinated by your assembling of facts and consequent interpretation.... This fascination certainly extended to your presentation of the future significance of the Prince of Wales [(now King Charles III)]. Any reader will ... absorb more knowledge than would be the case from nearly every prophetic manuscript which he has read....

I recommend the book to students of the Word of God everywhere and particularly those who desire an in-depth knowledge of the prophetic scriptures. ...I would quicken the interest of potential readers by reminding them that Cohen also suggests the possible identification of the anti-Christ. A reading of Messiah, History, and the Tribulation Period will be a worthwhile investment of time and intellectual energy.

— **Dr. Dave Breese**

And why do I say that ... the royal family [of Britain] has some dark secret about the lineage of their bloodlines—and whether or not the AntiChrist could be produced from Europe, and maybe even the [British] royal family itself? Well, I had a lot of good book reading [in the past]. And of course, Tim Cohen was one of the most inspiring guys, *ever,* to write a book. He wrote a book called *The AntiChrist and a Cup of Tea,* that I read. He's written several others too.... ... Well from his hard work, ... I'm willing to accept that Charles could be the AntiChrist....

— **Clyde Lewis** • Ground Zero (radio, 31 Aug. 2022)

...Tim Cohen has written a fascinating and quite amazing integration of the prophetic Scriptures. Its integration of the ages of history and the last days is ... unique and new.... The book is detailed and provocative. *[Messiah, History, and the Tribulation Period* is] ... a unique contribution to [the study of] prophetic history and eschatology.

— **Dr. Daniel Juster** • President, Tikkun Ministries
Author, *Revelation: The Passover Key*

Cohen has written a thought-provoking, riveting, [book on the] ... identity of the antichrist.... Could this be one of the mysteries Daniel speaks of, which will be revealed in the last days?

— A Customer

Mr. Cohen has made an important contribution to the ongoing prophetic debate with *Messiah, History, and the Tribulation Period*. His attempt to integrate the best points of virtually all major schools of prophetic interpretation is, as far as I know, unprecedented in modern times—and he carries it out with remarkable success. Not only that, but just when we thought there was nothing more that could be said about biblical prophecy, Cohen actually manages to plow some interesting new ground on several issues. Whether or not you agree with all of his conclusions, you will find the presentation to be logical, provocative, and thoroughly-researched.

    — **Dr. Gary Hedrick**[1] • President, The Christian Jew Foundation

Nothing today is as important as the truth of God's plan of redemption and salvation in the Messiah. Cohen has succeeded in not only summarizing very lucidly the many strands of theological Messiology and the Biblical end-times, but he has also given us a new and comprehensive presentation of the subject....

This challenging book fulfills a serious need for a detailed, balanced, informed and sober accounting of prophetic Biblical history. Cohen respectfully provides what I believe to be one of the best windows to glimpse accurately the centrality of the Person and work of Jesus Christ in history and apocalyptic prophecy.

I endorse *Messiah, History, and the Tribulation Period* and know that readers will find here an inspiring and reliable reference work on Christology, Israelology, Biblical Chronology, and Eschatology.... Clearly it is a bold help to the cause of Christ.

    — **Rick Drebenstedt** • Pastor and Director, Menorah Ministries

...Tim Cohen's *Messiah, History, and the Tribulation Period* ... is ... a ground-breaking, major eschatological "gem." ...Cohen's work ventures well beyond ordinary "Last Days" scenarios and controversies to chart new and illuminating territory, as in his unique harmony of Christ's Crucifixion/Resurrection Week with Scripture's History and Tribulation Weeks. This particular exposition's devotional value alone makes *Messiah, History, and the Tribulation Period* 'meat' doubtless to be profitably chewed on and digested by scholars, clergy and laity alike, for the remainder of this present age and perhaps throughout Eternity.

    — **Anton Marco**
    Author, *100 Jews Who Met Yeshua and Lived to Tell Others*

I ... found it full of [valuable] information.... I commend you for your tremendous [multi-]volume [series], *Messiah, History, and the Tribulation Period.* ...I will want to study it more.

    — **Dr. Ray Brubaker** • Director, God's News ... Behind the News

Tim Cohen has a mastery of the scriptures that few men in history have possessed. The depth of his research is unbelievable. Wow! I Have 28,000 hours studying the Bible and I felt like a little kid, when I met him and I am going to read everything this man writes. Do I believe his assessment of who the anti-Christ is going to be? Yes, Yes, YES I DO! Every true Christian and every true Christian warrior needs this info[rmation], NOW!

    — **C.M. Whittaker**

An incredible job of Research.... It has totally altered my view of the "End Times" scenario. I hope Hal Lindsay and company read Tim's book!... When you read the book, be sure to research the Bible footnotes he provides, [as] they will convince even the most skeptical mind if he is "open" to the truth.

    — **Michael Stevens**

I find Mr. Cohen's research and work to be very well thought out and intriguing. I have to say that ... I always sort of thought of the anti-Christ in terms of a bold,

---

1. Please note that Dr. Hedrick has declined either to read or endorse the present work out of a misguided belief that the Church cannot now know the identity of the AntiChrist. Nevertheless, his endorsement of the *Messiah, History, and the Tribulation Period* multi-volume series, stands.

charismatic wildly popular man. I never really thought of the idea that the anti-Christ could simply be a man totally immersed into every thought, philosophy, [and] theology and who has great influence. Mr. Cohen makes a very compelling argument ... regarding Prince Charles.
> — **R. Pichlik**

I love bible prophecy. Tim Cohen is such an exhaustive researcher. This book is very compelling ... [and] I couldn't put it down.... Every Pastor and/or prophecy buff MUST read this book.
> — **Krita Collier**

Tim Cohen writes as I have read few authors ... [and] he's not just 'repeating' what everybody else has said on this subject, [rather] he's shed a lot of new light on the mysterious subject of anti-Christ. It's so refreshing to read his insights.
> — A Customer

A 'conspiracy' book for non-conspiracists. Fascinating detail on Heraldry. Makes a lot of sense. Will this really end up more than symbolism? You can see how people of 'royal' breeding, with all that tradition and precedent to live up to, could sign on to an agenda that most people in the world would find objectionable. This is key.... Now we can see some of the mental profiles of those in positions of power and influence, and why they can stand by and allow tragedy to follow and do nothing. Just like Nazi Germany.
> — A Customer

This book is ... the best and most important information available on the subject of the Antichrist.... [It] ... is a must read for anyone who believes that we are living close to the time of the Great Tribulation.... It's not conspiracy theories, but historical facts that set this book apart. I find myself recommending it to everyone I know. Having read it, I find myself able to better understand what is the cause and political objective of our current world leadership, and who is the best equipped to be the "leader" of the "leaders".
> — **Paul B.**

I saw Mr. Cohen give a presentation of [t]his book. I was greatly impressed with the amount of research and documentation he presented and is included in [t]his book. I also purchased the genealogical chart, as it was very helpful in putting everything in historical prospective. I was so impressed with this book, I included it on my ... so others could also have the opportunity to read this amazing book. Those who pass up this book do themselves an injustice!
> — A Customer

This book certainly has a wealth of information concerning the Royal Family of England. I truly enjoyed this book, and it made me really start to think how close we are to the coming of the Lord. I pray many people will come to know the Lord because of it.
> — A Customer

Superb! This book draws reasonable conclusions from incredibly well-documented sources.... Indeed, anyone who has read the LaHaye and Jenkins "Left Behind" series will, upon reading Mr. Cohen's book, likely abandon that series as false prophecy (see the warnings against adding to or taking away from scripture, which apocalyptic fiction must inevitably do, in Revelation 22) in favor of an author [(Cohen)] and a title [(The AntiChrist and a Cup of Tea)] that offers real, credible information ... rather than fictional speculation and sensationalism.... If his first book leaves everyone else who has ever written on the subject of the antichrist in the dust

(and it does), just think what Mr. Cohen's upcoming title [(now a series)], *Messiah, History, and the Tribulation Period* ... will do. I for one can't wait to see.
— A Customer

A powerful, must-read book! Astounding and convincing! I couldn't put the book down. Cohen brought together a spectacular array of facts that not only identifies the probable AntiChrist but lays out in elaborate detail that person's credentials and the grooming that took place to shape that person into that [yet future] role. I wouldn't have thought of that person had it not been for Cohen. Thank you, Tim, for your excellent work.
— **Wilfred Mische**

I have spent months meticulously pouring over the book, and have come to the conclusion that it is the definitive and authoritative word on the coming of the Antichrist. You are truly blessed by God in expounding upon prophecy in these last hours.
— **Brett Wills**

Preface

In 1956, during the Suez Canal Conflict between Israel and Egypt, my mother and her family fled Egypt as secular Jewish refugees. I was born nine years later, in May 1965.[1] In July 1984, I enrolled in the class of 1988 at the United States Air Force Academy (USAFA), and in November 1986, I received Jesus as my Savior and LORD. When I received Jesus, I was a second-class cadet (junior) at USAFA. Although my experiences at the academy had rarely been what I would call "good," USAFA proved to be the cauldron of affliction from which God would give me the perseverance and strength to

---

1. The author's family on his mother's side, came from Alexandria in Egypt, which is near the ancient land of *Goshen*. His actual name, as given in Greek and Hebrew is *Timotheos Ya'acov Moshe Cohen*. *Timotheos* or "Timothy" means "honoring God", "in God's honor" or "honored by God." *Ya'acov* or "Jacob" means "prevailer" or "overcomer." *Moshe* or "Moses" means "drawn | saved from water." And finally, *cohen* is "priest." (The author is an actual *cohen*, genealogically descending from Aaron, Moses' brother. Moses gave waters from The Rock to Israel in the wilderness—yet Yeshua was that Rock, and He is our Well. It is He who gives us the living waters, which are drawn from Him. (Moses gave Israel the written Torah, but Yeshua is *The Living Torah.)*

   Like Timothy in the New Testament, the author was born of an Israelite mother and a Gentile father; the latter's side of the family apparently reached the United States from Ireland and/or England. Jacob, Moses and Aaron all experienced *On* or *Heliopolis* as well as the land of Goshen in Egypt. The motto on the author's historical family crest is *Fide et Marte,* meaning "fidelity and bravery" or "faithful and brave"—or alternately, "faith and martyrdom" or "faith and war;" His USAF Academy class motto—by divine appointment—is *Fides Intrepida,* meaning "fearless faith" or "bold faith."

   None of the author's parents or grandparents, nor *any* of his other living relatives, knew or served The God of Israel at the time of his birth or naming—yet *The Holy Spirit chose these names and mottoes for him.* (The author is a warrior of Christ—called to be "a general" in His "army.")

   The author's mother, Rebecca, through whom he descends from Moses' brother Aaron (as a Cohen), was born and raised in Alexandria, Egypt, until she turned fourteen. Though partially raised by an Italian nanny, Rebecca and her family (Maurice, Alba and Claude), whose main household language was French, fled Nasserism with little more than their lives during the 1956 Suez Canal Conflict, as the Egyptian government *confiscated and stole the family's then-significant wealth.* Egypt has never offered nor paid any restitution, despite family inquiries. As related to the author by his late grandmother Alba, her husband Maurice (Cohen-Hemsi), the author's grandfather, came from a "common" or poor Israelite family of French descent in Egypt, though he became a bookkeeper fluent in half a dozen languages. (The family also spoke Arabic.) Tragically, some years after arriving to the United States from Egypt ("Denver Receives Jewish Victims of Nasserism," *Dallas Texas Jewish Post,* 30 Oct. 1958, p. 6), by way of Italy, the author's grandfather suffered a debilitating stroke—apparently, due to an experimental medial drink meant to treat a brain tumor. That paralyzed Maurice across half his body, for the remainder of his life, so the author never could converse with him. Grandmother Alba, on the other hand, who also spoke French and other languages such as Arabic and English, never knew her womanizing Israelite father from Russia: a worthless man, he had abandoned her pregnant mother for England. Neither was Alba close to her Israelite mother from Egypt, who wasted much of her time as a wealthy socialite; it is through the latter that much of the family's past wealth had been inherited. Indeed, Alba's mother's own grandfather, or the author's great great grandfather, was an Israelite Baron from Germany. Following grandfather Maurice's stroke and paralysis, Alba started a successful seamstress business from their house, caring for her husband all his days. Though she lived a tragic life, the author's grandmother, he has been told, received Yeshua (Jesus) before her death. The author remembers fondly the many social gatherings and Jewish holidays at his grandmother's home as a boy and young man. (His mother also attends Church.)

   Due to the author's testimony, his Israelite children and several other family members have received Yeshua. The family knows of relatives in the United States, Israel, Canada and England.

proceed with this work. As a born-again Levite or "Jew," I soon realized that my calling in life had little to do with serving in the United States military. My life had been turned upside down.

After reading the entire New Testament, the five books of Moses (Torah), and many of the prophecies in the Old Testament, I found myself increasingly drawn to study the scriptures, to the point where I was unable to concentrate on my studies. One day in early 1987, while walking toward Arnold Hall, my thoughts settled on Revelation 13:18. That was the second day in less than a year that God turned my life upside down. On that day, I prayed for wisdom according to what is written in James 1:5-6 and Revelation 13:18. Within one month of that momentous prayer, a local pastor by the name of Monte Judah invited me to an unusual sabbath meal. While there, he showed me his preliminary information on what would become the main subject of this book—Charles, Prince of Wales, who is now King Charles III. That information included the then prince's English name calculation (first discovered in 1981) and a rather poor black and white photocopy of an unofficial version of his heraldic achievement. Through Monte, The LORD challenged me to (actually) examine what I had been taught to that point concerning eschatology or future events, much of which I subsequently concluded to be false.

I returned to my dorm room at USAFA following that sabbath meal, where I proceeded to tell various classmates that I was going to write a book. At the time, I knew only that the book was to concern biblical prophecy. With that revelation, however, I completely dropped my academic studies, and began the process of voluntarily resigning from the academy. While awaiting a decision from the Secretary of the Air Force, I pursued research on a wide variety of scriptural subjects. This research led almost immediately to a decent-quality color copy of the official version of Charles' heraldic achievement as Prince of Wales, which I found in a book on heraldry in the Cadet Library.

In November 1987, my resignation was accepted. Because I resigned in my final year at USAFA, however, I was required to enlist for a period of three years. While training for that enlistment in Texas, I met another man by the name of Steve Klein. Steve spoke of the fact that he and his wife were home-schooling their daughters, to which I made the off-the-cuff remark, "In a little over seven years, you won't have to worry about that." Steve oddly responded, "I hear you," and then invited my roommate and I to have dinner with his family that evening. When Steve arrived to pick us up, he brought with him a large copy of the official lineage of Queen Elizabeth II. Up to then, I had said nothing to Steve. The lineage later proved to be of great value in preparing this particular work.

Following the war with Iraq in 1990, I left the service. During my period of enlistment, The LORD not only provided me with a condominium, but enabled me to save sufficient funds to live for years without work. Over the next three years, I researched the subjects of biblical history and eschatology, and wrote, full-time. And now, in my later years, I have spent several more on those same endeavors —and several others God has added (e.g., the upcoming *Solar Apocalypse* multi-volume series, as well as the *Israel, "Peace" and the Looming Great Tribulation* multi-volume series, and yet more).

The first edition of this book, *The AntiChrist and a Cup of Tea,* was just the initial fruit of over ten years of research and writing. As such, it had originally been a part of *a much larger tome.* That multi-volume series, entitled *Messiah, History, and the Tribulation Period,* is foretold—from my perspective—by a childhood event.

At the age of ten, I enjoyed my only oceangoing fishing trip to date. The night before the "big event," unknown to me, my father and nine other adults—all family members who had prior experience—decided to add some excitement to the event. My father would contribute $6.00 for the two of us to a pot, while the other nine would each give $3.00, which they decided to divide in three. The person who caught the first fish would receive $11.00, as would the one who caught the largest and the one who caught the most. Almost from the moment we threw our lines in the next morning, I called to my father for help; something was pulling fiercely on my line, and as a child, I simply lacked the strength to reel it in. With my father's help, however, I was soon staring at a *large* and rare silver salmon. That day, my father caught the most fish, while I caught just one—the first *and* the largest![1]

---

1. At the same time that I was writing this introduction, my father was, unknown to me, publishing his own recollection of the event. As my father recalls: "'Hey Dad,' Tim whispered in my ear, 'isn't this unfair if we know we're going to take their money?' The subject of ten-year-old Tim's concern was a pool my brother and father were creating to add a little spice to our more-or-less annual salmon fishing charter. We were at Ilwaco, Washington, not far north of the mouth of the Columbia River. Eleven of us— all family—would kick in three bucks apiece. One buck each for the one catching the day's biggest salmon, the first salmon, and the most salmon. 'Yep,' I nodded to Tim. 'It's probably unfair.' I smiled and put our six dollars in the pot" (James L. H., "Salmon," *Wild Winds and Other Tails of Growing Up in the Outdoor West* {Washington: Reecer Creek Pub., 1997}, p. 123).

   Moses is a "middle" name of *this* author. Why? "As some sources [(see below)] compare Moses to a fish, a [Hebrew] *Nun* [glyph], because he was taken out of the water by [(a bent over)] Pharaoh's daughter, so is Joshua called *'ben Nun'* [(see below)]—the son (disciple) of this great fish (Moses). Torah [(i.e., the first five books of the Old Testament)] does not inform us about his intellect, but rather that he was Moses' disciple—that he was always at Moses' side and in Moses' tent. Why did he merit inheriting the leadership of the Jewish people from Moses? Because he embraced the quality of humility with his entire being" (Aaron L. Raskin, "Nun," Chabad.org, 1 Dec. 2020). On *Nun: "The Alef-Beit, op. cit.,* p. 217. Also see *Bereishis Rabbah* 97:4-5. Note that Moshe was born in the month of *Adar,* which corresponds to *mazal dagim* or Pisces. In addition, *Nun* means 'fish' in Aramaic" (ibid.)."

That event was, if you can receive it, prophetic of my future. From an allegorical standpoint, this book is a part of my childhood silver salmon. As a new edition, it has taken many more years to complete. May reading it bless you, as writing it has blessed me.

This work is dedicated to the only God and Savior, Christ Jesus — יֵשׁוּעַ הַמָּשִׁיחַ.

"The 'gematria' [(i.e., Hebraic value)] of *Nun* is fifty. There are fifty 'gates' or levels of *Binah*, understanding. That's [(here, allegedly)] why the Jews counted forty-nine days—seven complete weeks from Passover to Shavuos [(i.e., Pentecost)]—to ready themselves to receive the Torah. The famous question is: 'Why does the Torah tell us to count fifty days after Passover, when immediately afterwards it says to count seven complete weeks, which are only *forty-nine* days?' The [(here, claimed)] 'answer' is that an individual can only attain forty-nine levels of intellect on his own. The fiftieth level ... can only be provided by G-d. Therefore G-d [(here, allegedly)] says, 'You do yours and I will do Mine.' If you achieve the forty-ninth level, I will bless you with the fiftieth; the highest tier of *Binah*, understanding'" (ibd., and *Rosh Hashanah* 21b; also see *Pardes Rimonim, Shaar HaShaarim, Shaar 13,* ch. 1).

It is written: "Here is wisdom: Let him who has understanding calculate the number of the beast; for it is the number of a man, and his number is 666" (Rev 13:18, Gk.). *Today, this is fulfilled before your eyes and in your hearing—as you ingest the pages of this work.* Moshiach Yeshua soon *returns!*

Other Items and Social Media

For the author's other items (e.g., audio and video presentations, interviews, etc.), visit Prophecy House at "www.prophecyhouse.com" on the Internet. Relatively soon, you will find that this author has researched and written **dozens of books**—across nearly four decades —including at least three multi-volume series, together covering much of God's written Word—plus evidence of "aliens:"*

• O*vercoming Satan's Seed: A Last Days Polemic*

• *The Mark of the Beast*

• *The Great Reset: To Digitally Enslave, Depopulate, and Transhumanize*

• *North Korea, Iran, and the Coming World War: Behold a Red Horse*

• *Israel's Sojourn In, and Exodus from Egypt: The Real Dates and Pharaohs*

• *Israel, "Peace" and the Looming Great Tribulation* series

• *Messiah, History, and the Tribulation Period* series

• *Solar Apocalypse* series and related books

Social media.

YouTube: https://www.youtube.com/AuthorTimCohen
Odysee: https://odysee.com/@AuthorTimCohen
BitChute (playlists): https://www.bitchute.com/profile/CnCtAKrFlo4u
BitChute (videos): https://www.bitchute.com/AuthorTimCohen
Rumble: https://www.rumble.com/AuthorTimCohen

Facebook: https://www.facebook.com/AuthorTimCohen
Gab: https://gab.com/AuthorTimCohen
MeWe: https://mewe.com/i/AuthorTimCohen (there's a *free* Standard version)

Telegram (search for "Author Tim Cohen") :
https://t.me/antichrist_identity_proof   (on the AntiChrist)
https://t.me/red_horse_prophecy (on World War 3)
https://t.me/life_on_mars_proof (on Non-terrestrial Life)
https://t.me/life_on_the_moon_proof (on Non-terrestrial Life)

Twitter: https://twitter.com/AuthorTimCohen
Parler: https://parler.com/AuthorTimCohen (if use resumes)

Truth Social: *Look for it.*

For future newsletters, or to be notified when new items are released, please visit Prophecy House's web site. (Also, check for any mailing list of intereset. The company does not spam, nor does it share or sell your information.)

As Prophecy House becomes more "socially inclined," you may find additional information on Prophecy House's social media pages:
Facebook: https://www.facebook.com/prophecyhouse
Instagram: https://www.instagram.com/prophecyhouse
Twitter: @prophecy_house
Pinterest: https://www.pinterest.com/prophecyhouse

Support is needed and welcome. Your support is vital to this author's mission. Prophecy House's site provides a button to donate, but you may also calle *303-693-6399* in the U.S. Prophecy House desires to be able to place these items into various hands en-masse as inexpensively and quickly as possible. (Those could be provided to church pastors and leaders, politicians, etc.) We would be very grateful for any help you may offer.

This author has now spent most of his life researching and writing all these astounding books. To do so, he has sacrificed a great deal of personal livelihood, not just time. He could use your help financially to further these efforts. If you earmark a donation for Tim or Prophecy House, it will be received accordingly. Thank you.

*Please note that various books will not be mentioned on Prophecy House's site until they are actually published and available.

Introduction

Christians today are often unwilling to debate the possible identity of the AntiChrist, *no matter how compelling the evidence*. Many who are aware of past errors of various prophecy teachers, "scholars," and "authorities," have come to presume that no one can possibly know the AntiChrist's identity in advance. Others hold this view for what they, until now, have thought were valid theological reasons. These Christians are not the first to ignore, overlook, or misunderstand Revelation 13:18 and other passages related to the AntiChrist. Like many in the past, they have made precisely the opposite mistake of those mentioned above; they have gone to the other extreme of those who have—without proper biblical grounds—made unjustified, speculative, sensational, spurious, and, at times, even outrageous claims concerning the character and identity of the AntiChrist. Those who have erred and those who are mistaken will find *The AntiChrist and a Cup of Tea* to be fundamentally different.

The careful reader will discover that *The AntiChrist and a Cup of Tea* presents *the definitive treatise on the subject of the AntiChrist.* At the same time, *without* being overly sensationalistic, this work also distinguishes scripture's remarkably well-qualified "first beast"—*King Charles III, aka Prince Charles of Wales*—from the plethora of alleged "offers." Seriously, as you begin to delve into the vast material herein, bear the following in mind: Just as most were not expecting Christ to be as He was at His first coming, with many openly deriding the very notion that He could be The Messiah (e.g., see John 1:10-13, 7:25-44)—though they should have immediately *known* this true identity[1]—so too do most "scholars," "theologians," and other Christians presently expect an ultimate AntiChrist who in reality, *differs dramatically* from what's actually biblical. Also, these very individuals often presume to know *more than they really do* about *this* Charles. Ill-informed and insufficiently learned, they do not expect *the foretold AntiChrist* to be Charles. Yet, those who remain deceived by him to the end, serving him and taking his mark (i.e., the Mark of the Beast), *shall finally express their surprise and dismay when he, having been possessed by Satan (Lucifer), also is cast into Hell* (Isa 14:15-17; see Isa 14:1-23; cf. Rev 19:20 to 20:3).

Many, if not most, Christians are yet uncomfortable with the mere suggestion that a *known* individual—especially one like King Charles III—could be the AntiChrist. There are individuals who, as

---

1. For details, see the author's *Messiah, History, and the Tribulation Period* multi-volume series.

uncritical "newspaper exegetes," would sooner accept a convenient pulpit or media stereotype—regardless of its veracity—than permit themselves to undertake a genuine, biblical consideration or study of the evidence at hand, be it objective or circumstantial.[1]

As the scripture says, "He who answers a matter before he hears it, it is folly and shame to him" (Prov 18:13, AKJV; cf. John 7:50-51). Of such persons, it is written, "They have eyes to see, but do not see, and ears to hear, but do not hear; for they *are* a rebellious people" (Ezek 12:2*b-d,* NIV). To them, The Lord says, "I counsel you to buy from Me..., *that* the shame of your nakedness may not be revealed; and anoint your eyes with eye salve, that you may see" (Rev 3:18).

Sadly, there are many who speak foolishly even now, including in "Christian" pulpits. But this *extraordinary work* is for those who do have, or humbly would receive eyes to see, and ears to hear. Let's consider a couple (representative) examples of people who should know better, but simply *fail.* One pastor, for example, who has been heavily involved in the Pensacola "revival," for example (Michael L. Brown), told this author (in 1997), "[Prince] Charles has become an increasingly pathetic figure, and there is no possible way that the Jewish people, or the Muslims, or the Americans (to name just a few ethnic or religious groups) will ever look to him as their world leader." Another pastor (Norm Franz), who speaks and teaches as a prophecy "scholar," flatly stated (in 1997): "Nobody knows who the Antichrist is because he hasn't been revealed yet— maybe a *Nephilim....* To think the people around the world would follow Prince Charles is just ridiculous.... Every born-again believer will know it when the Antichrist has been revealed." (He ostensibly meant to write the singular *nephil.)* Such statements, as this work makes (painfully) obvious, are *precipitous.* Indeed they are the *opposite of scholarly.*

Few such "pastors" have been willing to hear anything God has shown this author—and fewer still have allowed any of it, to be shared from their pulpits. Instead, like so many "elders," they typically *only* permit speech from those who *reject* any notion of *already knowing the identity of the foretold AntiChrist,* "evidence be damned." Yet, per scripture (e.g., Rev 13:18), such rejecters *are manifestly wrong,* possessing *little to no* genuine understanding of the prophetic scriptures. *Christians can and must do better.*

---

1. Penny Junor, noting "the trivia and the lies" printed by the media, observes, "The simple fact of the matter was that their readers were more interested in reading about gossip from inside the Palace than about worthy schemes for the inner cities, and if people didn't get it in their usual paper they would change to another" *(Charles* {New York: St. Martin's Press, 1987}, p. 222). At best, this is merely a surface explanation.

When God first *showed* this author the identity of history's top AntiChrist, doing so with *staggering* material evidence (herein)— right after this author had asked The Father to explain and illuminate what is written concerning the "first beast" or AntiChrist, in Revelation 13—this author *presumed* that "Church" leadership everywhere would *want to know* and would then of course, *want to share* the information with their flocks. This author *assumed* that most "scholars," "teachers," "pastors," "elders" and the like, in the "Church," served God faithfully; this author *thought* they *would be excited* to have evidence in hand—actual *proof* that Jesus' return is impending. Yes, this author was *sure* that they would thus *want to immediately tell their congregants to begin to prepare, in whatever ways God would lead them, to serve their families, churches and communities under the very worst of circumstances to come. Truly, this author had convinced himself that the information you are about to read in this book would make their hair "stand on end" with excitement!* And that is what *absolutely should have occurred.*

Beyond troubling, however, this author met with somnambulance, lackadaisical attitudes, mass skepticism, shocking *unwillingness* to see *any* evidence whatsoever—despite the author stating that God Himself had provided the evidence, directly answering a specific prayer. Indeed, this author was everywhere, it seemed, met with obduracy, direct censorship, overt obstruction, and yes, even false accusations. All that came from the very people this author had most trusted—that is, "Church" pastors, elders and leaders! What was wrong? What did that mean? How could that possibly be? Why in the world were *these* folks—let alone those the author first approached, many of whom *had* taught on the "last days," as if *they themselves* wanted to be first in line to know and understand— *so turned-off to, so disinterested-in* what God Himself was now exposing, and seeking to share (e.g., through this author) about current reality and nearing events? After all, *there is literally nothing more salient to know, than the actual identity of the foretold AntiChrist*—period, full stop! That is *the* most serious "rubber meets the road" sort of material for modern Christendom! So why? Why wouldn't they listen? Why wouldn't they ear? Why did their eyes seem to glaze over and ears clog with wax upon approach? These people should have been *begging* this author to give them the information *as soon as humanly possible—or sooner even*—so that they could get the world out—*like yesterday, not tomorrow!* But they not only *didn't care*—they flat-out *refused to hear it, refused to see it, refused to consider it,* and instead proceeded to *malign* it and this author, to *dismiss* it and this author—to *shun* it and this author! What was or is *wrong?* Here's the bottom-line: such "Christians" are *unfaithful to God;* contrary to any claim they would make to the contrary, they do *not* genuinely know or believe His written Word. Do *not* be so. (This author provides a comprehensive biblical treatise on such matters, in his book titled *Overcoming Satan's Seed: A Last Days Polemic.)* Instead, believe God and *test* the provided evidence.

As a general rule, it is proper that the Church be wary of those who either *falsely* or *mistakenly* "claim to be able to identify end-time characters or dates"—who instead manage only to discredit Christianity in the eyes of unbelievers. We must point out, however, that the Church is not left without a *clear* means to discern the false from the genuine, something which most Christians, both today and in the past, have unfortunately overlooked. That is, the Apocalypse (i.e., what we generally call "Revelation") offers an unmistakable *test* for *anyone* who would claim to possess a true understanding of the apocalyptic eschatology, a test which, *in the specific context of Revelation 13:1-3,* is found in Revelation 13:18. Whoever legitimately and ultimately *passes* that test will differ from others who either sincerely, or for personal gain, daily misinterpret and sensationalize the eschatological scriptures.

The study of *biblical* eschatology has been obscured through the centuries by a wide variety of pretenders; in no time period has this proven more true than in ours, today. Several examples could be cited, not the least of which is the identity of the coming or prophesied AntiChrist. While many have tried and failed to identify the AntiChrist, the written Word of God clearly states that there will be at least one man—and perhaps others (cf. Dan 2:20-23, 11:32-35, 12:3; Matt 24:15)—who, according to Revelation 13:18, shall not only try, but *succeed:* "him who has understanding." To the extent that such a man shall have "understanding," *so shall he understand the eschatological scriptures in general.* That is, in fact, *demonstrated* reality.[1]

Friend, do not be *unwise,* but wise. Do not be like the *unfaithful-to-God* obstructionists and censors and censors who rashly assert or insinuate, contrary to the authority of the written revelation of God (cf. Rev 1:1-3), that such a preordained—even prophesied—call should be abandoned simply because others have gone astray and deceived the body of Christ; for the whole Church has this inspired admonition, "Here is wisdom: Let him who has understanding...." That is a *command*—yes, it is an *order*—to "allow," "permit," *not* hinder, etc. Truly, rather than obstruct, censor, *or in any other way hin-*

---

1. See *this author's* several other books, and various multi-volume series, to include the *Messiah, History, and the Tribulation Period* series, the *Israel, "Peace" and the Looming Great Tribulation* series, the *Solar Apocalypse* series, the *North Korea, Iran, and the Coming World War: Behold a Red Horse* book, and more (e.g., *Israel's Sojourn In, and Exodus from Egypt: The Real Dates and Pharaohs).*

der the critical effort this work represents, *every pastor* and every *teacher* before every body of believers, *who is faithful* to God, *will help this author get the information in this work (and even his other works) into the hands of God's saints throughout the world.* That particular conduct would demonstrate *actual obedience* to God and His written Word (e.g., per Rev 13:18*a*). But know this as well: those who would "run interference" *for the Devil,* while only *pretending* to be faithful to God, in a *pretense* to believing His written Word—including on the subject of the foretold Antichrist—*are unfaithful.* Thus, conducting oneself to *hinder* this author's *sacrifice*—his great effort to get the knowledge and information in his works, acquired and produced per God's calling over *nearly his entire adult life,* into the hands of the masses—also *is unfaithful.* Indeed, may God grant those who are *faithful* to believe the teachings of His written Word, *real wisdom and understanding*—and may he confound those who *dishonestly* or from *impure* motives insist they have understanding, but deceive and lie.

Hidden in plain sight: Satan's seed. Friend, there is a side to King Charles III, as well as to the British monarchy as a whole, that has been carefully hidden from the public and most media—a side that reveals power, influence, fame and wealth *totally unimagined* by the carefully led and spoon-fed public. It is this side, examined in the context of Bible prophecy, that *The AntiChrist and a Cup of Tea* addresses. (Even Netflix's recent *The Crown* TV "docudrama" series misses it.[1]) No one who has read this book will ever view the British

---

1. Likewise, the first four seasons of satanic Netflix's *The Crown* TV "docudrama" series (2016 to now, as of this writing) shows the public *no* more than it already knows generally, blatantly overlooking and outright ignoring *all* the extensive occult and globalist activities of the royals (esp. Prince Charles, now crowned King Charles III)—including their known satanism and paganism. We see nothing of the British monarchy's druidic, Wiccan, New Age, spiritualist or other satanic paganism in the *The Crown.*

   In fact, the red dragon—which is *central* to the power of King Charles III, and had been to his (now roasting) mother Elizabeth II (as herein exposed)—only briefly and incompletely features in the sixth episode of the third season (cf. 6 * 3), "Tywysog Cymru" or "Prince of Wales" in Welsh (ca. 36:55 to 43:24). That rather perfunctory (and *loosely* "6 6 6") episode does *not* show Charles' heraldic achievement as Satan's Prince. That stunning lapse was despite the reality that his official (artistic) "coat of arms"—produced by England's College of Heraldry, and seen on this book's front cover—was then formally granted; and that omission is likewise despite the fact that unofficial artists' renditions of that very satanic heraldic achievement, forever specific to Charles, were *commonly seen* among the *local* attendees. (Renditions of the Prince of Wales' full heraldic achievement was everywhere seen on investiture "souvenir" brochures—as well as there-sold porcelain cups, saucers, plates and bowls, besides certain fancy silver medals, which were serialized.) In "Tywysog Cymru," *only* the heir-apparent badge and Welsh dragon pieces (heraldic arms), from Charles' large official *graven* (and molded) "coat of arms" or heraldic achievement, which were painted to give mostly bronze appearances and originally hung over Caernarfon Castle's Queen's Gate for the real ceremony, are portrayed—while those (fundamentally similar arms) which were then also over the Eagle Tower's Water Gate, as well as Charles' badge (as the Black Prince) over the King's Gate, are entirely overlooked. (The graven arms are detailed at the bottom of this note, and actually shown later in this work.) Other than showing a number of the red dragon banners, to give Satan his "due," the heir-apparent's badge, which also happens to be the Prince of Darkness' badge, as well as the druidic round Welsh slate platform, three slate thrones and slate stool, most of the rest of the very obvious AntiChrist symbolism—on brash global display during

royal family, or the monarchy's sordid history, in that propagandized, even brainwashed, light again. As we'll see, the power, influence, fame and wealth of the British monarchy undergird the entire elitist push for global government, and have done so for centuries. This behind-the-scenes reality has made King Charles III arguably *the* central figure among elitists of every sort today. As Satan's seed (Gen 3:15), the former Prince of Wales, as difficult to fathom as it may be, is without peer or serious rival on the globalist stage.

This book is intended for those who will study to show themselves approved, who would sooner accept the Word of God than their own, or another's, predispositions; it is for those who desire *real* wisdom and *genuine* prophetic understanding. If you are in this latter category, then may God bless you and grant you discernment as you proceed. As you may now notice, *The AntiChrist and a Cup of Tea* requires some effort to fully digest. However, if you are like most Christians today, you will find it challenging, thought-provoking, and surprisingly informative. Be a noble Berean (Acts 17:10-12), and you may discover "a word fitly spoken," like "apples of gold in pictures [settings] of silver" (Prov 25:11).

In this book, we will first consider the *modus operandi* of the coming global government, along with the AntiChrist's probable rise to power in the United Nations Security Council by means of the European Union (chapter 1). Subsequently, we will examine the following:

✓ *who it is* whose royal hegemony over the European Union has already resulted in a request to be its king (chapter 2);

---

the investiture—are missing from *The Crown*.

Such shortfalls are just part of the *The Crown's* injustice to actual history, as a TV series that—like so many "approved" efforts—*grossly fails* to actually inform its viewers, who mostly just receive more monarchy-maintaining propaganda. (All the arms, along with some of the rather telling memorabilia, are shown in this edition of *The AntiChrist and a Cup of Tea*.) Those behind Netflix's *The Crown*, also try to make nearly everything revolve around feminist "dominatrix" perversions (e.g., the queens and princesses, as well as Margaret Thatcher)—flouting, as it were, original sin.

At the real July 1969 investiture, *two* fundamentally similar versions of Charles' *nearly full* heraldic achievement as Prince of Wales, were placed above the Queen's Gate and Water Tower Gate, respectively. Each of those was *missing* only 1) the topping "lion crest," above the prince's Tudor crown, 2) the overall "sovereign" helm, which is ordinarily seen beneath that crown (later detailed), 3) the accompanying silver and gold ermine mantle (or shroud), 4) the compartments containing the heir-apparent (Black Prince) badge and red dragon, respectively, and 5) Charles' arms as then Duke of Cornwall, with its black shield and overlaid gold bezants, at the bottom of the overall achievement. Yet, two versions were each *ostensibly completed* by 1) *not sure,* 2) the strange hat (in place of the helm) worn by the queen herself (below detailed), 3) the "ermine mantle" received and worn by Satan's Prince himself, which the (Satan-possessed) queen placed around his shoulders, 4) strategically-placed, yet separate red dragon and heir-apparent (Black Prince) badge banners and arms, and 5) medals or coins (silver and bronze) sold as memorabilia. That light golden yellow hat (or female Tudor bonnet) was embroidered with *seven vertical rows of pearls,* substituting for what would ordinarily be the *seven bars* of the sovereign's *(heraldic gold)* helm; indeed, understood as such, the queen then had it on *"backwards,"* since the "bars" were around her head rather than over her face.

✓ *who it is* whose name calculates to 666 in both English and Hebrew, using the scriptural system (chapter 3);

✓ *who it is* whose lineage places him at the head of the Merovingian dynasty, and asserts descendancy from Israel's King David, Jesus, and Islam's Mohammed (MuHammad), as well as the tribe of Dan and Satan (chapter 4);

✓ *who it is* whose royal ancestors have claimed to sit upon the throne of David for nearly two millennia (chapter 5);

✓ *who it is* whose heraldic achievement is a literal depiction of the satanic imagery associated with the AntiChrist in both the Old and New Testaments, whose oligarchical powerbase is behind the quest for a New World Order (chapters 6 and 7);[1]

✓ *who it is* whose current power, throne, and "great authority" *literally* derive from the "red dragon" or Satan, and whose *first advent* as the AntiChrist has already occurred (chapter 8);

✓ *who it is* whose agenda is specifically geared to address the many ominous and prophetic "signs of the times"—and what those signs are—through "global governance" (chapter 9);

✓ *who it is* whose multifaceted religious, political, and other ties are apparently set to position him as priest and prophet, not to mention king, to the world's major and minor religions—including apostate "Christianity," unregenerate Judaism, Islam, Hinduism, Buddhism, Sikhism, Zoroastrianism, Wicca, etc., or all satanism and paganism—and who is a global "mover and shaker" with vast potential wealth (chapter 10);

✓ *who it is* whose media exposure has already exceeded that of every other man in history, who exercises authority over Freemasonry and the Illuminati worldwide, who heads the United World Colleges, who instigated the rise in popularity of alternative medicine (good and bad) in the West, who is credited for the success of the watershed 1992 Earth Summit in Rio de Janeiro (which birthed the Kyoto Protocol and its successor agreements), who steers the environmental ethics and business agendas for as many as one-hundred or more of the world's largest multinational corporations, who is said to have personally initiated the

---

1. Dr. David Bay remarks: "This is the section of Cohen's book most intriguing to me, since I was totally unfamiliar with the British system of Heraldry—of Knighthood. That kind of "Country Club" living, believing, and acting was thoroughly rejected by Americans as we threw off the chains of Great Britain, and we have been sensitive to what we consider "nonsense" in the entire heraldry system. However, this very system is completely based on deep, abiding, and powerful Generational Witchcraft, and from this system, all the symbols foretold of Antichrist are present! If you are an average American, you will thoroughly enjoy this study of Heraldry."

United Nations' Global Security Programme, and who has already partnered with the World Bank and the United Nations Development Programme in an attempt to achieve a new form of global governance that emphasizes sustainable development and globalist education through public-private (government-business) partnerships worldwide (chapter 11);

✓ *who it is* whose New World Order agenda is reflected in his apparent personal instigation of the entire Mideast "peace process," which to date has resulted in Israel's Oslo I and II accords with the "Palestinians" as well as a peace treaty between Israel and Jordan (chapter 12);

✓ *who it is* whose life has already been threatened by "terrorists" on several occasions (chapter 13);

✓ *who it is* whose heraldic coat of arms may one day be associated with the image and mark of the "beast;" who has been sculpted as an angelic "winged god" and hailed as "Saviour of the World," "a man of such stature" who "is able to speak for all of us;" and who has already taken an electronic bio-chip implant for personal security (chapter 14); and, finally,

✓ *who it is* whose overall qualifications distinguish him as *history's only real candidate* to be *the* prophesied AntiChrist (chapter 17).

The evidence in this work is *beyond strong.* The above list, provides only a *taste* of what this work contains, which is substantial by any mortal definition. In fact, it is fair to say that *anyone claiming to have read this work,* but who then *denies* its conclusions, may—and should—be regarded as either false or "reading challenged" (i.e., lacking in comprehension). That may sound overly "confident." By the time you finish actually reading all the contents, however, you will *not* take issue. The gravity of this present work is simply *extreme*—both to the Church and the world at large.

Translations. Issues of translation are important to this work. At times, unfortunately, no currently extant English translation of a passage of scripture is sufficiently accurate or literal to convey a significant point of its underlying Hebrew or Greek text. In such circumstances, it is necessary to turn to the original autographs. Consequently, some of the best and most reliable Hebrew and Greek manuscripts and lexicons were consulted in the course of researching and writing *The AntiChrist and a Cup of Tea. Referenced* translations include the Authorized King James Version[1] and Baker's

---

1. Where AKJV or KJV is specified, the use of the King James Version is stressed.

Interlinear Greek-English New Testament. No references are made to other published translations. Another work consulted, but not referenced, for example, was Hendrickson's *Interlinear Bible.* All interlinear texts consulted are Strong's coded (see below). In several instances, for the sake of complete accuracy or to bring out some significant point, the author has taken the liberty of offering literal modern-English translations, taken from the Bible's original Hebrew and Greek autographs, as indicated. In an effort to make the original Hebrew and Greek of the Bible more accessible to most readers, *The AntiChrist and a Cup of Tea* employs Strong's reference numbers when examining specific Hebrew and Greek words.[1]

Your help and support are very much needed. This author is not an island unto himself! He *must* have your *help* to succeed in getting the proof herein contained—of the foretold AntiChrist's identity and more—into the hands of God's saints everywhere. That is likewise true for this author's other books and items, which are also weighty and important. Such help may be monetary, material, or by voluntary labor. The latter could include telling media and news personalities and sources about this, and the author's other works, to request they conduct interviews, which also are essential.

For decades, this author has labored *alone,* by God's *will,* to do all this; really, he has not just dedicated, but truly sacrificed much of his adult life to answer God's call. For that to continue, as it must, *your help is truly needed.* Anyone *familiar* with this author's works, to include those who hear his interviews and teaching, should confidently know that whatever is given will be used to reach "a great multitude which no one could number, of all nations, tribes, peoples, and tongues" (Rev 7:9; see 7:9-17). Christians have much fruit to yet bear for God's Kingdom, and you may share in this author's!

The first edition of *The AntiChrist and a Cup of Tea* was a "bestseller," with about twenty-five thousand copies sold (and many more stolen). That occurred with little to no marketing, and then God allowed a long hiatus of the work being out-of-print. That tiny number

---

1. Although various scholars dismiss Strong's system, in which most Hebrew and Greek words of the Bible are alphabetized and sequentially numbered, as insufficient and occasionally inaccurate, others find its reference numbers highly useful. Lexical works consulted, most of which are coded to Strong's numbering system, include *The New Englishman's HEBREW CONCORDANCE; The New Englishman's GREEK CONCORDANCE and LEXICON;* William Gesenius' *HEBREW-CHALDEE LEXICON of the OLD TESTAMENT; The New Brown-Driver-Briggs-Gesenius Hebrew-English Lexicon* (Francis Brown, S.R. Driver, and Charles A. Briggs {Massachusetts: Hendrickson Publishers, 1979}); the second edition of the revised *BAG* Greek-English Lexicon (Walter Bauer, William F. Arndt, and F. Wilbur Gingrich, *A Greek-English Lexicon of the New Testament and Other Early Christian Literature,* 2nd ed., rev. F.W. Gingrich and Frederick W. Danker {Illinois: The University of Chicago, 1979}); Joseph Thayer's *GREEK-ENGLISH LEXICON of the NEW TESTAMENT;* James Strong's "A Concise Dictionary of the Words in the Hebrew Bible" and "A Concise Dictionary of the Words in the Greek/New Testament" (*STRONG'S EXHAUSTIVE CONCORDANCE OF THE BIBLE*).

in sales, and that lengthy delay in availability of this edition, has all ensured that scripture is fulfilled without hindrance. Now, however, the time is come for this and the author's other works to reach *many millions* of hands, as the foretold AntiChrist is now taking his role. The necessary distribution cannot occur without your "word of mouth" sharing, dedicated support and help. Indeed, share what you learn with others, including those to whom you pay attention in media (e.g., reporters, journalists, editors, etc.), as well as hosts of your favorite radio, TV and Internet-based programs.

Friend—if you or someone you know is *able and willing* to cover the costs, be that in-part or in-full, of placing this work, and as possible the author's other books and items, into the hands of Church pastors, elders and teachers around the world, then kindly contact Prophecy House to that end. (For other languages, translators too are necessary.) Neither the author nor his publisher has the means, as of this writing, to solely accomplish what needs to occur, but we know God is able to move one who *does,* who *serves Him* (cf. Ps 50:10-12, 50:14-15, 50:23), or even many who collectively do. Please, pray seriously about what God would have *you* do—as the enormous gravity of this work, *is plain to see*—and then *obey* God. This is so that many who do not now know Him, may come to know Him. God rewards all faithfulness to Him, and this author thanks you in advance. Few in history have had an opportunity of *this magnitude* —to partake in fruit of such import to God's Kingdom. We here invite and request your participation as a fellow laborer.

Notice to the "establishment." The author has taken precautions appropriate to this work. Prior to publication, encrypted electronic copies of this edition of *The AntiChrist and a Cup of Tea* were placed in the hands of trustworthy individuals, around the world, who have the means at their disposal to distribute them widely. *Others* were given the necessary keys to decrypt those copies, which exist in Adobe Acrobat, and Internet formats. Should *any* significant harm befall the author (including a serious "accident"), or should the author or his publisher be threatened or subverted, so as to significantly hinder or effectively stop the publication, advertisement, marketing or distribution of *The AntiChrist and a Cup of Tea,* these individuals, who are *not* known to one another, will automatically provide their respective contacts with the necessary keys to decrypt the work for worldwide distribution. Furthermore, the author, who holds the copyright to said work, hereby grants explicit permission to any individual residing in any country where *The AntiChrist and a Cup of Tea* is **banned or disallowed** to **FREELY** copy—in a *non-digital* *and non-electronic format only*—and distribute said work **solely within that country;** all rights, however, are and shall remain reserved. Such explicit permission will be *irrevocable* upon any untimely demise of the author, or the start of the Great Tribulation, when half of Jerusalem is taken captive.

Acknowledgments. The author would like to thank the following individuals for their help, provision of research materials, prayers, and encouragement to persevere in this present work: Michael Bond, Jerry Carter, John Coleman, Patricia Collins, John Daniel, Gary Hansen, James H., (the late) Dave Hunt, Monte Judah, Gary H. Kah, Sally Moran, William Schnoebelen, Sam Schulstad, Fritz Springmeier, Ruiying W. and Juliah Y., (the late) Barbara Wiseman, Monte Judah, Steve Klein, and some who are unnamed.[1]

---

1. Certain individuals and certain last names have been omitted as necessary. To them, the author also extends his thanks.

1

The Footsteps of *the* AntiChrist

The AntiChrist and his denials of God's eternal Truth are explicitly mentioned just four times in the Bible, in only two epistles (1 John 2:18, 2:22, 4:3; 2 John 7). Nevertheless, the biblical identity of the foretold AntiChrist is a subject that has fascinated both Christians and non-Christians alike for nearly two millennia. Unfortunately, this fascination has often led to unwarranted speculation. The AntiChrist, when he takes up his role, will not be easy to spot. In fact, apart from the biblical criteria, he will be all but impossible to recognize. To most, he will not be an obviously evil man—at least not initially. Rather, he will live up to the dual meaning of the prefix, "anti," in his New Testament designation. He will be *against* the real Christ while at the same time setting himself *in His place*.[1] To set himself in The Messiah's place, the Anti-Messiah must ultimately be able to convince the unregenerate world that he *is* the "Messiah"—for *all* peoples and *all* religions. As Satan's unorthodox parody of Christ, he will be a counterfeit "Christ," and his disciples and followers, therefore, whatever their religious persuasions, will be counterfeit "Christians."

Although the false prophet is not a major subject of this treatise, some points are relevant. Many have held through the centuries that the false prophet and even the AntiChrist would arise from the Roman Catholic Church. Christians of all backgrounds recognize that while Roman Catholicism has historically advocated a Judeo-Christian morality, it nevertheless remains, in many respects, a pagan religion—a curious mixture of the holy with the profane. According to Revelation 13:11, the false prophet will have "two horns like a lamb," and speak like "a dragon." It is perhaps noteworthy, therefore, that Rome's prior pope, John Paul II, wore a "two-horned" miter which, around its base, depicts the pope as a lamb wearing the miter. This lamb, *because of the papal miter shown on its head,* actually looks like it has two horns.[2] This same pope, who had "two horns like a lamb," routinely proferred statements revealing his intolerance for true Christians, his antichristian ecumenism, and his worship of

---

1. For more information, see the section titled "Daniel 9:27 and the Latter Halves of the Weeks," in the volume titled *Messiah's Preeminence in History and Prophecy: The Heart of Israelology, Eschatology, and God's Holy Days,* of the *Messiah, History, and the Tribulation Period* series.
2. Associated Press photograph of the pope in Italy, *The Denver Post,* 29 Sept. 1997, p. 13A.

"Mary" and the dead, which Roman Catholicism euphemistically calls "saints." In other words, John Paul II spoke like "a dragon," even the red dragon or Satan (Rev 12:3, 12:9).[1] Roman Catholicism's latest pope, the Argentinian Francis (Jorge Mario Bergoglio), is no better. Given his "Marian devotion" (i.e., worship), it seems only appropriate to note that the author has encountered statements attributed to a Roman Catholic priest and theologian asserting that "Mary" is calling faithful congregants to receive a mark in their hand or forehead for protection from coming catastrophic judgments (cf. Rev 13:16-17). Based upon this and other information, the author agrees with those who have argued that the false prophet, who shall work to exalt the AntiChrist, could readily be Rome's final pope (see Rev 13:11-17, 16:13-14, 19:20; cf. 20:10).[2] Moreover, as we shall see, many of the ancestors of this book's subject—history's only real candidate for the role of the prophesied AntiChrist—were Roman Catholic. Indeed, the European Union (EU) has begun to actively promote Roman Catholicism to the exclusion of true Christianity.[3]

Past suggestions for the identity of the AntiChrist have included Judas Iscariot,[4] Antiochus IV,[5] Caligula, Charlemagne, Mohammed (Muhammad), Napoleon, and Nero. Suggestions in the twentieth and early twenty-first centuries, now mostly abandoned, have included (Mohammed) Yasser Arafat, Francisco Franco Bahamonde, George Bush Sr. (i.e., George Herbert Walker Bush), Juan Carlos I, William (Bill) Jefferson Clinton, Alister (i.e., Edward Alexander) Crowley, Boutros Boutros-Ghali, Mikhail Sergeyevich Gorbachev, Otto von Habsburg,[6] Adolf Hitler, Saddam Hussein (Abd al-Majid al-Tikriti), John Fitzgerald Kennedy, Ayatollah Sayyid Ruhollah Musavi Khomeini, Henry Alfred Kissinger, Javier Solana (de Madariaga), Sun

---

1. The Septuagint refers to Satan as the "apostate dragon" (Job 26:13, LXX). In quoting Job, therefore, Origen remarked: "That he is an apostate—that is, a fugitive—even The Lord in the book of Job says: 'Thou wilt take with a hook the apostate dragon' [(40:20, LXX)].... Now it is certain that by the dragon is understood the Devil himself" (*On Principles*, Bk. 1, Ch. 5, Par. 5; see *Ante-Nicene Fathers*, ed. Roberts and Donaldson, Vol. 4, p. 259).

2. For more information, see the chapter (or section) "The History of the Roman Empire and its Modern Thirst for Oil," in the volume titled, *The Prophetic Stage: Signs of the Times*, of the author's *Messiah, History, and the Tribulation Period* series.

3. See, for example, Adrian Hilton, *The Principality and Power of Europe* (England: Dorchester House Publications, Box 67, Rickmansworth, Herts WD3 5SJ; 1997).

4. There are strong biblical parallels between Judas Iscariot and the AntiChrist, each of whom is uniquely identified as "the son of perdition" in scripture. Some of these are touched upon in this work, and others are addressed in the author's *Messiah, History, and the Tribulation Period* multi-volume series. For example, Judas Iscariot was possessed by Satan and proceeded to betray Christ at the midpoint of the Crucifixion Week, whereas the AntiChrist will be possessed by Satan and proceed to betray Israel and the saints at the midpoint of the Tribulation Week. For more information, see the discussion on the son of perdition in ch. 7, at p. 203.

5. Antiochus IV claimed to be "God manifest," using the title *Epiphanies* of himself.

6. I.e., Franz Joseph Otto Robert Maria Anton Karl Max Heinrich Sixtus Xavier Felix Renatus Ludwig Gaetan Pius Ignatius von Habsburg, aka Archduke Otto of Austria. Someone forgot "illustrious!"

Myung Moon, Benito (Amilcare Andrea) Mussolini, Shimon Peres (i.e., *Szymon Perski),* Prince Philip (of Greece and Denmark, former Duke of Edinburgh, the biological father of King Charles III), Franklin Delano Roosevelt, Yitzhak Rabin, Joseph Aloisius Ratzinger (i.e., Benedict XVI), Ronald Wilson Reagan, Joseph (Vissarionovich) Stalin, Maurice (Frederick) Strong, and Karol Józef Wojtyła (i.e., John Paul II).

Current suggestions include Jorge Mario Bergoglio (i.e., Francis), Louis Farrakhan, the World Economic Forum's (WEF's) Klaus (Martin) Schwab or the Bill & Melinda Gates Foundation's William Henry Gates III (i.e., Bill Gates), both of whom are *knights* of King Charles III, Al Gore (i.e., Albert Arnold Gore Jr.), Ayatollah Sayyid Ali Hosseini Khamenei, Jared Corey Kushner (Donald J. Trump's son), Barack Hussein Obama II (i.e., "Barry" Soetoro), Recep Tayyip Erdoğan,[1] Xi Jinping, Vladimir V. Putin, Emmanuel Macron, Justin Trudeau, Yuval Noah Harari, the "Dalai Lama," and even Donald J. Trump, or some junior false prophet or fake "messiah" in Israel (e.g., Shlomo Yehuda aka "the Yanuka")—as well as Judas Iscariot, Nero (e.g., among errant "prophecy apostates" such as preterists), "Maitreya" (i.e., the Sanskrit *Maitreya,* Pali *Metteyya,* or Tibetan *Jampa).*

Of interest, there is "the Kushner Companies' 666 Fifth Avenue tower." Does this imply that Jared C. Kushner—the primary (public) architect of President Trump's *false* "peace" initiative (i.e., the "Peace to Prosperity: A Vision to Improve the Lives of the Palestinian and Israeli People" plan)—is in league with Satan? Arguably, *yes*—and that particular real estate is ostensibly harmful: "Kushner was chief executive of Kushner Companies when it acquired 666 Fifth Avenue in 2007.... It has been a drag on his family's real estate company ever since."[2] But any such address is *far from a name or title calculation,* and it is *not* Kushner who is actually over the false Mideast "peace" efforts (as later addressed), and there are other key criteria, of which Mr. Kushner meets *none.* So, Mr. Kushner is *not,* nor could he ever become, the foretold AntiChrist. Indeed, *none* of the above past or current suggestions seems (or is) truly plausible.[3]

---

1. Joel Richardson's effort to push Recep Tayyip Erdoğan as the AntiChrist of biblical apocalyptic prophecy, in his 2009 book *The Islamic Antichrist,* is *mistaken and false.* In fact, this author *handed* Richardson a first edition of *The AntiChrist and a Cup of Tea,* over a decade ago (ca. January 2012), at Congregation Roeh Israel in Denver, Colorado, which he clearly failed to read or heed. Richardson, even though he is *not* a pretribulationist, as *lacks* both credibility and biblical understanding. Yet, Charles as Prince of Wales—the actual foretold AntiChrist—reportedly converted to Islam *in Turkey* (see the footnote on p. 372).

2. Dmitry Zhdannikov, Herbert Lash and Saeed Azhar, "Qatar revamps investment strategy after Kushner building bailout," *Reuters,* 11 Feb. 2019.

3. In the particular context of the Crucifixion Week, Judas Iscariot is a special circumstance, as addressed and shown in the author's *Messiah, History, and the Tribulation Period* multi-volume series.

For Notes:

Curiously, former President Ronald Reagan, who was a knight of the British monarchy before his death, first met Prince Charles at the White House on May 1, 1981. That very day, Reagan wrote, "I swear I believe Armageddon is near."[1] Walvoord observes:

> An almost unlimited number of identifications of antichrist to specific historical characters can be found. Among the more prominent are Mohammed, the founder of the Muslim faith [(false religion)]; Caligula, a Roman emperor who claimed to be God; and Nero, a popular candidate for the title because of his burning of Rome and persecution of the Jews and Christians. To these can be added almost every prominent ruler of the past, including more modern characters such as Napoleon and Mussolini. In all these historical identifications, there is little more than evidence of being antichristian, but the variety of claims leaves the concept of [*the*] antichrist in considerable confusion.[2]

In our day, there continue to be multiple men on the world stage who, on character alone, would seem to be candidates to be the AntiChrist. Character alone, however, is *not,* and *cannot be,* the determining factor; to rely upon character as such, is *shallow* at best. Not only is character an *unreliable* "mainstay" criterion, it is an *unbiblical* one. (That's right, recognizing an evil character is *not* a scriptural way to identify the AntiChrist.) As always, the determining factor does and must come down to genuine, inspired scripture—that is, the written and inerrant Word of God. The author, in fact, would argue that *applying scripture* is the *only* legitimate approach (e.g., see 1 Cor 3:10-11; cf. 1 Cor 3:5-23; Col 2:8). Failure on the part of many— not a few of whom are called "experts" and "scholars"—to recognize *this truth* against an historical "cornucopia" of errors, or to give God His due as it were, is *the* main reason for all the misidentifications down through history.

Rejection of biblical truth, has always been is a primary cause of confusion over prophecy. Many today, due to a variety erroneous positions they yet embrace—just like some of the past—allege there will *not* be an individual who is *the* AntiChrist. To their detriment, they make themselves *mentally as well as spiritually blind and deaf* to much of what is *now* transpiring in fulfillment of Bible prophecy.

The "vaunted" Hank Hanegraaff, for example, is practically a "poster child" of prophetic heresy and apostasy—one whom this author is here going to display (just a little). Mr. Hanegraaff, as one who devotes himself to certain serious errors of preterism, vociferously disclaims Israel's *modern* place and role in scripture and prophecy—just as he disclaims a literal foretold AntiChrist, a literal

---

1. Christopher Hitchens, "The Reagan Diaries," *The Sunday Times,* 24 June 2007.
2. "ANTICHRIST," *The Zondervan Pictorial Encyclopedia of the Bible,* 1976 ed., Vol. 1, p. 179.

three-and-one-half-year Great Tribulation, a literal this and a literal that, *preceding* Jesus' Second Advent. That's literally *off.*

Others—mistakenly relying upon the claims of *false teachers,* who *contradict* the actual statements and teaching of God's written Word—are *so convinced* the Church will *not* be present on Earth during the Great Tribulation, that they—as *deceived* persons who are *not* hearing The Holy Spirit *prophetically*—will (stridently) dismiss *any possibility* of knowing beforehand (e.g., today) the identity of the foretold AntiChrist. Indeed, they are so trusting of those who have snookered them, and so sure of themselves, that they will *not* even countenance *unassailable evidence.* Their resulting proffered *anti*-scripture dismissals are *canards* or *misdirections* from the enemy. Those so-suckered are left *incapable* of recognizing *the real timing* of coming events. They *lack sufficient discernment,* harming any ability they might otherwise have exercised to be truly watchful. They generally see *more* than the likes of Mr. Hanegraaff, but *not nearly so much as God wants them to see.*

Jan Markell is a (sadly and tragically) popular woman who is a *false teacher continually fleecing God's flock* (e.g., on the *timing* of the rapture;[1] she is an *ardent pretribulationist liar).* In fact, the unrepentant Ms. Markell endangers her soul (Rev 15:1, 22:18-19).[2] That much being stated, Ms. Markell none the less *correctly* says of Hanegraaff: "He denies the 144,000 [Israelites of Revelation 7:1-8] are Jews [(i.e., genetic Israelites)] and denies the Two Witnesses are literal. He misses the essential apologetic of history: God has two distinct people[s]" (i.e., Israelites and Gentiles).[3] Yes, Hanegraaff also seems to *deny* a rapture is to occur—a mistake of which Ms. Markell is *not* guilty (though her sin is comparably serious)—yet Hanegraaff rightly affirms a resurrection at Christ's Second Advent.[4] But the saints' future "catching away" or "up" to God *is impending (not* "imminent"), and will transpire in at least *three posttribulational*

---

1. See the treatment on the rapture's timing in this author's book titled *Overcoming Satan's Seed: A Last Days Polemic,* starting with "Light versus dark, watchful versus inattentive, and prepared versus unprepared for the coming 'rapture.'" But if you are *not* a Christian, skip the rest of the polemic.

2. Pretribulationists continually use *slight of mind and slight of hand* to establish strawman arguments, while trying to leave tickled ears none the wiser. For example (one of many), some (e.g., Jan Markell) now speak of the "time of the signs," to obfuscate the fact that there *are* signs of the times, somehow imagining that aligns with their *immanency lie,* rather than reflecting the *actually impending* nature of Jesus' soon return! Similarly, Markell now speaks of the "shadow(s)" of coming tribulational events appearing, as if those were not themselves signs of the times! Not only is this *dishonest foolishness,* but demons are biblically (e.g., in the Hebrew text of Isaiah) called "shades" or "shadows," exposing the fact that *pretribulationism,* like so many other false eschatologies, *is a doctrine of demons!*

3. Jan Markell, "The Bible Answer Man Said What?," *Olive Tree Ministries,* 2 Feb. 2017. To see and hear Mr. Hanegraaff make such statements, visit "https://www.youtube.com/watch?v=Q51sL-2SOmo" ("Hank Hanegraaff: A Gospel Response to Christian Zionism") and "https://www.youtube.com/watch?v=eje2FjlAkVo&t=412s" ("Where is the Rapture Taught in Scripture?") on YouTube.

4. Ibid.

stages at Christ Jesus' return—starting with the two witnesses (Rev 11:12).[1]

A troublingly *obtuse and false* Mr. Hanegraaff, who *sullies* the legacy of the scripturally sound and true Dr. Walter Martin, whom Hanegraaff decades ago replaced on the "Bible Answer Man" program, becoming Dr. Martin's (non-preferred) successor at the Christian Research Institute (CRI), which Martin founded, has *fallen away* from God and His written Word. He has apostatized where Israel is concerned, while *explicitly denying and speaking against* correct interpretations of biblical prophecy. In fact, like other *heretics* who have written and created supposedly "Christian" works of apocalyptic fiction (e.g., such as Jerry B. Jenkins and deceased Tim LaHaye, or those behind the *Left Behind* propaganda and lies), Mr. Hanegraaff has authored a fictional apocalyptic series, based upon his own *grossly mistaken* interpretation of Revelation and history (as outlined in *The Apocalypse Code*). By all that, Mr. Hanegraaff is among those who effectively—whether by intent or not—*add to, and take away from scripture, including the Apocalypse.* In other words, he and they are *guilty of tampering with God's written Word.* (The penalties for such conduct are *very severe:* see Revelation 22:18-19.)

Though some allege Mr. Hanegraaff to be "one of the foremost apologists for the Christian faith," it is must be stated that he is *an apostate and a heretic.* Objectively arrogant and theologically false, he has transitioned (as a wolf, goat and tare) to the Greek Eastern Orthodox Church,[2] accepting its transubstantiation doctrine and heresy,[3] which is *not* good for that body. Hanegraaff effectively curses Israel directly by his associations (e.g., Stephen Sizer) and indirectly by his words, plain and simple—and he is eminently *unqual-*

---

1. For more information, see the volume titled *The Real Rapture and Other Prophetic Mysteries: Understanding the Revelation (Apocalypse),* in the author's *Messiah, History, and the Tribulation Period* series. A corresponding presentation called "The *Real* Rapture" is available on DVD and CD.

2. Brandon Showalter, "'Bible Answer Man' Hank Hanegraaff Leaves Evangelicalism, Joins Greek Orthodox Church," *Christian Post,* 11 Apr. 2017.

3. Contrary to the teaching of transubstantiation, any bread or wine used to partake in spiritual communion with Christ Jesus are strictly *symbols* of an ongoing spiritual reality to which we, as Christians, are joined by the indwelling of The Holy Spirit. We metaphysically partake in His crucifixion, death, burial and resurrection, which we acknowledge through communion, meaning we are literally crucified, killed, buried and resurrected in and with Him, having been joined to Him permanently through spiritual rebirth when we received the gift of The Holy Spirit. Bread and wine are *not* themselves transformed to become the literal physical body or physical blood of Christ Jesus; rather, we ourselves are spiritual partakers in His literal body much as cells, etc., are knitted together to constitute a complex biological organism. To extend these truths, going beyond what scripture says and teaches, by asserting that bread and wine, though they still look just like bread and wine, are suddenly the literal flesh and literal blood of Christ Jesus is heretical, and it is for this very reason, in fact, that Jesus, while speaking directly concerning communion, stated: "It is the Spirit who gives life; the flesh profits nothing: The words that I speak to you are spirit, and they are life" (John 6:63; see 6:28-64). That Mr. Hanegraaff now denies this is simply further evidence of his apostasy, and shows he is *no* scholar of God's written Word, but a *denier* of scriptural truth.

ified to guide *any* Christian, being a man who fails to recognize that God's calling and promises concerning Israel are irrevocable so long as the heavens and the Earth remain, so that all *surviving* Israel will one day become *Christian.* (The Universe and the Earth are still here, as is Israel.)

The God of Israel is *not* the God of Abraham *only,* as Hanegraaff or those like him might prefer, but He is The God of Abraham, Isaac and Jacob (Israel), even to this day. No one should pay heed to someone who comes up so short in biblical truth and understanding, but every Christian should call Mr. Hanegraaff and those like him *to repent of their falsehood, apostasy and even heresy* (as this author here does). Yet, Mr. Hanegraaff's presence on *Christian* radio continues unabated, revealing *the sad spiritual state of many in Christendom today.* In some very egregious ways, Mr. Hanegraaff has acted to *destroy* what Dr. Martin built.

Let the author also point out that the so-called World Council of Churches (WCC) similarly errs. Dexter Van Zile, for example, points out: "By broadcasting a narrative about Israeli intransigence and 'Palestinian' innocence, the WCC and its activists in Israel have helped legitimize violence against Israeli citizens.... The WCC got its bad reputation in Israel the old-fashioned way—it earned it. Now it's time for the organization to repent and stop using the cloak of [(supposed, but not actual)] peacemaking to provide cover for anti-Israel propagandists in the Holy Land."[1]

The above now stated, be forewarned that pretribulationism, midtribulationism, amillennialism, postmillennialism, and *historicist* posttribulationism are *all* to one degree or another, theological and prophetic errors *in their own right,* ones also producing mental and spiritual blindness; these too constitute apostasies, or *departures from* the prophetic truths of scripture. Here as well, this author is "him who has understanding" (Rev 13:18*a*). Let's continue.

It seems amazing that a decade after the release of the first edition of this work, which is *the most important extra-biblical work on apocalyptic prophecy this side of Christ's return,* and some may say even of all time, so many who know of it *still err in its arena,* stubbornly *clinging to their own private interpretations (see 2 Pet 1:19-21), unbiblical approaches, and clear—consider this work—misidentifications (i.e., of the AntiChrist).* More than amazing, it troublingly demonstrates a blatant disregard for sound doctrine and teaching—an indication of the arrogance and unsoundness of so many who fill modern pulpits, and who are heard on radio or television. Such individuals, who engage in "intellectual incest" with those who are

---

1. Van Zile, "Promoting hostility as 'peacemaking,'" *Israel Hayom,* 31 Jan. 2017.

similarly deceived, *face judgment*—lest they repent. From these, this author (led by The Holy Spirit), and this author's namesake Timothy (guided by The Holy Spirit), says *turn away* (2 Tim 3:5-9)—lest you too should be found guilty of their sins at Christ's return, not having endured sound doctrine and teaching.

Indeed, there must be far more than merely antichristian beliefs and activities on the part of a person to justify a consideration of him as *the* AntiChrist. Any individual under serious observation must not only have antichristian beliefs, but also be capable of fulfilling every biblical prophecy related to the AntiChrist, *without exception.* Such a person, for example, *must* be associated in some literal manner with the imagery of the "first beast," as described in the Apocalypse (chs. 12, 13, 17, and 18) and Daniel (ch. 7). Also, he *must* have a name or title that calculates to precisely six-hundred and sixty-six (666), preferably using a system that was recognized within Judaism—by both believers and unbelievers—when the Apocalypse was first penned (see Rev 13:18). Further, he *must* be a prominent ruler, presumably a prince, of Roman lineage (Dan 9:26-27). Some would even add that he *must* be a descendant of Israel's tribe of Dan (discussed later).

Before continuing, it is important to understand that association with the imagery *or symbolism* of the first beast on the part of the man of lawlessness and sin (2 Th 2:3)—*the* AntiChrist—is biblically *required.* It is not a mere possibility, nor is it just an interpretation or suggestion on this author's part. Why? Revelation 13:18 states that six-hundred and sixty-six (666) is "the number of the beast" *before* it states that it is "the number of a man." In other words, the actual presence of the *imagery* of this beast *in relation to a man* (i.e., the AntiChrist, a "Charles") is the biblical prerequisite to, and specific context for, the name calculation itself.[1] For this reason, any calculation for any person at any time who is not directly associated with the imagery or symbolism of the first beast is *invalid* and of *no use* in determining the real identity of the foretold AntiChrist. As we shall see, the Roman prince who is the topic of this book is *the only person in history* to actually have such an association. Indeed, the very image of the first beast of Revelation 13 itself, as well as the unicorn with human eyes of Daniel 7, *is shown on the front cover of this book*—and it belongs to, and heraldically represents, none other than the Roman prince in question. So he is not just the first biblical candidate ever for the role of the AntiChrist, as mentioned earlier, but really the *only* candidate. Indeed, this prince's own sons also

---

1. The name "Charles" *literally means* "man | strong man | manly | warrior | farmer." For details, see p. 482 of ch. 12, "Charles, Middle East 'Peace,' and Global Security."

lack complete and direct association with the imagery (i.e., it is *not* depicted on their heraldic achievements or coats of arms).[1]

Besides the biblical "musts" for qualification, there are, in this author's opinion, some prudent "shoulds." Any individual under consideration should have a prominent royal and religious lineage that will be viewed as proof-positive of his claims to world-leadership by all the world's major religions and cults. Also, he should have diverse royal, religious, political, military, and economic connections, as well as substantial wealth, to aid in his transition to power. Finally, he should be a man whom the world loves and desires to follow (despite any moral shortcomings he may exhibit), and who appears to be willing and able to cope with global problems and crises (e.g., the environment, religious and ethnic disputes, etc.).

Of course, there are also mistaken criteria. To these lists, for example, many prophecy teachers, "scholars," and "authorities" would add, *incorrectly,* that according to Isaiah 13, Jeremiah 50 to 51, and a host of other Old Testament passages and prophecies, the AntiChrist *must* be of Assyrian and/or Babylonian origin. Others would assert that he will be the King of the North prophesied in Daniel 11 who shall reject the "God of his fathers," meaning The God of Israel, as well as the "desire of women," being a homosexual. However, in their geographical, historical, and scriptural contexts, these prophecies all speak of an individual who shall reside in the "land of the Chaldeans," or what is today modern Iraq, where the late Saddam Hussein had been rebuilding the ancient capital cities of Nineveh and Babylon. The first capital geographically of the King of the North or the Seleucid dynasty, for example, was *Seleucia* on the Tigris River, or what we now call *Baghdad*.[2] In other words, a man from the region of modern Iraq will fulfill outstanding prophecies concerning the Assyrian, the Babylonian, *and* the King of the North.

Scripturally and historically speaking, the King of the North will *not* reject the "God" of his fathers, implying The God of Israel, but the "gods" (see below) of his fathers, meaning the particular pagan deities to whom his fathers bowed down. Likewise, the King of the North will *not* be a homosexual who wants nothing to do with women. He will *not* reject the "desire of women," meaning women

---

1. For more information, see ch. 3, "A Name that Calculates to 666," at p. 71.
2. Seleucia (on the Tigris River), the Seleucid dynasty's first capital, was located just a few miles north of Babylon and *barely south of modern Baghdad* (*The Harper ATLAS of the BIBLE*, ed. James B. Pritchard {New York: Harper & Row, Publishers, Inc., 1987}, p. 144). Soon thereafter, a second capital was set up at Syria's Antioch, though Seleucia Pieria (just north of the mouth of the Orontes River in the northeast corner of the Mediterranean Coast), one of nine cities bearing Seleucus' name, was also prominent ("SELEUCIA," Vol. 5, *The Zondervan Pictorial Encyclopedia of the Bible*, 1976 ed., p. 331). Today's Iraq, the capital of which is Baghdad, not only contains the ancient cities of Babylon and Nineveh, but it was the heartland of the Seleucid dynasty, from which arose Antiochus IV.

in general, but The Messiah, whom ancient Israel *and* the pagan world acknowledged as both "The Desire of women" (Dan 11:37) *and* "The Desire of all nations" (Hag 2:7)—the promised Seed whom women desired to bear from antiquity (Gen 3:15). In fact, Daniel 11:40-45 depicts the King of the North, or Iraq, in a future conflict with the King of the South, or Egypt, so that the King of the North shall overflow Egypt and overthrow other countries, come against Israel, and then ultimately be destroyed in connection with "news from the east and the north" (cf. Jer 51:33). The King of the North "shall regard neither the gods [Heb., *elohee*] of his fathers nor The Desire of women,[1] nor regard any judge [god; Heb., *eloha*]; for he shall magnify himself above *them* all. But in their place he shall honor a god of fortresses [munitions]; and a god which his fathers did not know he shall honor with gold and silver, with precious stones and pleasant things. Thus he shall act against the strongest fortresses with a foreign god, which he shall acknowledge, *and* advance *its* glory; and he shall cause them to rule over many, and divide the land for profit" (Dan 11:37-39, Heb.; cf. Rev 6:7-8). In their proper contexts, these prophecies all speak of what is now Iraq; they do not speak of the AntiChrist, but of a separate player who shall come upon the world scene during the seven-year *Tribulation Week* or Tribulation Period.[2] To conclude *on this basis* that the AntiChrist will be the King of the North, an apostate[3] Jew or a "Christian" who has rejected the "God" of his fathers, or a homosexual who rejects the "desire of women," is, in all candor, to show some ignorance of the subject matter. As a result of this kind of *eisegesis*, many Chris-

---

1. In the Zodiac, The Messiah is called "The Desired One" (cf. Hag 2:6-7). For details, see the chapter (or section) "The Gospel and the Zodiac," in the volume titled, *Conflict of the Aeons: Understanding the Protoevangelium,* of the author's *Messiah, History, and the Tribulation Period* series.

2. Modern scholars generally overlook the fact that Iraq, the heartland of ancient Assyria and Babylonia, is the historical land of the King of the North, whom the prophet Daniel predicted would conquer much of the Middle East and come against Israel and Mount Zion in the last four years of the Tribulation Period (Dan 11:40-45). When the first edition of this book went to press, Iraq's Saddam Hussein had been preparing to play the same role in modern history that Babylon's Nebuchadnezzar II played in the destruction of ancient Jerusalem.

    While the Mystery Babylon of the Apocalypse is a global, spiritual Babylon of the last days, possibly with Roman Catholicism at its heart, the Old Testament contains numerous prophecies that apply solely to the role of ancient Babylon (i.e., Babylon in the land of the Chaldeans) *in the Tribulation Period.* The last days, therefore, will see prominent roles for both the ancient Babylon of history under the King of the North and the worldwide, figurative Babylon under the AntiChrist. Unlike other works, this book and the author's forthcoming *Messiah, History, and the Tribulation Period* multi-volume series recognize these distinctions. For a balanced and thorough treatment of the different, but connected roles to be played by the literal Babylon of Iraq and the figurative Babylon of the world in the Tribulation Period, see the chapter "The Latter Halves of the Crucifixion, History, and Tribulation Weeks," in the volume titled, *Messiah's Preeminence in History and Prophecy: The Heart of Israelology, Eschatology, and God's Holy Days,* of the *Messiah, History, and the Tribulation Period* series.

3. The word "apostate" means "fallen away," and it's herein used to denote those who fundamentally abandon or reject the plain and clear truth of God's written Word, and in so doing, abandon both The God of Israel and the one true faith (i.e., biblical Judaism, which is generally known as Christianity). That word's use, like "heretic," is not meant as an aspersion, but as a description of spiritual state.

tians now have misguided expectations concerning the AntiChrist. Likewise, he is to be distinguished from the Assyrian king and the Babylonian king of various Old Testament prophecies that are as yet unfulfilled, or which have a greater future fulfillment.

We must be more careful in our handling of the Word of God. Our criteria for recognition of the AntiChrist, let alone understanding any other subject of Bible prophecy, must have a sure foundation. At best, the AntiChrist could *theoretically* be of Assyrian *and* Babylonian descent, as well as of Jewish extraction with "Christian" ancestors, but he must also be a prince of Roman lineage who shall come to rule over the modern Roman Empire (cf. Dan 9:27).[1] This makes the AntiChrist a fundamentally different personage from the King of the North; that is, prophecies given concerning the King of the North do not pertain to the AntiChrist. (Yet, the AntiChrist *could* also be a *sodomite*—even just to fulfill "expectations." It *is* so.)

What about Islam's Mahdi? Many comparing end times biblical prophecy with Islamic teachings, have come to view the *Mahdi* as the AntiChrist. In this, they have likewise *conflated* the *Mahdi* with prophecies concerning the King of the North, essentially making the same mistakes as those just addressed. *The Mahdi and the King of the North are demonstrably two different individuals.*

In Arabic, the root *hdi* of *mahdi* means "to guide."[2] Many Muslims refer to *the Mahdi* as "the Chosen One"—something Charles' parents called him.[3] Not all Muslims, however, accept the idea of *al-Mahdi* (i.e., "the *Mahdi*"), which is a non-Sunni concept. Common Shia teachings (e.g., in Iran) assert the following:

1. The *Mahdi* directly hails from Mohammed *(i.e., MuHammad)*, and bears Mohammed's name or some variant of it.[4]
2. He looks like an Israelite, and has a broad forehead with a prominent nose.
3. He revives or revitalizes the Muslim religion.[5]

---

1. Non-futurist methods of apocalyptic interpretation are generally beyond the scope of this particular work. However, for a detailed and reliable examination of the major views (i.e., the idealist or symbolic, preterist or contemporary-historicist, historicist, futurist, preterist-futurist, historicist-futurist, etc.), as well as the first true, *Messiah*-centered harmonization of them, see the volume titled *The Harmony of Weeks: God's Inspired "Grand Unified Theology" Unveiled,* in this author's *Messiah, History, and the Tribulation Period* series.
2. Charles refers to *himself* as a "pointer," someone who "guides mankind," who "leads" and "shows the way." As *the* foretold AntiChrist, King Charles III is a counterfeit "way" (cf. John 14:5-6). See ch. 10's coverage of pointers, starting at pp. 339 and 358.
3. Charles' parents called him "the Chosen One" from birth, believing that he "is the Chosen One—placed in line for the throne through a divine, preordained plan" (*Us,* 14 Jan. 1985, pp. 18-19).
4. King Charles III claims descent from "Mohammed, the Prophet of Islam." For more information, see ch. 4's section titled "Supposed descent from David, Jesus, and Mohammed," at p. 100.
5. This is a belief among Sunnis who accept the concept of *al-Mahdi.* These Sunnis hold that the *Mahdi* may not be connected with end-times or Jesus. *Most of the world's Muslims are Sunnis.* Note, therefore, that King Charles III while Prince of Wales, a) privately converted to Islam despite maintaining his facade of being "Christian," b) became "the most popular world leader in the Muslim community

4. He comes on a white horse, conquering.[1]
5. He ushers in "peace and security" or "peace and justice" as the Muslim deliverer or savior, the "promised one." During his rule, there will be good rain, with great harvests and crops.
6. He rules for seven years,[2] during the period of a treaty made with "Christian" Romans—one mediated by an Israelite[3] of Aaronic lineage. Within this period, he achieves global dominion. Subsequently, he dies.
7. He will appear at a time when earthquakes, disasters and great calamities are imminent, when there is great suffering among Muslims.
8. A Muslim army will attack Israel and reach Jerusalem, raising black flags. At that point, his appearance will be imminent.
9. His heart is to be changed "in a night" (i.e., instantly) to take up his responsibility.[4]
10. Allah[5] will cause the peoples of the world to admire and love him, but any who reject Allah are to be conquered by him.
11. He will govern according to the *Sunnah,* which is codified into Islamic Law *(i.e., Shari'a)*—and advocates beheading.
12. He will abolish Israel's corrupt leadership, and subject Israel like the world to *Shari'a.*
13. He will establish his seat of authority in Jerusalem, but also operate or rule from Iraq[6] or even Damascus.

---

throughout the world," c) openly promoted Islam, d) waded into matters of Islamic Law (e.g., with respect to capital punishment), e) received an honorary doctorate from Islam's oldest seat of learning in Cairo, Egypt, and f) accepted a Muslim [(satanist's)] prayer at Llandaff Cathedral, in Cardiff, Wales, following his mother Elizabeth II's death, which he attended: "We hold before you [Allah (i.e., a*l-Ilyah)*], our most gracious King Charles the Third. May your [anti-]wisdom inform him, your [anti-]illumination guide his heart and your [anti-]truth inspire his words and actions. May he serve in [anti-]righteousness and [anti-]truth, doing [anti-]justice" (Catherine Pepinster, "Charles's instincts are to be applauded — but 1,000 years of tradition are at stake. Is it wise for the Christianity of the Coronation to be so diluted in the name of diversity?," *Daily Mail,* 8 Apr. 2023).

Mixing the table of God with the table of demons (cf. 1 Cor 10:20-22), King Charles III, g) made overt satanism, including Islam which he still promotes, and paganism *central* to his May 6, 2023 *anti-Christian* coronation, as *Satan's son.* For more, see ch. 10, "Religious, Political, and Other Ties," at p. 289, and ch. 16, "King Charles III: History's Ultimate AntiChrist," at p. 561.

1. *Some* Muslims identify the rider of the white horse in the Apocalypse's first seal (Rev 6:1-2) as *al-Mahdi.* Others incorporate additional *twisted versions* of biblical events into their signs of *al-Mahdi.* Examples from Islamic scholar Moojan Momen ("Mahdi", *Wikipedia*): "Before his coming will come the red death and the white death. The red death is the sword and white death is the plague" (cf. Rev 6:1-4). (See *North Korea, Iran, and the Coming World War: Behold a Red Horse.*) "The Sun will rise from the West and a star will appear in the East giving out as much light as the Moon" (cf. Isa 30:26). "There will be a great conflict in the land of Syria until it is destroyed" (cf. Isa 17:1).
2. Some "less reliable" Islamic sources say he rules for eight, nine, or even nineteen years.
3. As history's ultimate AntiChrist, King Charles III was foretold and biblically identified (Rev 13:18) while yet an heir to a throne, a prince of Roman lineage (Dan 9:27), per Revelation 13. However, the former Prince of Wales is also of apparent Israelite lineage, via the tribe of Dan, though he claims multiple descends from Judah and King David (see ch. 4).
4. When the AntiChrist is possessed by Satan, he too shall embark on his prophesied mission.
5. Allah is *not* the God of Israel or Christianity; rather, he is *al-Ilyah,* "the Moon god" of pagan Arabia.
6. Note that British troops, not just those of the Untied States, currently operate in Iraq.

14. During his reign, Muslims will kill Israelites, slaughtering the Zionists, and they will likewise kill Christians.
15. He will bring the Ark of the Covenant to Jerusalem.[1]
16. He has *Isa* to assist him.[2]
17. He will convert some Israelites to Islam by means of a different Torah, and will persuade many Christians to leave Christianity by means of a different Gospel, which he discovers.[3] *Isa* too will persuade many Christians to become Muslims.
18. He will enrich Muslims, distributing wealth to them.
19. Allah will bring forth an animal or "beast of the earth" to mark Muslims on the face, so that it glitters, and to mark non-Muslims on the neck and noses, so they are black. This will distinguish Muslims from non-Muslims.[4]

---

1. There will not be an Ark of the Covenant in the Millennial Temple (Jer 3:16). Note, however, that King Charles III studied archaeology at Cambridge's Trinity College, while Prince of Wales.

2. Islam's *Isa* is a *counterfeit* Jesus who is a Muslim prophet. In terms of caricature, he is similar to Revelation's false prophet, who shall assist the AntiChrist. The apostle Paul warned: "But I fear, lest somehow as the serpent deceived Eve in his craftiness, so your thoughts should be corrupted from the purity [sincerity] *that is due* [pertaining] to The Christ. For if, indeed, the *one* coming proclaims another Jesus, whom we have not proclaimed, or *if* you receive another spirit which you have not received, or another gospel which you never *previously* accepted—you *might* well endure [bear with] *these*.... For such *are* false messengers [apostles], deceitful workers, transforming themselves into messengers [apostles] of Christ. And not marvelously! For Satan himself transforms himself into an angel of light. *It is* not *a* great *thing*, then, if his ministers [servants] also transform [disguise] themselves as ministers [servants] of righteousness, whose end will be according to their works" (2 Cor 11:3-4, 11:13-15, Gk.).

3. Concerning false gospels, the apostle Paul warned: "There are some who trouble you, and want to pervert the Gospel of The Messiah. But even if we, or an angel from Heaven, preach any other 'gospel' to you than what we have preached to you, let him be accursed. As we have said before, so now I say again, if anyone preaches any other 'gospel' to you than what you have received, let him be accursed.... But I make known to you, brethren, that the Gospel which was preached by me is not according to man. For I neither received it from man, nor was I taught *it,* but *it came* through the revelation of Jesus The Messiah" (Gal 1:6-12; see Gal 5 to 6; cf. 1 Cor 3:10-11, 9:24-27, 15:58).

4. These are Islamic counterfeits to the seal that 144,000 Christian Israelite men are to receive (Rev 7:1-8, 9:4, 14:1-5), and even counterfeits to the mark of the beast, which they intimate. Remarkably: "The Palestinian Authority Mufti of Jerusalem, Sheikh Mohammed Hussein ... warned of attempts by Jewish groups to establish a presence on the Temple Mount. [Liar extraordinaire] Hussein told the [so-called] Palestinian news agency *Khabar* that the entire holy site is Islamic and belongs only to Muslims. 'We affirm, time and again, that the blessed [(no, *cursed* by The God of Israel)] al-Aqsa Mosque, with its entire area of 144 dunams [144,000 sq.m.], is Islamic and only for Muslims,' he said. 'There is no place for non-Muslims ... in this mosque...'" (Khaled Abu Toameh, "PA mufti: No room for non-Muslims on Temple Mount," Jerusalem Post, 16 Dec. 2020). Jordan's Foreign Ministry similarly lies against Israel and God. For example: "Jordan ... again condemned visits by Jews to the Temple Mount.... Referring to visits by Jews..., the ministry [dishonestly] said: 'Under the protection of the Israeli forces, extremists recently stormed the holy site. These rejected and reckless provocations are a violation of [(illicit)] international law and the legal and [(falsely claimed)] historical status quo, which breach Israel's obligations as the [(not)] occupying power in east Jerusalem'" (ibid.). For more information, see ch. 14, "The Image, Statue, and Mark of the Beast," at p. 505. Also, see chs. "Seals in the Bible" and "144,000 Sealed Israelite Servants," in the vol. titled, *The Real Rapture and Other Prophetic Mysteries: Understanding the Revelation (Apocalypse),* of the *Messiah, History, and the Tribulation Period* series.

20. *Isa* will kill *ad-Dajjal*,[1] who supernaturally torments the world.[2]
21. Some Muslim sects believe the *Mahdi* and *Isa* to be the same person!

As you shall discover herein, there is one man today who could soon fulfill the role of *al-Mahdi* to the world's Muslims—the prophesied AntiChrist, who is the subject of this work. Yet *Shiite* scholars are not in total agreement regarding *al-Mahdi; in fact,* many contradictions permeate their religious *babel.*[3] The above list, therefore, represents only a core set of beliefs with which most Shiites would agree. Even so, Muslims will not expect a perfect fulfillment of the list—only something that seems "close enough."

Herein, you'll discover that King Charles III is not only a credible "shoe-in" for Shia Islam's Mahdi, but his popularity among Sunnis also is unrivaled: "Although some Britons may be bewildered at Prince Charles's infatuation with Islam, he has become a hero among Muslims. His February 1997 visit to Saudi Arabia '…was huge news…, [so that the] …. warmth of his welcome was extraordinary.' …John Casey of Cambridge University, warns that the British [(really, Western)] public lacks a clear understanding of Charles's standing in the Muslim world: 'The extent to which the Prince is admired by Muslims—even to the point of hero-worship—has not yet sunk into the consciousness of the … public. …' Casey concludes that the Prince of Wales's 'hero status' in the Arab world is permanent. 'No other Western figure commands this sort of admiration.' [In] …. May 1997, Prince Bandar bin Sultan of Saudi Arabia announced a donation by King Fahd of $33 million to Oxford University, to construct a new Centre for Islamic Studies at Oxford—a gift designed 'to establish Islamic studies at the heart of the British education system.' … Should Charles persist in his admiration of Islam and defamation of his own culture, it could be … that his accession to the throne will indeed usher in a 'different kind of monarchy.'"[4]

---

1. *Ad-Dajjal*, meaning "the deceiver" or liar, is Islam's *counterfeit* evil one or "antiChrist." *Ad-Dajjal* is a confused character in Islamic eschatology. On the one hand, he lines up with either of the New Testament's two witnesses, but on the other he lines up with the biblical AntiChrist. The *Dajjal* a) is one-eyed or only has sight in one eye (cf. Zechariah's idol shepherd {11:17, AKJV}, and the unicorn displaying just one [bulging] eye on Charles' (retained) heraldic achievement as Prince of Wales {p. 197}); b) is mistaken by unregenerate Israel as her true Messiah; and c) is possessed by Satan and worshiped as Allah (i.e., "God") by unbelievers (i.e., non-Muslims), until the trumpet heralding the Day of Judgment is blown (cf. Jesus' return at the last trumpet). Yet, like either of the two witnesses, the *Dajjal* a) is a non-Muslim; b) supernaturally torments the world; c) will invite the people "to a wrong religion" (cf. Christianity); d) has the power to raise the dead; e) commands rain and drought; and f) will be followed by tens of thousands (i.e., 70,000) of Persian Israelites.
2. Compare this with Jesus' two witnesses, who will be killed by the AntiChrist at the end of the Great Tribulation, when they have completed their testimony (see Rev 11:3-10).
3. Muslim writings and teachings, apart from Mohammed's plagiarizations from the Old Testament, are nothing like genuine scripture. In fact, they are riddled with confusion and self-contradictions, and often actually come across as demonic and hallucinatory, as if written while "stoned."
4. Ronni L. Gordon and David M. Stillman, "Prince Charles of Arabia," *Middle East Quarterly: Middle East*

Friend, have you heard the *footsteps* of the AntiChrist? Is there anyone in the world today who meets all these qualifications? Undoubtedly, many Christians would answer "yes," pointing to someone such as Rome's pope, the King of Spain, Klaus Schwab, Bill Gates or "the like"—just as many previously pointed to others, including some overtly wicked men. "The list goes on." Yet, while these individuals are and were antichristian, respectively, none of them meets the required qualifications or "musts," let alone the "shoulds." In fact, with just *one* exception, no human being has ever met more than half of them. Who is that exception? Before answering this question directly, let's first consider the method of the AntiChrist's eventual rise to political power in the light of history, apocalyptic prophecy, and a few current events.

Global government and the AntiChrist. The Roman Empire had its religious, political, military, and economic roots in ancient Babylon, which in turn had its own in the Tower of Babel. Offering no apologies and showing no shame, the modern European Union has depicted this very tower under construction below an inverted pentagram of twelve stars, a parody of its own counterfeit crown. The EU's purpose, therefore, is to preside over the construction of a final "Babylon project," or the much heralded New World Order. Of course, the Council of Europe began to show its true colors early on, when the president of its Consultative Assembly from 1949 to 1951, Paul-Henri Spaak, proclaimed: "What we want is <u>a man of sufficient stature to hold the allegiance of all people</u>, and to lift us out of the economic morass in which we are sinking. Send us such a man and, <u>be he god or the devil</u>, we will receive him."[1] Indeed, Mr. Spaak was curiously ahead of the game and its plan: **King Charles III, hailed as "a man of such stature" that he "is able to speak for all of us," is now idolized as an angelic "winged god" and presented to mankind as "Saviour of the World!"**[2] *Friend, this is **serious**!*

In the latter half of the fourth-century A.D., Emperor Valentinian split the Roman Empire into two divisions, as depicted by the two

---

Forum, Sep. 1997, pp. 3-7.

1. Hilton, *The Principality and Power of Europe*, pp. 19, 113 (emphasis added). The European Union's flag depicts a crown of twelve gold stars against a light blue field. It specifically took this imagery from the woman crowned with twelve stars in Revelation 12. The primary interpretation of that woman, in context, would be that she represents faithful or believing Israel, in which case her crown of stars represent at once the twelve tribes of Israel and the twelve apostles of Christ, to whom the woman gave birth. This is a complex apocalyptic metaphor, one that has important secondary interpretations. However, none of those interpretations may be harmonized with the EU's perversion of the imagery to represent itself. Indeed, the EU was more straightforward when it depicted those same stars in the arrangement of an inverted pentagram (ibid., pp. 49-50).

2. For more information, see ch. 10's section titled "Respect," at p. 388, and ch. 14's section titled "The Statue," at p. 506. Note that these events occurred four years *after* the first edition of this work (ISBN 0-9662793-0-1) was published.

legs in the statue of Nebuchadnezzar's prophetic dream (cf. Dan 2:33), not to mention the two horns of the false prophet (Rev 13:11). The Western Roman Empire retained Rome for its capital and maintained the Roman Catholic Church, whereas the Eastern Roman Empire adopted Constantinople (Byzantium) and formed the Eastern Orthodox Church.

Today, the most powerful country in the West, and perhaps the world, is the United States of America. It also happens to be the home of the United Nations—the embryo of a coming one-world government. The permanent member-states of the United Nations' Security Council currently include Russia, France, China, England, and the United States—the central powers in the Roman Empire over the past several centuries. Even so, the basic East-West division remains, with Russia representing the East and the United States representing the West. Soon, however, in preparation for a global government under the AntiChrist, ten horns or kings (representing nations or kingdoms—probably the world's most powerful and/or populous) will arise and supersede these divisions (cf. Dan 7:20a, 7:24a; Rev 12:3, 13:1, 17:3, 17:7, 17:12). Five will arise from each division (the statue had five toes per foot), being, it would appear, both autocratic and democratic (the feet and toes were a mixture of iron and clay; cf. Dan 2:41-43). This East-West group of ten will, in effect, govern the entire Earth.

Ten horns or kings will therefore constitute the governing body of the final form of the Roman Empire. These kings will be *contemporaries,* so that five shall arise from the East and five from the West. Notice, therefore, that three of the ten kings will be subdued, perhaps in an effort to consolidate power, by an unusual little horn (cf. Lam 2:17)—the AntiChrist—who shall come in among them as the eleventh (see Dan 7:8, 7:20-21, 7:24-25).[1] Thus, we are told in the Apocalypse that "the beast that was, and is not, is himself also the eighth, and is of the seven..." (Rev 17:11). That is, when counted with the seven contemporary kings who remain in direct power, the AntiChrist will be the eighth, while at the same time, perhaps genealogically, being "of the seven."[2] Nevertheless, the Apocalypse

---

1. In speaking of the rise of "the worthless shepherd" over Israel, Zechariah indicated that three other shepherds—presumably Lebanon, Bashan, and Jordan (according to context)—would be "dismissed ... in one month" (see Zech 11:1-9, 11:15-17, KJV; cf. Zech 10:2-3; John 10:12-13). This prophecy foreshadows the ultimate "worthless shepherd," or the AntiChrist, who will quickly subdue three of ten kings or "shepherds."

2. Some have observed that according to the *World Book Encyclopedia,* seven emperors of the "Holy Roman Empire" were named Charles. They then note that Satan's Prince is a descendant of Charles V, and that Charles would supposedly be Charles VIII. In the 1998 first edition of this book, the author stated, "This view is flawed, in that Prince Charles has said that he will one day be known as King Charles III (not VIII),"—and that is what's now occurred. Moreover, by the apostle John's day, the fifth king or kingdom had fallen (Rev 17:10), whereas Charles V was born over a millennium *after* John. Since 1998,

also indicates that there will yet be *ten* kings, not just seven, under the AntiChrist at the time of Jesus' posttribulational return (Rev 17:12-14). With this in mind, we have no choice but to conclude that the subdued kings will be retained and/or replaced, so that the total number of ten is maintained. If the AntiChrist is to keep his status as the eighth king, however, then these other three would necessarily become his vassals over their respective nations or kingdoms.

This can be a difficult scenario to envision, yet *there is a plausible means by which the AntiChrist's government could without suspicion or significant delay be so formed.* For example, should a *third* nation from the European Union (e.g., Germany), along with four other nations (e.g., Brazil, India, Japan, and Mexico), become a permanent member-state of the UN Security Council, as proposed (see below), and should the AntiChrist then arise over the EU *as its royal king or head,* the world would *suddenly* have just such a government. That is, the nations would awake one morning only to find that the AntiChrist had automatically acquired (been granted really) sovereignty over three of the ten permanent member-states—England, France, and presumably Germany—governing them, giving him a major or even decisive influence over the other seven. Such a scenario seems most feasible, in the author's opinion, should the AntiChrist be from England, the land that has given the modern world its most widely spoken language—English—and which opposed Nazi Germany and its French collaborators in World War II.[1]

At this point, we would do well, perhaps, to recall the infamous program falsely styled as "The Protocols of the Elders of Zion," which, having been circulated throughout much of the twentieth and early twenty-first centuries, states: "Certain members of the seed of

---

others have tried alternate though similar machinations around the name "Charles," but these arguments likewise fail under similar scrutiny. While the author gives the correct interpretation below, he does *not* suggest that the name "Charles" is prophetically *insignificant.* To the contrary, *the name "Charles" is intimated in the Hebrew text of Daniel 9:27,* which is a key prophecy concerning the AntiChrist, and as such, it is a very meaningful name indeed (see ch. 12, "Charles, Middle East 'Peace,' and Global Security," at p. 481).

The seven kings or *kingdoms* of Revelation 17:10-11, while serving as a prophetic introduction to the seven of ten *contemporary* kings, so that the AntiChrist "is himself also the eighth," as outlined above, are *first of all* the seven *successive* world *kingdoms* of history (preceding the Millennial Kingdom of Christ): "five have fallen" (i.e., Egypt, Assyria, Babylonia, Medo-Persia, and Greece), "one is" (i.e., Rome—from the apostle John's day until now—which constitutes a metamorphosed revival of the ancient Babylonian Empire), and "the other has not yet come, and when he [it] comes, he [it] must continue a short while" (Gk.; cf. Rev 12:12, 13:5). This seventh kingdom, which "has not yet come," will be the global kingdom under the AntiChrist centered at Mystery Babylon, which, although it shall scripturally represent the final form of the Roman Empire in world history (e.g., its ten kings derive from the East-West division of the Roman Empire), shall also be unique. The AntiChrist's global kingdom will, in both a literal and an historical sense, be "of the seven" (e.g., religiously, politically, and militarily).

1. For more information, see the chapter (or section) "The History of the Roman Empire and its Modern Thirst for Oil," in the volume titled, *The Prophetic Stage: Signs of the Times,* of the author's *Messiah, History, and the Tribulation Period* series.

David will prepare the Kings and their heirs.... Only the King and the three who stood sponsor for him will know what is coming." Note the phrase "the three who stood sponsor for him." These blasphemous "protocols" appear not to have originated with true Israelites, per se, but with the English-dominated, French-English oligarchical *Priory of Zion*. Consequently, as would be expected from the British monarchy's claims to supposed *Davidic* descent, they purport to plot the establishment of a worldwide "Masonic kingdom" with "an international church" under "the King of the Jews" who "will be the real Pope."[1]

As shown below, globalists have been planning their world government around a future UN Security Council consisting of ten permanent member-states. Following Gorbachev's revelation of the fact in 1992, a media blackout ensued. In 1997, however, a number of articles were suddenly released on the issue, indicating that the planned expansion may be just around the corner:

> What he seems to envision is a transition from the system of nation states, inherited from the 18th century, to a more internationalized system that can be more effective in many areas, from controlling nuclear weapons to protecting human rights. He wants a stronger United Nations, with new [permanent] members—including Japan, Germany, Mexico, Brazil and India—added to the Security Council. He wants ... to build on trends toward interdependence already set in motion.
>
> Gorbachev said the world's peoples face a turning point in history and need new ways to cope with the challenges, from pollution to economic disparities between rich and poor nations. One way to this end, he added, is to work for greater world integration of "all spheres of human activity," and to do so in the framework of a "democratically organized world community."
>
> Only by moving in this direction, Gorbachev said, can the world hope to control the deadly rivalries that have flared anew among nations and ethnic groups....
>
> [In fact,] ... many other political thinkers are embracing similar views. They cite growing world acceptance of treaties on nuclear proliferation and acid rain, and increasing respect for making basic rights globally enforceable....
>
> The former Soviet president is hardly alone in envisioning a strikingly new era of adjustment in the world order. Professor Joseph Nye of Harvard, in the current issue of *Foreign Affairs,* writes that the classic concept of sovereign national states is eroding under "the rapid growth in transnational communications, migration and economic interdependence." This suggests, he adds, that the ideas of "divisible and transferable sovereignty may play an increasing part in a new world order."

---

1. Michael Baigent, Richard Leigh, and Henry Lincoln, *Holy Blood, Holy Grail* {New York: Dell Publishing, 1983}, pp. 191-195. Please note that the authors of *Holy Blood, Holy Grail* are antichristian, and their works are contrary to God's inspired Word. For more information, see ch. 4, "Prince of this World—a *Diverse* Lineage," at p. 79.

....[Nye argues that] Americans should welcome it. Why? Because, says Nye, it promotes stability and security and reduces the risk of nasty surprises.[1]

UNITED NATIONS — A proposal to enlarge the United Nations Security Council from 15 to 24 members by adding five new members with permanent seats and another four serving a two-year term each, was presented Thursday by the chairman of a working group which has been studying council reform for the past three years.

The proposal was drawn up by Razali Ismail, Malaysia's representative, who is also president of this year's General Assembly.

It represents his best attempt to find a compromise on the immensely sensitive issue of the future composition of the organ charged with maintaining international peace and security acceptable to the largest number of United Nations' members.

"The underpinnings of this proposal are based on the need to enhance the representativeness, the credibility, the legitimacy and the authority of the Security Council," Razali told the working group Thursday, saying they would strengthen the council's ability "to deal with issues of peace and security."

The plan calls for the election of two new permanent council members drawn from the industrialized world.

The seats are likely to go to Germany and Japan, both of which are seeking permanent membership in recognition of their economic strength.

The three other new permanent members would be drawn from Africa, Asia and Latin America respectively.[2]

UNITED NATIONS — The United States will recommend that three permanent seats on the U.N. Security Council be given to developing countries to strengthen their role in global affairs, U.S. officials announced Thursday.

U.S. Ambassador Bill Richardson said the United States also would support permanent membership for Germany and Japan, raising the number of council members from 15 to 20. Currently, 10 of the 15 are chosen by region and serve two-year terms but do not have veto power.

---

1. Brian Dickinson, Scripps Howard News Service, "Gorbachev envisions warmer post-Cold War world," *Rocky Mountain News,* 11 May 1992, p. 53.

    According to (the late) Gorbachev, there is an "emerging [international] ... awareness of the need for some kind of global government—one in which all members of the world community would take part" (Lindsey, *Planet Earth—2000 A.D.,* p. 57). In establishing his "Gorbachev Foundation USA," he pontificated, "This is the symbol of our irreversible transition from an era of confrontation and militaristic insanity to a New World Order, one that promises dividends for all" (*The Los Angeles Times,* 17 Apr. 1993; see Lindsey, *Planet Earth—2000 A.D.,* p. 61). As the embryo of a world government, to complement a stronger World Court, Gorbachev advocated a greatly strengthened United Nations, one that would possess its own international police force and military structure, incorporating not only the conventional forces of its permanent member-states, but even their nuclear weapons. Such a government, Gorbachev held, could best serve the cause of peace in our day and have the power necessary to enforce the collective security of the world in the process. Regarding a stronger World Court, we may note the UN's *Genocide Treaty.* Signed even by the United States, this treaty has to date largely been ignored by the UN Security Council in the face of true ethnic atrocities and widespread infanticide. In the future, however, it could be used to imprison or execute Christians for a wide variety of "offenses," including opposition to cults, other religions, immorality, and the mark of the beast.
2. The New York Times, "Security Council expansion backed," *The Denver Post,* 21 Mar. 1997, p. 19A.

Richardson said a special U.N. committee studying Security Council reform should decide whether the new permanent members would have the same veto power as the United States, Britain, France, Russia and China.

In Washington, State Department spokesman Nicholas Burns said it was up to the developing countries from Asia, Africa and Latin America to decide whether to choose a permanent representative or rotate countries in and out of the seats.

Supporting an enhanced U.N. role for the developing world appeared to be designed at least in part to win their support for Secretary-General Kofi Anan's plan to restructure the U.N. bureaucracy.[1]

India is seeking a permanent seat on the Security Council when the U.N. expands its membership.[2]

UNITED NATIONS — After a crucial push from the United States, the United Nations is about to tackle the tough issue of expanding the 15-member Security Council, the most powerful single agency in the world body.

If the changes go through, Germany, Japan and three or more nations from the developing world will join the United States, Britain, China, France and Russia as permanent members of the council.

The result, supporters say, would be a group more reflective of today's balance of power and more authoritative in its efforts to maintain global law and order....

But the risk is that the power of authoritarian, antidemocratic states within the United Nations would increase and the influence of the United States diminish.

Bill Richardson, the U.S. envoy who has propelled the process forward...., views the challenge with characteristic optimism. "We're going all out to get (Germany and Japan) on the Security Council," he told reporters here before launching a 10-nation trip largely devoted to cultivating support in world capitals for council changes and other U.N. reforms....

While the United Nations is made up of 185 countries, each with an equal vote in the General Assembly, the real seat of power is in the elite membership of the Security Council.

And, to paraphrase George Orwell, in the Security Council, some countries are more equal than others, for the five permanent members are endowed by the U.N. Charter with veto power over any council action.

The U.S. goal is to win agreement on a framework for council expansion by year's end and postpone until later some of the toughest decisions, including which developing countries get to join Germany and Japan as new members and whether any get veto power....

Giving Germany and Japan permanent status, supporters say, would recognize their economic and diplomatic clout. Similarly, adding developing countries would grant recognition to the emerging importance of nations such as South Africa, Egypt, India and the "economic tigers" of Southeast Asia.[3]

---

1. Robert H. Reid, The Associated Press, "Developing countries posed for U.N. panel," *The Denver Post,* 18 July 1997, p. 23A. Also see "U.S. eyes expanded U.N. council," *Rocky Mountain News,* 18 July 1997, p. 52A.

2. Ved Nanda, "50 years of Indian independence," *The Denver Post,* 15 Aug. 1997, p. 7B.

3. Craig Turner, Los Angeles Times, "U.N. may expand Security Council," *The Denver Post,* 17 Aug. 1997,

2

A Man for Our Times

In *The English Constitution,* the Victorian constitutionalist Walter Bagehot made this tantalizing statement: "All the world and the glory of it, whatever is most attractive, whatever is most seductive, has always been offered to the Prince of Wales of the day, and always will be. It is not rational to expect the best virtue where temptation is applied in the most trying form at the frailest time of human life."[1] (It is *too late* for William, as only years from now, the British monarchy the world has known will be cast down to Hell.) At Buckingham Palace on November 14, 1948, just six months after the birth of modern Israel, Prince Charles was born; the following day, he was christened. Then the baby prince was circumcised by non-Christian "rabbi" Jacob Snowman—commencing Charles' (twice the child of Hell) "Israelite" life.[2]

In 1970, surrounded by undergraduates at Cambridge University, notwithstanding the fact that the British monarchy is "the largest constitutional monarchy remaining in the world, [and] ... the highest remaining office on earth attained by birthright,"[3] the then prince, whose worldwide popularity continues to increase, began to make his global aspirations known. Charles declared, "I want to be King of Europe!"[4] In 1990, *Majesty* magazine had this to say:

> As a new closeness develops between the member countries of the EEC [(European Economic Community, replaced by the European Union)], questions are being raised about the role that ... Charles might play in a future United States of Europe.... When he was at Cambridge, Prince

p. 4A.

1. Anthony Holden, *PRINCE CHARLES* (New York: Atheneum, 1979), p. xxiii. Royalty, 1994, Vol. 13, No. 2, p. 47.
2. "The London Jewish community's official Mohel Jacob Snowman performed the [circumcision] surgery on baby Prince Charles in Buckingham Palace, days after his 1948 birth" (Georgia L. Gilholy, "Why are male members of the royal family circumcised by a mohel?," *The Jewish Chronicle,* 10 Jan. 2023). "Extensive commentary has claimed that the [(recent)] circumcision of British royals [ostensibly] began due to Queen Victoria's [(alleged)] belief that she was descended from the biblical King David" (ibid.).
3. Alan Hamilton, *The Royal 100* (London: Pavilion Books Ltd., 1986), p. 22.
4. Media and others present presumed that then Prince Charles joked when he made this declaration. We're told: "Prince Charles's student joke might well become a reality. Of all the senior members of European Royal Families, Charles is undoubtedly the best qualified to lead a United States of Europe" ("The King of Europe," *Majesty* magazine, Nov. 1990, Vol. 11 – No. 11 {ISSN 0144-6932}, p. 29). However, as this work makes abundantly clear, Chalres could not have been more serious. Today, it is clear that King Charles III's aspirations go far beyond "merely" being the future monarch of Europe.

Charles was asked what he wanted to do after he left the university. He paused and then said, 'I want to be King of Europe.' ...

Sir William Rees-Mogg, a former editor of The Times and a leading constitutionalist, believes that, 'A natural role for the British monarchy in the next century would be as the leading royal house of Europe.' ... It is generally assumed that the House of Windsor would always come first in this [European royal] pecking order, both because of its ancient roots and continuity, and because of its unique standing in the world.

But there is another reason why the British Royal Family can put forward such a strong case. Prince Charles has personally made his influence felt throughout the European community in a way that no other royal [ever] has.... ...Charles focused his attention beyond Britain's shores long ago. In 1970, when he was 23, he chaired the Welsh steering committee for European Conservation Year.... He has been, in effect, a committed European for two decades.

His contacts have strengthened over those years. His family's German connections have helped Charles understand the nature of Europe's most economically successful nation. At the other end of the scale, the friendship he [(and his father Prince Philip)] forged with King Juan Carlos [I] of Spain ... has given him an insight into the problems of nations with less highly developed economies.[1]

His love of Italy, growing ever stronger as he returns to paint there each year, has taught him that there are cultures just as ancient as his own which need protection.... Perhaps it is in this sphere, above any other, that Charles has the most useful role to play: as a spokesman for the common man confronted by the system. It is a responsibility he has been eager to take on in Britain....

Even more fascinatingly, there is another important consideration to be made when viewing Charles's suitability as a pan-European figurehead. With the change in East-West relations, symbolized by the removal of the Berlin Wall, there is a group of once-royal countries who will soon be seeking to join the European Economic Community—Yugoslavia, Hungary and Romania spring immediately to mind....

....Their admiration of the British Royal Family can only serve to further Charles's cause. The Prince has made a particular hit in Italy and in France, and is rightly seen by those nations as a better bet than their own disenfranchised Royals when it comes to being the figurehead of a united Europe. Charles has earned respect because he has not been afraid to speak his mind [to defend the weaker and common man].... In particular, the Prince's outspoken attack on the wholesale destruction of villages and communities in Romania—made while the Ceaucescu regime was still at its most potent—won him millions of admirers in that country.

[A] ... number of political observers have suggested that it would be the Prince of Wales [(now King Charles III)] to whom Europeans would turn, rather than his mother. His track record has been one of constant forward thinking about the opportunities available in Europe....

....**If the seemingly impossible occurs, and member nations [of the EEC] grow closer through monetary, economic and political union, the Prince's assumption of the role of 'King of Europe' will happen auto-**

---

1. The British and Spanish royal families have vacationed together (Brian Hoey, *Charles & Diana: The Tenth Anniversary* {England: Colour Library Books Ltd., 1991}, pp.142-143, 152-153).

matically. No current member of any Royal Family in the world has such an impact as Charles. He is tailor-made for the job.[1]

In March 1995, in a passionate speech to the British Council, then Prince Charles stated, "We must act now to ensure that English—and that, to my way of thinking, means English English—maintains its position as the world language well into the next century."[2] King Farouk once said, "Soon there will be only five kings [in the world]—four in a pack of cards, and the King of England."[3]

Helen Cathcart observed, before he had even reached the age of thirty, that heredity had "already caused the personality of Prince Charles to be more assiduously studied and underscored by historians than that of any other young man of our contemporary world.... On his mother's side alone the compound is bewilderingly English, Scottish, Welsh, Danish, Germanic, Dutch, French and Russian, with traces of Spanish, Portuguese and other elements sufficient for the Common Market community to view him as a characteristic contemporary synthesis of European man.... Charles may claim to be the

---

1. Christopher Wilson, "The King of Europe," *Majesty* magazine, Nov. 1990, Vol. 11 – No. 11 (ISSN 0144-6932), pp. 26-29. In the July 11, 1994, broadcast of *Jack Van Impe Presents,* Mrs. Van Impe noted, "Here is the man who would *like to play* a prominent role in the E.U. and the New World Order; his name is Prince Charles." The late Jack Van Impe, who categorically asserted, "The AntiChrist will arise out of the European Union," responded, "Prince Charles has put in a request to become the King of the European Union—the head man!" While mistakenly touting Satan's Prince as a possibility for the false prophet (if King Charles III is anything, he is *the* AntiChrist), Mr. Van Impe also pointed out that Charles seeks to be the king and religious head of, among others, those who adhere to Zoroastrianism (see below), the *old Babylonian religion* (KDVR TV Fox 31, as well as TBN TV 47 and 57 {Denver, CO}). Zoroastrianism, which predicates itself upon the ancient struggle of good against evil, is believed to have originated with Zarathushtra among the Aryans of ancient Persia, whose antichristian religious philosophy may itself be traced back to the "Indo-Iranians," then to the "Indo-Europeans," and finally to the Tower of Babel. The Achaemenid dynasty, which ruled the later Medo-Persian Empire after Babylonia had been conquered under Cyrus the Great, spread Zoroastrianism to Babylonia and elsewhere. The main royal palace of the Achaemenids was Persepolis in Persia. The still later Parthian Empire, so-named after the region of Persia from which it arose, again took up the cause of Zoroastrianism, making it a major world religion by the first century A.D., when the ancient Roman Empire was at its zenith. Under subsequent Muslim persecution, some Zoroastrians left Persia in the tenth century for India, where they became known as the Parsis. While thousands of Zoroastrians remain in Persia, the Parsis now have Zoroastrian communities not only in India, but also in Pakistan, East Africa, Britain (primarily in London), the United States of America (primarily in New York), and Canada (*Eerdmans' Handbook to the World's Religions* England, 1982; rpt. Michigan: Wm. B. Eerdmans Publishing Co., 1987}, pp. 80-87, 221).

     Anthony Holden, in *King Charles III,* offered this "enticement" concerning Prince Charles' future: "The new King Charles III ... reigns over a proud but tired old Britain.... The monarchy is as popular as ever, thanks to Charles's hard work during the old age of his late mother.... [Prince] ... William ... has high hopes ... to ensure that his father's profile appears on the new 'Eurodollar' banknotes soon to be standardized throughout the EEC" ({London: George Weidenfeld & Nicolson Limited, 1988}, p. 203).

2. "Charles: Stop dissin' English," *The Denver Post,* 26 March 1995, p. 2A. After then Prince Charles first delivered this speech, the U.S. congress introduced and passed legislation "to declare English the official language of the United States and limit the federal government from conducting business in foreign tongues" ("Official English bill passes the House," *The Denver Post,* 2 Aug. 1996, p. 22A).

3. As Junor tells it: "King Farouk of Egypt, deposed by a military coup in 1952, once predicted that by the year 2000 there would be only five monarchs left in Europe: the four kings in a pack of cards and the King of England. He could yet be proved right" (p. 259).

most democratic Prince of Wales ever bred."[1] Cathcart, in a some-what remarkable allusion to Charles' early global aspirations, adds: "Chevening lies only twenty-two miles southeast from the heart of London.... [In] Chevening the heir to the throne saw a country house where he could visualise entertaining European and Com-monwealth heads of government in his own way, where world lead-ers of every clime would be able to meet in small groups while enjoying his hospitality, forging new friendships while beneath his roof. It would be entertainment without political or government strings, informal and eventually in a family atmosphere, like the Commonwealth itself.... ....In America, on meeting some ladies who called themselves 'Daughters of the British Empire', as members of an association by that name, he had pressed tender nerves.... 'It would make you more relevant,' he said, 'if you called yourselves "Daughters of the British Commonwealth". And when I come back next, I hope you'll be calling yourselves "Daughters of THE Com-monwealth".'"[2] Although Princess Diana had once said of Charles, "He is a doting daddy and does everything perfectly,"[3] his priorities are elsewhere: In 1991, as his son William was undergoing emer-gency surgery for a near-fatal head wound,[4] "Prince Charles left [the hospital] to go to Covent Garden opera house, where he was host to a party of European Community officials."[5]

Comprised of fifty-six nations and about one-third of the world's population and a quarter of Earth's land (cf. Rev 6:8), the Common-wealth of Britain represents all that is *overtly* left of Britain's once globe-encircling empire. ("Dubbed" individuals are yet styled "KBE," or Knights of the British *Empire.*) Meeting every two years, the Commonwealth remains linked by Britain's language (English), *monarchy, Illuminist (Luciferian) Freemasonry*—and cricket. As one writer put it, "Britain still presumes to wield a special sort of global influence."[6] (Actually, she does—and it is by no means benign.) Charles as Prince of Wales, for example, observed, "I am sure many people consider that the United Kingdom is in an ideal geographical

1. Helen Cathcart, *Prince Charles* (New York: Taplinger Publishing Co., 1977), pp. 1-3. As of 1998, perhaps more biographies and other biographical material had *already* been written on Charles Philip Arthur George than *any other contemporary figure,* living or dead, and yet the (then) prince has only *just be-gun* to make his mark in the annals of history. For more information regarding King Charles III's lineage, see ch. 4, "Prince of this World—a *Diverse* Lineage," at p. 79.
2. Cathcart, pp. 158-159. Daughters of the British Empire, which has about 5,000 members nationally, "is comprised of British immigrants, many of whom are war brides, English women who married American servicemen during World War II" (Stacie Oulton, "Denver-area residents pay respects to a princess," *The Denver Post,* 7 Sept. 1997, p. 15A).
3. *Charles & Diana: A Royal Family Album* (New York: Summit Books, 1991), p. 30.
4. As shown in ch. 3, "A Name that Calculates to 666," Prince William is *not* the foretold AntiChrist.
5. "Diana, Her True Story," *Good Housekeeping,* August 1992, p. 178.
6. Maureen Johnson, "Empire wanes, but Britons keep stiff upper lips," *The Denver Post,* 10 Oct. 1993, p. 21A.

and historical position to act as an interpreter and mediator between the United States and Europe."[1] From the British monarchy's standpoint, as we shall see, "all roads lead to London." Adrian Hilton states: "It is yet to be decided who will actually *play* Charlemagne in the new empire, but the political leaders—particularly of France and Germany—understand that monetary economics is the instrument of political leadership, and that the wider the currency's domain, the greater the power of those who control it.... The truth is that Britain is at the heart of the world."[2] "Charles," of course, is merely the modern form of "Charlemagne."

Concerning Satan's Prince, Jonathan Dimbleby adds, "it is only the very unwise who dismiss him as an anachronism." According to Dimbleby, Charles is "a man for all seasons and for none, a man for his time but not of his time," a man who "rages ... at the folly of the world.... Yet ... he stands outside the age in which he lives.... If there is always lingering about him an air of sadness, it springs in part from ... a sense of the sorrows which he believes the human race is storing up for itself."[3] Mankind, Charles asserts, faces "what could be a final settlement." As Junor puts it, Satan's Prince is a "leader of men, a potent force for good and for change."[4]

Whether or not King Charles III ever also becomes King of the European Union, he could fulfill the previous chapter's scenario. Consider, for example, the following. Should the EU choose to establish its own constitutional monarchy, as Charles appears to have already suggested, he could serve as king and wield control. As it is, Charles had long performed a wide range of functions on behalf of his late mother. If she—who, as "the world's most traveled woman,"[5] was "universally admired"—had been chosen to head such a monarchy rather than her son, the then Prince of Wales would nonetheless have been the one exercising that authority. How much more then, may Charles as king? Under today's circumstances, as herein exposed, King Charles III *will* readily gain control of a world government. Of course, what better way could the EU, which sees England as an essential but uncertain and somewhat unpredictable partner, strengthen—and following December 2020's "Brexit" or British exit from the union, *renew*—the United Kingdom's explicit commitment to it.

---

1. Junor, p. 271.
2. Hilton, *The Principality and Power of Europe*, pp. 125, 133.
3. Jonathan Dimbleby, *The Prince of Wales* (Great Britain: Little, Brown & Co., 1994), pp. 404, 565.
4. Junor, pp. 3, 273.
5. *Her Majesty The Queen* (Hong Kong: Purnell Books and Intercontinental Book Productions, 1980), p. 36. Before the death of Princess Diana, the queen perhaps had a rival.

As of June 2021, former British Prime Minister Gordon Brown yet seeks to *reverse* Brexit,[1] preferring European socialism and ostensible German dominance, or what we may construe as a "Fourth Reich." The UK and EU *remain* closely aligned—and Northern Ireland oddly remains in the EU's single market. Brexit is *not* a happy arrangement, however, and while the Satan-serving world pursues Jerusalem's division,[2] other nations and kingdoms are increasingly divided and on the brink. The UK, as but one example, struggles with nationalists from Scotland,[3] both Irelands,[4] and even Wales.[5]

Notably, in a very real sense, the British royal family *is* the royal family of France, Germany, and the other European nations.[6] Prince Philip, Charles' now roasting anti-Christian father and prior Duke of Edinburgh,[7] was fluent in French, German, English, and Greek.[8] Comparably, Charles speaks English, French, passable German and Welsh—as well as some Arabic. In March 2023, he even delivered the first-ever speech by a British monarch, to the German parliament, using English *and* German.[9]

With all this in mind, we should perhaps also observe that the EU, in its official publication *Europe's Star Choice,* had earlier singled out the United Kingdom's flag, or the Union Jack, for sharp criticism due to its failure to represent Wales.[10] Interestingly, the red dragon, or Satan (Rev 12:3, 12:9), is literally the national heraldic symbol of

---

1. Peter Walker, "Gordon Brown says he will not give up fight to reverse Brexit," *Guardian,* 10 June 2021.
2. See this author's *Israel, "Peace" and the Looming Great Tribulation* multi-volume series.
3. "Scottish nationalists vow independence vote after election win," *Reuters,* 8 May 2021.
4. "Brexit Is Probably the United Kingdom's Death Knell," *Foreign Policy (FP),* 3 Feb. 2021.
5. "Welsh independence: How worried should UK ministers be?," *BBC News,* 2 Feb. 2021.
6. The British monarchy has particularly strong ancestral ties to France, Germany, and Spain, as well as many other nations, through their former and current national monarchies. It is perhaps noteworthy that according to spokespersons for the Priory of Sion (Zion), "in the near future, there would be a dramatic upheaval in France—not a revolution, but a radical change in French institutions that would pave the way for the reinstatement of a monarchy" (Baigent, Leigh, and Lincoln, *Holy Blood, Holy Grail,* p. 225). For more information, see ch. 4, "Prince of this World—a *Diverse* Lineage," at p. 79.
7. Upon marrying then Princess Elizabeth, England's King George VI made the young Philip Duke of Edinburgh, Earl of Merioneth, and Baron of Greenwich. In 1957, after ten years of service to the realm, Philip's wife, Queen Elizabeth II, made him a prince (Junor, p. 23). In rebellion against God (Gen 3:16c-d), Philip served *under* his wife, who ruled him until April 9, 2021—when, as a (yet) unsaved man who had previously stated a desire to *reincarnate as a virus* to dramatically reduce Earth's human population, he finally *descended to Hell's roasting flames for his eternal "reward."* Remember this: with Elizabeth II, Philip raised *the* AntiChrist. Charles then became king and Duke of Edinburgh until March–April 2023, when he passed the latter title to Prince Edward.
8. Denis Judd, *Prince Philip* (New York: Atheneum, 1981), p. 65.
9. Charles is popular in Germany: "At the Brandenburg Gate, crowds were waving British and German flags as they waited.... Anja Wieting, 50, ... took time off [work] to drive five hours to Berlin with her daughter Lili, 18, for the spectacle. 'It's the visit of the king in Germany. We want to celebrate it, regardless...,' she told *AFP.* The joy of well wishers ... was palpable. ... 'The British royal family garners a lot of interest' in Germany, said Michael Hartmann, a sociology professor at Darmstadt Technical University. ... The late queen first visited Berlin in 1965, when the city was divided between a capitalist West and communist East.... Charles himself is a regular in Germany, having been in the country more than 40 times. He is fluent in German..." (AFP, "In Germany on 1st State Visit, Britain's Charles III Backs Kyiv," *NewsMax,* 29 Mar. 2023).
10. Hilton, *The Principality and Power of Europe,* pp. 50-51.

Wales, being central to the Welsh flag. It will take no genius, therefore, to realize that King Charles III could immediately rectify this "'unfortunate' oversight," since that same Welsh dragon is integral to his royal heraldic achievement (coat of arms) as Prince of Wales.[1]

Importantly, Klaus Schwab's and the WEF's "Fourth Industrial Revolution," aka "The Great Reset," which is and has always been *under King Charles III*—Schwab is one of Charles' knights—*is* the Fourth Reich at work! A great deal has been said and written about the WEF and Schwab's Great Reset, and this author has things to add, among his coming books. But what you must here understand is this: it is part of the creation of global governance, for the coming Great Tribulation, and it is *under* Charles. Of course, inasmuch as Satan's Prince has the media spotlight, there have been both sober, responsible statements and seemingly sensationalistic, irresponsible statements made about him. Herein, a relevant, proper balance in both regards will be presented.[2] Along the latter line, for instance, the *Sun* ran this article:

---

1. For more information, see ch. 7's section titled, "The red dragon, or Satan," at p. 188.

2. Certain well-meaning individuals and groups, who at one time or another spoke to firsthand sources such as the author or Monte Judah, or who got second-, third-, and even fourth-hand information, have made statements—and in some cases, published materials—showing that Prince Charles (now King Charles III) may be the AntiChrist. Statements have been made in radio and television programs, as well as before groups of prophecy buffs, and written materials have appeared over the internet and in print. Unfortunately, accuracy has often or even largely been substandard. When dealing with subjects of such gravity, reliability and credibility are imperative.

   The (late) Texe William Marrs in *Circle of Intrigue,* for example, asserted: "As a prime candidate [for the Inner Circle of the Illuminati and the role of the Antichrist,] we must consider Prince Philip.... Philip, who leads by default due to the stupidity and indiscretions of his son, Prince Charles, oversees Britain's powerful *United Lodge of Freemasonry,* and he presides over the secretive and monarchi[c]al *Order of the Garter.* The Prince [(Philip)] is also director of the *World Wildlife Fund"* (p. 70). In point of fact, Prince Philip *did not lead anything* due to "the stupidity and indiscretions of his son," nor did he *directly* oversee the United Grand Lodge of England. Although Prince Philip was offered the position of grand master of this lodge, he declined, instead allowing it to pass to Edward, the Duke of Kent, another Garter knight (Stephen Knight, *The Brotherhood* {London: Harper Collins Publishers, 1983}, pp. 211-212). Moreover, while Prince Philip was a mason and a companion knight of the Order of the Garter, Queen Elizabeth II and Charles, as the Prince of Wales, were the order's two highest-ranking members until his mother died. (Now Charles and son William are such.) Although Marrs never documented his sensationalist points, he was, however, at least partially correct in these observations: "Certain members of the Illuminati, including Prince Charles and [(now deceased)] Prince Philip, take part in the rituals and symbols of an odd secret society called the *Order of the Garter.* This Order, with its ceremonial magic, is thought to be a precursor to the coming establishment of the *Circle of the Round Table.* So demented are the leaders of the Illuminati that they fancy themselves to be the modern-day inheritors of the Arthurian legend. Upon the appearance, expected soon, of their great and divine king, or ruler, they would be knights of the Circle of the Round Table, noble and exalted co-rulers of Camelot" (pp. 70, 229). For information on the Illuminati, see ch. 3, "Prince of this World—a *Diverse* Lineage," at p. 71, as well as the discussion on the Garter in ch. 7, "The Heraldic Symbols in the Arms and their Interpretations," at p. 135.

   As another example, some have stated that Charles is a vegetarian, and tried to relate that (false) claim to tribulational events. However, King Charles III has never been a strict vegetarian, inasmuch as he occasionally eats red meat (e.g., Hoey, *Charles & Diana: The Tenth Anniversary,* p. 85). According to (late former wife) Diana: "[Charles] suddenly went all vegetarian and wouldn't kill. His family thought he had gone mad, ... but it all came back eventually in his own time. He does that—he has these crazes and then he drops them" ("Diana on the Family," *People* weekly, 20 Oct. 1997, p. 104).

Renowned psychic Sally Montefiore says she has seen "Charlie's angel" several times—and she's absolutely certain that it is watching over Charles. "Nothing bad can happen to Prince Charles despite the treacherous situations he places himself in," says Sally. "It's almost like he is defying the angel to withdraw its protective shield from around him. But the powers of Charlie's angel ... [are] extraordinary—and it won't let him down because he has a special destiny. Prince Charles will become King in 1994[1] and lead his nation back to greatness.... Under his leadership Great Britain will emerge as a true superpower, just as she was 150 years ago." ... .But the Prince has heard Mrs. Montefiore's claims about Charlie's angel—and he's starting to believe them himself.... "Charles ... right now ... is immune from death or permanent injury," says psychic Sally.... "Anyone else would have been crippled or killed by the injuries Charles has endured. But he will not be harmed because great things await him."[2]

As the first edition of this book was about to be printed, the popular press (often flippant or simply fake) began to latch onto "rumors" among Christians that then Prince Charles may prove to be the AntiChrist. *Imagine that!* On January 1, 1998, the *Rocky Mountain News,* showing pictures of Prince Charles, H.A. Kissinger, Saddam Hussein, Hitler, and King Juan Carlos I, observed, "Prince Charles ... is the latest world figure to be identified as the antichrist by some believers."[3] Jean Torkelson, in a related article, wrote:

Many today believe the Antichrist has already been born.... Others are naming names.

"Prince Charles [of Wales] is supposed to be the Antichrist, according to the latest rumor," says the [(ill-informed)] Rev. Chuck Wilkes, pastor of Highlands Ranch Community Fellowship.... "Last March was the last big date," says Wilkes. "That's when Prince Charles addressed the European congress, and that day, if you run out the mathematics (according to [those who say that] the Bible [in Daniel 9:27 is referring to the September 1993 Oslo I accord between Israel and the Palestinians]), ... was supposed to be the day he revealed himself as the Antichrist [(i.e., the start of the prophesied Great Tribulation)]. "Obviously, that day came and went." ...[4]

What disturbs end-timers is not meeting Jesus, but a predicted enslavement of humanity by satanic forces. Some end-timers see that happening now. They point to microchip tracking devices, which are being [im]planted in fish and cattle. Grocery store bar codes are said to contain a secret reference to 666, the biblical mark of the beast. Some suggest the

---

1. So much for the predictions of yet another false prophet(ess)! Nevertheless, while 1994 has come and gone, Charles has become king of the British Commonwealth, and may yet become Europe's king too.
2. Ken O'Hara, "Charlie's Angel," *Sun,* 10 March 1992, p. 2.
3. "RECOGNIZE THE ANTICHRIST?," *Rocky Mountain News,* 1 Jan. 1998, p. 5A.
4. For more information, see the chapters (or sections) titled "Is the Church already in Daniel's seventieth 'week?'" and "Identifying the covenant of Daniel 9:27" in the *Israel, "Peace" and the Looming Great Tribulation* multi-volume series.

common Internet prefix "www" refers to the sixth letter in the Hebrew alphabet, another mysterious stamp of 666 upon the world.[1]

Although much has been written regarding the AntiChrist's personality and his probable relationship to Rome's papacy, few Christians possess a satisfactory understanding of how such an individual could possibly rise to world prominence. In *GLOBAL PEACE AND THE RISE OF ANTICHRIST,* the late Dave Hunt not only offers relevant historical information, but presents a provocative scenario—one that, although entirely unintentional, points directly, as we shall see, to King Charles III:

SOMEWHERE, AT THIS VERY MOMENT, ... the Antichrist is almost certainly alive—biding his time, awaiting his cue.... Already a mature man, he is probably active in politics, perhaps even an admired world leader.... [He] could be ... of great wealth and behind-the-scenes influence, or a sports hero.... Somewhere he is being meticulously groomed....

....Even so, benevolence, prudence, integrity, and principle mark his circumspect public behavior. Certainly he seems to be no more evil than the accepted norm in today's amoral society. It may be that to this point in his life he is still convinced that his motives are altogether pure and unselfish.

....The Antichrist is so driven by his dream to rule—yes, perhaps in his own eyes, to *save*—the world, that he will pay any price, even satanic possession, to make his mark in history....

....But Hollywood caricatures play into the hands of the real Antichrist, since no suspicion will rest upon this one whose admirable qualities so well conceal his dark designs....

....He will oppose Christ while pretending to *be* Christ....

....In fact, he will be the closest counterfeit of Christ that Satan can produce. Completely deceived by this brazen masquerade, the world will hail him as its deliverer.

And right there is where the plot thickens. If the Antichrist will indeed pretend to be the Christ, then his followers must be "Christians"!...

The world must be primed both religiously and politically to embrace the Antichrist when he suddenly rises to power. If "Christianity" is to be the official world religion (which must be the case if the Antichrist claims to be Christ), then it must become broad enough to accommodate all of the world's faiths. As for the political climate, the world must be united in the twin causes of global peace and ecological rescue when this man appears....

The mystery of godliness ultimately involves Christ turning men from self to God and indwelling them in preparation for heaven. The mystery of lawlessness ultimately involves Satan turning men from God to self and indwelling them in preparation for hell. Satan's is a gospel of self.... It promises that we each have within ourselves the means of our own salvation.... We are not separated from God by sin; we are alienated from our-

---

1. Jean Torkelson, "Antichrist among us, according to believers," *Rocky Mountain News,* 1 Jan. 1998, p. 20A.

selves and our environment through ignorance of who we really are. We imagine ourselves to be weak mortals when in fact we are gods. We do not need a "Savior" external to ourselves, but simply need to learn to tap the infinite potential that lies within. It is the same appealing lie that seduced Eve.[1]

Suddenly secular leaders are declaring that not just religion but "Christianity" is the key to uniting Europe! Why is this so? Since the Antichrist pretends to be Christ, his followers must be "Christians" and his world religion must be a perverted form of "Christianity." Not only the Pope calls for a "spiritually united Europe," but numerous other leaders voice the same novel opinion....

In actual fact, neither the Pope nor Gorbachev has the least sympathy for "born-again" evangelical Christianity,[2] which John Paul II openly derides and warns his flock against. While encouraging dialogue with Buddhists, Muslims, and Hindus, the Pope warns Catholics "not to be seduced by Protestant fundamentalist sects...."[3] In fact, by "Christianity" both Gorbachev and the Pope mean *Roman Catholicism*. That just happens to have been the official world religion of the Roman Empire—the very religion which must recover that status in preparation for the Antichrist....

The ancient Roman Empire was a pluralistic society.... Any religion was tolerated. There was, however, one exception.... Christians were hated and persecuted and often killed, not because they believed in Christ, but because they believed *only* in Him....

....Tertullian's saying, "The blood of the martyrs is the seed of the church," was all too true. The Emperor Constantine decided that, to unify the Empire, Christians should be given the right to worship as they pleased....

---

1. Dave Hunt, *GLOBAL PEACE AND THE RISE OF ANTICHRIST* (Oregon: Harvest House Publishers, 1990), pp. 5-6, 8-9, 86. *All material from this author is quoted with his permission.*
2. Gorbachev, who (falsely) believed that Jesus was the "first socialist" and that religion should play a role in social progress, had stated that peace and social harmony in the Middle East "would have to be founded on the spirit of Jesus," in whose footsteps he claimed to follow (Allan Shapiro, "A disciple of Jesus, 'the first socialist,'" *The Jerusalem Post,* Int. Ed., 27 June 1992, p. 3). Of course, throughout his tenure as the Soviet Premiere, far from behaving like a Christian, Gorbachev's greatest concern was keeping Soviet Communism alive, finally liberalizing it, while allowing greater Israeli emigration, only because desperately needed Western aid, capital investment, and trade were conditioned upon such changes. Further, under Gorbachev, the Soviet Union's member-states continued to arm Israel's foes wholeheartedly (e.g., the PLO, Iran, Iraq, and Syria)—and some which were liberated still do, while Gorbachev himself, like Israel's enemies, foolishly and dishonestly equated Zionism with racism ("Gorbachev's visit," *The Jerusalem Post,* Int. Ed., 27 June 1992, p. 8).

    Calling environmental destruction "the central issue of our time," deserving "absolute priority above all other problems facing us today," Gorbachev, the "former president of the world's most polluted country," who openly advocated the creation of an "international government" to guard the world's "peace and security," announced his 1993 launching of the *International Green Cross* before an audience of politicians, religious leaders, and scientists at the Global Forum. Through it, he hoped to "increase the profile of environmental issues by lobbying world leaders," "prevent environmental disasters," bring about "a new international environmental law," and propose "reform of the United Nations." He stated: "We need an ecology of the soul. Without it, all our efforts to save mankind would be pointless. When science and rationality cannot help us, there is only one thing that can save us: our conscience and moral feelings" (Geoffrey Lean, London Observer Service, "Gorbachev launches crusade to save Earth from people," *Rocky Mountain News,* 6 May 1993, p. 36A).

    Whatever Gorbachev was, he gave *no* indication of being an actual Christian—only the opposite.
3. According to "Cardinal Joseph Ratzinger, Pope John Paul II's guardian of orthodoxy," "the only valid church community is that in which churches are linked through their bishops to the church in Rome and the pope" ("Vatican warns about straying from Rome," *Rocky Mountain News,* 16 June 1992, p. 4).

A brilliant military commander, Constantine also understood that there could be no political stability without religious unity. Yet to accomplish that feat would require a union between paganism and Christianity.... The Empire needed an ecumenical religion that would appeal to every citizen in a multicultural society.... Christianity had to undergo a transformation....

Constantine himself exemplified this expediency. He adopted Christ as the new god that had given him victory in the crucial battle at Milvian Bridge in 312 A.D.... Yet, as Caesar, he continued to function as the *Pontifex Maximus* of the Empire's pagan priesthood, known as the Pontifical College. Even as he endowed Christian churches, Constantine continued to support the construction of pagan temples. As a "Christian" Emperor, he automatically became the the de facto civil head of the Christian church and seduced her with promises of power. Thus began the destruction of Christianity and the process that created Roman Catholicism as it is today....

"Christianity" became a *means* for nearly everyone. Being a "Christian" was soon essential to anyone who wanted to advance in business, politics, or even the military.... Ecclesiastical posts, from priest to bishop, cardinal, and even Pope, went to the highest bidder....

So the "Christianity" of the Roman Empire, which became known as Roman Catholicism..., was not the same as the biblical Christianity of the early church and of the martyrs. Instead, it was the old paganism of Rome surviving under a thin veneer of Christian terminology and form....

As [the self-declared] head of the church, Constantine claimed two new titles...: *Vicar of Christ and Bishop of Bishops*.... *Vicar* comes from the Latin word *vicarius*. The Greek equivalent would be *anti*.... ...Constantine, as Vicar of Christ, was an Antichrist, and so are the Popes, for they bear the same title. Antichrist will be the new Constantine, the head of the ... Roman Empire worldwide, while the Pope will be his assistant, the second beast [or false prophet] of Revelation 13....

....It was Constantine who decreed that since Rome was the capital of the Empire, its Bishop should be the ecclesiastical head of the church....

....When the Empire later disintegrated *politically*..., it was held together *religiously* by the all-pervasive presence of the Roman Catholic Church with its ingenious ecumenical blend of paganism and Christianity still headquartered in Rome....

....That the Pope is almost universally recognized as the religious leader of the world [has] ... great significance.... Other world leaders are adding their voices to the call by former U.N. Assistant Secretary General [and New Ager] Robert Muller for the Pope to come "to the United Nations [to] speak for all the religions and spiritualities on this planet...." The picture becomes ever clearer and more ominous.[1]

....The heads of state in today's world all recognize that the Pope wields a power which in many ways is even greater than their own. ...Vatican City's citizens are found in great numbers in nearly every country. They constitute an international network that reaches into the inside circles of the world's power centers.... [Much like the Freemasons do for the British monarchy.]

It is not surprising, then, that all the major nations in the world, including the United States, have ambassadors to the Vatican.... When he

---

1. Hunt, *GLOBAL PEACE AND THE RISE OF ANTICHRIST,* pp. 104-111.

wanted to make his peace with the West, one of the first moves Gorbachev made was to journey to Rome.... That fact speaks volumes....

Certainly the rebuilt Babylon in Iraq ... does not fit John's description of the *woman*. She is "drunken with the blood of ... the martyrs of Jesus" (Revelation 17:6) and "in her was found the blood of prophets and of saints and of all that were slain upon the earth" (Revelation 18:24). Nearly a million martyrs died in the [Roman] Catholic Inquisition in Spain, France, and Holland alone. Yet the phrase "all that were slain upon the earth" indicates again that John is seeing the wickedness and idolatry that came from Babel and culminates in the false church of the last days. It will encompass all religions under the leadership of the Pope in Rome.

That this "last-days" Babylon is described as a *woman* again identifies her as the Roman Catholic Church, for whom a *woman*—"the Virgin Mary"—is the dominant deity....

When asked why they pray to Mary, most [Roman] Catholics will deny that they do so and will insist that they only ask her to intercede.... Yet prayers are addressed *to* Mary for everything from safety to forgiveness of sins and eternal salvation....

John Paul II made a solemn pilgrimage to Fatima on May 13, 1982, where he "prayed before the statue of Our Lady of Fatima. Thousands heard him speak and consecrate the world to Mary as she had requested." On at least three other occasions, ... he consecrated the world to our Lady" with "special mention" of the Russian people. She had promised that if the popes and bishops would consecrate the world and Russia to her Immaculate Heart, ... "My Immaculate Heart will triumph, Russia will be converted, and there will be peace!"

Such a statement is in the fullest opposition to the clear teaching of the Bible.... Global peace will only be established when Christ returns to reign from Jerusalem.... Yet "Mary" has taken the place of Christ as the one through whom peace will come, and the present Pope and his church support this heresy.[1]

....Since [Roman] Catholicism as it developed beginning with Constantine was paganism disguised as Christianity, it has consistently accommodated itself.... In Haiti, for example, every Voodoo ceremony begins with [Roman] Catholic prayers.... The frightening spiritist cult of Santeria exploding across America is also a blend of African paganism and "Christianity" carried on in the name of [Roman] Catholic saints who front for demons....

[Roman] Catholic retreat centers around the world mix "Christianity" with Hinduism, Buddhism, and all manner of New Age beliefs and practices....

....John Paul II takes a broad-minded view of Buddhism and all other religions. He considers the Tibetan Buddhist Deity Yoga of his good friend the Dalai Lama,[2] along with the prayers of witch doctors, spiritists, and every other "faith," to be generating "profound spiritual energies" that are creating a "new climate of peace." ...

Mindful of the mission that "Our Lady" has given him, the current Pope maintains contact with the world's leading religions. He accepts

---

1. Hunt, *GLOBAL PEACE AND THE RISE OF ANTICHRIST,* pp. 116-117, 120-122, 124-125.
2. The "Dalai Lama," who is worshiped in Tibet, Hollywood, and elsewhere as "a living god," is considered to be a reincarnation of "the divine Buddha."

them as worshiping the same God and their prayers as being as effective as those of Christians. Nor has he attempted to convert any of them. He simply wants everyone of every religion to acknowledge him as the moral and spiritual leader of the world.

....Already we are seeing leading Protestants working together with the Roman Catholic Church and adopting its ecumenism. A new spirit of compromise is sweeping the "Christian" church and the entire religious world today....

....In actual fact, the Roman Catholic Church is the most powerful and effective enemy of Christianity in history. Its teachings are masterpieces of deception.

....Yet today's "cult experts" rarely if ever include the Roman Catholic Church on their lists because it is now unacceptably "negative".... Partnership with Rome sets the stage for the rise of Antichrist....

....If the Pope identifies this impostor as the Christ, the obedience of ["faithful" Roman] Catholics is assured. Submission to the Pope is far broader than most people realize....

The Roman Catholic Church, as the sole interpreter of Scripture, seduces its members into embracing a different God, a different Jesus Christ, and a different plan of salvation from that taught in the Bible. Confusion arises because Rome uses biblical terms such as "justification by grace," the "Virgin Birth," the "blood atonement of the cross," and the "Resurrection of Jesus." Yet what Rome means by such language is entirely different from what evangelicals believe and the Bible teaches....

....One's own good deeds, obedience to the Church, and participation in its sacraments must be added to what Christ has done. The Rosary, the Confession to a priest, baptism into the Church, and indulgences earned are also required. And in addition to Christ's suffering on the cross the individual must also suffer for his own sins in purgatory, where the soul, though cleansed by the blood of Christ, must be more thoroughly "purged." Then there is the endless list of alms, good deeds, and Masses that others must engage in after one is dead in order to obtain his or her release from purgatory and entrance into heaven at last....

...Paul was very explicit: "There be some that ... would pervert the gospel of Christ. But though we or an angel from heaven preach any other gospel unto you than that which we have preached unto you, let him be accursed" (Galatians 1:7-9). The Roman Catholic Church, from the Pope down, preaches a far different gospel from that which the apostles preached.... Yet Rome boldly pronounces its own eternal curse upon those who dare to preach Paul's [true] gospel....

....Of course Mormons "name the name of Christ," as do Jehovah's Witnesses, Christian Scientists, and other cultists, occultists, and New Agers—and their "Christ" is a blasphemous counterfeit. So is the "Christ" of Roman Catholicism.[1]

The new Emperor..., the Antichrist, is not yet in position to accomplish the essential Constantinian strategy. In his absence, and in preparation for him, an ecumenical union of all religions is being aggressively pursued....

Indeed, the "engagement of the [Roman] Catholic Church in the ecumenical movement" was significant even before the present Pope took office. This fact may seem to be in conflict with its claims of being the only

---

1. Hunt, *GLOBAL PEACE AND THE RISE OF ANTICHRIST,* pp. 127-130, 136-137, 140-142, 145-146.

true and infallible church. However, while damning ex-Catholics and Protestants, [Roman] Catholicism allows for those outside its fold to be saved if ignorant of its claims and sacraments and if they are sincere in their own faith. Thus Mother Teresa and those who work[ed] with her never attempt[ed] to convert to Christ the dying people for whom they care[d]....

The Roman Catholic hierarchy has a long history of leadership in ecumenism. A book could be filled with examples, but a few must suffice. Popes John XXIII and Paul VI joined such notables as the Dalai Lama, Anwar el-Sadat (a Muslim), and [former] U.N. Secretary General U. Thant (a Buddhist), to form The Temple of Understanding, known as the United Nations of World Religions.... [Roman] Catholic Archbishop Angelo Fernandes was for its first eight years the President of the Geneva-based World Conference on Religion and Peace, organized to bring together "a growing network involving all the major religions of the world." ...

"His Holiness" the Dalai Lama, who is "God" to most Tibetan Buddhists, has been well-received by Roman Catholic leaders around the world. He ... has met five or more times with his good friend John Paul II. "Both of us have the same aim," says the Dalai Lama....

Encouraging such ecumenism, the Pope has declared that "Christians must work with other religions to secure peace." He has pledged that "the [Roman] Catholic Church intends to 'share in and promote' such ecumenical and inter-religious cooperation." ...

....Using his immense prestige and the emotional appeal of global peace, the Pope was able in 1986 to gather the leading figures of 12 world religions together in Assisi, Italy, to pray to whatever "God" each believed in, beseeching these deities to bring peace to the world. To justify honoring the prayers of even witch doctors and fire worshipers, John Paul II told participants..."the challenge of peace ... transcends religious differences."[1]

Prince Philip [of Britain] is representative of the growing numbers of nominal "Christians" who are turning back to paganism as a result of their ecological concerns....

....To speak of "spirituality" and "freedom of religion" is popular. To suggest that Jesus Christ as the Savior of sinners is mankind's only hope is not tolerated by those who preach tolerance. All religions must join together in a generic, pagan "spirituality" to rescue the planet....

Ecology and peace are the two great concerns that are sparking the new unity of all religions. Nothing else matters. Doctrinal beliefs are irrelevant....

....Satan's Messiah, with his seemingly unlimited psychic power, will be light-years ahead of any of today's gurus....

Since it is a key factor in establishing world peace, ecumenism will be unstoppable. Those who criticize it on the basis of biblical truth will seem to be small-minded. After all, as **Prince Philip** suggests, it hardly seems practical, when the survival of our species on earth hangs in the balance, to worry about heaven or hell. Environmental concerns and the need for peace at any price clearly take priority.[2]

[During the 1990-91 U.N. conflict with Iraq,] Muslims who protested the presence of "filthy foreigners" upon Islam's holy soil insisted that the

---

1. Hunt, *GLOBAL PEACE AND THE RISE OF ANTICHRIST,* pp. 149, 152, 155-156.
2. Hunt, *GLOBAL PEACE AND THE RISE OF ANTICHRIST,* pp. 168-169, 172, 174-176.

Arabs would work out a solution if left to themselves.... In actual fact, had the United States not stepped in immediately Iraq would have taken over Saudi Arabia and a few other countries as well....

Suddenly, thinking Arabs were forced to reevaluate their religion in ... that the territory containing the holiest Islamic shrines had to be defended by infidels against Muslims!...

It would be surprising if we did not see as great changes in the Arab world as in the Communist world as the stage is set for the rise of Antichrist.... Even the Bamboo Curtain around China must yield as well to worldwide pressures.[1] It is only a matter of time....

Confronted at last by some of the embarrassing questions about Islam, the faith of many Muslims is being shaken. Why did Muhammad with his "new revelation" give his God the same name, Allah, as the chief idol in the *kaaba*, the ancient pagan temple at Mecca? And why, although he destroyed the idols which it housed, did Muhammad retain the *kaaba* itself as a sacred shrine? And why did he keep and continue to revere the Black Stone that had long been worshiped along with the idols in the ancient religious ceremonies of Mecca? And why do Muslims consider the *kaaba* holy and kiss its Black Stone as an important part of their pilgrimage to Mecca?...

Painful though the admission may be, intelligent, thinking Arabs can no longer deny that Islam has been responsible for perpetuating a barbaric medieval mentality....

Unfortunately, the pressure for change is bringing a growing openness to ecumenism that is preparing the Muslim world to embrace the Antichrist....

....It is no longer so difficult to imagine that with a little more preparation Muslims too will be able to embrace and even worship the counterfeit "Christ"—while still professing allegiance to Islam....[2]

Throughout the world and in all ages there have been two general concepts of God: 1) pantheism/naturalism—that the universe itself is God; and 2) supernaturalism—that the Creator is distinct from His creation. Re-

---

1. For more information, see ch. 11's section, titled "Governor of Hong Kong?" at p. 443.
2. Hunt, *GLOBAL PEACE AND THE RISE OF ANTICHRIST,* pp. 227, 229-231.

   Charles, while as prince yet slated one day to head the Anglican Protestant Church, has not only long sought ecumenical rapprochement with the Vatican and popes John Paul II, Benedict XVI and now Francis, but he has also made extraordinary overtures toward Muslims and Islam. In fact, Satan's Prince has been called "the most popular world leader in the Muslim community throughout the world." Among other deeds, Charles as prince apparently "converted" to Islam, taking an Arabic title which has caused various Muslims to speculate that he intends to become the head of the Muslim world (for more information, see ch. 10's sections titled, "A so-called 'Christian' heritage" and "Ties to the New Age Movement, the occult, and false religions," at pp. 295 and 333, respectively).

   Various Islamic nations and other Muslim fundamentalists, as well as fundamentalist Christian organizations, joined the Vatican at the urging of then Pope John Paul II, in opposing and denouncing the sexually immoral, pro-infanticide agenda of the September 1994 United Nations' International Conference on Population and Development held in Cairo, Egypt. While the Vatican made overtures even to Iran and Libya, other countries, such as Saudi Arabia, the Sudan, and Lebanon, chose not to attend. As the *Associated Press* put it, "the controversy has made unlikely allies of the Holy See and Muslims" ("Catholics, Muslims protest abortions," *Rocky Mountain News,* 2 Sept. 1994, p. 63A). At the fourth UN Conference on Women, held in September 1995, the Vatican again collaborated with Islamic nations, including Syria and Iran, "to prevent what both perceived as a challenge to their dogma of purity and ban on extramarital sex" (Uli Schmetzer, "U.N. forum ends in dispute over women's sexual rights," *The Denver Post,* 17 Sept. 1995, p. 18A). Such efforts have continued.) ,John Paul II rightly said, "Every family must know how to resist the false sirens of the culture of death" ("Forum to focus on 'empowerment' as well as birth control," *The Denver Post,* 4 Sept. 1994, p. 12A).

lated to these are two more opposing views: 1) polytheism—that there are many gods...; and 2) monotheism—that there is only one God.

Antichrist's claims are built upon a pantheistic/polytheistic worldview. If everything is God and there are thus many gods, it then follows that every person is a god whether he realizes it or not.... The Antichrist, having apparently "realized" this inner potential, is in a position to help others to achieve their godhood also. Such is the great lie of the Serpent.

Supernaturalism/monotheism is divided into two rival beliefs: 1) that God is a single being; and 2) that God has always existed in three Persons [or Personalities] who are separate and distinct, yet [eternally united as] one [in the fullness of Deity]. Only Christians hold the latter view [(i.e., a single God who is Father, Word and Holy Spirit always)].... Yet it is the only biblical, logical, and philosophically coherent view of God possible.... All other views of God can be accommodated by the [polytheistic] Antichrist— but not the biblical doctrine of the [unified] Trinity.

....Just as Israel's misunderstanding of God's triune [or (more accurately) unified] nature caused her to reject her Messiah, so that same misunderstanding will allow her to be deceived into accepting the Antichrist....[1]

Satan transforms himself "into an angel of light" and inspires his emissaries to masquerade as "the ministers of righteousness".... He prevents his false theology from being unmasked by accusing those who attempt to expose it of being "negative" and "divisive."

The Serpent did not urge Eve to shake her fist at God and denounce Him, nor did he inspire her to practice overtly evil acts. On the contrary, he enticed her with promises of a better "self-image," of being a wiser and better person—of even becoming "like God." What could be wrong with that high ambition? Evil is far more seductive and effective when it is packaged as *good*. If he can encourage expressions of "man's basic goodness" that are high-minded, altruistic, and spiritual, but *without Christ*, Satan is very pleased.[2]

Satan's goal is to pervert the conscience to such an extent that his *lie* is embraced as God's *truth*. Far from desiring to destroy all religion, Satan seeks to be the leader of a *false religion* whose adherents unknowingly worship him. And of course that false religion, as we have seen, must be a perverted form of Christianity....

While raw Satanism is exploding, most people are repelled by it. Satan is most seductive when he masquerades as *God*....

The death, burial, and resurrection of Christ as historic events upon planet Earth make any kind of ecumenical union with the world's religions both impossible and abominable. A dead Buddha or Muhammad has nothing in common with the resurrected Lord Jesus Christ.... Christ alone paid the penalty demanded by the law, which He proved by His resurrection, and He alone can save....

The Antichrist won't even pretend to be Jesus.... On what basis, then, will he claim to be Christ? Almost certainly he will claim to be the latest *reincarnation* of the "Christ Spirit" that was allegedly in Krishna, Rama,

1. Hunt, *GLOBAL PEACE AND THE RISE OF ANTICHRIST,* pp. 233-234, 242, 245.
2. As one reviewer noted, "How similar is this to the morals, ideals and values that a great deal of the world's population embraces today?"

Buddha, Jesus, Muhammad, et al [or he will allow others to make that claim on his behalf]....

....Antichrist represents himself, not the God of heaven. Through him "Christianity" becomes the ultimate humanism. The satanic power manifest through Antichrist will be hailed as psychic powers of the mind and thus proof of man's innate Godlike potential....

In contrast to the Antichrist's religion, which exalts self, Christ taught that we must *deny* self and take up the cross to follow Him.[1]

After a honeymoon of peace, love, and brotherhood, the terror of Antichrist's rule will make Hitler's rule seem benevolent. Those who refuse to worship him and submit to the new world order will be summarily executed....

The most fascinating aspect of Hitler's deception was the heavy "Christian" element that was involved—an element that will be absolutely essential under Antichrist. Most of the church in Germany went happily along with the new order. Hitler promised "liberty for all religious denominations," much like the promises now being made in Eastern Europe.

In his March 23, 1933, speech, when he took over as dictator, Hitler praised the Christian faith and promised to respect liberty of conscience....

Thousands of German pastors joined the newly organized "German Christians' Faith Movement," which supported Nazi doctrines and promoted a "Reich Church" that would unite all Protestants under the state. A minority of pastors, ... realized at last that Hitler's "Positive Christianity" was in fact anti-Christian....

The "Reich Church," formed under leaders picked by Hitler, was formally recognized by the Reichstag on July 14, 1933. On November 13 a massive rally was held in the Berlin Sportpalast by the "German Christians' Faith Movement." Leaders of the rally proposed abandonment of the Old Testament and revision of the New Testament to fit National Socialism. Resolutions called for "One People, One Reich, One Faith," an oath of allegiance to Hitler to be signed by all pastors, and the exclusion of Jewish Christians by all churches. The Gestapo's reign of terror against followers of Christ began with the arrest of 700 pastors in the fall of 1935.

Always the justification under Hitler, as under Constantine, was ecumenical "unity." We are hearing the same appealing slogan today....

All the time that he was deliberately moving to destroy Christianity and replace it with his neopagan occultism, Hitler continued to pretend that he was the champion of real Christianity....

We are reminded by the homage afforded to cult leaders that the world remains vulnerable to delusion. The Dalai Lama, for example, is highly honored worldwide.... Yet his public claims are similar to those which will be made by the Antichrist.... He proposes to bring global peace through a heavily demonic Yoga visualization technique.... For this he was awarded the Nobel Peace Prize in 1989! This forerunner of the Antichrist continues to be feted by the Roman Catholic Church, which previously gave Hitler its blessing.

....**It is already a crime punishable under the Genocide Treaty, which was ... signed by the United States, to suggest that any religion is wrong. To be ecumenical and "positive" is required by international law. It is but a small step to Antichrist's harsh rule.**

---

1. Hunt, *GLOBAL PEACE AND THE RISE OF ANTICHRIST,* pp. 249-250, 252-254.

Today's "Positive Christianity"—which, like Hitler's, dresses occultism in Christian language—has virtually taken over in America and is now being exported into Eastern Europe. Those who promote Positive Thinking, Possibility Thinking, and Positive Confession are among the most influential radio/television preachers.... Any correction is rejected as "negative."[1]

....Many Charismatic leaders are now promoting the idea that the second coming is not the return of our Lord *personally* in His resurrected individual body to earth, but the attainment by His *spiritual body*, the church, to a higher spiritual state evidenced by great signs and wonders....

....And this thesis fits perfectly with the Antichrist's probable claim that he is the reincarnation of the Christ Spirit that was in Jesus—a "higher state of consciousness" into which he promises to lead the world....

....The general effect upon [Charismatic Roman] Catholics of the "baptism in the Spirit" has been to increase their heretical devotion to Mary.... The "spirit" that endorses such delusion will also endorse Antichrist....

On top of her heresies, the Roman Catholic Church consorts with "seducing spirits" such as those that have appeared at Fatima in the form of "Mary" and the *child* "Jesus." These apparitions ... have been embraced by every Pope in the past 60 years and thus by hundreds of millions of [Roman] Catholics. Similar appearances have increased around the world.... Always there are "miracles" and "warnings" to the world of coming judgment, with the promise that through the rosary and "Our Lady's" intervention peace can come....

....The message that comes from the "Virgin" is consistent with other demonic revelations and is important for the Antichrist: that all religions are basically the same and must come together for peace....

Through his pursuit of the occult and New Age medicine, **Prince Charles**, the next King of England and thus the next head of the Church of England, has concluded that all religions are basically the same. He considers himself to be psychic and believes in guidance from the spirit realm.[2] **The Queen** (also involved in spiritism) and **the Prince** both believe that he, Charles, "is the Chosen One—placed in line for the throne through a divine, preordained plan."[3]

Prince Charles is representative of many other prominent world figures who are also involved in the occult and anticipate the coming of a humanistic one-world religion....

One no longer need travel to a distant place where "Mary" has appeared. Visualization techniques are being taught, from kindergarten to top management seminars, which enable anyone to make contact with "Jesus" or the "Virgin Mary" or "extraterrestrials" or any person from the past or even the future. Through this ancient and powerful method of opening oneself to satanic delusion, demons posing as Jesus are being contacted for "inner healing" and "prayer" ....

....It is not difficult to see the day when untold millions of such spirit guides will identify the Antichrist as the Christ and will be believed. What a setup![4]

---

1. Hunt, *GLOBAL PEACE AND THE RISE OF ANTICHRIST*, pp. 266-268.
2. John Dale, *The Prince and the Paranormal: The Psychic Bloodline of the Royal Family* (London: W.H. Allen & Co. Plc, 1986), pp. 14-18.
3. *Us Weekly* magazine, 14 Jan. 1985, pp. 18-19.
4. Hunt, *GLOBAL PEACE AND THE RISE OF ANTICHRIST*, pp. 270-275, 277-278.

The "New Age Religion" of the coming "New World Order" is an intoxicating combination of pantheism and polytheism. Pantheists hold that a universal energy flows through, and thus unites, all life. They refer to this impersonal energy as a life- or god-force, and as an oversoul or universal spirit. New Agers alternately speak of it as their "Christ Consciousness," "Cosmic Consciousness," or "Higher Self." As pantheists, New Agers assert that this "energy," which they call "the Christ Energy," may be "channeled" or manipulated to "energize" an individual. An "energized" man or woman, as the teaching goes, not only partakes of the universal "god-force," but may realize his or her own "divine potential" or "godhood." According to pantheists, when an individual dies, he or she merely returns to, or unites with, the universal "force," and does not therefore cease to exist or experience divine judgment. Rather, a deceased person will at some point be reborn in another form—one that hopefully will be more attuned to the cosmic "life-force" and therefore more spiritually evolved. In other words, pantheists are not only natural polytheists, but they promote a kind of individual spiritual evolution through continual reincarnation. New Agers also teach a collective spiritual evolution, believing that when enough human beings have realized their "divine potential," mankind will suddenly take a "quantum spiritual leap" into "godhood" with all the "psychic powers" that it entails.

Many of today's New Age pantheists attempt to redefine and change orthodox Christian terminology and practice to conform with their occult beliefs. Often, these New Age cultists, who call themselves "christs," do not object to being viewed as liberal "Christians."[1] It should come as no surprise, therefore, to one day see the AntiChrist himself claim to be a "Christian." Yet the beliefs of New Agers and other occultists stem from Satan's ancient lie in the Garden of Eden, in which the serpent told the woman that she would not die by disobeying God, but that she would instead retain eternal life and even become "as *elohim* | God | gods, knowing good and evil [calamity, affliction]" (Gen 3:4-5, Heb.). Gary H. Kah, in *En Route to Global Occupation,* makes these astute observations,

> [Most] ... pantheists will automatically support the concept of a one-world government since global unity is essential to the proper flow of the god-force. Humanity will then, presumably, take a "quantum leap" to a higher level of [mystical] existence.... A new age of enlightenment—a New World Order—will be born.

---

1. For more information, see the chapter (or section) "The New Age and the spirit of the AntiChrist," in the volume titled, *The Prophetic Stage: Signs of the Times,* in the author's *Messiah, History, and the Tribulation Period* series.

Pantheism is Satan's religion....

....[A] New Ager who has embraced pantheism ... may, while in a trance, encounter a spirit which approaches under the guise of being a more highly evolved being....or "ascended master" ....

Those in the fields of philosophy and psychology who have delved into the occult, such as Carl Jung, have had similar experiences—only they refer to these beings as archetypal images or "Ideal Forms." Strict humanists, on the other hand, who do not believe in the existence of a spirit realm, are more commonly approached by beings posing as extraterrestrials....

Through willing or naive vessels who practice occult meditation, Satan is able to orchestrate his worldwide drive for a New World Order. Using secret occult hierarchies, he has systematically advanced his plans....

Tens of thousands of New Agers will appear on the world scene ... demanding that a one-world government be established .... to deal with existing global problems and to prevent any future catastrophes.... The international media will give full coverage....

....The most convincing arguments will have to do with the environment, global debt, world poverty, and the prevention of war....

The New World Order will appear to come from the bottom up, as something that the people of the world want. It will come in the name of democracy....

The AntiChrist will come to reside over an empowered United Nations or, perhaps, over a newly created global authority....

A World Constitution will be proposed, and a "democratic" World Parliament will be created. World citizens will believe they have a say in matters, not realizing that occult-based secret societies are really the ones in control....

Sovereign nations would [in essence] cease to exist. A single global economic system would be established.... Any real authority would now rest with an international body controlled by Satan himself.

The disputing world religions will become [largely] unified, and ... it is not inconceivable that, at some point during his ascent to power, he declares himself to be "the Christ." [He] ... might also claim to be the long awaited Messiah to the Jews. To the Buddhists he would be the fifth Buddha; to Moslems, the Imam Mahdi; to Hindus, Krishna. Those [so-called] Christians accepting this lie would unfortunately see in him the fulfillment of the second coming of Christ....

The Christianity represented by the AntiChrist will be a complete counterfeit, saturated with all the pantheistic teachings of eastern mysticism and the ancient mystery religions—the same beliefs held by New Agers and promoted by the secret societies....

The focus will be on elevating self rather than God.... The naive will actually be practicing occultism in the name of Christ, while worshiping the father of lies ...

The tragedy is that most people will voluntarily serve this man of lawlessness and his system, seeing him as their savior.... Evil will go forth in the name of goodness....

Christians who ... refuse to participate in this system will be seen as obstacles to world peace.[1]

---

1. Gary H. Kah, *En Route to Global Occupation* (Louisiana: Huntington House Publishers, 1991), pp. 69-70, 73, 75, 146-151.

3

A Name that Calculates to 666

Unlike English, ancient Hebrew and Greek did not use Arabic or Roman numerals to represent numbers. Instead, the characters of the respective alphabets were themselves used. The numbers historically applied to the Hebrew character set, which actually antedate the largely occult Cabala, are today called *cabalic*. With these numbers in mind, recall that the saints are told: "Here is wisdom: Let him who has understanding calculate the number of the beast; for it is the number of a man, and his number *is* 666 | χξς" (Rev 13:18, Gk.;[1] cf. Gen 7:6; 1 Sam 17:4, 17:7, 17:34-37; 2 Sam 21:19-20; cf. 1 Kin 10:14, 10:24; cf. Gen 7:6; Dan 3:1). As noted earlier, the name "Charles" literally means "man."[2]

Despite the arguments of some to the contrary, there is no compelling reason, biblically or otherwise, to believe that a correct identification of the AntiChrist through a proper calculation of his name, as Revelation 13:18 *calls us to do,* cannot *precede* the start of the Tribulation Period (i.e., Dan 9:27). In fact, if King Charles III is the AntiChrist (he *is),* then this is *already fulfilled* (see below).[3]

---

1. Two *false* claims regarding the original *Greek* text χξς in Revelation 13:18, as found in the Received Text *(Textus Receptus)* and most other ancient Greek manuscripts of the Apocalypse, are currently circulating among *biblical novices and liars.* First, some claim that χξς is actually *Arabic for "Allah"* (e.g., Walid Shoebat). That is patently *false.* These individuals try to shoehorn what are actually *very different* letter forms for Allah in Arabic, into Greek's χξς, and that is foolish as well as dishonest. Second, some alternately claim that the original Greek text has the equivalent of 616 (primarily pushed), 665 or 646 instead, but such claims are spurious, lacking both reliable and consistent manuscript support. A small number of *miscopied* manuscript fragments have those alternate numbers, but they are generally rejected as copying errors and unreliable. Moreover, this present chapter, in the context of the rest of this work, *proves* that χξς really is the original Greek text. There are many back-and-forth arguments in online forums, as well as errant presentations and videos elsewhere online. See, for example, "What is the original Number of the Beast?" in Stack Exchange's Biblical Hermeneutics forum at "https://hermeneutics.stackexchange.com/questions/11603/what-is-the-original-number-of-the-beast" on the Internet. All arguments against χξς and 666, are to be rejected as unlearned (novice) and false (lies); they come from "untaught and unstable people," who "twist to their own destruction," "some things hard to understand"—"as they do also the rest of the Scriptures" (2 Pet 3:16). *Indeed, this present book handily and unequivocally answers and nullifies all contrary arguments.*
2. See p. 482 of ch. 12, "Charles, Middle East 'Peace,' and Global Security."
3. Such knowledge in no way alters the fact that the general revelation of the AntiChrist—to both believers and apostate Israel—will not itself occur, in the manner spoken of in 2 Thessalonians 2, until just before the midpoint of the Tribulation Period. At that time, the son of perdition will sit in the Temple of God proclaiming his own deity (2 Ti 2:3-4, KJV), and the abomination that causes desolation, spoken of by both Daniel and Jesus, will be erected (see Matt 24:4-5, 24:15-26, 24:29; Mark 13:5-6, 13:14-25; cf. 2 Th 2:4-8, Gk.). For more information, see the discussion on the son of perdition (destruction) in ch. 7, "The Heraldic Symbols in the Arms and their Interpretations," starting around p. 203.

"Prince Charles of Wales" — or King Charles III's common name (and title) until his mother's death in September 2023[1] — is of the same form, for example, as "Messiah Jesus of Nazareth."[2] Unlike a manipulated or even contrived name or title (e.g., "Pope Caesar of Rome"), that long-employed real-life title not only calculates to six-hundred and sixty-six (666) using the cabalic numbers, but it does so in *more than one language!*

It does *not* matter that Charles has a new name as king — Charles III. Revelation 13:18 has been *fulfilled since the 1980s.* Simply put, the ultimate AntiChrist of biblical apocalyptic prophecy, is *already identified* scripturally — the name calculation (see below) is *already completed.* He is *known.* His name and the calculation thereof, *NO LONGER MATTER* — the purpose of identification, has already been achieved. Those who read any edition of *this* book (e.g., the first one from 1998), already recognize Satan's singular "seed" (Gen 3:15) as none other than Charles Philip Arthur George. Yes, the AntiChrist who is to be over a "global government," while possessed by the Devil, throughout the Great Tribulation, was *exposed to myriads of God's servants, decades ago.* Today, he is titled "King Charles III."

Below, we'll examine what this author broadly exposed in 1998, while Charles was Prince of Wales. The precise calculation method — first discovered and employed on "Prince Charles of Wales" et al. in 1981[3] — may be employed in English or Hebrew, through a simple procedure. First, *sequentially* apply the twenty-two cabalic numbers (one for each glyph or character in the Hebrew alphabet) to the first twenty-two letters in the English alphabet. Next, because Hebrew has only twenty-two characters, assign the null value (zero) to the last four letters in English (i.e., W, X, Y, and Z). Finally, obtain the

---

1. King Charles III's full name is Charles Philip Arthur George.
2. Acts 3:6 and 4:10 literally have "Jesus The Christ, The Nazarene" (Gk.), which is equivalent to "Christ Jesus, The Nazarene" (cf. Matt 26:71; Mark 1:24, 10:47, 14:67, 16:6; Luke 4:34, 18:37, 24:19; John 1:45, 18:5-7, 19:19; Acts 2:22, 6:14, 10:38, 22:8, 26:9).
3. This system is based upon an original English table from Monte Judah, given in 1987. Monte Judah and some friends of his, produced a simple computer program to calculate the value of names on this system, in *1981.* Having fed that program data containing the names of various world leaders and public figures, one name was exposed as 666—"Prince Charles of Wales." (Though Monte has now publicly stated he showed me his computer program in 1987, and that I keyed in Charles' name, I only recall being told of it, and being shown and given the English name calculation on a sheet of paper.)
  Much more recently, Monte Judah has *errantly alleged* "it is almost slander" to say that Charles *is* the foretold AntiChrist at this point, before he fulfills 2 Thessalonians 2! Such a statement is *false,* it is *error,* and it represents *weakness* (perhaps due to peer pressure) to even "go there." Those genuinely familiar with even "just" the hard evidence in the 1998 first edition of this book, *surely know better*—if their faith in God's written Word is *unwavering,* if they *really believe Him.* It is now clear why God chose this author, rather than someone else, to do the work of "him who has understanding" (Rev 13:18), as one who has "the spirit of prophecy," knowing and understanding "the Testimony of Jesus | Yeshua" (Rev 19:10)—never doubting, but by unwavering faith. Let this edition *crush* (cf. Gen 3:15) all such error, as "the just shall live by faith" (see Heb 10:37-39; cf. Hab 2:2-4; Rom 1:17-22).

sum of the values corresponding to each letter in "PRINCE CHARLES OF WALES" or נסיך צרלס מוילס (*modern* Israeli Hebrew).

The following system, for calculations in English, Hebrew or *(unusable)* Greek, shows the cabalic numbers as above described:

1	→	A	א	(A α)		50	→	N	נ ן	(N ν)
2	→	B	ב	(B β)		60	→	O	ס	(Ξ ξ)
3	→	C	ג	(Γ γ)		70	→	P	ע	(O o)
4	→	D	ד	(Δ δ)		80	→	Q	פ ף	(Π π)
5	→	E	ה	(E ε)		90	→	R	צ ץ	(Koppa)
6	→	F	ו	(ς)						
7	→	G	ז	(Z ζ)		100	→	S	ק	(P ρ)
8	→	H	ח	(H η)		200	→	T	ר	(Σ σ)
9	→	I	ט	(Θ θ)		300	→	U	ש	(T τ)
						400	→	V	ת	(Y υ)
10	→	J	י	(I ι)		0	→	W		500	→	Φ φ
20	→	K	כ ך	(K κ)		0	→	X		600	→	X χ
30	→	L	ל	(Λ λ)		0	→	Y		700	→	Ψ ψ
40	→	M	מ ם	(M μ)		0	→	Z		800	→	Ω ω
✍									900	→	*Sampsi*

In English, 'PRINCE' (70 + 90 + 9 + 50 + 3 + 5) = *227*, 'CHARLES' (3 + 8 + 1 + 90 + 30 + 5 + 100) = *237*, 'OF' (60 + 6) = *66*, and 'WALES' (0 + 1 + 30 + 5 + 100) = *136*. 227 + 237 + 66 + 136 = **666**. In Hebrew, נסיך (50 + 60 + 10 + 20) = *140*, צרלס (90 + 200 + 30 + 60) = *380*, and מוילס (40 + 6 + 10 + 30 + 60) = *146*. 140 + 380 + 146 = **666**.

Following 1998's publication of *The AntiChrist and a Cup of Tea*, some questioned the validity of this Hebrew spelling, and more recently, some note that the Hebrew version of Wikipedia spells Charles' name and title as Prince of Wales, differently (i.e., וויילס צ'ארלס, נסיך, in which "'" and "," are punctuation).[1] So, let's take a closer look. First, what many don't know is that there are actually *two* common ways to spell "Wales" in modern Israeli Hebrew. One involves a single י *(Yud or Yod),* whereas the other uses more than one Yod, as in יי; the former is what the author uses (i.e., וילס), while the latter is what we see in the Hebrew Wikipedia (i.e., וויילס). Second, use of מ *(Mem)* for "of" in front of וילס or "Wales" in "Charles, Prince of Wales" is *optional;* specifically, when מ is omitted that is only for "efficiency." When spelling "Prince Charles of Wales" (i.e., changing the word order), however, the מ for "of" *is* typically included (i.e., *not* optional). The author includes the מ (i.e., מוילס), which is proper, whereas the Hebrew Wikipedia omits it (i.e., וויילס),

---

1. Search for "Charles, Prince of Wales" at "https://he.wikipedia.org" on the Internet.

giving "Charles, Prince Wales." Third, "Charles" is optionally *translit-erated* with an **א** *(Aleph)* following the **צ** *(Tsadik);* the author does not use an **א** (i.e., the calculation employs **צרלס**), a character that is *unnecessary, silent and thus also useless in any transliteration,* though Wikipedia includes it anyway (i.e., **צ'ארלס**). Therefore, the Hebrew spelling employed herein is "typical" and certainly accept-able to all modern Israeli Hebrew (when using a single *Yod* for **ויליס** as opposed to two or **יי** for **ויילס**); indeed, there are those who would render it exactly as it is given in *The AntiChrist and a Cup of Tea.*[1] Tim McHyde, in a message to this author, rightly observes, "I would again argue that since there are various acceptable choices due to the variable nature of Hebrew transliteration, if it matches any of them, then that's good enough since the Bible does not specify what type of name, what type of transliteration, etc."

Over the years, the author has been surprised to see so many of his readers mistakenly infer that one of Prince Charles two sons—William or Henry (aka "Harry")—could be the foretold AntiChrist. Unlike their father Charles, whose name calculates to 666 in English and Hebrew, princes William and Henry *lack* the essential heraldic imagery—the symbolism of the first beast—mentioned earlier in this book,[2] and they additionally *lack* the required numerology, as no title

---

1. In March 2009, the author spoke by phone and corresponded by e-mail with Israelis in Israel, who are fluent in both modern Israeli Hebrew and English, to include Doram Gaunt, Night Editor at the English Edition of *Haaretz* in Israel (cited by permission), as well as an employee of *Ynet News*—and they con-firmed the above information.
2. See the discussion on the biblical requirements to be the AntiChrist in ch. 1, "The Footsteps of *the* An-tiChrist," at p. 30. Prince William was granted his heraldic achievement or coat of arms in June 2000, and Prince Henry (aka "Harry") received his in September 2002.
    Though both princes William and Henry had been *unofficially "styled"* "of Wales," neither was *ever* in any formal sense the "Prince of Wales," despite the *former* loose styling, *until Charles became king and "created" William as such.* Prince William as Duke of Cambridge, or "William Arthur Philip Louis Mountbatten-Windsor," was earlier *called* "of Wales" until marrying in 2011, whereas Prince Harry, Duke of Sussex, or "Henry Charles Albert David Mountbatten-Windsor," had likewise been so-called until he married in 2018. (See ch. 16, "King Charles III: History's Ultimate AntiChrist," on p. 561.)
    Neither William nor Henry bears the red dragon or possesses the ten horns (i.e., the seven-horned helm of the sovereign in conjunction with the three-horned label of the eldest son, as documented later in this book)—though some *mistakenly* think Scotland's *red lion* is Wales' red dragon. (Those who claim William or his brother have the red dragon on their heraldic achievements, are *ignorant*. They *conflate* Scotland's red *lion* with Wales' red dragon.) *Neither prince, therefore, receives* "his power, his throne, and great authority" from the red dragon or Satan (see Rev 13:2). *Both princes also lack* the imposition of the Shield of Wales, containing four lion-leopards, over the central royal shield; so each prince has six lion-leopards rather than ten (these are all *lion-leopard-bears* in the case of Charles' heraldic achieve-ment as Prince of Wales). Yet, the AntiChrist will be over ten "kings" or rulers. William did also lack, and *Harry yet lacks* the surrounding Garter of the Order of the Garter; as later clarified, this is actually very significant. From the relatively poor artistic renditions available, *it is unclear as to whether either* Prince William's or Prince Henry's heraldic achievement bears the normal lion (or lion-leopard) for Eng-land—as opposed to the first beast of Revelation 13:2 which is "<u>like</u> a leopard" with feet "<u>like</u> the feet of a bear" (a bear has five evident claws per foot, which is not always fully shown in heraldry) and a mouth "<u>like</u> the mouth of a lion." For the same reason, *it is also unclear as to whether either* actually bears a unicorn with human eyes (i.e., a little horn with eyes <u>like</u> those of a man; cf. Daniel 7:8, 7:11, 7:20-21). William's and Henry's heraldic achievements are primarily differenced by their *labels,* and the fact that William's as Prince of Wales, now also bears the Garter.

possessed or used now or previously by either of them—to include "Prince William of Wales" and "Prince Henry of Wales" (or "Prince 'Harry' of Wales," if you prefer), respectively—calculates to 666 on the biblical system.[1] While there are other criteria that ostensibly further disqualify King Charles III's *sons* (e.g., the *lack* of a key role in Mideast peace processes leading to imposition and enforcement of the covenant or treaty of Daniel 9:27), these two points—the *lack* of the requisite imagery or symbolism, and the *lack* of a name or title that calculates to 666, on the *biblical* system—*eliminate* princes William and Henry (Harry) from all consideration. Whoever lacks this genuine understanding, whoever disbelieves these points, *that person neither knows nor believes scripture in this area,* and is thus *not qualified* to speak to, nor address the identity of the foretold AntiChrist. Do not be misled. ***Neither William nor Henry (Harry) could be the foretold AntiChrist, but are "merely" his sons.*** Let's continue.

Three objections in particular might be raised to the above system, *as it pertains to English.* *First,* it may be argued that any name calculation should be done using the original Hebrew rather than the English, or some other alphabet.[2] *Second,* the cabalic numbers have been applied sequentially to the English alphabet, rather than phonetically as some might expect. *Third,* the last four letters in the English alphabet are left without numeric values, and are thus assumed to represent zero. However, as shown below, these objections are not entirely sound.

Some may also raise a further objection related to the Greek text of Revelation 13:18. We have seen that Charles' common name and title until Elizabeth II's death in September 2023—that is, "Charles, Prince of Wales" or "Prince Charles of Wales"—calculates to 666 in both English and Hebrew. However, the number 666 is explicitly

---

There are still other insurmountable disparities. All this serves, however, to reinforce the fact that *neither of King Charles III's sons is biblically qualified to be the prophesied AntiChrist.* Anyone who claims to have read this work, done his or her own "research," and/or "heard from God," who alleges that either Prince William or Prince Henry (Harry) could be the foretold AntiChrist, is a) lying, b) a very careless reader and "researcher," and/or c) just a "dime a dozen" false teacher—but irrespective of the applicable option, he or she is someone to whom Christians should pay *no* attention. In subsequent chapters, we will address the imagery or symbolism of the first beast of Revelation 13, and the little horn with eyes like the eyes of a man of Daniel 7, in great detail.

1. "WILLIAM" (0 + 9 + 30 + 30 + 9 + 1 + 40) = *119.* "HENRY" (8 + 5 + 50 + 90 + 0) = *153.* "HARRY" (8 + 1 + 90 + 90 +0) = *189.* Again, while many have referred to princes William and Henry as "Prince William of Wales" and "Prince Henry | 'Harry' of Wales," respectively, neither was ever officially invested as such, and therefore *neither of them has technically been an actual prince of Wales,* let alone *the* Prince of Wales. There is only one official Prince of Wales currently, and that is their father, Charles. Inasmuch as the red dragon is the national symbol of Wales, and as such was central to Charles' investiture as Prince of Wales in July 1969 (documented later in this book), we may rightly say that Charles was *and remains* the Prince of the Red Dragon or Satan (see Rev 12:3, 12:9), who *continues* to give Charles "his power, his throne, and great authority" (Rev 13:2).

2. See, for example, Arnold G. Fruchtenbaum, *The Footsteps of The Messiah* (California: Ariel Press, 1982), p. 173.

specified using the ancient biblical numbering system as applied to the Greek language, in the inspired *original* Greek text of Revelation 13:18. So what about modern Greek calculations? According to native Greeks in Greece, this is Charles as Prince of Wales' common name (and title) in uppercase modern Greek: ΠΡΙΓΚΙΠΑΣ ΚΑΡΟΛΟΣ ΤΗΣ ΟΥΑΛΙΑΣ (or "ΟΥΑΛΛΙΑΣ" in the recent past). The value or sum of the uppercase Greek text is at least 2,215 (i.e., ΠΡΙΓΚΙΠΑΣ = 504, ΚΑΡΟΛΟΣ = 491, ΤΗΣ = 508, ΟΥΑΛΙΑΣ = 712). The proper (i.e., upper- and lower-) case Greek is: Πριγκηπας Καρολος της Ουαλιας (or "Ουαλλιας" in the recent past). The value or sum of the proper-case Greek text is at least 1,437 (i.e., Πριγκηπας = 308, Καρολος = 297, της = 314, Ουαλιας = 518). (The sum of an all lower-case Greek calculation would, at least in this instance, have the same value as that of the proper-case calculation just performed.) In "high Greek," the word for "prince" in the nominative would be ΠΡΙΓΚΗΨ (upper-case) or Πριγκηψ (proper-case); these spellings, of course, would lead to different Greek calculations. We must conclude, therefore, that Charles' common name and title as Prince of Wales, "Prince Charles of Wales," does *not* calculate to 666 in Greek, and *cannot* therein be reliably calculated. Is that a problem? No, and *it should not surprise us:* capitalization in Greek affects calculations, making calculated values for Greek words suspect. This is not so, however, with English or Hebrew, where calculations are evidently reliable. Moreover, in 1976, Greece's socialist government "simplified" Greek, eliminating most double consonants to create "Standard Modern Greek," further complicating Greek calculations.

First, it may be counter-argued that the calculation of the AntiChrist's name should be performed in his own native language, thereby eliminating any possible need to transliterate and translate it into a different tongue, which would normally yield only an approximation. (We may also note that English is currently the world's most widely spoken language.) *Second,* a phonetic application of the cabalic numbers to the English alphabet would also be an approximation, just as the transliteration of a word from one language to another yields a word which sounds *approximately* like the original. Given these difficulties, it seems quite reasonable to use the most straightforward application of the cabalic numbers to the English alphabet (i.e., the sequential method) despite the aforementioned objections; such an application precludes all errors of approximation. Further, it must be pointed out that the ancient Greek numbering system was itself historically derived from the Hebrew system in precisely this manner. Yet unlike the unmodified, non-supplemented cabalic numbers used in our English system, the Greek system originally omitted 6 and 90, and added 500, 600, 700, and 800 (after 400). Also, provisions were later made for it to include 6 (final *sigma*) and 90 (arbitrary symbol *Koppa),* as well as incorporate 900 (arbitrary symbol *Sampsi). This very system, which the early Church fathers employed to calculate the values of Greek names and other words,*[1] *is the basis for the number 666 (i.e., χξς) in the original Greek text of Revelation 13:18.*[2] Therefore, apart from our omission of added numbers (i.e., 500, 600, 700, 800, and 900), the non-phonetic, sequential method used to apply the cabalic numbers to the English alphabet in our system is neither new nor unprecedented; rather, despite possible arguments to the contrary, it is *the* historically, biblically, and theologically accepted method. Indeed, it is also the method recognized by Ladd and others.[3] The authoritative weight of such a calculation in this system, scripturally speaking, is far greater than in any contrived system ever devised, and there are several.[4]

Finally, in the author's opinion, the weight of the evidence presented herein regarding King Charles III is so great that even if there were no known numbering system whereby his name as prince or otherwise calculated to 666, one would nonetheless be compelled to conclude that he is plausibly the AntiChrist. But above, we see that there are at least two languages—Hebrew and English—in which Charles' name as Prince of Wales, calculates to 666, and on the same numbering system, using entirely different combinations of numbers! With that reality, our "plausibility" really becomes a *statistical* certainty.[5] In fact, there is likely still not a *conventional* supercomputer, that is capable of accurately calculating the odds of such a multiple occurrence, among billions of name combinations, each compassing several different character values. Either way, we may be certain that if Charles Philip Arthur George is *the* AntiChrist, the man who is to ride as the Fourth Horseman (Rev 6:7-8)—and the combined evidence unambiguously shows King Charles III *is* that

1. Irenaeus, Against Heresies, Bk. 5, Ch. 30, Pars. 1 and 3; see *Ante-Nicene Fathers,* ed. Alexander Roberts and James Donaldson (1885-1886; rpt. Massachusetts: Hendrickson Publishers, Inc., 1994), Vol. 1, pp. 558-559.

2. With sexual satanism becoming so prevalent today, we may note that χξς read backwards, resembles "sex." These Greek letters, assigned to the numbers 600, 60, and 6, are used together in Revelation 13:18, to specify the numeric total 666, as seen in the Received Text (e.g., *Scrivener's Textus Receptus* 1894), the Greek NT used by the Greek Ortodox Church, and the *Greek NT: Tischendorf 8th Edition.* (Though Majority and NA or Nestle-Aland Greek texts are *unreliable* here, reflecting errors of modern "scholarship.") With the added exception of Revelation 7:4, for example, in which the number 144 is specified using this same system, most numbers in the Apocalypse are given using actual Greek words, not combinations of specific letters.

3. George Eldon Ladd, *A COMMENTARY on the REVELATION of JOHN* (Michigan: Eerdmans Publishing Co., 1972), p. 186.

4. For typical examples of interesting, but contrived systems, see Church, pp. 240-241.

5. Physicists view an event that is rarer than *one in ten to the fiftieth power* as so improbable as to be impossible. In our case, the odds depict an event that is *far less likely* to occur. In other words, it could only happen by God's sovereign intent.

man—then there must be such a system. The one herein presented, for lack of another which may seem more palatable, works.

4

Prince of this World
—a *Diverse* Lineage

Many have concluded that the AntiChrist will require some degree of authority over Jews, "Christians," *and* Muslims to achieve his eventual worldwide dominion. King Charles III, as documented below, may one day *openly and explicitly claim* literal descent from Israel's King David,[1] Jesus the Christ, *and* Islam's Mohammed, not to mention thousands of other historically influential individuals. Further, the "Merovingian" dynasty, as we shall see, appears to be central to such a "Christ Jesus" possibility. Beyond this, we may observe that the title "Prince of Wales" bears further import, as "Wales" actually means "foreigners" or "romanized foreigners." Thus, Charles is "prince" or ruler of this *romanized,* antiChrist world.

A Merovingian "conspiracy of destiny." Various researchers and others have come to recognize the fascinating existence of an historical conspiracy to establish a one-world government under a Merovingian descendant. We may begin our account with Merovée, a fifth-century king of the Sicambrians or Germanic Franks (now Germany and France),[2] who worshiped the bear in the form of the Roman *Diana*—the same goddess who is also known as the Greek

---

1. Per Robert Darby and John Cozijn: "This notion—that the British monarchy was somehow descended directly from King David—was not introduced until the 1860s, in England, [in] the *Remnant of Judah and the Israel of Ephraim: The Two Families Under One Head* (Glover, 1861, 1881), by a former 'chaplain to the consulate in Cologne,' Frederick Glover, and it was not until the 1870s that the myth took its final, elaborated form in J. C. Stevens' Genealogical Chart Showing the Connection between the House of David and the Royal Family of Britain (1877). Together with the wildly popular *Twenty-Seven Identifications of the British Nation With Lost Israel* by Richard Hines (1871), these texts spurred the formation of the [so-called] British Israelites as an organized movement, with newsletters, offices, meetings, and branches in other Anglo countries, including the United States" (Darby and Cozijn, "The British Royal Family's Circumcision Tradition: Genesis and Evolution of a Contemporary Legend," *SAGE Open*, October-December 2013, pp. 5-6; DOI: "10.1177/2158244013508960").

2. According to Baigent, Leigh, and Lincoln: "Between the fifth and seventh centuries the Merovingians ruled large parts of what are now France and Germany. The period of their ascendancy coincides with the period of [England's] King Arthur—a period that constitutes the setting for the romances of the Holy Grail." In the fifth century, the Sicambrian ancestors of the Merovingians "crossed the Rhine and moved en masse into Gaul, establishing themselves in what is now Belgium and northern France, in the vicinity of the Ardennes. A century later this region came to be called the kingdom of Austrasia. And the core of the kingdom of Austrasia was what is now known as Lorraine." The ancestors of the Merovingians may also be traced "to ancient Greece, and specifically to the region known as Arcadia," being "connected with Arcadia's royal house." The Arcadians, who, like the Sicambrian Franks, worshiped the bear, "supposedly migrated up the Danube, then up the Rhine, and established themselves in what is now western Germany" (*Holy Blood, Holy Grail*, pp. 234, 238-239).

Artemis, the "virgin-mother goddess" of the wooded hunt and the Moon (associated historically with the unicorn).[1] Although Merovée's son, Childeric I, practiced witchcraft, his grandson, Clovis I, converted to Roman Catholicism and became the "New Constantine."

Some Merovingians claim, however, that Merovée, their forefather, not only had a birthmark in the form of a red cross on his chest, but was a physical descendant of Jesus and Mary the Magdalene. Others allege that a sea monster (serpent)—or red dragon—*raped* Merovée's mother, making him a humanoid or *Nephil* (i.e., a human-angel hybrid, where *nephil* may be translated as "fallen liar").[2] (In a later chapter, we'll further address such claims.) According to the former sordid tale, Jesus didn't really die on the cross, but was stolen away from the tomb, only to survive and secretly wed Mary the Magdalene (as well as her presumed sister Martha), with whom he then fathered children. When the Romans temporarily lifted their siege of Jerusalem shortly before its destruction in A.D. 70, Mary the Magdalene fled with her children to France via the Mediterranean Sea, where they eventually married into the royal Frankish family. Viewing themselves as potentially divine, messianic descendants of King David and Jesus, as well as of the Roman emperors, these Merovingians have therefore sought clandestinely to place their offspring upon the thrones of Europe through intermarriage. Per the latter tale—that is, the one involving the alleged rape—the Merovin-

---

1. *Eerdmans' Handbook to the World's Religions,* pp. 393, 400. In the ancient Middle East, *Artemis* was otherwise known as the "Queen of Heaven," or the Babylonian *Ishtar,* the Egyptian *Isis,* the Canaanite *Ashtoreth* (Astarte), *Asherah,* and *Anath,* etc.—all of which originated with Semiramis. For more information, see ch. 6, "The First Beast and Prince Charles' Coat of Arms," at p. 115.

    In discussing the pagan priesthood of "Nemi" (i.e., Nimrod), who as the "dying god-king," is the "King of the Wood," James George Frazer held that "magic is a means of controlling nature and therefore an essential function of kingship," following from a "union of a royal title with priestly duties." According to Frazer, "No class of the community has benefited so much as kings by this belief in the possible incarnation of a god in human form." With this in mind, Frazer speaks of a union in a "sacred grove" of the "oak god," supposedly incarnated in Roman kings, and the "oak-nymph" or "oak-goddess" named "Diana" who, as the "goddess of fertility," is "a divinity of childbirth." The union "must have been intended to quicken the growth of vegetation by homoeopathic magic." The two thus became "King and Queen of the Wood in a solemn marriage, which was intended to make the earth gay with the blossoms of spring and the fruits of autumn, and to gladden the hearts of men and women with healthful offspring;" for "such kings were thought to ensure good weather and the fertility of fields and animals." Nemi, therefore, "embodied the great Aryan god of the oak; and as an oak-god he would mate with the oak-goddess, whether she went by the name of Egeria or Diana" (*The Illustrated Golden Bough,* ed. Mary Douglas {New York: Doubleday & Co., 1978}, pp. 19, 32, 52, 72, 76-78). It seems plausible that Charles, who had studied this particular mythology before his marriage to "Diana" (Cathcart, pp. 74-75, 81), had it in mind when he chose to court her, so that she could dutifully produce "an heir and a spare" and receive the "worship" of the masses. At the princess' funeral, her brother observed, "of all the ironies about Diana, perhaps the greatest is this; that a girl given the name of the ancient goddess of hunting was, in the end, the most hunted person of the modern age" (The Associated Press, "Brother extols Diana's humanity, commitment," *The Denver Post,* 7 Sept. 1997, p. 27A). Going overboard, Elton John eulogized, "Goodbye, England's rose, from a country lost without your soul."

2. For more information, see the author's *Solar Apocalypse* multi-volume series.

gians acquired their "'divine' right to rule" from an "alien" or even *Satan,* as the "'god' of this age" (see 2 Cor 4:3-4; cf. Eph 2:1-3, 6:11-12). Of course, most of Europe's royal families today are supposedly Merovingian in descent.[1]

Remarkably, the popular *Ancient Aliens* TV series claims the British monarchy descends from Woden (i.e., Wotan, Odin, etc., *aka Satan),* which *to that show's creators* suggests descent from an "ancient alien." At the same time, they allege that royalty among humanity generally have special bloodline(s), and that a supposed "alien" ancestry is the source of their "divine right to rule:" "Perhaps additional evidence can be found by looking at the extraordinary bloodline of one of the most powerful and enduring royal families in human history.... Is it possible that the British Monarch is an actual flesh-and-blood descendant of other-worldly beings? Tracing royal lineage back to a [(supposed)] 'god' [of extraterrestrial origin] implies great wisdom, almost celestial power, a connection to the divine, truly making the [('alien')] 'gods' on our side. Kings and Queens all over the world—particularly in Europe—believe they are from a special bloodline, and they make a big deal of that.... Might ancient royalties' possible extraterrestrial origins explain why monarchs have protected their bloodlines [(through familial interbreeding)] for centuries?.... One thing is certain, and that is, if it wasn't for these ancient peoples' believing that their kings and emperors were divine, there is [(supposedly)] very little to have held these early civilizations together—and believing that your leader was somehow a 'god,' or descended from a 'god,' [(may have at times)] kept people together.... Many of our greatest rulers were guided or influenced directly, according to what they say, by [(supposed)] celestial beings. Perhaps it is this influence that gave some of these rulers the capacity to change human history. Were there really extraterrestrial influences steering the emperors, kings and pharaohs of the ancient world? And if so, does this mean that the blood of the so-called 'gods' doesn't only flow throughout the veins of today's monarchs, but in the DNA of millions of people living throughout the world?.... Because it may not be that we need to wait for Earth's [(they falsely allege)] 'alien' ancestors to return; it may be they are already here."[2]

Ancient Aliens propagandists, while focusing on royal symbols and regalia (e.g., the "Stone of Destiny" and throne, as well as the scepter and crown, as later addressed), also juxtapose the British monarchy (e.g., Elizabeth II) with ancient Egypt's pharaohs, while at-

---

1. J.R. Church, *Guardians of the Grail ... and the men who plan to rule the world,* rev. ed. (Oklahoma: Prophecy Publications, 1991), pp. 12-14, 23, 25, 27, 62, 73, 101.

2. See 29:55 to 44:12 in Episode 7 of Season 6 of *Ancient Aliens,* titled "Emperors, Kings and Pharaohs," as aired in Nov. 2013. For more information, see the author's *Solar Apocalypse* multi-volume series.

tempting to connect both to "the gods" and "alien encounters."[1] But even these propagandists miss a lot, so the above is not all.

Legend has it, for example, that Joseph of Arimathea caught some of the blood of Jesus in the *cup* from which The Lord drank at the Last Supper with His disciples when His side was pierced by a *spear* upon the cross. Due to their contact with Jesus' blood, both the cup and the spear, called the "Spear of Longinus" and the *Spear of Destiny,* have since been associated with certain "magical" powers. The spear, which is said to confer upon its owner the ability to rule the world, but death to anyone who loses it, is currently in the Habsburg Treasure House (a family museum) at Vienna, Austria.[2] But what about the cup? Although some accounts hold that Mary the Magdalene took the *Cup of Destiny,* or the "Holy Grail," with her when she fled to France, others state that Joseph of Arimathea brought it "to England, where he and his offspring became the Guardians of the Grail."[3] It is noteworthy, therefore, that Queen Elizabeth II's lineage, while it shows the genealogies of both the virgin Mary and Jesus' adoptive father Joseph, as found in Luke 3:23c-33 and Matthew 1:3-15, seems to indicate that Merovée, rather than necessarily being a descendant of David through Jesus and Mary the Magdalene, was actually a descendant of David through Anna. Anna is referred to as a "cousin" of Jesus' mother Mary and depicted as a relative, apparently the daughter, of Joseph of Arimathea.[4] (We'll later address Elizabeth II's lineage.)

The Priory of Zion, the Knights Templar, and the Rosicrucians. By 1061, France's Roman Catholic Crusaders had captured Jerusalem. Upon doing so, they set Godfroi de Bouillon, the Merovingian leader of the First Crusade and the Duke of Lorraine,[5] who was the grandson of Eustache I and the son of Eustache II, upon the throne; for he claimed Davidic descent.

Later, in either 1090 or 1099, Godfroi founded the Order of Sion (Zion), a secret society.[6] In 1111, 1112, or 1118, Hugues de Payen instituted the Knights Templar (Temple Knights) as a "front organization"

---

1. "Aliens and Mysterious Rituals," *Ancient Aliens* (Seas. 3, Ep. 5), Aug. 2011.
2. According to Church, Constantine invoked this spear's "serpent powers" to "rise to the throne of the Roman Empire" and afterwards "held it to his breast" while declaring himself to be the "Thirteenth Apostle." Also, later Merovingian kings and emperors are thought to have used it "as a symbol of their power." From the time of Charlemagne, who "founded his whole dynasty on the possession of the Spear," until the fall of the last Habsburg emperor in 1806, "forty-five emperors claimed the Spear of Destiny." Later, Hitler invaded Austria at the start of World War II to obtain the spear, and committed suicide the day that the American military recovered it in Nuremberg (pp. 44, 54-57, 60, 63-69).
3. Church, pp. 53, 76.
4. In connection with the legend of the Grail, Baigent, Leigh, and Lincoln note that Joseph of Arimathea was supposedly also Perceval's mother's uncle (*Holy Blood, Holy Grail*, p. 290).
5. Baigent, Leigh, and Lincoln, *Holy Blood, Holy Grail*, pp. 268-269.
6. Baigent, Leigh, and Lincoln, *Holy Blood, Holy Grail*, p. 111.

for the Order of Zion,[1] and he appointed Godfroi's brother, Baudouin I, as its second grand master (after himself). Subsequently, around 1128, "Saint Bernard, abbot of Clairvaux and the age's [supposed] chief spokesman for Christendom," declared the Temple Knights to be "the epitome and apotheosis of Christian values." The "Church" then officially recognized and incorporated the Temple Knights as "a religious-military order" of "warrior-monks" and "soldier-mystics," and Hugues de Payen received the honorary title of grand master of the Temple Knights.[2] In 1188, the Temple Knights separated from the Order of Zion, which then changed its name to the Priory of Sion (Zion). Also in 1188, the *Priory* of Zion's first grand master, Jean de Gisors, founded the Rosicrucians.[3]

Originally known as the Order of the Poor Knights of Christ and the Temple of Solomon, the Knights Templar, according to tradition, built their quarters upon "the foundations of the ancient temple of Solomon."[4] Initially headquartered in France, however, the Temple Knights, who are thought to have found and plundered some of the hidden treasures of the destroyed Second Temple, adopted the Merovingian birthmark, a red cross, as their symbol. Introduced into England around 1140,[5] and ultimately threatened by the Roman Catholic Church, they found eventual refuge in Scotland, where the French Templars became the Scottish Rite of Freemasonry. The Templars are credited with having instituted a wealthy and influential "international banking system across Europe." All things considered, the supposed "Protocols of the Elders of Zion," appears not to be a Judaic work, but a modified work of the Priory of Zion,[6] possibly having been altered for public consumption with the complicity of the Illuminati.[7] Nevertheless, with much contrivance, the work was later advanced as proof of a "Jewish conspiracy." As such, it fueled the mass murder of millions of European Jews in the past century.[8]

From 1188 to the present day, the Priory of Zion has been the "benefactor" of a struggle for dominance between English and French royalty and nobility. Originally a French-English oligarchical order and secret-society, from which came the Knights Templar and

1. Baigent, Leigh, and Lincoln, *Holy Blood, Holy Grail,* pp. 86-87.
2. Baigent, Leigh, and Lincoln, *Holy Blood, Holy Grail,* pp. 67, 82, 117.
3. Church, pp. 15-16, 23, 25, 28-29, 86-88. For a brief outline of this historical development with additional details, see Baigent, Leigh, and Lincoln, *Holy Blood, Holy Grail,* pp. 117-118.
4. Baigent, Leigh, and Lincoln, *Holy Blood, Holy Grail,* pp. 66, 118.
5. Charles Boutell, *Boutell's Heraldry,* rev. J.P. Brooke-Little {London: Frederick Warne, 1978; ISBN: 0 7232 2096 4; LCCN: 73-75030}, p. 191.
6. See, for example, Baigent, Leigh, and Lincoln, *Holy Blood, Holy Grail,* pp. 193-195, 294.
7. Note, however, that various apostate Israelites have at times played prominent roles within the Illuminati. For more information, see ch. 7's section titled, "The Garter" at p. 147.
8. Church, pp. 23-29, 86-87, 167-169. Baigent, Leigh, and Lincoln, *Holy Blood, Holy Grail,* pp. 191-192.

the Rosicrucians, its control came to rest largely with the English side, even while a number of its grand masters resided in France.

Jean de Gisors, the priory's *first* grand master (1188-1220), for example, "was a vassal of the king of England—Henry II, and then Richard I." Note that Henry II was a French Anjou by birth (discussed below). Marie de Saint-Clair, the priory's *second* grand master (1220-1266) and possibly the second wife of Jean de Gisors, "was descended from Henry de Saint-Clair, Baron of Rosslyn in Scotland, who accompanied Godfroi de Bouillon on the First Crusade. Rosslyn itself was situated not far from the Templars' major preceptory in Scotland, and Rosslyn Chapel, built in the fifteenth century, became mantled with Rose-Croix and Freemasonry legends."[1] Today, of course, Scotland is an integral part of the United Kingdom under the English monarchy. The priory's *third* grand master was Guillaume de Gisors (1266-1307).

Edouard de Bar, the priory's *fourth* grand master (1307-1336), "was a grandson of Edward I of England and a nephew of Edward II.... Edouard's daughter married into the house of Lorraine.... ... Edouard was grand-nephew of Guillaume's wife, Iolande de Bar."[2] Jeanne de Bar, the priory's *fifth* grand master (1336-1351), was "the elder sister of Edouard" and "a granddaughter of Edward I of England and a niece of Edward II.... Jeanne ... seems to have enjoyed extremely cordial relations with the English throne .... [and] ... to have had similar relations with the king of France." Jean de Saint-Clair, the priory's *sixth* grand master (1351-1366) was not only "descended from the French houses," but "his grandfather was married to Jeanne de Bar's aunt." In other words, he also was a descendant of English royalty.[3] It was during this period, in 1348, that King Edward III founded the Order of the Garter, which, as will be shown later, established itself over the Priory of Zion, the Knights Templar, and the Rosicrucians! In other words, the Order of the Garter became the heart of the ultimate conspiracy for a Luciferic New World Order.[4] Note, therefore, that *the year 2014 on the Gregorian calendar will constitute 666 years since the founding of the Order of the Garter*. It will be interesting to see what of prophetic import, if anything, transpires in 2014.

René d'Anjou, the priory's *ninth* grand master (1418-1480), came to hold the titles "count of Bar" and "king of Jerusalem" (see below). René, who "seems to have had a particular preoccupation with the Grail," may have played a key role in the Renaissance. His influ-

1. Baigent, Leigh, and Lincoln, *Holy Blood, Holy Grail*, pp. 131, 415.
2. Baigent, Leigh, and Lincoln, *Holy Blood, Holy Grail*, pp. 131, 416.
3. Baigent, Leigh, and Lincoln, *Holy Blood, Holy Grail*, pp. 131, 417.
4. For more information, see ch. 7's section titled, "The Garter" at p. 147.

ence appears to have "prompted Cosimo de' Medici to embark on a series of ambitious projects ... destined to transform Western civilization," including the creation of "an academy of Pythagorean and Platonic studies."[1] "Cosimo's academy quickly generated a multitude of similar institutions throughout the Italian peninsula, which became bastions of Western esoteric tradition. And from them the high culture of the Renaissance began to blossom." One of René's daughters "married Henry VI of England and became a prominent figure in the Wars of the Roses." Henry VI also had Anjou blood. Iolande de Bar, another of René d'Anjou's daughters, was the priory's *tenth* grand master (1480-1483).[2]

Louis de Nevers, the priory's *fifteenth* grand master (1575-1595), "would have functioned in close concert with .... [the] treasurer of the military contingent sent by Elizabeth I of England to support the French king. ....In 1582, ... Louis was in England, consorting with ... John Dee, the foremost English esotericist of his age." Robert Fludd, the priory's *sixteenth* grand master (1595-1637), "inherited John Dee's mantle as England's leading exponent of esoteric thought." Fludd "warmly endorsed" the Rosicrucians, "declaring that the 'highest good' was the 'Magia, Cabala and Alchymia of the Brothers of the Rosy Cross.'" Enjoying the favor of England's King James I and King Charles I, Fludd "was among the conclave of scholars who presided over the translation of the [Authorized] King James Bible."[3] (It appears, then, that despite the claims of some, the AKJV translation was *not* accomplished entirely apart from the influence of heretics and apostates. In fact, it is a noteworthy twist that the British monarchy, which may well prove to have produced *the* AntiChrist, holds a copyright on the translation to this day.) Robert Boyle, the priory's *eighteenth* grand master (1654-1691), "was educated at Eton, where his provost ... was closely connected with the Rosicrucian entourage.... ...Boyle was among the first [English] public figures to offer allegiance to the newly restored Stuarts, and Charles II became patron of the Royal Society.... ...Boyle's two closest friends were [Sir] Isaac Newton and John Locke .... [who] ... shortly after making Boyle's acquaintance, embarked for a lengthy stay in the south of France." Locke "is known to have studied ... the history of the legends according to which the Magdalen brought the Holy Grail to Marseilles."[4]

---

1. For more information, see the discussion on the "Platonic ideal" in ch. 11's section titled, "The United World Colleges" at pp. 395 (note) and 401.
2. Baigent, Leigh, and Lincoln, *Holy Blood, Holy Grail*, pp. 131, 136, 138-139, 421-422.
3. Baigent, Leigh, and Lincoln, *Holy Blood, Holy Grail*, pp. 131, 425-426.
4. Baigent, Leigh, and Lincoln, *Holy Blood, Holy Grail*, pp. 131, 427-428.

Sir Isaac Newton, the priory's *nineteenth* grand master (1691-1727), who claimed descent from "ancient Scottish nobility," was elected president of the Royal Society in 1703. Newton, who "was militantly, albeit quietly, hostile to the idea of the Trinity" and who "questioned the divinity of Jesus," "more than any other scientist of his age, was steeped in Hermetic texts." "In addition to personally annotated copies of the Rosicrucian manifestos, his library included more than a hundred alchemical works." Newton, whose "works reflect interests shared by Masonic figures of the period," was sympathetic to those who "stressed the supremacy of gnosis, or direct knowledge, over faith." Moreover, he befriended "Jean Desaguliers, who was one of the Royal Society's two curators of experiments," and who "became one of the leading figures in the astonishing proliferation of Freemasonry throughout Europe." Desaguliers presided over the masonic initiation of Prince Francois, the Duke of Lorraine. Newton's closest friend, Nicolas Fatio de Duillier, "appears to have worked as a spy, usually against Louis XIV of France."[1]

Charles Radclyffe, the priory's *twentieth* grand master (1727-1746), was, as an illegitimate grandson of King Charles II, created an earl of Derwentwater by King James II. As such, he "devoted much of his life to the Stuart cause." **Charles V de Lorraine**, the priory's *twenty-first* grand master (1746-1780), was probably "exposed ... to a Jacobite influence;" for his father "had offered protection and refuge at Bar-le-Duc to the exiled Stuarts." (The Jacobites used three ostrich feathers, derived from Edward III's son, Edward the Black Prince, as their symbol.[2] In other words, Charles V de Lorraine was at least loosely associated with the Order of the Garter.) Charles was "Austrian field marshal in the eighteenth century, [and] brother-in-law to the Empress Maria Theresa." His court resembled that of René d'Anjou, his ancestor and another prominent Merovingian. Perhaps relevant, Maximilian de Lorraine, the priory's *twenty-second* grand master (1780-1801), "seems to have acted through cultural figures, as well as through certain of his own numerous siblings — Marie Caroline, for instance, who as queen of Naples and Sicily was largely responsible for the spread of Freemasonry in those domains."[3]

Charles Nodier, the priory's *twenty-third* grand master (1801-1844), appears to be the first of the priory's grand masters lacking "noble blood." Nevertheless, he published a "seditious tract" in London in opposition to Napoleon and claimed involvement in "two separate plots against Napoleon." Victor Hugo, the priory's *twenty-*

---

1. Baigent, Leigh, and Lincoln, *Holy Blood, Holy Grail,* pp. 131, 429-431.
2. For more information, see ch. 7's section titled, "The motto and the heir-apparent's badge," at p. 187. These resemble three *Vav's,* for 6-6-6.
3. Baigent, Leigh, and Lincoln, *Holy Blood, Holy Grail,* pp. 131, 134, 431-434.

fourth grand master (1844-1885), whose father "maintained very cordial relations with the conspirators involved in the plot against the [French] emperor," was a "fervent disciple" of Charles Nodier. "Like Newton he was militantly anti-Trinitarian and repudiated Jesus' divinity. [He] ... was immersed all his life in esoterica, in Gnostic, Cabalistic, and Hermetic thought.... And he is known to have been connected with a so-called Rose-Croix order." Jean Cocteau, the priory's *twenty-sixth* grand master (1918-?), decorated "such churches as Notre Dame de France in London."[1]

From the above documentation, it seems clear that the Priory of Zion has in fact been more an historical tool of the English monarchy and nobility than of the French. It is of significant interest, therefore, that the Priory of Zion, the Temple Knights, and the Rosicrucians, all of which ultimately derive from the earlier Order of Zion, together gave rise to English and French Freemasonry. Moreover, in 1348, as will be more fully documented later, the Order of the Garter became the major control point from which the English monarchy exercised its global influence.[2]

Recall that Godfroi de Bouillon, a Merovingian crusader, founded the Order of Zion in either 1090 or 1099. Upon Godfroi's death in 1100, Baudouin I (Baldwin I)—Godfroi's brother—assumed the title "King of Jerusalem." Following him, Baldwin II, Fulk V (the father of Geoffrey Plantagenet and grandfather of Henry II), Baldwin III, Amalric I, Baldwin IV, Baldwin V, and several others, all of whom were of Merovingian descent, held the title. Eventually it passed to Emperor Charles V de Lorraine, who, as a descendant the Merovingian Hildegarde and the twenty-first grand master of the Priory of Zion, married Eleonore Marie von Habsburg, daughter of Emperor Ferdinand III. The Habsburg (also spelled "Hapsburg") dynasty, which descends separately from Merovée through Alex, the sister of Godfroi and Baudouin I, has held it ever since. Currently, Karl von Habsburg of Austria, the titular "head of the House of Habsburg-Lorraine," who, under rosier circumstances, "would have been [called] Emperor of Austria, Apostolic King of Hungary and Holy Roman Emperor," could "pretentiously" hold the title like his late father Otto,[3] but politically states, "I don't refer to titles, I'm not that vain."[4] Meanwhile, King Felipe VI of Spain claims it. Like his late father Juan Carlos I, Felipe VI descends from Eleonore Marie and Charles V, who, as

1. Baigent, Leigh, and Lincoln, *Holy Blood, Holy Grail*, pp. 131, 434-438.
2. For more information, see ch. 7's section titled, "The Garter," at p. 147.
3. Baigent, Leigh, and Lincoln, *Holy Blood, Holy Grail*, p. 269.
4. "Karl von Habsburg," *Wikipedia.org*, 29 Mar. 2023; and Hilton, *The Principality and Power of Europe*, p. 16. According to Hilton, Otto von Habsburg as the titular Duke of Lorraine, had "long awaited the emergence of a new order. For any future united Europe, he advocates a strong religious role for the Roman Catholic Church, which he terms 'Europe's ultimate bulwark'" (ibid., p. 35). Karl succeeds him.

the grandson of the Spanish Isabella, also ruled Spain as King Charles I.[1]

We may connect the beliefs of the Priory of Zion and its offspring with ancient Zoroastrianism—and with the spiritual "enlightenment" represented in the Luciferic "all-seeing eye" of the Illuminati, which is depicted in the capstone at the top of their pyramidal "Great Seal" on the U.S. dollar bill (arguably, still the world's most important currency). We may also connect them with the modern New Age Movement. Interestingly, from 1188 to 1306, the Priory of Zion supposedly also called itself "Ormus," a name that "figures in Zoroastrian thought and in Gnostic texts, where it is synonymous with the principle of light," although masonic tradition would have us believe that the name derives from an ancient "Egyptian sage and mystic" who conferred a red cross upon his initiates, giving rise to the first Rosicrucians.[2] J.R. Church shows that the Temple Knights seem to believe that their world leader will appear following the alignment of the planets Jupiter, Saturn, Mars, and Mercury, and after a series of major world catastrophes. In 1981 and 1982, at the start of the so-called "Age of Aquarius," Jupiter, Saturn, and Mars conjoined, and in April 1982, Benjamin Creme and the Tara Center announced the supposedly imminent appearance of "Lord Maitreya," their New Age "Christ."[3] Interestingly, *Maitreya* (Sanskrit) in Hebrew, or מיתריאה, also calculates to 666 (i.e., 40 + 10 + 400 + 200 + 10 + 1 + 5), and there is reason to believe that this title actually pertains to King Charles III.[4]

Through his late father, Prince Philip, Charles III has Charles V de Lorraine as his ancestral uncle, and he descends from the House of Anjou and the Hapsburg dynasty. In this regard, King Felipe VI of Spain is not unique. (His father Juan Carlos I's former lineal claim to be the "King of Jerusalem"—now passed to Felipe VI—is the primary reason some had imagined him as a possibility for the role of the AntiChrist.) In the 1998 edition of this book, this author observed, "Prince Charles too could one day make this claim." In fact, when we consider the additional Merovingian lineage of his mother, the late Queen Elizabeth II, who, unlike both the Spanish royal line and von Habsburg "pretenders," apparently came even from *Godfroi de Bouillon* (through Henry the Black of the Guelph Line), it appears that Charles' claim, based upon essentially the same criteria, would

---

1. Church, pp. 13, 15-18, 20-22, 62, 86, 93-95, 313-314.
2. Baigent, Leigh, and Lincoln, *Holy Blood, Holy Grail*, pp. 122-123. Note that the Priory of Zion depicted the name "Ormus" as an anagram or acrostic containing the French words for "bear," "gold," and "elm" (ibid., p. 122).
3. Church, pp. 36-49, 165-166.
4. For more information, see the subsection *"Maitreya and King Charles III"* on p. 382, of ch. 10.

be considerably stronger. Additionally, as Cathcart had observed, "Among the unlikely ladies we find Melesende, Queen of Jerusalem, the second wife of one of Prince Charles' Plantagenet forebears."[1] As this author indicated decades ago, Charles would defeat Spain's king in a claim for the title. Crowned king in May 2023, the former Prince of Wales now *effectively has*—being anointed ("messiahed") with oil produced in Jerusalem, from Olives grown on the Mount of Olives, while seated upon "King David's" (satanic) throne![2]

The Merovingians and the Priory of Zion have long awaited what the *false prophet* Nostradamus referred to as "the Great Monarch," the ultimate "Prince of Lorraine" and "priest-king" *who would work with the pope* to establish a New World Order (NWO).[3] Neither *King* Felipe VI nor Karl von Habsburg is a *prince*—and Charles only ceased being one *after* initiating his "Great Reset," the *actualization* of the NWO, from the WEF. Baigent, Leigh, and Lincoln, baffled by an obscure Priory reference to the Prince of Lorraine's "sacred mission," have incorrectly asserted, "there is no known Prince of Lorraine today, not even a titular one."[4] Should the European Union seek a royal head having a strong Merovingian blood line, even one from the House of Lorraine, which seems plausible from the fact that the union's currency includes a portrayal of Charles V,[5] Charles, who already requested the job while prince, would yet be an *impeccable* choice. In fact, no stronger candidate exists.

Prince Philip's lineage. Robert Lacey remarks: "Philip, Prince of Greece, did not have a drop of Greek blood in his veins, and Princess Elizabeth's governess was right when she compared his ash-blond hair and angular features in July 1939 to those of a Viking. He was in essence a Dane, one of the exports to Greece of the most successful exporting dynasty of modern times, the Danish royal house, usually known to genealogists as the Schleswig Holstein Sonderburg Glucksburgs.... All [of] Philip's sisters had married Germans owning castles and the largest of them all was Schloss Salem, bigger than Buckingham Palace, the home of the Margrave of Baden." Lacey adds: "Apart from eighteen kings of Denmark this family has in recent history also supplied one king to Norway, four to Sweden, six to Greece, seven czars to Russia, and at the same time queen consorts for the Kings of Britain, Germany, and Rumania. So Prince Philip could boast more [recent] blue blood in his veins than Queen Eliza-

---

1. Cathcart, p. 3.
2. For details, see the chapter titled, "King Charles III."
3. Baigent, Leigh, and Lincoln, *Holy Blood, Holy Grail*, pp. 135, 170, 198-199.
4. Baigent, Leigh, and Lincoln, *Holy Blood, Holy Grail*, pp. 224-225.
5. Church, p. 227.

beth II. His ancestry can be traced back to Charlemagne through branches that wind diversely enough to include at one stage Henry Percy, ... the legendary Hotspur."[1] Denis Judd adds:

> The Duke of Edinburgh's genealogical background is woven into such a wide and complex tapestry.... Strands come together from such feudal residences as Frederiksborg Castle in Copenhagen, the Greek royal estate of Tatoi, and a Grand Duke's castle in Germany. They can be traced back to the Imperial Russian court at St Petersburg and to the ... palaces of the kings and queens of England. Even a cursory glance at Prince Philip's family tree ... is enough to show that the "unknown Greek prince" who ... came from nowhere to claim the hand of the heiress to the world's proudest and most stable throne had impeccable and impressive royal antecedents....
>
> Like Elizabeth, Philip is a great-great-grandchild of Queen Victoria; like her, he is a descendant of German ruling houses. On his father's side he comes from a Danish royal line that ... by 1947, boasted sixteen kings of the House of Oldenburg and three of the House of Glücksburg—and Beck.... Since 1947 there have been two more monarchs, one of them Queen Margrethe II who has reigned in Denmark.... Six kings of Sweden and seven tsars of Russia grew on the branches of the same tree, not to speak of the Glücksburg women who married into the British royal family....
>
> Equally formidable was the heritage of Philip's mother, Alice of Battenberg and Greece, whose brother ... [was] Earl Mountbatten [of Burma]....[2]

Queen Elizabeth II's lineage. According to Anglo-Israelites, the late queen came from King David (and Judah) through Solomon, Josiah, Zedekiah, and a woman named Tea Tephi. The queen's lineage, published in 1977 as "The Illustrious Lineage of The Royal House of Britain," not only concurs, but depicts her household as "The House of David—The Royal Line."[3] Indeed, in November 1985, President Ronald Reagan met at the White House with then Prince

---

1. Robert Lacey, *Majesty* (New York and London: Harcourt Brace Jovanovich, 1977), pp. 98-99, 102. Lacey adds: "[Philip's British mother] was born a Battenberg.... ...Philip was not born a Mountbatten, since his mother never anglicised her name.... [The] Act of Settlement of 1701 .... bestowed British nationality and royal status to the Electress Sophia of Hanover and all her descendants. So since he was numbered among these, Prince Philip had technically been a British Royal Highness from the moment of his birth" (ibid., p. 129).
2. Judd, *Prince Philip*, pp. 23-24. For a more detailed account of Prince Philip's lineage, including a "royal circle" going back six generations, which also covers Queen Elizabeth II, as well as a Mountbatten family tree going back even further, purporting that the "Mountbattens are a branch of one of the oldest traceable families in Christendom, the House of Brabant," see the covers, and pp. 22-30, 65-67, and 247 of the same work.
3. "The Illustrious Lineage of The Royal House of Britain."
   By AVCTORE GV. M. H. MILNER. A.M., S.G.R.Soc, I.V.ADSOC.
        E TYPIS EDD PRIOR R. FOLKARD ET FIL.
              ED. OCTAVA RENOVATA.
                 LONDINI: MCMXXIII.
   Published By: The Covenant Publishing Co. Ltd.
   6 Buckingham Gate, London SWiE 6jP
   (First published 1902. This edition 1977.)

Charles and his wife Diana, whom the then president referred to as "Princess David!"[1] Of even greater interest is the fact that in May 1996, Israel's Channel 2 television noted in a widely viewed program that Charles is connected to Israel by his supposed Davidic descent. (King Charles III is *very* popular in Israel.[2])

Ezekiel tells us that Zedekiah was a "profane, wicked prince of Israel" (21:25). Yet Elizabeth II's lineage shows that she not only had descent from *David* through **1)** Solomon, Josiah, Zedekiah, and Tea Tephi, but also through **2)** Nathan, Joseph of Arimathea (apparently), Anna (a so-called "cousin" of Jesus' mother Mary), and the House of Tudor (which eventually restored the red dragon to its ancient status as a royal device and supporter); through **3)** Anna, Penardim, Athildis, Clodomir IV, Pharamond (traditionally, France's first king), Clodion, *Merovée* (Merovic), Childeric I, Clovis I, Roger, etc., Eustache I, Eustache II, *Godfroi de Bouillon* (Godfrey of Bouillon), Henry the Black of the Guelph Line, etc.;[3] as well as through **4)** Penardim, Cadwalladr Frea, etc. (see below). Tea Tephi is represented as having borne the forefathers of the modern British monarchy through King Heremon (Lit., "Eochaidh, the Heremon"), an ancestor of subsequent Irish and Scottish kings.

Herbert W. Armstrong, a cultist, may have been correct when he sought to show that King Heremon's forefathers, and thus the comparatively recent British monarchs, were themselves descendants of Israel's seafaring Danites. In fact, Elizabeth II's lineage also shows descent from a man named *Dardanus* through **1)** Tros (Troes) and his descendants (i.e., the House of Troy), and **2)** Heremon and his forefathers. Although Dardanus is represented as descending from Judah (see below), he may have actually arisen from Dan.

---

1. Alstair Burnet, *In Private—In Public,* THE PRINCE AND PRINCESS OF WALES (New York: Summit Books, 1986), pp. 84-90. Maureen Johnson, "Private thoughts behind royal smile," *The Denver Post,* 2 Nov. 1994, p. 4A.

2. Today's Israeli population, apart from its relatively small number of true Christians, is entirely given to false Judaisms (Reform, Conservative, Orthodox, and Ultra-Orthodox), false religions and Christianities (Islam, Roman Catholicism, etc.), cults (e.g., Masonry), secularism, atheism, and all forms of "New Age" spiritualism and mysticism. Avi and Chaya Mizrachi, for example, observe, "More than 20% of the Israeli population consult with Kabbalistic Rabbis (who use mysticism and the occult) for decisions, or they go to astrologers or use tarot cards" ("Shalom from Israel" {Koinonia; P.O. Box 1491; Libby, MT 59923-1491}, Oct. 1997, p. 1). Further, Israel today accepts sodomy, other iniquitous sex, and infanticide (mass murder), and has little to *no* respect for The LORD's promises to our forefathers; like Esau before, many "Israelites" would sell their birthright for red lentil soup, if so much. This Israeli apostasy shall serve Satan's and the AntiChrist's interests, bringing God's swift judgment.

3. The queen also descends from the Merovingian Hildegarde. There is no clear indication, however, that while Baudouin I (Baldwin I), Baldwin II, Melisenda (the daughter of Baldwin II and a wife of Fulk V), Baldwin III, Amalric I, Baldwin IV, and Baldwin V are shown on her lineage, she actually descends from any of them. (A more detailed lineage than the one possessed by this author could conceivably show otherwise.) Geoffrey Plantagenet, the father of Henry II, who is in the queen's lineage, was himself the son of Fulk V and his first wife Matilda, not of Melisenda.

Besides through David, Elizabeth II's lineage shows separate descents from *Judah* (and possibly *Dan*) through **1)** Zerah, *Dardanus,* Tros (Troes), <u>Priam</u>, the House of Troy, the Sicambrians, and the Franks; through **2)** Tros, the ancient British, and the Byzantine emperors; through **3)** Priam's daughter, the Norse "god of thunder and lightning" *Tror (Thor;* cf. Rev 13:11-13), the Norse Line, and the Norse "god" *Odin,* who married Cadwalladr Frea; and through **4)** Heremon, who is represented as a descendant of *Dardanus.*

Cadwalladr Frea and *Odin* are together represented as the parents of the royalty of **1)** the latter Franks, **2)** the Anglo-Saxons, **3)** the Saxons, **4)** the Normans, **5)** the Merovingians, **6)** the French House of Anjou, **7)** the Spanish Line, **8)** the Guelph Line, **9)** the Russian Line, **10)** the Wettins, and **11)** the Skiolds. All of these royal families, as supposed descendants of David (through Cadwalladr Frea) and Judah (through *Odin* and David), are in Elizabeth II's lineage. Not only does the (dead) queen, therefore, supposedly descend from David and Judah through at least eleven additional lines, but much of Europe's royalty likewise supposedly descends from David and Judah. Nevertheless, the late queen's—and thus King Charles III's—lineal claims remain by far the most prodigious.

The day that Jesus was crucified, Wednesday,[1] is named after the Norse *Odin,* who is otherwise known as the Anglo-Saxon *Woden* and the German *Wotan,* as well as the Roman *Mercury* and the Greek *Hermes.* When the scriptures are considered, it becomes clear from ancient mythology that *Odin* is none other than Satan himself; for *Odin,* by his various names, is identified as the god of war, thieves, and merchants, and the prince of the power of the air (i.e., the "wild wind god" who leads the "spirits of the dead through the air"), who obtained his "wisdom" through the sacrifice of an eye (cf. the single "all-seeing eye" that remains) and to whom "victims were hanged on trees in sacrifice" (cf. Jesus' crucifixion).[2] As shown above, *Odin* is actually in Elizabeth II's official lineage. That is, this is what the British monarchy has said about itself. *Odin* may have been an historical personage, but in the context of the late queen's lineage, he represents Satan.

Church suggests that the name *Odin* is "a form of the word Dan." He also argues that the Merovingians, rather than being actual descendants of Judah and David, are really descendants of Dan, which, as one of northern Israel's ten tribes, not only "established an idola-

---

1. For more information, see the chapter "Jesus' Fourth-Day Crucifixion and Seventh-Day Resurrection," in the volume titled, *Messiah's Preeminence in History and Prophecy: The Heart of Israelology, Eschatology, and God's Holy Days,* of the author's *Messiah, History, and the Tribulation Period* series.
2. *Eerdmans' Handbook to the World's Religions,* pp. 119-121, 406, 419, 431. Somewhat in jest, Holden refers to the British monarchy as "the fount of all wisdom" (*PRINCE CHARLES,* pp. 312-313).

trous religion—the worship of the Sun and the Moon" (derived from the ancient Babylonian religion of Assyria), but may "produce the great usurper, the antichrist." From this, as well as other information, Church speculates that "most of the suffering of Israel down through the centuries has been plotted and perpetrated by ['Gentile' rulers who were themselves descendants of] the lost tribe of Dan."[1]

Henry II, whose parents were Geoffrey Plantagenet and Empress Matilda, was an Anjou by birth (through Fulk V, his grandfather). Henry II married Eleanor of Aquitaine, who bore him Richard I. Eleanor's former husband, Louis VII of France, formed a precedent-setting alliance with the Priory of Zion and the Temple Knights, having personally established ninety-five of the Priory's members in France, some of whom joined the Temple Knights, upon his return to France from the Second Crusade in 1152.[2] Subsequently, Richard I, a homosexual who reigned from 1189 to 1199 and was otherwise known as the "Lionhearted" (*Coeur de Lion*), was the second French Plantagenet (or Angevin) to occupy the English throne. While admitting of England's royal family, "from the Devil we sprang and to the Devil we shall go," he nevertheless defeated Saladin in the Third Crusade in 1191 and "secured a treaty to guarantee Christians safe pilgrimage to Jerusalem."[3] Like Louis VII before him, Richard I maintained an early alliance with the Knights Templar, which, from the times of the crusades to this day, have supposedly provided the British monarchy with "the oldest armed bodyguard in existence." Three members of this bodyguard, comprised of a group of twenty-four knights who are now referred to as "Serjeants-at-Arms," apparently stand-in for the Order of the Garter's twenty-four companion-knights during such functions as the State Opening of Parliament, where they attend the British sovereign and escort the royal heralds and pursuivants.[4]

King Charles III's lineage. All those mentioned above, who are in (now roasting) Prince Philip's and Queen Elizabeth II's lineages, are, of course, in Charles' lineage. Cathcart notes Charles' descent from William the Conqueror, Alfred the Great, Robert the Bruce, Mary the Queen of Scots, the Bowes-Lyons, Charles I, Electress Sophia, a "powerful line of Scandinavian counts and dukes and kings," the

1. Church, pp. 87, 102, 108-114, 117-129. As Queen Elizabeth II's son, King Charles III also descends from all these individuals. The underlying significance of his possible Danite ancestry will be examined in the next chapter, "Anglo-Israelism, David's Throne, and the AntiChrist," at p. 103.
2. Baigent, Leigh, and Lincoln, *Holy Blood, Holy Grail*, pp. 118-119.
3. Plantagenet Somerset Fry, *The Kings & Queens of England & Scotland* (London: Dorling Kindersley; New York: Grove Weidenfeld of Grove Press, Inc.; 1990), pp. 22, 37, 42.
4. James and Russell, *At Home with the Royal Family*, pp. 141, 146-147, 206; and Baigent, Leigh, and Lincoln, *Holy Blood, Holy Grail*, p. 121. For more information, see ch. 7's section titled, "The Garter," at p. 147.

Dukes of Normandy and the House of Anjou, the "Anglo-Danish kings to Canute, grandson of Harald Blue-tooth, King of Denmark," King Cole or Ceol, Sweyn Forkbeard, Rollo the Ganger (a cattle thief and pirate who captured the dukedom of Normandy), Vladimir Monomakh the "Great Prince of Kiev," the Battenbergs, as well as "through Henry Tudor—from Llewellyn-ap-Gruffyd[d], the last native Prince of All Wales." Cathcart also remarks that Charles is related to George Washington, Robert E. Lee, and Alice Liddell, known as Alice in Wonderland. Moreover, the king is "the most Scottish prince [(now king)] since Charles I and perhaps the most English ... since Henry VIII."[1] In *Prince Charles,* Anthony Holden gives the following information regarding King Charles III's unusually diverse lineage:

> ....The odds against being born to his fate are incalculable....
>
> ....His ancestors include Charlemagne and Genghis Khan,[2] El Cid and George Washington [(through John Smith)], Shakespeare and Count Dracula....[3]
>
> ....As [Sir Iain Moncreiffe] ... says, "HRH's [(His Royal Highness's)] breeding is the most important in the world ... [and] he is heir to the world's greatest position that is determined solely by heredity...."
>
> In ... **Charles's veins runs the blood of emperors and kings,** Russian **boyars,** Spanish **grandees, noblemen of every European nation,** bishops and judges, knights and squires, and tradesmen.... ... Charles is a cousin or nephew, in varying degrees, of all six wives of Henry VIII; ... **he has many descents from the royal houses of Scotland, France, Germany,**[4] Austria, **Denmark, [Greece,]** Sweden, **Norway, Spain,** Portugal, **Russia,** and **the Netherlands.** Many of his ancestors died bloodily, in battle or by the ax....
>
> ....Moreover, he descends many times over from Llewellyn the Great, Prince of Wales [and grandfather of Llewellyn ap Gruffydd], and all Welsh kings and princes by way of Hywel Dda back to Cunedda and Old King Coel himself, who reigned ... soon after the Romans left Britain [in 410 A.D.]....
>
> ....Among his celebrated Viking ancestors were King Sven Forkbeard of Denmark and King Harold Haardrade of Norway, but **he also springs from the ancient "Peace Kings,"** whose vast grave mounds can still be seen at Uppsala in Sweden....

---

1. Cathcart, pp. 1-4.
2. Aga Khan gifted Elizabeth II, while yet princess, a filly for her wedding (*Her Majesty The Queen,* p. 50).
3. Charles has shown strong interest in preserving Romania's Transylvanian countryside, successfully opposing placement of a Dracula theme park, and may now be associated with "Ottomar Rodolphe Vlad Dracula Prince Ketzulesco ... [who] had himself [been] adopted in 1987 by Prince Ketzulesco, ... a descendant of the Transylvanian-born Vlad the Impaler, the Romanian prince notorious for impaling Turkish prisoners on wooden stakes, and on whom Bram Stoker based his fictional villain Count Dracula" ("Dracula seeks blue-blooded English heir," *The Sunday Independent,* 17 April 2002).
4. In 1917, England's King George V, King Charles III's great-grandfather, changed his last name from the German *Saxe-Coburg-Gotha* to the more innocuous "Windsor," with his family following suit. Battenberg was then also anglicized to Mountbatten, the name adopted by Prince Philip in 1947 (Junor, p. 22). Since a 1960 British "Order in Council," Queen Elizabeth II's grandchildren, besides Princess Anne and princes Andrew and Edward, are styled "Mountbatten-Windsor." The British monarchy, therefore, has a comparatively recent German extraction. For the backdrop to these name changes, see Judd, *Prince Philip,* pp. 45-46, 195-197.

In Russia, he is descended through Czar Nicholas I from both Catherine the Great and Peter the Great. He also has innumerable descents from the Grand Princes of the House of Rurik, who originally founded "all the Russias," among them St. Vladimir of Kiev, who Christianized the Russians....

In what was the Holy Roman Empire, he descends over and over again from Charlemagne and [crusader] Frederick Barbarossa and all the great dynasties, Habsburg and Hohenstaufen, **Guelph** and Hohenzollern, Bavaria and Saxony, Hesse and Baden, Mecklenberg and Wurrttemberg, Brunswick and Anhalt, the Electors Palatine and other Wittelsbachs, plus many of the historic houses such as Hohenlohe and Galen, Moltke and Sickingen, Schwarzenberg and Trauttmansdorff. **Otto the Great and Phillip of Hesse were his direct forefathers. Frederick the Great and the Emperor Charles V were his ancestral uncles....**

In Italy, his forefathers include Dukes of Savoy and the Emperor Frederick II, "Stupor Mundi," and the medieval kings of Sicily, as also the Orsini of Rome (Pope Nicholas III was his ancestral uncle)....

....**The prince's [(now King Charles III's)] Anglo-Saxon and Danish royal forefathers [and others] sprang from Dark Age kings who incarnated the storm-spirit Woden.... Through the Lusignan crusader kings of Cyprus, titular kings of Jerusalem, ...** Charles descends a millennium farther back from King Tiridates the Great, the first Christian monarch of all (under whom Armenia was converted in AD 314, before even Rome itself), and thus **from the divine Parthian imperial House of Arsaces (247 BC), which reigned over Persia and Babylonia** and was in its time the mightiest dynasty in the ancient world.[1]

Alan Hamilton adds:

He boasts a pedigree that is frightening in its extent. In 1977, ... Mr Gerald Paget ... produced ... *The Lineage and Ancestry of HRH Prince Charles, Prince of Wales.* Mr Paget ... traced and enumerated 262,142 ancestors of ... Charles. It was a slight cheat, for as a result of cousin marriages many of that number are in fact the same person appearing several times; **inbreeding has always been a strong strand in royal pedigrees.** Nevertheless Mr Paget showed that ... **Charles was in some way descended from just about everybody who was anybody, anywhere, ever.**

Among his more direct forbears are the royal houses of Scotland, France, Germany, Austria, Denmark, [Greece], Sweden, **Norway, Spain,** Portugal, **Russia,** and **the Netherlands.** He can trace a connection to Alfred the Great, Hereward the Wake, William the Conqueror and every English monarch since.... He is descended no fewer than 22 times over from Mary Queen of Scots, and at least once from the Welsh prince Owen Glendower, **the Irish high king Brian Boru,**[2] Robert the Bruce of Scotland, Sven Forkbeard the Viking, Catherine the Great of Russia, Good King Wenceslas of Bohemia, **the emperors Charlemagne and Frederick Barbarossa,**

---

1. Holden, *PRINCE CHARLES*, pp. xxv, 330-335.
2. As Fritz Springmeier has documented, the Illuminati appear to be organized around certain leading occult bloodlines, of which the Merovingian lineage is by far the most prominent. Another Illuminati bloodline is the Boru (Kennedy) bloodline.

Frederick the Great of Prussia, Pope Nicholas II, and last but far from least among mere commoners, George Washington....

Charles is the twenty-first Prince of Wales, yet strangely only 13 of the previous holders of the title ever became king, and one of those was Edward VIII, who did not stay at his post long enough for his [public] Coronation....[1] ....He himself has said that he will reign as King Charles III,[2] although he would be quite entitled to call himself King Philip, King Arthur II, King George VII, or indeed any other name he cared to choose.[3]

Judd remarks: "Charles Philip Arthur George. Why those names? Philip was obvious. So was George, on both sides of the family. Arthur has quite often been used by British royalty. But Charles? Was it an unfashionable tribute to the troubled House of Stuart, which had produced Charles I and Charles II? (When the couple's second child was christened Anne it seemed to confirm this theory.)"[4] Actually, King Charles III has a significant Stuart lineage. We should, however, point out that there are other reasons for the prevalence of certain of his names. Charles refers to Charlemagne, for example; Philip may be in reference to Philip II of France; Arthur is in reference to the legendary King Arthur;[5] and George may be in reference to England's "St. George" or, as we shall see later in this book, France's Merovée.[6] Charles could just as well have been fully named "Charlemagne Philip Arthur Merovée." Yet, that would have been too telling. When asked why Queen Elizabeth II and Prince Philip chose "Charles" as their son's first name, Buckingham Palace responded that is was for "personal and private reasons."[7]

As the AntiChrist must be, Charles is a prince of Roman ancestry, in line to be on a throne (see Dan 9:26-27)—which he now has as King Charles III. Yet while Holden notes that Charles descends from "crusader kings of Cyprus, titular kings of Jerusalem," he and others

---

1. King Charles III is now the *fourteenth* coronated (as king) Prince of Wales.
2. In the first edition of this book, the author noted, "If this is so, it seems unlikely that Prince Charles will succeed his mother to the English throne. King Charles III does *not* calculate to 666 using the scriptural system." To this author, it had seemed superfluous and potentially contradictory for Charles to become king, to fulfill his prophesied role as history's ultimate AntiChrist—the Fourth Horseman of the Apocalypse (Rev 6:7-8). Still, what this author did not then state, but really should have, is that Charles was *already identified* as that AntiChrist, in unassailable fulfillment of Revelation 13:18. In other words, any subsequent name or title change with any attending calculation loss would really be immaterial: that is, Charles is *already proven* to be the foretold AntiChrist. That being stated, a few things have become clear, to include this: as king, Charles now formally claims to sit upon the throne of King David, and being anointed with oil produced in Jerusalem, makes him a "shoe in" to be *Israel's Anti-Messiah!* For more information, see the preceding chapter, "A Name that Calculates to 666," at p. 71, and ch. 16, "King Charles III: History's Ultimate AntiChrist," at p. 561.
3. Hamilton, *The Royal 100*, pp. 17-18. For more information on Charles' amazingly diverse lineage, see Appendix B, or pp. 222-227, of *King Charles III* by Holden.
4. Judd, *Prince Philip*, p. 144.
5. According to Baigent, Leigh, and Lincoln, the name "Arthur" derives from the Welsh word for "bear" (*Holy Blood, Holy Grail*, p. 239).
6. For more information, see ch. 7's section titled, "The Garter," at p. 147.
7. Junor, p. 21.

curiously neglect to mention Charles' apparent claims to *Davidic* descent as well, not only through the Merovingians, but also through other, non-Merovingian royalty in the lineage of his mother, Queen Elizabeth II. As shown later, King Charles III also supposedly descends from Mohammed, Islam's false prophet and founder![1]

Therefore, assertions such as these are *incorrect:* "As we study the personality of the AntiChrist, we often run into people who want to consign him to a Jewish heritage.... And usually their reasoning goes like this: He makes a covenant with the Jewish people, and therefore that covenant demonstrates the fact that they consider him to be the Messiah, and certainly no Jew would ever consider a non-Jew to be the Messiah, so the AntiChrist must be a Jew. And yet, as you study the scripture, there's no evidence anywhere in the bible for determining that the AntiChrist is a Jew. In fact, there's evidence to the contrary. The fact of the matter is that the bible does not teach that the league of the AntiChrist with the Jewish nation is based upon their idea that he is the Messiah. It is simply a political maneuver on his part to gain control over Israel, the center of military power. But we do learn in the bible that the AntiChrist arises out of the fourth empire, out of the Roman Empire. Daniel 9 says he is the prince [(or royal ruler)] that will come, he comes out of that great empire that is reigning in the last days; he is a Roman. Some have said that he is a Roman by citizenship and a Jew by race or ... religion, and of course, we can't demonstrate that either. We simply know that he comes out of the final form of the final empire, and he is nationally identified with that empire, and I believe his ancestry will be within the Roman ten-confederation final form."[2] The AntiChrist is both Roman and Israelite, and yes, he must be able to demonstrate an Israelite lineage—whether it is contrived or not—before Israel would consider him to be the Messiah. Satan's Prince is both Roman and of the tribe of Dan simultaneously, as we have seen.

An "illuminated" lineage. The British monarchy has strong lineal ties to the Illuminati. Fritz Springmeier, who has studied the Illuminati extensively, states:

> The Illuminati are powerful elite bloodlines of generational satanists who manipulate the world from behind the scenes. Some people have already heard about the Illuminati, but I have been involved for several years in a venture perhaps never before done; I have been extricating members of the Illuminati, or deprogramming them. In doing so, I have taken a

---

1. For more information, see this chapter's later section titled, "Supposed descent from David, Jesus, and Mohammed," at p. 100.
2. Dr. David Jeremiah, "The Reign of Terror," *Turning Point,* 12 March 2009.

topic that was very nebulous and theoretical, that of "the Illuminati," and exposed it in detail, something which remains an ongoing effort. Some of this information specifically involves the British royal family.

The people with whom I have worked, who were members of the Illuminati, can testify full well that the British royal family is part of the Illuminati. In 1995, I combined selected articles that I had written in previous years about these Illuminati bloodlines into the book *The Top 13 Illuminati Bloodlines*. These bloodlines are the Astor, Bundy, Collins, DuPont [(du Pont)], Freeman, Li, Onassis, Kennedy, Rockefeller, Rothschild, Russell, Van Duyn, and Merovingian (the 13th bloodline). The British royals are members of the Merovingian dynasty, the 13th and most prominent Illuminati bloodline, the "Holy" bloodline.

Prince Charles [(King Charles III)] is related to the following American Presidents: Washington, Jefferson, Madison, both Harrisons, Tyler, Taylor, and George Bush [Sr. and George Bush Jr.], as well as [the senior] Bush's vice-president Dan Quayle. Moreover, the prince is a known descendant of the Kennedy bloodline, and as such, he is a distant relative to John F. Kennedy. Prince Charles is also related to Robert E. Lee and Mrs. Woodrow Wilson, not to mention some others. The British royal family is closely related to the Virginia Tidewater plantation aristocracy, which ran the United States in its first decades. These aristocracy were the Carters, the Lees and Randolphs and the Smiths and Ironmongers who had so much power and wealth in Virginia. And they are Prince Charles' ancestors.

When Prince Charles married Lady Diana Spencer, Illuminati covens and other witchcraft covens in many countries recognized that this was a very important occult marriage. The marriage was observed with great interest by these covens. The media have occasionally made the mistake of telling the public that Prince Charles married a commoner. Lady Diana Spencer's ancestry is not so common.[1] Who are some of Princess Diana's ancestors and kinsmen? They include the following persons: William Vincent Astor, McGeorge Bundy and also Mrs. McGeorge Bundy, Amelia Earhart Putnam (Putnam is of the Collins family), Pierre Samuel ["Pete"] DuPont IV, J.D. Rockefeller (I, II, III, and IV) and David Rockefeller, Franklin Delano Roosevelt (and Teddy), Brigham Young (a prominent Mormon of the Merovingian dynasty) and one of his wives Louisa Beeman, Bertrand Arthur William Russell and his fourth wife Edith Finch, John Pierpont Morgan, Henry Cabot Lodge and many other people written about in *The Top 13 Illuminati Bloodlines*.[2] No blood ties between Diana and the Chinese Li Illuminati family, the Turkish Onassis bloodline, or the Reynolds-Dukes Illuminati bloodlines are evident. With such a bloodline, Diana was not supposed to have married a Dodi Fayed, an Egyptian playboy. (Although nothing, of course, has been heard of it in the press, their car accident just happens to have occurred at an important Merovingian ritual site.)[3]

---

1. As one columnist put it: "Diana didn't just become a princess; she was carefully chosen for the role. The royal selection process was as cold and prosaic as any thoroughbred auction. At 20, she had the lineage, the upbringing and the docility to appear to meet the requirements for a future Queen of England" (Alessandra Stanley, The New York Times, "Struggle for happiness touched women deeply," *The Denver Post*, 7 Sept. 1997, p. 22A).
2. For the genealogical information relating these individuals to Princess Diana, see Gary Royd Roberts and William Adams Reitwiesner, *American Ancestors and Cousins of The Princess of Wales* (Baltimore, Maryland: Genealogical Publications Co.).
3. For more information, see ch. 10's section titled, "Death of a princess," at p. 320.

Many Americans couldn't care less about their own genealogy. But bloodlines are very important to the Illuminati. There is no question that the Prince of Wales [(now King Charles III)] (who is related to all of Europe's aristocracy including the Russian Romanov family [whom his own abandoned to die]) and his ex-wife Princess Diana are related to some very powerful blue-blood bloodlines. Some of these connections may seem meaningless to the average reader. For example, Prince Charles is related to Genghis Khan, who was a type of the AntiChrist. Genghis Khan's relatives live in Europe and America. Due to having interviewed one of the descendants from this family, I know that most of the family is working for the New World Order, and that it still has a great deal of power. These families connect in unexpected ways too. Genghis Khan married a Jewish (Israelite) woman. Likewise, although the Romanov family dropped out of sight, I know an Illuminati slave (someone under the influence of powerful Illuminati mind-control programming) in Oregon who is a Romanov. Persons with the Romanov name are not ruling countries anymore, but the bloodline still carries occult power within the Illuminati.

There is no way to fully convey to the reader all the hidden connections of these satanic occult bloodlines. It must suffice to say that Prince Charles is well connected with them. The most important occult bloodlines are interwoven. For instance, William II (Prince of Orange) was from the occult Orange lineage, and his wife Mary from the House of Stuart (another occult lineage). Their son William III, therefore, had two strong occult lineages in his veins, making him more powerful in the occult, according to Illuminati thinking, than either of his two parents. As it turns out, this Dutch Freemason William of Orange (William III), who took the British throne in 1688, was a significant part of the Mystery Religions' conspiracy to bring in a New World Order. In fact, many of the important people of the conspiracy trace back to William of Orange. He started the Order of Orange patterned after Freemasonry, which is still strong in Ireland. He also got the Scotsman William Paterson to start the mother of all central banks, the Bank of England. The Paterson family still has descendants who are Illuminati. Later, the Bank of England was put under the direction of the Rothschild Illuminati bloodline. Along with this, another Scottish occultist, John Law, started the French central bank in 1716, which he modeled after the Bank of England.

In the book *The Very Rich: A History of Wealth,* by Joseph J. Thorndike, Jr., one reads on page 170, "The British Rothschilds became ardent hunters, famous hosts, and members of the inner circle of the Prince of Wales." If one examines the lives of the British royal family, one will find that they have a lot of contact with the Astors, the Greys, and the Rothschilds, as well as other Illuminati families. Just one example of many to illustrate this is Higham's description of the Prince of Wales' life during the 1930's and '40's, when, as the Duke of Windsor, he married Wallis Warfield Simpson and abdicated his throne and title as King Edward VIII.[1] As the Prince of Wales, Edward was a close friend of Eugene de Rothschild, and spent much time at his Schloss Enzesfeld castle near Vienna. While the prince visited the Rothschilds in 1937, another guest at the castle was Fritz Mandl, a Jewish armament maker who supplied Hitler with weapons. ... Edward [VIII] was involved in all kinds of pro-Nazi activity, and was widely

---

1.   Charles Higham, *The Duchess of Windsor* (New York: McGraw-Hill Book Co., 1988).

viewed as pro-Nazi, and yet here he was visiting with a Jewish Rothschild and a Jewish arms dealer who apparently supplied Hitler with arms. When Louis Rothschild was arrested by the Nazi's, the Duke of Windsor negotiated his release in 1939. Later, on August 15, 1940, Edward sailed with Baron Maurice Rothschild to the Bahamas. And when Wallis Simpson, ultimately styled the Duchess of Windsor, came out of seclusion in December of 1973, it was to attend an Onassis Party in Paris. All these families were above (presided over) World War II.

I have sought to demonstrate that if one understands the hidden occult lineages, history takes on an entirely new shape and meaning.... When we start to understand the Illuminati, we not only need to understand their lineages, but also their HIDDEN lineages. These people have large numbers of hidden bastard lineages, through children who themselves are the result of secret satanic ceremonies.[1]

Supposed descent from David, Jesus, and Mohammed. At times, King Charles III (Satan's Prince or ruler) looks, talks, and acts as though he were a Christian, and he certainly seems to have at least a few Christian ancestors. Further, today's British monarchy alleges itself to be the legitimate genealogical line of Israel's King David, and to sit upon the David's throne. Charles' seemingly Christian veneer, combined with an adherence to Anglo-Israelism, enables leveraging both "Christianity" and anti-biblical Judaism—as *the* AntiChrist. Jesus told unbelieving Israel, "I have come in My Father's name, and you do not receive Me; if another comes in his own name, him you will receive" (John 5:43). We see that it is so.

But what about Islam, another major religion? Believe it or not, King Charles III also supposedly descends from Mohammed. In her book, *Invitation to a Royal Wedding,* Kathryn Spink remarks, "[Charles'] ancestors included such unlikely figures as Mohammed, the Prophet of Islam, and George Washington, the first President of the United States, and he was born to bear a range of titles which are at the very least impressive."[2]

Where presidents of the United States are concerned, consider this somewhat chilling (alleged) revelation regarding the true reach of the British monarchy: "According to those presidential-race watchers obsessed with blood links to royalty and nobility, Bill Clinton is the blue-blooded winner. 'The presidential candidate with the greatest number of royal genes has always been the victor, without exception, since George Washington,' said Harold Brooks-Baker, director of Burke's Peerage publishing house in London. 'Only the

---

1. Written correspondence, quoted by permission, from Fritz Springmeier. Regardless of Springmeier's status as "Christian," the above material is, as far as this author knows, accurate. For more information, see the discussion on the Garter at p. 147 in ch. 7, "The Heraldic Symbols in the Arms and their Interpretations."

2. Kathryn Spink, *Invitation to a Royal Wedding* (England: Colour Library International Ltd., 1981), p. 19.

merest drop of royal blood flows in the veins of Sen. Dole,' he added. Both men can trace their ancestry to England's King Henry III, but Clinton's lineage is much more royally rooted, with loose links to Britain's reigning royals, Brooks-Baker said."[1] Like Franklin D. Roosevelt, who was related to the British monarchy and acted on its behalf, Clinton, of course, won the election. The same was claimed for Bush Jr.[2] (and Bush Sr. before him), Obama and even Donald J. Trump.

According to Church, the Priory of Zion is comprised of thousands of nominal (unfaithful) "Protestants, Roman Catholics, Jews, and Moslems."[3] These individuals believe that Jesus didn't really die on the cross, but was stolen away from the tomb and survived. No matter how bizarre, the elements that make up this view are not particularly unique, nor are they repulsive to most non-Christians.[4] In fact, many non-Christians, regardless of their ethnicity, would readily accept such a lie over the truth, which condemns their false religious beliefs and reveals their less than pleasant eternal destiny.

We see, therefore, that King Charles III, by virtue of his lineage alone, may claim for himself royal heirdom to much of the world, including the three major religions that have historically vied for control of Jerusalem (i.e., Judaism, Roman Catholicism, and Islam).[5] Indeed, the unregenerate Yona Metzger, Israel's former Ashkenazi "Chief Rabbi," emphasizes Abraham—as the alleged "father" of (false) Judaism, apostate as well as genuine Christianity, and antiChristian (satanic and pagan) Islam—as "a starting point for a dialogue of peace between them"—while calling for the creation of a "United Religious Nations" (URN): "The word 'Abraham' ... is constructed from the words 'father of many nations.' So, if Muslims associate themselves with Abraham's son Ishmael, or Christians ... with Abraham's grandson Esau,[6] or we ... with his other grandson

---

1. "Royal roots? Clinton gets edge," *The Denver Post,* 29 Oct. 1996, p. 2A.

2. Former President Bush (Jr.) first met with then Prince Charles at the White House in 2005. During the visit, Satan's Prince, who "wants [to see] a greater tolerance and understanding of ... other religions" to "promote better relations between faiths," tried to persuade Bush Jr. of the merits of Islam, having "voiced private concerns over America's 'confrontational' approach to Muslim countries and its failure to appreciate Islam's strengths" since 9-11 (Andrew Alderson, "Prince Charles to plead Islam's cause to Bush," *Telegraph.co.uk,* 1 Nov. 2005). (In truth, *Islam is among the most intolerant of religions.*) Around that, Charles also attended a Georgetown University seminar on faith and social responsibility, received the Vincent Scully Prize for architecture at the National Building Museum, showcased his organic farming products, and gave a speech on environmental issues.

3. Church, p. 11.

4. E.g., see Josh McDowell, *The Resurrection Factor* (California: Here's Life Publishers, Inc., 1981), pp. 92-102.

5. For more information, see ch. 10, "Religious, Political, and Other Ties," at p. 289.

6. *No Christian associates himself with Esau.* In asserting that Christians do, however, Mr. Metzger is upholding a rabbinic teaching that the city of Rome or its emperors had Edomite origins (Edomites descended from Esau) while simultaneously equating Christianity to *Roman* Catholicism. This is actually quite an aspersion, as Mr. Metger is surely aware of the fact that Obadiah, a Hebrew prophet, tells us

Jacob, then three great monotheistic religions were born from him.... My dream is to create a United Religious Nations.... The diplomats did not succeed in bringing peace to the world. They need help. And this can come through religious language. Because a Muslim does not respect a person who is secular; he will only have respect if you are religious. This Religious United Nations would also include Hindus and Buddhists. We ... speak the same language."[7] Charles has similarly emphasized Abraham.[8]

Short of repenting and receiving Jesus, many will get along (in)famously with *the* AntiChrist! Lineage, however, is not King Charles III's only advantage where such heirdom across the world is concerned: there is, for example, also the British Commonwealth.[9]

---

that God is going to *exterminate all Edomites* (Obad 10-18). (This will occur at Jesus' return.) It is not uncommon for unregenerate Israelites to say one thing but mean another, any more than it is for the average unbeliever to do so. Perhaps Mr. Metzger believes that Christianity will have an end, when in reality *all of surviving Israel* will soon be *Christian* (Rom 11:25-27).

7. Christoph Schult, "'My Dream Is to Create a United Religious Nations,'" *SPIEGEL ONLINE*, 24 Dec. 2008.
8. For more information, see ch. 10's section titled "Respect," at p. 388.
9. For more information, see ch. 2, "A Man for Our Times," at p. 51.

5

Anglo-Israelism, David's Throne, and the AntiChrist

According to the doctrine of Anglo-Israelism, which the author fully *rejects,* Great Britain and the United States are both significantly populated by the so-called "lost" ten tribes of Israel. Although it is Jesus, not a usurping British monarchy, who truly sits upon David's throne (Isa 9:6-7), the statement at the bottom of Queen Elizabeth II's official Anglo-Israelite lineage nevertheless reads, "David shall never want a Man to sit upon the throne of the house of Israel" (cf. Jer 33:17)! In this vein, on June 2, 1953, with the participation of the world's top heralds (including Rouge Dragon, meaning "red dragon" and symbolizing Satan, as well as Unicorn Pursuivant of Arms), and then four Knights of the Garter carrying and holding the canopy over her head,[1] Elizabeth II was anointed and crowned at her coronation as "Queen" of "Thy people Israel" (i.e., God's people Israel).[2] The 1953 coronation service may be watched on the Internet.[3]

Various Anglo-Israelites, including King Charles III and previously his mother, hold that the throne upon which British monarchs are crowned—that is, the famous Coronation Chair (commissioned by King Edward I) at Westminster Abbey in London, which bears the Luciferian "all-seeing eye" at its *top-back* (i.e., engraved behind its triangular headrest, as seen during the 1953 coronation)—is the rightful throne of Israel's King David. (A golden arch in Westminster Abbey itself, overtly bears *the same Luciferian imagery.*) Until recently, most asserted that the "throne" had "Jacob's head-stone," on which he supposedly rested his head at Bethel, for its base. Legend has it that the prophet Jeremiah took this 336-pound stone, called the *Stone of Destiny,* to Ireland. Used there for a coronation throne (and presumably, as a *druidic* "Throne Stone"[4]), it was then brought

---

1. For more information, see the discussion on the Garter at p. 147 in ch. 7, "The Heraldic Symbols in the Arms and their Interpretations."
2. Both Prince Albert, who became King George VI, and his daughter Elizabeth, who became Queen Elizabeth II, were nearly bypassed in the royal succession, due to alleged concerns over the need for "personalities dynamic enough to win back the lustre of the monarchy, after [Edward VIII's] abdication" (Lacey, *Majesty,* pp. 72-74). Cathcart adds, "if he had unexpectedly arrived a week earlier, [before a change to the laws of succession,] Charles would not have been born a Prince at all" (pp. 8-9). In light of this work, however, it is crystal clear that Charles has an ignominious destiny to fulfill.
3. See, for example, "BBC TV Coronation of Queen Elizabeth II: Westminster Abbey 1953" on YouTube, as posted at "https://www.youtube.com/watch?v=52NTjasbmgw".
4. See ch. 8, "The Red Dragon and Prince Charles' Investiture as Prince of Wales," at p. 207.

to Scone (pronounced "skoon") in Scotland, where for a millennium —until 1296—Scottish kings were crowned. Edward I, who apparently viewed King Arthur as a *hero*,[1] is purported to have then taken the stone by force to England, where it was placed in Westminster Abbey, to then be used since 1308 for English coronations. Indeed, it would seem that Edward I tied his Coronation Chair *to legendary King Arthur.*

In 1278, Edward I "visited Glastonbury Abbey to open what was then believed to be the tomb of Arthur and Guinevere, recovering 'Arthur's crown' from Llywelyn [ap Gruffudd (grandson of Llywelyn the Great)] after the conquest of North Wales, while ... his new castles drew upon the Arthurian myths in their design[s] and location[s]. He held 'Round Table' events in 1284 and 1302, involving tournaments and feasting, and chroniclers compared him and the events at his court, to Arthur."[2]

Lacey similarly comments: "This statuesque and elaborately carved high-backed oak chair was built by order of King Edward I (reg. 1272-1307, not to be confused with St. Edward, Edward the Confessor, who ruled from 1042 to 1066) to enclose the Stone of Destiny on which Scottish Kings used to sit when they were crowned, and which Edward had stolen from its resting place in the Abbey of Scone in 1296. The stone was said, by legend, to be the pillow on which Jacob slept."[3]

Regarding Elizabeth II's coronation, Lacey records: "Queen Elizabeth II's view of her own function in the summer of 1953 was infused with mysticism.... 'I was glad when they said unto me, We will go into the House of the Lord,' rang out the notes of the opening anthem.... As Handel's setting of 'Zadok the Priest and Nathan the Prophet' [(who millennia ago, had anointed Solomon King of Israel)] carried through the church [via singing, and then prayer,] the text which had been recited at every crowning in England from the coronation of King Edgar the Peaceful in 973, the Queen's jewellery and robes were lifted.... Her ceremonial train made a rich crimson pile.... 'Be thy hands anointed with holy oil, be thy breast anointed with holy oil, be thy head anointed with holy oil,' proclaimed the

---

1. Edward I appropriated Welsh myths and legends when presenting himself as Wales' ruler. Building at Caernarfon, and especially the additional construction at Caernarfon Castle, was Arthurian symbolism he employed to impress the Welsh. For all practical purposes, as well as historically, that particular castle *is* the legendary one of King Arthur and occult wizard Merlin. It had also been near the site of Segontium, a first-century Roman fort—one under *dracones* or *draco* military standards, or Satan's *red dragon* symbol. For more information, see ch. 8, "The Red Dragon and Prince Charles' Investiture as Prince of Wales," at p. 207.
2. "Edward I of England," *Wikipedia.org,* 17 Dec. 2020.
3. Lacey, *Majesty*, p. 161.

[apostate] Archbishop of Canterbury,[1] 'as Kings, Priests, and Prophets were anointed.' Enthroned in King Edward[I]'s Chair..., Elizabeth II received the elaborate tokens of the responsibility with which she was being invested, the Orb—'remember that the whole world is subject to the power and empire of Christ'[2]—the Sceptre [of Justice] with the Cross, ensign of power and justice, the Rod of Mercy, and also the Royal Ring with a sapphire and ruby cross—'the Wedding Ring of England.'"[3] She also received the Bracelets of Sincerity and Wisdom, as "wisdom" and "knowledge" were frequently claimed. The Archbishop of Canterbury then placed St. Edward's Crown upon Elizabeth II's head, the congregation proudly sang "God Save the Queen" (Britain's National Anthem), and the queen took communion.[4] "Saint" Edward's Staff, an uncertain recreation, was *not* held by the queen during her coronation. The Sword of State, which was used, is maintained in "St." Edward's Chapel, aka the Chapel of Edward the Confessor.

Still, some historians have questioned whether Edward I obtained the real Stone of Scone, which may have had a Hebrew inscription, and whether the stone he did obtain is the one that England reluctantly returned to Scotland, in November 1996 from Westminster Abbey—which appears to be nothing more than a Scottish "slab of reddish-grey sandstone"[5] (apparently quarried in Perth). There is also an Irish claim or myth that the original Stone of Scone, was taken from the Hill of Tara—where an Irish "Stone of Destiny" (aka *Lia Fáil*) yet "somehow" resides—to Scotland,[6] and that this stone would "roar" for the chosen king. Thus, at the base corners of Westminster Abbey's Coronation Chair or "throne," we find lion supporters. In any case, the alleged "real" stone is now on display in the Crown Room of Edinburgh Castle, Scotland.[7] Significantly, this stone is also a druidic *Logan Stone* (later addressed)!

Solomon served as a type of Christ in the first half of his reign, but the AntiChrist in the second half.[8] Such reference to Solomon in

---

1. For a synopsis on the spiritual fornication of various archbishops associated with the British monarchy, see ch. 10's section "Of archbishops and fallen seeds," at p. 289.
2. The Orb is actually a gold sphere having a Templar or Merovingian cross at its top. For more information, see the discussion on the Garter at p. 147 in ch. 7, "The Heraldic Symbols in the Arms and their Interpretations."
3. Lacey, *Majesty,* pp. 160-162. For a photograph of Michael Ramsey, former Archbishop of Canterbury, wearing a miter and a crucifix, and holding an opulent Templar cross-tipped staff, see Frazer, p. 46. It is reminiscent of the Roman pontiff for its pomp, with a caption comparing "Christian priests and bishops" to "magicians in primitive societies."
4. Junor, pp. 27-28.
5. "Palace of Destiny," *Realm,* Sept./Oct. 1994, No. 58, pp. 24, 27.
6. For more details on this "lower Old Red Sandstone," see "Stone of Scone," *Wikipedia.org,* Apr. 2023.
7. William D. Montalbano, "Scots get the Stone but not at Scone," *The Denver Post,* 16 Nov. 1996, p. 4A. "Royal relic returns to Scottish castle," *The Denver Post,* 22 Nov. 1996, p. 26A.
8. See the section (or chapter) "The Messiah, David, Solomon, and the AntiChrist," in Vol. I, *Biblical Inter-*

British coronations of their antiChristian kings and queens, who have so often historically only made *a pretense* to being "Christian," seems curiously apropos. Samuel Tuominen asked, "Is the Queen of England a born-again Christian or the greatest pretender in history?"[1] As this author later exposes, *Elizabeth* Alexandra *Mary* Windsor was given *to Satan* in 1946, to become his pagan (druidic) "handmaiden," while still just a princess. As queen, Elizabeth *II* then publicly *reaffirmed* that choice multiple times: *following* her 1953 coronation (i.e., at Caernarfon Castle in August 1953), at Charles' July 1969 investiture as Prince of Wales (later addressed), and at other such events (e.g., a Welsh Assembly in 1999, with princes Charles and Philip).[2] It is *not* coincidental that this woman's given name contains "Elizabeth" and "Mary," recalling the names—as a wealthy and opulently adorned antithesis to the persons—of the mothers of John the Baptizer and Christ Jesus, respectively. Yes, Princess Elizabeth ... Mary ... was beforehand *chosen to be the mother of the foretold AntiChrist!*

In the 1953 coronation service, we see dignitaries of Muslim and Hindu nations (e.g., Pakistan and India),[3] besides an ostentatious display of opulence. The coach in which Elizabeth II arrived is laden with *four tons* of gold, lion heads (cf. Gen 4:7, Heb.) and four pagan "tritons," two of which seem to "pull" the coach, suggesting mythological Neptune / Poseidon (cf. Rev 13:1*a-b* and 6:7-8) or *prostitute* Venus as its occupant.[4] Listening, we may also hear the (late) queen make multiple *promises*—disobeying Christ Jesus in the process (e.g., see Matt 5:33-37). She said, "I solemnly promise," for example, when asked by Canterbury's (surprisingly) *apostate* Archbishop Geoffrey Fisher, "Will you solemnly promise and swear to govern the peoples"—including "Pakistan" and at the time, India—"according to their respective laws and customs." But Islam and Hinduism are satanic false religions, and both India and Pakistan have been *horrible offenders* against Christians and The LORD! *No* thinking *Christian* would agree (e.g., see Ex 34:12-16), let alone "solemnly promise" "to govern" such peoples "according to their respective [(satanic)] laws." Truly, those who serve God may *not* "drink the cup of The Lord and the cup of demons; you cannot partake of The Lord's table and of the table of demons" (1 Cor 10:21 {see 10:14-32}; cf. 1 Tim 4:1-3).

---

pretation (Hermeneutics), of the author's *Messiah, History, and the Tribulation Period* series.

1. Samuel Tuominen, "An overview of Elizabeth II's annual Christmas messages. Is the Queen of England a born-again Christian or the greatest pretender in history?," *SamuelTuominen.com*, 13 Dec. 2015.
2. See the information starting with the section, "Princess Elizabeth: Satan's 'handmaiden,'" at p. 212.
3. For a relatively comprehensive list of *participants* in the 1953 event, see "List of participants in the coronation procession of Elizabeth II," *Wikipedia.org*, 16 Nov. 2020.
4. See, for example, "Neptune (mythology)," *Wikipedia.org*.

It is written: "'No servant can serve two lords | masters; for either he will hate | detest the one and love | greatly esteem the other, or else he will be loyal | devoted | cling to the one and think little of | disregard | despise | scorn | insult the other. You cannot serve God and mammon | {riches | property | possessions | money}.' Now the Pharisees, who were lovers of money, also heard all these things, and they turned up their nose at Him. And He said to them: 'You are those who justify yourselves before men, but God knows your hearts. For what is highly esteemed among men is an abomination in the sight of God'" (Luke 16:13-15, Gk. and Aram.; cf. Matt 6:24, 6:31-34, 17:24-27, 22:15-22; Mark 4:13-19; Luke 20:21-26; Phil 3:18-19; 1 Tim 6:9-12 {cf. Luke 22:2-6; John 12:4-6, 13:26-30, 17:12; 2 Th 2:3-12}; 2 Tim 3:1-9; 1 John 2:15-16; cf. Matt 19:16-30; Mark 10:17-31; Luke 18:18-30).

But then the British monarchy really is *all about compromise with the devil!* They desire to serve *two* "gods" — that is The Creator of the Universe plus a fallen angel, Satan. But the former, or The God of (real) Christians, *does not, nor ever shall* accept such wicked duplicity and gross unfaithfulness (e.g., see Ex 20:3-7, 34:14-16; cf. Josh 24:14-24). Spiritual light *cannot* fellowship with darkness, nor righteousness with unrighteousness, nor Christ with Satan (e.g., see 2 Cor 6:14-17)! Those who attempt such are *lukewarm,* rather than hot or cold, and they shall be *vomited* from Jesus' mouth in the Day of Judgment (see Rev 3:14-19). Those who serve God *cannot* seek to please the non-Christian world and also then please their Creator: such conduct is both double-minded and insincere (Gal 1:10; cf. Rom 8:1-17). Remember this: God knows all and *cannot* be fooled, nor is He finally mocked (Gal 6:7-8)!

Those who believe the British monarchy serves God are misled and deceived. They, in fact, *hate our Creator and despise Jesus in whom He is incarnate,* but love Satan and parade the latter. Yes, they are of their "father ... the Devil" (cf. John 8:38-47).

Anglo-Israelism received new life in the past century through its popularization by the late Herbert W. Armstrong's Worldwide Church of God.[1] As a cornerstone of his theology, Armstrong adopted Anglo-Israelism. Bob Larson comments:

> It was Armstrong's belief in Anglo-Israelism that drew the most theological attention. Though Herbert denied it, his doctrine closely resembled

---

1. The Worldwide Church of God had *until recent decades* rejected the biblical doctrine of The Godhead (i.e., God as continually Father, Word and Holy Spirit) and denied the existence of Hell. It has held instead that the believer would ultimately be absorbed spiritually *into* God, thereby becoming a part of God, and that the unbeliever or wicked would be annihilated rather than suffer eternal punishment. Also, it had ardently promoted Anglo-Israelism.

the theory expounded by Canadian Richard Brothers, a psychic visionary who lived in London in the eighteenth century.... Ignoring sound rules of linguistics and hermeneutics, the theory suggests that England ([supposedly the superior] Ephraim) and the Untied States ([supposedly the inferior] Manasseh) are what is left of the so-called Ten Lost Tribes of Israel. Ancient Judah and Israel are believed to [still] be two separate entities.... After the Assyrian captivity, Israel [presumably] migrated northward to eventually become the Anglo-Saxons of British heritage.

Armstrong taught that the promises of God due to his chosen people have been transferred to America and the United Kingdom. He also declared that Queen Elizabeth [II] sits on the throne to which Christ will return. [The] ... WCG maintains that the British Coronation Stone of Scone was actually brought to the Emerald Isle by the prophet Jeremiah....

Perhaps the most dangerous Armstrong doctrine is the contention that deity is an attainable goal of man. A recent WCG publication insists "We are to be changed from physical to spiritual [(a denial of the bodily resurrection)] ... into the spirit of God. We must be God. Blasphemy? No. Believe it or not, you are a potential omnipotent power. You were born to become God!" Note, the writer doesn't say *a* god. He says *God*. This view, of course, robs Christ of his unique position as eternal God.[1]

Consider also the following brief excerpts from the late Dr. Walter Martin's refutation of Anglo-Israelism:

> The basic premise of the Anglo-Israelite theory is that ... these so-called "lost" tribes are, in reality, the Saxae, or Scythians, who surged westward through Northern Europe and eventually became the ancestors of the Saxons, who later invaded England. The theory maintains that the Anglo-Saxons are the "lost" ten tribes of Israel and are substituted, in Anglo-Israel interpretation and exegesis, for the Israel of the Bible.
>
> In the heyday of the British Empire, when their colonies spanned the globe under Victoria, Anglo-Israelites were in their glory, maintaining that, since the British were the lost tribes and, therefore, inheritors of the covenants and blessings of God, it was obvious that God was honoring His promises and exalting His children in the latter days.
>
> In light of recent history, however, and the loss by Britain of virtually all her colonial possessions, Anglo-Israelites are content to transfer the blessings of the Covenant to the United States, maintaining as they do that Ephraim is Great Britain and Manasseh, the United States. The fact that Ephraim is called "the exalted one" in Scripture and that Manasseh is designated as the inferior of the two, creates both historical and exegetical problems for the Anglo Israelites. This is particularly true because the United States, the inferior (Manasseh), has now far surpassed the allegedly superior Ephraim....
>
> ...Anglo-Israelism maintains that Judah represents the Jews who are still under the divine curse and are not to be identified with Israel at all....
>
> Moreover, it should be noted that the Anglo-Israelite theory and the Worldwide Church of God both maintain that the throne of England is the

---

1. Bob Larson, *Larson's New Book of Cults,* rev. (Illinois: Tyndale House Publishers, 1989), pp. 469-471.

throne of David. In the June 1953 issue of *The Plain Truth* [(a WCG publication)] appears the statement:

> Herman L. Hoeh now reveals the astonishing fact that Elizabeth II actually sits on the throne of King David of ISRAEL—that she is a direct descendant, continuing David's dynasty—the VERY THRONE on which Christ shall sit after his return.... Elizabeth II was crowned "Queen of thy people Israel." Turning to the article by Hoeh, it clearly states that the throne upon which she was crowned (i.e., the "Stone of Scone," lodged in Westminster Abbey) is really the stone which Jacob used for a pillow, which he took with him when he departed from Bethel, and which later came under the care of Jeremiah the Prophet, who took it with him to England, where it became the Coronation Stone for the British (Davidic) dynasty.

The disturbing scientific fact that the Stone of Scone has been examined and analyzed, and found to be ... "... of Scottish origin" does not deaden the enthusiasm of Anglo-Israelites....

The Anglo-Israelites' school of interpretation claims more than 3,000,000 adherents in England, Canada, the British Commonwealth and throughout the world, including the United States. They are found in many already-established denominations in Christian Churches and so do not constitute a separate denomination, preferring to work through all groups, instilling its propaganda....[1]

Martin goes on to quote the following material from pages 37 to 38 of David Baron's, *A Letter to an Inquirer*:

> ....There is not the least possibility of doubt that many of the settlements of the Diaspora in the time of our Lord, north, south, and west, as well as east..., were made up of those who had never returned to the land of their fathers since the time of the Assyrian and Babylonian exiles, and who were not only descendants of Judah, as Anglo-Israelism ignorantly presupposes, but of all the *twelve tribes scattered abroad* (James 1:1)....
>
> To summarize the state of things in connection with the Hebrew race at the time of Christ, it was briefly this:
>
> I. For some six centuries before, ever since the partial restoration in the days of Cyrus and his successors, the descendants of Abraham were no longer known as divided into tribes but as one people, although up to the time of the destruction of the second temple tribal and family genealogies were for the most part preserved, especially among those who were settled in the land.
>
> II. Part of the nation was in [the land]..., but by far the largest number were scattered far and wide, and formed innumerable communities in many different lands, north and south, east and west. But wherever dispersed and to whatever tribe they may have belonged, they all .... anticipated the same future. They had one common center of worship in Jerusalem ... and they made pilgrimages thither annually in great numbers at high festivals.

---

1. Dr. Walter Martin, *The Kingdom of the Cults* (Minnesota: Bethany House Publishers, 1985), pp. 307, 309-310. Quoted by permission of CRI.

The name of "Jew" and "Israelite" became synonymous terms from about the time of the Captivity....

"That the name 'Jews,'" writes a Continental Bible scholar, "became general for all Israelites who were anxious to preserve their theocratic nationality, was the more natural, since the political independence of the ten tribes [from the two] was destroyed." ...

Anglo-Israelism teaches that members of the ten tribes are never called "Jews," and that "Jews" are not "Israelites," but both assertions are false....

Now note, Anglo-Israelism tells you to identify the ten tribes with [just two nations]..., but if you are on the line of scripture and true history, you will seek for them "among all nations." ...

My last words on this subject must be those of warning and entreaty. Do not think, as so many do, that Anglo-Israelism, even if not true, is only a harmless speculation. **I consider it nothing short of one of the latter-day delusions by which the Evil One seeks to divert the attention of men from things spiritual and eternal....**

And finally, it not only robs the Jewish nation, the true Israel, of many promises in relation to their future by applying [them] to the British race in the present time, but it diverts attention from them as the people in whom is bound up the purpose of God in relation to the nations, and whose receiving again to the heart of God after the long centuries of unbelief, will be as life from the dead to the whole world.[1]

It is evident that the counterfeit theology of Anglo-Israelism lacks any legitimate basis. However, there is an early Church teaching which, if correct, lends substantial support to the contention of Armstrong, some Anglo-Israelites, and others that the British monarchy is related to the tribe of Dan.

Dan and Ephraim are not mentioned in the apocalyptic list of the twelve tribes, from which the 144,000 sealed Israelites are to come during the Great Tribulation[2] (see Rev 7:5-8, 14:1-3). While these saints are to be spiritually chaste (Rev 14:4-5, Gk.), Dan and Ephraim led ancient Israel into idolatrous worship, after the manner of the Gentiles, causing Israel to become spiritually defiled (see Judg 17 to 18; 1 Kin 12:26-30; Hos 4:17-19; cf. Deut 29:18-21). Nevertheless, the

---

1. Martin, *The Kingdom of the Cults,* pp. 310, 312-314.
2. What Jesus referred to as "great tribulation" in the New Testament Gospels, is really the latter half of Daniel 9:27's contextual *seven-year period* (i.e., seven 360-day years, or just under six years and eleven months by a *post-Flood* solar-year or secular reckoning). Christians often generically refer to that seven-year period as the "Tribulation Period | Week," though in scripture, only its latter half is scripturally designated "tribulation | birth pangs"—specifically, what Christ called "great tribulation" (see Matt 24:21; Mark 13:14; cf. Rev 2:22, 7:14). Thus, Christians also (formally) recognize that week's latter half—which is 42-months (reckoned as 30 days each, per the *pre-Flood* solar year reality delineated in Genesis 7:11, 7:24 and 8:3-4), 1,260-days, as well as 3.5-years long (e.g., see Rev 11:2-3, 12:6 and 12:14)—as the "Great Tribulation" (cf. Dan 12:1 {Heb.} and 12:7). Both the Tribulation Week (of years) or Tribulation Period, as well as the compassed Great Tribulation, immediately precede Jesus' return to Earth from Heaven. This author commonly addresses the Tribulation Period or Tribulation Week (Dan 9:27), as well as the *second-half* Great Tribulation, under those terms. For more information, see this author's *Messiah, History, and the Tribulation Period* multi-volume series.

list alludes to the half-tribe Ephraim through its inclusion of Joseph (cf. Ezek 37:15-19), evidently signifying that those from Ephraim who are in The Son of Joseph (an ancient rabbinic designation for the suffering-Servant Messiah) are eligible. (The half-tribe Manasseh is listed separately from Joseph.) Unlike Ephraim, however, Dan is entirely excluded from the 144,000 sealed Israelites, even though it will inherit its allotted portion of the Land of Israel in the Millennial Kingdom (see Ezek 48:1-2; cf. Josh 19:40-48).[1] While some of northern Israel's Ephraimites apparently repented under Judaea's Hezekiah and Josiah, there is no indication of such repentance among the Danites (see 2 Chr 30:1-11, 30:18-23, 31:1, 34:6-9). Finally, notice that the tribe of Levi, which is omitted from certain Old Testament lists because it has no territorial inheritance in the Land of Israel, is included in the list of the 144,000 sealed Israelites.

Based upon Dan's exclusion from the apocalyptic list, as well as certain Old Testament prophecies and parallels, Irenaeus concluded that the AntiChrist would arise from that tribe,[2] and Hippolytus, observing that both Judah and Dan are called "a lion's whelp" (Gen 49:9; Deut 33:22) and that "the deceiver seeks to liken himself in all things to the Son of God," wrote, "as the Christ springs from the tribe of Judah, so the AntiChrist is to spring from the tribe of Dan."[3] Jacob prophesied, saying: "Dan shall be a red dragon [serpent][4] by The Way [the way], a *horned* serpent [viper] by the path, that bites

---

1. A few scholars (e.g., Walvoord) have made the suggestion that Dan is classified with his brother Naphtali who was born to the same mother. Yet no biblical support exists for this position. Indeed, all of Israel's tribes came from just four mothers, and none of them is categorized in such a manner in other lists of the twelve tribes found in the scriptures.

2. Irenaeus, *Against Heresies*, Bk. 5, Ch. 30, Par. 2; see *Ante-Nicene Fathers,* ed. Roberts and Donaldson, Vol. 1, p. 559.

3. Hippolytus, *Treatise on Christ and AntiChrist*, Pars. 6-7 and 14-15; see *Ante-Nicene Fathers,* ed. Roberts and Donaldson, Vol. 5, pp. 206-207.

4. The first Hebrew word translated as "serpent" in Genesis 49:17, which is also found in Genesis 3:1-4 and 3:13-14, Numbers 21:6-9, Deuteronomy 8:15, Job 26:13, Psalms 58:4 and 140:3, Proverbs 23:32, Isaiah 14:29, 27:1, and 65:25, Jeremiah 8:17 and 46:22, Amos 5:19 and 9:3, and Micah 7:17, is Strong's number 5175. In Arabic, this word is used to refer to "the constellation of the serpent or dragon in the northern part of the sky" (William Gesenius, 5175, *HEBREW-CHALDEE LEXICON of the OLD TESTAMENT* {Michigan: Baker Book House Co., 1979}, p. 545). Further, this word is related to another Hebrew word, Strong's number 5153, which refers to the "*red* color of the throat of a serpent [5175, as denom.] when hissing [(cf. Prov 23:31-32)]" (James Strong, 5153, "A Concise Dictionary of the Words in the Hebrew Bible," *STRONG'S EXHAUSTIVE CONCORDANCE OF THE BIBLE* {Tennessee: Abingdon Press, 1986}, p. 102). Therefore, Genesis 49:17, like most of the other verses mentioned above, not only refers to a serpent, but it can also be taken as a reference to a red-colored dragon (i.e., Satan; cf. Num 33:11). In fact, Philo, writing in the first century A.D., not only identified the serpent of Genesis 49:17 as a "dragon," but he also addressed *the* dragon who in the form of a serpent deceived Eve in the Garden of Eden (*On Husbandry* {*Agr.*}, secs. 95-96; see *The Works of PHILO,* trans. C.D. Yonge {Massachusetts: Hendrickson Publishers, Inc., 1993}, p. 182). Likewise, the Greek Septuagint renders this Hebrew word as "dragon" in Job 26:13, where it refers to the "apostate dragon," as well as in Isaiah 27:1 and Amos 9:3. Moreover, the creature represented by this word is actually defined as a "dragon" in Isaiah 27:1, so that most English translators not only represent it as such, but some even occasionally render the word itself as "dragon" (e.g., in Job 26:13 or Isaiah 14:29). Finally, the Apocalypse itself explicitly calls this very serpent a "fiery red dragon" (Rev 12:3-4, 12:9; cf. Gen 3:13-15).

the horse's heels so that its rider falls backward. I have waited for your Yeshua [Salvation],¹ *O* LORD!" (Gen 49:17-18, Heb.; cf. Jer 8:16-17, Heb. and KJV). Understood literally, Jacob's prophecy refers to the mortal conflict between the red dragon or Satan, as represented by Dan (cf. Rev 13:2-4), and The Messiah (see Gen 3:15; Rev 12:3-5; cf. Rev 1:18, 20:1-3), who is The Way (John 14:6), as well as the saints in Him (cf. Rev 12:9-17, 20:4), who in the first century were referred to collectively as "the Way" (see Acts 9:2, 19:9, 19:23, 24:14, 24:22, Gk.; cf. 22:4)! We are also told in the pseudepigraphic (Jewish) *Testament of Dan* (found in the *Testaments of the Twelve Patriarchs*) that Dan's prince is Satan (5:6).² Ever since the days of Jacob, Israel's twelve tribes have been individually represented by the signs of the twelve houses of the Zodiac. With this in mind, one writer observes, "To Judah was given the insignia of Leo, the Lion, and to Dan was given the insignia of Scorpio, the seed of the serpent."³ Morris comments, "Dan's bad reputation may be quite old, for this tribe (along with Zebulun) is omitted from the genealogies in the early chapters of 1 Chronicles."⁴

According to Anglo-Israelites, Tea Tephi (a supposed descendant of Solomon) bore the forefathers of today's British monarchy through a man named Heremon, who was himself an ancestor of later Irish kings. Armstrong endeavored to show that these kings, to whom the British monarchy is related, were themselves descendants of the Danites:

> The tribe of Dan occupied two different districts, or provinces, in the Holy Land before the Assyrian captivity. One colony lived on the seacoast. They were principally seamen, and it is recorded Dan abode in ships (Judges 5:17).
>
> When Assyria captured Israel, these Danites struck out in their ships and sailed west through the Mediterranean and, as we shall now note, north to Ireland....
>
> Some historians see a connection between those Danites and the Danoi in Greece and the Tuatha De and Tuatha De Danaan [(meaning "people of the goddess Danu"] of Ireland. *Tuatha De* means "people of God." The name Dunn in the Irish language, for example, means the same as Dan in the Hebrew: judge....

---

1. Targum Jonathan and the Jerusalem Targum both paraphrase the meaning of *Yeshua*—Jesus' Hebrew name—in Genesis 49:18 as "the redemption of the Messiah, the Son of David" (C.F. Keil and F. Delitzsch, "THE FIRST BOOK OF MOSES," Vol. 1 of *Commentary on the Old Testament* {1986; rpt. Massachusetts: Hendrickson Publishers, Inc., 1989}, p. 404).
2. *The Old Testament Pseudepigrapha*, ed. James H. Charlesworth, Vol. 1 (New York: Doubleday, 1983), p. 809. Ante-Nicene Fathers, ed. Roberts and Donaldson, Vol. 8, p. 26.
3. Church, pp. 113, 116-117.
4. Leon Morris, *REVELATION*, Tyndale New Testament Commentaries, No. 20 (Michigan: Eerdmans Publishing Company, 1987), pp. 112-113, n. 2.

The real ancient history of Ireland is very extensive.... ...Long prior to 700 B.C. a colony of mixed ancestry called "Tuatha De Danaan" arrived in ships, drove out other tribes, and settled there. Later, in the days of David, a colony of Milesians, apparently of the line of Zarah [(presumably Zerah, a descendant of Judah)], arrived in Ireland from the Near East.

Later still, an elderly, white-haired patriarch [(i.e., Jeremiah)], sometimes referred to as a "saint," came to Ireland. With him was the princess daughter of an eastern king [(i.e., Zedekiah)] and a companion called "Simon Brach," spelled in different histories as Breck, Berech, Brach, or Berach. The princess was named Tephi or Tea-Tephi....

This royal party included the son of the king of Ireland [(i.e., Heremon)] who had been in Jerusalem at the time of the [Babylonian] siege. There he had become acquainted with Tea-Tephi. He married her shortly after the city fell. Their young son, now in his late teens, accompanied them to Ireland.

....The son of this ... king [Heremon] and the Hebrew princess [Tea Tephi] continued on the throne of Ireland and *this same dynasty continued unbroken* through all the kings of Ireland; was *overturned* and transplanted again in Scotland; again *overturned* and moved to London, England, where *this same dynasty continues today* in the reign of Queen Elizabeth II [(now King Charles III)]....

Besides the royal family [of Israel], the prophet [Jeremiah] is thought by some to have brought with them certain remarkable things, including a harp, and a wonderful stone called ... [the] "stone of destiny." ...

Another strange coincidence—or is it just coincidence?—is that many kings in the history of Ireland and England have been coronated sitting over this stone—including the present queen. The stone rests today in Westminster Abbey in London, and the Coronation Chair is built over and around it. A sign once beside it labeled [it] "Jacob's pillar-stone" (Gen 28:18)....

In view of the linking together of biblical history, prophecy, and Irish history, can anyone deny that this Hebrew princess was the daughter of King Zedekiah of Judah and therefore heir to the throne of David? That the aged patriarch was in fact Jeremiah, and his companion was Jeremiah's scribe, or secretary, Baruch?[1]

Is it plausible that certain seafaring Danites really did travel to Ireland? Could the tribe of Dan have even been aware of Ireland's existence? It is known that King Solomon traded heavily with the merchants of *Tarshish* (2 Chr 9:21). Regarding *Tarshish,* R.F. Gribble comments,

[The] ships of Tarshish were symbolic of Mediterranean trade and traders, being well-known in Mediterranean and Red Sea waters, and carrying merchandise of great value.

The genealogical list of Genesis 10, in connection with 1 Chronicles 1:7, gives an intimation that these special Tarshish ships did business with

1. H.W. Armstrong, *The United States and Britain in Prophecy* (U.S.A.: Worldwide Church of God, 1986), pp. 98-102.

the Greek isles. Such commerce, carried on in the 6th and 7th centuries B.C., is noted by Herodotus (1.163; 4.152)....

....Evidently [Tarshish] ... developed trade in minerals (Jer 10:9; Ezek 27:12).... A Phoenician inscription of the 9th cent. B.C., found in 1773 in Sardinia, notes a Tarshish in the island.[1]

In the first century, what now constitutes the United Kingdom — Great Britain and Northern Ireland — was a Roman province, the head of the Roman Empire in the West. Before the Roman Empire, however, today's United Kingdom was known as *Tarshish* (cf. Jonah 1:3).[2] Further, based upon the above mentioned inscription, it appears that *Tarshish* may have established a base on the island of Sardinia, which lies due-west of Rome in the Mediterranean Sea. If so, Dan's merchants could have heard about Ireland's location from the merchants of *Tarshish,* and some of them could have eventually sailed there.

---

1. "Tarshish," *The Zondervan Pictorial Encyclopedia of the Bible,* 1976 ed., Vol. 5, p. 598. For more information, see ch. 7's section, "The royal shield and the arms of the Principality of Wales," at p. 137.

2. For more information, see the section (or chapter) titled "The Last Four Seals of the Tribulation Week (and the Second Advent)," in the volume titled, *Messiah's Preeminence in History and Prophecy: The Heart of Israelology, Eschatology, and God's Holy Days,* in the author's *Messiah, History, and the Tribulation Period* series. Also, see the related note on p. 138, in ch. 7, "The Heraldic Symbols in the Arms and their Interpretations."

6

The First Beast
and
Prince Charles' Coat of Arms

By the age of *thirteen,* Prince Charles was granted his own heraldic achievement,[1] or what many loosely identify as a "coat of arms,"[2] and at nineteen, one year before his public investiture as Prince of Wales (discussed later), he was granted his own Welsh standard (right).[3] Below, we'll thoroughly examine the

heraldic symbols found in the Charles' official achievement as Prince of Wales,[4] as well as some unusual variations between it and at least

---

1. Boutell, *Boutell's Heraldry,* rev. C.W. Scott-Giles and J.P. Brooke-Little (London: Frederick Warne, 1963), pp. 217-218. The design of then Prince Charles' heraldic achievement as Prince of Wales (and the red dragon or Satan), was finalized by 1962 (e.g., see Boutell, plate V). Indeed, as Norroy and Ulster King of Arms, John P. Brooke-Little participated in Charles' July 1969 investiture as Satan's Prince, where the full heraldic achievement, in both graven and printed forms, was first publicly unveiled.

2. Although we may refer to each of Charles' full heraldic achievements (he now has more than one) as a "coat of arms," Boutell correctly observes that this term, while "frequently used as synonymous with achievement," embracing not only the shield but also the crest, supporters (if any) and other accessories," actually applies in a strict sense "only to the heraldic insignia now normally displayed on the shield." According to Boutell, a coat of arms originally consisted of "a coat, or tunic, which a man wore over his armour, and on which were painted or embroidered the same devices as appeared on the wearer's shield" (Boutell, 1978 ed., pp. 21-22). Such a coat or tunic served as a graphic and unmistakable way of identifying an individual in a contest or battle.

3. Holden, *PRINCE CHARLES,* p. 156. Boutell, 1978 ed., p. 258. This standard is based upon the personal banner for Llewellyn the Great, Prince of Wales: "These arms, differenced with a small green inescutcheon [(i.e., shield)] bearing The Prince's Crown in the middle (illustrated on the cover of this [investiture album] sleeve) are borne today by Prince Charles as his Personal Banner for use in Wales" (Rodney Dennys, O.B.E., F.S.A., Somerset Herald of Arms, *The Investiture of H.R.H. Chalres, Prince of Wales,* album cover inset). Notably, on the album sleeve, all four of these heraldic beasts are shown with *five claws per foot;* this is clearly evident for each of their front paws, though only four of the five claws per foot are visible on each of their back paws.

4. For a quality color representation of Charles' official heraldic achievement as Prince of Wales, see Boutell, 1970 or later ed., between pp. 174-177. According to Brooke-Little: "This is the approved design of the arms of the heir-apparent for use by H.R.H. Charles Philip Arthur George, Prince of Wales, Duke of Cornwall and Rothesay, Earl of Chester and Carrick, Baron of Renfrew, Lord of the Isles and Great Steward of Scotland. Worked into the compartment are H.R.H.'s badge as heir-apparent..., the red dragon badge for Wales differenced by a label argent and the arms of the duchy of Cornwall. (This illustration is from an original painting by Mr. Geoffrey Mussett [who is a Herald Painter at the College of Arms].)" For a close unofficial version of the same, see *Burke's Guide to the Royal Family,* 1st ed. (London: Burke's Peerage Ltd., 1973), p. 104. The author has been told that this achievement may also

one later, unofficial version.[1] However, before doing so, the words "herald" and "heraldry" should be defined.

A herald may be a messenger who proclaims important news, or a harbinger who gives a sign or an indication of something to come. The heralds of medieval history, for example, communicated challenges and made proclamations at tournaments and battles while recognizing armored combatants by their distinctive insignia, or "devices." These artistic and beastly devices, which were likewise used on seals as a means of personal identification,[2] formed the basis for modern, or institutionalized heraldry. Of such, God's saints—particularly today—should not be unaware (cf. 2 Cor 2:11). "While still associated with the knightly shield, helm and banner, heraldry was no longer a practical ancillary to the warrior's equipment, but became rather a decorative art.... [The] ... heralds began to weave a mystery about their craft, deliberately complicating its nomenclature and language, and introducing unnecessary rules and conventions."[3] The purposes and functions of heraldic arms, designed and produced through the ancient and modern "arts" of heraldry (armory), are not unlike those of heralds. Indeed, those officials whose specialty is heraldry, are called "heralds" (as well as "armorists"). According to *Boutell's Heraldry,*

> In its widest sense, heraldry means all the duties of a herald....
>
> ....True heraldry does not boast—it aspires. For some, indeed, it possesses a spiritual value.
>
> In various ways, therefore, heraldry appeals to the mind.... Some [early princes and knights] took a lion or other beast characterizing strength or valour; **some took a religious symbol; and many placed on their shields figures forming a play on their names**. Symbolism of a rudimentary kind was present in early heraldry, and in this respect there is a link between it and the insignia which appeared on the shields and banners in previous periods of history.
>
> At pre-heraldic insignia we need only glance. At all times, and in all parts of the world, men have used symbols to focus ideas and sentiment and express them in visual form. Warriors, and particularly leaders, have

---

be found on p. 141 of *Burke's Guide to the British Monarchy,* although he could not verify it. As a knight of the Order of the Garter, Charles' Prince of Wales heraldic stall-plate, containing his actual *graven* achievement, was supposedly displayed in St. George's Chapel along with all the stall-plates of the other Garter knights. As sovereign, however, Charles III's is ostensibly *absent.* Likewise, as a knight of both the Order of the Thistle and the Order of the Bath, Charles could have had his Prince of Wales stall-plate displayed in the chapel of St. Giles church in Edinburgh, Scotland, as well as in Henry VII's Chapel in Westminster Abbey (Boutell, 1978 ed., pp. vi, 194, 196).

1. Unofficial versions of an achievement may reflect an emphasis on the part of the herald that differs from the officially accepted (legal) version of an achievement. In the case of the particular version of Charles' "unofficial" arms as Prince of Wales, with which this work deals, the deviations—which are both occult and intended to be prophetic—suggest some very salient points, as we'll soon see.

2. Boutell, 1978 ed., pp. 176-178.

3. Boutell, 1978 ed., pp. 10-11.

been accustomed to display such symbols on shields and standards.... The legions and cohorts of Rome had their insignia....

These insignia of antiquity are [generally] to be regarded as the predecessors and not as the ancestors of medieval heraldry.... [Yet] some of the emblems found in ancient symbolism have survived to take their place as devices in heraldry. For example, **the British tribal emblem of a [red] dragon [which was formerly displayed upon the standards of Roman cohorts] became a supporter of the Royal Arms in Tudor times and is still the badge of Wales**.... In more remote times personal insignia may sometimes have been used to establish identity.... In the 12th century it became purposefully distinctive and consistently hereditary....

A modern herald has defined "true heraldry ... as the systematic use of hereditary devices centered on the shield."

....Heralds have [also] drawn on classical and medieval mythology, and on their own creative imaginations, to add a number of monsters and hybrids to the animals of nature.[1]

In heraldry, these monsters and hybrids are called "beasts." Stephen Friar states,

The vigorous medieval interpretation of beasts, birds, fish, reptiles and chimerical monsters is for many the very quintessence of heraldry.

The magnates of the Middle Ages often possessed one or more distinctive beasts as personal devices, culled from the pages of the bestiaries or from the shadowy traditions of ancestral crusaders. Many of these devices were incorporated into the shield of arms, but a far greater number were adopted as personal badges and were later translated into crests and supporters....

The use of beasts as emblems of authority pre-dates armory [(institutionalized heraldry)] by many centuries.... From the reign of Richard I [the Lionhearted] (1189-99) beasts became increasingly popular as royal devices, and by the fifteenth century the English kings had accumulated a variety of devices as the result of alliance or inheritance. Collectively these, with a number of later additions, are known as the Royal Beasts....[2]

Like heralds, each "coat of arms" makes certain proclamations about its owner. To some extent, these proclamations may be determined by "reading" the shield and the devices surrounding it. To read a coat of arms, one should be familiar with the heraldic terminology used to identify specific points or locations on, or relative to, an armorial shield. The shield itself is usually central to the arms. The upper one-third of the shield is sometimes referred to as the *Honor* point, the middle one-third as the *Fess* point, and the lower one-third as the *Nombril* or Navel point. More frequently, however, a combination of the terms *chief, base* (or *ground*), *dexter,* and *sinister* is used. *Chief* means the *top* of the shield, or the area above it,

---

1. Boutell, 1978 ed., pp. 2-4, 81; and "Wales, Principality of," *A Dictionary of Heraldry,* ed. Friar, p. 373.

2. "Beasts," *A Dictionary of Heraldry,* ed. Stephen Friar (New York: Harmony Books, 1987), pp. 55-56.

whereas *base* and *ground* mean the *bottom* of the shield, or the area below it. (The area below the shield, at the base of the heraldic achievement, is the location of the *Compartment* and a related *Motto*. The motto, which is usually given in Latin, expresses an idea, goal, or admonition.) From a frontal viewpoint, *dexter* means the *left*-hand side of the shield, or the area to the shield's left, whereas *sinister* means the *right*-hand side of the shield, or the area to the shield's right. The four quadrants, or quarters, of the shield are specified through combinations of these terms. Chief-dexter (or dexter-chief), for example, means the top-left quarter of the shield. As a general rule, armorists (heralds) read a coat of arms, relative to its central shield, from top to bottom and left to right.[1]

As we shall see, Charles heraldic achievement as Prince of Wales, comprises a literal, graphic representation of the beast described in Psalm 22:21, Daniel 7:2-24, and the Apocalypse (e.g., see Rev 12:3, 13:1-4). The Apocalypse describes the dexter beast, the center of the arms, and the red dragon, whereas the book of Daniel describes the center of the arms and the sinister beast. Psalm 22:21, on the other hand, describes the dexter and sinister beasts, as well as the red dragon (see below). Also, there are descriptions of other parts of the arms elsewhere in the scriptures.

Revelation 13 describes two beasts: the AntiChrist and the false prophet. Regarding the former, referred to as "the first beast," we read "the beast which I saw was like a leopard, his feet were like the feet of a bear, and his mouth like the mouth of a lion" (Rev 13:2). Over the years, a number of readers of the first edition of this work have mistakenly read the above as if it said "the beast which I saw was a leopard, his feet were the feet of a bear, and his mouth the mouth of a lion." *That is **not** what the scripture says!* Rather, we see the word "like" three times, clearly denoting that the reader should *not* expect this first beast to have the body of a leopard, feet of a bear, and mouth of a lion. What should you, the reader, then expect? *Exactly what the scripture actually says, of course.* So, what does the scripture actually *say?* We are told that the first beast has a body *like* that of a leopard, feet *like* those of a bear, and a mouth *like* that of a lion. This strange and awful beast is based upon *similes to parts* of real creatures—*not the actual parts themselves. To miss this subtle but clear distinction is to miss a major point of the prophecy.* No one should look at the dexter beast in Charles' arms as Prince of Wales, and expect to see a creature that has a leopard's body, a bear's feet, and a lion's mouth. What we see instead is a beast with a body evincing proportions similar to that of a leopard's, feet and

---

1. "Shields, Points of the," *A Dictionary of Heraldry,* ed. Friar, p. 316. Also see Boutell, 1978 ed., p. 21.

claws similar to those of a bear's feet and claws, and a mouth similar to the mouth of a lion. *That is precisely what the prophecy indicates.* Some have stumbled regarding King Charles III's true identity over this one point alone. You should not.

The dexter beast in Charles' achievement as Prince of Wales, rather than being the "normal" heraldic lion for England, has a body *like* a leopard for *Germany,* feet *like* the feet of a bear for *France,* and a mouth *like* the mouth of a lion for *England*. In other words, it fully represents the Merovingian dynasty, which originated and prospered historically in Germany, France, and England.[1] The sinister beast, a unicorn, faces the dexter beast, stands above the red dragon (see Rev 13:2; cf. 12:3, 12:9), and has eyes *like* those of a man. This beast is restrained (cf. 2 Th 2:6-7, Gk.) by means of a chain (cf. Ezek 7:23, AKJV). In heraldry, as well as in many New Age circles today, the unicorn is said to represent "the Christ," and in ancient Babylonian artwork, as well as in the book of Daniel, it was portrayed as a beast having a *little horn* (see Dan 7:8, 7:11, 7:20-21, 8:9-11; cf. Dan 8:5-8; Lam 2:17). Irenaeus, Tertullian, Justinus, and others, likened the horn of the unicorn to the central beam of the cross upon which Jesus was crucified.[2] (The unicorn's horn may also be compared to the spikes that were used to pierce Jesus.) Like certain Renaissance artwork,[3] ancient Babylon's Ishtar Gate incorporates depictions of lions, dragons, and unicorns (or bulls).[4] At His crucifixion, Jesus prayed,

> Many bulls | unicorns have surrounded Me; strong *ones* of Bashan have encircled Me. They have opened their mouth at Me as a raging and a roaring lion.... You have brought Me to the dust of death. For dogs have surrounded Me; the assembly of the wicked has enclosed Me. Like a lion, *they pierced* My hands and My feet.... Deliver Me from the sword, My only one from the dog's paw. **Save Me from the lion's mouth and from the horns of the unicorns—***the* **affliction**[5] **of the dragon [sea-**

---

1. For more information, see ch. 4, "Prince of this World—a *Diverse* Lineage," and ch. 7's section titled, "The dexter (left-hand) supporter," at pp. 79 and 192, respectively.
2. Odell Shepard, *The Lore of the Unicorn* (New York: Avnel Books, 1982), pp. 80-81.
3. Nancy Hathaway, *The Unicorn* (New York: Avenel Books, 1980), pp. 47, 104-105.
4. *The Thompson CHAIN-REFERENCE BIBLE,* 4th ed., 4334 (Indianapolis, Indiana: B.B. Kirkbride Bible Co., Inc., 1982), p. 318.
5. Strong's no. 6040, עֲנִי or *onee*.

monster]![1] (Ps 22:12-13, 22:15c-16, 22:20-21, Heb.; cf. Ps 22:21, AKJV; Rev 13:1-2)

In 1603, following the death of England's Queen Elizabeth I, Scotland's King James VI took England's throne as James I. Upon uniting Scotland's crown with England's, James I added Scotland's red lion to England's royal shield of arms, as well as replaced Elizabeth I's *sinister* lion supporter with Scotland's unicorn. Rüdiger R. Beer remarks: "By far the best known unicorn in heraldry is part of the British coat of arms. When England and Scotland united at the beginning of the seventeenth century and James VI of Scotland became James I of the United Kingdom, a unicorn replaced one of the pair of lions supporting the shield. The menacing lion and antagonistic unicorn from Psalm 22 thus became fortuitously reunited in heraldry."[1] *Queen Elizabeth II's* coat of arms, as currently displayed in the Garter Throne

---

1. Strong's no. 8577, תני or *tanee*. The translation of this last phrase in Psalm 22:21 (v. 22 in Heb.), "*the* affliction of the dragon [sea monster]," is derived from a concatenation in the Hebrew of two words, Strong's numbers 6040, עני or *onee*, and 8577, תנין or *taneen*. Strong's no. 8577 is represented with the final *nun* having been dropped or omitted, giving תני or *tanee*. This *nun* may have been dropped inadvertently through a copyist's error, or purposely omitted to create a poetic rhyme with the last word, יחידתי or *y'chee-datee* (tr., "My only one"), of the preceding verse (cf. *Onee-tanee*).

   In the Masoretic Text, the Hebrew phrase *onee tanee* appears as one word, עניתני or *anee-tanee*. In English, this text is commonly translated as "You have answered [rescued] Me," though some render it simply as "poor," which comes from the same Hebrew word as "afflicted" (cf. the Greek *Codex Sinaiticus*). Along the latter line, the Revised Standard Version (RSV) has "My afflicted soul" (the *New* RSV uses "You have rescued Me"). Yet all these translations are *dubious*. In the case of "You have answered [rescued] Me," *anee-tanee* is alleged to be Strong's number 6030, which in reality bears only a weak resemblance to it, whereas in the other translations, it is viewed as a combination of Strong's number 6041 (for "poor" or "afflicted") and an *inexplicable* or *nonexistent* word (e.g., for "soul"). Further, none of these translations agrees with the immediate context or poetic form of verse 21, a plea for deliverance from *beasts,* and, with the lone exception of the RSV, they ignore verse 24 (v. 25 in Heb.), which clearly addresses an earlier "affliction."

   In this author's opinion, therefore, it is best to understand the Hebrew as a concatenation of two words that do exist (i.e., Strong's numbers 6040 and 8577, where the root for 8577 appears to be 8565, תן or *tan*), thereby obtaining "*the* affliction of the dragon [sea-monster]." Inasmuch as Jesus' crucifixion upon the cross was typical of the swallowing of Jonah by a "sea monster" (e.g., see Matt 12:40, Gk.), this is a viable translation; moreover, it perfectly fits the immediate context and poetic form of verse 21.

2. Rüdiger Robert Beer, *Unicorn: Myth and Reality,* trans. Charles M. Stern (New York: Van Nostrand Reinhold Company, 1972), p. 138.

Room, is shown above.[1] A remarkable graven version of the royal achievement adorns the gates of Buckingham Palace. It displays the dexter lion and the sinister unicorn, each resting upon a base of palm branches that curve around their backsides (perhaps indicating millennial aspirations), as well a "George Pendant" dangling from the central royal shield, over which, in place of the normal helm, there is a lion's head. Moreover, its shield contains the pagan version of the Irish harp, which shows the upper body of a bare-breasted harlot. A photograph of this achievement is shown in *The Illustrated Golden Bough,* with a caption that reads: "In many cultures, the souls of dead kings in particular are thought to migrate into animals, and sometimes living kings may be embodied in them. A trace of this idea survives in European heraldry."[2]

Taken together, the symbols in Charles' heraldic achievement as Prince of Wales, represent his ultimate dominion. It is Interesting, therefore, that the organization of the dexter and sinister beasts in British royal arms, including Charles', appears to have Babylonian origins. Barbara G. Walker states: "[The unicorn is the classic] symbol of the phallic horse deity, or sacred king incarnate in a horned horse.... A source of the unicorn myth may have been the Babylonian dragon-beast made up of a horselike body ... and a flat [single] horned head.... One theory proposes that the unicorn was originally the bull of spring, rearing up and struggling with the lion of summer. Babylonian art showed both animals in profile so the bull appeared to have only one horn. The British coat of arms still has 'the lion and the unicorn' contending in just such a manner."[3]

The pagan lion, dragon, and unicorn symbols were prominent in ancient Babylonia and Assyria, as well as subsequent world empires

---

1. As sovereign of the Order of the Garter, Queen Elizabeth II's coat of arms was (ostensibly, yet is) prominently displayed above her Garter Throne in the Garter Throne Room. For a color photograph of the Garter Throne Room, see p. 64 of *Royalty,* Vol. 12, No. 2 (1993). Unlike Charles' heraldic achievement as Prince of Wales, the queen's was (may yet be) readily seen. In fact, her Garter stall-plate, containing her actual *graven* achievement, rather than being displayed in St. George's Chapel along with the stall-plates of other Garter knights, had been located above her throne in the British parliament, where she presided annually over the state opening. (Those "honors" now pertain to King Charles III and his new royal heraldic achievement, which we'll later address.) For a color photograph of the late queen's Garter stall-plate, as well as certain other heraldic symbols and badges discussed in this book, see the state opening of parliament shown on p. 50 of *Royalty,* Vol. 11, No. 3 (December, 1991). Other color pictures of Elizabeth II's arms may be seen, for example, on p. 83 of *Debrett's Book of the Royal Wedding* by Hugo Vickers (New York: The Viking Press, 1981); the jacket, inside front cover, and p. 96 of *The Royal Family* by Jane Masterson (New York: Crescent Books, 1991); pp. 82, 83, and 94 of *Royalty,* Vol. 13, No. 2 (1994). Artistic renditions of the queen's arms may also be found in the various editions of *Boutell's Heraldry,* although the rendition in the 1963 ed. is more accurate than that in later editions (Plate I, facing title page). Likewise, heraldic descriptions of both her arms and Prince Philip's arms may be found on pp. 218 or 219-220 of the same work.
2. Frazer, p. 110.
3. Barbara G. Walker, "Unicorn," *The Woman's Encyclopedia of Myths and Secrets* (New York: Harper Collins Publishers, Inc., 1983), pp. 1027-1028.

(e.g., the Medo-Persian, Greek, and Roman empires). Today, however, their greatest applications are to the AntiChrist and his coming worldwide kingdom, with its capital at Mystery Babylon (Rev 17:4-5, 17:18). Inasmuch as the United Kingdom was *Tarshish*, this neo-Babylonian capital will be intimately associated with "Tarshish, and all its young lions" (e.g., see Ezek 38:13; Rev 13:2; cf. Jer 2:14-15, 4:5-7, 5:6).

As will be shown, the mythological unicorn was initially derived from Babylon's spring bull. When considered, this fact should lay to rest the arguments of many modern scholars that the Hebrew word רְאֵם or רֵים, which is pronounced *re'em* or *rêm* and translated as "unicorn" throughout the Authorized King James Version of the Old Testament, should instead be translated as "wild ox." Given the historical association of the unicorn with the AntiChrist, this matter is significant.

With the lone exception of Deuteronomy 33:17, in which the singular *re'em* must be translated as "wild ox" (due to the fact that Moses ascribed a plural number of horns to it in the original Hebrew), this word may be rendered as "unicorn" (referring to a beast having just one horn) throughout the Hebrew Bible. One could perhaps, however, reasonably argue that the word *re'em* in Numbers 23:22 and 24:8 must also refer to some kind of "wild ox" (since Moses likewise penned Numbers). Nevertheless, besides Psalm 22:21, the following passages, based upon the original Hebrew text, remain:

> Will the **unicorn** [wild ox] be willing to serve you? Will he bed by your manger? Can you bind the **unicorn** [wild ox] in the furrow with ropes? Or will he plow the valleys behind you? Will you trust him because his strength *is* great? Or will you leave your labor to him? (Job 39:9-11)

> The voice of The LORD breaks the cedars; yes, The LORD splinters the cedars of Lebanon. He makes them also skip like a calf, Lebanon and Sirion like sons of **unicorns**. (Ps 29:5-6)

> "But You, LORD, *are* on high forevermore. For behold, Your enemies, O LORD—for behold, Your enemies shall perish; all the workers of iniquity | Awen[1] shall be scattered. But You have exalted like **unicorns** My horn. My eye also has seen *My desire* on My enemies, ... on the wicked who rise up against Me." *The* Righteous One shall flourish like a palm tree; He shall grow like a cedar in Lebanon. (Ps 92:8-12; cf. Num 23:22, 24:8; 1 Sam 2:10*d-e*, Heb.; Ps 89:17-29, 132:17-18, Heb.; Zech 14:10, Heb.)

> "For My sword shall be bathed in heaven; indeed, it shall come down on Edom, and on the people of My curse, for judgment." The sword of The

---

1. See ch. 8, "The Red Dragon and Prince Charles' Investiture as Prince of Wales," at p. 207.

LORD is filled with blood, it is made fat with fatness, with the blood of lambs and goats, with the fat of the kidneys of rams. For The LORD has a sacrifice in Bozrah, and a great slaughter in the land of Edom. The **unicorns** shall come down with them, and the young bulls with the mighty bulls; their land shall be soaked with blood, and their dust made fat with fatness. (Isa 34:5-7; cf. Isa 63:1-6; Rev 14:17-20, 19:11-21; Obad 15-18, 21)

In the third century B.C., when composing the Greek Septuagint, at least seventy of Israel's rabbis (according to rabbinic tradition) together translated the word *re'em* in all of the above passages as *monoceros* (i.e., a beast having one horn projecting from its head). Various scholars have argued that these rabbis, unfamiliar with the beast, mistakenly translated *re'em* as *monoceros*. Yet even Isaiah distinguished the *re'em* from "the young bulls with the mighty bulls" (34:7).

Although the *re'em* spoken of in the scriptures almost certainly *was* a ferocious wild ox, perhaps even the now extinct aurochs, it was the very bull of spring depicted in Babylonian artwork. The significance of this lies not in the fact that the biblical *re'em* was originally a wild ox, but rather in the fact that by the time the Septuagint was produced, this Babylonian bull had long been superseded by its earlier artistic depiction as a unicorn. It seems plausible that the rabbinic translators of the Septuagint had this in mind when they chose to render the Hebrew *re'em* as *monoceros* in Greek (Lat., *unicornis*), the beast that by then had replaced the ancient Babylonian bull in pagan mythology. Consequently, the unicorn is now a symbol that represents both Satan and the AntiChrist. (More will be said on this in the discussion of the sinister unicorn supporter.) Regarding the *re'em* and the lion, Odell Shepard gives this helpful discourse:

> ...[It has been discovered] that *rimu* was the Assyrian name of the gigantic aurochs or *Bos Primigenius*, a species of wild buffalo which became extinct in the sixteenth century. Cuvier, basing his measurement upon remains of the aurochs much smaller than others since discovered, estimated that this animal was twelve feet long and almost seven feet high; its teeth have been found in a cave on Mount Lebanon; ... Layard identified the animal with the majestic sculptured bulls of Nineveh. The *Bos Primigenius* now holds the field. Its bulk, speed, and savage ferocity ... make it clear why the Hebrews always spoke of the *Re'em* with bated breath....
>
> Before the accession of James I to the throne of England a great variety of "supporters" had been used for the Royal Arms, but a lion had for several generations been one of the two.... On the Royal Arms of Scotland the unicorn had been employed as consistently.... It is often said that the lion and unicorn were chosen as supporters of the British Arms because of the belief in the natural animosity of these two beasts and as a symbol of the reconciliation between England and Scotland.... James kept his Scot-

tish unicorn and he chose the English lion merely because it had been the most persistent supporter of the English Arms before his time. He kept the lion dexter as it had been on Elizabeth [I]'s Arms....

....It is certain that the presence of the unicorn on the British Royal Arms, reproduced as they are millions of times in every year and scattered throughout the world, has tended to maintain interest in the animal and to develop a curiosity about its tradition....

One recalls in this connection several Biblical references to horns, apparently single....

Thus far we have paid no attention to the total scene ... at Persepolis,[1] in which a beast resembling a powerful lion attacks an apparently one-horned animal.... ...I shall call these animals the lion and the unicorn. The delineation of their conflict was remarkably popular over a great extent of territory and of time. One sees it continually and with only slight variations on cylinder-seals of Babylon[ia] and Assyria, on coins of Mycene, and on *objects d'art* of uncertain origin that were spread through Europe and Asia during the Middle Ages by Scythian traders. The inference is that it had more than a decorative value and was widely recognized as a symbol. But a symbol of what?

Here and there in the unicorn literature of Europe one finds references to a clever ruse employed by the lion in capturing unicorns [via a tree]. [This lion-capture fable] ... seems to have been crowded out by the story of the virgin-capture [in which a unicorn (cf. The Messiah) is meekly lured by a virgin (cf. the Church) to his death under a tree (cf. the cross) before a huntsman and his dogs (cf. Satan and those who perpetrated the crucifixion)], yet it may be much older than the Holy Hunt allegory and may have served for ages as a religious symbol in the East....

...Edward Topsell ... says of the unicorn: "He is an enemy to Lions, wherefore as soon as ever a Lion seeth a Unicorn, he runneth to a tree for succour, that ... he may not only avoid his horn but also destroy him; for the Unicorn in the swiftness of his course runneth against a tree, wherein his sharp horn sticketh fast. Then when the Lion seeth the Unicorn fastened by the horn, without all danger he falleth upon him and killeth him."
...

As I have pointed out, the one-horned figures at Persepolis were imitations, both in subject and treatment, of others [found] at Nineveh and Babylon. These in their turn were by no means original, for recent diggings at Ur of the Chaldees have shown ... precisely the same conventional treatment of horned animals....

Looking at these objects from the city of Abraham, one realizes that .... the pattern or theme of the lion and unicorn conflict can be shown to have endured in art for at least twenty-five hundred years.... Is it possible to make a plausible guess at the meaning these objects had for their makers?... Is it possible that the lion and the unicorn ... were solar and lunar emblems?...

That there is some kind of connection between the Moon and the unicorn is not a theory but a fact.... On ancient cylinder-seals the crescent moon frequently appears in conjunction with figures of animals which ...

---

1. Persepolis was the main royal palace of Medo-Persia's Achaemenid dynasty and a major center of Zoroastrianism, which predicates itself upon the ancient struggle of good against evil (*Eerdmans' Handbook to the World's Religions,* p. 82).

are represented with single horns. ...The unicorn is commonly, though not always, thought of as white in body; it is an emblem of chastity; it is very swift; according to the best authorities it cannot be taken alive. The animal is most readily associated with the new or crescent moon, which might indeed seem to dwellers by the sea to be leading the stars down to the water and to dip its own horn therein before they descend. The crescent moon has been used for ages to represent both celestial motherhood and virginity, whether of Ishtar, Isis, Artemis, [Ashtoreth (Astarte), Asherah, Anath, Diana,] or the Madonna.[1] In all his pictures of the Assumption ... Madrid Murillo painted the crescent moon over Mary's head. Old alchemical charts commonly designate the figure of Luna by placing in her right hand a single horn. The ki-lin, or unicorn of China, is commonly represented in bronze, bearing a crescent moon among clouds on his back....

....For is not the [pagan] belief in the Moon's power to absorb poisons rising from earth during the darkness closely similar to the belief in the unicorn's water-conning? Does it not recall the vivid picture of the three-legged ass dipping his golden horn into the waters of the firmament and dispelling their corruption?...

If the unicorn [in the lion-capture story] is to represent the Moon, then the lion, a common solar emblem, should of course represent the Sun, and we have only the tree left to be explained.... Unicorned animals are often found on Assyrian cylinder-seals grouped with a single conventionalized tree in symbolical arrangement. This tree of the cylinder-seals is usually called the Tree of Fortune, but it seems to be ultimately indistinguishable from the Cosmogonic Tree ... springing from the nether darkness and holding the earth and heavenly bodies in its branches, familiar in the myths of many peoples.... If the lion and the unicorn are to represent the Sun and the Moon they will need no less a tree than this as the scene of their encounter.

We are now prepared for a bald statement of the solar-lunar theory concerning the lion-capture [of the unicorn]...: "The Lion-sun flies from the rising Unicorn-moon and hides behind the Tree or Grove of the Underworld; the Moon pursues, and, sinking in her turn, is Sun-slain." In other words, just as the lion of our story slips behind the tree to avoid the unicorn's onrush, so the Sun goes behind the Tree...; and as the unicorn is caught by the [lodging of its] horn [in the tree] so the Moon is held fast during the interlunar period—at which time, many myths assert, the Sun eats it up....

Brown also finds significance in the fact that many of these [one-horned] creatures are shown touching or nearly [touching] the symbolic tree with their horns, and that their heads are invariably turned toward this tree.[2]

Before its ancient perversion and corruption, the Zodiac apparently represented the Gospel of Jesus in symbolic form.[3] Could the

1. Not only has the unicorn likewise been used to represent the Virgin Mary, but past Pope John Paul II and other Roman Catholics are known to have prayed and said the Mass before the "Black Madonna." Located in the shrine of Czestochowa at Jasna Gora, Poland, this demonic image is taken as a depiction of the Virgin Mary holding the Child Jesus.
2. Shepard, pp. 44-45, 75-79, 240-244, 247-249.
3. For more information, see Ethelbert W. Bullinger, *The Witness of the Stars* (Michigan: Kregal Publications, 1967); D. James Kennedy, *THE REAL MEANING OF THE ZODIAC* (Florida: Coral Ridge Ministries,

explanations put forth to date for the combined mythological symbolism of the lion and the unicorn also be corruptions of an original,
divine theme? What if the tree whereby the unicorn in the lion-capture fable is slain originally represented the Tree of Life, or Jesus, as
well as the cross upon which He was hung? The entire universe is
under Jesus' dominion and power, and the stars, planets, moons,
etc., rest in His branches (cf. Gen 3:22; Matt 13:31-32; Luke 13:18-19).
What if the unicorn pictured Jesus' adversaries—Satan and those in
him (e.g., Judas Iscariot and the AntiChrist; see Ps 75:4-5 {KJV},
75:10a)—who in piercing both Jesus and the tree (cross) upon which
He hung, became lodged in that tree and were themselves vanquished thereby, along with guilt and sin (though certain victories
are yet to come)? Besides representing Satan who personifies sin,
the unicorn would then also have represented the sins of the redeemed world, Jesus' bride, for whom Jesus was to be pierced. Finally, what if the lion depicted The Lion of the tribe of Judah (see Rev
5:5; cf. Gen 49:8-12; Num 23:24), who, having veiled Himself upon
the cross as the Lamb of God (cf. hiding behind the tree), slew Satan
in Satan's attempt to slay Him (see Rev 5:6-14)?

As God's Mighty Messenger (Rev 10:1, Gk.), Jesus will shout
aloud "with a great voice, as *when* a lion roars," and then "seven
thunders" will speak "their voices" (Rev 10:3; cf. Rev 11:19, 16:17-18).
Further, He will "roar *over* His enemies" (Isa 42:13, Heb.; see Jer
25:30-38, 50:44; Hos 11:8-12; Joel 3:13-16)! As God's Lion, Jesus will
slay the AntiChrist, or Satan's unicorn, ending Satan's dominion.

What about the Sun and the Moon? In paganism, the Sun has
long been represented by a lion (cf. Hos 5:13-14), and the Moon by a
unicorn (cf. Hos 5:7, 5:13). Biblically, however, the Sun is a symbol of
The Bridegroom, Jesus (see Num 24:17; Ps 19:4-6, Heb.; Isa 62:1;
Mal 4:2; Matt 17:2; Rev 1:16, 10:1, 22:16; cf. Ps 89:36), whose glory
will be seen upon His saints (e.g., see Judg 5:31, Heb.; Isa 58:10;
Matt 13:43; 1 Th 5:5; 2 Pet 1:19; cf. Isa 30:26). Also, the Moon is a
symbol of Jesus' bride, the saints (e.g., see Ps 89:35-37; Rev 12:1; cf.
Gen 37:9-11; Song 6:10; Isa 24:23), who reflect His light in the midst
of the darkness of an unregenerate world (cf. Matt 25:5-10;
2 Cor 3:18). Therefore, the Sun, representing Messiah Jesus, is associated with the symbol of the lion, whereas the Moon, representing
His bride, for whom and by whom He was pierced, is associated
with the symbol of the unicorn.

1989); or Troy Lawrence, *The SECRET MESSAGE of the ZODIAC* (California: Here's Life Publishers, Inc.,
1990). Also see the chapter (or section) "The Gospel and the Zodiac," in the volume titled, *Conflict of
the Aeons: Understanding the Protoevangelium,* of the author's *Messiah, History, and the Tribulation
Period* series.

Recall that God warned Cain, saying: "If you do well, is there not exaltation? And if you do not do well, Sin is crouching *like a lion* at the door, and his desire is toward you, but you should rule over him" (Gen 4:7, Heb.). Unable to better Him, Satan has always sought to counterfeit the things of God. *The lion and unicorn symbols, besides representing Jesus and His adversaries, respectively, also have counter-applications.* Just as Jesus is The Lion of the Tribe of Judah, Satan too is viewed as a lion (1 Pet 5:8; cf. 2 Tim 4:17). Similarly, just as Satan, in the person of the AntiChrist, is represented as a unicorn, God, in the person of His Son, is represented as The Horn of David (Ps 132:17-18, Heb.; see 1 Sam 2:10*d-e,* Heb.; Ps 75:6-7, 89:19-29, 92:8-12; Luke 1:68-75; cf. Ps 75:10*b;* Ezek 29:21). Having been lured to His death by a virgin under a tree (i.e., the cross), as in the virgin-capture story, Jesus shall yet trample His adversaries beneath His feet; for it is written, "You shall tread upon *the* roaring *lion* and *the* asp, *the* young lion and *the* dragon You shall trample underfoot" (Ps 91:13, Heb.; cf. AKJV).[1] Indeed, as a type of His Son (e.g., see Num 23:21-22, 24:7-8, Heb.; Hos 11:1; Matt 2:14-15), God likens redeemed Israel to a conquering unicorn around the time of Armageddon, stating, "Arise and thresh, *O* daughter of Zion; for I will make your horn iron, and I will make your hooves bronze [brass], and you shall crush [beat in pieces] many peoples" (Mic 4:11-13, Heb.; see Deut 33:26-29; Ps 44:4-5, 89:17-18; Mic 7:8-10; Zech 10:3-5, 10:12; Mal 4:1-3). Further, according to Zechariah 14:10, in which the Hebrew word for *re'em* is generally translated as "raised up" or "rise," Jerusalem itself will be exalted as upon the tip of a unicorn's horn in the Millennial Kingdom (cf. Ps 75:10*b*); that is, she will sit atop *one mountain,* then Earth's highest, which can be likened to the *single horn* of a majestic unicorn.

In The Messiah, who is God's and Judah's Lion, the saints will be victorious in their war against the AntiChrist, Satan's and Britain's counterfeit lion-beast, even though it will cost most of them their physical lives (e.g., see Rev 6:7-11, 12:17, 13:3-17, 15:1-4, 20:4-6). The Horn of David, not the little horn, shall be eternally exalted; for Satan and those in him will be utterly crushed (e.g., see Ps 75, KJV)! It is written,

> How lovely are your tents, *O* Jacob—your dwellings, *O* Yisra-El!... He shall pour water from His buckets, and His Seed *shall be* in many waters. His King shall be higher than Agag, and His kingdom shall be exalted. God brings Him out of Egypt. He has strength like a wild ox [unicorn]. He shall consume the nations, His enemies. He shall break their bones and pierce

---

1. According to Shepard, the Talmud records that Adam's first sacrifice was an ox having just one horn on its forehead (p. 45). This would constitute a unique parallel to the sacrifice of The Messiah.

them with His arrows. He bows down, He lies down as a Lion, and as a Lion, who will rouse Him? Blessed *is* he who blesses You, and cursed *is* he who curses You. (Num 24:5-9, Heb.; cf. 23:21-24)

Unfortunately, if these interpretations are correct, the biblical lion and unicorn symbolism went the way of the Zodiac, having been transformed and incorporated into pagan mythologies. Further, this pagan symbolism has become central to the rise of the AntiChrist.

"In Medieval art, ... chimerical figures appear as embodiments of the deceptive, even satanic forces of raw nature.... Virgil, in the *Aeneid* (book 5) employs Chimaera for the name of gigantic ship of Gyas in the ship-race, with possible allegorical significance in contemporary Roman politics."[1] Importantly, Charles' heraldic achievement as Prince of Wales, could ostensibly also be seen as a corporate representation of the classic chimaera (chimera) of Greek mythology, where a beast having a lion's head, goat's body and dragon's tail arises from a sea. (The horse-bodied unicorn has a *goat's beard* and boar's hoofs.) In "the earliest surviving literary reference," this monstrosity is represented as "a thing of immortal make, not human, lion-fronted and snake [(or dragon)] behind, a goat in the middle, and snorting out the breath of the terrible flame of bright fire."[2] Reading Charles' heraldic achievement as Prince of Wales, from left to right and top to bottom, we encounter the "lion-leopard-bear" dexter beast as the "lion front," the human-eyed unicorn as the "'goat' in the middle," and the fiery red dragon as the "snake behind." Indeed: "Hesiod's *Theogony* follows the Homeric description: he makes the Chimera the issue of Echidna: 'She was the mother of Chimaera who breathed raging fire, a creature fearful, great, swift-footed and strong, who had three heads, one of a grim-eyed lion; in her hinderpart, a dragon; and in her middle, a goat, breathing forth a fearful blast of blazing fire.'"[3] Again, the foretold AntiChrist's heraldic achievement corporately bears these particular heads: that of "a grim-eyed lion," "a 'goat'" in the "middle," and "a dragon" at its "hinderpart."

We may, therefore, relate the classic chimera to ancient Assyrian and Babylonian religious seals, with all their meanings intact. Thus, it seems that God through the Apocalypse, would have us recognize and understand that the first beast—and thus, the foretold AntiChrist himself—embodies spiritually at least, Greece's terrible mythological chimera. Such were also the symbols of Charles' July 1969 (this year intimates 666 if we invert each 9) investiture as Prince of Wales.

---

1. "Chimera (mythology)," *Wikipedia.org,* 5 Sep. 2019.
2. Ibid.
3. Ibid.

C.W. Scott-Giles and J.P. Brooke-Little, in the somewhat cryptic, occult, and often obscure language of heraldry, summarize the symbols in *Charles'* arms as Prince of Wales, as follows:

> H.R.H. The Prince of Wales bears the Royal Arms differenced by a label of three points argent and with an escutcheon [(small shield)] of the arms of the Principality of Wales ensigned by the Heir Apparent's coronet.... His shield is encircled with the Garter. He also bears the Royal Crest and Supporters, all differenced by a label as in the arms and also by the substitution of his coronet for the crowns in the crest and the supporting lion. His motto is ICH DIEN. His badge as Heir Apparent is, *a plume of three ostrich feathers argent enfiled by a coronet of crosses paty and fleurs-de-lis or, with the motto,* ICH DIEN.... In his full achievement this badge is placed below the shield together with the red dragon of Wales, differenced by a label as in the arms, and the arms of the Duchy of Cornwall: *Sable fifteen bezants*, the shield ensigned with the Heir Apparent's coronet.[1]

Of Charles *(not* William), Friar adds:

> The badge of the Prince of Wales is *y ddraig goch*, the red dragon, upon a green mount and with a white label of three points about its neck. The so-called Prince of Wales' Feathers' badge, which comprises three white ostrich feathers enfiling a gold coronet ... and, on a blue scroll, the motto 'Ich Dien', is the badge of the heir apparent to the English throne....
> The Prince of Wales bears the arms of the sovereign differenced by a label of three points argent [(white)] on a shield, crest, and supporters. His crown is similar to that of the Queen but without the arch from front to back. On his shield of arms he bears the arms of the Principality [of Wales] on an inescutcheon ensigned by his crown. His achievement may include the shield of arms of the Duchy of Cornwall *Sable [(Black) with] fifteen Bezants*, and this is usually placed below the principal shield of arms and ensigned by the crown.[2]

It is perhaps interesting to observe at this point that then Prince Charles has shown at least a cursory knowledge of, and interest in, heraldry: "While awaiting his posting [to the H.M.S. *Norfolk*] the Prince noted, with an inherited touch of King George VI's interest in heraldry, that the ship's crest was 'a silver ostrich feather with a gold quill ensigned by a gold prince's coronet, the pen piercing a scroll bearing the motto *Ich Dien*.'"[3] In the next chapter, we will examine each symbol on Charles' heraldic achievement as Prince of Wales. This examination will include the historic origins, heraldic and biblical meanings, and in several instances, the overall message conveyed.

---

1. Boutell, 1978 ed., pp. 218-219. This same heraldic description may be found in editions of Boutell's Heraldry going back to 1963.
2. "Wales, Prince of," *A Dictionary of Heraldry*, ed. Friar, p. 372.
3. Cathcart, p. 128.

The *Official* Heraldic Achievement of Charles, as Prince of Wales*

(as ostensibly described in Daniel and the Apocalypse)

*See the cover of this book for the full-color achievement.

An *Unofficial* Version

Official *Graven* Heraldic Arms of Satan's Prince—Eagle Tower's Water Gate, Caernarvon Castle, July 1969

Official *Graven* Heraldic Arms of Satan's Prince—Queen's Gate, Caernarvon Castle, July 1969

133

7

The Heraldic Symbols in the Arms
and
their Interpretations

The heart of every heraldic achievement is the shield (e.g., see the center of Charles' heraldic achievements). Shields, like other unique devices in British arms, may not legally or ethically be imitated for use by others, except as set forth in the laws of the United Kingdom and the British Commonwealth. In this regard, laws governing the use of heraldic devices and other symbols, which are a recognized form of property, are similar worldwide. Consequently, just as no two snowflakes are the same, no two achievements are ever legally identical. James and Russell remark: "Heraldry is basically a picture language developed by knights to make them recognizable in battle. Dressed in armour they all looked identical, so they began to wear sleeveless coats over their armour with obvious symbols on them. Shields bore colours, helmets had crests to show their rank and family. As no two families have the same crest, heraldry became the method of identification and the individual records going back five centuries are still kept up to date by the heralds."[1]

As previously mentioned, there are various later, unofficial versions of Charles' arms as Prince of Wales, that differ somewhat from his official, granted achievement as such. Below, and in the subsequent discussions on the dexter and sinister supporters, we will compare the official version of his "princely" achievement with what may now be the most prevalent rendition among his unofficial versions (both versions appear to be addressed in scripture). While examining the devices in Charles' achievement as Prince of Wales, we will proceed from top to bottom, and then from left to right.

The top of the arms. At the top of then Prince Charles' arms, there is a gold "lion" crest. The "lion" itself, which represents the dexter beast, is in a "guardant" posture (i.e., its head faces the observer).[2] It has four or five claws per foot, like a heraldic bear, as

---

1. James and Russell, *At Home with the Royal Family,* p. 144.
2. A similar crest is found in the arms of the Life Guards, which is the senior regiment of the British Army and one of the two armored regiments of the Royal Household Cavalry (James and Russell, *At Home with the Royal Family,* pp. 123-124). For more information, see this chapter's later section titled, "Related orders and royal guards," at p. 183, as well as the related note in this chapter's section titled, "The

well as a body with leopard's proportions. Like the dexter beast, it has a copy of the heir-apparent's crown upon its head, and the three-horned label of the eldest son (i.e., Charles) is around its neck.

The lion crest in the official achievement of Charles as Prince of Wales, differs from the one in the unofficial version. For example, in the official version, both of the lion's eyes are open, whereas in the unofficial version, the lion looks as if it is winking its right eye (see Job 15:12-16; Ps 35:17-21; Prov 6:12-19, 10:10; cf. Zech 11:17, KJV).[1] Indeed, the single open eye in the unofficial version is perhaps intended to suggest as well the single "all-seeing eye" of Lucifer in the capstone of the Seal of the Illuminati.[2] Further, the lion's tail in the unofficial version is substantially longer. In heraldry, the presumed magic of a lion is proportional to the length of its tail.[3] For Charles as the foretold AntiChrist, this lengthy tail—ostensibly, like the loosed re-strainer (discussed later)[4]—may signify his coming satanic possession. Finally, with the exception of this beast, and the dexter beast from which it came, all the beasts in Charles' *official* achievement as Prince of Wales, have protruding tongues. In the unofficial version, however, this beast and the dexter beast also have protruding tongues (see Ps 10:7-9, 12, 52:1-7, 57:4, 64, 73, 120; Isa 54:17, 57:3-4; cf. Job 5:19-23; Jer 9:8; Rev 6:7-8).

There is a second copy of the heir-apparent's gold crown below the lion crest, followed by the silver (white) ermine wreath (or torse), and the silver and gold ermine mantle (or shroud). At the center of these devices, and above the royal shield, is the gold helm. The helm in then Prince Charles' arms is that of the British sovereign, though princes of royal blood (in the succession) may also use it.[5]

---

dexter (left-hand) supporter," at p. 192.

1. On June 28, 1990, then Prince Charles nearly shattered his right arm in a polo fall. Compare this, and the winking of the beast, with Psalm 10:15 and Zechariah 11:17 (KJV).

2. For more information, see this chapter's later subsection entitled, "Garter development in history," at p. 178.

3. Margaret Young, "Lion," *A Dictionary of Heraldry,* ed. Friar, p. 215.

4. For more information, see the discussion on the restrainer in this chapter's later section titled, "The sinister (right-hand) supporter," starting around p. 203.

5. Child, *Heraldic Design* (London: G. Bell and Sons, 1965), p. 92.

Notice that the helm has seven curved bars. Interestingly, the word that Daniel used to describe the horns in the fourth beast's head may refer to an object that resembles an elephant's tooth (i.e., a banana-shaped object—like the horn of an ox), a flask (e.g., a test-tube), or a cornet (i.e., a cone-shaped, pointed object).[1] Therefore, it may be applied to these bars. Further, this word is also applicable to the three horns of each eldest-son label (discussed later) and to the horn of the sinister unicorn. Finally, notice that just as each beast on a coat of arms has its own head, so also does the overall coat of arms. That is, *the region near the top of the shield, around the location of the gold helm, is the head of the overall coat of arms* (cf. Dan 2:31-32, 2:35-39, 7:20). This (unseen) head, which in our context may be construed as a sort of satanic antithesis to "The Godhead" (i.e., The Deity), will be discussed in greater detail later.

A second copy of the eldest-son label lies immediately below the helm, with a third copy of the heir-apparent's crown imposed over its middle horn. Before looking further at this label and the crown imposed over it, let's discuss the royal shield over which both the label and the crown are themselves imposed.

The royal shield and the arms of the Principality of Wales. The royal shield, which is central to Charles' arms, has four quarters. Imposed over those as Prince of Wales, besides the second eldest-son label and the third heir-apparent crown, we find yet another quartered shield, itself representing the arms of the Principality of Wales. This small shield (escutcheon) helps to differentiate Charles' royal shield as Prince of Wales, from a similar design granted to 1890's Prince of Wales.[2] Further, Charles' arms are *here* essentially identical, setting aside artistic details of representation, to those of Edward VIII, when the latter served as Prince of Wales.[3] The shields of the princes of Wales of 1890 and 1962 are contrasted at right.

---

1. Strong, 7161/7162, "A Concise Dictionary of the Words in the Hebrew Bible," p. 139.
2. For a color representation of these royal shields, see Boutell, plate V, pp. 20-23.
3. Boutell, 1978 ed., p. 221.

In heraldry, the quarters on quartered shields are numbered from left to right and top to bottom as one through four.[1] Quarters one and four on the royal shield contain six lions in guardant postures, each one stretching forth its right-front paw. Called the "lions of England," they represent England and its empire[2] (cf. Ezek 38:13, "the merchants of Tarshish, and all its young lions;" see Ps 35:11-26, 57:3-6, 58; Isa 5:5-7, 5:26-30; cf. 2 Chr 9:16-22; Job 29:17; Jer 2:14-15, 50:17; Nah 2:11-12).[3] In Job 15:25-26, we read, "he stretches out his hand against God, and acts strong against the Almighty; he rushes at Him with a *bound [stiff]* neck [defiantly], with his thickly bossed [embossed] shields" (Heb.). Representing Scotland, the second quarter contains a red lion *holding a sword in its paw,* surrounded by a

---

1. According to Boutell: "If there are only two coats of arms to be quartered, the more important is placed in the first and fourth quarters, and the other in the second and third.... In the case of three coats of arms, the principal one (normally the paternal coat) is placed in the first quarter and repeated in the fourth, the others being placed in the second and third in order of their importance or acquisition" (1978 ed., p. 136).
2. According to Boutell, there is "no direct evidence as to the insignia of the Norman kings, but there are several indications that a lion was a royal badge long before the emergence of the three lions as the English Royal Arms." By 1198, the royal shield of Richard I, who was otherwise known as the "Lion-hearted," contained three passant-guardant lions, referred to collectively as "England." This shield was subsequently borne by all the Plantagenet kings until 1340, when Edward III quartered them with the arms of France, resulting in the six lions since called the "lions of England." Although these lions now occupy the first and fourth quarters of the royal shield, they were originally in the second and third quarters with the lilies (fleurs-de-lis) of France occupying the first and fourth quarters (Boutell, 1978 ed., pp. 206-208, 275).
3. As mentioned earlier, the United Kingdom was *Tarshish,* and it eventually came under Roman jurisdiction. Those who assert that the United Kingdom is not *Tarshish* typically point to the area of Gibraltar, sometimes called "the Rock," as more likely. However, we must point out that Gibraltar was relinquished to Britain by the Treaty of Utrecht at the conclusion of the War of the Spanish Succession in 1713, and Gibraltar's populace remains loyal to Britain. *The debate is entirely academic.* Indeed, Gibraltar is the point from which Charles and Diana embarked upon their honeymoon (Dimbleby, *The Prince of Wales,* pp. 23, 165, 174-175, 292-293; Hoey, *Charles & Diana: The Tenth Anniversary,* p. 69).

   Today, the United Kingdom is positioned to become an integral part of the final, worldwide form of the Roman Empire. Therefore, it seems plausible that the phrase "Tarshish, and all its young lions" (Ezek 38:13) is not just a reference to Great Britain, or to the United Kingdom as a whole, but also to England's historical offspring, including the United States of America, Canada, Australia, and New Zealand. The companion phrase, "the merchants of Tarshish" (Ezek 38:13), on the other hand, undoubtedly applies in a somewhat broader sense to the United Kingdom's prominent trading partners, including other members of the European Union. J.R. Church, taking a less restrictive view, commented: "The mother lion was eventually to become Great Britain, whose insignia is a lion. The young lions, then, could include the United States, Canada, Australia, New Zealand, and all the former colonies of Great Britain" (p. 220). The late Jack Van Impe identified *Tarshish* as England and the "young lions" as her English-speaking offshoots, but Peter Lalonde, borrowing from the others, thinks that "Tarshish" likely refers to Great Britain (*This Week in Bible Prophecy,* TBN TV 57 {Denver, CO}, 1 April 1993). As is evident from a list of (late) Prince Philip's (mostly past) titles, which are similar to those of (late) Queen Elizabeth II and King Charles III, the monarchy practically runs Canada, Australia and New Zealand (Judd, *Prince Philip,* p. 249). By other means, it now controls the United States.

   One of Charles' titles as Satan's Prince had been "Lord of the Isles," now passed to Prince William. Regarding the coming Millennial Kingdom, Psalm 72:10 states, "The kings of Tarshish <u>and of the isles</u> will bring presents; the kings of Sheba and Seba will offer gifts" (see Ps 48:7; cf. Isa 60:9, 66:18-21). In this light, it is noteworthy that Sheba and Dedan (i.e., modern Yemen and Saudi Arabia), which are also mentioned in Ezekiel 38:13, are now located in territory that Great Britain controlled as recently as the twentieth century, and that they are associated with Great Britain and its monarchy through British Petroleum. In fact, before the 1948 birth of the modern nation-state of Israel, Great Britain controlled much of the territory of the Middle East.

frame bearing the French *fleur-de-lis* (discussed later). Symbolically, this red lion arguably also *represents* the dexter beast of the overall heraldic achievement— while *standing-in* for the sinister beast or the unicorn having a man's eyes, as the eleventh "horn" among ten (cf. Dan 7:7-8, 7:20 and 7:24). (Both the dexter and sinister supporters represent Charles.) The third quarter contains the seven-stringed Irish harp for Ireland, as seen on Ireland's Royal Badge (left).[1] Its design, which supposedly originates in a Davidic harp brought from Israel (cf. Ps 33:2, 144:9), is not only identical to that of the harp that is being prepared for Israel's next Temple, but also to cave drawings found at Megiddo which may date to shortly after Noah's Flood.[2]

Notice that the dexter beast in then Prince Charles' achievement, is shown pawing the upper left-hand corner of the harp. *In heraldry, the specific positions of a beast's limbs are both meaningful and intentional* (e.g., cf. Prov 6:13). It is written: "A worthless | 'beliya'al' person, an Awen | wicked man, walks with a perverse |deceitful mouth: he winks with his eyes, he signals with his feet, he points | directs with his fingers; with perverse things in his heart, he devises with all evil continually, sowing discord. Thus, his calamity shall come suddenly upon *him;* he shall be broken instantly, and without remedy. These six *things* the LORD hates, even seven *are* loathsome | abominable to His Soul | Mind: haughty eyes | a proud look, a tongue of falsehood | lies | deception | 'shah'ker,' hands that shed innocent blood, a heart engraved with thoughts of Awen | iniquity, feet that are quick to run to evil | 'Ra-ah,' a false witness *who* utters lies | falsehoods | deceptions | 'kezabim,' and one who sows | sends discord | strife among brethren | between brothers" (Prov 6:12-19, Heb.; cf.

---

1. Boutell, 1978 ed., pp. 215-217. The red lion of Scotland and the Irish harp were both introduced to the royal shield with the accession of the Stuart kings (following the reign of Elizabeth I), before England's union with either of those countries. Later, in connection with the union with Ireland in 1801, the arms of France were omitted (Boutell, 1978 ed., p. 215). Interestingly, this omission took place not long after the Order of the Illuminati was founded (for more information, see this chapter's later discussion on the Order of the Garter at p. 147). From the reign of George I through that of William IV, the fourth quarter of the royal shield bore the arms of Hanover, which contained the "golden crown of Charlemagne." With the accession in 1837 of Victoria, who did not succeed to the throne of Hanover, that kingdom's arms were removed from the royal shield, which then assumed its present form (Boutell, 1978 ed., pp. 215-217). For color representations of the royal shield in its historical transitions, as well as a brief description of those transitions, see Boutell, plate V, between pp. 20-23.

2. Haim Shapiro, "TREASURES OF THE TEMPLE," *The Jerusalem Post,* Int. Ed., 30 July 1988, p. 9.

11:18, Heb.) Indeed: "Treachery | deceit *is* in a heart engraved by 'Ra'.... The righteous avoid all | do not seek any Awen, but the wicked | 'reshaim' are full of 'Ra'" (Prov 12:20-21, Heb.; see Prov 12:20-23, Heb.; Mic 2:1-3, Heb.; cf. Isa 58:9, Heb.). Then Prince Charles' own Royal Regiment of Wales,[1] was among the very first battalions of the Royal Army to be deployed to Northern Ireland, serving there following his 1969 investiture as Prince of Wales.[2] Not only has Britain pawed Ireland ever since, but at Satan's bidding, the beast will persecutes and seeks to destroy Israelite Christians (e.g., see Rev 12:1, 12:5-6, 12:13-16), with whom harps are associated (see Rev 14:2-3, 15:2-3), and then Christians generally.

Now, we might supposed that the noted signaling is purely a "heraldic" phenomena or practice. But it is not. Let's digress briefly for a salient real-world lesson. Freemasonry—as a disguised, covert form of *Luciferian satanism* (nothing more and nothing less)—sits beneath Charles (and now also William) globally. At the 33rd degree level (and above), Lucifer (i.e., Satan) is explicitly worshiped, which is obviously incompatible with Christianity. (Later, we'll examine all that in some significant detail.)

In fulfillment of the same passage in Proverbs 6, which we above detailed, Freemasons commonly "vice signal" (contrary to outward appearances, they have *no* virtue and many are pedophiles *or worse).* Such signaling occurs in a variety of ways: They frequently cover their right eye and/or hide a hand (often with a portion of their corresponding arm) under a shirt or below a lapel; by that, they associate with Zechariah 11:17's "idol | worthless shepherd" (i.e., the foretold AntiChrist). They also commonly place a finger over their mouth to warn fellow satanists to maintain their silence and thus secrecy (the opposite of speaking God's written Word)—while others move a flat hand in an obvious horizontal slicing motion across the neck to warn their fellow satanists of the death penalty (e.g., being bled to death, gutted and/or beheaded), for violating their Freemasonic oaths and talking, etc. Additionally, they place their thumb and forefinger together while spreading out their remaining three fingers, to intentionally signal three sixes, or 6-6-6. Other's will place a lightning bolt tattoo or mark on their bodies, especially across or around an eye—not unlike neo-Druidry's use of the same symbol, as we'll later see—to signify Satan's fall from Heaven (Luke 10:18; see 10:17-20); angelic manifestations, including of the Devil, may resemble "a flash of lightning" (e.g., see Ezek 1:13-14).

---

1. For more information, see ch. 8, "The Red Dragon, and Prince Charles' Investiture as Prince of Wales," at p. 207.
2. "Royal Regiment of Wales," *Wikipedia.*

Freemasons *know* they are worshiping the Devil; despite any contrary statement or disavowal they might make, they know whom they serve—the "father of lies." (In fact, Anton Szandor LaVey, the *forever roasting* founder of the modern "Church of Satan," was an idiot *Freemason* under Charles, as seen in LaVey's use of that order's symbolism.) Satanists consider themselves free *to sin,* caring *not* to be free *from sin!* Yet, Christians know that Christ Jesus, whom Freemasons and other satanists objectively and often overtly *reject,* is the actual God "of thunder | lightning" (Ex 19:16-17, 20:18; Dan 10:5-6; Matt 24:27, 28:3; Luke 17:24; cf. 2 Sam 22:14-15; Job 36:32-33, 37:2-4; Ps 18:13-14, 77:17-18, 97:3-5, 135:7, 144:6; Jer 10:13, 51:6; Zech 9:14; Rev 4:5), whom the Devil always seeks to counterfeit and malign. Though Lucifer's "light" is spiritual darkness only, God formerly covered His Light with "thick darkness"—so that Israel would not perish (e.g., Ex 20:21; cf. 19:9, 19:16-21); though Satan masquerades as "an angel of light" (2 Cor 11:14-15), he spreads spiritual darkness to condemn mankind—but our Creator actually cloaks His infinite Light just enough to prevent our annihilation from His holy Presence. To the servants of Satan, whose realm is built upon lies and darkness, everything is supposed to be kept secret, even upon oath-based death penalties—contrary to Christ Jesus' commandments (e.g., see Jas 5:12). But what God does, He first reveals to His servants the prophets (Amos 3:7)—so that nothing is secret that shall not be revealed (Luke 8:17; see 8:16-18).

Something most satanists, including Freemasonry's Luciferians, neither know nor realize, is that the devils and demons to whom they prostitute their lives, have a very betraying plan: they desire to supplant humanity *entirely* with (e.g., beastly) chimeric hybrids, or so-called "aliens," especially humanoids—just as soon as they reach a bioengineered point where one or more corporeal humanoid "species" is able to "reliably" self-reproduce![1] Satanists are, therefore, *ultimate fools;* they do not realize that in Lucifer's "economy," they are to be made obsolete, and would be eliminated. Yet, per God's sure Word, satanists' spiritually fallen "masters" have themselves *already lost their war,* so that Satan and the rest of them *will indeed spend eternity roasting in Hell's flames.* In fact, anyone who dies having rejected Christ Jesus as God and Savior, never could "rule in Hell"—neither on, nor in the Earth—contrary to the lies satanists embrace; in the end, they burn forever. Okay, let's get back to the details of the heraldic arms of Charles as Prince of Wales.

---

1. For more information, see this author's uniquely important and revealing *Solar Apocalypse* multi-volume series.

Imposed over the center of the royal shield, we find then Prince Charles' heir-apparent crown, as well as the quartered shield of arms of the Principality of Wales, known as the Shield of Wales, with each quarter containing one guardant lion.[1] This Welsh shield, first borne by Llywelyn the Great, has *never before* been included in the royal arms. Now derived from Llewelyn ap Gruffydd (i.e., "the Last"), Llywelyn the Great's grandson and a late native Welsh prince,[2] it is "quartered gold and red, with four passant [guardant] lions counter-coloured, *i.e.* red on the gold quarters and *vice versa*."[3] Further, it constitutes Charles' standard as Prince of Wales, flown when he as prince, was in Wales.[4]

Besides Scotland's red lion, there are ten lions at the center of then Charles' coat of arms (i.e., the six lions of England and the four similar lions of Wales), as Prince of Wales. These ten lions, like the red dragon, have a "passant" heraldic posture (as opposed to a "rampant" posture), in which just the right, front paw is raised. Historically speaking, any lion that was passant-guardant (or even earlier, not rampant) was known as a *lion leopardé*. Thus, we have the heraldic phrase "the lions (leopards) of England."[5] Each of the ten beasts in the center of Charles' coat of arms as Prince of Wales, is a "lion leopardé." But they are *not* "normal" lion-leopards. In harmony with the dexter beast, they each, like a heraldic bear, have five claws per foot, with only four being visible. In other words, they actually represent *lion-leopard-bears*.[6] The same may be said for the red lion of Scotland,[7] which substitutes for the dexter beast on Charles' royal shield. The ten lions represent royal dignitaries: according to the Apocalypse, the AntiChrist will eventually give power

---

1. Boutell, 1978 ed., p. 218.
2. "Wales, Principality of," *A Dictionary of Heraldry,* ed. Friar, p. 373.
3. C.W. Scott-Guiles, *The Romance of Heraldry* (Published by J.M. Dent & Sons; New York: E.P. Dutton & Co., Inc., 1957), p. 74.
4. "Wales, Prince of," *A Dictionary of Heraldry,* ed. Friar, pp. 372-373. According to a royal warrant dated May 21, 1968, Charles' personal flag as Prince of Wales, is "to be flown and used in Wales by His Royal Highness upon all occasions" (Boutell, 1978 ed., p. 258). For a picture of Charles' flying Welsh standard, see Hoey, *Charles & Diana: The Tenth Anniversary,* p. 6.
5. "Leopard," *A Dictionary of Heraldry,* ed. Friar, p. 213.
6. Notice that the four lion-leopards on Charles' fabric (cloth) standard as Prince of Wales, shown in the previous chapter, each have three claws per foot. However, as evidenced from the gold and red cover (sleeve) of the official album of Charles' Investiture as Prince of Wales on July 1, 1969, each of those lion-leopards are actually *lion-leopard-bears* with *five* claws per foot clearly evidenced. Likewise, this section's earlier depictions of the shields of the prince's of Wales of 1890 and 1962 shows all the lion-leopards with three claws per foot, whereas Charles' official achievement as Prince of Wales, actually has five claws per foot, with four being visible. For more information, see this chapter's later section titled, "The dexter (left-hand) supporter," at p. 192.
7. Film footage of the funeral procession of King George VI, King Charles III's grandfather, shows a cloth royal shield draped over the king's coffin; it bore the red lion of Scotland *with five claws per foot.*

to ten kings under his authority for one hour (see Rev 17:12-14; cf. Dan 7:7-8, 7:19-21, 7:24-25; Rev 13:1-9). Further, notice that of these ten lions, only seven have relatively unobscured heads (cf. Rev 12:3, 13:1, 17:3). Finally, excluding either the dexter beast or Scotland's red lion, there are a total of twelve lions in then Prince Charles' coat of arms (cf. 1 Kin 10:14-20).

Since 1603, the dexter and sinister supporters in British royal arms, called "royal beasts," have been "the lion for England and the unicorn for Scotland."[1] However, the dexter supporter in Charles' coat of arms as Prince of Wales, is altogether unique in heraldry; it is *not* the normal lion or (ostensibly atypical) lion-leopard for England. After looking at the eldest-son label, the crown of the heir-apparent, the Garter that encircles the royal shield, and the devices found at the shield's base, we will examine this evil beast.

The label of the eldest son and the crown of the heir-apparent. The eldest-son label and heir-apparent crown are both found five times in the achievement of Charles as Prince of Wales, in each instance directly associating the given part of his arms with him. Therefore, with the possible exception of the ten lions (i.e., lion-leopard-bears) just discussed, all the heraldic beasts on Charles' arms pertain specifically to him *and* his authority.

The eldest-son label has the appearance of three parallel horns which are, in a manner of speaking, "plucked out by the roots" (i.e., turned upside down). This particular mark of cadency also derives from the Black Prince, being "the distinctive mark of all succeeding Princes of Wales,"[2] and should remain on Charles' arms only while his father is alive. Yet, it *remained* despite Prince Philip's death.[3] Notice that this label on Charles' royal shield, is directly below the helm, which contains seven more horns. Recall, therefore, that the region near the top of the shield, around the location of the helm, is the head of the overall coat of arms. In other words, the three horns of this eldest-son label, along with the seven horns in the helm, comprise a total of ten horns that are in the head of the overall coat of arms. Moreover, to the right of this cluster of ten horns "in a head," we find an eleventh

---

1. Kay W. Holmes, "United Kingdom, Royal Heraldry," *A Dictionary of Heraldry,* ed. Friar, p. 359.
2. Boutell, 1978 ed., p. 119.
3. The labels of all other members of the British royal family (i.e., all but the eldest son), which are borne on their respective shields of arms, have more than three descending horns. Unlike permanent marks of cadency, the eldest son's label is to be removed from his arms if and when his father dies, so that he becomes the family head. So, it normally remains only while his father is living (Boutell, 1978 ed., pp. 117, 131; "Label," *A Dictionary of Heraldry,* ed. Friar, p. 212). For Charles, this was *not* done.

horn, or the little horn which has eyes like those of a man (i.e., the unicorn).[1] Regarding the first beast, it is written:

> And another sign appeared in heaven. And, behold, a great, fiery red dragon having seven heads and ten horns *in a head,*[2] and seven diadems near[3] his heads.... And the great dragon was cast out—the old serpent, called the Devil and Satan, who deceives the whole world—was cast out to the Earth, and his angels were cast out with him. (Rev 12:3 {Gk.}, 12:9 {Gk.}; cf. 20:2)

> And I stood upon the sand of the sea. And I saw a beast rise up out of the sea, having seven heads, and ten horns *in a head,* and near its horns *in a head,* ten diadems,[4] and near its heads, names[5] of blasphemy[6] [*a slanderous motto*]. (Rev 13:1, Gk.; cf. Dan 7:2-7)

> Then one of the seven angels, of those having the seven bowls, came and spoke with me, saying to me, "Come, I will show you the judgment of the great harlot who sits on many waters, with whom the kings of the Earth committed fornication, and those inhabiting the Earth were made drunk with the wine of her fornication." And he carried me away into a desert [wilderness] by The Spirit, and I saw a woman sitting on a red [scarlet, crimson][7] beast, full of names of blasphemy [*a slanderous motto*], having seven heads and ten horns *in a head.* And the woman was arrayed in purple and red [scarlet, crimson], and adorned with gold and precious stone and pearls, having a golden cup in her hand, full of abominations and uncleanness of her fornication. And on her forehead a name *was* written: Mystery, Babylon the Great, the Mother of the Harlots and of the Abominations of the

---

1. For an explanation of this terminology, see the discussion on the sinister supporter.
2. Strong's number 2768, which *literally speaks of "the hair of the head"* (James Strong, 2768, "A Concise Dictionary of the Words in the Greek/New Testament," *STRONG'S EXHAUSTIVE CONCORDANCE OF THE BIBLE* {Tennessee: Abingdon Press, 1986}, p. 54), may be "a projecting extremity in shape like a horn, a point, apex" (Joseph H. Thayer, 2768, *GREEK-ENGLISH LEXICON of the NEW TESTAMENT* {Michigan: Baker Book House, 1977}, p. 344). Like nails and claws, animal horns are made of compressed hair. By implication, therefore, this word (Strong's no. 2768) refers to ten horns which are in a particular head. Moreover, this is perfectly consistent with Daniel 7:20. According to C.F. Keil and F. Delitzsch: "[The] beast must represent not merely the last world-power, but at the same time the last world-ruler .... its personal head. The ten horns are to be conceived of as on one of the heads..." ("THE BOOK OF DANIEL," Vol. 9 of *Commentary on the Old Testament* {1986; rpt. Massachusetts: Hendrickson Publishers, Inc., 1989}, p. 277).
3. Strong's number 1909, which, as a preposition, may be translated as "among," "near," "by," "beside," or "below," as well as "on" (Strong, 1909, "A Concise Dictionary of the Words in the Greek/New Testament," p. 39; Thayer, 1909, p. 232).
4. A diadem, according to *The American Heritage Dictionary,* may be a "royal power or dignity." Biblically, it is the crown of a sovereign or royal personage. Given these definitions, consider the ten lions, apart from the red lion of Scotland, at the center of Charles' achievement as Prince of Wales.
5. Strong's number 3686 refers to a person's distinguishing name, title, or phrase (motto), and its use invokes everything which the name, title, or phrase (motto) covers, to include "rank, authority, interests, pleasure, command, excellences, [and] deeds" (Thayer, 3686, p. 447). Given this definition, consider the Garter motto that surrounds the heads of the eleven lions—six for England, four for Wales, and one for Scotland—on the royal shield and the shield of the Principality of Wales.
6. Strong's number 988, which refers to "impious and reproachful speech injurious to the divine majesty," or slander (Thayer, 988, p. 102).
7. The Greek word translated as "red," "scarlet," or "crimson," Strong's number 2847, refers to particular berries which, "when collected and pulverized produce a red which was used in dyeing" (Thayer, 2847, p. 352).

EARTH. And I saw the woman drunk with the blood of the saints and with the blood of the witnesses [martyrs] of Jesus. And I marveled, seeing her, with great amazement. But the angel said to me: "Why did you marvel? I will tell you the mystery of the woman, and of the beast which carries her, which has the seven heads and the ten horns *in a head*.... Here *is* the mind which has wisdom: The seven heads are seven mountains, where the woman sits on them....[1] And the ten horns which you saw are ten kings who *have* not yet received a kingdom, but *who* receive authority *for* one hour as kings with the beast. These have one mind, and their power and authority they shall cede to the beast. These will make war with The Lamb, and The Lamb will overcome them...." And he said to me: "The waters which you saw, where the harlot sits, are peoples and multitudes, and nations and tongues. And the ten horns which you saw on the beast, these will hate the harlot, and shall make her desolate and naked, and will eat her flesh and burn her down with fire. For God has put it into their hearts to do His mind [will], and to act *in* one mind, and to give their kingdom to the beast, until the words of God are fulfilled. And the woman whom you saw is the great city which has a kingdom [kingship] over the kings of the Earth.[2] (Rev 17:1-7, 17:9, 17:12-18, Gk.)

The ten horns described thus far in Charles' arms as Prince of Wales, could well represent the ten horns in the head of the apocalyptic beast. Unlike seven of the ten horns (recall our previous discussion regarding the seven bars in the helm, which forms the head of the overall coat of arms), three are to be "plucked out by the roots" (see Dan 7:8, 7:24; cf. the eldest-son label over the shield). Charles' arms do in fact depict such an arrangement (above right). Further, the little horn that has eyes like those of a man (i.e., the sinister unicorn—discussed later) is to come up among them (see Dan 7:8, 7:20).

The design of the heir-apparent's crown is based upon the Imperial State Crown (worn by the monarch, during state functions), which "embodies many historical gems, including the Black Prince's

---

1. Rome, which began on the left bank of the Tiber River as a group of seven communities on seven hills, was known among ancient Roman writers as "the city on seven hills."

2. London, through the British Commonwealth (formerly the British Empire), appears to be the *only* city today which has a *literal* kingdom, as well as kingship, over other kings of the Earth. Although Rome has a pope, she does not have a king or a queen. Should the British monarchy be adopted as the monarchy of the European Union, however, so that King Charles III gains hegemony in the United Nations Security Council in New York, then London—which had been ruled by Elizabeth II and now has Camilla (cf. "the mother of harlots")—would effectively have kingship over *all* the kings of the Earth, much as the king of Babylon was "a king of kings" and "ruler over them all" (Dan 2:37-38). Moreover, in partnership with the pope, London (the British monarchy) would rule over Rome. Of course, during King Charles III's May 6, 2023 coronation, every watching human being *globally* was invited to "swear" to "pay true allegiance to Your Majesty"—and to his "heirs and successors!"

ruby."[1] Other than its lack of bowed arches and an arch from front to back, the heir-apparent's crown is also similar to the St. Edward's Crown (so-called after Edward the Confessor who allegedly believed that he had supernatural healing powers), with which the last forty British monarchs, including the present queen, were coronated: "The St. Edward's Crown ... is the official Crown of England and the one with which the Sovereign is usually crowned. Elizabeth II decided she could wear no other.... Then in the Abbey she was crowned with St. Edward's Crown, made in 1661 for Charles II to replace the crown of St. Edward the Confessor destroyed ... after the Civil War. This solid gold crown set with pearls and precious stones is most easily identified by its generously bowed arches. On leaving the Abbey modern sovereigns have exchanged this for the Imperial Crown of State whose silver arches are less baroque."[2] The heir-apparent's crown, like that of "St. Edward," has a gold Templar cross and a sphere, called a "mound" or "orb," at its top. While this sphere or globe was formerly "green banded with gold," apparently representing the Earth under Merovingian rule,[3] it is now depicted as gold banded with gold.[4]

Crosses on the heir-apparent and state crowns generally have a central pearl. Although gold and silver, respectively, they are identical to the red cross paty of the Temple Knights (right) from which they

were derived. The Templar cross, like the modified Templar cross euphemized as "St. George's cross" (discussed below), is often depicted in a circular shield or "roundel." Regarding

---

1. Timothy B. Benford, *The Royal Family Quiz & Fact Book* (New York: Harper & Row, Publishers, 1987), p. 235. Also see "Coronation, Symbols of," *A Dictionary of Heraldry,* ed. Friar, p. 110.
2. Lacey, *Majesty,* p. 159. "On the day of the ceremony itself Queen Elizabeth II wore Queen Victoria's diadem on her way to the Abbey. This low diamond circlet, originally made for George IV, featured the Cross of St. George and the emblems of the other component parts of the United Kingdom" (ibid., p. 159). One such "emblem" is the *fleur-de-lis.*
3. Lacey notes the "tokens of responsibility" with which British monarch's are invested, including "the Orb —'remember that the whole world is subject to the power and empire of Christ'" (*Majesty,* p. 162). Illustrating some of the intrigue of the Order of the Garter, this same royal Orb is depicted in a French drawing dating to around 1615 that depicts Abraham's near-sacrifice of Isaac (Frazer, p. 114). A photograph of Queen Elizabeth II carrying the former royal Orb, which was green banded with gold and about the size of a human head, was taken following her coronation in 1953 (*Her Majesty The Queen,* p. 9). The royal Orb is now gold banded with gold, having a diamond and emerald Templar cross at its top. Interestingly enough, according to Baigent, Leigh, and Lincoln: "Many ... [crystal] balls have been found in Merovingian tombs. Their use is unknown" (*Holy Blood, Holy Grail,* caption 29, between pp. 240-241). For more information, see ch. 8, "The Red Dragon and Prince Charles' Investiture as Prince of Wales," at p. 207.
4. For color representations of these and other crowns, see Boutell, plate XVI, between pp. 178-181.

crosses, Scott-Guiles comments: "Foremost among the emblems of the Holy Wars was, of course, the cross.... Pope Urban II, the preacher of the First Crusade, decreed this practice.... But when the English adopted St. George as their patron saint they made his red cross their own.... Certain families which have crosses in their shields claim that they signify some ancestor's participation in a crusade."[1] Actually, *St. George*—despite the often *messianic* Arthurian legends concerning a knight by that name—has long been a Garter synonym for *Merovée* (see below).[2] Per tradition, St. George was ostensibly born of a Greek father and a "Palestinian" mother.

The French *fleur-de-lis* or lily is interspersed with the Templar crosses on the British royal crowns. Some have suggested that the French lily is actually a derivation of the Judaean lily depicted on an ancient Jewish coin, whereas others think that it came from royal bee of Charlemagne and subsequent French kings (e.g., Merovée's son, Childeric I, who practiced witchcraft and whose grave contained 300 such bees).[3] However, it actually has more significant meaning: it represents the druidic *Awen.*

In addition to the five heir-apparent crowns in Charles' arms as Prince of Wales, there are two more crowns, one around the neck of the unicorn and the other around the three ostrich feathers in the heir-apparent's badge, for a total of seven crowns (otherwise known as coronets or diadems). Recall that the beast has "seven diadems near his heads" (Rev 12:3).

The Garter. England has long had various orders of knights, called knighthoods, of which the most prominent is the Most Noble Order of the Garter. Elizabeth II was installed on April 23, 1948—her birthday and "St. George's Day"—as a "Lady of the Order," and upon becoming queen, as the order's sovereign.[4] King George VI, emphasizing his daughter's "precedence and seniority," installed Prince Philip as a Garter knight eight days after installing Elizabeth II as a Lady of the Order.[5] Ten years later, on July 26, 1958, the year that the red dragon became the official heraldic symbol of Wales, Charles as Wales' new prince automatically became a knight of the Order of the Garter—though his formal installation as such did not occur until June 17, 1968.[6] Cathcart, speaking of this event, shows that, like the

---

1. Scott-Guiles, pp. 52-54.
2. For more information, see ch. 4, "Prince of this World—a Diverse Lineage," at p. 79.
3. Manly P. Hall, *The Secret Teachings of All Ages* (San Francisco: H.S. Crocker Co., Inc., n.d.), p. lxxxvii. Baigent, Leigh, and Lincoln, *Holy Blood, Holy Grail*, captions 30 and 33, between pp. 240-241. For more information, see ch. 4, "Prince of this World—a *Diverse* Lineage," at p. 79.
4. *Her Majesty The Queen,* p. 12.
5. Judd, *Prince Philip*, pp. 131-132.
6. Holden, *PRINCE CHARLES*, pp. 174, 326.

public generally, she misunderstands the true nature of the Order of the Garter: "But the ceremonies of chivalry are to be taken seriously, with their prayers for steadfastness in the Christian faith. In the procession to the chapel [of St George] there walked such figures of lasting history as Earl Alexander of Tunis, Earl Mountbatten of Burma and Viscount Montgomery of Alamein."[1]

Cathcart adds, "In the Dorset manor of Fordington, villagers roast a sheep on the village green every St George's Day and supposedly send a leg of mutton to Prince Charles wherever he may be."[2] On this same day, April 23, in an act of apparent druidic tree-worship, a tree is cut down, decked with "flowers and garlands," and then carried in a procession "accompanied with music and joyful acclamations," with "the chief figure in the procession being the Green George, a young fellow clad from head to foot in green birch branches." The "Green George," or an effigy of him, is then dunked in a river or pond in hopes of bringing forth a year of plentiful rain.[3]

Established in 1348 by King Edward III, a descendant of the French Plantagenets, and his son, Edward the Black Prince, the Order of the Garter is England's (and Europe's) most prestigious and exclusive "Christian" order of chivalry.[4] Originally called "The Order of [the Company of] St. George,"[5] it is the oldest surviving order of chivalry in the world, having absorbed the essential aspects of its few predecessors, including "the Society of St. George in Hungary (1325/6)," "the Order of the Band or Sash in <u>Spain</u> (before 1330)," and, after it was first proposed by the Duke of Normandy in 1344, who later became King John II of <u>France</u>, the Company of the Star (1352). In Garter literature, Edward III is sometimes called "the Founder," and the Order of the Garter is referred to as "the Foundation."[6] John Campbell-Kease asserts:

> Several historians are of the view that at first the 'order' was quite casually formed, perhaps at a tournament [in 1344]—24 knights in two bands of twelve, one under the king, the other under the prince, and only later did it become a permanent institution....
>
> The symbol of the blue garter seems [according to some] to have been suggested by an incident at a ball at Calais in the autumn of 1347, when the young countess of Salisbury, Joan of Kent (later to be Princess of

1. Cathcart, p. 83. Junor, p. 74.
2. Cathcart, p. 105.
3. Frazer, pp. 62-63.
4. Benford, p. 100.
5. James and Russell, *At Home with the Royal Family*, p. 36. Laurence R. Taylor, *Indiana Monitor and Freemason's Guide*, 15th ed. (Indiana: Grand Lodge of the State of Indiana, 1993), p. 59, n. 1.
6. Peter J. Begent, *The Most Noble Order of the Garter, Its History and Ceremonial* (Slough: Delworth Printing Ltd., n.d.—1990 or later), p. 2. For a copy of this self-published work, which is copyrighted by the Dean and Cannons of Windsor and illustrates the Order of the Garter and its insignia, write to: St. George's Chapel Bookshop, Ltd.; 8B, The Cloisters; Windsor Castle; Windsor Berks; SL4 1NJ; England.

Wales), dropped her garter, which the king picked up and tied round his knee with the now famous words, Honi soit qui mal y pense, 'shame on him who thinks evil of it', and the promise that the garter would become highly honoured. And so it was. The informal creation of the Round Table after the great tournament at Windsor in 1344 was translated, in 1348, into the Order of the Garter—24 young men plus the king and his eldest son....[1]

The armorial bearings (heraldic achievements) of Garter members, both past and present, are emblazoned on their respective stall-plates, and their banners are also hung in the Chapel of St. George at Windsor.[2] Edward III, "inspired by the English legend of King Arthur and the Knights of the Round Table," originally constructed St. George's Chapel in 1350, not to mention St. George's Hall, while making Windsor Castle "one of the most magnificent castles in Europe." (Recall Edward I's earlier alleged "Round Table" events in 1284 and 1302.) In 1472, King Edward IV demolished the original Chapel of St. George and began construction on its famed replacement, which was completed under King Henry VII. His son, King Henry VIII is credited with developing "much of the Order of the Garter ceremony, in which the" monarch "participates annually."[3] Interestingly, Henry VII, who added Welsh blood to the British monarchy, "restored the red dragon to its ancient status as a royal device," and Henry VIII and King Edward VI subsequently used it.[4]

June is a major month for royal ceremonial, to include coronations and parades. It is also significant to pagan worship. June, for example, is the month in which pagans historically mourned the death of Tammuz, the ancient Babylonian perversion of the Zodiac's original symbolic prediction of a future virgin-born Messiah who would suffer, die, and rise from the dead to redeem mankind. June also is the month of Midsummer Eve (the 23rd), when the druids culled "certain magic plants, whose evanescent virtue can be secured at this mystic season alone." This same eve, now dubbed the "Eve of St. John" for John the Baptizer, "was the day of all days for gathering the wonderful herbs by means of which you could combat fever, cure a host of diseases, and guard yourself against sorcerers and their spells."[5]

Each June, new knights, when required and available, are admitted to the Order of the Garter in an annual ceremony at Garter

1. John Campbell-Kease, "Garter, The Most Noble Order of the," *A Dictionary of Heraldry,* ed. Friar, p. 160. Also see James and Russell, *At Home with the Royal Family,* pp. 37, 155.
2. Boutell, 1978 ed., pp. 193-194. The royal standard is hung over the queen's pew.
3. James and Russell, *At Home with the Royal Family,* pp. 36-37, 40.
4. For more information, see this chapter's section titled, "The red dragon, or Satan," at p. 188.
5. Frazer, pp. 124, 133, 135, 229, 234.

Chapel—called St. George's Chapel—in Windsor Castle.[1] As prince, Charles opined: "I would change nothing. Besides ceremony being a major and important aspect of monarchy, something that has grown and developed over a thousand years in Britain, I happen to enjoy it enormously."[2] (Yet, Charles *unreservedly destroyed* every *Christian* aspect of his May 2023 coronation.[3]) According to James and Russell: "Every June on the Monday of Ascot week[4] the" monarch "as Head of the Order, assembles with twenty-four Companion Knights and walks down the hill from St George's Hall to St George's Chapel for a special service. Each knight wears a dark blue velvet mantle with crimson velvet hood, a black velvet hat with white ostrich plumes, a blue riband with the cross of St George, [a Garter Star,] plus a gold collar of twenty-six intertwined garters [around roses],[5] one for each of the knights and the" monarch "and Prince" of Wales, "as 'constituent member of the Order'. Each also wears a dark blue velvet garter [(Elizabeth II's was light blue)] embroidered with the motto in gold thread.... [The] Garter ceremony takes place with all the theatrical aplomb of an heraldic festival, and [it] ... would not look out of place in a re-make of *The Three Musketeers*."[6]

What is publicly known of the Garter ceremony evidences the fact that it remains a mixture of the holy with the profane, overseen by unfaithful and apostate "Christians" (e.g., the Bishop of Winchester and the Dean of Windsor). James and Russell observe,

1. Benford, p. 101. *Her Majesty The Queen*, p. 12. For color photographs of the order's annual procession to the chapel, including (the late) Queen Elizabeth II wearing her dark blue Garter Mantle (cloak) with the Garter Star and Collar, see *Her Majesty The Queen*, p. 17. For similar photographs of Satan's Prince, see *Charles & Diana: A Royal Family Album*, p. 45; and Hoey, *Charles & Diana: The Tenth Anniversary*, p. 115. Such for King Charles III et al., are now also readily available online.
2. *Charles & Diana: A Royal Family Album*, p. 44.
3. For details, see ch. 16, "King Charles III: History's Ultimate AntiChrist," at p. 561.
4. Apart from royal permission, only royalty, and perhaps the very wealthy, are permitted to attend the annual Ascot races at the Ascot Race Course. These races may serve as a cover for the presence of foreign royals during that week, who attend not just for the races themselves, but to participate in the Order of the Garter ceremony and other meetings.
5. The "Marlborough Great George," which depicts "St. George" slaying the dragon, hangs from the front-center of the pure gold Collar; hanging down both back and chest from a knight's shoulders (like an excessively-wide collar), the gold chain may seem to resemble a necklace in front. Its enamel red roses are encircled with enamel blue Garter Belts bearing the motto *Honi soit qui mal y pense*, all overlaying gold; interleaved gold knots separate one from the next.
6. James and Russell, *At Home with the Royal Family*, pp. 37, 155. Apparently standing-in for the Order of the Garter's companion-knights, "twenty-four knights who are Serjeants-at-Arms form the oldest armed bodyguard in existence." During the crusades, these twenty-four knights, *who were Templars*, are "supposed to have formed a bodyguard for King Richard I." Three of the twenty-four Serjeants-at-Arms participate in the State Opening of Parliament, where they attend the sovereign and escort the royal heralds and pursuivants, who, with "a vast knowledge of royal ceremony ... assist the Earl Marshal in planning state ceremonies" and "function in any regal parade ... to ensure that everyone is in the right place at the right time, in the right order and dressed correctly" (ibid., pp. 141, 146-147, 206; Baigent, Leigh, and Lincoln, *Holy Blood, Holy Grail*, p. 121).

The whole ceremony [originally] took three days with the sovereign and knights meeting on the first day for a general discussion in a room guarded by Black Rod;[1] day two being the main processional day, Garter Ceremony and state banquet; and the closing day, in contrast to the earlier pomp, being a day of remembrance and prayer, with a requiem mass to end the proceedings.

Just over a century later the College of Arms was founded and the heralds became an intrinsic part of the Garter Ceremony, now presided over by Garter King of Arms....

....Lacking none of the dignity of bygone days, the ceremony [now] begins in the morning in the Throne Room of Windsor Castle, where the Queen [(now Charles as king)] buckles the garter onto the leg of the knight elect in a private ceremony, the knight having first been ritually summoned by Black Rod and the Garter King.

'To the honour of God Omnipotent,' proclaims the Prelate [(now the Bishop of Winchester)], 'and in Memorial of the Blessed Martyr, Saint George, tie about thy leg, for they Renown, this Most Noble Garter. Wear it as the symbol of the Most Illustrious Order never to be forgotten or laid aside, that hereby thou mayest be admonished to be courageous, and having undertaken a just war, into which thou shalt be engaged, thou mayest stand firm, valiantly fight, courageously and successfully conquer.'

....After the garter the collar of twenty-six buckled garters in gold surrounding enamelled Tudor roses is placed around the knight's neck by the Queen [(now Charles as king)]. The prelate continues:

'Wear this Collar about thy Neck, adorned with the image of the Blessed Martyr and Soldier of Christ, Saint George, by whose imitation provoked, thou mayest so overpass both prosperous and adverse encounters, that having stoutly vanquished thine enemies, both of body and soul, thou mayest not only receive the praise of this transient Combat, but be crowned with the Palm of Eternal Victory.'

Finally the mantle is placed around the shoulders.

'You being chosen to be of the Honourable Company of the Most Noble Order of the Garter, shall promise and swear, by the Holy Evangelists, by you here touched, that wittingly or willingly you shall not break any Statutes of the Said Order, or any article in them contained (except in such from which you have received a Dispensation from The Sovereign), the same being agreeable, and not repugnant to the Laws of Almighty God, and the Laws of this realm, ... so God help you, and His Holy Word.'

Following this historic but never publicly witnessed ceremony the Queen [(now Charles as king)] ... leads the way into the Waterloo Chamber for lunch, a simple meal compared to the former banquets of wild boar, duckling, pheasant, rabbit, lobster, quail, pigeon, salmon and crab....

At 2:30 p.m. the public procession starts out from the royal apartments to St George's Chapel; thousands of people apply every year to the Lord Chamberlain's Office to ... witness the most historic of all processions. The governor of Windsor Castle heads the Military Knights of Windsor in their red uniforms, followed by the heralds and pursuivants wearing royal crested tabards, then the Knights of the Garter themselves in the full

---

1. For brief descriptions of the "Gentlemen User of the Black Rod," who "was once responsible for the security of the sovereign" and now "carries a black rod made of ebony in 1883, with a gold sovereign set into the base dated 1904," see James and Russell, *At Home with the Royal Family*, pp. 148, 194.

uniform of the Order.... Lastly come the officers of the Order—the Garter King of Arms, the Gentleman Usher of the Black Rod, the Secretary, the Register [(now the Dean of Windsor)] and the Prelate—and the Queen [(now Charles as king)]....

In St George's Chapel a simple service takes place, the Garter King of Arms presenting any newly installed knights for a blessing, and the service ending with a prayer: 'God save our gracious Sovereign and all the Companions, living and departed, of the Most Honourable and Noble Order of the Garter.'[1]

Garter "placement." Garter membership now includes King Charles III (formerly as Prince of Wales), Prince William of Wales,[2] Princess Anne, the current Duke of Kent,[3] chosen members of *other European and non-European royal families (e.g., the now deceased Japanese Emperor Hirohito),*[4] some of the most powerful *former and*

1. James and Russell, *At Home with the Royal Family,* pp. 155-158. To apply for tickets to attend the procession of the Order of the Garter (for research purposes), write to: The Lord Chamberlain's Office, St James's Palace, London SW1, England (ibid., p. 241).

2. On June 16, 2008, Prince William was invested as a "Royal Knight Companion of the Most Noble Order of the Garter," the order's 1000 knight. Robert Hardman, reporting beforehand, noted that it would "be exactly 40 years since the Prince of Wales was invested as a member." New appointments to the order, which "owes its origins to both King Arthur and St George," are always announced by the monarch on April 23, St. George's Day. Hardman observes, "with a black ostrich-plumed hat, a red hood, a blue velvet cloak lined with white satin, a silver star, a priceless miniature of St George and the Dragon dangling from a chain of solid gold and a garter strapped just below his left knee, it will probably be the biggest dressing-up exercise this side of his own coronation" ("Prince William to join Britain's most exclusive club as Knight of the Garter," *Mail Online,* 11 June 2008).

3. A color picture of the prior Duke of Kent (Snowdon) wearing the Garter Star may be seen in *Majesty* magazine, July 1994, Vol. 15, No. 7, p. 27. The Dukes of Kent and Beaufort sponsored then Prince Charles' introduction to the "House of Lords" in 1970 (Cathcart, opposite p. 57). The late Duke of Kent was a womanizer and overt homosexual (i.e., a "bisexual").

4. The kings of Norway, Bulgaria, Portugal, Germany, Greece, Belgium, Spain, England, and Denmark, respectively, a number of whom were members of the Order of the Garter, were photographed together, wearing their Garter stars (e.g., the kings of Germany, Greece, England, and it appears Norway, Denmark, and possibly others), at Windsor for the funeral of Edward VII (Lacey, *Majesty,* between pp. 126-127). These same kings of Norway, England, and apparently Denmark were also members of the Committee of 300, whereas some of the other kings mentioned above, besides other royal households (e.g., the Netherlands), had family representatives who were committee members (John Coleman, *The Committee of 300,* 3rd ed. {Nevada: Joseph Publishing Co., 1994}, pp. 314-315). Their heirs now carry-on in their place. King Haakon of Norway was one of eight "godparents" to the infant Prince Charles (Junor, p. 21; Judd, *Prince Charles,* p. 144). In 1983, King Carl Gustav XVI of Sweden was appointed as a stranger-knight to the Order of the Garter; as such he is supernumerary to it (Begent, p. 14). Anthony Eden, the former Earl of Avon, was also a Garter knight (Begent, p. 1), as were Earl Mountbatten of Burma, Earl Alexander of Tunis, and Viscount Montgomery of Alamein (Cathcart, p. 83; Judd, *Prince Philip,* p. 24).

   A color photograph taken in 1971 at Buckingham Palace shows Japanese Emperor Hirohito wearing the Garter Star: "The Emperor is seen wearing the Order of the Garter, which was removed during the Second World War and only restored to him a few months before his visit" (*Her Majesty The Queen,* p. 34). On a visit to Japan in 1970, Satan's Prince dined with the late Emperor Hirohito, preparing the way for a 1975 state visit by Queen Elizabeth II and Prince Philip (Cathcart, p. 112). Apparently, Charles was also restoring Hirohito to the Order of the Garter, preparing the way for the emperor's own 1971 visit to Buckingham Palace. Other Garter members are shown in the same photograph, all but Princess Anne wearing their Garter Stars, to include Queen Elizabeth II, then Prince Charles, Prince Philip, Princess Anne (who was elevated from the status of "lady" to become a knight-companion of the order), the then Duke of Kent, and Queen Elizabeth the Queen Mother (who appears to have also been elevated from her original status as a lady of the order). Oddly enough, the same photograph also clearly shows Queen Elizabeth II, then Prince Charles, Prince Philip, and Emperor Hirohito all wearing the star of an-

current world leaders,[1] and a few prestigious public figures.[2] (Prior to their deaths, Queen Elizabeth the Queen Mother and Prince Philip were members, while Queen Elizabeth II was the top knight.) James and Russell state, "The number of knights remains constant although the Queen [(now the king)] has the authority to create 'Stranger Knights' if she [(he)] wishes, a[n] honour offered only to those held in great esteem."[3] Campbell-Kease adds: "Foreign royalty have been appointed as members: 'Stranger Knights and Ladies of the Garter', and they are additional to the twenty-six companion knights[, thus called 'extra knights and ladies']. Membership was often used for diplomatic purposes, though today membership of both the Garter and the Thistle is in the personal gift of the sovereign." Garter members are sworn to befriend and defend one another, in both peace and war, throughout the course of their lives: "In 1348 the Black Prince was just eighteen years old, and several other founders not much more.... Thus ... the Order of the Garter ... was a brotherhood..., a fellowship, in which all were equal 'to represent how they ought to be united in all Chances and various Turns of Fortune, co-partners in both Peace and War, assistant to one another in all serious and dangerous Exploits and through the whole Course of

other order, one almost certainly Japanese in origin—probably the "Supreme Order of the Chrysanthemum," of which Prince Philip was then Grand Cordon (Judd, *Prince Philip,* p. 252). Hirohito's heirs likely then took his place in both orders.

For a color photograph of Satan's Prince, Queen Elizabeth the Queen Mother, and the Duke of Kent wearing their Garter insignia "at the service of the Most Noble Order of the Garter in June 1986," see Burnet, *In Private—In Public,* THE PRINCE AND PRINCESS OF WALES, pp. 126-127.

1. On June 14, 1954, for example, Queen Elizabeth II installed Winston Churchill as a knight of the Order of the Garter (James and Russell, *At Home with the Royal Family,* p. 156). Later, the queen likewise installed Margaret Thatcher, John Major and Tony Blair as such.

2. Hardman adds: "Inside the chapel, every knight takes his seat or 'stall' — beneath his own banner — for a service of thanksgiving. This year, [2008,] there will be some extra ceremonial because there are new knights to be welcomed. Before lunch, they will gather in the Garter Throne Room to see a private investiture for three new additions — Prince William plus Lord Luce, the former Lord Chamberlain, and Sir Thomas Dunne, Lord Lieutenant of Herefordshire. The Queen will give each of them a garter, inscribed: 'Honi Soit Qui Mal y Pense', which will be attached below the left knee over the trouser leg. Reciting ancient words of welcome, she will place the blue riband of the order over the knight's shoulder, followed by the velvet robes. 'I fear that knights are not as useful as we once were — we don't joust any more — but it is a tremendous honour,' says Lord Carrington (the former Foreign Secretary).... It's extraordinary that the order has existed since 1348 and Prince William is only the 1,000th member,' says Lord Butler, adding that all the knights feel 'a special sense of obligation' to the Sovereign. That was not always the case. To this day, any knight who wrongs the Monarch can be 'degraded'. This involves having one's banner torn down from St George's Chapel and kicked into the gutter. The miscreant's [coat of] arms must be painted over in St George's Hall while the words 'Out upon thee, Traitor' are added next to their name in the Garter register. There has not been a full-scale degradation since the Duke of Ormonde was kicked out in 1716 for supporting the Jacobite Rebellion, although George V did remove the banners of eight German cousins during World War I [and Japan's Emperor Hirohito had his membership revoked during World War II, only to have it later restored].... Winston Churchill famously turned down a Dukedom and remained plain 'Mr' until 1953, when the new young Queen offered the stubborn old man one title which he could not refuse. It is the same title Prince William" received ("Prince William to join Britain's most exclusive club as Knight of the Garter").

3. James and Russell, *At Home with the Royal Family,* p. 37. Note that the Central Chancery "maintains records of the holders of the Orders of Chivalry" (ibid., p. 205).

their lives to show Fidelity and Friendliness towards one another.'"[1] "In the early days, knights of the Garter were expected to join their Sovereign in battle and, when not at war, to meet up for feasts and jousting. Today, most knights are too old for jousting, but they still have an appetite. Every year, on the Monday following the Queen's official birthday [(now ostensibly Charles', as king)], they come for lunch in Windsor Castle, where the seating plan rotates to ensure no one sits next to the same person more than once in a decade. After lunch, the knights put on their elaborate robes. They then join a spectacular procession through Windsor to St George's Chapel, 'marching' ahead of the Queen [(now Charles as king)]. In deference to their age (many are in their 80s), the pace is gentle."[2] It is perhaps noteworthy that Charles and now son Prince William are, and while alive Queen Elizabeth II and Prince Philip were, *almost always* photographed wearing their Garter Stars, except when in suits, regardless of uniform or other attire. They are occasionally also shown wearing the Garter Collar with its pendant, and the blue Garter Riband with its Lesser George.[3]

The Order of the Garter is not only responsible for the creation of the modern Illuminati, as will be shown in the following pages, but it also heads and controls the shadowy "Committee of 300."[4] Not all

---

1. Campbell-Kease, "Garter, The Most Noble Order of the," *A Dictionary of Heraldry*, ed. Friar, p. 160.
2. Hardman, "Prince William to join Britain's most exclusive club as Knight of the Garter."
3. A formal portrait of Queen Elizabeth II and Prince Philip wearing their respective Garter Collars may be seen on p. 11 of *Her Majesty The Queen*. The same portrait, taken following the queen's coronation, also shows her wearing the Imperial State Crown and the Commonwealth Bracelets (allegedly representing "sincerity and wisdom"), with Prince Philip wearing the Garter Star. A larger portrait of the queen wearing the Garter Collar and State Crown, or a photograph of her wearing the Garter Mantle, Collar, Star, and hat, may be seen on pp. 13 and 17, respectively, of the same work. Similar photographs of then Prince Charles may be seen on p. 126 of Burnet, *In Private—In Public, THE PRINCE AND PRINCESS OF WALES*, and between pp. 150-151 of Junor. The Collar and/or Riband are also worn for various official functions, including the State Opening of Parliament and certain funerals (e.g., see *Her Majesty The Queen*, pp. 18-19; *Charles & Diana: The Tenth Anniversary*, pp. 36-37). The insignia of the Order of the Garter will be described in detail later in this section.
4. While alive, in Coleman's words, Queen Elizabeth II was "the head of the Committee of 300"—a role now pertaining to King Charles III. Speaking of the news media, Coleman adds: "These media change artists and news manipulators report directly to the Club of Rome, which, in turn, reports to the Committee of 300, at whose head sits the Queen of England [(now Charles)]. She rules over a vast network of closely-linked corporations who never pay taxes and are answerable to no one else; who fund their research institutions through foundations whose joint activities have almost total control over our daily lives" (*The Committee of 300*, pp. 22, 102-103). Elsewhere Coleman states, "The Committee of 300 is for the most part under the control of the British monarch" (ibid., p. 239). Coleman, in defense of the existence of the committee, besides tracing its membership, organizations, holdings, and dealings, states: "But there is some proof: Walter Rathenau, a prominent Socialist politician and financial advisor to the Rothschilds..., wrote an article in the WIENER PRESS, which it published on December 24, 1921. In the article, Rathenau made this astonishing comment: 'Only three hundred men, each of whom knows all others, govern the fate of Europe. They select their successors from their own entourage. These men have the means in their hands of putting an end to the form of State which they find unreasonable.' ... Further proof that the Committee exists, is found in the vast number of powerful institutions owned and controlled by it...., all of which come under THE MOTHER OF ALL THINK TANKS AND RESEARCH INSTITUTIONS, THE TAVISTOCK INSTITUTE OF HUMAN RELATIONS with its far-flung network of hundreds of branches" (ibid., pp. 108-109). This super-institute is "owned and controlled by the

knights of the Order of the Garter, however, are a part of the Committee of 300, whose members are usually chosen from among apostate Anglican Protestants. Loosely speaking, we may think of the Order of the Garter as the board of directors for the British monarchy, which King George VI once described as the "Royal Firm."[1] According to Springmeier, who has studied the Illuminati extensively and claims to have deprogrammed and debriefed former members of the order, the Illuminati are organized around the world's thirteen most prominent occult—generational satanic—bloodlines, the thirteenth and most powerful being the Merovingian, or "Holy" bloodline.[2] The Committee of 300 is similarly organized. John Coleman, a former British intelligence analyst and political science officer,[3] states:

> The Committee of 300 has a major bureaucracy at its disposal made up of hundreds of think tanks, and front organizations that run the whole gamut of private business and government leaders....
>
> The Committee of 300, although in existence for more than 150 years, ... was always given to issuing orders through other fronts, such as the Royal Institute for International Affairs. When it was decided that a superbody would control European affairs, the RIIA founded the Tavistock Institute, which in turn created NATO....
>
> The Committee is the ultimate secret society made up of an untouchable ruling class, which includes the Queen of England [(ostensibly, now King Charles III)], the Queen of the Netherlands, the Queen of Denmark and the royal families of Europe. These aristocrats decided at the death of Queen Victoria, the matriarch of the Venetian Black Guelphs,[4] that in order

---

Royal Institute for International Affairs [(RIIA)]" (ibid., p. 240). Coleman also observes: "The drug trade [worldwide] is controlled by the Committee of 300 from the top down. The drug trade started with the British East India Company and was closely followed by the Dutch East India Company. Both were controlled by a 'Council of 300'" (ibid., p. 141). *All material from this author is quoted with his permission.* China now plays *fentanyl* and other roles.

1. Hoey, *Charles & Diana: The Tenth Anniversary,* p. 30.
2. Fritz Springmeier, *The Top 13 Illuminati Bloodlines,* Vol. I (Oregon: 5316 S.E. Lincoln, Portland, OR 97215; 1995), pp. 228-236. For more information, see ch. 4, "Prince of this World—a *Diverse* Lineage," at p. 79.
3. According to Coleman: "All the information that I provide in this book comes from years of research, and is backed up by impeccable intelligence sources. Nothing is exaggerated. It is factual and precise, so do not fall into the trap set by the enemy that this material is 'disinformation.' For the last two decades, I have provided information which has proved to be highly accurate, and which has explained a lot of puzzling events" (*The Committee of 300,* p. 107). Although the author can personally verify the veracity and accuracy of significant aspects of Coleman's work from the author's own research, and can verify much of the rest of Coleman's work from the writings of other authors, the author does not agree with Coleman on all points, particularly where a number of his clearly biased and scripturally unbalanced views and statements concerning Israel and Christian fundamentalists are concerned. Moreover, Coleman's work is to be faulted in that it is poorly documented and loosely organized. Nevertheless, if one is willing to look past these shortcomings, one will find a vast amount of particularly incriminating and damning material where the British monarchy is concerned. For this reason, *The Committee of 300* is well worth examining in relation to *The AntiChrist and a Cup of Tea.*
4. According to Coleman, "The 'Windsors' are in reality of the House of Guelph, one of the Venetian Black Nobility's oldest dynasties" (*The Committee of 300,* p. 321). Recall that King Charles III, like his (roasting) mother, descends from *Godfroi de Bouillon* through Henry the Black of the Guelph Line. By that lin-

to gain world-wide control, it would be necessary for its aristocratic members to "go into business" with the non-aristocratic, but extremely powerful leaders of corporate business on a global scale. And so, the doors to ultimate power were opened to what the Queen of England [(Elizabeth II while alive)] likes to refer to as "the commoners."[1]

From my days in the [intelligence] field, I know that the heads of foreign governments refer to this all-powerful body as "The Magicians." Stalin coined his own phrase to describe them: "The Dark Forces," and President Eisenhower ... referred to it in a colossal understatement as "the military-industrial complex." Stalin kept the USSR heavily armed with conventional and nuclear forces, because he did not trust what he called "the family." His ingrained mistrust and fear of the Committee of 300 proved to be well-founded....

Political and financial control ... is exercised through a number of secret societies, most notably, the Scottish Rite of Freemasonry, and perhaps even more importantly, through the Venerable Order of St. John of Jerusalem, an ancient order consisting of the British monarch's hand-picked executives, chosen for their expertise in areas vital to the continued control of the Committee. In my work "The Order of St. John of Jerusalem," published in 1986, I described The Order in the following manner: "... It is therefore not a secret society, except where its [original] purposes have been perverted in the inner councils like the Order of the Garter, which is a prostituted oligarchical creation of the British royal family.... As an example, we find the [(late)] atheist Lord Peter Carrington, who pretends to be an Anglican Christian, but who is a member of the Order of Osiris and other demonic sects, including Freemasonry, installed as a Knight of the Garter at St. George's Chapel, Windsor Castle, by Her Majesty, Queen Elizabeth II of England, of the Black Nobility Guelphs, also head of the Anglican Church, which she thoroughly despises." ...

We have been so brainwashed that we believe the British royal family is just a nice, harmless and colorful institution, and so we fail to realize just how corrupt, and therefore highly dangerous is this institution called the British Monarchy. The Knights of the Order of the Garter are the INNERMOST circle of the most corrupt public servants who have utterly betrayed the trust placed in them by their nation and their people.

The Knights of the Order of the Garter, is Queen Elizabeth's [(now King Charles')] most trusted "privy council." ... [The] Knights of the Garter are the inner sanctum, the elite of the elite of Her Majesty's Most Venerable Order of St. John of Jerusalem....

....Like the present royal family, [Lord] Palmerston, [one of the founders of the opium dynasty in China,] like so many of his kind, was not only a Freemason, but also a dedicated follower of Gnosticism. Like the present royal family, Palmerston made a pretense of being a Christian, but was in fact a practicing Satanist. Many satanists became leaders in the hierarchy of the British aristocracy....

....[It] was the power of the Order of the Garter which saved [Japan's] Emperor Hirohitho from most probably being executed as a war criminal.

---

eage alone, Charles could have claimed the Merovingian crusader title "King of Jerusalem." But on May 6, 2023, he was anointed with oil produced in Jerusalem and crowned king, obviating any "need." For more information, see ch. 4, "Prince of this World—a *Diverse* Lineage," at p. 79.

1. For concrete examples, see ch. 11's sections titled, "The World of Business and Finance" and "The United Nations and public-private partnerships," at pp. 440 and 446, respectively.

Queen Elizabeth II had maintained a close relationship with the late Emperor Hirohitho (formerly Crown Prince Akihito), and [(ostensibly) King Charles III] still does with his family [(e.g., current Emperor Naruhito)]....

Every "royal" and [all] so-called European "noble" dynasties past and present, have seats on the Committee of 300, most often by way of nominees. For instance, the Hohenzollern dynasty might be represented by Edward the Duke of Kent; the Braganzas by the Duke of York, and so on. There are just too many of these "royal" families for them all to have direct seats on the Committee of 300.... But the thing to remember is the order of rank; first the royal family members, then dukes, earls, marquises and lords, then finally the "commoners," who usually get the title of "Sir".[1]

The Committee of 300 is a supranational organization whose express purpose, like the Illuminati, is to facilitate the creation of a Luciferic New World Order. This overarching committee, working through world leaders of virtually all backgrounds and persuasions, the Illuminati, Freemasonry, the intelligence services, all types of or-

---

1. Coleman, *The Committee of 300,* pp. 84-85, 231, 269-271, 322. For lists of most past and present (as of 1998) members, institutions, and organizations of the Committee of 300, see pp. 311-350 of the same work. Just a few of the more easily recognized names of yet-living members, most of whom are on Coleman's decades-old list, include King Charles III, Queen Sofia, Queen Margreta [(i.e., Margrethe II)], Queen Beatrix, Princess Maria Beatrice of Savoy, Prince Richard the Duke of Gloucester, Prince Edward the Duke of Kent, Lord Salisbury (the current Robert Gascoyne-Cecil, presumably), Battenburg (family Designate), DuPont (family Designate of Pierre S. du Pont, presumably), John Forbes (ostensibly John F. Kerry) and Ted Turner. Deceased members (in order) allegedly include: Henry Kissinger, Queen Elizabeth II, Prince Philip, George Pratt Shultz, Baron Rothschild, George Herbert Walker Bush (Bush Sr.), David Rockefeller who donated the land in New York City on which the Untied Nations' buildings were constructed, Maurice Strong, Angus Ogilvie (Ogilvy), Queen Juliana of the Netherlands, Cyrus Roberts Vance, Paul Culliton Warnke, Francois Mitterand, W.E. McClaughlin (presumably, this is supposed to be William Earle McLaughlin), Robert Runcie (a *pagan* former Archbishop of Canterbury, who was personally selected by Elizabeth II), Aurelio Peccei who founded the Club of Rome (from which came the 1957 "Treaty of Rome" that established the European Economic Community, which is now the European Union), Louis Mountbatten, David *ben* Gurion (modern Israel's first Prime Minister), Alfred P. Sloan, Winston Churchill, Aldous Leonard Huxley, Earnest Oppenheimer, Chaim Azriel Weizmann (modern Israel's first President who has now been superseded by his nephew Ezer Weizmann), Duke of Devonshire Victor Cavendish, H.G. Wells, Lloyd George, "Colonel" Edward Mandel House, Arthur Balfour, John Pierpont Morgan, and Cecil Rhodes.

According to Coleman, membership in the Committee of 300, "which has a 150-year history," includes top representatives from the old families of the European Black Nobility, the Illuminati, the Order of St. John of Jerusalem, the Order of Skull and Bones, Lucis Trust, the Vatican, the United Nations (UN), the International Monetary Fund (IMF), the Bank of International Settlements (BIS), NATO, the Central Intelligence Agency (CIA), the Nine Unknown Men, the Club of Rome, the World Wildlife Fund (WWF), Greenpeace, the Sierra Group, Socialist International, Anenherbe-Rosicrucianists, the National and World Council of Churches, the One World Government Church, the Thule Society, "and literally HUNDREDS of other organizations." This membership involves "some of the most brilliant intellects assembled to form a completely totalitarianist, absolutely controlled 'new' society" (ibid., pp. 216-218, 237).

ganized crime, including global banking,[1] the worldwide drug trade,[2] the media (noted later), and many other agencies, has vast wealth at its disposal[3] and has literally shaped the course of events over the past century, to include fomenting World Wars I and II, and creating the League of Nations and then the United Nations on their ruins. The committee itself is not a monolith; when the British monarchy finds its control or operations threatened, it quickly acts to eliminate the threat, be it internal or external.[4] A more recent example of the committee's tampering was Desert Storm, or the 1991 war against

1. In discussing the committee's structure, Coleman again notes the Tavistock Institute and then states: "The EAGLE STAR GROUP, which changed its name to the STAR GROUP after the close of the Second World War, is composed of a group of major international companies in overlapping and interfaced areas (1) Insurance, (2) Banking (3) Real Estate (4) Entertainment (5) High Technology.... Banking, while not the mainstay, is vitally important, especially in the areas where banks act as clearing houses and money launderers of drug money. The main 'big name banks' are: The Bank of England, The Federal Reserve Banks, Bank of International Settlements, The World Bank, The Hong Kong and Shanghai Bank, and American Express bank.... Each of these banks is affiliated with and/or controls hundreds of thousands of large and small banks throughout the world. Banks large and small in their thousands are in the Committee of 300 network.... ...Nothing happens on Wall Street that is not controlled by the Bank of England, whose instructions are relayed through the Morgan Bank and then put into action through key brokerage houses, whose top executives are ultimately responsible for carrying out Committee directives" (*The Committee of 300*, pp. 240-241, 246). Honored "for his contribution to global economic stability," Alan Greenspan, Chairman of the Federal Reserve (i.e., the banks to which Coleman refers), was knighted by Queen Elizabeth II on September 26, 2002 ("Call him Almost Sir Alan Greenspan," *Rocky Mountain News*, 27 Sept. 2002). Remarkably, the Federal Reserve is in reality *not* federal, but is instead *a private and largely English international banking concern*—one that yet exercises major influence over the U.S. economy.
2. As quoted earlier: "The drug trade [worldwide] is controlled by the Committee of 300 from the top down. The drug trade started with the British East India Company and was closely followed by the Dutch East India Company. Both were controlled by a 'Council of 300'" (Coleman, *The Committee of 300*, p. 141). To this, Coleman adds: "[The] British Crown, or the Royal Family, ... levied a tax on all producers of opium duly registered with the state authority who were sending their opium to China.... Britain has been involved in the China opium trade for more than two centuries. No one is going to be so foolish as to rock the boat when millions upon millions of dollars flow into the bank accounts of the British oligarchists.... Every British monarch since 1729 has benefited immensely from the drug trade and this holds good for the present occupant of the throne. Their ministers saw to it that wealth flowed into their family coffers.... By the turn of the century, ... [their] income from the China opium trade exceeded David Rockefeller's income by SEVERAL BILLION DOLLARS PER ANNUM.... F.S. Turner's book, 'British Opium Policy,' published in 1876, shows how the British monarchy and its hangers-on family relatives were deeply involved in the opium trade" (ibid., pp. 152, 155, 161, 183, 200). The British monarchy apparently also controls today's *heroin* trade through Canada, which in turn is controlled by the Canadian Institute for International Affairs, another child of the London-based Royal Institute for International Affairs (ibid., pp. 253-256). Per Coleman, the worldwide drug trade may be traced from the Tavistock Institute to 1) the British East India Company, 2) the Hong Kong London Council, 3) the Medellin Cartel, and 4) the Cali Cartel (ibid., p. 368).
   Coleman is not alone in his assertions concerning the origins of the modern drug trade. It is a known fact that Britain acquired Hong Kong and its surrounding territories as a result of its Opium Wars with China in the nineteenth century. What is perhaps not so well known is that the British monarchy still have very strong "business" ties to Hong Kong. Coleman, John Daniel (author of the *Scarlet and the Beast* trilogy), and others have shown that those ties continue to involve the drug trade. Anyone who pays attention to the news media will recall that the monarchy, through Satan's Prince, personally officiated at Britain's handover of Hong Kong to communist China, at the start of July 1997. Could this have been more than just the next major international media-blitz for Satan's Prince, since his extravagant wedding to Diana? One must seriously wonder. For more information, see ch. 11's section titled, "Governor of Hong Kong?," at page 443.
3. Besides its wealth from the worldwide drug trade, the British monarchy controls the metal and mineral wealth of South Africa. Coleman states: "The [Arthurian MI6] Round Table was established in South

Iraq, which was intentionally misled by the Bush (Sr.) administration to believe that the Untied States would merely blink if Iraq invaded Kuwait in 1990. On the ruins of this *multinational* war, then President George Bush proclaimed the dawning of a "New World Order," publicly floating the committee's goal as a "trial balloon" (see below).[1] Gorbachev—who, upon meeting the pope at the Vatican in December 1989, "realized that the pope had also played a role in what we [communists] came to call the new political thinking,"[2] and who became clearly associated with the committee *as well as* then Prince Charles[3]—earlier did so publicly in a 1988 speech, before the

Africa by Cecil Rhodes and funded by the English Rothschild family. Its purpose was to train business leaders loyal to the monarch, who would secure the vast gold and diamond treasures for the British Crown.... By the early 1930s, the British Crown had a stranglehold on the biggest gold and diamond fields ever found in the world. NOW THE COMMITTEE OF 300 HAD AT ITS DISPOSAL BOTH THE VAST FORTUNE COMING FROM THE DRUG TRADE AND THE EQUALLY VAST FORTUNE OF THE MINERAL AND METAL WEALTH OF SOUTH AFRICA. Financial control of the world was complete" (*The Committee of 300*, pp. 207-208). We may trace "the spokes of the drug wheel, including terrorism, production of opium, the gold markets, dirty money laundering and banking, to its central core, the British Crown" (ibid., p. 256). Note that as a Rhodes Scholar, President Clinton is similarly subservient to the British monarchy.

4. One conspiracy-theorist view of the start of World War II, for example, is as follows: Hitler, after having been groomed in Masonry and other areas of the occult, decided that his masonic masters and Masons generally, many of whom were apostate Jews, were a threat to his own "Aryan" aspirations. He therefore determined that the Jews were not just a convenient scapegoat on which to cement his power base, but that both they and the masonic influence in Europe had to be eliminated. Consequently, the British monarchy itself came to feel threatened, and World War II ensued. Is this plausible? *Yes.*

1. Coleman asserts that Bush, "another member of the Committee of 300," acted on behalf of "the Royal Institute for International Affairs (RIIA) who received its mandate from the Committee of 300, also known as the 'Olympians.'" Coleman adds: "the war was fought by American troops to protect the interests of British Petroleum (BP), which is one of the most important companies in the Committee of 300 in which members of Queen Elizabeth's immediate family have a big stake.... ...Britain is in charge of our government.... The plain truth is that the United States has fought in 5 wars this century, for, and on behalf of the infamous Committee of 300" (*The Committee of 300*, pp. 22, 64, 79, 180, 192, 214).

2. Mikhail Gorbachev, "Pope played significant role in changing world," *The Denver Post,* 9 Mar. 1992, p. 7A. This article was reproduced by Gary Kah in *Hope for the World Update,* Fall 1995, p. 6.

3. On October 19, 1994, in what was billed as a "major policy speech" and delivered "to 300 distinguished members of the New York Council on Foreign Relations" (a veiled reference to the U.S. C.F.R.'s master, the supranational Committee of 300, only some of whose members were actually present), Gorbachev "unveiled the final report of the Global Security Project." Called "The Global Security Programme" (non-American English), the report called for "measures to strengthen the authority of the United Nations and regional security institutions." According to the traitorous Senator Alan Cranston, head of the U.S. delegation for the project and Chairman of the Board of the Gorbachev Foundation USA, not to mention a member of the masonic Bohemian Club, "This initiative represents a major step forward in building consensus for the emerging global security system for the coming century, an era where cooperation among nations and peoples must replace our outmoded and dangerous aggressive brinkmanship" ("Mikhail Gorbachev unveils new *Global Security Programme,*" Gorbachev Foundation USA, as reproduced by Gary Kah in *Hope for the World Update,* Fall 1995, pp. 3-4). It is perhaps noteworthy that the effort was strongly supported by the Carnegie Corporation of New York, another Committee of 300 organization (Coleman, *The Committee of 300,* pp. 85-86, 290, 316). In fact, Gorbachev, as President of the Gorbachev Foundation, and at his 1995 State of the World Forum conference in San Francisco, had worked not just with some of the world's most prominent New Agers, but directly with such past Committee of 300 members as George Bush Sr., George Shultz, David Rockefeller, Maurice Strong, Francois Mitterand, and yet-living ones like Ted Turner (Kah, "Gorbachev Calls For World Tax ... While Wooing Spiritual Leaders," and Samatha Strong, "Gorbachev Forum Highlights World Government," *Hope for the World Update,* Fall 1995, pp. 1-5), all of whom are listed by Coleman (*The Committee of 300,* pp. 312, 317, 319-320). A co-sponsor of Gorbachev's State of the World Forum was The

UN General Assembly. Just after the ground war against Iraq, in January and March of 1991, Bush Sr. asserted,[1]

> We [Americans] can find meaning and reward by serving some higher purpose than ourselves—a shining purpose, the illumination of a thousand points of light....
>
> What is at stake is more than one small country [like Kuwait]; it is a big idea—a New World Order, where diverse nations are drawn together in common cause to achieve the universal aspirations of mankind....
>
> With few exceptions, the world now stands as one.... [For] the first time since World War II, the international community is united. The leadership of the United Nations, once only a hoped-for ideal, is now confirming its founders' vision....
>
> The world can therefore seize this opportunity to fulfill the long-held promise of a New World Order.... Yes, the United States bears a major share of the leadership in this effort. Among the nations of the world, only the United States of America has had both the moral standing and the means to back it up. We are the only nation on this Earth that could assemble the forces of peace.[2]

> "Our commitment to peace in the Middle East does not end with the liberation of Kuwait," Bush said. "The time has come to put an end to the Arab-Israeli conflict."
>
> ....Bush re-emphasized longstanding American policy that Israel must trade territory it seized during Arab-Israeli wars for peace and secure borders.[3]

> ....Bush pledged a "new and vigorous determination" to push a land-for-peace in the Arab-Israeli conflict. He called for finally implementing U.N. Security Council resolutions 242 and 338, which call for Israel to withdraw from occupied territories in exchange for secure borders.[4]

As a member of the Committee of 300, former Prime Minister David *ben* Gurion of Israel, who created the Mossad with the help of MI6, made these remarkable, yet twisted, predictions in 1962: "With the exception of the USSR, as a federated Eurasian state, all other

---

Red Rose Collection, a globalist Rosicrucian organization that promotes New Age ideology (Kah, "World Federalists Call for U.N. Empowerment," ibid., p. 3). Coleman adds, "The Committee of 300 is filled with members of British aristocracy which has corporate interests and associates in every country of the world, including Russia" (ibid., p. 240).

The punch line to the Global Security Programme "unveiled" and trumpeted by Gorbachev, however, is that it was initiated *not* by Gorbachev in 1994, but years earlier at Cambridge University with then *Prince Charles'* involvement. See ch. 11's section titled, "Global Governance, the Global Security Programme, and a possible 'Economic Security Council,'" at p. 451.

1. This material is excerpted from the author's forthcoming *Messiah, History, and the Tribulation Period* mutli-volume series.
2. "State of the Union—Bush Seeks to Inspire Support for his Persian Gulf Mission," *Congressional Quarterly*, 2 Feb. 1991, pp. 308-310. Also see Kah, p. 63.
3. Denver Post Wire Services, "Pledge made to maintain Mideast role," *The Denver Post*, 7 Mar. 1991, p. 1A.
4. G.G. LaBelle, Associated Press, "Baker's peace bid faces battle lines," *The Denver Post*, 9 Mar. 1991, p. 6A. For more information, see ch. 12, "Charles, Middle East 'Peace,' and Global Security," at p. 481.

countries will become united in a world alliance, at whose disposal will be an international police force. All armies will be abolished, and there will be no more wars. In Jerusalem, the United Nations will build a shrine to the Prophets to serve the federated union on all continents, as prophesied by Isaiah. Higher education will be the right of every person in the world. A pill to prevent pregnancy will slow down the explosive natural increase in China and India."[1] Indeed, apart from Israelite Christians, modern Israel is almost entirely apostate, and under Satan's grip.

To be more precise, as Coleman essentially charts it, under the *Committee of 300,* we may place **1)** the royal families of Europe, **2)** British Intelligence or MI6, **3)** the Royal Institute for International Affairs (RIIA), **4)** the United Nations and its member nations, and **5)** Communism, Fabianism, Zionism (in an effort to control Israel and Jerusalem), Liberalism, Socialism, and Right Wing Parties. Under *British Intelligence,* we may place **1)** the CIA, **2)** the Mossad, and **3)** other intelligence agencies worldwide (detailed below). Under the *Royal Institute for International Affairs (RIIA),* we may place **1)** the Tavistock Institute of Human Relations and **2)** the Executive Arm of the RIIA; **3)** the Rhodes/Milner Group and its Round Table; **4)** Freemasonry and other secret societies, as well as the Nine Unknown Men; **5)** international terrorism; **6)** control of the world's banking, petroleum, mining, insurance, commerce, and industry; and **7)** religious organizations, including the One World Government Church.[2] Under the *Tavistock Institute for Human Relations,* we may place **1)** the Club of Rome, from which came **2)** NATO and today's U.S. military; **3)** the worldwide drug trade, to include the British East India Company, the Hong Kong London Council, the Medellin Cartel, and the Cali Cartel; and **4)** the major institutions, to include the Stanford Research Institute, the Massachusetts Institute of Technology, the Institute for Policy Studies, RAND, the Hudson Institutes, and the Wharton School of Economics.[3] Under the *Executive Arm of the RIIA,* we may place **1)** the various Councils on/for Foreign Relations (e.g., U.S., Canadian and Israeli), **2)** the *private* "Federal Reserve System," with its many banksters (and primary control under the British

1. Coleman, *The Committee of 300,* pp. xlll-xiv, 235-236.
2. *The Committee of 300,* p. 367.
3. *The Committee of 300,* p. 368.

Crown),[1] **3)** the U.S. Trilateral Commission,[2] and **4)** the Bilderbergers. Under the *U.S. Council on Foreign Relations,*[3] we may place control of **1)** the United States Government, which, at least in the United States, involves education, the environment, abortion (the U.S. also promotes infanticide worldwide through "aid" to developing countries), gun control (i.e., satanic efforts to disarm *law-abiding citizens),* congress, the senate, and FEMA, as well as **2)** the U.S. media, to include ABC, CBS, NBC, CNN, UPI, the New York Times, the Washington Post, etc.[4] The RIIA, having literally been *conceived to establish global dominion (governance) under the British Monarch,* works with British Intelligence and its offspring to further **a)** nefarious religious activities, to include so-called "Christian" publishers promoting one-world government and the humanist religion of Darwinism

---

1. On the heels of the first world war, the British RIIA arose from an original idea (via Lionel George Curtis) of an elitist Anglo-American "victors'" think tank—one that would provide "libraries, research facilities and group discussions" for an "English-speaking 'common market of ideas'" (Katharina Rietzler, "The Hotel Majestic and the Origins of Chatham House," Chatham House, 30 May 2019). Initially, the RIIA concerned itself with reformation of the British Empire, leading to the British Commonwealth—while the original "Anglo" component then led to the U.S. Council on Foreign Relations (CFR). L.G. Curtis had then advocated federalism for the British Empire, but later wanted a world state or global government —under the British Monarch! The RIIA and the world's various CFRs (e.g., U.S., Canadian and Israeli) are ultimately about global governance under *the* AntiChrist. As elsewhere mentioned, King Charles III as Satan's Prince, seeks *the* Commonwealth of Nations, or a global Commonwealth.

   "Colonel" Edward Mandell House, son of the Civil War's Rothschild agent Thomas W. House, conspired as a member of the RIIA, while working for Rothschilds, to enable creation of the Federal Reserve System in the U.S., through 1913's Federal Reserve Act. Not coincidentally, E. House was behind the formation of the U.S. CFR—*under* the RIIA—on July 29, 1921. "The ... [U.S.] Council on Foreign Relations, took a slightly different direction, and did not manage to rival Chatham House's [(the RIIA's)] research programme on international questions until the era of the Second World War" (ibid.).

   As history would have it, the conspiratorial murders of presidents Abraham Lincoln and JFK Jr., as well as multiple other politicians and private individuals, besides "ordinary" tampering in various major U.S. elections to install treasonous traitors (e.g., Woodrow S. Wilson, Barack Hussein Obama II, aka Barry Soetoro, and Obama's puppet Joseph "Manchurian" Robinette Biden Jr.) and co-conspirators, factually trace to the British Monarchy and entities it directly controls or otherwise indirectly influences heavily. The U.S. Senate, Congress, and Presidency (other than Donald J. Trump and ostensibly Ronald S. Reagan) have been, and still are severely compromised by treasonous traitors beholden, knowingly or not, to Britain's Crown. Notably, L.G. Curtis was made a Companion of Honour (CH).

2. For "information" on the Trilateral Commission, including its current leadership and membership, visit "https://www.trilateral.org" on the Internet.

3. For "information" on the U.S. Council on Foreign Relations, visit "https://www.cfr.org".

4. *The Committee of 300,* p. 369. Note that Ted Turner, owner of CNN, is on the Committee of 300 (ibid., pp. 236, 320). Coleman adds: "Going back to RCA, we find that its directorate consists of British-American establishment figures, who feature prominently in other organizations such as: the CFR, NATO, the Club of Rome, the Trilateral Commission, Freemasonry, Skull and Bones, Bilderbergers, Round Table, Milner Group, Cini Foundation, Mont Pelerin Society, and the Jesuits-Aristotle Society.... All three major [U.S.] television networks came as spinoffs from RCA, especially the National Broadcasting Company (NBC), which was closely followed by the American Broadcasting Company (ABC), in 1951. The third big television network was Columbia Broadcasting System (CBS), which like its sister companies, was, and still is, dominated by British intelligence. William Paley was trained in mass brainwashing techniques at the Tavistock Institute prior to being passed as qualified to head CBS. Thus, if we the people of the United States but knew it, all our major television networks are subject to British oversight, and information they provide first goes to London for clearance.... All three major networks are represented on the Committee of 300 and are affiliated with the giant of the mass communications business, Xerox Corporation" (ibid., pp. 248-249).

(e.g., macroevolution) in education,[1] as well as socialist and humanist ideas such as "respect"[2] and "tolerance;" **b)** the World Council of Churches and its hierarchy, Liberation Theology, and Socialism; and **c)** secret societies, religious foundations, "church" research groups, the Rockefeller Riverside Church, apostate seminaries and left-wing religious groups, and, finally, schools for indoctrination into one-world government ideas.[3]

Like King Charles III now, one of Queen Elizabeth II's and Prince Philip's titles had been "Colonel-in-Chief, the Intelligence Corps."[4] According to Coleman, the Committee of 300 "possesses a super-intelligence service that has corrupted the KGB, the Vatican Intelligence, the CIA, the ONI, DGSE, U.S. military intelligence, the State Department intelligence service, and even the most secret of all U.S. intelligence agencies, the Office of National Reconnaissance."[5] He asserts: "There is no entity the Committee cannot reach and control, and that includes the organized religions of the world. This [committee] then, is the [so-called] all powerful OLYMPIAN GROUP, whose power base is in London, and the City of London financial center, with its grip on [South Africa's and the world's] minerals, metals and precious gems, [tobacco,] cocaine, [heroin,] opium and pharmaceutical drugs, rentier-financier bankers, cult promoters and founders of rock music. The British Crown is the control point from which all things [related to the creation of a Luciferic New World Order] radi-

---

1. For more information on the *royal-blooded* Charles Darwin, see p. 286 in ch. 9.
2. While yet Prince of Wales, Charles started his own religious movement called "Respect." For more information, see p. 388 in ch. 10.
3. *The Committee of 300,* p. 370.
4. Judd, *Prince Philip,* p. 249. Prior to their deaths, Elizabeth II and Philip held this title, besides Charles.
5. "The existence of the National Reconnaissance Office (NRO) was known only to a handful of people outside of the Committee of 300, until Truman stumbled upon it quite by accident. Churchill had a hand in setting up the NRO, and he was reportedly livid when Truman [who was controlled through Freemasonry] discovered its existence.... [The NRO] is a creature of the Committee of 300, to whom its reports are routinely sent every few hours" (*The Committee of 300,* p. 237).
    To his earlier statements regarding the committee's Star Group (formerly known as the Eagle Star Group), which controls banking worldwide, as well as Wall Street (ibid., pp 240-241, 246), Coleman adds: "The English companies controlled by the British royal family are: Eagle Star, Prudential Assurance Company, and the Prudential Insurance Company, which own and control most American insurers, including Allstate Insurance. At the head of the list is Eagle Star, probably the most powerful 'front' for Military Intelligence Department Six (MI6). Eagle Star, although nowhere near as large as Assicurazioni Generale, is perhaps equally important simply because it is owned by members of the Queen of England's family, and as Queen Elizabeth [II] is the titular head of the Committee, Eagle Star is tremendously important. Eagle Star is more than a major 'front' for MI6; it is also a front for major British banks.... It can be said with a great degree of accuracy that the most powerful British oligarchical families created Eagle Star as a vehicle for 'black operations' against those who oppose Committee of 300 policies" (ibid., p. 244). Coleman elaborates: "As giant-sized as Xerox is, it is dwarfed by the Rank Organization, a London-based conglomerate fully controlled by members of Queen Elizabeth's immediate family.... The best proof I can offer of the existence of the Committee of 300, is the Rank Organization, which, in conjunction with Eagle Star IS THE BRITISH CROWN. It is also the black operations center of MI6 (SIS)" (ibid., pp. 250, 253).

ate. As the saying goes, 'They have a finger in every pie.'"[1] Recall, of course, that the Order of the Garter is *the* central organ to all this.

Garter symbols. As today's *first and second ranking* Garter knights, King Charles III and Prince William of Wales wear the order's insignia. These include the blue velvet Garter itself, the gold motto of which is *Honi soit qui mal y pense,* the Collar (from which dangles the Marlborough  Great George pendant depicting St. George on a white horse slaying a spotted green dragon), the Star, and the blue Riband with its Lesser George pendant medallion. Like the larger pendent on the Collar, the Lesser George also depicts "Saint" George slaying a spot-

---

1. Coleman, *The Committee of 300,* p. 248. Coleman outlines the aims of the "Olympians," who "believe they are equal in power and stature to the legendary gods of Olympus." These aims include the creation of a New World Order; the elimination of national identities; the destruction of major religions—especially Christianity—through the introduction of new cults and the furtherance of existing ones ("most cults operating in the world today, are the product of British intelligence acting for the oligarchical rulers" of the Committee of 300); mass mind control; drastic depopulation through the deaths of about three billion people and a subsequent zero-growth society with abundant "slave labor;" the creation and management of major crises and resulting chaos to maintain and increase control of populations and governments (FEMA—the Federal Emergency Management Agency—in the U.S., exists for this purpose); the legalization of illegal drugs to increase profitability (hence, the Bush and Clinton administrations' so-called "war on drugs" drug-legalization agenda); and to keep the nation of Israel apostate and under masonic hegemony (ibid., pp. 42-47, 230).

   With the above objectives in mind, "Britain's MI6 (SAS) promotes a wide variety of kookery such as the New Age, Yogaism, Zenn Bhudism, Witchcraft, Delphic Priesthood of Apollo and hundreds of small 'cults' of all kinds" (ibid., p. 237). Coleman observes that most of today's "Christian" churches "have become little more than social clubs run by the infinitely evil World Council of Churches (WCC), whose beginnings lie not in Moscow but in the City of London.... This body was set up in the 1920s to serve as a vehicle for One World Government policies, and stands as a monument to the long-range planning capabilities of the Committee of 300" (ibid., pp. 289-290; for a chart, see p. 372). (The author does not fully share Coleman's pessimism, and finds his point exaggerated. We must always remember that God is stronger than Satan, and that in Christ, we shall have the final victory.) Coleman adds: "The war on drugs which the Bush administration was allegedly fighting, but which it was not, was for the legalization of ALL types and classes of drugs. Such drugs are not solely a social aberration, but a full-scale attempt to gain control of the minds of the people of this planet.... THIS IS THE PRINCIPAL TASK OF THE COMMITTEE" (ibid., pp. 204-205). "Both prohibition and the distilleries who met the demand for alcohol were creations of the British Crown.... It was an experiment which became the forerunner of today's drug trade, and the lessons learned from the prohibition era are being applied to the soon to be legalized drug trade" (ibid., p. 272).

   According to Coleman: "Summarized, the intent and purpose of the Committee of 300 is to bring to pass the following conditions: A One World Government and one-unit monetary system, under permanent non-elected hereditary oligarchists, who self-select from among their numbers, in the form of a feudal system as it was in the Middle Ages. In this One World entity, population will be limited by restrictions on the number of children allowed per family, diseases, wars and famines, until 1 billion people who are useful to the ruling class in areas which will be strictly and clearly defined, will remain as the total population of the world.... Satanism, Luciferianism and Witchcraft, shall be recognized as legitimate One World Government curricula with no private or church schools. All Christian churches have already been subverted [so far as the oligarchists are concerned], and Christianity will become a religion of the past in the One World Government." Of the remaining 1 billion, "500 million will consist of Chinese and Japanese races, selected because they are people who have been regimented for centuries" (ibid., pp. 218-219, 222). King Charles III by the way, is *pro*-infanticide.

ted dragon.[1] (Could this intimate Satan *in the AntiChrist,* when the latter is mortally wounded by "a sword?" Reportedly, Edward VI called this dragon "Satan," despite its not being red, and he wondered why "George" slew it with a spear, rather than a sword.[2])

"The Collar [now] consisting of twenty-six red [Tudor] roses each enclosed by the Garter interspersed with twenty-six gold knots and having pendant a representation of St George and the [spotted] Dragon was introduced during the reign of Henry VII, probably shortly before 1500. The Garter Star, a badge which the Companions were to wear upon their coats or cloaks dates from 1626/9. The blue Riband with its Lesser George, a representation of St George slaying the Dragon within the [encircling] Garter, was first ordered to be worn by Henry VIII."[3] Actually, the twenty-six red roses of the Collar were originally, at the time of Henry VIII, twenty-six roundels of St. George's cross (see below).[4]

The eight-pointed Star of the order, which is made of chipped silver, enamel, and gold, has a central red cross—representative of the emblem of the Merovingian birthmark historically adopted by the Temple Knights and then the Priory of Zion—encircled by the Garter.[5] That is, the Merovingian cross—now euphemistically called the arms of "St. George"—appears as the red quartering device of a white shield surrounded by the Garter, which is imposed over the center of an eight-pointed star. "Companions" and "priests"[6] of the order wear **a)** the white shield with the Merovingian cross encircled by the Garter, called the Garter Badge of St. George's Cross (companions),[7] or **b)** a "roundel" similar to it but circular (priests), upon the left shoulder of either **a)** the dark blue velvet Garter Mantle (cloak), which has a crimson velvet hood (companions), or **b)** a crimson or murrey (dark purple) robe (priests). Since around 1911, the Sovereign of the Order, unlike the other companions, has worn the Star it-

---

1. For color representations of the insignia of the Order of the Garter, see Boutell, plate XVII, between pp. 184-187. Note, however, that the depiction of the formerly light blue Garter (before George I's reign, but still worn by the present queen) is defective in that rather than being edged with two rows of 169 miniature gold buckles each, as on the actual deep blue Garter in primary use since George I's reign, it is edged with two gold chains. (The author has a color photograph of a deep blue Garter dating to around 1813, in which the buckles are evident. For more, see the later related note.)

2. H F (Toby) Rance, ed. Adrian Rance-McGregor, "Chapter 10 The Most Noble Order of Saint George named the Garter," as posted at "https://insearchofsaintgeorge.com/chapter-10-the-most-noble-order-of-saint-george-named-the-garter". (John Foxe, *Foxe's Book of Martyrs,* cited by Heylyn op cit Part 3.)

3. Begent, p. 11.

4. Begent, p. 3.

5. For more information, see ch. 4, "Prince of this World—a *Diverse* Lineage," at p. 79.

6. For more information, see the discussion on the College of St. George in ch. 10's section titled, "A so-called 'Christian' heritage," at p. 295.

7. For a color picture of Charles' Garter Badge, see Burnet, *In Private—In Public,* THE PRINCE AND PRINCESS OF WALES, p. 127.

self on the left shoulder of the Mantle.[1] Likewise, the "habit" of the Temple Knights, originally a priestly order of apostate Roman Catholic soldiers, "was white with a red cross of eight points worn on the left shoulder."[2] *A version of the Merovingian cross encircled by the Garter, which thus constitutes a roundel, is the central symbol of the Order of the Garter.* As such, it is not only imposed over the center of an eight-pointed silver star to compose the Garter Star,[3] but it is also prominently displayed on the forehead of the black velvet Garter hats worn by King Charles III and Prince William (formerly Queen Elizabeth II and Charles[4]). *The same red cross is likewise hidden in the straight horizontal and vertical edges of the two red quarters of the royal shield, and is similarly surrounded by the Garter.*[5]

In other words, the Temple Knights, having been thrust out of France and supposedly the rest of Europe in 1309, being "abolished" by Papal Bull in 1312,[6] had actually become so powerful and influential in Scotland and England that by 1348, if not earlier, the English monarchy had not only joined their cause, but taken up their leadership in the form of the newly constituted Order of the Garter.[7] Indeed, it was the Knights of the Garter who held the canopy over Elizabeth II as she was anointed and crowned queen during her 1953 coronation.[8] In 2023, those Garter knights likewise served Charles III. Furthermore, the modified Templar cross of the Order of the Garter is prominently displayed on the Union Jack and the arms of the British Commonwealth. The Union Jack combines the cross of St. George for England—having a white fringe representing the field of St. George's banner—with the saltires of "St. Andrew" and "St. Patrick" for Scotland and Ireland.[9] Occupying the place of the lions of Eng-

---

1. Begent, pp. 1, 9, 13.
2. Boutell, 1978 ed., p. 191.
3. For a color photograph of Charles' Garter Star, see Burnet, *In Private—In Public, THE PRINCE AND PRINCESS OF WALES*, p. 124.
4. *Her Majesty The Queen*, p. 17; and Burnet, *In Private—In Public, THE PRINCE AND PRINCESS OF WALES*, p. 127.
5. A round seal of the English Knights Templar dating to 1303 is comparably encircled by a motto (Baigent, Leigh, and Lincoln, *Holy Blood, Holy Grail*, just above caption 16b, between pp. 240-241).
6. Boutell, 1978 ed., p. 192.
7. The Garter Seal of Henry VII depicts a shield quartered by the Merovingian cross, as on the Garter Star, "marshaled" with the quartered arms of England and France (no doubt taken from the Black Prince's "shield for war"). The modern version of this seal, which is further marshaled with the Irish harp and another device (possibly the red lion of Scotland), now constitutes the badge of the "Garter, Principal King of Arms" (Begent, pp. 9, 17). Similarly, the Merovingian cross is the primary device in the shield of arms belonging to the Garter King of Arms, which is marshaled with a lion of England, the Garter, and a *fleur-de-lis* (lily) for France (Boutell, 1978 ed., pp. 232-233). For more information, see this chapter's later discussion on the Black Prince, at p. 204.
8. Begent, p. 1. Previously, Queen Mary wanted to borrow the Duke of Windsor's "diamond-studded Garter Star" for Edward VIII's coronation (Lacey, *Majesty*, p. 85).
9. Boutell, 1978 ed., p. 255. "Except when they bore royal devices, the English standards of the Tudor period always had the cross of St. George at their head" (Boutell, 1978 ed., p. 254). The white ensign of the Royal Navy, which bears the Merovingian cross and shows the union in a canton, is a version of St.

land on the royal shield, the first and fourth quarters of the Commonwealth's shield each contain the Garter Badge of St. George's Cross. Its second quarter contains the saltire of St. Andrew for Scotland, rather than Scotland's red lion, and the third quarter has a pagan version of a harp, displaying a harlot's breasts, for Ireland (as opposed to the Davidic harp on the royal shield).[1] Likewise, versions of the Garter Badge of St. George's Cross have not only been central to the achievement of the city of London since the middle of the fourteenth century,[2] but also are now flown over Anglican Protestant churches[3] and serve as the symbol of the Red Cross organization, seen throughout the world. In fact, the Merovingian cross is among the most prolific of symbols in British and Commonwealth heraldry.[4] Similarly, since Henry VIII in 1534 took the inflated and blasphemous title of "Supreme Head on Earth of the Church of England," not only has the English monarch's *coat of arms* or achievement been "prominently displayed in many English churches as tokens of loyalty to the crown and obedience to the sovereign as head of the Church," being required by a statute for "all churches" under Charles II in 1660,[5] but it too has been propagated throughout the Commonwealth.

That is not all, however. A quick search of the Internet, for example, will reveal that there are numerous churches of several denominations besides Anglican Protestant, not to mention other organizations, that are named after "St. George" or have selected "St. George" as their patron "saint." Indeed, like the antichristian "Hiram Abiff" of Freemasonry, "St. George" is said to have died and been resurrected. Since Satan cannot beat Christians, he attempts in a host of ways to co-opt them. To this end, satanic parodies of

---

George's banner (Boutell, 1978 ed., p. 256). For a picture of Charles and Princess Diana sitting in front of a large Union Jack, see Hoey, *Charles & Diana: The Tenth Anniversary,* p. 96.

1. Boutell, 1978 ed., pp. 213, 215. A crowned lion and a dragon serve as the dexter and sinister supporters in the full achievement of the Commonwealth. With this arrangement in mind, we might imagine that a heraldic achievement of Charles', could one day take the place of the Commonwealth's current arms.

2. Boutell, 1978 ed., p. 235.

3. According to Brooke-Little, the proper banner or flag to be used by Anglican Protestant churches was declared by the Earl Marshal in 1938 as follows: "The Banner or Flag proper to be flown upon any Church within the Provinces of Canterbury and York to be the Cross of St. George and in the first quarter an escutcheon of the Arms of the See in which such Church is ecclesiastically situate" (Boutell, 1978 ed., p. 257).

4. As yet another instance, Jamaica's shield of arms, granted by 1661, consists of the Garter Badge of St. George's Cross charged with five golden pineapples (Boutell, 1978 ed., pp. 243, 245-246). "For visits to other Commonwealth Countries the Queen has adopted a special flag consisting of the arms of the Government of the country in question with the central motif on her personal flag over all. For example, the Queen's personal flag for use in Jamaica consists of a banner of the [shield of] arms of Jamaica ... with the motif from her personal flag in the fess point" (Boutell, 1978 ed., p. 258).

5. John E. Titterton, "Royal Arms in Churches," *A Dictionary of Heraldry,* ed. Friar, p. 288. For more information, see ch. 10's section titled "A so-called 'Christian' Heritage," at p. 295.

Christ, preached in a plethora of false gospels, have made the rounds, not just among cultists, but also among ignorant and apostate Christians. Over the centuries, the British monarchy has played a *defining* role in this satanic activity.

The first three degrees of Freemasonry, the Blue Degrees, are common to both the York Rite and the Scottish Rite. These degrees, which are collectively referred to as the Blue Lodge, originated in what is now the United Grand Lodge of England, which is acknowledged by advanced Masons worldwide as the *Mother Lodge* of all Freemasonry.[1] Although few seem to be aware of it, the British monarch, who may serve personally as the grand master of this lodge before *his* coronation as king, installs its grand master, and is, like the Prince of Wales (see below), *over* Freemasonry worldwide.[2]

---

1. The United Grand Lodge of England "has powers to revoke the charter of any Lodge found to be conducting itself in an unworthy, immoral or criminal way." However, "this provision is never implemented" (Knight, *The Brotherhood*, p. 307).

2. The British monarchy has a long history of deep involvement in Freemasonry. Descriptions of some of the masonic involvement and activities of Queen Elizabeth I (1533-1603), Prince Frederick (1737), King George III (1738-1820), King George IV (1762-1830), Duke Edward Augustus (Duke of Kent, 1767-1820), Augustus Frederick (1813-1843), President George Washington (1797), King Edward VII (1841-1910), Greece's King George I (1845-1913), King George V (1865-1936), Greece's Constantine I (George I's son), Alexander Albert Mountbatten (1st Marquess of Carisbrooke, 1886), Greece's King George II (1890-1947), King George VI (1895-1952), Prince George (Duke of Kent, 1902-1942), King Edward VIII (1936), and Queen Elizabeth II may be found on pp. 8-9, 16, 102-105, 107, and 181 in the four volumes of *10,000 Famous Freemasons* by William R. Denslow (1957). Prince Philip and Louis Mountbatten were likewise involved in Freemasonry; their "family name was changed from Battenberg to Mountbatten in 1914 at the outbreak of WW1" (ibid., p. 181). In reading these descriptions, it is interesting to note "Prince of Wales Lodge No. 259, the lodge connected with the royal family" (ibid., p. 181), as well as other "Prince of Wales" lodges, are frequently mentioned, and that a number of the royal personages mentioned above are said to have reached the 33-degree.

   "George, Prince of Wales (later George IV and grand master) [was] initiated in 1787, in a special lodge at the Star and Garter, Pall Mall.... He was initiated in a special lodge, Feb. 6, 1787, meeting at the Star and Garter at London.... He served as grand master of the Grand Lodge of England for 23 years, and in 1805 was grand master of the Grand Lodge of Scotland. When he became king, the Duke of Sussex was elected grand master, and the king took the title of grand patron. The Duke of Sussex, his younger brother, was able to bring about a union of the two English [(actually, English and Scottish)] grand lodges in 1813," thus forming the United Grand Lodge of England (ibid., pp. 102-103). On April 28, 1875, Edward VII was elected grand master of the [United] Grand Lodge of England, and, having been installed by the Earl of Caernarfon, served as such until his ascension to the throne in 1901, when he assumed the title, "protector of the craft" (ibid., p. 8). George V, of the "house of Saxe-Coburg-Gotha, which in 1917 changed its name to the house of Windsor," "became grand patron of the three Masonic charities of the Grand Lodge of England" (ibid., p. 103). Before becoming king, Prince Edward of Wales "was a Freemason and supported the application of Ernest Simpson for admission to a masonic lodge.... [He] was told that it was against the masonic law for the husband of his mistress to be admitted. The Prince gave his word that this was not in fact the situation and Ernest Simpson was admitted" (Lacey, *Majesty*, p. 48). As king, Edward VIII became grand master of the United Grand Lodge of England in 1936 (*10,000 Famous Freemasons*, p. 9). Prince George, Duke of Kent, had ascribed the "commoner" Wallis Simpson's enchantment of Edward VIII, who subsequently abdicated the throne to marry her, "to something approaching sorcery" (Lacey, *Majesty*, p. 47). George VI, who was formerly Prince Albert, as king "accepted the rank of past grand master of the [United] Grand Lodge of England, and was ceremonially installed at the Albert Hall in London before an audience of Masons from all parts of the world.... **He** created the precedent of the English sovereign's active participation in Masonic ceremonies, and **personally conducted the installation of three grand masters —the Duke of Kent at Olympia in 1939; the Earl of Harewood in Freemason's Hall in 1943; and the Duke of Devonshire in Albert Hall in 1948.** Only his last illness prevented his installing the Earl of Scarbrough in 1951.... He held the rank of past grand master, and of knight commander of the Temple,

We should not be surprised, then, by Elizabeth II's and now Charles III's direct oversight of various masonic institutions and activities.[1] With these things in mind, note that the Star and *blue* Garter are specifically referred to in the first degree (Entered Apprentice) of the *Blue* Lodge: "The Lamb-skin ... is ... the badge of a Mason; ... [it is] more honorable than the Star and Garter."[2] According to Albert Pike, who wrote Freemasonry's preeminent work *Morals and Dogma:* "Masonry conceals its secrets from all except the adepts and sages, or the elect, and uses false explanations and misinterpretations of its symbols to mislead those who deserve to be misled, to conceal the truth, which it calls light, from them, and to draw them away from it.... The Blue Degrees are but the outer court or portico of the [masonic] Temple. Part of the symbols are displayed there to the Initiate, but he is <u>intentionally misled by false interpretations</u>. It is not intended that he shall understand them; but it is intended that he shall imagine he understands them. Their true explication is reserved for the Adepts, the Princes of Masonry."[3] *The Royal Masonic Cyclopaedia* defines an Adept as "a name given to the Order of the Illuminati."[4] In other words, the Star and Garter are actually considered to be *more* noble, not less, than Freemasonry.[5] Recall, therefore, that the Duke of Kent, who is currently the most powerful Mason in the world by virtue of being the grand master of the United Grand

was a 33-degree [Mason], and grand inspector general in the Ancient and Accepted Rite of Rose Croix [(meaning, "Red Cross"—of Merovée—and associated with the Rosicrucians)]. Said he of Masonry: 'The world today does require spiritual and moral regeneration. I have no doubt, after many years as a member of our Order, that Freemasonry can play a most important part in this vital need'" (*10,000 Famous Freemasons,* p. 104). **Prince George, Duke of Kent, on "July 19, 1939 ... was formally installed grand master of the Grand Lodge of England by his brother, King George VI. He was killed, August 25, 1942, in an airplane accident"** (ibid., p. 105). His son Edward, the current Duke of Kent, is the grand master of the United Grand Lodge of England today (Knight, *The Brotherhood,* p. 212), and, like his father before him, remains subservient to the British monarch. All this continues (e.g., see "The royal connection: John Hamill examines the link between masonry and royalty," *FreemasonryToday.com,* 14 Dec. 2012).

1. Queen Elizabeth II was, among other things, Grand Patroness "of each of the three Royal Masonic Benevolent Institutions conducted by the Grand Lodge of England—one for old people and one each for boys and girls [(e.g., the Royal Masonic Institution for Boys)]" (*10,000 Famous Freemasons,* pp. 16, 181). (King Charles III is ostensibly now Grand Patron of the same.) A picture of Queen Elizabeth II congratulating a 32-degree Mason, Donald M. Dinning, "upon his receiving The Most Excellent Order of the British Empire in a ceremony held at Buckingham Palace ... on October 25, 1995," is in the May 1996 *Scottish Rite Journal* (Washington: Southern Jurisdiction USA), Vol. CIV, No. 5, p. 41. "It is an interesting anomaly that the Queen, as a woman, is banned from entering a masonic temple—yet she is Grand Patroness of the movement. Her two younger sons are already marked down by the elders of Great Queen Street as possible future Grand Masters" (Knight, *The Brotherhood,* p. 215). Of course, the queen had also headed the Committee of 300, and "only Freemasons of highest rank had any hope of being selected by the Committee of 300" (Coleman, *The Committee of 300,* p. 191).
2. Taylor, *Indiana Monitor and Freemason's Guide,* pp. 58-59. Also, see Albert G. Mackey, *A Manual of the Lodge* (New York: Clark & Maynard Publishers, 1878), pp. 32-33.
3. Albert Pike, *Morals and Dogma,* pp. 104, 819.
4. Kenneth MacKenzie, *The Royal Masonic Cyclopaedia* (England: The Aquarian Press, 1877), p. 18.
5. The Star of the Order of the Garter is eight-pointed with a central red cross. The last three degrees of the York Rite of Freemasonry are Knight of the Red Cross, Knight of Malta, and Temple Knight. Knight Templar corresponds roughly to the thirty-second degree in the Scottish Rite of Freemasonry.

Lodge of England, is subservient to the Monarch of England and the Prince of Wales through his membership in both the Order of the Garter and the Committee of 300.

Regarding *1998's* British monarchy and its participation in the Illuminati and satanism, Springmeier adds:

> Some of what follows may exceed the understanding of the average reader, and will approach the British monarchy from an uncommon angle. This account constitutes an insightful overview of the British royal family and their participation in the Illuminati....
>
> Of great importance in understanding the Illuminati is their mind-control. The Illuminati intentionally create multiple personality disorder (DID) among their people. This means that what the outside world sees is not the whole story. I have firsthand reports from insiders that clearly show that Prince Charles [(now King Charles III)] has a hidden satanic side to him. The British royalty, the Swedish royalty, the Dutch, Belgium and Luxembourg royalty, have all been leading secret satanic lives apart from the awareness of the general public. The insider reports that I have received are simply too accurate and numerous to discount. Where's the proof? That is the difficult part; these people are masters of deceit and have all the finances and power they need to pull off long-term programs of secrecy. In fact, it is required of Illuminati members that they do their rituals from memory, and not write down the things that they do in secret.
>
> The British royal family have long been involved with the occult.[1] They have also been actively involved with Freemasonry. In the early history of the Scottish Rite it served as a front for the Stuart cause. The Stuarts/Stewarts have been closely connected with the leadership of both Freemasonry and the Illuminati.[2] Stillson and Hughan's *History of Freemasonry and Concordant Orders* talks about the leadership the Prince of Wales (later King Edward VII) gave to modern English Templarism, and its masonic orders. A host of masonic sources have given the memberships and some of the details of the British Royal family's masonic activities. Queen Elizabeth II, for example, holds [(did hold, as she's perished)] the position of Grand Patroness of Freemasonry.[3] Sixty-two Lord Mayors of London [(now more)] have been Masters of the Guildhall Masonic Lodge. This lodge has many of the important officials of the City of London, which is the financial capital of not just greater London, but the world. Queen Elizabeth II's [(presumably, now King Charles III's)] coat of arms is one of the 4 coats of arms appearing in the ritual at the crypt inside the Guildhall building to install the lodge's Master.[4]
>
> Ex-Illuminati informants have revealed that the Queen of England *does* [(did)] participate in the Satanic rituals of the Illuminati. [(With Elizabeth II in Hell, King Charles III *continues* to participate.)] In fact, Great Britain is

---

1. For more information, see ch. 10's section titled, "Ties to the New Age Movement, the occult, and false religions," at p. 333.

2. For more information, see the discussion on the Priory of Zion's grand masters in ch. 4, "Prince of this World—a *Diverse* Lineage," at p. 79.

3. Knight, *The Brotherhood,* p. 26. Although Springmeier cites Stephen Knight, much of what Knight had to say reflects only a superficial knowledge of the British monarchy's masonic connections, activities, and roles.

4. Knight, *The Brotherhood,* pp. 216-218.

the mother country of Satanism, and is the center for generational satanism.[1] This is widely known among generational satanists. Obviously then, whoever rules the United Kingdom must tie in powerfully with that satanic power. This explains why Cecil Rhodes and others of the Round Table, like the Rothschilds,[2] wanted to make the world subservient to Great Britain. Note also that the national symbol of Wales is the red dragon (the snake), and for years the chief of Wales was called the dragon. The Gaelic language, which Prince Charles had to learn for his 1969 investiture,[3] is an important language for Satanism, although English and French are also used extensively by the Illuminati; various planning sessions for world dominion, which some ex-Satanists have experienced, were held in French.

The queen [(now King Charles III)] also presides over the Knights of the Order of St. John of Jerusalem, the British Protestant part of the Knights of Malta. Interestingly, the masonic reference book *History of Freemasonry and Concordant Orders,* written by a British masonic board of editors and published in London in 1891, states on page 767 that the Knights of St. John are the real lineal descendants of the original Knights of Malta.

Prince Philip plays [(did play)] a role in Freemasonry, having been initiated into Freemasonry on December 5, 1952. There are conflicting claims as to how important the prince's role is [(was)].... However, when the Grand Master of the United Grand Lodge of England was named in 1966, Prince Philip had allowed the Queen's cousin, the 30-year old Duke of Kent, to have the position, even though he could have had it.

Prince Charles' private secretary, the [(late)] Hon. Edward Adeane, son of Lt-Col. the Rt. Hon. Lord Michael Adeane, is [(had been)] a devoted Freemason, but Charles has not publicly joined Freemasonry. The prince [(now King Charles III)] has participated in satanic rituals, had Druids at his investiture, etc., but has not publicly made statements which would unequivocally confirm that he is a Freemason.[4] Prince Charles travels all over the world participating in important behind the scenes meetings, and, like Queen Elizabeth II [(before she died)], he is a central member of the Order of the Garter, which is, among other things, an elite group of satanic aristocratic Knights of the Illuminati who control the plans for bringing in the New World Order. The American branch of this is the Society of the Cincinnati. There is also an Irish, Scottish and French counterpart to the Order of the Garter. Charles, who was taught at the important elite school of Gordonstoun, used by the Illuminati,[5] was close to Lord Louis Mountbatten, another major Illuminati figure,[6] until he was assassinated. The prince has

---

1. Brought out in interviews by Fritz Springmeier with numerous ex-witches and ex-satanists.
2. "The Rothschilds have been Freemasons for generations" (Knight, *The Brotherhood,* p. 222).
3. Of Charles' investiture, Junor remarks, "His triumph had been the Welsh, a difficult language..., which he had spoken easily and fluently," being "the first English Prince of Wales ever to speak and understand Welsh." The president of Plaid Cymru commented: "His performance was amazing. I have never heard anyone who has taken to Welsh so recently master the language so well" (pp. 78, 88).
4. Actually, Charles has made indirect statements in favor of masonic beliefs, statements which clearly show that his own world-view harmonizes with that of the most occult Masons. For more information, see ch. 10's section titled, "A so-called 'Christian' heritage," at p. 295.
5. A symbol that may be a precursor to the capstone of the Seal of the Illuminati forms the relief over an entrance to the Gordonstoun grounds (see Junor, between pp. 86-87). For more information, see the discussions on Gordonstoun in ch. 10's section titled, "Ties to the New Age Movement, the occult, and false religions," and in ch. 11's section titled, "The United World Colleges," at pages 333 and 394, respectively.
6. Junor notes that Mountbatten "was the man charged with giving India her independence in 1947, and who presided over some of the bloodiest religious massacres in history, that resulted in the partition of

rubbed shoulders with the Rothschilds [(some of whom married into his family)], Juan Carlos [I], the Pope, Israeli leaders, etc., and he appears to play some type of major role for the Illuminati behind the scenes, besides his public role....

The British royalty have served as important figureheads to British Freemasonry, lending credibility and respectability. British Freemasonry has managed to keep itself free from much of the criticism that the other national masonic groups have brought on themselves. However, much of the credibility of British Freemasonry is undeserved. True, it is what it portrays itself to be to the public for the lower levels. But the lower level Masons, by their dues and activities, are unwittingly supporting an organization that is led by satanists at the top.

An example of the subterfuge constantly exercised on the public by Freemasonry is a book purportedly written by a non-Mason entitled *The Unlocked Secret Freemasonry Examined*. The book portrays itself as an unbiased and complete exposé of Freemasonry. It states unequivocally that the masonic order called *Societas Rosicrucian in Anglia* [sic] is only open to Christians and is a "Christian Order." However, Edith Starr Miller reprints copies of a number of letters from the chief of the *Societas Rosicrucian in Anglia* (SRIA) which show that the English Grand Masonic Lodge (United Grand Lodge of England), the SRIA, the *Ordo Templi Orientis* or Order of Oriental Templars (also known as the OTO or *Ordo To Ov*), and the German Illuminati are all working together. She briefly explains how she obtained the letters.[1]

Barons, Dukes, Counts, Earls and Knights have been getting involved with the European secret occult societies for centuries. These secret societies are not only being manipulated to serve as fronts for the Illuminati to bring in their New World Order, but also to enrich these Illuminati kingpins through criminal activities. Allow me to give just a brief peek at some of the characters who tie in with the British royal family, who are participating in all this secret activity.

James H. Carey [(now deceased)], one of the Rockefeller's Chase Manhattan Bank officers, is [(was)] also a Knight of the Order of St. John, which Queen Elizabeth II heads [(now under King Charles III)]. The queen likewise

---

the sub-continent into India and Pakistan" (p. 139). He "was a dynamic, tyrannical figure, full of energy and drive and wisdom.... He was a national hero, he had been Supreme Commander in South East Asia during the Second World War, the last Viceroy and first Governor General of India, First Sea Lord, and finally Chief of the Defense Staff. He had spent twenty-three years at the top, he had traveled all over the world.... Charles had been devoted to him ever since he was a small boy.... Obsessed with the concept of the Royal Family, Mountbatten saw it as his role in life to keep it going as a healthy popular institution. He was one of Queen Victoria's great-grandchildren, like George VI.... [When] the name Mountbatten finally became hyphenated to Windsor in 1960 he was a happy man." In determining then Prince Charles' future education and his Naval service, it was Mountbatten's recommendation that prevailed (ibid., pp. 62-64). Yet Mountbatten was a womanizer and known sodomite (i.e., a "bisexual"), just like the Duke of Kent, as well as a pedophile interested in teenage boys. According to Satan's Prince, although Mountbatten "could certainly be ruthless with people when the occasion demanded, ... people would have followed him into Hell, if he had explained the point of such an expedition." (We may wonder, "Did Mountbatten explain it to Charles?") Having planned his own epitaph and funeral, "a blend of military and international, attended by dignitaries from all over the world," in advance, Mountbatten wrote, "His personal leadership, as long ago as 1945, helped to set the line on which the British Empire changed itself into the Commonwealth of sovereign states" (ibid., pp. 143-145). We may add, "Mountbatten made it to Hell, but not back!"

1. Edith Starr Miller [Paget] (aka Edith Queenborough), *Occult Theocracy* (1933), Appendix IV, pp. 8-35.

knighted Sir Y.K. Pao, who also sits [(did)] on the board of Chase Manhattan. Pao is a major figure in the Illuminati Asian drug smuggling.[1]

Another key figure for the British Crown is Louis Mortimer Bloomfield, a third Knight of St. John. Bloomfield has been [(was)] the Crown's top secret intelligence man in North America, operating out of Jamaica. He was an intermediary between Winston Churchill and FDR, and was instrumental in merging American and British intelligence operations during World War II. *They have never been unmerged.* Bloomfield was part of the American OSS. As such, he set up a long list of corporations which were used as fronts to invest in Permindex, a "trade organization" hiding one of the Illuminati's most powerful assassination groups. Bloomfield has been [(was)] instrumental in helping draft UN regulations against hijacking and terrorism. (The fox guards the chickens.)

Eagle Star Insurance Company has been one of the Illuminati's top Canadian financial institutions. N.M. Rothschilds & Sons, Barclay's Bank, Hill Samuel, and Lloyds are all involved with it. MI-6's two top men, Sir Kenneth Keith and Sir Kenneth Strong, were Eagle Star directors. Behind the guise of Great Britain's and Canada's Official Secrets Act, MI-6 has run drugs worldwide for the Illuminati.

British MI-6 has been a major vehicle for the Satanic hierarchy working behind the secret veil of Freemasonry to control world events.[2] It is the most secret large intelligence organization in the world.[3]

Finally, it should be noted in this overview, which shows how England is the center for the Illuminati, that the AntiChrist is claimed to have his present-day throne in a London suburb.... In a nutshell, this article has tried to give an overview of how deeply enmeshed the British royal family is within the Illuminati, as well as of the extent of the monarchy's activities at the highest levels of the occult hierarchy. The British royal family is extremely wealthy and extremely powerful, much more so than people imagine. The queen [(now the king)], for a typical example, appoints Canada's Governor-General. Also, there is no question that Prince Charles plays an important role in the World System from behind the scenes.[4]

Further occult ties. Garter knights are now permitted to compass their shields with the Garter, outside of which they may also place the Collar and its pendant.[5] Like the arms of other British royalty since 1837, the deep-blue Garter encircles the royal shield in Charles' arms.[6] There is more to this satanic arrangement than we have so far discussed. As noted earlier, a roundel of the Merovingian cross is hidden on the royal shield with its encircling Garter. What we have not until now pointed out, however, is that the two ends of the

---

1. Sir Y.K. Pao's drug overlord role has been discussed in publications from *Executive Intelligence Review.* See, for example, *Dope, Inc.* (Washington, D.C.: EIR, 1992), pp. 215-218.
2. Confidential interviews conducted by Fritz Springmeier.
3. David Wise and Thomas B. Ross, *The Espionage Establishment,* p. 79. British MI6 is properly known as the British Secret Service, and should not be confused with the U.S. agency by the same name, which performs a different function entirely.
4. Written correspondence, quoted by permission, from Springmeier.
5. Boutell, 1978 ed., p. 193.
6. Boutell, 1978 ed., p. 217.

Garter are joined and folded in such a way as to give the impression that one end is swallowing the other, like a "serpent swallowing its own tail." As shown below, this is intentional, and has Templar and Rosicrucian origins. Likewise, the Collar's original twenty-six roundels of St. George's cross and its current Tudor roses, each surrounded by the Garter as above, as well as the Garter Star itself, were derived from the earlier symbolism of the Temple Knights and the Rosicrucians: "The god of the Rosicrucians is symbolized by the 'zero': a circle created by <u>the serpent swallowing its own tail</u>. This symbol was superimposed on the [Merovingian, anti-]Christian cross with a sunburst surrounding the circle. The circle also represented the sun, as well as the 'eye' of Osiris, the Egyptian sun-god."[1] The eight-pointed chipped-silver and enamel Garter Star, besides representing the "sunburst surrounding the circle," is similar in design to the "Knights Templar star jewels" of English Freemasonry, which, in place of the central red cross surrounded by the Garter, bear a central cross intertwined with a serpent in front of a brilliant light, a skull and crossbones, a casket, and a dagger lying in what appears to be a pool of blood, all circumferenced by a motto bearing the Latin *Memento Mori,* meaning "death warning."[2] The point, of course, is that all this is directly or indirectly associated with the Garter on Charles' heraldic achievements.

We may also note that similar imagery—what appears to be a serpent intertwining a pole intersected by the perpendicular side of a triangle (cf. the central cross intertwined with a serpent) in front of a half-darkened sun representing the Zoroastrian concept of the conflict between good and evil (cf. a brilliant light), and a large, seemingly casket-shaped, black natural magnet (cf. a skull and crossbones, a casket, and a dagger), perhaps intended to act as a hallucinogenic catalyst like a drug—comprises the occult Meditation Room at the United Nations, where "followers of all religions, who visit by the hundreds of thousands each year, may [currently] awaken the 'god within.'"[3] This room, which is designed to look like a pyramid lying on its side with the above three-dimensional imagery in place of the capstone (i.e., at the front of the room), has just enough seats to accommodate eleven individuals—the AntiChrist and ten kings.[4] Recall that the red lion and ten other lions—*Tarshish*

1. John Daniel, *Scarlet and the Beast,* Vol. I, 2nd ed. (Texas: Jon Kregel, Inc., 1995), p. 30.
2. For a picture, see Michael Baigent and Richard Leigh, *The Temple and the Lodge* (New York: Arcade Publishing, Inc., 1989), above caption 32, between pp. 194-195.
3. Hunt, *GLOBAL PEACE AND THE RISE OF ANTICHRIST,* p. 275. For a picture of this room, see Church, p. 47, or John Daniel, *Scarlet and the Beast,* Vol. I, 2nd ed. (1995), p. 749.
4. Describing the United Nations' Meditation Room and one related to it in Washington, Church observes: "It ... represents a pyramid turned over on its side. The room is very dimly lit. The only source of light comes from a special lens recessed in the ceiling which focuses a beam of light on the altar in the center

and all its young lions—are represented *within the Garter* on Charles' heraldic achievement as Prince of Wales.[1] Lucis Trust (for "Lucifer Trust") published this advertisement, originally giving the organization's return address as "866 United Nations Plaza," in *Reader's Digest* in October 1982 and again in December 1991: "From the point of Light within the Mind of God, Let light stream forth into the minds of men. Let Light descend on Earth. From the point of Love within the Heart of God, Let love stream forth into the hearts of men. May Christ return to Earth. From the centre where the Will of God is known, Let purpose guide the little wills of men—The purpose which the Masters know and serve. From the centre which we call the race of men, Let the Plan of Love and Light work out, And may it seal the door where evil dwells. Let Light and Love and Power restore the Plan on Earth." According to Lucis Trust, "The Great Invocation belongs to all humanity," and "millions ... daily use this prayer to invoke peace on earth .... for only through humanity can the Plan work out." This blasphemous advertisement, which has non-American English spelling, prominently displays a rose inside a circle.[2] We may note that in 1988, along with a few other men wearing red roses, then Prince Charles visited the *Pyramide du Louvre* in Paris, France.[3]

"Organizational" ties to witchcraft. In witchcraft, a coven consists of 13 persons, including a high priest or priestess. Early members—knights, officers, etc.—of the Order of the Garter, which

of the room. The altar is four feet high; it is a dark gray block of crystalline iron ore .... the largest of its kind ever mined .... described as a lodestone or magnetite. It is strongly magnetic and possesses polarity. On April 24, 1957, the late Dag Hammarskjold, UN Secretary General, described this pagan stone as an altar to universal religion. He said, 'The altar is the symbol of the god of all.' The picture or mural at the front of the room ... was painted to open up the wall, to give a feeling of space, of the void—in effect, to extend the room farther out to another dimension. The theme of the mural is infinity.... The circle near the center of the painting represents the All-Seeing Eye. There is a vertical line down the center of the mural with waving lines around it. It is said to represent the tree of life. It may also represent the serpent in the tree. [According to Spenser, 'the] .... Meditation Room is constructed in the shape of a wedge .... [a] pyramid with the apex cut off.' Another prayer room dedicated to the All-Seeing Eye can be found in the United States Capitol building in Washington, D.C.... The lighting in this Meditation Room is subdued. The concealed light focuses on a white oak altar, similar to the light in the U.N. Meditation Room. There are ten chairs facing the altar, just as there are ten chairs in the United Nations Meditation Room. Ten?... Above the altar in the stained glass window the unfinished pyramid with its capstone containing the All-Seeing Eye is prominently displayed. The New Age Movement, with its roots in the ancient Order of the Knights Templar, has been 'working to set up a universal theocratic state. Already the high priests, the prayers, and the temples of this universal cult are with us'" (pp. 151-153). Church mentions a third meditation room at the Pentagon, which again contains the Luciferic "all-seeing eye" (p. 166).

1. For more information, see this chapter's earlier section titled, "The royal shield and the arms of the Principality of Wales," at p. 137.
2. For pictures of this advertisement, see John Daniel, *Scarlet and the Beast,* Vol. I, 2nd ed., pp. 742-743. An earlier satanic invocation, given by a "spirit guide" to Alice Bailey (the founder of Lucis Trust) in 1940, reads: "Come forth, O Mighty One, The hour of service of the Saving Force has now arrived. Let it be spread abroad, O Mighty One. Let Light and Love and Power and Death Fulfill the purpose of the Coming One" (Brian E. Weiss, "World Goodwill Update," *Hope for the World Update,* Fall 1995, p. 5).
3. *Charles & Diana: A Royal Family Album,* p. 55.

included several of the first heralds of England's *College of Heraldry,* engaged in various covert activities throughout France. Originally established by Edward III for use by the order, and later made an official part of the Royal Household by Richard III's charter in 1484,[1] the College of Heraldry is organized into a *coven* of 13 heralds, including pursuivants (assistant-heralds who aspire to the office of Herald), and is the oldest and most powerful heraldic body in the world.[2] The college's senior heralds (Garter, Clarenceux, and Norroy *and* Ulster) are each styled "King of Heralds" or "King of Arms," with the most powerful among them being called the "Principal King of Arms." A version of the Garter Badge of St. George's Cross, with a blue (azure) dove placed in each of its four quarters, serves as the arms of the Herald's College.[3] The college's reach extends throughout the British Commonwealth and beyond, to include even the United States.[4] The highest ranking herald in the college, and therefore the world, is the *Garter, Principal King of Arms.* His office as Herald dates to 1415.[5] It was this herald—Sir Anthony R. Wagner at the time—who (with heralds under him) created Charles' heraldic achievement as Prince of Wales, though the design was clearly not one of his own imagination.[6] Today, as it has been ever since the decline of feudalism, "her-

---

1. Boutell, 1978 ed., p. 262. James and Russell, *At Home with the Royal Family,* p. 144.
2. More specifically, officers of the College of Arms or Heralds' College consist of "three [Herald] Kings of Arms—Garter, Clarenceux, and Norroy *and* Ulster; six Heralds—Lancaster, Somerset, Chester, Richmond, Windsor and York; and four [Herald] Pursuivants—Rouge Dragon, Rouge Croix, Portcullis and Bluemantle," for a total of thirteen heralds. Indicating the importance of the Heralds' College to the Order of the Garter, Rouge Dragon Pursuivant is named for the red dragon of Wales, Rouge Croix Pursuivant is named after the red cross of "St. George," and Bluemantle Pursuivant is named after the dark blue Garter Mantle. "From time to time officers of arms who are not members of the corporation of the College of Arms are appointed by warrant under the [King's or] Queen's sign manual. The duties of these officers, styled 'extras ordinary' [(i.e., extraordinary)], are purely ceremonial.... Frequently such officers are appointed at the time of a coronation and in many cases people so appointed become offer-in ordinary when vacancies occur." Extraordinary *offices* are currently those of Norfolk Herald, Arundel Herald, and Fitzalan Pursuivant. In 1963, for the first time since the end of the fourteenth century, an appointment was also made to the extraordinary office of Wales Herald (Boutell, 1978 ed., p. 263). Extraordinary heralds and pursuivants are not part of the Heralds' College. The thirteen heralds and pursuivants of the College of Arms precede the English monarch in various ceremonies, including the State Opening of Parliament (James and Russell, *At Home with the Royal Family,* pp. 141, 145-146, 197).
3. Boutell, 1978 ed., pp. 231-233, 260-261.
4. Boutell, 1978 ed., p. 268.
5. Although he is "associated particularly with the Order of the Garter," the Principal King of Arms is "empowered also to exercise a general supervision over the other Herald Kings" (Boutell, 1978 ed., p. 262). James and Russell, *At Home with the Royal Family,* pp. 144, 196.
6. Genealogy plays a major role in the determination and creation of an individual's heraldic achievement. For this reason, the early heralds "inevitably ... had to concern themselves with genealogy in connection with cadency and the marshalling of arms" (Boutell, 1978 ed., pp. 261-262; see also pp. 269-270). (The genealogical research of the College of Heraldry is perhaps rivaled only by that of the more recent Mormon cult.) "Since at least 1418, it has been impossible to acquire a legal title to armorial bearings by any other method than inheritance according to the laws of arms, or a grant or confirmation of arms from the duly constituted authorities.... Conjectural descent is inadmissible. A person who bears a device of heraldic appearance invented by himself or an ancestor, and neither granted nor confirmed by the King of Arms, is in fact not armigerous, and the device is not a legal coat of arms." From the fifteenth century to 1686, the laws of arms were periodically enforced by the heralds, through the re-

alds are found only in the Royal service;" for "more than 500 years ago, the Crown assumed the full control of armorial bearings, and has ever since exercised it through Officers of Arms appointed for the purpose."[1]

The high priestess of a coven wears a garter to which at least one horseshoe-shaped buckle is attached—one for each coven over which she presides. When two or more covens have "hived off" from a high priestess' coven, she attains the title of "Witch Queen." The Garter of the Order of the Garter is edged with two rows of 169 miniature gold buckles of the type described above, each representing a coven of 13 witches for a total of 169 x 13, or 2,197, witches.[2] That is, it depicts two covens of covens of a coven (2 x 13 covens x 13 covens x 13 witches = 4,394 witches)—one coven of covens of a coven (1 x 13 x 13 x 13 = 2,197) for the sovereign and another for the Prince of Wales. The order's primary membership consists of twenty-six "companion knights," or the sovereign plus twelve knights (13) and the Prince of Wales plus twelve knights (13). Each Garter knight, therefore, is represented as the priest or priestess of a coven of covens (26 x 13 x 13 = 4,394), making each a Witch King or a Witch Queen. The British sovereign, then, is depicted as a Witch King or Witch Queen of Witch Kings and Witch Queens, as is the Prince of Wales. A *witch*—Joan of Kent, the Countess of Salisbury, who later became the Princess of Wales—played a prominent role in Edward III's selection of the Garter as a central symbol of the order.

Interestingly, Charles is the *thirteenth* Prince of Wales to be formally invested. Despite being over Freemasonry worldwide, he was once rumored to have been "secretly initiated into a north London Lodge that practised Black Magic."[3] Moreover, he married *Diana,*

---

moval and/or defacement of unlawful arms and other heraldic devices, under the authority of various royal commissions (Boutell, 1978 ed., pp. 262-263, 264). James and Russell make similar points (*At Home with the Royal Family,* p. 146). Nevertheless, the heralds have historically dealt with armorial disputes through the "Court of Chivalry," over which the Constable and Earl Marshal, the Duke of Norfolk, preside. Although the Marshal, "styled Earl Marshal since 1386," ultimately became recognized, since his office is hereditary, as the Officer of State to whom all the heralds were responsible, Scotland's Lyon King of Arms was granted independence from both the Constable and Marshal early on, and, being separate from the College of Arms, receives his office directly from the sovereign. The Lyon King of Arms possesses his own judicial powers and status through the "Court of the Lord Lyon." Today, disputes regarding armorial matters continue to be addressed in the Court of Chivalry and, for Scotland, in the Court of the Lyon King of Arms (Boutell, 1978 ed., pp. 261, 263; see also pp. 231-232). For more information related to the ancient and modern laws of arms, see, for example, Boutell, pp. 261-265.

1. Boutell, 1978 ed., pp. 261, 264.
2. For a color picture of the deep-blue Garter, as well as the Collar with the Marlborough Great George suspended from the center, Star, and Lesser George, see Begent, *The Most Noble Order of the Garter, Its History and Ceremonial,* cover and p. 3.
3. Knight, *The Brotherhood,* p. 5. Knight's information is to be taken with a grain of salt. For example, he wrote that then Prince Charles, due to being "a committed (as opposed to nominal) Christian," like his grandmother, refused to "be initiated and take over from the Duke of Kent" on his twenty-first birthday. However, Satan's Prince has *never* been a Christian, let alone a committed one. Nor ever was his grandmother, the "Queen Mother." Knight, recognizing at least some limits to his own information, admit-

whose namesake is the patron "goddess" of witchcraft (representing chastity, fertility, the Moon, and hunting among other things), "whom all Asia and the world worship" (Acts 19:27; cf. 19:23-36), *on the one day that witches are "sealed" each year*—July 29![1] Indeed, since her death *or sacrifice*,[2] Diana has literally been "deified" on the Internet, where wiccan and other pagan prayers (e.g., Buddhist, "Christian," Hindu, Islamic, Jewish, New Age, and Sikh) have been posted not just on her behalf, but *to her!*[3] As if this were not revolting enough, idols of Diana have even begun to join those of Mary in Nativity scenes, and a cult of Diana worship is taking shape to rival that of Roman Catholicism's Mary worship: "But a new figure has joined those in the crib: a large statue of Princess Diana. Italy is not alone in ... stirrings of Diana worship.... At first glance, <u>Diana prophecies</u> appear to be Christian. They promise a spiritual millennium, the working of the Lord's spirit through the world and an overcoming of sorrow—all familiar themes.... Christian fundamentalists may only see Diana as a minor saint, if that, but she may appeal much more strongly as a goddess to the pagan unbelievers who make up the majority of Western society.... Mohammed.... Buddha.... Christianity.... Now, ... our society is threatened by science, machines and rationalism. The cult of Diana offers compassion, a war on machines and beauty linked with femininity. Will Diana be our next goddess? We can only guess. But a feminine goddess seems a safe prediction. It may not be Diana; she may be only a John the Baptist coming to announce a new earth. It might be Gaia, the new goddess of the earth worshipped by ecologists, but it will be female.... It may then be a thousand years before we begin to think for ourselves again."[4]

Garter development in history. In 1337, King Edward III commenced a protracted war with France, claiming the right to the French throne through his French mother Isabella, and in 1340, he assumed the title, "King of France." His son, Edward the Black

---

ted: "There was talk that Charles 'was not strictly against Freemasonry', but that he simply had no wish to become involved.... I failed miserably to ascertain more clearly Charles's current thinking on the subject.... Even Sir George Young, former Vice Chief of MI6, told me that the extent of his knowledge about Freemasonry was that 'the Royal Family are all in it'" (ibid., pp. 212-214, 290). Actually, Charles' beliefs perfectly accord with those of masonry (see ch. 10's section titled, "A so-called 'Christian' heritage," at p. 295). Moreover, whether or not he is a mason is, practically speaking, irrelevant. That is, Charles has *no* great need to fraternize with the masonic rank and file, especially when one considers the fact that he is already over Freemasonry worldwide, by virtue of his position within the Order of the Garter.

1. Where the media and the public are concerned, Diana certainly personified such a role.
2. For more information, see ch. 10's section titled "Death of a princess," at p. 320.
3. When the first edition of this book came out, such pagan prayers to the late Princess Diana were posted under a web page titled "Into the Light". That is now archived at "https://web.archive.org/web/20000226102918/http://www.royalnetwork.com/hearts/light.html".
4. Myles Harris, "I predict Diana will be a goddess," *International Express,* U.S. Ed., 16 Dec. 1997, p. 8.

Prince, whose title ostensibly derived from his black heraldic sur-coat, later carried the war on in his stead. Concerning this war and the Order of the Garter, Scott-Guiles comments,

> Of the origin of the Most Noble Order we know little. According to its historian, Ashmole, it commemorated an occasion when King Edward [III] had "given forth his own garter as the signal for a battle"....
> So the order may have been intended as a revival of the mythical Round Table.... Even so the symbolism of the Garter itself remains ob-scure.... Ashmole regarded the Garter as an emblem of "unity in society."
> ....The motto of the Order is a denunciation of those who think ill of some specific project, and not a mere pious invocation of evil upon evil-thinkers in general. "Shame be to him who thinks ill *of it*" was probably directed against anyone who should oppose the King's design on the French crown.... All things considered, it seems highly likely that the Order originally represented the assembly of chivalry to aid King Edward of Eng-land to become King Edward of France.[1]

Scott-Guiles' understanding is only partially correct. The Order of the Garter was founded not only as a continuation of the legend of King Arthur's Round Table, with all the mysticism and occultism that entails, but also as the overseer of the inner circles of the Priory of Zion, the Knights Templar, and the Rosicrucians, with the Temple Knights having just been thrust out of France and Europe.[2] Very loosely speaking, where French Freemasonry tends to be atheistic, and was a precursor to Socialism and Communism,[3] English Freemasonry is more spiritualistic, and was a precursor to Capital-ism and Fascism.[4] The Order of the Garter, already having had the secret advantage of the Priory of Zion, the Templars, and the Rosicru-cians, wanted clear control not just of English, but also of French Freemasonry. By the order's reasoning, this would enable it to play the two sides of masonic dominion against one another, as often as necessary, to consolidate its own power structures, such as the more recent Committee of 300, *at the top*—in its own hidden, amoral thrust for world domination *at nearly any price*.[5] Moreover, it would enable the order to experiment with different systems of govern-

---

1. Scott-Guiles, pp. 93-96. Contrary to the Garter motto, the apostle Paul admonished the saints, saying, "See that none render evil for evil unto any *man*" (1 Th 5:15).
2. For more information, see ch. 4, "Prince of this World—a *Diverse* Lineage," at p. 79.
3. Bruce Lockhart, in *Memoirs of a British Agent*, however, shows that the Bolshevik Revolution was con-trolled from London (Coleman, *The Committee of 300*, p. 357).
4. According to John Daniel, English Freemasonry currently dominates "Great Britain, Canada, Northeast USA (Eastern Establishment), most oriental countries, Hong Kong, Australia, and South Africa," whereas French Freemasonry dominates "[the] Continent of Europe, southern and Western U.S.A., former U.S.S.R., Pacific Islands, Philippines, Latin and South America, [and] Africa (has recently taken over South Africa) [sic]" (*Scarlet and the Beast*, Vol. I, 2nd ed., pp. 56-57).
5. As mentioned earlier in this section, the world can thank the British monarchy—with its Order of the Garter and Committee of 300—for fomenting World Wars I and II, much of the Arab-Israeli conflict, and more, in the past century alone.

ment on a vast scale, all the while improving the implements of war, in a secondary effort to discover those elements most useful to the final construction of a New World Order, which, it has now been determined, is to constitute a global slave state after the *Platonic ideal*.[1]

It was in this vein that the modern Illuminati began—when Adam Weishaupt, under the apparent indirect influence of the Order of the Garter, infiltrated the masonic lodges of France starting on May 1, 1776.[2] According to Coleman, "the French Revolution was organized and run out of England by Jeremy Bentham and William Petty, the Earl of Shelburne," by means of "the secret Quator Coronati Lodge in London, and the Nine Sister Lodge in Paris."[3] Christians have heard that the Illuminati had certain outward goals, among which were the abolition of oligarchies and governments, the destruction of the major religions, and the elimination of the family unit, patriotism, and private ownership, along with a parallel introduction of communal education for children.[4] What has perhaps not been realized, however, is that the real agenda of the Illuminati appears not to have been to introduce total societal chaos, as is so commonly believed; rather, it was to eliminate and subdue *all* the British monarchy's potential competition and opposition, while simultaneously aiding its rise to global dominance!

The British monarchy clearly *is* on top. In fact, the pyramidal Seal of the Illuminati had a combined Templar and Garter *precursor*, dating to no later than the early fourteenth century. In this precursor, the capstone containing a roundel of the "all-seeing eye" of Lucifer was instead shown as a roundel of "St. George's cross"—or, according to the Rosicrucian view, the "eye" of the Egyptian sun-god Osiris, as well as a serpent swallowing its own tail superimposed on the Merovingian cross—with the whole placed over a shield having a

---

1. For more information, see ch. 11's section titled, "The United World Colleges," at p. 394.
2. The creation of the Illuminati was as much the British Crown's answer to the Declaration of Independence of the United States as it was an attempt to continue the quest for control of France. In fact, through the sublime and covert tools of Freemasonry, the Illuminati, and the Committee of 300, as well as several other secret agencies, the Order of the Garter has gained significant control of far more, including not just France and the United States, where it still "calls the shots," but also the entire British Commonwealth. Moreover, in key respects—such as environmentally and financially—the Order of the Garter controls the machinery of the United Nations, a Committee of 300 creation and stepchild. Should the British monarchy succeed in becoming the monarchy of the European Union, it will undoubtedly seek world hegemony through direct "democratic" control of the United Nations' Security Council. For more information, see ch. 2, "A Man for Our Times," at p. 51.
3. Coleman, *The Committee of 300*, p. xii.
4. Arno Clemens Gaebelein, *The Conflict of the Ages* (Windward Islands, British West Indies: Pryor N. Russell, 1968), p. 72.

serpentine banner (right).[1] This symbol may be seen today just above the piscina in the south chapel of the Templar church at Garway, Herefordshire (near the Welsh border)—where, in a foreshadowing of Scottish Rite Freemasonry,[2] it unites a fish for Christianity and a serpent for Satanism beneath its banner.[3]

We see then that the encircled Merovingian cross is *a* symbolic origin of, and directly represents, the "all-seeing eye" of Lucifer (e.g., in the capstone of the pyramidal Seal of the Illuminati). As discussed earlier, the red Merovingian cross is hidden in the straight horizontal and vertical edges of the two red quarters of the royal shield. Moreover, it is surrounded by the Garter, one end of which is folded to represent a serpent swallowing its own tail. In other words, the satanic "all-seeing eye" is symbolically central to British royal coats of arms, and is depicted at the very heart of Charles' heraldic achievement as Prince of Wales. Notice as well that the overall layout of Charles' heraldic achievement as Prince of Wales, which is somewhat "pyramidal," bears two interesting similarities to the layout of the Seal of the Illuminati. *First,* at the achievement's base, we find a "scroll" bearing a German motto; heraldically, this motto plainly states that he serves the red dragon or Satan.[4] Above the ends of this scroll, and artistically connected to them, we see the outer legs and tails of the dexter and sinister supporters, respectively. Likewise, at the base of the modern achievement or Seal of the Illuminati, we find a scroll with a Latin motto that translates as "New Order of the Ages" or "New World Order"; attached to the ends of this scroll, are tail-like "serpents heads." A side by side or superimposed comparison of the two achievements makes the visual resemblance apparent. *Second,* just as the pyramidal Seal of the Illuminati is comprised of a small pyramid containing the "all-seeing eye" (i.e., the capstone) above a larger pyramid (i.e., the pyramidal base without its capstone), so too is the presence of the "all-seeing

---

1. The triangular capstone on the Seal of the Illuminati also bears a resemblance to the counter-seal of Mary de St. Paul, who, as the granddaughter of Beatrice (Edward I's sister) and John de Dreux (the Duke of Brittany), founded Pembroke College in 1373. Besides displaying a triangle containing a roundel (like the capstone), this seal has three adjacent roundels which contain the arms of England, France, and De Dreux (Boutell, 1978 ed., pp. 132-133). The Seal of the Illuminati, which forms the counter-seal of the Great Seal of the United States (as shown on the dollar bill), conforms *precisely* to the design of early *British* seals (Boutell, 1978 ed., pp. 273-274).

2. For more information, see ch. 4, "Prince of this World—a *Diverse* Lineage," and ch. 10's section titled, "A so-called 'Christian' heritage," at pp. 79 and 295, respectively.

3. For a picture of this scene, see Baigent, Leigh, and Lincoln, *Holy Blood, Holy Grail,* just below caption 32, between pp. 240-241. Although these authors seem to have no clue as to the heraldic derivation or meaning of the image, they were helpful enough to show it. For other information, see Baigent and Leigh, *The Temple and the Lodge,* captions 8-10, between pp. 66-67.

4. For more information, see this chapter's later sections, "The base of the coat of arms" through "The red dragon, or Satan," beginning on p. 185. Also, see ch. 8, "The Red Dragon and Prince Charles' Investiture as Prince of Wales," at p. 207.

eye" suggested at the top of Charles' *unofficial* heraldic achievement as Satan's Prince, in which a smaller version of the dexter lion-leop-ard-bear beast, representing Charles himself, has *just one open eye.*[1] *Will King Charles III one day lose or sacrifice an eye as the An-tiChrist?*

In 1801, not long after 1776, by an interesting "coincidence," the arms of France were omitted from Britain's royal shield, the conve-nient occasion being the union with Ireland, though they remain on the badge of the "Garter, Principal King of Arms." In this capacity, the Garter motto alludes, historically, to an attempted takeover of France—something that perhaps bears an interesting message for us now. France, like the United Kingdom, is an integral part of the modern European Union. Could it be, therefore, that in the appear-ance of the Garter on Charles' coats of arms, there is an allusion to the eventual takeover of the EU by the AntiChrist, whose intent will appear to be to promote "unity in society"? Should King Charles III one day exercise authority over the EU, he will have achieved that which Edward III and the Black Prince presumably sought. Today, it appears that the Order of the Garter essentially controls the Illumi-nati not just in the West, but also in the East through the Committee of 300 and other means.

Garter mimicry of God's heavenly order. Of course, there is more to be said about the Order of the Garter, particularly regarding the composition of its membership, which as mentioned above, pri-marily consists of twenty-six "companion knights." These twenty-six knights first-of-all include the sovereign and his (or her) eldest son, the Prince of Wales. Further, when the sovereign or, as has occasion-ally occurred, the sovereign's eldest son, invests a new knight, two supporting knights are present. Stephen Slater remarks,

> When a new knight is invested, the sovereign presides over the Chapter of the Order in the Throne Room at Windsor Castle.... Knights Elect are pre-sented to the sovereign by Black Rod, Garter King of Arms and two sup-porting knights. The sovereign personally secures the Garter, places the Riband and Lesser George over the left shoulder, affixes the Star and in-vests the knight with the Mantle and Collar. At the same time the Admoni-tion is read. This takes the same form as in the time of the Tudors, and possibly earlier. The Admonition upon Putting on the Mantle, for example, is:
>
> > Receive this Robe of heavenly colour, the Livery of this Most Excellent Or-der in Augmentation of thine Honour, ennobled with the shield and red Cross of our Lord, by whose power thou mayest safely pierce troops of thine enemies, and be over them ever victorious, and being in this tempo-

---

1. For more information, see the discussion on the lion crest in this chapter's earlier section entitled, "The top of the arms," at p. 135.

ral warfare glorious, in egregious and heroic actions, thou mayest obtain eternal and triumphant joy.[1]

Like the true origins of the Order of the Garter, the organization of its membership is thought to be somewhat mysterious. Yet it seems plausible that, among other things, it actually represents a satanic mimicry of God's heavenly organization. We read in the Apocalypse that John saw twenty-four elders in heaven before the throne of The Father and His Son. Similarly, there are twenty-four companion knights in the Garter, in addition to the sovereign and his (or her) eldest son. Also, just as God has appointed two witnesses to prophesy and torment the nations during the Great Tribulation, and then to stand to the left and the right of Jesus in His Kingdom, so also are two supporting knights present at the investiture of a new knight. If these things are so, then they are a sad commentary on what in reality is a satanic (Luciferic), non-Christian order. Considering the order's motto, one cannot help but wonder what "power" President Woodrow Wilson of the United States once had in mind when he remarked, "There is a power, so organized, so subtle, so watchful, so interlocked, so complete, so pervasive that prudent men better not speak above their breath when they speak in condemnation of it."[2]

Related orders and royal guards. While this section represents a pause in our discussion of Charles' heraldic achievement or coat of arms as Prince of Wales, it helps inform what comes next. Besides the insignia of the Order of the Garter, as well as those of the Order of the Thistle (Scotland's ancient Caledonian counterpart to the Garter), Charles also wears the insignia of the Order of St. Patrick (Ireland's counterpart to the Garter),[3] and those of the Order of the Bath, including the badge of its Military Division (see below).[4] The Order of the Thistle, officially founded in 1687 by Scotland's King James VII (or England's King James II), but going back at least a century earlier to James V, consists of just sixteen knights and bears the motto *Nemo Me Impune Lacessit,* meaning "No one Provokes Me with Impunity." The Scottish "Green Rod" serves as the Thistle's counterpart to the Garter's Black Rod. Possibly going back to the ninth century, the Order of the Thistle's roots may actually pre-date the Order of the Garter.[5]

---

1. Stephen Slater, "Garter, The Most Noble Order of the," *A Dictionary of Heraldry*, ed. Friar, p. 161.
2. Steven Wright, "Environmental Warfare" video (P.O. Box 8426; Clearwater, FL 34618).
3. For a sketch of the Order of St. Patrick's Star, see James and Russell, *At Home with the Royal Family*, p. 126. For a color photo of Charles wearing the St. Patrick Star, see *Her Majesty The Queen*, p. 15.
4. For a color representation of this badge, see Boutell, plate XVIII, between pp. 192-195. For more on these orders, see ch. 10's section titled, "A so-called 'Christian' heritage," at p. 295.
5. James and Russell, *At Home with the Royal Family*, pp. 52, 126, 158-159. To apply for tickets to attend the procession of the Order of the Thistle (for research purposes), write to: The Dean of St Giles, St

Although Queen Elizabeth II was "Sovereign of the British Orders of Knighthood and Sovereign Head of the Order of St John,"[1] then Prince Charles, as the "principal knight" (see below), may have been the highest-ranking knight of the Order of the Bath. As king, he surely is. Based upon the order's heraldic symbolism, it appears either to exist to safeguard the other three British orders—the Order of the Garter, the Order of the Thistle, and the Order of St. Patrick—or to be a super-order of them. If the Order of the Bath is a super-order, and it may not be, Charles in the final analysis, is yet the highest-ranking knight of the most elite orders in the world. This may or may not be significant. For purposes of public consumption, all these orders hold their official annual meetings in church chapels.[2]

Like the Order of the Garter, the Order of the Bath has a star, a collar with a pendant, and a robe. An eight-pointed Templar cross not only serves as the enameled white and gold pendant of the Bath Collar, but is also imposed in gold over a silver sunburst to comprise the Bath Star. As the Sovereign and former "Great Master"—a blasphemous title similar to "grand master" (cf. Matt 23:10, AKJV)—Charles wears the order's insignia over a crimson robe.[3] Attached to a crimson ribbon, the badge of the Bath's Military Division depicts the gold lions of England along with a "conjoined rose, thistle, shamrock, and sceptre," and has a central circlet bearing the motto, *Tria Juncta in Uno* (i.e., "three joined in one"), below which is the Prince of Wales' motto *Ich Dien*[4]—which King Charles III yet *wears* on his left pinky finger (discussed later). This particular combination of the Tudor Rose for England, the thistle for Scotland, and the shamrock for Ireland, all sharing a common stem (cf. the scepter above), bears a semblance to the Rosicrucian symbol of the conjoined rose and cross, and is also used as the badge of the United Kingdom.[5] The conjoined rose and cross, interestingly enough, constituted the original cover design of *The New Age Magazine*, now renamed as the *Scottish Rite Journal*.[6]

Giles's Cathedral, Edinburgh Scotland (ibid., p. 241). For a color picture of Prince Charles' Thistle Star, see Burnet, *In Private—In Public, THE PRINCE AND PRINCESS OF WALES*, p. 124. For a brief description of the Order of the Thistle, as well as a black-and-white representation of its insignia, see Boutell, 1978 ed., pp. 194-195. Prince Philip also was a Thistle knight and "GBE 1953 (Grand Master of the Order)" (Judd, *Prince Philip*, p. 248).

1. For a list of the late Queen Elizabeth II's official "titles and distinctions," see James and Russell, *At Home with the Royal Family*, pp. 214-215.
2. See ch. 10's section titled, "A so-called 'Christian' heritage," at p. 295.
3. For color photographs of Charles as prince wearing his Bath insignia, see Burnet, *In Private—In Public, THE PRINCE AND PRINCESS OF WALES*, p. 125; and *Charles & Diana: A Royal Family Album*, p. 44.
4. For an outline of the Order of the Bath and its insignia, see Boutell, 1978 ed., p. 196.
5. Boutell, 1978 ed., p. 218. For color representations of the badges of England, Scotland, Ireland, Wales, and the United Kingdom, see Boutell, plate XII, between pp. 164-167.
6. For pictures of the original and current cover designs of what is now called the *Scottish Rite Journal*, see John Daniel, *Scarlet and the Beast*, Vol. I, 2nd ed., pp. 746-747.

The Order of the Garter's motto, *Honi Soit Qui Mal y Pense,* is shared by the Life Guards, Blues and Royals (so-named from the lst Royal Dragoon Guards), Grenadier Guards, and Coldstream Guards. Moreover, the Garter Star serves as the emblem of the Coldstream Guards, who also wear the Tudor Rose on a shoulder as a part of their uniform. The Order of the Thistle's motto, *Nemo Me Impune Lacessit,* is shared by the Scots Guards. Likewise, the Thistle Star serves as the emblem of the Scots Guards. Similarly, the Order of St. Patrick's motto, *Quis Separabit,* meaning "who shall separate," is shared by the Irish Guards, and the St. Patrick Star serves as their emblem. Interestingly, the French Imperial Eagle, surrounded by the Garter, serves as the emblem of the Blues and Royals, and the gold eagle itself remains a part of the Crown Jewels Collection used in the British monarchy's coronation ceremonies.[1] Being armored regiments, the Life Guards and the Blues and Royals comprise the Royal Household Cavalry. Also, the Grenadier Guards, Coldstream Guards, Scots Guards, Irish Guards, and Welsh Guards comprise the Royal Foot Guards, who perform sentry duty outside Buckingham Palace. Together, the Royal Household Cavalry and the Royal Foot Guards make up the Royal Household Division.[2] Like the orders, these are subject to the monarch and the Prince of Wales.

The base of the coat of arms. At the base of Charles' heraldic achievement as Prince of Wales, there is a fourth copy of the heir-apparent's crown, below which is the shield from the arms of the Duke (and Duchy) of Cornwall. This shield is centered upon the Black Prince's *Ich Dien* motto. Above the *Ich,* in the left-hand (dexter) compartment of the base, we find the heir-apparent's badge (which bears the *Ich Dien* motto). Finally, above the *Dien,* in the right-hand (sinister) compartment of the base, there is the red dragon of Wales. As shall become clear, the overall message conveyed at the base is "*Ich,* the Black Prince, *dien* the red dragon," or "I, the Black Prince, <u>serve</u> Satan." After addressing these devices in the given order, we will deal with the two supporters of the royal shield (i.e., the dexter beast and the sinister unicorn).

Satan as *Molech* is often symbolized by the owl or an owl's head. Significantly, the base we're here addressing, intimates the eyes (cf. the two compartments) and beak (cf. the central shield), with Satan as the fiery red dragon reflecting off one eye and the Prince of Darkness' badge off the other, all intimating a horned owl or *Molech.* A resemblance to "male reproductive parts," also has been noted.

---

1. For a color photograph of a set of miniature replicas of the "crown jewels," see *Majesty* magazine, June 1993, Vol. 14, No. 6, p. 2.
2. James and Russell, *At Home with the Royal Family,* pp. 123-127.

The arms of the Duke and Duchy of Cornwall.

The arms of the Duke and Duchy of Cornwall also belonged to Charles as Prince of Wales, who had then likewise been the Duke of Cornwall (see the duke's arms at right). According to Campbell-Kease, the rank of duke is the most senior rank in Britain's peerage. (Though William is now Prince of Wales, Charles' heraldic achievement as such remains his, *unaltered.)* Further, Campbell-Kease states: "The word 'duke' is derived from the Latin *dux*, meaning 'leader'. The rank was introduced in England in 1337, when Edward the Black Prince was made Duke of Cornwall.... The duke (in common with other peers) has certain armorial privileges: he employs a silver helm with gold bars facing the dexter,[1] his coronet of rank ensigns his arms, and he normally has supporters."[2]

Two ostrich feathers adorn the Duchy of Cornwall's arms, each adjacent to the shield— forming an *invoking* druidic *Awen* (later discussed). This basic design, to which two Cornish chough[3] supporters were added in June 1968 by a royal warrant, comes from two of the seals of the Black Prince, who set his quartered shield of arms between two ostrich feathers.[4] The shield itself is "surmounted by the coronet [(actually, crown)] of the Heir Apparent" and "shows [fifteen] besants, gold coins brought back by the Crusaders" (whose loyalties were all too often toward the Roman Catholic Church and its heretical clergy, rather than to God).[5] We will refer to this shield as the Shield of the Black Prince or simply the Black Prince shield. The *Houmout* motto at the base of the arms may mean "magnanimous" (see the later discussion on the Black Prince), "high minded," or "high spirited" (cf. *prideful).*[6]

---

1. In the case of Charles as Prince of Wales, ostensibly because he was the heir-apparent to the throne, his heraldic achievement employs the gold sovereign helm.
2. Campbell-Kease, "Duke," *A Dictionary of Heraldry,* ed. Friar, p. 130.
3. The Cornish chough is a black "crow" with red legs and a red bill.
4. Boutell, 1978 ed., pp. 165-166, 219.
5. Burnet, *In Private—In Public,* THE PRINCE AND PRINCESS OF WALES, p. 118.
6. Boutell, 1978 ed., p. 219. For a black-and-white representation of the same duchy arms, see Boutell, 1970 ed. or later, p. 219.

The base of Charles' achievement as Prince of Wales, bears his then arms as the Duke of Cornwall. The flags—burgee and ensign—of the Royal Fowey Yacht Club, as well as the arms of the Cornwall County Council,[1] similarly contain the shield from these arms.

The motto and the heir-apparent's badge. The left-hand compartment of Charles' achievement as Prince of Wales, contains his badge as the heir-apparent to the British throne.[2] Derived from, and possibly first used by the Black Prince,[3] the badge not only forms the seal on the gold signet ring that Charles *always wears* (even as king) on the leftmost finger of his left hand everywhere he goes, but it is front and center on his personalized *kippah* or *yarmulke* (Jewish scullcap). Indeed, the Black Prince badge is also found imprinted on many British coins. The three elements of the badge are: **1)** three ostrich feathers (resembling ווו, or the specific Hebrew glyphs corresponding to 6-6-6, and looking a bit like *three serpent's heads),* **2)** Charles' crown as the then heir-apparent (surrounding the feathers), and **3)** the *Ich Dien* motto (taken from the defeated King of Bohemia after the Battle of Crécy).[4] Recall the judgment upon Babylonia's Nebuchadnezzar, when "his hair had grown like eagles' *feathers,"* perhaps through his crown (Dan 4:33).

Like its motto, the badge's three ostrich feathers came from the "shield for peace," in the Black Prince's arms (discussed later).[5] In *The Bestiary of Christ,* Louis Charbonneau-Lassay remarks: "In [ancient] Nubia, Arabia, Persia, Sumeria, Mesopotamia, Assyria, and Asia Minor, the learned scholars and teachers looked upon the ostrich as one of the birds most favored by various astral influences and as possessing in itself elements of the divine" (cf. Job 39:13-18; Lam 4:3).[6] Ostrich's and heron's feathers now adorn the black velvet hats of Garter knights.

The meaning of *Ich Dien* has been disputed. While Charles understands it to mean "I serve," there are those who believe that *Ich*

1. Scott-Guiles, p. 71.
2. For another color representation of this badge, see Boutell, plate XII, between pp. 164-167.
3. "Wales, Prince of," *A Dictionary of Heraldry,* ed. Friar, p. 372. According to Boutell, Edward VI may have been the first to place the Black Prince's group of three ostrich-feather badges within a coronet, "the form in which they are used today" (see 1978 ed., pp. 165-166).
4. Junor, p. 88.
5. Boutell, 1978 ed., pp. 77, 165.
6. Louis Charbonneau-Lassay, *The Bestiary of Christ,* trans. D.M. Dooling (New York: Parabola Books, 1991), p. 275.

Dien "is not German but a corruption of the old Welsh *Eich Dyn*, meaning 'Your man.'"[1] Scott-Guiles comments: "If *Ich Diene* is German, as is generally supposed (despite Welsh claims), it means 'I serve,' and is thought to refer to the Prince's duty to the King, his father...: 'The heir, while he is a child, differeth nothing from a servant.'"[2] Charles once said, "I believe it best to confine myself to three basic aims at the start: to show concern for people, to display interest in them as individuals, and to encourage them in a whole host of ways."[3] Holden recalls this comment from Charles: "Of *Ich Dien* ('I serve'), the motto he had inherited from Edward, the Black Prince, he said: 'It means just that. It is the basis of one's job: to serve other people. If you have a sense of duty, and I like to think I have, service means that you give yourself to people, particularly if they want you—and sometimes if they don't.'"[4]

What, therefore, might be the implied message of the heir-apparent's badge, and is a satanic message conveyed by the *number* of ostrich feathers within it? Interestingly, each of those feathers resembles a Hebrew *Vav* glyph (i.e., ן), which has a value of six, suggesting three sixes or *6-6-6*. Could it be that Charles, who claims to view himself as a servant of others, whose man he says he is, seeks to proclaim a false, antichristian peace to the world? Is Charles not one of three members of Satan's counterfeit "trinity" (i.e., Satan, the AntiChrist, and possessing fallen spirits in the False Prophet et al.)? (This book answers such questions.) Holden observes that at Charles' formal investiture as Prince of Wales, the badge's *Ich Dien* motto was "the dominant motif of the day."[5] In fact, the badge itself was prominently displayed on the clear canopy over Charles, while his mother Elizabeth II placed the coronet on his head, as well as being shown elsewhere at the event.[6] But there is more to the arrangement of the badge itself, as the three feathers specifically *invoke* the druidic *Awen,* and in so doing, indicate satanic *possession.*[7] Hereafter, we will refer to this badge as the Badge of the Black Prince or the Black Prince badge.

The red dragon, or Satan. In 1911, the red dragon of Wales was "assigned to the Prince of Wales to place over the royal arms as a central escutcheon [(shield)], to symbolize the Principality."[8] Shortly

---

1. "Wales, Prince of," *A Dictionary of Heraldry,* ed. Friar, p. 372.
2. Scott-Guiles, pp. 89-91.
3. Holden, *PRINCE CHARLES,* p. 270.
4. Holden, *PRINCE CHARLES,* p. 195.
5. Holden, *PRINCE CHARLES,* p. 181-182.
6. "Memories of the Day," *Majesty* magazine, July 1994, Vol. 15, No. 7, p. 35.
7. See ch. 8, "The Red Dragon and Prince Charles' Investiture as Prince of Wales," at p. 207.
8. "Beasts," *A Dictionary of Heraldry,* ed. Friar, p. 57.

before his death in February 1952, when then Prince Charles was just three years old, King George VI *allowed* the red dragon added to his grandson's future coat of arms—years *before* Wales made that dragon (and Satan) its *national symbol* (in 1958). A.C. Fox-Davies recorded: "The red dragon upon a mount vert, which forms a part of the Royal achievement as the badge of Wales, is known as the red dragon of Cadwallader,[1] and <u>in deference to a loudly expressed sentiment</u> on the subject, His Majesty the King has recently added the Welsh dragon differenced by a label of three points argent [(i.e., the eldest-son label and druidic *Awen)]* as an additional badge to the achievement of His Royal Highness the Prince of Wales. The red dragon was one of the supporters of the Tudor kings, being used by Henry VII, Henry VIII, and Edward VI."[2]

Not only did George VI participate in spiritism, psychic healing, and homeopathy,[3] but as the former head of Freemasonry worldwide, he "held the rank of past grand master, and of knight commander of the Temple, was a 33-degree [Mason], and grand inspector general in the Ancient and Accepted Rite of Rose Croix."[4] The king and his wife, Queen Elizabeth, were also druids, and were photographed in druidic robes while attending Eisteddfod events in Wales (e.g., the 1926 Eisteddfod in Swansea). As a *satanist,* King George VI, surely knew that his grandson Charles was destined for evil—being per daughter Princess Elizabeth and son-in-law Prince Philip, Satan's "Chosen One."[5]

This author is *on-record* stating that Charles' family—that is, his parents, grandparents, etc.—were *not* invovled in the creation of his heraldic achievement as prince, and that in fact, they could *not* have intentionally caused it to match the first beast of Revelation 13, for example, specifically due to the national and international laws and rules of hearldry. All that is *true.* But apparently it does *not* mean that the Sovereign *must* agree—that he has *no* choice—as we're told George VI *deferred* to "a loudly expressed sentiment" (e.g., from Satan's heralds), concerning the red dragon's addition.

Until May 2008, the Royal Badge of Wales consisted of the British monarch's crown, the red dragon, and an encircling riband with the motto *Y Ddraig Goch Ddyry Cychwyn,* meaning "The red dragon

---

1. Cadwallader is now identified as the legendary King Arthur.
2. A.C. Fox-Davies, *Complete Guide to Heraldry* (Nelson Publishers, n.d.), p. 225. For example, Prince Arthur, Henry VII's son, used a version of the Black Prince's ostrich-feather badge in which the feather was held up by a Welsh dragon (Boutell, 1978 ed., p. 166).
3. John Dale, *The Prince and the Paranormal: The Psychic Bloodline of the Royal Family* (London: W.H. Allen & Co. Plc, 1986), pp. 79-82, 89, 96-97, 132, 163, 171-172.
4. Denslow, *10,000 Famous Freemasons,* pp. 104-105. For more information, see the related note in the earlier discussion on the Garter.
5. For more information, see "King Charles III: Satan's 'Chosen One,'" at p. 220.

gives the lead" or "inspires action."[1] Calling the 1953 addition of this profane motto "an honourable augmentation," Scott-Giles and Brooke-Little note that the Welsh badge had previously consisted of the red dragon only.[2] Brooke-Little adds: "The Dragon is a monster with a horny head and forked tongue, a scaly back and rolls like armour on chest and belly, bat-like wings, four legs ending in talons, and a pointed tail. It is ... rarely displayed. A dragon gules [(red)] occurs in the royal badge for Wales..., and is a common charge in the civic heraldry of the Principality."[3] Fox-Davies similarly comments,

> ....The head of a dragon is like nothing else in heraldry.... It is like nothing else in heaven or on earth. Its neck is covered with scales not unlike those of a fish. All four legs are scaled and have claws, the back is scaled, the tongue is barbed, and the under part of the body is likewise scaled, but here, in rolls of a much larger size. Great differences will be found in the shape of the ears, but the wings of the dragon are always represented as the wings of a bat, with the long ribs or bones carried to the base.... The dragon is one of the most artistic of heraldic [beasts]..., and lends itself very readily to the genius of any artist. In nearly all modern representations the tail, like the tongue, will be found ending in a barb....
>
> Whilst we have separate and distinct names for many varieties of dragon-like creatures, other countries in their use of the word "dragon" include the wyvern, basilisk, cockatrice, and other similar creatures [(cf. Job 41; Isa 14:29, 27:1, AKJV)]....[4]

The red dragon in Charles' arms as Prince of Wales, has a third copy of the eldest-son label around its neck, thereby associating it with him. In fact, the unique presence of this label around the red dragon's neck actually seems to indicate that at some point the dragon shall *possess* the eldest son—Charles (cf. Rev 17:8, 17:11, KJV). Indeed, there is more to this label: like the feathers in the Badge of the Black Prince, it too represents the druidic *Awen*.[5]

Per Friar, this particular dragon came from the Roman Empire:

---

1. For a color representation of this badge, see Boutell, plate XII, between pp. 164-167. A new design for the Royal Badge of Wales was approved in May 2008. The red dragon is now replaced by the Shield of Wales (ordinarily bearing four lions or lion-leopards), and the motto has been changed from "the red dragon gives the lead" (or "the red dragon inspires action") to *Pleidiol Wyf I'm Gwlad*, meaning "I am true to my country." "Its predecessors have all been variations on either the Red Dragon, an ancient emblem revived by Henry VII, or the arms of Llywelyn" the Great ("Royal Badge of Wales," *Wikipedia*, 29 June 2020). Wales satanic national flag, however, remains *unchanged*.
2. Boutell, 1978 ed., p. 218.
3. Boutell, 1978 ed., p. 81.
4. Fox-Davies, pp. 224-225.
5. See ch. 8, "The Red Dragon and Prince Charles' Investiture as Prince of Wales," at p. 207.

Y ddraig goch, the red dragon, is the royal badge for Wales and is properly depicted on a grassy mount or on a shield ... within a riband ensigned with the Royal Crown and bearing the motto 'Y Ddraig Goch Ddyry Cychwyn' (The red dragon gives the lead). The dragon appears in the arms or as the badge of several old Welsh families, notably the Tudors who, when they ascended the English throne through Henry VII, restored the red dragon to its ancient status as a royal device, together with the white and green liveries worn by Welsh archers who served under the Black Prince in the previous century.

The dragon is believed to have entered British armory through the standards of the Roman cohorts and to have been adopted by the shadowy Celtic warriors of post-Roman Britain, Arthur and Cadwallader among them.[1]

Due to its apparent Roman history, and the fact that it has been incorporated into an image matching the beast described in Daniel and the Apocalypse, there can be little doubt that what is now known as the red dragon of Wales is the specific dragon that is identified in Genesis (3:1-4, 3:13-14, 49:17, Heb.), the Apocalypse (12:3, 12:9, 20:2), and elsewhere (e.g., Isa 14:29, 27:1, Heb.; Amos 5:19, Heb.; cf. Ps 22:21, Heb.; Rev 13:2) as a symbol of Satan himself. Indeed, the Apocalypse is rich in imagery that early Christians, who were severely persecuted under Rome's satanic yoke, would have understood as direct references to Rome and its evil empire. Therefore, *to the extent that the "red dragon gives the lead," Satan controls King Charles III, formerly known as Prince Charles.*

The logo of *Peace on Earth* depicts a huge *Welsh* dragon sitting upon and guarding the sphere of the Earth, whereas one of the organization's brochures proclaims, "as we enter what has been described as the Aquarian Age, we are entering a time of cooperation between the spiritual and the material realms, so it is time for us to make peace with the [red] dragon and work in partnership with the wisdom and the power of the earth that the dragon represents."[2] In ancient Babylonia, dragons were similarly worshiped. One writer comments: "The *dragon*, or serpent, was the symbol painted on the great Gate of Ishtar that travelers passed through as they entered ancient Babylon.... The New Age must take particular delight in its portrayal of the dragon as a creature to be loved and taken to heart.... One finds the dragon gracing everything from newsletters to jewelry. There are also crystal dragons as ornaments and idols...."[3] Today, many New Age parents openly promote dragons

---

1. "Wales, Principality of," *A Dictionary of Heraldry,* ed. Friar, p. 373.
2. Hunt, *GLOBAL PEACE AND THE RISE OF ANTICHRIST,* pp. 44-45.
3. Texe Marrs, *Mystery Mark of the New Age* (Illinois: Good News Publishers, 1988), p. 115.

and serpents, like unicorns, lions, and bears, as good, lovable creatures to their children. In such a vein, Charles and Princess Diana
provided their children "furniture with hand-painted animals from
Dragons, a posh London furniture store."[1]

More remains to be said, however, concerning these beasts and
their uses in ancient and modern cultures around the world—*over
which Charles could have sway merely by virtue of the symbolism in
his arms.* Charbonneau-Lassay, for example, notes that "granite lions, crouched and ferocious, ... [stand] guard in the company of
dragons at the threshold of India's temples...."[2] Regarding China, he
adds: "The Chinese see the sacred image of the dragon nearly everywhere.... Among these many dragons, some are good spirits,
others are fearsome and maleficent.... The greatest of them all 'is a
mysterious, supernatural creature, the reptile-spirit specifically designated in Chinese books as the Dragon above all others.' ... The image of the Great Dragon in China is like the symbol of sovereign
nobility and divine power...."[3] Over the past century, largely due to
communist China, the red dragon has become loosely associated
with Communism (cf. "reds," "the red peril," etc.).

The dexter (left-hand) supporter. *The guardant, dexter supporter
in Charles' arms as Prince of Wales, is a beast that has a body like a
leopard's, ferocious feet like those of a bear,[4] and a "mouth like the
mouth of a lion."* With the exception of its ferocious red claws,[5] as
well as its white fangs and red tongue, this beast is entirely brass (or
bronze) in color. The fifth (and last) copy of Charles' heir-apparent
crown is upon its head, and a fourth copy of the eldest-son label is
around its neck. Due to its guardant posture, this beast's left ear is
facing the mouth of the sinister unicorn (see Prov 17:4). It is written,

> And I stood upon the sand of the sea. And I saw a beast rise up out of the
> sea.... Now the beast which I saw was <u>like</u> a leopard, his feet were <u>like</u> the
> feet of a bear, and his mouth <u>like</u> the mouth of a lion. And the dragon
> gave him his power, his throne, and great authority. (Rev 13:1-2; see Prov
> 28:15-16; Jer 5:6; Lam 3:10-11; Hos 5:14-15, 13:4-9; Joel 1:6; Amos 5:16-
> 19, Heb.; 1 Pet 5:6-9; cf. Gen 49:17, Heb.; 1 Sam 17:34-37; Ps 22:13,
> 22:21, Heb.; Jer 4:5-7; Dan 7:2-8, 7:20-25; Rev 12:3)

---

1. Bonnie Johnson, "Growing Up Royal," *People Weekly,* 1988, p. 117.
2. Charbonneau-Lassay, p. 8.
3. Charbonneau-Lassay, p. 414.
4. Typically, heraldic lions have three claws per foot, whereas bears have four or five; the dexter supporter
   in Charles' official achievement as Prince of Wales, has five claws per foot, with all the fifth claws hidden. For a close *unofficial* version of this achievement, in which the dexter beast's feet are less exaggerated and perhaps even more bear-like, with the red dragon likewise having four claws per foot, see
   Burke's Guide to the Royal Family, 1st ed. (London: Burke's Peerage Ltd., 1973), p. 104.
5. See the notes on Daniel 7:19 in the later discussion on the sinister unicorn.

This beast is said to "rise up out of the sea." As we have seen, Charles' coat of arms as Prince of Wales, represent not only England, but also Scotland, Ireland, and Wales (via the red lion and unicorn, harp, and red dragon, respectively). In other words, it represents the United Kingdom, which in every way—physically, economically, militarily, and religiously—rises "out of the sea." Indeed, it was through its seafaring prowess that Britain built its empire and constituted its Commonwealth. But the AntiChrist will eventually receive worldwide power during the Tribulation Period. It is perhaps noteworthy, therefore, that ships from all the major military powers, including the United Kingdom, have in this century and the last patrolled, as well as exercised influence over, the coastal areas of both Israel and her Arab adversaries from the Mediterranean Sea.

Although it is traditionally supposed to represent England,[1] the dexter beast in then Prince Charles' heraldic achievement is totally unique in history and heraldry. The dexter supporter in the vast majority of current and former coats of arms, including Elizabeth II's (right), has the appearance of a normal lion, with a lion's body and feet. In limited exceptions, this supporter has a lion's mouth and a body with similar proportions to a leopard's. Charles' as Prince of Wales, however, bears the *first* and *only* true heraldic representation of this combination—anywhere ever—with ferocious feet such as those of a bear.[2] His lineage, apart from royal military

---

1. Boutell, 1978 ed., p. 214.
2. Each June, "for the Queen's Birthday Parade," in the same month as the annual ceremony at Garter

uniforms,[1] offers perhaps the best explanation for this anomaly. As mentioned earlier, the leopard-like body is for *Germany,* the bear-like feet are for *France,* and the lion-like mouth is for *England,* giving a unique beast that fully represents the Merovingian dynasty, which historically originated and prospered in Germany, France, and England.[2] Through parents Prince Philip and Queen Elizabeth II, King Charles III is of German, French, and Russian descent, and his ancestors include rulers of Greece, ancient Persia and Babylonia. While the lion was associated Babylonia historically (Dan 7:4), it is today representative of England. Likewise, the leopard and the bear, besides being associated historically with the Greek and Medo-Persian empires (Dan 7:5-6), are today viewed as representative of Germany and either France or Russia.

Germany, France, and Russia, like England, are major powers within Europe and in the United Nations. But that is not all. We may further assert that these particular nations have for centuries been among the world's most menacing powers. England has been one of the greatest colonial powers the world has ever known (and through her Commonwealth may still be), Russia fomented the Cold War and still threatens the world with nuclear annihilation, and Germany is largely responsible for World Wars I and II. It seems noteworthy that Prince Philip, King Charles III's roasting father—who was once voted "first choice for a national dictator," and whose "brother-in-law, Prince Christopher of Hesse, was certainly an active and influential Nazi"—was himself, as some other members of Britain's royal family *still may be,* viewed as a Nazi sympathizer.[3] Indeed, Prince

---

Chapel, Charles as Prince of Wales, wore his red uniform as then Colonel-in-Chief of the Welsh Guards (cf. the red dragon of Wales), which includes a bearskin (Burnet, *In Private—In Public, THE PRINCE AND PRINCESS OF WALES,* p. 127; *Her Majesty The Queen,* pp. 14-15). This is now William's role.

1. Although the royal guards were discussed earlier, more remains to be said regarding their symbols and uniforms. The Royal Household Cavalry, which serves both at Windsor and in Germany, is comprised of the Life Guards, which is the senior regiment of the British Army and bears the royal *lion* as part of its crest, as well as the Blues and Royals. The uniforms of the Royal Household Cavalry, like those of the five regiments of the Royal Foot Guards (i.e., the Grenadier Guards, Coldstream Guards, Scots Guards, Irish Guards, and Welsh Guards), who perform sentry duty outside Buckingham Palace, include *bearskins.* In other words, the royal lion and bearskins are directly associated with the guards of the British monarchy (James and Russell, *At Home with the Royal Family,* pp. 123-127). As we have seen, Charles as prince wore the insignia of a number of these regiments. As king, he's over them. For more, see this chapter's earlier section titled, "Related orders and royal guards," at p. 183.
2. For more information, see ch. 4, "Prince of this World—a *Diverse* Lineage," at p. 79.
3. Judd, *Prince Philip,* pp. 14, 66-67, 73, 89. Despite Judd's attempts to gloss over Prince Philip's thinking regarding the Nazis, and his attempts to show the prince's loyalty to World War II Britain (ibid., pp. 89-90), certain statements reveal at the very least Philip's weak moral fiber: "Hitler's march into the Rhineland in 1936 was welcomed by most of the German side of his family but disturbed his British relatives. Where did Philip's loyalties lie? One of his Gordonstoun schoolfellows recalls that he was careful and diplomatic in his comments—'intelligently non-committal' was the phrase used" (ibid., pp. 79-80). Prince Philip's close relations were similarly sympathetic towards the Germans around World War I (ibid., pp. 45-47), and the prince himself had a strong German education. For more information, see the brief discussion on "outcome-based education" (OBE) in ch. 11's section titled, "The United World Colleges," at p. 394.

Henry (Harry), Prince Philip's grandson and Charles' youngest son, wore a Nazi swastika armband while dressed as a Nazi soldier to a "colonial native" costume party in January 2005.[1] Prince William, on the other hand, dressed as a *lion* for the same party,[2] though he was present and said nothing when his younger brother, "'Harry' the Nazi," chose his attire.[3]   France, of course, gave rise to its own menace—Napoleon.

In the near future, Gog (Russia), Persia (Iran), and Gomer (Turkey or Germany), in apparent opposition to the United Kingdom's merchants and offspring (i.e., "the merchants of Tarshish, and all its young lions"), may well trigger Armageddon (Ezek 38 to 39).[4] Sraya Shapiro remarks, "devising a millennium in the Middle East with the British Lion looking on benevolently, suggesting practical solutions for the well-being of all concerned," as Winston Churchill envisioned, "would just have been too good to be true."[5]

---

1. Alan Cowell, "A Prince Who Forgot History Angers Many," *The New York Times,* 14 Jan. 2005.
2. "Harry says sorry for Nazi costume," *BBC News,* 13 Jan. 2005.
3. Christine Lagorio, "Charles to Harry: Visit Auschwitz," *CBS/AP,* 14 Jan. 2005. Lest this confuse you, know that Charles is really *anti-Israel and pro-Islam,* and Prince Henry (Harry) did *not* visit Auschwitz.
4. For more information, see the section (or chapter) titled "The Last Four Seals of the Tribulation Week (and the Second Advent)," in the volume titled, *Messiah's Preeminence in History and Prophecy: The Heart of Israelology, Eschatology, and God's Holy Days,* in the author's *Messiah, History, and the Tribulation Period* series.
5. Sraya Shapiro, "Slouching towards the millennium," *The Jerusalem Post,* Int. Ed., 15 Feb. 1992, p. 23.
   In this author's opinion, Great Britain, next to Rome, Nazi Germany, and Russia, bears perhaps the greatest responsibility for the persecutions, sufferings, and slaughter of Israelites over the past century. In the November 1917 Balfour Declaration, Britain's Lloyd George government promised to use its "best endeavors" to establish a "national home for the Jewish people" (i.e., an Israeli state) in the Middle East. The promised homeland was to include not only the territory that Israel now possesses, but also all of modern Jordan. In 1922, Herbert Samuel, then high commissioner for Palestine, and John Shuckburgh, head of the Middle East Department of the Colonial Office, issued a "White Paper," in then Colonial Secretary Winston Churchill's name, that all but revoked the provisions of the Balfour Declaration while suggesting the partitioning of what was to have been the Jewish National Home. Further, the Lloyd George government adopted this new "interpretation" of the Declaration (H.G., "The real author of the Churchill White Paper," *The Jerusalem Post,* Int. Ed., 20 June 1992, p. 11). According to Coleman, Lloyd George and Arthur Balfour were both members of the Committee of 300, as were Israel's first Prime Minister and first President, David *ben* Gurion and Chaim Weizmann (*The Committee of 300,* pp. 235-236, 311, 314, 321).
   Britain's broken promise prevented the establishment of an Israeli state before World War II, greatly reduced the flow of Israelites to the Promised Land, and resulted in the formation of modern Jordan— which was originally intended to be a Palestinian state. Further, it led to another White Paper in 1939 that severely restricted Israelite immigration to the Promised Land ("1922: Britain sets the stage for conflict," *The Jerusalem Post,* Int. Ed., 20 June 1992, p. 11). Consequently, the British Navy forcibly sent many European Israelites who were fleeing Hitler's death camps back to Europe—to their deaths, thereby contributing greatly to the Holocaust. Moreover, ... "The British [government] knew as early as mid-1941—more than a year earlier than previously acknowledged—that Jews were being systematically slaughtered by the Nazis.... By late 1941 'it was perfectly obvious' to the British 'that the Nazis were executing every Jew they could lay their hands on' (Associated Press, "Britain apparently knew about slaughter of Jews," 19 Nov. 1996, *Rocky Mountain News,* p. 23A).
   Had the British government kept its word to Israel, as given in 1917, the Nazi Holocaust might not have occurred, and even if it had, the toll on Israelite lives would have been significantly reduced. Surely God will recompense those who are myopic in their view of the Arab-Israeli conflict, who conveniently forget their own blood-stained past while ignoring the Arab and Muslim wickedness toward Israel resulting from it.

Mythologically, all heraldic beasts have certain attributes. Regarding the bear, Margaret Young remarks, "In the heavily wooded areas of some of the central European countries the bear was a familiar animal, and ... it took the place of the lion, in their heraldry, for boldness, courage and majesty."[1] What about lions? Charbonneau-Lassay notes that the lion was adopted "as insignia by the legions of Rome," and that it "shares with numerous animals ... the negative role of serving ... as an allegorical image for the Antichrist, for Satan."[2] According to Walker, the lion was "usually a symbol of the Sun god in Greece and Rome," but it was "more commonly associated with the Goddess in the Middle East and Egypt."[3] Young states,

> **The lions of mythology have magic in their tails.** By sweeping them over their tracks they obliterate their footprints and make their ways unknown. By swinging them over their bodies they render themselves invisible. **Thus the longer the tail, the greater the magic.**
>
> The lion is always alert and sleeps with his eyes open. **It was also believed that the cubs were born dead and remained so for three days, whereupon their father came and breathed into their faces to give them life.** Many other strange beliefs concerning the lion have come down the ages.... **The lion is regarded as the embodiment of courage, strength and nobleness. He is the King of the Beasts, and a fitting symbol of kings and kingdoms.**[4]

In the official version of Charles' heraldic achievement as Prince of Wales, the lower jaw of the dexter beast has a normal shape, with its mouth's front fangs evident. However, in the unofficial version, the beast appears to have something shaped like a partial rectangle atop its lower jaw, virtually concealing its lower fangs. In other words, it appears to have taken a three-sided, frame-like object into its mouth (cf. the "three ribs" of Daniel 7:5)—over which its sharp tongue protrudes (see Job 20:4-29; Ps 10:2-12, 22:21 {AKJV}, 35:11-26, 50:16-21, 52:1-7, 57:2-4 {KJV}; Isa 5:29-30; cf. Job 29:17). The heraldic *ostrich* has a similar mouth configuration. Regarding its depiction, Scott-Giles and Brooke-Little note that the ostrich is "usually

---

1. Young, "Bear," *A Dictionary of Heraldry,* ed. Friar, p. 55.
2. Charbonneau-Lassay, pp. 8, 13.
3. Walker, "Lion," p. 544.
4. Young, "Lion," *A Dictionary of Heraldry,* ed. Friar, pp. 215, 218.

shown with a horseshoe or other metal object in its beak, <u>apparently in exaggerated reference to its digestive powers."</u>[1] Recall that during the Great Tribulation, unregenerate Gentiles will devour Judaea and half of Jerusalem.[2] Finally, notice this beast's bulging eyes (see Ps 73:7).

The sinister (right-hand) supporter. The sinister supporter in Charles' heraldic achievement as prince of Wales, is a *pale-green gray* unicorn. With a single twisted or spiraled horn, it has a horse's main body, eyes like those of a man, a (billy) goat's beard and tufts, and boar's hoofs, besides an unusual and long tail. That deathly coloration is specifically prophesied in the *Greek* text of Revelation 6:8, being attributed to the apocalyptic fourth horseman's "horse"[3]—and it resembles, not coincidentally, rotting human flesh.[4] (It's also in the ermine and feathered areas of the same achievement.) This unicorn—which in heraldry represents not only Scotland,[5] but also a counterfeit Christ—also has the fifth (and last) copy of the eldest-son label around its neck. Prophetically, *this unicorn is the "horse" of the Apocalypse's*

---

1. Boutell, 1978 ed., p. 77.
2. As addressed in the *Messiah, History, and the Tribulation Period* multi-volume series, Persia was by far the greater power in the ancient Medo-Persian alliance, providing it as a bear-like beast, its lopsided appearance (Dan 7:5, 8:3, 8:20). The "three ribs" held in its mouth (Dan 7:5), are typically thought to have represented Babylonia to Medo-Persia's west, Lydia to its north, and Egypt to its south—all of which Persia conquered historically (cf. Dan 8:4). Yet, those three ribs may also relate to *Israel:* When the modern nation-state is devoured at the start of the coming Great Tribulation, for example, she will be a prey and a spoil taken in the mouth of the beast (2 Kin 21:12-15; Isa 5:13-15, 5:29, 10:6 {KJV}; see Ezek 34:8, 34:28, 38:1-17). Indeed, Israel may be allegorically represented by the three ribs in the mouth of the bear-like beast (see Dan 7:5; cf. Ps 50:19), which it shall tear from *Israel's rib cage,* using its feet (see Rev 13:2; cf. Hos 13:8). If so, we may view these ribs as the descendants of Abraham, Isaac and Jacob, who were taken from The Last Adam to be made in His image (see 1 Cor 15:22, 15:41-47 {see Gen 2:21-24}). In the specific "first beast" context of Charles' heraldic achievement as Prince of Wales, we might also liken Scotland, Ireland and Wales to "three ribs."
3. The Greek word used for "horse" compasses a normal horse, a horse-bodied unicorn, and a Pegasus.
4. The "green" of ecofascism's "green agenda," is one of *rotting human flesh.* That is, it *produces death and depopulation*—contrary to the life-giving verdant green of plants, etc. Ecofascism is *anti*-green.
5. Boutell, 1978 ed., p. 214.

fourth horseman—who, while possessed by Satan, shall *be* "Death" (see Rev 6:7-8; cf. 1 Cor 15:21, 15:26, 15:54-55; Rev 20:6-15; cf. John 11:9-44). Yes, *Charles will become Death—and Hell shall be in his wake.* Young comments:

> The mystery and magic of the unicorn has been known to all civilizations.... In the world of heraldry it became known as an elegant and beautiful animal, like a horse but with cloven feet, a lion's tail and a goat's beard [(a relatively recent addition)], and a delicate spiraling horn on its forehead. To earlier civilizations it had been known with a different appearance, the flamboyant *ki-lin* of China, and the *kirin* of Japan. In Arabia and Persia it was the *karkardanh*, sometimes a violent and blood-thirsty creature, sometimes more graceful. The mount which Alexander the Great tamed and called Bucephalus was said to be a *karkardanh*.
>
> In medieval times the unicorn became the [mythological] symbol of Christ because of its purity and virtue. Besides these qualities it was believed to possess medicinal powers. The horn was an antidote to poison and no animal would drink from a pool until the unicorn had stirred the water with its horn, thus rendering innocuous any poison that a dragon or serpent had deposited therein. Powdered unicorn horn was [allegedly] used as a cure for many ills....[1]

The earliest known depictions of unicorns are those found in the artwork of Mesopotamia. In ancient Chaldean and Babylonian artifacts, unicorns are portrayed as beasts having a single, little horn projecting from their foreheads. The book of Daniel, written while the prophet was in Babylonia, not only represents Alexander the Great as an unstoppable one-horned goat, or *unicorn* (Dan 8:5-8), but in that immediate context, it depicts his most profane successor —Antiochus IV "Epiphanes," who had claimed to be "God manifest" and was typical of the AntiChrist—as a beast having a single, little horn (Dan 8:9-11). Yet the beast representing the AntiChrist, besides having such a horn, will also have eyes like those of a man (Dan 7:8, 7:11, 7:20-21). Daniel, in other words, pictures the AntiChrist as a rather exotic unicorn. (Recall that the meaning of the name "Charles" is "man.")

This chimera's goat-like features (beard and tufts) arguably have further import: *a goat, for example, served as Charles' July 1969 investiture mascot, led as it was by official satanic standards (flags)—one portraying Satan himself as Wales' red dragon and the other bearing Wales' four lion-leopards or, in Charles' case, lion-leopard-bears!* (Horses too were part of the investiture's "train.") We will have more to consider in relation to this symbolism, when we reach the next chapter, "The Red Dragon and Prince Charles' Investiture as

---

1. Young, "Unicorn," *A Dictionary of Heraldry,* ed. Friar, pp. 353-354. Cf. Ps 75:4-8, NKJV or NAS.

Prince of Wales." For now, however, be sure to grasp everything in this one. Johanna Michaelsen remarks:

> The myth of the unicorn probably originated in ancient Babylon and spread to numerous civilizations around the world, its form and interpretation varying depending on where it found itself [and] in which century. It has ... been regarded as a symbol of purity, despite the fact that ancient legends ascribe to it some decidedly impure and unvirginal activities. It is seen as a symbol of opposites, rather like the [Chinese] *yin/yang*.... New Agers have, in fact, adopted the unicorn as one of their major symbols, viewing it as "the spark of divine light in the darkness of matter and evil," and as a symbol of the great world leader whom they expect to bring peace on the earth in the New Age. The Bible identifies this leader as the Antichrist, the little horn that rises in the midst of the ten horns which Daniel saw....[1]

New Agers often uphold unicorns as "spirit guides," telling children that they should have their own "special unicorn" to imagine, call upon, and "love." It is interesting to note in this context that in "Christian" symbolism, the unicorn is sometimes taken to represent the "Virgin Mary."[2] One wonders, then, to whom it is that tens of millions of Roman Catholics are really praying when they call upon the "Virgin Mary." One writer observes,

> The *unicorn* is today pictured as a friendly and loving, gentle creature with great appeal to kids. But his origins are occultic. Nimrod, the "Great Hunter" and man-god of Babylon, wore a headdress with a single horn protruding from the front. According to *The Lore of the Unicorn*, the unicorn ... was worshiped as sacred in pre-Christian Persepolis.... In ancient China, statues of human heads with a horn were thought to keep demons away from homes.
> Odell Shepard ... also wrote that the unicorn was a common idol in ancient Babylon and Nineveh where it was used as a charm and a talisman.[3]

Regarding the mythological beliefs of pre-communist China, Charbonneau-Lassay wrote, "it is unicorns that bring human babies to their mothers, and their images are much used luck-bringers in the family." He continues, "In any case, before our era people of almost all countries thought of the unicorn, in spite of the elegance of form generally attributed to it, as an invincible and very dangerous animal."[4] Recognizing the unicorn as a symbol of destruction, death, and transformation, Nancy Hathaway writes,

---

1. Johanna Michaelsen, *Like Lambs to the Slaughter* (Oregon: Harvest House Publishers, 1989), p. 221.
2. "Christian Symbols," *A Dictionary of Heraldry*, ed. Friar, p. 91.
3. Marrs, *Mystery Mark of the New Age*, p. 116.
4. Charbonneau-Lassay, pp. 365, 367.

In the twentieth century the unicorn, after centuries of obsolescence, has emerged in an unexpected guise. Its re-emergence was partially inspired by nineteenth-century investigations into mythology—including such peculiar and wonderful books as *The Unicorn: A Mythological Investigation* by Robert Brown, which approached the unicorn in terms of solar symbolism.... In the beginning of this century, the unicorn began to appear as a symbol of strength. William Butler Yeats, who was fascinated by symbols of all kinds, published a play in 1908 called *The Unicorn from the Stars*. In it the one-horned beast becomes once more a complex and paradoxical symbol:

> *Martin:* There were horses ... white horses rushing by, with white shining riders ... there was a horse without a rider, and someone caught me up and put me upon him, and we rode away, with the wind, like the wind.... Then I saw the horses we were on had changed to unicorns, and they began trampling the grapes and breaking them.... They tore down the wheat and trampled it on the stones, and then they tore down what was left of the grapes and crushed and bruised and trampled them. I smelt the wine, it was flowing on every side ... everything was silent.... I saw a bright many-changing figure ... it was holding up a shining vessel ... (holds up arms) then the vessel fell and was broken with a great crash ... then I saw the unicorns trampling it. They were breaking the world to pieces ... when I saw the cracks coming, I shouted for joy! And I heard the command, "Destroy, destroy; destruction is the life-giver; destroy." ...I am to destroy; destruction was the word the messenger spoke.
> *Father John:* To destroy?
> *Martin:* To bring again the old disturbed exalted life, the old splendour.

The unicorn here is once again a symbol of transformation, for this unicorn seeks a better world—or a return to a better world—through the purifying, purgative powers of destruction. Its purpose, like that of the Hindu god S[h]iva, is to tear down and to renew....

....Dylan Thomas, in his poem "And death shall have no dominion," refers to "unicorn evils...." The creative powers of the artist and the destructive powers of death are cut from the same cloth as the powers of the unicorn—that is, they are transforming.[1]

Constance Cumbey remarks, "The *Satanic Bible* of Anton Szandor LaVey mentions the name 'Shiva' as a synonym for Lucifer or Satan."[2] Among other things, early Christianity viewed the unicorn as a symbol of Satan and Death (recall the earlier discussion on Psalm 22:21). Beer states,

> At a very early date, ... [the unicorn] became an ideograph for Christ, yet it stood also for Death and the Devil; in this last case Asiatic influences were powerfully at work.... Becoming associated with the Virgin through the Son of Man, the unicorn was, further, a symbol of chastity. But because of its boundless strength it also embodied unlimited licentiousness:

---

1. Hathaway, pp. 159-163.
2. Constance Cumbey, *A Planned Deception* (Michigan: Pointe Publishers, Inc., 1985), p. 70.

the horn as aphrodisiac in yet another guise. The contradictory nature of the creature is manifold.... And though the lion symbolizes Christ's sovereignty, the devil, too, roams like a roaring lion....

....The unicorn was identified by the Church Fathers with everything resisting the domination of Christ and contrary to the Church.... Finally, the Devil himself is represented as a unicorn in patristic works and Coptic incantations....

Pope Gregory the Great called the Prince of Darkness a unicorn....

The so-called Basil version [of *Physiologus* ... states]: "The unicorn is evilly inclined toward man. It pursues him, and when it catches him up it pierces him with its horn and devours him." What a contrast that makes to the figure of the Redeemer! The author purported to be Basil in his commentaries pushes this contradiction to its full extent: "Take care then, O Man, to protect thyself from the unicorn, that is to say from the Devil. For he is ill-inclined toward man and skilled in doing him harm. For he stands by the way day and night and by permeating man with his sophistries severs him from God's commandments." Thus the same creature that denotes the Redeemer is also a symbol for his adversary....

The later *Physiologus* of the Waldenses (a twelfth-century Roman Catholic sect) identifies the unicorn with Satan, but the Basilian volume allows an alternative; as we have seen, the unicorn there is concurrently a symbol for Satan and for the Savior.[1]

Eyes like those of a man. Like the dexter beast, the sinister unicorn on then Prince Charles' coat of arms is unique. It not only has a little horn, and brass (or bronze) colored hoofs (hooves) and nails, but it also has eyes like the eyes of a man. Most unicorns, in history and heraldry, have round horse-like eyes, with no visible eye-whites, including Queen Elizabeth II's (shown at left). Yet in the official version of this achievement (and in King Charles III's new ones, as later addressed), the unicorn's one visible eye—its left eye (cf. Zech 11:17, KJV)—is not only similar in shape to a man's eye, but it also has a clearly defined eye-white around its cornea. In Charles' unofficial Prince of Wales arms, this eye looks like the eye of a man when the man is viewed from the left side of his face. As a captive prophet in Babylon, Daniel wrote:

---

1. Beer, pp. 9, 24, 50-52.

After this I watched in the night visions, and behold, a fourth beast, dreadful and terrifying, and exceedingly strong. And it had huge iron teeth; it devoured and crushed, and *the* residue it trampled with its feet. And it *was* different from all the beasts that *were* before it, and it had ten horns *in its head*. I was considering the horns, and behold, another horn, *a* little *one,* came up among them, before whom three of the first horns were plucked out by the roots [uprooted]. And behold, in this horn, *were* eyes like the eyes of a man, and a mouth speaking great things.... Then I desired to know the truth about the fourth beast, which was different from all of them, exceedingly dreadful, *with* its teeth of iron and its nails [hoofs, claws]¹ of brass [bronze, copper, red],² *which* devoured, crushed, and *the* residue it trampled with its feet; and about the ten horns that *were* in its head; and about the other *horn* which came up, before whom three fell, even that horn having eyes and a mouth which speaking great things, whose appearance [aspect] was greater [stouter] than his fellows. I was watching; and this *same* horn made war with the saints, and prevailed against them.... ....And he shall be different from the first *ones*, and shall subdue [humble] three kings. And he shall speak words against the Most High, and shall wear-out the saints of the Most High, and shall intend to change times and law. And they shall be given into his hand for a time and times, and half a time. (Dan 7:7-8, 7:19-21, 7:24-25, Heb.; cf. Ps 22:21 {AKJV}, 75:2-7a {KJV}, 144:11; Rev 6:7-8).³

A restraining chain. In the original, official version of then Prince Charles' coat of arms (e.g., as seen on cups and plates made for his wedding to Diana),⁴ we see a chain—one that heraldically functions

---

1. This Hebrew-Chaldee word, Strong's number 2953, is used just once more in the Old Testament, where it refers to the nails of a man (Dan 4:33). However, it may be translated as nails, hoofs, or claws. Besides having a body like a horse, the unicorn in Charles' achievement as Prince of Wales, has cloven feet and nails like those of a boar (cf. goat), whereas the feet of the dexter beast have claws.

2. This Hebrew-Chaldee word, Strong's number 5174, can be translated as "brass," "bronze," "copper," or "red." The possible translation as "red" derives from another Hebrew word, Strong's number 5153, that is directly related to 5174. Strong's number 5153 refers to the "*red* color of the throat of a serpent [5175, as denom.] when hissing" (Strong, 5153, "A Concise Dictionary of the Words in the Hebrew Bible," p. 102).

    Strong's number 5175, which is identical to 5174 (though its pronunciation differs), is used in Arabic to refer to "the constellation of the serpent or dragon in the northern part of the sky" (Gesenius, 5175, p. 545). By implication, therefore, the beast described by Daniel may have bronze- or brass-colored nails or hoofs, or it may have red, serpent- or dragon-colored nails or claws. The unicorn on Charles' heraldic achievement as Prince of Wales, fits the former description, whereas the dexter beast matches the latter (i.e., it's claws are identical in color to the red dragon).

3. Notice that the apocalyptic description of the first beast ascribes multiple heads to it, not just one (see Rev 13:1-3). Further, it is the specific head which is to be wounded of that corporate beast that is to make war against the saints for forty-two months, or three and one-half years (Rev 13:3-8; cf. 11:2-3). In describing this beast, Daniel identifies the little horn that has eyes like those of a man as being the individual who will make war with the saints. Therefore, it appears that this little horn represents the head of the first beast that is to receive the deadly wound. Further, this association clearly implies that the little horn actually protrudes from a particular head on the corporate first beast, and that the given head has eyes like those of a man. Consequently, it should not surprise us to learn that the Hebrew word used in Daniel 7:8 and 7:20 for "horn," Strong's number 7161/7162, most literally refers to a beast that has a single horn which projects from its head (Gesenius, 7161, p. 744). In other words, taken in conjunction with the Apocalypse, Daniel clearly portrays the AntiChrist as a unicorn having human eyes.

4. Spink, p. 60.

as a restrainer (cf. 2 Th 2:6-7, Gk.: "the thing restraining .... until *it* comes out of *the* way"). It holds the unicorn to the base of the arms (directly above the red dragon). Also, the unicorn's two hind-feet are touching the base. "The verb *restraineth* (*katechó*) quite literally means 'to hold down'...."[1] In conjunction with this, notice that the red dragon is nowhere touching the base's associated rim.

In the later, unofficial version of Charles' achievement as Prince of Wales, the chain is detached from the base, and no longer restrains the sinister unicorn. Further, its reared-back countenance looks fierce, and its right-rear *boar's (swine's)* hoof is suddenly elevated off the base, evidently lifted against The LORD (see Ps 41:9, Heb.; cf. Prov 6:13). Not co-incidentally, the red dragon's wing-tips, tongue, and front feet are now

touching the associated rim (cf. Gen 49:17, Heb.). Interestingly, Jesus quoted Psalm 41:9, which literally speaks of the lifting of a hoof,[2] when referring to Judas Iscariot (see John 13:18), whom he called the "son of perdition" (John 17:12, KJV; see Acts 1:15-20; cf. Ps 109). Yet in the context of taking a restrainer "out of *the* way" (see 2 Th 2:6-7, KJV and Gk.; cf. Job 30:10-13), the apostle Paul spoke of the future revelation of another son of perdition (2 Th 2:3-4, KJV).[3] Satan

---

1. D. Edmond Hiebert, *The Thessalonian Epistles* (Chicago: Moody Press, 1971), p. 311.
2. Strong's number 6117/6119, translated as "heel" in Psalm 41:9, can also be rendered as "hoof" (e.g., see Gen 49:17; Judg 5:22). Further, Strong's number 6117 can be translated as "restrain."
3. Regarding the coming "son of perdition" (2 Th 2:3, KJV), Paul wrote, "And now the thing restraining you know, for him to be revealed at his *own* time; for the mystery of lawlessness is already working, only He [he] is restraining *him* presently, until *it* comes out of *the* way" (2 Th 2:6-7, Gk.). Notice that both a "thing" and a Person (or person) are involved in the process of this restraint (*The Wycliffe Bible Commentary*, ed. Charles F. Pfeiffer and Everett F. Harrison {Chicago: Moody Press, 1962}, p. 1364). In other words, this passage not only speaks of a *thing* restraining the son of perdition (who lifts his hoof against Messiah Jesus and Israel), but also a *Person*, God, or person (e.g., the archangel Michael; cf. Dan 12:1, Heb.) who controls it. Although God may control the restrainer by the power of His Spirit, or The Holy Spirit may Himself do the restraining, there is nothing in Paul's statements, explicitly or implicitly, that would allow us to presume that he was in any way referring to the removal of the Spirit-filled Church from the Earth before the completion of the Great Tribulation (Robert H. Gundry, *the church and the tribulation* {Michigan: Zondervan Publishing House, 1973}, pp. 125-128).

will likewise possess this son of perdition, the AntiChrist (e.g., see Rev 17:8, 17:11, KJV)— only to later himself be *"bound" with "a great chain"* (Rev 20:1), after the AntiChrist and False Prophet are "cast alive" into fiery Hell (Rev 19:20). Therefore, this unicorn appears to represent not only "the Christ" in heraldry, but also the biblical son of perdition—the foretold AntiChrist. Compared to Charles' July 1969 arms, whether official or unofficial, the countenance of the unicorn on his mother's achievement (left), is tame.

The Black Prince and then Prince Charles' arms. Finally, as we have seen, a number of the devices in Charles' arms as Prince of Wales, associate him with Edward the Black Prince, who became a feared military commander throughout Europe following his victory in the Battle of Poitiers in 1356. As a grandson of Isabella of France and Edward II, who was a homosexual satanist, the Black Prince expired one year before his father, King Edward III, having served as the Prince of Wales from 1330 to 1376. To the mind of Froissart, the Black Prince was the "chief flower of chivalry of all the world."[1] The medallion here shown (opposite page), encircled by the Garter, allegedly represents the Black Prince before God's Judgment Throne,[2] in "Mary's" presence. But the apparent frog and cat held by what can only be construed as a witch, like the prevalence of the occult five-fingered hand, tells a different story, clearly exposing the scene as occult. Notice also the shield held by an angel crowned with a cross, presumably Merovin-

---

In fact, 2 Thessalonians 2 is entirely posttribulational in nature; for the "gathering together" of the saints to Jesus (2 Th 2:1) at the start of the "Day of The Christ" (2 Th 2:2, Gk.)—which is likewise called the "Day of The Lord, Jesus The Christ" (1 Cor 1:8, Gk.), the "Day of The Lord, Jesus" (1 Cor 5:5, KJV; 2 Cor 1:14), etc., or simply the "Day of The Lord [LORD]"—will be *preceded* by both "the apostasy" (i.e., the worldwide falling away from God, His Word, and His Truth by unbelieving Israelites and those who falsely profess to be Christians) and the revelation of "the man of sin | lawlessness, the son of perdition" (2 Th 2:3, Gk.). However, as discussed in ch. 3, "A Name that Calculates to 666," the revelation of the son of perdition will not itself occur, in the manner spoken of in 2 Thessalonians 2 (i.e., name calculations and the like excepted), until just before the *midpoint* of the Tribulation Period. Around that time, he will proclaim his deity in the Temple of God (2 Th 2:4), and the abomination that causes desolation, spoken by both Daniel and Jesus, shall be erected (see Matt 24:4-5, 24:15-26, 24:29; Mark 13:5-6, 13:14-25; cf. 2 Th 2:4-8, Gk.). Further, according to this same passage in 2 Thessalonians, Jesus will return to destroy the impostor "with the brightness of His coming" *after*, not before, he is revealed (see 2 Th 2:8; cf. Matt 24:27-28, 24:30-44; Mark 13:26-33; 1 Th 1:9-10; 2 Th 1:3-10; Rev 1:7, 11:13-19). For more information, see the chapter titled "The Tribulation Period, the Day of The LORD, and God's Wrath" in the volume titled, *The Real Rapture and Other Prophetic Mysteries: Understanding the Revelation (Apocalypse)*, of the *Messiah, History, and the Tribulation Period* series. Also, see the author's DVD presentation set titled "The *Real* Rapture."

1. "Black Prince, The," *A Dictionary of Heraldry,* ed. Friar, p. 60.
2. "Christian Symbols," *A Dictionary of Heraldry,* ed. Friar, p. 89.

gian, above the Black Prince. Created by Edward III in 1340 to express England's claim upon the French throne,[1] this shield, later known as the Black Prince's "shield for war," depicts the quartered arms of England and France.[2]

Just as the Black Prince wore a black surcoat, which showed his arms, the Garter cap which Charles wears to Garter services, is, apart from its white feather, black.[3] Interestingly, the so-called *Epistle of Barnabas,* which likely dates to the early second century A.D. (cf. 16:3-5), refers to Satan, in the guise of the AntiChrist, as "the Black One" (4:9, 20:1).[4] Charles embodies the modern Black Prince, gold signet ring and all, so we may surmise that he *is* the "Black One" to whom Barnabas refers—the very "Prince of Darkness."

Indeed, the "staff at Camilla's home knew Charles as the 'Prince of Darkness', as he never arrived in daylight."[5] On April 9, 2005, that Prince of Darkness and divorcée Ms. Parker Bowles wed—in a likely *illegal* civil ceremony (under the 1836 Marriage Act of Parliament).[6] In light of Princess Diana's sacrifice (murder),[7] note that Camilla in the *Aeneid,* was "a queen of the Volsci, who was given as a servant to the goddess Diana and raised as a 'warrior virgin' of the Amazon

1. Boutell, 1978 ed., between pp. 22-23 and pp. 119, 130, 165, 207-209.
2. For an outline of this medallion, see Scott-Guiles, p. 95. Edward III's "noble" (gold coin) shows an image of the King bearing this shield and standing in a ship having at its mast-head St. George's pennon or flag (Boutell, 1978 ed., p. 278).
3. Burnet, *In Private—In Public, THE PRINCE AND PRINCESS OF WALES,* pp. 126-127.
4. *The Apostolic Fathers,* ed. and rev. Michael W. Holmes, eds. and trans. J.B. Lightfoot and J.R. Harmer, 2nd Ed. (Michigan: Baker Book House, 1992), pp. 283, 323. *Ante-Nicene Fathers,* ed. Roberts and Donaldson, Vol. 1, pp. 139, 149.
5. See 1999's "Profile: Camilla Parker Bowles," as now posted at "https://web.archive.org/web/20011220 222043/http://www.royalreport.com/camilla.html" and "https://web.archive.org/web/2008112210154 6/http://sunnybrits.com/british/features/camilla.htm" on the Internet.
6. E.g., see "Panorama: Lawful impediment?", *BBC News,* 14 Feb. 2005; Andy McSmith, "Charles's civil ceremony may not be legal," *The Independent,* 20 Feb. 2005; and Allison Yee, "Camilla's marriage to Charles might not be valid," *Yahoo Lifestyle,* 22 Aug. 2017. Queen Elizabeth II did *not* attend, being the Church of England's "Supreme Governor," though "in 2005, the Palace argued that Charles' rights to a civil marriage were covered by the European Convention on Human Rights" (Anna Kretschmer, "Why Queen said 'I had to put Church before Charles,'" *Daily Express,* 26 May 2020).
7. See ch. 10's section titled "Death of a Princess," at p. 320.

type."[1] Part of Diana's sacrifice or not, as a "helper," Camilla is *no* "Wonder Woman."

Regarding the Black Prince of history, Scott-Guiles comments:

Following the example of the three foregoing Edwards, who all adopted badges from their mothers' devices, the Black Prince took these arms as his "shield for peace"..., while his "shield for war" was, of course, the royal coat-of-arms [(i.e., the royal shield)] differenced by a silver label....

These two shields appear on the sides of his tomb in Canterbury Cathedral. The "shield for peace" is surmounted by a scroll with the motto *Ich Diene*, which also appears on the scrolls pierced by the pens of the feathers....

Accompanying the "shield for war," is the old German *Houmout*, meaning "Magnanimous," or, as rendered by "Toc H," who have made it their motto, "Hearts High." It has been suggested that those two mottoes should be read in together as "I serve with a high heart."

The effigy of the Black Prince on his tomb ... shows him with a surcoat of the Royal Arms. Since the shield with the three feathers is definitely described as his "shield for peace," we may assume that on his peaceful occasions he wore a corresponding surcoat, the ground of which was, of course, black like the field of the shield. His nickname was therefore due to his black heraldic surcoat, and not to any habit of wearing black armour as is popularly supposed....[2]

---

1. "Camilla (given name)," *Wikipedia.org*, 2 June 2023.

2. Scott-Guiles, pp. 89-91. An outline of the Black Prince's shields for war and peace may be found on page 90 of the same work. Also, see Boutell, 1978 ed., p. 77.

The Red Dragon
and
Prince Charles' Investiture as
Prince of Wales

In the first edition of *The AntiChrist and a Cup of Tea,* this was an Earth-shaking, but small chapter. There was a great deal, however, that this author did not address, particularly in the area of occult connections and imagery. Of particular interest, there is much in the imagery that relates not only to satanism and witchcraft, but also to druidry and the British monarchy's connections to it. Indeed, many will be shocked—and I do not say that lightly—to learn about Queen Elizabeth II's druidic history and the role the red dragon (i.e., Satan) played in her life, from an early age. Yes, as Queen of the United Kingdom, she was a satanist and a druid, among other things. The same had been true of Charles' father Prince Philip, as well as his grandparents on Elizabeth II's side. This satanism is *so extensive* in fact, that *a goat* served as the mascot for Charles' July 1969 investiture as Prince of Wales. To adequately cover what's just been stated, which was not formerly done, we are going to take a "deep dive" into relevant symbolism, addressing druidry in the context of both scripture and—you may be surprised to learn—some (basic) Hebrew language characters or glyphs.

Like what is found in this author's other books, much of the material herein is beyond primary research—it's scholarship which *surpasses* even most doctoral levels. While you may find some of it challenging, theologically or otherwise, the more you are able to grasp, the broader and deeper shall be your understanding of the overall import of Charles' July 1969 investiture as Satan's Prince—as *the* foretold AntiChirst of biblical apocalyptic prophecy. (The author seriously weighed placing a considerable portion of this—that is, the more theological and in some cases, esoteric information—in his *Messiah, History, and the Tribulation Period* multi-volume series instead, as that is a particularly advanced systematic theology and work on biblical history and prophecy. Really, that series' tome on interpretation (hermeneutics), in which some related material re-

mains, and so is *not* herein included, seemed ideal. However, this information is so salient to our present topic, that it seemed best to provide it in this chapter, where it may be most impactful.) Much effort has been devoted to making what follows understandable to the *careful* reader; those who do digest it, will be blessed. There are *stunning* things to see and learn all the way around.

As we proceed, you'll encounter some theological "deep dives," particularly in relation to druidry and how its paganism counterfeits certain things of God. On theological and pagan contrasts, we'll be talking about a two-horned goat, throne stones, throne circles, druidic versus biblical symbolism and the nature of the satanic "trinity" (i.e., Satan, the AntiChrist, and possessing fallen spirits in the False Prophet et al.) versus God or *Elohim,* and more. These have a direct bearing upon the *druidic* British monarchy, its history, and certain core symbolism of Charles' investiture as Prince of Wales. (Druidry is thoroughly Anti-God and antiChristian, not "just" pagan; indeed, it is *overtly* satanic.) Do strive to pay particular attention to all the imagery—and there's a lot—even when the meaning may not be immediately apparent. Generally, we will "circle back" to illuminate and clarify. OK, "buckle your seat belt!"

Enter the red dragon. 2002's *Reign Of Fire* movie portrays a large *fiery dragon,* having, arising from beneath the heart of *London,* after its disturbed by a subsurface mining operation which inadvertently penetrates its lair. We are told that the "millions of years" old, dormant creature is (somehow) a survivor of a past species *responsible* for the demise of the dinosaurs, which were "burned ... to dust;" indeed, "in eons past," as this evolutionary delusion would have it, such dragons "had scorched the world clean of life, and starved and slept, waiting for the Earth to replenish itself, waiting to start their cycle again" (ca. 0:09:15-36). Not only does the species emit a natural napalm-like stream of fire from its mouth as a weapon (ca. 0:56:09-21), but it multiplies extremely rapidly, and together with its *millions* of hatched carnivorous and flying offspring, which "swarmed like locusts, burning everything in their path" (ca. 0:08:54 to 0:09:04), it destroys and eats the world and mankind—with the "help" of a *failed* global nuclear holocaust to try to stop the monsters—so that there are few survivors among humanity (ca. 0:09:36 to 0:10:24). At about 1:07:36-50 into the movie, we see a dangling street sign originally bearing "London 66," but scratched to say "NO London 666" and an "X" or two. Eventually, some brave "Kentucky irregulars" and their British "conscript"—the very individual who, as a boy, saw the first dragon slay his mother as it emerged from a mining shaft beneath London, and is now "holed up" in a *castle* with dozens of others (ca. 0:02:10 to 0:08:34 and 0:56:51 to 1:00:50)—manage to slay the presumed-*only* male dragon, which yet resides in London (ca. 0:55:40 to 0:56:51) and is much larger than the still very large females, so that the dragons, having consumed most life on Earth, ostensibly then starve to death, and again die out. (The American dragon slayer tosses an apple at one point, to a boy who will join his ranks, perhaps to remind us of the original "forbidden fruit.") A few pockets of small numbers of humans are left with a decimated and radioactive world, to try to "pick up the pieces" and eventually repopulate the planet. Thus, we see London, an actual (fictional) fiery red dragon, and the number 666 connected, in a *false and thus cursed* (Rev 22:18-19) apocalyptic scenario, as disturbingly entertaining as it may be to watch.

Earlier (setting fiction aside), we learned, "The [red] dragon is believed to have entered British armory through the standards of the Roman cohorts and to have been adopted by the shadowy Celtic warriors of post-Roman Britain, Arthur and Cadwallader among them."[1] In fact, ruins from the Roman fort Segontium, apparently founded between A.D. 77 and 80, lie just hundreds of meters from the site of Caernarfon Castle.[2] Let's look a bit deeper, shall we?

Historian Rupert Matthews outlines how the red dragon entered British armory or heraldry: "Roman cavalry units carried a standard known as the 'draco', or dragon. This took the form of a metal dragon's head with an open mouth, through which the wind would blow. The body of the dragon was made up of a tube of fabric, rather like a modern windsock. The [red dragon] banners were used to serve as markers on which the riders formed into different formations, and to give orders by means of some vigorous waving. The British militias [later] adopted many aspects of Roman military gear, and the impressive looking *draco* was among those.... Following the fall of Rome, British princes continued to use Roman-style *dracos* as battle standards .... until about 1250, after which the red dragon of Wales began to be embroidered onto a flag.... The green and white background, incidentally, comes from the family colours of the Tudor Dynasty, and was added in 1959."[3]

That's interesting, but where did the Romans themselves get the dragon "device?" We are told: "From the conquered Dacians, the Romans in Trajan's time borrowed the dragon ensign, which became the *[draco]* standard of the cohort.... It consisted of a bronze dragon

---

1. "Wales, Principality of," *A Dictionary of Heraldry,* ed. Friar, p. 373.
2. See, for example, "Segontium," *Wikipedia.org,* 9 Dec. 2020.
3. Rupert Matthews, "Why does the Welsh flag feature a red dragon?," *BBC History Revealed Magazine* (HistoryExtra.com), 18 Dec. 2020.

head, with a fabric body similar in shape to a tail.... Wind flowed through the gaping mouth and billowed out the cloth tail.... It is thought that some form of whistle was mounted in the dragon's neck to make a terrifying noise when galloping."[1]   "The *draco* ("dragon" or "serpent," plural *dracones)* was a military standard of the Roman cavalry. Carried by the *draconarius,* the *draco* was the standard of the cohort as the eagle *(aquila)* was that of the legion...."[2] The Greek military writer Arrian describes the *draco* in his passage on cavalry training exercises, calling it 'Scythian' [(cf. Persian)]: 'The Scythian banners are *dracontes* held aloft on standard-length poles. They are made of colored cloths stitched together, and from the [base of the bronze dragon] head along the entire body to the tail, they look like snakes. When the horses bearing these devices are not in motion, you see only variegated streamers hanging down. During the charge is when they most resemble creatures: they are inflated by the wind, and even make a sort of hissing sound as the air is forced through them.'[3] ... The Gallo-Roman Latin poet Sidonius Apollinaris offers a similar, if more empurpled, description."[4] (Today, Wales' red dragon-bearing flag blows in the wind!)

So, two origins are alleged: "conquered Dacians" and Scythians or Persians. In fact, historians tell us that Romans acquired the *draco* from Dacians, who in turn had assimilated it from ancient Sarmatians (e.g., Scythians or Persians). Those Dacians were comprised of peoples now addressed as Daco-Mysian, Daco-Thracian, Daco-German, Daco-Celt and Daco-Sarmatian. In other words, we are talking about the ancestors of modern Turkey, Europe (e.g., Germany) and the Balkans, as well as Iran (e.g., Persia).[5] These severely persecuted both Israel and Christians historically. Moreover, crucifixion originated with Persia (cf. Iran). "According to Vegetius, in the 4th century a *draco* was carried by each legionary cohort."[6]

From the above, we see that Rome really received the *draco* military standards from the *Persians* (i.e., Sarmatians who had replaced Scythians). Moreover, historians admit Rome began using those by the late first- or early second-century A.D. (i.e., in Trajan's time). Yet, based upon the Hebrew text (and prophecy) of Psalm 22:21 (v. 22 in Heb.), which is below shown, this author suggests that Roman cohorts ostensibly employed *draco* military standards *decades prior—*

1. "Draconarius," *Wikipedia.org,* 5 Apr. 2019.
2. "Draco (military standard)," *Wikipedia.org,* 9 Nov. 2020. Yust 1953, p. 570.
3. Ibid. Arrian, *Technē Tacita* 35.2–4.
4. Ibid. Sidonius, *Panegyric on Maiorianus* 5; Southern and Dixon, *The Late Roman Army,* p. 126. Search for "roman cavalry draco standard [history]" on the Internet, to see some examples.
5. See "Dacia," *Wikipedia.org,* 9 Dec. 2020; "Dacians," *Wikipedia.org,* 28 Nov. 2020; etc.
6. "Draco (military standard)," *Wikipedia.org,* 9 Nov. 2020. Vegetius 2.13; Pat Southern and Karen R. Dixon, *The Late Roman Army* (Yale University Press, 1996), p. 98.

so that the very soldiers who crucified Jesus could have even carried one. If correct, there could have been a *visible* red dragon symbol before Jesus, while He suffered upon the cross. There, He indeed prayed, "Save Me from the lion's mouth and from the horns of the unicorns—*the* affliction of the <u>dragon</u>."[1]

Under Constantine, fourth-century Roman Catholics started using the *Chi-Rho* or labarum military standard in battle, described as "a Christogram formed from the first two Greek letters of the word 'Christ' (Greek: ΧΡΙΣΤΟΣ, or Χριστός) — Chi (χ) and Rho (ρ)."[2] Notably, *Chi* and *Rho* (i.e., Χρ) total 700 on the Cabalic numbering system. That is certainly an interesting contrast to the foretold AntiChrist's 666, but it also serves as a somewhat remarkable confirmation of early Christianity's use of the cabalic numbers to calculate the values of names and words.[3] (This author might have preferred 777, but 700 is much better than 666!)

Without belaboring, nor really addressing the points here, ask yourself these *insightful* questions: "Will the world (e.g., the United Nations) under the foretold AntiChrist, act to deliver *national* Israel to crucifixion and death, claiming that it is to "save" the world— much as first-century Israel's substantially corrupt priesthood acted under Judas Iscariot to deliver Christ Jesus to crucifixion and death? As Jesus suffered "birth pangs" upon the cross (Acts 2:24*b*, Gk.), does the looming Great Tribulation—or period of forty-two months of great "birth pangs"—represent the modern nation of Israel's corporate crucifixion? Will all the same torments attend her suffering, but on a national scale? Will unregenerate (i.e., to date, unsaved) Israel finally reap what she sowed all those centuries ago, toward her own incarnate God? You may find *definitive answers* to such questions in the *Messiah, History, and the Tribulation Period* multi-volume series. Let's continue.

The British monarchy: Satan's druidic servants. On August 3, 1926, King George VI and Queen Eilizabeth, as the Duke and Duchess of York, joined themselves to Wales' *Gorsedd* (or *Gorseth,* meaning "Throne") of Bards. The Gorsedd Archdruid—who wears a crescent "Breastplate of Judgment" (Welsh *Iodhan Moran),* and "wields" a "Grand Sword" topped with a (metal) Welsh dragon guarding a large occult crystal—conducted the ceremony. That of course, makes him the world's most prominent *neo*-druid.

The ceremony in Swansea, at that year's druidic Eisteddfod, prominently displayed Wales' red dragon. Everyone saw it on the

---

1. For more information, see p. 119.
2. "Labarum," *Wikipedia.org,* 12 Dec. 2020.
3. For more information, see ch. 3, "A Name that Calculates to 666," at p. 71.

paraded "Gorsedd Banner" (i.e., "Throne Banner"),[1] and hanging from each *Corn Gwlad* or trumpet. It was also on the "Hirlas Horn" from which the Archdruid drank wine early in the event, as part of *"communion" with the red dragon or Satan!* (We'll consider these and other involved druidic items a bit later.) As part of his particular regalia, Archdruid "Elfed" (i.e., Howell Elvet Lewis) wore a stole or sash that prominently displayed the satanic "all-seeing eye" as the "dot" above an "evoking" Awen (i.e., "/|\")—symbolism *later* explained. (The more recent sash bears the red dragon beneath the evoking Awen, *without* the "all-seeing eye.")

In the royal couple's group photo with the Archdruid, we may also see an attending druid wearing a Welsh dragon necklace (below detailed). Simply put, therefore, Wales' druidic ceremonies center on the red dragon—*the* biblical symbol of Satan—and thus, we may truly state that Britain's former king and queen were *satanists*.

Princess Elizabeth: Satan's "handmaiden." On August 6, 1946, in the midst of an ash glade in Mountain Ash, Glamorgan, then Princess Elizabeth—born Elizabeth Alexandra Mary Windsor—was initiated into the Gorsedd of Bards by the then Welsh Archdruid "Crwys" (i.e., William Williams), at the National Eisteddfod (a druidic festival).[2] Wearing an "emerald green robe," this was twenty-year-old Elizabeth's "enthronement" as an "Honorary Ovate."[3] (Ovate implies "egg," referring to an oval outline.) Druids, as worshipers of spirits (i.e., fallen angels and demons), often in the midst of nature— irrespective of any *false* claims or protestations they may or do make to the contrary—do themselves admit that Ovates, historically speaking, were (pagan) prophets, seers, healers and diviners, whereas *today,* they may study or practice herbalism, healing and divination.[4]

As occurred when her parents were initiated in 1926, the Archdruid drank wine in communion with Satan.[5] Regarding the in-

---

1. See 0:10-14, 0:31-50, 1:53-57 and 2:13-34, "Royal Bards (1926)," *British Pathé,* at "https://www.you tube.com/watch?v=uDzoLQTP-Co" on YouTube. Photos of the Gorsedd Banner show the red dragon.
2. The Welsh word *gorsedd* means "throne," "seat," or "chair," and the Gorsedd of Bards is an assembly of druidic bards that directs Wales' National Eisteddfod, the largest "folk" event in Europe. (Such events may be held up to four times in a year, at solstices and equinoxes.) It is the Gorsedd of Morganwg (Glamorgan) that the Welsh Gorsedd of Bards preserves, which in druidic lore, represents the esoteric or occult "secret wisdom" of *Merlin* and the druids. Thus, *it is King Arthur's throne and the "wisdom of Merlin,"* both satanic, that were bestowed upon then Prince Charles in 1969. Indeed, the Welsh dragon is the "red dragon of Cadwallader," with the latter being identified as King Arthur. However, druids also equate the *Gorsedd* or druidic Throne with *the Garden of Eden,* and thus *the one bearing its authority, to them, rules the world.* The Gorsedd is also viewed as a High Court.
3. See, for example, "Princess A Welsh Bard (1946)," *British Pathé,* at "https://www.youtube.com/watch? v=2WUtGN2rdyw" on YouTube.
4. See, for example, "What is an Ovate?," *Druidry.org,* 22 Dec. 2020.
5. See 0:03-07, "Princess A Welsh Bard (1946);" and 0:05-11, "The Princess A Welsh Bard (1946)," *British Pathé,* at "https://www.youtube.com/watch?v=s5h8eJrAlyw" on YouTube.

volved horn, we are told: "The Hirlas Horn is a symbol of the wine offered by *Mam y Fro* (the Mother of the area) hosting the National Eisteddfod to welcome the [druidic] Gorsedd.... It isn't certain when the rite was first enacted, but it is mentioned at Conway (the Chair of Gwynedd) in 1861.... The Hirlas Horn was presented to Archdruid Hwfa Môn by Lord Tredegar [(Ifor Hael yr Ail)] in Cardiff in 1899. It is described as an ox's horn ... set in silver and resting on a huge silver [(metal)] dragon, which holds a large crystal ball in one claw. The coat of arms of the Tredegar family, [(a shield bearing the red dragon in its first and fourth or upper-left and lower-right quadrants,)] is emblazoned on it. The Hirlas Horn was carried on a bier [(normally used to carry a coffin or corpse to a grave)] in Gorsedd processions, during the first half of the twentieth century. In 1923 Arlunydd Pen-y-garn designed a beautiful red cloak for the presenter and a headdress of gold lace was donated by Oswyn Afan."[1]

Although Wales had yet to formally adopt the red dragon as its national symbol, something that occurred in 1958, Satan has none the less *always* been central to druidry. Use of a glade is meant to symbolize the Garden of Eden—and by that, *Satan* intimates authority over the heart of ancient Israel, to include the Temple Mount on Zion, beneath which *may be* extant remains of the pre-Flood Garden of Eden.[2] (Charles III now allegedly sits upon the throne of Israel's King David, per the British Monarchy's official and fraudulent claim, making Charles the first "Davidic"—in reality, Danite—*king* of the modern nation-state.) Such ostensible authority is *not* insignificant, as shall become even clearer when we examine the history and nature of then Prince Charles' investiture castle.

Everything about the event was pagan, from the music and children's earth-worship dance, to the presence of the red dragon—the apocalyptic symbol of Satan. The then princess—wearing a green robe and standing next to one of the stones of the "Gorsedd Circle" (i.e., "Throne Circle"), and between her two female sponsors (i.e., bards Mrs. Coombe Tennant and Mrs. Maud Thomas, in blue robes) —appeared perfectly at ease. The sponsor to the princess's right, wore a typical chained druidic necklace bearing a *salient* (i.e., "leaping") dragon of Wales—as it grasps and guards a "mystic egg" or "serpent's egg," which is overlaid with an evoking Awen (usually above two also-overlaid crossing swords, apparently representing the Gorsedd's "split swords" or "peace" motif). An ostensible gold lightning bolt supports both the emerald (or sometimes white) egg,

---

1. "Scrolls, swords and mystic marks: Gorsedd symbols and regalia," Amgueddfa Cymru — *National Museum Wales*, 25 July 2010.
2. For more information, see the *Messiah, History, and the Tribulation Period* multi-volume series.

perhaps also meant to represent Earth under the (red) dragon's control, as well as the dragon (made of gold metal) itself. Others present (e.g., some of the druids) also wore this necklace, including the druid who—following the pagan dance of young girls in green dresses, to druidic harpists, in the midst of the Gorsedd Circle—then led the young Elizabeth by the hand, to the Archdruid of Wales. The latter stood atop the *flat* "Logan Stone," also called the "Throne Stone" *(Maen Gorsedd)* or "Compact | Altar Stone" *(Maen Llog),* in the center of the circle. (The Stone of Scone, atop which Elizabeth was later crowned queen, and then Charles recently crowned king, while seated on King Edward I's Chair, is a Logan Stone! Consider the occult implications as we proceed.)

While the above transpired, the red dragon *Corn Gwlad* (i.e., a trumpet from which hangs a white banner bearing the red dragon atop a green field) was blown—just a few feet behind the princess and also within the Gorsedd or *Throne* Circle. The Archdruid then placed one hand upon the princess while holding "the sword of King Arthur" with the other, and so initiated her as his future queen druid and a member of the Order of Ovates (honorary druids), naming her "Elizabeth o (from) Windsor!" Did you catch that? The Gorsedd Circle is *Satan's Throne Circle*—about which the author shall have much more to say!

Then Princess Elizabeth's 1946 druidic initiation was, in fact, entirely under the auspices of the red dragon: the "Gorsedd Banner" (i.e., "Throne Banner") shows the red dragon within a Sun-like roundel, from which the three rays of the druidic *Awen* (Cornish), called the *Nod Cyfrin* (Welsh) or **"Secret | Mystical Mark,"**[1] descend, with the encircling Welsh words *yn wyneb haul* and *llygad goleuni*, translated as "In the Face of the Sun, the Eye of Light."[2] Adding to their blasphemy, these words are followed by *y gwir yn erbyn y byd*, meaning "the truth against the world." Importantly, this topmost Awen on the Gorsedd Banner is in an *evoking* occult orientation ("/|\"), which symbolically means "to *request* or *converge* a deity's presence, as by awakening it from within the universal self or cosmic consciousness, to *receive* that deity." Thus, an "evoking" orientation is an *invitation* to demonic and satanic spirits. Beneath this evoking orientation, the Awen is again shown on the Gorsedd Banner in an *invoking* orientation ("\|/"), where the "three rays of light" ascend from a second, dark green roundel, which acknowledges *possession* by calling upon a demonic or satanic spirit that is seen as *already present,* as later discussed. This latter roundel bears the Welsh word *heddwch*, meaning "peace," indicating that satanic possession brings peace!

In druidry, an encircled Awen also represents a "serpent's egg" — so that giving birth to the encircled red dragon may be construed as a female druid's *highest goal*. Recall that Elizabeth became a druidic

---

1. The "666" "guard-bar" pattern of United Parcel Code (UPC) bar-codes (i.e., barcodes) *is based upon the Mystical Mark, or the three rays, of the Awen*. For more information, see ch. 14's subsection titled "The Mark," at p. 518.
2. In this design, we see a parody of the Seal of the Illuminati, where the "three rays of light" of the Awen form the pyramid and the red dragon roundel forms the "all-seeing eye."

Ovate—or "egg"—in 1946, years before giving birth to Charles. So, were her eggs then effectively *dedicated* to Satan? Certainly, when Satan one day *possesses* King Charles III, as scripture's foretold AntiChrist, that wicked goal will have been *achieved*.

Describing the Gorsedd Banner, its designer and Herald Bard, T.H. Thomas, wrote: "In the upper part is seen the sun symbolising celestial light, bearing upon it the golden [roundel with its red] dragon, at once a symbol of energy and the badge of Cambrian [(Welsh)] nationality; from the [dragon in the] sun emerge golden rays, three of which are prolonged downwards forming the 'Nod Cyfrin' of the 'Awen'.... The lower part of the design represents, in [roundel] symbol, the Gorsedd of the Bards of the Isle of Britain.... Around the 'Maen Llog' are the twelve 'meini gwynion' [("blessed | sacred | white stones," or "stones *of* testimony")].... Upon the 'Maen Llog' may rest a sheathed sword.... Around the Gorsedd Circle are deposited the plants representing the 'Alban'—trefoil, vervain, corn and mistletoe. The whole design is surrounded by a wide decorative border of oak leaves with acorns from which at parts mistletoe arises."[1] In other words, these druids worship Satan as the source of light and truth, above all others, as well as the guarantor of peace, thereby putting "darkness for light, and light for darkness," calling "evil good, and good evil" (Isa 5:20)—yet they shall receive neither light nor truth, nor peace, but woes of judgment from Israel's God (cf. Isa 5:11-23).

You may be wondering if the (earthly) husband of Satan's royal handmaiden, or the now-roasting former Duke of Edinburgh, also finally became an "Honorary Ovate." In fact, on August 5, 1960, as Queen Elizabeth II approvingly watched, Prince Philip was initiated at Sophia Gardens, Cardiff, during Wales' annual druidic Eisteddfod. The Gorsedd of Bards' Archdruid "Trefin" (i.e., Edgar Phillips), whose sash *did* bear the red dragon beneath the evoking Awen, there gave the Greek prince the Welsh bardic title "Philip Meirionnydd." Thus, King George VI and Queen Elizabeth, as well as Queen Elizabeth II and Prince Philip, all *spiritually fornicated* with the red dragon, or Satan.

Shin and Awen, or Good and Evil, Light and Darkness. The Welsh *llog* or "logan" relates to the Greek *logos,* which means "word." (Jesus is The *Logos* or Word of God incarnate.) In druidic thought, the presence of the bard makes the Logan Stone "vocal," and this is in combination with the purported name of God found in the *Nod Cyfrin* or "Mystical Mark" of the Awen. In reality, though,

1. "The Gorsedd Banner," *National Museum of Wales,* 2009 (see "https://web.archive.org/web/20130624 053211/http://www.museumwales.ac.uk/en/909" on the Internet).

the Awen is *a pagan and satanic perversion* of the Hebrew letter *Shin* (**ש**), which is taken to mean "teeth," but by extension means "sound" and intimates "voice." The Awen is a falsehood. *Hieroglyphically,* **ש** represents the spiritual unity and nature of God, who is Father, *Word,* and Holy Spirit; specifically, *Shin* portrays what Christians may call "The Godhead" (i.e., the fullness of Deity). The early *Shin* looked just like a letter "E" rotated ninety degrees counterclockwise, so that its vertical lines pointed up—or much like an inverted eldest-son label.

Shin or **ש** may be described as the harmonization or unification of two parts or opposites, such as male and female, by an intervening mediator. In the case of The Godhead, The Mediator is God The Word, now and forever incarnate in Christ Jesus, the "male" or masculine is God The Father, and the "female" or "feminine" is God The Holy Spirit, who, though generally identified as "He" (e.g., John 14:16-17), is, *for limited purposes,* also personified in scripture as "Her" (e.g., Prov 1, 8). In other words, to save us, God The Father united with God The Holy Spirit, who enveloped Jesus' mother Mary to enable the latter's divine impregnation, giving us all Christ Jesus, who, as The Mediator and Word of God incarnate, unites God The Father and God The Holy Spirit. (There are *not* three "Gods," but *one* God who is *always* Father, Word *and* Holy Spirit, where God The Word.) Indeed, Jesus is indwelt by God The Holy Spirit *without measure* (i.e., completely and infinitely; see John 3:34), and God The Father is known through Jesus; for He revealed, "He who has seen Me, has seen The Father" (John 14:9; see 14:6-13). Truly, in The God-man, Christ Jesus, "dwells all the fullness of The Deity | Godhead bodily" (Col 2:9, Gk.; cf. 1:19). **ש** is, therefore, *fully embodied in Jesus!* In The Godhead, God The Father, God The Word, and God The Holy Spirit are united or "one." *Shin,* among other things, is also viewed as representing the unity of body, soul, and spirit, or the *unified (and triune) nature of man* created in God's image:[1] for He said, "Let Us make man in Our image, according to Our likeness" (Gen 1:26), and thus "God created man in His image, ... male and female He created them" (Gen 1:27). Yes, it *is* all very exciting, but our lesson continues.

As The God-man who is the one and only Mediator between God and man (1 Tim 2:5), Jesus paid the ultimate price for our sins, willingly giving His life upon the cross—*at the midpoint of the Crucifixion Week, on the fourth day* (i.e., Wednesday). So, we should not be

---

1. The Hebrew words for man and woman, or *ish* and *isha* (Strong's nos. 376 and 802), both have *Shin* in them, which indicates mankind's own unified (and triune) nature, where each human is comprised of a body, a soul (mind) and a spirit. *Antithetically,* Awen also (confusedly) represents these three—body, soul and mind—but as *disconnected or disconnectable* (cf. astral projection).

surprised to discover that *Shin* also compasses a division of seven, or a week, into four and three. With His self-sacrifice, Jesus became The Savior (cf. 1 Tim 2:3-6), and this too is embodied in שׁ; those who believe have peace with God, as Jesus redeems and reconciles us to Him (e.g., see Col 1:13-23). Again, the *Shin* is taken to represent the act of raising one's hands to God in prayer (cf. 1 Tim 2:5, 2:8), and seeking divine deliverance (cf. Ex 17:11). The *menorah* of seven branches, and the *chanukiah* of nine branches based upon it, each derive from three branches of שׁ. The outermost branches of the *menorah* and *chanukiah*, derive from the outermost branches of the שׁ, and in all three, the middle branch represents The Messiah, who is the Source of all Light and Truth, and our High Priest. By ancient tradition, Israel's high priest would divide the fingers of his hands, such that each hand would resemble *Shin,* while raising his arms to bless Israel (see below), and in so doing a third, "macro," *Shin* would be manifest between the high priest's head and raised arms (i.e., arm, head, and arm). So, the high priest would display the seven branches of the menorah, with himself central to it. This very tradition continues among Hebrew Christians, when a pastor divides the fingers of his hands and raises his arms to God, forming a "macro" *Shin* and the overall menorah. As the *Shin* and *menorah* are thus displayed for all to see, the pastor emphasizes the unity of God by reciting the "Shema" (Duet 6:4-9), and then he proceeds to bless the saints of God in Messiah, in His Name, stating: "The LORD bless you and keep you. The LORD make His face shine upon you, and be gracious to you. The LORD lift up His countenance upon you, and give you peace" (Num 6:22-26). By this, God says, "So they shall put My Name on the children of Israel, and I will bless them" (Num 6:27). From שׁ, The Godhead, the saints receive The Messiah, who is The Light of God, The Word of God, and The Peace of God.[1]

Shin is found in a number of God's names and titles, to include *Mashiach Yeshua* (Christ Jesus), which in Hebrew is מָשִׁיחַ יֵשׁוּעַ, and

---

1. The Hebrew hieroglyph שׁ, in the pattern of the *menorah*, is much more. In fact, it represents the centrality of Messiah to the pattern of seven, encompassing the physical creation (e.g., the seven valence levels of an atom, and seven scales in music) as well as time itself (e.g., seven "days" in a "week"). In terms of the latter, there are three major "days" in the "week"—the first, fourth, and seventh. As the author demonstrates in the *Messiah, History, and the Tribulation Period* multi-volume series, *all the weeks of scripture are patterned after the Crucifixion Week,* making The Person and Work (i.e., the crucifixion, death, burial and resurrection) of Messiah, or His testimony (cf. Rev 19:10), central to them all. Of these commonly patterned weeks, *three are major,* in which there is death on the fourth day and resurrection at the end of the seventh or sabbath day; these are the Crucifixion, History, and Tribulation Weeks. (The *Messiah-centered* theology, or *Messianic view,* underpinning all this, which permeates *Messiah, History, and the Tribulation Period,* is advanced and largely intended to serve as the core theology of the Millennial Church—not just to enlighten *today's* saints, although it also serves that purpose. As advanced as it is, the author has also made it very understandable.) And this brings us back to the שׁ and the *menorah:* the bulk of scripture focuses on the first, fourth, and seventh days of these three weeks.

El Shaddai, meaning "Almighty Judge" or "All-Sufficient Judge," which is אֵל שַׁדַּי. It is likewise found in many Hebrew words, such as *shalom* or שָׁלוֹם for "peace." Indeed, true peace comes from the true God, and so *Shin* likewise serves as an acronym for *shalom. Shin,* in fact, represents the voice and holy nature of God. Thus, שׁ is typically inscribed on the cases of the *mezuzot* that Israel places, by commandment, on her doorposts and gates (Deut 6:4-9, 11:13-21).

Again, *Shin* has been associated with the three primary colors of the rainbow, with some likening these to refracted "rays" of the flaming spiritual Light of God. While this may seem to stretch the real symbolism and meaning of *Shin,* it is fascinating to recognize the strong parallel it presents to the perversion that is "\|/", or the druidic Awen. The perversion of שׁ by man without understanding is represented in the Hebrew word for "falsehood"—that is, *sheh'ker (i.e., shah'ker)* or שֶׁקֶר—which is essentially a combination between *Shin, Qoph,* ק, for "monkey," and *Resh,* ר, for "head." In other words, a *beastly* (cf. "monkey head") treatment of *Shin*[1]—a hieroglyph representing The Person of God (i.e., God The Father, God The Word *and* God The Holy Spirit), as well as His work or the "Testimony of Jesus" (Rev 19:10)—*produces counterfeit truth (and counterfeit prophecy),* leading to falsehood and deception. Awen leads to dishonesty, compassed as "monkey head." The corrupted *Shin,* known as the occult Awen, is a satanic distortion and unregenerate half-truth, a full-blown usurpation of The Godhead by Satan, the red dragon of old. In *Shin,* we find the Voice of God in the Person of Christ Jesus, but in the Awen, we find the voice of Satan masquerading as "god" in the person of the AntiChrist.

The *orientation* of the Awen, whether its three rays reach *upward* as "\|/" (invoking) or *downward* as "/|\" (evoking) is a symbolic "message" to the spirit being addressed; in the case of the Gorsedd, that spirit is the red dragon, or Satan himself. Of course, druids who don't wish to be forthright concerning the antiChrist meaning of the Awen, will try to water it down; a typical explanation would be that it represents the "inner light" or "spirit" that "inspires and illuminates poets, prophets, and diviners." We must ask, therefore, "Is it not now obvious that Queen Elizabeth II and Prince Philip both belonged to the Gorsedd 'Druid Circle,' *as* satanists?"

---

1. Original Hebrew *is inspired.* Combining "monkey head" (קָר) with *Shin* (שׁ) for "falsehood" (שֶׁקֶר; e.g., see Ps 7:14 and 101:7-8, Heb.) *is a divine indictment against the lie that is called "evolution,"* both physical (i.e., Darwinism) and spiritual (cf. "you shall be as 'gods'" or "you shall be like God," Genesis 3:5 {Heb.}). Is it any wonder, then, that Charles Darwin, who claimed that mankind came from monkeys rather than God our Creator, should be related to King Charles III, the foretold AntiChrist? For more information, see the related note in ch. 9, "Signs of the Times and the Rise of 'Global Governance,'" at p. 286.

King Charles III: Satan's "Chosen One." In November 1948, just two years later, Charles was born the "Chosen One," according to then Princess Elizabeth and her husband, Prince Philip, who likewise was then a member of the Gorsedd druids. Referring to Christ Jesus (Messiah Yeshua) as Eve's (i.e., "the woman's") and His own "Seed," in whose body *all* His saints are *collectively* represented and found by The Holy Spirit, God told the Devil, "I will put enmity | hostile conflict between you and the woman, and between your seed and her Seed; He shall crush your head, and you shall strike His heel" (Gen 3:15). That is the very first prophecy regarding the (then to come) Messiah in history and the Hebrew Old Testament. But who is Satan's "seed," who wars against Jesus and those in Him? Collectively speaking, the Devil's seed (a collective noun) compasses *all* who are do not know nor serve The God of Israel and Christians, including *every* antiChrist of history, of whom there have been quite a few. But just as the woman had a *specific* Seed—that is, Christ (Messiah)—so too does Satan have a *specific* seed (spiritually)—the foretold AntiChrist.[1]

Does Genesis 3:15, therefore, also suggest that King Charles III's mother, as a Satan-serving princess, *engaged in sexual intercourse with Satan,* so that the Devil—rather than her "traditional" husband Prince Philip—impregnated her to produce Charles? As the foretold AntiChrist, is Charles a humanoid *Nephil,* and *not* fully human?[2] (If it were so, Charles would then actually be an *adoptee* of a human father—like Jesus.) Or is it that King Charles III is "merely" Satan's ultimate *spiritual* "seed?" While some allege female members of the British monarchy, including Charles' mother, have engaged (or do engage) in satanic rituals, *to include such sex,* there is *no (i.e., zero) known credible evidence* (beyond hearsay at best) to support such allegations. Also, we have *no* evidence that Charles, or Satan's Prince, is anything other than biologically human. So, the "protoevangelium"—that is, Genesis 3:15—*may* be limited to a spiritual view of Satan's "seed," where the foretold AntiChrist is concerned.

Yet, unnatural (i.e., unintended by God) satanic and chimeric humanoid hybrids, including human-angel humanoids or Nephilim (the plural form of Nephil), *do exist and have existed* historically. Such *abominable* creatures (e.g., fake or counterfeit hominid "aliens"), which *are* also part of Satan's collective seed spiritually, are obvi-

---

1. See the volume entitled *Conflict of the Aeons: Understanding the Protoevangelium,* in the *Messiah, History, and the Tribulation Period* series.
2. For shocking, but historically true information on the human-angel hybrids known as Nephilim and what they wrought in our solar system and perhaps beyond it, before and after Noah's Flood, see this author's *Solar Apocalypse* multi-volume series.

ously *not* fully human. They are encountered as corporeal (and thus mortal) reptoids, insectoids, etc.[1]

In fact, counterfeit "aliens"—except alleged "Nordics," who would most likely be (longer-lived) descendants of humans removed from Earth before Noah's Flood by Nephilim,[2] assuming so-called Nordics really exist—do *not* appear fully human, nor are they biologically compatible with humans. But they are generally hominid, and some of them are close enough to humans in appearance, to where they are able to interact directly, without being recognized as non-human, while temporarily disguised. Such chimeric hybrids generally have reptilian and or insectoid DNA, besides human DNA—and this is the "bandwagon" upon which certain dishonest sensationalists have jumped headlong to allege that various human leaders, including British royals, are reptilians, claiming that those "reptoids" have been caught on "film" with eyes (e.g., corneas and pupils) shifting between human and reptilian forms. But anyone who knows anything about digital manipulation of images in "aliens"-related science fiction TV shows and movies, knows that Hollywood and other producers of such content have been able to convincingly fake "live" eye changes since the 1980s, and were using contact lenses prior to such digital capabilities. In other words, even photographs and film "showing" reptilian eyes in the heads of world leaders and royalty are not reliable and cannot be viewed as "evidence," let alone "proof."

Despite *a total lack of any actual evidence* to support alleged "reptoidhood," for example, the so-called "news" media have none the less (disgustingly) been "all over it!" *The Daily Express'* Jon Austin cites (infamous) conspiracy "theorist" David Icke as believing "the Queen of England is actually a shape-shifting reptilian lizard from outer space:" "Icke subscribes to the ... conspiracy theory that a secret society made up of the royals, political and business leaders, actually pulls the strings of world, seemingly democratic governments, from behind the scenes. But, he adds to this that members of the Illuminati, including all world royal families, and high powered business, and political families are the descendants of ancient hybrids between reptilian aliens and humans.... He said people all over the globe had provided the same evidence..., including CIA insiders. He said: 'It took the form of meeting people who tell of experiences of seeing people, often in positions of power, change from human form to a reptilian form and back again in front

---

1. See the *Solar Apocalypse* multi-volume series for *hard evidence* of their existence and activities.
2. Ibid.

of their eyes.'"[1] Well, that must make it true then, and not just (demonic) deceptions, right? Sadly, Icke mistakes fallen angels and demons for reptilian "aliens." (Reptoids *do* exist, however.)

Of course, Icke and those like him never bother to cite even *a single* reputable individual who would *go on-record* to admit to "seeing people … change from human from to a reptilian form and back again." But we are told he claims "people all over the globe had provided the same evidence…, including CIA insiders." Really? Icke also makes a number of other leaps in relation to scripture and history, which are *inaccurate and false.* Somehow, though, such allegations, without even the slightest bit of actual support, pass for "worthwhile reporting" at outfits like the *Daily Express.*

Now, this author has just "downgraded" Icke and those who would listen to him. But that's *not* the end of the story—far from it. Earlier in this work, we addressed the Merovingian dynasty.[2] This author noted two radically different tales—both sordid and wicked—behind the Merovingians' lineal claims. The first one alleges that they descend from Jesus through Mary the Magdalene—a highly blasphemous *satanic contradiction* to God's written Word. The second one would have us believe that the Merovingian dynasty derives from a sea monster (serpent)—or red dragon—who *raped* Merovée's mother—in which chase, he would necessarily be a humanoid or Nephil. (We'll set aside the conventional explanation for a moment, which would assert that Merovée's parents were just ordinary humans, even if they dabbled in the occult or had been satanists.) Those who "accept" the first tale could then attribute a "divine right to rule" to Merovée's descendants, alleging descent from The Christ. Those who would go with the second tale, on the other hand, could allege such a "right" as well, but theirs would be *"alien-"* or even *Satan-based.* Accepting *either* tale obviously results in *an anti-Christian and satanic world view.*

But what if one accepts *both tales?* What if elite members of the British monarchy, in fact, do so? In that case, Merovingians among them would allegedly be *physical* descendants of Jesus and Mary the Magdalene, *as well as* descendants of an "alien" or red dragon (Satan)! Wouldn't such derangement further explain the conduct of British royals like Queen Elizabeth II and her son, Charles? Would that not indeed explain their *feigned* loyalty to God through Jesus and their *actual* loyalty to Satan? Would it not even enable the great confusion—and sensationalism—of individuals like Icke?

---

1. Jon Austin, "David Icke explains his infamous theory why 'Queen IS a shape-shifting reptile,'" *Daily Express,* 17 Feb. 2017.

2. See the subsection titled "A Merovingian 'conspiracy of destiny,'" starting on p. 79.

Among "'aliens' enthusiasts," the sea monster that purportedly raped Merovée's mother to give mankind the Merovingian lineage—as opposed to the blasphemous and false claim that Christ Jesus impregnated her—*is* interpreted to be an "alien" in a "royal" line. To their misinformed thought processes, Merovée's descendants—of whom King Charles III is *key*—may hang their imagined "divine right to rule" on a "superior" hybrid or "alien" genealogy and inheritance. With that in mind, some Merovingians believe they are destined, as a family, to inherit the Earth and rule it—both now *and* if mankind is supplanted by a fully-hybridized successor. Incredibly, achieving a "race" of humanoids capable of ordinary sexual reproduction—that is, without further use of "materials" taken from human men and women—who could then *entirely replace and usurp mankind on Earth,* is a *core agenda* behind "alien" abductions of humans for abominable *biological use* in chimeric "reproduction" efforts and hybridization experiments.[1] Perhaps the British monarchy's deep interest in the occult, UFOs and "aliens,"[2] while simultaneously claiming to be "Christian," is now a bit more understandable.

Speaking of antigravitic saucers, *they too were symbolized at the 1969 investiture.* Indeed, that "modern" symbolism was *central* to the entire event! Though we'll have much more to consider regarding the round gray Welsh slate platform on which Charles was invested as Prince of Wales, its concentric pattern *should* remind us of the sort of *craft*—that is, antigravitic spacecraft, where each ship was called *ha-Galgal* or "the 'Wheel'" (Ezek 10:13, Heb.)—which the prophet Ezekiel watched four *cherubim* actually employ. Notably, each *cherub* is a powerful *four-faced as well as four-winged* angel (see Ezek 1:5-11, 1:23-25, 10:5, 10:7-8, 10:12, 10:14, 10:21-22).

Ezekiel tells us: "Look, ... one *concentric* 'wheel' *was* on the ground beside *each of* the living creatures, with its four faces. The appearance of the wheels and their workings was like the color of beryl [(Heb., *tarshish,* which *precisely matches* the shimmering colors produced with antigravitic propulsion)], and *all* four had a *concentric* pattern; and their appearances, and their workings *was* like that comprising the wheel in the center of the wheel.... And as for their rims, they *were* high and they *were* awesome; and their rims

---

1. For more information, see the author's *Solar Apocalypse* multi-volume series.
2. Reportedly: "Gordon Creighton, a Foreign Service official and Intelligence officer, concluded his story about a reported 1960s UFO landing on the estate of Prince Philip with: 'So there had been a landing on the estate of Mountbatten, and there was Mountbatten's great interest.' The entire testimony was made during an interview with the Disclosure Project [(of demonized New Age occultist Steven M. Greer)] in September 2000. Prince Philip supposedly had a drawer full of sketches and information on different types of UFOs" ("Bohemian Grove: Historical Membership List Plus Biographies," *Institute for the Study of Globalization and Covert Politics,* July 2020). For more information, see this author's *Solar Apocalypse* multi-volume series.

were full of eyes [(cf. lights and illuminated windows)], round about |
all around.... And when the living creatures went, the wheels went
with them; and when the living creatures were carried up from the
Earth, the wheels were lifted up. Near wherever the spirit wanted to
go, there they went—*because* there the spirit went; and the wheels
were lifted together with them, for the living creature's spirit *was* in
the wheels" (Ezek 1:15-20, Heb.; see 1:15-25; cf. 10:2, 10:6, 10:9-10,
10:12-13, 10:16-17, 10:19, Heb.).

Ezekiel's use of the word *tarshish* to describe the colorful glow
(e.g., green, blue, red, yellow and white) produced by the above
craft, seems all the more remarkable in our context, given that
Tarshish *also is the ancient Hebrew name for what we now call the
United Kingdom.* Not only do antigravity craft produce *those very
same colors across their metallic skin when operating,* but these particular colors also may remind us of the colors of four horses of the
Apocalypse in Revelation 6:1-8. Never the less, we may be surprised
to learn that the four *four*-winged *cherubim* Ezekiel saw are *not* the
same as the four *six*-winged *seraphim* of Isaiah 6:1*b*-2 and 6:6-7,
where the latter may actually comprise the "four living creatures"
(i.e., apparent *seraphim)* of Revelation 4:6-9, 5:6, 5:8, 5:14, 6:1 and
6:6. Indeed, it is those *six*-winged angels who *show* us the judgments of the Apocalypse's first four seals (Rev 6:1-8), which summarize the first four years or so of the Tribulation Week—*not* the earlier
four-winged *cherubim* Ezekiel saw.[1]

Now, the round gray Welsh slate investiture platform also served
as the druidic Throne Stone and inner Throne Circle, as we've already
begun to address. Isn't it also remarkable, then, that Ezekiel simultaneously speaks to seeing The *(Non-*Created) Angel of The LORD (i.e.,
Yahveh Himself, or The God of Israel, as a colorful theophany) seated
on His stunning *throne,* "above the firmament" (see Ezek 1:26-28; cf.
10:1, 10:4, 10:18-19)!

Now, returning to this author's earlier assertion that Merovée
was just an ordinary non-Christian, there remains the question of the
foretold AntiChrist being Satan's actual "seed"—that is, in more than
just a "mere" spiritual sense. We may wonder, "Could it be that one
or more persons in the combined genealogy of Queen Elizabeth II
and Prince Philip have been slightly hybridized—via past abductions
by humanoids?" *We just do not know.* Should we *allow for that* as
a possibility, even from a purely theological perspective? *Yes, that is
reasonable.* If such were reality, then at least *some* support could
hypothetically be found for "reptoidhood" claims. Genetic testing,
predictably, *should then expose them as not quite human.* Still, *no*

---

1. For more information, see the *Messiah, History, and the Tribulation Period* multi-volume series.

such test or information has come to light. Ultimately, such "arguments" from silence are *not* really very helpful. Remember, Satan's kingdom is built upon *lies.*

Torn between two "lovers:" God and Satan. In February 1952, King George VI, also a druid, had the red dragon added to his grandson's then future coat of arms. But this symbol of Satan is not without an accompanying Awen. In fact, *the Awen is throughout Charles' heraldic achievement as Prince of Wales*—in its eldest-son labels and fleur-de-lis, some of which are "hidden" in the design.[1] Significantly, *the invoking Awen is even the macro pattern of British royals' full heraldic achievements*—most importantly including those of Charles. In the case of the latter, it is likewise the macro pattern for the top of the arms (mantle included) as well as the base of the arms as Prince of Wales (motto, compartments, and Black Prince shield included). Thus, the invoking Awen macro pattern appears three times on Charles' heraldic achievement as Prince of Wales.

On June 2nd, 1953, with specially-created red dragon statues bearing the Shield of Wales placed outside a temporary annex attached to *Westminster Abbey,* where dignitaries prepared and preened themselves before entering the abbey itself, the princess was coronated Queen Elizabeth II. Just six weeks later, on July 16th, 1953, Queen Elizabeth II, with her husband Prince Philip at her side, made a "Coronation visit" to greet Wales from Caern-Arfon Castle—infamous and better known among some as *druid wizard Merlin's home*[2] *castle*—in an elaborate ceremony that was a clear precursor to her son's future (not then yet announced) investiture as Prince of Wales;[3] In fact, there were four-thousand seated guests, and many more surrounding the castle.

While walking to the central covered platform within Caernarfon Castle, from the Eagle Tower, the queen and Prince Philip passed a shielded *triquetra* of three serpents.[4] This triquetra was *clearly satanic;* with its three heads showing forked tongues and three tails extended from its three corners, one could easily discern it as three intertwined sixes, or 666.

---

1. On Charles' heraldic achievement as Prince of Wales, the *fleur-de-lis* is repeatedly shown interspersed with Templar crosses on coronets and crowns. It is also incorporated into the design of the sovereign helm and the mantle around it, the tails of the dexter and sinister beasts, the frame surrounding the red lion-leopard-bear, and the arrangement of the three ostrich feathers in the Black Prince badge.
2. "Caernarfon" derives from the Welsh *Caer Myrddin,* meaning "Merlin's town" or fortress.
3. The choice of Caernarfon Castle was a means of gaining occult "credibility" among the Welsh people.
4. The *triquetra* is a symbol which some Christians have used to signify The "Trinity" or to try to represent the unified nature of God, *yet pagans also use it.* Some Christians believe that 666 is hidden within the triquetra, even though its loops are outwardly pointed. It is, therefore, a symbol with dual usage—just like the lion, unicorn, and red dragon.

From that central platform within the castle, where Satan's Prince (Charles) would himself be invested (several years later), the queen and Prince Philip greeted a long line of dignitaries, with the queen personally shaking their hands. Fascinatingly, as Elizabeth II did so, she held a program booklet in her left hand—openly displaying the Royal Badge of Wales and its central red dragon, to all. But that was not the major highlight.

Following those above greetings, the queen and Prince Philip proceeded to Queen Eleanor's Gate, otherwise known as the "Queen's Gate," where both stood before a huge Royal Badge of Wales, with its encircled red dragon, to greet the Welsh standing below, outside the castle itself.[1] The profane motto, *Y Ddraig Goch Ddyry Cychwyn,* meaning "The red dragon gives the lead,"[2] was highly visible. In this, the queen and Prince Philip acknowledged being led by the red dragon, or Satan himself. *This was the most significant event at the start of the queen's reign.* Following this event, the queen and Prince Philip attended the 1953 Royal National Eisteddfod, where they were both seated and warmly greeted by the Archdruid of Wales, and then other dignitaries.

In 1958, just as the eagle on the dollar bill is the heraldic symbol of the United States, the red dragon became the official heraldic symbol of the nation of Wales—though it had long been used.[3] On

---

1. Six shields were also mounted on the castle walls to their left and right, with the Shield of Wales being to the queen's right.
2. For more information, see the discussion on the red dragon at p. 188 in ch. 7, "The Heraldic Symbols in the Arms and their Interpretations."
3. "The red dragon is popularly believed to have been the battle standard of [(legendary)] Arthur and other ancient Celtic/Romano-British leaders. There is considerable evidence to suggest that ... the [red] dragon was a symbol of the Romano-British monarchy and possibly Romano-British society more broadly.... The dragons of Arthur and Cadwaladr [(i.e., the king of Gwynedd from ca. 655 to 682)] were ... based on the *draco* standards carried by [earlier] Roman cavalry units.... Despite the close link throughout early Welsh history, the [red] dragon was not [then] used exclusively as a symbol for Wales..., and it was used throughout Britain [only] as a symbol of authority. In 1138, it was adopted by

July 26 of that year, at the conclusion of the Commonwealth Games in Cardiff, Queen Elizabeth II "created" (made) her *absent* son, Prince Charles, the Prince of Wales.[1] At that time:

> ....After Prince Philip's opening remarks, they heard the Queen's voice say: "I want to take this opportunity of speaking to all Welsh people, not only in this arena, but wherever they may be.... I intend to create my son Charles Prince of Wales today."
>
> ...36,000 Welsh voices broke into "God Bless the Prince of Wales." When the clamor died down, the Queen's voice continued: "When he is grown up, I will present him to you at Caernarvon...."
>
> In the headmaster's study that afternoon, Charles automatically also became Earl of Chester and Knight Companion of the Most Noble Order of the Garter.... The monarch and the Prince of Wales are the only two ex-officio of the twenty-six Knights of the Garter...; the Prince of Wales's pew, by ancient tradition, is the second in rank (though the first on the left) in St George's Chapel at Windsor, but may not be occupied until he has been formally dubbed and installed by the sovereign. The Queen, perhaps having reflected on her son's reaction at the age of nine years and eight months, did not perform this ceremony (which also entitled him to wear the Garter's resplendent robes and insignia) for another ten years. By that time, June [17,] 1968, it was part of the buildup to his [formal] investiture at Caernarvon and his emergence into full-time public life.[2]

---

the Scottish as a royal standard, and Richard I took a [(presumably red *draco* or)] dragon standard to the Third Crusade in 1191. Henry III fought under the [red] dragon at the Battle of Lewes and it was used later by Edward III at the Battle of Crécy.... [Around 1416,] ... the English crown, under the rule of Henry V, used the red dragon standard itself during the Battle of Agincourt. The English forces during the battle utilised Welsh longbowmen, along with their own archers. In 1485,...Henry Tudor flew the red dragon of Cadwaladr during his invasion of England. Henry was of Welsh descent and after leaving France with an army of 2,000, landed at Milford Haven on 7 August.... Henry met and fought Richard III at the Battle of Bosworth Field, and in victory took the English throne. After the battle, Henry carried the red dragon standard in state to St Paul's Cathedral, and later the Tudor livery of green and white was added to the flag" ("Flag of Wales," Wikipedia.org, 18 Dec. 2020).

Per the BBC: "The Laws in Wales Acts, passed in 1536 and 1543 during the reign of Henry VIII from the Welsh Tudor dynasty, created a single state and legal jurisdiction, effectively annexing Wales to England. Henry [VIII] did, however, use the red dragon on green and white as an emblem on many Royal Navy vessels. It was also used by Queen Elizabeth I.... It didn't return to the Royal Badge of Wales until 1807" ("Wales history: an official emblem," BBC, 8 Aug. 2008).

From 1807 to 1953, Wales' flag consisted of a white background with a central red dragon over a green (grass) mount. "In 1901 the dragon became the official symbol of Wales, and in Caernarfon in 1911, at the investiture of Edward, Prince of Wales, the flag appeared in its current form, helping its rise to prominence" (ibid.). In 1953, that was changed to a horizontally-oriented half white, half green background with a textually augmented royal badge—that is, the (now former) Badge of Wales containing the red dragon—at its center. "In 1959, after successful lobbying by the Gorsedd of Bards and others [(e.g., in Wales)], Queen Elizabeth II made the [enlarged] red dragon on a green and white background [(in place of the former Badge of Wales)] the official flag for Wales. It was announced that the flag to be flown on government buildings would consist only of the red dragon on a green and white flag, rather than the 1953 badge, which was still in occasional use. The 1959 design can today be seen right across Wales" (ibid.). Also, from 1936 to 2006, the symbol of the Party of Wales, or the Welsh National Party, consisted of an evoking Awen, called a "Triban," in the form of three green triangular mountains, over which portions of the red dragon were centrally imposed.

1. Holden, *PRINCE CHARLES,* p. 325.
2. Holden, *PRINCE CHARLES,* pp. 119-121, 174.

Just over six months later, in February 1959, Queen Elizabeth II approved a change to the design of the Welsh Flag. On February 23, the Minister for Welsh Affairs, Henry Brooke, announced, "I now have it in command from the Queen to say that Her Majesty has been pleased to direct that in [the] future only the Red Dragon on a green and white flag, and not the flag carrying the augmented Royal Badge, shall be flown on Government buildings in Wales and, where appropriate, in London ... [but] the augmented Royal Badge will, of course, continue in use for other purposes."[1] Recall that the augmented flag, approved in 1953, like the Royal Badge of Wales, bore the profane motto *Y Ddraig Goch Ddyry Cychwyn*, or "The red dragon gives the lead."

In mid-August 1963, on the second day of a two-day tour, Queen Elizabeth II and Prince Philip went to Caernarfon Castle a second time, where they were greeted by Lord Snowdon, then Princess Margaret's "bisexual" sodomite playboy "commoner" husband—and Constable of the Castle. Following this, the queen and Prince Philip once again attended the Wales' Royal National Eisteddfod, where the red dragon took center stage. By this point in time, then Prince Charles too had been made an "honorary" bard or druid.

Charles: Satan's Prince globally exposed. In July 1969, modern mankind first publicly walked on the Moon.[2] That same month, on

---

1. Boutell, 1978 ed., pp. 258-259.
2. Questions are yet raised over the Apollo 11 and other NASA Moon landings. Some evidence *does* suggest that the U.S. faked the event, or that elements within the country had prepared to do so, going as far as to actually produce fake footage and photos beforehand—just in case. Apparently, some of that fake stuff *has* been aired, leaked and published (e.g., see "Rare NASA footage of Apollo 11 Astronauts Staging Part of Moon Mission" at "https://youtu.be/ZNOyRnOziPc" on YouTube). Many question "strangeness" such as film which allegedly shows a U.S. flag "blowing" in impossible lunar "wind"—arguing against simple astronaut-induced motion from wrist rotation of the attached pole.

   We may *see* (even with errant "flat Earthers") compelling evidence that NASA created and prepared fake footage and photographs for the Apollo program's missions and events, complete with fake lunar sets, fake Moon backgrounds, fake props, "creative" film editing, and scripted dialogs, involving actual (foul-mouthed and blasphemous) astronauts. In fact, considerable incriminating fake footage and photos *were released* through incompetence and mix-ups—or just secretly leaked—to the public. That is *not* speculation: see, for example, the six-part "Richplanet – Apollo Conspiracy" documentary on YouTube, starting with "https://www.youtube.com/watch?v=RnZAhG-fBpQ". (Search for "Richplanet – Apollo Conspiracy – PART 1 OF 6", to locate the remaining five parts.)

   Lunar conspiracy "theorists" note apparent contradictions in NASA's released Apollo-era material, and tend to remain dissatisfied with provided explanations. Factually speaking, NASA *cannot* deny producing arguably incriminating material—and so has been *unable* to offer *credible* refutations.

   As exposed in this author's *Solar Apocalypse* multi-volume series, from its inception, NASA has engaged in an overt pattern of boldly *lying* to the whole world, seeking to hide what astronauts and other personnel have seen and/or imaged on the Moon, Mars and elsewhere. Whether NASA ever had any intent to release fake footage and photos, or to leak classified genuine imagery, is unknown. But we have available to us a fascinating and troubling mixture of real and fake Apollo-era imagery (motion films and still photographs), which NASA has at times, actively worked to hide and obfuscate. NASA's very real history of "air brushing," to obfuscate and remove certain objects from its photos taken of celestial bodies in our solar system—undertaking such extreme measures before releasing those to the public—is well-known. But that has often been haphazard, incomplete and inconsistent.

   Despite all the above, it is certain that Apollo Program astronauts *were* on the Moon's surface,

the morning of July 1, before an estimated worldwide television audience of five-hundred million—the largest ever, before Charles' 1981 marriage to Diana—his investiture as Prince of Wales took place.[1] Situated at Caernarfon Castle, which looks as though it *rises "out of the sea" (cf. Rev 13:1),* and is the "birthplace of the first Prince of Wales" and the site of the old stone castle of Llewellyn ap Gruffydd, the much-hailed event followed the charter that "created the Black Prince, Edward III's son, Prince of Wales in 1343" (the insignia of which were a coronet, a gold ring, and a silver rod).[2] "The ritual had lain defunct for three hundred years until revived with romantic Celtic enthusiasm by Lloyd George in 1911 .... for a quasi-religious service mixed with improbable pageantry.... [The] 1911 investiture was little more than an extra ceremonial.... Yet, when attending his own first investiture committee, Prince Charles was astonished at the number of people who had come to be involved.... The assembly ranged from Lord Lieutenants to an Archdruid [(i.e., a top pagan)]—even including a woman Catholic Welsh Archbishop.... Slowly, and ultimately with remarkable efficiency, across a sixteen-month task schedule, the whole operation, dragon-like, lumbered forward."[3] For the investiture, both Charles and Prince Philip wore the Garter Collar with its George Pendant and the blue Garter Riband with its Lesser George.[4] Upon then Prince Charles' arrival at the castle, as if to underscore their ignorance and sad scriptural illiteracy, Welsh voices again sang "God Bless the Prince of Wales."[5] Holden summarizes:

> Charles's procession was more splendid than anything he will know again before his own coronation. Flanked by the secretary of state for

---

where they took many stunning photos and shot some amazing videos. Japan's Kaguya probe speaks to Apollo 15 (see "Japanese SELENE (Kaguya) Lunar Mission Spots Apollo 15 Landing Site (Images)" at "https://www.universetoday.com/15579/japanese-selene-kaguya-lunar-mission-spots-apollo-15-landing -site-images" on the Internet)—even though fake materials for this mission *could likewise* have been produced. (Consider the "Moon Landing Hoax: Apollo15 Hadley Rill Was Left For Apollo16" clip, at "https://www.dailymotion.com/video/x7n4bq" and "https://www.dailymotion.com/video/x2w9lqe" on the Internet.) Claimed footage and photos of supposed artificial structures and ancient ruins—as well as saucers, triangles and other craft—on the lunar surface, may also be found.

In the realm of objective reality, there is *no legitimate question* that mankind *has* been to the Moon —including through NASA's Apollo program. Indeed, *no room remains for doubt.* **For more information, see the author's explosive *Solar Apocalypse* series.**

1. Cathcart, p. 93. Junor, pp. 84, 88. See Holden, *PRINCE CHARLES,* photo before p. 163. For more information, see ch. 10's section titled "Marriage, ascension, and politics," at p. 314.
2. Fry, *The Kings & Queens of England & Scotland,* p. 56.
3. Cathcart, pp. 89, 92-93.
4. For color photographs of the investiture, including Charles' and Prince Philip's attire, see "The 25th Anniversary of the Investiture of the Prince of Wales" and "Memories of the Day," *Majesty* magazine, July 1994, Vol. 15, No. 7, pp. 33, 35, 37, 39. For additional color photographs, see *Her Majesty The Queen,* p. 18. For more information, see ch. 7's section titled, "The Garter," at p. 147. Several video segments and images of the event are also freely available over the internet.
5. Holden, *PRINCE CHARLES,* p. 189. Junor, p. 86.

Wales, the Welsh Herald Extraordinary, and two lords-in-waiting, he was followed by five Welsh peers carrying his insignia. Earl Lloyd George of Dwyfor bore the same silver-gilt sword used by the last Prince of Wales, Lord Heycock the golden rod, Lord Maelor the gold ring embellished with two dragons and an amethyst,[1] Lord Harlech the mantle of purple velvet and ermine, and Lord Ogmore the coronet....

The Queen handed the letters patent to the Home Secretary, James Callaghan.... Almost entirely lacking punctuation,[2] they were something of a mouthful:

> "Elizabeth the Second, by the Grace of God, of the United Kingdom of Great Britain and Northern Ireland, and of Our other Realms and Territories, Queen, Head of the Commonwealth, Defender of the Faith. **To all Lords, Spiritual and Temporal**, and all other Our Subjects whatsoever to whom these Presents shall come, Greeting. **Know ye that we have made and created, and by these Our Letters Do make and create, our most dear Son Charles Philip Arthur George**, Prince of the United Kingdom of Great Britain and Northern Ireland, Duke of Cornwall and Rothesay, Earl of Carrick, Baron of Renfrew, Lord of the Isles, and Great Steward of Scotland, **Prince of Wales and Earl of Chester**. And to the same, Our most dear Son Charles Philip Arthur George, have given and granted, and by this Our Present Charter, do give, grant, and confirm the name, style, title, dignity and honor of the same Principality and Earldom. And Him, Our most dear Son Charles Philip Arthur George, as he has been accustomed, We do ennoble and invest, with the said Principality and Earldom, by girding him with a Sword, by putting a Coronet on his head and a Gold Ring on his finger, and also by delivering a Gold Rod into his hand, that he may preside there and may direct and defend those parts—To hold to him and his heirs, Kings of the United Kingdom of Great Britain and Northern Ireland and of Our other Realms and Territories, Heads of the Commonwealth, for ever...."

As Callaghan struggled on, **the Queen formally invested Charles with the insignia**, and both waited while the Charter was read again in Welsh.... Then came the climax of the ceremony. Kneeling before his mother, the Prince of Wales intoned the oath.... **Placing his hands between the Queen's, he declared: "I, Charles, Prince of Wales, do** become your liege man of life and limb and of earthly **worship**, and faith and truth I will bear unto you to live and die against all manner of folks."[3]

Cathcart similarly remarks: "[Charles was] preceded by the Wales and Chester heralds of arms, by the Secretary of State for Wales and by Garter King of Arms.... In ritual closely based on the Westminster investiture of King Charles I, Prince Charles received from the Queen, his ermine mantle in token of leadership, the sword as a symbol of justice, the new-made crown as a token of rank, the ring of Welsh gold in token of duty [and marriage to the Principality of Wales] and the golden verge of pity. Then, to his mother, the

---

1. Among occultists, amethyst is associated with psychic abilities and healing.
2. The author has taken the liberty of inserting such punctuation.
3. Holden, *PRINCE CHARLES*, pp. 191-192.

Queen, he gave the same pledge of homage given by his father, the strange oath of fealty he had been too young to utter at the Coronation: 'I, Charles, Prince of Wales, do ... worship, and faith and truth I will bear unto you to live and die against all manner of folks.'"[1] Michèle Brown adds: "Dressed in the [dark] uniform of the Colonel-in-Chief of the ... Royal Regiment of Wales, Charles appeared bareheaded, flanked by the Secretary of State for Wales, the Wales Herald Extraordinary and two attendant peers. Behind him walked five Welsh peers bearing the insignia of Investiture: the silver-gilt sword, the golden rod signifying authority, the ring, with which the Prince would be married to his country, the mantle of purple silk velvet and ermine, and the coronet. As the Queen invested her son with these insignia, the Letters Patent which created Charles Prince of Wales were read."[2] Of import, Charles' *marriage* to Wales signifies that *he is Satan's*—the antithesis to Christians' marriage to The Christ.

The clothing Charles wore that morning, besides his various Garter insignia (e.g., the gold "chain" or Collar), consisted of a Welsh military uniform with an ermine-trimmed dark-purple surcoat draped over it.[3] Apart from the coronet, the insignia of the investiture included "the ring, formed of two dragons grasping an amethyst;[4] the golden rod or verge of government derived from a shepherd's staff; the sword [bearing the etched phrase *Ich Dien* across its blade], with its [Welsh] dragons guarding the crown, [as held by] the [purple velvet-covered belt and] scabbard, [also] with the motto *Ich Dien,* I Serve.... As the watchdog of tradition, the Duke of Norfolk [pronounced]...., 'The heraldic devices are ancient, traditional and correct. There will be no monkeying about.'"[5] When placed, the purple belt was slung across Charles' right shoulder, going to the front of his left hip, where it held the sword in the attached scabbard. Although (now) King Charles III has not yet entirely fulfilled it, and it may not even pertain to the foretold AntiChrist, the author is here reminded of the prophecy: "Woe to the idol shepherd that leaveth the flock! The sword shall be upon his arm, and upon his right eye: his arm *shall be* clean dried up | completely wither, and his right eye shall be utterly darkened | blinded" (Zech 11:17, KJV; cf. Ps 10:15). Besides Charles' "golden rod" derived from a "shepherd's staff" and

---

1. Cathcart, p. 96.
2. Michèle Brown, *PRINCE CHARLES* (New York: Crown Publishers Inc., 1980), pp. 96, 133.
3. Holden, *PRINCE CHARLES,* p. 186.
4. The gold ring, called the "William Goscombe John Investiture Ring" and originally made for the Prince of Wales in 1911 by Garrard, consists of two gold (metal) instances of the dragon of Wales, clutching a round purple Amethyst between its claws, tail and mouth.
5. Cathcart, pp. 91, 93. Recall that the Duke of Norfolk is the Earl Marshal over the Court of Chivalry, through which the heralds deal with armorial disputes. Bernard Marmaduke served as the Earl Marshal for this investiture (Junor, p. 85).

the dragon-laden sword and ring, we find parallels to the darkened right eye in his arms as Prince of Wales, as shown earlier,[1] and on June 28, 1990, Charles nearly shattered his right arm in a polo fall.[2] Notably, these are biological locations of the coming Mark of the Beast (Rev 13:16, 14:9), so might this "idol shepherd" prophecy even relate to the False Prophet who promotes Charles?

Trimmed with platinum, the coronet itself was made of gold, containing seventy-five diamonds and twelve emeralds.[3] Cathcart observes: "The designer conceded that there was a hint of the crown of thorns in the interweaving fragile shapes of fleur-de-lys and crosses-patées. But was that not the humblest of all crowns?"[4] Having been fashioned specifically for then Prince Charles, the coronet depicts four gold, diamond-studded Merovingian crosses—one to the North, one to the East, one to the West, and one to the South—as well as four gold *fleur-de-lis* around its circumference. The crosses themselves were fashioned from gold *nails* (cf. thorns). The coronet also bears the gold "mound" or globe, representing the Earth, with a *fifth* gold Merovingian cross above it, at the top-center.[5] A banded gold globe with a cross is similarly depicted at the top-center of the *five* heir-apparent crowns on Charles' heraldic achievement as Prince of Wales. (He is meant to be "ruler | prince of this world," under Satan.) Interestingly, the earliest surviving register of the Order of the Garter (ca. 1534), known as the Black Book from its black velvet cover, contains an illustration of the Order of the Garter's twenty-six companion knights. This illustration shows King Henry VIII seated in the Garter Throne Room surrounded by the remaining twenty-five Garter knights, *five* of whom, including the king, are holding a gold scepter in one hand and a gold globe (mound or "orb") with a gold Merovingian cross at its top-center in the other.[6]

---

1. For more information, see ch. 7's sections titled, "The top of the arms" and "The sinister (right-hand) supporter," at pp. 135 and 197, respectively.
2. Hoey, *Charles & Diana: The Tenth Anniversary,* pp. 85, 89, 150.
3. Holden, *PRINCE CHARLES,* p. 187. Cathcart, p. 91.
4. Cathcart, p. 91.
5. For relatively clear color photographs of Charles wearing this coronet, see "The 25th Anniversary of the Investiture of the Prince of Wales" and "Memories of the Day," *Majesty* magazine, July 1994, Vol. 15, No. 7, pp. 33, 36. Photographs are also available on the Internet.
6. Begent, p. 11.

Notably, all that regalia, those "insignias of office," in which Charles' found himself arrayed, while being invested as Satan's Prince—that is, the blood-red sash of (in his case) *lies* around his waist (cf. Eph 6:14*a),* the (chained) Collar and blue Riband of *unrighteousness* across his chest (cf. Eph 6:14*b,* 6:20*a),* black-shod feet prepared for evil (cf. Eph 6:15), the anti-Christian Garter Star "shield" (cf. Eph 6:16), the encircling "helmet" (cf. Eph 6:17*a,* Gk.) or coronet symbolizing dominion over all the Earth, and the sword of Satan (cf. Eph 6:17*b),* the gold ring representing his marriage to Satan, the "gold rod" (countering a shepherd's staff), and the dark-purple silk-velvet ermine mantle (cf. robe)—may also be construed as *counterfeiting the things of God.* Indeed, they are antithetical to the "armor of God," which His saints are instructed to "put on" (cf. Eph 6:10-20).

At the investiture's center, there were three "utility" thrones: "Made of [grey] Welsh slate, those of Prince Philip and Prince Charles were backless, for the benefit of the TV cameras, while the Queen's had a low back for reasons of status...."[1] Indeed, the backrest of Elizabeth II's throne had the dragon of Wales on it, signifying her service to the Devil. When Charles' mother visibly placed the coronet upon his head, not only was this dragon directly behind her and adjacent to her son's throne,[2] but Elizabeth II was then possessed by Satan (captured as "X lightning" on film[3]). Red cushions, representing the red dragon, decorated all three seats—as well as the slate stool, the druidic *Maen Y Gyfamod* or "Covenant Stone," upon which Charles knelt to *worship* before Satan. The round

1. Holden, *PRINCE CHARLES,* p. 181.
2. For color photographs of the investiture, including the queen's regalia, see pp. 35 and 37 of *Majesty* magazine, Vol. 15, No. 7 (July 1994), and p. 18 of *Her Majesty The Queen.* For other photos showing the thrones, see Jeannie Sakol and Caroline Latham, *An Intimate Look at The Lifestyles of Britain's Royal Family, The Royals* (Chicago: Congdon & Weed, Inc., 1987), p. 151; and Brown, *PRINCE CHARLES,* p. 98. Much may now be seen via the Internet.
3. For further details as well as a captured image of this "X lightning," see p. 256.

grey Welsh slate platform itself, *evoking King Arthur's Round Table* and upon which all this transpired, represented, *among other things,* the roundel filled with the red dragon on the Throne (Gorsedd) Banner. Indeed, with the druidic Throne Stone—known otherwise as the Logan Stone or Altar Stone—at its center, it would be perfectly at ease in the center of Stonehenge, a pagan monument ostensibly *relocated* to Salisbury Plain, from an ancient Welsh circle in Pembrokeshire.[1]

Of the AntiChrist, it is written, "And the dragon gave him his power, his throne, and great authority" (Rev 13:2). *As Prince of Wales, Charles received (and as king continues to receive) his power, his throne, and great authority from the red dragon of Wales—"that serpent of old, called the Devil and Satan, who deceives the whole world" (Rev 12:9).* Interestingly, unlike Revelation 12:3, verse 13:2 does not call the apocalyptic dragon "red," and indeed, the normally red Welsh dragon was depicted in grey on the queen's investiture throne. This fulfilled scripture literally. That Charles, like his late parents, is a *Gorsedd* or "Throne" druid, whose Throne (Gorsedd) Banner bears the red dragon centrally, is just a further confirmation.

Junor, noting that the Earl of Snowdon "created a perfect theatre in the round," comments, "The soaring walls of the castle were emblazoned by tall, white banners bearing red dragons," overlooking "banks of flame-red seats and a carpet of bright green grass in the middle; and at the focal point, beneath a canopy of clear Perspex bearing the Prince of Wales feathers [with his 'Ich Dien' motto]..., stood three thrones of riven Welsh slate on a 28-foot circular slate dais." As Snowdon put it, "You wouldn't be surprised to see them at [druidic] Stonehenge, would you?" Indeed, the appearance of the three feathers in the Badge of the Black Prince are intentionally arranged reflect *the druidic Awen,* in an *invoking* occult orientation, which means "to disperse *possession* through ascent" (in this case, by Satan); such a "dispersion" of possession, like watering a spiritual lawn with a spiritual sprinkler, is typically made by *ceremony!* Regarding the restoration of "the old Eisteddfod" in 1857, Charles de Gaulle wrote: "The bardic *Awen* was <u>invoked</u> to re-animate the Gorsedd. The popular [red dragon] spirit was appealed to for the support of a gathering designed for the vindication, not less than for the pleasure, of the people."[2] In other words, the Eisteddfod is satanically inspired, motivated, and animated, and always has been.

---

1. Franz Lidz, "Was Stonehenge a 'Secondhand' Monument?," *New York Times;* and Andrew MacAskill, "Second time lucky? Stonehenge first erected in Wales, archaeologists say," *Reuters,* 12 Feb. 2021.
2. Charles De Gaulle, "The Celts of the Nineteenth Century," *The Cambrian Journal,* p. 58.

Moreover, this is central to the very idea of the so-called "Black Prince."

Now that we have learned *a little* (so far) about the Awen, consider the fact that the Perspex canopy itself was formed as an *invoking* Awen! Not only so, but the arrangement of the three thrones *and stool* beneath it also formed an *evoking* Awen—just as both an invoking and evoking Awen are shown together on the Gorsedd Banner. In the case of the latter Awen, then Prince Charles' position on the slate stool corresponds to the Welsh word *heddwch,* or "peace," in the aforementioned banner, thereby placing him symbolically as the "Prince of Peace"—a title that in reality belongs only to Christ Jesus (cf. Isa 9:6-7). For both of these Awens, centered as they were over the round Throne Stone at the center of the round platform,[1] the three thrones and their royal occupants represented the three so-called "rays of light" or the "Mystical Mark." (As will be shown later, an actual "ray" of light—part of a strange "X" pattern—appears on *an official* reel of film, over the queen's satanic throne.)

Importantly, there is more: "Iolo [Morganwg (Edward Williams)] ... propounded that 'God created the world by the melodious utterance of his holy name, and that the form and figure of that name was /|\, being the rays of the rising sun at equinoxes and solstices conveying into focus the eye of light'.... This symbol [(i.e., the three rays of the Awen)] was known as the 'Nod Cyfrin' (Mystical Mark) and is represented within the Great Circle of the Gorsedd.... The 'Maen Y Gyfamod' (Covenant Stone) stands a few feet outside the actual circle [(cf. the slate stool on which Charles knelt)], marking as it does the ... cardinal point, within the main circle [(cf. the central circle, or Throne Stone, beneath the queen's satanic throne)].... This alignment in relation to the position of the 'Maen Llog' [(i.e., the Logan or Altar Stone, which is one and the same as the Throne Stone)] mark out the three rays of the 'Nod Cyfrin', bestowing the circle with the voice of God and the vibration of his Holy name."[2]

Upon hearing then Prince Charles speak at his investiture, the most knowledgeable or astute druids would have concluded that his was "the voice of god and the vibration of his holy name!" Yet, this druidic "god" was, again, none other than Satan himself. (Recall that the Awen is actually a perversion of the Hebrew ש, which relates to the true voice of The God of Israel.) Lucifer, who was the anointed or "messianic" *cherub,* the most powerful of the *cherubim* (a special class of angels, perhaps the most powerful) before his transgression

---

1. The overall platform is patterned as four concentric rings encircling a central round Throne Stone.
2. Kristoffer Hughes, "The Stones and The Chair – A History of the Gorsedd of Bards," *The Druid Network*, 20 Feb. 2009, as now archived at "https://web.archive.org/web/20120322232740/http://druidnetwork.org/articles/meiniachadair.html" on the Internet.

and fall, then spoke in the person of the foretold AntiChrist. Did Satan temporarily possess his "chosen one?"

Notably, Lucifer had been *musical* before he sinned. It is written: "Thus says The Lord LORD: ' ... your heart *is* lifted up, and you say, "I *am* God, I sit *in* the seat of God, in the midst of the seas" — yet you *are* a man, and not a 'god,' though you set your heart as the heart of God. (....With your wisdom and your understanding, you have gained riches....) ... Thus says The Lord LORD: 'You *were* the seal of perfection, full of wisdom and perfect in beauty. You were in Eden, the garden of God; every precious stone *was* your covering.... The workmanship of your timbrels and pipes was prepared for you on the day you were created. You *were* the messianic cherub who covers; I established you. You were on the holy mountain of God; you walked back and forth in the midst of fiery stones [(cf. stars)]. You *were* perfect in your ways from the day you were created — till iniquity was found in you. By the abundance of your trading, you became filled with violence within, and you sinned. Therefore, I cast you as a profane thing out of the mountain of God, and I destroyed you, *O* covering cherub, from the midst of the fiery stones. Your heart was lifted up because of your beauty; you corrupted your wisdom for the sake of your splendor. I cast you to the ground; I laid you before kings, that they might gaze at you" (Ezek 28:2-4, 28:12-17; see 28:1-19).

As to light, the name Lucifer literally means "Day Star" (Isa 14:12, Heb.; see 14:12-20), and this was appropriate before his fall. Yet, "Day Star" is now a title of Jesus, The Messiah (2 Pet 1:19, Gk.), who is The Bright and Morning Star (Rev 22:16; cf. Num 24:17) and whose face shines like the Sun (e.g., see Matt 17:2; Rev 1:16). But Satan is a usurper, and his seed Charles is *the* foretold AntiChrist.

Of the investiture ceremony, Satan's Prince affirmed, "Perhaps it's symbolizing 'Ich Dien', if you like, in some way."[1] Notice the arrangement. Charles' motto, meaning "I serve" and "your man," stood directly over the central throne, which bore the Welsh dragon atop slate encircled by green grass.[2] As the queen's and indeed the world's "liege man," the arrangement's message was "I serve the red dragon" or "I serve Satan" — essentially the same message conveyed at the base of Charles' achievement as Prince of Wales.[3] Tim Heald recalls: "[The] investiture was a keynote occasion because it was one of the first royal spectaculars which seemed to have been designed almost entirely for television.... After the ceremony, ...

---

1. Junor, pp. 84-85.
2. The red dragon is typically shown standing on a mount of green grass in Welsh heraldry.
3. For more information, see ch. 7's section titled, "The base of the coat of arms," at p. 185.

[there were] little knots of Welsh matrons gathered by the roadside waving flags, usually the Welsh Dragon of Wales, and crying out 'Ooooh, isn't he lovely!' ... We all felt that we were in at the beginning of something special that day in Carnarvon Castle."[1] These same flags, depicting the red dragon, were also waved during the ceremony inside the castle.

Ironically, a short Welsh Bible reading followed the investiture, after which the queen presented her son.[2] Junor recounts: "Next there followed a short interdenominational religious service, conducted in both English and Welsh. This, with the participation of Roman Catholic prelates, was one of the most important innovations since Prince Edward's investiture, and although it was not Prince Charles's own doing he has been very much in favour of ecumenical worship ever since. All that was left was for the monarch to present the Prince of Wales to the people.... [It] had been a glorious, colourful, spine-tingling day. But it was not the pageant that had conquered the Welsh.... It was Prince Charles."[3] As "Prince of the Red Dragon," Charles serves Satan, not God. This is especially disturbing when we consider the fact that, contrary to God's Word, his mother currently is, and he is in line to be, the "Supreme Governor" of the Church of England—the Anglican Protestant Church. Junor, and others like her, could not be more confused in referring to "state ceremonial involving the monarchy" as "the foremost Protestant ceremonies in the land."[4]

In listening to the album (LP) of Charles' investiture as Prince of Wales, and watching available film of the event and preparations for it,[5] there are several more salient points to make. *Some of these are plainly astounding.* So, let's uncover and unpack these *formerly hidden* points as we recap, and afterward discover what then Prince Charles himself had to say about it all.

The first advent of the AntiChrist: Prince Charles' Investiture as Prince of Wales. At Christ's first coming, He did not make war, destroy the world's armies, conquer the world, cast His enemies down to Hell, nor judge all the survivors of mankind and then save the sheep among them, etc. Rather, He manifest Himself as The Lamb of God to pay the penalty for our sins, and to make Himself personally

1. Tim Heald, "When hope was born," *International Express*, US Ed. No. 132, 29 June–5 July 1994, p. 34.
2. Holden, *PRINCE CHARLES*, p. 193. A picture of "the Queen leading Prince Charles through the King's Gate to be presented to the people of Wales" may be found on p. 39 of the July 1994 issue of *Majesty* magazine (Vol. 15, No. 7). Also see Junor, between pp. 86-87.
3. Junor, p. 89.
4. Junor, p. 85.
5. Several low-quality investiture video segments are available over the internet, and original videos and raw footage, while costly, can be purchased in a number of instances. (Prophecy House may produce its own detailed video in the future, so look for that *and express your interest to the publisher.*)

known to those whom He would save. You may have begun to notice a similar pattern in the life of Charles Philip Arthur George, who
seeks to save mankind apart from the true and real Christ. If not,
you now shall — *as this is what Charles' investiture as Satan's Prince
was all about.* In fact, there was a carefully crafted and enacted
amalgamation of satanic parodies to **a)** the false prophet; **b)** the sign
of the cross and the crucifixion of Christ, with import to our blood-
red sins being made white like snow;[1] and **c)** Christ's marriage to His
saints, the Church (cf. Principality of God).

Charles' investiture was, quite literally, *a satanic initiation and
rite* for the estimated eighty-thousand present in and around the castle, and intended to be so for the hundreds of millions who watched
by television. "The investiture of the Prince of Wales was designed
for the camera.... Lord Snowdon worked ... to show the ceremony
to the widest possible public. 'It was very important to make it into a
television production that was going to be viewed at home, in peoples' sitting rooms, so that when you were sitting alone watching it,
you thought you were there.... I wanted to design it for the four or
five hundred million viewers, rather than like it was in 1911, when it
was just for an elitist few of maybe four thousand people.'"[2] This
was the AntiChrist's *first advent* — when he was in fact "brought signally before the world."[3] His second advent will transpire when he is
possessed by Satan[4] and commences to rule the world during the
Great Tribulation, which is yet future. (Yes, the AntiChrist, like Christ,
has *two advents,* but unlike Christ, they are not separated by nearly
two millennia, and in the latter's case, the mortal wound is at his *second advent* rather than his first!) We shall see all this and more in
the pages that follow.

Paying homage to the goat, the investiture mascot. In early 1969,
months before his investiture, then Prince Charles received his first
army appointment as Colonel-in-Chief of the new Royal Regiment of
Wales — *a regiment employing a two-horned billy (male) goat as its
ceremonial mascot.*[5] It was his uniform as *Colonel-in-Chief of the*

---

1. Where the red dragon banners were concerned, both their color and contrast were like oxygenated
   blood against pure white snow.
2. "BBC Colour Television 1969," as posted at "https://www.youtube.com/watch?v=scar4bwXXFI".
3. Some mistakenly teach that the AntiChrist would not begin his ministry in such an overt manner: "He is
   not brought signally before the world and announced, and then we are caused to see him. But he in-
   conspicuously begins his ministry, behind the scenes, before finally he is brought out to center stage"
   (Dr. David Jeremiah, "The Reign of Terror," *Turning Point,* 12 March 2009). Hindsight is 20-20.
4. One sensational but equally erroneous teaching is that "the AntiChrist is nothing more nor less than Satan incarnate; he is ... Satan walking around in the flesh" (Dr. Jeremiah, ibid.). No, the AntiChrist shall
   be *possessed* by Satan; he is not and will not be Satan incarnate any more than was Judas Iscariot!
5. The Royal Regiment of Wales was one of two British regiments having a goat as mascot. The second,
   The Royal Welch Fusiliers, was likewise part of the Prince of Wales' Division; it too incorporated the
   Badge of the Black Prince. These goats, each named "Taffy" followed by a roman numeral indicating its

Royal Regiment of Wales, with its *Ich Dien* Cap Badge (i.e., the Badge of the Black Prince), that Charles selected for his investiture. With his Garter Star pinned over his heart, Charles also wore his Garter Collar with its George Pendant and his blue Garter Riband or sash with its Lesser George. (Prince Philip too wore these Garter regalia.)

Thus, while Charles' Royal Regiment of Wales lined the route to Caernarfon Castle,[1] its *goat—his goat—would soon serve as the investiture mascot* (see the later photo)! Yet, there was considerably more to this satanic choice: it was, in fact, an unambiguous symbol of the false prophet—the second beast of Revelation 13: "Then I saw another beast rise up from the Earth, and it [he] had two horns like a lamb and spoke as if a dragon. And it [he] produces [brings about] all the authority of the first beast in its sight, and causes the Earth and those dwelling therein *to think* that they should worship [revere, honor, do homage to, defer to] the first beast, whose deadly wound was healed" (Rev 13:11-12, Gk.). Earlier, the author noted that the three ostrich feathers (intimating 6-6-6) in the Black Prince badge, derive from the original Black Prince's "shield for peace," and the author asked if these three feathers might in some way also intimate Satan's unholy "trinity." In fact, that appears to be so, as suggested by this goat mascot. Moreover, the inbuilt message, "I serve the red dragon" or Satan, includes, therefore, an implication that Satan gives "peace." False prophets, however, are known to *disingenuously* say "peace, peace"[2] and "peace and security" (e.g., cf. 1 Th 5:3, Gk.).

On June 11, 1969, *two* Welsh regiments (cf. two horns), The South Wales Borderers (red uniforms) and The Welch Regiment (olive green uniforms) were "amalgamated" into the new Royal Regiment of Wales; at the Prince of Satan's subsequent investiture, the two sub-regiments wore their original red and green uniforms, respectively. The amalgamation event—at which Charles, his father Prince Philip, the red dragon and the goat were center-stage, on a large *green grass* parade ground known as the Cardiff Castle Green—was widely publicized and televised; also, a large in-person audience surrounded the grassy field. The ceremony began with The Welch Regiment taking the field, followed by the The South Wales Borderers, as Charles and Prince Philip observed; each of these regiments wore the *Ich Dien* Cap Badge, as did Charles and Prince Philip. Unlike the

---

succession, are selected from the royal goat herd. On March 1, 2006, The Royal Welch Fusiliers amalgamated with the Royal Regiment of Wales to form the two battalions of The Royal Welsh.

1. "Royal Regiment of Wales," *Wikipedia.* Caernarfon Castle was designed to evoke thoughts of Constantinople, and to remind England's adversaries of the imperial power of Rome.

2. God has warned His people concerning the presence of false prophets and sirens (Ezek 13:17-23), who would come in among them clothed as sheep, falsely saying, "Peace, peace!" (Jer 6:13-14, 8:8-11; Ezek 13:1-16; see Deut 13:1-3, 18:20-22; 1 John 4:1-6; cf. Isa 48:22; Jer 23:1-2, 23:16-40).

latter, Satan's Charles also wore his Garter Star and blue Garter Riband with its Lesser George.

The Goat Major, a corporal of The South Wales Borderers (red uniforms), *led the goat* of The Welch Regiment (olive green uniforms), bearing its original red goat-coat and silver *Ich Dien* (Black Prince badge) head plate, as well as The South Wales Regiment marching band, through a castle archway and *onto the field*—directly between The Welch Regiment and Charles. Green contrasted against red throughout (suggesting the contrast of the red dragon on a grassy field), and all active-duty military personnel present, *including the goat,* bore the *Ich Dien* or "I serve" motto along with the three *Vav*-like ostrich feathers (cf. 6-6-6) of the Badge of the Black Prince.

A number of standards and flags were flown. The Prince of Wales standard flew from a castle tower, while Charles and Prince Philip stood between two flag poles at the dais (platform) opposite the goat and regiments; the pole to their right bore the Union Jack, and that to their left bore the Flag of Wales with its red dragon against a green and white field. The regiments with the goat in front of them, bearing its original red goat-coat, were facing Charles and Prince Philip, and in turn the red dragon immediately adjacent to them (on the Welsh flag). Behind the goat and the regiments themselves, and below the castle tower flying the Prince of Wales standard, there were three more flag poles; the one in the middle was used to fly a new black regimental flag displaying the Badge of the Black Prince with its *Ich Dien* motto, while a pole next to it—the one closest to the castle—bore the previous Welsh flag (displaying the red dragon). Charles and Prince Philip were facing these flags from all the way across the Cardiff Castle Green—as they faced the goat and the regiments in front of them. These flags were all in addition to the original and new regimental colors, which soldiers paraded. Also, the Land Rover taking Charles and Prince Philip onto, and then from the field bore the Prince of Wales standard on its hood—even as a few onlookers flew the red dragon Flag of Wales.

Charles, with Prince Philip just behind him, then proceeded from the platform to inspect the troops *and meet Taffy, the goat, in the midst of the grassy field*. There, Charles stretched forth his hand as the goat stretched forth its neck, until Satan's Prince placed his hand on the goat's forehead. Charles, with Prince Philip following, then returned to the dais and faced the goat. Upon doing so, as the Goat Major stood at the goat's side, a soldier of The Welch Regiment removed the original red goat-coat from the goat and replaced it with the new Royal Regiment of Wales goat-coat—a dark forest green coat with a red border *that bore the red dragon inside a white wreath at its center on both sides of the goat.* This was the official point of formation of the new Royal Regiment of Wales. With the two-horned goat now bearing the motto "I serve" on its head, and the

red dragon—the symbol of Satan—at its sides as it stood on the grassy field, *Charles and Prince Philip saluted the two-horned goat* (and the two sub-regiments behind it). In other words, once "I serve the red dragon" or "I serve Satan" had been symbolized with the goat, Charles and Prince Philip paid homage to Satan.[1]

Following the salute from Satan's Prince and Prince Philip, the new regimental colors were consecrated or "blessed," and sprinkled with "holy water," by the apostate Chaplain General, Archdeacon J.R. Youens, as he faced Charles, Prince Philip, and the Flag of Wales to their left, and made the sign of

the cross in the air before them. Afterward, the goat, servant to Satan, led the sub-regiments around the Cardiff Castle Green, as they paraded before Charles as Prince of Wales. Therefore, *the red dragon gave the lead, the goat acted as the false prophet, and the soon-to-be presented (to the world) foretold AntiChrist, then Prince Charles, was proclaimed.*

Now, let's fast forward to the day of Charles' investiture as Prince of Wales, *just three weeks later.* The royal family, having arrived aboard the Britannia at Holyhead (henceforth, *un*-Holyhead) the prior evening, proceeded by train to Caernarfon.[2] *Before riding in*

---

1. All this was a satanic parody of Israel's ancient high priest placing his hand upon the head of the *Azazel* or Scapegoat at Yom Kippur each year to symbolically transfer the sins of the nation to the goat. At that time, the goat bore a white cord dipped in sacrificial blood, which God would subsequently turn white—signifying that He had accepted the sacrifice for the nation and forgiven the nation's sins that year. Yet, at this ceremony involving then Prince Charles, the goat was made to signify "I serve Satan," after Satan's Prince placed his hand upon its head.

2. This was despite warnings that Welsh patriots intended to attack the royals, as well as actual attempts on Charles' life. Indeed, a bomb had been discovered on the Holyhead pier where the Britannia was to

separate carriages, from a nearby railway station to Caernarfon Castle, for the awaited investiture ceremony, both Satan's Prince and Prince Philip took care to first render salutes to this same goat—doing so as a regimental officer faced them *in turn,* and held the goat steady by its collar in his right hand.

Charles was first to exit the Royal Train, where he met George Thomas, then Secretary for Wales, on the train's red-carpeted disembarkation platform. With Secretary Thomas at his right side, Charles faced the goat to salute. Satan's Prince, Secretary Thomas, and a squadron leader of the Royal Regiment of Wales then descended the red-carpeted stairs, boarded the initial royal carriage and departed to the castle.

Following Charles' departure, as the raised royal standard waved overhead in the breeze, Prince Philip stood upon the disembarkation platform—*along with Queen Elizabeth II at his right side, and Princess Anne, the Queen Mother and Princess Margaret, Countess of Snowdon, behind.* Philip then moved to attention *with the queen and the others mentioned,* directly faced the goat just below and before the platform's stairs, and formally saluted—just as Charles had done. Thus, Queen Elizabeth II, Prince Philip, the Queen Mother, Princess Anne and Princess Margaret *all paid homage to the goat! That was of course, entirely pre-orchestrated and intentional.* The queen then descended the stairs and walked in front of and behind the goat, effectively *encircling it,* while Prince Philip and the others remained on the platform above, awaiting their royal carriages. (There were *four* royal carriages.) As they waited, two more royals— Princess Alice, the Duchess of Gloucester, and Kathleen Hamilton, the Duchess of Abercorn, Mistress of the Robes to the Queen Mother, who then was the senior lady of the British Royal Household —joined them from behind on the platform.

The queen, Prince Philip, and Princess Anne then boarded and departed in the *second* royal carriage; the Queen Mother and Princess Margaret boarded and departed in the *third* royal carriage; and finally, the Duchess of Abercorn and Princess Alice, who would later accompany Lord Louis Mountbatten at the castle, boarded and departed in the *fourth* royal carriage.

Each carriage among the four, as it traveled to the castle—just as when they later departed the castle to return to the Royal Train—was

---

dock, and two Welshmen of the "Movement for the Defence of Wales"—who allegedly had earlier bombed the Snowdonia Country Club at Penisarwaun, Caernarfon, as a repudiation of Lord Snowdon and the royals generally—were killed while planting another bomb on the railway at Abergele on the eve of the investiture, and thus beneath the train that would carry the royals to Caernarfon. (Hywel Trewyn, "Prince bomb Martyrs 'also blasted club', book claims," *DailyPost.co.uk,* 6 Nov. 2008.) Still, the time for one of this beast's heads to be mortally wounded remains future.

surrounded by soldiers of the Welsh regiment on horseback. Finally, the goat itself departed to the castle—walked by the very soldier who had stood at attention with the animal at his right side as Satan's Prince and then the other royals saluted the creature. Such was the epitome of satanic symbolism.

Through all this, the goat wore its silver *Ich Dien* head plate, *but not its green goat-coat bearing the red dragon*. So where was the red dragon, and how did Satan then "give the lead?" And who wore the "missing" dark emerald green of the absent goat-coat? Another soldier, a squadron leader of the Royal Regiment of Wales, went ahead of Charles and the Secretary for Wales *on foot,* preceding even the mounted regimental soldiers who surrounded Charles' carriage—while the goat trailed them all. *That squadron leader marched the red dragon banner all the way to the Water Gate, at the base of the Eagle Tower—so-named for the three large stone Roman Eagles perched atop its three turrets—where then Prince Charles would arrive to depart the first carriage, and enter the castle (ahead of all the other aforementioned royals).* Immediately adjacent to the squadron leader, a second soldier, also on foot, marched the standard of the Prince of Wales with its four lion-leopard-bears and central green coronet. Lord Snowdon waited at the Water Gate to meet Charles and the Secretary for Wales; Snowdon wore his custom-designed dark emerald green uniform, with its *Ich Dien* lapel pin, the badge of the Black Prince.[1] Thus, Satan led Charles, his ultimate AntiChrist—and the two-horned goat, symbolic of his false prophet—all the way to the Water Gate of the roman Eagle Tower![2] The order of arrival then was 1) Satan as the red dragon, 2) the foretold AntiChrist, and 3) the "False Prophet" as the two-horned goat! But this was just the start.

Prince Charles' arrival at the castle. Led by Satan, as previously addressed, Charles was the first royal to arrive by royal carriage at Caernarfon Castle. In that carriage, George Thomas, then Secretary of Wales, as well as another squadron leader of the Royal Regiment of Wales, rode with Satan's Prince. At the Water Gate, Charles met Lord Snowdon, the Mayor of Caernarfon, and the Town Clerk.

---

1. Snowdon and all others who displayed the Badge of the Black Prince, were there as servants not just of Satan, but of Charles himself as the Black Prince or *Prince of Darkness*.
2. These two standards, that of the red dragon and that of the Prince of Wales, also led then Prince Charles from the Water Gate to the Chamberlain Tower, from the investiture platform to the Queen's Gate, from the Queen's Gate to the King's Gate, and then from the King's Gate back to the Water Gate (i.e., throughout the pattern of the cross that Satan's Prince traced). The two soldiers bearing these standards, having brought them outside the Water Gate (from which they had originally entered the castle ahead of Charles), then posted themselves to meet Charles as he emerged from the Eagle Tower to board the Royal Carriage, for the return trip to the Royal Train. The red dragon likewise, of course, led the queen and Prince Philip as they accompanied Satan's Prince.

"The Procession of the Prince of Wales is formed up just inside the Castle, and as he emerges from the Eagle Tower a [trumpeted] Fanfare is sounded.... This Procession includes the Archdruid[, chief pagan].... <u>The Banners of Llywelyn ap Gruffydd and of the Red Dragon are carried after them</u>, followed by ... the five [Welsh] Lords who will shortly carry the [investiture] Regalia, with Chester Herald and Wales Herald Extraordinary immediately before The Prince of Wales, who is accompanied by his two Supporters."[1] That is, Charles was preceded by the "Red Dragon Banner" as well as his own Welsh standard, which itself is based upon Llewellyn the Great's banner and bears four lion-leopard-bears differenced by his coronet on a central green shield. Specifically, these two standards preceded the Secretary of Wales; five Welsh lords (peers), who would later carry the investiture regalia; the Wales Herald of Arms Extraordinary, Francis Jones, and the Chester Herald of Arms, Walter Vecko; Charles himself; and two more lords-in-waiting, who would serve as his "two witnesses." Therefore, seven of the *thirteen ceremonial lords*, a "coven" of twelve lords under Lord Snowdon effectively, were in Charles' procession.

Evidently referring to the red dragon or Satan as "God"—whose banners adorned the stone walls of Caernarfon castle and whose flag ignorant Welsh men and women inexcusably waved all around —the Welsh people blasphemously sang the words to "God Bless:" "God bless the Prince of Wales!... Till Britain's name and glory, resounds from shore to shore.... God bless the Prince of Wales!... May God's strong arm protect us, May heav'n still on us smile! Above the throne of England may fortune's star long shine.... God bless the Prince of Wales!... God bless the Prince of Wales!" Religious, lost, and *without* spiritual understanding,[2] they did this as Charles entered Caernarfon Castle's amphitheater, proceeding from the Eagle Tower to the Chamberlain Tower. Likewise, apostate heads of various church bodies participated.[3]

The arrival of the remaining royals. The royals in the remaining three royal carriages—including Queen Elizabeth II, Prince Philip, Princess Anne, the Queen Mother, Princess Margaret, and Princess Alice—arrived at Caernarfon Castle as then Prince Charles, and those lords and heralds with him, entered the depths of the Chamberlain

---

1. Dennys, ibid. These "two Supporters" *were the mentioned banners.*
2. Men without *godly* understanding are "like the beasts *that* perish" (Ps 49:12, 49:20); they go to Hell.
3. Such biblical illiteracy, ignorance and even outright rebellion toward The God of Israel, *has few parallels in history.* For a people who claim to be "Christian," it was beyond inexcusable. With symbols of Satan *everywhere*, they arrogantly acted as though God Himself should be pleased. Yet, in their magnificent hypocrisy, they were actually there to encourage and abet the crowning of Satan's Prince!

Tower. They were met by Lord Snowdon, as they gathered together at the base of the Eagle Tower.

"When The Queen arrives at the Water Gate...., the Constable [of the Castle, Lord Snowdon,] surrenders the Key of the [Devil's] Castle to The Queen, who returns it to him, and enters the Eagle Tower. As she emerges into the [(red dragon's)] Castle, a Fanfare is sounded [with trumpets]...."[1]   Queen Elizabeth II, upon arriving to the Water Gate with Prince Philip and Princess Anne, received from Lord Snowdon the symbolic fifteen-inch key to Satan's castle, which the queen symbolically touched. Then, with Prince Philip, the queen entered through the Water Gate's iron door, passing beneath the first huge version of their son's graven heraldic achievement (discussed and shown later), followed by the remaining royals. Once inside the Eagle Tower, Elizabeth II's procession made ready.

In this second procession, the queen, Prince Philip, Lord Louis Mountbatten, and Princess Alice moved east—past the center of the castle and the Chamberlain Tower, where the foot-soldiers bearing the red dragon and Prince of Wales standards then stood guard. They were preceded by Princess Anne, the Queen Mother, Princess Margaret, and the Duchess of Abercorn; the Kings of (Heraldic) Arms, to include the Garter, Principal King of Arms—as well as other heralds and participating pursuivants—with Lord Snowdon in their midst; and three other lords—the Lord Great Chamberlain, the Earl Marshal, and the Sword of State. The queen, Prince Philip, Lord Mountbatten, and Princess Alice were immediately followed by two more lords, for a total of six *ceremonial* lords in the queen's procession. "The Heralds and Pursuivants of Arms come next.... The Kings of Arms form the next group, with the Lord Great Chamberlain, the Earl Marshal, and the Sword of State borne immediately before The Queen, who is accompanied by [her husband, Prince Philip,] The Duke of Edinburgh. The Queen proceeds to the Dais [(i.e., the round platform)] and takes her place on the [red dragon's central grey Welsh slate] Throne, when the Ceremony itself begins."[2]   As the queen and other royals entered the castle's interior, the many pagans and apostates present loudly sang "God save the Queen!"[3] Then, as the queen prepared to touch her foot to the green field on which the round platform sat (and *still sits,* between the southern Black Tower and northern Granary Tower), all the royal standards, including that of the red dragon, were tipped to the ground—perhaps signifying subservience not just to the queen, *but to Satan who ani-*

---

1.   Rodney Dennys, O.B.E., F.S.A., Somerset Herald of Arms, *The Investiture of H.R.H. Chalres, Prince of Wales,* album cover inset.
2.   Rodney Dennys, *The Investiture of H.R.H. Chalres, Prince of Wales,* album cover inset.
3.   To that, the author can only say, "Elizabeth II appears to have served Satan, to the end!"

mated her. The royals, other than the queen, Prince Philip, and later Charles, took seats near the round platform. Other royals present included the Duke and Duchess of Kent.

Charles' heraldic achievement as Prince of Wales, the symbolism of the investiture, and 666. Throughout the investiture ceremony, the symbolism on Charles' official heraldic achievement, which heralds him as *the* AntiChrist, was presented to the world by means of *convergence*. A key aspect of this convergence involved the regalia worn by the kings of arms, heralds and pursuivants. Each wore a *tabard,* which is a colorful garment—typically of red, gold, and blue or black—that is emblazoned with the arms of the royal shield upon its back and front. These emblazoned arms consist of six lions or lion-leopards, which are best understood as lion-leopard-bears in the context of Charles' investiture, in the first and fourth quarters; the red lion of Scotland, itself representative of the dexter beast in an overall heraldic achievement, in the second quater; and the Davidic harp for Ireland in the third quarter. The tabard of a King of Arms is velvet, that of a herald is satin, and that of a pursuivant is damask silk. The kings of arms each wore a black hat, which is feathered from the forehead to the back of the head, while the other heralds and the pursuivants wore black berets.[1] Finally, the participating kings of arms and other heralds each carried a scepter or wand, with that of the Garter King made of gold and bearing the sovereign's arms on the sides of a crowned cube at its top; historically, these arms included a roundel of St. George's cross encircled by the garter of the Order of the Garter.

Sequentially speaking, the first whole or complete example of such symbolic convergence occurred at the Eagle Tower's Water Gate, where Charles was greeted by Lord Snowdon—clothed in a dark emerald green outfit and wearing the badge of the Black Prince. Upon arrival, Satan's Prince was also met by the red dragon and four lion-leopard-bears—upon the standards borne by the two aforementioned soldiers who had preceded him. Simultaneously, to then enter the castle, Charles, arrayed in his Garter regalia (i.e., the Star, Collar and Riband), faced the Water Gate, *over which was hung the first of two huge special versions of his graven heraldic achievement; each of these bore the dexter lion-leopard-bear beast and the sinister unicorn having human eyes—with the other "components"*

---

1. Although the Garter King of Arms has a gold coronet, and the Scottish and other English kings of arms have silver gilt coronets, none were worn. These crowns are typically comprised of sixteen encircling leaves (Oak in the case of the Garter King), with nine being visible in profile, and they bear the words *"Miserere mei Deus secundum magnum misericordiam tuam,"* meaning "Have mercy upon me, O God, according to Thy great mercy." Yet their craft is satanic and occult.

or arms of Charles' overall heraldic achievement as Prince of Wales, being strategically placed (see below). As Charles entered the Eagle Tower via its Water Gate, heralds bearing the royal arms greeted him, and his standard as Prince of Wales was raised over its turrets to announce his presence to the world. (At a later point, the Welsh flag with its central red dragon, was likewise raised over the Eagle Tower.) So, in this first convergence, all the symbols of Charles' official heraldic achievement, were displayed. Indeed, all who entered the castle through the Water Gate, including the queen and Prince Philip, were not only *preceded* by Wales' red dragon standard as well as the Prince of Wales' personal standard, but they also immediately saw the red dragon banners on the opposite castle wall (behind the gray slate platform and thrones), and even on the adjacent or side walls—and of course, they saw the Badge of the Black Prince atop the clear Perspex canopy.

More such examples would follow. Indeed, similes of the lion, leopard, and bear were repeatedly combined with the red dragon and the Black Prince's or heir-apparent's badge,[1] which bears the motto *Ich Dien* or "I Serve," just as they also were with the unicorn having human eyes, and the royal and welsh shields. Even a large Irish or Davidic (and druidic) harp was present,[2] near the Queen's Gate, which then Charles, Prince of Wales, faced as he was invested. Importantly, the arms of two large special versions of then Prince Charles' actual, graven heraldic achievement—besides the official rendition of his achievement or coat of arms, that was then publicly unveiled to the world on memorabilia—were also *central* to the ceremony's satanic symbolism.[3] These graven versions of Charles'

---

1. For more information, see ch. 6's sections titled "The motto and the heir-apparent's badge" as well as "The Black Prince and Prince Charles' arms," at pp. 187 and 204, respectively.

2. The harpist was a Gorsedd druid and bard. Indeed, then Prince Charles' Royal Harpist, Claire Jones, who played the instrument at Caernarfon Castle for the twenty-fifth anniversary of his investiture, is likewise a druid. Her web site ("https://www.clairejones.co.uk") shows her in a blood-red dress, formerly bearing the red dragon against a green and white field.

3. There were *two* variants of this huge graven coat of arms, each made of bronze and possibly cast iron. One was hung over the *exterior* archway (i.e., outside the Castle) of the Eagle Tower's Water Gate, and the other was hung over the *exterior* archway of the Queen's Gate. The latter gate saw six of the sixteen huge red dragon banners—four directly behind it, imposed over an interior castle wall, and two directly surrounding it, on the exterior castle wall—that is, one to its left and one to its right.

   One fascinating point: these two graven variants—each of which bore the same overall set of symbols—lacked the badge of the Black Prince, the lower-central Shield of the Black Prince (see below), and the dragon itself at their base, and they also lacked the copy of the dexter beast at the top. Why? Because these symbols were to be conjoined in the events of the investiture itself, as a *living spiritual experience*. That is, red dragon banners, bronze Welsh dragons, the flag of Wales (e.g., over the Eagle Tower), and the badge of the Black Prince surrounded these graven variants (e.g., on the castle walls). Specifically, the red dragon itself was "moved" from the graven arms to the backrest of the queen's throne, at once reinforcing and pointing out the fact that it was this dragon, or Satan himself, who was giving Charles his power, his throne (or seat), and his great authority (cf. Rev 13:2). Yet the two bronze copies of Charles' graven coat of arms as Prince of Wales, were not without their corresponding bronze Welsh dragons. Indeed, those were placed over the railing at the Queen's Gate, and like the red dragon heraldic arms—which placed upon Caernarfon Castle's stone walls (see pp. 132-133), presaged the "first beast" "rising up, out of the sea" (Rev 13:1, 13:12)—unambiguously show very exaggerated, bear-like feet on the dexter beast, with each foot having five bear-like claws, besides a slender body like that of a leopard and a mouth like the mouth of a lion. They also indicate human eyes in the head of the sinister unicorn.[1]

At the castle, there were apparently eighteen representations of the red dragon, or six, six and six (6-6-6), ostensibly *placed to invoke*

on the full heraldic achievement, each bore the label of the eldest son (cf. the Awen), around its neck—thus representing Charles as satanically possessed. Likewise, the two bronze copies of Charles' graven coat of arms as Prince of Wales, were not each without their corresponding bronze Black Prince badge! One of these *Ich Dien* badges was hung at the King's Gate, just inside the top of its exterior archway, while the other one was incorporated into the center of the clear Perspex canopy that stood above Charles', the queen's, and Prince Philip's heads as the queen invested her son. What about the mostly black Shield of the Black Prince? Recall that the shield from the arms of the Duke (and Duchy) of Cornwall (i.e., the Shield of the Black Prince) employs fifteen gold besants or crusader coins. Druids from the Duchy of Cornwall were present with this shield. Moreover, not only was then Prince Charles dressed mostly in black *as the Black Prince* or Prince of Darkness, but a number of commemorative proof and regular medals or "coins"—"gilt bronze," "bright bronze" and near-pure silver—were minted specially for the occasion, where they were sold. These bronze and silver pieces typically have Charles' profile or head on the front or obverse face, as Satan's Prince, and the Welsh dragon, Black Prince badge, or Charles' full heraldic achievement as Prince of Wales, on the reverse face—sometimes encircled by the words "DRAIG GOCH CYMRU," translated as "red dragon, Wales," or even "Y DDRAIG GOCH DDYRY CYCHWYN," meaning "The red dragon gives the lead." Since the July 1969 investiture, a number of similar proof coins have likewise been minted.

A third, smaller Black Prince badge was necessarily placed between the two bronze Welsh dragons at the Queen's Gate. With this, the overarching message of Charles' investiture as Prince of Wales, as conveyed at the base of his corresponding full heraldic achievement, was once more clearly given—though with a different heraldic arrangement. At his first presentation as Prince of Wales to the Welsh people, Charles stood behind the Black Prince's badge, itself imposed over a red background, effectively stating in part, "I, the Black Prince, serve the red...." Simultaneously, he stood behind and between the two graven Welsh dragons, thereby completing that statement with "dragon" for the masses. Charles' heraldic message remained, "I, the Black Prince, serve the red dragon" or Satan.

As just intimated, within the top of the exterior archway of the King's Gate, instead of the special version of Charles' graven coat of arms, a huge version of the Black Prince badge was there hung, and it likewise was directly compassed by two of the sixteen huge red dragon banners—one to its left and the other to its right; also, *behind* the King's Gate, a third such banner could be seen hung on the interior castle wall. Upon departing Caernarfon following the investiture, Satan's Prince passed directly in front of the King's Gate, as his carriage traveled down *Pen Deltish*, and then, subsequently, beneath multiple "Black Prince-red dragon" banners lining the *Lon Crwyn* road or "'blessed love' lane."

1. A black-and-white photo of the graven coat of arms that was over the Water Gate of the Eagle Tower, is available from Getty Images. Go to "https://www.gettyimages.com" on the Internet, search for "3286766", and click on the image displayed. A colorized version had been available through Corbis (under "U1633251"), but is now found at Getty Images: select "EDITORIAL" and search for "U1633251". (The author licensed the highest resolution of "U1633251," from Corbis.) A color photograph was also published on the back cover of—or in another edition, inside—the booklet *Charles, 21st Prince of Wales* (Pitkin Pictorials Ltd., 1969).

For the graven version that was over the Queen's Gate, go to "https://www.britishpathe.com", select film (reel) 2217.05 (from then Prince Charles' investiture), which is titled, "EXTRA - INVESTITURE PREPARATIONS (1969)" (see "https://www.britishpathe.com/asset/89477") Once on reel 2217.05, click the "View as Stills" button, to display a frame per second. The frames of greatest interest are 64 and 89–90, with the numbers being visible upon hovering over individual stills (see "https://www.britishpathe.com/asset/stills/89477"). Click on the frame you want to see, to enlarge its image. The lion-lepard-bear "first beast" actually has five claws per foot. Per frames 64 and (e.g.) 89, three each are evident on the top-right foot and both bottom feet (we see two inner claws plus the middle claw on on the bottom-left foot), whereas only the two inner claws are evident on the top-left foot. (The author licensed

the biblical number of the beast, or 666, to the careful observer. Of these, sixteen were tall red dragon banners draped from the castle walls, each bearing the three-pronged label of the eldest son, also properly recognized as the evoking druidic Awen, around the neck.[1] The other two were bronze-colored "graven" Welsh dragons, situated just below the handrail at the Queen's Gate. Now, those eighteen were placed specifically for Satan's Prince.[2] Besides all those, there were *several* overhead wide (what we'll here describe as) "Black Prince-red dragon" banners, each bearing the invoking druidic Awen,[3] beneath which *Charles* and the other royals passed in

frame 89. That and similar images, some likewise licensed, are herein shown.)

    In the "U1633251" image of Charles' arms above the Eagle Tower's Water Gate, the rear left foot exposes four if its five claws, and the right right foot shows only two of its five, but the other two feet have the same exposed claws as the version over the Queen's Gate. In both versions, the claws are thicker and somewhat longer than those of lions, are *without* sheaths and *only extended* (like those of bears), and the legs themselves evince something (like what is seen on a "fishing" bear, *not* a lion) and larger and longer than what is seen on actual lions.

1. Each of these resembled an ornamentally cut tall white sheet with a large red dragon at its top. Note that to an informed druid, the appearance of the evoking Awen around the neck of the red dragon essentially indicates that the red dragon is "God." But to one familiar with royal heraldry, it effectively implies and declares that the eldest son, or Charles in this case, is the druidic "'God' incarnate!"

2. Upon arriving by carriage at Caernarfon Castle, to be invested, Charles entered by the Water Gate at the base of the Eagle Tower, where two huge red dragon banners hung. He then proceeded to the Chamberlain Tower, passing three more huge red dragon banners on the Queen's Tower, and then encountering another three around the Chamberlain Tower, all on the interior castle walls. Upon exiting the Chamberlain Tower, when summoned by the Queen through the Garter Herald King, Charles proceeded to the round platform to be invested.

    Immediately following the investiture, the queen, Satan's Prince, and Prince Philip proceeded from the round platform to the Queen's Gate, passing a huge Irish or Davidic harp along the way. There, at the Queen's Gate, which Charles had faced as he was invested and which was itself surrounded by six huge red dragon banners (four inside the castle, two outside), the queen first presented Charles as Prince of Wales—or Satan's Prince—to Wales and the world. (The Queen's Gate was just behind the investiture platform.) Besides the six large red dragon banners surrounding the Queen's Gate (four behind and two in front), also displayed were two bronze-colored "graven" renditions of the red dragon. These two bronze Welsh dragons, each against a white background and bearing the label of the eldest son, faced one another and a central bronze Black Prince badge, itself against a red background, placed between them. (Perhaps one loosely stood for Queen Elizabeth II and the other for Prince Philip, as the biological parents of Charles, who would now acknowledge Satan's Prince as their own Prince of Darkness.) These two dragons, with the *Ich Dien* (Black Prince) badge between them, covered the railing of the metal fence at the end of the exterior plank of the Queen's Gate—on which the queen, Satan's Prince, and Prince Philip stood while she presented Charles as *Satan's* son. Indeed, these dragons were immediately in front of the queen and Charles, at waist level.

    Next, proceeding from the Queen's Gate, in the opposite direction, the queen presented Charles as *Satan's son* for the second time at the King's Gate—as she and "their" son emerged from the castle beneath the huge *Ich Dien* badge of the Black Prince that sat between two of the sixteen large red dragon banners, with another one seen on the interior wall behind them. From there, the queen walked Satan's Prince to the Water Gate—the place where he had first entered the castle to be invested—for his third presentation as *Satan's son*. From there, they boarded the carriage with Prince Philip and Princess Anne, and proceed back to the Royal Train.

    Now, consider that throughout these movements, from beginning to end, *Charles was preceded—and thus led—by the red dragon*. Indeed, two soldiers of the Royal Regiment of Wales went before Satan's Prince on foot, one carrying the red dragon banner or *standard,* and the other carrying the Prince of Wales standard!

3. Each of these other four banners, which were stretched overhead—across *Lon Crwyn*—consisted of **a)** two Black Prince badges (on either end); **b)** two depictions of the Eagle Tower, with the red dragon standing on its three turrets and the three ostrich feathers of the Black Prince imposed over the Water Gate beneath them (toward the banner's center); and **c)** a large red dragon (at the banner's center). In

their royal carriages, as they traveled to and from the castle. That's not all. Recall the Welsh dragon on the slate backrest of Elizabeth II's throne (above its red seat cushion), and the red dragon standard preceding Charles—besides the innumerable small Welsh flags (bearing the red dragon on a green and white field) waved by attendees to the investiture.

The red dragon gives the lead. The red dragon standard, or the *past* flag of Wales—which had preceded Charles and the other royals from the Royal Train, all the way to the Water Gate at the base of the Eagle Tower—likewise *preceded Satan's Prince throughout the day and ceremony,* still carried by a squadron leader of the Royal Regiment of Wales. This standard is the one that *previously* served as the Welsh flag on government offices in London, for example, and is recognized by the College of Arms as one carrying the "augmented Royal Badge of Wales," in which the red dragon stands atop a grassy field with a bright green patch in the midst of a dark emerald green area, and is against a pure white background. Thus, it matches the red dragon depicted at the base of Charles' official achievement as Prince of Wales.[1] This, of course, is where the imagery of the *four-thousand red chairs* commissioned by Lord Snowdon for the event, each bearing the badge of the Black Prince in gold on their backrests and sitting atop bright green grass, come into their own. All the seated ceremony participants and invited "guests," *as those seated for a most royal wedding* (i.e., Charles' *marriage* to the Principality of Wales or Satan), represented the body of the red dragon standing atop a green field, as they encompassed Satan's Prince and the pattern of the cross he walked (see below). Due to the *Ich Dien* motto these chairs bore, these people effectively proclaimed themselves servants of the red dragon throughout the ceremony! Ignorance was not bliss. The dark emerald green area on which the red dragon stands was likewise behind Snowdon's choice for the color of his uniform as Constable of the Castle, which he designed himself for the occasion: dark emerald green, which appropriately contrasted with the bright green grass beneath the thousands of red chairs.[2]

The pattern of the cross. In four "movements," Charles traced out the pattern of a cross through the length and breadth of Caernarfon Castle—all while making the red dragon or Satan central. We may think of the castle itself as being laid out like the handle of a

---

the three ostrich feathers and the three castle turrets, the invoking druidic Awen was again seen.

1. On the current Flag of Wales, the red dragon is shown against a white and green field only.

2. As we shall see, there was *no point* within the investiture where Satan's Prince was not facing the red dragon. The same can be said for Queen Elizabeth II and Prince Philip. Indeed, this would also have been true had there *not* been Welsh men and women throughout the audience waving their flag.

sword, with its length going from West to East, and its breadth from North to South. The Eagle Tower and its Water Gate are *West*. The Queen's Gate is *East,* opposite the Water Gate. The King's Gate is *North,* at the castle center. The Chamberlain Tower is *South,* also at the castle center—opposite the King's Gate. Between the three "gates" and the Chamberlain Tower, Satan's Prince walked four right-hand "L" patterns, forming the sign of the cross.

Upon entering the castle by the Water Gate at the Eagle Tower, where two of the sixteen huge red dragon banners surrounded the gate's exterior, Charles proceeded from West to East (symbolic of rejecting The God of Israel and favoring the false "gods" of the East)—all the while facing red dragon banners in front of him and to his right as he traversed the central walkway toward the King's Gate and Chamberlain Tower. (He directly faced four red dragon banners on the interior of the opposite castle wall, behind the inner "Throne Circle" (dais) or "marriage" platform. As he walked, toward the center of the castle's interior, he passed three more red dragon banners draped on the Queen's Tower *(not* to be confused with the separate Queen's Gate). From the area of the King's Gate, Satan's Prince turned to his right or *South* to proceed *into* the Chamberlain Tower, which itself was surrounded by three more red dragon banners (one of which could be seen from outside the castle, when looking through the King's Gate to the interior); with this, Charles effectively entered *the first of three of the red dragon's (Satan's) "lairs!" This was the first "L" pattern.*

So far, we've noted twelve huge red dragon banners: two around the Water Gate outside the Eagle Tower; four behind the dais inside the castle, or on the wall directly behind the Queen's Gate; three on the Queen's Tower inside the castle; and three around the entrance to the Chamberlain Tower, also inside the castle. What about the other four? Of those, two surrounded the King's Gate outside the castle, and two surrounded the Queen's Gate, likewise outside.

Next, Charles did an "about face" and ascended from within the Chamberlain Tower—as if coming out of a dungeon or pit—exiting toward the King's Gate or *North.* Once exposed, Charles moved straight toward the castle's center and then again turned to his right, or *East* this time to proceed to the round "marriage" platform (and "Throne Circle"), at the "womb" (center-East) of the castle. There, Charles would kneel upon *a red cushion* to be invested as Satan's Prince, marrying his satanic Principality (see below) and figuratively the Devil's servants—all while directly facing four of six huge red dragon banners around and over the archway of the Queen's Gate, besides the Welsh dragon engraved on the backrest of the queen's throne.[1] Upon being invested, Satan's Prince proceeded *further east,* to the Queen's Gate, or *the second of three red dragon lairs*—where he found himself surrounded by six of the sixteen red dragon banners (two around the gate outside the castle, plus the four immediately inside)—besides the two graven bronze Welsh dragons in front of him, at waist level. *This was the second "L" pattern.*

From the Queen's Gate, Satan's Prince did an about face and proceeded *West* down the walkway toward the center of the castle. Upon again reaching the area of the Chamberlain Tower, he turned to his right to proceed *North* through the King's Gate, itself "backed" by a visible *interior* red dragon banner (on the Chamberlain Tower) and surrounded by two more exterior red dragon banners. Thus, the King's Gate was *the third of three red dragon lairs—and all this served as the third "L" pattern.*

From the King's Gate, Charles did a final about face, proceeding *South* toward the Chamberlain Tower while reentering the castle. Upon reaching the central interior walkway from the King's Gate, Satan's Prince once more turned to his right, this time heading *West—* back to the Eagle Tower and its Water Gate. *This was the fourth and final "L" pattern.* Thus, Charles completed the sign of the cross—*as he acknowledged and worshiped Satan at every point.* By this as well, he accepted Satan's offer of this world (West, South, East, North); he <u>*already is*</u> the prophesied AntiChrist.

Satan foolishly sought to tempt Jesus by showing Him "all the kingdoms of the world in a moment of time," telling Him: "All this authority I will give you, and their glory; for this has been delivered to me, and I give it to whomever I wish. Therefore, if You will worship before me, all will be Yours." Indeed, referring to "all the kingdoms of the world and their glory," Satan told Jesus, "All these things I will give You if you will fall down and worship me" (Matt 4:8-9). What hubris! What insanity! Here was Satan, a created being, a fallen angel, and by comparison a *peon,* trying to tempt The Creator Himself. To this, Jesus simply replied: "Get behind Me, Satan! For it is written, 'You shall worship The LORD your God, and Him only you shall serve'" (Luke 4:5-8; cf. Matt 4:10). Where Christ triumphed, however, the AntiChrist has now transgressed. Jesus rejected Satan's offer outright, but Charles as Prince of Wales, fully accepted it without the slightest hesitation! This too is what then Prince Charles' investiture as Prince of Wales, was all about.

---

1. These four red dragon banners were hung upon four poles—each in the form of a cross—before an interior castle wall, surrounding the Queen's Gate. From Charles' vantage point, they were above and behind his mother's grey Welsh slate throne, with its engraved dragon of Wales.

Now, all this was while Charles, as Satan's "Chosen One," was receiving a crown designed to *both* evoke thoughts of Christ's crown of thorns *and* symbolize global hegemony as "ruler | prince of this world"—though the thorns on this abominable coronet were a bit more upscale, having been fashioned from gold nails, with no intent to draw blood. Satan's Prince has yet to fatally suffer (cf. the mortal wound to be received by the AntiChrist)! All this was decidedly *counterfeit Christ;* it was *antiChrist* from start to finish.

The association of the red dragon with the sign of the cross was not new. In fact, the children of Israel were to look at a "fiery *red*" "bronze serpent" that Moses placed upon a pole in the wilderness to live (Num 21:6-9, Heb.). That bronze serpent, or *fiery red dragon,*[1] was representative of Christ at His crucifixion upon the cross. Indeed, it was Jesus Himself who made the point: "And as Moses lifted up the serpent in the wilderness, even so must The Son of man be lifted up, that whoever believes in Him should not perish, but have eternal life.... He who believes in Him is not condemned; but he who does not believe is condemned already, because he has not believed in the name of the only begotten Son of God. And this is the condemnation, that The Light has come into the world, and men loved the darkness rather than The Light, because their deeds were evil.... Now is the judgment of this world; now the ruler of this world will be cast out. And I, if I am lifted up from the Earth, will draw all *peoples* to Myself" (John 3:14-15, 3:18-19, 12:23-32). We must all look to Jesus for eternal life with Him, with God. So, what shall we say? "For He made Him who knew no sin *to be* sin for us, that we might become the righteousness of God in Him" (2 Cor 5:21). Upon the cross, Christ became "sin for us" — *bloody red* as he took *our sins* upon Himself; in *that state,* God likened Jesus to the red dragon, or Satan. Our enemy is a counterfeiter, having counterfeited the lion and unicorn symbolism that pertains to Christ, who is The Lion of Judah and The Horn of David—for the AntiChrist. Understand, therefore, that God took the symbol of the red dragon, which pertains to Satan, and used it to represent Christ's work upon the cross for all His redeemed, having made that point forcefully to a rebellious Israel many centuries ago!

Of marriage, special effects, and supernatural activity. A clear Perspex canopy, bearing one of two large Black Prince or *Ich Dien* badges (bronze and graven), stood over the round grey Welsh slate platform where Charles was invested. The canopy, supported by four spear-like poles with red-tasseled tips, represented a wedding,

---

1. For more information, see the related note in ch. 5, "Anglo-Israelism, David's Throne, and the AntiChrist," on p. 111.

and was reminiscent, in a satanic and intentional way, of a Jewish *chuppah*.[1] It was here, beneath this canopy with its "I serve" motto, that the gold ring, consisting of a single smooth amethyst held in place by the heads and claws of two interlaced Welsh dragons, was removed from the top of a *pyramidal* mold on a pillow and placed upon Charles' ring finger—signifying the "marriage of the prince to the Principality [of Wales]." Indeed, the ring itself, symbolizing the world in Satan's grip, here constituted a roundel at the top of a pyramid (i.e., on the pillow from which it was removed), thereby invoking the "all-seeing eye" of Lucifer (e.g., in the capstone of the pyramidal Seal of the Illuminati). This ring was just one of *five* items of the investiture regalia. Thus, the AntiChrist married his bride (i.e., the Principality of Satan) at his first advent, whereas Christ *will* marry His bride (i.e., the Church) at His *second advent.*

With the Secretary of Wales, Charles and seven of the ceremonial lords, including those who would bear the investiture regalia, still in the Chamberlain Tower, Queen Elizabeth II sent the Garter (Principal) King of Arms to the tower to summon her son—and the other key members of his procession—to the platform for these events. Indeed, the queen had commanded the Duke of Norfolk, *as the Hereditary Earl Marshal who planned, organized and marshaled the investiture*—with the assistance of the kingdom's heralds, who themselves acted as his staff officers for this purpose—to direct the "Garter, Principal King of Arms," Sir Anthony R. Wagner,[2] to summon Charles to her presence, and that of Satan, on the "center disc" to be invested.

As Queen Elizabeth II and Prince Philip stood beneath the canopy that was over the round platform—with the Garter King having *just* passed between the red dragon and Prince of Wales' standards posted on either side of the entrance to the Chamberlain Tower (in the hands of the two foot soldiers), as well as beneath and between the six huge red dragon banners surrounding that tower's entrance, to retrieve their son, Charles—the worldwide television audience was treated to *a clue*. This particular clue was one that significantly enhanced the extreme prominence already afforded Satan. Specifi-

---

1. The womanizing sodomite (i.e., "bisexual") Lord Snowdon, who "had a major role in designing the physical arrangements for the 1969 investiture of his nephew Prince Charles, as Prince of Wales," "was born of minor Welsh gentry and Jewish banking heritage" ("Anthony Armstrong-Jones, 1st Earl of Snowdon," *Wikipedia,* 2009; see "https://en.wikipedia.org/wiki/Lord_Snowdon" on the Internet).

   Indeed, there were other homosexuals, besides Lord Snowdon, with whom Charles had already been close to this point in his life. Recall that Lord Mountbatten and the Duke of Kent were both also womanizers and known homosexuals, and the former was a pedophile interested in boys.

2. It was this herald, the most powerful in the world, who superintended the creation of Charles' official heraldic achievement, as Prince of Wales, yet he is technically under the Duke of Norfolk. For more information, see ch. 7's subsection, "'Organizational' ties to witchcraft," at p. 175.

cally, by a special effect, the large red dragon in the center of the waving flag of Wales—possibly the one blowing in the wind over the Eagle Tower—was then imposed semi-transparently over the standing queen and Prince Philip, and then, just as suddenly, over the large graven badge of the Black Prince mounted in the center of the Perspex canopy. The latter instance was done so that the dragon's hindmost red foot touched the top of the *Ich Dien* badge itself as the audience watched and faced the Chamberlain and Eagle towers from behind the canopy. So, it was the red dragon or Satan himself, who was summoning Charles through the queen! As the red dragon fades out, we then see Satan's Prince, already retrieved by the Garter King of Arms, kneeling in front of the queen as he is about to receive the final investiture regalia, the dark purple velvet and ermine mantle or cloak.[1]

In the real world, of course, the transition was not so quick. Exiting the Chamberlain Tower or dragon's lair, and proceeding to the central grey Welsh slate platform, were the Secretary of Wales, the Garter King, Charles, the then prince's two lords-in-waiting, and the five lords bearing the investiture regalia. This bit was skipped during the television "wizardry." Something else, rather strange (circled at right, in frame 229 of reel 2217.18[2]), is evident in available footage, which was presumably *not* by special effect. The *instant* before the then Prince of Wales began to emerge from the Chamberlain Tower,

with the Garter King a short distance in front, *four fiery "paw prints,"* *with "claws," suddenly appear vertically up the right edge of the*

1. Go to "https://www.britishpathe.com", select film (reel) 3391.08 (from then Prince Charles' investiture), which is titled, "(INVESTITURE AT CARNARVON CASTLE) (1969)" (see "https://www.britishpathe.c om/asset/104874" on the Internet) Once on reel 3391.08, click the "View as Stills" button, to display a frame per second. The frames of interest are 199–200, 209, and 214–219, with the numbers being visible upon hovering over individual stills (see "https://www.britishpathe.com/asset/stills/104874"). Click on a frame to enlarge its image.
2. It's been said, "Seeing is believing." So, *to actually see these,* follow the above directions, but choose reel 2217.18, and view frames 229-230. (Click a frame and then click again on the image displayed to further enlarge it.) For a nearly identical image—one that varies by only the slightest instant, if at all, in time—that is *from a different film reel and camera,* but which *lacks* these fiery prints, choose reel 2219.08 and view frame 216. Whether these prints are occult or not, Satan himself was present.

tower's entrance—just to Charles' left and opposite the posted red dragon banner. That is not all. As the queen and others present held the cloak to wrap it around Charles, something *stranger still,* likewise an improbable effect (it occupies *more than one film frame),* suddenly occurred: One beam of an "X"-patterned blast-wave of

light—which we'll simply call "X lightning"—centered immediately above the dragon backrest of the queen's throne and just in front of its red cushion, shot through the queen's right shoulder and hand, through the ermine-clad top of the cloak, and then through Charles' head (and the head of the Lord who had carried the cloak, who stood to Charles' left), after which it "dissipated." At the same instant, the *other* beam of this "X lightning" shot directly over or even through the head of Prince Philip, who remained seated, and in the opposite direction, shot through the microphones where Prince Charles would later speak.[1] Might these bizarre satanic "effects" represent supernatural activity surrounding Satan's Prince—and was that actually caught on film as "X lightning?" Did those frames capture an instance of satanic possession or animation *in progress,* as it occurred. In fact, *Charles himself* intimated that *Lucifer—*as his spiritual "father"—*had possessed his mother,* as we'll soon see.

Of regalia. Various Lords bore the investiture regalia to the platform, having followed Satan's Prince from the Chamberlain Tower. The Letters Patent were then delivered by the Garter King of Arms to the Home Secretary, Mr. James Callahan, who took them to the lectern—adjacent to the 1588 William Morgan Bible (the first Welsh translation)—to read them aloud: "Elizabeth II, ... Queen, Head of the Commonwealth, Defender of the Faith. <u>To all Lords, spiritual</u> and temporal, ...<u>Greeting</u>...."

Subsequently, (Lucifer or Satan via) the queen placed the coronet on Charles' head; Satan's Prince also received a dragon-laden sword and the dragon-laden gold marriage ring. Next, Charles re-

---

1. To see this "live," follow the above directions, but choose reel 2217.18, click the "Download Video" button (open or save the video), and watch the segment near 5 minutes and 49 seconds (5:49).

ceived the golden rod, having at its head three winged *cherubim* supporting the unique crown, of which the cap is formed of a large single amethyst; derived from a shepherd's staff, this was placed in the Charles' right hand. Then came the mantle or cloak, which the queen placed around Charles' shoulders, as he cracked a grin. With his hands placed firmly between those of *Satan's (possessed) emissary, his mother the queen (and spiritual father the Devil),* in an attitude of homage and prayer, Satan's Prince recited, "I, Charles, Prince of Wales, do become your liege man of life and limb, and of earthly worship, and faith and truth I will bear unto thee, to live and die against all manner of folks." *Charles, by this one defining act, effectively pledged his lifelong loyalty and worship to Satan.* By the sealing Kiss of Fielty on his cheek, the "Overlord"—that is, Lucifer in the body of the queen—then pledged to protect his (her) "Vassal" or Charles; *this kiss was the ceremonial focal point of the investiture:* "Everything else in the lengthy Ceremonial on that day builds up to this and flows away from it."[1] In fact, as each item of investiture regalia was given to Charles in turn, and as he then took the Oath of Fielty (earthly worship) and subsequently received a kiss from Satan's emissary, he was facing the dragon on the backrest of her throne, as well as the red dragon banners above and behind it.

Charles then stood, for the first time since arriving on the center disc, to receive the letters patent from his mother. Having received his authority as "Prince of the Red Dragon," Charles took his throne at the right hand of Satan's emissary the queen, whose own throne bore the engraved dragon of Wales. "Homage was the most significant act which could be performed in the Middle Ages, going back to the earliest origins of Western European society, to the dark ages following the ... [division] of the Roman Empire [into East and West], when the personal tie between a man and his lord came before all other obligations.... This oath, taken with joined hands held between those of the overlord, was completed by the exchange of the Kiss of Fealty, which placed the lord and his vassal on the same social level. Having taken his homage and allegiance the overlord would invest his vassal with his honours and lordships, handing over to him some symbolic object."[2]

While the guidance of "The Holy Spirit" was then invoked, with alleged recognition to the William Morgan Bible—and while "Jesus" (so-called) was asked to "bless" *Satan's Prince* by the apostate Archbishop of Cardiff, John Murphy—the blatantly satanic context of the

---

1. Dennys, ibid. Though claimed to be largely historical, much of this investiture's ceremony was actually contrived specifically for Charles. Welsh nationalists saw this as unabashed English imperialism.
2. Dennys, ibid.

red dragon banners and flags unambiguously demonstrated that *these men (goats, wolves and tares) were not of God.* Indeed, the Archdruid of Wales—for whom the rectangular stone stool upon which Charles knelt to receive Satan's coronet, as well as the round platform upon which that stool (and three stone thrones) sat, together served as a *Logan Stone* and *inner Gorsedd Circle,* respectively, all in the midst of what could be viewed as the larger *Throne Circle,* itself comprised of the castle's "encircling" towers—also prayed for Satan's Prince. Likewise, the apostate President of the Free Church Council of Wales, Gwilym Owen, in his long black gown, pronounced the benediction in Welsh. In every sense, this was a satanic mixing of the profane, with the holy, so that poison substituted for healthful, evil was called good and darkness proclaimed as light![1] *Gehenna's* torments punish such *hypocrites*—for eternity.

As the invested Charles headed towards the castle's royal exits, to be presented in turn by his mother the queen at the Queen's Gate and then also at the King's Gate,[2] the Welsh commentator (of the official investiture album's audio) remarked, "And now I can see the flutter of union jacks and red dragons, as the children [who are] nest[ed] in front of the gate get the first glimpse of the Queen and the Duke and the Prince of Wales approaching." Satan's Prince, when traversing to the King's Gate from the area of the investiture platform or inner Throne Circe, was preceded by the heralds and flanked by his Satan-worshiping mother (the queen) and biological father Prince Philip; at that time, not only did the other high ranking members of the royal family all face Charles' left side as he passed, but the religious leaders of the UK—all pagans, heretics and apostates (e.g., the Archdruid of Wales and Archbishop of Canterbury)—faced his other or right side. The audience was all around, and everywhere anyone looked, red dragon banners and rapidly waving (and thus "hissing") Welsh flags were evident! As the queen, attended by her son and Prince Philip, departed from the green field bearing the round investiture platform, to then enter through the King's Gate, all the royal standards, including that of the red dragon, were once more tipped to the ground.

While Elizabeth II presented Satan's Prince, "their" son, at the King's Gate, the two soldiers posted at the Chamberlain Tower (i.e., those bearing the red dragon and Prince of Wales' standards), then

---

1. Jesus will *not* bless Charles Philip Arthur George, and he shall *not* come into Christ's eternal joy *nor* His Kingdom. Instead, our LORD will literally and figuratively crush the head of Satan's Prince, beneath His feet (cf. Gen 3:15). So shall The Christ, our High Priest, slaughter the AntiChrist, Satan's beast. Like Judas Iscariot who betrayed Christ, *it would be better for this man, had he never been born.*

2. As the royals departed the Queen's Gate to go to the King's Gate, the crowds received further imperial entertainment: cannon were fired from a hill across the waterway, directly opposite the Water Gate, and sixteen fighter aircraft flew in formation overhead.

marched away from it and past the King's Gate, toward the Eagle Tower. With this, they and others paused to await the return of Charles, the queen, Prince Philip, the Garter King of Arms, and others with them, from the King's Gate presentation—after which, they then marched (behind two royal guards at the head of the procession, various heralds, and the other royal women) to the Eagle Tower's Water Gate.

The investiture then concluded, Satan's Prince and his mother, followed by the other royals, finally exited through the Water Gate, passing beneath Charles' graven coats of arms (i.e., the lion-leopard-bear beast and unicorn with eyes like those of a man). At the Water Gate, they awaited the royal carriages to return to the railway station, and to *un*-Holyhead.[1] Both the red dragon and Prince of Wales standards were posted—with the red dragon of the former standard being to the royals' right, and the four lion-leopard-bears of the latter standard to their left, as they exited the castle. That is, the two soldiers who had carried them before Satan's Prince throughout the investiture ceremony, also bore them ahead of the royal procession from the King's Gate to the Water Gate, where they took positions to the right and left at the bottom of the Water Gate's stone stairs. The Garter King of Arms then stood next to the red dragon banner, with five other heralds and pursuivants behind him, while a second King of Arms stood next to the Prince of Wales standard, with four other heralds and pursuivants; in fact, all the participating kings of arms, heralds, and pursuivants, preceded Charles and other royals to the Water Gate. Thus, these banners were on either end of the first royal carriage as Satan's Prince, Queen Elizabeth II, Princess Anne, and Prince Philip, having descended the stairs, *passed between them,* or between the red dragon and four lion-leopard-bears, to board it. Likewise passing between these banners, the Queen Mother and Princess Margaret boarded and departed in the second royal carriage, while Lord Louis Mountbatten, the Secretary of Wales, Princess Alice, and the Duchess of Abercorn boarded and departed in the third royal carriage back to the Royal Train.

With this event, Charles' official heraldic achievement as Prince of Wales, reproduced on the front cover of this book, was first unveiled publicly to the world—though quite amazingly, nearly the whole Church failed to recognize it. Official memorabilia sold at the investiture, to include porcelain cups and plates as well as medals ("coins") and other items, bore Charles' heraldic achievement as

---

1. While beneath Charles' graven arms as Prince of Wales, he, his mother, Prince Philip, and Princess Anne, as well as others, looked skyward to catch the sixteen fighter aircraft making another pass.

Prince of Wales, the Black Prince badge, or Wales' (red) dragon.[1] Yet, as previously shown, at two of the castle's gates (i.e., the Water Gate and the Queen's Gate), huge bronze versions of those arms, were visible to all. Given such ceremonial prominence, few if any attending the investiture that day could have missed both of these. It bears repeating that on each of them, the feet of the dexter beast were not only hugely exaggerated, but they evinced truly striking bear-*like* claws that were both thick and long—*five each per paw* being discernible or even apparent. This same beast, in each instance, had a body *like* that of a leopard and a mouth *like* that of a lion. Likewise, the unicorn on each had eyes *like* those of a man. Still, of all the symbols paraded at Charles investiture, the red dragon, representing Satan himself, was by far the most prominent, though others, such as the goat mascot, stand out as similarly satanic.[2]

The following day, Charles toured Wales in the back of a Rolls Royce that bore his standard as Prince of Wales as well as the Shield of Wales, each showing four *lion-leopard-bears*. Welshmen lined the roads to see Satan's Prince and wave as he passed, several of whom held Wales' satanic national flag with its red dragon.

During an October 1981 tour of Wales, Satan's Prince and the late Princess Diana visited Caernarfon Castle. There, they enjoyed outdoor air from atop his 1969 investiture platform—as they sat across from one another on the original two matching (no backrests) grey Welsh slate thrones. Today, those and Elizabeth II's dragon-engraved throne, as well as some of the red chairs, are housed inside Caernarfon Castle, now recognized as a World Heritage inscribed site.

Charles' take. Intimating <u>Lucifer's possession of his mother the queen</u>, at his 1969 investiture, Charles clearly recalled: "Within the vast ruin of Caernarfon Castle, ... <u>my father invested me</u> as Prince of Wales. Upon my head <u>he</u> put a coronet cap as token of principality, and into my hand the

dragon of Wales

---

1. Many imitations have now been sold with unofficial renditions of Charles' heraldic arms, so that today it can be challenging to find an article bearing his genuine achievement, as Prince of Wales.

2. Besides the major heraldic arms covered herein, others also decorated the walls of Caernarfon Castle. Among them were the shields of the ancient kings and princes of Gwynedd and Powys, as well as those of the founders of the sixteen noble tribes of North Wales and Powys. Also present was the Coat of arms of Caernarfonshire County Council, which bore at its top the three ostrich feathers of the Black Prince (as the invoking Awen), and *fish-tailed* Welsh dragons for its supporters.

gold verge of government, and on the middle finger the gold ring of responsibility. Then leading me by the hand through an archway to one of the towers of the battlements, <u>he</u> presented me to the people of Wales."[1] Either this is a gross misquotation—saying "father," "he" and "he" again—or Charles referred to someone other than his mother and Prince Philip as his "father" in connection with his investiture. It was not Prince Philip, Charles' biological father—who lacked such authority since he was never the British sovereign—but Elizabeth II who placed the coronet upon Charles' head; also, it was not Philip, but the queen who led then Prince Charles by the hand to present him to the Welsh people!

If we accept the above quote as accurate, we must conclude that the Prince of Wales could only have been referring to another "father"—that is, the red dragon or Satan. As Charles put it: "One could be so cynical about this sort of thing, and think, 'Well it's only a ceremony and some people are against it, ... and you know it's just a show.' Yes, one could think that. But I like to think it's something a little bit more than that—that perhaps it is symbolising *Ich Dien,* if you like."[2] Years later, while flying helicopters in the Royal Navy, Charles was known as "the Red Dragon."[3] (Like father, like son?)

We may note that each June, in the same month as the annual ceremony at Garter Chapel, the British monarch (now Charles), the monarch's consort (now Camilla), and the Prince of Wales, preside over the annual Trooping *the Colour* military parade outside Buckingham Palace, in which all—though Prince William now serves as Colonel-in-Chief of the Welsh Guards—are dressed in bright *red* and have bearskin hats.[4] As knights of the Order of the Garter, the king, Prince William, etc., also wear the blue Riband with its Lesser George.[5]

King Charles III and other British royals would like us to believe that they are Christians, yet the apostle Paul warned the saints, saying, "grievous [savage] wolves will come in among you, not sparing the flock" and "from among yourselves men will rise up, speaking

1. Holden, *PRINCE CHARLES*, p. 176.
2. "BBC Colour Television 1969," as posted at "https://www.youtube.com/watch?v=scar4bwXXFl".
3. A March 10, 1975 wired *Associated Press* photograph, taken in Devenport, England—one listed for sale on eBay in July 2022—bears this typed sidebar text: "Prince Charles, nicknamed the Red Dragon, is welcomed aboard the aircraft carrier HMS Hermes by Captain Derek Raffell, right, Monday. The 26-year-old prince, who is a lieutenant in the Royal Navy, made a perfect landing on the carrier to start active service as a navy helicopter pilot. As Prince of Wales, his banner bears a rampant red dragon, hence his nickname in the navy. (AP WIREPHOTO) (dt21915pP) 1975". eBay item no. 304354599651: "Historic Images Part Number: saa10096" — "an original [8 x 10.25 inches] press photo."
4. For a color photograph of this uniform, see Burnet, *In Private—In Public, THE PRINCE AND PRINCESS OF WALES,* p. 127. The Duke of Kent also is present in red uniform for this ceremony (*Her Majesty The Queen,* pp. 14-15). Occasionally, Charles as Prince of Wales also wore a predominantly black uniform, with some red, as Colonel of the Welsh Guards (*Charles & Diana: A Royal Family Album,* p. 87).
5. Hoey, *Charles & Diana: The Tenth Anniversary,* p. 36. *Her Majesty The Queen,* pp. 14-15.

the perverted things, to draw away the disciples after themselves" (Acts 20:29-30, Gk.; cf. Matt 22:11-12; Rev 16:15). To this, Paul added: "But I fear, lest somehow as the serpent deceived Eve in his craftiness, so your thoughts should be corrupted from the simplicity and the purity | integrity which *pertains* to The Christ. For if, indeed, the *one* coming proclaims another Jesus, whom we have not proclaimed, or *if* you receive another spirit which you have not received, or another gospel which you never *previously* accepted— you *might* well endure | bear with *these....* For such *are* false messengers | apostles, deceitful workers, transforming themselves into messengers | apostles of Christ. And not marvelously! For Satan himself transforms himself into an angel of light. *It is* not *a* great *thing,* then, if his ministers | servants also transform | disguise themselves as ministers | servants of righteousness, whose end will be according to their works" (2 Cor 11:3-4, 11:13-15, Gk.). Similarly, Jesus said: "Then if anyone says to you, 'Look, here is the Christ!,' or 'Here!,' do not believe *it;* for false christs [messiahs] and false prophets shall arise, and will give great signs and wonders, so as to lead astray [deceive], if possible, even the elect. Look, I tell you beforehand" (Matt 24:23-25, Gk.; cf. Mark 13:21-23).

Let there be no obfuscation: Queen Elizabeth II, Prince Philip, and Charles, like Lord Snowdon and some other British royalty, as well as all the involved heralds and Welsh leadership, were (some now roast) and are *satanists*—by any other "word." (Philip is in Hell.) When any of them says he or she is a "Christian," they lie; in reality, they are savage wolves in sheep's clothing! As Jesus stated: "Beware of false prophets, who come to you in sheep's clothing, but inwardly are ravenous wolves. You will know them by their fruits.... Every tree that does not bear good fruit is cut down and thrown into the fire" (see Matt 7:15-20; cf. Matt 24:4, 24:11, 24:24-26; Mark 13:5, 13:22-23; Luke 21:8). Indeed, the queen, as the mother of the historically wicked man who received (and yet receives) "his power, his throne, and great authority" from Satan, dressed entirely in off-white for the occasion; and with her stylish hat covering all her black hair, she looked truly *sheepish!* Charles, rather than choosing the symbolism of a lamb, overtly followed a dragon-clad goat.

Awen and Satan's Prince. The Awen (e.g., "\|/" in an invoking orientation), which some call the "Bardic symbol," while actually deriving from ancient Egypt (i.e., the Hebraic *Awen* or Grecian *Heliopolis),* has been associated with Welsh Arthurian legends by more recent, historically speaking, *neo*-druidry. *Awen* is said to represent "the entirety" of the pagan Celtic *Ogham* or "Tree alphabet." According to legend, this druidic alphabet hails from the ancient Philistines (i.e., "a people originating in the Aegean, called 'the people of the sea' by the Egyptians"). Yet, the Philistines themselves, irrespective of what the ancient Egyptians may have called them, were in fact descendants of Egypt or *Mitzraim* itself, perhaps as grandchildren (Gen 10:13-14, Heb.). Moreover, scripture reveals that *Awen* had a pre-Flood origin, so that it even predated the Tower of Babel (see Job 22:15-17, Heb.; cf. 21:19-20, Heb.); consequently, that which Awen has represented to the *post-Flood* world, as actually delineated within the Hebrew scriptures,[1] including what it now represents to neo-druidry, encapsulates some portion of the religious philosophy and beliefs of the fallen, *pre-Flood* world—indeed, *perhaps a very large portion.*

Legend has it that the *Ogham* or "Tree alphabet" was created as the actual combination of the "best" of all the confused languages that God brought at the Tower of Babel, in the years immediately following the tower's fall, and that the new language derived from this combination was what is now known as *Goidelic*—the forerunner to *Gaelic,*[2] and thus to Irish, Scottish, Manx (spoken on the Isle of Man), and, more distantly, Welsh! If this legend holds any seeds of truth, it would certainly be that that Awen and its corresponding "mystical mark" represent confusion concerning God and His nature, as the author will below show. If, on the other hand, the Awen (i.e., the Awen mark) actually can be traced historically to the ancient Egyptians or even their Philistine grandchildren, it would supplement the author's evidence, presented herein, that it is a perversion of the Hebrew letter or glyph *Shin* (שׁ), even though neo-druidry is only able to demonstrate historical druidry's existence at a much later date; both the ancient Egyptians and the Philistines had close contact with ancient Israel. In fact, the Awen symbol traces to ancient Egypt's sun cult in *On* or *Awen* (Heb.), otherwise known as *Heliopolis* (Gk.), the "City of the Sun." So, the Awen symbol dates to at least the days of Israel's enslavement in Egypt, and is a paganized version of *Shin,* where the latter represents the The Godhead.[3]

With the *Awen* symbol or mark ("\|/" and "/|\") as a perversion of *Shin* (שׁ)—where the Awen glyphically represents the nature of Satan, the False Prophet, and the AntiChrist, including the latter's name, and *Shin* glyphically represents the unified nature of The

---

1. For a detailed study on this, see the chapter (or section) "Egypt, Awen and Satan Versus Israel, Shin and The LORD," in Vol. I, *Biblical Interpretation (Hermeneutics),* of the author's *Messiah, History, and the Tribulation Period* series.
2. For example, see "Ogham", *Wikipedia,* July 2009.
3. Again, see "Egypt, Awen and Satan Versus Israel, Shin and The LORD," in Vol. I, *Biblical Interpretation (Hermeneutics),* of the *Messiah, History, and the Tribulation Period* series.

LORD, including His Name—there is much to discover. Because these glyphs, the Awen and *Shin,* pertain to the AntiChrist verses The Messiah, a study of one in relation to the latter sheds some very significant new light on our understanding of both the name *and the number* of the "first beast" or the foretold AntiChrist, and as we shall see, tells us *a great deal more* about Charles' investiture as Satan's Prince. In a later chapter within this work, the author shall demonstrate that this greater light also enables considerable new insight regarding the nature and origin of the foretold mark of the beast! Bearing all this in mind, let's proceed.

The three vertical "lines" of the Awen are known in Welsh as *Y Nod Cyfrin,* "The Mystic Mark," or *Y Nod Pelydr Goleuni,* "The Mark of the Shaft of Light." In a Triban (Tribann) pattern, the Awen is also revealed in the *fleur-de-lis.* The word *awen* in Middle Welsh means "muse," "inspiration" or "essence," referring to spiritual illumination and representing "the creative powers in action." *Awen,* like the Welsh word *awel* for "breeze," also derives from the Indo-European root *uel,* which means "to blow;" thus, the Awen is said to represent the "breath of the divine, the wind of the spirit." A parallel Irish word, *ai,* similarly means "poetic inspiration," compassing not only poetry, but also sorcery and divination—all of which are common to druidry. Embodying a "harmony of opposites," the Awen is rightly viewed as being akin to the Taoist yin-yang symbol.

The Awen is also equivalent to the Sanskrit *Aum* (or *Om*) of the pagan Indian religions, and in Tibetan script, as perhaps the best example, the *Aum* bears at least a loose resemblance to *Shin.* That resemblance certainly is not lost on heretic "rabbi" Ariel Bar Tzadok, who basically exposes himself as a (New Age) *pantheist,* claiming: "There is an ancient book called *Perek Shirah,* with a chapter of song, wherein which is revealed that everything in nature, has its own vibration, which means it has its own consciousness.... Everything is alive."[1] Along with other "regulars" on the *Ancient Aliens* TV series,[2] Mr. Ariel Bar Tzadok connects *Aum* to "divine" connections and creation.[3]

Indeed, some modern druids use the word *awen* as the Celtic equivalent to *aum,* intoning it during "trance work" as "aah-ooo-enn" (i.e., "awen"). (The Sanskrit *Om* similarly corresponds to the Hebrew *On.*) In the pagan Indian religions (e.g., those that rely upon

---

1. Ca. 33:25-42, "The Harmonic Code," *Ancient Aliens* (Seas. 16, Ep. 10), 12 Mar. 2021.
2. For thorough treatments of the many (often false) claims made in the "History" Channel's *Ancient Aliens* TV series—along with evidence for the real nature, historical and modern origins, and agendas of so-called "aliens," plus *beyond-extraordinary proof of seeded (from Earth) microbial and complex chimeric life elsewhere in our solar system*—see this author's *Solar Apocalypse* multi-volume series.
3. "The Harmonic Code," *Ancient Aliens.*

lies such as reincarnation), which are ancient perversions of the true understanding of the real God, The God of Israel, the *Aum* (or *Om)* is said to represent the power of "God" to create ("a"), preserve ("u"), and destroy ("m") the universe *(aum),* thereby encompassing the "supreme and most comprehensive name of all names of God," bearing no other meaning. "God" in Hinduism, then, is known as Brahma, or "creator" (the "a" of *aum),* Vishnu, or "preserver" (the "u" of *aum),* and Shiva, or "destroyer" (the "m" of *aum).*[1]

Druids wear the "Mystical Mark" or "Mark of the Shaft of Light" of the Awen, otherwise known as the "Three Rays" or "three bars of light," on their bandeaus and plastrons (breastplates); that is, ***the three "rays" or "bars" of the Awen comprise and are themselves the druidic "mark."***[2] As the most important of all druidic symbols, the Awen is often drawn with either three stars (dots) or one star (dot) above or below its mystical mark (i.e., the three *concentered* "rays"), with the three stars or one star representing the "divine" light(s) or flame(s) or the "Supreme Being;" indeed, the three "rays" are said to emanate from the three stars or "points of light," which themselves are said to represent "the aspect of triple deity." (Compare this to the satanic "trinity," bearing in mind that angelic beings are referred to as "stars" in scripture.) Also, the Awen may be enclosed within three concentric circles, which are sometimes called the "Triple Circle." Druidic explanations for the "rays," "stars" and "circles" abound, and show two things: first, the Awen (like the *Aum)* is a pagan—and at points—satanic perversion of *Shin,* and thus a direct affront to The God of Israel, and second, the Awen represents witchcraft and satanism.

Druidism attributes a variety of meanings and interpretations to the three "rays" or "bars" of the Awen's "mark," which, like the three stars, do not themselves necessarily meet; we again see polytheistic and pantheistic, as opposed to unified monotheistic, interpretations. (Like *Shin,* the Awen is actually a hieroglyph.) One may be surprised to learn that this, in fact, bears upon the very use of three sixes to represent the AntiChrist in scripture. Among Christians to date, the three sixes are invariably related to the fact that mankind was created on the sixth day, intimating that six is the "number of man." However, as the author will now show, there is a far more sinister reality and intent behind the use of six six six. In Hebrew, *Vav* (i.e., ו) has a value of six, and its appearance is very much like that of a railroad spike; in fact, the *Vav* represents a piercing spike, nail or thorn.

---

1. In Hebrew, *Shem* or *Shin-Mem* (i.e., שמ), meaning "Name," may bear similar import.
2. The three bars of the "guard bar" or "security bar" pattern of UPC and related barcodes are scanned with light. *These barcodes directly relate to the druidic "mark" or Awen*—as detailed in ch. 14 and its section entitled, "The real history of the UPC barcode symbol and standard."

Vav Vav Vav, then, represents six six six. Notice, therefore, that Jesus was pierced in his hands, feet, and head by spikes (nails) and thorns, or effectively by six six six, and this was at the midpoint of the Crucifixion Week, which, as the author demonstrates in his *Messiah, History, and the Tribulation Period* multi-volume series, serves as the base pattern for the Tribulation Week![1] Now, if one looks hieroglyphically at *Vav Vav Vav* (וּוּוּ) versus *Shin* (שׁ), one will notice as well that the appearance between three adjacent *vavim* (plural form of *Vav)* versus one *Shin* is relatively similar, with the primary difference in appearance residing in the fact that the *vavim* are *disjoined* and individual, whereas the three branches of the *Shin* are joined to a common base. (Satan actually *lacks* unity.) In other words, *Vav Vav Vav,* or six six six, represents not just the "number of man," where man was created on the sixth day, but in fact it suggests a polytheistic and pantheistic counterfeit of *Shin* (because the *vavim* are disjoined)!

Consequently, we discover that the use of three sixes may have even more to do with counterfeiting God and His nature than they do with the day of mankind's creation. Moreover, we find a corresponding indication elsewhere, in today's fallen world: the first Greek letter used in Revelation 13:18 to represent six-hundred (in the number six-hundred and sixty-six), or *Chi* (i.e., X or χ), is itself a hieroglyph and bears the appearance of an X or cross on its side (in this context, representing denigration of Christ's cross), so "XXX" or triple-X, which in our time causes so many to stumble and sin, would then signify *six*-hundred *six*-hundred and *six*-hundred. Being yet another version of six six six (see below), "XXX" likewise represents the denigration of the crucifixions of Christ, Israel, and the saints in Christ (i.e., Christians) at the midpoints of the three major weeks of God's redemptive plan: the Crucifixion Week, the Week of History, and the Tribulation Week![2] (Substituting "X-mas" for "Christmas" may seem or even be spiritually similar.)

Indeed, when one considers Goliath, Nebuchadnezzar's statue, and Solomon's throne or Solomon himself in the latter half of his reign, one sees the three sixes associated not only with multiple biblical types of the AntiChrist, but with those who, animated by Satan historically, would counterfeit the true God Himself. Likewise, in the foreseeable future, when human beings begin *en masse* to receive the mark of the beast on their forehead or right hand, men shall blasphemously establish themselves as their own "gods" in place of

---

1. That is, the Crucifixion Week is the base pattern for the Tribulation Week, besides other "weeks."
2. Thus, this author anticipates that the *Messiah, History, and the Tribulation Period* multi-volume series may be similarly denigrated by the Adversary. For more information, see that series.

the only real God, The God of Israel. This, of course, brings us back to the Awen and its inbuilt mark.

The Awen mark's three "rays" or "bars" are said to **a)** be columns of "light and sound at the same time," where "Word and Light produced Life" *(Men Heim),* and thus "the three fundamental principles from which all the Forces of Creation stem," rendered as the first three letters of he Ogham alphabet, or "I", "O", and "U";[1] **b)** represent the primal sound and light caused by the "Supreme Being" pronouncing "His" name to create the universe; **c)** represent the harmony of opposites, or male energy or forces called "E" in the physical realm (e.g., the left "ray" of an invoking orientation), the harmonious natural balance of male and female called "Ah" (i.e., the center ray), and female energy or forces called "O" in the physical realm (e.g., the right "ray" of an invoking orientation), respectively ("E-Ah-O" is actually then viewed as a "sexual moan"); **d)** "open the gates of *Annwyn,* the doorway to the Otherworld" "at the time of the midsummer sunrise;" **e)** be a symbol of the "divine" name; **f)** symbolize "divine" inspiration; **g)** signify truth, love or knowledge, and peace or justice; and finally, **h)** relate to earth, sea, and air or spirit (i.e., elements of paganism and witchcraft). Unsurprisingly, there are even druids who speak of "three foundations of Awen: love of truth, the understanding of truth, and the maintaining of truth." Their version of "truth," however, is sadly bound to Satan—the father of lies!

According to Iolo Morganwyg, an early Unitarian cultist and father of mesopagan (neo-) druidry, the Triple Circle represents the "three stages of existence" or creation. The Triple Circle, when used to encompass the Awen, is likewise said to represent a) three Celtic realms of Earth, sea, and sky, and b) light, fire or energy, and spirit. In this, of course, we see all the "elements" of witchcraft: earth, water, sky or air or wind, fire or energy or light, and spirit. As such, the Triple Circle, which is also a wiccan ritual or "sacred circle," is said to speak to existence and passage of the soul from this world to the next. In fact, the wiccan ritual circle is associated with their "horned god" *(Cernunnos* or *Cern,* the ancient Celtic horned deity, said to be the "god" of fertility, wealth, and the underworld), who is otherwise known as their anti-Christian dying and "rising" (natural or "recycled" life from death) "Green Man" and "horned moon."

Charles as the modern "Green Prince" and eco-fascist globalist leader, has been referred to as "the Green Man," and is a secret Muslim under the sign of the crescent moon. In fact, at his behest, the official invitation to King Charles III's May 6, 2023 coronation, most

---

1. This may make governmental "I.O.U.s" seem even more perverse.

prominently features the Green Man—to represent *Charles himself*—at the bottom-center. (Later, we'll further address this.)

Among Muslims, "al" means "the," and "al-lah" means "the god." Yet, the name *Allah* or *Al-lah* actually derives historically from *al-Ilah* or *al-Ilyah,* where *Ilah* or *Ilyah* referred to the ancient Arabian "Moon god" *Hubal* (otherwise known as *Baal* and *Tammuz,* for example)—chief "god" in a pantheon of pagan "gods." In this version of the pagan pantheon, the "Moon god" *Hubal,* generically referred to as *Ilah* or *Ilyah,* was male rather than female, and because *al-Ilah* was the chief "god," its pagan adherents worshiped the Moon by night over the Sun by day—effectively favoring darkness over light. (The idol of *Hubal* in the Arabian *Kaaba* or pantheon is said to have been a red statue "in the form of a man." Might this have been blood-red, like the red dragon?) Later, the false prophet Mohammed discarded use of the name *Hubal* for this "Moon god," calling him simply "the god" or *Allah* (a title, not a true proper name) within "Islam," his new monotheistic religion—while retaining and incorporating most aspects of the pagan worship of *Hubal* in Islam.[1]

Remarkably, this *"Ilah,"* or the "Moon god" of Mohammed and Islam, *is actually a perversion of the Hebrew "Elah" or "elah," which is both a title of The God of Israel* (e.g., see Ezra 5:11, 7:19, 7:23, etc., Heb.; cf. Jer 10:11, Heb.) *and the primary word for an oak or other strong tree* (e.g., elm, terebinth, etc.; see Gen 35:4, Heb.; Judg 6:11, 6:19, Heb.; 2 Sam 18:9, 18:14, Heb.; 1 Kings 13:14, Heb.; Isa 1:30, 6:13, Heb.; Ezek 6:13, Heb; Hos 4:13, Heb.; cf. 1 Sam 17:2, 17:19, 21:9). In other words, *Elah* or *El-ah,* when used of The God of Israel, is a variant of *El*—one that imputes strength like an oak tree, and in its variant *Eloah,* actually intimates piercing (e.g., crucifixion) upon a "tree."[2] Yet, there is another pronunciation in the Hebrew scriptures, *according to the Masoretes,* for an oak tree: *alah* (see Josh 24:26, Heb.; cf. 19:26, Heb.)![3] (Though rare, it is found in Joshua.)

---

1. Mohammed was not accused of "preaching a different Allah" than that one pagan Arabians already knew and worshiped; rather, he sought to eliminate the astral worship of all the other pagan "gods."

2. *El-o-ah*—a variant of *Elah*—includes a *Vav* (for "o" or even "u") between the *Lamed* and *Hey,* and is most frequently used of God in Job. The added *Vav* in *Eloah* hieroglyphically represents piercing, and so correlates the sufferings of The Savior, or Jesus who is The God of Israel, to Job's sufferings—as well as to the suffereings of Israel nationally and the saints. Indeed, we see the same difference in Hebrew between *Moshiach* for "Savior" and *Mashiach* for "Messiah;" Savior *(Moshiach)* includes a *Vav* following its *Mem,* whereas *Mashiach* (Messiah) omits it, showing that The Savior is The Messiah pierced! Jesus had to be pierced to the death to be The Savior, and this was done upon a "tree."

3. *Elah* and *alah* have the same spelling in Hebrew—*Aleph, Lamed, Hey;* only the vowel and accent marks —or the pronunciation—differs, at least in the Masoretic Text. Now, this could easily have been a Masoretic error, as it was the Masoretes who added the vowel and accent marks to the inspired Hebrew scriptures, thereby producing the "Masoretic Text," from which most translations of the Hebrew scriptures—including those in English—derive. If the responsible Masorete erred in the vowels he chose for the word meaning "oak" in Joshua 24:26, which is possible, then that would mean that it should read *elah* as opposed to *alah;* just a single vowel change would make that difference. On the other hand, perhaps God wanted that Masorete to show a relation between "oak" and *alah* (i.e., Allah). Still, nei-

Given the above, we could assert that *Elah,* in reference to the God of Israel as opposed to an oak tree, with a simple vowel change, could everywhere be translated as *Alah,* and that *El* could just as well be translated as *Al.* No doubt, such a change would gratify Muslims the world over, who have long asserted that *Allah* or *Alah* is the name of God even in the Hebrew scriptures. However, all we (and they) would really be accomplishing through this alteration of Masoretic vowel markings, is to establish the existence of a connection between *Alah* or Allah and "oak." *Yet, this is actually quite significant.* Recall our earlier discussion of the "dying god-king" of witchcraft or Wicca, who is also known as the "oak god" and the "god of the wood" of both witchcraft and Druidism, dating to ancient Nimrod. (Charles is intimately familiar with the mythologies and occultism surrounding the "oak god," etc. At "the most sacred moment" of his later May 2023 coronation as king, Charles III used an "anointing screen" having four wooden poles "hewn from an ancient windblown Windsor oak"—two topped by gold leaf-gilded bronze eagles,[1] like Babylon and Rome.) Were we to grant Islam's assertion that *Alah* is the name of God in the Hebrew scriptures, *which we could do,* then we would also have to conclude that *Alah* or Allah, apart from being the ancient Arabian "Moon god," is the "oak god" who marries and "fertilizes" the "goddess of the wood"— otherwise known as *Diana* and the "goddess of fertility"—only to become the "dying god-king" (cf. the AntiChrist who shall receive a mortal wound, and paganism's anti-Christian "Green Man").[2]

Allah, then, is a complete pagan perversion of *Elah,* The God of Israel, so that Allah bears little to no resemblance to Him. *Such a connection, which can only confound Muslims, necessarily implies that witchcraft, including its "goddess of fertility," is itself endemic to the very root of Islam.* Consider, for example, the many fertile virgins Islam promises to its "martyrs" and other adherents for Allah, who, in accord with the "dying god-king," may sacrifice themselves. Is this not about the "goddess of fertility?" Surely, it is—despite the fact that the Koran, albeit as a highly confused "blind guide" (see Matt 5:33-37, 23:16-22; cf. Koran 74:32, 84:16), rejects worship of the Sun and the Moon (Koran 41:37). Not only that, but this "Moon god" *Ilah* was also known as the Semitic (i.e., *Akkadian) Sin* (not to be confused with the Hebrew glyph *Sin)*—the supposed controller and illuminator of the night.[3]

---

ther *elah* nor *alah* would refer to God, but only to a mere oak tree in this particular verse.

1. Caroline Davies, "Anointing screen to be used in King Charles coronation revealed," *The Guardian,* 28 Apr. 2023.
2. For more, see ch. 4's section "A Merovingian 'conspiracy of destiny,'" and ch. 10.
3. Recall that the Hebrew *Shin* and Phoenician *Sin* are effectively the same *hieroglyph,* and that *Shin*

This same Semitic *Sin* "is commonly designated as *En-zu*, or 'lord of wisdom.' During the period ... that Ur exercised a large measure of supremacy over the Euphrates valley, *Sin* was naturally regarded as the head of the [pagan] pantheon. It is to this period that we must trace such designations of *Sin* as 'father of the gods', 'chief of the gods', 'creator of all things', ['illuminator'] and the like. The 'wisdom' personified by the moon-god is likewise an expression of the science of astrology, in which the observation of the Moon's phases is an important factor.... The bull [(unicorn)] was one of his symbols, through his father, *Enlil*, 'Bull [(Unicorn)] of Heaven', along with the crescent and the tripod [(cf. the Awen)].... On [ancient] cylinder seals, he is represented as an old man with a flowing beard and the crescent [moon] symbol [(cf. Merlin)].... The cult of the moon-god spread to other centers, so that temples to him are found in all the large cities of Babylonia and Assyria."[1]

We may properly conclude, therefore, that Charles here (at his 1969 investiture as Satan's Prince) personified Allah, or the "Moon god" of Islam (and the wiccan "horned moon"), and that he even relates to Allah as the "dying god-king" and "oak god" of witchcraft and Druidism! In fact, Islam strictly maintains its historical connection to the Arabian "Moon god:" the crescent moon symbol is atop every mosque, and adorns the flags of Arab nations. Moreover, the word "druid" literally means "oak" or "oak man," being cognate with the Greek word for "oak," and druids, naturally, worship the pagan "oak god;" indeed, they see in oak leaves a repetition of the Awen's "Mystical Mark" pattern. This very "oak god" is otherwise known as the Roman *Jupiter*, Greek *Zeus*, Teutonic (Norse) *Thor*, Slavic *Perun*, Lithuanian *Perkunas* or *Perkuns*, Islamic *Allah* (as just shown), etc., and is viewed by pagans as "the god" of the sky, the rain, and the thunder, and a "god" of the Earth—or all the "elements" (sky, water, fire, and earth)! Consider, therefore, the fact that Charles' investiture was in an open-air castle, under a fully visible sky on a day that included both a mild rain (the queen carried an umbrella) and "thunder" (cf. cannon and jet fighters overhead); and, by all means, do not forget the manifest "X lightning" over the dragon throne (p. 256), nor the fiery dragon paw prints that appeared for an instant to the left of Satan's Prince as he emerged from the Chamberlain Tower

---

specifically represents The God of Israel. Referring to the pagan "Moon god" as *Sin*, or by the same name as the Phoenician hieroglyph just mentioned, as the ancient Mesopotamians and their forebears did, is perhaps a perversion. Similarly, Islam perversely associates The God of Israel with its "Moon god" Allah—for that's what Allah really is—when it uses the Arabic version of the hieroglyph *Shin* to represent and spell Allah's supposed name in Arabic. In fact, visually speaking, the Arabic spelling of *Allah* is not unlike a *Shin* with a sword next to it!

1. "Sin (mythology)", Nov. 2009, *Wikipedia*.

(see the provided investiture footage frames).[1] Is it any wonder that Charles has, since his July 1969 investiture, become enormously (and abnormally) popular among satanists (e.g., Muslims) and pagans everywhere? And, should we be surprised to learn that this man is over Druidism, like organized witchcraft, globally? As the foretold AntiChrist, today's King Charles III is the very embodiment of *Sin* (pun intended), and is to be possessed by Satan himself.

This "horned god" is also none other than the androgynous Baphomet to satanists, which is depicted as a goat-headed winged beast with a "transgender" body.[2] Thus, as the author has shown, a two-horned goat wearing an invoking Awen over its forehead—in the form of the badge of the Black Prince—served as the investiture mascot, representing Satan, Charles as the foretold AntiChrist, and the coming False Prophet, all rolled into one. Joined to the red dragon, Satan's Prince also represented the classical red devil, which itself derives from Baphomet. To satanists, Baphomet is the first beast of Revelation 13, the AntiChrist! He is their "Sun God," their "Dual Accursed-One." Anton Szandor LaVey, in his Satanic Bible, states: "The symbol of Baphomet was used by the Knights Templar to represent Satan. Through the ages this symbol has been called by many different names. Baphomet represents the Powers of Darkness combined with the generative fertility of the goat."[3] *Charles, then, is this Baphomet, the AntiChrist, to satanists.* (Pagans call this same "horned god" by a variety of names.) In fact, photos showing the investiture coronet on Charles' head, while he as prince faces forward, reveal a truly striking parody of Baphomet's goat-head, to include protruding nail-based crosses and a central gold "planet Earth" (orb), from which another nail-based cross rises, in place of Baphomet's two horns (cf. the top-left and top-right crosses) and central torch (cf. the orb with its cross). Indeed, the investiture crown itself also exposed oval holes over Charles' forehead, where one would otherwise expect to see Baphomet's eyes. Yet, that is not all. The two horns and central torch in the head of Baphomet are actually arranged in the pattern of an invoking Awen—as were the gold crosses and central orb on Charles' investiture crown. (Recall that a "beam" or "wave" of supernatural light appears to have been captured on-film proceeding from just above the seat of Elizabeth II's dragon throne, and this light passed through Charles' head, as he wore the "Baphomet" coronet!) Going back in time, one would also

---

1. Of course, the reader may wish to know more. Zeus, for example, is alternately said to have been raised by a goat, *Gaia,* and a nymph—all rather accurate for Charles, one might say! Other myths surrounding "Zeus" placed him as a serpent "god" of the underworld!
2. "Transgenders" are the *apex predators* of sexual satanists (i.e., so-called "LGBTQIA+ whatever" loons).
3. Anton Szandor LaVey, *The Satanic Bible,* p. 136.

discover that Babylon's *Tammuz,* Egypt's *Horus,* Greece's *Zeus,* Rome's *Jupiter,* etc., and now the modern European Union's bull (cf. unicorn), each one a perversion of the real Savior (i.e., Messiah Yeshua or Christ Jesus), were all religious types of the AntiChrist or first beast of Revelation 13, and imagery pertaining to each one of these false pagan deities was compassed within then Prince Charles' investiture as Prince of Satan.   (The queen, then, corresponded to Babylon's *Semiramis* or *Ishtar,* Egypt's *Isis,* Greece's *Rhea* or *Demeter* her daughter, Rome's *Ops* or *Ceres* her daughter, and now the EU's *Europa,* each a perversion of Jesus' mother, Mary or *Miriam.*)

The Triple Circle also relates to the wiccan "Triple Goddess," or Diana "whom all Asia and the world worship" (Acts 19:27; see 19:23-38; cf. Charles' sacrificed late wife, Diana), who is the complement to the "horned god." The "Green Man" and "Triple Goddess" combine in the druidic "Triple Circle," therefore, to represent both "male" and "female."   Indeed, the investiture sword, one of the items of Charles' investiture regalia, served as the wiccan *"athame,* a director of energy," which "the male high priest" (Charles himself) pushed "into a scabbard held by the high priestess" (i.e., the queen, once she placed the sword on her son), representing the "sexual energy" and "union" between male and female.   (Yes, in the case of the then prince and his mother, Queen Elizabeth II, this really *was* incestuous symbolism.) That same sword also served as the Sword of Allah, the "Moon god," and Islam.

All this, of course, played to a world filled with pagans, which Satan hopes to further paganize.   Consider, therefore, this article entitled, "'Everyone's a pagan now:'"

> Look out, here come the pagans. It's late May in central London and a man dressed as a tree, a witch in a velvet robe and a woman pretending to be a raven with a long black beak are dancing through the streets.... They could wake the god of thunder with their noise but it's OK, the people at the back with the broadswords and shields are followers of Thor. This is a parade to celebrate pagan pride [(like sexual-wickedness pride)]....
>
> Paganism is casting its spell over more people now than ever before in the modern age....
>
> ....At Stonehenge at least 30,000 people were expected to watch the sun rise in the company of the druids who see themselves as practising the ancient faith of pre-Christian Britain. For them, the sun is symbolic of one aspect of the "universal force which flows through the world and which can be encouraged to flow through us", according to Philip Carr-Gomm, founder of the Order of Bards, Ovates and Druids and author of the new Book of English Magic. The druids are only a small part of modern paganism, which encompasses a bewildering number of traditions or "paths", but central to them all is this idea of a divine force inherent in nature....

Away from Stonehenge, much smaller groups of people celebrate the summer solstice by gathering before sunrise in gardens or woods, on beaches or hilltops....

"What we believe is suddenly everywhere," says Bantu, a dreadlocked 29-year-old who planned to be on a hill in Wales when the moment came. He started to worship Gaia, the earth goddess, after going to a workshop at a climate camp. "Everyone's a pagan now."

Not quite, maybe, but the rise has been dramatic....

[Ronald Hutton, a professor of history at Bristol University,] adds that there has been a much greater acceptance of pagan ideas among the wider public. "It is best to think in terms of concentric circles," he says, "from those who are initiated members of a group such as a coven, out to those who go to Stonehenge for a drink and a party."

The Pagan Federation's membership list includes druids as well as wiccans, practising modern witchcraft; shamans, engaging with the spirits of the land; and heathens, worshipping the gods of the north European tribes (including Thor). But then there are the neopagans such as Bantu, always visible at environmental protests, who ... pursue a rainbow of revived, recreated or invented beliefs with nature at their heart.

All you have to believe to be a pagan, according to the federation, is that each of us has the right to follow our own path (as long as it harms no-one else); that the higher power (or powers) exists; and that nature is to be venerated. If you asked everyone in Britain if they agreed with those three statements, millions would put their hands up. At its loosest, paganism is beginning to look like our new national faith.

The circles can be seen widening in the most unlikely places....

These public events usually include a re-enactment of whatever stage of the pagan cycle is being marked. In Eastbourne they needed some dancers to perform the cutting down of the male sun god, represented as the mythical character John Barleycorn, and so a Morris-dancing group [(represented by the Morris Ring)], Hunters Moon [whose members wear pentagrams], was born....[1]

Witchcraft is another driving force in the rise of paganism [(and is of keen interest to Charles as the foretold AntiChrist)].... Their version of the divine force is embodied in a horned male god and a mother goddess,[2] and their response to its energy all around us involves the casting of spells and incantations to influence real events....

....Wiccans believe in the ability to communicate directly with the divine by calling down the god or goddess to enter the body, which can involve going into a trance and allowing them to speak through you. The most common wiccan symbol is the pentagram, whose points represent the elements essential to life: air, fire, water, earth and the spirit that ties them all together. They see themselves as inheritors of the "wise craft"....

"It is a mystery religion," says [Chris Crowley, a wiccan high priest who speaks for the Federation]. "You do have to be initiated." ...

Jeanette Ellis is not a wiccan but a "traditional" witch.... She is not so shy about ritual and is able to explain why so many people on the parade

---

1. This, of course, is the old Babylonian religion, in which the Sun is represented by the lion and the Moon by the unicorn; it is embodied on the heraldic achievements of British royals, including the AntiChrist.

2. From the day of his July 1969 investiture as Satan's Prince, where Charles wore a horned crown, the "horned male god" has been none other than *Charles*—even before his coming possession by Satan—with Elizabeth II then serving as the "mother goddess."

are wearing knives, including those broadswords (with the police turning a blind eye). "That is the *athame,* a director of energy. It must not touch blood. There are no sacrifices going on." The knife is placed in a chalice to bless wine. She also describes the male high priest pushing the athame into a scabbard held by the high priestess. Hang on, this is all about sex, isn't it?

"There is a sexual energy [(between male and female)], I wouldn't deny it," says Ellis.... "The sexual union happens within every ritual, usually symbolically." ...

Some wannabe wizards did go on to take an adult interest in the esoteric after reading Harry Potter, but the boy wizard's bigger impact has been in the adoption of pagan ideas into the mainstream: the BBC uses pagan spirituality as a source of inspiration even for children's shows such as Raven and Merlin....

It is in pop culture that witchcraft meets the other main force behind the rise in paganism: environmentalism. James Lovelock made the link explicit in his influential 1979 description of the earth as a single, living organism, which he named after the Greek goddess Gaia.[1] Some take this more theologically..., but it remains the most famous example of ... turning away from the established, patriarchal faiths towards new forms of spirituality. Of course, you don't have to be a pagan to be a green [(i.e., an eco-fascist environmentalist)].... But the two movements have given each other energy, as each has grown.

For many pagans, becoming a green campaigner is a way of demonstrating faith with practical action. For many activists who come at it from the opposite direction, the pagan idea of an ancient and universal spirit that animates the earth gives their actions a personal, spiritual framework. Not that you have to read eco-theory to get it these days, just watch Teletubbies. "The indoctrination into things like recycling starts at an early age," says Catherine Hosen, a druid from Kent.... "If you start off trying to be environmentally aware, it is not much of a step to seeing all of nature as sacred, and from there to becoming a pagan."

Perhaps. This, don't forget, is mostly a loose faith. That is why it is so popular in these individualistic, iconoclastic times. Wander towards the centre of Hutton's concentric circles where the covens wait and you will be asked to pass tests, obey priests, follow rituals and keep secrets; but on the outer edges, at festival times such as the summer solstice, there is none of that — just a dance, a beer and a "Merry meet, merry part and merry meet again". Just watch yourself with those knives [and broadswords].[2]

At Charles' investiture as Prince of Wales, the three slate thrones and slate stool were arranged (intentionally) *to represent four points of an Awen* concentered upon the latter (i.e., the stool); this Awen pattern was then fully encircled by three of four concentric slate circles of the round slate investiture platform. The outer two investiture thrones, and the slate stool Satan's Prince would use, sat directly atop the innermost or fourth concentric circle, while the queen's

---

1. Charles as prince and now king, along with Al Gore, have done much to popularize Gaia worship.
2. Cole Moreton, "'Everyone's a pagan now'," *guardian.co.uk,* 22 June 2009.

throne sat atop the round Throne Stone at the very center of all these circles. Thus, a total of four concentric circles compass the Throne Stone to comprise the overall platform, which is further subdivided into pyramidal "slices," with the three outermost circles having encompassed the arranged Awen. Put yet another way, for clarity's sake, the queen's satanic dragon throne rested atop the round Throne Stone at the very center of the platform, while the other two thrones and the stool, upon which Charles worshiped and which formed the converged area of an Awen, were atop the slate circle immediately around the Throne Stone, and all these, representing a complete Awen converged on Satan's Prince, were themselves encircled by three more slate circles. In every way, therefore, the design of the esoteric investiture platform was distinctly druidic and occult, being as it were an astonishing sigil, with the round Throne Stone encircled by four concentric slate circles, the innermost of which was for the stool and the backless thrones of Charles and Prince Philip. That is still not all. The particular design of the round investiture platform, which is divided into sixteen major "slices," may also represent the wiccan "Spirit Wheel"—four wooden "spears" on the platform supported the Perspex canopy, signifying earth, wind or air, fire and water—and the "Sun wheel" or "Solar cross" or "Year Wheel," which marks the "sabbaths," equinoxes and solstices of the wiccan ritual calendar, thereby delineating pagan times and seasons. The very same platform likewise represents the druidic "Year Circle," Buddhist "Dharma Wheel," and Native American "Medicine Wheel." Indeed, the central Throne Stone, itself encircled by sixteen radiating lines (delineating the platform's sixteen major "slices"), even represents the Sun itself and, corporately, the satanic "all-seeing eye."[1]

Each pair of these sixteen "slices," or even each individual "slice," moreover, when viewed with the round Throne Stone at their top, represents the pyramidal Seal of the Illuminati, with its "all-seeing eye" of Lucifer, discernible from every direction. Likewise, each individual "slice" represents an Awen concentered on the round Throne

---

1. The investiture platform as a whole is highly reminiscent of many solar petroglyphs found throughout the ancient pagan world—precisely matching some—besides Sumerian-Akkadian and Mesopotamian depictions of the Sun and stars. In that latter context, Satan's Prince, wearing his horned investiture crown, represented the "Moon god." Yet, *there are several other important "contexts" to consider.* For example, we may also discern the ancient eight-pointed rosette petroglyph depicting the star of Ishtar, or the "goddess Ishtar" and the "Moon goddess," who is known by a variety of other names, including Diana, within the design of the platform; indeed, we could even see the core outline of an eight-pointed Garter Star. *Thus, pagan astral worship, with Satan and the AntiChrist at its heart, figured prominently in the investiture: a mother, a father, and a son, representing the Sun, Moon, and male "morning star," were all present; Charles is Satan's counterfeit "morning star," and these three stood as a counterfeit "trinity." In fact, the three stars (dots) often portrayed in the Awen actually represent this astral trinity.* (Charles has been likened to his great uncle David, aka Edward VIII, who was called "Chief Morning Star.") The LORD strongly condemns astral worship (see Deut 4:19, 17:2-5; 2 Kin 21:1-12, 23:2-28; Jer 8:1-3, 19:13; and Zeph 1:4-5).

Stone, where the queen sat on her satanic dragon throne! Finally, the position of four "spears" on the round investiture platform, in combination with the position of Charles at the slate stool as he faced the red dragon and was invested, formed the five tips of a pentagram within a circle, thereby constituting a wiccan "Pentacle." (The five tips of the wiccan pentagram represent the "elements" of witchcraft.) Therefore, the major symbols of, and participants in Wicca, or the religion of witchcraft, were all depicted at the investiture platform, to include the pentacle, "horned god" or "Green Man," "Triple Goddess," "sun wheel" or "solar cross" or "year wheel," "spirit circle," high priest, high priestess, and "athame." (Recall that Charles is a Witch King of witch kings, and then living Queen Elizabeth II was a Witch Queen of witch queens.) Don't forget either that, in concert with the simultaneously present druidic, Buddhist and Native American symbolism, all the "elements" of witchcraft, to include "male" and "female," were likewise well and unmistakably represented.[1]

The directional layout of the two middle rays of the two Awens converged on the investiture platform was East-West, in agreement with the directional layout of a Gorsedd Circle. These two Awens together formed, as well, the points of the square and compasses symbol of freemasonry, in which the Throne Stone bearing the queen upon her satanic dragon throne sat in the place of the "G" for "Grand Architect of the Universe" ("GAOTU") or "god."[2] They also constituted a "macro" version of the Seal of the Illuminati!

Consequently, we may see that satanism, Druidism and witchcraft (Wicca) and paganism, esotericism and freemasonry, Islam (followers of the Mesopotamian "Moon god," *al-Ilyah),* and even apostate Christianity and Judaism, were *all* simultaneously represented—with every important detail "hidden in plain sight"—upon the investiture platform itself! (Recall as well that the Awen is equivalent to the *Aum* of the pagan Indian religions, and they too were thus encompassed in the religious symbolism and spirituality of Charles' investiture.) This web of symbolism and ceremony was most intricately orchestrated—so that each religion could discern its own presence, seeing what it "desired," and each person watching throughout the world could "recognize" his or her own spirituality in Satan's Prince. It was all one satanic lie after another, and "perfection itself" for *the* AntiChrist! Lucifer has indeed given his "glory"—

---

1. Notice as well similarities to "flying" discs (aka "flying saucers" or disc-shaped antigravity craft).
2. Charles, who has had much to say regarding architecture, created his own Institute of Architecture, which itself is now succeeded by his "Foundation for the Built Environment."

all the glory of the non-Christian world—to his seed and "son" Charles, who becomes the spiritual "ruler | prince of this world."

9

Signs of the Times
and
the Rise of "Global Governance"

King Charles III as *the* foretold AntiChrist, is the *fourth* horseman of the Apocalypse, *only.* However, he sums up, within himself, *all* the antiChrists of history—*to include the first three horsemen* (Rev 6:1-6); he combines their elements. (Thus, Charles' heraldic achievement as Prince of Wales contains *all* the colors of the first three horses and their riders as well.) Indeed, Charles will fulfill elements pertaining *to them all,* so that some are *confused* and think that the four horsemen are really *just one* individual who rides four different "horses" in succession." Yet, they are *distinct* actors and spirits who precede, and then later also ride alongside or in tandem with Charles. The October 2023 conflagration in the Middle East, which began with Edomite Muslim-led Hamas' October 7th satanic genocidal attack upon Israel, is leading to the imposition and enforcement of the treaty of Daniel 9:27, under Charles as Satan's Prince.

Though King Charles III is the wholly evil fourth horseman, he also is active *throughout* the Tribulation Week. (This also helps to explain the imposition and enforcement of the covenant or treaty of Daniel 9:27, as being *under* the Roman prince or ruler—that is, Charles himself!) Indeed, Charles wraps elements of the *first three* apocalyptic horsemen within himself (Rev 6:7-8)—though as stated, they are *distinct.* For example, Charles received the victor's crown (e.g., of thorns, on the Green Man's head, as *later addressed)* as well as the royal diadems at his coronation; Charles is associated with the Tower of Babel and Nimrod, via what happened during the 2022 Commonwealth Games (later addressed), and thus he is associated with Nimrod's bow—not just the Devil's Edomite-led "Palestinian" "baby" in Gaza and elsewhere; Charles has received the UK's nulcear arsenal as king and its other ballistic missiles; his "intelligence"-controlled government is *against* peace with Russia, supporting and promoting war (e.g., between Russia and Ukraine, and then what comes next[1]), so Charles is actually *against* peace (cf.

---

1. For more information, see the author's *North Korea, Iran, and the Coming World War: Behold a Red Horse* book, as well as his *Israel, "Peace" and the Looming Great Tribulation* multi-volume series.

2nd seal); and Charles' actual agenda is one of anti-energy and famine, and thus death and depopulation (cf. third seal).[1]

This chapter, which derives from one of the volumes in the author's forthcoming series, *Messiah, History, and the Tribulation Period,* constitutes a helpful background to the rest of this book. As we shall see, Charles not only champions, but *leads* much of the elitist and globalist agenda below outlined.

When various Pharisees and Sadducees came to Jesus to tempt Him, wanting Him to show them a sign from Heaven, He replied: "*When* evening arrives, you say, 'Clear weather—for the sky is red;' and at morning, 'Today, *there will be* a storm—for the sky is red, being overcast.' Hypocrites! Indeed, you know *how* to discern the face of the sky, but you cannot *discern* the signs of the times. A wicked and adulterous generation seeks a sign, but no sign shall be given to it, except the sign of Jonah the prophet" (Matt 16:2-4, Gk.; cf. Luke 12:54-56). The Greek word that Jesus used for "hypocrites" most literally means "actors" or "pretenders."[2] Although it may sound unnecessarily insulting, according to Jesus, those who actually claim that they are God's "well-informed" servants, but who are unable or unwilling to discern the signs of the times, are in reality "pretenders" or disingenuous.

Among many in today's Church, this is certainly not a popular message. Yet it is central to our time. Though the "Judaeans request a sign, and the Greeks seek after *worldly* wisdom" (1 Cor 1:22, Gk.; cf. Matt 12:38, 16:4; Mark 8:11; Luke 11:29), we, as true Christians, should be able to discern and recognize the signs of the times that precede Jesus' return. Concerning the signs of His coming, and of the completion of the age (Matt 24:3), Jesus forewarned His disciples, saying,

> See *that* no one misleads you. For many will come in My name, saying, 'I am the Christ [Messiah],' and will deceive many.[3] But you will hear of wars and rumors of wars. See that you are not troubled; it is right for all *these things* to happen, but the completion [end] is not yet. For race [ethnic group] will rise against race [ethnic group], and kingdom against kingdom.[4] And there will be famines[5] and pestilences[6] and earthquakes

---

1. See the author's book titled, *The Great Reset: To Digitally Enslave, Depopulate, and Transhumanize.*
2. Strong's no. 5273.
3. Cf. the many cults in which men claim themselves to be God, gods, Christ, and/or christs.
4. Cf. the numerous wars of the past century (e.g., WW I, WW II, the Arab-Israeli wars, etc.).
5. Consider the mass starvations in Angola, Ethiopia, Somalia, Sudan, the Ukraine, and elsewhere. For typical documentation, see for example, Hal Lindsey, *Planet Earth—2000 A.D.* (California: Western Front, Ltd., 1994), pp. 93-94, 123-129.
6. Consider the increase in pestilences such as AIDS, various cancers, Cholera, Ebola, Hepatitis, Hanta (e.g., the Four-Corners disease), Legionnaires disease, Malaria, Tuberculosis, etc., not to mention the many horrific biological weapons that may yet be unleashed. For some typical documentation, see Lindsey, *Planet Earth—2000 A.D.*, pp. 103-116.

against places.[1] But all these *things are* a beginning of sorrows [birth-pangs].[2] Then they will deliver you up to tribulation [affliction], and will kill you, and you will be hated by all the nations for My name. And then many will be offended, will betray one another, and will hate one another. And many false prophets will arise and deceive many. And because law-lessness shall be increased, the love of many will grow cold. But the *one* who endures to the completion, that one shall be delivered [protected, res-cued, saved]. And this Gospel of the Kingdom will be proclaimed in all the inhabited world, for a testimony to all the nations, and then the comple-tion will have come.... Immediately after the tribulation of those days the Sun will be darkened [obscured], and ... the stars will fall from the heaven [sky].... (Matt 24:4-14, 24:29, Gk.; cf. Mark 13:4-13, 13:24-25; Luke 21:7-19, 21:25)

As true students of eschatology acknowledge, the above passage best characterizes, and most literally pertains to, the Tribulation Pe-riod. In it, Jesus not only summarized the major events of the first four seals of the Apocalypse (Rev 6:1-8), but He reached forward to the completion of the tribulation under its seventh seal (Rev 6:12*b*-17).[3] Without belaboring the point, let it be said that every reason-ably informed Christian should recognize and understand that many, if not all, of Jesus' last-days predictions have not only historically been, but are even now being, foreshadowed through contemporary happenings. Moreover, the prophetic scriptures, by their repeated use of the birth-pangs metaphor, clearly indicate that such events will occur on an even greater scale—at an ever increasing frequency and magnitude—as the time of Jesus' return draws near.

These tribulational events, rather than working to prevent the rise and formation of a world government, as some suppose, are ac-tually the particular disturbances that make such a global authority seem truly necessary and justifiable to the minds of secular men and women for the ultimate survival of mankind. In other words, they really serve to accelerate such a government's impending develop-ment. Combined with the often exaggerated and even fabricated en-

---

1. Compare this prophecy with worldwide high-magnitude earthquake data for the past few centuries, and especially the last six decades. A decade ago, Lindsey offered some typical documentation for the prior ten decades (*Planet Earth—2000 A.D.,* pp. 83-85, 89-90, 96-98).

2. Jesus' point here is not that ethnic conflicts and wars, famines, pestilences, and earthquakes, in various places, are peculiar, but that *all these things occurring simultaneously and increasingly,* so that even the world seems ominously aware, will signify the approach of the Tribulation Period, as well as the start of the birth-pangs of the Great Tribulation. Matthew 24:8, like its parallels in Mark and Luke, does not point to the *first half* of the Tribulation Period, but to the Great Tribulation itself (cf. Rev 6:7-8).

   Unlike any time in history past, life on Earth today, even in its waters, could be extinguished virtually overnight. Not only that, but the simultaneous occurrence of *all* the outlined events is now, *for the first time ever,* actually transpiring. Mankind is experiencing a taste of each of the tribulations of which Je-sus and the prophets spoke. From a strictly prophetic view, our generation really is unique.

3. For information on the sixth and seventh seals, see the chapter "The Order of the Seals, Trumpets, and Bowls," in the volume titled, *The Real Rapture and Other Prophetic Mysteries: Understanding the Reve-lation (Apocalypse),* of the author's *Messiah, History, and the Tribulation Period* series.

vironmental and ecological claims and other elitist propaganda, not to mention their intentionally manufactured and subsequently "managed" crises and societal ills, of various one-worlders (globalists)—who push their insidious, multifaceted agenda on an often ignorant, gullible, and at times eager pagan public—such events undoubtedly constitute an effective catalyst for the appearance of the AntiChrist. Coleman, for example, observes: "Today, we find that some of the largest companies, allegedly 'polluting' the earth, are the largest contributors of funds to the environmentalist movement. The big names send forth their message: Prince Philip is [(i.e., was)] one of their heroes, yet his son Prince Charles, owns a million acres of forested land in Wales from which timber is regularly harvested, and in addition, Prince Charles is one of the biggest owners of slum housing in London, where pollution thrives."[1]

As pantheists and polytheists, globalists and other elitists assert that humanity is "tired of wars and threats of wars;"[2] that "the greatest hope for the survival of life on earth is the establishment of a democratic world government," which alone "can provide the security and authority necessary;" and that "we are on the threshold of a new world order which promises to usher in an era of peace, prosperity, justice and harmony" through "the principle of unity in diversity."[3] Regarding the increasing frequency and violence of earthquakes and volcanic eruptions, which they take as further indications of the need for a world government, they even suggest that we "read all about it in the daily news."[4] While often suppressing unfavorable scientific data and other detrimental information, they emphatically cite the following needs in arguing for the urgent establishment of a world government to take charge of "world affairs" at "this time of extreme global crises":[5]

Wars, ethnic and non-ethnic

(1) to contain and prevent current and future local and regional wars;

(2) to reduce the threat of war generally through the enforcement of world peace and security;

(3) to reduce the growing threat of a nuclear war, including

---

1. *The Committee of 300,* p. 192.
2. Kah, *En Route to Global Occupation,* p. 182.
3. Kah, pp. 175 and 210. Compare this "principle" with the phrase *E PLURIBUS UNUM,* meaning "from pluralism, unity," in the heraldic coat of arms of the United States. For more information, see the section (or chapter) "A Place in the Wilderness, Petra, and the United States of America," in the volume titled, *Messiah's Preeminence in History and Prophecy: The Heart of Israelology, Eschatology, and God's Holy Days,* in the author's *Messiah, History, and the Tribulation Period* series.
4. Kah, p. 199.
5. Kah, p. 170.

its radioactive fallout and possible subsequent nuclear winter;

(a) to safely dispose of nuclear and toxic wastes;

(4) to contain the spread of nuclear weapons;

(5) to control and eventually eliminate weapons of mass destruction (nuclear, chemical, and biological);

(6) to disarm national entities and halt the international trade in arms;

(7) to prevent international terrorism;

(8) to ensure tolerance of ethnic, religious, racial, political, and cultural differences;

(a) to enforce a core set of tolerant, non-fundamentalist, beliefs and values, as determined by international consensus, which is conducive to a world government and the maintenance of international peace and security;

(9) to protect human and minority rights, halt rampant rights violations and discrimination (including sexual), and prevent national governments from becoming dictatorial and tyrannical;[1]

(10) to reduce supranational language barriers through the choice of an official world language (e.g., English, the world's foremost language of commerce);

(11) to indoctrinate and initiate people as Luciferic planetary citizens and world patriots for the common good of humanity;[2]

(12) to peacefully settle all supranational problems;

(13) to help the world's numerous refugees;

Famines and radical climate changes

(14) to halt the current decrease in agricultural productivity, which has led to a dwindling world food supply and numerous famines;

(15) to improve world food distribution mechanisms;

(16) to prevent impending universal crop failures, widespread famines and starvations, and a possible mass starvation of hundreds of millions or even billions of people in the near future through

(a) population control in overpopulated regions using

---

1. Contrary to their serpentine double-talk, globalists actually plan to achieve a multicultural, internationally interdependent, New World Order through a tyrannical dictatorship masquerading as a benign "democracy." As a typical example, see the late Mikhail Gorbachev's telling statements in the chapter titled "New York City and the United Nations—the Heart of Political Babylon/Rome," in the volume titled *The Prophetic Stage: Signs of the Times,* of the *Messiah, History, and the Tribulation Period* series.

2. Lindsey, *Planet Earth—2000 A.D.,* p. 43.

readily available, highly encouraged, and even mandatory abortion practices and infanticide, as well as various forms of birth control;[1]

(b) the reduction and eventual prevention, for all practical purposes, of the current supranational environmental pollution of the world's air, water, and land resources, which has resulted not only in radical climate changes such as increasingly frequent and destructive floods and hurricanes, but also in atmospheric ozone depletion, acidic rainfall and snowfall, increasing drought conditions, spreading and expanding deserts, soil erosion, and the rapid loss of topsoil and soil fertility; and

(c) reforestation of the Earth and remineralization of its topsoil;

(17) to reduce the wasteful use of land in producing tobacco and satisfying meats (non-vegetarian) diets;

(18) to halt the worldwide use of harmful pesticides;

(19) to prevent mental malfunctioning resulting from malnutrition, which is a threat to civilization;

(20) to prepare for possible mass migrations of people due to unlivable conditions;

Pestilences and drugs

(21) to stop the modern proliferation of virulent, drug-resistant diseases;

(22) to control and eventually eliminate biological weapons;

(23) to improve human welfare and health;

(24) to prevent the use of harmful drugs and alcoholism, and stop the drug trade;

Earthquakes and volcanic eruptions

(25) to effectively deal with the increasing frequency and magnitude of earthquakes;

(26) to address the increasing frequency and violence of volcanic eruptions, which spread smoke and dust over wide areas and thus reduce sunlight reaching the Earth's surface;

---

1. At the fourth UN Conference on Women, which concerned itself largely with "a woman's right to use the birth-control methods of her choice" and lesbian "rights," the female head of the Vatican delegation voiced this dire warning regarding the "Beijing Declaration" (named for the conference's location in China, the child-murdering capital of the world): "This document is obsessed only by the sexual reproductive aspect of women.... It could be turned into a license of coercive population control [as in China] and the practice of the unspeakable crime of abortion" (Uli Schmetzer, "U.N. forum ends in dispute over women's sexual rights," *The Denver Post,* 17 Sept. 1995, p. 18A).

The sea and the waves roaring
(see Luke 21:25-26)[1]

(27) to deal with increasingly frequent and destructive floods and hurricanes, and address the threat of a new ice age or melting polar ice caps;

Falling Stars
(nuclear war, and comet and asteroid strikes)

(28) to internationalize efforts, such as those of the United States, to defend against limited nuclear missile threats;

(29) to internationally coordinate nuclear arsenals, and possibly create a specific arsenal, to defend the Earth against limited comet and asteroid threats;[2]

Other—environmental

(30) to protect dwindling and jeopardized energy resources such as Mideast oil;

(31) to develop safe (environmentally friendly) and sustainable energy supplies;

(32) to eliminate pollution and other dangers from nuclear power plants, and safely dispose of radioactive waste;

(33) to save the environment and world ecology from current and impending environmental crises;

(34) to avert or minimize extreme global climatic, environmental, ecological, and social catastrophes for everybody;

(35) to halt the current massive deforestation of the world, and reduce forest fires and oceanic pollution, all of which threaten the world's oxygen and fish supplies;

(36) to prevent the extinction and loss of species;

Other—political, economic, and legal

(37) to integrate differing political and economic systems, and overcome the sovereignty of each nation, to solve supranational problems;

(38) to enforce international law through world courts having mandatory jurisdiction;

(39) to implement and enforce world legislation;

(40) to handle the transition to a new world economic order;

(41) to retire the massive world debt, for which a new global

---

1. For some related documentation, see Lindsey, *Planet Earth—2000 A.D.*, pp. 86-91.
2. For more information, see the section (or chapter) "Blood, Fire, and Palm-Trees of Smoke," in the volume titled, *The Prophetic Stage: Signs of the Times,* and the chapter "Falling Stars," in the separate volume titled, *The Real Rapture and Other Prophetic Mysteries: Understanding the Revelation (Apocalypse),* of the author's *Messiah, History, and the Tribulation Period* series.

system of finance and credit, including a world currency, is imperative;

(42) to address the inequitable use of natural resources, and plan globally for their wise use and necessary preservation as a common heritage;

(43) to guarantee full employment in the face of widespread poverty, unemployment, and social unrest;

(44) to reduce and eventually eliminate the vast disparities between economies, as well as the primitive lifestyles of many peoples; and

(45) to determine who owns the atmosphere and stratosphere, and facilitate space exploration as a global project.[1]

From the above information, we should realize that those who claim to be enlightened while simultaneously denying or even ridiculing the contemporary existence of eschatologically significant events, whether they be laymen or distinguished seminary professors, are *perhaps* much akin to the *hypocrites* of Jesus' day (see Matt 16:2-4, KJV; cf. Luke 12:54-56), being in reality insufficiently grounded in The Word of God. Indeed, their thinking is not too unlike that of the prophesied scoffers who say: "Where is the promise of His coming? For since the fathers fell asleep, all things remain [continue] as from the beginning of creation" (2 Pet 3:3-4, Gk.). Although Peter forewarned the saints in this very context, saying, "But beloved, <u>do not</u> let this one thing be hidden from you, that with The Lord one day *is* as a thousand years, and a thousand years as one day" (2 Pet 3:8, Gk.; cf. Ps 90:4), these individuals are yet unmindful of the Bible's seven-millennia—or seven-day—chronology, to which the writings of the entire early Church, and ancient Israel, attest. Consequently, they fail to discern that inasmuch as the world is now demonstrably close to the end of the sixth millennium, Jesus' return and the ensuing Sabbath Millennium—the Millennial Kingdom (cf. Heb 4:3-11)—*must* be quite near.[2] This blindness and confusion, for which the *royal-blooded* Charles Darwin is blameworthy,[3] is one of

---

1. Kah, pp. 43, 170-182, 192-200, 210. Also see Lindsey, *Planet Earth—2000 A.D.*, pp. 43-44, 47-48.

2. For more information, see the volume entitled *Biblical Chronology: The Young Creation* in the author's *Messiah, History, and the Tribulation Period* series.

3. Charles Darwin, the man whose legacy has done so much to harm Israel and true Christianity over the past century, was a relative of the British royal family; indeed, his remains are buried in Westminster Abbey, the "heart" of Britain's establishment church, to this day. On February 12, 2009, Darwinist Prince Philip, a "viral" mass-murderer, blasphemously unveiled a "young Darwin" statue at Cambridge University's (misnamed) "Christ's College." Shockingly, anti-Christian humanists who willfully delude themselves and the world through false, fraudulent and fake "evolutionary science," now promote "Darwin Day" as a "global celebration" of "science and reason" on Darwin's (above) birthday.

the unwholesome fruits of a replacement theology that has generally rejected Israel in scriptural eschatology in favor of *a supplanting Church* (see Hos 6:1-2; cf. Ps 90:12-17). Moreover, it foreshadows the frog-like spiritual deception that is to engross the world—through Satan, the AntiChrist, and the false prophet—before Christ's return (see Rev 16:13-14). That is, just as a frog cannot detect a gradual increase in heat, so that it would sooner boil to death in a formerly cool pot of water than leap to safety, the blind cannot see how markedly the present differs from the past, indicating Christ's soon return. They fail to discern the signs of the times.

10

Religious, Political, and Other Ties

King Charles III's possible claims to leadership of the Jewish and Muslim populations of the world, as well as the final form of the Roman Empire, through his purported lineage, were addressed in chapter 4, "Prince of this World—a *Diverse* Lineage." Below, we will consider Charles' so-called 'Christian' heritage; his marital infidelity —including Princess Diana's death—and its potential impact upon his future; his political affiliations, aspirations, and privileges; and his ties to the New Age Movement, the occult, and false religions, including Islam. We will also look at Charles' personal religious movement, entitled "Respect." Although this is a *large* chapter, it is vital.

Of archbishops and fallen seeds. While the author shall focus primarily on the archbishops of Canterbury of the past century in this section, know that the spiritual condition of most other "archbishops" within the sphere of the British monarchy has been and remains similar—and not just over the past several decades.

The position of Archbishop of Canterbury is that of the symbolic head of the Anglican communion—though the British Monarch is considered to be its "titular head on Earth." The history between the British monarchy and what for many, sadly passes as "Christendom" is one of *continual compromise, spiritual adultery and fornication, or apostasy.* This is made no clearer than among the many archbishops of Canterbury themselves—as may be seen from even a cursory examination, of those who served from the end of the twentieth century, to now. Let's look.

Frederick Temple, 1896 to 1902. Mr. F. Temple was deeply involved in the early Tractarian Movement and the "Oxford Liberal Movement" that derived from it. This, in turn, led to "Anglo-Catholicism," itself an effort to subvert Anglican Protestantism or "Low Anglicanism" through a reincorporation, historically speaking, of many of the unscriptural traditions, teachings, and practices of Roman Catholicism. F. Temple was quick to embrace Darwinism or the *religion* of evolution, which is *falsely* and erroneously called a "theory," actively promoting it in his writings and speeches—even though it is contrary to Christ and all scripture, and opposed by all genuine, nonfraudulent science. In this, F. Temple directly aided Satan in his long efforts to undermine and destroy the Church through "science falsely so called, which some professing have erred concerning the faith" (1 Tim 6:20-21, KJV). Like other archbishops of Canterbury, F. Temple frequently appealed for Anglican "unity"—as he busily sowed the seeds of apostasy and thus disunity from Christ Himself.

Randall Thomas Davidson, 1903 to 1928. Mr. Davidson was an active ecumenicalist, though otherwise unremarkable. (This is a remarkable statement in itself.)

Cosmo Lang, 1928 to 1942. Mr. Lang held that the humanity of Christ so masked His essential Deity that He was not infallible, contrary to scripture. Previously, as Archbishop of York in 1926, Lang baptized then Princess Elizabeth at Buckingham Palace, and in 1928 was made Archbishop of Canterbury. Lang viewed supposed communication with the dead, or spiritual mediumship and spiritualism, favorably—despite the fact that scripture soundly condemns such communication.

William Temple, son of Frederick Temple, 1942 to 1944. Mr. W. Temple was a socialist and an ecumenicalist in the broad, interfaith sense, and thus an apostate. As such, he was effectively the founder of the largely apostate British Council of Churches and World Council of Churches.

Geoffrey Fisher, 1945 to 1961. Mr. Fisher was a committed Freemason. Many Church of England Bishops of his day were also Freemasons. (We'll delve into why this is *entirely incompatible with Christianity* a bit later.) Fisher served as Grand Chaplain in the United Grand Lodge of England. Exposing further apostasy, he also advocated decriminalization of abominable homosexuality. (Remember, this abominable departure from biblical orthodoxy *was under the foretold AntiChrist's mother, Elizabeth II!)*

Arthur Michael Ramsey, 1961 to 1974. Mr. Ramsey enjoyed warm relations with Roman Catholicism's Pope John Paul VI despite being pro-sodomite (pro-homosexual). Ramsey believed that "honest" agnostics and atheists would be saved, and accepted female "priests" within the Anglican Communion, even receiving sacrament from a female "priest" in the US in retirement! "Oddly," Billy Graham became friends with this apostate![1]

Donald Coggan, 1974 to 1980. Mr. Coggan strongly supported the ordination of women, in contravention of all scripture, having personally proposed it to the Anglican communion in 1970.

Robert Alexander Kennedy Runcie, 1980 to 1991. Mr. Runcie sought reconciliation with the Roman Catholic church—despite its false claims to primacy over all other churches. As a "liberal," Runcie did not oppose the ordination of women as priests nor their conse-

---

1. "Michael Ramsey," *Wikipedia*.

cration as bishops, in contravention of all scripture. Going even further, and contrary to doctrines upheld within the Anglican communion at the time, Mr. Runcie intentionally ordained sodomites as "priests."[1]

George Leonard Carey, 1991 to 2002. Under Mr. Carey's tenure and with his strong support and advocacy, women were ordained in the Anglican communion, contrary to God and Christ, and *Anglicans apostatized to the point of actually debating whether sodomites should also be ordained.* (Scripture is unequivocal that their conduct is abominable and worthy of death.) While Carey opposed ordination of sodomites, he shamefully supported sodomite "partnerships," thereby aiding sodo-fascism. At the same time, Mr. Carey worked for unity between the Anglican communion and the unbiblical Roman Catholic church. Active in interfaith work, Mr. Carey also sought "deeper dialogue" and better relations with the world's unsaved Muslim community.[2] While denouncing "extremist" Muslims, Carey yet supported the Philistine and Edomite (i.e., "Palestinian") "cause" against Israel,[3] and in so-doing, effectively cursed Israel.

Rowan Douglas Williams, 2003 to 2012. Charles as Prince of Wales, himself influenced this selection, knowing that Mr. Williams was previously Bishop of Monmouth[4] and Archbishop of Wales (i.e., Archbishop of Satan). Williams, who represents "liberal" Anglo-Catholicism, which originally had its roots in the conservative but Roman Catholic favoring Oxford Movement, is the first Archbishop of Canterbury to serve as primate of two provinces of the Anglican Communion (cf. "two horns like a lamb" while speaking "like a dragon" in relation to the coming false prophet). Even before being appointed Archbishop of Canterbury, Williams was known for his ardent support of "gay rights," or what Christians, Muslims and others have come to know as "sodofascism." Williams, contrary to all scripture and in direct opposition to The God of Israel, promotes sodo-fascist and feminist (ungodly female) causes, to include the *antiChristian* ordination and consecration of sodomites and women in

---

1. "Robert_Runcie," *Wikipedia*.
2. <u>All Muslims are unsaved</u> because they follow a false "god," not knowing The God of Israel. They are, however, beloved by *Yhvh* for the sake of Abraham and Ishmael, and the author is grieved to say, they are often more righteous than unsaved Israel, which rejects her own true Messiah and God; infanticide and sexual perversion are comparatively rare among Muslims. Indeed, *their birth rates far exceed those of Israel because unregenerate Israel is busy murdering her unborn,* sacrificing them to *Molech* (Satan). The fearsome tribulational judgments God is about to mete out to unsaved Israel are *well-deserved.*
3. "George Carey," *Wikipedia*.
4. Geoffrey of Monmouth, in 1136, wrote *Historia Regum Britanniae,* or the History of the Kings of Britain, in which he popularized the reign, legend and myth of King Arthur and druid wizard Merlin. The Welsh "Black Book of Caernarfon," from 1250, has bardic poems and stories related to Arthur and Merlin.

the offices of bishop, priest, and deacon (see 1 Tim 2:11-14). He is also a New Ager.

Fluent in the Welsh language, which Charles' had to learn for his July 1969 investiture, and a well-known poet in his own right, the multilingual Williams supports the pagan Gorsedd of Bards, and has joined the organization *as a satanist* (red dragon) druid. (It matters not that Williams would refute such a charge: he serves the red dragon or Satan, and as satanists delight in lies and liars, so too does Williams.) While Archbishop of Wales (Satan), Williams, "joined by members of the fourteen faiths represented on the Peace Mala bracelet" (discussed below), personally launched the Peace Mala Youth Project For World Peace charity from the Welsh National (UNA) Temple of Peace and Health, having served as the organization's patron between 2002 and 2008. Concerning this New Age "charity," we read:

> Peace Mala ... is ... dedicated to fostering inter-cultural and inter-faith tolerance through the manufacture, distribution and wearing of a symbolic mala (bracelet) whose beads represent various faiths.
>
> The organisation's aims are "promotion of understanding, respect, friendship, tolerance and peace between all communities, cultures and enlightened, compassionate faiths". Peace Mala promotes global citizenship and invites all people to treat each other with respect and compassion regardless of race, colour, religion, gender, sexuality, ability, size or age....
>
> A Peace Mala is a symbolic bracelet used to promote the message of the Golden Rule of mutual respect recognised by many spiritual paths. It consists of 16 beads, forming a double rainbow, which represent Christianity, Buddhism, Sikhism, Islam, [unregenerate] Judaism, Bahá'í, ISKCON, Zoroastrianism, Tribal and Native Religions, Jainism, Earth Religions [(Pagans)], Taoism, Hinduism and Yungdrung Bön [(meaning "Eternal Light" or "Enlightened Teaching," promoting "indiscriminate love and compassion for all sentient beings")]. The central white bead represents the wearer and whatever path they follow, with two knots on the elastic thread: one symbolising the wearer's uniqueness, the other a reminder of causality and the path of peace and friendship to follow. Peace Malas [are] hand-made in Wales....
>
> [Peace Mala arose in response] to Islamaphobia, racism, religious intolerance and fundamentalism worldwide....
>
> Through the promotion of peace, tolerance and respect, Peace Mala has received numerous awards for their work, notably [starting with] The Prince's Trust Millennium Award in 2003....
>
> The Peace Mala website [("www.peacemala.org.uk")] was created in 2002 using money granted by the Princes Trust Millennium Award.... The website includes ... endorsements from prominent religious leaders, political dignitaries and celebrities including ... Pope John Paul II ... [and] the 14th Dalai Lama....
>
> [Peace Mala focuses on] issues of peace, justice, tolerance and friendship, ... equality, human rights and global citizenship....

Attached to the Registered Office is a peace garden ... [which] has many features including a shrine to Saint Francis of Assisi, Buddhist statues and prayer flags, a miniature Zen-style stone garden, water features, and a tree area which has been blessed in a ceremony lead by Witches, and Druids. There is also a tranquil area facing Mecca, which is dedicated to the Muslim faith....

Peace Mala had outlined its "Main Aims" as: Education for global citizenship through the promotion of understanding, respect, friendship, tolerance and peace between all communities, cultures and enlightened, compassionate faiths; Peace Mala supports human rights, confronts bullying and all forms of prejudice; Peace Mala raises awareness of issues of global interdependence and encourages active compassion by learners that will effect positive changes locally and globally....

In 2007, the Peace Mala Awards for Youth became an international competition with youth groups in the USA taking part in the project.[1]

In line with his immediate predecessors, Williams asserts, contrary to God and Christ, that the pagan religion of evolution is compatible with Christianity; *it is not.* Moreover, Williams openly opposes Christians who support the modern state of Israel (i.e., so-called "Zionists"). Also, he is wishy-washy on Freemasonry, which is Luciferian satanism. (Again, we'll get to that a bit later.) In short, Williams, perhaps more than any of his predecessors, *other than being ostensibly pro-life,* is antiChrist, and as Satan's archbishop, had been a perfect sidekick to the foretold AntiChrist, Charles. While the false prophet seems likely to arise from the Roman Catholic church, this former Archbishop of Canterbury, Mr. Rowan Williams, would have made an intriguing candidate for the role. With the pointed style he chooses for his eyebrows, Williams very much resembles a goat—altogether in line with his spirituality.[2]

Justin Portal Welby, February 2013 to now. Is he too an apostate? In July 2015, Welby's bestial head and queen, Elizabeth II, signed a law in the UK to permit and thus enable homosexual marriages *in Anglican churches!* With that, a hihgly political Welby suddenly became "'much less certain' about his [former] stance on human sexuality," adding, "I don't do blanket condemnation of people."[3] (Really? Such antiChristian equivocation is *damnable!)*

The faithless evils of sexually satanism, as seen in sodomite and female consecration and ordination by *anti*-Christians, the wilfull turning of a general blind-eye toward spiritualism while embracing ecumenicalism and/or ecumenism, as well as acceptance and even promotion of the lie that is called "evolution" (i.e., macroevolution), have all become endemic to the Anglican "communion" and many

1. "Peace Mala," *Wikipedia,* May 2009.
2. "Rowan Williams," *Wikipedia,* May 2009.
3. "Justin Welby," *Wikipedia,* 15 Feb. 2021.

of its key leaders—in direct association with the British monarchy. Indeed, it is this great and particular combination of apostasy—in which *truth is suppressed* and *lies are embraced*—that has enabled the rise not just of many false teachers and antiChrists, but of *the* foretold AntiChrist in their midst; it has also facilitated the apparent ability of the British royals to continue to deceive the ignorant masses into accepting their claim to be "Christian."

Indeed, "the repeated [sexually satanic] failure of the [apostate] Archbishop of Canterbury and the other Instruments of Communion (the Lambeth Conference, the Anglican Consultative Council and the Primates' Meetings) to offer godly leadership, have now led to a vote of 'no confidence' by the majority [(about 85%)] of the world's Anglicans. ... [Now,] the GAFCon [(Global Anglican Futures Conference)] Primates ... recognise new orthodox jurisdictions for faithful Anglicans, including the Anglican Network in Europe, ... to welcome those who ... can no longer remain in the Church of England or Church in Wales, because of the failure of the leadership."[1] Unlike GAFCon, the Global South Fellowship of Anglican Churches (GSFA), is yet seeking to correct the Anglican Communion's course *from within*—a futile endeavor, clearly, while the foretold AntiChrist from a royal family that has long been anti-Christian, serves as that communion's earthly "supreme" governor or "head."[2] Meanwhile, the "Church of England Evangelical Council (CEEC) has made an urgent appeal to bishops to reverse course on blessings for same-sex couples," fearing that "in the event of the General Synod endorsing blessings for people in sexually active relationships outside of heterosexual marriage, the Church of England will confirm she has 'chosen to impair her relationship with the orthodox provinces in the Communion,'" thereby ensuring "that the Anglican Communion will cease to exist in anything like its current form." Yet, the *political* CEEC likewise seeks *unbiblical compromise* by its *oxymorinc* call for "structural re-organisation without theological compromise,"[3] as

---

1. Susie Leafe, "Majority of world's Anglicans formally reject leadership of Archbishop of Canterbury," *Christian Today*, 22 Apr. 2023. GAFCon states: "We have no confidence that the Archbishop of Canterbury nor the other Instruments of Communion led by him (the Lambeth Conference, the Anglican Consultative Council and the Primates' Meetings) are able to provide a godly way forward that will be acceptable to those who are committed to the truthfulness, clarity, sufficiency and authority of Scripture. The Instruments of Communion have failed to maintain true communion, based on the Word of God and shared faith in Christ. Successive Archbishops of Canterbury have failed to guard the faith, by inviting bishops to Lambeth who have embraced or promoted [sexual and ministry] practices contrary to Scripture. This failure of church discipline has been compounded by the current Archbishop of Canterbury, who has himself welcomed the provision of liturgical resources to bless these [abominable] practices.... This renders his leadership role in the Anglican Communion entirely indefensible" (ibid).
2. John Sandeman, "Conservative Anglicans Reject Church of England and Archbishop of Canterbury," *Christianity Today*, 21 Apr. 2023.
3. Staff writer, "Church of England bishops urged 'to step back from the brink' on same-sex blessings," *Christian Today*, 25 Apr. 2023.

such would *lack repentance and discipline.* Unsurprisingly, a broad decline of Christendom in the United Kingdom, Europe, the United States and elsewhere, particularly evident in "Western culture," is well underway, so that what now so often passes for "Christian" is *not.*

Christianity in many places, now faces open assault—seemingly everywhere—by satanic sodomites, feminists, and *detached-from-reality* (e.g., lunatic) "transgenders" and "non-binary genders," who would pose as "priests," "pastors," "bishops," "Christians," "rabbis," "religious Jews," and "tolerance and diversity experts" (see 1 Tim 2:11-14; cf. Gen 3:16); and among such *satanists* "by any other name" (or title), we see those who promote and commit the mass-murder of unborn children in the womb. Truly, *these are those whom Christ shall condemn to the fiery pits of Hell* (i.e., *Gehenna)*—despite all their false protestations of "Lord, Lord!" At His return, Jesus will not listen to, nor reason with these adversaries, but *He will answer them plainly,* commanding, "Depart from Me, you cursed, into the everlasting fire prepared for the devil and his angels [messengers]" (Matt 25:41)—*and though they call Him "Lord, Lord,"* begging "Have we not prophesied in Your name, cast out demons in Your name, and done many wonders in Your name?," *He will say to them:* "I never knew you! Depart from Me, you who practice lawlessness!" (Matt 7:21-23, 25:44; see 7:13-27, 25:31-33, 25:41-46). These, who without genuine fear of God and Christ, bring shame upon The Name above all names—that of Messiah Yeshua (Christ Jesus)—these, who so misrepresent God, shall forever be shamed, as *wolves in sheep's clothing.* God is not mocked, nor is He a fool.[1]

A so-called 'Christian' heritage. Although then Prince Charles was only nineteen at the time, Dermot Morrah wrote, "No British prince since the Stuarts has cared more sincerely for the things of the mind and the spirit."[2] We may view Morrah's statement as a veiled and somewhat gross reference to King James I, who gave us the Authorized King James Version translation of the Bible. Satan's Prince, of course, has Stuart blood.[3] Of Charles' supposed Christian roots and convictions, Holden notes that Charles opposes racial prejudice and actively campaigns on behalf of the environment, and that he differs from his father in that he is "circumspect, gentle, and kind-

---

1. Those who are Christians must not tolerate unfaithfulness to The God of Israel and His written Word within the Church—neither from pulpit nor pew. Yes, we are all sinners, but when a Christian sins, he or she may only—and must always—exercise perfect fealty to God and His Word, demonstrating both truthful testimony and genuine repentance.
2. Holden, *PRINCE CHARLES,* pp. 250-251.
3. For more information, see ch. 4, "Prince of this World—a *Diverse* Lineage," at p. 79.

hearted."[1]   In fact, Satan's Prince appears to be a bit of a "social worker," endeavoring to help the poor and the disadvantaged.[2]   As the former "Great Master" (cf. Matt 23:10, AKJV) and Principal Knight Grand Cross of the Order of the Bath, which supposedly ranks third to England's Garter and Scotland's Thistle among British knighthoods and is the "premier meritorious Order of the Crown,"[3] and now as Sovereign, Charles has "vowed 'to defend maidens, widows, and orphans.'"[4]   Charles, as Alstair Burnet puts it, "has a list of good causes to support that far outnumber the regiments whose uniform[s] he wears...."[5]   Like the Order of the Garter, which meets in St. George's Chapel, knights of both the Order of the Thistle and the Order of the Bath meet in a church's chapel to provide those orders a "Christian" veneer in the eyes of the public, and to cloak their private antichristian and even outright satanic activities. The Order of the Thistle, officially instituted by Scotland's King James VII, who was otherwise known as England's King James II, in 1687, meets in the chapel of St. Giles' Church in Edinburgh, Scotland. Similarly, the Order of the Bath, founded by Henry IV in 1399 and later revived by George I in 1725, has met in King Henry VII's Chapel in Westminster Abbey since 1725.[6]

With "water from the River Jordan," the infant Prince Charles was christened in December 1948.[7]   (That presaged of course, his May 2023 anointing as King Charles III, with oil produced in Jerusalem, from olives grown on the Mount of Olives.[8])   In 1953, at the age of four, Charles observed his mother's coronation as queen at Westminster Abbey, which included an extravagant Anglican Protestant service.   In 1965, at sixteen, he received his Anglican Protestant confirmation, having supposedly had a "keen interest" in Scripture.[9]   According to Holden, the Dean of Windsor was "gratified to find the prince unassailed by doubts."[10]   (Sycophants.)

Yet, Charles' father Prince Philip, being of a "corrupt" mind and "disapproved concerning the faith," never really ceased to "resist The Truth" (2 Tim 3:8). Indeed, like Charles' mother who was *never* a

---

1. Holden, *PRINCE CHARLES*, pp. 18-19, 72.
2. Holden, *PRINCE CHARLES*, pp. 270-282.
3. Conrad Swan, "Bath, The Most Honourable Order of the," *A Dictionary of Heraldry*, ed. Friar, p. 48.
4. Holden, *PRINCE CHARLES*, pp. 216-217.
5. Alstair Burnet, *In Person, THE PRINCE AND PRINCESS OF WALES* (New York: Summit Books, 1985), p. 8.
6. Boutell, 1978 ed., pp. 194, 196; and James and Russell, *At Home with the Royal Family*, p. 52. Similarly, "In 1484 the Kings, Heralds and Pursuivants [of the College of Heraldry], while remaining officers of the Royal Household, were incorporated by Charter, ... called 'Coldearber' in the Parish of All Saints the Less in the City of London" (Boutell, 1978 ed., p. 262).
7. Cathcart, p. 11.
8. For details, see ch. 16, "King Charles III: History's Ultimate AntiChrist," at p. 561.
9. Holden, *PRINCE CHARLES*, pp. 141-142. Cathcart, p. 37.
10. Holden, *PRINCE CHARLES*, p. 18.

real Christian, Philip—though a man—could easily have reminded us "of gullible women loaded down with sins, led away by various lusts, always learning and never able to come to the knowledge of The Truth" (see 2 Tim 3:6-9). We're told: Philip found the "ritualistic Greek Orthodoxy of his childhood, Salem's austere German Protestantism, and the social conventions of ... Anglicanism as practiced in the navy and by the royal family all combined to make him cynical of Christianity for some time—agnostic, atheist even. Friends have known him to phone at odd hours to discuss some philosophical abstraction, and he can revel in theological arguments with the clerics who are official—and personal—guests of the Queen.... But from his own uncertain spiritual quest came misgivings that Prince Charles should be confirmed as early as sixteen."[1] Prince Philip, who had been "Master of the Bench of [the] Inner Temple" since 1954, honorary member of the Goat Club and the Danish Dragon Club, and Patron of the Lucifer Golfing Society, clearly remained antichristian *for life.*[2]

An outward contrast to Prince Philip, Satan's Prince for his twenty-first birthday, "rose early ... to visit the Chapel Royal of St John in the Tower of London in the company of Princess Anne and the Queen Mother to make 'an act of thanksgiving and dedication for his future life.'"[3] Charles has observed, "Where Christianity is new it must be much easier to enter into the whole spirit of it wholeheartedly."[4] Junor, evincing the *wool pulled over her eyes,* commented: "He had been to church regularly throughout his childhood, and ... he had been confirmed by the Archbishop of Canterbury, Michael Ramsey, in St George's Chapel, Windsor. One day, as heir to the throne, he would be Head of the Church of England; a belief in God

---

1. Lacey, *Majesty,* pp. 254-255. Speaking of a Christian veneer, James and Russell add: "One regular but little-known event is the Royal Epiphany Service held on 6 January every year in celebration of the Three Kings' arrival in Bethlehem.... Originally it was the time when the Sovereign gave alms to the poor and needy, and although the ceremony still takes place in the Chapel Royal, the monarch has not been present since ... the Hanovarian King George III curtailed many English customs.... The Gentlemen Ushers take the Queen's [(monarch's)] gifts in procession to the high altar: twenty-five gold sovereigns, frankincense and myrrh carried on silver gilt.... [Elizabeth II] ... does not attend the Epiphany Service mainly because it coincides with her winter retreat.... Like the Epiphany Service, the Royal Maundy has a Christian significance, representing as it does the Last Supper.... King George VI only personally attended seven times, but Elizabeth II ... distributed the Maundy [money] every year of her reign, other than when prevented by pregnancy" (*At Home with the Royal Family,* pp. 151-153). "Ever since the Reformation there have been clergymen in the Royal Household, headed by the Clerk of the Closet, since 1096 the private confessor of the sovereign. There are thirty-six chaplains who are appointed by the Clerk of the Closet.... There are [also] Extra Chaplains, clergymen who have reached the age of 70 and are appointed for their long and distinguished service. There are two Priests in Ordinary who attend services on a rota basis and with the Domestic Chaplain attend to the pastoral care of the Household and Her Majesty's staff" (ibid., p. 195; for details, see pp. 211-213).
2. Judd, *Prince Philip,* pp. 251-252.
3. Cathcart, p. 99. Speaking of the "Queen Mother," Junor notes: "Prince Charles is utterly devoted to his grandmother. It was she who virtually brought him up" (p. 14).
4. Cathcart, p. 65. Junor, p. 57.

and an acceptance of the teachings of the Church were fundamental to his existence. He did, nevertheless, have a genuine faith—one which has remained strong to the present day.... Prince Charles was and still is ... an extremely moral and religious man, and fundamentally conservative."[1]

Since the *exceedingly* lewd as well as "titilating" "Camillagate" conversations between Charles and then mistress, Camilla Parker Bowles, were aired, however, Junor has admitted, "I thought he was better than that." Of course, Charles was just *twenty* when he *married* Satan, as represented by Wales' red dragon symbol; on that day, he became Prince of Satan, as we earlier saw![2] Likewise, his mother Elizabeth had also given her own life *to Satan*—having done so in 1946, in a Welsh druidic ceremony, which she then reaffirmed as queen, during her 1953 coronation visit to Wales![3] That's right, having undergone her ostensibly Christian coronation in England, Queen Elizabeth II then *publicly demonstrated her fealty to Satan* at Caernarfon Castle, overtly employing the red dragon as *the central symbol to the affair,* which thousands of sycophants, including many dignitaries from Wales and elsewhere, attended! The British royals are *pagan to the bone*—and yet somehow, they largely continue to fool the world into thinking they are "Christians."

Subsequently, on July 29, 1981, Satan's Prince and Lady Diana Spencer were married in what appeared to be a generally orthodox Christian wedding, one that was filled with pomp and pageantry.[4] However, like other symbols that may have a dual interpretation—as pagans who favor a Zoroastrian (Babylonian) approach to spirituality, religion, and religious terminology, prefer—the red cross of Merovée, as opposed to the true cross of Christ, was, from the oligarchists' perspective, central to the entire proceeding.[5] In other words, what the British monarchy saw and heard in the ceremony, for example, differs tremendously from what true Christians would have gotten from it. The wedding featured prayers from "representatives of four different churches," including the Roman Catholic Cardinal Hume.[6] A similar ecumenicalism was seen in the earlier wedding of Princess Elizabeth [II] to Prince Philip, in which Roman Catholic bishops participated.[7] Prayers then became a part of the Wales' family routine: "Prince Charles and his wife involve their children in almost everything they do at Highgrove, so before they eat

1. Junor, pp. 58, 72.
2. See ch. 8, "The Red Dragon and Prince Charles' Investiture as Prince of Wales," at p. 207.
3. Ibid.
4. Spink, pp. 6-7, 91-113.
5. Hoey, *Charles & Diana: The Tenth Anniversary,* p. 17.
6. Ibid., p. 64.
7. Judd, *Prince Philip,* p. 131.

their evening meal together they join ... in the nursery for family prayers. This has been the custom since the children were old enough to take part and both parents regard it as an important end to the day and it is something they try never to miss."[1]

While yet a "mere" prince slated to one day head the over eighty million members of the Anglican Protestant Communion,[2] Charles was "anxious to use his position to encourage rapprochement with Rome"[3]—something he now pursues "full boar" as King Charles III. The history of interactions between the Vatican and the British monarchy is replete with twists and turns, as well as alliances at different points. A *partial* brief history, relating to Charles, follows.

Edward III formed the College of St. George at Windsor Castle in 1348 "as parallel and supportive to his foundation of the Order of the Garter." Yet the Roman pontiff authorized its formation in 1350. Originally, the organization of the college was to include "thirteen Canons, one of whom should be the Warden, a title later changed to Dean, together with thirteen Priest Vicars, later to be Minor Canons, making twenty-six priests in all"—one priest for each of the twenty-six Garter knights. Besides the priests, the college was to include twenty-six beadsmen (aka bedesmen), now called "military knights." The beadsmen "were to pray daily for the Sovereign and the Knights Companion [of the Order of the Garter] during life and for their souls after death." In other words, the college was to have a coven of 13 priests and a coven of 13 beadsmen for the sovereign and twelve Garter knights, as well as an identical arrangement for the Prince of Wales and twelve Garter knights. Currently, the college consists of the Dean, four Canons, and two Minor Canons, for a total of seven *secular* priests, besides a significant choir. Elizabeth I reduced the number of military knights, who today take part in the ceremonies of the order at St. George's Chapel, to thirteen, leaving just one coven of military knights. Although secular, "[they] have, through the centuries taken part in the religious observances of the Order as well as praying daily for the Sovereign and the Order....: 'God save ... all the Companions, living and departed, of the Most Honourable and Noble Order of the Garter.'"[4] This arrangement of covens is in harmony with the Order of the Garter itself.[5] Years later, Pope Leo X gave Henry VIII, who used the red dragon (symbolic of Satan) as a royal device, the title *Fidei Defensor,* or "Defender of the Faith," in connec-

---

1. Hoey, *Charles & Diana: The Tenth Anniversary,* p. 148.
2. The Associated Press, "Church of England approves ordination of women priests," *The Denver Post,* 23 Feb. 1994, p. 2A.
3. Holden, *PRINCE CHARLES,* p. 18.
4. Begent, pp. 2, 13. See James and Russell, *At Home with the Royal Family,* pp. 158, 201.
5. For more information, see the discussion on the Garter at p. 147 in ch. 7, "The Heraldic Symbols in the Arms and their Interpretations."

tion with Roman Catholicism (see below). Cathcart observes, "At St George's Chapel, Windsor, it was noted that Charles became a frequent communicant."[1]

Following World War II, the British government "recognized the temporal authority claimed by the Pope." It is unlikely that such a recognition could have occurred apart from the approval of the monarchy. Later, in 1980, Queen Elizabeth II and Prince Philip, dressed entirely in black, visited Pope John Paul II, dressed entirely in white, at the Vatican: "Since 1980, the Royal Court of St. James has had a Papal Nuncio (a Vatican ambassador to a foreign court). Relations were improved further when the Queen visited the Pope at the Vatican and willingly wore black in order to be received by him. Perceived by successive popes as a heretic, the Queen would not have been granted an audience unless she had symbolically submitted herself to the radiance of his whiteness. This she did, to the dismay of many Christians back home, and to the insult of those Protestant martyrs who died during the reigns of her forebears."[2] (Notice the *Zoroastrian contrast* between the forces of darkness and those of "light.")

During their "historic visit," in an *unprecedented and remarkably blatant* overture, Elizabeth II not only openly wore her Garter Star and Riband, but was even photographed wearing and fully exposing her light blue Garter just above the elbow on her left arm before the pope. The same photograph also shows, less clearly, Prince Philip wearing and exposing his Garter, just below his left knee.[3] Bear in mind that this was *not* a Garter ceremony. In purposely exposing their garters to the pope, the queen and Prince Philip were, as far as the occult symbolism is concerned, suggesting the possibility of an alliance between the Order of the Garter and the Vatican (cf. the AntiChrist and the false prophet). To the author's knowledge, this is the only published photograph of any Garter member so-exposing the Garter, let alone in a high-level setting. Clearly, the monarchy wished to send a message.

Since at least the early 1980s, Charles as Satan's Prince, apparently following the same agenda, has been at the forefront of those advocating rapprochement between the Roman Catholic and Anglican Protestant churches. (Such an occasion, if it were to occur, would no doubt affect other liberal denominations as well.) In 1982,

---

1. Cathcart, p. 66.
2. Hilton, *The Principality and Power of Europe,* pp. 52-53.
3. "A Snapshot in Time: An Informal Pictorial History of the Queen's Reign," *Majesty* magazine, Feb. 1992, Vol. 13, No. 2, on p. 12 of special insert between pp. 34-35. Of the Garter, Begent states, "It is worn by the Knights below the left knee and by Ladies above the left elbow" (p. 3). For more information, see ch. 7's section titled, "The Garter," at p. 147.

Pope John Paul II visited Britain, where he participated in an ecumenical service under the authority of Robert Runcie, then Archbishop of Canterbury and a member of the Committee of 300. The two "knelt together in prayer in an historic act of reconciliation" at Canterbury Cathedral. "The Prince, as heir apparent and prospective Supreme Governor of the Church of England, sat in the place usually occupied by the sovereign and was later photographed in conversation with the Pope before a brief private audience with him in the Deanery. The 'Celebration of Faith', as the service had been ecumenically entitled, was a resounding triumph" involving Christians and non-Christians alike. "This rapprochement reached its culmination when Pope John Paul II visited Britain in 1982, the first Pope to do so since the Reformation. He held joint services with the Archbishop of Canterbury and was received by the Queen. Since then, there have been further meetings between the Pope and prominent members of the Royal Family, and also between the Pope and the present Archbishop of Canterbury, Dr George Carey. In former times, such a series of happenings would have been unthinkable."[1] "By 1985, relations between the Vatican and Lambeth Palace were warmer than ever. In this climate, the Prince wanted to use his visit to Italy to make a further gesture of reconciliation towards Rome.... The Archbishop favoured 'a special service' in St Peter's to celebrate what would have been the first formal act of reconciliation between the papacy and the royal family since the excommunication of Henry VIII.... Instead, it was agreed that the Prince and Princess should attend the Pope's domestic eucharist in his private chapel. As the Prince would not partake of communion, ... only 'the extreme minority' who rejected the Pope's spiritual and ecclesiastical position could dissent.... [The] ... Archbishop declared that by attending a private mass in the Vatican, the Prince would be far more effective ... in moving the Pope more firmly in favour of ecumenism.... [The] Prince would cause scandal in Britain only to 'a few on the lunatic fringe.'"[2] Those on the "lunatic fringe," by such a claim, would include true Christians. Nevertheless, it is Runcie, the late queen's late pet priest, who was apostate: "The Archbishop of Canterbury, Robert Runcie, has hosted in Canterbury Cathedral the 'Canterbury Festival of Faith and the Environment' featuring 'joint prayer and worship ... with Buddhists, Muslims, Baha'is, Jews, Sikhs, and Hindus.'"[3] Hell bound "Runcie ... knowingly ordained practising homosexual clergy."[4]

1. Hilton, *The Principality and Power of Europe*, p. 52.
2. Dimbleby, *The Prince of Wales*, pp. 348-351.
3. Hunt, *GLOBAL PEACE AND THE RISE OF ANTICHRIST*, p. 173.
4. Hilton, *The Principality and Power of Europe*, p. 52.

On April 29, 1985, then Prince Charles and Princess Diana, each dressed in black, approached the Vatican for their audience with John Paul II, dressed in white (a Zoroastrian contrast).[1] Describing the pope's as "the ultimate presence," Charles had intended to celebrate mass with the pope privately, only to be thwarted at the last moment. While Dimbleby asserts that the queen had not been previously informed of the plan, Junor correctly states, "He was prevented, not by the Queen, as was reported at the time, but by politicians and the church hierarchy."[2] The audience itself, however, proceeded nonetheless. Satan's Prince and the pope "talked about unity between the different branches of the Christian faith," the pope noting that "the Anglican Church was in fact closer to the Catholics than the Orthodox at the present time." Charles went on to express his admiration for "the spiritual leadership he so clearly provided in such a difficult and uncertain world." Although Charles did not get to celebrate mass with the pope, an unprecedented gesture from the then future head of Anglican Protestantism, he nevertheless "asked the Pope to bless them—'which he did very briefly by making the sign of the cross over us.'" The Vatican, for its part, asserted that were it not for "a last-minute cancellation, the Prince would have taken part in an historic act of reconciliation with the Church of Rome." Various protests occurred, and one Christian even observed that Charles had been "ill-advised in spiritual matters by some who have departed from the true teaching of the inspired, infallible and inerrant way of God"—to which Charles wrote a reply denouncing "bigotry and prejudice in all its forms," adding that such attitudes were "the main cause of so much human suffering and misery."[3] Put more mildly, Charles feels that doctrinal disagreement among Christians causes "needless distress."[4]

Remaining without discernment, Junor commented: "Charles is naturally tolerant of other people's views.... It was no surprise, therefore, that he should have wanted to attend a private Mass with the Pope ... in 1985—not because of any weakness in his own Anglican faith, but because he believes that by demonstrating religious tolerance himself he might in some way be able to ease the tension between Anglicans and Catholics, especially in Northern Ireland.... [The] Prince was nevertheless bitterly upset and angry. A year later,

---

1. For a photograph of this event, see Hoey, *Charles & Diana: The Tenth Anniversary,* p. 131.
2. Junor, p. 260.
3. Dimbleby, *The Prince of Wales,* pp. 347-348, 352-354. While studying at Trinity College, Cambridge, then Prince Charles, along with "several of his friends," was "thoroughly inspired" by the apostate "Reverend" Harry Williams, who, as a Fellow of the college, "had written several lively and provocative books including *Objections to Christian Belief and The God I Want*" (Junor, pp. 75-76).
4. Holden, *PRINCE CHARLES,* p. 287.

while staying privately with some Catholic friends, ... he accompanied them to a little country church and heard Mass."[1]

Hilton, who starts from the mistaken view that the British monarchy has *ever* been, and is supposed to be a truly Christian institution —something which it has *never* been—comments,

> After the Reformation and the adoption of the 39 Articles of the Church of England, the Church and State laid their foundations upon the authority of the Bible and a Protestant monarchy. However, the present Queen, in 1996, appointed an influential Roman Catholic as her chaplain, and attended Vespers in Westminster Cathedral to celebrate the centenary of the building of Britain's Roman Catholic centre. Further, Prince Charles, the [(then)] Heir to the Throne, is professing an allegiance not to biblical Christianity but to all faiths. The Coronation Oath is clearly being ignored and undermined through these changes, in a prelude to the removal of the *Act of Settlement* of 1701, which does not permit a Roman Catholic, or a monarch married to a Roman Catholic, to accede to the throne. If this happened, for the first time since the Glorious Revolution of 1688, Rome would be provided with a vassal monarch with sovereignty over 'Mary's dowry' [(i.e., the United Kingdom)]. This would inevitably lead to the ascendancy of Roman traditions over the authority of Scripture which lies at the heart of Protestantism and the institution of the Monarchy....
>
> ....The prospect of the removal of the *Act of Settlement* from the Statute Books, a change which the Queen and other senior members of the Royal Family are reported to favour, would be the crowning glory of the Anglo-Roman Catholic International Commission. The signs are already evident. On the significance of **Prince Charles' bedside rosary, a gift from the Pope**, The *Sunday Telegraph* reported: 'How changed is our country. Even 30 years ago, the news that the future Supreme Governor of the Church of England practised what would have been considered a Popish superstition would have provoked outrage. A century before it might have provoked revolution....'
>
> ....Lord St John of Fawsley, a devout Roman Catholic ... seems to have become the Queen's personal spokesman. The fact that the Supreme governor of the Church of England is surrounded by such influential Roman Catholics highlights the progressive Anglican subjection to the Papacy....
>
> It is curious that with an ecumenical climate in which it is not supposed to matter which denomination one belongs to, the recent high-profile conversions to Rome of leading politicians and members of the Royal Family have enjoyed huge media attention, as have the conversions of members of the Anglican clergy.[2]

The British monarchy's apparent agenda to "break down the walls" between Roman Catholicism and not just Anglican Protestantism, but Christianity generally, has taken hold of some of Chris-

---

1. Junor, p. 260.
2. Hilton, *The Principality and Power of Europe*, pp. 53, 55, 173. Junor adds, "According to the Act of Settlement of 1701, which was drawn up to prevent descendants of the [Roman] Catholic King James II from returning to the throne, those who inherit the crown are forbidden 'to be reconciled to or hold communion with the See or Church of Rome'" (p. 260).

tianity's most prominent spokespersons. The (too) late Paul and Jan Crouch of Trinity Broadcasting Network (TBN) fame, as well as the late Christian apologist Charles Colson, for example, were among the suckered. (Indeed, TBN also owns a Roman Catholic network.) Although ostensibly sincere in their desires and efforts to serve Christ, despite significant deviations from sound and true doctrine, some have *unwittingly* allowed themselves to be compromised throgh a direct association with British royals (e.g., Charles, Andrew, William, and now roasting Elizabeth II and Philip).

Charles (Chuck) Colson—who like so many, confusedly identified (arguably) *pagan* "Mother Teresa" as a "Christian," perhaps unaware that she *openly* accepted (and apparently endorsed) *false spiritual beliefs* as *potentially leading to salvation)*—stated on Christian radio that he had received his Templeton Prize for Progress in Religion award money, on behalf of Prison Fellowship, *from the hands of Prince Philip* at Buckingham Palace! (Imagine that.) A moving and (admittedly) often tremendous apologist for the faith, Colson was awarded the prize, the monetary value of which "exceeds every other established award, including the Nobel prizes," for having "shown 'extraordinary originality in advancing humankind's understanding of God.'" Named as the recipient of the Templeton Prize in March 1993, just one year later—in March 1994—Colson (a Protestant), along with Richard John Neuhaus (a Roman Catholic), rocked evangelical Christianity with the release of a joint Protestant and Roman Catholic declaration entitled, "Evangelicals and Catholics Together: The Christian Mission in the Third Millennium." Although mostly sound in its statements, the declaration put aside major differences of belief to leave the *general public* with the *intended misperception* that the declaration's "Roman Catholic" participants and signers represented typical Roman Catholic belief, and vice versa, which they do not. The net effect, of course, was to leave the public with the false view that true Christian belief and typical Roman Catholic belief are not really all that far apart, and that the two really should join ranks. Whether or not this had been the understanding of Colson, it is an important goal of the British monarchy, which has been happy to employ his talents in accomplishing it. If and when the pope partners as the false prophet with the AntiChrist, so that one represents Roman Catholicism and the other *supposedly* Protestantism and the Reformation, such public confusion will only harm the Church by tending to leave it in the middle, where *both* Roman Catholicism and apostate Protestantism *may be accepted*, rather than polarizing it squarely on the side of the truth of the Reformation. Hunt, in *A Woman Rides the Beast*, states: "The most significant event in nearly 500 years of church history was revealed as a *fait accompli* on March 29, 1994. On that day leading American evangelicals and [Roman] Catholics signed a joint declaration titled 'Evangelicals and Catholics Together: The Christian Mission in the 3rd Millennium.' The document, in practical effect, overturned the Reformation and will unquestionably have far-reaching repercussions throughout the Christian world for years to come. This startling development was the culmination of careful planning and negotiations over the previous two years. Each step was continuously monitored and approved by the Vatican."[1] All this, of course, is *not* meant to detract from Colson's eloquent, inspiring, and at times, even *brilliant* defense of Christianity—including on September 2, 1993, at the University of Chicago, before an ecumenist audience having "many delegates of the Parliament of the World's Religions."[2]

TBN, on the other hand, has now made famous its own heraldic crest, which, perhaps from ignorance, parodies the opposing lion and unicorn arrangement of the ancient Assyrian and Babylonian religious seals.[3] TBN's unicorn, however, differs markedly from the pagan unicorn of standard heraldry; although its eyes have a human profile, like those of the unicorn on Charles' achievement as Prince of Wales, and its horn is blended into the crest's mantle, it otherwise looks like a horse.[4] Nevertheless, its arrangement seems to derive from the same source as that of the British monarchy's heraldic achievements. When the author approached Paul Crouch (now deceased), who was then head of the world's largest Christian television broadcasting network, for support in disseminating this work, Mr. Crouch foolishly replied, "TBN does not promote materials outside of those that we use for our own ministry purposes."[5] While wondering how it could be that *credibly* revealing the plausible identity of the AntiChrist fails to accord with then TBN's "ministry purposes," the author learned that Paul and Jan Crouch, as aired on TBN itself, had (at that time) *recently met with Queen Elizabeth II and Prince Philip* to brief them on plans for various future TBN activities! *To date,* TBN still *ignores* all this—remaining *unfaithful* to God's written Word.

1. Dave Hunt, *A Woman Rides the Beast* (Oregon: Harvest House Publishers, 1994), p. 5. For more information, see *A Woman Rides the Beast.*
2. Charles W. Colson, "The Enduring Revolution: 1993 Templeton Address," *SOURCES,* No. 4, p. 2; Colson and Richard John Neuhaus, "Evangelicals & Catholics Together: The Christian Mission in the Third Millennium," *First Things,* May 1994; and "Evangelicals & Catholics Together," 15 June 1994. For these and other materials, contact Prison Fellowship.
3. See ch. 6, "The First Beast and Prince Charles' Coat of Arms," at p. 115.
4. See ch. 7's section titled, "The sinister (right-hand) supporter," at p. 197.
5. Correspondence from Paul F. Crouch, dated December 9, 1997.

305

That the British monarchy sits at the top of a global neo-Babylonian system seems evident. That as Satanists "by any other name," they so-influence "Christianity," is not just troubling, but extraordinarily dangerous to the Church. Additional illustrations may be offered. John Daniel, for example, observes:

> In January 1983, the Queen and her consort toured the United States. There seemed to be no apparent reason for her visit, other than the honor bestowed on her by the Bohemian Club.... The Bohemian Club is a West Coast center [(having both a city clubhouse in the Nob Hill district of San Francisco, California and the infamous Bohemian Grove)] for the inner elite of Templar Scottish Rite Freemasonry in the United States. Some of its members are Senator Alan Cranston, [former] FBI Director William Webster, [and] former secretaries of state George Shultz and Henry Kissinger.[1]
>
> On February 3, 1983, a five minute segment of the Bohemian Club's extravaganza in honor of Queen Elizabeth was aired on all three television networks. The event began with a view of the Queen sitting slightly high in the middle of the auditorium, as if on top of a pyramid. Two dancers entered the stage wearing huge hats hanging from cables. The cone of the first hat was representative of a walled city with a pyramid, or ziggurat towering in the middle. Obviously, it portrayed ancient Babylon. At the base of the pyramid two doors continuously flapped open and shut displaying inside a large picture of Prince Charles, successor to the British throne, and his wife, Princess Diana.... The cone on the second hat portrayed the city of London, with Big Ben towering in the center. [Then] ... a voice bellowed, "Oh Queen, you have traversed the ages from Babylon to London!" Ever so slightly, and without a smile, Queen Elizabeth nodded as if in agreement to the statement.
>
> That night the Bohemian Club, an arm of Templar Scottish Rite Freemasonry, [apparently] acknowledged London as the seat of Mystery Babylon. Queen Elizabeth accepted that acknowledgment.[2]

As Hilton puts it, "The Vatican recognises that the defeat of Protestantism here would weaken it throughout all Europe." Noting a *Catholic Herald* prediction that the "days of the Anglican Church are numbered, and most of its worshipers will return to the true faith of their distant medieval forebears," he observes,

> It is almost a symbolic fulfillment of that prophecy that the 20 pence coin of the British colony Gibraltar, issued by Parliament and approved by

---

1. The late Senator Alan Cranston was a lead U.S. participant in the Global Security Programme, initiated by then Prince Charles, and also was Chairman of the Board of the Gorbachev Foundation USA. The late Kissinger and the late Shultz were prominent members of the Committee of 300. Finally, recall that Charles' *Ich Dien* motto was originally taken from the defeated King of *Bohemia* by the Black Prince, after the Battle of Crécy. For more information, see the related notes in the discussion on the Committee of 300 in the subsection titled "Garter 'placement'" in ch. 7's discussion on the Garter, as well as ch. 11's section titled "Global Governance, the Global Security Programme, and a possible 'Economic Security Council,'" beginning at p. 152 and 451, respectively. Also, see ch. 7's section titled, "The motto and the heir-apparent's badge," at p. 187.
2. John Daniel, *Scarlet and the Beast*, Vol. II, 1st ed. (Texas: Jon Kregel, Inc., 1994), pp. 25-26.

the Queen, bears an engraving of Mary crowned "Queen of Heaven" and titled "Our Lady of Europa". The head of the Queen on the other side is simply titled "Elizabeth II—Gibraltar", without her usual titles of D.G. REG. F.D.—Queen by the Grace of God, Defender of the Faith. As portentous as such obvious Roman Catholic symbolism is [in connection with Europe's "goddess worship" (and Queen Elizabeth II)], the British postage stamps issued in 1984 to commemorate the second election to the European Parliament went even further. They depicted a whore riding a beast over seven mounds or waves. Such imagery has startling similarities to passages from the book of *Revelation* which a succession of theologians from Wycliffe to Spurgeon has identified as representing Papal Rome.

Roman Catholic imagery is endemic in Europe, and has been wholeheartedly embraced by the European government. The design of the European flag was inspired by the halo of 12 stars around pictures of the [Black] Madonna [which, the Vatican claims, represents the glorified woman of Revelation 12 rather than a demonic impostor], and appears prominently on the Council of Europe stained-glass window in Strasbourg Cathedral.[1]

Charles' ecumenicalism is not limited to Protestant Christianity and Roman Catholicism. As an ecumenist and Garter Illuminist who, as the British Monarch, is *over* Freemasonry (and thus, Luciferian satanism) worldwide,[2] he also embraces the occult, cults, and false religions in general:

> He believes that racial and religious differences, and a lack of understanding of other people's cultures and traditions, are the most explosive issues of the day. They are the cause of tension, bloodshed and misery not just on the streets of Britain but all over the world; and have been for centuries…. In opening the Tenth International Council Meeting of UWC [(United World Colleges)] in 1985 he said, 'It is a great pity that there aren't enough students from the Middle Eastern countries. There aren't enough Moslem students. One of the great problems, it seems to me, is the increasing degree of misunderstanding between the Islamic approach to life and indeed the misunderstanding between different branches of the Islamic faith. To … improve understanding in Britain, where large numbers of Moslems live, the Prince suggested to Sir Richard Attenborough that he should produce a series for Channel 4 television to explain a variety of different religious beliefs. The Prince contributed a foreword….
> ….The Prince is unlikely to abandon his ecumenical lead. He sees it not as a failure to uphold the Protestant reformed religion, but as another pragmatic step to meet the needs of modern society.[3]

---

1. Hilton, *The Principality and Power of Europe*, pp. 48-49. This window shows the "goddess" "holding the 1000-year-old symbol of political unification—the crown of the Holy Roman Empire" (ibid., copyright page). Actually, it is the crown of Charlemagne or "Charles." According to Hilton: "Europe was consecrated to Mary by the Vatican in 1309, and placed under her patronage. The shrine of 'Our Lady of Europa', in Gibraltar, was instituted at the consecration. This shrine is being renovated" (ibid., p. 35).
2. For more information, see the discussion on the Garter at p. 147 in ch. 7, "The Heraldic Symbols in the Arms and their Interpretations."
3. Junor, pp. 260-261. According to Satan's Prince, "Tolerance and patience are what is needed, the simple effort to try to understand the other person's point of view and his idealism, and not to condemn it

The Prince has said he wants to be called "defender of faith" and not "defender of THE faith" when he becomes king. The move, making him a figurehead for all religions and denominations in Britain, would end a 450-year tradition.... The Prince says: "I happen to believe that the Catholic subjects of the sovereign are as important as Protestants, not to mention the Islamic, Hindu and Zoroastrian." ...

One of Charles's friends added: "... What the Prince is saying is not out of step with some senior churchmen. "What is so wrong about the future head of state defending the faith of his subjects, whatever their faith is?"

Charles, although a regular churchgoer, is a radical thinker who has worked to achieve an understanding and tolerance of a wide variety of religions. He has researched beliefs ranging from Buddhism and Hinduism to Jungism and shown admiration for their teachings....

Charles's remarks were welcomed by Roman Catholic leaders and spokesmen for other religions.[1]

This week, in the much-heralded Jonathan Dimbleby programme on his 25 years as the Prince of Wales, broadcast on ITV, Charles rejected the present exclusive association between the monarchy and the Church of England. "I happen to believe," he is quoted as saying, "that the Catholic subjects of the sovereign are as important (as the Protestants), not to mention the Islamic, Hindu and Zoroastrian subjects." ...

Charles wishes to ... [become], as he puts it, not Defender of the Faith, but Defender of Faith.[2]

Some clergy have attempted to gloss-over Charles' blasphemies and heresies, including his above statements. Dimbleby, however, quoting the latter more fully, lays such falsehood to rest:

...."[Charles] had not only explored Hinduism and Buddhism but remained unwilling to dismiss the idea of reincarnation. He had also decided that it was important to understand Islam and ... was drawn towards some of that great religion's guiding tenets; he identified strongly with those who saw in Islam, Judaism and Christianity a common belief in a monotheistic creation which was of greater significance than the doctrinal hostilities which ... had pitted each faith against the other.

He was dismayed by the schisms within the Christian communion. In particular, as he had demonstrated so forcibly in his attempt to attend mass in the Pontiff's private chapel during his official visit to Italy in 1985, he was contemptuous of doctrinal and liturgical disputes that divided the Roman from the Anglican Church....

....[All this] had come to form the bedrock of his conviction that salvation springs less from religion than from faith....

---

outright" (ibid., p. 80). For more information, see the next chapter's section titled, "The United World Colleges," at p. 394.

1. Robert Jobson, "Queen's Rift With Charles," *International Express*, U.S. Ed. No. 132, 29 June – 5 July 1994, pp. 1-2.
2. David Starkey, "If Church and Crown divide," *International Express*, U.S. Ed. No. 132, 29 June – 5 July 1994, p. 8.

His attitudes are not bounded by ecumenicism. Although he has long deplored the schisms within the Christian Church and has been scathing about the exclusive forms of evangelism represented by Protestant sects like the Free Presbyterians.... 'I've always felt that the Catholic subjects of the sovereign are equally as important as the Anglican ones, as the Protestant ones. Likewise, I think that the Islamic subjects or the Hindu subjects or the Zoroastrian subjects [(or the Jewish and other non-Christian subjects)] of the sovereign are of equal and vital importance.' ...

To this extent he finds himself at ease walking between and within all those religions in addition to being a practising Christian.... To be Defender of the Faith was for him to be 'Defender of the Divine in existence, the pattern of the Divine which is, I think, in all of us but which, because we are human beings, can be expressed in so many different ways.' ...

After the publication of the Prince's interview, ... the Archbishop [of Canterbury, George Carey,] allowed himself to be tempted into remarking on BBC Radio that the Prince had 'intended' to say that he wanted to be Defender of the *Christian* Faith.... According to the Archbishop, what the Prince had said 'was perfectly compatible.... As heir, he has to be concerned with every citizen, regardless of creed.... I believe that that is what he intended to say.... What can be changed is the Coronation Service which can reflect the multicultural society in which we live' [by giving prominence to leaders from other faiths].

The Archbishop's minimalist interpretation ... was not easy to reconcile with the Prince's words.... [The] Prince amplified his perspective thus:

> I feel, you know, that certainly the great Middle Eastern religions—Judaism, Islam, Christianity, all stemming from the same geographical area —all have a great deal in common. And I think Christianity had a great deal more in common a long time ago than it does now—sadly in my opinion. And I think a lot of that is due to the great schism between the Orthodox Church and the Roman Church before the Reformation produced Protestantism. But I also think there are aspects of Hinduism and Buddhism, again further east, which are attached by very profound threads to Islam, Christianity and Judaism. And when you begin to look at what these religions are saying you find that so much of the wisdom that is represented within these religions coincides. [All the great prophets, all the great thinkers, all those who have achieved an awareness of the aspects of life which lie beneath the surface, all have showed the same understanding of the universe or the nature of God or of the purpose of our existence—and that is why I think it so important to understand the common threads which link us all in one great and important tapestry.] ...

....The Archbishop also welcomed the drift of the Prince's comments about the importance of faith in an increasingly secular society.... [The] participation by the leaders of other faiths in his coronation would be an ecumenical gesture that the Prince favoured, but it seemed unlikely to meet the full challenge of the Prince's faith....

....Some advisors believe that .... it should be possible to include in the coronation a supplementary declaration affirming the Prince's belief in the divinity of other religions and, in the process, diluting the 'exclusive' character of the Oath ... which so disturbs the Prince....

As sovereign, the Prince would have to meet three other legal requirements.... He would have to declare himself to be a faithful Protestant...;

that he was in communion with the Church of England...; and that he would 'maintain' the Church of England and the Church of Scotland.... In themselves, none of these three would cause him any anxiety.[1]

In 1521, England's King Henry VIII, whose heraldic arms were supported by the red dragon,[2] published *Assertio Septem Sacramentorum,* "In Defence of the Seven Sacraments" (of Roman Catholicism). As a polemical response to Martin Luther's writings, it upheld Rome's spurious papal authority and called for obedience. Widely debated in Europe, the work was warmly received in Rome, and prompted Pope Leo X to formally confer on Henry VIII the title *Fidei Defensor,* or as since commonly rendered in English, "Defender of the Faith." Henry VIII later abandoned Roman Catholicism, while, in 1534, blasphemously asserting himself to be "the Supreme Head [on Earth] of the Church of England," so that he could divorce and re-marry. Although Leo X had not authorized the king to "pass the title to his heirs," the English Parliament chose to do so in 1543 in "The Act of the King's Style," which "declared that the words *Fidei Defensor* were 'united and annexed for ever to the imperial crown'." While the title was originally granted for Henry VIII's defense of the *religion of Rome,* "FD", for *Fidei Defensor,* has since been placed by the head of the reigning monarch on British coinage. Ironically, Westminster Abbey, the "shrine" of Anglicanism, remains "vested in a family of Roman Catholic dukes."[3]

Under Charles, as with the late Elizabeth II, "annual Commonwealth Day services held in Westminster Abbey," "have been relaxed affairs, engaging different [(satanic and pagan) anti-]faiths, because the Abbey is a Royal Peculiar, answerable directly to the Sovereign" — though "for a coronation, the Abbey comes under the ... [monarch's appointed] Archbishop of Canterbury, not its Dean."[4] In Dimbleby's biographical documentary titled, "Charles: The Private Man, The Public Role," Satan's Prince stated: "I personally would rather see it as Defender of Faith, not *the* Faith, because it means just one particular interpretation of Faith, which I think is sometimes something that causes a [great] deal of a problem.... [We're] all actually aiming for the same ultimate goal, I think. So I would much rather it was seen as defending faith itself."[5] As discussed here and

---

1. Dimbleby, *The Prince of Wales,* pp. 526-528, 530-533.
2. For more information, see the discussion on the red dragon at p. 188 in ch. 7, "The Heraldic Symbols in the Arms and their Interpretations."
3. Junor, p. 85.
4. Pepinster, "Charles's instincts are to be applauded — but 1,000 years of tradition are at stake. Is it wise for the Christianity of the Coronation to be so diluted in the name of diversity?"
5. "How Hal muddied the holy waters for Charles," *Independent on Sunday,* No. 231 (London), 3 July 1994, p. 16. Also see Dimbleby, *The Prince of Wales,* p. 528.

in the later section titled, "Ties to the New Age Movement, the oc- cult, and false religions," Charles has, perhaps more than any other contemporary figure, sought to ingratiate himself to the world's many "faith traditions."

It has been well-documented by others, and is beyond *knowl- edgeable* dispute, that *at their highest degrees and levels,* Freema- sonry and its plethora of cult and occult branches, which include Mormonism, Theosophy, the New Age Movement, and even Anton LaVey's "Church of Satan," not only openly deride Christ and His work, but explicitly advocate the worship and adoration of Lucifer (Satan) as a means to achieve individual "godhood" and world "peace." Illuminist Freemasonry, which itself originated with the Rosicrucians and the Temple Knights, and from there Gnosticism,[1] Cabalism,[2] and the ancient mystery religions, especially Zoroastrian- ism, has long conspired to infiltrate, subvert, and co-opt, the major oligarchic, religious, military, financial, economic, political, govern- mental, educational, informational, and medical bodies and institu- tions of the world, including the Church, at their upper echelons, so as to eventually foist a full-fledged, Luciferic New World Order con- sisting of a "democratic" world government and a unified world reli- gion upon mankind. Italy (Rome), France (Paris), England (London), Germany (Berlin, Hamburg), Russia (Moscow), and the United States (Washington D.C. and especially New York City) are among the major international bases of operation for this massive conspiracy (Eng- land being the most prominent currently), which is working heavily through the United Nations, the World Constitution and Parliament Association, and many other organizations and institutions to achieve its insidious aims.[3]

---

1. Gnosticism is an occult view and explanation of the New Testament, and is largely predicated upon the Cabala.

2. Cabalism is essentially an occult view and explanation of the Old Testament, having much in common with the ancient mystery religions.

3. Kah, *En Route to Global Occupation*, pp. 9, 13-14, 16, 20-21, 30-40, 46, 48-65, 76-79, 83-85, 88-119, 133-136, 139-140, 164-168, 175-176, 182, 192-210. Regarding the Church, Kah observes: "Another or- ganization collaborating with [Philip] Isely's World Constitution and Parliament Association is the World Council of Churches.... This organization has come to represent the leadership of most of the mainline Protestant church denominations in America and has privately been pushing for unification with the Church of Rome. But it appears that the WCC is only trying to 'unite' Christianity in order to bring it into the New World Order. [The council actively promotes] interfaithism—the merging of all the world's religions under one umbrella" (*En Route to Global Occupation*, p. 84). James Shaw, a former American thirty-third degree Mason, adds, "I knew of many ministers and preachers who were Masons, particu- larly those associated with the National Council of Churches" (Kah, *En Route to Global Occupation*, p. 138). Besides a few individual churches, collaborating "Christian" organizations also include Christian Youth Fellowship in Nigeria, the Federation of Christian Churches in Pakistan, the National and Interna- tional Councils of Christian Churches as well as Gospel Faith Mission in the Ivory Coast, and Save the Children in Austria (Kah, *En Route to Global Occupation*, pp. 186-187). (Note that Princess Anne is Pa- troness for Save the Children.) For a cogent history of this international conspiracy and an outline of its progress prior to 1998, see Kah's *En Route to Global Occupation*.

Jesus stated: "No servant can serve two masters.... You cannot serve God and mammon [riches]" (Luke 16:13; cf. Matt 6:24). Much of Freemasonry's control over governments and nations has been achieved financially, through the establishment of national and international banks and monetary institutions. As the late Joan Veon points out, according to Dr. Carroll Quigley (whom President Clinton admires): "The powers of financial capitalism had another far-reaching aim, nothing less than to create a world system of financial control in private hands able to dominate the political system of each country and the economy of the world as a whole.... The apex of the system was to be the Bank for International Settlements in Basle, Switzerland, a private bank owned and controlled by the world's central banks which were themselves private corporations.... The B.I.S. is generally regarded as the apex of the structure of financial capitalism whose remote origins go back to the creation of the Bank of England in 1694 and the Bank of France in 1803.... It was set up rather to remedy the decline in London as the world's financial center by providing a mechanism by which a world with three chief financial centers in London, New York, and Paris could still operate as one [from London]."[1] London's financial district remains "Europe's pre-eminent center of financial services."[2]

Luciferian Albert Pike, who wrote Freemasonry's preeminent work *Morals and Dogma,* in which he blasphemously referred to God (i.e., The Father, The Word and The Holy Spirit, or *Elohim)* as "the Demons," had this to say in his delusional and satanic "Instructions" to Masonry's Supreme Councils:

> If Lucifer were not God, would Adonay (The God of the Christians) whose deeds prove his cruelty, perfidy, and hatred of man, barbarism and repulsion for science, would Adonay and his priests calumniate him? Yes, Lucifer is God, and unfortunately Adonay is also God. For the eternal law is that there is not light without shade, no beauty without ugliness, no white without black, for the absolute can only exist as two Gods...., the divine dualism.... That is why the intelligent disciples of Zoroaster, as well as, after them, the Gnostics, the Manicheans, and the Templars have admitted, as the only logical metaphysical conception, the system of the two divine principles fighting eternally, and one cannot believe the one inferior in power to the other. Thus, the doctrine of Satanism is a heresy; and the true and pure philosophic religion is the belief in Lucifer, the equal of Adonay; but Lucifer, God of Light and God of Good, is struggling for humanity against Adonay, the God of Darkness and Evil.[3]

---

1. Carroll Quigley, *Tragedy and Hope* (Macmillan, 1965), p. 324. For more information, see Joan Veon, "Economic Globalization, Glass Steagall and the DOW" (Veon Financial Services, Inc.; P.O. Box 1323; Olney, MD 20830-1323), Dec. 1996, Vol. 10, No. 4, pp. 2-3.
2. Fred Barbash, The Washington Post, "Europe begins move toward common currency," *The Denver Post,* 13 Feb. 1997, p. 36A.
3. Kah, *En Route to Global Occupation,* pp. 124-125; see also pp. 113-116. Although the names of many

Freemasonry, as a Luciferic religion of "good works" arising from the ancient mysteries—against which The LORD warned Israel, saying, "Woe to those who call evil good, and good evil; who put darkness for light, and light for darkness; who put bitter [poisonous] for sweet, and sweet for bitter" (Isa 5:20; cf. 5:18-21)—advocates the same kind of ecumenism sought by Satan's Prince (King Charles III). Freemasonry finds its foundation in Satan's ancient lie, which denies the existence of absolute, unchanging, eternal truth. On pages 37, 226 and 525 of *Morals and Dogma,* for example, Pike asserted:

> [A]ll truths are *"Truths of Period,"* and not truths for eternity.... Masonry, around whose altars the Christian, the Hebrew, the Moslem, the Brahmin, the followers of Confucius and Zoroaster, can assemble as brethren and unite in prayer to the one God who is above *all* the Baalim, must needs leave it to each of its Initiates to look for the foundation of his faith and hope to the written scriptures of his own religion.... It reverences all the great reformers. It sees in Moses, the Lawgiver of the Jews, in Confucius and Zoroaster, in Jesus of Nazareth, and in the Arabian Iconoclast, Great Teachers of Morality, and Eminent Reformers, if no more: and allows every brother of the Order to assign to each such higher and even Divine Character as his Creed and Truth require.[1]

Lance Gay notes that "history shows that high-living hedonism and amorous escapades are embedded firmly in the British monarchy. Extramarital affairs and royal licentiousness are more the rule than the exception."[2] (Even though the Church of England has condemned Freemasonry as "blasphemous" and "positively evil,"[3] it too, as graphically illustrated in what are presumed to be the monarchy's bloody "Jack the Ripper" murders,[4] has been firmly embedded.) From then Prince Charles' unrepentant promiscuous and adulterous lifestyle before[5] and after[6] his marriage to Diana, his avid

---

false gods are routinely invoked in Freemasonry, one is forbidden to publicly pray in the name of Jesus. In the York Rite's Royal Arch degree, the god of Masonry is revealed as a blasphemous combination of *Yah* (The God of Israel), Baal, and Osiris, called Jah-Bul-On or J.B.O. (Kah, *En Route to Global Occupation,* pp. 134-135, 140).

1. Kah, *En Route to Global Occupation,* pp. 125-127.
2. Scripps Howard News Service, "Antics normal for British royalty," *Rocky Mountain News,* 10 Dec. 1992, p. 58.
3. Kah, *En Route to Global Occupation,* pp. 134-135.
4. Coleman notes: "The Committee of 300 is for the most part under the control of the British monarch.... Queen Victoria is believed to have been quite paranoid about keeping it secret and went to great lengths to cover up MASONIC writings left at the scene of 'Jack the Ripper' murders, which alluded to the Committee's connections with 'experiments' carried out by a family member who was also a highly-placed member of the Scottish Rite of Freemasonry" (*The Committee of 300,* pp. 239-240).
5. Holden, *PRINCE CHARLES,* p. 223.
6. Nigel Dempster and Peter Evans, "Mayhem in the monarchy, Royal scandals crack foundation of the House of Windsor," *The Denver Post,* 6 June 1993, pp. 1A, 8-9A.

"pursuit of the occult and New Age medicine,"[1] and his "openness" to, willing participation in, and overt defense of, false spiritualities and religions, including now as King Charels III, it is evident that his Anglican confirmation never was representative of a genuine belief in The God of the Bible. The antichristian acting role Satan's Prince chose at the age of seventeen, less than a year after his confirmation, was therefore revealing: "[For] the school play at Christmas 1965, Prince Charles undertook the role of Shakespeare's Macbeth.... Charles' satanic thane ... raised an impromptu buzz in the audience only when the three witches cried: 'All hail, Macbeth, that shalt be king hereafter!'"[2] We may add that the apple does not fall far from the tree: Elizabeth II and Prince Philip, like King George VI and Queen Elizabeth, were all druidic *Satanists*.[3]

Marriage, ascension, and politics. Although King Charles III has been strongly contrasted with his (roasting) father Prince Philip, particularly as personalities go,[4] Charles has been and reamins, as we shall see, very much the activist in his father's mold: "Prince Philip's public life is, at first sight, amazingly varied and exciting. If the ambition of most aspiring beauty queens is 'to travel', he out-travels them all, averaging something like 75,000 miles a year. He also [annually] delivers sixty to eighty major speeches and gives an even larger number of shorter talks.... The number of hands shaken ... and crowds gratified make up a programme that is as exhausting and daunting as that of any American presidential candidate on the stump.... Not only is he another pair of eyes and ears for the Queen, but he believes he has a creative mission as well: to present the monarchy as a dynamic, involved and responsive institution.... This means being seen to react to certain situations, to produce alternative proposals, to exhort, advise, warn, and sometimes to rebuke."[5] That was Prince Philip, while yet alive in this world—though it sounds a lot like Charles too.

Charles' 1981 marriage to Diana took place before an estimated worldwide television audience of seven-hundred and fifty million,[6] with a total combined audience of nearly two billion in 141 coun-

---

1. Hunt, *GLOBAL PEACE AND THE RISE OF ANTICHRIST,* p. 275.
2. Holden, *PRINCE CHARLES,* pp. 142-143.
3. See ch. 8, "The Red Dragon and Prince Charles' Investiture as Prince of Wales," at p. 207.
4. Prince Philip was rightly called "bluff, outspoken, hearty, tough and something of a bully." Charles' great desire for power and influence may derive in part from the fact that Prince Philip "spent a lifetime criticizing him and quietly undermining his self-esteem" (Junor, p. 13).
5. Judd, *Prince Charles,* p. 214.
6. The London Bureau of People, "Once upon a Time...," *People Weekly,* 22 July 1991, p. 28. Michelle Green, Lydia Denworth, Terry Smith, and Margaret Wright, "PRINCE-LESS DIANA," *People Weekly,* 11 Mar. 1996, p. 80.

tries,[1] making it by far the most widely viewed event in history—that is, until the untimely death and burial of Diana in August–September 1997, during which Satan's Prince also received substantial coverage. The princess' death and burial were followed by as many as two-and-one-half billion, covering at least 44 languages (discussed later).[2] (Recall that the third most widely viewed event was Charles' 1969 investiture as Prince of Wales.) Upon her marriage to Satan's Prince, and for that sole reason initially, Diana became "the world's most famous woman," having to "cope with the unbearable attention and lack of privacy."[3] Subsequently, it was said: "The Princess of Wales has done more to popularize the concept of monarchy throughout the world than any other member of the Royal Family.... She has not only become perhaps the most famous and most frequently photographed woman in the world, but she has helped to bring the institution of monarchy to a new peak of popularity and boosted the image of Britain worldwide."[4] "When Prince Charles was single, he was considered to be the most eligible bachelor in the world.... However, nothing he had experienced in previous years compared with the mass adulation and widespread fascination he and his wife attracted at and after their wedding.... Together they were ... the most sought-after couple on earth, and within a short period the Princess of Wales became the most photographed woman in the world, eclipsing every other member of the Royal Family.... Throughout the world, presidents and prime ministers vied with each other in their efforts to persuade the royal couple to visit them. Politicians of every hue wanted to be photographed in their presence.... [Due to the princess,] London has all but eclipsed Paris and Rome as the fashion centre of the world."[5] *TIME* magazine stated, "Charles and Diana are arguably the most famous, the most glamorous couple in the world."[6]

Eventually, goaded by the media, the public became increasingly disillusioned with the obviously troubled marriage between Charles and Princess Diana—later ended in divorce and death (sacrifice)—

---

1. Hoey, *Charles & Diana: The Tenth Anniversary,* p. 60. With the advent of global television, "Nearly 2 billion people saw her make those wedding vows, and most of them continued to pay attention as she and Prince Charles went about breaking them" (Martin Walker, "Can Charles grasp Diana's legacy?," *USA Today,* 2 Sept. 1997, p. 13A).
2. George Jahn, The Associated Press, "Billions worldwide take time to tune in," *The Denver Post,* 7 Sept. 1997, p. 17A. Pre-funeral estimates ranged from one-billion up to "several billion," which exceeds the limits even of possibility. The day before the funeral, William D. Montalbano of the *Los Angeles Times* asserted that the ceremony was "expected to draw ... more than 2 billion television watchers around the globe" ("Ceremony symbol of change in stoic Britain," *The Denver Post,* 5 Sept. 1997, p. 11A).
3. *Charles & Diana: A Royal Family Album,* p. 11.
4. *Charles & Diana: A Royal Family Album,* pp. 58, 94.
5. Hoey, *Charles & Diana: The Tenth Anniversary,* pp. 10-11, 92-94.
6. *Charles & Diana: A Royal Family Album,* p. 72.

besides the Charles' seemingly bizarre activities. Of course, then Prince Charles' rhetorical statement, "whatever 'love' is," made about Diana and marriage in a televised pre-ceremony interview, should have given the public some early apprehension. We're told Charles is "a serious-minded man who regards duty as a sacred trust to be preserved above all other emotions—including love."[1]

Due to the highly publicized marital woes and infidelities of both Charles and Diana, there were frequent rumors asserting that Queen Elizabeth II might one day abdicate the British throne, or that she might consider bypassing Charles in the royal succession. Such statements, however, were just hype. Still, it had seemed doubtful that Prince Charles would become King of England, as opposed perhaps to Prince or King of the European Union, any time soon. As this author stated in original edition of this book, "If the prince is the AntiChrist, he will soon attain worldwide authority in the most elite of Earth's occupations, and then be utterly crushed by The King of kings and LORD of lords in a fiery judgment (see Rev 13:1-4, 13:18, 19:11-20; cf. 1 Sam 17:4, 17:7, 17:34-54; 2 Sam 21:19-20; Isa 9:6-7; Zech 12:1-10)." Now, yet before constitution of formal global governance, we may discern that *Charles already possesses worldwide authority* —and increasingly has since July 1969.

Appealing to the chain of succession as a "divine right of kings," Holden points out that those encouraging abdication "fail to understand the nature of the British monarchy's popular appeal."[2] Nicholas Davies, for example, had (incorrectly) speculated:

> The state of Charles' and Diana's marriage was one of the prime reasons the queen clearly indicated in her Christmas broadcast of 1991 that she intended to continue as monarch until her death.... ....[If there were a formal separation or divorce], Charles would find it all but impossible to take the [current] religious vows at his coronation as king and head of the Church.... If those events did indeed unfold, then the throne would pass directly to young Prince William.... And if the queen should die before William reached the age of 21, then Prince Charles would act as regent, ruling in the name of his son....[3]

"The prince, who [formally] separated from Princess Diana in December [1992], ... pursued his interests more intently—'no longer walking in the shadow of his estranged wife,' said one of his aides."[4] Before the royal divorce, the British public generally considered Di-

---

1. Hoey, *Charles & Diana: The Tenth Anniversary*, p. 16.
2. Holden, *PRINCE CHARLES*, pp. 312-313.
3. "Charles' wrecked marriage forces queen to make a fateful decision," *Rocky Mountain News,* 7 July 1992, p. 18.
4. Nicholas Davies, "More dirty linen? It's environmental," *The Denver Post,* 22 May 1993, p. 2A.

ana, who had obscenely denounced Charles before the queen and Prince Philip,[1] and who was herself an adulteress,[2] to be an ideal choice for a future queen. There are, and had long been, however, those questioning Charles' suitability to be king:

> [In 1993]..., Charles began courting the press—albeit in a stately way. Eager to establish himself as a player on the world stage, he made high-profile visits to [Western Europe,] Poland, Mexico and the Persian Gulf.... ....Few [though] who read the transcript of Charles's 1989 phone conversation with Camilla [Parker Bowles] will ever forget his adolescent crudeness.[3]

> In truth, one year after the Waleses' separation, the Palace seems bent on removing Diana from the spotlight—and in pushing her estranged husband onto the stage.... [The] .... Archdeacon of York ... questioned whether Charles's affair with Camilla Parker Bowles renders him unfit to become Defender of the Faith.... Still, ... [the prince] and his handlers are said to be determined to make 1994 the Year of Charles....[4]

> ...Just as his great-uncle Edward [VIII] had given up his throne for the woman he loved, Prince Charles, 45, was said to have given up his love for the throne he covets.... "After months of heart searching," reported [Nigel] Dempster, Charles had [(allegedly)] vowed to "remove any obstacle to his succession," by breaking off his [(then) 24-year] relationship with Camilla Parker Bowles....
>
> Royal watchers quickly smelled a scam.... While the ploy [to "remain morally eligible for the throne,"[5]] seemed to work in some quarters—the Archdeacon of York, who had characterized Charles as morally unfit to be king, praised his apparent repentance—it may yet backfire.[6]

> ...[George] Austin seemed to change his mind..., declaring that if the affair was over, "I don't think there is a problem for the future. All Christians make mistakes...."
>
> But the Rev. Tony Highton, a leading member of the General Synod, disagreed...: "From what I understand, there does not appear to be any hint of penitence.... I, therefore, do not think he is fit to become Defender of the Faith and Supreme Governor of the Church of England." "I also think he is going to be in trouble over his remarks of wanting to be 'defender of all faiths,'" Highton added.[7]

> Prince Charles is seeing his popularity **soar** in Britain since his TV admission that he wasn't faithful to Princess Diana after their marriage "irretrievably

---

1. Nicholas Davies, "Shooting becomes a bone of contention," *Rocky Mountain News,* 8 July 1992, p. 23.
2. Michelle Green and Terry Smith, "Diss and Tell," *People Weekly,* 17 Oct. 1994, pp. 38-45.
3. Michelle Green, Terry Smith, and Margaret Wright, "The Outsider," *People Weekly,* 6 Dec. 1993, pp. 111-112, 114.
4. Michelle Green and Terry Smith, "Di Drops Out," *People Weekly,* 20 Dec. 1993, pp. 39-40.
5. "Charles ends relationship?," *The Denver Post,* 30 Jan. 1994, p. 20A.
6. "Age of Chivalry," *People Weekly,* 14 Feb. 1994, p. 56.
7. William Tuohy, "Charles' adultery admission, church stance raise firestorm," *The Denver Post,* 29 June 1994, p. 16A.

broke down." ... At the palace, "switchboards have been jammed with people ringing in to say nice things"..., says press secretary Richard Aylard. "People are saying that they appreciated the opportunity to see what the prince is really like."[1]

[The (apostate)] Archbishop of Canterbury [is now] ... supporting the future head of the Church of England in his desire to be not just the defender of the Anglican faith, but of <u>all the others</u> that are now a part of the <u>multicultural society</u> over which Charles will eventually reign. And ... the opinion polls showed that most of the British public thought that he ... would make a good king![2]

Suddenly, **the world**—and what it thought of **its future King**—had been stood on its head as poll after poll showed that these future subjects, who had been told for two years that he was *not* fit to be King...., felt that the television programme had improved his image and that he was fit to be King—and would probably turn out to be a very good King.[3]

...Charles ... shocked the nation by confirming rumors that he had committed adultery, but that was only the beginning. In Dimbleby's ... biography, ... the prince is [(craftily)] portrayed as an emotionally deprived pawn abandoned by his mother, bullied by his father and tortured by a paranoid wife whom he may never have loved....

....Neither the constitution nor the Church of England forbids a divorcé from becoming monarch, though remarriage is not normally allowed by the church.... ....Charles's partisans assert that he is determined to become King....[4]

The British press went so far as to suggest that Satan's Prince might stoop to self-removal from the royal succession.[5] It seemed far more likely to many, however, should the circumstances have required it, that the queen would herself have chosen to bypass him, for her eldest grandson (William) instead. As stated in the 1998 edition: "Either way, if Prince Charles is removed, or the British constitution is altered or bypassed, or his mother continues into the next century as queen, it could result in a substantial *expansion* of his role as a social crusader—and perhaps actually clear the way for him to rise to world prominence."[6] That rise *has now transpired,* as this updated edition exposes. As of 1998, others had opined:

1. "Mea culpas a coup for the prince," *The Denver Post,* 6 July 1994, p. 2A.
2. "Royalty Today," *Royalty,* 1994, Vol. 13, No. 2, p. 4. *Emphasis added.*
3. *Royalty,* 1994, Vol. 13, No. 2, p. 44. *Emphasis added.*
4. Michelle Green, Margaret Wright, Lydia Denworth, and Elizabeth Terry, "Prince of Pique," *People Weekly,* 31 Oct. 1994, pp. 47, 56.
5. For the order of succession to the British throne, see Lacey, *Majesty,* p. 309. For details of the royal household in addition to the succession, see James and Russell, *At Home with the Royal Family,* pp. 192-213, 216-217.
6. Following 1998, the world saw a substantial expansion of Charles' role as a social crusader. As Prince of Wales, he also increasingly assumed his aging mother's duties as monarch.

The possibility that Charles even would remove himself from the succession —an abdication of sorts—was floated in [1991].... [This] ... would free Charles to carry on as a social critic.... ...Charles's stepping aside could be put forward as a noble sacrifice to allow him to complete his lifelong mission as an activist in a way that would not be possible if he were King [of England (as opposed to Europe)].[1] [(Yet, Charles does as he pleases.)]

"The prince has great popularity in the country," one of Prime Minister John Major's men told me sourly. "His views are taken seriously...."

"The Prince of Wales feels very clearly that Walter Bagehot's out the window, and that he can participate, if he wishes, in making his country a better place," says Harold Brooks-Baker, editorial director of Burke's Peerage. "The right to be consulted, the right to encourage, the right to warn" is Bagehot's endlessly quoted dictum for royals. But **Charles is not king yet and, technically, says Brooks-Baker, he can do whatever he wants.**[2] [(Charles' lawlessness and thus activism have *increased* as king.)]

[Charles] does not react kindly to anyone who threatens his position. Diana became a threat because she became a rival for the public's attention.... Separation or even divorce would not in any way stand in the path of his becoming King.... There is, as yet, not the slightest indication that he has fallen from public favour, in spite of ... attempts to blacken his name with his wife's [(Diana's)] approval. He still enjoys enormous goodwill, because he is still perceived as an essentially good man.... [He] should be aware that attempts to besmirch his character, and to upstage him, have singularly failed so far to turn his future subjects against him.[3]

The idea of abdication is of course a nonstarter. The Queen accepts her role as a sacred trust to which she is committed for life and, when she was anointed with holy oil at her coronation..., the religious aspect of the ceremony was real to her in every sense. There is no question of her 'opting out' in favour of her son.... He ... wants nothing more than that his mother should reign until the twenty-first century.[4]

British Prime Minister John Major said ... Prince Charles ... has been ... waiting for his mother to step down from the throne.... [Meanwhile, the] ... 45-year-old prince will meet with a trade minister to discuss stepping up his role as a roving cultural and commercial ambassador for Britain.[5]

Princess Anne, eighth in line to the British throne, is being groomed by ... Queen Elizabeth II, to become a surrogate queen consort to the wifeless Prince Charles, said reports ... in the London *Daily Express....* ...."The queen wants Princess Anne to be elevated to such a rank, that when Prince Charles becomes king, she can be first lady of the land."[6]

---

1. The London Bureau of People, pp. 34-35.
2. Adam Platt, "What's it all about, Charlie?," *Esquire*, June 1992, pp. 114, 116.
3. "A Sense of Duty," *Majesty*, Nov. 1992, Vol. 13, No. 11, pp. 14-17.
4. Hoey, *Charles & Diana: The Tenth Anniversary*, pp. 97-98.
5. "Britain seeks real job for prince," *The Denver Post*, 25 Nov. 1993, p. 2A. As Charles himself had put it, "I'm just a roving ambassador for Britain" (*Charles & Diana: A Royal Family Album*, p. 56).
6. "Princess readied for new status?," *The Denver Post*, 14 June 1994, p. 2A. When Satan's Prince divorced Diana, she lost all hope of becoming queen.

[In] 1981, [their marriage] captivated Britain and the world as a once-in-a-century storybook romance. But ... the fairy tale has been replaced by a reality in which the union appears to have been loveless, passionless and hollow from the first post-nuptial kiss.... The only remaining question would be whether a divorced person could be the monarch...."[1]

Ultimately ... the biggest beneficiary of the split ... may be Charles. "It was very clever that it was the Queen who seemed to run the divorce.... Charles is being portrayed as a Mr. Nice Guy." ... As for the royal family, the task now at hand is to rehabilitate its soiled image....[2]

Death of a princess. The death of Princess Diana on August 31, 1997, was attended by unparalleled media coverage. Much of that coverage, however, was superficial and incomplete. Strange circumstances, hinting at a possible conspiracy, surrounded the princess' death. Further, it seems clear that the British monarchy had come to see Diana as an increasing, rather than decreasing, public rival and threat. Regarding then Prince Charles, Junor comments: "He was being eclipsed by her, and ... the frustration was unbearable.... The wife who had at first given him so much confidence and pride now appeared to have emasculated him. The more obsessive the media grew, the more Diana became obsessed with reading what they had to say about her. She was elated by being a superstar, she loved the adulation, delighted in the stir she caused, and revelled in being the most famous, most photographed, most sought after woman in the country, if not the world. But it was too much, too soon, and she began to believe her own publicity and enjoy the power of her position."[3] As Diana saw it: "Everybody always said when we were in the car, 'Oh, we're [on] the wrong side, we want to see *her,* we don't want to see him.' Obviously he wasn't used to that, and nor was I. He took it out on me. He was jealous."[4] The following information should aid the public discourse concerning the princess' death.

Strange circumstances. Henry Paul, driver of the Mercedes S-280, was, we are told, quite drunk (over three times beyond the legal limit) as well as drugged with an "antidepressant" (possibly Prozac), yet he was apparently not detected as such by Dodi al-Fayed or Diana. At the same time, the drunken and drugged Paul was forced to drive rapidly (between 90 and 121 m.p.h.) in an effort to flee a gang of "paparazzi" in hot-pursuit on motorcycles: "If driver Henri Paul, 41, the deputy head of security at the luxurious Hotel Ritz, was

1. Louis J. Salome, "Pressure grows for royal divorce," *The Denver Post,* 19 Oct. 1994, p. 6A.
2. "The Big Kiss-Off," *People Weekly,* 29 July 1996, pp. 42-43.
3. Junor, pp. 221-222.
4. "The Diana Tapes," *People* weekly, 20 Oct. 1997, p. 104.

legally drunk—his blood reportedly contained nearly four times the legal limit of alcohol concentration—how did he negotiate the seven sweeping turns before finally losing control of the car? Was he distracted by the photographers on motorcycles who had followed him, also at high speed, from the moment he picked up his passengers?" Not only did a witness describe the Mercedes as "surrounded by so many motorcyclists that he believed it was an official cortege," but "France 2 TV reported that a witness saw one photographer zigzag in front of the car before it crashed." The Mercedes then impacted a second vehicle, reportedly a black Fiat Uno, just before it hit a support pillar in the tunnel under *Place de l'Alma* in Paris.[1] The Fiat fled from the scene, suggesting that the Mercedes may have been run off the road. The motorcyclist and the Fiat weaved "in front of the Mercedes moments before it went out of control." CNN aired an early telephone call from a "witness" who claimed that Dodi was walking around looking dazed after the crash; the call was later said to be a "prank." Mohamed al-Fayed, Dodi's father, contended "that their deaths were caused not by the recklessness of a drunken driver employed by the Ritz, but by the paparazzi who pursued them." Following the crash, the paparazzi continued to hound the dying princess with incessant photographs, rather than offering assistance, even as the princess told them to leave her alone: "All around her, there were photographers who were machine-gunning (taking rapid-fire photographs). They were only a few centimeters from her face, taking her picture from every angle." Indeed, "within 30 seconds of the crash, photographers were taking pictures and tried to push rescuers and police away." "Le Monde reported ... that, within 30 seconds of the crash, some photographers were taking pictures of the bleeding victims. Citing at least a dozen unnamed witnesses, it said some photographers actually pushed away rescuers and two policemen who arrived on the scene, saying they were ruining their pictures.... Her head was twisted to one side, and the photographers were taking pictures from just a few inches away." Several of the photographers are "under formal investigation for involuntary homicide and failing to come to the aid of the victims or impeding rescue efforts.... [Romuald] Rat had been one of the first to arrive on the accident scene and had interfered with rescue attempts. But Rat told the authorities that he had taken Diana's pulse to determine whether she was still alive." (Or, perhaps, whether she had yet died!)

A *six-mile* trip to *La Pitie-Salpetriere* Hospital in Paris by ambulance "took <u>an hour</u> to get from the crash site," so long that "waiting officials feared it was lost." Doctors attempted heart-massages on

---

1. According to Fritz Springmeier, *Place de l'Alma* is "an important Merovingian ritual site."

Dodi at the crash scene, and on Diana at the hospital. During the trip to the hospital, the "ambulance had to halt suddenly when the princess's heart stopped beating so she could be given a massive dose of adrenaline." At the hospital, Diana's heart again stopped, when the doctors discovered a broken pulmonary vein that resulted in "almost a gallon and a half of blood spilled into her rib cage area." However, instead of placing the princess on a heart-lung bypass machine to pump her blood and provide oxygen to it while attempting to repair the vein, doctors continued with heart massage "for two hours, long after the critical period had passed." According to "Robert Shesser, chairman of emergency medicine at George Washington University Medical Center in Washington, D.C.," "doctors could have tried something else: placing Diana on the heart-lung bypass machine that stands in for those organs during heart surgery. 'That would give you time to repair what was broken, and hopefully get the heart started.'" (Removal of the heart is a part of masonic ritual murder.) Finally, Rees-Jones, the sole survivor of the accident, was given such large doses of anesthesia that his memory was affected, having "told investigators that he does not remember the crash."[1]

The case for a conspiracy. A possible marriage between Diana and a non-Anglican Protestant, particularly the Muslim Dodi al-Fayed, would have been construed as a potential threat to the royal succession due to Diana's influence over princes William and Henry (Harry). Prince William had suggested that Diana "leave Britain to escape the paparazzi," whereas the princess' brother, Charles, the Earl of Spencer, had even earlier asserted that the paparazzi would one day bring about the princess' death. Following her death, the earl affirmed: "I would say that I have always believed the press would kill her in the end." (Was it a scenario just waiting to be exploited by the monarchy?) Indeed, according to Egyptian sources, "Diana was already pregnant with [Dodi] Fayed's baby."

Several Muslim news sources have suggested that the British monarchy had Diana assassinated to prevent a marriage to Dodi,

1. "Charles publicly discusses how sons dealing with loss," *The Denver Post*, 20 Sept. 1997, p. 16A. John-Thor Dahlburg, Los Angeles Times, "Diana's last moments," *The Denver Post*, 11 Sept. 1997, p. 2A. Fred Coleman and Jack Kelley, "Report: He taunted the photographers," *USA Today*, 2 Sept. 1997, p. 1A. Marco R. della Cava and Maria Puente, "Alcohol, pursuit, speed are factors in probe," *USA Today*, 2 Sept. 1997, p. 3A. Craig R. Whitney, "Princess's driver drunk, speeding," *Rocky Mountain News*, 2 Sept. 1997, p. 3A. Craig R. Whitney, The New York Times, "Diana's car apparently collided with Fiat, then hit pillar," *The Denver Post*, 3 Oct. 1997, p. 2A. Steve Sternberg, "Questions raised over injuries, care at scene," *USA Today*, 2 Sept. 1997, p. 16A. Christopher P. Winner, USA Today, "Many questions still unanswered after accident," *The Denver Post*, 7 Sept. 1997, p. 24A. Anne Swardson, The Washington Post, "Fayed family denies driver drunk," *The Denver Post*, 7 Sept. 1997. Craig R. Whitney, The New York Times, "Ruling begins probe of paparazzi," *The Denver Post*, 3 Sept. 1997, p. 1A. Jocelyn Noveck, *Associated Press*, "Di's chauffeur legally drunk," *The Denver Post*, 2 Sept. 1997, pp. 1A, 7A.

who had helped to bring down the Conservative government of John Major in an apparent act of revenge for his not having been granted British citizenship. "Al-Fayed has been denied citizenship ever since he took over Harrods, and the wags guessed that he was taking his revenge on British society by having his son woo the mother of the future King William." "The ultimate revenge against the establishment would have been a marriage between Diana and Dodi. That would have made the Fayeds step-parents and grandparents to a likely future King of England—Diana's son, William. Before their untimely death, British newspaper commentators had written acidly of the Fayeds' seduction of Diana and compared Dodi to a 'toad' kissed by a princess. Some observers believe revenge was partly a motive on both sides for the sudden romance, with Diana seeking to annoy the royal establishment that rejected her." "No other celebrity courted and manipulated the media with as much savvy and charm.... Only six hours before she died, Diana called her favorite royal correspondent [from the Ritz].... Maybe she would marry her new love, Dodi Fayed. Then again, maybe not." Supposedly, "she planned to give up her role in public life." "Arab news media raised the theory that her life was ended instead by a conspiracy.... [From] the Persian Gulf to Libya, the theme was the same: Diana's affair with Dodi Fayed, an Arab and Muslim, went against the prejudices of the British establishment. Columnist Anis Mansour ... put it directly in the Cairo daily Al-Ahram: 'She was killed by British intelligence to save the monarchy.... Nobody since Cromwell, who called for a republic in the 17th century, has been able to shake the royal family as Princess Diana did.' ... Libya's official JANA news agency .... accused Britain of 'setting up the accident' and France of carrying it out."

Although Diana was supposed to fade from the royal limelight with the divorce, she maintained her popularity through "good works," continuing to upstage Charles and the monarchy generally: "She learned to use her fame to do good works—and also to punish the royal family she felt had abused and abandoned her." According to Diana, "I'm much closer to the people at the bottom than the people at the top, and the latter won't forgive me for it." However: "Whenever public attention shifted to Charles, Diana upstaged him with a photo-op.... Charles was toast. Diana was so skillful at manipulating media coverage that she fell into a common trap of great celebrity: She thought she could turn it off when she chose." Diana had actually embarked on a "campaign to paint Charles as unsuitable for the throne," "doing serious damage to the institution of England's royal family." "Others hint at unspeakable motives—such as race, class, and Royalist fervor—in blaming Britain's MI5 or others for Diana's death." (Of course, all the MI#s report to the monarchy.) Mohamed Al Fayed, for example, believes that MI6 assassinated Princess Diana and his son, Dodi, "because she was pregnant and they were about to announce their engagement."[1]

While Diana would steal the limelight in death as well, at least it would be temporary and transitory. Of course, the monarchy would receive substantial press as well: "This is a funeral that has mobilized an entire people, even the people of the whole world," said one observer. Indeed, it also served Charles' ecumenist goals; for example, "A hastily arranged service at St. Paul's Cathedral, where Charles and Diana married in 1981, drew 2,000 mourners from all faiths." Moreover, it was said that it could free Charles to "marry again, in the eyes of the Anglican Church, of which he will be the titular head if he becomes king." (Obviously, Satan's Prince felt so and *did*—like a "tampon.") A columnist had this to say: "Unless I want to get thrown out of the Global Media Conspiracy of Pundits, Commentators & Sundry Scurrilous Knaves, I must write about the death of Diana, Princess of Wales.... [If I were editing a mass-market magazine,] ... I'd be among those waving big money at photographers, which leads to stakeouts and pursuits, and, perhaps, a gruesome auto accident."

To avoid or deflect any implication or claim of impropriety, the Firm at Charles' behest, treated Diana's corpse royally, even draping the royal standard over her casket. Moreover, Queen Elizabeth II protested that "the initial shock of Diana's death was followed by 'disbelief, incomprehension, anger and concern for those who remain,'" adding: "I want to pay tribute to Diana myself. She was an exceptional and gifted human being.... I admired and respected her for her energy and her commitment to others, and especially for her devotion to her two boys." Really? Oddly, princes William and Henry (Harry), attending "regular Sunday church services in Scotland" with father Charles, amazed their vicar "at how dry-eyed and controlled they were." One reporter earlier observed: "National mourning was punctuated by sharp criticism of the British royal family as cold, remote and unfeeling. Amid perhaps the greatest outpouring of public grief in British history, anti-royal anger echoed across newspapers.... 'Not one word has come from a royal lip, not one tear has been shed in public from a royal eye. It is as if no one in the royal family has a soul,' said Britain's largest newspaper, *The Sun*.... 'From the outside looking in, the House of Windsor seems a

---

1. Tom Kelly, "'My husband is planning an accident in my car': Diana's sensational letter is revealed in full," *Mail Online*, 20 Dec. 2007.

cold, compassion-free zone where duty and protocol push emotions into a dark corner,' the popular tabloid said."[1]

Diana's death stands in stark contrast to the subsequent decommissioning of the royal yacht Britannia: "It was one of the most powerful public displays of emotion by the Royal Family in ... years. Stiff upper lips were forgotten as the Queen and even Prince Philip were reduced to tears.... Just three months ago, the Royal Family stood accused of not showing enough emotion in public ahead of Princess Diana's funeral. For the Royal Yacht Britannia, it was a Royal Family transformed. On the rain-swept dockside the Queen choked back tears as she paid an emotional tribute to the vessel and the sailors who had looked after her for the past 44 years. Then, when the Royal Standard was lowered for the last time, the tears flowed — an amazing finale...."[2]

Princess Diana's own testimony. The above information is not materially changed from the 1998 edition of this book. Five years later, in 2003, relevant pre-death testimony from the princess herself began to come to light.

On October 30, 1995, the princess informed Lord Victor Mishcon, who acted as her personal legal representative and general advisor, that she believed her life to be in danger, and that there was a plot to severely injure her *head* or even kill her by means of a car accident; Diana cited "reliable sources." According to Diana, Ms. Tiggy Legge-Bourke, a former royal nanny and now Mrs. Alexandra Pettifer, had her unborn baby murdered, with the child presumably being that of Satan's Prince. Then, ten months before her death, in a handwritten letter dating to October 1996 which she gave to her butler Paul Bur-

1. Larry Kaplow, Cox News Service, "Diana's death a 'conspiracy,'" *The Denver Post,* 18 Oct. 1997, p. 31A. "Aggressive intrusion," *The Denver Post,* 1 Sept. 1997, p. 11B. "Diana's advice: 'Lead from the heart,'" *USA Today,* 2 Sept. 1997, p. 2A. Barbara Slavin, "Diana, Dodi shared sense of not belonging," *USA Today,* 2 Sept. 1997, p. 18A. Marco R. della Cava, "Reassigned a royal status stripped away in her life," *USA Today,* 2 Sept. 1997, p. 2A. Trey Graham, "Flood of conspiracy theories surges through on-line world," *USA Today,* 2 Sept. 1997, p. 18A. George Jahn, The Associated Press, "Billions worldwide to take time to tune in," *The Denver Post,* 7 Sept. 1997, p. 17A. Ed Quillen, "Sometimes lightning strikes," *The Denver Post,* 7 Sept. 1997, p. 2F. Alessandra Stanley, The New York Times, "Struggle for happiness touched women deeply," *The Denver Post,* 7 Sept. 1997, p. 22A. Roxanne Roberts, The Washington Post, "In death, Diana the victor in media war against royals," *The Denver Post,* 7 Sept. 1997, pp. 22A-23A. "Interview believed to have been Diana's last," *The Denver Post,* 7 Sept. 1997, p. 25A. Swardson, "Fayed family denies driver drunk." "Charles, young princes move among mourners," *The Denver Post,* 7 Sept. 1997. Ray Moseley, Chicago Tribune, "What's next for Charles?," *The Denver Post,* 1 Sept. 1997, p. 7A. "Britons mourn loss of 'people's princess,'" *The Denver Post,* 1 Sept. 1997, p. 13A. "Diana emulated, never duplicated," *The Denver Post,* 1 Sept. 1997, p. 14A. David Von Drehle, The Washington Post, "World dazzled by soap opera of icon's life," *The Denver Post,* 1 Sept. 1997, p. 18A. The Associated Press, "Arab media sense plot in Diana's death," *The Denver Post,* 3 Sept. 1997, p. 19A. Dean E. Murphy, Los Angeles Times, "Stiff upper lip prevails," *The Denver Post,* 2 Sept. 1997, p. 4A. William D. Montalbano, Los Angeles Times, "Royals bow to public, expand funeral access," *The Denver Post,* 4 Sept. 1997, p. 1A.
2. Robert Jobson and Sean Rayment, "For Britannia, tears that the Royals couldn't hide," *International Express,* U.S. Ed., 16 Dec. 1997, p. 7.

rell, the princess stated: "This particular phase in my life is the most dangerous—my husband is planning 'an accident' in my car, brake failure & serious head injury in order to make the path clear for him to marry Tiggy. Camillia is nothing but a decoy so we are being used by the man in every sense of the word."[1] According to Burrell, "She certainly felt that 'the system' didn't appreciate her work and that for as long as she was on the scene Prince Charles could never properly move on."[2]

On September 18, 1997, after the princess' death: "Lord Mishcon met with the then Commissioner Sir Paul (now Lord) Condon and then Assistant Commissioner (now Sir) David Veness at New Scotland Yard (NSY), in order to bring the note to their attention. He read out the note (Operation Paget Exhibit VM/1) and emphasised that he was acting in a private capacity rather than on behalf of his firm or the Royal Family."[3] If Diana had it right, that would indicate that Charles, as the "god-king of the wood," sacrificed her as the "goddess of fertility" at a Merovingian and Illuminati ritual site.[4]

Speaking of "most widely viewed" events, there have been several more involving Charles, a number of which, are separaely addressed. Among them, are Yitzhak Rabin's funeral on November 7th 1995; Charles' November 30th 2015 opening of, and central presence at COP21 (i.e., the twenty-first Conference of the Parties UN climate talks) in Paris, France; *knight* Shimon Peres' funeral on September 30th 2016,[5] where Charles wore not only his gold signet ring bearing the Black Prince badge, but also a custom blue *kippah* or "yamaka" (Jewish head covering) bearing it, which due to the badge's three *Vav*-like ostrich feathers, represents 6-6-6; Charles' January 23rd 2020 speech at the Fifth World Holocaust Forum, held at Yad Vashem in Jerusalem; Charles' June 3rd 2020 announcement of Satan's global "Great Reset"—a project *Charles himself* launched the prior month —before the World Economic Forum (WEF); Charles' infamous November 1st 2021 speech at COP26 in Glasgow, Scotland, where he

---

1. Kelly, "'My husband is planning an accident in my car': Diana's sensational letter is revealed in full." For the full letter, see the article at *Mail Online's* web site ("https://www.dailymail.co.uk").
2. Jane Kerr, "Diana Letter Sensation: 'They will try to kill me'," *Mirror.co.uk*, 20 Oct. 2003.
3. "The Operation Paget inquiry report into the allegation of conspiracy to murder Diana, Princess of Wales, and Emad El-Din Mohamed Abdel Moneim Fayed Report," otherwise known as "The [Lord] Stevens Report," Dec. 2006, p. 96.
4. For more information, see the related note and discussion in ch. 4's section, "A Merovingian 'conspiracy of destiny,'" and ch. 7's subsection, "'Organizational' ties to witchcraft," at pp. 79 and 178, respectively.
5. Then Prince Charles stated: "I have always had the greatest admiration for the constancy and determination of [(now deceased)] President Peres' [(anti-God)] work for [(a false satanic)] peace over so many years. I pray that his [chivalrous] legacy will inspire future generations to continue this [(evil)] work." Charles, who "is the Patron of a number of [(unregenerate)] Jewish charities, and is the first member of the Royal family to attend the inauguration of the [UK's (non-Christian)] Chief Rabbi," then "met with current [(at the time)] Israeli President Reuven Rivlin" ("The Prince of Wales attends the funeral of President Shimon Peres in Israel," *PrinceOfWales.gov.uk*, 4 Oct. 2016).

called for "trillions [(ostensibly, of dollars)] at his [(i.e., Satan's)] disposal" (and thus, *Charles' own disposal* once he's satanically possessed); the opening ceremony of the 2022 Commonwealth Games on July 28th, in Birmingham England; the Sptember 10th 2022 Accession Council ceremony, where King Charles III was formally declared; Elizabeth II's funeral and procession on September 19th 2022; and of course, Charles III's own May 6th 2023 coronation and formal crowning. No doubt, there shall yet be others. Who among men may "complete" with all that?

Political affiliations, aspirations, and privileges. King Charles III now is, and Elizabeth II had been, monarch not just of the United Kingdom, but also of Canada, Australia, and New Zealand—though the monarchy's affiliation with Australia has been weakened. By virtue of service to Satan and Charles' position in the monarchy, even as Prince of Wales, he came to enjoy significant authority over those nations, not to mention the British Commonwealth as a whole. Brian Hoey, before Diana's death, stated:

> ....Almost every day ... a large number of people have been 'received by the Prince and Princess of Wales'. These people could range from the commanding officers of service units associated with Their Royal Highnesses, who arrive to be formally presented..., to leaders of Commonwealth countries who personally brief the Prince on matters concerning their particular country. Others who are summoned to the royal presence include businessmen, social workers, artists and politicians, all with one purpose in mind: to keep the Prince and Princess fully informed on the widest variety of issues. Each visitor has his or her own place in the royal scheme of things and, when the day comes that Prince Charles ascends the throne, he and his wife will surely be the most widely informed couple the British monarchy has ever known. This is in part what has given rise to the claims that there is a separate court, but the Queen is fully aware of what is taking place in St James's Palace and she has gladly given her approval....
> Even Margaret Thatcher found that there is no such thing as a free lunch where the Prince and Princess are concerned. When Prime Minister, she was frequently a guest only to find that her influence was needed.... However, no one seems to object to being manipulated in this way....
> ....Many Asians have become very successful and extremely rich businessmen, and the Prince of Wales has not been slow in involving them in his pet projects.... They knew when they accepted the royal invitation that there was going to be a price to pay—and they were delighted to be associated with a project headed by the future king.[1]

Speaking of "the ordinary man in the street," Junor comments: "He cares about them and tries to improve their lot.... He goes to

---

1. Hoey, *Charles & Diana: The Tenth Anniversary,* pp. 102-104, 108.

the trouble spots to ... ask people ... what they think.... Then he gathers together architects, builders, youth unemployment officers —anyone whose services he thinks he can manipulate to good effect —and tells them what he thinks should be done. Prince Charles entertains widely, but as the many top businessmen, media executives and corporation bosses flattered by an invitation from His Royal Highness have soon realized, there is no such thing as a free lunch, not even at Kensington Palace. The Prince dispenses with formalities early on in the meal, and gets straight down to what he would like his guest to do or provide.... His sheer presence turns a mundane event into a major celebration, swamps a factory with orders, ensures that a charity gets a sudden flush of donations." In the words of Satan's Prince: "I can go to all the dinners and banquets on earth, but it's not going to make any difference to the world. What I want to do is be a part of something that does."[1] In fact, Charles, who is "more than capable of carrying off the ritual diplomacy required of him," has traveled worldwide as a "seasoned ambassador" (of sorts) for the United Kingdom.[2] Holden adds:

> Elizabeth II ... has encouraged her son from his earliest adulthood to take an active part in the constitutional process; he reads cabinet papers, and **since becoming a privy councillor in 1977 meets politicians of all hues on an intimate and confidential footing....** ...Prince Charles is constantly exploring new routes toward a more positive role.[3]

> He is the first Prince of Wales [(and now UK monarch)] to have grown up in the era of mass communications, and he has taken pains to master its dominant medium. With a growing list of credits behind him, he is quite at ease in front of the cameras.... Prince Charles likes using television to promote his own multifarious activities and enjoys watching himself on the video cassettes he keeps of all his appearances.[4]

The *International Express* comments: "The Prince's views certainly have a contemporary ring to them. He may not have his heart in defending the faith. [Yet] it appears he would have no trouble at all defending political correctness."[5] Adam Platt tells us, "On issues close to his heart," Satan's Prince, who [(yet)] "meets regularly with members of the cabinet," has been known to "barrage government ministers with unsolicited advice," giving them "memos and position papers."[6] That is not all: Charles has also exercised the obscure

---

1. Junor, pp. 12-13, 247, 249.
2. Holden, *PRINCE CHARLES,* p. 268.
3. Holden, *PRINCE CHARLES,* p. 38.
4. Holden, *PRINCE CHARLES,* p. 241.
5. "Keeping faith," *International Express,* U.S. Ed. No. 132, 29 June — 5 July 1994, p. 8.
6. Platt, pp. 113, 116.

"Queen's consent" procedure (now "King's consent") "to alter legislation to benefit" his or the royal family's "private interests"—using it, for example, "to compel government ministers to secretly change a proposed law to benefit his landed estate." "Ministers must obtain the consent of the Queen and the prince [(now the King and Prince William)] before relevant legislation can be approved by parliament. This procedure is different than the better known procedure of royal assent, a formality.... During her [(Elizabeth II's)] reign, ministers have been required to secure approval from the Queen or her son [Charles] for more than 1,000 parliamentary acts, before they were implemented."[1] (Who among the public knew? Not many.) Now, they must do so from Charles or William. The former, per Junor, "detests bureaucracy and red tape above practically everything else."[2]

In July 1970, one year after his formal investiture as Prince of Wales, he met with then President Richard Nixon at the White House in Washington. Mr. Nixon recorded this account:

> From news accounts in the British and American press I expected to meet a rather callow, superficial youth with no particular interest in or understanding of world affairs. His conduct completely dispelled that image.
>
> He was serious without being dull, dignified without being pompous, respectful without being deferential. We discussed the whole range of East-West relations, NATO, the Third World countries, and the attitude of young people toward government in the US and Britain.
>
> His perception and knowledge with regard to developments in the Commonwealth nations was greater than that of many State Department professionals. Without crossing the line of interfering in British governmental policies, he expressed agreement with my long-held conviction that Britain must continue to play a role on the world stage—particularly in NATO and in those nations in Africa and Asia where the legacy of the British parliamentary system and the common law is so essential if ordered freedom is to survive.
>
> I told Mrs. Nixon after our meeting that the British and American media greatly underestimated him as a student of world affairs and as a man....[3]

King Charles III is the most accomplished Prince of Wales, and is perhaps one of the most accomplished men, in history. He "has had a far broader education than any of his predecessors, attending school and university [as Prince of Wales,] and mixing with a large number of ordinary people."[4] In fact, few men could ever hope to ri-

1. Rob Evans, David Pegg and Severin Carrell, "Revealed: how Prince Charles pressured ministers to change law to benefit his estate," *Guardian,* 28 June 2022.
2. Junor, p. 117.
3. Holden, *PRINCE CHARLES,* pp. 262-263, 327.
4. "A Sense of Duty," *Majesty,* Nov. 1992, Vol. 13, No. 11, p. 14.

val the sheer magnitude and diversity of what Charles, had by 1998, already accomplished. In this regard, King Charles III again takes after (now roasting) Prince Philip, who, despite his lack of a university education, was himself remarkably accomplished, having a list of "various presidencies, decorations, patronages, foreign honours, membership of a host of clubs and associations, university honours, and so on," that "is a staggering, even awesome, testimony to his involvement in hundreds of organisations."[1] To call the *pre*-king Charles a "renaissance man," almost seems like a "punishable" understatement: As a royal ambassador, public speaker, university graduate, naval commander and ship's captain, frogman and commando, colonel-in-chief of *ten* army regiments, air force wing commander, pilot of military fighter jets and helicopters, as well as civilian aircraft, parachutist, race-car driver, international polo-player and national team's captain, jockey, steeplechaser, skier, hunter, painter, would-be actor, dancer, singer, and musician, not to mention knight and "Doctor of Laws," "the Prince of Wales has won the respect of the world."[2] (As king, Charles III is *over* the entire UK military, including its nuclear and other WMDs.) Hoey remarks, "Prince Charles is also one of the world's great communicators, being able to converse easily with youngsters from deprived inner-city ghettos or with farm labourers…, and making them feel that what they have to say is worth listening to."[3] A fawning Junor comments: "His ideas are sound, his heart is in the right place, and he has a remarkable gift for communicating with the man in the street and understanding his needs. Furthermore, he cares about those needs, and has the clout among businessmen and politicians to make mountains move."[4] Of then Prince Charles, Holden adds:

> He is Earl of Chester, Duke of Cornwall, Duke of Rothesay, Earl of Carrick and Baron of Renfrew, Lord of the Isles and Great Steward of Scotland, Knight of the Most Noble Order of the Garter, Knight of the Most Ancient and Most Noble Order of the Thistle, Great Master and Principal Knight Grand Cross of the Most Honorable Order of the Bath. He is personal aide-de-camp to Queen Elizabeth II; commander, Royal Navy; wing commander, Royal Air Force; colonel-in-chief of ten regiments; member of a dozen international orders of chivalry; president, patron, or member of some two hundred clubs, charities,[5] committees, and learned organizations.

---

1. Judd, *Prince Philip,* p. 248. For an amazing yet abridged list of Prince Philip's (mostly former) titles, patronages, presidencies, honorary citizenships, foreign honors, honorary degrees, and past publications, see pp. 248-252 of the same work.
2. Spink, p. 24. Hoey, *Charles & Diana: The Tenth Anniversary,* p. 43. Junor, p. 65.
3. Hoey, *Charles & Diana: The Tenth Anniversary,* p. 116.
4. Junor, p. 16. *Charles & Diana: A Royal Family Album,* p. 54.
5. As of 2023, Satan's Prince was patron of *over four-hundred* "charitable organizations" globally.

A thousand years of history merge in this ... desperately well-meaning man.... He has a quick wit, a talent for mimicry, a sharp tongue.... He is a countryman at heart, but would rather like to have been an actor. He is proud, ambitious, romantic, and anxious to carve himself a place in history.

....He expects the deference due to his office, takes its pomp and circumstance very seriously, [and] enjoys the archaic rituals of royal ceremonial....

....His birthright provides incomparable material comfort and international respect, adulation, even awe. Government departments look after various aspects of his business.... On his birthday flags fly, guns sound, and judges don their scarlet robes....

....Every word he speaks is remembered or written down. His presence unnerves people..., they lose the power of speech..., they fight to touch him as if he were divine.[1]

Indeed, according to Burnet, there are those who expect Prince Charles to "walk on water."[2] (Will recovery from a fatal wound suffice?) Cathcart remarks: "Enter a dragon, a dragon in a red coat. Throughout the summer of 1974, Prince Charles told anyone who would listen how much he was looking forward to flying helicopters.... Hence the dragon, the call-sign from Cranwell dredged up in new guise as the Red Dragon of Wales. The Prince approved the scarlet and gold dragon arm-flashes of his training unit with much pleasure."[3] While a lieutenant and helicopter pilot in the Royal Navy, then Prince Charles' uniform included a "Red Dragon" patch bearing both that text and the Welsh dragon, which he wore and displayed on his right shoulder.[4] Indeed, as earlier mentioned, Charles was himself nicknamed "the Red Dragon."

Likewise, reported U.S. Secret Service *code names* assigned to Satan's Prince, from 1971, are "Unicorn," "Principal," and ostensibly "Daily."[5] Might President Reagan also have referred to Charles as "Unicorn," or submitted to Charles as the "Principal," when Satan's Prince visited the White House? We are speaking of *the* AntiChrist.

Brown, in her decades-old biography on Charles, adds: "Whenever Prince Charles is photographed or filmed, he is almost invariably surrounded by people. He meets as many new people every

---

1. Holden, *PRINCE CHARLES*, pp. xxv-xxvii.
2. Burnet, *In Private—In Public, THE PRINCE AND PRINCESS OF WALES*, p. 84.
3. Cathcart, p. 147. Opposite p. 121, Cathcart shows a black-and-white photograph of Charles wearing such an arm-flash (cf. a patch) in a Wessex 5 Commando helicopter.
4. See, for example, picture id "592623067" at GettyImages.com (on the Internet), described thus: "Prince Charles (left) gesturing upwards as he sits in the cockpit of a Royal Navy Wessex helicopter with his instructor, Lieutenant Commander Alan McGregor, during a flying lesson at the Royal Naval Air Station in Yeovilton, Somerset, September 9th 1974." In color (see "https://www.telegraph.co.uk/ multimedia/archive/02727/Charles65_1974_2727157k.jpg"), the patch itself is red, with the text and dragon ostensibly embossed in an off-white color.
5. E.g., "Prince Charles," *NNDB.com*, 2019; and "Secret Service code name," *Wikipedia.org*, 1 July 2022.

week as most of us meet in a year, and he must rate as one of the most widely recognized men in the world today."[1]

Accustomed to receiving red-carpet treatment,[2] Charles and his family are also quite wealthy. Though we'll later see current estimates versus likely reality, here are some from the early 1990s:

> By FORTUNE's calculation, the Queen is the richest woman in the world and No. 4 overall, behind only the Sultan of Brunei ($25 billion), Saudi Arabia's King Fahd and his family ($18 billion) and America's Mars candy-bar clan ($12.5 billion). FORTUNE estimates Elizabeth's worth at $11.7 billion, but other appraisers believe it to be much higher, given such personal assets as her race-horses, stamp collection and art acquisitions. Charles, meanwhile, is believed to be worth about $536 million, which would still place him among Britain's 40 wealthiest people.[3]

> As one of the richest men in the world, Prince Charles can afford anything he or his family wants, and they do not stint themselves. Their homes ... contain every conceivable luxury, and everything that they eat, drink, wear or otherwise use is the very best that money can buy.[4]

> ....Elizabeth II is reputed to be the world's richest woman. But royalty has its privileges.... Consider that ... Prince Charles, voluntarily pays 25 percent of his estimated $5 million annual income in tax. Also, that queenly $11 billion net-worth figure is misleading. Some $10.5 billion of it, including the $4.5 billion royal art collection and $500 million in crown jewels, is controlled by the state and therefore belongs to the queen in name only. Her five official residences too are owned by the government.... Some royal watchers argue that the [queen's] portfolio's true value is nearer $700 million.[5]

According to Lacey, "It is quite possible—probable indeed—that Queen Elizabeth II has private investments now worth tens of millions of dollars whose precise nature and size is known to a very small group of people indeed, and whose identity, shrouded in a complex pattern of nominees and holding companies, is effectively beyond the reach of any outside enquiry through existing legal—or even illegal—channels without her cooperation."[6] But are such estimates even real? Might they serve as part of a massive con for public consumption? What if the British Monarchy substantially *owns* the land and resources of the nations that fete it as their own?

---

1. Brown, *PRINCE CHARLES*, p. 155.
2. *People Weekly*, Extra: Summer 1988, p. 46.
3. Richard Lacayo and Jonathan Cooper, "Are These Folks Loaded, or What?," *People Weekly*, Extra: Fall 1990, p. 118.
4. Hoey, *Charles & Diana: The Tenth Anniversary*, pp. 20-23.
5. John Sims, *Money Magazine*, "Queen's 1993 tax bill no small matter," *The Denver Post*, 7 Feb. 1993, p. 4G.
6. Lacey, *Majesty*, p. 279.

Actually, the above claims are so *grossly low,* as later seen, that they may not even begin to convey the true nature and scope of the wealth—amassed across multiple centuries through succeeding generations of royals—actually pertaining to the British monarchy. In the 1990s, Lyndon H. LaRouche Jr.'s *Executive Intelligence Review* alleged the "real" figure to be in the vicinity of *nine trillion* dollars! That is, the British monarchy may have (vastly) more "riches" at its disposal, through its "complex pattern of nominees and holding companies," than the combined wealth of *all* of *Fortune* magazine's listed billionaires. (Later, we'll dive a bit deeper.)

The power of the British monarchy goes well beyond influence, fame and wealth. Although it heads the most elite of international orders, the Order of the Garter, it also plays significant behind-the-scenes roles in several other pagan and occult orders. Prince Philip, as a typical example, holds or held the following foreign honors:

> Order of the Superior Sun, Afghanistan; Grand Cross of the Order of San Martin, Argentina; Grand Cross of Honour, Austria; Grand Cordon of the Order of Leopold, Belgium; Hon. Member of the Most Esteemed Family Order, Brunei; Medal of the Order of Dogwood, Canada; Knight of the Order of the Elephant, Denmark; Chain of the Most Exalted Order of the Queen of Sheba, Ethiopia; Grand Cross of the Order of the White Rose, Finland; Grand Cross of the Order of George I, Greece; Grand Cordon of the Supreme Order of the Chrysanthemum, Japan; Chevalier-Grand-Croix, Order of the Golden Lion, Luxembourg; Commander of the Order of the Golden Ark, Netherlands; Grand Cross of the Order of St Olaf, Norway; Grand Collar of the Order of Prince Henry the Navigator, Portugal; Member of the Distinguished Order of Izzuddin, Republic of Maldives; Hon. Member, Darjah Utama Temasek, Singapore; Member of the Order of the Seraphim, Sweden; Grand Cross, Yugoslav Star; Grand Cordon, National Order of the Leopard, Zaire; 1st Class Order of the Brilliant Star, Zanzibar.[1]

Ties to the New Age Movement, the occult, and false religions. Is it reasonable, given what we know so far, to think that the unbelieving world might one day hail Charles as the "cosmic Christ" of the "New Age," having succeeded to a "second coming" as defined by Merovingian cabalists? At least one small group of Melanesian villagers, the Iounhanan tribe in the New Hebrides' [(i.e., Vanuatu's) island of Tanna], has already succumbed to similar cases of "mistaken identities," starting with Prince Philip: "A group of villagers in the New Hebrides islands in the Pacific Ocean believe that the Duke of Edinburgh is their Messiah [(i.e., the incarnation of Tanna's Mount Yasur 'volcano spirit')] and that he will soon return to them to cure all sickness and to make the old young once more. The two- [(now

---

1. Judd, *Prince Philip*, p. 252.

over four-)] hundred followers of the cult expect the Duke to restore paradise on earth, and to resume his rightful place as a Melanesian.... The villagers also believe that Prince Philip runs the Commonwealth and has deliberately kept his true identity a secret from the Queen. They are convinced that when the royal yacht *Britannia* passed close to their island in 1974, the Duke confessed to his wife that 'he was really a Melanesian Messiah and that the marriage could not last'. There has even been an authenticated exchange of gifts between the worshippers and the object of their veneration.... On 19 November 1979, a Buckingham Palace spokesman admitted the exchange...."[1] With that prince's April 2021 relocation to Hell, many of those confused pagans—who under Chief Charlie, feasted on a cooked pig to mourn (their island's allegedly) "black man ... turned white" Philip, in a "papal conclave-like ceremony"—may through their "magic and spiritualism," now so-honor his "successor" son: Charles Philip Arthur George.[2] For such spiritual suckers, Satan's stars are now finally "aligning."

As pointed out earlier, the AntiChrist and his antichristian denials are explicitly mentioned only four times in the Bible. Based upon the scriptures, whoever denies the unique divinity of The Father and The Son, who are eternally united as One, is antichristian (1 John 2:18-29). Further, any spirit or person who denies that Jesus has come—and indeed will return—in the flesh (i.e., in the physical body in which He was resurrected from the dead), is antichristian (1 John 4:1-6); for this is the "doctrine of The Christ [Messiah]" (2 John 6-11). All cultists (e.g., Freemasons, Mormons, Jehovah's Witnesses, New Agers, etc.), participants in false religions and counterfeit "Christianities" (e.g., those who adhere to rabbinic Judaism, Buddhists, Hindus, many or even most Roman Catholics, Muslims, Christian Scientists, Scientologists, Unitarians, etc.), agnostics, and atheists are antichristian *by definition*.

Besides his prominent roles in the Order of the Garter, the Illuminati, and the Committee of 300, rumors about Charles' occult activities and his interest in various forms of eastern and New Age mysticism abound. Indeed, even Diana, who felt "centered" (e.g., through *tai chi*), was involved in occultism and New Age philosophies (e.g., acupuncture, aromatherapy, astrology, healing crystals, homeopathy, hypnotherapy, and shiatsu massage), and she was said to engage in "reflections on The Prophet by Kahlil Gibran," having

---

1. Judd, *Prince Philip*, p. 227. For a photograph of a member of the Iounhanan tribe holding a picture icon of Prince Philip, see ibid., no. 61, between pp. 224-225.
2. Levi Parsons (for Daily Mail Australia and AFP), "Remote South Pacific tribe who worship Prince Philip debate replacing him as their god with his son Charles in papal conclave-like ceremony and mourn their fallen deity for 100 days," *Daily Mail*, 14 Apr. 2021.

herself supposedly "come to rival Shirley MacLaine."[1] In other words, she had "an obsessive interest in astrologers [(e.g., Penny Thornton)], mystics, and clairvoyants."[2] "The New Age Princess," that is, "was enmeshed in a shallow world of psychics, astrologers, fashion, aromatherapy, colonic irrigation, bulimia, self-mutilation, adultery, TV confessions, tell-all books, tapped phones, international playboys and Furies swooping down on her with cameras;" she was "the fallen goddess."[3] Likewise, Prince Andrew and his ex-wife Fergie support "Fergie's alternative health guru Jack Temple .... [who uses] energy inducing rocks and poison detecting pendulums."[4] Fergie has also enjoyed the services of "one Madame Vasso—a psychic who once performed 'healing sessions' for her client under a blue plastic pyramid," and Fergie's personal trainer, Josh Salzmann, likes to think that "her exercise sessions have helped her to center herself."[5]

In March 1977, Charles visited Ghana, where "<u>he sat on a throne while he was crowned *Charles Naba Nampasa*—which [is] translated as *Charles Who Helps Mankind*.</u>"[6] Then in July 1977, while on an official visit to Alberta, Canada, to "commemorate an 1877 treaty with Blackfoot Indians near Calgary,"[7] *a Red Indian tribe made Charles an honorary chieftain.*[8] Brown comments: "As a non-smoker Charles must have been relieved when the traditional peace-pipe rather ominously refused to smoke. But he willingly agreed to don the traditional costume of a tribal chief for the second time in four months. On this occasion it was not 'Naba Charles Mampasa' who appeared, but 'Chief Red Crow' of the Kainai tribe. Complete with buckskins, feathered head-dress and war-paint, the new chief joined in the tribal dances <u>in honour of the Sun, the Moon, the Grass and, inexplicably, the Chicken.</u>"[9] Heald and Mayo Mohs add: "Charles as Chief evokes an eerie echo of another Prince of Wales, his great-uncle David (Edward VIII). When David visited Canada in 1919, he was acclaimed 'Chief Morning Star'" (cf. Rev 22:16).[10]

---

1. Robert Lacey, "Diana, What Happened and Why," *LIFE,* Aug. 1992, pp. 31-32; Susie Pearson, "Diana," *Ladies' Home Journal,* June 1991, p. 132; and "The Diana Tapes," *People* weekly, 20 Oct. 1997, pp. 106, 108. **Please note that although much is, not *all* acupuncture, aromatherapy, homeopathy, or hypnotherapy is occult.**
2. "Princess Di will rebound, new book says," *The Denver Post,* 8 Nov. 1994, p. 2A.
3. Maureen Dowd, "Princess a prisoner of New Age," *The Denver Post,* 4 Sept. 1997, p. 11B.
4. Janice Min, "ROYAL WATCH: Navy Blues", *People Weekly,* 5 Aug. 1996, p. 66.
5. Michelle Green and Simon Perry, "Rue, Britannia", *People Weekly,* 25 Nov. 1996, pp. 52-55. For more information, see *Fergie: The Very Private Life of the Duchess of York* by Madame Vasso.
6. Dale, pp. 9, 12.
7. Tim Heald and Mayo Mohs, *The Man Who Will Be King, H.R.H.* (New York: Arbor House, 1979), n. pag.
8. Holden, *PRINCE CHARLES,* p. 329.
9. Brown, *PRINCE CHARLES,* p. 138. Actually, inasmuch as chickens lay eggs, the chicken here represented the *giver of life.*
10. Heald and Mohs, n. pag.

In August 1984, "Prince Charles visited Papua New Guinea ... to open the new Parliament building and was made 'supreme chief' on the island of Manus."[1] During his installation as the new "supreme chief," Satan's Prince wore a headband and necklace composed of wild-boars' teeth, while holding forth a carved chieftain's spear in his right hand. Besides wild-boars' teeth, the headband had a central cross.[2] Charbonneau-Lassay wrote: "In all the ancient literature the wild boar appears as typical of ferocity, independence, and fearless brutality.... But the Middle Ages recognized only the wild boar of David, who ravaged the Lord's vineyard [(Ps 80:13; see 80:8-19)]. It was regarded as the 'evil beast' of the Apocalypse, the Antichrist."[3] Previously, in 1966, Satan's Prince had visited Papua and New Guinea, "so that the native tribesmen might see 'the Great Son of the Queen.'" While there: "He shook thousands of hands, hiked through the jungle, waded rivers not immune from leeches and crocodiles, downed mysterious liquid concoctions at native feasts and was then rightly decked with necklaces of dogs' teeth as a symbol of courage.... One festive evening he watched dancers, as he noted, 'in magnificent head-dresses of bird of paradise feathers, cassowary feathers, hornbill beaks and chicken feathers' and then joined in, with his party."[4] Like boars (swine), dogs are not favored in scripture (see Matt 7:6; cf. Ex 11:7; Ps 22:16, 22:20, 59:5-7, 59:14-15; Prov 26:11; Isa 56:9-11, 66:3-4; Jer 15:3; Phil 3:2; 2 Pet 2:22 {see 2:18-22}; Rev 22:15). Charles of course, revels in being associated with both swine and dogs. (Who is thinking of Camilla? Be honest.)

More recently (in 2011), Tanzania's Maasai cattle herders (and rustlers) named Charles "The Helper of the Cows." "Charles's new name in the tribe's language is Oloishiru Ingishu, which literally translates as 'the one who makes cows cry'. According to Mathayo Rimba Olemirai, a village elder..., the animals would cry, or call, for their helper because of the support he gives them. His fellow herders were less impressed, though, when they heard later that Charles's cow empire stretched to only 800 cattle. 'We'd expect a rich man around here to have about 2,000 cattle,' said Thomas Lelboko, 48."[5] In reality, rather than helping cows, Charles makes them —and hungry humans—"cry," by seeking a global reduction in their numbers, alleging that the methane they exhale harms Earth's climate! (Yes, Satan's servants are fools.)

---

1. Burnet, *In Person, THE PRINCE AND PRINCESS OF WALES,* p. 20.
2. For a color photograph of this event, see *Charles & Diana: A Royal Family Album,* p. 48; or see Junor, between pp. 150-151.
3. Charbonneau-Lassay, pp. 143, 145.
4. Cathcart, pp. 64-65.
5. Richard Palmer, "Prince Charles becomes Maasai tribesman," *Daily Express,* 9 Nov. 2011.

In 1985, after asking Charles about his interest in spiritualism and mysticism, Burnet gave this account of his response:

"....I've seen articles shown to me saying that I play with Ouija boards. I don't even know what they are. I've never seen one. I spend my entire time, apparently, trying to get in touch with Lord Mountbatten, and all sorts of other things. The answer is I don't, nor would I necessarily want to. I might as well say it, I might as well emphasize it, because I'm fed up with getting letters from people all the time saying 'Don't touch the Ouija boards'."

The Prince believes the reports about him on this began as a result of his admiration for the late Arthur Koestler, the author who was greatly interested in parapsychology [(the study of demonic powers)] and left a bequest for a professional chair for its study in a British university.... Told that no British university might take up the offer, the Prince, as Chancellor of the University of Wales, wrote to the Vice-Chancellor saying it would be a great pity to lose the bequest.... The Prince thinks that the publicity began with just that scientific proposal.

"What I find so annoying is that it should be reduced to this level of absurdity. I'm not interested in the occult, or dabbling in black magic or any of these kinds of things or, for that matter, strange forms of mysticism. I'm purely interested in being open-minded."[1]

Of false prophets, Jesus said, "You will know them by their fruits." Charles' fruits are very clearly not those of a Christian, but of a pagan who is "open-minded" to the world's false religions and cults. During a five-day stopover in Japan in 1970, for example, then Prince Charles "dined with Emperor Hirohito—forging one of the many links of statecraft that culminated in the Queen and Prince Philip's 1975 state visit to Japan—and was ready [the] next day for ... a round of temples, castles and palaces in the ancient Imperial capital.... The abbot who showed him around the temple of the great bronze Buddha [in Kyoto,] was equally impressed by his intelligent questions on Shinto philosophy. 'I found that what the old man was saying I had believed, without realising it, all my life,' Prince Charles said afterwards—encouraging words ... not inexplicable to a younger generation, who seek the common truths of religion rather than the differences.... [Of course,] ... four years later the Prince opened a new Sony factory in [Welsh] Glamorgan."[2] In November 1980, as yet another example, Satan's Prince toured India and Nepal, where "he undertook a three-day trek in the Himalayas ... and also

---

1. Burnet, *In Person, THE PRINCE AND PRINCESS OF WALES*, p. 45. Also see Dale, pp. 225, 227-229. Junor, rather ignorantly, states: "Stories appeared saying that he had become a vegetarian, that he had given up shooting, that he was dabbling in spiritualism and had been attempting to reach Lord Mountbatten with a ouija board.... It was all fantasy" (p. 221). The ouija board claim *continues*.
2. Cathcart, pp. 112-113. Dale notes the same experience, adding that Satan's Prince "told an interviewer that [in Japan,] 'he felt he'd come home' at last" (pp. 200-201).

visited the Golden Temple at Amristar," at which he did homage.[1] In 1988, Charles and Princess Diana "visited the Temple of the Emerald Buddha," and "in 1989, Prince Charles reached to touch a special statue of Buddha in the world's oldest Buddhist temple."[2] On the evening of February 28, 1996, Satan's Prince visited "a Hindu temple in North London," happily taking a red mark on the center of his forehead![3] (Much more like the above, has since transpired.)

John Dale, who has been an authority on the occult beliefs, practices, and activities of Britain's Royal Family, and Satan's Prince in particular, wrote a relatively thorough book titled, *The Prince and the Paranormal: The Psychic Bloodline of the Royal Family*. The following several pages of information are quoted from Dale's book:

> On March 6, 1977, one of the world's best-known amateur aviators bounced the tyres of his trusty Andover down onto the overheated runway of [Kenya's] Nairobi Airport....
>
> For this was no ordinary safari. It was something much more than that—an exploration into Africa's soul and, simultaneously, into the soul of the Prince of Wales.
>
> So, on March 16, it was a handsome, bronzed and fit Charles who emerged from nine days in the wilderness, reassured, rejuvenated and spiritually refreshed....[4]
>
> Thus a new Prince was born, with a drive to challenge long-respected orthodoxy and to become the torch-bearer of radical, revolutionary ideas about how every one of us should live....
>
> ....For, there is evidence that deep inside himself, the Prince has become a super-ecumenist—somebody who believes that each of the world's religions—including Christianity—contains a relative truth, rather than an absolute one.
>
> For some time members of the Royal Family, especially his parents, had been growing anxious about the way he was making this clear to those who could read the signs and recognize the codewords. At first, for more than two years, the Prince seemed oblivious of the very real dangers that were awaiting him. Then, late in 1985, the menace to his own position and potentially to the Crown was brought home to him. As the truth

1. Burnet, *In Person*, THE PRINCE AND PRINCESS OF WALES, p. 45.
2. Hoey, *Charles & Diana: The Tenth Anniversary*, pp. 108-109.
3. Green, Denworth, Smith, and Wright, "PRINCE-LESS DIANA," *People Weekly*, 11 Mar. 1996, pp. 76-78. For a picture of then Prince Charles walking barefoot in a Hindu temple in India, see *Charles & Diana: A Royal Family Album*, p. 48.
4. John Dale, *The Prince and the Paranormal: The Psychic Bloodline of the Royal Family* (London: W.H. Allen & Co. Plc, 1986), pp. 9, 11. Neither the London-based publisher nor the Australian author of *The Prince and the Paranormal* could be contacted to obtain permission to quote the work's material, despite several calls to the United Kingdom and Australia. Dale's book was officially **banned** in the UK by Queen Elizabeth II, and its publisher went out of business. However, due to the important nature of the material for this work, it was deemed a necessary risk nonetheless to quote it. As stated in 1998, "The author apologizes if having done so results in any copyright infringement or hardship to Mr. Dale, and he wishes to thank Mr. Dale in advance for his gracious support in this endeavor." Although the work is officially banned in the UK, the reader may find a copy on Amazon or eBay. Copies may also be available at a local library, or through an inter-library loan.

dawned, he belatedly began a damage-limitation exercise and tried to play the matter down.

He resorted to ridicule. 'It really is quite extraordinary,' he said. 'As far as I can make out, I'm about to become a Buddhist monk, or live halfway up a mountain or only eat grass. I'm not quite as bad as that.'

He employed flat denials. 'I'm not interested in the occult, or dabbling in black magic or any of these kind of things or, for that matter, strange forms of mysticism,' he replied to the 'approved' questions of Sir Alastair Burnet in a television interview.

But the truth is that the Prince has come to hold beliefs that many of his future subjects will find strange and questionable. They allow him to put aside rationalism, for instance, and to surrender to psychic influences. In a word, he has become absorbed in the *paranormal*—that is, phenomena which cannot be explained by modern science.

Here are some of the beliefs that this book will show he holds:

Coincidences are *signposts*—when he encounters one, he analyses it to see which path it is directing him along.

Dreams can foretell the future—for this purpose, he has tried keeping a dream diary and pen at his bedside.

Modern medicine must incorporate the psychic, spiritual and the paranormal.

Much can be learned from ancient prophecy systems such as I-Ching, astrology, and divination by pendulum.

All religions are ultimately one.

In addition the Prince appears to believe himself to be psychic.

It was in 1982 that the Prince first hinted publicly at such unusual spiritual beliefs. Then followed a period in which he attempted to discuss them as openly as possible. He saw himself as a sort of missionary, lending his prestige to a neglected but very worthy cause. The outcome, however, left him disappointed and even a little bitter....

The plain truth was that his intellectual and spiritual concepts were way above the heads of his audience, with the result that instead of being greeted as **a 'pointer'**—his word for someone **who guides mankind**[1] onto the right path—he was treated as a crank. The tabloid press looked upon him as a freak and his personal reputation was put at risk....

....After all, this was not a joke to the Prince. It was religion—and on that subject, as always, he was deadly serious....

'It was the most extraordinary thing,' he [(then Prince Charles)] told the writer Anne de Courcy. 'I was sitting at my desk at the time and I happened to look at my bookshelf and my eyes suddenly settled on a book about Paracelsus.' (Paracelsus was a sixteenth century physician who believed in an occult cosmic unity and, like the Prince, considered that all religions were part of a greater whole.) 'So I took the book down and read it and as a result I tried to make a speech around Paracelsus and perhaps a re-look at what he was saying and the ideas he propounded—wasn't it time to think again about the relationship between mind and body, or body and spirit?' ...

....It is a long sentence but, because of its half-hidden meanings, an important one. 'Perhaps,' he said, 'we just have to accept it is *God's will* that the unorthodox individual is doomed to years of frustration, ridicule

---

1. The title *Mahdi,* for Islam's coming deliverer, means "to guide."

and failure in order to act out his role in the scheme of things until his day arrives and mankind is ready to receive his message[1]—a message which he probably finds hard to explain himself, but which he knows comes from *a far deeper source than conscious thought.'* (Author's italics.) The irony is that the Prince could easily have been talking about himself.

....At one stage Prince Charles, although committed to Christianity, was also somewhat unsure about certain aspects of such matters, feeling there was a lack of positive evidence. Then, beginning in 1977, he began to climb off the fence and to line up with the mixed bag of visionaries, intellectuals, cranks and lunatics who say there are other planes of existence tangled inside and around the one which we inhabit.

The person who helped convince him was a writer and explorer, and a former political adviser to the Prince's favourite uncle, Lord Mountbatten. He is Renaissance Man reborn, a benign intellectual and the major single influence in the Prince's stage by stage spiritual development over the last ten years. His name: Laurens van der Post....[2]

Through all his rich and sometimes perilous experience, van der Post had never lost touch with what he considered to be the African side of his mind. He continued to cling to his belief that dreams contained, in effect, messages. He was sceptical of the way Western people placed too much reliance upon reasoning. He considered that intuition could sometimes offer much more valuable guidance than rational thought. He also believed that coincidences should not be ignored but warranted careful interpretation.

....[He] was introduced by his wife Ingaret to a man whose ideas would come to dominate much of the remainder of his life and, through him, radicalize the mind of the future King of England. That man was Carl Gustav Jung....[3]

What was it [that] van der Post believed?

First, ... he ... believed that dreams offered guidance as to future decisions. They were incapable of falsehood and were the true source of mythology, religion, legend and art.

Second, he considered coincidences to be equally meaningful, that they should not be ignored and that they indicated man's relationship with the cosmos.

Third, he thought that psychic intuition—listening with his 'inner ear'—was sometimes a better basis for decision-making than reasoning. He considered that Western man had come to rely too heavily upon rationalism.

Fourth, he believed in a world of spirit gods, able to aid or hinder ordinary mortals, sometimes even threatening their lives. Evidence for this lat-

---

1. E.g., ca. 44:45, "Inside The Mind Of King Charles III | The Madness of Prince Charles," *Absolute History,* 11 Oct. 2019, at "https://www.youtube.com/watch?v=2FNoNVXnSjo&t=2675s" on YouTube.
2. Dale, pp. 13-19.
3. Dale, p. 25. Junor too notes "the important part that intuition played in his life" (p. 2). According to Junor, van der Post "knew more about the African people and their spiritual heritage not only than any European alive, but more than most Africans themselves. He spoke several native dialects and loved Africa." Then Prince Charles was captivated by "the wise thoughts on man and nature that spilled forth from the elderly man." Satan's Prince was taken by van der Post's "fascination with the inner self," as well as his "inordinate interest in dreams" and Jungian interpretation. Van der Post's grandfather had taught him about Joseph's deliverance of Egypt and Israel through "his dreaming." Van der Post therefore "encouraged Charles to trust his intuition, to listen to his dreams and to pay attention to coincidence" (Junor, pp. 110-112, 220).

ter conviction—that such benign and malign spirits existed—was displayed before him while he was in the Kalahari Desert in southern Africa in the 1950s making a documentary about the native Bushmen living there.

Van der Post witnessed how his filming party became jinxed because one of its members shot dead a steenbuck, thereby breaking a promise not to spill blood on sacred territory. After that, they were viciously attacked twice by huge swarms of stinging bees which he sincerely came to suspect were dispatched by angry spirit gods. Then perfectly reliable equipment began to fail for no reason whatsoever. And evidently their Bushman guide, Samutchoso, was tossed over backwards by an unseen force when he knelt to pray. Finally, van der Post feared that even their Land-rovers might be cursed and they would be stranded in the desert to die.

He described how he watched Samutchoso go into a trance. The Bushman apparently contacted the spirit gods who conveyed the message that they were offended by the lack of respect shown by the party.

In all seriousness, van der Post decided to try to make amends. Before leaving, he wrote a letter to the spirits—a letter which, even to those accompanying him, seemed rather strange.

The letter began by begging for the pardon of spirits for any unintended display of disrespect. Van der Post flattered and praised them, saying how a cave painting of an eland—the Bushmen's most important religious symbol—showed the spirits could make flesh and blood create beyond their own physical constraints. Then, virtually as a penitent, he offered them his profound contrition and asked for forgiveness. Finally, he hoped that others who followed in his party's footsteps might not make their mistakes and would show the spirits the respect they deserved....

From that moment, noted van der Post later, his feeling of frustration lifted as he seemed to break through into another dimension of life.

On other occasions with the Bushmen, van der Post encountered additional paranormal phenomena, these seemingly connected with telepathic powers....

These then were some of the stories that Prince Charles learned about van der Post during the period when the two men spent many hours sitting together at Buckingham Palace....

And yet they were not the most astonishing stories in the Afrikaner's repertoire, the stories that must have seized the attention of Prince Charles. These were the ones concerning Jung....[1]

....Over many years Jung had analysed 67,000 dreams. In addition to living with the Elgonyi in Kenya, he had spent much time interviewing Red Indians and Negroes in the United States. He toured the world in order to study mythology and religious development, particularly of the Chinese, Tibetans, Indians, Greeks and Babylonians.

From all this work he deduced that the minds of people completely separated by space, time and culture still contained much material in common. He said that some of this material came from outside the personal experience of those who possessed it. If it was not part of the *personal* unconscious, he asked, then where was it from? To his own question, Jung answered that it must come from somewhere else, from a force equally influencing all mankind—a force which he labelled the Collective Unconscious.

---

1. Dale, pp. 28-30.

In a letter to van der Post, Jung told him that although he could not say what God was, his work proved empirically that the pattern of God existed throughout all mankind.

Jung became positive that the Collective Unconscious contained all the fundamental religious symbols and was the repository of all religious aspirations....

Van der Post's encounter with Jung ended the feeling of spiritual isolation that the Afrikaner had suffered all his life. At long last, he was able to share the inner core of his being with another person.

Even before going to Kenya in 1925, both men, independently of each other, had already learnt through personal experience the importance of dreams. Then both, in their separate explorations of Africa became further convinced of the existence of psychic forces and the paranormal....

Thirty years later, van der Post tried repeatedly to persuade the ageing Jung to return with him to Africa.... But Jung always refused. He told him that witchcraft also existed in Zurich and in the Swiss mountains—and until he had understood that, he had no right to go back to Africa....

Van der Post was also led into other realms of the paranormal by Jung. He came to share with Jung a belief in the I-Ching, a book of Chinese philosophy arguing that mankind and his cosmic and earthly environments made up an interacting unity. In this it is believed that the universe is composed of two equal and complementary forces, yin and yang. Yang is light and positive, and yin is dark and negative. Through the use of the I-Ching, a person can determine a course of action and consult a high form of moral guidance from, in effect, the cosmos....

So, to sum up, what does all this establish?

We know that in March, 1977, Prince Charles paid a secret visit to Africa, inspired by the ideas of Laurens van der Post.

The Prince chose to disappear into a wilderness that was a particularly meaningful part of Africa for both van der Post and Carl Gustav Jung. He would have found himself near, and probably among, the Elgonyi whose dreams and witchcraft had so influenced Jung. These were the very dreams and witchcraft which convinced Jung of the truth of religious relativism, an essential component of his theory of the Collective Unconscious. It helped him understand coincidence, dreams and intuition....

So when Prince Charles went there in 1977, it was not a randomly chosen destination. It was an area which possessed a deeply spiritual association for van der Post.... It had played a crucial role in the development of the Afrikaner's own spiritual views....

It was during this period that I believe the Prince underwent a spiritual transformation.

After Charles's return van der Post was quoted in *Harpers and Queen* magazine as saying that the Prince had had some sort of profound religious experience in Kenya, though he has since categorically denied making this statement.

If this were really so, then the Kenyan expedition represented Prince Charles's own 'road to Damascus and blinding flash'—an intense religious experience of the kind which van der Post certainly believes can happen. On that basis, it would truly amount to a turning point in his life....[1]

---

1. Dale, pp. 33-37.

In 1981, Laurens van der Post read a book called *Something is Happening*, written by one of his good friends, Dr Winifred Rushforth, then aged 97. She was a Jungian analyst practising in Edinburgh....

Through this work, which she considered her true vocation, she met Jung himself and also van der Post and, of course, became a firm believer in the existence and influence of the Collective Unconscious. Her own gift was for interpreting the dreams through which the unconscious expressed itself and she set up numerous dream therapy groups. She argued strongly that dreams could be a guide to the future.

All this she explained in her book which was read by Prince Charles. For instance, in 1979, she had had a 'big dream'—a Jungian term for a dream which is prophetic. This one dealt with the unity between psychology and religion....

She also described her belief in telepathy.

These then were some of the ideas which so impressed Prince Charles as he read the pages of *Something is Happening* from start to finish. It left a profound mark upon him and he wrote to Dr Rushforth about it. As a specialist in the interpretation of dreams, she would have recommended that he keep a dream diary. This he did—later admitting he was 'remembering and recording dreams'. He added: 'I think one can probably learn a considerable amount from them.' ...

The correspondence with Dr Rushforth was private and the Prince's letters came to rest safely in the hands of her daughter, Dr Diana Bates, who had properly maintained their complete confidentiality. But the Prince was sufficiently impressed by the answers to make a private visit to Dr Rushforth in 1983, accompanied by Princess Diana....[1]

One crucial question remains: to what extent did van der Post and Rushforth—these two followers of Jung—come to influence the Prince? Did they persuade him to believe in the radical religious concept of the Collective Unconscious? In my view the only answer is *yes*....

[In] ... quotes which he formally approved—the Prince ... openly [declared] ... his trust in intuition, dreams and coincidences.

[In] ... mid-1985, the Prince was asked about Jung in another interview and said: 'I think [Jung] makes a great deal of sense in many, many areas, and particularly what is written in the Bible and Indian religions, and in Islam, and many others ... definitely a pattern develops, I think, where we are all ultimately trying to explore, to go along the same path, to answer the same questions. We all approach it from different paths but ultimately, the paths meet somewhere in infinity, and that's the important thing.'

These were dangerous words from a future head of the Church of England. The Prince was taking the Jungian view that all religions are of equal value.

[The] ... Prince selected Laurens van der Post as godfather to Prince William. It is a fact that van der Post believes all religions—Christianity, Islam, Animism or whatever—are components of the same force....

It seems highly likely that the Prince knew this was van der Post's religious position. Yet he still selected him for an important role in a Church of England ceremony for a child who might one day head that church. It is surely a proper question to be asked, whether Prince Charles fully agrees

---

1. Dale, pp. 39-42.

with van der Post. If so, then Charles, the future head of the Church of England, may be a super-ecumenist. It would cause tremendous trouble in almost every country in the world....

Taken as a whole, I believe the evidence proves beyond reasonable doubt that Prince Charles accepts the concept of the Collective Unconscious and is a follower of Carl Jung. More than that, it shows that his interest is not merely academic: it has already had tangible repercussions. It reveals that on occasions he is even willing to let the Collective Unconscious take over the decision-making process for him—through intuition, dreams and coincidences—in preference to rational thinking....[1]

Whatever the Royal Family discuss behind closed doors about the paranormal, they maintain the highest standards of discretion in public. But occasionally, by complete accident, they let something slip that gives the rest of us an insight.

One such slip that occurred in March, 1980, can be attributed to Prince Charles, a full two years before he began to express himself publicly on such matters....

The occasion was a visit he was making to an orphanage in south-west London. Among the assembled spectators was a group of people wearing lapel badges that announced: 'Healing is a Gift of the Spirit.'

As the Prince went through his usual handshaking routine, one such badge caught his eye. 'Are you a Spiritualist [(i.e., spiritist)]?' he asked its wearer, Mr Derek Robinson.

'Yes,' replied Mr Robinson.

'How lovely,' said the Prince. 'Do you know Mr Fricker? I am reading his book. It is amazing.'

He then turned to Jean Bassett, a Spiritualist medium, also in the group. 'There's a lot of you about,' he joked.

Quite spontaneously and accidentally, the Prince had revealed several very personal features about himself. Firstly, by his immediate recognition of the lapel badge, he had showed himself familiar with Spiritualism, the religion which claims direct communication with the dead via the séance room. Secondly, he believed that being a Spiritualist, like Mr Robinson, was 'lovely'. Thirdly, he disclosed that at that very moment he was reading a book about Spiritualism, one of the most astounding ever written.

Ted Fricker, the author of the book the Prince found 'amazing', was a well-known Spiritual healer practising in London. He claimed to have once been a little boy in the Holy Land at the time of Christ. He had later been trained in Heaven before being sent back to earth, via Tottenham, to conduct his healing mission.

'It's not the first time I've been here,' Fricker told an interviewer. 'I used to run after Jesus, touching his clothing because I loved him so much. That's why God sent me back to earth as a miracle worker, just like Christ.'

In his book—*God Is My Witness*—Fricker explained more:

Every night after I've gone to bed I'm surrounded by spirit people who come to talk to me, not only the doctors who advise me but many others who help me to solve the various problems which my patients bring to me....

Among his early patients was a businessman named M.H. Tester....

---

1. Dale, pp. 45-47.

'Fricker is a gifted healer,' he wrote in a review, 'but as a spiritual philosopher I think he is naive and does himself injustice by the facile way he attempts to explain his gift.'

Tester added: 'The image of the boy walking in the wake of Jesus, the golden ring with the cross lit and a wreath of thorns burned into his inner face by a lightning bolt, the thinly-veiled comparison with Moses, and the general suggestion that he is one of the spiritual elite —about all this I'm sceptical.'

Tester was not alone in his scepticism. His was the widespread judgement in the Spiritualist world. Anyone who treated Fricker's claims seriously was thought naive. Yet here was Prince Charles, with all the other demands upon his time, sitting down and reading this book and raising the subject matter in an impromptu street conversation. Why was he even interested in it?...[1]

Why would Prince Charles spend his time reading a particularly bizarre Spiritualist book which was dismissed by most Spiritualists as outrageous rubbish, and by most Christians as offensive? Was he interested in the healing career of Edward Fricker? Did he think it possible that Fricker had once been a boy on the Holy Land following in the wake of Jesus, or that he entertained the spirits of the dead at night in his bedroom?

To the outsider, the Prince's behaviour might appear inexplicable. But to the insider, to someone with knowledge of the Royal Family, these questions come as no surprise. There is evidence that by the time the Prince began to read Fricker's book, he was not only familiar with the religious concepts of Jung, but he may already have been initiated into the secrets of Spiritualism.

But equally important was that the Prince came from a family with profound, if concealed, interest in several aspects of the paranormal. It went back six generations and was part of the bloodline. It was something which the royals kept very much within their own circle....

The strong likelihood is that Prince Charles received his introduction to Spiritualism in the early 1950s, when he was at the impressionable age of about seven. It appears that he was introduced to the Spiritualist faith by his mildly eccentric great-great-aunt, Princess Marie Louise, then in her eighties. She was a grand-daughter of Queen Victoria.

There can be no doubt that she was very much involved in Spiritualist practices. She was a very regular patient of Harry Edwards, probably the most celebrated of all spiritual healers. The list of clients journeying into the North Downs to receive Edwards's healing touch included even more of the rich, famous and powerful than attended Fricker's clinic. Of course, many of these did not appreciate that Edwards believed his powers came from the dead....

How did this sweet old lady introduce Prince Charles to Spiritualism? The answer is that she almost certainly gave him a book on the subject, entitled *Spirit Stories for Children*. Edwards was a Spiritualist medium, able to go into trance and contact the Other Side. He believed his healing power came from the spirits of two dead medical pioneers....

'One day she purchased a copy of Mrs Burton's book,' wrote Edwards later. 'Some time afterwards she asked for another copy for, as she said, "a little boy you know very well".'

---

1. Dale, pp. 49-50, 52.

As far as Edwards was aware, there was only one possible candidate for this role....

'She did not specifically say it was for his Royal Highness Prince Charles,' he added, 'but the imputation was there.' What would the book have told the infant Prince?...

In the book's introduction, Mrs Burton, a medium herself, explains to the child readers that she has written down the stories as related to her by a spirit personality with whom she has been in contact. To that extent, she denies authorship.

'For each of you, there is someone in the spirit world or "Heaven" who tries to look after you, to help you do the right thing,' she says....

From the book, one's first impression is that the contents came through Mrs Burton's own mediumship. But this was not the case. The real source was Harry Edwards himself and one of his spirit guides, Reuben....[1]

As the Prince began to forge his radical spiritual views, he recognized that the process held some danger for him. The problem was that one day, when he succeeded to the throne, he would also become head of the Church of England. Some church leaders would undoubtedly welcome his enlightened opinions. But there would be many others, both in the pulpits and the pews, who would not.

They would find it difficult to accept that all the world's religions were one, that Christianity was neither more nor less important than the spirits of African witchcraft. As for Spiritualism itself, it had already split the Anglican church.

In 1937, the Church of England had mounted a systematic inquiry in which the investigators sat in séances with mediums. It had then suppressed the majority report. This was eventually leaked and found to be quite favourable to the Spiritualists.

Although the report was signed by seven of the ten committee members, the then Archbishop of Canterbury Dr Cosmo Lang was on the side of the minority. 'Spiritualism and spiritualistic services,' he said, 'are not countenanced or encouraged in the Church of England.' ...

During the war years, the Scottish medium Helen Duncan was arrested during a séance in Portsmouth, tried at the Old Bailey and jailed for an allegedly fraudulent spirit materialization. It was the movement's *cause célèbre*. This caused Spiritualists to live in fear of the Witchcraft Act, the instrument of law employed....

As Spiritualism frequently involved the very practices which outsiders argued must be fraudulent—such as materialization of the dead—Spiritualists understandably felt they were a persecuted minority. However, in 1951 their persistent campaigning was rewarded when the Witchcraft Act was repealed—a move that would open the floodgate to Britain becoming the occult capital of the Western world by the 1980s....

In the circumstances, it is not surprising that the Prince realized that his views could propel him into a head-on collision with some Church of England leaders and many of its members.

He had a very wide choice of clerics to consult but the one he most favoured happened to be the most unorthodox: Dr Mervyn Stockwood, the

---

1. Dale, pp. 53-56, 58.

Bishop of Southwark, and a man as interested in the paranormal as he was.

'If you were to cut out psychic occurrences from the Bible,' declared Stockwood, 'you would have to cut out a great deal. It is irritating when people dismiss the whole thing as black magic and roguery.'

Stockwood was the most senior Church of England cleric to have openly supported Spiritualism....

Now, in his adulthood, the Prince turned to Dr Mervyn Stockwood seeking answers to matters of faith—important to him, the Church and, ultimately, the nation....

Thus, if Prince Charles had suffered doubts and anxieties over the direction of his beliefs, they would have been alleviated by his discussions with the Spiritualist Bishop....[1]

In 1976 the now defunct weekly newspaper *Reveille* discovered that an unregistered medical practitioner had been visited separately by the Queen, Princess Margaret and Princess Alexandra. At once a cover-up was mounted to conceal the actual nature of the treatment.

The stress was laid upon the fact that the treatment, although unorthodox, was purely mechanical. this was the substance of the items published in the press. *It was untrue.*

The person visited was Kay Kiernan who runs the Bluestone Clinic in Harley House, near Harley Street, London. She offers several kinds of therapies—some physical, and others psychic and Spiritualist. She is a medium able to go into a trance.

The Queen went to see her because of recurring pain she suffered in a shoulder which she had sprained while chopping wood on one of her country estates. It was slow in healing. What Miss Kiernan offered were sessions on an American machine called a Diapulse, which transmitted pulses of high frequency electro-magnetic waves through the body....

The truth is different. The interesting fact about the Diapulse is that in the hands of Miss Kiernan, it is more than merely mechanical. When it is switched on, Miss Kiernan tunes into it with her mind and uses it as a channel for her psychic and Spiritual powers. She admitted as much in an article later, saying she believed she was 'spirit-guided' to buy the machine while on holiday in New York.

Then she explained how her healing worked. 'I believe it is the perfect instrument to be used with psychic power,' she added....

The combination of royalty and horses brings us to Mrs Lavender Dower.... She has two roles.

Second only to Prince Charles, she is the most important figure in the rapid transformation of alternative medicine from the marginally disreputable to the reasonably respectable. Since 1962, when she was way ahead of her time, she has been the driving force in trying to unite the many different therapies in order that they should become self-policing. She did this by founding the Institute for Complementary Medicine.... With her in the chair, it has established strong links with Prince Charles and other intimate members of the royal circle....[2]

As the driving force behind the Institute..., she has met Prince Charles. 'He's a great support,' she said.

---

1. Dale, pp. 61-65, 67.
2. Dale, pp. 69, 71, 73.

The Institute is the most important body in making alternative medicine acceptable to the public....

Mrs Dower stressed that Prince Charles was not directly involved in supporting the Institute financially although he had expressed strong sympathy with its aims. But what is surprising—and quite unexplained—is the heavy involvement by members of the royal circle.[1] Its patrons, for instance, include [(i.e., while living)]:

Angus Ogilvy, husband of Princess Alexandra.

Major John Wills, whose wife Jean is a cousin of the Queen and one of her ladies-in-waiting.

Dr Charles Elliott, homoeopathic doctor to the Queen.

Lord Oaksey, racing friend of the Queen and the Queen Mother.

Sir Antony Acland, Permanent Under-secretary at the Foreign and Commonwealth Office and head of the Diplomatic Service— the man responsible for all executive-level royal staff.

Also involved is Dr Alec Forbes who, through the public endorsement by Prince Charles, has become Britain's best-known practitioner of alternative medicine....

He [(Anthony Baird, the Institute's administrator)] added: 'We have had letters from America saying we can hardly realize the effect Prince Charles's speeches have caused. It's reverberated throughout the Western world....'[2]

I believe that Canon W.H. Elliott, who served as chaplain to George V, George VI and the present Queen was effectively a Spiritualist medium. He attended séances with the result that he came firmly to believe in communication with the dead. However, he recognized Spiritualism to be a major source of dispute within the Church of England and, bearing in mind his position, he scrupulously avoided supporting the movement as such— while taking little care to conceal his views.

'Why should anybody think it uncanny and wrong that a "sensitive", such as I am, can hear voices from the Other Side? I will not renounce my experience,' he said....

Was the royal chaplain a Spiritualist?

The answer is that although he never openly supported the Spiritualist movement as far as we know, he espoused the Spiritualist cause in a way which challenged Anglican orthodoxy head-on.

He believed that 'sensitives'—that is, mediums—such as himself could communicate with the dead. He spoke of the Other World being all

---

1. In 1992, Princess Anne "visited two Tibetan refugee camps." While doing so, the "personal representative of the Dalai Lama ... welcomed the Princess and showed her the feeding centres, clinic and school and, most interesting of all, the Tibetan medical centre. The centre uses herbal remedies—a great favourite with all the Royal Family, including the Princess—and works hand in hand with the Save the Children [Fund's] doctors and local hospitals" ("The Top of The World," *Majesty*, Nov. 1992, Vol. 13, No. 11, p. 8). **Please note that herbal remedies, when they work and are provided by non-occultists, are, even in the author's opinion, to be preferred to modern drugs, inasmuch as they are a natural provision from God.**

2. Dale, pp. 76-77. In one such speech, as a typical example, Charles observed: "More working days are lost because of back pain than for any other reason. It is a chronic problem.... Surely we should be investigating every method that might reduce that number, and there are two forms of alternative treatment, chiropractics and osteopathy, which have proved to be successful in a great many cases of back pain. Even doctors consult them. So what is there to lose by giving them a try?" (Junor, p. 259).

around us, interpenetrating the world we see. He thought that the dead could come to the aid of the living.

This is Spiritualism, not Anglicanism....

So, what was Elliot's influence upon the Royal Family during the 31 years in which he served them?

First, I believe that they must have been aware of his views because they were made public in broadcasts and in print. The fact that they were tolerated, at the very least, says something about the sympathies of George V, George VI, and the Queen.

Second, in my opinion, he would not have opposed members of the Royal Family turning to clairvoyance, spiritual healing and the comfort of the séance room. Indeed, it seems likely he would have encouraged it—in the way he tried to encourage a deeper sense of spiritual awareness in the public at large.[1]

In the late 1950s, a well-known but ailing medium named Lilian Bailey told an astonishing story to her family.

In 1953, at her home in Wembley, North London, she had received a telephone call from a stranger, asking her for her services. He wished to hold a séance. He arranged with Mrs Bailey for her to visit an address in Kensington at a set time. She agreed....

She arrived at the location as planned, was led inside and was carefully blindfolded. Then she was taken to another house. There, she sat on a chair ready to begin the séance, hearing the rustle of skirts as the sitters took their places around her.

Despite the difficult setting, she quickly went into a trance and made contact with her spirit guide....

Eventually Mrs Bailey emerged from her trance, the lights were raised and her blindfold removed. Then she saw who her sitters were—the Queen Mother, the Queen, Prince Philip, the Duchess of Kent and the latter's daughter Princess Alexandra....

Was Lilian Bailey bolstering her own importance by telling a tall story? The evidence suggests: *no*....

After the first séance, according to Morrow: 'There were several private sessions with the medium for the Queen Mother....'[2]

Another medium has also claimed to have served the Royal Family at this time. She was Bertha Harris....

'What I can tell you,' she said in 1976, 'is that the Royal Family have always had a deep interest in Spiritualism—but it would not do for them to admit it.'

She claimed she was summoned by George VI in the late 1930s. In an interview she agreed she had visited him 'many times' but refused to disclose details of their exchanges. 'That would be breaking faith,' she said. 'Their secrets are safe with me. I can only tell you he came to me about lots of things.' ...

In fact, other reasons exist for believing Spiritualism is very familiar to the [(anti-Christian)] Queen Mother. Her devoted Extra-Woman-of-the-Bedchamber, Lady Elizabeth Basset, who has served her many years, is deeply interested in communication between the living and the dead.

---

1. Dale, pp. 79-82.
2. Dale, pp. 91-92.

She shows this in an anthology she compiled, *The Bridge of Love*, in which she quotes approvingly from Spiritualists....

Equally revealing are her lengthy quotations from Sir George Trevelyan, often called the high priest of the British psychic movement and a man much admired by Prince Charles....

And, in 1980, another well-known British clairvoyant Robin Stevens was quoted as saying: 'One has to keep some secrets but on occasions I have been called to Windsor Castle.' ...

Nowadays, the Queen Mother is careful to avoid controversy, preferring her public image to be that of the 'nation's favourite grandmother', a role she plays to perfection. She leaves the contentious issues to various offspring, especially to the ... willing Prince Charles.[1]

As far as Prince Charles is concerned, royal fascination with the paranormal and Spiritualism is not confined to his mother's side of the family. It also comes from his father's side through the Greek Connection....

According to his biographer Philip Ziegler, [Prince Charles's favourite 'uncle', Lord] Mountbatten was open-minded about the Theosophical Society—which is spiritualist and occultist....

Ziegler adds: 'Mountbatten was fascinated by the theory of reincarnation....' ....

This is not surprising. Mountbatten was a secret member of the Ghost Club which, despite its frivolous-sounding name, is a serious organization, founded in 1862, for the pursuit of psychical research. [He] ... would have met many of the most distinguished Spiritualists and occultists of the last half century....[2]

So what effect did this Greek fascination with the paranormal have on the young Philip Mountbatten, one day to step from relative obscurity to be Consort to the Queen of England? His mother was deeply committed to the Spiritual world and his two cousins, George and Paul, were practising Spiritualists. His Uncle Dickie believed in flying saucers, and another close Greek relative, the Duchess of Kent was also apparently turning towards the séance room....

It would have been unsurprising if Philip, too, [who (until his April 2021 death), believed in flying saucers and (foolishly) the essential divinity of nature,] had become intrigued with the subject....

As we have seen, Prince Charles is deeply religious and firmly committed to a belief in spiritual forces that affect daily life.... ....To Prince Charles, a student of Jung, the mind is in contact with the Collective Unconscious....[3]

1. Dale, pp. 96-100.
2. Dale, pp. 113-114.
3. Dale, pp. 120-122.

Accepting Prince Philip to be the exception that proves the rule,[1] the fact is that whichever other part of the Royal Family one scrutinizes, there is evidence of unusual interest in the paranormal....

....It is part of the bloodline. It runs like a secret thread through the House of Windsor. It was the backcloth against which Prince Charles's mind was made receptive to the ideas of Laurens van der Post.

The only difference in his case was that he insisted upon being true to himself, stepping out of the royal confines and telling the world about it, whether that world was prepared or not. If he is criticized for honestly held beliefs, then he must also be congratulated for displaying the guts to speak out where others have remained silent....

In speaking out, Prince Charles must have known that he was embracing six generations, reaching back to his great-great-great grandmother, Queen Victoria. For it was Victoria herself who set her descendants firmly upon this path, as she did for other European royalties of which she was also effectively grandmother....[2]

If there is one unusual enthusiasm for which the Royal Family is known, then that enthusiasm is homoeopathy. It is used regularly by the present generation of Royalty, particularly the Queen. And the royal bloodline reaches right back to the discipline's founder, Samuel Hahnemann....

This is where it differs completely from orthodox medicine.... [Homoeopaths] say that their remedies rely upon a *spiritual* force, not a material one. In this way, homoeopathy is unquestionably paranormal....

....Edward VIII, George VI and the Duke of Gloucester—all appointed a homoeopathic doctor.

The man who won this honour for homoeopathy was Dr John Weir. For this achievement alone, which many believe saved homoeopathy from virtual extinction, Weir is probably the discipline's most important figure since Hahnemann....

How much did the Royal Family use homoeopathic remedies? On the day of George V's funeral, Weir loved to recall, he wrote prescriptions for

---

1. "Philip co-founded .... the Interfaith consultations between Jews, Christians, and Muslims in 1984 [(having learned from Charles)], together with Crown Prince Hassan of Jordan and Sir Evelyn de Rothschild, at Windsor Castle" ("Bohemian Grove: Historical Membership List Plus Biographies," July 2020).

   At a National Press Club speech, Prince Philip proclaimed, "It is now apparent that the ecological pragmatism of the so-called pagan religions such as that of the American Indians, Polynesians, [and] Australian Aborigines, was a great deal more realistic in terms of conservation ethics than the more intellectual monotheistic philosophies of the revealed religions" (Hunt, *GLOBAL PEACE AND THE RISE OF ANTICHRIST*, p. 168). According to the (now roasting) prince, who had been the International President of the World Wide Fund for Nature—a role for which he had previously recruited former Nazi Party member Prince Bernhard of the Netherlands—"If God is in nature, nature itself becomes divine" ("A Wing and a Prayer," *Majesty* magazine, June 1994, Vol. 15, No. 6, p. 29).

   While the Committee of 300 continues to plot the deaths of much of the world's population, so that "nature" may survive and thrive, Prince Philip, one of the inner-circle members of the committee, played the hypocrite as well as anyone: "since he was appointed 1951's president of the British Association for the Advancement of Science, he has hammered at the themes ... that commercial laboratories pursuing profitable ends in secret are starvers of the national good; the need to maintain humane priorities in science since 'we can either set the world free from drudgery, fear, hunger and pestilence, or obliterate life itself'; and the importance of preserving the world's wildlife" (Lacey, *Majesty*, p. 253). Indeed, Prince Philip is on record as stating, "In the event that I am reincarnated, I would like to return as a deadly virus, in order to contribute something to solve overpopulation" (West German *Deutsche Press Agentur*, Aug. 1988).

2. Dale, pp. 123-124. James and Russell note, "Recent evidence reveals the possibility that John Brown was in fact a medium, his clairvoyant powers keeping [Queen] Victoria in touch with her 'beloved Albert' beyond the grave" (*At Home with the Royal Family*, p. 50).

three kings and four queens. And in 1946 George VI, in a letter to his brother the Duke of Gloucester, wrote revealingly: 'I've been suffering from an awful reaction to the strain of war.... Medicine, not even Weir's, is of any use as I really want a rest...'....

The present Queen carries a small box of homoeopathic remedies with her on her travels; belladonna for her sinusitis, and arsenic to prevent her sneezing in mid-speech. And more recently Prince Charles has been following closely the experimental use of homoeopathic remedies on pigs and cattle at the Elm Farm Research Centre, near Newbury....[1]

By their selection of Dr John Weir as royal homoeopath, the Royal Family allied themselves with a particular wing of the homoeopathic discipline; Kentian homoeopathy.

Named after an American homoeopath, James Tyler Kent (1849-1916), it is the most extreme metaphysical form, a kind which is even further removed from orthodox medicine than standard homoeopathy.

'In 1950, the British Homoeopathic Society became the Faculty of Homoeopathy, established by Act of Parliament. This remarkable degree of official recognition makes Britain unique in the world....

Kent had been one of the first to paint word pictures, indicating the kind of personality which matched a particular medicine. These word pictures now became central to homoeopathy. Through links with a form of Spiritualism called Swedenborgianism, they showed that its practitioners believed homoeopathy to be divinely revealed.

It is in this form that the discipline has been accused of being a religious cult.

On one level, it seems to have descended from the 'doctrine of signatures', as endorsed by Paracelsus—the very figure whose principles were recommended to BMA doctors by Prince Charles in December, 1982....

'Since renouncing homoeopathy as occult, I have found my relationship with Jesus much more real and effective,' he [(Dr Douglas Calcott)] wrote in 1983. 'I am seeing Him heal as I pray against sickness in His name, something I had come to accept I could never experience. Homoeopathy, though producing results, had robbed me of faith in the highest source of healing, Jesus Christ the Son of God. Although the truth may offend some, I trust that for many it will be the truth that sets them free. Satan is desperate to deceive us on this issue and has raised up many counterfeit physicians and methods of treatment.'[2]

---

1. Dale, pp. 169-173. Lacey similarly observes: "Her faith in homeopathy was another token of her preference for the traditional and unsophisticated. Sir John Weir had introduced the royal family to its folk remedies in the 1920s, and after his retirement as Elizabeth II's personal physician he was succeeded by another homeopath, Margerie Blackie.... The homeopathic remedy for sinus trouble, Elizabeth II's one recurring problem in a remarkably healthy life, involves arsenic, to prevent sneezing, onions, to deal with a running nose, and deadly nightshade, for the sore throat" (*Majesty*, p. 240). James and Russell add: "she has her own homeopathic remedies: pills made from deadly nightshade for a sore throat, arsenic for cold symptoms, and half an onion (inhaled) to clear the nasal passages. The Queen has her own homeopathic physician to prepare the remedies" (*At Home with the Royal Family*, p. 114). Junor remarks: "[Prince] Charles had grown up with complementary medicine, particularly homeopathic cures, which both the Queen and Queen Mother have been using for years. One of the oldest of the healing arts, it involves treating the person as a whole, looking at his or her medical history to find the cause of the specific illness, then administering [often toxic] remedies that are so dilute as to be scientifically indiscernible" (Junor, p. 214). **Again, not *all* alternative medicine is occult or witchcraft; for example, taking belladonna for sinusitis is reasonable.**
2. Dale, pp. 175-178.

Before her death Dr Blackie—niece of one of the most famous homoeopaths, Dr James Compton-Burnett—paid tribute to the Queen in her book *The Patient, Not the Cure.* 'Our homoeopathic cause has the enormous privilege of having the Queen as patron of the Royal London Homoeopathic Hospital. May I, on behalf of homoeopathic doctors and patients, pay tribute to our Royal Family who for three generations have given their encouragement and support to homoeopathy.' ....

The current royal homoeopath, appointed in 1980, is Dr Charles Elliott, who is more reticent in print about his beliefs. Because of his royal connection, he has also stopped giving interviews. However, he is very much an admirer of Dr Blackie, to the extent of being the joint editor of her written estate. [He is] ... a follower of the Kentian tradition.[1]

[In] ... 1971, Prince Charles made his first public gesture towards a psychic healer. He sent a message of good will to Paul Daws who had just completed a 240 mile 'healing hike' through Wales....

One day, more than a decade later, the Prince would reveal: 'Ever since I was a child, I've been interested in medical matters and in the business of healing—I've always wished that I could heal...'

Then came March, 1977, and his private expedition into the Kenyan wilderness inspired by Laurens van der Post.

But the Prince kept quiet about it.

That is, until June 30, 1978, when he was addressing the Salvation Army.

'What we should be worried about now,' he said, 'is whether people are going to become atheists ... whether they are going to be given an idea of right or wrong ... whether they are going to be given an awareness of the things of the spirit and the meaning of the infinite beauty of nature...'

This was hardly sensational but the liberal theology of other parts of the speech, condemning doctrinal bickering, created a furore.

And the reference to 'things of the spirit' was open to more than one interpretation.

The chance was seized by Maurice Barbanell, the respected founder and editor of *Psychic News.* One has to remember that for more than 20 years he had sat dumbly upon what he believed to be the greatest secret of Spiritualism: that medium Lilian Bailey had held séances for the Queen Mother, the Queen and others. Now, prompted by Prince Charles, he had to blurt out something.

In his diary notes of the issue of July 15, 1978, he ran the following headline: PRINCE CHARLES KNOWS ...

The following text read, 'One phrase used by Prince Charles in his address on the futility of orthodox religious dogma was virtually unnoticed by those who have joined in the furore.

'The Prince of Wales said that to him it was more important that instead of arguing about theological dogmas, people should be given an awareness "of the things of the spirit and of the meaning and infinite beauty of nature".

'This suggests that he has some inkling of psychic matters. *The suggestion, as I know, is founded upon fact, but I cannot tell you why I make this statement. What I can say is that he, like many members of our Royal*

---

1. Dale, pp. 182-184.

Family, has an acquaintanceship with mediumship and its implications' (author's italics).[1]

As far as the public were concerned, the main task facing Prince Charles in the late 1970s was the one of choosing a bride.... They were well pleased when his eye stopped roving and settled upon the radiantly pretty Lady Diana Spencer.

The press and television insisted on treating their courtship like some modern-day fairy-tale.... The couple's wedding in St Paul's in 1981 ... was the world's biggest-ever media spectacular.

In the gush of money-spinning verbiage, no one stopped to ask what, if anything might be going on behind the Prince's smiling mask.

Eighteen months passed before he gave the first clue—a clue that most observers failed to appreciate. It happened on his installation as President of the British Medical Association, the doctor's 'trade union'.

To understand the background, we need to refer briefly to the first Medical Act of 1858.

The conventional view has been that it was this Act that elevated medical science, separated it from superstition and quackery, and enabled it to 'blitz' many illnesses and disorders almost out of existence. Belief in this interpretation was the rock on which the BMA was built.... Yet with the installation of Prince Charles, this edifice began to fall apart....

As we now know, Prince Charles was already taking a great interest in Jungian psychology, particularly the Collective Unconscious. His mentor was probably Laurens van der Post who had been Jung's close friend. And he had just encountered the book *Something Is Happening* by the Edinburgh Jungian analyst Winifred Rushforth. In this she dealt with the way that coincidences could also be *signposts* from that spirit world.

While in his library, wondering what to speak about to the BMA, the Prince's eye alighted upon a book by Paracelsus, the sixteenth-century German physician who, like Jung, believed in an occult cosmic unity.

As we have seen, the Prince interpreted this as his *signpost*.

....The result was the biggest jolt the BMA had ever received....

These were the most challenging words that the BMA had ever heard from a President.

'Perhaps,' continued the Prince, 'we just have to accept it is God's will that the unorthodox individual is doomed to years of frustration, ridicule and failure in order to act out his role in the scheme of things, until his day arrives and mankind is ready to receive his message; *a message which he probably finds hard to explain himself, but which he knows comes from a far deeper source than conscious thought'* (author's italics).

Not only was he espousing the cause of the unscientific, he was implying, in my view, that unorthodoxy might be divinely inspired, that the things opposed by the medical establishment might possibly be messages from the Collective Unconscious....

'Through the centuries,' said the Prince, 'healing has been practised by folk healers who are guided by traditional wisdom that sees illness as a disorder of the whole person, involving not only the patient's body, but his mind, his self-image, his dependence on the physical and social environment, *as well as his relation to the cosmos....* I would suggest that the

---

1. Dale, pp. 200-202.

whole imposing edifice of modern medicine, for all its breath-taking successes is, like the Tower of Pisa, slightly off balance.'

That speech—delivered on December 14, 1982—can be seen today as the turning point for what is now promoted and marketed as alternative medicine.[1] It was reported worldwide. Its impact was not restricted to the doctors it attacked. The meaning was absorbed by a public not just in Britain but throughout the West.

If that had been the Prince's last word on the subject, he would still have achieved more than anyone else. But it was not his last word, far from it.

'Don't over-estimate the sophisticated approach to medicine,' he told an increasingly rattled BMA the following summer. He lectured them on taking note of 'what lies beneath the surface of the visible world ... and those ancient, unconscious forces which still shape the psychological attitudes of modern man.'[2]

The weight of postal deliveries to Buckingham Palace following his challenges to the British Medical Association soon convinced the Prince that his *signpost* had been right. He found himself receiving a great deal of public support.

'It was unbelievable,' he said. 'I have *never—ever*—had so many letters.'

He added: 'I was riveted by this. While I was pretty sure I was going to stir up a hornet's nest—which I did, I think—I also realized there was a great deal more interest in and awareness of this aspect than I'd imagined, particularly among lay people—although many doctors, especially the younger ones, also seemed to feel the same way.'

In the face of a seething medical establishment, he needed to be borne along by this sense of purpose, that **here was a mission for which he had been chosen by the very forces for which he was now a spokesman**....

Among the letters was one that particularly caught the Prince's attention and which came from a man who asked a favour of the Prince: would he open the new ... centre which he was helping to set up.

The Prince knew that to lend his authority to such an enterprise would be the greatest gift he could give. He had no hesitation in accepting the invitation.

That is how on July 15, 1983, he came to be sharing the platform at the Bristol Cancer Help Centre with Dr Alec Forbes, the centre's unpaid medical director....

Then the Prince referred to the methods of treatment. 'It may be described as psychotherapy, or religion, or the power of prayer, or whatever,'

---

1. Junor, in quoting then Prince Charles' speech, oddly omits his most "controversial" statements, with *no* indication. Nevertheless, she quotes Satan's Prince as having remarked: "What is taken for today's unorthodoxy is probably going to be tomorrow's convention.... [Paracelsus] maintained that there were four pillars on which the whole art of healing rested. The first was philosophy; the second astronomy (or what we might now call psychology); the third alchemy (or biochemistry) and the fourth virtue (in other words the professional skill of the doctor). Paracelsus believed that the good doctor's therapeutic success largely depends on his ability to inspire the patient with confidence and to mobilize his will to health.... It is frightening how dependent upon drugs we are all becoming and how easy it is for doctors to prescribe them as the universal panacea for our ills. Wonderful as many of them are it should still be more widely stressed by doctors that the health of human beings is so often determined by their behaviour, their food and the nature of their environment" (Junor, pp. 213-214).

2. Dale, pp. 203-206.

he said, 'but it represents that invisible aspect of the universe which although unprovable in terms of orthodox science, as man has devised it, nevertheless cries out for us to keep our minds as open as possible and not to dismiss it as mere hocus-pocus.' ...

[It] ... is surprising that so few have stopped to discover the beliefs that Forbes really holds, especially considering the amount of publicity the Prince has generated for him:

SPIRITUAL HEALING: Forbes says there are two kinds of beings in the spirit world. One group are unpleasant and untrustworthy; the others possess great understanding. Healers use the latter benign spirits to balance the emotional and mental energies of the sick.

It is a rare gift unconnected with religious faith....

PSYCHIC SURGERY:....

ANTHROPOSOPHICAL MEDICINE:.... It involves maintaining harmony between four fields of force [which are affected by the Earth, Sun, Moon, Mercury, Venus, Mars, Jupiter, and Saturn, and which can be treated through the use of those bodies's respective metals—gold, silver, mercury, copper, iron, tin, and lead]....

HOMOEOPATHY:....

BACH FLOWER REMEDIES:.... [These] remedies consist of the dew precipitated on the leaves of plants. Different plants ... impart different curative powers, though these are not bio-chemical....

RADIONICS (WITH PSIONICS): Here the practitioner holds a pendulum over a hair or blood sample of the patient—who is not present—and 'dowses' for the diagnosis. Then the remedy is 'transmitted' to the patient over any distance ... by using psychically 'tuned' instruments....

OUT OF THE BODY EXPERIENCES: Forbes says that the healer's mind may leave his body and travel any distance to heal an ill person....

COLOUR AND GEM THERAPY: Here colour is said to represent chemical potencies in 'higher octaves of vibration'. Forbes ... seems to agree that water can be charged by leaving it in sunlight in suitably coloured containers. It can then be drunk as medicine. Similarly, small gems can be left in alcohol, thereby conferring their curative imprint....

ORGONE THERAPY:....

[This employs] ... the fundamental life force of the Universe—Orgone—which is everywhere and in everything....

VITA FLORUM: This is an ointment produced from water in which certain live flowers have been held in sunlight, until their curative power is believed to have passed into the fluid....

ASTROLOGY:....

REINCARNATION: He [(Forbes)] says that perhaps one third of all illness is Karmic—that is, inherited from a previous life....

There is no evidence, however, that any of these healing methods have ever been used at the Bristol Cancer Help Centre, other than the fact that the Centre states in its brochure that 'healing by touch, sometimes called spiritual healing, is available.'[1]

....Never before had the Prince provoked such a response. But his post also included criticism, especially from those who said he was dabbling with the occult.

'The establishment of the Bristol Cancer Help Centre is an extraordinary milestone in the progress of alternative medicine,' declared evangelist Roy Livesey.

He then took a sharp prod at the Prince. 'This range of therapies—and the support received from *so many places*,' he said, 'is a measure of the longing on everybody's part to find some right answers. Nothing should be taken away from their sincerity, commitment, care and willingness. My plea is for the discernment of the spirits.'

Livesey quotes in full Prince Charles's support for Paracelsus. Then he adds: 'No Paracelsian philosophy, no royal or clerical approval, no measure of care or concern, can counter the great and inevitable dangers in store for those who fall for the wiles of Satan.' ...

But by then, it was already too late, for **the Prince, in a bout of enthusiasm for the new health boom, had given the most unusual interview of his life....**

He used crucial expressions and described revealing behaviour which were highly significant to anyone well versed in the works of Carl Jung, especially those dealing with the Collective Unconscious. But to the relief of the Royal Family, it so happened that his interviewer, the highly respected journalist Anne de Courcy, was not particularly prepared for a discussion in this esoteric field of psychology...; neither were the references understood by the various editors who published her article all over the world....

'To me, it is very interesting to see how primitive societies—though I think "primitive" is a complete misnomer anyway—are the whole time *subconsciously* far more aware of their instinctive relationship with the things and people round them than we are in the so-called civilized world.'

Without naming them, he went on to agree with Jung and van der Post in supporting the African side of the mind, in saying in effect that man should use the Collective Unconscious in making decisions. Of this subconscious awareness he said:

'It's still there but buried under a mountain of ... what?—anxieties, fears, worries, a feeling that it's something we should be ashamed of as though *rational* thinking is the only acceptable process. Yet I believe instinct, sensitivity, call it what you will, is enormously important.'

He told Anne de Courcy that, as a result of this, **he was trying to teach himself to become more aware by 'listening with his inner ear'....**

---

1. Dale, pp. 207-212. Junor, observing that the "Bristol Centre treats cancer patients not by drugs but by a combination of diet, positive attitudes and support from everyone around," once again offers a sterilized version of Charles' "controversial" remarks: "What they claim is that you have to put a great deal of effort as a patient into attacking your own disease, and that those who have the willpower, who are able to adopt the very strict diets ... who are able to learn the relaxation and imagery techniques and who perhaps have a natural inclination to fight, are likely to do better." On another occasion, while attending a Royal Society of Medicine seminar on alternative medicine, Satan's Prince stated: "Many, many people in this country are predisposed towards various types of complimentary medicine.... Increasingly, I think, they are not getting all they want from orthodox medicine" (p. 215).

'Today,' said the Prince, 'the knowledge that Man is capable of harnessing nature to his own ends—that he even has the capability to destroy the whole planet—has given the feeling that *we* are masters of our fate; which is so far from the truth it makes one cry sometimes.'

With this statement he raised, but did not answer, the obvious question. Who, or what, did he believe was in charge of the planet?

He also spoke of modern societies need for 'pointers'—that is, figures who could teach a new understanding of morality and metaphysics. [A pointer is] ' ... someone to lead us, to show us the way.... Once you have been pointed in a direction, you can follow it if it is a philosophy or way of thinking that suits you,' he said. 'But I don't think we have that many people who are "pointers". That's one problem. Another is a lack of awareness....'

It was at this time that the Prince made another move that confirmed his interest in the paranormal.

His attention was caught by reports of a large bequest left by the author and psychic researcher Arthur Koestler for the establishment of a chair of parapsychology at a British university.

Like the Prince, Koestler was fascinated by Jung's theory of the Collective Unconscious and particularly by the meaning of coincidence.... He certainly believed in the power of psychic forces and, apparently, in a spirit world. The Prince admired him very much indeed.

When he heard of the bequest, the Prince wrote to the University of Wales, of which he was Chancellor, and asked the Principal: 'Why don't we have a go at taking up this scheme?' ... [1]

Since the first hints of the Prince's spiritual predilections, several stories [about Windsor Castle] have appeared in the popular press which are unverifiable. Normally, they would not warrant serious scrutiny. But because of the Prince's interest in the paranormal, they become more credible....

Why should Windsor be the scene of so much supernatural activity? The reason may be that the Long Walk lies upon an ancient ley line—a route that was established in pre-Christian days for astronomical and mystical purposes.

In fact, according to some researchers, Windsor Castle stands at the very centre of such a network, making the adjacent area particularly susceptible to paranormal activity.

The well-known writer Colin Wilson says: 'It seems likely that the whole Windsor Park area is a site of the ancient religion associated with the horned god of the witches and with Diana. Since the area is associated with the kings of England, it is even conceivable that the park was *the* centre of the old religion.' ... [2]

---

1. Dale, pp. 213-217.
2. Siân Ellis remarks: "The longer history of the Buckingham Palace site is even more fascinating, conjuring up unusual ghosts where guards parade today. In medieval times a witch, Margarie Gourdemaine, lived in a hut where the present courtyard stands. She was burned at the stake, accused of sorcery against King Henry VI. When the guards change at the palace they are probably marching upon the very spot where the witch's hut once stood" ("Secret City," *Realm* magazine, Sept./Oct. 1997, No. 76, pp. 31-32). James and Russell comment: "Most Guards prefer sentry duty at Windsor Castle..., despite the tales of George III's ghost which is said to appear periodically. From where the Guards stand they can count twelve statues but, strangely, sometimes there appear to be thirteen. Sentries have also heard the sound of someone tapping on a window, and on looking up they have seen the ghostly King's wild eyes staring blankly out at them, as if imploring to be let out of his prison" (*At Home with the Royal Family,*

[Tom Johanson, secretary of the Spiritualist Association of Great Britain,] who has given regular healing displays in Trafalgar Square, promoted the phrase, 'Prince of Psychics'—a label which the Prince detests. He also quoted a friend of the Prince as saying: 'Charles is very definitely creating a problem in the family by insisting on the infallibility of working things out by psychic methods.'

And—implying he was on surprisingly intimate terms with royalty—Johanson wrote: '....**The fact is that the Prince is such an avid researcher in all aspects of the psychic field and is speaking so openly about it that many within his group of close friends refer to him as the "Prince of Psychics".'** ...

It was after Johanson published the ouija board story that it was taken up by the tabloid press, both in Britain and abroad. It was this one item that most infuriated the Prince and provoked him to speak out. By safely attacking it as untrue, he attempted to cast doubt upon the credibility of all other allegations concerning himself and the paranormal. In his interview with ITN, he went so far as to say: 'I'm not interested in the occult, or dabbling in black magic of any of these kinds of things or, for that matter, strange forms of mysticism.'

This was rather over the top, a blanket denial which probably revealed more about his own anxieties than about the facts of the matter. His mother was reported to have been against the interview in principle, afraid that he would say something which could later be pulled to pieces. In this instance, her fears appear to have been fully justified. Indeed, in the very same broadcast, he also described how he had campaigned for the Arthur Koestler chair of parapsychology to be adopted by the University of Wales. As parapsychology is the study of the paranormal—from Uri Geller's spoon-bending to the mechanics of the occult and black magic—then the Prince must therefore be interested in such matters, no matter how vehement his denials. This is in addition to all the other evidence [thus far] revealed....

Such is also the view of people who have talked to him on the subject.[1]

Royal patronage has helped turn Britain into the occult capital of the Western world. Paranormal practices which are illegal in other countries can be promoted without hindrance. Seemingly inexplicable treatments such as radionics or orgone therapy—which were chased out of the United States, for instance—can be structured into professional bodies, advertised openly and awarded a scale of fees. British Spiritualists are probably the most celebrated on earth as they tour the globe, applying their healing powers. London possesses the finest facilities for homoeopathy, a discipline which was virtually saved from extinction by royal support. The National Health Service experiments with alternative medicine. And the British Government fends off Common Market regulations which would inhibit some paranormal therapists.

This all constitutes a wonderful tribute to British freedom. There is no other developed nation so tolerant of occult and paranormal practices when they are being performed seriously, for money, sometimes in life-and-death circumstances....

---

p. 128). Recall that George III was a Mason.
1. Dale, pp. 225, 227-229.

The evidence shows that Prince Charles believes firmly in the existence and power of paranormal forces governing our health and welfare. In doing so, he has hitched his reputation—and that of the Royal Family—to the credibility of the phenomena he has so carefully endorsed.

If, at some time, the occult and the unscientific are shown to be worthwhile and of benefit, then the Prince will be vindicated and hailed as a prophet. He will be seen as a man who was ahead of his time, a natural leader ... perhaps, even, what he calls a *pointer*.

If, on the other hand, they are deemed wasteful, ineffective, harmful and demonic, the result for the Prince will be the gravest crisis of his public life. From one side he will be labelled a crank and from the other an occultist....

....[Having] ... **drawn his conclusions, the Prince is equipped to defend them forcefully.**

During 1983 and 1984, this is what he tried to do, feeling that there was a general benefit to be spread by open discussion of such matters. He saw it as part of his leadership role to introduce these ideas at large, to act as one of society's 'pointers'.

But by the middle of 1985 his optimism had been replaced by disillusionment as he witnessed himself being turned into an object of ridicule, at least by some. At that point, both surprised and hurt by the cruelty of the attacks, he changed his position quite dramatically. Urged on by family and advisers, he adopted a wholly defensive posture and began to say he had been misunderstood—that he had only ever advocated an 'open' mind, nothing more radical than that.

Overnight he forgot all about his support for the unproven and how he had said he was trying to interpret dreams and coincidences. No longer did he refer to Winifred Rushforth or Carl Jung or his challenges to the British Medical Association. Suddenly, from having supported the unscientific, he wished to pose as an objective investigator.

Increasingly impatient with criticism, he categorically denies any interest whatsoever in the occult or strange forms of mysticism.

His claim was, however, inconsistent with the facts. At best, it might be said the Prince was confused; at worst, that his nerve had [at least temporarily] snapped. If '83 and '84 had been the years of the public transformation, '85 was the year of the public turnaround and recantation.

But there is one thing worth remembering: at no time did the Prince flatly contradict or deny the detail of his earlier statements in support of psychic and paranormal matters. From this fact alone it may be assumed that he still held such views but, for personal reasons, was no longer espousing them. The cause—family pressure and public relations....

It is the Prince's eternal misfortune that his religious faith can never be a private matter.... What he believes is of proper concern to all Anglicans worldwide, as well as to most British subjects, for whom, as monarch, he would also serve as spiritual leader. And this is bound to create problems.

Firstly, many church-goers, of all denominations, will find the Prince's apparent super-ecumenism unacceptable. He apparently considers all religions—Christianity, Islam, African spirit worship—to be parts of the same whole. More than that, there is the specific difficulty of reconciling his opinions with those of the Church of England, of which the monarch is head. Anglicanism is noted for its ability to accommodate many different interpretations of the gospels. But if the Prince were unable to reach such an accommodation—one in which both sides felt their integrity to be protected—then a real obstacle would block his path to the Succession....

It may be weakness which prompts some people to be drawn towards unusual spiritual beliefs....

But there are other individuals, often deeply impressive ones, who take up a spiritual quest not out of inadequacy, but in order to seek the ultimate religious truth, feeling such a mission is the sole cause able to instill their life with purpose.

In my opinion, it is into this latter category that Prince Charles falls; it is from a sense of mission, perhaps of destiny, that he has been driven to explore the mysteries of the spirit.

He is idealistic and compassionate. **He concerns himself with the state of the world. He obviously frets over what he sees as its physical and spiritual deterioration. Whereas many might surrender to the inertia of despair, he seeks an understanding of what is wrong in order that he might help find a cure and better serve mankind.**

That sense of vocation has led him to his present beliefs....

'Today's unorthodoxy is tomorrow's convention,' Prince Charles will no doubt repeat in his own defence.

And, in my opinion, he will be left with a choice, one that will decide his future and, perhaps, that of the [British] nation—to disguise his views, live a lie and preserve the constitutional peace, or be true to himself, his Church and his subjects, and face the consequences.[1]

Despite occasional public denials, whether or not he cares to admit it ("thou doth protest too much"), Charles who would like to have been an actor, is a dedicated New Age adherent and spiritist. Further, as we shall see, he may be loosely associated with Peter LeMesurier's *The Armageddon Script.* Holden writes:

[The] ... face before you is a contemporary icon. You have seen it not just on a thousand news-stands, but on stamps and coins, T-shirts and dishcloths....

....Charles has become a disciple of Jung, who believed, among other things, in a "collective unconscious," the premise that diverse cultures share basic myths and symbols. Earlier this year, the prince took a trek into Africa's Kalahari Desert with his Jungian guru, Sir Laurens van der Post, who holds that the life and values of the "lost tribes" of the African desert have much to teach the civilized world.

....[He] has shown an interest in the occult, participating in primitive rituals, dancing beneath the stars with dusky African beauties and summoning up the spirits of the dead.... ...Charles believes the world is on a downhill slope and thinks it only logical to explore alternative solutions.

....Visitors ... hear little but the long catalogue of his concerns: unemployment, housing, race [relations], drugs, the decay of the inner city, the environment and family life....

There is an unworldliness ... about his otherwise admirable yearning to tackle the problems of Britain and the Third World....

---

1. Dale, pp. 231-238.

....[Having studied world-history, archaeology, and anthropology, as well as pursued amateur theatrics, he] is an honors graduate of [Trinity College at] Cambridge....[1] The books he reads ... are weighty ones about modern problems.... [(Consider *knight* William Henry Gates III.)]

While Diana's presence can make a room glow, his tends to breed stiffness and formality....

....[When] puttering about his country estate, Highgrove in Gloucestershire [Scotland,] ... he talks to his plants....[2]

Brad Darrach adds:

[Prince Charles] ... has a record of achievement unmatched by any other Prince of Wales .... ruddy good health, scorching charm, lively wit, ever-ready virility and a flair for the arts.... ....Charles has championed scholarships for the poor, raised financing for start-up businesses and launched a nationwide campaign to protect the environment.... "I want to be involved in something that makes a difference." ...

....As the world has learned, ... he has advocated alternative medicine and blithely admitted that he talks to plants, to make them grow. He has even found a guru, ... Sir Laurens van der Post..., who plunged Charles into the archetypal world of psychologist Carl Jung, where for several years the prince has been paddling like a metaphysical fly in symbol soup.... But often Charles transcribes the night's dreams on a bedside notepad and in the morning telephones van der Post to discuss his collective unconscious.

....[He is] affable, sincere, generous, devoted to his people. But he can also play the arrogant aristocrat....[3]

Junor states: "[Charles] has a magnetism about him which sets him apart, and such a talent for listening that even the toughest kids ... cheer him when he leaves. His charm is extraordinary.... He is straightforward, direct and sincere.... Inefficiency and bureaucracy make him angry, as does the popular press sometimes.... His entire being is subjugated to duty." Although Charles "is hugely caring and concerned for everyone," displaying "genuine humility, humor and sheer vulnerability," he "can be selfish and spoilt."[4] Cathcart comments:

Prince Charles is ... the first prince in history ever to have undertaken a systematic academic study of his craft, of the primitive roots of awe and the deep human need of tribal leadership that upholds the prestige of princes and the majesty of kings. These elements of his profession all arose in his year of social anthropology, 'from the origins of man through Stonehenge to Julius Caesar'....

---

1. Fry, *The Kings & Queens of England & Scotland*, p. 216.
2. Anthony Holden, "Man in a Gilded Cage," *LIFE*, Sept. 1987, pp. 32, 34-35.
3. Brad Darrach, "Prince Charles: A Dangerous Age," *People Weekly*, 31 Oct. 1988, pp. 97-98, 100.
4. Junor, pp. 3-4, 78.

His studies involved the folk mysteries of Frazer's *Golden Bough*[1] as well as modern theories of social behaviour. As he worked it out, 'if more people can be assisted to appreciate and understand their own social behaviour, the better and more healthy our society will be.... We should have a shrewd idea why we react to various situations and stimuli in the way we do.' ... For Charles, anthropology ... explained something of his own role in the world.... 'But I think it helps to illustrate the useful application of anthropology to modern existence.' ...

....[He] stayed at a hotel in Les Eyzies, sallying forth to see the reindeer paintings in the local honeycomb of caves, and the primitive carvings.... [He also] made a point of visiting the tombs of his Plantagenet ancestors at the Abbey of Fontrevault and, in Brittany, he examined the mysterious avenues and circles that are equated with Stonehenge....

....At an R.A.I. [(Royal Anthropological Institute)] dinner, Prince Charles had eloquently spoken of the need to popularise anthropology as a source of knowledge of the motivations of mankind. The sequel was, of course, a race of television companies to secure him for their cameras, and his agreement to take part in a series to feature himself and others giving a personal view of 'the values of Man'....[2]

Charles' enthusiasm for archaeology and anthropology is made clear by the possibility that had he continued those studies, "instead of changing in his second year to history, he might even have come away with a first." Nevertheless, Satan's Prince sees history as being "of paramount importance and relevance to us all," having stated: "I honestly believe that the only real way one can hope to understand and cope with the present, is by knowing and being able to interpret what happened in the past.... I don't think that's true of modern

---

1. James George Frazer's *Golden Bough* is a significant work for Charles as prince to have studied. In 1914, Frazer was knighted for his work, and in 1920, he became a Fellow of the Royal Society. Then, in 1925, he received the Order of Merit. Frazer's work is a famous study in paganism and witchcraft, which centers largely on the "slain god" of various pagan mythologies. Frazer, not surprisingly, relates virtually all pagan customs back to *Tammuz* in Babylon (*Adonis* in Greek). What is significant from the perspective of this work, however, is that according to Frazer, Christianity derives from the ancient pagan mythologies, rather than the mythologies themselves deriving from early pagan corruptions of the Zodiac. (In reality, before its ancient perversion, the Zodiac represented the complete Gospel message in a symbolic form.) Any reader who accepts Frazer at face value will come away with an historically twisted and completely perverted understanding of true Christianity—one that ties in well with the occult beliefs of the Merovingian dynasty. Frazer's accepting reader will see Christianity as merely a more sterile version of the ancient pagan mythologies. Mary Douglas, editor of *The Illustrated Golden Bough*, comments: "Frazer believed in a process of social evolution that had by now passed an irreversible judgment against all ritual slaying, whether the victim be animal or human being, or the god himself slain [only] to be offered to himself on behalf of his people. The full ambition of *The Golden Bough* is to place the sacrificial doctrines of Christianity, together with the doctrines of the Incarnation and of the Virgin Birth and of the Resurrection into the same perspective as totemic [(nature)] worship, together with the lusty antics of the Greek pantheon and with the burnt or bleeding carcasses on ancient altars of the Israelites. Whatever the stories were, they would be regarded as partial, imperfect versions.... But for the enlightened scholarship the task ahead ... would be the adducing of more and more evidence for that worldwide evolution towards a purer spirituality.... Yet for all this, Frazer cannot escape the charge of superficiality. He chose to deal with reflections on life and death, humanity and animality, divinity and immortality" (Frazer, pp. 9, 11, 13). King Charles III, no doubt, considers himself to be a part of "the enlightened scholarship."

2. Cathcart, pp. 74-75, 81, 170.

politicians."[1] Consider also these excerpts from Peter Davis' "real-life fiction" which explores the "fact and fantasy" of Charles' life:

> How indeed prepare a king? Let him know history...., science..., culture..., enough religion to know that he, like God, exists only if people believe he does....
>
> ....He sees a "dark side to man's psyche" and urges people to study psychology. He walks the Kalahari desert in Africa, meditating with his latest octogenarian guru.... He writes a children's book, *The Old Man of Lochnagar,* about a magical old man living in a cave on the Balmoral estate, where he can turn plants and animals into his friends and make himself vanish when he feels threatened by civilization.... PC .... goes to vegetables and talks to flowers....
>
> ....Methodically, usefully, he writes down his dreams.
>
> ....PC ponders [the meaning of a dream].... On an archetypal level, one strives to reunite with some dynamic harmony in nature as represented by the trees, plants, and deer, perhaps some unconscious wish to be them, mirrored by their own collective wish to be oneself....
>
> In a dream his grandfather's gold watch appears to PC. Instead of ticking, it talks to PC about healing an army of the disabled so that, cured, they can arise from their wheelchairs....
>
> ....His books are by the Greek philosophers, John Ruskin, Carl Jung, Alexander Solzenitsyn....
>
> ....When PC starts to walk off, a young black reaches out to touch him, saying, "You are the man, you are the man." ...
>
> Nature has inspired PC.... "I feel that deep in the mirror of mankind is a reflection of the beauty and harmony of the universe. Through the outer manifestation of that reflection we can attain the kind of peace for which we yearn...."[2]

The "Highlands" of Balmoral Castle in Scotland are perhaps Charles' favorite place on Earth—Romania ostensibly being a close second—and Lochnagar is his favorite place at Balmoral. Lochnagar means "Goat Lake." Maybe it should not surprise us then that it was at Balmoral (cf. *Ba'al*-moral) "where in solitude he would lose himself entirely, entering into ... intimacy with nature."[3] Recall, therefore, the earlier discussion concerning the tail of the dexter (left-hand) supporter, as well as other lion beasts, in Charles' heraldic achievement as Prince of Wales. We learned that the lions of mythology have magic in their tails, and that by waving them across their bodies, they are able to vanish. Such lions also have the power to resurrect their dead cubs.[4] Considering this, the "magical old man"

---

1. Junor, pp. 90-91.
2. Peter Davis, "Prince Charles Narrowly Escapes Beheading," *Esquire,* Apr. 1988, pp. 98, 100, 103, 106, 108, 111.
3. Dimbleby, *The Prince of Wales,* p. 30. Junor, between pp. 150-151. As Colonel-in-Chief of the 2nd King Edward VII Own Goorkhas, then Prince Charles wore, as part of that unit's insignia, what appears to be a goat's-head symbol (*Charles & Diana: A Royal Family Album,* p. 87).
4. For more information, see ch. 7's sections titled, "The top of the arms" and "The dexter (left-hand) sup-

in the then Prince Charles' book appears, at first glance, to be a veiled allusion not just to the Goat or *Satan*, but to Charles himself (e.g., when possessed), and his presence suggests Charles' own familiarity with the mythological meanings of various symbols in his coat of arms. (We may here also note a popular occult series of movies and a corresponding TV series, about a "highlander" from Scotland—who has a bloody mission as the "chosen one" to "save" the world. These movies enjoyed great success in Western Europe, and to an extent in the United States.)

"As a small boy he had imagined himself running away, escaping to the mountain of Lochnagar that loomed over the Balmoral estate <u>and hiding in a secret cavern</u>.... Contemplating the notion of the 'Wise Old Man', an archetypal figure representing that 'superior insight' which Jung discovered within himself, the Prince was encouraged by van der Post to believe that this 'guru' was, in his case, represented by the Old Man of Lochnagar—the mythical figure created by the Prince who inhabited the mountains at Balmoral and who was the subject of the children's book which he had written for his younger brothers when he was twenty."[1] Given this description, one has to wonder whether the "Wise Old Man" is not also an allusion to Merlin, the ancient "guru" and druid wizard of King Arthur's Round Table; for Merlin, who legend has it was born in a cavern outside Caernarfon, likewise could be viewed as Satan. King Charles III's full name remains, of course, Charles Philip *Arthur* George—and, as we saw earlier, it is Merlin's "wisdom" and King Arthur's "throne" that Charles received at his July 1969 investiture as Satan's Prince, at Merlin's home castle of Caernarfon.[2]

Before continuing, we must briefly look at northern Scotland's Findhorn Foundation. As a "prototype New Age community ... that offers an ongoing educational program in the principles of New Age spirituality and world service," this foundation "emphasizes the sacredness of everyday living."[3] Elliot Miller calls Findhorn "an almost legendary New Age community."[4] Yet, as with other New Age organizations, the spirituality of Findhorn (cf. "find the little horn") is a form of Satanism. David Spangler, a popular New Ager who cofounded and once led the Findhorn Foundation, makes the following statements concerning Lucifer in *Reflections on the Christ:*

---

porter," at pp. 135 and 192, respectively.
1. Dimbleby, *The Prince of Wales*, pp. 89, 252.
2. See ch. 8, "The Red Dragon and Prince Charles' Investiture as Prince of Wales," at p. 207.
3. Dr. Walter Martin, *The New Age Cult* (Minnesota: Bethany House Publishers, 1989), p. 116.
4. Elliot Miller, *A Crash Course on the New Age Movement* (Michigan: Baker Book House, 1989), p. 32.

The true light of Lucifer cannot be seen through sorrow, through darkness, through rejection. The true light of this great being can only be recognized when one's own eyes can see with the light of Christ, the light of the inner sun. Lucifer works within each of us to bring us to wholeness and as we move into a new age, which is the age of man's wholeness, each of us in some way is brought to that point which I term the Luciferic initiation, the particular doorway through which the individual must pass if he is to come fully into the presence of his light and wholeness....

Lucifer comes to give to us the final gift of wholeness. If we accept it then he is free and we are free. That is the Luciferic initiation. It is one that many people now, and in the days ahead, will be facing, for it is an initiation into the New Age.[1]

Larson informs us: "New Age proponents like the Findhorn Foundation ... communicate with plants, believing them to be inhabited by elemental spirits called *devas.* Plant communicators seek wisdom and guidance from the spirits, whom they believe possess feelings and intelligence."[2] Miller adds, "The former luminaries of Scotland's famed Findhorn community ... have channeled everything from nature spirits, to fairies, to elves, to the Greek god 'Pan,' to angels, to 'God.'"[3] As mentioned, Charles frequently travels to Scotland, where he talks to plants, to make them grow. (This is the opposite of Christ Jesus' purpose, when he *spoke to an unfruitful fig tree:* see Matthew 21:18-20). Also, Charles has traveled to the Kalahari desert with Sir Laurens van der Post, a personal friend of the late Jung, to learn the "values of the 'lost tribes' of the African desert." Among these "values," which Sir Laurens himself adheres to, is doing homage to demonic spirits.[4]

Charles as Satan's Prince supports not just the satanism and witchcraft of the *Harry Potter* series, but the Luciferianism of fool Philip Pullman's *Dust* trilogy, where: "'The Fall' is to be celebrated as the defining moment of mankind, rather than the source of all worldly evil.... Essentially, the trilogy is about the transition of innocence to experience, the triumph of knowledge over [(alleged)] ignorance.... Only later do we find that Dust is good — 'the totality of human wisdom and experience' is Pullman's description. It's the religious zealots trying to prevent the spread of [Luciferian] wisdom who are the bad guys [per Pullman], even if they wear clerics' robes."[5] Pullman confesses: "I've been surprised by how little criticism I've got. Harry Potter's been taking all the flak. I'm a great fan

1. David Spangler, *Reflections on the Christ* (Moray, Scotland: Findhorn Publications, 1981), pp. 44-45. Also see Michaelsen, p. 323.
2. Larson, p. 328.
3. Miller, p. 157.
4. Laurens van der Post and David Coulson, *The Lost World of the Kalahari* (New York: William Morrow and Company, Inc., 1988), pp. 167-170; Dale, pp. 29-30.
5. "The shed where God died," *Sunday Morning Herald,* 13 Dec. 2003.

of J.K. Rowling, but the people — mainly from America's Bible Belt — who complain that Harry Potter promotes Satanism or witchcraft obviously haven't got enough in their lives. Meanwhile, I've been flying under the radar, saying things that are far more subversive than anything poor old Harry has said. My books are about killing God.... I think I'm writing realism."[1] Tuominen comments:

> Many Christians are startled to hear [that] Charles supports the witchcraft of the *Harry Potter* books, but in fact, much more worrying is his support for Philip Pullman.... In Pullman's books, the biblical account of good and evil, God and Satan, is described in symbolic form, but ... things are turned upside down. The serpent in Adam's and Eve's paradise was not the villain..., but its hero who came to redeem mankind and deliver it from the tyranny of God—who is not, in fact, The Creator, but the fallen angel who hijacked His throne and pretends to be The Creator.
>
> Is this what Prince Charles [(now King Charles III)] really believes — that The God worshiped by Christians is not The Creator, but a fallen angel pretending to be Him, and that the true God is indeed the serpent of paradise, Lucifer himself? Pullman's books also describe the demonic ... as ... positive.... If we scroll through the pages of [Charles' 2012 book] *Harmony*, we end up with occult symbols traditionally associated with witchcraft and Satanism: triangle, [all-seeing] Eye of Horus and pentagram — these symbols, according to the prince himself, constitute the "grammar of harmony" at the heart of his [(architecture) vision and] message, the understanding of which contains the key to the unification of the whole world, from the destruction brought to us by materialist philosophy.[2]

It appears, therefore, that a connection may exist between Charles, who is a disciple of the teachings of Carl Jung, *as well as being a Luciferian,* and Scotland's Findhorn Foundation.

What makes this possibility most intriguing is the fact that Peter LeMesurier, author of *The Armageddon Script,* has, as Cumbey notes, a "publishing relationship with the Findhorn Foundation in Northern Scotland" (see below). LeMesurier's script is based upon "Jungian archetypes," so-called after psychiatrist Carl Jung, whose occultist ideas have heavily influenced the New Age Movement (not to mention modern psychiatry and certain heretical elements in the "Christian" Church). As Hunt points out, in the ecumenism of so-called "Christian" psychology: "Christ becomes the partner of Freud, Jung, Rogers, Maslow, and a host of other anti-Christians.... Such false 'Christianity' no longer holds truth to be important and thus can be embraced by the followers of all religions...."[3] With T.A. McMahon, he adds,

1. Ibid.
2. Samuel Tuominen, "Book Review: Prince Charles' Harmony," *SamuelTuominen.com,* 10 Oct. 2015.
3. Hunt, *GLOBAL PEACE AND THE RISE OF ANTICHRIST,* p. 158.

....Psychiatrist C.G. Jung, whom Morton T. Kelsey raised to the level of a Christian leader and saint, believed that images originating within the mind were as real as those coming from external objects. Heavily involved in the occult, including seances for communicating with the dead, Jung explained the "ghosts" he saw on more than one occasion as "exteriorizations" of archetypal images within his mind originating in the deep psyche of the human race. Refusing to believe in a real spirit world of demons or angels, psychologists play mind-games with visual images....

Miraculous cures, ecstatic experiences of universal love and personal transformation have been effected not only through visualizing "Jesus," but also by visualizing spirits of the dead, the great saints, ascended masters, and religious leaders from the past such as assorted ancient Hindu gurus or Buddha. What is the difference? Jung would say there is none; and this seems to be the teaching not only of Kelsey but of a number of other Christian leaders....

If it doesn't matter whether we visualize Jesus or Buddha, then it must not matter whether we *believe* in Jesus or Buddha.... Although it may be denied by some who practice it, that is the only premise upon which inner healing can be said to rest. *Imagination* is the Creator of a whole new past, present, and future; and is somehow confused with *revelation* from God.[1]

One writer comments,

The late occult Swiss psychiatrist Carl Jung ... is the modern-day father of symbology and also of visualization and inner healing. Jung admitted to possession by various spirits (demons), and one of his books was written through his hands by a demonic author. Jung believed that man could create reality with his thoughts. *Therefore, man can use thought-power to give life to symbols.*

Jung based his beliefs on his study of ancient Eastern religions such as Hinduism and on gnosticism. New Agers practically worship Carl Jung, and they .... are convinced that through visualization and meditation they can make symbols [and images] come alive and that these symbols will ever after have life, living on in the Collective Unconscious of the universe....

Scores of Catholic priests would agree with ... Jung.[2]

In an article on dreams, New Age enthusiast Cate Terwilliger states,

Chuck Specht, a deacon and pastoral administrator in St. Francis Parish, is a Christian Jungian dream worker[3] who occasionally uses his expertise in spiritual counseling....

---

1. Dave Hunt and T.A. McMahon, *The Seduction of Christianity* (Oregon: Harvest House Publishers, 1985), pp. 135, 177.
2. Marrs, *Mystery Mark of the New Age*, pp. 133-135.
3. Did you catch the oxymoron (i.e., "Christian Jungian")?

Jung believed in archetypes—universal patterns in the unconscious that emerge in dreams, art, legends and myths. A snake in a dream, for example, represents man's deepest awareness of the life energy of nature. A mandala (a combination of a four-sided figure and a circle) represents the self, or what Christians would think of as the Christ within, Specht says.[1]

Concerning *The Armageddon Script,* and the staging of a counterfeit "Christ," Cumbey writes,

> *"Their script is now written, subject only to last minute editing and stage-directions. The stage itself, albeit as yet in darkness, is almost ready. Down in the pit, the subterranean orchestra is already tuning up. The last-minute, walk-on parts are even now being filled. Most of the main actors, one suspects, have already taken up their roles. Soon it will be time for them to come on stage, ready for the curtain to rise...." ....*

....The above quote is the summation of *The Armageddon Script* by Peter LeMesurier a noted pyramidologist/occultist. It is a how-to manual for New Agers and intellectuals interested in staging a simulated second coming of Christ. The script they write, if successfully staged, could deceive "even the very elect."

It is logical and proper to question why one might expect the average person of intelligence to support such a scheme. To the contrary, it is precisely the intellectual whose support is being courted *and won* for this undertaking....

LeMesurier is a man with strong New Age connections, including a publishing relationship with the Findhorn Foundation in Northern Scotland. His books are widely promoted and sold in New Age bookstores. They show that he strongly supports and promotes the New Age philosophies....

....Crombie was **a dedicated patron of the Findhorn Foundation. He thought he frequently communed with "nature spirits."** ...

Analogies of an actor on the stage are common among occult initiates.... As a matter of fact, the 1914 issue of *The Theosophist* carried a similar analogy. In 1914 the Theosophical Society was, as are the occultists of today, engaged in preparing the world to receive their New Age "Christ." ... An article appearing in that magazine entitled "Why the World Does Not Understand" made it clear that what Theosophy was really all about was preparing the world to receive a myth—that the underlying actor was always the same....

....LeMesurier also says in effect that visualization is necessary for the manifestation of the Kingdom—for the kingdom of their deliberately staged false Christ!

> "In the meantime the new world-leader must prepare himself for his role. He must study the scriptures and the Dead Sea Scrolls, immerse himself in current Jewish messianic expectations, thoroughly survey the general locality and familiarize himself with all the major prophecies and the best in New Age religious thought. *In short he must create in his own mind a*

---

1. Cate Terwilliger, "Dreams," *Gazette Telegraph* (Colo. Springs, CO), 20 Oct. 1987, p. F3.

> crystal-clear idea of the vision which he has to fulfill. For only in this way can that vision be guaranteed to come into manifestation."[1]

In effect, *The Armageddon Script* and other, related New Age writings, advocate the introduction of a major world figure—one who is familiar with the significant prophecies and other teachings of the major religions—upon the world stage, so that, at the proper time, he could step forward to seemingly "fulfill" those prophecies. In other words, this individual, through a grandiose bit of acting, is to fool the bulk of the world's populace into thinking that he is their man, their "divinely" preordained leader who will finally usher in a spiritual new age of peace, security, and prosperity on Earth. When that time comes, in an effort to unite all mankind and ultimately eliminate religiously and ethnically motivated warfare, he is to claim to be the 'Coming One' for all the world's religions. Does such a scheme sound outlandish? Inasmuch as Britain's monarchy "has long enjoyed an association with entertainers and actors," and then Prince Charles was a personal acquaintance of the late actor Peter Ustinov,[2] consider this article:

> Groups led by Academy Award-winning actor Peter Ustinov and former presidential candidate John Anderson are plotting world government—a goal they say is not far-fetched. [(Satan's hypocrites are players.)] Ustinov is president of the World Federalist Movement, an international group that wants to transform the United Nations into a powerful federation able to protect the environment, end war and curtail international terrorism. "If all goes well, it's a logical ending to a long road of intolerance and battle and all sorts of wretched things in the past," said Ustinov, who is British. He met at Wellesley College in Massachusetts with other members of the group and its sister organization in the United States, the World Federalist Association, headed by Anderson.[3]

Burnet recalls a 1985 speech given by Satan's Prince, at a White House gala dinner in Washington:

> The Prince decided to take on the critics. In a speech at the dinner he hit back: 'What I want to know is what actually is wrong with being elite, for God's sake?' And 'how on earth do they expect us to get anything done without money?'
> He went on: '**How are we to have any hope of balanced and civi-lized leadership in the future unless there are some people who have learned about** service to others, about compassion, about understanding, as far as is humanly possible, **the other man's religion, the other man's**

---

1. Cumbey, *A Planned Deception*, pp. 7-8, 116-117, 180.
2. Ross Benson, "Stars in Their Eyes," *Majesty* magazine, July 1995, Vol. 16, No. 7, pp. 19-20.
3. AP and Reuter, "Actor plots world government," *Rocky Mountain News*, 14 June 1992, p. 150.

customs, and his history, about courage to stand up for things that are noble, and for things that are true?

'After all, there's so much to be done in this world—so much famine exists, so much disease, so much poverty, so much conflict, bigotry and prejudice, and there are so many people who are crying out for help, for their own simple dreams to come true.'[1]

Islam, and Overtures to Muslims. Satan's Prince, of course, goes well beyond trying to understand the other man's religion and customs. Note, for example, the following excerpts from an article captioned, "Prince Charles calls for millennium money to be spent on mosques and temples to bridge some of the divisions in society:"

...Prince Charles, writing in *The Guardian* ... says that ideas [in Britain] to mark the millennium have 'not focused on its spiritual importance and the potential it holds for personal and national renewal'....

Now our 20th-century Prince ... wishes to ensure that this Christian celebration is made 'relevant' to other faiths....

Of course the Heir to the Throne has been here before when, in a statement of equal eccentricity, he talked of his unconstitutional hope to be 'defender of all the faiths'....

...Charles talks about renewing Christian landmarks, for which I suppose we should be grateful even if it does mean, in his words, turning abandoned churches into 'health and healing centres which link together body and spirit in a complementary approach to healing'.

But the man who will one day head the Church of England goes on to say that the millennium can be harnessed by 'those of all faiths and creeds' ... and says the millennium funds should be used to build non-Christian places of worship....

[This] ... is a complete contradiction of the true spirit and meaning of the millennium, not a reaffirmation of it....

What Britain should be doing, as a [supposed] Christian nation, is concentrating on how to spend the money to reinforce and celebrate our Christian heritage. ....what better way to 'make people's lives better in a way which will have real meaning for them', as the Prince put it.[2]

Charles' advocacy of building mosques and temples is fascinating enough. Yet his overtures toward the world's one-billion-plus Muslims have become far more extreme. According to a few Muslim sources on the Internet, Satan's Prince underwent the ceremonies necessary to "become a Muslim by the name of 'Abdus-Salem Hafidh ad-Deen,'" which means "The Guardian of faith." Perhaps due to the fact that Islam's top Muslim clerics are referred to as "guardians," or due to its similarity to the traditional Anglican title "Defender of the Faith," formerly held by Queen Elizabeth II as the "head" of the Church of England—Charles changed it at his May 6th

1. Burnet, *In Private—In Public, THE PRINCE AND PRINCESS OF WALES*, pp. 88-90.
2. Simon Heffer, "God save us from politically correct Princes," *Daily Mail*, 26 Jan. 1996.

2023 crowning, to be "inclusive" and openly anti-Christian—*this title has prompted speculation among Muslims that Charles intends to "become the leader of the Muslims."*[1] Note that as a schoolboy, then Prince Charles, like Prince Philip before him,[2] was given the similar Platonic title of "Guardian" as *head boy* at Gordonstoun,[3] an Illuminati-run school that practices a form of what we now know as "outcome-based education" (OBE). At Gordonstoun, the "Guardian" had ten "helpers," just as the AntiChrist shall command ten world leaders.[4] In fact, Gordonstoun is situated on a satanic site.[5] (There are also druidic "guardians.")

Satan's Prince is said to take "regular advice on Islamic issues from a group of 12 religious leaders and academics." This is in harmony with other instances in which royals and their secret societies form groups of *thirteen* individuals, and likely parodies, in a satanic or Luciferic way, Jesus' calling of the twelve apostles. As the result of studied speeches made in October 1993 and December 1996 on Islam and the West, *Charles became and has apparently remained the most popular Westerner in the Muslim world.*[6]

---

1. Othman The Italian, *Is Prince Charles a Muslim?*, p. 1. The author possesses an HTML copy of this *formerly on-line* Muslim book (at "www.sinet.it/Islam/dwnload/charles.zip"), which addresses Charles, Prince Philip, and Freemasonry. An October 15, 1996 Internet article from *Londoner's Diary*, titled "Charles 'is a Secret Islam Convert,'" informed us: "The man making the claim is a respected religious leader—the Grand Mufti of Cyprus, Shaykh Nazim Adel, leader of Turkish Northern Cyprus' Muslims. He says Charles converted during a trip to Turkey. The Mufti is quoted in *The Riddle and the Knight: In search of Sir John Mandeville,* by Giles Milton.... 'Did you know,' the Mufti is reported as saying, 'that Prince Charles has converted to Islam. Yes, yes. He is a Muslim.' Milton, naturally, expressed astonishment. 'I can't say more,' responded the Mufti. 'But it happened in Turkey. Oh yes, he's converted all right. When you get home, check up on how often he travels to Turkey,' Milton says. 'He certainly wasn't joking.'" Others have noticed: E.g., Gordon and Stillman, "Prince Charles of Arabia;" Rayhan Uddin, "King Charles III: Five things the new British monarch said about Islam and Muslims," *Middle East Eye,* 13 Sep. 2022; and Paul Serran, "Charles III at an Impasse With Church of England Over His Coronation – Wants Participation of Non-Christian Clerics in Defiance of Tradition – Globalist King Previously Accused of Secretly Being a Muslim," *Gateway Pundit,* 10 Apr. 2023.

2. Judd, *Prince Philip,* p. 77.

3. Dimbleby, *The Prince of Wales,* pp. 43 and 61, 89. "Charles had passed through this selection process stage by stage until the post of Guardian became a definitive recognition of merit imposed directly by his school fellows" (Cathcart, p. 69).

4. For more information, see ch. 11's section titled, "The United World Colleges," at p. 394.

5. "In 1638..., Sir Robert Gordon, 1st Baron of Gordonstoun, bought the estate.... The next significant building work was carried out by the 3rd Baronet, known as Sir Robert the Wizard, who constructed ... the [non-traditional] Round Square. According to legend ... the reason for its odd shape arose from the fact that Sir Robert had struck a bargain with the Devil while a student in Padua. The Devil agreed to teach him 'the hidden secrets of the universe that the King of Heaven has denied to men' in return for his soul.... As the years passed Sir Robert brooded on the awful fate that approached. He finally hit on the idea of constructing a circle of magical proportions, a mathematical sanctuary in which the Devil would never be able to catch him.... The Round Square now houses the library, several classrooms, teachers' accomodation[s] and a few sleeping quarters, and it is said that the ghost of Sir Robert can be seen to this day" (Junor, pp. 39-40). Note, therefore, that when then Prince Charles was made Guardian at Gordonstoun, "he moved out of Windmill Lodge and into a room in Bob Waddell's flat in the Round Square" (ibid., pp. 64-65). Also, recall that Charles was invested as Prince of Wales, upon a circular platform of Welsh slate, at the center of which Satan was represented by the Welsh dragon. This, no doubt, emphasized the fact that Satan has also gained Charles' soul.

6. Additional information on King Charles III and Islam is readily available on the Internet. See, for exam-

That's what the author shared in the *first edition* of this work. Prior to its 1998 publication, "Prince Charles was photographed ... at the Grand Opening of a new Ahl as-Sunna masjid in London," where, dressed in Muslim garb and "accompanied by two shaikhs wearing traditional Sunni turbans, he waters [(watered)] a newly planted tree symbolizing the spread of [(satanic)] Islam in England."[1]   Dr. Mohamed Aboulkhair Zaki Badawi, who before his 2006 death had been among the globe's prominent Muslim scholars, described Charles as "the most popular world leader in the Muslim community throughout the world...., a man of such stature, and is able to speak for all of us."[2]   Later, then Prince Charles was awarded an Honorary Doctorate from Egypt's Al-Azhar University, Islam's "most ancient seat of learning."[3]   *Evidently, Charles is viewed as an Islamic scholar!*   While Charles freely quotes from "memorable passages" in the Koran, and from other Islamic sources, calling Mohammed "the prophet"—and though he has even studied Arabic "so he can read [and study] the Koran" itself "in its original form," and "decipher Arabic script on visits to mosques and museums"[4]—Charles yet pauses over Christian sources, stating, "I hesitate to speak with any authority on a subject as important and central as the [Anglican] Book of Common Prayer."   Notably, despite that "hesitation," Charles *presumes to do so anyway,* and that as a New Ager and satanist![5]

Excerpts from Charles' highly compelling and manipulative early speeches,[6] made as prince before hand-picked audiences including some of the world's most prominent Muslim clerics, follow:

> ....Unlike many of you, I am not an expert on Islam—though I am delighted ... to be a Vice Patron of the Oxford Centre for Islamic Studies. The Centre has the potential to be an important and exciting vehicle for promoting and improving understanding of the Islamic world..., like the Oriental Institute and the Middle East Centre....

ple, "Is Prince Charles a Convert to Islam?" at "https://www.danielpipes.org/blog/2003/11/is-prince-charles-a-convert-to-islam.html".

1. "Prince Charles Praises Islam," Al Ummah Newsletter, Vol. 1, No. 4, *As-Sunna Foundation of America,* January 1997. Re-titled as "Prince Charles' Latest Speech on Islam," see the article at "https://web.archive.org/web/20191124040212/http://www.sunnah.org/nl/v0104/prince.htm" on the Internet.
2. Stephen Bates, "Prince calls for respect between faiths," *The Guardian,* 30 April 2002.
3. For more information, see this chapter's later section titled "Respect," at p. 388.
4. Rebecca English, "'It goes in one ear and out the other': Prince Charles reveals he's been having Arabic lessons for six months so he can read the Koran," *Daily Mail,* 14 Mar. 2013.
5. "A speech by HRH The Prince of Wales at the anniversary reception for the Prayer Book Society, St James's Palace, London," 28 April 1997. See "https://web.archive.org/web/20120523225554/http://www.princeofwales.gov.uk/speechesandarticles/a_speech_by_hrh_the_prince_of_wales_at_the_anniversary_recep_1142669666.html" on the Internet. Also, see the example of Charles' 1999 eulogy to Jordan's King Hussein in the "1993-2001: The Clinton Era" chapter (or section) of the author's *Israel, "Peace" and the Looming Great Tribulation* multi-volume series.
6. Cathcart notes, "Like his father, he takes pains with his speeches, drafting and revising, memorising and often seeming to speak extempore, though a copy lies to hand" (p. 168).

....I believe wholeheartedly that the links between these two worlds matter more today than ever before, because the degree of misunderstanding between the Islamic and Western worlds remains dangerously high, and because the need for the two to live and work together in our increasingly interdependent world has never been greater....

....There are one billion Muslims worldwide. Many millions of them live in countries of the Commonwealth. Ten million or more live in the West, and around one million in Britain. Our own Islamic community has been growing and flourishing for decades. There are nearly 500 mosques in Britain. Popular interest in Islamic culture in Britain is growing fast. Many of you will recall—and I think some of you took part in—the wonderful Festival of Islam which Her Majesty The Queen opened in 1976. Islam is all around us. And yet distrust, even fear, persist. In the post-Cold War world of the 1990s, the prospects for peace should be greater than at any time in this century. **In the Middle East, the remarkable and encouraging events of recent weeks [(i.e., signing of the "Declaration of Principles," or the Oslo I "agreement," developed as part of the "security" negotiations of the Oslo "peace" process[1])], have created new hope for an end to an issue which has divided the world and been so dramatic a source of violence and hatred.** But the dangers have not disappeared. In the Muslim world, we are seeing the unique way of life of the Marsh Arabs of Southern Iraq, thousands of years old, being systematically devastated and destroyed. I confess that for a whole year I have wanted to find a suitable opportunity to express my despair and outrage at the unmentionable horrors being perpetrated in Southern Iraq. To me, the supreme and tragic irony of what has been happening to the Shia population of Iraq—especially in the ancient city and holy shrine of Kerbala—is that after the Western allies took immense care to avoid bombing such holy places (and I remember begging General Schwarzkopf when I met him in Riyadh in December 1990 to do his best to protect such shrines during any conflict) it was Saddam Hussein himself, and his terrifying regime, who caused the destruction of some of Islam's holiest sites. And now we have had to witness the deliberate draining of the marshes and the near total destruction of a unique habitat, together with an entire population that has depended upon it since the dawn of human civilization. The international community has been told the draining of the marshes is for agricultural purposes. How many more obscene lies do we have to be told before action is taken? Even at the eleventh hour it is still not too late to prevent a total cataclysm. I pray that this might at least be a cause in which Islam and the West could join forces for the sake of our common humanity.... Elsewhere, the violence and hatred are more intractable and deep-seated, as we go on seeing every day to our horror in the wretched suffering of peoples across the world—in the former Yugoslavia, in Somalia, Angola, Sudan, in so many of the former Soviet Republics. In Yugoslavia the terrible sufferings of the Bosnian Muslims, alongside that of other communities in that cruel war, help keep alive many of the fears and prejudices which our two worlds retain of each other. Conflict, of course, comes about because of the misuse of power and the clash of ideals, not to mention the inflammatory activities of unscrupulous and bigoted leaders. But it also arises, tragically, from an inability to understand, and from the powerful

---

1. For more information, see the *Israel, "Peace" and the Looming Great Tribulation* multi-volume series.

emotions which out of misunderstanding lead to distrust and fear. Ladies and gentlemen, we must not slide into a new era of danger and division because governments and peoples, communities and religions, cannot live together in peace in a shrinking world.

It is odd, in many ways, that misunderstandings between Islam and the West should persist. For that which binds our two worlds together is so much more powerful than that which divides us. **Muslims, Christians —and Jews—are all 'peoples of the Book'.** Islam and Christianity share a common monotheistic vision: a belief in one divine God, in the transience of our earthly life, in our accountability for our actions, and in the assurance of life to come. We share many key values in common: respect for knowledge, for justice, compassion towards the poor and underprivileged, the importance of family life, respect for parents. 'Honour thy father and thy mother' is a Quranic precept too. Our history has been closely bound up together. There, however, is one root of the problem. For much of that history has been one of conflict: fourteen centuries too often marked by mutual hostility. That has given rise to an enduring tradition of fear and distrust, because our two worlds have so often seen that past in contradictory ways. To Western school children, the two hundred years of Crusades are traditionally seen as a series of heroic, chivalrous exploits in which the kings, knights, princes—and children—of Europe tried to wrest Jerusalem from the wicked Muslim infidel. To Muslims, the Crusades were an episode of great cruelty and terrible plunder, of Western infidel soldiers of fortune and horrific atrocities, perhaps exemplified best by the massacres committed by the Crusaders when, in 1099, they took back Jerusalem,[1] the third holiest city in Islam.... The point, I think, is not that one or other picture is more true, or has a monopoly of truth. It is that misunderstandings arise when we fail to appreciate how others look at the world, its history, and our respective roles in it.

The corollary of how we in the West see our history has so often been to regard Islam as a threat—in medieval times as a military conqueror, and in more modern times as a source of intolerance, extremism and terrorism.... With the fall of the Ottoman Empire, Europe's triumph over Islam seemed complete. Those days of conquest are over. But even now our common attitude to Islam suffers because the way we understand it has been hijacked by the extreme and the superficial. To many of us in the West, Islam is seen in terms of the tragic civil war in Lebanon, the killings and bombings perpetrated by extremist groups in the Middle East, and by what is commonly referred to as 'Islamic fundamentalism'. Our judgment of Islam has been grossly distorted by taking the extremes to be the norm. That, ladies and gentlemen, is a serious mistake....

For example, people in this country frequently argue that the Sharia law of the Islamic world is cruel, barbaric and unjust.... The truth is, of course, different *[(no, it is not)]* and always more complex. My own understanding is that extremes, like the cutting off of hands, are rarely practised. The guiding principle and spirit of Islamic law, taken straight from the Qur'an, should be those of equity and compassion. We need to study its actual application before we make judgements. We must distinguish between systems of justice administered with integrity, and systems of justice

---

1. Note Charles' veiled reference to Godfroi de Bouillon. For more information, see ch. 4, "Prince of this World—a *Diverse* Lineage," at p. 79.

as we may see them practised which have been deformed for political reasons into something no longer Islamic.... Women are not automatically second-class citizens because they live in Islamic countries. We cannot judge the position of women in Islam aright if we take the most conservative Islamic states as representative of the whole....

We in the West need also to understand the Islamic world's view of us. There is nothing to be gained, and much harm to be done, by refusing to comprehend the extent to which many people in the Islamic world genuinely fear our own Western materialism and mass culture as a deadly challenge to their Islamic culture and way of life.... The fact is that our form of materialism can be offensive to devout Muslims—and I do not just mean the extremists among them. We must understand that reaction, just as the West's attitude to some of the more rigorous aspects of Islamic life needs to be understood in the Islamic world. This, I believe, would help us understand **what we have commonly come to see as the threat of Islamic fundamentalism.** We need to be careful of that emotive label, 'fundamentalism', and distinguish, as Muslims do, between revivalists, who choose to take the practice of their religion most devoutly, and fanatics or extremists who use this devotion for political ends. Among the many religious, social and political causes of what we might more accurately call the Islamic revival is **a powerful feeling of disenchantment,** of the realisation that Western technology and material things are insufficient, and that a deeper meaning to life lies elsewhere in the essence of Islamic belief.

At the same time, we must not be tempted to believe that extremism is in some way the hallmark and essence of the Muslim. **Extremism is no more the monopoly of Islam than it is the monopoly of other religions, including Christianity.** The vast majority of Muslims, though personally pious, are moderate in their politics. Theirs is the 'religion of the middle way'. The Prophet himself always disliked and feared extremism. Perhaps the fear of Islamic revivalism which coloured the 1980's is now beginning to give way in the West to an understanding of the genuine spiritual forces behind this groundswell. But if we are to understand this important movement, we must learn to distinguish clearly between what the vast majority of Muslims believe and the terrible violence of a small minority among them which civilized people everywhere must condemn.

Ladies and gentlemen, if there is much misunderstanding in the West about the nature of Islam, there is also much ignorance about the debt our own culture and civilisation owe to the Islamic world.... The mediaeval Islamic world, from Central Asia to the shores of the Atlantic, was a world where scholars and men of learning flourished.... The contribution of Muslim Spain to the preservation of classical learning during the Dark Ages, and to the first flowerings of the Renaissance, has long been recognised.... Not only did Muslim Spain gather and preserve the intellectual content of ancient Greek and Roman civilisation, it also interpreted and expanded upon that civilisation, and made a vital contribution of its own in so many fields of human endeavour—in science, astronomy, mathematics, algebra (itself an Arabic word), law, history, medicine, pharmacology, optics, agriculture, theology, music....

Islam nurtured and preserved the quest for learning.... Cordoba in the 10th century was by far the most civilised city of Europe.... That was made possible because the Muslim world acquired from China the skill of making paper more than four hundred years before the rest of non-Muslim Europe. Many of the traits on which modern Europe prides itself came to it from Muslim Spain. Diplomacy, free trade, open borders, the techniques of academic research, of anthropology, etiquette, fashion, alternative medicine, hospitals, all came from this great city of cities. **Mediaeval Islam was a religion of remarkable tolerance for its time, allowing Jews and Christians the right to practise their inherited beliefs, and setting an example which was not, unfortunately, copied for many centuries in the West.** The surprise, ladies and gentlemen, is the extent to which Islam has been a part of Europe for so long, first in Spain, then in the Balkans, and the extent to which it has contributed so much towards the civilisation which we all too often think of, wrongly, as entirely Western. Islam is part of our past and present, in all fields of human endeavour. It has helped to create modern Europe. It is part of our own inheritance, not a thing apart.

More than this, **Islam can teach us today a way of understanding and living in the world which Christianity itself is poorer for having lost. At the heart of Islam is its preservation of an integral view of the Universe. Islam—like Buddhism and Hinduism—refuses to separate man and nature, religion and science, mind and matter, and has preserved a metaphysical and unified view of ourselves and the world around us. At the core of Christianity there still lies an integral view of the sanctity of the world, and a clear sense of the trusteeship and responsibility given to us for our natural surroundings....**

But the West gradually lost this integrated vision of the world with Copernicus and Descartes and the coming of the scientific revolution. A comprehensive philosophy of nature is no longer part of our everyday beliefs. I cannot help feeling that, if we could now only rediscover that earlier, all-embracing approach to the world around us, to see and understand its deeper meaning, we could begin to get away from the increasing tendency in the West to live on the surface of our surroundings, where we study our world in order to manipulate and dominate it, turning harmony and beauty into disequilibrium and chaos. It is a sad fact, I believe, that in so many ways **the external world we have created in the last few hundred years has come to reflect our own divided and confused inner state.** Western civilisation has become increasingly acquisitive and exploitive in defiance of our environmental responsibilities. **This crucial sense of oneness and trusteeship of the vital sacramental and spiritual character of the world about us is surely something important we can relearn from Islam.... ...I am appealing for ... a wider, deeper, more careful understanding of our world: for a metaphysical as well as material dimension to our lives, in order to recover the balance we have abandoned, the absence of which, I believe, will prove disastrous in the long term. If the ways of thought in Islam and other religions can help us in that search, then there are things for us to learn in this system of belief which I suggest we ignore at our peril.**

Ladies, and gentlemen, **we live today in one world, forged by instant communications, by television, by the exchange of information on a scale undreamed of by our grandparents. The world economy functions as an inter-dependant entity. Problems of society, the quality of life and the environment, are global in their causes and effects, and none of us any longer has the luxury of being able to solve them on our own.** The Islamic and Western worlds share problems common to us all: how we adapt to change in our societies, how we help young people who feel alienated from their parents or society's values, how we deal with **Aids, drugs, and the disintegration of the family**. Of course, these problems vary in nature and intensity between societies. But the similarity of human experience is considerable. **The international trade in hard drugs is one example, the damage we are collectively doing to our environment is another. We have to solve these threats to our communities and our lives together.... [We] have to learn to understand each other, and to educate our children ... so that they understand too. We have to show trust, mutual respect and tolerance.... The Islamic and Western world can no longer afford to stand apart from a common effort to solve their common problems.... We have to ... understand and tolerate, and build on the positive principles our cultures have in common.... Each of us needs to understand the importance of conciliation....**

If this need for tolerance and exchange is true internationally, it applies with special force within Britain itself. **Britain is a multi-racial and multi-cultural society.... Where there are failings of understanding and tolerance, we have a need ... for greater reconciliation among our own citizens.** I can only admire, and applaud, those men and women of so many denominations who work tirelessly ... to promote good community relations. **The Centre for the Study of Islam and Christian-Muslim Relations in Birmingham is one especially notable and successful example.** We should be grateful for the dedication and example of all those who have devoted themselves to the cause of promoting understanding.

....These two worlds, the Islamic and the Western, are at something of a crossroads in their relations. We must not let them stand apart. I do not accept the argument that they are on a course to clash in a new era of antagonism. I am utterly convinced that our two worlds have much to offer each other. We have much to do together.... The further down that road we can travel, the better the world that we shall create for our children and for future generations.[1]

....I start from the belief that **Islamic civilisation at its best, like many of the religions of the East—Judaism, Hinduism, Jainism and Buddhism—has an important message for the West** in the way it has retained an integrated and integral view of **the sanctity of the world around us**. I feel that we in the West could be helped to rediscover the roots of our own understanding by an appreciation of the Islamic tradition's deep respect for **the timeless traditions of the natural order**.

I believe that process could help in the task of bringing our two faiths closer together. It could also help us in the West to rethink, and for the better, our practical stewardship of man and his environment—in fields such as health-care, the natural environment and agriculture, as well as in architecture and urban planning....

1. Charles, Prince of Wales, "Islam and the West," 27 Oct. 1993. For the full text of this speech, given at the Sheldonian Theatre, Oxford, when Satan's Prince visited the Oxford Centre for Islamic Studies, see "https://eweb.furman.edu/~ateipen/pr_charles_speech.html" or "https://web.archive.org/web/20120115080941/http://www.princeofwales.gov.uk/speechesandarticles/a_speech_by_hrh_the_prince_of_wales_titled_islam_and_the_wes_425873846.html" or "https://web.archive.org/web/20080704062532/http ://www.islamicsupremecouncil.org/bin/site/wrappers/media-pr_show-238A.html" on the Internet.

Modern materialism ... is unbalanced and increasingly damaging in its long-term consequences. **Yet nearly all the great religions of the world have held an integral view of the sanctity of the world. The Christian message with, for example, its deeply mystical and symbolic doctrine of the Incarnation, has been traditionally a message of the unity of the worlds of spirit and matter, and of God's manifestation in this world and in mankind.**

....Science has tried to assume a monopoly—even a tyranny—over our understanding. Religion and science have become separated.... Science has attempted to take over the natural world from God; it has fragmented the cosmos and relegated the sacred to a separate and secondary compartment of our understanding, divorced from practical, day to day existence.

We are only now beginning to gauge the disastrous results. We in the Western world seem to have lost **a sense of the *wholeness* of our environment, and of our immense and inalienable responsibility to the whole of creation**. This has led to an increasing failure to appreciate or understand tradition and the wisdom of our forebears....

In my view, a more holistic approach is needed now. Science has done the inestimable service of showing us a world much more complex than we ever imagined. But in its modern, materialist, one-dimensional form, it cannot explain everything. God is not merely the ultimate Newtonian mathematician or the mechanistic clockmaker. As science and technology have become increasingly separated from ethical, moral and sacred considerations, so the implications of such a separation have become more sombre and horrifying—as we see in genetic manipulation....

I believe there is a growing sense of the danger of these materialist presumptions in our increasingly alienated and dissatisfied world.... Some scientists are slowly coming to realise the awe-inspiring complexity and mystery of the universe. But there remains a need to rediscover the bridge between what the great faiths of the world have recognised as our inner and our outer worlds, our physical and our spiritual nature. That bridge is the expression of our humanity. It fulfils this role through the medium of traditional knowledge and art, which have civilised mankind and without which civilisation could not long be maintained. After centuries of neglect and cynicism the transcendental wisdom of the great religious traditions, including the Judaeo-Christian and the Islamic, **and the metaphysics of the Platonic tradition which was such an important inspiration for Western philosophical and spiritual ideas is finally being rediscovered**.

I have always felt that **tradition is not a man-made element in our lives, but a God-given intuition of natural rhythms, of the fundamental harmony that emerges from the union of the paradoxical opposites that exist in every aspect of nature. Tradition reflects the timeless order of the cosmos, and anchors us into an awareness of the great mysteries of the universe**, so that, as Blake put it, we can see the whole universe in an atom and eternity in a moment. That is why I believe Man is so much more than just a biological phenomenon.... ...I nevertheless believe that the survival of civilised values, as we have inherited them from our ancestors, depends on the corresponding survival in our hearts of that profound sense of the sacred and the spiritual.

Traditional religions, with their integral view of the universe, can help us to rediscover the importance of the integration of the secular and the sacred. The danger of ignoring this essential aspect of our existence is not just spiritual or intellectual. It also lies at the heart of that great divide between the Islamic and Western worlds over the place of materialism in our lives. In those instances where Islam chooses to reject Western materialism, this is not, in my view, a political affectation or the result of envy or a sense of inferiority. Quite the opposite. And the danger that the gulf between the worlds of Islam and the other Eastern religions on the one hand and the West on the other will grow ever wider and more unbridgeable is real, **unless we can explore together practical ways of integrating the sacred and the secular in both our cultures in order to provide a true inspiration for the next century**.

This rediscovery of an integrated view of the sacred could also help us in areas of important practical activity. In Medicine, whatever some scientists might say, the rupture between religion and science, between the material world and a sense of the sacred, has too often led to a blinkered approach to healthcare, and to a failure to understand the wholeness and the manifest mystery of the healing process. Hospitals need to be conceived and, above all, designed to reflect the wholeness of healing if they are to help the process of recovery in a more complete way. Modern medicine remains too often a one-dimensional approach to illness which, however, sophisticated and miraculous in some of its achievements, cannot of itself understand more than a fraction of what there is to know, and can still be enriched and enlightened by more traditional approaches. There are, I am glad to say, beacons of light seeking to integrate the modern and traditional approaches which I have come across over the years, such as the Marylebone Health Centre in London, or the Bristol Cancer Help Centre....

Look also at urban planning. The great historian, Ibn Khaldun, understood that the intimate relationship between city life and spiritual tranquillity was an essential basis for civilisation. Can we ever again return to such harmony in our cities? As civilisations decay, so do the crafts, as Ibn Khaldun again wrote.

....Islamic culture in its traditional form has striven to preserve this integrated, spiritual view of the world in a way we have not seen fit to do in recent generations in the West. There is much we can learn from that Islamic world view in this respect....

....There are many ways in which mutual understanding and appreciation can be built. Perhaps, for instance, we could begin by having more Muslim teachers in British schools, or by encouraging exchanges of teachers. **Everywhere in the world people want to learn English. But in the West, in turn, we need to be taught by Islamic teachers how to learn with our hearts, as well as our heads. The approaching millennium may be the ideal catalyst for helping to explore and stimulate these links, and I hope we shall not ignore the opportunity this gives us to rediscover the spiritual underpinning of our entire existence.** For myself, I am convinced that we cannot afford, for the health and sustainability of a civilised existence, any longer to ignore these timeless features of our world. A sense of the sacred can, I believe, help provide the basis for developing a new relationship of understanding which can only enhance the relations between our two faiths — and indeed between all faiths — for the benefit of our children and future generations.[1]

---

1. Charles, Prince of Wales, "A Sense of the Sacred: Building Bridges Between Islam and the West," The

According to Satan's Prince, Islam represents "one of the greatest treasuries of accumulated wisdom and spiritual knowledge available to humanity."[1] *Yet, Islam's forever-roasting false prophet Mohammed was an Edomite—not just an Ishmaelite—and Islam is an Edomite religion; Charles also descends from Mohammed.* Satan's Prince has made a definite impact not just among Muslims, but also in the West. Major themes of his speeches concerning Islam and the West, have for decades, been echoed in the popular press:

> ....With the demise of communism, Islam has emerged as one of the world's most powerful ideologies, a religion that embraces more than 1 billion adherents who make up a majority in about 45 countries.
>
> Yet, as a new century dawns, Islam is undergoing change potentially more important than any time since the death of the Prophet Mohammed.... That change—a quest to determine its role in a modern world —poses a challenge to the West and to Islam itself.
>
> Its impact is vast, with implications for the flow of oil, trade, nuclear proliferation, even war. While Muslim countries account for just 4 percent of the world's economy, they make up one-fifth of its population—a potentially explosive mix.
>
> Already the revival has witnessed terrorism in Algeria, a battle over women's rights in Afghanistan, militancy in Iran. Its flip side has been grassroots work that has bettered the lives of millions.
>
> For the West, the renewal may mean confrontation or co-existence with Islam, depending on attitudes on both sides at their many points of contact.[2]

In 1996, after the Muslim "holy" month of Ramadan, then Prince Charles visited a London mosque where, attired "in traditional Islamic cap and shawl," "he met with the Muslim worshippers including followers of Mawlana Shaykh Mohammed Nazim Adil al-Haqqani, Grand Mufti of Cyprus and world leader of the Most Distinguished Naqshbandi Order of Sufis."[3] On November 12, 1996, while in Uzbekistan, Satan's Prince wore a square skull cap and traditional Islamic wedding gown given to him as a gift by "the country's religious leader, the Mufti Mukhtar Abdullaev," which, according to the *Evening Standard*, "ended up looking like a marriage between East and West." From there, after "meeting with the Mufti at the nearby

Wilton Park Seminar, 13 Dec. 1996. For the full text of this speech, which Satan's Prince delivered to a private audience of seventy religious leaders, academics, and businessmen, see "https://web.archive.org/web/20110805202536/http://www.princeofwales.gov.uk/speechesandarticles/a_speech_by_hrh_the_prince_of_wales_titled_a_sense_of_the_sa_1083050310.html" on the Internet.

1. Rayhan Uddin, "King Charles III: Five things the new British monarch said about Islam and Muslims," *Middle East Eye*, 13 Sep. 2022.
2. "Islam evolves, seeks to define role in modern world," *The Denver Post*, 23 Jan. 1997, p. 20A.
3. Afdhel Aziz, "Celebrations for Eid- Ul- Fitr," 8 Feb. 1998, as posted at "https://sundaytimes.lk/98020 8/mirrorm.html" on the Internet.

Baraka-Khan Madrassah, a 16th-century Islamic seminary, ... [in] a small, white-washed room," Charles went to Tashkent's Tellya Sheikh Mosque "to see the Osman Koran, said to be the world's oldest Islamic holy book," in which he "showed great interest," stating 'I'm so thrilled at having a chance to see this great Koran.'" In Uzbekistan, typifying his ecumenism, Satan's Prince also met the Patriarch of Russia, who "told him of a 'very considerable' revival in the Russian Orthodox Church."[1] Many more such events have since transpired!

Maitreya and King Charles III. Many New Agers are not currently looking for a "Coming One." Yet some New Age organizations *are,* and they have stated that he lives *in London,* where he has supposedly resided since 1977. Calling him "Maitreya Buddha," "The World Teacher," "the Avatar for the Age, the Representative of God, the Messiah of the Jews, the Imam Mahdi of the Muslims, Krishna returned," Benjamin Creme announced on May 14, 1982: "He is in England and has been in England for all these years since July 1977. The large town is London.... The community is the Pakistani-Indian community of South London.... The christ comes not really to save —he comes to teach."[2] Ernest Ramsey, a New Ager who has written about the approaching *"Reappearance of the Christ and his Executives, the Masters of Wisdom,"* traveled "to London to try and see 'The Christ.'"[3] According to Dale, it was in 1977 that Satan's Prince "began to climb off the fence and to line up with the mixed bag of visionaries, intellectuals, cranks and lunatics who say there are other planes of existence tangled inside and around the one which we inhabit," and "[it] was in 1982 that the Prince first hinted publicly at such unusual spiritual beliefs.... He saw himself as a sort of missionary...." Indeed, Dale credits a highly publicized speech that then Prince Charles delivered on December 14, 1982, "as the turning point for what is now promoted and marketed as alternative medicine."[4] With these things in mind, consider the following comments:

> ....Light-years ahead of anyone else on earth, he will teach marvelous new revelations and bring peace and prosperity. He will come as a savior, arriving just as the world is sliding into chaos and destruction to lead man into a bright, shining, glorious New Age.
> ....The New Age "Christ" is a blasphemous imitation of the true Christ of the Bible....
> Lola Davis identifies the New Age "Christ" as "the One for whom all religions wait, called Lord Maitreya by some in the East, Krishna, Messiah,

---

1. "Blood, Charles and the murdered Caliph," *Evening Standard,* 12 Nov. 1996.
2. Church, pp. 258, 261-262.
3. Cumbey, *A Planned Deception,* p. 171.
4. Dale, pp. 9, 13-19, 33-37, 175-178, 200-206. For more information, see Dale's documentation starting around p. 354 of this chapter.

Bodhisattva, Christ, Immam Mahdi." She promises, he "will bring new revelations and further guidance for establishing the World Religion."

Currently, Davis explains, the New Age "Christ" resides on a different plane of consciousness from that which we experience. There he directs the Masters, "a group of advanced souls, most of them discarnate ... known variously as the White Brotherhood, The Great White Lodge, the Masters of Wisdom, the Hierarchy, and the Angels around the Throne." ...

Alice Bailey, head of both the Arcane School and the Lucis Trust, has written a number of books which detail The Plan.... Bailey's *The Externalization of the Hierarchy* predicts that the New Age will be in full bloom soon after a global crisis occurs and in desperation the world turns to the "Christ" for leadership. This New Age "Christ" will affirm the essential divine nature of humanity, says Bailey, and a New World Religion will come about.... Christianity will be eclipsed by the new religion....

The New Age holds that the term Christ can be applied to any person who reaches an elevated state of consciousness and thereby achieves divine status. It is said that we are all simply Christs-in-the-making. Nevertheless, historically only a few souls have found enough favor with the spiritual hierarchy of reincarnated ancient Masters to be chosen to return to earth as an *avatar*.

The concept of the avatar is derived from the Hindu religion, which teaches that avatars are reincarnations-in-the-flesh of the god Vishnu, messengers sent to the living from the "gods." ... This corresponds to the New Age belief in the hierarchy of reincarnated ancient Masters.

....In the New Age scheme of things Jesus is not the Son of God, but just another enlightened, reincarnated spirit.

New Age disciples claim that in the near future we can expect an avatar to come who is far greater than either Jesus, Buddha, Krishna, Mohammed, or Gandhi. Rather than just *another* "Christ," this is to be the "Christ." He will be god realized, god incarnate.

Lord Maitreya, avatar and world teacher, is now claimed to be living in London, preparing himself for his eventual reign at the world's helm....

"Lord Maitreya" is identified by most New Age groups as their coming "Christ." However, to deflect criticism, many refrain from naming him. Instead, such general titles as "the enlightened one to come," the "Cosmic Christ," the "Universal One," or the "New Age World Teacher" are used.[1]

New Age leaders can't imitate Jesus' mind-boggling coming in the clouds with all power and glory, so they claim that their "Christ," the Lord Maitreya, *has already appeared* on Planet Earth. Benjamin Creme says that the New Age "Christ" is now in London living in a Pakistani community, though he has not as yet revealed his identity to everyone.[2]

On the basis of God's inspired Word, we can be certain that the Tribulation Period and the events preceding it will not unfold in precisely the manner foretold by the false prophets and prophetesses of the New Age Movement. Nevertheless, it is noteworthy that Buck-

---

1. Texe Marrs, *Dark Secrets of the New Age* (Illinois: Good News Publishers, 1987), pp. 56-59.
2. Marrs, *Mystery Mark of the New Age*, p. 247.

ingham Palace is near London's Southall, where a number of Pakistani and Indian families live. Therefore, some statements from New Age circles (e.g., that their so-called "Christ" lives in London) definitely do bear consideration.

As shown, Charles openly airs his concerns about various social ills: "the Prince and Princess have shown great social concern, involving themselves in the problems of the underprivileged in a way that few others of their generation and class have done."[1] According to Satan's Prince, "The first function of any monarchy is the human concern for people."[2] It is interesting, therefore, that the very issues which Charles has addressed publicly with the most zeal and repetition are the very same ones that the mentioned New Age organizations allege to be the primary concerns of their coming "Christ." Not coincidentally, they are likewise among the pressing reasons pushed by today's one-worlders to try to justify global governance.[3] Consider these statements from a full-page Tara Center advertisement in the January 12, 1987 edition of *USA Today*:

> *Drugs ... A.I.D.S.... poverty ... rampant crime ... mass starvation ... nuclear threat ... terrorism.... Is there a solution? In answer to our urgent need ... THE CHRIST IS IN THE WORLD. A great World Teacher for people of every religion and no religion. A practical man with solutions to our problems. He loves ALL humanity.... Christ is here, my friends. Your Brother walks among you.*[4]

It has never been coincidental that Charles routinely makes his views regarding these and other, related issues known. Subjects not mentioned in this Tara Center advertisement, in which Satan's Prince likes to involve himself, include architecture[5] and the environment:

> ....Charles [(now King Charles III)] pursues his ambitions to improve architecture, the state of the English language and the environment through his public speeches and the making of films for television....
> ....Charles ... has become the voice of the people in his stand against pollution; pollution of the old values, represented by the falling standards of spoken English and modern architecture and by inner-city decay, as well as the pollution, in real terms, of the very air we breathe, the food we eat and the items we use in our everyday lives. The "greening" of the Royal Family owes much to ... Charles. He grows his own vegetables organically

---

1. Hoey, *Charles & Diana: The Tenth Anniversary*, p. 155.
2. *Charles & Diana: A Royal Family Album*, p. 55.
3. For more information, see ch. 9, "Signs of the Times and the Rise of 'Global Governance,'" at p. 279.
4. Marrs, *Dark Secrets of the New Age*, p. 66.
5. For insight on Charles' seemingly disconsonant and overbearing interest in architecture, see ch. 11's section titled, "Architecture," at p. 479.

and refuses to allow any aerosol containers to be used in any of his homes. In other words, he practises what he preaches.[1]

....The prime requisite for a good architect [(per Charles)] should be 'to be concerned about the way people live—about the environment they inhabit and the kind of community that is created by that environment.' ...

....'Those who recall it [(i.e., London before he was born)] say that the affinity between the buildings and the earth, in spite of the city's great size, was so close and organic that the houses looked almost as though they had grown out of the earth, and not been imposed upon it—grown, moreover, in such a way that as few trees as possible were thrust out of the way.' He faintly sugared the pill by praising some of the work that had been done in designing for the disabled,[2] but the burden of his speech [to the Royal Institute of British Architects] was damning....

The Prince was not so very out of step, however, as he discovered from the letters of support that poured in. Indeed he had put his finger most succinctly upon precisely what a great many people felt.... The issue of community architecture was based on more than just instinct; it was soundly based on what he had learned from talking to people who had to live in the buildings and environments that planners had created for them. Charles is a great listener....

Community architecture was not a new concept—enlightened architects had been practising it from time immemorial.... The Prince ... had simply discovered that one of the biggest difficulties for people living in the inner cities was that their housing was unsuitable for their needs....

The result was that people became despondent. If they didn't like their surroundings they didn't look after them.... [They then] ... reached rock bottom and hit out at society.... If people are happy in their homes and their environment they will become involved in looking after it and take a pride in what they are doing; this in turn will restore their own self-confidence and alter their entire outlook on life. This surely was the solution, and with this in mind Charles sought out architects who were already working in the field.[3]

Prince Charles attacked modern British architecture again ... with a television documentary.... The heir apparent ... wrote his own script [in which he spoke of the "Great Fire of 1666"].... He narrated it with grace, humor, and occasionally self-deprecating wit.... The queen, as monarch, is

---

1. Hoey, *Charles & Diana: The Tenth Anniversary,* pp. 110, 150-151.

2. Charles ostensibly takes his concern for the disabled seriously. In 1981, for example, the then prince served as Patron of the International Year of Disabled People. According to Junor: "Prince Charles had been eager to make a contribution [to the disabled] himself.... [He] had been camping and canoeing with them—and had come to appreciate the problems of living in a world designed for the able-bodied.... [So] it was suggested that Prince Charles should set up an advisory group which would not duplicate the good work already being done by other organizations in the field, but rather support them, pinpoint areas of weakness and act as a catalyst in getting things done.... [Consequently,] the Prince of Wales's Advisory Group on Disability had been formed.... [The advisors] have highlighted the five major areas of neglect: access, housing, employment, independent living and prevention, and are systematically working through them" (pp. 219, 230). In the booklet *Living Options,* Charles as prince states: "Recognize that those who are affected by disability are people first and disabled second, and have individual attitudes, likes, aspirations, fears and abilities. Understand that although there may be special areas of need, people with disabilities wish to have the opportunity to live in the same way as other people" (ibid., p. 232).

3. Junor, pp. 216-218.

constitutionally forbidden from publicly expressing political views and does not give interviews, let alone make documentaries. But the prince is emerging as a public spokesman in his own right....[1]

In the television program, his main message was deeply serious: "Man is more, much more, than a mere mechanical object whose sole aim is to produce money.... Above all he has a soul, and the soul is irrational, un-fathomable, mysterious. Throughout history our ancestors have derived their inspiration from the infinite richness of the natural world."[2]

Prince Charles, who banned aerosol sprays from his household out of con-cern for the ozone layer, is to write and present a TV documentary on envi-ronmental threats, the British Broadcasting Corp. said.... The 60-minute program ... is expected to focus on global issues such as the destruction of the rain forests and the ozone layer.... The program is to be broadcast ... as part of a project called One World, in which European stations are col-laborating on ... programs about world problems.[3]

Prince Charles announced ... in London the establishment of an interna-tional task force to promote self-help projects in the developing world.... The Business Leaders Forum, a charity the Prince sponsored in 1990, will oversee the project. The group will promote projects in communities to help them overcome hunger, poverty, homelessness and environmental degradation.[4]

Prince Charles urged Saudi and British oil merchants ... to address the threat of global warming at once. "This is an issue which we have to ad-dress now, not in 10 or 20 years' time," he said in a [November 1993] speech in Saudi Arabia's oil-producing Eastern Province. "The penalty for failure will affect our children and grandchildren dramatically, not just here in the Gulf region, but in the world at large."[5]

Our Environment has suffered beyond our worst nightmares, in part because of a one-sided approach to economic development which, until very recently, failed to take account of the inter-relatedness of creation. Little thought was given to the importance of finding that sustainable bal-ance which worked within the grain of nature and understood the vital ne-cessity of setting and respecting limits. This, for example, is why protection of our environment is a relatively recent concern; and why or-ganic and sustainable farming are so important if we are to use the land in a way which will safeguard its ability to nourish future generations.

A third area in which this separation of the material and spiritual has had dramatic consequences is Architecture. I believe this separation lies at the heart of the failure of so much modern architecture to understand the essential spiritual quality and the traditional principles that reflect a cosmic harmony, from which come buildings with which people feel comfortable

1. For decades, there have been rumors that the British Constitution may be altered to permit changes to the monarchical system. One change could involve freedom to express political views, even as king.
2. The New York Times, "Prince Charles thrashes recent British architecture," *Denver Post*, 30 Oct. 1988, p. 13A.
3. "Prince Charles promotes environment," *The Denver Post*, 24 Oct. 1989, p. 14A.
4. "Prince Charles announces international aid project," *Rocky Mountain News*, 11 July 1992, p. 102.
5. "Prince urges action on global warming," *The Denver Post*, 9 Nov. 1993, p. 9A.

and in which they want to live. That is why I started my own small Institute of Architecture some five years ago. Titus Buckhardt wrote: "It is the nature of art to rejoice the soul, but not every art possesses a spiritual dimension". We see this spirituality in traditional Christian architecture which incidentally was also inspired by a far more profound symbolic awareness than could ever be imagined by those who categorise such architecture as a question of mere style. This spiritual dimension also infuses the intricate geometric and arabesque patterns of Islamic art and architecture, which are ultimately a manifestation of divine Unity, which in turn is the central message of the Qur'an. The Prophet Mohammed himself is believed to have said: "God is beautiful and He loves beauty".[1]

Recall that Charles traveled to Africa's Kalahari desert with a man who openly paid homage to demonic spirits. With this and earlier information in mind, consider these excerpts from another full-page Tara Center advertisement—one printed on April 25, 1982, in various newspapers globally:

THE WORLD HAS HAD *enough* … OF HUNGER, INJUSTICE, WAR. IN ANSWER TO OUR CALL FOR HELP, AS WORLD TEACHER FOR ALL HUMANITY, THE CHRIST IS NOW HERE.

HOW WILL WE RECOGNIZE HIM?

Look for a modern man concerned with modern problems—political, economic, and social. Since July, 1977, the Christ has been emerging as a spokesman for a group or community in a well-known modern country. He is not a religious leader, but an educator in the broadest sense of the word—pointing the way out of our present crisis. We will recognize Him by His extraordinary spiritual potency, the universality of His viewpoint, and His love for all humanity. **He comes not to judge, but to aid and inspire.**

WHO IS THE CHRIST?

Throughout history, humanity's evolution has been guided by a group of enlightened men, the Masters of Wisdom. They have remained largely in the remote desert and mountain places of earth, working mainly through their disciples who live openly in the world. This message of the Christ's reappearance has been given primarily by such a disciple trained for his task for over 20 years. At the center of this "Spiritual Hierarchy" stands the World Teacher, *Lord Maitreya* known by Christians as the *Christ*. And as Christians await the Second Coming, so the Jews await the *Messiah*, the Buddhists the fifth *Buddha*, the Moslims the *Iman Mahdi*, and the Hindus await *Krishna*. These are all names for one individual. **His presence in the world guarantees there will be no third World War.**[2]

---

1. Charles, Prince of Wales, "A Sense of the Sacred: Building Bridges Between Islam and the West," *The Wilton Park Seminar,* 13 Dec. 1996.
2. Constance Cumbey, *The Hidden Dangers of the Rainbow* (Louisiana: Huntington House, Inc., 1983), p. 13 and the back cover.

387

Respect. In April 2002, less than two months after being hailed "Saviour of the World" and depicted as an angelic "winged god,"[1] then Satan's Prince took it upon himself to launch his own *multi-faith new-age religious movement* called "Respect":

> The Prince of Wales is to launch a multi-faith campaign that is being seen as a move to take on an expanded royal role.... He has held a summit for Britain's religious leaders at St James's Palace to combat a "dangerous" breakdown of tolerance in society. He will make public their proposed solution on the eve of the Queen's golden jubilee address to parliament..., flanked by a cardinal, two archbishops and the chief rabbi.
>
> The multi-faith campaign coincides with plans to increase his royal profile. He ... will ... hold bi-monthly meetings with ... prime minister [Anthony (Tony) Charles Lynton Blair]. Charles is also to conduct more ceremonial duties, including investitures, and take over from the Queen some of the duties of receiving foreign ambassadors in London.... His plan [is] to enlist millions of people in a movement to bridge the religious divide in schools.... Schemes ... include opening Muslim faith schools to other religions ... and joint Christian-Muslim aid <u>for the West Bank</u>.
>
> Charles has moved rapidly since an initial meeting with religious heads on March 11[, right after returning from Brazil and Mexico].[2] It was first inspired by a suggestion to the prince from Jonathan Sacks, the chief rabbi [(an unregenerate "Jew" with whom Charles became very close)].[3]
>
> He will launch his movement, called Respect, alongside the leaders of all of Britain's principal religions ... on April 29, at an event co-ordinated by the Prince's Trust. The leaders will include the Archbishop of Canterbury, the Cardinal Archbishop of Westminster and the Archbishop of Wales. Also present will be Zaki Badawi, a leading Muslim; Indarjit Singh,

---

1. For more information, see ch. 14's section titled, "The Statue," at p. 506.
2. This was *less than one week* after Charles was publicly proclaimed "Saviour of the World!"
3. Jonathan Sacks, the apostate ecumenical chief "rabbi" of the orthodox United Hebrew Congregations of the Commonwealth, who does not believe in biblical inerrancy and promotes interfaith openness and tolerance, was knighted in June 2005, for "for services ... to interfaith relations" ("Faith leaders knighted in honours," *BBC News*, 10 June 2005). Yes, he was Elizabeth II's and thus *Charles'* knight.
   One likewise spiritually lost "rabbi" (Yisrael Meir Lau), called Sacks "the bridge between the Jewish Nation and the diaspora, and all nations of the world." No doubt Charles, who had earlier honored Sacks (e.g., see "Tribute to Chief Rabbi Jonathan Sacks | Speech by HRH The Prince of Wales" at "fXUd-fYzuzNo" on YouTube), saw him as a means to an end, one targeting Israel. After Sacks' 2020 *descent to Hell*, Charles as Satan's Prince said: "He and I were exact contemporaries, born in the year of the foundation of the State of Israel and, over many years, I had come to value his counsel immensely. He was a trusted guide, an inspired teacher and a true and steadfast friend. I shall miss him more than words can say. With ... innate sense of the power of the story, he defined the moral challenges and the choices our society faces, speaking with conviction across the boundaries of the sacred and the secular, across the generations, and across all barriers of culture and religion. He taught us how to listen to others, and how to learn from them without compromising the convictions of either party; ... and through it all, he taught us the need to respect the integrity and harmony of God's Creation" (Sandy Rashty, "Prince Charles leads Lord Sacks memorial: I'll miss him more than words can say," *Jewish News*, 6 Dec. 2020). Calling Sacks "a leader whose wisdom, scholarship and humanity were without equal," Charles added, "His wise counsel was sought and appreciated by those of all faiths and none, and he will be missed more than words can say" (Clarence House). Besides the above tribute, which may be fully heard in "HRH The Prince of Wales | Shloshim for Rabbi Lord Jonathan Sacks," at "sGtYIcN_xfk" on YouTube, Charles gave a second one the following year, in "HRH The Prince of Wales Honors Rabbi Lord Sacks" at "nQhT8wisbH0", also on YouTube.

of the Sikh Council for Interfaith Relations; and Barnabas Leith, of the Bahai faith. There will also be Hindu, Buddhist and Jain representatives.

The prince's plan ... will be the first time that he has sought to implement his ideas on the religious role of the monarch in a multi-faith society. He declared his intention to reign as "defender of faith" in 1994. Charles ... hosted a dinner at his Highgrove home for leading Muslim figures shortly after September 11.

One religious leader said: "His view is that we have had dialogue between the faiths ... and now it is time for a new stage...." Iqbal Sacranie, a member of the advisory council of Respect, said British Muslims should co-operate with Christians and Jews in providing overseas aid.... Other proposals ... included a plan for faith schools to share lessons with schools from other religions....[1]

BIRMINGHAM, England — Launching a campaign to promote religious understanding, Prince Charles on Monday urged Britons to return to the values of love, forgiveness and good neighborliness.

"Over the past year, we have seen, internationally, nationally and locally, all too many examples of intolerance to others," the heir to the throne told a gathering of more than 20 religious leaders, including Christians, Muslims, Jews and Hindus, at Birmingham's National Exhibition Center.

Charles said tolerance is "an easy word to pronounce, but it seems to be very difficult to enact in our lives...." Although the prince did not mention specific examples of intolerance, his remarks were widely read as a reference to the Sept. 11 terrorist attacks on the United States, [and] the ongoing Mideast conflict.... ...Britain's [heretical so-called] chief rabbi, Jonathan Sacks, said that anti-Semitism in Britain has not been worse since the Holocaust....

Most religious leaders have welcomed the tolerance campaign, entitled "Respect," which is an initiative by ... the Prince's Trust.... [It] ... will encourage Britons to spend more time with others from different backgrounds.

The prince said ... that love and forgiveness are "the only means of breaking the cycle of hatred, vengeance and conflict" between groups. His vision of good neighborliness, he said, embraces "the young Muslim mowing the lawn for the elderly Hindu lady down the street. Or the choir from the Catholic church singing to entertain the Jewish old people's club."

Religious tolerance is an issue that has long concerned Charles, who will become supreme governor, or temporal head, of the Church of England when he assumes the throne. In 1994, he declared his intention to reign as "defender of faith" rather than "defender of the faith" ....[2]

The Prince of Wales found himself smothered with praise by a British Muslim leader..., as he launched an initiative to promote greater tolerance between cultures. Prince Charles, surrounded by 23 religious figures, called on members of different religious faiths to help each other in launching the plan, called Respect, during a visit to Birmingham.

---

1. "Charles gears up to be the prince of faiths," *The Sunday Times,* 16 April 2002. Reproduced in *The Times of India Online,* 21 April 2002. For the full article, visit "https://web.archive.org/web/200610040 72556/http://www.forf.org/news/2002/pcrespect.html" on the Internet.
2. Sue Leeman, "Prince Charles launches campaign to promote tolerance," *AP,* 29 Apr. 2002.

...[Dr Mohamed Aboulkhair] Zaki Badawi, [the founder and] principal of the Muslim College [in London, and chairman of the Imams and Mosques Council of the United Kingdom since 1984],[1] described him [(then Prince Charles)] as "the most popular world leader in the Muslim community throughout the world". Dr Badawi said: "He is a committed and believing Christian,[2] a man of such stature, and is able to speak for all of us...."

The prince replied: "I feel very flattered and embarrassed."

Only the Archbishop of Canterbury was absent from the launch, due to a clash of commitments. A spokesman said the [(apostate and heretical)] archbishop fully supported it.

Moves by the royal family to show their appreciation of different religious faiths — the Queen is to visit a mosque during this summer's jubilee tour — have already attracted criticism from some Protestant[s]....

The prince said: "Over the past year, we have seen all too many examples of intolerance to others. Tolerance is an easy word to pronounce and yet it is such a tragedy that when the various faith communities have so much in common, its members should so often be divided by the different ways we have of interpreting the inner meaning of our existence." ...

The chief rabbi, Jonathan Sacks, said, "There could not be a more necessary project at a more important time." Indarjit Singh, chairman of the Sikh Network, said: "God is not the least bit interested in our different religious stables. He is interested in our contribution to society."[3]

---

1. The Egyptian-born Zaki Badawi, whose college "stresses a broad knowledge of Islam as well as the importance of a clear understanding of Western society and world religions," is now roasting. Before dying in January 2006, he was considered to be a leading liberal Islamic scholar and ecumenical "global Muslim": "In 1997, Badawi established the Three Faiths Forum with Sir Sigmund Sternberg and the Rev Marcus Braybrooke. The idea of encouraging friendship, goodwill[, tolerance] and understanding amongst 'people of the book'[—Muslims, Christians, and Jews—]appealed to the halal globetrotter who always envisioned himself as a bridge-maker of peace and understanding. Badawi was for many years until his death a leading member of the Tripoli-based World Islamic Call Society which shared his conviction of Muslim benevolence across the world. He was Vice-Chairman of the World Congress of Faiths and a founder director of the Forum Against Islamophobia and Racism (FAIR). Perhaps the most ambitious project Badawi initiated was the setting up in London in 1986 of the Muslim College, of which he remained Principal until his death.... Long before it became an obsession of desperate civil servants faced with radical Islam, Badawi had realised the significance of a home-grown Islam in Britain — 'free of the cancer of Muslim culture, neurosis and ignorance.' ... The network he developed over the years included laymen and scholars, presidents and priests, [prime ministers such as Tony Blair,] politicians and academics[, and Charles (as Satan's Prince)].... As British Islam enters what augurs to be difficult times, it will miss ... its most vociferous proponent. However, they are many signs that Badawi's idea of an Islam based in tradition, yet not afraid of modernity ... has made deep roots" ("Zaki Badawi: 'Grand Mufti of Islam in Britain,'" The Independent, 27 Jan. 2006). Still, even according to Badawi, who in 1997 "established, with Sir Sigmund Sternberg and the Rev Marcus Braybrooke, the Three Faiths Forum 'to encourage friendship, goodwill and understanding amongst people of the three Abrahamic monotheistic faiths in the UK and elsewhere,'" "the Koran emphasised that those who disturbed the peace of society and spread fear and disorder deserved the severest punishment that could be imposed;" Sir Badawi, knighted by Queen Elizabeth II in 2003, was appointed Knight Commander of the British Empire or "KBE in 2004" ("Zaki Badawi," The Times OnLine, 25 Jan. 2006). Islam views true Christians, whose faith is exclusive and not tolerant of spiritual lies, as those who disturb the peace of society. "Prince Charles, who had developed a friendship with Mr. Badawi through his interest in Islam, said his death was 'a devastating blow to this country and to me personally.... His brand of wisdom, scholarship, [and] farsightedness ... has ensured that Zaki played an extraordinarily important role ... amongst the Muslim community,' the prince said" ("Zaki Badawi; Leading Muslim Scholar," Associated Press, 26 Jan. 2006).
2. Like so many today, Zaki Badawi clearly had no idea of the true meaning of the word "Christian."
3. Stephen Bates, "Prince calls for respect between faiths," The Guardian, 30 April 2002. For the full article, visit "https://www.theguardian.com/uk/2002/apr/30/religion.world" on the Internet.

Following the death of Mr. Badawi, as well as denigration of Islam's false prophet and founder in the Danish press, Satan's Prince spoke out. He delivered a speech, titled "Unity of Faith," before a crowd of thousands of Muslims—including Egypt's most prominent dignitaries (e.g., "Usama El-Baz, political advisor for Egyptian President Hosni Mubarak; Esmat Abdul-Magid, former Arab League Secretary General; Egypt's Minister of Waqfs Hamdy Zaqzouq; Egypt's Mufti Ali Goamaa; [and] representatives of the Egyptian Church, in addition to a host of other politicians and Al-Azhar heavyweights")— *at Islam's "most ancient seat of learning"* (i.e., Al-Azhar University in Cairo, Egypt). There, as a *Muslim, "Charles was awarded an Honorary Doctorate from Al-Azhar:"*

> British Crown Prince Charles [(now King Charles III) on] ... March 21, [2006,] harped on the fact that Islam, Christianity and Judaism share the same origin, urging wise men and women to help restore mutual respect between faiths and criticizing Danish cartoons lampooning Prophet Muhammad ... and the ensuing violence. "The recent ghastly strife and anger over the Danish cartoons shows the danger that comes of our failure to listen and to respect what is precious and sacred to others," Prince Charles told an audience of some 3,000 people at Al-Azhar University [in Cairo], Islam's most ancient seat of learning.
>
> "I think of the experience of Muslims living in Europe who are subject to varied and continuous expressions of Islamophobia." He asserted: "The true mark of a civilized society is the respect it pays to minorities and to strangers."
>
> Twelve cartoons, including one showing the Prophet with a bomb-shaped turban, were first published by Danish daily *Jyllands-Posten* in September [2005] and reprinted by European newspapers.... The drawings, considered blasphemous under Islam, have triggered massive and sometimes violent demonstrations across the Muslim world.
>
> Prince Charles paid tribute to late prominent British Muslim scholar Zaki Badawi, an Egyptian-born graduate of Al-Azhar who died last January, calling him "a man of wisdom and learning." ...
>
> The Prince of Wales also reserved harsh criticism for some Muslim countries over the treatment of non-Muslims. "I think of Christians living within some Muslim nations, who find themselves fettered by harsh and degrading restrictions, or subject to abuse by some of their fellow citizens," he said.
>
> Prince Charles underlined the need for the followers of all three Abrahamic religions — Judaism, Christianity and Islam — to speak with courage of the enduring values of faith and to "affirm them again and again to a world troubled by change and dissension." He expressed his conviction that "our beliefs and values call out for peace, not conflict." Prince Charles called on wise men and women to respect the religion of others. "I believe with all my heart that responsible men and women must work to restore mutual respect [and understanding] between faiths...," he said.... "History shows that giant leaps of creativity in knowledge — in science, literature

391

and the arts — have occurred when the members of the Abrahamic family have worked together." Quoting the Qur'anic verse ... Al-Hujurat 49:13..., Charles highlighted the fact that differences do not erase chances for unity.... "[We] have a duty to speak for the principles of our religious faiths", ... [and] need to "protect our traditions — Muslim, Christian and Jewish — acknowledging and celebrating our rich diversity...."

After his speech, entitled "Unity of Faith", **Prince Charles was awarded an Honorary Doctorate from Al-Azhar.**[1] **In a brief speech, Grand Imam of Al-Azhar Sheikh Mohamed Sayed Tantawi hailed the significant role played by Charles in the field of inter-faith dialogue.** Ahmed Al-Tayeb, president of Al-Azhar University, then announced the decision to grant the Prince of Wales the Honorary Doctorate from the prestigious university. ....Sheikh Tantawi repeatedly cited from Prince Charles Oxford speech and described the prince's ideas as the fruit of "serious study." When the doctorate — in a maroon leather folder — was handed over, there was a surge of applause from the audience. A visibly moved Charles bowed slightly to the crowd and waved in thanks....

Before the speech, Sheikh Tantawi accompanied Prince Charles and his wife Camilla, the Duchess of Cornwall, who donned a headscarf, in a tour of the oldest functioning mosque in Egypt, Al-Azhar Mosque. The royal couple ... were briefed on the great role of Al-Azhar and its engagement in Islamic studies.[2]

About a decade earlier, Charles reportedly "set up a panel of twelve 'wise men' (in fact, eleven men and one woman) to advise him on Islamic religion and culture.[3] This ... group was reported to have met in secret."[4] Speaking of the Arab-Israeli conflict, Mr. Barack Obama claimed "that he wanted to adopt 'a new emphasis on respect.'"[5]

---

1. This is a university at which (now roasting) Zaki Badawi studied, and at one time also taught.
2. "Prince Charles Urges Unity of Faith, Slams Cartoons," *Daily News,* 22 Mar. 2006. For the full article, see "https://web.archive.org/web/20080408085353/http://www.turks.us/article.php?story=200603220 74725845" on the Internet. For the full text of Charles' speech, "Unity in Faith," visit "https://web.archive.org/web/20120809064530/http://www.princeofwales.gov.uk/speechesandarticles/a_speech_by_h rh_the_prince_of_wales_titled_unity_in_faith_at_94.html" on the Internet.
3. Richard Kay, "Charles and the 'Wise Men' of Islam," *Daily Mail,* Jan. 6, 1997.
4. Gordon and Stillman, "Prince Charles of Arabia."
5. Steven Gutkin, "Israel finds itself at crossroads in Gaza invasion," *The Associated Press,* 12 Jan. 2009.

11

Power Plays

Some of what follows is merely outlined. Because the points have significant import, however, they are nevertheless mentioned.[1]

The Order of the Garter, the Committee of 300, the Illuminati, and Freemasonry. The British monarch and the Prince of Wales are the two highest ranking knights in the Order of the Garter. As such, both head the Committee of 300, and both have authority over the Illuminati and Freemasonry worldwide.[2]

Other orders of knighthood are likewise used to wield influence. Current American knights of the British monarchy, for example, include former Presidents Ronald Reagan and Bush Sr.; former Federal Reserve Chairman Alan Greenspan; former Secretaries of Defense Caspar Weinberger and Colin Powell; retired generals Norman Schwarzkopf, Colin Powell (the same, and former Chairman of the U.S. Joint Chiefs of Staff), and Wesley Clark (a Rhodes Scholar and former NATO commander); retired Admiral Leighton W. Smith Jr.; former New York mayor Rudolph (Rudy) William Louis Giuliani (Mayor of New York on 9/11); software mogul Bill Gates; former Speaker of the House of Representatives Thomas S. Foley; deceased entertainer Bob Hope; film director Steven Spielberg; composer Andre Previn; and actor Peter Falk. That certain of these knighthoods violated the Emoluments Clause of the U.S. Constitution—which reads, "No title of nobility shall be granted by the United States, and no person holding any office of profit or trust under them shall, without the consent of the Congress, accept of any present, emolument, office, or title of any kind whatever from any king, prince, or foreign state"—has been handily swept under the rug *by the U.S. Department of Justice!* Indeed, the *original* 13th Article of Amendment to the U.S. Constitution reads, "If any citizen of the United States shall accept, claim, receive, or retain any title of nobility or honour, or shall without the consent of Congress, accept and retain any present, pension, office, or emolument of any kind whatever, from any emperor, king, prince, or foreign power, such person shall cease

---

1. Such may be further documented in a later edition of this work. Meanwhile, should you desire to know more, you may see *The Prince of Wales* by Jonathan Dimbleby, as well as other biographies on Satan's Prince, besides doing research on the Internet.
2. For more information, see the discussion on the Garter at p. 147 in ch. 7, "The Heraldic Symbols in the Arms and their Interpretations."

to be a citizen of the United States, and shall be incapable of holding any office of trust or profit under them, or either of them."

The United World Colleges. Charles as Prince of Wales, was President of the United World Colleges (UWC) until 1995, having taken the role upon the death of his uncle, Louis Mountbatten. Thinking of the "UWC's great aims" and "ordinary people," Charles "realized he had to keep going for their sake, to carry on where his great-uncle had left off, to work towards [(supposed)] democracy and ['woke'] justice in the world, and to strive towards peace [(cf. 1 th 5:3, Gk.)] through [(presumed)] knowledge and understanding. 'The United World Colleges movement,' he said in his address at the memorial service, 'was a particular passion of his in the final years, because he saw within the scheme a means of bringing peace and international understanding through students from many countries, to a world that he had seen pull itself to pieces twice in twenty-five years....'"[1] (Jordan's Queen Noor now has the role.)

The elitist UWC exist "to promote international understanding through education; and to provide a pattern of education adapted to meet the special needs of our time." According to Satan's Prince: "My acceptance of the Presidency was based really on a deep and personal conviction of the intrinsic merits of the UWC concept, which I think in many ways is close to the Gordonstoun ideal which essentially is the belief in the importance of human relationships in world affairs.... And last but not least the Presidency does provide me, in particular, with an ideal topic of discussion with Heads of State and so on, throughout the world." Naturally, Charles used his position as such to promote globalism and multiculturalism, emphasizing the importance of "meeting people from all over the world and thus forming a more comprehensive picture of the things that unite us all, rather than those which divide us." As a Finnish student put it: "You start to see the truth from other people's points of view. That is how you change the world."[2] In other words, anything goes, except what's actually true and good (i.e., biblical Christianity and serving The God of Israel, the actual Creator of the Universe).

Where elitist "experimental learning" is concerned, we should point out that Charles himself, like Prince Philip before him (see below), was subjected to a form of "outcome-based education" (OBE): "The Gordonstoun authorities were just then preparing their 'Final Report to Parents', an unorthodox document providing comment not only on the standard reached in a pupil's studies but also giving judgment on his public spirit and sense of justice; his ability to fol-

1. Junor, pp. 148-149.
2. Junor, pp. 133-135, 137-138.

low the right course in the face of discomfort, boredom, scepticism or impulses of the moment; his ability to plan and organise, to deal with the unexpected, and on his imagination and fighting spirit."[1] Gordonstoun, under the strong German influence of Kurt Hahn, a Jewish Illuminist who was indirectly and ironically instrumental in Hitler's rise to power,[2] was closely associated with Salem in Germany, where Prince Philip experienced "the most formative educational experience of his life." Having been described as "the man who made Philip," Hahn's educational ideas were "partly based on one of Hahn's principal inspirations, Plato, and his distinctly élitist philosophy,[3] and partly on the principals of Sparta, the austere soldier state of Greek antiquity." The German Salem, founded in 1918 by Prince Max of Baden with Hahn, "was on one of the family's estates," residing in part of Prince Max's castle at Salem. The school offered "an excellent, liberal German education." Earlier, Prince Philip had been educated at Cheam in England, a "progressive" school that Winston Churchill had also attended. The prince "hardly excelled, except in French, which he spoke as well as English and German and better than Greek." From 1953, Philip, in the experimental learning vein, became Patron of the Outward Bound Trust in Britain, Canada, and Australia.[4] Of Salem, Judd comments:

---

1. Cathcart, pp. 69-70.
2. Kurt Hahn was the personal secretary and advisor to Max von Baden, Germany's last Imperial Chancellor. As such, the German case at the Versailles peace negotiations "owed a good deal of it substance to Hahn, a brilliant scholar." As a Rhodes Scholar at Christ Church of Oxford when World War I began, Hahn returned to Germany to serve as an intelligence expert on Britain and as a Liaison Officer with the Imperial army. Hahn later authored "Brockdorff-Rantzau's impassioned speech repudiating Germany's 'war guilt.'" Consequently, "Hahn helped to coin the explosive slogan ... which was to lead to the [German] clamour for revenge, rearmament, the Nazi regime and, finally, the Second World War" (Judd, *Prince Philip*, p. 68; also, see Junor, p. 35).
3. Having read Plato's *Republic* as a young man, Hahn fell in love with the Platonic philosophy that "any nation is a slovenly guardian of its own interests if it does not do all it can to make the individual citizen discover his own powers; and further, that the individual becomes a cripple from his or her own point of view if he is not qualified by education to serve the community." In other words, "Ask not what your country can do for you, but what you can do for your country." Based upon this same philosophy, Charles has strongly advocated a kind of *compulsory* voluntary service to the community, or involuntary volunteerism (an oxymoron for forced servitude or slavery), for the youth of society. The Clintons' Americorps "volunteer" program, which Bill and Hillary would like to make compulsory for U.S. youth, is likewise in this vein. Junor, observing that Socrates, in Plato's *Republic*, "asserts that his citizens, if they are to be guardians of the state, must be 'spirited, swift and strong' and yet, at the same time, gentle and swayed by 'beauty and truth,'" ignorantly states: "The fundamental divergence from Plato's philosophy, however, was in religion. Gordonstoun was a Christian school, whereas Plato's *Republic* was a pagan slave state. Hahn, who was himself Jewish, simply took the best from Plato" (Junor, pp. 35-36). In fact, Hahn, the British monarchy, and the Clintons advocate "a pagan slave state," one trained for service, not an enlightened Christian state. Moreover, it is this philosophy which is to form the glue, so to speak, between East and West in the New World Order. The *Platonic ideal* will enable the elite to merge what *they* have determined are the "best" aspects of Communism-Socialism and Capitalism-Fascism into a global system made "partly of iron and partly of clay" (cf. Dan 2:41-43). For more information, see ch. 7's section titled, "The Garter," as well as this chapter's later section titled, "The United Nations and public-private partnerships," at pp. 147 and 446, respectively.
4. Judd, *Prince Philip*, pp. 65, 67, 69, 250. Also, see Junor, p. 35.

Achievement through struggle, an aristocracy of accomplishment, it is not surprising that Hahn, who disliked socialism, believed in a form of leadership not unlike the Nazi *Führer* principle; indeed, he once called his system a kind of non-Jew-baiting Nazism. He denounced Hitler for "making good things look bad", and was horrified by Nazi violence, yet, predictably, Nazi influences permeated his school....

....The New regime could not appreciate that the children at Salem were being brought up in a fiercely patriotic spirit; nor could it understand how implicitly Hahn believed in the greatness of Germany, and even thought that "Hitler's cause could be good or made good". To the Nazis the most significant fact about Hahn was that he was a Jew....[1]

By a curious twist of fate, as Hahn was bound for Britain, the young Philip of Greece was on his way to Salem.... The official family line was that after his French and English schools, Philip would benefit from a spell of liberal German education....

"Prince Philip of Greece", as a foreigner, was exempt from the Hitler Youth activities....

The Duke of Edinburgh remembers the Nazis of Salem with distaste....

Ironically, while Philip's brother-in-law Berthold von Baden was battling against the Nazis at Salem, another brother-in-law, Prince Christopher of Hesse, was serving the Nazi regime as an S.A. officer.... An ideal alternative now existed, and, less than a year after entering Salem, Prince Philip returned to Britain.

His destination was Kurt Hahn's new school at Gordonstoun in Scotland, which opened in 1934. [Hahn had already] ... assembled a board of governors of extraordinary distinction and authority. The board included William Temple, Archbishop of York, and later Archbishop of Canterbury, Claude Elliot, the Headmaster of Eton,[2] John Buchan ... who [being pro-apartheid] ... was subsequently to become Governor-General of Canada....

...Hahn's ideas were a strange amalgam of the revolutionary and the reactionary.

....What did emerge at Gordonstoun was a system of education which blended the expected with the unconventional, while containing a good deal that was downright quirky.

....A heavy emphasis in fact on life-saving of all sorts which ... was an intrinsic part of Hahn's philosophy....[3]

....According to Gordonstoun school reports to parents, pupils were expected to develop the ability "to state facts precisely", "to take the right course in the face of Discomforts, Hardships, Danger, Mockery, Boredom, Scepticism, Impulses of the Moment", and "to plan, organise, and deal

---

1. Hitler imprisoned Hahn and took over Salem's chancellorship. By that time, the school had become so famous and important to the elite that Britain's Prime Minister, Ramsay MacDonald, intervened directly to gain Hahn's release, at which point Hahn fled to Britain to establish Gordounstoun, "a school in the mould of Salem" (Junor, p. 36).

2. Like Gordonstoun, Eton has "a similarly self-elected hierarchy, which gives the school a limited form of self-government" (Junor, p. 36).

3. According to the anti-Christian Hahn, "He who drills and labours and encounters dangers and difficulties all to be ready to save his brother in peril," "he experiences God's purpose in his inner life." Much like the counterfeit Christianity of psychologists who push "self-esteem," Hahn preached "the good in man, and in particular the capacity of the young to produce their best when confronted by the challenge of responsibility for others." "It was this belief in the good in man and the means by which it could be drawn out that Prince Charles took ... from Gordonstoun" (Junor, pp. 66-67).

with the unexpected".... Gordonstoun also demanded "Mental Concentration", "Conscientiousness" and "Manners"....

But, as Hahn's critics never tired of pointing out, studies in English, ancient languages, modern languages, history, natural science and mathematics, came rather low on the list of requirements, only just above practical work, art work..., fighting spirit and endurance....

....He has remained solidly loyal to Hahn and his methods, once remarking...: "For some reason it is perfectly respectable to teach history and mathematics, electronics and engineering. But any attempt to develop character, and the whole man, tends to be viewed with the utmost suspicion."[1] ...

He had graduated in the quasi-military hierarchy of Gordonstoun from Room Leader to Captain to Colour Bearer to Helper (one of the ten boys in charge of particular activities...) and now, in his last year, he was elected Guardian or head boy, a distinction conferred on the school's most responsible and authoritative young man. Impatience and intolerance were his chief faults, and ... they remain so."[2]

Speaking of the UWC, Hahn, and Charles, Junor comments:

....Prince Charles was and is [(e.g., now as King Charles III)] a truly international man; and he subscribed to Hahn's vision, shared by Earl Mountbatten, of a harmonious world where nations are so educated that they understand, and so tolerate, one another.

The belief that national barriers could be reduced and international cooperation fostered by education had been the principle behind an organization first called Atlantic College, and subsequently the United World Colleges, which Hahn cofounded in 1962.... Situated at Donat's Castle[3] in South Wales it was a sixth form college which now has [over] three hundred international students, most of whom are on scholarships, combining two years of academic study with physically demanding activities and service to the community. The idea is that by living, studying and putting their lives in the hands of fellow students of every race, colour and creed under the sun, they will take the message of racial harmony home to their own countries, and bit by bit mankind will learn.... The students ... study

---

1. Gordonstoun strongly emphasizes self-improvement, as is implied in the school's motto, *Plus est en vous*, which is translated, "There is more in you" (Junor, p. 37). "[Hahn,] saw the young exposed to a series of decays: 'The decay of fitness, the decay of self-discipline, the decay of enterprise and adventure, the decay of skill and care that goes to make the craftsman, and, most shattering of all, the decay of compassion.' He attributed these decays to defective education, concerned 'too exclusively with the transmission of knowledge ... than with the development of character which is basic and fundamental'. The sacred purpose of education was to 'arrest these decays, to restore, to defend, to develop human strength in the young'" (ibid., p. 66). Charles has praised "Hahn's principles" and "an education which tried to balance the physical and mental with the emphasis on self-reliance to develop a rounded human being." According to Satan's Prince, who credits Gordonstoun with having developed his "willpower and self-control," "giving shape and form and tidiness to your life, ... is the most important thing your education can do" (ibid., p. 65). That is, as in a military academy, education should regiment students.

2. Judd, *Prince Philip*, pp. 70-75, 77, 83.

3. Junor observes, "The round tower, with a sumptuous room at the top where Prince Charles stays if he needs a room overnight, overlooks the jousting field to one side and to the other the Beast Garden, where no matter in which part of the garden you stand one of the mythological stone creatures has its eye on you" (p. 137).

for an international school-leaving examination, the International Baccalaureate now recognized by most universities in the world, including Oxford and Cambridge.

Lord Mountbatten had become chairman of the College in 1968, and one of his first acts had been to change its name to United World Colleges.... After ten years ... not only had the College got well and truly off the ground in Wales, but new colleges had been set up in Canada and Singapore....

Of all the colleges, the Prince of Wales is probably particularly proud of the Venezuelan one.... At the Simon Bolivar United World College of Agriculture in Venezuela, however, they have broken away from the traditional curriculum. They are teaching young people agricultural skills specially designed for the developing countries of the world; trying to tackle the problems of poverty, [under-productivity,] famine and disease; providing a practical training at [the] grassroots level to meet a fundamental need.... [(How is Venezuela doing today?)]

....[Colleges] had been opened in Singapore—the UWC South East Asia—and in Canada—the Lester B. Pearson UWC of the Pacific on Vancouver Island—but there was nothing in the pipeline for America. Prince Charles took up the search and in 1980 tentatively approached Dr [Armand] Hammer, [(then) chairman and chief executive of the giant multinational Occidental Petroleum Corporation, and] a noted philanthropist. He told him about the movement..., and less than two years later a magnificent new college opened in Montezuma, New Mexico, aptly named the Armand Hammer UWC.... [It] ... had opened the doors to 102 students from forty-six nations....

Another college opened in 1982. Waterford Kamhlaba in Swaziland which joined in 1981, the College of the Adriatic in Italy. With the Venezuelan college that opened in 1986, and the original Atlantic College in Wales, the total is now seven....[1]

In 1992, the *Jerusalem Post* reported: "Leaders of the United World College[s] (UWC), an institution dedicated to promoting world peace and international brotherhood, are planning to set up a branch in the Negev, which would concentrate on desert ecology, according to Batya Gershoni, a graduate of a branch of UWC abroad. She said that the institution, which has seven branches throughout the world [(at that time)], is headed by Britain's Prince Charles."[2] Junor elaborates:

[Prince Charles] ... believes that change in emerging countries must come from the villages and not from well-educated leaders....

...Prince Charles is still keen to try to get something going in India, convinced that UWC can contribute to the problem of food production and agricultural development in the Third World. 'I believe most strongly,' he said while visiting the Canadian college in 1980, 'that better food pro-

1. Junor, pp. 131-132, 136, 202-203. Armand Hammer had worked closely with then Prince Charles and Al Gore. Hammer's father was a founding member of the Communist Party in the United States.
2. Itim, "New desert ecology college planned for the Negev," *The Jerusalem Post*, daily, 8 Dec. 1992, p. 3; accession no. 920001175 on the *Jerusalem Post* CD-ROM.

duction and the development of the rural economy in many of the developing countries is vital to the future of the whole world.'

During his various tours of Commonwealth countries, the Prince had become increasingly preoccupied by the problems of the Third World. [He] ... is concerned for the people there no less than for the people of the United Kingdom. He had read around the subject extensively, and had been particularly impressed by a book called *Small is Beautiful*, written by the late economist and philosopher E. F. Schumacher, who to propound his views had founded in the 1960s ... the Intermediate Technology Development Group. Although Charles was always the guest of the President or Head of State when he traveled to developing countries, and was therefore restricted in what he saw, he was well aware of poverty, sickness and the devastating results of drought and mismanagement. His sister [Anne] had been able to tell him even more from her visits on behalf of the Save the Children Fund. He was convinced that the problem was not a local but a global one, for which we should all share responsibility. Integrating students in United World Colleges was one way....

....What was needed [according to Schumacher] ... was technology appropriate to the people for whom it was intended: not giant machines that needed specialist knowledge to operate, but simple tools that anyone could use. When Schumacher first set up the group it was dismissed as the eccentric brainchild of an over-idealistic visionary, but since his death ... quite a number of the mainstream charities such as Oxfam, Christian Aid and the Save the Children Fund now turn to Intermediate Technology for advice.[1]

In his speech to the 1985 UWC International Council Meeting, Satan's Prince stated: "If the world could see that, in addition to our more conventional educational efforts, we were playing a significant part in educating [(i.e., indoctrinating)] young people from across the globe to tackle some of the huge survival problems facing the developing world, e.g. hunger, poverty, conservation of our resources and health, we would surely the more easily and quickly attract the global attention and awareness which are two of our most obvious deficiencies.... [There is a] level of support from Governments which we need to achieve." Charles, of course, is succeeding. Junor opines: "They are truly integrated. You cannot fail to go there and talk to the students without coming away convinced that there is hope for the world."[2]

In a remarkably poignant and sublimely manipulative speech, delivered in 1986 at the Harvard 350th Commemoration Ceremony, "the real Prince of Wales, stripped bare," touched upon a number of themes, even defining motives, which have since proved to be central to his globalist and elitist agenda, and international prominence:

1. Junor, pp. 136, 203-205.
2. Junor, pp. 136-137.

Perhaps, too, as parents you may be wondering, like I do on frequent occasions, whether the educational system you are confronted with is the right one to produce the kind of balanced, tolerant, civilized citizens we all hope our children can become?...

I cannot help feeling that one of the problems which is gradually dawning on the western, Christian world is that we have for too long, and too dangerously, ignored and rejected the best and most fundamental traditions of our Greek, Roman and Jewish inheritance. I would suggest that we have been gradually losing sight of the Greek philosophers' ideal, which was to produce a balance between the several subjects that catered for a boy's moral, intellectual, emotional and physical needs. While we have been right to demand the kind of technical education relevant to the needs of the twentieth century it would appear that we may have forgotten that when all is said and done a good man, as the Greeks would say, is a nobler worker than a good technologist. We should never lose sight of the fact that to avert disaster we have not only to teach men to make things, but also to produce people who have complete moral control over the things they make.... [The] emphasis has been too one-sided and has concentrated on the development of the intellect to the detriment of the spirit....

....All the best thought in Greece, Rome and Judea emphasized the interdependence of moral and intellectual training if we are to escape from the leadership of clever and unscrupulous men. There is no doubt in my mind that the education of the whole man needs to be based on a sure foundation [of faith and psychology].... That of course does not mean we have to deny the validity of other men's traditions. We should indeed look for those elements that unite us rather than concentrate on the things which make us different.... [It] is perhaps possible to learn to equate human rights with human obligations. It is possible then to see a relationship between moral values and the uses of science.... Surely it is important that in the headlong rush of mankind to conquer space, to compete with Nature to harness the fragile environment, we do not let our children slip away into a world dominated entirely by sophisticated technology, but rather teach them that to live in this world is not an easy matter without standards to live by.

And yet, at the same time, how do we guard against bigotry; against the insufferable prejudice and suspicion of other men's religions and beliefs which have so often led to unspeakable horrors throughout human history and which still do? How do we teach people to recognize that there is a dark side too to man's psyche [besides the "Zoroastrian" light side] and that its destructive power is immense if we are not aware of it?... There is in existence a proved and tested natural science dedicated to the study of the soul of man and the meaning of his creation. As in the past religious teaching was an essential part of the curriculum, perhaps there is now a need in universities for some introductions to the natural science of [Jungian] psychology? We are, to all intents and purposes, embarked on a perilous journey. The potential destruction of our natural earth; the despoliation of the great rain forests (with all the untold consequences of such a disaster); the exploration of space; greater power than we have ever had or our nature can perhaps handle—all confronts us for what could be a final settlement. But if we could start again to re-educate ourselves the result need not be so frightening. Over Apollo's great temple was the sign 'Man know thyself'. This natural science of psychology could perhaps help to lead us to a greater knowledge of ourselves; knowledge enough to teach us the dangers of the power we have acquired and the responsibilities as well as the opportunities it gives us. Could man, at last, begin to learn to know himself?[1]

In passing, we should note that Satan's Prince has created and spurred other projects that have similar elitist aims to the UWC. One such project, Operation Drake, resulted in the creation of the Drake Fellowship. Taking youth who had "hit rock bottom," the fellowship thrust them "into team work, survival training, community service and the sort of outdoor activities that they had never even dreamt about." "At the end of six or eight months broken up into a series of short courses, between 70 and 80 per cent found jobs. The Fellowship now handles about 4500 young people a year."[2] Operation Drake subsequently gave rise to Operation Raleigh, the "most ambitious international expedition ever mounted:" "Operation Raleigh was very similar to the previous expedition, but on a far bigger scale than Drake, as Charles had wanted. It was still fully international, but instead of taking four hundred applicants there were to be four thousand, each spending up to three months in the field; in addition the whole venture was to last not two years, as before, but four. The expeditions comprised the same blend of scientific and community projects and adventure, designed to give the participants the 'challenges of war in peacetime', and to bring out the latent potential for leadership in people who came from all sorts of backgrounds, including the inner cities."[3] There have been more such projects under Charles.

Based upon Plato's philosophy, or the "Platonic ideal," as earlier *noted* in this section (i.e., on p. 395), Charles strongly advocates a kind of *compulsory* "voluntary service" to the local community, or involuntary volunteerism (an elitist oxymoron for *forced servitude or slavery),* for society's "1984" (Orwellian) youth:

> Soon after Operation Raleigh was on its way, the Prince of Wales had another idea—a dream that he wanted to put into practice, an opportunity for young people to give service to their country.... Why was Britain the only country in Europe that did not have some form of [compulsory] national service? There must be a way [thought Charles].... ....Discussions were held with ... industry, the employers and the unions, the voluntary organizations, the government and the local councils....
>
> It was called the Prince of Wales Community Venture, and the literature and application forms briefly explained his philosophy: 'I believe that

1. Junor, pp. 270-273.
2. Junor, p. 207.
3. Junor, pp. 225-226.

we should all have the opportunity at one stage in our lives to make a *[required]* contribution to our community. It is also vital that we find ways in which people from all walks of life and backgrounds can operate together for a limited period in their lives. Ours is one of the very few countries where this does not happen.' ....Unlike Operations Drake and Raleigh this scheme was not looking simply for potential leaders....

....["Volunteers"] are paid [to] ... do a mixture of community service and adventure activity, with a strong accent on teamwork.... On day one they go off on an outward bound type of course with the Drake Fellowship, which involves camping and hiking.... The next two weeks are spent visiting community centres like old people's homes, the Salvation Army, spastics' schools, and fire and police stations—all places where they will be seconded later in the year for an eight-week stint. They are shipped off to Atlantic College in Wales for a week's course in first aid, coastguard and lifeboat service, and cliff rescue. They work with the fire brigade for a month; they clean up and improve some derelict site within the city; work in some branch of the local health authority; and for two months go away again to work in a distant community, such as Pembrokeshire in South Wales, where the first team did conservation work like fencing, scrub clearing and tree planting. Three-quarters of the year is taken up with community service, but the remainder is adventure and enterprise....

The original idea was that the venturers would be interviewed by a personnel manager at the beginning and end of the year.... They now have one manager looking after every three volunteers; he introduces them to the world of business, gives them a visit to the works, teaches them how to fill in job application forms and how to present themselves in interviews....

So far the scheme has been a resounding success: it has been described as the finest project [of its kind] in the country.... Nobody could have been more delighted than the Prince of Wales, not just that another group of young people had been taught to care about others and to taste some adventure in their lives, but because he has been proved right to all those bureaucrats and negative thinkers [whose attitude he hates] who at the outset said it would never work.[1]

Alternative medicine. Charles is credited by various biographers with having personally brought about (spurred) the rise in popularity of alternative forms of medicine, some of which are overtly occult while others are truly beneficial and needed, in the United Kingdom —and from there, throughout the western world.[2]

Environmentalism, the Rio Earth Summit, and the Kyoto Protocol. As Henry Lamb has pointed out, the whole environmental movement for the past two centuries can be traced back to Britain, largely beginning with the British Fauna and Flora Protection Society (founded in 1903). From this society came the International Union

1. Junor, pp. 226-230.
2. For more information, see the previous chapter's section titled, "Ties to the New Age Movement, the occult, and false religions," starting around p. 354.

for the Conservation of Nature (IUCN), which has now been renamed the World Conservation Union (still IUCN). The World Conservation Union or IUCN is the most influential of all environmental organizations. In 1961, the IUCN created the World Wildlife Fund (WWF) and designated Prince Philip as its international head.[1] Until his death in April 2021, he continued to serve the WWF as its President Emeritus, with the organization renamed the World Wide Fund for Nature *(retaining* WWF as its acronym) outside Canada and the U.S. Russel Train, a former President of the WWF USA, created the World Resources Institute (WRI). The WWF manages many environmental and other projects on behalf of the United Nations. These three organizations—the IUCN, the WWF, and the WRI—provide the impetus for the world environmental movement. Naturally, Satan's Prince has also played a major (even storied) role in these organizations, having been personally introduced to them by his father, Prince Philip, as well as by others. Indeed, Charles (even as king) has been President of WWF-UK since September 2011.

In 1968, as his July 1969 investiture before the world was being planned, Charles "was asked to chair the Welsh steering committee for European Conservation Year, designated for 1970."[2] In February 1970, Prince Philip took Charles as Prince of Wales, "to Strasbourg to attend a conservation conference under the auspices of the Council of Europe, initiating his son into a sphere of wider international statesmanship."[3] At the Conservation in 1970 Conference, Satan's Prince, as chairman of the Countryside in 1970 Committee for Wales, "touched prophetically on 'the horrifying effects of pollution in all its cancerous forms,'" brashly insisting that we "must be prepared" to "discipline ourselves to [environmental] restrictions and regulations that we feel we ought to impose for our own good." At the same time, Charles "announced the Prince of Wales's Countryside Award for individual enterprise in protecting the environment."[4] Junor, connecting Charles as the modern Prince of Wales to the modern Lady

---

1. In 1961, Prince Philip was designated President and "International Trustee of the World Wildlife Fund" (now named the World Wide Fund for Nature outside Canada and the U.S). Indeed: "Philip co-founded the WWF International in 1961 with Julian Huxley and Prince Bernhard. He has been the longtime president of WWF UK. Co-founded the 1001 Nature Trust and 1001 Club from 1971 to 1974, together with Anton Rupert and Prince Bernhard." ("Bohemian Grove: Historical Membership List Plus Biographies," July 2020). Before his descent to Hell, the prince was also Patron of the Norfolk Island Flora and Fauna Society, and President of the Royal Agricultural Society of the Commonwealth. Due to his participation in blood sports, something that his son Charles likewise avidly enjoys, (now roasting) Philip has been accused of hypocrisy. Prince Philip's publications include *Wildlife Crisis, Dilemmas in Conservation,* and *The Environmental Revolution: Speeches on Conservation* (Judd, *Prince Philip,* pp. 13-14, 250-252, and picture no. 44 between pp. 192-193).
2. Junor, p. 162.
3. Cathcart, p. 107.
4. Dimbleby, *The Prince of Wales,* pp. 421-422. Junor, p. 162.

Salisbury, whose ancestor was used to create the Order of the Garter, as well as to the English Rothschilds, elaborates:

....In this case he sought the advice of a family friend, Lady Salisbury, who had designed several gardens.... What Lady Salisbury ... does not know about plants is probably not worth knowing. She ... has gardened without the use of chemicals all her life.... ....Side by side, ... he and Lady Salisbury made the garden; and in those early weeks and months Charles discovered a new passion in life. He began to read gardening books rapaciously, and .... in a short time has become very knowledgeable....

One of the organizations that was pleased to find the Prince of Wales taking an interest in conservation [in 1970] was the Society for the Promotion of Nature Conservation (now the Royal Society for Nature Conservation), founded in 1912 by Nathaniel Charles Rothschild....

....[Miriam Rothschild, having inherited her father's passion,] does not conduct her campaign just for the aesthetic value of the result.... A vast range of plants are used in medical preparations, and as research continues new species are found to have beneficial properties. If a species is allowed to become extinct, however insignificant it may have appeared to be, that is one potential medication lost to mankind for ever.

Prince Charles, ... when he acquired Highgrove ... asked Miriam Rothschild if she would come and plant some wild flowers there. She too had known him since he was a child—she was an old friend of Lady Salisbury's —and so ... she descended on the garden....

....Wearing his other hat, as Patron of the Royal Society for Nature Conservation, [Charles] ... is a passionate conservationist, angered by the way man has plundered the natural habitat of plants and animals all over the world and caused the extinction of so many species as a result, and dismayed by the rape of the land due to the excessive use of chemicals and the fashion for tearing out hedgerows.[1]

In 1982, then Prince Charles sent this influential message to the Royal Agricultural College's first organic food conference:

For some years now modern farming has made tremendous demands on the finite sources of energy which exist on Earth. Maximum production has been the slogan to which we have all adhered. In the last few years there has been an increasing realisation that many modern production methods are not only very wasteful, but probably also unnecessary. The supporters of organic farming, bio-agriculture, alternative agriculture and optimum production are beginning to make themselves heard, and not before time.

I am convinced that any steps that can be taken to explore methods of production which make better and more effective use of renewable resources are extremely important. Even if it may be some time before they are commercially acceptable, pioneer work is essential if our planet is to feed the teeming millions of people who will live on it by the twenty-first century. I hope that you will seek solutions which can have practical and economically viable results within a comparatively short space of time. I

---

1. Junor, pp. 160-163, 237.

shall be watching the practical results with interest to see what might be applicable to our work in the Duchy of Cornwall....[1]

Not only has Charles played *the* pivotal role in popularizing environmentalism—including organic farming, which is generally *good* —in Britain and Western Europe, since making his seminal 1970 remarks as Prince of Wales, but *he is personally credited for the success of the seminal Earth Summit in Rio de Janeiro* (see below). This summit is considered by many environmentalists and others worldwide to have been a *watershed* event in the modern thrust for global government, which often takes the form of rabid environmentalism.[2] According to Lamb, two very important documents to emerge from the Rio Earth Summit, which are related to Agenda 21 (the UN global environmental agenda), are the Framework Convention on Climate Change and the Convention on Biological Diversity. Additionally, the Rio Earth Summit produced the UN Commission on Sustainable Development, with which he Prince of Wales [International] Business Leaders Forum (PWBLF, BLF, PWIBLF, IBLF) worked through its core participation in Business as Partners in Development.[3] (IBLF Global now succeeds the PWBLF et al.) Regarding then Prince Charles and the Rio Earth Summit, Dimbleby observes:

> By 1991, the momentum generated by the Prince's speeches on the environment had secured him an international reputation. In the run-up to the Rio summit which was planned for 1992, the Prince was determined to have his own input by bringing together key international figures in an attempt to achieve a degree of harmony between the conflicting attitudes of Europe, the United States and the developing nations, led by Brazil.[4] He

---

1. Junor, pp. 237-238. Junor comments, "Thus the Prince of Wales's decision to experiment with an eighty-acre block at Broadfield Farm [which the Duchy purchased] was a massive boost to the organic movement [in Britain]" (ibid., pp. 241-242).
2. For more information, see *Cloak of Green* by Elaine Dewar.
3. For more information, see this chapter's later section titled, "The United Nations and public-private partnerships," at p. 446. The PWBLF became the PWIBLF, or Prince of Wales International Business Leaders Forum, then the IBLF, and now IBLF Global (see "https://www.iblfglobal.org" on the Internet).
4. "Brazil, the world's fifth-largest nation in area, is the most biologically diverse country, with more species of plants, insects, freshwater fish, monkeys and amphibians than anywhere else. Altogether it has 20 percent of the world's plant species and 30 percent of the planet's tropical rain forest.... In second place is Indonesia, a small country but the world's fifth most populous, with the greatest marine life diversity on Earth and large numbers of unique animals and plants.... Altogether, Latin American countries—Brazil, Mexico, Columbia, Peru, Venezuela and Ecuador—hold the planet's greatest diversity, with Asian nations—Indonesia, China, Malaysia and the Philippines—close behind, the data show. The United States also makes the list, one of only two developed countries, the other being Australia. Three African nations—South Africa, Madagascar and the Democratic Republic of the Congo—are included, as well as Papua New Guinea and India. The 17 countries, which cover just 25 percent of the planet's land surface, contain 80 percent of the planet's endangered species. 'These countries play a fundamental role in efforts to conserve life on Earth,' said Russell Mittermeier, the president of Conservation International.... Environmental organizations, including Conservation International, have tried to preach the benefits of biodiversity, from eco-tourism to biological prospecting for medicines, to countries such as Brazil and Indonesia for years. So far progress has been slow.... Madagascar, for instance, ... has over the past decade attracted large amounts of international funding for sustainable development it would

alighted on the idea of using the royal yacht as the base for a two-day international seminar at the end of an official tour of Brazil in April 1991. Among others, he invited [then U.S.] Senator Albert Gore; senior officials from the World Bank; chief executives from companies such as Shell and BP; the principal non-governmental organizations [(NGOs)]; European politicians...; and ... President Fernando Collor of Brazil.

....At the last moment, the Brazilian President threatened to cut short his appearance.... The Prince wrote to him...:

> ...I was so keen to arrange this seminar, following our first meeting just before your inauguration as President ... to reconcile conservation requirements with development pressure. [A] ... great deal of time and effort has been expended ... to attract the most influential and effective participants.... I, personally, would be disappointed and disheartened by your absence because ... many people ... are looking towards the importance of the 1992 United Nations Conference....

Written in longhand, it was a characteristic letter with a characteristic effect: the President yielded to the Prince.

According to some of those present, the *Britannia* seminar played a crucial role in preparing North and South for the accommodation in their positions which would be needed if the Rio summit were not to be a diplomatic fiasco. [The] ... participants ... moved towards a much closer understanding of the predicament facing them all.[1]

On a Prophecy Club radio broadcast, Rod Lewis asserted, mistakenly, that Al Gore "has been commissioned as the next world leader."[2] In fact, Al Gore and the "Clintonistas" practically work for the British monarchy, whether or not they care to admit it. Before the Rio Earth Summit, for example, then Prince Charles made a television documentary titled *The Earth in the Balance,* "in which he warned against the accelerating depredation inflicted on the planet by human greed and folly," having been "deeply engaged in a struggle to develop his own 'model' village on the outskirts of Dorchester" and having pleaded "for the rainforests."[3] The documentary was aired in May 1990, well before the publication of Al Gore's similarly titled book, *Earth in the Balance.*[4] Moreover, Satan's Prince was

---

not have gotten if not for its biodiversity, he said" (Laurie Goering, Chicago Tribune, "Study takes stock of biodiversity," *The Denver Post,* 12 Dec. 1997, p. 60A).

1. Dimbleby, *The Prince of Wales,* pp. 497-498.
2. The Prophecy Club, 31 July 1997, multiple times on multiple A.M. radio stations.
3. Dimbleby, *The Prince of Wales,* p. 404.
4. An analysis of Gore's book reveals that the former Vice President is a New Age pantheist who endorses goddess worship and feminist views of "god" as "mother," and displays his twisted presumption that such perversion is somehow linkable to Christianity, besides Hinduism, Buddhism, Native American spirituality, Islam and counterfeit or rabbinic Judaism. *(Biblical or scriptural Judaism is Christian.)* In all this, Gore also promotes an earth-centric goddess-based "new faith" for mankind's future. Mr. Gore is *anti-Christian.* Berit Kjos comments: "Vice President Gore's 'faith-friendly' campaign hides beliefs that oppose Christianity ... on every point. The evidence is in his 1992 book, *Earth in the Balance — Ecology and the Human Spirit.* It calls for a 'panreligious perspective' that would conform Christianity to the UN vision of social and religious solidarity. The old biblical absolutes simply don't fit the new global spiritu-

working on a "village" concept long before Satan-serving Mrs. Hillary Clinton. Not only does it appear that Al Gore, a New Age satanist and top member of the Illuminati, took the title for his popular antichristian book from Satan's Prince, but Hillary too jumped on that bandwagon. Notably, following his 1969 investiture: "Charles and Anne held a dinner party for the younger set aboard the royal yacht anchored at Holyhead. Percys and Pagets, the Ormsby-<u>Gores</u>, the Nevill cousins, Kerrs and Soames's were there, among other close personal friends."[1]

By 1990, then U.S. Senator Al Gore had worked closely with (roasting) Canadian Maurice Strong, who himself had worked closely with (roasting) Prince Philip and was a member of (roasting) Queen Elizabeth II's Privy Council for Canada. Strong served as the Undersecretary General of the UN Earth Council, being a WWF vice president—and had also pushed the population control agenda of the "elite" through international environmental conferences, starting with the Stockholm Conference of 1972. While a U.S. Senator, Gore worked with Strong to establish the Association of Global Parliamentarians; in turn, Strong aided Gore's staff in the preparation of Gore's book. Around this same time, in 1990, Gore met Prince Philip in Washington, D.C. This is the background to Gore's invitation to participate aboard the *Britannia* in April 1991, where he met then Prince Charles. Since that time, Gore has openly called for "population stabilization" (i.e., infanticide and genocide), arguing that an "overcrowded world is inevitably a polluted one."[2]

Before its 1997 decommissioning,[3] Charles regularly used the royal yacht "to host seminars or conferences, or to entertain the rich and powerful." Having previously argued unsuccessfully against its abandonment, Satan's Prince remarked, "I believe the aim should be to ... keep the Yacht in service until the year 2000—and whatever happens next is in the lap of the Gods...."[4]

In December 1997, the same month that the royal yacht was decommissioned, another item of great international interest came out of the Rio Earth Summit—the *Kyoto Protocol:*

---

ality needed as a foundation for a new earth-centered ethic. [Each] ... model for this blended spirituality must be: Pantheistic: god is all, god is in everything; Monistic: all are one, all are spiritually interconnected; [and] Evolving: always ready to adapt to the changing requirements of our globalist leaders" (see "https://www.crossroad.to/articles2/Gore.html" on the Internet).
1. Cathcart, p. 97.
2. Scott Thompson and Nancy Spannaus, "Al Gore: Britain's Malthusian Agent," *Executive Intelligence Review,* 25 Apr. 2008.
3. A new royal yacht is in the works.
4. Dimbleby, *The Prince of Wales,* pp. 511-513. There is only *one* God, of biblical Israel and Christians.

KYOTO, Japan — Negotiators from around the world agreed today on a package of measures that for the first time would legally obligate industrial countries to cut emissions of waste industrial gases that [a few elitist and globalist] scientists say are warming Earth's atmosphere....

The agreement reached by delegates from more than 150 nations creates a landmark environmental policy to deal with global warming....

The nations would have a year to ratify the treaty, starting in March [1998]. Talks on "trading" of emissions are expected take place in November 1998.

Despite the uncertainties, some environmentalists hailed the agreement as a remarkable political and economic innovation, in that it would establish a global system for dealing with what many scientists believe [(this is an outright lie designed to seduce the public—see below)] is the overarching environmental concern.

Opponents of the treaty condemned it as economically ruinous.

The accord—known as the Kyoto Protocol—would require the industrial nations to reduce their emissions of carbon dioxide and five other heat-trapping greenhouse gases to 5.2 percent below those of 1990....

Some countries may be allowed to increase emissions, but globally, emissions are to be reduced by 30 percent from the levels currently projected for 2010.

After an all-night session..., the protocol was approved by representatives of more than 150 countries. The countries were modifying an agreement, negotiated in Rio de Janeiro in 1992, that called for voluntary efforts to limit emission of greenhouse gases.[1] [Such efforts will now be compulsory.] The burning of fossil fuels like coal and oil is responsible for most emissions of carbon dioxide [(another lie—see below)], the most important greenhouse gas.[2]

The treaty, though, contains at least two worrisome flaws. Most significantly, it doesn't impose restrictions on rapidly developing countries like China, India, Brazil and Mexico.... Moreover, it's not certain how the emission trading credits will be implemented.[3]

....Like the little boy who cried "wolf," environmental alarmists and scaremongers have exhausted their credibility.

Add the Great Global Warming Scare of 1997 to the list. This is more than a dispassionate debate over a questionable theory. To the greenies, global warming dissenters are heretics, challenging their religion. This is a blasphemy on Gaia, the goddess of the earth. It's like saying trees are not our equals.

Global warming hysteria is a convenient vehicle for the radical enviro political agenda. Energy use and economic growth are inherently "bad," as are their byproducts: suburban development, cars, RVs, SUVs, power boats, snowmobiles, materialism in general, and its handmaiden, capital-

---

1. The six gases are carbon dioxide, methane, nitrous oxide, and three halocarbons. Carbon dioxide, of course, is essential to plant life, as oxygen is to us. The likely result of increased carbon dioxide emissions would actually be lusher and more plant life, which in turn would churn out more oxygen into the Earth's atmosphere—a healthy and commonsense prospect.
2. William K. Stevens, New York Times, "Global emission accord gets nod," *The Denver Post,* 11 Dec. 1997, pp. 1A, 29A.
3. "A treaty to warm to," *The Denver Post,* 12 Dec. 1997, p. 7B.

ism. We must simplify our lives and return to nature. If that's the goal, then a false crisis, like global warming, is better than no crisis at all.

How can you help but be skeptical when the global warmers have quotes like these on their record:

✓ Stephen Schneider, Stanford University atmospheric scientist: "We have to offer up scary scenarios, make simplified, dramatic statements.... Each of us has to decide what is the right balance between being effective and being honest."

✓ Tim Wirth, outgoing Undersecretary of State for Global Affairs: "We've got to ride the global warming issue. Even if the theory of global warming is wrong, we will be doing the right thing in terms of economic policy and environmental policy."

✓ Vice President Al Gore: "Minor shifts in policy, marginal adjustments in ongoing programs, moderate improvements in laws and regulations and rhetoric offered in lieu of genuine change ... are all forms of appeasement, designed to satisfy the public's desire to believe that sacrifice, struggle and a wrenching transformation of society will not be necessary."

....I choose to believe that, as we've demonstrated throughout our history, we can solve tomorrow's problems with tomorrow's technology. And that we can do so without sacrificing our economic well-being....

In any event, 96 percent of all greenhouse gas emissions occur naturally; only 4 percent are attributable to human industrial influence. Solar activity alone, dwarfing human influence, could account for all of the [(alleged)] recent global warming—which, incidentally, in moderate doses can be of net benefit to the planet.

Contrary to the assertions of the greenies, there is no scientific consensus on the exaggerated claims of global warmers. When members of the Meteorological Society and the American Geophysical Society were asked in a Gallup poll whether they thought human actions are causing global warming, only 17 percent agreed. Greenpeace likes to brandish the names of scientists who believe that current patterns of energy use will cause catastrophic climate change in the future. What they don't tell you is that their doomsayers represent only a small fraction of those surveyed.[1]

The outspoken host of "Lou Dobbs Tonight" observed that global warming activists treat their belief in global warming like a religion following a segment about the issue by CNN correspondent Ines Ferre. "The one issue here [is] ... they bring this thing to a personal belief system," Dobbs said. "It's almost a religion without any question."

Dobbs noted how "minuscule" man's impact on the climate is compared to other factors, specifically sunspot activity. "And ... we're in the second year of the solar sunspot activity cycle—an 11-year cycle and many scientists are saying, 'My gosh, compared to what our Sun can do, man has minuscule influence,'" Dobbs said.

Dobbs also said that data is cherry-picked to make the case for global warming alarmism. "Well ... we're all concerned about this planet.... But, there seems to be such a crowding out of facts and objective assessment of those facts...." The climatologist Dobbs referenced from Ferre's report was Joseph D'Aleo—the executive director of International Climate and Environmental Change Assessment Project (ICECAP).... "We are too short-

---

1. Mike Rosen, "Global warming is hot air," *The Denver Post*, 12 Dec. 1997, p. 7B.

sighted or certainly ... those who believe in it, are not looking at the big picture, which needs to include other factors, the natural cycles in the ocean and the Sun that are the real drivers, [not to mention volcanic activity,[1]]" D'Aleo said.

Ferre alluded to the $175 "cow tax" that some farmers feel is a possibility and could increase their operating costs. "Some farmers fear future regulations on greenhouse gas emissions could include ... a cow tax," Ferre said. "The United Nations calculates that livestock are responsible for 18 percent greenhouse gas emissions worldwide.... The Environmental Protection Agency says methane, a greenhouse gas associated with livestock, is not being considered for regulation <u>at this point</u>," Ferre said. However, Rick Krause, senior director of congressional relations for the American Farm Bureau, told the Business & Media Institute it is a possibility—especially based on the rhetoric of ... Barack Obama....[2]

The founder of the Weather Channel is ridiculing Al Gore over his calls for action on global climate change.... John Coleman,[3] now a weatherman at San Diego's KUSI, wrote ... that Gore refuses to acknowledge the faulty research on which the idea of global warming is based. Coleman's lengthy scolding came as the former vice president and [ignoble] Nobel Peace Prize winner addressed the Senate Foreign Relations Committee and urged lawmakers to pass a bill that would put caps on heat-trapping gases and take the lead on a [forthcoming] global climate treaty. Coleman wrote that the [U.S.] Environmental Protection Agency is "on the verge" of naming CO_2 (carbon dioxide[, which plants breathe and require to live, and which humans and animals thus require *to live*]) as a pollutant, and that seemingly all of Washington is on board with such [insidious] "CO2 silliness." "I am totally convinced there is no scientific basis for any of it.... Global Warming: It is *the* hoax; it is bad science; it is a 'high jacking' of public policy; [and] it is no joke. It is the greatest scam in history," Coleman wrote.[4]

---

1. A *normal* volcanic eruption can cause a global reduction in average temperatures for *years*. What would happen if multiple volcanoes *simultaneously* erupted? Indeed, what would happen if just *one* supervolcanic eruption, equivalent to *hundreds* of normal volcanic eruptions, were to occur? Wyoming's Yellowstone Basin is perhaps the most dangerous of a number of *active* super-volcanoes around the world (e.g., in the United States, Indonesia, New Zealand, Japan and elsewhere in Asia), and may actually be ready to blow *now*—with an eruption equivalent to as many as *one-thousand or more* Mount St. Helens. "Volcanic eruptions can have a huge impact on the climate, but unlike as with coal plants, they tend to cool the planet down. That's what happened in 1991, when Mt. Pinatubo in the Philippines erupted, spewing millions of tons of energy-deflecting sulfur dioxide into the atmosphere, which caused the world's average temperatures to fall by about 3.8 degrees Fahrenheit that year. The devastating 1883 eruption of Indonesia's Krakatoa, produced a similar effect, cooling the globe by about 4.2 degrees and producing spectacular sunsets around the world.... Even more dramatic was an eruption of another Indonesian volcano, Mt. Tambora, in 1815. This explosion, thought to be four times larger than Krakatoa's..., resulted in snow and frost in New England and Europe in May, June, and July, causing widespread crop failures and famine. That year became known as 'The Year Without a Summer'" (Eoin O'Carroll, "Do volcanoes change the climate?", *The "Christian" Science Monitor,* 29 Jan. 2009). Such effects are *minor and short-lived* compared to those likely to ensue from just a single supervolcanic eruption; for a genuine and scary illustration of this very real threat, see the docudrama movie *Supervolcano* as well as the corresponding documentary program, *The Truth about Yellowstone*.
2. Jeff Poor, "CNN's Dobbs on Global Warming Hysteria: 'It's Almost a Religion without Any Question,'" *Business & Media Institute*, 6 Jan. 2009.
3. This is a different "John Coleman" from the one who wrote *The Committee of 300*.
4. "Weather Channel Founder Blasts Gore Over Global Warming Campaign," *Fox News*, 29 Jan. 2009.

So, as of the second edition of this work, nothing has changed in this elitist fraud; the real scientific evidence continues to contradict their eco-fascist claims of (predominantly) anthropogenic (i.e., human caused) "global warming,"[1] which has become a form of *religious* hysteria among global elitists.[2] As fools who claim to be "wise," the "elite" commonly delude even themselves. This is *not* about saving the world or mankind—but quite the opposite.[3] No, it *is* really about power and money—the power to control a dwindled global population, and the money to pay off whomever they must to impoverish, starve, and kill everyone else.

Under President Bush (Jr.), the greatest foreign policy damage to the image of the U.S. worldwide, apart from the second war in Iraq, came from the U.S. refusal to sign the Kyoto Protocol. This was something for which then Prince Charles in November 2005, chided Bush (Jr.),[4] and something Mr. Barack Hussein Obama—as a *British*

1. Some scientists argue the opposite—that Earth is on the brink of a new Ice Age: "The reason that global CO2 levels rise and fall in response to the global temperature is because cold water is capable of retaining more CO2 than warm water. That is why carbonated beverages lose their carbonation, or CO2, when stored in a warm environment.... The earth is currently warming as a result of the natural Ice Age cycle, and as the oceans get warmer, they release increasing amounts of CO2 into the atmosphere.... [Anthropogenic Global Warming] theory is based on data that is drawn from a ridiculously narrow span of time and it demonstrates a wanton disregard for the 'big picture' of long-term climate change. The data from paleoclimatology, including ice cores, sea sediments, geology, paleobotany and zoology, indicate that we are on the verge of entering another Ice Age, and the data also shows that severe and lasting climate change can occur within only a few years. While concern over the dubious threat of Anthropogenic Global Warming continues to distract the attention of people throughout the world, the very real threat of the approaching and inevitable Ice Age, which will render large parts of the Northern Hemisphere uninhabitable, is being foolishly ignored" (Gregory F. Fegel, "Earth on the Brink of an Ice Age," *Pravda*, 11 Jan. 2009). *Is Earth really about to enter another Ice Age? No, but Jesus shall soon return; after judging the world, He will heal it.*

2. As but one of many such examples, in an article attributing cyclones, earthquakes, severe cold, typhoons, low-pressure systems and storms to "global warming," we read: "Natural disasters killed more than 220,000 people in 2008, making it one of the most devastating years on record and underlining the need for a global climate deal, a large reinsurer has said. Although the number of natural disasters was lower than in 2007, the catastrophes proved to be more deadly and more expensive, Germany-based Munich Re said in its annual assessment. 'This continues the long-term trend we have been observing. Climate change has already started and is very probably contributing to increasingly frequent weather extremes and ensuing natural catastrophes,' Munich Re board member Torsten Jeworrek said.... The world needed 'effective and binding rules on CO2 emissions, so that climate change is curbed and future generations do not have to live with weather scenarios that are difficult to control,' Mr Jeworrek said" ("Natural disasters 'killed more than 220,000 in 2008,'" *Telegraph.co.uk*, 30 Dec. 2008). Really? Since when do *we* control weather? *This elitist nonsense has become a fools' fad, mixed in with a clear globalist agenda.*

3. The truth is that a natural *increase* in atmospheric carbon dioxide would result in an *increase* in global plant life; this would then result in an *increase* in atmospheric oxygen and humidity, and that would lead to an *increase* in animal and other life. It would also move the world toward a tropical climate with a thicker atmosphere globally—all necessary ingredients to make Earth a global "Eden."

4. In November 2005, after meeting with then UN Secretary-General Kofi Annan and visiting the site of the 9/11 terrorist attacks in New York to dedicate the "British Memorial Garden," Satan's Prince personally chided then President Bush (Jr.) at the White House: Having stated previously that "global warming" is among "the most crucial issues that face our planet," Charles warned the President, saying, "the burden of the world rests on your shoulders" ("Charles asks US to lead on planet," *BBC News*, 3 Nov. 2005). "The Prince of Wales used a speech during a White House dinner to administer the politest of warnings to George Bush to shoulder the burdens of world leadership in tackling environmental and climate change issues.... Prince Charles, who last week described climate change as the most important issue

"manchurain" electee,[1] treasonous traitor (e.g., via sedition against duly-elected President Trump), socialist criminal, Muslim "jihadist," bent sexual satanist, etc.—had vowed to "rectify." Clearly, Queen Elizabeth II's and Prince Philip's May 2007 visit to the White House, which was "not only the social event of the year, but also of the entire Bush [(Jr.)] presidency,"[2] did *not* itself suffice.

But Satan's Prince could not totally fault Bush (Jr.): The infamous September 11, 2001 terrorist attacks against the United States in New York City and Washington D.C. were (evidently) undertaken with the *conspiratorial complicity* of high-level Bush (Jr.) administration officials, who *intentionally and traitorously acted to ensure their success.*[3] Indeed, this *treason* enabled the entire "Homeland Security" apparatus and related initiatives, some of which severely undermine and destroy the constitutional nature of U.S. governance, facilitating preplanned entry into a coming global government. (We may view this as a new "Pearl Harbor.") Implicated officials include then Vice President Dick Cheney, former Secretary of Defense Donald Rumsfeld, and US Air Force General Richard Myers, who was acting chairman of the joint chiefs on 9/11, among others.[4]

---

facing the world, told the 100 guests: 'So many people throughout the world look to the US for a lead on the most crucial issues that face our planet.... Truly the burden of the world rests on your shoulders.' The [Bush (Jr.)] White House is famously sceptical about the importance of climate change and the US has refused to implement the Kyoto protocol on greenhouse gas emissions.... Among the guests were ... former president George Bush [(Sr.)], Nancy Reagan, ... Donald Rumsfeld, ... Condoleezza Rice, ... [Senator Joseph Lieberman, Chief U.S. Supreme Court Justice John Roberts, NBC's Tom Brokaw, United Methodist Church pastors Kirbyjon Caldwell and Kathleene Card, Marie-Josee Kravis who is President of the blasphemous Museum of Modern Art, top military and Homeland Security brass,] and a smattering of stars" (Stephen Bates, "Prince issues gentle rebuke to Bush on climate change," *The Guardian,* 4 Nov. 2005).

1. Barack Obama may *not* have met the U.S. Constitutional requirements to be President, having *never* publicly produced *valid* (i.e., non-fraudulent) evidence or documentation of "natural born" citizen status. Obama is not only supports infanticide (e.g., abortionists and women who murder their unborn children), sexual satanism (e.g., lunatic "transgenderism," sodomy and lesbianism), but apparently he also was a socialist "manchurian" presidential electee who a) appears to have been born in Kenya in 1961, actually making him *a British citizen*—because his natural father, Barack Obama Sr., was then a Kenyan citizen *subject to British jurisdiction,* automatically conferring British citizenship, while B. Obama's mother, a minor, was herself too young to confer U.S. citizenship; b) was an adopted or otherwise acknowledged *Indonesian citizen* and declared *Muslim* child named Barry Soetoro—by Lolo Soetoro, his Indonesian stepfather—at a time when Indonesia did *not* provide for dual citizenships; c) may not have even become a "naturalized" U.S. citizen later; and d) traveled to Pakistan as an apparent Indonesian citizen in 1981, when U.S. Citizens could *not* legally enter Pakistan. The U.S. Democratic National Convention (DNC) illegally colluded with Obama to conceal all those facts and suppress the truth from the public, as have the establishment "news" media and U.S. Courts. That so much of the public remained *willfully ignorant* only aided the illicit conduct. For quick information, see videos like "Obama Is Not A Natural Born U.S. Citizen And Is Ineligible For The Presidency," as posted at "https://www.youtube.com/watch?v=pWTs1YyhFRg" on YouTube; and articles like "Watch Obama commercial they don't want you to see," *WND Staff,* 8 Jan. 2009. Obamanation's lawlessness continues and has only increased with the Mr. Pedo-Joe "Manchurian" Biden et al.
2. "For Queen and First Lady, Bush Will Try White Tie," *New York Times,* 5 May 2007.
3. In July 2001, President Bush (Jr.) visited Queen Elizabeth II and Prince Philip at Buckingham Palace.
4. A great deal of information convincingly demonstrates both a major conspiracy and ongoing cover-ups by government officials and agencies in connection with the 9/11 attacks. Some individuals have taken legal action. Notable among them is former career Army Major April Gallop, who was present

In the run-up to 2008's U.S. Presidential election, Powell, a (late) knight of the British monarchy, and "Chicken Little" Gore, who is yet personally close to Charles,[1] both strongly endorsed Obama. In fact, Obama consulted Gore on a bi-weekly basis for much of his campaign, with Gore having stated, "I intend to do whatever I can to make sure he is elected president of the United States."[2] Close on their heels, from the floor of the New York Stock Exchange, Henry Kissinger, who had been a key globalist and elitist under the British monarchy,[3] revealed: "His task will be to develop an overall strategy for America in this period when, really, a New World Order [(NWO)] can be created. It's a great [global] opportunity, it isn't just a crisis [of economics]."[4] According to Gordon Brown, Britain's Prime Minister: "We could allow this crisis to start a retreat from globalisation.... Or we could view the threats and challenges we face today as the difficult birth-pangs of a new global order—and our task now as nothing less than making the transition through a new internationalism to the benefits of an expanding global society."[5] Well, Sa-

at the Pentagon on 9/11 when one or more (alleged) bombs were detonated nearby, contradicting claims of an aircraft strike. (Other evidence could support an alternately alleged cruise missile impact.)

Major Gallop, who began working at the Pentagon in 2000 with a top secret clearance, filed suit against Dick Cheney, Donald Rumsfeld, Richard Myers et al., claiming conspiracy, high treason, and other crimes against the United States and its citizens. The lawsuit, filed on December 15, 2008, is extensive and available to read in full on the Internet. Paragraph 2 of the Complaint's Preliminary Statement reads, for example: "The defendants' purpose in aiding and facilitating the attack, and the overall object of the conspirac(ies), was to bring about an unprecedented, horrifying and frightening catastrophe of terrorism inside the United States, which would give rise to a powerful reaction of fear and anger.... This would generate a political atmosphere ... in which the new Administration could enact and implement radical changes in the policy and practice of constitutional government in our country.... By helping the attack succeed, defendants and their cohorts created a basis for the seizure of extraordinary power, and a pretext for launching the so-called Global War on Terror, in the guise of which they were free to pursue plans for military conquest, 'full spectrum dominance' and 'American primacy' around the world." (For example, see Stephen C. Webster, "Career Army Specialist sues Rumsfeld, Cheney, saying no evacuation order given on 9/11," *Voltaire Network*, 26 Dec. 2008.)

Gallop's account is uncertain: "April Gallop ... had an office in wedge 2 over 150 feet from the impact hole. Gallop's office structure did collapse and the lights went out, but Gallop was [(supposedly)] too far away to smell jet fuel. She, with her child and others, exited through a window near the Heliport. Once outside, Gallop collapsed, was apparently unconscious, and was moved to the outer lawn area, and then to a hospital. Gallop [(allegedly)] had no opportunity to see aircraft debris inside or outside the building" (John D. Wyndham, "Bringing Closure to the 9/11 Pentagon Debate," *Foreign Policy Journal*, 7 Oct. 2016). Sadly, Gallop's lawsuit was *corruptly dismissed*.

For the record, this author considered that a conspiracy was underfoot *the moment the second airliner struck the second World Trade Center tower in New York City*. From his military perspective, it was *extremely unlikely*, apart from actual high-level government and military complicity, for in-the-air US fighter jets to have failed to down, let alone intercept even the *first* off-course civilian plane, to say nothing of a later one. Indeed, given the *known* civilian and military air traffic and other safeguards that had *long been in place*, against such eventualities within the continental United States, that subsequent planes were somehow not intercepted and stopped before further terrorist impacts. These facts *beg all credulity and support objective conspiracy claims*.

1. For more information, see ch. 14's section titled "The Statue," at p. 506.
2. "Gore Endorses Obama, Says U.S. Must Change Direction," *The Associated Press*, 16 June 2008.
3. Kissinger was a prominent Committee of 300 member, an original member of the Trilateral Commission, and also was the head of the U.S. CFR, when the first edition of this book went to press.
4. Cliff Kincaid, "Kissinger, Obama and the communist Chinese," *World Tribune*, 8 Jan. 2009.
5. "Brown warns against 'pessimism,'" *BBC News*, 26 Jan. 2009.

tan's Mr. Obama always aims to please his NWO masters: indeed, as iniquitous occupant of the White House, he appointed no fewer than eleven Trilateral Commission members to key administration positions—in the State Department, national "intelligence," the Treasury Department, and even as Ambassador to the United Nations.[1]

The Kyoto Protocol itself was "destined" to be *replaced* by an even more stringent and far reaching global environmental treaty in the 2009 to 2010 time frame—one for which Charles had again set the tone: "A global partnership must be formed to tackle the problem of climate change, the Prince of Wales told the European Parliament today. Prince Charles called on the public and private sectors as well as non-governmental organisations to make 'corporate social responsibility truly global and truly effective'. 'We are simply not reacting quickly enough. We cannot be anything less than courageous and revolutionary in our approach to tackling climate change. If we are not, the result will be catastrophe for all of us, but with the poorest in our world hit hardest of all,' he said. His royal highness warned that a failure to reduce global warming will increase instability and urged the European Parliament to give 'determined and principled leadership'. His speech has been warmly welcomed by Friends of the Earth (FoE).... 'The Prince of Wales has today raised issues of urgent importance that demand immediate political action,' said FoE director Tony Juniper."[2]

Celestial Signs (a Blood Moon Tetrad) and the COP21 Accord of 2015. Certain past "rabbis" claimed that "when the Sun is in eclipse, it is a bad omen for the whole world," because idolaters reckon seasons "by the Sun," but "when the Moon is in eclipse, it is a bad omen for Israel, since Israel reckons [seasons] by the Moon" (*Succah*

---

1. These include Secretary of Treasury, Tim Geithner; Ambassador to the United Nations, Susan Rice; National Security Advisor, General James L. Jones; Deputy National Security Advisor, Thomas Donilon; Chairman, Economic Recovery Committee, Paul Volker; Director of National Intelligence, Admiral Dennis C. Blair; Assistant Secretary of State, Asia and Pacific, Kurt M. Campbell; Deputy Secretary of State, James Steinberg; State Department, Special Envoy, Richard Haass; State Department, Special Envoy, Dennis Ross; and State Department, Special Envoy, Richard Holbrooke. Some other Trilateral Commission members who do or did figure prominently with Obamanation include: Zbigniew Brzezinski, a co-founder of the Trilateral Commission, who served as Obama's principal foreign policy advisor; Al Gore; former President Clinton, whose satanic treasonous wife Hillary was then Secretary of State; informal Geithner advisors Alan Greenspan and Henry Kissinger; Brent Scowcroft, a U.S. CFR member who served as an unofficial advisor to Obama and had mentored Defense Secretary Robert Gates; Robert Zoellick, former President of the World Bank; and Laurence Summers, former White House Economic Advisor, whom past Treasury Secretary Robert Rubin mentored (Patrick Wood, "Obama: Trilateral Commission Endgame (Update 1)," *The August Review*, 30 Jan. 2009). Mrs. Clinton chose Anne-Marie Slaughter, then a member of the World Economic Forum's (WEF's) "Council on Global Governance," Dean of Princeton University's Woodrow Wilson School of Public and International Affairs, and author of *A New World Order,* to run the State Department's Office of Policy Planning (Cliff Kincaid, "Global Taxes and Global TV Now on the Agenda," *AIM Report*, 26 Jan. 2009).
2. "Prince of Wales calls for global effort to help climate," *Energy Saving Trust,* 19 Feb. 2008. Note that the Friends of the Earth logo is a green serpent swallowing its tail.

29a). But how much, really, have Israel's teachers understood? (On May 6, 2023, Charles was crowned king—including of *Israel,* and with "rabbinic" participation—right after a lunar eclipse.) How much does today's Church understand?

For years, a great deal of talk and sensationalism, including false prophetic speculations, surrounded a "rare" tetrad of blood-moons —on Passover of April 15, 2014, *Sukkot* or the Feast of Tabernacles of October 8, 2014, Passover of April 4, 2015, and finally *Sukkot* of September 28, 2015—all intersected from an intervening solar eclipse. What made this particular tetrad unusual is that it perfectly coincided with multiple scriptural High Holy Days. Some speculated that we would see Jesus' return. (But this author has *proven* since the 1980s that *Christ's return will be posttribulational,* and that *the rapture itself will occur in at least three posttribulational stages,* with the final stage occurring *after* the fifth and sixth bowls of wrath in Revelation 16 are outpoured.[1]) Many others anticipated some disaster to befall Israel or the world instead—only to find themselves later seriously wondering what it was really all about, if anything.[2]

Something significant *did* later occur, however—in December 2015. For our purposes, here, Passover and *Sukkot* reflect a) Christ's crucifixion at Passover (on a Wednesday) and then His resurrection as The Firstfruit to God (i.e., the first-ever harvest unto eternal life, at the very end of the *weekly* sabbath), as well as b) national Israel's coming crucifixion at the midpoint of the Tribulation Week (e.g., cf.

---

1. For concrete details on the saints' rapture, see *The Real Rapture and Other Prophetic Mysteries: Understanding the Revelation (Apocalypse),* the fifth volume of the author's *Messiah, History, and the Tribulation Period* series. Also, get the author's "The *Real* Rapture" teaching from Prophecy House.

2. Notably, though Pastor Mark Biltz of El Shaddai Ministries receives credit for bringing this particular tetrad to the world's attention, even he has neither known nor understood their actual meaning. Indeed, like so many, he only loosely speculated. In 2014, for example, Biltz stated: "I'm just saying there's a good chance there could be a war with Israel.... I'm also saying there's a good chance there could be economic calamity. And I'm basing that on the Bible and patterns." (These events will come, but they are *not* what this particular celestial tetrad portended.) Biltz has also been *less* sound in his prognostications at times, mentioning Russia and Ukraine, ISIS terrorists, the Ebola plague, etc. Moreover, Biltz *errantly* asserts that lunar eclipses relate only to Israel, when in fact, scripture clearly shows they also relate to the Church generally (e.g., cf. Rev 12). *Biltz might do better reading tea leaves!*

Others, such as the sometimes sensationalist and—certainly on the timing of the rapture—*false as well as errant* prophecy "teacher" John Hagee, also did much to advertise the celestial tetrad in question: "Of course, many blood moon believers, including megachurch pastor John Hagee, believe that this particular blood moon closely precedes the [(claimed)] pretribulational] Rapture of Christians [(but it will *not* be pretribulational)], Armageddon and the second coming of Christ." Hagee first heard of the tetrad from Biltz—but then claimed discovering it himself (Abby Ohlheiser, "Everything you need to know about the 'blood moon' apocalypse debate," *Washington Post,* 3 Apr. 2015). And, many news outlets sensationally promoted these and other errors to the world.

Mr. Hagee has time and again shown himself to be *dishonorable* toward this author, conducting himself as *a false accuser and censoring liar.* Indeed, heretic Hagee is *an ardent false teacher,* both on prophecy and the (critical) matter of salvation for Israel—which *contrary* to Hagee, is *only* through belief in Christ Jesus (i.e., Messiah Yeshua). Popularity and any support for Israel aside, false prophecy teachers such as Hagee ought to be avoided—for they know *not* whereof they speak.

Rev 6:7-8), and then the nation's resurrection[1] or translation[2] at the "last trumpet," which shall begin to sound at the very end of the Tribulation Week's "sabbath" or seventh apocalyptic seal. So, these two feasts point to sacrificial death at the midpoint of the week (Passover), on the fourth day or in the fourth year, followed by resurrection at the end of the week *(Sukkot),* at the end of the seventh day or year. The tetrad then portends events related to judgment and then redemption, respectively, that are coming. Now, if that was *all* we could say, it would still be quite significant. However, there is much more that we'll here bring to light (uniquely).

Something both portended and foretold occurred—filling the anticipatory global "news" media's pages for many months. More saliently, *it all ties to Charles as the foretold AntiChrist.* To see and understand, though, a little scriptural background is essential. Pay *close attention.* Jesus foretold, "And there will be signs in the Sun, in the Moon, and in the stars, and on the Earth distress of nations, with perplexity, the sea and the waves roaring—men's hearts failing them from fear and the expectation of those things which are coming on the Earth; for the powers of the heavens will be shaken" (Luke 21:25-26). Consider Christ's words carefully, re-reading them.

Notice all this: First, celestial signs involving the Sun, Moon and stars (e.g., comets, asteroids, meteors, etc.) are to *precede,* we are told, "distress of nations, with perplexity, the sea and the waves roaring—men's hearts failing them from fear and the expectation of those things which are coming on the Earth." Mankind has, of course, saw a remarkable celestial tetrad in 2014–15, coinciding as it did with major High Holy Days (themselves centered on Christ's crucifixion, death and resurrection). Second, the noted distress and confusion ("perplexity") of nations seems to revolve around Earth's oceans and waters ("the sea and the waves roaring"), such that the fearful could experience heart failures ("men's hearts failing them"). What we've just read is *now* (i.e., currently) being fulfilled (e.g., via satanic fraudulent climate alarmism). Before we get to that, however, notice that *third,* "the powers of the heavens will be shaken."

Simply put, "things" (keep reading) *will* come from on-high, accentuating mankind's *environmental and earthly fears.* These involve much of what is foretold in the apocalyptic scriptures—to include comet and asteroid strikes, the destructive activities of fallen angels (cf. "powers of the heavens" and "stars"), and Messiah Yeshua's / Christ Jesus' (i.e., The Power's) subsequent return (Luke

---

1. The resurrection will be *spiritual* for a newly-regenerate surviving nation of Israel, as indicated in Romans 11:15 (cf. 11:25-27), but *physical* (literal) for deceased tribulational Christians.
2. For example, the 144,000 believing and sealed Israelite males of Revelation 14:1 (see 7:2-8).

21:27) to both judge and save the world (e.g., see Mark 13:24-26; Rev 6:12b-17, 8:1 to 10:7; cf. Joel 2:30-32).[1]

To summarize, couched between the celestial signage of the noted tetrad (to say nothing of yet coming solar and lunar signs), and the approaching "powers of the heavens" being "shaken," we find this remarkable foretelling: "on the Earth distress of nations, with perplexity, the sea and the waves roaring—men's hearts failing them from fear and the expectation of those things which are coming on the Earth." It is *this and similar* "sandwiched prophecies" that we may here recognize as transpiring in our day (i.e., now), and for which *Charles is again and again front and center.* Indeed, not only are Jesus' words being fulfilled, but the associated core wording (below quoted) is an unmistakable *expansion* of Luke 21:25b-26a.

Satan and the other fallen angels have long endeavored to use Christ's foretelling *against Him*—as they subsume and twist His words to try to further deceive fallen mankind. Thus, the noted celestial tetrad (2014–15), which many misunderstood, *really did* portend something momentous—and the "devil is in the details."

The COP21 Accord. Well, as it happened, *then Prince Charles,* a long-term advocate of population control through infanticide—aka "abortion," or the genocidal mass murder of unborn children—for alleged "sustainability," *personally opened* the likewise much-hyped Paris climate talks on November 30, 2015, as he spoke in French and English.[2] Globally, those talks are known as "COP21," or "the 21st Conference of the Parties to the 1992 UN Framework Convention on Climate Change." (Recall 1992's Rio Earth Summit.) *Nearly all the world's leaders,* including the likes of Obama and Bill Gates, Vladimir Putin and Xi Jinping, and any other who could readily be named, *followed Charles' lead*—specifically attending to promote and pursue, Satan's fraudulent global climate agenda.[3]

---

1. The author addresses all these coming events elsewhere, particularly in his multi-volume *Messiah, History, and the Tribulation Period* series.

2. Although Charles' speech *technically* followed the various opening remarks of Peru's Manuel Pulgar-Vidal, who (as Peru's environment minister) served as President of COP20 in 2014, Laurent Fabius, the President of the current COP21 in Paris, and Christiana Figueres, the United Nations Framework Convention on Climate Change Executive Secretary or so-called "climate [change] chief"—those three—Charles' speech was the very first *not dictated by international protocol;* indeed, *Charles preceded all international heads of state and other dignitaries.* Thus, Satan's Prince *did* open COP21, being *the real head of the entire effort.* For more information, see "Statements in connection with COP 21" at "https://unfccc.int/meetings/paris_nov_2015/items/9333txt.php" on the Internet.

3. Consider this 2015 finding: "Climate models used by scientists to predict how much human activities will warm the planet have been over-predicting global warming for the last six decades, according to a … working paper by climate scientists…. [Patrick] Michaels and [Chip] Knappenberger, [climate scientists at the libertarian Cato Institute,] compared observed global surface temperature warming rates since 1950 to what was predicted by 108 climate models used by government climate scientists [around the world] to predict how much carbon dioxide emissions will warm the planet. What they found was the models projected much higher warming rates than actually occurred…. To further bolster their case

Indeed, even Rome's socialist pope Francis, a lying heretic who *embraces* sexual satanism[1] and pagan Gaia or "Mother Earth" worship,[2] also now perpetrates satanic ecofascist fraud—as one who directly and explicitly entangles the Vatican and Roman Catholic cult with it, *while partnering with Satan's Prince.* As he (Charles) bemoaned "an increasingly crowded planet," apostate Francis simultaneously warned that without such a worldwide "climate" agreement —whereby "wealthy" nations would transfer their monies and technologies to poorer nations—mankind would face a collective ecological "suicide:" "Francis [(cf. Rome's 'patron saint of nature')] said ... the world is 'at the limit of suicide' if it doesn't reverse course and move away from its fossil fuel-based economy.... Paris' conference on climate is so crowded with world leaders that some of them are having to wait hours for their turn at the podium [(and all behind Satan's Prince)]—a highly unusual situation for the most powerful people in their respective countries. About 150 [world] leaders [and delegates from 195 countries] showed up, each giving a speech about their plans to fight global warming."[3]

Such was the imagined importance of the talks that even Israel's Netanyahu deigned to shake wicked "Palestinian" Abbas' hand "for the first time in years," at the lead of Satan's Prince.[4] (Pray that Netanyahu's eyes and ears are opened to Messiah Yeshua.)

---

that climate models are over-predicting warming rates, Michaels and Knappenberger looked at how climate models fared against satellite and weather balloon data from the mid-troposphere. The result is the same, and climate models predicted way more warming than actually occurred.... Satellite temperatures, which measure the lowest few miles of the Earth's atmosphere, show <u>there's been no significant global warming for the last two decades despite rapidly rising carbon dioxide levels in the atmosphere</u>" (Michael Bastasch, "Climate Models Have Been Wrong About Global Warming For Six Decades," *The Daily Caller,* 28 Dec. 2015). Generally, those "liberal" climate scientists cited by Charles' international followers, are either incompetent or professionally compromised.

1. "Pope Francis has revealed his views on sex.... Francis was quizzed ... on a variety of topics, including LGBT rights, abortion, the porn industry, sex, and faith and sex abuse within the Catholic Church. The [Disney+ documentary] film [*The Pope: Answers*] by ultra-woke Disney, has the 'aim of talking and conveying to [Francis] the main concerns of their generation'. While he did [partially] denounce abortion..., ... he [none the less] had to pander to [satanic] gender ideology, insisting that that LGBT people *must be welcomed* by the Catholic Church: 'All persons are the children of God, all persons. God does not reject anybody, God is a father. And I have no right to expel anyone from the Church'" (Paul Serran, "Pope Francis' Easter Address Overshadowed By His Appearance in Disney Documentary Discussing Sex, Porn and Transgenderism," *Gateway Pundit,* 10 Apr. 2023).

2. In his June 2015 encyclical, heretic Francis, speaking as an unambiguous *pagan,* claimed: "Everything is related, and we human beings are united as brothers and sisters on a wonderful pilgrimage, woven together by the love God has for each of his creatures and which also unites us in fond affection with brother Sun, sister Moon, brother river and Mother Earth" (Michael Bastasch, "'Mother Earth': UN Draft Global Warming Treaty Promotes Gaia Worship," *The Daily Caller,* 7 Dec. 2015). Francis here uses language akin to pantheism—where he addresses strictly *inanimate* objects (i.e., the Sun, Moon, "Mother Earth" and "brother river," as if they were somehow religiously alive and spiritually active. That is *not remotely* Christian, but Francis evidently promotes the false pagan religion of Gaia, or "Mother Earth" (i.e., nature) worship, as promulgated by the likes of Satan's Prince and Al Gore.

3. "The Latest: US House Leader Won't Pay for Climate Deal," *Associated Press,* 30 Nov. 2015.

4. Ibid.

"The last climate deal, the 1997 Kyoto Protocol [(which derived from 1992's Rio Earth Summit, for which the key international stakeholders personally credited Charles as Satan's Prince)], only required developed countries to cut man-made emissions. Western countries say this time all countries must chip in.... [But at 2015's COP21,] Britain's Prince Charle has issued a rallying cry to world leaders to address climate change, describing it as the greatest threat faced by humanity. Delivering the keynote [address] to the U.N. climate conference, Charles [(deceptively)] urged world leaders ... to think of their grandchildren in seeking a deal.... The ... champion of green causes [who is *for* infanticide,] told delegates: 'I urge you to consider ... the youngest generation, because none of us has the right to assume that for our today, they should give up their tomorrow.'"[1]

Ignoring pre-birth death by mass-murder: "'On an increasingly crowded planet, humanity faces many threats—but none is greater than climate change. *[(Liar, liar, you will be on fire!)]* It magnifies every hazard and tension of our existence,' the Prince of Wales told the summit, as he opened it.... 'It threatens our ability to feed ourselves, to remain healthy and safe from extreme weather, to manage the natural resources that support our economies, and to avert the humanitarian disaster[s] of mass migration and increasing conflict.'[2]

---

1. Ibid.
2. Then Prince Charles states: "Some of us were saying 20 something years ago that if we didn't tackle these issues, you would see ever greater conflict over scarce resources and ever greater difficulties over drought.... And in fact there's very good evidence indeed that one of the major reasons for this horror in Syria, funnily enough, was a drought that lasted for about five or six years, which meant that huge numbers of people in the end had to leave the land, but increasingly they came into the cities" (Michael Holden, "Climate change root cause of Syrian war: Britain's Prince Charles," *Thomson Reuters,* 23 Nov. 2015). As Satan's Prince would have it, then, evil conduct by ungodly Muslims is the result of climate chaos rather than their false and innately barbaric religion.

Obamanation and others pushing the anthropogenic global warming scam, foolishly follow Satan's Prince on that as well: "Barack Obama doubled-down on arguments that global warming is the greatest national security threat facing America, arguing global warming causes the rise of 'dangerous' ideologies.... Obama and his environmentalist allies argue global warming will cause more frequent and intense extreme weather events, like droughts, that will strain the resources of poor countries and allow extremist groups to rise. Secretary of State John Kerry even argued global warming was a cause of the Syrian civil war and the rise of ISIS [(even though he, Obama and other 'administration' cronies *intentionally acted to destablize the Middle East by promoting the anarchist 'Arab Spring' and Muslim terrorism via Satan's Muslim Brotherhood, destruction of Libya, etc.)]....* [But] Donald Trump [righly] lambasted Obama calling global warming the country's greatest national security threat as 'one of the dumbest statements I've ever heard in politics'" (Michael Bastasch, "Obama: Global Warming Causes 'Dangerous Ideologies,'" *The Daily Caller,* 4 Dec. 2015). Thankfully, there are leaders (e.g., Trump) who are *not* sold-out to Satan's NWO agenda.

Alexander Boot aptly comments: "It's hard to keep pace with the runaway train of [Prince] Charles's [(lying)] thought.... Our wanton disregard for the environment [(per Satan's Prince)] caused 'five or six years of drought' in Syria; the drought caused the 2011 uprising; the uprising caused the civil war; the civil war caused 250,000 deaths; the deaths caused 11 million to run away from home; and the combined effect of all those disasters presumably caused the hundreds [(i.e., *hundreds of thousands)]* of massacres perpetrated by Muslims over the last 20 years [(as of 2015)].... All this is traceable back to anthropogenic climate change, believes our future king.... However, [note that] .... since Israel is right on Syria's border, her climate has to be roughly the same. Israel, in other words, must be suffering the same effects of [alleged] climate change ... as those [supposedly] driving so many Syrians and other

He echoed comments by [Christiana] Figueres, [United Nations Framework Convention on Climate Change Executive Secretary,] saying, 'Rarely in human history have so many people [around the world] placed their trust in so few.' ... 'The whole of Nature cries out at our mistreatment of Her.... You, Ladies and Gentlemen, have the power to put her on life support, and you must surely start the emergency procedures [now!].... In damaging our climate, we become the architects of our own destruction. While the planet can survive the scorching of the earth and the rising of the waters, the human race cannot.'"[1] Having opened by admitting the he was "enormously touched to have been invited ... to say a very few words at the start of this crucially important Conference"—perhaps reminding the world that he had formerly been "touched and deeply amazed" upon receiving the statue of himself as a "winged god" while being hailed as the (environmental) "Saviour of the World" in March 2002—eco-fascist Charles concluded with these sentiments: "If, at last, the moment has arrived to take those long-awaited steps towards rescuing our planet and our fellow man from impending catastrophe, then let us pursue that vital goal in a spirit of enlightened and humane [(i.e., murderous)] collaboration."[2]

Muslims to mass migration and mass murder. Yet ... [the] only thing Israel seems to be suffering from is the same [jihadist] Muslim aggression that has been with us for 1,400 years" ("The madness of [would-be] King Charles III," *Jerusalem Post,* 23 Nov. 2015).

    Some rightly note: "The alleged [direct] link between [presumed] global warming and terrorism has been repeatedly debunked. Research shows terrorism is far more closely associated with separatist movements, [non-Christian] religious extremism [(especially among fundamentalist Islamic sects)], weak governing systems, and a lack of political legitimacy over [any claimed] environmental conditions ostensibly caused by [alleged] global warming [or actual climate instability]" (Andrew Follett, "Sanders: 1 Percent Are 'Hell-Bent' on Causing Global Warming," *The Daily Caller,* 7 Dec. 2015). For more information, see Linda Qiu, "Fact-checking Bernie Sanders' comments on climate change and terrorism," *PolitiFact,* 16 Nov. 2015.

1. "Prince Charles opens Paris climate talks and calls on world leaders to act now," *The Guardian,* 30 Nov. 2015.

2. For Charles' complete and unjumbled speech, see "Speech by HRH Charles, Prince of Wales: For COP.21 Opening Session, Monday, 30th November 2015" at "https://unfccc.int/sites/default/files/cop21cmp11 _opening_speech_prince_of_wales_fr.pdf" on the Internet.

"<u>More world leaders</u> are <u>in the same place at the same time than</u> <u>ever before</u> [and] at a critical global climate conference.... The French organizers say 151 heads of state and other leaders are at the talks.... U.N. climate agency spokesman Nicholas Nuttall said it is the largest such gathering of world leaders on the same day [ever] .... French President Francois Hollande, hosting the talks [in Paris], said 'no conference has ever gathered so many leaders from so many countries ... but never before have the international stakes been so high.'"[1]

"Prime Minister [David Cameron] painted an apocalyptic vision of the Earth's plight, as he joined almost 150 leaders in Paris for the start of a UN climate conference, described by organisers as <u>the largest gathering of heads of state the world has [so far] known.</u>"[2] The noted one-hundred and fifty or so world leaders posed for a top elitists' "family photo" — *with the then Prince of Wales in the exact center,* directly beneath the background words "Paris, France." Yes, Satan's Prince stood next to Cameron, and above and behind

China's premiere, France's president and the UN's Ban Ki-Moon.[3]

"Cristopher Loeak, Prime Minister of the Marshall Islands, told the congregation: 'Everything I know, and everyone I love, is in the hands of those of us gathered here today.' ... Indian PM Narendra Modi [arrogantly claimed]: 'Over the next few days, we will decide the fate of this planet. We do so when the consequences of the industrial age powered by fossil fuels are evident, especially on the lives of the poor.' He says the world's 'prosperous [polluters] still have a strong carbon footprint,' while billions of people remain at the 'bottom of the development ladder'.... Developed countries

---

1. "The Latest: US House Leader Won't Pay for Climate Deal."
2. Emily Gosden and Henry Samuel, "Paris climate summit: David Cameron warns 'earth is in peril' — as it happened," The Telegraph, 30 Nov. 2015.
3. Gosden and Samuel, ibid. For the group photo, see "https://www.occupy.com/sites/default/files/field/i mage/499249230-world-leaders-pose-for-a-family-photo-during-the-cop21.jpg.CROP_.promo-xlarge2.j pg" on the Internet.

must meet their [initial] $100-b[illio]n-a-year climate finance pledge [(i.e., transfer their populations' resources and money to the 'elite')], he says.... [Cameron stated] a 'good deal' should [include] ... finance [and] ... transfers [of] technology from the richest countries to the poorest countries.... [The] President of Micronesia says...: 'We know that there is danger in the air'.... The UN secretary-general should 'declare a global emergency to show that the world is in peril'. 'This world is in trouble.' ... President Benigno S. Aquino III of the Philippines warns that extinction of small island states will be a certainty unless we acknowledge climate change is a matter of survival for many countries....["1]

"20 [(twenty) countries'] leaders, along with those of the world's five most populous, ... are launching an initiative [called Mission Innovation] to 'dramatically accelerate public and private global clean energy innovation to address global climate change'.... Mission Innovation is linked to a parallel private sector-led effort spearheaded by Bill Gates [(one of the British monarchy's 'let's save the world' via global mass-murder knights,[2])]—a coalition of over 28 significant private capital investors from 10 countries, which will be called Breakthrough Energy Coalition. This grouping has pledged to invest huge amounts of private capital in clean energy....["3]

"The President of Kiribati, the low-lying island nation—one of those most at risk of climate change—says, '....[our] very survival is at stake'.... [Marxist] Evo Morales [asserted] ' ... the dramatic effects of climate change ... are threatening our existence and the existence of mother earth. Saving mother earth to save life—that is our endeavour.' ... [He made an] 'urgent appeal to the Governments of capitalist powers of the world, for them to stop destroying our planet irreversibly'.... Putin, [the] Russian president, ... says climate change is one of the "greatest challenges humanity is facing.... Obama [stated]..., 'There is such thing as being too late, and when it comes to climate change the hour is almost upon us,' ... [adding, we] must work to build 'a world worthy of our children, ... a world that is safer, more prosperous, more secure and more free.'"[4]

---

1. Gosden and Samuel, ibid.
2. In March 2005, Queen Elizabeth II made William Henry Gates III an honorary "Knight Commander of the Order of the British Empire," with his wife Melinda present and right after he met with Prince Philip. Under the influence of his nominally Roman Catholic wife, the Gates Foundation satanically promotes *infanticide*—that is, *the mass-murder of unborn children*—as part of its Orwellian "family planning" (obviously, an oxymoron) around the world. (We'll later consider their harmful "vaccines.") Neither Bill nor Melinda Gates is actually Christian, but both would surely say they seek to *save lives*, improve mankind's future and otherwise do good, perhaps pointing to their very real track record of seeking to provide clean water and sanitized toilets to billions, eradicate polio and develop *safe* nuclear-*fission* energy (TerraPower). Yet, they are anti-Christian (as I write this), so please pray for their *repentance* unto salvation.
3. Gosden and Samuel, libd.
4. Gosden and Samuel, ibid.

"[UN Secretary-General Ban Ki-Moon stated:] 'This is a pivotal moment for the future of our common home, our planet. You can no longer delay. The future of the people of the world, our planet is in your hands. We cannot afford indecision, half-measures or merely gradual approaches. Our goal must be a transformation.' ... [French President Hollande tweeted,] 'essentially what is at stake at this climate conference is [world] peace [(cf. 1 Th 5:3)].' He stated, 'My thoughts go to those islands that could very soon, purely and simply disappear, ... because the very diversity of our planet is at stake.' ... 'Today is an historic day. Never has a conference received so many authorities from so many countries. Never, I say never, have the stakes of an international meeting been so high, for this is about the future of the planet and the future of life [on Earth].... We must leave our children ... a planet protected from [environmental] disasters, a viable, livable planet.'"[1]

At COP21, then Prince Charles additionally reiterated the importance of "sustainable energy, farming and fishing," as opposed to the use of "fossil fuels, deforestation and over-exploitation of the seas."[2] On forests and deforestation, which actually are critical to the world (like fish in our seas),[3] Satan's Prince again leads: "Charles also called for large-scale restoration of forests, warning the world would need much more forest 'as all the horrors' of global warming started to bite. On the issue of saving the forests, he told a packed audience, which included the King of Sweden, ... that 'there can be no room for failure'.... 'It is very simple: we must save our forests, for there is no Plan B to tackle climate change or many of the other critical challenges that face humanity without them'.... While some companies had taken steps to transform their supply chains so they did not damage forests, he urged a redoubling of efforts to ensure a shift in global markets.... All companies should be committed to stopping destruction of forests, [the prince said,] with zero net deforestation becoming the norm rather than the exception...."[4]

"Charles also called for [accelerated] action to to bring about large scale forest landscape restoration, pointing to the need ... in the face of the loss of 500 million hectares (1.2 billion acres) of tropical rainforest since 1950. It should be an equal priority to halting deforestation, not an afterthought, he said.... At the start of the two-week [Paris] conference, [seemingly heeding the prince's warnings,]

---

1. Gosden and Samuel, ibid.
2. See then Prince Charles' full COP21 speech.
3. Half-truths, or mixtures of truth with falsehood, often prove to be the most effective lies, and in half-truths, Charles excels. Such lies are among Satan's primary approaches to mass deception.
4. Press Association, "No plan B for climate change without forests, Prince Charles tells Paris summit," *The Guardian*, 1 Dec. 2015.

leaders from 20 countries including [Australia, Brazil, Canada, Colombia, Democratic Republic of Congo, Ethiopia, France, Gabon, Germany, Indonesia, Japan, Liberia, Norway, Peru, the UK and the US,] put out a joint statement recognising the 'essential' role forests play in protecting the planet and avoiding dangerous climate change. 'We are committed to intensifying efforts to protect forests, to significantly restore degraded forest, peat and agricultural lands, and to promote low-carbon rural development,' they said."[1]

"Saying that the world has 'the knowledge, the tools and the money' [(only *ninety-trillion dollars* are demanded!, as below seen)] to make a difference, Charles said it was essential that global warming be restricted to 2 degrees Celsius (3.6 Fahrenheit) ['to avoid catastrophe, beyond which there is no recovery']. At a similar climate conference in Copenhagen six years ago, Prince Charles had [(falsely of course)] warned that within 100 months, or a bit more than eight years, the world would reach a point of no return on climate change. He referred to those remarks in his speech...: 'Have we really reached such a collective inertia that ignores so clear a warning? Eighty of those 100 months have now passed, so we must act now.' [(Satan's Prince is a *liar.*)] Addressing the leaders and delegates at the conference, he said, 'You are all here to set us on the road to a saner future.'"[2] "The ... Red Cross is calling for delegates at the Paris conference to make a priority of helping poor and vulnerable people [(via wealth transfer using 'carbon taxation,' or global theft)] to deal with the impact of climate change."[3]

"Warnings from climate scientists, demands from activists and exhortations from religious leaders like Pope Francis have coupled with major advances in cleaner energy sources like solar power to raise pressure for cuts in carbon emissions [(fraudulently)] held responsible for warming the planet. Most scientists [(who become biased via governmental doles)] say failure to agree on strong measures in Paris would doom the world to ever-hotter average temperatures, bringing with them deadlier storms, more frequent droughts and rising sea levels as polar ice caps melt.... [(Cf. Luke 21:25b-26a.)] 'What should give us hope that this is a turning point —that this is the moment we finally determined we would save our planet—is the fact that our nations share a sense of urgency about this challenge and a growing realization that it is within our power to do something [real] about it,' said Obama, one of the first leaders to

---

1. "No plan B for climate change without forests, Prince Charles tells Paris summit."

2. Madeline Kruhly, "Prince Charles Asks for End to 'Collective Inertia' on Climate," *New York Times*, 30 Nov. 2015.

3. "The Latest: US House Leader Won't Pay for Climate Deal."

speak at the summit [after (then) Prince Charles]."[1] "[Per Obama,] there's no greater rejection to those who want to tear down the world than to mount best efforts to save it.... [Obama envisioned, like some other world leaders,] submerged countries, abandoned cities and fields that won't grow .... [while 'creatively' attempting to draw] a link to the refugee crisis [as] ... desperate peoples seek sanctuaries outside their home nations."[2] But while there is ample evil in the "global warming" mix, there are likewise some laudable efforts to promote the development of viable alternative energy sources that are environmentally friendly, renewable, and affordable—including by Gates (e.g., TerraPower, and nuclear fusion).[3]

Preparing for COP21. Only days earlier, on November 27, 2015, Charles prepared the British Commonwealth at a Malta summit: "[According to the Prince of Wales (now King Charles III),] 'This [upcoming Paris climate] meeting falls at a very important, indeed critical moment for the future of mankind and our planet.... Countless concerned people around the world' are <u>banking</u> on global leaders to come up with an ambitious long-term goal for the rapid reduction of carbon emissions.... 'We face an unprecedented set of interlocking challenges, all of which are creeping up on us in the shape of perfect storm,' he added, from unsustainable population growth to migration, rapid globalisation, and social economic and energy insecurity.... The Commonwealth family of 53 nations [(now 56)] is gathering in Malta ... with a focus on reaching agreements that will open doors for wider deals at the COP21 climate talks in Paris, [with Satan's Prince playing a critical role, as he did for the 1992 Rio Earth Summit].... Born out of the British empire, the Commonwealth of Nations brings together around a quarter of the world's countries [(cf. Rev 6:7-8)] and a third of its population.... [Then] Prince Charles said the influence of the Commonwealth should not be underestimated.... 'If there is one thing other than taxes and death of which we can be certain, it is that <u>there is never going to be enough public money to implement the SDGs (Sustainable Development Goals) or Paris agreement</u>,' he said. '<u>Billions of dollars will need to become trillions of dollars</u>,' he insisted, with an '<u>estimated 90 trillion dollars needed for infrastructure development alone over the next 15 years</u>, in order to have any hope of keeping us in a world only 2.0 degrees warmer.' ... The outcome of the Paris talks [(*not* God)] would [(allegedly)] 'determine the survival of our species and all those who share this precious planet with us,' Prince Charles said. 'We do not

---

1. "World Leaders Attend COP21 Climate Change Conference," *TruNews.com*, 1 Dec. 2015.
2. "The Latest: US House Leader Won't Pay for Climate Deal."
3. Ibid.

have the right to test to destruction the planet's tolerance to our in-discretions. We do have a responsibility to act now,' he said."[1]

Also on November 27th, in the above context, Queen Elizabeth II strongly recommended to the British Commonwealth that her son, Satan's Prince, soon be received as that organization's new head—while she would remain monarch: "The Queen has given Common-wealth leaders a heavy hint that they should vote for the Prince of Wales as her successor as head of the organisation ... of the 53 [(now 56)] member countries. In a speech to declare the summit open, the Queen said she could not 'wish to have been better sup-ported and represented in the Commonwealth than by the Prince of Wales who continues to give so much to it with great distinction.'"[2]

Compassing COP1. On December 12, 2015, or almost two weeks after the Paris climate talks began and years after the failed 2009 Copenhagen conference—and longer still to follow the Kyoto Proto-col and Rio Earth Summit of the 1990's from which both derive—the world (i.e., nearly two-hundred nations) agreed to a landmark "COP21" accord, and thus unregenerate mankind again sees Satan's Prince acting as Earth's environmental "savior!" In 2009, then Prince Charles, continuing to spread fear of "a defining moment in the world's history," warned Brazilians: The "threat of catastrophic cli-mate change calls into question humanity's continued existence on the planet.... It will result in vast movements of people escaping ei-ther flooding or droughts, in uncertain production of food and lack of water and in increasing social instability and potential conflict.... We have very little time left if we want to sustain life on Earth as we ac-

---

1. "Prince Charles warns of 'perfect storm' should Paris climate talks flop," *Associated Free Press,* 27 Nov. 2015. No one could point out the fraud of anthropogenic (i.e., human-caused) global warming, or its true intent to facilitate unimaginable global monetary theft, all to actually finance and enthrone a com-ing global government, any more clearly than to say that "90 trillion dollars" are required within the "next 15 years" if the world is "to have any hope" of avoiding an otherwise inevitable proverbial frying pan of an atmosphere! Think about that.

    One should wonder if Charles himself really understands just how much wealth transfer (aka scam-based theft) he is suggesting—as the numbers are hardly credible to the thinking person. (At a later ecofascist event, while yet Prince of Wales, Charles spoke of "trillions at his disposal," leaving many scratching their heads who did not understand that Charles referred to *himself*—once he's possessed by Satan.) In fact, for vastly *less* money—vastly less—*every* supposedly "threatened" individual, anywhere and everywhere on the face of the planet, could be "resettled" into *brand new* and *completely modern* "metropolitan paradises," with global food production also being dramatically increased through *achievable* vast new agricultural investments and initiatives. Consider this: *Ninety trillion dollars is* ninety-thousand-billion dollars, which would actually equate to *one-hundred-eighty-thousand dollars for each and every member of half the world's human population, on an Earth of nine-billion men, women and children,* which is still well beyond mankind's current Earth population.

    Satan's globalists are talking about so much money that Charles' statement is ludicrous on its face. Satan's Prince and those under him would have to rob humanity blind, to achieve such a wealth trans-fer. But hey, it's just humanity's survival that's at stake—*according to the prince ... of lies.*

2. Gordon Rayner, "State visit to Malta: Queen hints to sceptical leaders that Prince should be next Head of the Commonwealth," *Valletta,* 27 Nov. 2015. The British Commonwealth now compasses about one-third of the world's population, though still about one-quarter of Earth's land.

tually know it.... We have less than 100 months to alter our behaviour before we risk catastrophic climate change."[1]

Of greater import to the average man or woman on the street, however, globalists and other elitists under King Charles III would commence their theft in earnest, helping to pave the way for global governance under the foretold AntiChrist—evidently, Charles himself. France's Hollande, having called the talks a "decisive moment for the planet," slyly "tweeted" (via Twitter): "History is written by those who commit, and not those who calculate [(the real meaning and global impact of ninety-thousand-billion dollars to be *confiscated* from the alleged 'rich')]. Today, you [(gullible people)] committed; you did not engage in [(sensible)] calculations."[2] Yes, Hollande is a thief extraordinaire—just like the rest of these international sycophants to Satan's Prince. Communist China's red dragon-worshiping dictator Xi Jinping cited Victor Hugo: Supreme resources spring from extreme resolutions."[3]

"'Whereas [in 2009,] we left Copenhagen scared of what comes next, we'll leave Paris [in 2015,] inspired to keep fighting,' said David Turnbull of Oil Change International, a research and advocacy organization opposed to fossil fuel production.... In the United States, many Republicans will see the pact as a dangerous endeavor that threatens to trade economic prosperity for an uncertain if [presumably] greener future."[4] Satan's "green religion," which is pagan and antiChristian by definition, is all about mass deception, fraud and theft—as well as *implemented mass death.*[5]

---

1. Tom Phillips, "Human race threatened by climate change, Prince Charles warns Brazilians," *The Guardian*, 12 Mar. 2009. Phillips reminds us: "In 2007, he founded the Prince's Rainforests Project, a group that seeks to combat climate change by protecting the world's tropical rainforests. The last time Prince Charles visited Brazil, in 2002, he traveled to the northern state of Tocantins, where the state governor presented him with a bronze statue ... replete with a pair of angelic wings. 'This represents Prince Charles saving the world,' the governor said." We earlier addressed this idol.
2. "The Road to a Paris Climate Deal," *New York Times*, 12 Dec. 2015.
3. "Paris climate summit: David Cameron warns 'earth is in peril' — as it happened."
4. Alister Doyle and Barbara Lewis, "With landmark climate accord, world marks turn from fossil fuels," *Reuters*, 12 Dec. 2015. The greater the Christian presence in a nation, the less susceptible it is to Satan's lies, including the anthropogenic global warming scam. Thus, the U.S. and UK, despite lying elitists' efforts, continue to have many who see through these lies.
5. On Earth, carbon dioxide is actually *life-producing*—and contrary to elitists' lies, its reduction is *life-killing*. More atmospheric carbon dioxide would lead to more photosynthesis and thus more plant life— as it did prior to Noah's Flood thousands of years ago—and that in turn, would again result in more plant-produced oxygen for mankind and other life forms; this would increase health, strength *and longevity*. More CO_2 and O_2 together lead to a thicker, higher-pressure, warmer and more humid atmosphere. (Regarding fire hazards, the higher atmospheric pressure and greater humidity would *partially offset the extra oxygen.* That is, higher oxygen levels *without* the pressure and humidity offsets, would be harmful and catastrophically dangerous.) *All* these factors, in combination, however, are life-increasing and healthier in many ways. While much of modern science has yet to reach this understanding, it is sensible—and would also closely resemble the atmosphere of the pre-Flood world, where life was not just everywhere more abundant, but enjoyed much longer average lifespans and, in many cases, achieved greater average physical sizes (e.g., giant insects).
   Pre-Flood men and women lived *about eight times longer than today.* The biological mechanisms

Scripture versus ungodly tools. Coming back to Luke 21:25-26, and what we earlier saw in that (i.e., 21:25*b*-26*a),* consider this well-reported major highlight of the COP21 Accord, and its typical public interpretation: "It calls for 'holding the increase in the global average temperature to well below 2°C above pre-industrial levels and to pursue efforts to limit the temperature increase to 1.5°C above pre-industrial levels, recognizing that this would significantly reduce the [(fraudulently alleged)] risks and impacts of climate change.' This language recognizes the [(supposedly)] scientific conclusions that an increase in atmospheric temperatures of more than 2 degrees Celsius, or 3.6 degrees Fahrenheit, would lock the planet into a future of

behind that past reality are not yet well-understood, though we may speculate. For example: Might there be more available energy, due to more available oxygen, at the cellular level, resulting in slower metabolisms? Notably, following Noah's Flood, mankind and animals consumed oxygen while surface plant life had to regrow globally, taking decades and even centuries; *as Earth's atmospheric oxygen simultaneously decreased, so did the lifespans of subsequent generations of mankind*—until a new equilibrium, or what we have now known for millennia, was finally reached.

Recently, Israeli scientists showed that *very substantial age reversal* occurs when external oxygen and presssure are increased: "Scientists ... successfully reversed the human ageing process in a group of elderly adults.... Oxygen treatment altered the elderly people's bodies at a cellular level to how they were 25 years earlier.... In a unique study, scientists used oxygen therapy to reverse two key indicators of biological ageing—telomere shortening and an accumulation of malfunctioning senescent cells.... Senescent cells, or so-called zombie cells, prevent regeneration as they build up in the body over time. The study used ... Hyperbaric Oxygen Therapy.... ...35 healthy adults aged 64 and older were placed in pressurised oxygen chambers [(above one 'absolute atmosphere')] in Israel, and breathed in pure oxygen through a mask. The sessions lasted for 90 minutes each and took place five days a week for three months. The pressurised chamber mimics a state of 'hypoxia', or oxygen shortage, enabling tissues to dissolve more oxygen, which has well-known regenerative effects. Results show the trial enabled telomeres to regrow by more than 20 per cent, while their senescent cells had been reduced by up to 37 per cent. This is the equivalent to how their bodies were at a cellular level 25 years earlier.... 'The significant improvement of telomere length shown during and after these ... protocols provides the scientific community with a new foundation of understanding that ageing can indeed be targeted and reversed at the basic cellular-biological level,' [Professor Shai] Efrati, [a Professor at the Faculty of Medicine at Tel Aviv University, and co-author of the study] added" (Rachael Bunyan for *Mail Online*, "Scientists claim they have reversed the human ageing process in study," *Daily Mail*, 20 Nov. 2020). "Every 20 minutes, the participants were asked to remove their masks for five minutes, bringing their [breathable] oxygen [(but not external pressure)] back to normal levels. However, ... researchers saw that fluctuations in the free oxygen concentration were interpreted at the cellular level as a lack of oxygen—rather than interpreting the absolute level of oxygen. In other words, repeated intermittent hyperoxic (increased oxygen level) exposures [seemingly] induced many of the mediators and cellular mechanisms that are usually induced during hypoxia (decreased oxygen levels)—something Efrati explained is called the hyperoxic-hypoxic paradox. 'The oxygen fluctuation we generated is what is important,' he [(mistakenly, this author would suggest)] told *The Jerusalem Post.*. 'During this process, a state of oxygen shortage resulted, which [later] caused cell regeneration'"—that is, upon restoration of higher oxygen (Maayan Jaffe-Hoffman, "Israeli scientists claim to reverse aging process," *Jerusalem Post*, 21 Nov. 2020).

Clearly, more carbon dioxide would engender a *superior* world for life, including mankind, whereas its reduction ends up mitigating populations and shortening life. *Those who promote the "global warming" fraud are helping Satan harm life on Earth, and keeping our lifespans shorter!*

There are other interesting studies and speculations on the Internet, some of which offer valuable information, though *none* were found to account for *the complete combination of pre-Flood factors* the author above mentions. Understand as well that some helpful *biological* nutrients have likely *perished from Earth.* Some helpful articles and blogs, which remain current, include Jeremy Michael Van Raamsdonk et al., "Decreased energy metabolism extends life span in Caenorhabditis elegans without reducing oxidative damage," *Genetics.org,* 2 Apr. 2010; "What would be the effects on the human body if the oxygen level increased by a lot?," *Worldbuilding Stack Exchange;* and "What would happen if the amount of oxygen in Earth's atmosphere was doubled instantly?," *Quora.com.*

catastrophic impacts, including rising sea levels, more devastating floods and droughts, widespread food and water shortages and more powerful storms. But it also recognizes the [(dominance- and greed-driven faux)] scientific conclusions that warming of just 1.5 degrees Celsius, or 2.7 degrees Fahrenheit, could present an existential threat to low-lying island nations that would be inundated by sea level rise at that rate of increase. But while those nations celebrated the inclusion of that 1.5 degree target, it is more aspirational than practical. The national plans submitted for the [Paris] conference would probably result in an increase above 3 degrees Celsius."[1]

Indeed, deceived and compromised global warming "scientists," many of whom dishonestly depend upon public doles, warned that world leaders may still not be doing enough. "[Fearmongering] scientists warned ... that the [propagandistic COP21] deal could be ... leaving humanity flirting with extreme danger—rising seas that could swamp island nations and flood many of the world's coastal cities, intensified droughts and storms, and possibly a collapse of food production as the planet warms to intolerable levels.... [They say that time is] running out, particularly for a chance of meeting the tighter target of 1.5 degrees Celsius—a limit on global warming that could preserve many island nations, as well as the coral reefs on which hundreds of millions of people depend for food."[2] We have just read whining elitist sound bites, or core tenets, from what are sometimes much lengthier texts. Yet, as earlier indicated, such vociferous claims essentially and remarkably align with Jesus' foretelling that there will be "distress of nations, with perplexity, the sea and the waves roaring—men's hearts failing them from fear and the expectation of those things which are coming on the Earth." Such alignment is *not* coincidental. Clearly, Luke 21:25-26 is being fulfilled in our day (e.g., in the touted celestial tetrad).

Under President Trump, the United States *sensibly* backed away from ecofascist claims of damaging anthropogenic global warming —so much so that all the above conspirators clamored to see Satan's Prince try to get Trump in line: "Further complicating matters, ... tensions were mounting ... because Trump, a climate change skeptic, did not want a 'lecture' during his [planned future] visit by ... Prince Charles, a passionate environmentalist."[3] However, Trump being at least a nominal (turned evangelical) Christian, like a number of others in his administration—seriously questioned, if not outright dismissed such elitist and globalist *lies*.

1. "The Road to a Paris Climate Deal: Key Points of the Paris Climate Pact," *New York Times,* 12 Dec. 2015.
2. "The Road to a Paris Climate Deal: Scientists See Catastrophe in Latest Draft of Climate Deal," *New York Times,* 11 Dec. 2015.
3. "Britain: 'Don't let Trump Embarrass our Queen,'" *TruNews.com,* 30 Jan. 2017.

Among his early actions as President, Trump signed an "Energy Independence" order to largely reverse Obamanation's misguided and fraudulent "Clean Power Plan," which required U.S. states to very substantially reduce carbon emissions. With that executive action, Trump effectively negated the corresponding U.S. COP21 pledge: "It will also rescind a ban on coal leasing on federal lands, reverse rules to curb methane emissions from oil and gas production, and reduce the weight of climate change in federal agencies' assessments of new regulations.... Trump campaigned on a promise to sweep aside green regulations he said hurt the economy, and vowed to pull the United States out of the Paris climate accord...., [(allegedly)] meant to limit the planet's warming by reducing carbon emissions."[1] In any case, the United States no longer officially complied under Trump et al. (see below)—though unofficially, the country actually *exceeded* the carbon-emissions *reduction goals* set under COP21. (To satanic elitists, the real issue is *not,* and *never has been* emissions of "greenhouse gases," but serving massive taxation to achieve anti-Christian global governance *and depopulation.*[2])

AntiChristian cult leader "Francis ... has placed environmental causes at the heart of his papacy, denouncing what he sees as a throwaway consumer culture ... [in capitalist] economies. 'Economics and politics, society and culture cannot be dominated by thinking only of the short term and immediate financial or electoral gains,' Francis said.... Francis welcomed the Paris accord, but urged voters everywhere to make sure their governments did not backtrack. 'It is up to citizens to insist that this happen, and indeed to advocate for even more ambitious [(ecofascist)] goals,' he said. He asked the world's one billion Roman Catholic to embrace a green agenda.... 'May the works of mercy also include care for our common home,' Francis said."[3] Knowing that Trump's wife, Melania professes to be Roman Catholic, "Francis entered the fray ... by making the case to Mr. Trump that combating global warming is a moral imperative." Indeed, Francis "presented the [(now-elected)] president with a signed copy of his 2015 encyclical on climate change, and [(then)] Secretary of State Rex W. Tillerson later said that Vatican officials privately lobbied the administration to remain in the Paris deal.... Mr. Trump is sure to face similar calls at the G-7 summit. Analysts said the heads of state of Japan, Canada, Britain, France, Germany and Italy will seek to educate [(i.e., satanically indoctrinate)] the U.S. president about the true [(no, *imagined)]* dangers of [fraudulently-alleged an-

1. "Trump to reverse Obama-era climate policies," *TruNews.com,* 28 Mar. 2017.
2. For more information, see the author's book titled *The Great Reset: To Digitally Enslave, Depopulate, and Transhumanize.*
3. "Pope Francis urges Christians to back Agenda 2030," *Reuters,* 1 Sept. 2016.

thropogenic (i.e., human caused)] climate change while stressing that the Paris deal represents a key opening shot in the international fight against global warming."[1] (So, demanding *ninety trillion dollars* to enable globalists' control and fraud under Satan, is just their "opening shot.") Thankfully, on June 1, 2017, President Trump formally announced the United States' intention to exit the accord, despite almost total global condemnation and many childish liberal rants at home—though Satan's minions continued to vow to *rejoin* COP21, magnifying their malign agendas and efforts.

Indeed, moralizing unregenerate and misguided Israelites and Roman Catholic cultists, as well as some (apostate) "evangelical" Christians, joined the condemnation chorus, failing to discern that they are promoting a satanic, antiChrist fraud based upon invalid (i.e., fraudulent and actually-junk) so-called "science." A particularly strong and slanderous judgment came from Young Evangelicals for Climate Action. That organization's scripturally *misguided* and *scientifically uneducated or simply illiterate* national organizer and spokesperson was unacceptably disrespectful to President Trump: "We will continue to take hopeful action to address climate change and to love our neighbors both here and around the world. As we do, we reject your [(i.e., the President's)] disdain for the well-being of those suffering from the impacts of a changing climate. We bear witness to your moral failure, and we will not forget it." John Gehring (Twitter: "@gehringdc") similarly hyperventilated, falsely assessing, "Trump's rejection of Paris accord should offend pro-life Christians."[2] Yet, God Himself controls global climate using natural occurrences, including solar and volcanic activities and events, tsunamis and hurricanes, and even by meteor impacts; at times, He even intervenes supernaturally. Factually, one is *not* genuinely educated on this topic, in *any* sense, if swallowing the anthropogenic global warming fraud and related scaremongering.

The pagan and antiChristian Parliament of the World's Religions (PWR) summed up the deluded world's incorrect and remarkably *hysterical* sentiments, stating: "The decision is wrong from every relevant perspective. Scientifically, it is unsound and indefensible. Economically, it undermines the ability of the United States to build a competitive economy for the future.... Medically, it condemns hundreds of thousands to unnecessary sickness and premature death." (Of course, they have nothing negative to say about the mass murder of unborn children around the world!) The PWR is

---

1. Ben Wolfgang, "G-7 leaders prepare to go face to face with Trump over Paris climate accord," *The Washington Times*, 24 May 2017.
2. Madeleine Buckley and Jerome Socolovsky, "Strong Religious Reaction to Trump Climate Accord Decision," *Religion News Service*, 1 June 2017.

somewhat correct, however, in *this:* "Politically, it [(seemingly)] undermines the United States' credibility and trustworthiness with its strongest allies as well as its fiercest competitors, and thus strikes a self-inflicted blow against national security." Indeed, with the U.S. swayed by the likes of Al Gore and the Prince of Wales, a complicit Obamanation (i.e., Obama with suitably wicked VP Joseph Robinette Biden Jr.) then substantially led the charge for the COP 21 Accord— but then it was the U.S., as perhaps the major *patsy,* that also seemingly threatened (under President Trump and Vice President Pence) to bring down that same ecofascist house of cards. Not everyone, however, is fooled by a power-seeking "climate" agenda. For example, the Cornwall Alliance (Twitter: "@CornwallSteward") stated, "Many thanks to @realDonaldTrump for making the best decision for the poor, the economy, *and* the environment by withdrawing #ParisAgreement."[1] Those who inadvertently or intentionally align with Satan's, the foretold AntiChrist's and the False Prophet's global governance agenda, *now often redefine "sin,"* so that per them, it consists of a *perceived* (real or not) transgression against creation (or *anti-science* "evolution")—rather than a transgression against God's law (1 John 3:4). (There is a world of difference.)

Then-President Trump made the *right* call. UN Secretary General Antonio Guterres reacted: "It is absolutely essential that the world implements the Paris agreement [(e.g., under Satan, the foretold AntiChrist and the False Prophet)] and that we fulfill that duty with increased ambition"[2] (to fund "global governance"). "Scientists [(working with fraudulent and faulty data, while proffering unreliable analyses and ignoring *vastly worse* offenders like China, India, etc.) *dishonestly]* say Earth is likely to reach more dangerous levels of warming sooner if the U.S. retreats from its pledge because America contributes so much to rising temperatures …. [as to] melt ice sheets faster, raise seas higher and trigger more extreme weather."[3]

In a January 2018 WEF (World Economic Forum) survey: "Some 79 percent see a heightened risk of state-on-state military conflict. In addition to the threat of a conflict on the Korean peninsula,[4] the report highlighted risk of new Middle East military confrontations.[5] It cited a rise in 'charismatic strongman politics' across the world and said political, economic and environmental risks were being exacer-

---

1. Buckley and Socolovsky, ibid.
2. "It's official: President Trump withdraws U.S. from Paris climate accord," *The Washington Times,* 1 June 2017.
3. "Paris agreement on climate change: World reaction to US pullout," *Fox News,* 1 June 2017.
4. For more information, see the author's book, *North Korea, Iran, and the Coming World War: Behold a Red Horse.*
5. For more information, see the author's multi-volume series *Israel, "Peace" and the Looming Great Tribulation.*

bated by a decline in support for rules-based multilateralism. The report noted Trump's decisions to withdraw from the Paris climate and
the TPP [(Trans-Pacific Partnership)] trade agreements, as well as his
intent to pull out of a [(silly) JCPOA] deal between Western powers
and Iran.... 'The risks ... require multilateral solutions but we are
moving in the other direction,' said [Marsh's] John Drzik.... While
geopolitical worries rose sharply, ... extreme weather events [are]
seen as the single most prominent risk ... after a year of unusually
frequent Atlantic storms [in 2018], including Hurricane Maria, which
devastated Puerto Rico."[1]

In January 2021, Joseph (Joe) R. Biden Jr., who is a (horrific)
mass-murderer of unborn children, criminal traitor to the United
States, pathological liar and serial plagiarizer, relentless promoter of
sexual abominations and literal lunacies (e.g., sodomy, lesbianism,
so-called "transgenderism" and alleged "non-binary 'genders'"),
then re-occupied the White House—to the everlasting shame of the
U.S. Constituting an "Obamanation 'reboot'"[2] while hysterically
claiming to represent "science," Mr. Biden—with comparably unethi-
cal Ms. Kamala Devi[l] Harris—*recommitted the U.S. to COP21, as
one of his very first acts:* "In the most ambitious U.S. effort to stave
off the worst effects of climate change, ... [a lawless Mr.] Joe Biden
issued [(illicit)] executive orders ... to cut oil, gas and coal emissions
and double energy production from offshore wind turbines. The orders target federal subsidies for oil and other fossil fuels and halt
new oil and gas leases on [U.S.] federal lands and waters. They also
aim to conserve 30 percent of the country's lands and ocean waters
in the next 10 years and move to an all-electric federal vehicle fleet.
Biden's sweeping plan is aimed at slowing human-caused global
warming.... 'We can't wait any longer' to address the climate crisis,
Biden said.... 'We see with our own eyes. We know it in our bones.
It is time to act.' He said his orders will 'supercharge our ... ambitious plan to confront the existential threat of climate change.' Biden
has set a goal of eliminating pollution from fossil fuel in the [U.S.]
power sector by 2035, and from the U.S. economy overall by 2050....
The aggressive plan is aimed at slowing [(alleged)] human-caused
global warming that is magnifying extreme weather events such as
deadly wildfires in the West and drenching rains and hurricanes in
the East.... Biden also is elevating climate change to a national security priority.... Biden also will direct all U.S. agencies to use [(alleged)] science and [(alleged)] evidence-based decision-making in

1. Noah Barkin, "As Trump heads to Davos, survey points to rising risk of war," *Reuters*, 17 Jan. 2018.
2. See this author's material on the first horse and horseman of the Apocalypse (Rev 6:1-2). (The book to include that, and its title, has not been determined as of this writing, but please look for it.)

federal rule-making, and announce a U.S.-hosted climate leaders summit on Earth Day, April 22."[1]

That authoritarian *anti-science* "re-commitment" was formalized on February 19, 2021: "The US officially rejoined the Paris Climate Accord ... almost a month after ... Biden declared that the US again accepted the agreement's terms. Former President Donald Trump ... said it was ineffective because it allows countries to voluntarily restrain their own pollution and seeks to hold the US and other [mostly Western] industrialized countries to a higher standard.... No. 1 carbon emitter China also is a member of the 2016 accord — but Trump scoffed at the idea that the authoritarian state would voluntarily curb its own pollution.... 'What we won't do is punish the American people while enriching foreign polluters,' Trump said in 2019...."[2] But that—along with facilitating taxation "by any other nomenclature" for future global governance under the AntiChrist—is precisely what Mr. J. Biden *does want,* as China has enriched the whorish "bought and paid for" Biden[ista] clan.

In the midst of the above, God brought such a severe cold snap to Texas, that the state's wind-driven "green energy"—the largest such supply in the United States—*seized,* leading to cascading power grid failures that literally brought Texas to *within "seconds and minutes" from a months-long statewide power grid loss;*[3] simultaneously, many of that state's water and natural gas lines froze and broke, creating one of the costliest natural disasters in U.S. history— and leaving many Texas without heat, without clean water to drink, without near-empty grocery stores, etc., for days to over a week. Yup, pushing the anthropogenic *"*global warming" lie "can be a real 'Bid-Ch'"—and more now realize that ecofascist elitists' "green jokes" are *on them!* Few are laughing. (Yet, the U.S. as a whole is threatened by *a national grid failure that could last for many months, fry and thus destroy most "unhardened" electronics, and result in the deaths of perhaps a third of the U.S. populace within a year,* should it occur.[4]) That disaster was just a start, with more to follow (e.g., Afghanistan). But hey, at least Mr. J. Biden—along with "leaders of some of the world's richest nations"—got to dine with Satan's Prince, his mother the queen, and other British royals for his treachery, eating of "Eden's" permissive "fruit:" "The ... monarch was joined by the other most senior members of the British royal

1. Matthew Daly and Ellen Knickmeyer, "Biden: 'We Can't Wait Any Longer' to Address Climate Crisis," *Associated Press,* 27 Jan. 2021.
2. Steven Nelson, "US officially rejoins Paris Climate Accord," *New York Post,* 19 Feb. 2021.
3. Erin Douglas, "Texas was 'seconds and minutes' away from catastrophic monthslong blackouts, officials say," *Texas Tribune,* 18 Feb. 2021.
4. See the author's book *North Korea, Iran, and the Coming World War: Behold a Red Horse.*

family with son and heir Prince Charles.... At the reception, held at the Eden Project, the world's largest indoor rainforest, the queen met Joe Biden as U.S. [(coup)] President for the first time...."[1]

Biden's *delusional* definition of "science," which he may have picked up while fondling some poor person around a bonfire, is just hair-brained: "We see with our own eyes. We know it in our bones." That of course, *is* how Satan's poorly-educated and deceived "left" approaches its "green religion"—adding faux-"science" or *anti-science.* Thus, they allege human-caused "climate ... changes" "are driving devastating storms, wildfires and rising seas...."[2] Per such blind *fools,* The Creator is somehow *not* in control. Of course, they gleefully overlook many "inconvenient" facts, as their real interest is *money,* not saving our planetary environment: "In 2017, the [Trump-Pence] White House said ... 'compliance with the terms of the Paris Accord and the onerous energy restrictions it has placed on the United States could cost America as much as 2.7 million lost jobs by 2025....' Instead, the U.S. continued decreasing its greenhouse gas emissions <u>faster than any other major polluter</u>, and ... without the Paris agreement."[3] (That's *inconvenient.*) But hey, Satan's Prince and his mother like their regurgitated White House drone: "Queen Elizabeth will host new U.S. President Joe Biden and other world leaders at Buckingham Palace before a summit of the G7 big economies in June [2021].... Describing it as a 'soft power' reception, the *Sunday Times* said the Queen would be joined by the Prince of Wales...."[4]

In April 2021, the climate liars became more shrill, as *anti*-science and macroevolutionary *Scientific American* spurred the ecofascist "climate change" fraud and delusion to new heights: "'Journalism should reflect what science says: the climate emergency is here,' ... senior editor Mark Fischetti said.... 'A hurricane blasts Florida. A California dam bursts because floods have piled water high up behind it. A sudden, record-setting cold snap cuts power to the entire state of Texas,' Fischetti wrote.... A study published ... in *Science* magazine found [(i.e., claims)] that the massive ice shelf stemming from Antarctica's Thwaites Glacier is even more unstable than previously thought, thanks to warming water melting the ice that connects it to land. A collapse of this single ice shelf would translate into a global sea level rise of up to 3 feet, the study

1. Thompson/Reuters, "Queen Elizabeth Hosts Biden at G7 Reception," *NewsMax,* 11 June 2021.
2. Zack Colman and Ben Lefebvre, "Biden pitching a much vaster climate plan than Obama ever attempted," *Politico,* 27 Jan. 2021.
3. Ellen R. Wald, "The U.N. Says America Is Already Cutting So Much Carbon It Doesn't Need The Paris Climate Accord," *Forbes.com,* 10 Dec. 2020.
4. "Queen Elizabeth to Host Biden Before G7 Summit in June," *Thomson Reuters,* 31 Jan. 2021.

concluded.... If ... global average temperatures do rise by 7.2 degrees (4 degrees Celsius), over one-third of the entire Antarctic ice shelf will be at risk of collapse, said a second study conducted by researchers at the University of Reading, submerging whole countries and states like Florida.... 'Failure to slash the amount of carbon dioxide in the atmosphere will make ... extraordinary heat, storms, wildfires and ice melt ... routine and could 'render a significant portion of the Earth uninhabitable'....'[1] With all that, Mr. Fischetti adds: "These are also emergencies that require immediate action. Multiply these situations worldwide, and you have the biggest environmental emergency to beset the Earth in millennia: climate change.... The planet is heating up way too fast.... To preserve a livable planet, humanity must take action immediately."[2] Of course, such prognostications are really just anti-God, *satanic* propaganda.

But God is certainly in the picture: With Mr. J. Biden having also just pronounced "climate change" an "existential threat" to humanity, the Southeastern U.S. then faced a weeks-long *shut down and disruption* of the Colonial Pipeline—in a May 2021 "ransomware cyberattack"—leaving several states starving for gasoline and jet fuel. (Such events show that energy infrastructure fragility is an *actual* existential threat.[3])

"China and the U.S. ... represent as much as 45% of global [carbon] emissions. 'The Chinese-U.S. relationship will largely determine the success or failure of climate mitigation globally,' said Paul Bledsoe, who ... is ... with the Progressive Policy Institute."[4] John Kerry, Mr. Biden's "climate envoy," now prostitutes the U.S. to China's wicked regime "to cooperate on combating climate change,"[5] not discerning that global war looms.[6]

While the elitist "party line" of anthropogenic global warming has only *ever been* a massive satanic fraud, largely perpetrated under the British monarchy, with a historical global governance conspiracy at its heart, it remains that "God is not mocked" (Gal 6:7)—and *He will subject these thieving liars (and willful idiots) to their most expressed fears: from His hand, they shall know thirst and famine, and shall escape neither heat nor fire;* some will even *drown* (e.g., see Rev 8:8-9). In the coming Great Tribulation, there will be those among them whose skin will be "hot as an oven, because of

---

1. David Knowles, "Citing grave threat, Scientific American replaces 'climate change' with 'climate emergency,'" *Yahoo News*, 12 Apr. 2021.
2. Ibid.
3. For the EMP threat, see *North Korea, Iran, and the Coming World War: Behold a Red Horse*.
4. Josh Siegel, "Kerry bets on setting aside confrontation with China to combat climate change," *Washington Examiner*, 9 Feb. 2021.
5. Ibid.
6. See this author's book, *North Korea, Iran, and the Coming World War: Behold a Red Horse*.

the fever of famine" (Lam 5:10). After that suffering, a day shall come "burning like an oven" (Mal 4:1*a-b).* At that time: "'All the proud, yes, all who do wickedly will be stubble. And the day which is coming shall burn them up,' says The LORD of hosts. 'That *burning* will leave them neither root nor branch. But ... you who fear My Name .... shall trample the wicked—for they shall be ashes under the soles of your feet, on the day that I do *this,*' says The LORD of hosts" (Mal 4:1-3).

We who serve God rightly decry mankind's very real destruction of the world's forests, natural biodiverstiy, and depletion of its resources (e.g., ocean-going fish)—recognizing that Yeshua Himself will "destroy those who destroy the Earth" at His return (Rev 11:18; see 11:15-19, 16). But for Satan's Prince and those who follow him, a time will come between Lamentations 5:10 and Malachi 4:1-3, when one-third of the world's trees and *all* green grass shall simply be "burned up"—as fiery frozen water ("hail and fire") mixed with blood, or ostensible comets in lieu of giant hail stones, strike Earth's surface (Rev 8:7). Yet, even as The God of Israel *mocks the Devil and those who serve him by such judgments,* given their inability to stop or even avoid those strikes, His sealed Israelite servants will *not,* it appears, be harmed by these or other similar events (see Rev 7:1-4, 8:1-2, 8:6; cf. Isa 24:23). The apparent comets will be followed by an apparent asteroid strike that turns "the third part of the sea" to "blood," destroying all corresponding sea life and ships (Rev 8:8-9). But for all that, still *another* "great star" will fall "from heaven, burning like a torch, and" dispersing "on a third of the rivers, and on the springs of water"—so that ultimately, "a third of the waters became wormwood; and many of the men died from the waters, because they were made bitter" or fatally poisonous (Rev 8:10-11)—and arguably radioactive as well, considering that "wormwood" is *chernobyl* in the Russian and Ukrainian translations.

We also read in Revelation that a *personified* star (i.e., an angel) shall "fall from heaven unto the Earth" to open "the bottomless pit," so that "there arose a smoke out of the pit, as the smoke of a great furnace—and the sun and the air were darkened by reason of the smoke of the pit" (Rev 9:1-2). The "creatures" that emanate from this "bottomless pit" (cf. the center of Earth's molten core), which certainly *sound* strikingly like modern military attack helicopters, will "not hurt the grass of the earth, neither any green thing, neither any tree—except those men not having the seal of God on their foreheads," whom they shall torment physically for "five months" (Rev 9:4, Gk.; see 9:3-11).

Compounding those terrifying judgments from falling "stars," following the resurrection (of deceased) and translation (of living) saints at the last trumpet (Rev 10:6-7, 11:15), just before Armageddon itself transpires (Rev 16:10-16), "the sea" will become like "the blood of a dead [man]," so that unbelievers receive "blood to drink," being those who wickedly "shed the blood of saints and prophets" (see Rev 16:3-7).

Many non-Christians will then be "scorched with great heat" and "with fire" — but rather than quickly repenting, their degenerates will continue to blaspheme God our Creator (Rev 16:8-9). The "extinction of small island states" will also transpire, though *not* due to any direct anthropogenic global warming, but rather from God's anger and shaking of the planet (see Isa 24:17-22). With the seventh bowl of wrath (see Rev 16:17-21), which is to be outpoured following Jesus' *posttribulational* return (see Rev 16:10-16; cf. 1 Th 5:1-10),[1] "every island fled away," and the mountains shall not be found (Rev 16:20; cf. 6:14-17); for "every mountain and island was moved out of its place" (Rev 6:14*b).*[2]

We may conclude that as mankind further accepts Satan's frauds (plural) and those of his supplicant prince, the more God's divine judgment shall surely manifest. In truth, mankind has *little* control over Earth's climate, but God controls all nature — and He will fully demonstrate that, to the shame of fools. (Unregenerate mankind, like Al Gore at COP21, offers only noxious hot air.) How will those who continue to reject Jesus as LORD, Savior, and Messiah explain these fearsome occurrences? As unrepentant deceivers, they may proceed to claim that not enough was done "in Paris" or wherever, so that the world has "failed!" These are they who magnify Satan's lies, rather than repent and receive Christ Jesus, who alone saves!

Though not speaking to environmentalists or their concerns, whether fake or real, even leaders like Russia's Putin fear what they perceive: "He said the [global 'Coronavirus Disease 2019' or COVID-19] crisis had increased social stratification, populism, right- and left-wing radicalism, adding that domestic political processes were becoming more violent. 'All of this cannot but impact international relations, making them less stable and predictable,' he said.... 'In the 20th century, the failure and inability to centrally resolve such issues resulted in the catastrophic World War II. Of course, nowadays such

---

1. See the author's material on the rapture.
2. The frequently nutty *Ancient Aliens* TV series postulates that "aliens" and spirits have established subsurface bases and presences among the world's islands, and within tall or otherwise venerated mountains and volcanoes (see Episodes 9 and 11 of Season 6 of *Ancient Aliens,* titled "Aliens and Forbidden Islands" and "Aliens and Mysterious Mountains," as aired on 28 Nov. and 12 Dec. 2013, respectively). Regardless, God would here completely eliminate such.

a heated conflict ... would mean the end of our civilization. But I would like to reiterate, that the [('plandemic')] situation might develop unpredictably and uncontrollably if we will sit on our hands doing nothing to avoid it. And there is a possibility that we may experience an actual collapse of global development that might result in a fight of all against all.'"[1]

Clearly, there will be more celestial signs, followed by more earthly catastrophes, as Jesus' return draws ever closer. As the author details elsewhere in his works,[2] the Apocalypse, and biblical prophecy generally, are structured to be both telescoping and repetitious, so that the Testimony of Christ is foundational and central to all history and prophecy.

Christianity, Judaism, Islam, etc., and a unified world religion. As previously discussed, Satan's Prince (now King Charles III) has a very wide range of religious and spiritual activities; there seems to be almost nothing in which he will not participate. He clearly has sought, and continues to seek to ingratiate himself to the world's major religious communities. More than that, however, it appears that Charles ultimately wants to head apostate Christianity, apostate Israel, *and* the Muslim world.[3] In this vein, before his 2021 death, Prince Philip had been in charge of the "Sacred Literature Trust," a United Nations project which seeks to distill and document the common tenets of the world's various religious systems and to revive what Al Gore refers to as the *Gaia* principle—"Mother Earth" worship. This project's findings are to serve as the basis for a new, unified world religion. Springmeier adds: "An example of how Gentile and Jewish Satanists collaborate together could be seen when Prince Philip of England's representative Martin Palmer and Rabbi Arthur Hertzberg jointly announced their plans at the United Nations in 1989 for the Sacred Literature Trust, which is a major project to revive Mother Earth worship. Moreover, Palmer has written on Gnostic and pagan themes which have been published by Lucis Trust, and in 1986, Rabbi Hertzberg, an aide to Jewish Illuminatus Edgar Bronfman, publicly advocated revival of Cabalism at Assisi, Italy."[4]

The European Union. Charles' activities, as described throughout this book, have served to help him make great inroads among EU elites. Not only does he have a strong Merovingian lineage, but

---

1. Holly Ellyatt, "Putin warns of 'all against all' fight if global tensions are not resolved," *CNBC*, 27 Jan. 2021.
2. See, for example, the *Messiah, History and the Tribulation Period* multi-volume series.
3. For documentation, see the previous chapter's sections titled, "A so-called 'Christian' heritage" and "Ties to the New Age Movement, the occult, and false religions," at pp. 295 and 333, respectively. Also, see the next chapter, "Charles, Middle East 'Peace,' and Global Security," at p. 481.
4. Written correspondence, quoted by permission, from Springmeier.

he has all the other qualifications that the EU would seek in a future leader or monarch. As things currently stand, King Charles III yet awaits a reply to his request to be King of Europe.[1]

Race (ethnic) relations. In 1984, Satan's Prince, being already "woke," called a conference "on race and employment, known as the Windsor Conference." Junor comments: "Gathered under one roof were the chairmen of sixty major companies in Britain and a crowd of bright, articulate members of the black community. For two working days and a night they mixed.... That conference is widely regarded as one of the most significant advances in race relations ever made [in Britain], and is still talked about today. The black community ... had no idea that there were people in the white hierarchy who were seriously interested in their unemployment problems; and the white establishment, on the whole, admitted they had never realized there were intelligent members of the black community. Without the Prince of Wales such a confrontation would almost certainly never have taken place." It was this event that led to Charles' initial 1985 presidency of Business in the Community (BiC): "Charles wanted to see what good had come out of the conference in Windsor.... So a special unit called the Black Economic Development Secretariat was set up at the BiC offices in City Road, to report back to the Prince every six months...; and progress was noticeable.... Prince Charles was [also] eager to have a black face on his staff.... [Charles (as a *racist*)] has an affinity for black people."[2]

The world of business and finance. Over the past four decades, Charles has become one of the most influential men, if not *the* most influential man, in the global business world. A primary vehicle is the Prince of Wales | International Business Leaders Forum (PWBLF | IBLF), an organization that Charles created and over which he yet presides. The IBLF is highly connected with multinational and other companies around the world:

> By the end of the eighties, the Prince had become ambitious to take BITC's [(Business In The Community's)] message to other countries. Enthused by the thought of inspiring **the world's most powerful multinational companies** to share his perspective, he and his team decided to hold an international forum in the American town of Charleston, South Carolina. They invited **more than a hundred senior executives** from the United States, Britain, Europe, Japan and Australia for a two-day meeting at which they talked freely about the responsibilities of international industry to the environment and to the community. Led by the Prince, ... they broke up into small groups for intense debate about the issues raised by

---

1. For more information, see ch. 2, "A Man for Our Times," at p. 51.
2. Junor, pp. 248, 251.

the Prince through BITC in Britain. The event was a success. Within a few months, [in 1990,] ... what soon became know[n] as the Business Leaders Forum (BLF) was in operation. Over the next few years, [BITC executive Robert] Davies was to organise seventeen similar international meetings [(as of early 1994)], timed where possible to coincide with the Prince's official tours abroad, involving more than 4,000 [top] business leaders in North America, Latin America, Europe and Asia.

....With the opening of Eastern Europe, ... the BLF was to form partnerships with more than ninety businesses working in Russia, Poland, the Czech Republic and Slovakia, setting up a range of [education,] training and environmental projects, forming a task force to help regenerate the cultural [and economic] life of St Petersburg, and transforming the Red Army Barracks outside Budapest into a series of units for small businesses.[1]

In a separate initiative, more than 7,000 international hoteliers, responsible for more than two million rooms, have been mobilised to set new environmental targets for their industry worldwide. In the autumn of 1994, as president of the BLF, the Prince is due to launch a new project called 'Inter-City Action', linking community leaders in the United States and other western countries to their counterparts in the developing world to tackle jointly their shared problems of youth unemployment, ethnic minority conflicts, shortages of housing and skills, and environmental degradation.[2]

Although it sounds breathtaking in scope, that outline merely scratches the surface of a host of successful related initiatives by Prince Charles in Britain, the British Commonwealth, and now the world at large, leading to the ultimate formation of the IBLF and more. *Books* could literally be written on these initiatives alone.[3] As of early *1994,* the PWBLF involved as many as one-hundred of the world's top multinational corporations. Consider, therefore, the following past information from a study "written by Sarah Anderson and John Cavanagh using statistics largely drawn from charts published by *Forbes"* magazine and titled "The Top 200:"

The global economic power of giant companies has grown to the point that they have become bigger than most of the countries where they do business.... In fact, more than half of the 100 biggest economies in the world are corporations.... Taken together, the world's 200 biggest companies control no less than 28 percent of the globe's economic activity. These companies are the powerhouses of [economic] globalization.... The multinational companies have the power to go anywhere to make or buy anything to be sold anywhere else in the world.... For most [small countries,] ... the might of the big companies challenges their sovereignty.... The global firms ... can wring concessions from governments eager to cre-

1. Dimbleby, *The Prince of Wales,* pp. 372-373, 569-570.
2. Dimbleby, *The Prince of Wales,* p. 570.
3. For a current but brief summary, see Dimbleby, *The Prince of Wales,* pp. 567-574.

ate jobs.... The 21 biggest economies in the world still are countries, with the United States at the top, Japan second, [and] Germany third...."[1]

With such statistics in mind, one can only conclude that then Prince Charles, through the highly influential PWBLF, had *already become* a major, if not *the* major, behind-the-scenes economic "mover and shaker." Consider, for example, these excerpts from a November 1996 article: "Arriving in Kiev at the start of a nine-day, five nation tour [including Ukraine and central Asia], the Prince was soon ensconced in a seminar of his Business Leaders Forum together with what he called the 'movers and shakers' of Ukraine's fledgling market economy. [In that corrupt country, the] ... Prince listened to the aspirations of local executives as they spoke of the need for ethical business conduct and better business education. 'It is only too clear to all of us,' the Prince concluded, 'that the countries of the former Soviet Union are at an historic crossroads and urgently need the partnership of the West to tackle environmental problems and to alleviate the disillusionment of their young people.... If what we call free market systems are to be sustainable in the long run, international management must share its management skills.... For business to be actively involved in matters of social concern does help the reputation of business.' [At Mohlya Academy, a] ... large crowd of students blocked the doorway brandishing photographs of the Prince and banners of greeting. 'Dear Prince Charles, You Are The Best Prince We Have Ever Seen,' said one."[2]

Junor, in a very brief summary of his youth-related activities, states: "He has not just put his name to other people's schemes, and taken on patronages. He has initiated projects, found the people to run them, provided the funds to get the ideas off the ground, and reaped the rewards. Some schemes have sent young people round the world, working as part of an international team in areas of need [(e.g., operations Drake and Raleigh)]. Others have taken them off the dole and given them a year's paid work, combining community service, teamwork and physical challenge. Yet others have given unemployed young people the chance to set up in business on their own by providing not just a grant to get them started, but professional guidance to help them over early problems."[3] *The Economist,*

---

1. R.C. Longworth, Chicago Tribune, "Global companies control large part of world economy," *The Denver Post*, 13 Oct. 1996, p. 10A. Recall that Japan and Germany are among the small group of nations being considered as possible new permanent member-states of the UN Security Council (see ch. 1, "The Footsteps of the AntiChrist," at p. 30).
2. Robert Hardman, "Ukrainians need West's help, says Prince," *The Electronic Telegraph*, 5 Nov. 1996, No. 531, p. 1.
3. Junor, p. 12.

in a 1996 article on Charles' Youth Business Trust, one of the initiatives above mentioned, made these observations:

> AN AVERAGE annual compound growth rate of 25% over ten years; 30,000 businesses launched, 60% of which have survived at least three years: for any venture-capital fund, this would be a remarkable result. The brains behind this one is an unlikely financial whizz, a man with no job.... He is the Prince of Wales.
>
> The Prince's Youth Business Trust was launched a decade ago to help young people who have the motivation, but not the means, to start a business.... Alongside the cash, it provides the services of a business advisor for three years, or sometimes longer. It employs 300 people full-time and finances around 4,000 businesses a year.
>
> ....But, according to James Morton, in "Investing with the Grand Masters"..., the trust looks like a widely-diversified conglomerate.... "The return on capital employed," says Mr Morton, "is off the charts. It puts the professionals to shame."
>
> The trust is well managed and .... benefits from an elaborate network of marketing, legal and financial advisers, some of whom are paid, some of whom are not.[1]

Governor of Hong Kong? In an effort to satisfy "the [then] heir apparent's worldly vanity," former Prime Minister Margaret Thatcher, recalling Charles' "frustrated ambition to become Governor-General of Australia," decided that he should become "Governor of Hong Kong for the last year of its life as a British dominion." It was "a chance for Charles to hold conspicuous, quasi-monarchical sway, while showing himself a man of his times." To Satan's Prince, "the remnants of what was his grandfather's empire, and will one day be his own global kingdom [as *The* Commonwealth], are of paramount importance."[2] While Chris Patten, not Charles, became Governor of Hong Kong, Satan's Prince officiated for the queen and Britain at Hong Kong's turnover to bloody China at the start of July 1997, a highly publicized event. A bit reminiscent of the queen's "dotting the eye of a dragon," at which point it "is said to be alive and able to take part in a colourful procession," during her 1975 visit to Hong Kong,[3] Charles' handover of the cosmopolitain city was attended by, among other things, dragon dances throughout the night.

We have already seen that Satan's Prince was center-stage for the three most publicized events in the history of the world to date:

---

1. "Princely performance," *The Economist,* 23 Nov. 1996, p. 64. Speaking of then Prince Charles' Youth Business Initiative (YBI), Junor offers similarly amazing statistics: "In contrast to the usual pattern of small businesses, which have a failure rate of 80 per cent, 85 per cent of the businesses funded by YBI are still trading; 20 per cent of those have employed other people; and of the 15 per cent that failed, half of those people who were unable to run a business of their own found jobs with employers soon afterwards. The type of businesses they have started could not be more diverse" (p. 210).
2. Holden, *King Charles III,* pp. 210-211.
3. *Her Majesty The Queen,* p. 40.

1) the untimely death and burial of Princess Diana, with an overall estimated audience of up to two and one-half billion viewers and listeners; 2) the then prince's 1981 marriage to Diana, with seven-hundred and fifty million viewers and a total audience of nearly two billion; and 3) his July 1969 investiture as Prince of Wales, with five-hundred million viewers.[1] Although the author has not seen any estimates as to the actual size of the viewing audience, it seems highly likely that Charles' handover of Hong Kong to communist China was then among the top *four* most publicized and viewed events to that point in world history. Additionally, as noted even in the first edition of this book, perhaps more biographies and other biographical material had already been written on Charles, than *any other contemporary figure,* living or dead, and yet he had only *just begun* to make his mark in history's annals.[2] Apart from the reality of this book's core premise, such circumstances would seem to be *inexplicable.* Other than the two witnesses of the Apocalypse (Rev 11), this incredible degree of publicity could reasonably be expected for just one person before Christ's return—the AntiChrist. Falling in line, the World Economic Forum's "'The Global Agenda 2009' report urges [the] creation of a global television channel."[3]

As we have seen throughout this book, where Satan's Prince and the British monarchy generally are concerned, there is inevitably, it seems, a story behind the story. More often than not, that hidden story is both shocking and sordid. In fact, the British monarchy's amazing duplicity and hypocrisy give new meaning to the phrase "spin doctor." Charles' involvement in Hong Kong is no different. Holden, as quoted earlier regarding the then prince, states, "Visitors ... hear little but the long catalogue of his concerns: unemployment, housing, race, drugs, the decay of the inner city, the environment and family life." In his own words, Charles has remarked: "The Islamic and Western worlds share problems common to us all: ...how we deal with Aids, drugs, and the disintegration of the family.... The international trade in hard drugs is one example.... We have to solve these threats to our communities and our lives together."[4]

---

1. For more information, see ch. 8, "The Red Dragon and Prince Charles' Investiture as Prince of Wales," and ch. 10's section titled, "Marriage, ascension, and politics," at pp. 207 and 314, respectively. The wedding of Spain's Princess Cristina de Borbon to Inaki Urdangarin in Barcelona reportedly had a pre-ceremony estimated television audience of nine-hundred million ("Royal rites put spotlight on Barcelona," *The Denver Post,* 4 Oct. 1997, p. 2A). This, however, seems to have been a gross exaggeration of the true public interest.
2. For more information, see ch. 2, "A Man for Our Times," at p. 51.
3. Kincaid, "Global Taxes and Global TV Now on the Agenda."
4. Then Prince Charles, "Islam and the West," 27 Oct. 1993. For the full text of this speech, made at Oxford's Sheldonian Theatre on a visit to the Oxford Centre for Islamic Studies, as well as Holden's statement in context, see ch. 10's section titled, "Ties to the New Age Movement, the occult, and false religions," at p. 333.

Still, as shown earlier, both the development and the continuance of the modern global drug trade—to include opium, cocaine, heroin, tobacco, and pharmaceutical drugs—traces largely and directly to the British monarchy![1] Britain is well-known, for example, to have acquired Hong Kong and its surrounding territories as a direct result of its Opium Wars with China in the nineteenth century, wars that greatly enriched its monarchy's coffers. Little has changed. The monarchy, and Satan's Prince in particular, retain strong "business" ties to Hong Kong, ties which yet involve the worldwide drug trade. Perhaps the monarchy's key participation in Hong Kong's handover, therefore, constituted more than just the next major international media-blitz for Charles since his extravagant wedding to Diana.[2] We have little choice, it seems, but to conclude that Charles' litany of alleged "concerns" is really just one more clever oligarchical ploy to manipulate the world's thinking toward a perceived need for "global governance"—under the very purveyors of the mankind's greatest decadence themselves. As Satan's Prince has stated, "I don't want to be a figurehead, but one can reasonably hope to underline influence people to do what you think is good and useful"[3] (i.e., evil and destroying).

Today, communist China uses Mexican drug cartels to engage in wicked *chemical warfare and thus genocidal murder,* via Fentanyl poisoning (e.g., of hundreds of thousands of foolish youth), against the United States. Indeed, that transpires with the *satanic complicity*

---

1. To the extent that the British monarchy runs Great Britain, consider the following example from the tobacco industry: "SANTA CRUZ DO SUL, Brazil—Freakish tobacco plants that explode from the soil in the remote river valley grow huge leaves on stalks as thick as Louisville Sluggers. The growers here call it *fumo louco.* Crazy tobacco. Crazy not just because it grows so big and so fast. Crazy because it has been genetically altered by one of the world's largest tobacco companies to pack twice the nicotine of other commercial leaf. The farmers of Brazil's southernmost state are growing it by the ton for the world market.... *Fumo louco*—the farmers' generic term for several related strains of high-nicotine tobacco—is the offspring of a genetically altered plant created in U.S. laboratories for Brown & Williamson Tobacco Corp., the third largest U.S. cigarette maker.... *Fumo louco* blends give cigarette makers a new tool for adjusting nicotine levels in their products. They may also provide the U.S. Food and Drug Administration with a new argument for the assertion that the tobacco industry intentionally manipulates nicotine levels to 'hook' smokers.... 'It's weird stuff,' Neury de Oliveira said in his native Portuguese. The nicotine content is so high that 'just the crazy smell of it gets you dizzy. But, sir, it comes up like nothing you've ever seen.' The farmers said **they sell their high-nicotine tobacco to Souza Cruz, a Brazilian company owned by B.A.T. Industries, the same British conglomerate that controls Brown & Williamson**.... The FDA learned in 1994 that Brown & Williamson had developed a nicotine-rich plant, code-named Y-1.... Y-1 cultivation began in Brazil in 1983, according to former Souza Cruz agronomists.... Souza Cruz, according to its own figures, shipped nearly 8 million pounds of Y-1 to the United States for Brown & Williamson between 1990 and 1994.... Grower David Moraes led a reporter to his sorting barn.... Bitter air buffeted the senses. A queasiness spread from the pit of the stomach up through the chest. 'That,' said Moraes, 'is the bite of *fumo louco*'" (Todd Lewan, The Associated Press, "'Crazy tobacco' packs a punch in world market," *Rocky Mountain News,* 21 Dec. 1997, p. 56A). But the tobacco story runs deeper. Notice, for example, that most cigarette brands bear a British heraldic achievement on their packaging!
2. For more information, see the discussion on the Committee of 300 in ch. 7's section titled, "The Garter," starting around p. 154.
3. Cathcart, p. 92.

and *direct help* of Washington, DC's *treasonous and traitorous* Joe "Manchurian" Biden *coup regime* of *domestic enemies.*

The United Nations and public-private partnerships. For decades now, Satan's Prince has "partnered" with the United Nations. The PWBLF, for example, collaborated with the World Bank and the UN Development Programme (UNDP) to form **Business as Partners in Development (BPD)**, an organization which has long had an *enormous* impact on business, government, and education around world (see below).[1] (The PWBLF is now "replaced" by IBLF Global.[2]) Indeed, BPD is now *leading* mankind into a new form of global governance based upon the "Platonic ideal," as modeled in public-private (government-business) partnerships, that employ *elitist* sustainable development concepts. First floated years ago in Pittsburgh, such partnerships combine (mix) what so-called *elites* (i.e., *elitists)* have now determined are the "best" and most useful aspects of Communism-Socialism and Capitalism-Fascism. That "unnatural" mixture is to constitute a new global system made "partly of iron and partly of clay" (cf. Dan 2:41-43).[3] Through such public-private partnerships, power is literally shifting away from national, state, and local governments—at all levels—and toward Business as Partners in Development. For multiple decades, Charles has been *steadily and quietly taking control.*

In a related effort, Charles through his own Internet presence (e.g., via the PWBLF, which became the PWIBLF, then just the IBLF, and is now IBLF Global), has also long used the *w*orld *w*ide *w*eb (cf. *Vav-Vav-Vav* or 6-6-6) to "get his message out." As a former *OneWorld Online* "partner," Charles' homepage as Prince of Wales, like that of other British royals, had been incorporated into the more extensive OneWorld Online homepage of One World Broadcasting Trust, a British "charity."[4] As of May 1996, Charles' "Millennium Agenda" message, offered in the form of a brief electronic video showing himself in front of a background displaying his badge as heir-apparent, stated, "It seems to me, ... that the next challenge for *all international business leaders* is to develop a *new world vision,* a

---

1. For more information, see the PWBLF's publication titled "Business as Partners in Development." In 1998, this publication could be obtained by contacting The Prince of Wales [International] Business Leaders Forum; 2) The World Bank Group (1818 H. Street N.W., Washington DC 20433); or 3) The United Nations Development Programme (Division for the Private Sector in Development; One United Nations Plaza; New York, NY 10017).
2. For IBLF Global, see "https://www.iblfglobal.org".
3. See the discussion on the "Platonic ideal" in this chapter's earlier section titled, "The United World Colleges," at pp. 395 (note) and 401, as well as ch. 7's section titled, "The Garter," at p. 147.
4. Since publication of the first edition of this work, the OneWorld Online site has become defunct.

form of business ethic which sees this international commitment to good corporate citizenship as a natural part of business practice."[1]

Jane Nelson, speaking for the PWBLF, states: "Business as Partners in Development offers a global perspective on the evolving role of business in a complex and rapidly changing world.... This debate is likely to be one of the defining themes of the 21st Century, as both nation-states and corporations struggle to adapt to a world in which greater efficiency and effectiveness must be combined with more responsible and accountable governance; and in which economic competitiveness must be combined with social cohesion and environmental sustainability."[2] As this introduction to "the first stage in a series of consultations and case studies which The Prince of Wales Business Leaders Forum will be conducting in collaboration with the World Bank and UNDP" would imply, Business as Partners in Development is a major player in the push for global governance. "The next stages in the PWBLF- World Bank- UNDP programme will be focused on ... the impacts of about 20 major multinational companies in selected countries; interviewing some 150 stakeholders...; and carrying out a series of roundtables and consultations in different countries around the world."[3] The organization seeks to "develop new types of consultation and partnership[, having social objectives,] between companies and their secondary stakeholders—communities, governments, non-governmental organisations and the general public."[4] It wishes to encourage "multi-stakeholder partnerships between multinational companies and international NGOs; between business and multilateral and bilateral development agencies; and between groups of companies."[5]

Nelson asserts that there is "a growing recognition ... of the crucial linkages between economic growth, human development, social cohesion and environmental sustainability .... [as] summed up in the concept of sustainable development," and that "these challenges can no longer be tackled by yesterday's rules of governance." "Fundamental to this is the growing importance of the private sector, ranging from large multinational corporations to millions of small and micro-enterprises; and of civil society, ranging from international and professionally managed non-governmental organisations, to grassroots community-based organisations and individual citizens." Moreover, in "most cases, the debate is no longer about extreme al-

---

1. Tokyo, Nov. 1990.
2. Jane Nelson, *Business as Partners in Development: Executive Summary* (United Kingdom: The Prince of Wales Business Leaders Forum, 1996; ISBN: 1 899159 94 0), p. 1.
3. Nelson, *Business as Partners in Development: Executive Summary,* p. 12.
4. Nelson, *Business as Partners in Development: Executive Summary,* pp. 4, 7.
5. Nelson, *Business as Partners in Development: Executive Summary,* p. 1.

ternatives—about communism versus capitalism, the free market versus state control, democracy versus dictatorship—but about finding common ground. It is about developing co-operative, integrated and inclusive solutions ... both within nations and between them. It is about finding a balance."[1]

The organization's seal mentions environmental sustainability, human development, social cohesion, economic growth and participation, education, training, health, nutrition, soil, atmosphere, water, wetlands, cultivated natural assets, physical infrastructure, goods and services, finance, technology, and formal and informal associations (e.g., NGOs). The seal also portrays national wealth as a combination of natural or environmental capital, human capital, social capital, and man-made or economic capital between companies, communities, and countries.[2] A brief overview of related first-stage key-ideas, phrases, and words would include the following: *the environment (atmosphere, soil, water, wetlands, and natural assets)*—environmental protection, improvement, and accountability, not just sustainability, in the face of current degradation; maintaining biodiversity; *human development*—setting and spreading international ethics standards and business practices; enforcing laws, and tackling crime and corruption; promoting youth and community development, with volunteerism (e.g., utilizing university students for community work); *social cohesion, health, and nutrition*—increasing participation in child-care and health-care; addressing the problems of world poverty and its alleviation, unemployment, economic insecurity, rising inequality, child labor, and social dislocation and disintegration; supporting and strengthening humanitarian efforts for emergency and disaster relief and rehabilitation after natural and man-made disasters, including earthquakes, famine, and war; *global economic growth and participation, education, and training (goods and services, finance, technology)*—economic globalization, regionalization, and development; national wealth creation; promoting good governance and competitiveness; political transition and geopolitical transformation; technological transformation, and the current transition from an industrial to a knowledge-based society (e.g., through the Internet); and *physical infrastructure*—urban renewal and rural development.

Examples of "good" corporate action cited, to name just some through the late 1990s, include several involving Charles, directly and indirectly: the Prince's Youth Business Trust (PYBT) in the United Kingdom, India, and South Africa; his International Youth Founda-

---

1. Nelson, *Business as Partners in Development: Executive Summary*, p. 2.
2. Nelson, *Business as Partners in Development: Executive Summary*, p. 3.

tion; his International Hotels Environment Initiative (IHEI); the PWBLF in Poland and the PWBLF's St. Petersburg Partnership; his Business in the Community (BiC), which led to the PWBLF, in the UK;[1] the UK's Investors in People programme; the UK government's Advisory Council on Business and the Environment; Aim High in the UK; Groundwork in the UK; the Mega-Cities project; the World Business Council for Sustainable Development; the World Environment Centre; the World Wildlife Fund (WWF); Conservation International; President Clinton's Principles of Corporate Citizenship, and his Council on Sustainable Development; and Goals 2000 in the United States.[2]

Could it be that Satan's Prince is not just influencing, but actually *setting* the U.S. government's agenda? A number of the past Clinton administration's pet projects, three of which we've noted, fall directly into above-listed categories. As yet another example, in a significant strategy reversal,[3] the altogether corrupt Clintons came to suggest that "a large-scale federal program" was *not* the answer to that administration's socialist child-care agenda: "Instead, they explored solutions that relied more on public-private partnerships and efforts by businesses to help make child care more available to ... workers. In addition to the scholarship program, the president ... announced the formation of a group of business leaders to spur private investment in child care, and said volunteers in the Corporation for National Service would help improve after-school care programs."[4]

Nelson concludes: "The purpose of Business as Partners in Development [(BIPD)] is to profile good practice; to emphasize the positive and the possible.... There is no time for complacency when more than a billion people still live in absolute poverty. When millions of others are out of work and when inequality and social exclusion are increasing in many countries. There is no time for complacency when climate change, environmental degradation, loss of biodiversity and declining food and water supplies threaten the ecological carrying capacity of our planet. And there is no time for

---

1. Business in the Community (BiC) was initially modeled after similar successful initiatives already underway in the United States (e.g., see Junor, pp. 249-250).
2. Nelson, *Business as Partners in Development: Executive Summary,* pp. 7, 10-11.
3. Linda Chavez, for example, had commented: "if Clinton has her way, Thursday's White House conference on child care will usher in a new era in which Uncle Sam takes on primary responsibility for minding the nation's children.... For years, Hillary Rodham Clinton has worked for greater government involvement in the lives of children. From her early law-review articles arguing that courts should recognize the full legal rights of minor children (including the right to sue their parents) to her work on the board of the Children's Defense Fund, ... Clinton has championed a greater government role in dictating how families function" ("Family feminism puts Uncle Sam in charge of our kids," *The Denver Post,* 22 Oct. 1997, p. 7B).
4. Barbara Vobjeda, The Washington Post, "Clinton unveils child-care plan," *The Denver Post,* 24 Oct. 1997, p. 2A.

complacency when crime and corruption are still growing.... The core issue is about changing attitudes and approach. It is about thinking and acting in non-traditional ways. It is about a new way of [global] governance—at both a societal and corporate level."[1] To this end, the organization sees the "need to activate a sense of common purpose on behalf of all sectors of society," which may be accomplished through "communications campaigns to inform, educate, motivate and in some cases mobilise the general public around specific ... issues."[2]

The *Executive Summary* of Business as Partners in Development "recommends that corporate leaders and their counterparts in international NGOs and development agencies work more closely together" to 1) "encourage national governments to develop ... partnership between the public and private sector," 2) "undertake joint awareness-raising and educational campaigns," 3) "identify and/or establish joint 'demonstration projects,'" 4) "support joint education and capacity-building exercises, based on [(e.g., 'woke')] experimental learning," 5) "invest in joint efforts to educate [(i.e., indoctrinate)] some of tomorrow's leaders by working with schools, universities and student organisations and developing teaching materials, mentoring programmes and other opportunities for today's decision-makers to inspire and inform tomorrow's."[3] "In this new world, the private sector has become the principal motor of [(e.g., socialist-fascist)] development and its [(satanic)] growth the test of [(e.g., communist-capitalist)] economic strength [(collapsible brittleness)].... [The] private sector can, and in numerous cases already is, playing a leadership role in moves towards sustainable development.... The growing strategic commitment to this new partnership [(with the Devil)] approach by leaders in business, government and international institutions, and the growing ... support from communities and NGOs, is a strong indication that we are witnessing the beginning of a new way of doing business. This way ... needs to be understood and strongly encouraged by governments and international institutions at all levels."[4]

Perhaps unsurprisingly, Satan's Prince was chosen to provide the opening message at the June 4, 1996, award ceremony of Habitat II, the UN Conference on Human Settlements. Awards, sponsored by the Tokyo Metropolitan Government and the Dubai Municipality, were presented for "best practices," which "represent solutions to pressing social, economic and environmental problems," as well as

---

1. Nelson, *Business as Partners in Development: Executive Summary,* p. 12.
2. Nelson, *Business as Partners in Development: Executive Summary,* p. 6.
3. Nelson, *Business as Partners in Development: Executive Summary,* p. 12.
4. Nelson, *Business as Partners in Development: Executive Summary,* back cover.

"a different approach to defining problems and finding solutions in true partnership between civil society, public and private enterprise." "Conferees said that the partnerships should include State and non-State actors—local authorities, the private sector, parliamentarians and non-governmental, community-based and international organizations," noting "the need to develop broad partnerships to tackle the growing problems of urban centres." The 'Best Practices' Initiative "was officially launched at the first substantive session of the Habitat II Preparatory Committee in Geneva in April 1944." According to Boutros Boutros-Ghali, recipients "demonstrate that positive change and sustainable human settlement development are indeed possible."[1]

Global Governance, the Global Security Programme, and a possible "Economic Security Council."

As the then-future "Head of the Armed Forces" of Britain, Charles stated, "We delude ourselves if we think that humanity is becoming ever more civilised, ever more sophisticated and ever more reasonable."[2] Rather: "There will always be dangerous, evil people, and people who will seek to take advantage of others in a weaker condition.... You only have to look at the way the world is now. It's becoming a far more dangerous place.... [The] one certainty is that we have to face the unexpected. Look at the [(then recent) Persian] Gulf War."[3] To Charles, as to so many governments, military forces constitute an "insurance policy."

Of greater interest, is the fact that **Satan's Prince envisions the need for a permanent standing UN army—*with himself as its head:*** "The Prince was tempted to argue for British troops to play a permanent role within the United Nations as a standing army, financed by member states. 'I foresee that we will have to play a policeman's role all over the world.' ... [The] Prince became the first public figure to suggest openly but tentatively that Britain might be 'paid' to provide its military services overseas. Knowing that to advocate openly a 'mercenary' role for the British armed forces was to court the charge that he was ready to see British soldiers die on foreign battlefields for alien causes, he countered that..., in any case, to play a leading part in a permanent United Nations force was an entirely honourable prospect. 'It wouldn't be an entirely mercenary army,' he insisted.... As head of the armed forces, the [(then)] Prince of Wales would inherit the Queen's role as a focus for their loyalty and

---

1. "Twelve Awards Presented for 'Best Practices' by Secretary-General" (Habitat II – 2 – Press Release HAB/IST/8 4th Meeting), pp. 1-2.
2. Dimbleby, *The Prince of Wales,* pp. 524-526. King Charles III holds *the topmost ranks* in each of the UK's armed services, and he wears their various military uniforms. He also is displays his Garter Star on them, as when prince (e.g., see Hoey, *Charles & Diana: The Tenth Anniversary,* pp. 74-75).
3. Ibid.

unity.... The Prince ... as King ... would be quite at ease in the role."[1] Charles III now is king—and the GreatTribulation *looms!*

Given the above, it should perhaps not surprise us to learn that Satan's Prince is said to have *personally* initiated the UN's **Global Security Programme**, which came out of Cambridge University, via Maurice Strong and others.[2] This program involves three agendas, one of which is a global neighborhood watch [(mass surveillance)] using the Internet. While one might be tempted to dismiss Charles' idea of mercenary UN forces, it meshes with what the Gorbachev Foundation advocated, in its 1994 "Global Security Programme" (non-American English) report, which Gorbachev himself delivered "to 300 distinguished members of the New York Council on Foreign Relations:" "Effective [(e.g., totalitarian)] measures are essential for restricting transfers, stockpiling and production of conventional arms [(e.g., private U.S. handguns, rifles, etc.)] through the establishment of an international authority and the imposition of a tax on their production and sale. The proceeds of the tax should go to the UN and, where appropriate, to [(Fourth Reich)] regional security organizations for their peace-keeping operations."[3]

In June 1995, Sir Shridath Ramphal, knighted co-chairman of the Commission on Global Governance, which is based at the University of Cambridge,[4] *stated that Satan's Prince personally inaugurated the Global Security Programme's lecture series established by his commission in 1993*, when he (Ramphal) then delivered the second "Global Security Lecture:" "Security in the Global Neighbourhood." More than that, however, Ramphal stressed the fact that both the commission and the programme are "at one with ... the Prince of Wales—in taking a broad, inclusive view of security." At the same time, Ramphal recommended the establishment of "an Economic Security Council as an apex global economic body within the UN system, but reaching beyond governments in its functioning," or "a global forum that can provide leadership in economic and social fields." But we know that is *already* more than one such forum, not least of which are the IBLF and the WEF (recall that Klaus Schwab likewise is Charles' knight), and *they* report to King Charles III. Other

---

1. Ibid.
2. For more information, see *Our Global Neighbourhood*, a two-volume UN book published by the Oxford University Press. It's free online: "https://en.wikipedia.org/wiki/Our_Global_Neighborhood" (see "https://www.gdrc.org/u-gov/global-neighbourhood") and "https://web.archive.org/web/20111227100 749/http://actrav.itcilo.org/actrav-english/telearn/global/ilo/globe/gove.htm". For Henry Lamb's "summary analysis" on *Our Global Neighborhood*, see "https://web.archive.org/web/20130130172538/ http://www.sovereignty.net/p/gov/gganalysis.htm" on the Internet.
3. "Mikhail Gorbachev unveils new *Global Security Programme*," Gorbachev Foundation USA, as reproduced by Gary Kah in *Hope for the World Update*, Fall 1995, pp. 3-4.
4. Recall that Charles is an honors graduate of Trinity College at Cambridge, where as prince he studied world history, archaeology, and anthropology.

early commission members included Maurice Strong, who was "a member of the Queen's Privy Council of Canada," as well as Barber Conable, Jacques Delors, Adele Simmons, and Brian Urquhart, all of whom, like Ramphal,[1] have or had direct or indirect associations with the British monarchy.[2] According to Ramphal:

> Nation states are not about to disappear, or the nation state system to lose its centrality. Yet something has happened on the way to the 21st century.... It is a transition to a new order and, as in all transitions, there is contention between old habits and perceptions and new realities and needs. All I say in this Lecture about security in our global neighbourhood is conditioned by this awareness....
>
> But I run ahead of myself. I must start truly by expressing my warm appreciation to the University [of Cambridge] and to the Global Security Programme for providing me this very special opportunity to speak to the theme of global governance. I thank particularly the Vice-Chancellor, Professor David Williams, and the Director of the Programme, Dr Prins. To be asked to give the Second Global Security Lecture is a great honour. I look on it as recognition of the work undertaken by the Commission on Global Governance, which I have had the privilege of serving as co-chairman together with Ingvar Carlsson, the Prime Minister of Sweden. **To give such a lecture is under any circumstance a challenge, but to have to follow His Royal Highness the Prince of Wales, who inaugurated this series of lectures two years ago,[3] both enlarges the honour and heightens the challenge....**

---

1. Ramphal has an impressive *monarchy-centered* background: "Shridath Ramphal, Guyana Secretary-General of the Commonwealth from 1975 to 1990, and Minister of Foreign Affairs and Justice of Guyana from 1972 to 1975. Currently the Chairman of the International Steering Committee of LEAD International—the international Leadership in Environment and Development Program; Chairman, Advisory Committee, Future Generations Alliance Foundation; and the Chancellor of the University of the West Indies and of the University of Warwick in Britain. Member of each of the five independent international commissions of the 1980s, and chairman of the West Indian Commission, which issued its report in 1992. President of the World Conservation Union-IUCN from 1991 to 1993, and author of *Our Country, The Planet,* written for the Earth Summit" (original source: "www.cgg.ch/members.htm"; current information on Ramphal and the Commission on Global Governance is available on the Internet).
2. "**Maurice Strong**, ... Chairman of the Earth Council. **Has received the Order of Canada and is a member of the Queen's Privy Council of Canada.** Secretary General of the 1992 UN Conference on Environment and Development in Rio, and of the 1972 Stockholm Conference on the Human Environment. Member of the World Commission on Environment and Development." "**Barber Conable**, United States President of the World Bank from 1986 to 1991.... Has served on the boards of multinational corporations...." "**Jacques Delors**, France President of the European Commission from 1985 to January 1995.... Member of the European Parliament and President of its Committee on Economic and Monetary Affairs (1979-81)." "**Adele Simmons**, ... an elected member of ... the Council on Foreign Relations. In 1993, appointed by the Secretary General of the UN to the High Level Advisory Board on Sustainable Development. From 1977 to 1989, ... she developed new programmes in population and health and in peace and international security. From 1978 to 1980, served on President Carter's Commission on World Hunger and from 1991 to 1992, on President Bush's Commission on Environmental Quality." "**Brian Urquhart**, United Kingdom.... Involved in the formation of the United Nations ... and served as Under Secretary General for Special Political Affairs from 1972 to 1986" (original source: "www.cgg.ch/members.htm"; current information on Ramphal and the Commission on Global Governance is available on the Internet).
3. Charles Gunawardena, speaking for the Commission on Global Governance, states, "The Prince of Wales inaugurated the Global Security Lecture series, established by the Cambridge Global Security Programme, in 1993" (written response to inquiry from the publisher).

The central theme of Global Security Studies, the quintessence of the Global Security Programme is 'survival' .It is on this note that I should like to start, because all too often the very notion of 'survival' with its connotations of apocalypse invites disbelief and dismissal as hyperbole. And yet those who framed this Programme did in my judgement dare to face up to the most vital issue of our time—humanity's most clear and present danger, and the prospects for those who should follow us....

The most inviolable of human rights is the right to life....[1]

We have already so depreciated our stock of ecological capital that we cannot deliver the planet to our heirs in pristine condition. That is the magnitude of our offence....

....Certainly, a new generation understands better than we ever did that the world is more than an assortment of sovereign states and separate peoples; that there is a human society beyond frontiers; that each of us does belong to two countries, our own and the planet....

The Commission on Global Governance was established in September 1992 [just months before Charles inaugurated its Global Security Programme lecture series], but the seeds were planted a few years earlier, in fact about the same time that the Global Security Programme was being set up in Cambridge. It was in 1989 that Willy Brandt, reflecting on the changing, post-Cold War landscape of international relations, began to give thought to the possibilities of arrangements to advance cooperation in a world freed of superpower tensions. Discussions at a meeting he convened in Konigswinter in January 1990 and at a somewhat broader gathering in Stockholm in April 1991 paved the way for the constitution of the Commission, with 28 members from almost as many countries....

We published our report in January—at the start of the UN 50th anniversary—calling it *Our Global Neighbourhood*: a signal we thought, of the kind of world that globalisation and technological change were creating.... **Security was high on our agenda of concerns as we viewed the state of the world and its people. But from the outset the Commission was at one with the Global Security Programme—and with the Prince of Wales—in taking a broad, inclusive view of security.** We were concerned with security in its conventional sense, of course, with **peace and security** and related issues such as disarmament and nuclear weapons on the one side and with such matters as peacekeeping on the other. We were also concerned about security in its economic and environmental dimensions, because our starting point was the security of people. But, beyond this, we were concerned with survival. 'Unprecedented increases in human activity and human numbers', we said, 'have reached the point where their impacts are impinging on the basic conditions on which life depends'.

....What the end of the post war era both allowed and required was work on 'how' we were going to manage human affairs so that in these and other fields of global endeavour we could answer the challenge of 'survival'. Our central task was to suggest how world governance could be developed and improved to enlarge the probabilities of success.

The present framework of global governance is essentially what was put in place around the end of World War II: at Dumbarton Oaks, at Bret-

---

1. Ramphal is referring not to the unborn here, but to the born.

ton Woods and finally at San Francisco.... The architecture of the global system is of the mid-1940s....

Consistent with the world of embattled states that shaped their ends at San Francisco, the UN's founders saw future dangers to peace and security arising essentially from conflict between nation states. It was the scourge of war between countries against which the United Nations would stand guard. Iraq's bid to grab Kuwait and its war against Iran are warnings that wars between states are not becoming extinct. But is it just the security of states and the integrity of frontiers that must concern us, when the higher probability today is that threats to the security of people will arise instead from situations within countries? Liberia, Rwanda, Somalia, the former Yugoslavia are all contemporary examples. There are others in the making. Is this not the very crux of our transition from a world of states to a world of people?...

....We must insist that, save only for self-defence, the use of force against countries is permissible only under the authority and control of the United Nations acting for our global community. That must be the basic norm of global security.... ....The Commission on Global Governance has attached critical importance to the <u>reform of the Security Council</u>; we have proposed ... to enlarge the Council in respect of both long- and short-term (or rotating) members to make it more representative of UN members without making it unwieldy.... We ... strongly ... favour ... strengthening the UN's peace-keeping and peace-making role and, as I have said, of forming a UN Volunteer Force to enable the UN to respond more promptly in emergency situations....

But we have gone further in our Report and called for concerted action to diminish accumulation and dispersal of conventional arms through treaty agreement to restrict arm sales and to prohibit the manufacture of a particularly insidious weapon that (as last week's conference in Cambodia highlighted) has brought death and suffering to hundreds of thousands of innocent people, namely landmines. And we call for a Demilitarization Fund to assist countries towards further demilitarization of the global neighbourhood....

....There is little moral difference between the legitimized sale of weapons of mass destruction [(WMDs)] to impoverished countries and the illegitimate sale by impoverished [(or communist)] countries of addictive drugs in the market places of the rich. [(For example: Mexico, China and Fentanyl.)] Our global neighbourhood would be a better one, and global security more realisable, without each of these evil traffickings....

....The global neighbourhood is not a mirage. Like all other neighbourhoods, it has to be good for all its people if in the longer term it is to be good for any....

The time has come, the Commission believes, to establish an Economic Security Council [(ESC)] as an apex global economic body within the UN system, but reaching beyond governments in its functioning. It is palpable that the world needs a global forum that can provide leadership in economic and social fields.... We envisage that the essential function for an Economic Security Council would be to continuously assess the overall state of the world economy and the interaction between major policy areas; provide a long-term strategic policy framework in order to promote stable, balanced and sustainable development; and secure consistency between the policy goals of

the major international economic organizations, particularly the Bretton Woods bodies and the World Trade Organization....[1]

The Group of 7 might claim to be such an apex body. However, the G7 a self-constituted club of the nominally richest countries created to look after their own rather than global interests. But there are other reasons which go to the heart of the G7's inadequacies as a world economic directorate. ...China is the third largest economy after the United States and Japan; India is the fifth, ahead of France, Italy and Britain, with Brazil, Russia, Mexico and Indonesia in the first twelve, ahead of Canada.... The rich have yet to come to terms with the reality of economic multipolarity. An Economic Security Council will both reflect that reality and respond to its new challenges, which are at heart the challenges of globalisation. The Economic Security Council, we believe, has now become an essential part of the structure of global governance.

In the ultimate analysis global security, the security of people, of countries and of civilisation itself rests on planetary security.... Global security at its most basic level is now about survival on an endangered planet. The cumulative consequences of global warming, ozone shield depletion, rising consumption, population explosion, and other emerging critical stresses could lead to human extinction....

....More apposite is the analogy of a tree dying from acid rain. For humanity, it is the tree of life that is endangered. Whether it dies altogether, or withers but clings to life, or loses its leaves and branches yet survives to bloom again, depends on our responses to the blight that afflicts it in the form of the crisis of environment and development—the crisis of global security.

As with other forms of global security there is a governance dimension to planetary security, and we have begun to acknowledge this. **Ever since the UN's Stockholm Conference on the Human Environment in 1972, and with sharpened intensity since the Brundtland Commission's Report** *Our Common Future* **in 1987 and the Earth Summit in Rio** five years later, **we have been addressing some of these governance issues**.[2] But, as the [(then)] recent Conference in Berlin on the Climate Change Convention shamefully demonstrated, we have done so invariably in half measure, wanting to both have our planet and devour it. We espouse sustainable development as a virtue, but find it too demanding a creed to live by....

The Commission on Global Governance calls for a new level of response. We propose that the Trusteeship Council created in 1945 to administer territories in transition to independence be given a new mandate —to be trustees of the global commons and of the planet's life support systems....

We see the Trusteeship Council in its new role becoming the principal world forum for environmental matters, with its functions including the

---

1. While such an Economic Security Council could be formed from the existing UN Economic and Social Council—as suggested on January 26, 2000 by its outgoing President, Francesco Paolo Fulci of Italy— one would likely be hard-pressed to better describe the Prince of Wales [International] Business Leaders *Forum* (now "replaced" by IBLF Global) or even Business as Partners in Development. Either one could instead serve in the described capacity. Additionally, in many ways, Business as Partners in Development is an offshoot of the Prince of Wales Business Leaders *Forum*.

2. Recall that Charles as Prince of Wales, was personally credited for the success of the Rio Earth Summit. For more information, see this chapter's earlier section titled, "Environmentalism, the Rio Earth Summit, and the Kyoto Protocol," at p. 402.

administration of environmental treaties in such fields as climate change, biodiversity, outer space and the oceans. There is no higher trusteeship than that of planetary security. Our systems of governance must reflect this primacy and provide authority for fulfilling it.

....The rule of law has been a critical civilising force in every free society. It is what distinguishes an authoritarian from a democratic society, what secures liberty and justice against oppression, what elevates equality above dominion....

....When the founders of the United Nations drew up the Charter they genuflected at the altar of the rule of law.... ....The development of international law could have been a major chapter of the post-war era; it was to be a mere footnote. The era was characterised instead by the rule of military power and economic strength.... We must strive to ensure that the global neighbourhood of the future is characterised by law not lawlessness; by rules which all must respect; by the reality that all, even the weakest, are equal under the law; that none, even the most powerful, is above the law. We made proposals to that end.

For 45 years the Cold War held humanity in thrall threatening 'mutual assured destruction'—our 'double-speak' for human survival.... [The] threat itself arose out of human failure to devise saner approaches to global security.

And now, released from the compulsions of the nuclear arms race and the larger tensions of the Cold War, we are failing to capture the 'peace dividend'. Five years after the end of the Cold War, the world is more tense, more fragile, more unstable, and its people more fearful and uncertain. Humanity remains an endangered species.... On the eve of a new century and a new millennium, we probably have less reason for assurance than our ancestors had ... that we are passing on to future generations the right to life....

That we urgently need a new universal ethic of survival and a reordering of global priorities appears no longer to be in doubt. That ethic of survival will require us to recognize how we have ravaged the planet and endangered its life forms, including our species. It will require us to acknowledge that we could nullify all of humanity's incomparable achievements unless we change course. It will require us to consider how we stand poised between a new globalism, heralding a more civilized society governed by the rule of enforceable law worldwide, and a return to old instincts of power, arbitrariness, and selfcentred nationalism.

Does it matter if we fail to rise to the challenge of survival? In cosmic terms, perhaps not. Whatever the manner of our going, Earth will heal her wounds, however grievous; our planet's flora and fauna, however transfigured, will have a better chance to survive and flourish because we have gone....

But surely that cannot be our conclusion. What of our duty to humanity itself, to our own worthiest qualities and the highest purposes of human existence; what of our trust to the generations that should succeed us? Homo sapiens has a duty to sustain life that transcends our capacity to destroy it.... As the Cambridge Global Security Programme, as your Global Security Studies dictate, it is time we 'begin to find ourselves'.[1]

---

1. Sir Shridath Ramphal, "Security in the Global Neighbourhood: The Second Global Security Lecture," June 1995.

Wow. That is just *one* global security lecture. We may well ask, "What exactly is Satan's Prince unleashing upon the world?"

Insanity by design. We live in "a world going mad." But how is that occurring? Actually, it is largely perpetrated through surreptitious use of intelligence apparatuses, *turned inward.* The U.S., for example, has its CIA, NSA, etc. But those tie to British "intelligence," which is under the Crown. (Later, we'll look more closely at the Crown.) We'll here use the CIA as one example of "how things work," under Satan—where those who serve God, get *no* security.

Since before 1952, the CIA has been "controlling an individual to the point where he will do our bidding against his will."[1] This is accomplished through Operation Mockingbird as well as other media and entertainment controls, whereby propaganda (e.g., *provided* "stories and biases") are peddled not only to the world, but to the U.S. public as well. The CIA employs compromised, amoral, and even possessed and outright satanic individuals (e.g., Demon-rat politicians and their controlled "opposition"), to direct or even effectively control influential and powerful companies.

Operation Mockingbird initially served to print fake stories and fake interviews the CIA wanted to feed the public. From there, it morphed to try to completely control the "news" narrative on any and every subject, about which "they" cared. As past CIA director Willaim J. Casey put it, "We'll know our disinformation program is complete when everything the American public believes is false." (Operation Mockingbird is ongoing.)

Of course, Satan's minions "forget" that The Truth finally prevails (always), and He is greater than their master. So long as Christians remain alive in the world, the Devil's lies *cannot* fully prevail. (This may be a reason that under *the* AntiChrist, Christians will find themselves being wholesale slaughtered.)

In 1996, the CIA established the Entertainment Liaison Office to penetrate Hollywood, which is ostensibly named after "Christmas holly" (i.e., toxic holly bushes bearing toxic red berries). With that done, every form of spiritual wickedness was portrayed and ostensibly used, to include druidry, satanism, mind-altering drugs, and perhaps even some clandestine mind-affecting weapons. Words having dual meanings and applications became common, such as programming (brainwashing), entertainment (entrainment), and television (tell a vision).

---

1. Ca. 0:31:49 to 0:32:28 (see 0:28:43 to 0:36:49), Brian Rose, "Plandemic – Indoctrination," *London Real,* 18 Aug. 2020, as published at "https://freedomplatform.tv/plandemic-indoctornation-world-premiere" on the Internet.

Operation Mockingbird has always gone far beyond Hollywood, compassing every form of "news" entity in the U.S. In fact, former military personnel, including intelligence officers, directly or indirectly founded the major U.S. TV "news" organizations, and their successors control them still. Compromise and control has always been "the game," whether through politicians, sex "honeypots," entertainment (TV shows, movies), publishing (books, "news," magazines, comics), video games (violence, "aliens," etc.), or music.

This is one means the Crown employs to influence and control the U.S. public—including by "divide and conquer" strategies. There are additional means (as herein seen), and the U.S. is not unique globally in that the Crown employs similar tactics around the world. We may come across something like this: "'It's cancel culture coming to our news media and our sources of information,' said David Johnson, CEO of Strategic Vision PR Group. 'It's an orchestrated attack, not just by Democrats, but also by other left-wing networks to silence conservative voices completely. It's an attempt at almost outright censorship.'"[1] But what we are dealing with, is vastly more complex, vastly larger.

The WEF—with its implementation of *Charles'* Great Reset agenda—is a major example not only of steering the public, but of actively seeking to control the whole world. The WEF pushes a toxic mixture of global socialism, fascism and communism under Charles, as *the* AntiChrist; elitist totalitarian global governance is the real aim of the Great Reset or NWO. And they are succeeding among those who parrot their satanic "build back better" mantra. The faux problems they allege, and the ones they actually foment or create, serve only to enable faux "solutions," so that they may further enslave.

Like Satan's Democratic Party in the U.S., WEF elitists seek to 1) take away your defenses (e.g., personal guns, by which to protect oneself against tyranny), 2) inhibit and destroy national safety (e.g., by removing all sensible border controls, so as to enable Muslim terrorists, Latin American murderers, rapists, pimps, prostitutes, child traffickers, drug dealers and violent gang members to flood and irreparably harm western societies, in addition to adding "cheap" labor to *illicitly and criminally* steal identities, and take needed jobs and public resources from lawful citizenry), 3) undermine, destroy and then supplant all free press and discourse (e.g., by silencing truth-tellers through fake "news" media and controlled anti-social "social networks" like Fakebook and Twitster) and curated (e.g., by AI) Internet search results and even censorship of "offending" pages,

---

1. Marisa Herman, "House Democrats Target Newsmax, Fox News for De-platforming From Cable," *News-Max*, 22 Feb. 2021.

4) take away our free speech rights (e.g., by declaring conservatives and Christians to be the new "domestic terrorists"), 5) suppress all "disagreeable" freedom of conscience, undermining and eliminating actual religious and spiritual freedoms simultaneously (e.g., by imposing sexually-abominable homo-fascist "equality" and the literal lunacy that is so-called "transgenderism"), 6) severely curtail freedom to peaceably assemble (e.g., by arresting peaceful protesters while tolerating or even *endorsing* BLM and fascist "Anti-Fa" criminal thugs, who are actual domestic terrorists), 7) take away freedom to work (e.g., by imposing dishonest and illicit, as well as unconstitutional in the U.S., "lockdowns") and incentive to work (e.g., with "public" money providing everyone a "basic income"), 8) take away school choice as well as freedom to be schooled, while suppressing real history (e.g., by canceling the Trump Administration's 1776 Commission) to push lies, 9) take away freedom of movement (e.g., by mandating "green" or immunization "passports" or "documents") and even public exercise, 10) take away freedom to *responsibly and cleanly* employ land to produce goods and get buried resources (e.g., by *unnecessarily* nationalizing excessive territories to "protect" the environment and wildlife), 11) take away individual and family freedoms to grow food to consume or sell (e.g., by acquiring all the best farmland on Earth, so that someone like Bill Gates is now a—or the—top U.S. farmland owner), 12) eliminate freedom to actually control one's own body (e.g., by mandating potentially deadly DNA-altering mRNA therapeutics, besides ostensibly unsafe actual vaccines), 13) curtail freedom to breath (e.g., by mandating unhealthy long-term use of face masks and coverings) and tax *our* "carbon pollution," and 14) take away your moral authority (e.g., by using your tax dollars to finance infanticide, promotion of bestial sex such as sodomy and lesbianism, "sex change" mutilations, and insanities like "transgenderism"). No doubt, the above list is *incomplete.* Oh yes, they want to eliminate your financial security as well, by printing money backed by nothing while "drugging you" with ever-increasing government "cares-for-you" "largess"—until you spend your last pence for a fallen crumb, and no longer own anything! But hey, they assure, you'll "be happy!" Who could ask for more?

Satanic globalists and other elitists are often *total-control freaks and psychopaths.* Why? To start, *many of them objectively serve Satan,* having rejected God in Christ Jesus. Beyond that, they also suffer from *extreme insecurity,* putting *no* faith in God our Creator. But God is love, and *faith is intrepid,* being *without fear.* (This author was divinely called from the "crucible" of USAFA's class of 1988 —whose motto is *Fides Intrepida,* or "Faith Has No Fear," as inscribed on his class ring.) It is written: "But without faith *it is* impossible to please *Him,* for he who comes to God must believe that He is, and *that* He is a rewarder of those who diligently seek Him" (Heb 11:6). God's saints exercise such faith: "There is no fear in love; but perfect love casts out fear, because fear involves torment. But he who fears has not been made perfect in love" (1 John 4:18). Yet, the Devil's pathological "leaders" and sycophants cannot find, buy or provide enough "safe spaces"—or "liberal" (i.e., freakishly totalitarian) places where their oh-so tender ears are not offended by The Truth, or by (pretty much) *any* real modicum of spiritual or moral truth. Yes, such *anti-social* "socialists" (and Marxists and neo-fascists) insist upon *silencing* those with whom they disagree—*because actual debate of issues, let alone in public, is beyond their capacities: the real facts actually defeat them!*

Paul Joseph Watson observes, "While society is handed over to deranged, infantilized cry babies, who think 'hate speech' is challenging their stupid opinions, hysterical authoritarian clowns have seized control of the new public square—and conservatives did nothing to stop it!"[1] Yes, we are talking about the most serious of moral retards, spiritual idiots, and satanists "by any other name." Most of them *mean to do, what they do.* These are they who *invert, pervert and mock reality* (see Isa 5:18-21, 5:23), "who practice lawlessness" (see Matt 7:15-22), who *choose* to ignore God and His righteousness (cf. Isa 5:23-24), who increasingly *insist* that *you and your family* believe and behave *as they do.* They may even demand that "agreement" upon severe penalties, up to and including death. Indeed, increasingly as The LORD's return draws near (see Matt 24:12), such lawless "moral retards," and the vicious "packs" in which they (often rancorously) cavort as "ravenous wolves" (cf. Matt 7:15), are *willfully irrational*—even *willfully insane.* Theirs is a world of "rules for thee, not for we," "rules for you, not for us;" "rules for the 'outs,' not the 'ins.'" To them, laws are solely to manipulate and control their "enemies," defined and identified as whomever they view as "disagreeable," because *they are superior* and part of the oligarchic "in crowd"—an oligarchy of *sin and satanism.* In their minds, Truth is *only* valid when it is convenient *to them,* and their "conveniences" may and do "acceptably" shift with the weather, winds and sands (cf. Matt 7:24-27).

For the sort of people we've just been addressing, there is a "new" word—one long ago foretold by Christ Jesus, as we're going to see. It's the word "woke." Today, being "woke" means *fomenting societal divisions through racism*—such as the kind embodied in

---

1. Paul Joseph Watson, "Banned by Facebook & Instagram," *YouTube.com,* 2 May 2019.

Marxist-fomented "divide and conquer" "Critical [Race] Theory" (CT and CRT) and sexual satanism's "Gender Identity" (GI). In Orwellian terms, CRT and GI are also called "Social Emotional Learning" (SEL).[1] Some might want to skip the discussion on "wokeness" and SEL—except for the fact that they are employed to upend "free" countries—ultimately, to try to force them into the coming "global government" of the foretold AntiChrist. So, let's take a hard look, to better recognize, and thus more effectively resist, what the Devil is trying so hard to accomplish in our midst (e.g., in the U.S.).

Sexual satanism, which compasses GI, is something this author addresses in troubling detail in his book titled *The Great Reset: To Digitally Enslave, Depopulate, and Transhumanize.* So we won't here significantly do so, but will instead focus our attention on CRT.

Adhering to CRT's major tenets, which derive from CT, is now "trendily" called "wokeness"—a term with surprising *scriptural import,* as this author below reveals. But CRT or social "wokeness" is demonstrably just *an extension of Critical Theory's or CT's "rules for thee, not for me" mentality.* Many have witnessed its increase in popularity among individuals who are (literally and bizarrely) *detached from reality,* objectively irrational and spiritually deluded, who (often openly) act as *racist bullies and even Marxist "change agents"*—while hypocritically imagining themselves, despite being *amoral, godless and unthinking rebels,* to somehow represent "enlightenment." We are talking about people whose intellectual *and* emotional intelligence and development have been spiritually *sabotaged* or even *outright truncated and broken* by the Devil's "invert everything" minions. As anarchists who reject objective truth, they are morally bankrupt and mentally compromised—and under their spiritual father the Devil, they now do everything to push a redefined and outright Orwellian (e.g., Marxist and otherwise bullying) version of "equity." In that, what they really proffer is differing and thus *unjust* "weights and measures"—something The LORD plainly calls "abominable | detestable" (see Prov 20:10, Heb.; cf. e.g., Lev 19:11-18 and 19:34-36).

The "rules for thee" crowd often believes they may do *anything* (morals do *not* apply to them), with "the rule of the jungle" (i.e., fallen nature) or "anything goes" carnality, simply so long as they are *not* caught—or those who do apprehend them, *approve of their*

---

1. Christopher Alexander observes: "The ultimate goal of SEL, as with CRT and GI, is to replace parents with the State, individual dignity with the "collective consciousness", and equal rights under the law with notions of institutional racial and gender victimhood. Every one of Louisiana's earliest learners will fit neatly into either the class of "oppressors" or the class of "victims" based solely upon race or gender" ("Top Louisiana Education Board Must Protect Children from CRT and Anti-American Lies — Window of Opportunity Coming Up," *Gateway Pundit,* 5 Jan. 2023).

evil (cf. Rom 1:32). Through criminal conduct, they work to destroy whole societies—from undermining the family unit, education, work environments, and governance, to (literally) looting, burning and destroying the same; their goal is nothing less than to "bring down the whole system," so that they may supplant it with their own satanism and totalitarianism.

But their CT-based "change" efforts will often *start mildly, and thus under the radar of all but the most observant.* They may lead their assault with vague claims of in-place "systems of power and oppression," or unjust hegemonies that must be overcome—and then escalate from there, to criticizing, shaming and ostracizing.[1] That's just to start. Deflection, redefinition of language and whatever revisionism, historical or otherwise, suits their aims, is all just part of their evil playbook. Though ostensibly "earnest," what we see is that honesty and basic sense give way to categorizing people, entities and even nations into "oppressor" and "oppressed," creating division where there had been little to none—and then enacting (often harsh) "consequences." Eventually, their victims may realize that the dishonest accusers and judges are *not* playing with a genuine or even "full deck," but using one purpose-built to cheat, steal and destroy, in which little is as it may outwardly seem.

Of this *dystopian* ideological subversion, Grace Daniel explains:

> "These ["divide and conquer" Marxist] theories basically divide society into two groups: oppressor and oppressed. If you are white, straight, male, and/or wealthy, you are an oppressor. If you are a racial minority, [sinful] gay or trans, a woman or [delusionally] identify as some 'other' [alleged] gender, and financially not wealthy, you are oppressed. The objective of Critical Theory is to defeat oppressors and overturn the system that benefits them.
>
> Those who have embraced the tenets of Critical Theory are colloquially referred to as "social justice warriors," or simply "woke." (It's important to note that most … wouldn't identify themselves as "critical theorists"). Whatever they are called…, they share the conviction that they have acquired a "critical consciousness" that enables them to rightly perceive systems of power and [(racial)] oppression unseen by others (hence, being "woke"). This [anti-facts, irrational] belief governs all of their actions. …
>
> [Theirs] … is an anti-objectivity ideology: One of its fundamental assertions is that there are no objective truths, only "positional" truths. … Bearing that in mind, you can throw out your notions of engaging in classical discourse where the best idea will emerge victorious. Your ideas are not on trial—*you are.*
>
> Your "woke" assailants will accuse *you* of ineptitude, the inability to perceive reality, or even immorality based on your identity—by which I mean, the characteristics you can't change about yourself. Your identity

---

1. Grace Daniel, "My Woke Employees Tried to Cancel Me. Here's How I Fought Back and Saved My Nonprofit," *Daily Signal*, 7 June 2021.

can even disqualify you from talking about certain subjects. For example, they will demand your silence in conversations on race if you are deemed "white" or even "white adjacent." They will suggest you do "harm" or "violence" if you are "cis-gendered" [(i.e., identify with your birth sex)] and attempt to engage in conversation on "gender identity." This ... is a result of the presupposition ... that all truth is "positional." Therefore, only those who have a certain "social position" due to their [actual or claimed] identity can perceive or speak truth on [related] topics.... Don't take the [prejudged we-win, you lose] bait....

Keep the dialogue on the faultiness of their ideas.... Your opponents will cry foul no matter your speech or behavior. Claims of "harm" [or "violence"] will be made simply on account of certain ideas being brought into the conversation or [imagined] sacrosanct commitments ... being challenged. ... Insist that terms be defined clearly from mutually agreed upon authoritative sources or fruitful engagement will be impossible.

It was revealing to me that our ["woke"] team members not only resisted the traditional definition of science, but indicated our adherence to it was a symptom of "white supremacy" that contributed to the disenfranchisement and harm of entire groups of people. ... As soon as I insisted ... on evidence-based principles, many of the emotional and irrational attacks ... lost their effect. ... The [(unrepentant)] staff members who disagreed ... ultimately left the organization, [falsely] accusing us of perpetuating ongoing harm. ...

It's not a [practical] matter of "agreeing to disagree." As our cultural and academic institutions are captured..., the [real-world] impacts will be on the most vulnerable. ... Wherever you have a sphere of influence, you have an important role to play in combatting the toxic effects of <u>ideological subversion</u>.[1]

The satanic CT and CRT "cabal" represents the rebellious "broad ... way that leads to destruction" (see Matt 7:13-14)—that is, to eternal damnation and punishment in Hell. In Satan's realm, "woke" "cabal" members, or CT and CRT adherents, feel they have the right or *privilege* to *negatively* judge as well as falsely accuse others whose *skin color,* and thus *presumed* ethnic "bent," differs from their own—especially if the other's physical color is "white." When the "woke" accusers fallaciously allege and denounce so-called "white privilege," for example, it is really *they* who, as brazen hypocrites and actual racists, are disturbingly guilty.

Despite its moral and spiritual destructiveness and falsehood, intentionally-divisive CRT is being surreptitiously *forced* upon school children—a process that has been underway in the United States, for years. This damaging and damnable CRT indoctrination is now largely achieved through intentionally *falsified* historical accounts (e.g., those of the "1619 Project")—virtually as a form of planned Marxist propaganda. Such dishonest accounts in the U.S., for exam-

---

1. Ibid.

ple, deride and defame major historical aspects of the nation from its inception, undermining its very foundation while employing revisionist confabulations and racially-motivated "liberal" indoctrination (e.g., under Marxist and socialist so-called "progressives").

Parents who question or reject CRT's lies and "whiteness" race-baiting, wherein "law" *allegedly* institutionalizes social, economic and political inequities between "whites" and non-whites, are (often) bullied into silence or submission. They face orchestrated smear campaigns *designed to destroy,* wherein they are scandalously accused of racism (e.g., being "white supremacists")—and whatever else comes from thinking-deficient, but "creative" hypocrites, many of whom have been (foolishly) entrusted with the safety, well-being and education of children in the nation's public schools.[1] This "cooked up" opposition to imagined "whiteness," which has gone largely unchecked by inattentive and easily led masses, now spoils all levels and many institutions of society.

Is all this really about racism? Or are these things *part of a coordinated attack up the Judaeo-Christian ethos of Christianity*—and thus Christianity itself? What about "Jews" and Israel? Is it also an attack upon God as Creator and Judge? Indeed, "wokeness" correspondingly attacks the very ethical foundations of "Western" civilizations—and special (divine) creation. Let's take a closer look.

A North Korean escapee came to the U.S. to experience a quality college education, but instead encountered a "woke" agenda that makes even the most brutal communist regime on Earth—that of North Korea—seem sane by comparison:

> Yeonmi Park knows what real oppression looks like. ... "Yeonmi Park attended Columbia University and was immediately struck by what she viewed anti-Western sentiment ... and a focus on political correctness that had her thinking 'even North Korea isn't this nuts.' ... "Park, 27, transferred to Columbia University from a South Korean university in 2016.... 'I expected that I was paying this fortune, all this time and energy, to learn how to think. But they are forcing you to think the way they want you to think,' Park said.... 'I realized, wow, this is insane. I thought America was different, but I saw so many similarities to what I saw in North Korea, that I started worrying.' ... 'You guys have lost common sense to [a] degree that I as a North Korean cannot even comprehend,' she said. ... 'There's no rule of law, no morality, nothing is good or bad anymore, it's complete chaos.' 'I guess that's what they want, to destroy every single thing and rebuild into a Communist paradise.'" In those few short sentences, she brilliantly

---

1. As but one of several citable examples at this point, see William A. Jacobson, "Update: Smear of Mom Nicole Solas Was Prepared By Public Relations Firm Hired By South Kingstown (RI) School Committee," *Legal Insurrection,* 9 June 2021, at "https://legalinsurrection.com/2021/06/update-smear-of-mom-nicole-solas-was-prepared-by-public-relations-firm-hired-by-south-kingstown-ri-school-committee" on the Internet.

summed up where we are as a society. ... A big reason why most Americans can't see the bigger picture is because the brainwashing is not just limited to our schools. The left has completely taken over big media ... too.... At this point, America has become an "idiocracy," where most people just willingly accept whatever they are told to think. Those that choose to think for themselves are considered to be "troublemakers," and ... we have witnessed an unprecedented campaign of censorship that is designed to shut such people up. What the elite want are vast herds of mindless "sheeple" that will never be capable of standing up for themselves....."[1]

Her professors gave students "trigger warnings," sharing the wording from [class] readings in advance..., Park told The *[New York] Post.* "Going to Columbia, the first thing I learned was 'safe space,'" she said. "Every problem, they explained [to] us, is because of 'white men.'" Some of the discussions of "white privilege" reminded her of ... her native country, where people were categorized based on their ancestors.... Cancel culture and shouting down opposing voices is ... self-censorship.... "Voluntarily, these [U.S.] people are censoring each other, silencing each other, no force behind it," she said. "Other times (in history) there's a military coup d'etat, like a force comes in taking your rights away and silencing you. But this country is choosing to be silenced, choosing to give their rights away." Park said she knows what a country could become with rights and discourse stripped away. "North Korea was pretty insane," she said. ... Park ... said Americans are obsessed with oppression, even though there is not much oppression they've witnessed firsthand. ... "I don't know why people are collectively going crazy like this, or together at the same time. ... In some ways they (in the US) are brainwashed. Even though there's evidence so clearly in front of their eyes, they can't see it."[2]

Truth, objectivity, and sanity in society, are now at stake in ways formerly almost unimaginable. STEM (Science, Technology, Engineering and Mathematics) disciplines are being dumbed-down to satisfy the lazy and incompetent "woke" crowd. This is occurring even at "vaunted" institutions. Harvard's "wokies," for example, allege "racism is embedded in science," and so seek to promote "equity" in mathematics. How? By *dumbing-down tests* of course, so that those who have failed to study and do their homework may "pass" them anyway—as if "racism" were somehow the reason for their (actual) failing scores! Christopher Sanfilippo, adding women to the mix, comments: "It's both condescending and an open admission that diversity is more important than rigorous education. Is it lamentable that some years Math 55 has no women? Perhaps. But that is preferable to encouraging students to take it who may not succeed, or lowering the standards for all."[3] The School of Engineer-

---

1. Michael Snyder, "A North Korean Defector Says That The Brainwashing In U.S. Schools Is Similar To The Brainwashing In North Korean Schools," *The Most Important News,* 14 June 2021.

2. Mark Moore and Mark Lungariello, "North Korean defector slams 'woke' US schools," *New York Post,* 14 June 2021.

3. Christopher Sanfilippo, "Is Harvard Sacrificing Science for Wokeness?," *RealClear Science,* 30 June 2021.

ing and Applied Science (SEAS) wants "a comprehensive training program" for all members of SEAS to address "bias, privilege, inclusive leadership, gender identity, etc."[1] Sanfilippo rhetorically asks, "But what does this have to do with engineering?," concluding that ensuring "wokeness" has become "more important than rigorous education" at Harvard, adding, "Rational inquiry and the scientific method will be sacrificed to the new idols: [(racist)] diversity, equity, and inclusion."[2] Of course, Harvard is at best just a "canary in the coal mine" of today's "woke" (and often sexually perverse) indoctrinating "education" establishments.

> As Manhattan Institute's Christopher Rufo explains..., "critical race theory" reformulates the Marxist dialectic of oppressor and oppressed, "replacing the class categories of bourgeoisie and proletariat with the identity categories of white and Black". In simple terms, critical race theory can be seen as a form of "race-based Marxism". This appears to be why these exiles, who have known Marxism in their own countries, are alarmed by seeing how its racial version of "oppressor and oppressed" is spreading....
>
> According to [Lei] Zhang, [Professor of Physics at Winston Salem State University]: "When they tell [young] kids ... that they are bad because they are in this race, or they are oppressed if they are in this group, and children cannot disagree, this is very bad because they cannot change their skin color or where they are from. They did not choose to be this..., [but] we are all Americans, and if we are fighting each other over this [ludicrous] ideology, I agree ... that this will destroy America." ... Fast forward to ... 2021. ... "The USSR is no longer on the map," [Anna] Krylov, [who though born in the Soviet Union, is now a chemistry professor at the University of California,] recalls. "But I find myself experiencing its legacy..., as if I am living in an Orwellian twilight zone. I witness ever-increasing attempts to subject science and education to ideological control and censorship. Just as in Soviet times, the censorship is being justified by the [alleged] 'greater good'. Whereas in 1950, the 'greater good' was advancing the [communist] World Revolution, in 2021 the greater good is 'Social Justice'.... We are told that in order to build a better world [(cf. Satan's 'build back better' or '6-6-6' mantra and anti-God platitude)] and to address societal inequalities, we need to purge our literature [(and remove or destroy statues, art, etc.)].... We can succumb to extreme left ideology and spend the rest of our lives ghost-chasing and witch-hunting, rewriting history, politicizing science, redefining elements of language, and turning STEM (Science, Technology, Engineering, and Mathematics) education into a farce. Or we can uphold a key principle ... —the free and uncensored exchange of ideas— and continue our core mission, the pursuit of truth, focusing attention on solving real, important problems of humankind."
>
> It is vitally important to listen to what those who have escaped from repressive governments say and write. They have lived through personal intimidation, political propaganda, brainwashing at schools and universities, and intellectual terror for a "wrong" word, book or idea. Today, those

1. Ibid.
2. Ibid.

who fled from Communist regimes see — most dangerously — the same censorship and totalitarian suppression repeated in America's democracy.[1]

Today's anti-truth "wokeism" extends beyond the United States. Similar satanic agendas are at play in other nations, even ones which have historically stood against, and overcome communism, fascism and totalitarianism. In fact, we are now also seeing the fruits of communist plots in, and activities against the West, for example, in the United Kingdom and much of Europe.

You may be surprised to learn that "wokeism" and its attendant CRT madness *literally fulfill Jesus' prophetic warning:* He told us, "ethnicity shall waken | awaken | be woke | rise against ethnicity," as recorded in Matthew 24:7, Mark 13:8 and Luke 21:10, Gk. Isn't that amazing? It suggests that "woke" racism is to become *global.*

Today, that malevolence arguably starts against Israel, and then it turns toward God's Church, which is being and has been infiltrated by tares, wolves in sheep's clothing, and goats. As we know, those are counterfeit "brothers" and "sisters" sown by the enemy of our souls, whose real purpose is to foment anti-scripture and antiChristian divisions and destructions, undermining and greatly damaging biblical "family units" (i.e., families who would serve God faithfully) and indeed whole church bodies. Eventually, though, it becomes a direct attack upon God as Creator—something that may surprise many.

Indeed, we also now see and experience an epidemic of children who wickedly dishonor and abandon their parents, often in great falsehood,[2] while other parents do not provide for, but in comparable evil, abandon their children. Such sin may be *worse* than murder, as God's commandment to honor one's parents, *precedes* His commandment against murder (Ex 20:12-13)—while one who "does not provide for *their* own, and especially for those of *their* household, has denied the faith and is worse than an unbeliever" (per 1 Timothy 5:8). Consider the mission of Elijah, who shall soon return as one of God's two apocalyptic witnesses: see Malachi 4:5-6.

Of the modern nation of Israel, Michael Mostyn comments:

> There are ever-mounting efforts underway, including by people who consider themselves part of a "progressive" movement asserting human rights for minorities — a noble aim in principle — to single out only one country, Israel, and its national movement, Zionism, for [international] vilification. Delegitimizing rhetoric seeking to portray Israel as a "settler-colonialist" enterprise imbued with "white supremacy" is hurled with feverish abandon

---

1. Giulio Meotti, "'If You Do Not Have Free Speech You Are Not Free:' Refugees from Communism Horrified at America," *Gatestone Institute,* 18 July 2021.
2. This author's own daughters have done this, and he knows other parents who similarly suffer.

— but is unhinged from fact and history. We're in the realm here not of reason, but of a quasi-religious cult of incantation.... One doesn't "colonize" one's [historically] native [(and scripturally promised)] land. One returns home.... [The] ... obsessive anti-Israel crowd abroad is doubling down on its [(virulently evil)] determination — delusional as it may be — to see things move in the opposite direction: the imposition of discriminatory, hostile measures, leading to the destruction of Israel. As to this crowd's ludicrous linking of Zionism with "white supremacy," consider this — the majority of Jewish Israelis come from the Arab and Muslim Middle East [(and their skin is not white)].... The challenge to those "social justice warriors" who are intent on sweeping up others, in their anti-Israel mania, is this: How ... can you deny that Jews are a people with the right to self-determination in their ancestral homeland? What is that refusal other than [actual] bigotry and hatred?[1]

In great irony, some unregenerate and degenerate (i.e., non-Christian) Israelites are foolishly at the forefront of pushing Satan's racist anti-"whiteness" agenda—just as they have been and are pushing anti-God and death-worthy infanticide, abominable sexual perversions, like reproduction-destroying and mutilating "transgender" lunacies, packaged as "LGBTQI+," where "I" apparently stands for "non-binary" "genders!"[2] (If left to their childish "devices," these folks would eventually run out of letters and numbers to twist, with which to further confuse the world's other dunces and dupes.) Yes, there are those anti-God "Jews" who both engender and promote those who are "twice the children of Hell" (cf. Matt 23:15; Jude 1:12 {see 1:10-19}).[3] (Instead of turning to God our Creator through Messiah Yeshua / Christ Jesus, they prostitute themselves to the Devil's minions and their evil agendas, as if embracing such could somehow "benefit." They *lack* spiritual discernment, while foolishly rejecting The Truth. Israel's national crucifixion fast approaches.[4])

What about the Church? Todd Starnes speaks to the recent history of one well-known denomination, thus:

For a decade now, a number of young pastors have been indoctrinated in some Baptist seminaries with their minds filled with ideas like "social justice." Conservatives [(i.e., Christian baptists)] made a crucial mistake during those years; they ... ignored the problem. Had they taken the time to attend annual meetings and engage..., [Christian] conservatives might

---

1. Michael Mostyn, "We Are Entering a New Era of Jew Hatred," *The Algemeiner,* 11 June 2021.
2. Suzanne Goldberg, DOE's "Acting Assistant Secretary for Civil Rights," is an anti-Creator example from Mr. J. Biden's criminal cabal: see Milton Quintanilla, "Biden Administration Warns School Employees against Trans-Discrimination in 'Dear Educator' Letter," *Christian Headlines,* 25 June 2021.
3. E.g., see Vincent James, 27:40 to 30:48, "Liberal Plants Attempt TAKEOVER of 'Critical Race Theory' Narrative in Conservative Media," 22 June 2021, as posted at "https://tv.gab.com/channel/realredeleph ants/view/liberal-plants-attempt-takeover-of-critical-60d1658da049561caf1e0681" on the Internet.
4. For more information, see this author's multi-volume series *Messiah, History, and the Tribulation Period,* and *Israel, "Peace" and the Looming Great Tribulation.*

have been able to snuff out the wokeness before it infected the SBC [(Southern Baptist Convention)]. In response to the leftward drift, thousands of Christians joined the Conservative Baptist Network. They mustered a noble fight, but … it was too little, too late. The other [(only nominally Christian)] side [(i.e., spiritual tares, wolves and goats who've infiltrated the SBC and its churches)] rallied mean-spirited [(nominally)] Baptist Twitter bullies and heathen journalists … to wage a disgusting political smear job on … [Christian] conservatives. They were brutally slandered by their woke [(alleged)] brethren while being [falsely] accused of being misogynists, racists, and xenophobes. Baptist 'Deplorables.' It's an ugly business when Christians behave more like [Satan's] political operatives than ambassadors for Christ. When Baptists have problems with one another they should go to the Gospel of Matthew [(e.g., 18:15-22)], not the [fake] news [media].[1]

Would you believe that ecofascists now cynically employ CRT to further Satan's "climate change" fraud? "The U.S. Department of Health and Human Services (HHS) … is creating …. the Office of Climate Change and Health Equity … to operate around social justice ideology claiming minorities … are disproportionately affected by climate change."[2] So, to CRT suckers, "white" "carbon pollution" is "racist," while that of "non-whites" somehow isn't.

Of "ultra progressive" Anglicans, under the foretold AntiChrist and other royals, Julian Mann tells us this:

Church of England leaders are increasingly taking on the mantras of the radical Left about "systemic racism" or "alarmist calls for a climate emergency", a new report from religion think tank Civitas claims. The report [is] titled "Rotting from the Head: Radical Progressive Activism and the Church of England [(CofE)]".... …

The researchers found that 70 per cent of the CofE's 42 dioceses have appointed [ecofascist] clergy who "promote climate activist warnings". Over half of all … warnings occurred within 12 months after the CofE hierarchy urged support for climate protests during Holy Week in 2019.... They also found that 87 per cent of claims by clergy of "systemic or institutional racism" occurred within the first six months of the UK racial justice campaigns in May 2020, following the [communist] Black Lives Matter [(criminal)] 'protests' in the United States. …

Civitas trustee and practising Anglican, Tom Harris, argues....: "The focus on racism sits awkwardly with its [(i.e., CofE leadership's)] apparent silence on things which a truly caring Christian Church might be expected to care deeply about. … A Church informed by its Gospel mission rather than by Marxist ideology would surely not behave this way." …

The report says ….: "Thus, ideologically, institutions like the Church are increasingly taking on the mantras of ultra-progressivism, such as the notion of 'systemic racism' or alarmist calls for a 'climate emergency'. These ideas are reinforced by new policies to achieve structural change …

1. Todd Starnes, "Starnes: Southern Baptists Take Dangerous Turn Left," *NewsMax*, 16 June 2021.
2. Jeremy Frankel, "HHS Opens Office to Deal With Climate Change," *NewsMax*, 30 Aug. 2021.

and rewriting education curriculums. That has, in turn, impacted the spirit and ideals of the Church's mission. ... There is a common denominator of leadership acquiescence or ... laziness in objecting to questionable claims and narratives, often to appease relentless and large-scale agitators."[1]

So, after Israel or the original (post-Flood) House of God, the satanic world's racism attacks and undermines the Church. (The latter, as God's heavenly "ethnicity" and born-again family in Christ Jesus, are "strangers" to this world, as our citizenship is in our heavenly Father's eternal Kingdom.) Unregenerate and rebellious Israelites, who neither know nor serve The Creator, but who abide evil toward Yeshua (Jesus) and persecution of Christians, are *not* God's children, but Hell's (e.g., Matt 23:15; see 23:13-15).

We may readily surmise and often see that *all* the *unregenerate* (i.e., non-Christian) ethnicities or races of the world—including today's Israelite non-Christians—are biased or "woke" against the Church. "Woke" degenerates and racists oppose the Church's *collective heavenly "ethnicity" or "race,"* or our *spiritual descent from God* through Christ Jesus—and rebel "Jews" are "in-lumped:"

> Student employees at James Madison University in Virginia are receiving training to recognize that people identifying as male, straight, cisgender or Christian are "oppressors" engaging in the "systematic subjugation" of other social groups.... According to a training video required to be viewed by student staff..., oppression is described as "the systematic subjugation of one social group by a more powerful social group...." The video says an "oppressor" group is one with power to define reality for themselves as well as others. As a result, the "target" groups "take in and internalize the negative messages ... and end up cooperating with the oppressors (thinking and acting like them)." ...
>
> Among the races and nationalities listed as "privileged" or "agents" are those identifying as male, cisgender, ... heteroromantic, Christian, white, Western European, American, upper to middle class, thin/athletic build, able-bodied or ages 30s to early 50s. The "oppressed" or "target" groups include those identifying as Black, Asian, Latinx, non-Western European, LGBTQ+, homoromantic, Muslim, <u>Jewish</u>, working class, overweight or disabled.[2]

The "wokeness" of such spiritual liars and lunatics compasses murderous, frothing (e.g., foamed mouth) hatred toward God's children and servants, because we *oppose the world's wickedness.* We do *not* embrace cold-blooded and grisly murder, human sacrifice to the Devil (e.g., infanticide or so-called "abortion," euthanasia and

---

1. Julian Mann, "Church of England leaders increasingly embracing 'ultra-progressive values' – report," *Christian Today,* 28 July 2021. Things continue to get *worse,* even from these appalling numbers.
2. Jack Gournell, "Report: James Madison U Trains Students That Christians, White Males Are 'Oppressors,'" *NewsMax,* 19 Aug. 2021.

godless eugenics), sexual abominations (e.g., sodomy and lesbian-ism, bestiality, pedophilia, etc.), anti-Creator lunacies (e.g., "trans-genderism" and alleged "non-binary 'genders'"), the anti-science lies and delusions of alleged macroevolution, etc. Those who em-brace such things "think it strange that" we "do not run with them in the same flood of dissipation," and so they are heard "speaking evil of" those who fear and serve God (1 Pet 4:4).

What about the British Monarchy? They have long presided over many predominantly non-white nations—often as racists. (Across the centuries, the monarchy embraced slavery—like so much of the world—and then apartheid, as well as sympathized with Hitler's Nazis and their eugenics.) While today's British royals may down-play or deny being "slavers" and racists, that has not stopped their anti-Israel biases or conduct—nor familial accusations of racism. Al-legedly facing racism,[1] Prince Harry and mulatto wife Meghan seem to have gone "woke," uncritically embracing racial (e.g., "anti-white") biases. As king, Charles "has said he's trying to deepen his understanding of 'slavery's enduring impact' ... in the [nations of the] Commonwealth," having "referred to 'the darkest days of our past and the appalling atrocity of slavery, which forever stains our history.'"[2] Yet, as we're going to see, *liar* Charles really seeks to *enslave all mankind to the Devil*, meaning the entire world!

True Christianity *counters* racism. An Afghan pastor, asked about future prospects for the Gospel in Afghanistan, stated: "Chris-tianity is what makes it possible to live at peace with other ethnici-ties. If this can happen, it will have a great impact."[3] Yes, and Satan *hates* that impact, which is *love!* Howard Sachs remarks:

> This is part of an old, throw-back, pervasive, and relentless attack on Western, Judeo-Christian values—even our view of reality. The name-amenders will argue the "he/his/him" stuff is just part of their Leftist Democrat Weltanschauung of peace, love and kindness—the same kind of love and peace they aim at our culture, history and founders with things like the vile 1619 Project. It's the love and peace of destroying our liberties like free speech; the hate they show our girls with boys running around their shower-rooms; the poison they spread with the racism of "black dorms" and Critical Race Theory. It's the kindness and tolerance they spew by trashing the [scriptural] Western notion of marriage, [trashing] the nu-clear family, their hate-filled defunding [of] our police and military, destroy-ing our borders, the plundering of our kids future with mountains of debt,

1. Jane Ridley, "Book: Prince Charles is the one who asked about baby Archie's skin tone," *Page Six*, 28 Nov. 2021.
2. Associated Press, "King Charles III Supports Probe into Monarchy's Slave Ties," *NewsMax*, 6 Apr. 2023.
3. Jayson Casper, "Dari TV Host: Afghanistan Will Now See 'Pure Christianity,'" *Christianity Today*, 30 Aug. 2021.

and destroying the greatest wealth production machine in human history—capitalism.

These 'progressive' loving ones amend, they argue, in order to show solidarity with the Marxist lie that America is structured on the notion of oppressed against oppressor. The lie is that the heterosexual, capitalist, Christian white man with a European heritage is the oppressor. The atheist, trans, beige-colored, socialist, bisexual with a great grandfather from El Salvador, is [somehow] the oppressed. And beneath the lie is the core of darkness—that of radical, unabashed Marxism, out to tear apart this country from within, and destroy every aspect of Western, American, Judeo-Christian civilization.

These American Marxists flat out reject the City on the Hill concept from our Bible—the fact that the America 'City' is structured not on oppressed vs. oppressor, black vs. white, rich vs. poor, gay [sodomite and lesbian] vs. straight [heterosexual], but on liberty vs tyranny, good vs. bad, virtue vs. non-virtue, character vs lack of, merit vs. non-merit, God-fearing vs Government worshiping. [Mid-July 2021's Senate Resolution 153] … amendment comes from the same Leftist poison…, commanding we [now] alter reality itself by calling women "birthing people" and demanding we fear and focus on 75 million non-existent white supremacists [(i.e., all U.S. Republican voters)] so they may be rooted out, by our now corrupt justice institutions.[1]

Macroevolution, like Marxism, has its roots in atheism. Among the "woke" crowd, we see "Black Lives Matter" communists and socialists, "Anti-Fa" fascists, and atheist fools, nearly all of whom, embrace macro-evolution. We should not be surprised to see, then, that they directly attack God as Creator—or that such lunatics would allege that rejecting macroevolution represents "white supremacy." The now disreputable *Scientific American,* a left-wing *anti*-science magazine and venue, has "gone there," publishing a July 2021 propaganda piece by the title, "Denial of Evolution Is a Form of White Supremacy." Ms. Hopper, a CRT radical, whose foolish lies we'll shortly dissect, acrobatically alleges and asserts:

> I want to unmask the lie that evolution denial is about religion and recognize that at its core, it is a form of white supremacy that perpetuates segregation and violence against Black bodies. Under the guise of "religious freedom," the legalistic wing of creationists loudly insists that their point of view deserves equal time in the classroom. Science education in the U.S. is constantly on the defensive against antievolution activists who want biblical stories to be taught…. In fact, the first wave of legal fights against evolution was supported by the [Ku Klux] Klan in the 1920s. Ever since then, entrenched racism and the ban on teaching evolution in the schools have gone hand in hand. …
>
> At the heart of white evangelical creationism is the mythology of an unbroken white lineage that stretches back to a light-skinned Adam and Eve. In literal interpretations of the Christian Bible, white skin was created

---

1. Howard Sachs, "Pronouns as weapons against America," *Arutz Sheva,* 23 Jul. 2021.

in God's image. Dark skin has a different, more problematic origin. As the biblical story goes, the curse or mark of Cain for killing his brother was a darkening of his descendants' skin. ...

Fundamentalist interpretations of the Bible are part of the "fake news" epidemic that feeds the racial divide in our country. For too long, a vocal minority of creationists has hijacked children's education, media and book publishing. ... My hope is that ... we make the connection between creationism and racist ideology clearer.... Science deniers are pumping money into a well-funded antievolution machine. ...

In the Adam-and-Eve scenario, the Creator bestows both physical and cultural humanity on the first people. From the get-go Adam knows how to name the animals. No one has to invent language or figure out how to make tools. Science, of course, tells us otherwise.[1]

Okay, that's more than a little disgusting. Let's bring Ms. Hopper and her ilk *up* to Earth, out from their hellish mire. Truthfully, macroevolution is a relatively recent *anti*-science and highly religious *lie*—and *the most evil mass-murderers and racists in modern history all embraced it* (e.g., Lenin and Trotsky, Hitler, Stalin, Mao, etc.). It takes very little research or education to become aware. But reality would escape those who embrace half-truths and lies to pursue nefarious agendas. Are murderers and racist thugs *Ms. Hopper's heroes?*

Scripture says *nothing* about skin color in relation to Adam and Eve, nor even in relation to their direct descendants—and we know relatively little about the specifics of the mark God placed upon murderer Cain. Also, *actual white racists (e.g., those of the KKK) are primarily responsible for the false skin-color narrative Ms. Hopper proffers* and *stupidly* attempts to attribute to scripture: yes, *she* is repeating *the KKK's* racist lies. (How dumb and propagandized does one really have to be, to do that?) Indeed, as an *anti-Christian fool,* Ms. Hopper *epitomizes* the very "fake news" and *science denial* she only *pretends* to oppose, as *macro-evolutionists*—not creationists—are those who (demonstrably) have "hijacked children's education, media and book publishing." Of course, real science and data—to include the second law of thermodynamics, provable catastrophism, and information theory and genetic programming—*incontrovertibly* back special and direct creation.[2]

Ms. Hopper further alleges that Adam and Eve did not have to "figure out how to make tools," but is again met with *scriptural silence.* She brazenly asserts, "science ... tells us otherwise." But Ms. Hopper is *no scientist*—just an anti-Christian and anti-God loon and editorializer. Real scientists (e.g., *this author),* for example, realize

---

1. Allison Hopper, "Denial of Evolution Is a Form of White Supremacy," *Scientific American,* 5 July 2021.

2. Many sources of information and evidence are available, including through organizations like the Institute for Creation Research (ICR) and Answers in Genesis. Many creationists, with doctorates spanning every scientific discipline, have produced books and periodicals refuting macr-evolutionism.

that even the most simple device or machine must be "taught" (e.g., designed or programmed), even initially in the case of A.I. (though that's hardly simple), as devices and machines are incapable of doing anything useful, short of that. So, a calculator, for example, let alone a vastly more complex computing system, *must have "know how" from the "get go," provided by its creator!* God, as mankind's Creator, accomplished something similar, though in an almost infinitely more complex and advanced manner, in relation to the first two humans. Such is not "rocket science," but an easily understood reality—at least it is to those who engage in even a modicum of basic science. (Macro-evolutionists are *anti*-science where *biological origins and divine "object oriented" programming* are concerned, being *satanically brainwashed idiots,* literally.)

Satan-serving cheap-shot propagandists, blasphemers and hypocrites have infiltrated global society. Shockingly, for example, atheist Scarlet Jones, whose sins are as blood, organized a public "Global Middle Finger to End Christianity" Facebook event, in which thousands of self-worshiping fools were called upon to "give a big middle finger to the sky to end Christianity and create more Atheists, while fighting the Global Prayer so their sky daddy won't snatch us up." Reaching out to her to suggest she read this book (on August 9, 2021), garnered a fool's "clever" response: "You're a nut. Books written by *men* is why you are psychotic ... and ... like a child who thinks his imaginary friend is being hurt by his parents." (Say what?) Back to Jerusalem's Eugene Bach wryly observed: "To be certain, the silent gesture of giving the middle finger to the sky would be a blessing compared to what Atheists usually do when they gain power. More Christians have been slaughtered in the name of Atheism in the last 100 years than any by any other religion. It is also good to know that Atheists are being somewhat sensible..., because they were too cowardly to ... include giving the finger to [false 'god'] Allah to end Islam."[1] Yes, atheists are *cowards*—and as such, they are also *first among the condemned* (Rev 21:8)! Really, that's infinity for the "nuts," and zero for the foul finger pointers—but who's keeping score. Reprobates, whose fantasies rely upon brazen lies, "straw man" arguments, and gross ignorance, *must be rebuked, corrected, and called to repentance and receipt of Christ Jesus.*

"Wokeness" is a multi-pronged "last days" satanic attack upon truth and rationality. It targets Israel, the Church and Christians, and ultimately, God Himself as Creator. Under Satan and his spiritually fallen minions, the violent "woke" (e.g., terrorists and thugs) are a

---

1. Eugene Back, "Today is 'Global Middle Finger to End Christianity' Day," *BackToJerusalem.com,* 12 Aug. 2021.

direct threat to the lives of Israelites and Christians. *We now face multiple mass psychoses—deadly spiritual and mental breakdowns—under fallen angels, demons and satanists globally.* When rational discourse becomes manifestly impossible, understand that such people are *objectively insane.* (Pray, fast, expose, *and* speak truth.)

As blasphemers of God, non-Christians also include murderers, general evildoers and busybodies (cf. 1 Pet 4:14-15), who "will give an account to Him who is ready to judge the living and the dead" (1 Pet 4:5). Yes, many among them shall finally be cast down to Hell's flames for eternal punishment, as those who disbelieved and cursed God's saints *without* repentance unto life, being cursed in turn by The Judge (see Gen 12:1-3; Matt 25:31-46; Gal 3:5-29; cf. Matt 15:3-9, Mark 7:6-13). Real "social justice" is near, even though we *bless* our enemies in the face of their cursing, persecution and spiteful use of us (see Luke 6:27-49; Rom 12:14-15 and 12:17-21; cf. Jas 3:5-18).

Fallen spirits (e.g., via the U.S. Demon-rat Party) seek to impose racist "CRT" indoctrination, severely harming morale and cohesion—all to expose and remove those who hold to Judaeo-Christian and conservative, or truth-based, values. Predictably, actual threats, such as "Anti-Fa," "BLM," and "radical" Islam, are mostly *ignored.*[1]

So, there is an active "under-the-table" attempt to purge U.S. military branches of Christians and conservatives—all to further the globalist coup's efforts to ensure a totalitarian takeover of the U.S. Specifically, it is to enable and ensure the U.S. "component" of *Charles'* "Great Reset" and NWO under Satan. (It is *not* incidental: the U.S. ostensibly has the most powerful and dangerous military capability on Earth.) Simultaneously, the Obamanation cabal has compromised every branch of the U.S. Federal Government, besides state governments it effectively controls. Nowhere is that more evident than in the organs of "justice" (e.g., the FBI, DOJ and the courts) and elections theft. At the DOJ, for example, race-baiting is used to impose *permanent fraud* in U.S. elections, so that globalists may ensure their U.S. coup's long-term viability and "success."[2]

Today, "woke" and "wokeness" are euphemisms for ethnic discrimination, canards behind satanic totalitarianism. Treacherous and dishonorable "woke" racists are not truly about "[critical] social justice" as they allege, but injecting objective falsehoods which serve to create social divisions leading to destructions—up to and including murders and rapes, other assaults and destructions, as well as thefts

---

1. See, for example, Emily Caldwell, "Two lawmakers say they're getting hundreds of whistleblower complaints from troops," *Stars and Stripes,* 16 June 2021.
2. See, for example, Solange Reyner, "Ex-Rep. Collins to NewsMax: DOJ Lawsuit 'Cover-Up' for Dems Failing to Pass Voting Act," *NewsMax,* 25 June 2021.

and general criminality. All those things are actual fruits of satanism (cf. John 10:10) and spiritual delusion.

In fact, we are witnessing a growing *mass psychosis,* which manifests as a radical and, increasingly often, violent rejection of rational thought and truth. Suddenly, falsehood and lies are "truth," truth is "abuse" and "violence" (or worse); evil is "good," good is "evil;" spiritual darkness is "light" or "enlightenment," light is "darkness;" and poison is "healthful," and that which is healthful is "poisonous" (cf. Isa 5:20). Reality is inverted. As foretold, these "woke-tards" are they "who draw | drag iniquity with cords of vanity | falsehood, and sin as if with a cart rope" (Isa 5:18), being "wise in their own eyes, and prudent in their own sight" (Isa 5:21): "Professing to be wise, they became fools .... deserving of death..." (Rom 1:22, 1:32; see 1:18-32).

The "woke" crowd allows—and even invites—Satan to take them spiritually and mentally *captive* "through philosophy and empty deceit, according to the tradition of men, according to the basic principles of the world, and not according to Christ" (Col 2:8). Because "they did not like to retain God in *their* knowledge, God gave them over to a debased mind, to do those things which are not fitting..." (Rom 1:28). In lieu of actual social justice, these spiritually dead men and women "justify the wicked for a bribe, and take away justice from the righteous man!" (Isa 5:23). As the Devil's children, his bidding *they want to do.* To them, Jesus stated: "You are of *your* father the Devil, and the desires of your father you want to do. He was a murderer from the beginning, and does not stand in the truth, because there is no truth in him. When he speaks a lie, he speaks from his own *resources,* for he is a liar and the father of it" (Rom 8:44).

"Politically correct" language among "cognitively challenged" individuals and (willful) "certifiable" lunatics has reached *hitherto unimaginable* "heights." As one example, on a growing list, childbearing women (i.e., mothers) are now being called "birthing people"—in deference to those who say they have "non-binary" genders.[1] How much mental compromise does it take to *embrace* such nonsense—or to assert that conceding the truth that *biological females alone give birth among humans,* is somehow "a complex issue?" Is their "reality" some sort of "twilight zone?" Have they long been so *infantile,* experiencing a bizarre form of "extended adolescence"—or is their *moral disorder* also a *highly spiritual one?*

Should we be surprised to see that the bizarre "birthing people" obsequiousness has arisen through Mr. J. Biden's "ranks" (e.g., the

---

1. See, for example, "Tucker obtains 'shocking' government document on bias-free language," *Fox News* channel, 10 June 2021, at "https://youtu.be/beFYv8ZwT2U" on YouTube.

Office of Management and Budget or OMB), infecting the U.S. Federal Reserve and other organs of government—only to further extend the "reign" of anti-truth, morally-unhinged Obamanation. (J. Biden and B. Obama are close.) In the very name and nature of bias, these same folks allege they are imposing "bias-free language!" In other words, up is down and down is up to this anti-Creator cabal. They seek to *impose avoidance* of terms like "founding fathers," "man made" and gender-based pronouns (e.g., "he," "her," "him," "she") and titles (e.g., "Mr," "Ms," "Mrs," "sir," "mam"), etc. We're told: "The State Department ... is ... updating ... to allow [(sexually satanic)] Americans to have their passports include a gender marker 'for non-binary, intersex, and gender non-conforming persons'...."[1]

Paul warned: "And for this reason"—"because they did not receive the love of The Truth"—"God will send them strong delusion, that they should believe the lie, that they all may be condemned who did not believe The Truth, but had pleasure in unrighteousness" (2 Th 2:10*b* and 2:11-12; cf. Gen 3:4-13). That "strong delusion" is arguably now active, but how far could it go?

This author will now *mock*—just a little—the Devil's deluded servants: Left to their own "devices," would non-Christians eventually be directed toward "self" identification as "dog," "cat," "lion," "leopard," "bear," "dragon," "pig," "microbe," "toad," and so forth? Or perhaps a toddler or a turd? Or maybe something less understated, like "beast without understanding?" Should we who serve God all just make things easier for everyone? Perhaps we could be plain-spoken, rather than genteel, and simply identify such loons as "bull[shitter][s]" and "bitch[es]?" It's *true,* you know: scripturally, as anti-Creator individuals, the "woke-tards" *are* spiritually-affected *"dogs;"* yes, we may truthfully assert that they amount to tongue-wagging *animals,* prepared for Hell's open mouth (cf. Ex 11:7; Ps 49:20; 2 Pet 2:12-22). George Orwell himself could perhaps have embraced such labeling, given that this age's "progressive" lunatics have now managed to "out progress" even his legendary creativity; yes, he might even have (disturbingly) taken notes. Okay, "fun" aside, we must recognize that fortunately, some or even quite a few among today's pathological "dogs," *may yet come to their senses, repent and so be saved* (cf. Matt 15:21-28; Mark 7:25-30), converting to sheep. Notably, many already *have*—and for that, we all praise God. (As Christians may attest, it's a truly wonderful and blessed change!)

Clearly, the Devil's servants have evil agendas, and in those, they work to impose their satanic *confusions and delusions* upon the rest

---

1. Adam Kredo, "State Department Says Passports Can Include Any Gender," *Washington Free Beacon,* 30 June 2021.

of society and mankind generally, often now starting with children, so that the insane asylum they work to run and feed, metastasizes. But though they disbelieve, they face this factually insurmountable reckoning: *the future.* What is that? Simply this: *Christ Jesus shall shortly crush their heads (cf. Gen 3:15; Hab 3:13, Heb.) and cast them down to Hell's flames* (e.g., Rev 19:11 to 20:3). They will perish as brute beasts, yet suffer for all eternity as imprisoned and tormented souls and spirits. Will they timely "catch a clue," to repent? No one in Hell, calls it "heaven"—and even "animals" *seek to live.*

Friend, that "strong delusion" from God, is arguably all around us today, where men and women routinely try to act as *their own* "gods" (cf. Gen 3:4-5). When the Great Tribulation itself finally commences, only years from now (as this author writes), unrepentant "woke" reprobates shall "believe the lie," being spiritually lost rebels and idiots, only to serve Satan and the foretold AntiChrist (e.g., see Rev 13:3-4, 13:8, 13:11-17)! But Christians are to *pray for them,* that those who do *not* receive the coming Mark of the Beast, may find grace to repentance—and so receive forgiveness of their sins, renewal of their minds, and eternal salvation. Praying for the lost who are yet alive in this world, is every Christian's duty before God.

Architecture. Through much maneuvering, Satan's Prince as of 1998, had already become perhaps the most influential man in Britain regarding architecture, having even authored a book on the subject and started his own Institute of Architecture.[1] Despite appearances, there is method to King Charles III's past and present "madness." As will be discussed in the next chapter, his activities in this area significantly contributed to the city of London's renewed international prominence. But we should understand this: Satan's Prince takes a *Luciferian approach to architecture* generally, and by that, he pursues a carnal "unity" of the world's religions.[2]

Terra Carta and Astra Carta. On January 11, 2021—just months after Charles' launched his evil Great Reset effort from the WEF—the then Prince of Wales, unveiled his Terra Carta framework. With a logo showing flora, fauna and insects, as well as the phrase, "For the Harmony of Nature, People, and Planet," what could go wrong? (Of course, the logo shows *no people.*)

We're told: "The Prince of Wales's Sustainable Markets Initiative today announced the 'Terra Carta'—a charter that puts sustainability at the heart of the private sector. Marking a year since The [(i.e., Sa-

---

1. For more information, see the previous chapter's section titled, "Ties to the New Age Movement, the occult, and false religions," at p. 333.
2. Tuominen, "Book Review: Prince Charles' *Harmony.*"

tan's)] Prince announced his Sustainable Markets Initiative at Davos, the Terra Carta offers the basis of a recovery plan to 2030 that puts Nature, People and Planet at the heart of global value creation. Terra Carta (Earth Charter) will provide a roadmap to 2030 for businesses to move towards an ambitious and sustainable future; one that will harness the power of Nature combined with the transformative power, innovation and resources of the private sector. The Prince of Wales virtually delivered remarks at the One Planet Summit in Paris...: 'Today, I am making an urgent appeal to leaders, from all sectors and from around the world, to join us in this endeavour, and to give their support to this 'Terra Carta' – to bring prosperity into harmony with Nature, People and Planet over the coming decade.'"[1]

But an Earth Charter under Satan's Prince—even with a decidedly ecofascist bent and appeal—simply wouldn't prove to be enough. As later addressed, in June 2023, Charles also launched *Astra Carta* (Space Charter)—ostensibly representing our solar system *and* the Universe, also under the Crown! Buckle up, there's *more* to come.

---

1. "The Sustainable Markets Initiative announces the Terra Carta," *Royal.uk*, 11 Jan. 2021.

12

Charles,
Middle East "Peace,"
and
Global Security

In the first edition of this work (1998), this chapter occupied about sixty pages. While updating it for the second edition, it became clear that much of the material in it, really belonged in the author's new *Israel, "Peace" and the Looming Great Tribulation* multi-volume se-ries—formerly titled, *Israel, "Peace" and the Coming World War: The Great Tribulation is Near.* (Though re-titled, the series remains a "companion" work to *North Korea, Iran, and the Coming World War: Behold a Red Horse.)*

Despite moving the above-mentioned material, it is still germane and certainly salient to *this* work, that you be aware that since the 1980s, *Charles as Satan's Prince* has played *the* central role, behind the scenes and now sometimes publicly, *in the entire Mideast false "peace" process.* Without Charles, *the whole world would be a very different place today.* He is Satan's emissary and "prime mover." So, some of the material from the first edition is herein helpfully re-tained and updated. For the full picture, however, you will want to read *Israel, "Peace" and the Looming Great Tribulation*—a work of major importance, in its own right.[1]

Charles (as prince or king) in Daniel 9:26-27. Besides telling us that the AntiChrist is either a "prince" (e.g., Charles, Prince of Wales) or ruler (Heb., נָגִיד) such as a king (e.g., King Charles III), of Roman lineage,[2] verses 26 to 27 of Daniel 9, indicate that he will act to "strengthen"—meaning to "confirm," "enforce," and/or "impose"

---

1. To facilitate understanding, a small number of paragraphs (fewer than a dozen) from this material are replicated in *Israel, "Peace" and the Looming Great Tribulation.*
2. Daniel 9:26 states "the people of *a* coming prince | ruler shall destroy the city and the sanctuary" (Heb.), which the Romans accomplished when they destroyed Jerusalem and its Temple around A.D. 70. This same "coming prince | ruler" is referred to as "he" in Daniel 9:27. Having said this, preterist inter-pretations that assert the "he" of Daniel 9:27 is actually Jesus are also addressed in the author's *Mes-siah, History, and the Tribulation Period* multi-volume series. In fact, *in the right context* (i.e., that of scripture's and the author's *Messianic view*), this is a *valid* alternate interpretation; that is, there is a re-markable duality of meaning within Daniel 9:27, such that the verse apparently refers to, as well as en-folds *both* the Crucifixion and Tribulation Weeks.

(Heb., *g'bor* or גביר)—"a covenant" *(b'reet | brit* or ברית) "with many | archers | rabbis" (Heb., *l'rabim* or לרבים) for "one 'seven'" (Heb., *shavua echad* or שבוע אחד)—שבוע אחד ברית לרבים.

An extended definition for the Hebrew word *g'bor* (i.e., גביר) in Daniel 9:27 would be "arrogantly, audaciously, or tyrannically exert, impose, compel, cause to prevail, secure or accomplish," while alternate meanings are "man" or "strong man," or implicitly, "warrior." Indeed, Keil and Delitzsch, commenting on Daniel 9:27, correctly observed, "the two contracting parties are not viewed as standing on an equality, but he who concludes or who confirms the covenant prevails, and imposes or forces the covenant on the other party."[1] Joyce G. Baldwin similarly sees in Daniel 9:27 "the implication of forcing an agreement by means of superior strength."[2] The alternate translation of *g'bor* as "man" or "strong man" (cf. "manly") is based upon the strength of a man, versus that of a woman, and is thus also translated as "warrior" in various Old Testament verses. This is emphasized in Revelation 13:4, where the question is posed, in reference to the first beast or the AntiChrist, "Who is able to make war with him?" Yet, this question in conjunction with Daniel 9:27, is far more meaningful than it may appear on the surface. The name "Charles" is a Germanic word meaning "man" or "manly," for example, though it also derives from the Germanic element *heri,* meaning "army" or "warrior."[3] In English, French, German and Latin, "Charles" is also said to mean "strong," "strong man," "man" and "farmer" (cf. Zech 13:5, KJV). We find, therefore, what amounts to a perfect match between the various meanings attributed to the name "Charles" and the Hebrew word *g'bor,* as found in Daniel 9:27. It cannot be coincidence, then, that the AntiChrist bears the name "Charles"—nor that *g'bor* is central to this particular prophecy.[4]

This covenant that is to be strengthened, enforced, imposed, pushed, secured, etc., is generally understood to be a "peace" treaty between Israel and her several adversaries. Central to it, will be the theme of "peace and security" (and variants of the same), for both apostate Israel and the unbelieving world (1 Th 5:3, Gk.). We must not overlook, therefore, the fact that UN Resolutions 242 and 338, to

1. C.F. Keil and F. Delitzsch, "THE BOOK OF DANIEL," Vol. 9 of *Commentary on the Old Testament* (1986; rpt. Massachusetts: Hendrickson Publishers, Inc., 1989), p. 366.
2. J. G. Baldwin, "Daniel: An Introduction and Commentary," *Tyndale Old Testament Commentaries,* No. 21 (Illinois: Inter-Varsity Press, 1978), p. 171.
3. For example, see "Charles: Meaning & History" at "https://www.behindthename.com/name/charles" on the Internet. Regarding attempts to relate the name "Charles" to Revelation 17:10-11, see the related note in ch. 1's section titled "Global government and the AntiChrist," at p. 44.
4. In some languages (e.g., Czech, Hungarian, and Polish), the words for "emperor" derive from the name "Karl," which in turn comes from the same Latin root as that for "Charles"—*Carolus* (e.g., see "Charles – Meaning of Charles" at "https://www.babynamespedia.com/meaning/Charles").

which this theme is central, have served as the basis for *all* peace negotiations and treaties with modern Israel, since the nation regained sovereignty—for the first time in nearly 2,600 years—over the old city of Jerusalem, otherwise known as East Jerusalem, in 1967's Six Day War.[1] In fact, *many thousands* of articles have been written over the past three decades alone using the exact phrases "peace and security" and "security and peace," as well as variants of them, in relation to Israel and the Mideast peace process.[2]

Who will sign? Importantly, Daniel 9:27 is *silent* on the issue of whether the AntiChrist will actually sign the covenant *or not*. Although many have taught that he will do so, that is a *presumption*. Likewise, Daniel 9:27 is silent on whether Israel as a nation will even *agree* to the covenant; in fact, the Hebrew text suggests that the Roman prince, in collusion "with many" (i.e., the world in opposition to God and Israel), *who are apparently even proceeding in (Yitzhak) Rabin's name,[3]* will externally *impose* the treaty upon Israel. Indeed, the treaty *could* be enacted **without Israel's consent**. This is an *important point,* and may explain how it is that when half of Jerusalem is taken captive by force in war, *nearly three-and-one-half years after the treaty is initiated* (see Zech 14:1-2; Matt 24:15-28; Mark 13:14-23; Luke 21:20-24; Rev 11:1-4; cf. Dan 7:24-25, 9:27, 11:40-45a, 12:6-11), that event is somehow *not* construed to be an abrogation of, and end to the treaty itself, *which remains in force for another three-plus years.*

Consider what has just been said carefully. Since the rhetorical question is asked, "Who can make war with him?," we may well surmise that unregenerate Israel will feel she has *no choice but to comply*—even though she will *yet refuse* to cede the Old City, the City of David (i.e., East Jerusalem). Israel may go along with Rabin's four

---

1. *UN Resolution 242* (passed on the November 22, 1967, following the war), emphasizes "the inadmissibility of the acquisition of territory by war and <u>the need to work for a just and lasting peace in which every State in the area can live in security</u>...." It also affirms that "the fulfillment of [UN] Charter principles <u>requires the establishment of a just and lasting peace in the Middle East</u>...." According to the resolution, this should include the withdrawal of "Israeli armed forces from territories occupied in the ... conflict" as well as "respect for and acknowledgment of the sovereignty, territorial integrity and political independence of every State in the area and their right to live in peace within secure and recognized boundaries free from threats or acts of force." Additionally, it affirms the "necessity" for "<u>guaranteeing the territorial inviolability and political independence of every State in the area</u>, through measures including the establishment of demilitarized zones" and for "achieving a just settlement of the ['Palestinian'] refugee problem" (Leonard J. Davis, *MYTHS AND FACTS 1989, A Concise Record of the Arab-Israeli Conflict,* ed. Eric Rozenman and Jeff Rubin {Washington, D.C.: Near East Research, Inc., 1988}, p. 294). Resolution 338 is essentially a reaffirmation of 242.
2. This figure does not include the many additional articles employing the same phrases in relation to various United Nations and NATO operations, activities, and agendas. We should remember that the United Nations, and before it the League of Nations, is literally chartered to maintain international "peace and security."
3. See the further exegesis of Daniel 9:27 in the *Israel, "Peace" and the Looming Great Tribulation* series.

major "peace" parameters, which he outlined as Prime Minister shortly before his assassination: "In his last Knesset speech, delivered on Oct. 5, 1995, Rabin underscored four guiding principles: (1) 'We aspire to establish the State of Israel as a Jewish state with at least 80% of its population Jewish'; (2) 'first and foremost, a united Jerusalem, including [the suburbs of] Maaleh Adumim and Givat Ze'ev, as the capital of Israel, under Israeli sovereignty'; (3) 'for Israel's security, the border will be drawn in the Jordan Valley, in the broadest interpretation of this term'; (4) touching on the [(so-called)] Palestinian political entity that will be established alongside Israel, west of the Jordan River, 'This entity will be less than a state and will independently manage the lives of the Palestinians under its rule.'"[1] But, Israel will not agree to cede East Jerusalem or the Temple Mount for any "peace" treaty. Indeed, Israel's "Palestinian" foes may themselves, *for a while,* likewise feel that they have *no choice* other than to submit to such an arrangement.

What, then, are we really talking about when it comes to this prophesied treaty? Clearly, it may bear little resemblance to what "scholars" and "experts" have generally asserted. In reality, it is likely be quite different. We know that the duration of the treaty is to be seven years. We know today that the entire world, including the United States, has for decades demanded that, as part of any treaty or "solution," Israel allow the "Palestinians" to govern their own "state" from East Jerusalem, *Israel's ancient capital,* in accord (so it is falsely claimed) with the original British Mandate. (Yes, this final "two-state solution" also has its origins in Buckingham Palace with the satanic British monarchy.) We also know—and it bears repeating —that regardless of the vacillations of unregenerate Israeli governments preceding Christ's return, *Israel will not cede East Jerusalem to the nations, and certainly not to the "Palestinians"*—no matter the demands of Israel's "friends" in the United States, Europe or elsewhere. To the contrary, at the midpoint of the Tribulation Week, around the start of the Great Tribulation, East Jerusalem will be taken from Israel *by force*—in an internationally waged war, when "all the nations" gather "to battle against Jerusalem" (Zech 14:1-2). Therefore, *the prophesied treaty, as the vast majority of prophecy teachers have envisioned it, is quite <u>impossible</u>.*

In fact, for about three-and-one-half years preceding this massive attack upon Israel, which shall occur with the acquiescence of the AntiChrist, the prophesied treaty will be imposed and enforced, just as it shall be for the remaining three-and-one-half years of East

---

1. Maj. Gen. (res.) Gershon HaCohen, "Ehud Barak: Blatantly Ignoring Danger," *Begin-Sadat Center for Strategic Studies,* 31 May 2017.

Jerusalem's captivity. In other words, *Israel's enemies will not in reality be satisfied with the "solution" brought under the AntiChrist, and they will bide their time until, having conspired together, they feel Israel is sufficiently vulnerable to take what they wanted all along—the City of David with the Temple Mount and Israel's very life.* At that time, Israel's Muslim adversaries will attack her full-force, and the international community under the AntiChrist *will allow them to take East Jerusalem captive—cutting the baby, Jerusalem, in two.*[1] God's determined response, following the Tribulation Week, will be to "go forth and fight against those nations," and so Armageddon shall come, as shall Jesus' global rule from Jerusalem and a newly regenerate and faithful Israel (see Zech 14).

Today, a bit over two decades after the first edition of this work went to press, many more "peace and security" articles have been written and "professions" made, as violence has all the while continued to unfold and escalate throughout the Middle East and beyond.

London's centrality to Mideast peace initiatives. Does London *excite* you? For at least the past three decades, the city of London has been undergoing a modern environmental and architectural "renaissance," another seemingly disconsonant event that Charles as Prince of Wales, through continual active prodding of the architectural community and government of England concerning a myriad of his own environmental and architectural concerns, personally set in motion. This renaissance is now being recognized in fascinating ways. In the words of one writer: "As the 21st century approaches, their denizens boast that London can lay claim to being the world's most exciting city. 'There has been a culture change here in mindset and environment. This is a new way to make a city,' said Camilla Cavendish, who heads a consortium of businesses and residents recasting[—under a wide-scale program initiated and overseen by Charles (starting as Prince of Wales)—]a once-shabby neighborhood south of the Thames, that now houses Europe's largest cultural center. 'This is a good time to be in London. It's become a magnet for creative people. Other European cities don't seem to have the critical mass or the flexible attitude.' ... London is a fine place for architects."[2]

Architecture, though, just scratches the surface of Charles' hand in London's renewed prominence. As now documented in *Israel, "Peace" and the Looming Great Tribulation* multi-volume series,

---

1. We may speculate that they will go no further than this due to a very real threat of global nuclear war.
2. William D. Montalbano, Los Angeles Times, "New London a millennium high, City is celebrating renaissance," *The Denver Post*, 6 Nov. 1996, p. 31A.

those dignitaries addressing Mideast "peace," who are allegedly trying to resolve the Israeli-"Palestinian" conflict, at least apart from
threatening war and massive destruction, invariably pass through
London.

Since 2002, a *global* "Quartet" (cf. the four cardinal directions)
comprised of all the nations of the world (i.e., the UN, EU, U.S. and
Russia), has spearheaded the false "peace" process, which centers
on demands to further divide and take the heart of the Promised
Land from Israel—especially Jerusalem's Old City or the City of
David (i.e., East Jerusalem). Israel's now-deceased Ariel Sharon had
endorsed the Quartet's "Road Map for Peace," or the antiChristian
world's false "peace" approach, in May 2003—and was afterward
judged by God, put in a Coma, and cast down to Hell.

From its inception, the Quartet's "representative" or envoy has
been someone who reports to, or is subject to Satan's Prince. Until
June 2015, that was former British Prime Minister Tony Blair. From
June 2015 to June 2017, the England-educated and formerly London-
employed (at McKinsey & Co.) "Dutch" Kito de Boer served as "Head
of Mission" (the envoy's updated title), in the Office of the Quartet
(OQ). Since then (and as of this writing), part-Irish and Cambridge-
educated Canadian John N. Clarke serves as the Head of Mission or
Quartet envoy.

As of September 2021, the so-called "Palestinian Authority" (PA)
"prime minister" Mohammad Shtayyeh, "'stressed ... working ... to
end the [(imagined) Israeli] occupation through the Quartet, ... on
the basis of [(anti-God)] international law and [(non-)] legitimacy and
[(satanic)] United Nations resolutions,' according to [the PA's 'news'
agency] Wafa." We've been told, "The PA ... is ready to resume
[(false and entrapping)] peace talks with Israel only under the leadership of all the Quartet members, and not the US alone."[1] Again, all
that is actually under King Charles III!

A Commonwealth gambit. In August 1997, the Secretary General
of the British Commonwealth approached Israel, seeking her *membership*. Previously, the PA, which evolved from the earlier British-
created Supreme Moslem Council, had asked about the possibility of
its own future "associate" membership:

> Israel is actively considering joining the British Commonwealth, following
> an "unofficial approach" to its ambassador in London from the secretary-
> general of the 53-member organization. The approach was made earlier
> this month in a meeting between Ambassador Moshe Raviv and the Com-

---

1. Khaled Abu Toameh, Tovah Lazaroff, "Shtayyeh urges US to hurry and reopen Jerusalem consulate,"
   Jerusalem Post, 4 Sep. 2021.

monwealth's secretary-general, Chief Emeka Anyaoku. The move is being seen as especially significant at a time when Israeli ties with the European Union and other international bodies have been strained over the stalled Middle East peace process. A spokesman for the Commonwealth confirmed that a meeting had taken place between Chief Anyaoku and Mr. Raviv, but declined to provide further details. The approach came in the wake of a visit to London earlier this month by Yasser Arafat, during which the Palestinian Authority chief asked Commonwealth officials whether a future [(so-called)] Palestinian state could have associate membership of the organization.[1]

Many actors have changed since 1997, relations between Israel and *two-faced* Europeans have mostly further strained, and Israel has not (thus far) joined the British Commonwealth or the like. On November 20, 2008, Queen Elizabeth II knighted then Israeli President Shimon Peres at London's Buckingham Palace. Awarded a "Knight Grand Cross of the Most Distinguished Order of St. Michael and St. George," Peres was dubbed "a Knight Commander in the Order of St. Michael and St. George [(KCMG)], a title usually reserved for British ... foreign-service officers and high-ranking diplomats in Commonwealth countries."[2] Afterwards, Peres—a Nobel Peace Prize laureate—met privately with the queen to discuss "the Middle East in general," and the security situation between Sderot and Gaza in particular. Peres "presented the Queen with a letter written by her father, the late King George the VI, in which he recognizes the independence of the State of Israel."[3]

Afterward, Peres also met with then Prince Charles to request help with *Hamas!* Seriously. Were it not for information disclosed in this book, one could well struggle to discern, let alone understand the extraordinary influence Charles wields, even over "Palestinian" terrorists. Upon exchanging a *masonic* handshake at Clarence House in London, Peres later told Satan's Prince, "I know you have warm ties with many leaders in the Middle East." Peres then "urged him to help [with Hamas, so] the Red Cross visit [to then kidnapped Israeli soldier Gilad Shalit, held captive by Hamas, could] take place. The two also discussed the current situation in Israel, the ongoing peace process with the Palestinian Authority, the Iranian nuclear

1. Middle East Digest (MED), "Israel could join British Commonwealth," *Weekend News Today,* 25 Aug. 1997.
2. "Shimon Peres to be knighted by Queen Elizabeth," *Israel Today Magazine,* 24 Oct. 2008.
3. Anshel Pfeffer, "Peres receives honorary knighthood from Britain's Queen," *HaAretz,* 20 Nov. 2008. Pfeffer added, "Peres joins a long and distinguished list of international philanthropists and social figures given the title over the last few years, including Microsoft founder Bill Gates, U2 singer Bono, former French president Francois Mitterrand, former German chancellor Helmut Kohl and former New York mayor Rudolph Giuliani." *A homosexual sympathizer, Giuliani later unsuccessfully campaigned to become President of the United States—and remarkably, from April 2018, had served as likewise-sympathetic President Donald J. Trump's personal attorney.*

threat, and cooperation on various environmental projects Prince Charles is promoting."[1]

Until just a few years ago, Charles as Prince of Wales—owing to his strong Islamic ties, severe and ongoing (even when "private") anti-Israel (e.g., anti-Zionist) bias, and the UK's desire to continue to take advantage of Charles' ties politically and economically—had refused to officially visit Israel, doing so only "privately" for certain occasions (e.g., the auspicious and highly visible gathering of world leaders attending the funerals of Rabin and later Peres). In fact, to further pressure Israel's leadership, Charles for decades indicated that he would *not* officially visit the nation before resolution of the ongoing Arab-Israeli conflict, particularly the "Palestinian situation" in the "occupied territories."

Like other British royals, however, Charles as Prince of Wales, had little to no apprehension related to visiting Israel's Muslim enemies all around. Indeed, in February 2004, Charles even traveled to Iran, Israel's arch-foe, to meet with its Islamofascist regime (e.g., then President Mohammad Khatami)—doing so on behalf of Britain, France, and Germany for the European Union—to counterbalance the United States in a classic "god-cop, bad-cop" scenario over Iran's nuclear weapons ambitions.[2] According to then Iranian president and madman Mahmoud Ahmadinejad, who sermonizes on *al-Mahdi,* "even for the supporters of the occupying regime and its leaders, it has become clear that the continuation of the Zionist regime's life in the region is not feasible."[3] (More recently—in March 2016—Charles let it be known that he "is very keen to visit Iran."[4]) It is thus remarkable, given the *clear deference* of British royals to Israel's *adversaries,* let alone significant UK responsibility for the deaths of so many Israelites in the twentieth century, that Peres *allowed himself* to be knighted by the British monarch.

The big picture. It seems only fair to ask at this point, "Could the prophetic picture be any clearer?" That is, are those prophecy teachers, "scholars," and "authorities" who *fail* to recognize the significance of the Oslo peace process, and all that yet derives from it, to the covenant of Daniel 9:27, simply missing the boat? How could they be so ignorant and thus *materially* wrong? Aren't they *supposed to know?* What about their near universal *failure* (so far) to

1. Hagit Klaiman, "Peres praises Britain as democratic role model after being knighted," *Ynet news,* 20 Nov. 2008.
2. Paul Reynolds, "Charles's goodwill visit to Iran," *BBC News,* 9 Feb. 2004. Officially, then Prince Charles went to Iran to visit survivors of the devastating Bam earthquake, which killed over 25,000 Iranians. He also visited Iraq, where he met with Basra's governing council, as well as Saudi Arabia.
3. Sarah El Deeb, "Iran president: 'Not feasible' for Israel to live," *The Associated Press,* 15 Jan. 2009.
4. Rachael Pells, "Prince Charles 'plans' historic royal trip to Iran," *The Independent,* 27 Mar. 2016

recognize Charles as Prince of Wales, for who he really is? It is *not* as though the Church lacks readily available hard evidence.

Since the first edition of this book became available in 1998, *no one* may continue to make such a claim, which *only* reflects a) ignorance, b) a lack of fidelity toward, and faith in God's Word (e.g., a failure to believe Him), and/or c) brazen dishonesty. Now, over two decades later, ignorance must end, disbelief of God's written Word must be exposed, and liars must hear the Gospel faithfully preached. We must no longer tolerate those who do or would continue to censor the truth from those who line their church's pews, listen to their "biblical" programs, etc. Of course, *the non-Christian world itself will soon face The Truth*—and so we who are genuine and faithful Christians in His service, may clearly state that those false teachers, fake "scholars" and pretend "authorities" who reject repentance, are going to be exposed—and then judged as *dishonorable* and perhaps even cowardly (cf. Rev 21:8) before both God and His Church.

The European Union—through France and Germany (and apart from Brexit, also England)—seeks to play a major role in the Mideast peace process. (The British monarchy is also the royal family of France and Germany, even if not formally acknowledged as such today—and it maintains hegemony over a variety of Mideast rulers and leaders through its global control of Freemasonry.) At multiple points, their various approaches have been especially obnoxious and offensive. Consider France, for example: "French Foreign Minister Herve de Charette said it was crucial for Europe to have a role in the region.... France has a long history of influence in the Middle East, especially in Lebanon and Iraq.... French President Jacques Chirac ... tried to play the power broker in the region. In a visit to Israel, he shouted at protective Israeli security guards and became the first Western leader to address the [(so-called)] Palestinian parliament.... ...Germany thinks 'Europe should not overestimate its role.' And British Foreign Secretary Malcolm Rifkind could not resist a dig at Chirac.... 'Our involvement could be slightly less romantic, slightly less colored, slightly less dramatic than that of other countries, but it could be in fact more effective,' he said.... Charette shot back, calling Rifkind's remarks 'misplaced ... [and] based, no doubt, on some old Franco-British rivalry.'"[1] "President Jacques Chirac has boldly gambled..., hoping for a payoff in power, prestige and, eventually, lucrative [Arab] defense contracts.... The specter of French meddling in the delicate peace talks discomfited European Union partners [(at that time)] such as Britain, as well as the United States.... Israel issued a flat 'no' to Chirac's push for greater involve-

---

1. Elizabeth Wise, "Europe seeks niche in Middle East," *USA Today,* 29 Oct. 1996, p. 4A.

ment.... Defying Western wisdom, Chirac lauded Syrian President Hafez Assad, called Iraq a 'great country' and snubbed Israel with his failure to address the Knesset. The address would have balanced his speech before the [(so-called)] Palestinian Legislative Council—the first by a Western leader. He also called for a [(so-called)] Palestinian state and the return of the Golan Heights to Syria."[1]

We may note that despite historically recent attempts to unite France and Britain through such machinations as the amazing underwater "Chunnel," which runs between the French city Coquelles and the British city Folkestone, the simmering Mideast diplomatic row between the two countries demonstrates that the centuries-old Merovingian struggle for supremacy, between the British monarchy —using the Order of the Garter and its control of Illuminist Freemasonry—and the French leadership, continues unabated. French government officials, for example, worry that "the Internet could overwhelm the French language," noting that (as of 1997) some "85 percent of Internet sites are in English, while about 2 percent are in French."[2] It appears that the British monarchy has the upper hand.

Clearly, not all the Rabin government's conflicting commitments could have been honored. This realization led the PLO to assert that there is an "Armageddon Plan" afoot. A London-based "Palestinian" journalist commented: "Do you think Hussein would ever have signed the treaty if Israel didn't secretly give him future control of the Moslem holy sites in Jerusalem? [(So-called)] Palestinians are opposed to the agreement because we know we lost out. And if Hussein did get control, then the Masons got their foothold on the Temple Mount."[3] The same journalist elaborated, "Hussein's Masonic ties are well known to Arab reporters, and we believe Hussein is being used to give his friends in London a foothold in the city by the year 2000."[4] (Arguably, they *already* had it and still do.)

If the Israeli government is to attempt to fulfill the promises made by Peres and Rabin, as part of the latter's "legacy," it would ap-

---

1. Elaine Ganley, *Associated Press,* "France adopts a risky role as Middle East negotiator," *The Denver Post,* 27 Oct. 1996, p. 9A.

2. *Los Angeles Times,* "Integrity of language an issue," *The Denver Post,* 7 Feb. 1997, p. 33A.

3. Chamish, *Traitors and Carpetbaggers in the Promised Land,* pp. 115-117, 169. Arafat, enraged by the "special status" that the Israeli-Jordanian treaty grants to Jordan as custodian of Jerusalem's Muslim "holy shrines," openly threatened Hussein, declaring "in Gaza, to Hamas and Islamic Jihad supporters, that anyone who didn't agree that Jerusalem is 'Palestinian' and that the custodianship of the holy places should be in the hands of [(so-called)] Palestinians, could go and drink Gaza sea water." As Hussein saw it: "Jerusalem remains a trust with the Hashemites, who are resolute on its patronage and reconstruction and on the supervision of its holy sites.... We will never relinquish our religious responsibilities toward the holy sites under all circumstances" (Alon Pinkas, *Associated Press,* "Hussein: Our religious role in Jerusalem is everlasting," *The Jerusalem Post,* daily, 23 Oct. 1994, p. 1; Moshe-Zak, "Hussein and Arafat in Conflict," *The Jerusalem Post,* daily, 28 Oct. 1997, p. 6; accession nos. 940003526 and 940003890 on the *Jerusalem Post* CD-ROM).

4. Ibid.

pear that the Vatican and the Masons—or, loosely speaking, the French and English sides of the (false) peace process conspiracy—must ultimately partner with one another. Such a scenario, in which the final Roman pontiff joins forces with the head of the masonic hierarchy—that is, *Charles as the foretold AntiChrist*[1]—is precisely what the Apocalypse seems to indicate; that is, the false prophet and the "first beast" of Revelation 13, shall work together to deceive and dominate mankind. Moreover, it perfectly agrees with the overtures Charles, who now "titularly" heads apostate Anglican Protestantism, toward Roman Catholicism's popes and their *anti-Christian cult*.[2] Such partnership would go beyond a mere return to "the old European order, in which the pope rules the spiritual realm and the emperor the secular."[3] That spiritual alliance would also represent a significant coming home, in both historical and religious contexts, for the Temple Knights and the Rosicrucians—who originally split off from Roman Catholicism, only to give rise to Freemasonry and the vast British Empire and Commonwealth. It would perhaps also surprise many Christians, who have (mistakenly) been taught that the foretold AntiChrist would arise not stealthily from a Protestant denomination, but obviously from the Roman Catholic Church.[4]

Charles—Islam's choice ambassador from the West, and Israel's counterfeit Davidic prince and king. Of Charles' 1981 honeymoon, we're told: "The royal couple also paid a courtesy call on President Sadat of Egypt. Less than two months later, Prince Charles would return to Cairo to walk in the funeral procession of the assassinated Egyptian...."[5] Subsequently, in 1989, while on a "six-day visit to Kuwait and the United Arab Emirates," Satan's Prince enjoyed a relatively quiet "desert picnic at an oasis in Abu Dhabi."[6] Much, as we have seen, has since then occurred.

Charles, whom *Majesty* magazine foolishly dubbed the "Prince of Peace" (cf. Isa 9:6-7),[7] has already played a somewhat visible Mideast role: "Eager to establish himself as a player on the world stage, he made high-profile visits to [Western Europe,] Poland, Mexico and the Persian Gulf [in 1993], and he delivered a hard-hitting

---

1. For more information, see ch. 7's section titled, "The Garter," at p. 147.
2. See ch. 10's section titled, "A so-called 'Christian' heritage," at p. 295.
3. Hilton, *The Principality and Power of Europe*, p. 16.
4. Recall that shadowy Committee of 300 members are usually chosen from among apostate Anglican Protestants. Just as being a "Christian" became essential for advancement in the still-pagan Roman Empire of Constantine, who knowingly mixed the holy and the profane to give the world Roman Catholicism, so an ecumenist "Christianity" is perhaps the major means by which the British monarchy, down through the centuries, has deceived the world.
5. Hoey, *Charles & Diana: The Tenth Anniversary*, p. 69.
6. *Charles & Diana: A Royal Family Album*, p. 56. Hoey, *Charles & Diana: The Tenth Anniversary*, pp. 30-31, 70-71 and 154-155.
7. Alan Hamilton, "Prince of Peace," *Majesty* magazine, July 1995, Vol. 16, No. 7, p. 14.

speech at Oxford in which he decried the 'unmentionable horrors' perpetrated by Saddam Hussein."[1] After denouncing that former Iraqi strongman, and calling for "greater understanding between Christians and Muslims" in his Oxford speech, Satan's Prince found himself greatly esteemed in the eyes of the Middle East's allegedly more moderate Sunni Muslims. During his six-day, 1993 tour of the region, the then Prince of Wales enjoyed the lavish hospitality of Saudi Arabia, Kuwait, the UAE, and Jordan, while repeating his verbal attack on Saddam Hussein, likening the (now deceased) Iraqi leader to a lunatic. Charles' statements, combined with Great Britain's part in the 1990 war against Iraq, have given him "immense popularity in the region."[2] That of course, was Charles' goal, and since then it's just been more of the same.

In April 1993, the then Prince of Wales, who "pontificates on how to save the world," also gave "an earnest speech about global security."[3] Kah, remarking on Mideast peace and the AntiChrist's rise to power, observed and suggested:

> The Gulf War ... was only the latest tactic used by [elitist] insiders [such as President Bush (Sr.) and his cabinet][4] to accomplish their goal.... [It] would unite the nations of the world against a common enemy—which was necessary to take humanity the final step into a one-world system. [Saddam] Hussein played the [unwitting] role of the perfect villain....
>
> The war would also ... [show] other countries what they would encounter if they opposed the emerging world system. It would make true patriots who opposed the concept of a New World Order appear to be unpatriotic, while making globalists ... appear as patriots....
>
> The [(then)] recent war with Iraq might have been only a dress rehearsal for something much larger yet to come.... If there is another Middle East conflict, it could result from, or start out very similar to, the recent crisis; only this time, the chances of it escalating into a regional, or even a global conflict would be much greater....
>
> Two world wars have already been fought.... In each case, an aggressive power was used [as a pawn by one-worlders] to ignite a crisis that drew in the rest of the world.... After each war, a supranational organization was established for the alleged purpose of promoting world peace [and security]—first the League of Nations, then the United Nations....
>
> The United Nations today is the closest thing to world government that humanity has ever known.... The U.N. [currently] lacks only the power to implement and enforce its strategies.... The mere threat of a major world conflict could be enough to scare the public into accepting such a change....

1. Green, Smith, and Wright, "The Outsider," *People Weekly,* 6 Dec. 1993, p. 111.
2. Alan Hamilton, "Prince Charles visits the Gulf," *Majesty* magazine, January 1994, Vol. 15, No. 1, pp. 13-17.
3. Leslie Shepherd, *Associated Press,* "Diana most likely to succeed with press," *The Denver Post,* 1 May 1993, p. 22A.
4. Kah, *En Route to Global Occupation,* pp. 51-55.

> At some point, the [first] beast [of Revelation 13 (i.e., the AntiChrist)], or one of his representatives, will step forth with what will appear to be a brilliant plan for Mideast peace.... The agreement would probably guarantee Israel's security and would allow the Jews to rebuild their long-anticipated [(i.e., third and new)] temple.... The beast will succeed where others before him have failed. His appearance will most likely be as a democratic leader, ... appearing as a genuine man of peace.[1]

On a 1995 trip to Egypt and Morocco, then Prince Charles, who continues to be "held in high esteem in the Arab world," was met by several Muslim and Greek Orthodox dignitaries, including Egypt's Hosni Mubarak. Indeed, a "large portrait of the royal guest was lifted aloft by balloons alongside another of President Mubarak, the signal for mass cheering all around." Satan's Prince not only visited several mosques, the great pyramid of Cheops, the Sphinx, and "the dark, scented labyrinths of Fez, the greatest medieval city in the Arab world," but also received a clipping from what is alleged to be the ancient bush from which God, at the base of Mount Sinai, spoke to Moses. When asked, "How would you like to be Pharaoh?," Charles replied: "I don't know. I haven't been anything else." As yet another indication that "Charles is rapidly becoming Britain's most accomplished ambassador to the Arab world," "the Moroccan Crown Prince ... heaped further praise on his Islamic initiative."[2] Perhaps in a similar vein to receiving the "burning bush" clipping, Satan's Prince once drove "through the trick parting of the Red Sea at Universal" Studio, Hollywood.[3]

Since the first edition of this book went to press, Satan's Prince has continued a meteoric rise in popularity among the world's religious communities. Not only has Charles been hailed as "the most popular world leader in the Muslim community throughout the world" and received an Honorary Doctorate from Islam's "most ancient seat of learning" in Egypt, but he is portrayed as "Saviour of the World," being depicted as an angelic "winged god," and has even started his own multi-faith religious movement.[4]

King Charles III is also very popular among today's unregenerate Israelis, and as mentioned in chapter 4's discussion on his lineage, Israel's Channel 2 television noted in May 1996, that the then Prince of Wales is connected to Israel by his supposed Davidic descent. In fact, on May 6th of 2023, King Charles III was crowned sitting upon Britain's alleged throne of King David—not just King of the United Kingdom and several British Commonwealth nations, but as King of

---

1. Kah, *En Route to Global Occupation*, pp. 64-65, 141-143, 147.
2. Robert Hardman, "Desert Prince," *Majesty* magazine, May 1995, Vol. 16, No. 5, pp. 41-42.
3. Cathcart, p. 146.
4. For more information, see ch. 10's section titled "Respect," at p. 388.

Israel.[1] Indeed, he will be the *first British monarch* to visit the Holy Land. *Should Israel one day join the British Commonwealth, as earlier proposed, King Charles III would if not earlier, literally be acknowledged as her Davidic monarch.*

Yesef Berger, who is in charge of King David's Tomb, along with other unregenerate "rabbis" in Israel, have specially prepared both a Torah Scroll[2] and a golden crown for Israel's "Messiah"[3]—or the one we Christians call *the* AntiChrist or Anti-Messiah. (Berger et al. intend to present those to him, when he arrives to Jerusalem!) That

---

1. For more information, see ch. 16, "King Charles III: History's Ultimate AntiChrist," at p. 561.

2. Adam Eliyahu Berkowitz, "Torah Scroll Being Written to Present to Messiah Upon His Arrival," *Israel365 News*, 15 Dec. 2015; and A.E. Berkowitz, "Special Torah Scroll Written for Messiah Completed [PHOTOS]," *Israel365 News*, 22 Mar. 2016.

    "Yosef Berger, one of the [heretical so-called] rabbis in charge of King David's Tomb in Jerusalem's Old City, has been dreaming of … one Torah scroll to unify all of Israel. Recent global events have forced … Berger to move … quickly, … as he wants to be able to personally present this Torah as a gift to the [(Anti-)]Messiah. Many prominent [heretical (unregenerate) so-called] rabbis and [heretical occult] Kabbalists have told … Berger that may be very soon…. The inspiration for the project came from … Hosea (3:4-5)…. … 'In the end of days, when Israel realizes that all hope is lost and they have no solution or salvation from their plight, the people of Israel will be wise enough [(non-Christians are *not)]* to seek the three things which our ancestors despised: the Kingdom of Heaven, the Kingdom of David, and the building of the Temple," he [(Berger)] said. 'It is taught in the Yalkut Shimoni (a collection believed to have been arranged in the 13th century) Samuel 1: 106, "[(Heretical so-called)] Rabbi Shimon Ben Monsia said, 'No signs of redemption will be shown to Israel until they seek these three things — the kingdom of heaven, the dynasty of King David, and the building of the Temple.'"' …Berger believes that by <u>bringing all of Israel together in the writing of a single Torah scroll</u>—housed on Mount Zion, where King David is interred, and adjacent to the Temple mount—he will accomplish all three goals…. … 'The [(Anti-)]Messiah will also take part…,' [heretical so-called] Rabbi [David Hai] Abuhatzeira explained. 'The nation of Israel will give him this Torah…, as it is written 'Whither kings shall bring presents unto Thee' (Psalms 68:29) and 'Bring presents unto Him that is to be feared' (Psalms 76:11). … Berger realizes that preparing a gift for the [(Anti-)]Messiah is not a normal type of charity.… '…I want all … Israel individually to have a part in this Torah,' he explained…. Berger plans on having a parade through Jerusalem to dedicate it. The parade will go through every corner of the city, … to include as many people as possible, and will finish at the Tomb of King David, where the Torah scroll will be kept. 'We want … all … Israel … praising God and asking for him to come and redeem us'" ("Torah Scroll Being Written to Present to Messiah Upon His Arrival").

    "Berger finished this stage of the project, …. [and] the ceremony to consecrate the new Torah scroll began at the Kotel (Western Wall) in Jerusalem, and moved to the adjacent Ohel Yitzchak Synagogue, where the final letters were written by … [heretical] honored [so-called] rabbis. The ceremony was on … both the birth date and the … anniversary of the death, … of Moses. [(Will Moses prophesy and torment alongside the prophet Elijah, per Malachi 4:4-6 and Revelation 11:2-12?)] … Berger announced…, 'Moses was truth, and his Torah was truth, and this Torah will never change.' … The … celebrants then paraded around the walls of Jerusalem, which were lit [in Hebrew, with the words "David the King"]…. Thousands … accompanied the Torah scroll to its new home at David's Tomb, on Mount Zion. The momentous occasion was attended by several of Israel's leading [heretical so-called] rabbis [(e.g., Yitzchak Shtern, Shalom Berger, Reuven Elbaz, Dov Lior, and Shalom Ber Sorotzkin)]…, among many other honored rabbis and participants. The ceremony was immediately followed by a global recitation of the Shema prayer [(Deut 6:4)]. The organizers … were hoping that having all … Israel join together in reading the entire Shema, would save Israel from the terrifying wave of terror that has plagued the Jewish state…. [(Those who do *not* pray in Messiah Yeshua | Christ Jesus, who is The Way, The Truth and The Life, do *not* pray to The LORD God of Israel, but to a *false* "*god*" of their own *imagining*, which *cannot save.)*] …Berger has also initiated a new … project: a book of Psalms, which were written by King David, hand-written on parchment. When completed, the scroll [of David's psalms,] will be on display in a special case at David's Tomb…. Reading David's prayers at his burial site, will be especially fitting when the [(Anti-)Messiah, David's [alleged] descendent, finally arrives" (Special Torah Scroll Written for Messiah Completed [PHOTOS]").

3. Adam Eliyahu Berkowitz, "BIN Exclusive: Campaign to Construct Messianic Golden Royal Crown," *Is-*

crown is distinct from the one prepared by the Temple Institute, for the anticipated (unregenerate) high priest—also likely at some point, to be the Anti-Messiah.[1]

Unregenerate Israel, to whom Charles ingratiates himself, in the UK and in the nation-state—besides flattering Satan's "Palestinians," such as terrorist murderer Mahmud Abbas aka Abu Mazen[2]—is ready to give silver *half-shekels* too.[3] This brings us to another point. Not only was David Israel's king, but he also functioned as a prophet and high priest[4]—typifying Messiah Yeshua, whom the Anti-Messiah counterfeits. Unlike Levites and *cohenim* (priests) currently training for the resumption of Levitical duties, at a Tabernacle-like structure and/or a rebuilt "Temple" in Israel, Charles possesses the scripturally required documentation, spurious or not, to make the necessary claims. A priesthood without a registered genealogy is considered unclean; for this reason, many Israelites will *not* accept Temple worship until "Messiah"—that is, the Anti-Messiah—comes. Regarding the issue of Temple worship, we should also note that the Priory of Zion, looking for the "Prince of Lorraine" (i.e., Charles), claims to possess "the lost treasure of the Temple of Jerusalem," which it says will be "returned to Israel when the time is right."[5]

Is the Anti-Messiah, Lucifer's counterfeit Davidic king, (ecofascist) prophet, and ("all faiths" and beliefs) priest, about to massively fool Israel? Will Israel also crown King Charles III? Might he even one day sacrifice in heretical Israel? All shall soon see.

Might he—though an Israelite himself (e.g., a Danite)—even be *worshiped* by unregenerate "Jews?" We already know the answer is *YES* (see Rev 13:3-4, 13:8, 13:12, 13:15). Indeed, unregenerate Judaism itself does *not* oppose worshiping the *"right" Israelite,* even if he is just a man! Israeli "rabbi" Chaim Richman (ostensibly Orthodox), following Satan's Edomite Muslim-led October 7, 2023 Hamas attack upon Israel, stated: "You have to understand [that] *what's going on, here in Israel, ... will determine the fate of all humanity.* And ... I just want to say this to our Christian friends...: You guys are

---

rael365 News, 7 Dec. 2018.

1. E.g., see "Israel is waiting for the 3rd temple – Golden crown is ready," *Frankiy Sen.,* 25 May 2008, as posted at "https://www.youtube.com/watch?v=LqGvIyMZwH4" on YouTube.

2. Itamar Sharon and TOI Staff, "King Charles III: A friend to UK Jewry, with special and historic ties to Israel," *Times of Israel,* 10 Sep. 2022.

3. Adam Eliyahu Berkowitz, "Modern Revival of Lost Biblical Commandment Paving the Way for the Third Jewish Temple," *Israel365 News,* 8 Sep. 2023.

4. As stated in (a draft of) the *Messiah, History, and the Tribulation Period* multi-volume series, "David was not only the King of Israel, as well as a prophet of God, but at times he also exercised certain responsibilities of the high priest (e.g., see 1 Sam 23:6, 23:9-12, 30:7-8; 2 Sam 6:13, 6:17-18; 1 Chr 15:11-12, 16:1-4), while wearing the high priest's garments (e.g., see 2 Sam 6:14; 1 Chr 15:27; cf. Ex 28:2-15, 28:25-31, 29:4-5; Lev 8:6-7; 1 Sam 2:18, 2:28, 14:3, 22:18...)."

5. Baigent, Leigh, and Lincoln, *Holy Blood, Holy Grail,* p. 225. For more information, see ch. 4, "Prince of this World—a *Diverse* Lineage," at p. 79.

worshiping one Jew [(i.e., Christ Jesus / Messiah Yeshua)]. That's a mistake. <u>You should be worshiping every single one of us—because we [as God's collective or national firstborn son,] all die for your sins, every single day</u>, and that's exactly what's going on here. <u>We're all God's firstborn [son, Israel collectively and biblically], and we're dying for your sins right now—because the Jewish people and the Land of Israel, are the [sacrificial and sacrificed] bulwark against the Orcs</u> [(i.e., satanic and demonic evil, à la the *Lord of the Rings* books)]. Okay, the Orcs are coming, not to a theater near you, but to your home."[1]

---

1. 20:14 to 21:03, Chaim Richman, "Jerusalem Lights Podcast # 176 : Israel at War," *Jerusalem Lights,* 9 Oct. 2023, at "https://www.youtube.com/watch?v=rpGqkbrYzFE&t=1214s" on YouTube.

Except for the parts about a need to worship Israel and the latter's payment for the rest of mankind's sins, where Richman's spiritual arrogance and biblical illiteracy lead him astray, it is otherwise true that *the nation of Israel is God's firstborn son, being typologically conformed to Messiah himself, who is Israel*—and accordingly, Israel as a collective entity also suffers the equivalent of a national crucifixion, death, burial and resurrection. For extraordinary theological evidence, see this author's *Messiah, History, and the Tribulation Period* multi-volume series.

13

Potential for a Fatal Wound

And I stood upon the sand of the sea. And I saw a beast rise up out of the sea.... I saw one of its heads as *though he* had been slain to death, and the wound of his death was healed. And all the world marveled after the beast. So they worshiped the dragon who gave authority to the beast; and they worshiped [revered, honored, did homage to, deferred to] the beast, saying: "Who *is* like the beast? Who is able to make war with it?" And it was given a mouth speaking great things and blasphemies, and he was given authority to continue for forty-two months.... And it was granted to it [him] to make war with the saints and to overcome them. And authority was given to it [him] over every tribe and tongue and nation. And all those dwelling on the Earth—whose names have not been written in the Book of Life of the Lamb slain from the foundation of the world—will worship it [him].... Then I saw another beast rise up from the Earth, and it [he] had two horns like a lamb and spoke as if a dragon. And it [he] produces [brings about] all the authority of the first beast in its sight, and causes the Earth and those dwelling therein *to think* that they should worship the first beast, whose deadly wound was healed. And it [he] produces great signs, so that it [he] even makes fire come down out of the heaven [sky, atmosphere] onto the Earth in the sight of men. And it [he] deceives those dwelling on the Earth by the signs which it [he] was granted to do in the presence of the beast, saying to those dwelling on the Earth to make an image to the beast who had the wound of the sword and lived. (Rev 13:1, 13:3-5, 13:7-8, 13:11-14, Gk.)

Since 1979, past Pope John Paul II and former President Ronald Reagan received nearly fatal wounds, and each recovered. In April 1985, Satan's Prince and Princess Diana had a "private audience with Pope John Paul II at the Vatican."[1] Also, in November 1985, Charles met with then President Reagan at the White House, and then Vice-President Bush (Sr.) at the British Embassy,[2] and later, in February 1990, with then President Bush (Sr.). In 1991, Charles' son William sustained a fractured skull when he was "accidentally struck with a golf club," an injury that might have been, if not for modern surgical procedures, a deadly wound.[3] In fact, other than Gerald Ford, with whom Queen Elizabeth II met, Satan's Prince has met with *every* U.S. President since Richard Nixon—in person.

---

1. Burnet, *In Person, THE PRINCE AND PRINCESS OF WALES,* p. 8.
2. *Charles & Diana: A Royal Family Album,* pp. 50-51.
3. The London Bureau of People, p. 34. Prince William's injury required a seventy-minute operation to fix a depressed fracture on his skull. But William is *not* qualified scripturally to be the foretold AntiChrist.

What about King Charles III? In May 1969, shortly after his arrival as prince in Aberystwyth, Wales, for a two-month term that was to conclude with his formal investiture as Prince of Wales: "Gelignite was found in disused chimneys, hastily dumped machine-guns were retrieved from a lake dredged by the police, a time-bomb blew up at an R.A.F. radio post, and a fanatical plan for an armed uprising ran far beyond the scope of student japes.... On the final day of his visit [to Wales] a booby-trap bomb exploded in Caernarvon and gravely injured a young schoolboy playing with a football close by; he had to have a leg amputated."[1] Two men also died while attempting to plant a bomb on a railway line the prince was to use the morning of the investiture. In all, "There were fifteen bomb attacks before the investiture was over, the last one on the morning of 1 July itself, which was to have repercussions for years to come."[2] One week after a 1973 diplomatic stopover at Bermuda, during which Charles conferred with Sir. Richard Sharples regarding the "forthcoming independence of the neighbouring Bahamas," Governor Sharples and an aide were "shot dead."[3]

There has been speculation that Satan's Prince might one day be "targeted by IRA assassins," and "Di has confided to friends her belief that Charles 'has a death wish.'"[4] In fact, an IRA "killer-turned-informer" disclosed that "he was involved in an aborted plot to kill Prince Charles and Princess Diana," as "the Irish Republican Army [had] asked him to kill the couple at a rock concert at London's Dominion Theater on July 20, 1983."[5] Recalling the IRA's successful assassination of Mountbatten, Charles decried the death, "through the agency of some of the most cowardly minds imaginable," of "a man who was desperately trying to sow the seeds of peace for future generations." To Charles, Mountbatten became "a lifeless reminder of that dark, inexplicable side of man's nature, which brings death and misery to countless people all over the world."[6]

On January 26, 1994, a crowd of several thousand watched as a university student in Australia interrupted an outdoor ceremony at which Charles was about to speak. Lacking evident concern for his own safety, Satan's Prince hardly reacted when the student "ran out of a crowd, lunged at him and fired two blank shots from a starter's pistol...."[7] "Noted the *Daily Mirror:* 'Ice-cool Prince Charles shrugged

---

1. Cathcart, pp. 87, 98.
2. Junor, pp. 80, 86.
3. Cathcart, p. 138.
4. The London Bureau of People, p. 35.
5. The Associated Press, "IRA member tells of plot in '83 to kill royal couple," *The Denver Post,* 29 Nov. 1992, p. 3A.
6. Junor, pp. 145-146.
7. "Charles shows his princely cool under attack," *The Denver Post,* 27 Jan. 1994, p. 8A.

off the attack that could have cost him his life.' *Independent Television News* said the incident 'may have done more for the prince's reputation than a legion of public relations staff.'"[1] Then, on February 8, 1994, a New Zealander sprayed air-freshener at Charles while he "chatted with well-wishers ... in Auckland, the country's largest city."[2] As the guarantor of Israel's security, or in some other internationally prominent capacity, Satan's Prince would be an even more enticing target. (Consider, for example, the Muslim terrorist attempts on the life of the then UN Secretary General, the late Boutros Boutros-Ghali.)

After his 1981 wedding to Diana, Charles took some precautions. What was the couple's Highgrove home has "a steel-lined room for use in the event of an attack by terrorists. This is on the first floor, and measures twenty feet square; the staff at Highgrove call it the 'iron room'—though it is made entirely of steel. The room has been constructed in such a fashion that, if necessary, the whole room can fall intact onto the ground floor, even if the rest of the house is destroyed. Inside are medical supplies, long-lasting food and drinks, radio transmitters, air purifiers and special lavatories, all of which would enable the occupants to survive inside the 'iron room' for several months." It was at Highgrove that Satan's Prince held his "board meetings," where "the directors of what is known (behind his back) as 'Prince Charles Limited'" gathered.[3]

Decades later, in January 2002, *The Sunday Times* of London reported: "Fears of an Al Qaeda terrorist attack prompted Queen Elizabeth [II] to install ... panic rooms at Buckingham Palace and Windsor Castle.... The high-security rooms are encased in 18-inch-thick steel walls and are designed to protect senior members of the royal family from poison gas [(e.g., a chemical weapon)], bomb attacks and other assassination attempts.... The shell of each new room is bullet-resistant and fire-retardant, and the rooms themselves could withstand a mortar attack and even possibly a direct hit by a small airplane.... Windsor Castle is on the flight path for London's Heathrow Airport. The rooms are equipped with secure communications, beds, washing facilities and enough food and hot water for the royals to survive at least a week. The rooms were built following a security review after the Sept. 11, 2001, terror attacks in the U.S."[4] Likewise, Karnataka's *Deccan Herald* stated: "A similar safe room is expected to be constructed at Clarence House [(as of 2002)], the

1. "Attack gives career boost to Charles," *The Denver Post,* 28 Jan. 1994, p. 2A.
2. "Anti-royalist charged in attack on Charles," *The Denver Post,* 8 Feb. 1994, p. 6A.
3. Hoey, *Charles & Diana: The Tenth Anniversary,* pp. 136, 143.
4. "Gaffco technology to protect the UK Royal Family," *New York Daily News,* 12 Jan. 2002. Also see Associated Press, "'Panic rooms' to protect royal family," *The Tribune India* Online Edition, 12 Jan. 2002.

Queen Mother's former residence.... The shell of each room is a bullet-resistant and fire-retardant steel core made of reinforced metal with an inner layer of carbon fibre. It is capable of withstanding a mortar attack and, possibly, a direct hit by a light aircraft. ...Windsor lies in the Heathrow flight path.... Although the details are secret, Tom Gaffney, owner of Gaffco, a leading manufacturer of 'panic rooms', said he expected that the ... secure rooms would have their own air supply and filter system to keep out poison gases. Lighting and heat in the room would be powered by a submarine-style battery system.... A back-up electricity system would be run from a generator hidden outside. The emergency larder might be stocked with enough supplies of tinned, non-perishable meat and vegetables to last a fortnight. 'Together with the filtration system, the command and control system and the other accessories, we could be looking at 600,000 pounds [cost] each,' Gaffney said."[1]

Satan's Prince has also experienced and witnessed potentially fatal accidents, and is viewed as a bit of a "daredevil." In 1972, although he "had been driving fast sports cars since the age of nineteen, and was good at it," the then prince, at "the invitation of world champion racing driver Graham Hill to have a spin," "nearly killed himself in a Formula II racing car," having ignorantly run dry tires on a wet track.[2] Charles then witnessed the death of a close friend and the injury of that friend's wife in an avalanche—one that the then prince very narrowly escaped—during an off-course skiing adventure. Recall that in 1990, Charles nearly shattered his right arm in a polo fall. All that is just a partial *early* list.

What would have been construed as a fatal wound at the time of John's apocalyptic vision and writing, is often survivable today with prompt and proper medical care. Yet, the Apocalypse states clearly that the AntiChrist will be wounded "to death" (Rev 13:3, Gk.); at a minimum, we may reasonably expect that wound to ordinarily result in death. It seems plausible, therefore, that the anti-Christian world shall choose to view Charles' subsequent recovery as some sort of "resurrection." As one preacher put it: "Satan realizes that if he's going to get the acclaim of the people, he's got to do just what God The Father did, so what does he do? He gets the beast to be killed, or at least to appear to be killed.... And his [(seeming)] resurrection causes his great following by ... the world."[3] We have already seen

---

1. "Queen installs £1-million 'Panic Rooms' in Palace," *Deccan Herald,* 13 Jan. 2002, as seen at "https://web.archive.org/web/20031014135647/http://www.deccanherald.com/deccanherald/jan13/f6.asp" on the Internet. Also see: "Panic rooms installed in royal homes" at "https://www.telegraph.co.uk/news/1418658/Panic-rooms-installed-in-royal-homes.html".
2. Junor, pp. 119-120.
3. Dr. David Jeremiah, "The Reign of Terror," *Turning Point,* 12 March 2009.

that Charles and the royal family, besides supporting good forms of alternative medicine, also favor various forms of demonic healing.

Actual magicians partner with demons, to exhibit some actually supernatural (or *invisible-to-us,* technological) feats. These may include passing "objects" of different composition through one another (e.g., plant-based cloth, rope, metal, differing plastic or glass through an operating electronic device or human being), without harm or disruption to either (e.g., counterfeiting Christ Jesus passing through construction into a room); almost instantly (too fast for eyes) shrinking objects dramatically (e.g., a metal key, a *functioning* cell phone, etc.), and then just as suddenly restoring their sizes; destroying (e.g., tearing) and (invisibly) reassembling an "object" (e.g., paper); *telepathy* (i.e., remotely scanning another person's brain for thoughts, accurately); *perfectly controlled bidirectional teleportation* (e.g., swapping the interiors of two fruits while conforming to the smaller one's size and shape), *ostensible transmutation* (turning water into wine, juices and other drinks, via the noted teleportation capability), *remote heating, directed antigravitic movement of fiery objects or "balls of light"* (ostensibly, these are visible demonic manifestations) resembling miniature non-corporeal "UFOs."[1]

As impressive as those feats are—and they are *very impressive* indeed—they are *not* here salient. No, it is this next feat—which has been captured on film multiple times, before live audiences, and from multiple such magicians—that "takes the cake:" *mortal wounding* with *unseen angelic or demonic (aka "psychic") healing.* Some partnered (demonized and ostensibly possessed) magicians (e.g., Arnold Gerrit Henskes aka Mirin Dajo,[2] and David Blaine who "traffics" in frogs, a snake[3]) have publicly demonstrated being impaled and even fully thrust through, by swords, skewers and knives, including through vital organs and nerve bundle areas (e.g., a lung, heart or hand). The nature of such a piercing through a heart or a lung, where a sword for example, is thrust completely through their

---

1. See, for example, Xendrius, "SPIRIT Magicians: PART 1 - Reveal THIS - Criss Angel, Hans Klok, David Blaine & More" at "https://www.youtube.com/watch?v=ml7uHl1x09A"; "SPIRIT Magicians: Part 2 - Reveal THIS - (Cyril, Yif, Hans Klok)" at "https://www.youtube.com/watch?v=O3YLneFhr60"; "Demon Magicians: Part 3 (2015) Criss Angel Mind Reading, Live Show Levitation & More" at "https://www.youtube.com/watch?v=mirGPEfA68c"; "SPIRIT Magicians: PART 4 - Reveal THIS (Water to Wine)" at "https://www.youtube.com/watch?v=I5VV_FaEIFo"; etc. *Expand the description under any one of these, to also see parts 5 through 8, for more types and examples of satanic "magic."*

2. See "Mirin Dajo" at "https://www.youtube.com/watch?v=LFoctXxfs_A" on YouTube. Some allege this was a trick of employed internal "scar tissues," where the same spots were repeatedly impaled after healing (e.g., see "Sword Impalement - 1940" at "https://www.youtube.com/watch?v=KUl1LtrzWul" on YouTube). Such *conjecture* is *not* credible, and spots in fact, were clustered and/or differed.

3. See "Ricky Gervais Sees Pierced Arm: Real or Magic | David Blaine" at "https://www.youtube.com/watch?v=oLAs11gkqKE"; "Watch David Blaine Push an Ice Pick Through His Hand for Alec Baldwin" at "https://www.youtube.com/watch?v=VOzckvynDPw"; and "The Best of David Blaine | The Tonight Show Starring Jimmy Fallon" at "https://www.youtube.com/watch?v=k2FIFQIYBvA" on YouTube.

body from back to chest or side to side, and completely through vital organ(s), is expected to be fatal—and yet, rather than bleeding or seeming to feel any real level of pain, the weapon is then withdrawn and magician has *no material bleeding or even debilitating injury!* You may *watch real-life examples* on YouTube.[1] *(Do* watch at least one of these if you can.) So, could it be that the Devil or one of his underling fallen angels or demons, heals Charles of a (possibly non-bleeding) fatal wound? Years from now, we'll know.

Tom Horn would have us believe that the AntiChrist's seeming "resurrection" will occur in a crypt beneath Washington D.C.:

> I personally believe that AntiChrist is going to be revived from his deadly head-wound in the crypt that's beneath the floor of the rotunda in the U.S. capital dome. [The] ... U.S. capital dome is actually an antiChrist [(freema-sonic)] parody of the death, burial and resurrection of Jesus Christ. Jesus dies, [and] according to the [(apocryphal and mostly false)] scripture [of Enoch,] He goes into the underworld, [and] He presents Himself there, to those seventy-two fallen watchers that are bound, according to the book of Enoch.... Well, when you look at .... the base of it [(i.e., the capital dome)], there are seventy-two pentagrams; it ... forms .... the most power-ful stargate on planet Earth.... And it is the stargate that allows for traversing into, um, the pagan heaven of Osiris, but also coming back from the pagan heaven of Osiris, into this current world. Seventy two. Jesus dies, [per the book of Enoch,] He presents Himself to the seventy-two [fallen] angels, um, and yet its parodied ... in the U.S. capital dome.... But then beneath your feet, in the U.S. capital dome, is the [empty] crypt.... All of it is an antiChrist parody of Jesus.[2]

Wow. While interdimensional time-space portals or "stargates" *may* exist, and could peerhaps be technologically producible,[3] and though the described freemasonic crypt really exists, there is *zero (no)* evidence to support the rest of what Horn alleges, *nor may we rely upon fake scripture (e.g., the book of Enoch) or esoteric sources.* (In Charles' 2012 book *Harmony: A New Way of Looking at Our World,* for example, Satan's Prince notably *reveres* Osiris as a hero "god," intimating a false mythological connection to Christ Jesus.) Moreover, the very notion that Jesus would present Himself to fallen angels, especially after His crucifixion and before His resurrection, is *false.* Biblically, Jesus went to Paradise—a place beneath Earth's surface, which is separated from Hell by an impassable gulf (cf. Luke 16:23-26), a place where there are *no* fallen angels—before He rose

---

1. See, for example, "SPIRIT Magicians: PART 1 - Reveal THIS - Criss Angel, Hans Klok, David Blaine & More" at "https://www.youtube.com/watch?v=ml7uHI1x09A" on YouTube.
2. Ca. 1:19:19 to 1:22:05, "Tom Horn & Steve Quayle — The Imminent Alien Disclosure & Deception."
3. For more information, see the volume dealing with alleged Secret Space Programs and whistleblowers in the author's *Solar Apocalypse* series.

(Luke 23:43). If we are to accurately understand God's written Word, we must stick to the facts, and avoid such sensationalism.

14

The Image, Statue, and Mark of the Beast

Then I saw another beast rise up from the Earth, and it [he] had two horns like a lamb and spoke as if a dragon. And it [he] produces [brings about] all the authority of the first beast in its sight, and causes the Earth and those dwelling therein *to think* that they should worship [revere, honor, do homage to, defer to] the first beast, whose deadly wound was healed. And it [he] produces great signs, so that it [he] even makes fire come down out of heaven [the atmosphere] onto the Earth in the sight of men. And it [he] deceives those dwelling on the Earth by the signs which it [he] was granted to do in the presence of the beast, saying to those dwelling on the Earth to make an image to the beast who had the wound of the sword and lived. And it [he] was granted to give a vibration of air[1] to the image of the beast, that the image of the beast might *both* utter sound [speak] and cause as many as would not worship the image of the beast to be killed. And it [he] makes [compels] all, both small and great, rich and poor, free and slave, so that it[2] might give to them a mark [stamp] on their right hand or on their foreheads, and that no one *should* be able to buy or sell except one who has the mark, or the name of the beast, or the number of his name. Here is wisdom: Let him who has understanding calculate the number of the beast; for it is the number of a man, and his number *is* 666....

Then a third angel followed them, saying with a loud voice: "If anyone worships the beast and its [his] image, and receives [lays hold of, takes possession of, obtains, accepts] *its [his]* mark on his forehead or on his hand, even he shall also drink of the wine of the fury [indignation, wrath] of God, having been mixed without dilution in the cup of His wrath. And *he* shall be tormented in fire and brimstone in the presence of the holy angels and in the presence of The Lamb; and the smoke of their torment ascends forever and ever. And those worshiping the beast and its [his] image, even if anyone receives [lays hold of, takes possession of, obtains, accepts] the mark of its [his] name, *shall* have no rest day and night." Here is *the* patience [endurance] of the saints; here *are* those who keep the commandments of God and the faith of Jesus. (Rev 13:11-18, 14:9-12, Gk.)

How will we recognize the coming image and mark of the beast for what they truly are?

---

1. Compare "a vibration of air" with today's electronic speakers and speech synthesis. Interestingly, the two most popular commercial speech-recognition software packages bear the satanic titles "Dragon NaturallySpeaking" and "DragonDictate | Dragon Dictate" (now just "Dragon"). Originally from the U.S.' Dragon Systems, but now the UK's Nuance, both products had employed a red dragon logo as of 1998. *PC World* then wrote, "The accuracy of the program was almost scary."
2. This may refer to the image of the beast.

The image. What is already known about the image of the beast? *First,* it will represent the AntiChrist in some manner. As shown, Charles' heraldic arms as Prince of Wales, compass that "first beast." *Second,* the image will speak, though not necessarily understand speech. *Third,* unregenerate men will worship it. Per scripture, worship may include prostration before (lying face down on the ground), kneeling before, stretching forth a hand toward, kissing a hand (e.g., as is done to Roman Catholicism's pope), or bowing of the forehead. *Fourth,* the image will be associated with buying and selling, and with a mark or stamp (e.g., a tattoo).

The Greek text *might* additionally allow for the possibility of an implantable electronic bio-chip, which, in the fashion of integrated circuits generally, is made through a technological process involving a series of photographic plates or "stamps" (i.e., photolithography). What makes this particular possibility both fascinating and insidious is the little-known practice of *chip heraldry,* in which circuit designers and engineers actually incorporate *nano-scale* text (i.e., smaller than microscopic print), images,[1] and *heraldic achievements* onto the surface's of the integrated circuits themselves: "We have seen just about everything you can imagine on the surface of integrated circuits, so it was no great surprise when we discovered a *coat of arms* on a Hewlett-Packard microprocessor."[2] Finding such images within a chip is not easy: besides needing a powerful microscope, if you don't already know precisely where to look on the surface of a given unpackaged circuit, it is *at best,* like searching for a needle in a proverbial hay stack. While chip heraldry could ultimately prove to relate to the mark of the beast, the topic of the mark itself is vast, and so the author covers it in a separate book.

The statue. Earlier, we saw that the name "Charles" is indicated in the Hebrew text of Daniel 9:27, to include its meaning "man."[3] There is yet more to this verse, however, than meets the eye. Daniel 9:27 contains the word כָּנָף, typically pronounced *kan'p;* for many centuries, its correct or intended translation has been a subject of scholarly debate, disputation and speculation. Indeed, while perusing the translations of different Old Testament passages containing this Hebrew word, we find *kan'p* variously translated as "wing,"

---

1. Discovered images include the starship Enterprise, Excalibur sword, company and sports logos, cartoon creatures, an Illuminati pyramid, serpents, mythological gods (Thor, Anubis, and Godzilla), etc.
2. Michael W. Davidson, "Chip Heraldry," *Florida State University (in collaboration with Optical Microscopy the National High Magnetic Field Laboratory),* 22 March 2004 (emphasis added). For more information, see "Molecular Expressions: Silicon Zoo" at "https://micro.magnet.fsu.edu/creatures/index .html" and "Chip Heraldry" at "https://micro.magnet.fsu.edu/creatures/pages/spectrum.html" on the Internet.
3. See p. 383.

"winged," "wings," "pinnacle," "corner," "edge," and even "skirt"[1] (i.e., "loincloth"). In Daniel 9:27, this word is sometimes viewed as indicating where the abomination of desolation will be placed in the yet future tribulational Temple. At other times, *kan'p* is thought to describe the idol or statue comprising that abomination. In fact, its usage within Daniel 9:27 is even more meaningful. Keil and Delitzsch, in seeking to address this, state that Daniel 9:27 "can be rendered as such: 'on the wings of abomination he comes desolating.' ... The connection ... permits us, however, with Reichel, Ebrard, Kliefoth, and Kranichfeld, to think on nothing else than that wings ... are attributed to the [idol-image]," adding that the singular *kan'p* "does not oppose this, since it is often used collectively in a peculiar and figurative meaning."[2] Let's take a closer look.

What does Daniel 9:27 really tell us regarding the idol or statue associated with its roman prince? Might it actually be *winged*—as in a flying "man" (cf. "Charles")? Indeed, Daniel 9:27 literally speaks to a "[covering] wing," where "wing" or *kan'p* is a collective singular, rather than explicitly plural, and implies a "covering" or "overshadowing" (e.g., from the covering wing of a winged idol), *or* it speaks to an "[overspreading] winged [covering]," where we may again view *kan'p* in a collective and thus plural sense, as Keil and Delitzsch have done.[3] Thus, we may render this portion of Daniel 9:27 as *"an overspreading winged covering of* abominations *of* [a] desolator | destroyer | horror-causer | desolation." *Kan'p,* however, which is translated as "wing," "winged" or "wings" above, *may likewise be rendered as "loincloth."* Could this be an oxymoron, a contradiction in terms—or are *both* translations correct? If we are to accept both translations, then the Hebrew of Daniel 9:27 enfolds an unmistakable and truly remarkable description of a winged statue bearing a loincloth—just as it speaks to a prince of Roman lineage who is tallied in the name "Charles." This statue is a kind of *phoenix,*[4] and as such, it alludes, in an occult sense, to the apparent resurrection of the AntiChrist, after he receives a mortal wound.[5]

---

1. See, for example, Gesenius, 3671, p. 406.
2. C.F. Keil and F. Delitzsch, "THE BOOK OF DANIEL," Vol. 9 of *Commentary on the Old Testament,* p. 371.
3. Indeed, the Syriac or Middle Aramaic *Peshitta* renders *kan'p* as "wings" in Daniel 9:27. Also, consider the Roman eagle standards that were erected in the Temple during Christ's first advent.
4. Ancient Egyptians at times represented the winged phoenix with a man's body and face.
5. Earlier, when addressing the Hebrew text of Daniel 9:27 in the context of a covenant to be imposed and enforced over a seven-year period, the author noted that the "he" of Daniel 9:27 could alternately be understood as Jesus in the Crucifixion Week—a preterist interpretation that covers a period of seven days for the week rather than seven years (see ch. 12, "Charles, Middle East 'Peace,' and Global Security," at p. 481). While this is compassed within scripture's, and thus the author's Messianic view, as set forth in the *Messiah, History, and the Tribulation Period* multi-volume series, it is important and fascinating to recognize here that under such an interpretation, the phoenix enfolded within Daniel 9:27 would represent an allusion to the resurrection of Christ, the true Prince of Peace, in a verse that also then speaks to His prior death upon the cross, where He may have been covered only in a loincloth (e.g., see

Should any of this surprise us, really? The image described in Daniel 9:27—that of a winged man and prince—is strikingly similar to the appearance of Lucifer, who was the "messianic <u>cherub who covers</u>" prior to his fall (see Ezek 28:12-15). Before apostatizing (see Isa 14:12-14; Ezek 28:15-18*b),* when he became God's Adversary (i.e., *Satan* in Hebrew), he guarded God's Throne, *stretching his wings over it* as the "<u>covering cherub</u>" (Ezek 28:16). Thus, the AntiChrist takes after his father, Satan. If that were the end of the matter, it would be remarkable enough, but it isn't.

Indeed, the AntiChrist is also the successor to the very worst Egyptian pharaohs of history. So it is noteworthy, then, that there are many depictions of pharaohs wearing only loincloths—besides their necessary head gear (e.g., a false beard, headdress or crown, etc). Of course, the Greeks did the same thing. Athletes and soldiers under Greece's Antiochus IV, were *not* always completely nude, but often wore loin cloths. This brings us to the abominable statue of Zeus (cf. Rome's Jupiter) that wicked Antiochus IV placed in ancient Israel's Holy of Holies, defiling the Second Temple: Zeus was *customarily* so-attired—that is, *dressed only in a loincloth* (or a "robe" that was often worn only around the waist and legs, thereby resembling a skirt)! As the Satan-like "sky 'god,'" Greek mythology also holds that Zeus once appeared as a swan, while Roman mythology relates the eagle to Jupiter (cf. Obad 3-4; Rev 12:14 {cf. Isa 40:31}).[1] Such history *agrees* with a determination that *kan'p* in Daniel 9:27 compasses a winged *loincloth-attired* desolating idol.

In March, 2002, the secular press revealed that a 4.59 meters-high statue (15.06 feet)—one portraying Satan's Prince as a "winged god" dressed only in a loincloth and bearing the inscription "Saviour of the World"—would be fashioned in central Brazil:[2]

> LONDON – The [(then)] Prince of Wales is to be immortalized in bronze as a muscular, winged god.... Although the Prince is destined to become Defender of Faith..., the inscription on the statue in Brazil will honor him as "Saviour of the World." He is shown naked, apart from the loincloth, with giant, angel-like wings protruding from his back. His arms are extended as if offering comfort and security....
>
> The statue will dominate the town square, to be named after the Prince, in Palmas, the state capital of Tocantins on the edge of the rainforest [in central Brazil]. The sculpture, which will invite comparisons with the

---

Matt 27:28, 27:31; cf. Mic 1:8). Christ is generally represented on the cross wearing only a loincloth, with outspread arms and hands (cf. wings), and above the masses.

1. God associates His care for His people with the eagle (e.g., see Ex 19:4; Deut 32:11-12; cf. Isa 40:31; Jer 49:22; Rev 12:14). But the eagle symbol is also used in reference to Edom, Assyria, Babylonia and even Egypt (Jer 48:40-42, 49:16-17; Ezek 17:1-21; Hos 8; Obad 1-4; Hab 1:6-8; cf. Dan 4:33).

2. Some sources seem to say the full-sized statue will be about "four" meters, or perhaps twelve feet high, whereas others, which are likely more accurate, say its height will be 4.59 meters, or fifteen feet.

statue of Christ overlooking Rio de Janeiro from Corcovado, is set on a marble base. At its feet is an untidy mass of human bodies, one drinking from a bottle of wine, which is said to represent the world in a mess which the Prince is busy saving. Jose Wilson Sequeira Campos, the Governor of Tocantins, in central Brazil, said: "It is Prince Charles saving the world. We think he is deserving of it." Civic leaders commissioned the work in honor of the Prince's efforts in highlighting the threat to the rainforests from [(falsely alleged)] global warming. The Amazon contains about 40 per cent of the world's dwindling tropical rainforest. It also has the world's highest absolute rate of forest destruction, averaging nearly 8,000 square miles a year.

While the muscular physique of the statue, complete with bulging pectorals, may not immediately shout Prince Charles [(now King Charles III)], the facial features are unmistakable.... Mauricio Bentes, the sculptor, modeled the features on images taken from the Internet.

When presented with the miniature copy, the Prince ... said: "I am amazed and deeply touched." He had just emerged from the Cangacu [global warming] research station, which is situated in thatched wooden buildings perched on stilts in a swamp.

The royal party, having flown to Palmas from Rio, took a helicopter and motor launch ride along the piranha-infested Javaes River. The Prince had been welcomed to the region by a group of Karaja Indians who performed a traditional dance and presented him with gifts of a hunting club and a beaded garland.

The miniature statue no doubt will take pride of place on one of the mantelpieces at Highgrove, the Prince's home in Gloucestershire.

....An official at St James's Palace said: "It is very special to have a statue carved in your honor. Prince Charles is chuffed to bits...." ...

The Prince has regularly courted controversy with his views on the environment. In 2000, he was branded arrogant and ignorant by scientists after he blamed mankind's arrogance and disregard for the delicate balances of nature for severe weather conditions buffeting Europe.

He said that mankind had to learn the lesson of the effects of global warming so that "advances in technology do not just become the agents of our own destruction."[1]

A giant bronze statue of Prince Charles [(now King Charles III)] as a winged hero "saving the world" is to become the centrepiece of a remote Amazonian town. The Prince was presented with a model of the sculpture, which shows him with bulging muscles, pinned back ears and only a loin cloth to protect his modesty. During his visit to Tocantins state in central Brazil the Prince was told the full size piece would be erected in a square named in his honour in the main town of Palmas....

Charles arrived in Tocantins from Rio, where [(as a 'very good dancer'[2] and an impressive football player)] he showed his appreciation for Brazilian culture by doing the Samba with street dancers and playing football with children at a community centre [in the Baixada Fluminense slum, which has

1. Andrew Pierce, "Winged Prince is 'Savior of the World'," *Fox News Network*, 7 March 2002. Evidently, the statue has *not* been placed in a renamed square, but is hidden in a crate. Notice that Pierce said "Defender of Faith," and *not* "the Faith," saying Charles would get his wicked way.

2. "Charles dances samba in Rio," *BBC News*, 5 March 2002. For more information, see "https://news.bb c.co.uk/2/hi/americas/1856478.stm" on the Internet.

the highest population density in Latin America]. [In this, Satan's Prince "defied both health and safety scares" (i.e., a dengue fever epidemic and armed drug traffickers) to highlight British funding of a local community police programme to change "the face of policing in Rio," central to an effort to stem the murders of impoverished street children by corrupt Brazilian police.[1]....

Apart from the angel-like wings and muscular physique he also gave Prince Charles a full head of hair. At his feet are human bodies, one of whom is drinking a bottle of wine.... Accepting the scale model of Mr [Mauricio] Bentes' work the Prince said he was "amazed" and "deeply touched". Explaining its significance, Tacantins state governor Jose Wilson Sequeira Campos said: "It is Prince Charles saving the world".

Charles, dressed for the trip in a khaki safari shirt, is in the region for a visit to a global warming station. The Cangacu research station consists of thatched wooden buildings perched on stilts in a swamp.... ... The Prince was welcomed ... by Karaja Indians, who performed a traditional dance and presented him with gifts of a hunting club and a beaded garland.[2]

A giant bronze statue depicting a winged Prince of Wales [(now King Charles III)] "saving the world" is to take pride of place in a Brazilian town square named in his honour. A foot-high [(18 inches)] replica of the sculpture was presented to the Prince as he went deep into the Amazonian rainforest. ... With royal permission, the statue will be recreated in a full-size version to be erected in the state capital Palmas in a place to be named Prince Charles Square.

The statue, whose face bears more than a passing resemblance to the Prince, shows him reaching out with arching wings.... "It is Prince Charles saving the world," explained Jose Wilson Sequeira Campos, the governor of Tacantins state, in the centre of Brazil. The 53-year-old Prince professed himself "amazed" and "deeply touched" with the idea. ....[The] face is unmistakably that of Charles as [artist Mauricio] Bentes, who is well known in the region, studied pictures of the Prince on the Internet to capture his likeness.[3]

A remote Brazilian town in the Amazon is honouring [(then)] Prince Charles with a giant bronze statue depicting him as a winged hero "saving the world". The lean and muscular figure, dressed only in a skimpy loin cloth, will dominate a town square to be named after Charles, who in the sculpture has a huge pair of angel-like wings sprouting from his back....

A ... plaster model of the [4.59 metres-high] statue was presented to Charles during his foray into the jungle yesterday to visit a global warming research station. ...[Satan's] Prince was told that, with his permission, it would be recreated full-size [in bronze] in a newly-named Prince Charles Square [in the state capital Palmas]. [The Prince ... gave his permission for the move — which recognises his work for the environment....[4]]

1. "Charles draws crowds in Rio," *BBC News,* 5 March 2002. For more information, see "https://news.bbc.co.uk/2/hi/americas/1853730.stm" on the Internet.
2. "Prince Charles 'the winged hero'," *BBC News,* 6 March 2002. For the full article, go to "https://news.bbc.co.uk/2/hi/americas/1857482.stm" on the Internet.
3. "Prince 'saving the world' statue will go in Brazilian town square," *Ananova Ltd,* 6 March 2002.
4. St. James's Palace and the *Press Association Ltd,* 5 March 2002.

The statue shows him naked, apart from the loin cloth, and reaching out with his arms as if to offer comfort and security. (…Mauricio Bentes … is a well-known artist in Tacantins state.) When he was presented with the [miniature] replica, Charles, wearing a khaki safari shirt, declared himself "amazed" and "deeply touched".

The delicate and somewhat unwieldy [miniature] model was entrusted to his equerry, Commander William Entwistle, for the journey out of the jungle and back to the royal plane, a British Airways charter jet.

The sculpture is set on a marble base. At its feet is an untidy mass of human bodies, one of whom is downing a bottle of wine, that perhaps is supposed to represent the world in a mess — which the Prince of Wales [(now King Charles III)] is "saving". The statue was presented during the Prince's tour of the Cangacu [global warming] research station….[1]

Prince Charles has agreed to allow a four-metre [(apparently, 4.59 metres)] high bronze statue to be erected in the middle of Brazil's Amazon rainforest depicting him as "saviour" of the world in a loincloth with arms outstretched and suspended by giant wings.

The statue is a tribute from the people of Tocantins State, the remote Amazon region. It was the region's affinity with Prince Charles' [global] eco-friendly campaigning that inspired local sculptor Mauricio Bentes.

The statue showed him hovering over a sea of humanity, casting a benign look downwards with his arms in open embrace. "It is Prince Charles saving the world," said Tocantins' governor, Jose Wilson Sequeira Campos, who sprang the gift on Prince Charles as he toured a [global warming] research station in the middle of the rainforest swamp.[2]

The head bore a passing resemblance to the Prince of Wales [(now King Charles III)], since Mauricio Bentes, the sculptor, was basing it on images from the internet. But then there were the wings. They sprouted from the bronze figurine making it look like a Gothic batman and almost completely encapsulating the statuette.[3]

"This represents Prince Charles saving the world," said Jose Siqueira Campos, the governor of the Amazonian state of Tocantins. He looked thrilled. Charles, next to him, looked a little bemused. Mr Siqueira Campos then asked royal permission to build a life-size version of the winged prince and install it in Palmas, the state capital, in a square to be named after his illustrious guest.

"I am very touched," smiled the prince, who was wearing a safari shirt and Indian bead necklaces, as he looked around for help from his advisers. "And amazed." The prince's head of protocol gracefully accepted the statuette and then, holding it like a plate of strange local soup, walked across the wooden passageway to the royal speedboat.

---

1. Sam Greenhill, "Prince 'saving the world' statue for town square," *The Age* ("*www.theage.com.au*") / *John Fairfax Holdings Ltd,* 6 March 2002.
2. Ilha do Bananal, "Prince Charles as world's saviour," *AFP, Telegraph,* 8 March 2002. For the full article, see "https://web.archive.org/web/20170513000137/http://www.theage.com.au/articles/2002/03/07/10 15365728733.html" or "https://www.theage.com.au/world/prince-charles-as-worlds-saviour-20020308 - gdu13l.html" on the Internet.
3. The comparison to the black-clad batman of modern comic lore is appropriate given that Charles is rightly called the "Prince of Darkness," and his authority stems from Edward the Black Prince of history (i.e., the founding Prince of Wales of the Order of the Garter, who dressed entirely in black).

Palmas ... is Brazil's fastest growing town, attracting those drawn to the generations-old dream of finding fortune at the Amazon frontier. But with development comes the threat of environmental destruction, and the issue of protection was the reason for the prince's trip yesterday.

He visited an ecological centre on the Ilha do [(island of)] Bananal, the world's largest fluvial island, to be explained research on [(supposed)] climate change and to inaugurate a turtle sanctuary that is funded by a £50,000 donation from the Foreign and Commonwealth Office. By that time the prince had made Brazil, the world's fifth largest country, appear the size of a European principality since he had danced samba on the outskirts of Rio in the morning 1,000 miles away. The itinerary was a type of Cannonball Run in which the royal entourage visited both the most densely populated [first world] part of South America and one of its remotest [third world] areas within the space of only a few hours.[1]

WITH arms outstretched and suspended by giant wings, this is the [(then)] Prince of Wales in a loin cloth and, as the Brazilians will remember him, as "Saviour" of the world. This 2ft [(18 inches) miniature] statue depicting Prince Charles [(now King Charles III)] as an angel is the model for a 12ft [(or more likely, 15ft)] high bronze [statue] which, with the Prince's permission, will be erected in a town square in the middle of the Amazon rainforest and named Prince Charles Square in his honour.

The statue is a tribute from the people of Tocantins State, the remote Amazon region, which prides itself on its enlightened attitude to environmental issues. Its capital, Palmas, where the statue will be placed, likes to call itself the "eco-city of the third millennium". It is the region's affinity with Prince Charles's eco-friendly campaigning that inspired local sculptor Mauricio Bentes, who studied the facial features of his royal subject on the internet in an attempt to capture a true likeness.

The depiction ... is ... a sculptural metaphor for the Prince's almost evangelical stance on environmental issues.... The statue shows him hovering over a sea of humanity, casting a benign look downwards with his arms in open embrace. There is a passing resemblance facially.[2]

Recall that then Prince Charles received personal credit for the success of the 1992 Rio Earth Summit, from world leadership. Later, the summit led to the Kyoto Protocol, an international environmental treaty tied to the United Nations Framework Convention on Climate Change (UNFCCC or FCCC). The Kyoto Protocol was then essentially supplanted by more stringent and broader global environmental "agreements," or United Nations COP "accords" (e.g., 2015's COP21), for which Satan's Prince himself more than set the tone. These

---

1. Alex Bellos on the Ilha do Bananal, "Charles, winged and saving the world," *The Guardian Unlimited,* 6 March 2002. For the full article, visit "https://www.theguardian.com/uk/2002/mar/06/monarchy.alexbellos" on the Internet.

2. Caroline Davies in Ilha do Bananal, "Amazon tribute to Charles, the model environmentalist", *Telegraph.co.uk,* 7 March 2002. For the full article, see "https://web.archive.org/web/20220815085805/ht tps://www.telegraph.co.uk/news/worldnews/southamerica/brazil/1387048/Amazon-tribute-to-Charles-t he-model-environmentalist.html" or "https://www.telegraph.co.uk/news/worldnews/southamerica/braz il/1387048/Amazon-tribute-to-Charles-the-model-environmentalist.html" on the Internet.

treaties and (thieving) "agreements"—the Rio Earth Summit, the Kyoto Protocol, and the UN COP accords—are all the result of *an immoral push for taxing global governance by any and all means,* to include the propagandistic use of environmental and scientific fraud, leading to delustional "global warming" hysteria and *anti*-science ecofascism.[1] Scripture warns: "Professing themselves to be wise, they became fools .... who exchanged [traded] the truth of God for the lie, and worshiped and served the creation [creature] rather than [before | in the presence of | more than] The Creator, who is blessed forever" (Rom 1:22-25, Gk.).

A fantastic example of this fraudulent propaganda comes from fat-faced liar Al Gore, who as an unlearning cohort of Satan's Prince at the 1992 Rio Earth Summit, put forth "An Inconvenient Truth"[2]—a 2006 global warming "docudrama" that is appropriately viewed as a *convenient elitist fabrication* from start to finish[3]—as well as his *lies-based* book, *The Inconvenient Truth: The Planetary Emergency of Global Warming and What We Can Do About It.* These, just like the above mentioned treaties and accords, can be traced directly to Charles. Indeed, around December 2006, Gore met privately with then Prince Charles at Highgrove to strategize on environmental issues and Charles' upcoming "Accounting for Sustainability" project, which promotes so-called "carbon emissions offsetting" schemes for

---

1. Al Gore, for example, is on record as stating: "Adopting a central organizing principle—one agreed to voluntarily—means embarking on an all-out effort to use every policy and program, every law and institution, every treaty and alliance, every tactic and strategy, every plan and course of action—to use, in short, every means to halt the destruction of the environment.... Minor shifts in policy, moderate improvement in laws and regulations, rhetoric offered in lieu of genuine change—these are all forms of appeasement, designed to satisfy the public's desire to believe that sacrifice, struggle and a wrenching transformation of society will not be necessary" (Gore, *Earth in the Balance,* p. 274). This extremism includes manipulation of oil and gas availabilities and prices in the United States to try to force a reduction in driving automobiles, as well as provide the impetus to invest in new technologies to power transportation that would reduce greenhouse-gas emissions: "We now know that their cumulative impact on the global environment is posing a mortal threat to the security of every nation that is more deadly than that of any military enemy are ever again likely to confront.... I [therefore] support new laws to mandate improvement in automobile fleet mileage, but much more is needed.... It ought to be possible to establish a coordinated global program to accomplish the strategic goal of completely eliminating the internal combustion engine over ... a twenty-five-year period" (ibid., pp. 325-326). Gore's eco-fascism extends to a "mother earth goddess worship" global education program: "The fifth major goal of the Global Marshall Plan should be ... to organize a worldwide education program to promote a more complete understanding of the crisis. In the process, we should actively search for ways to promote a new way of thinking about the current relationship between human civilization and the Earth" (ibid, pp. 354-355). For more information, see ch. 11's section titled, "Environmentalism, the Rio Earth Summit, and the Kyoto Protocol," at p. 402.

2. For more PC (Politically Correct | Prince Charles) propaganda, see Al Gore's former "ClimateCrisis" site: "https://web.archive.org/web/20121127235544/http://www.climatecrisis.net", and *give it time to load.*

3. Several sources of solid information regarding the errors, falsehoods, and outright fabrications and lies that are evident in Al Gore's "An Inconvenient Truth," are readily available on the Internet. As Christians, we must not fail to recognize that the environmental and other natural catastrophes that are manifesting around our world are all subject to the sovereignty of God; only He can intervene to stop their continued, and indeed exponential, escalation. Scripture is clear, however, that God will not do so before Jesus returns; in that regard, Jesus Himself stated, "unless those days were shortened, no flesh would be saved; but for the elect's sake those days shall be shortened" (see Matt 24:21-22).

513

companies![1] Then, on January 28, 2007, at the Harvard Club in New York City: "Gore presented Charles with the Global Environmental Citizen Award, given by the Center for Health and the Global Environment at Harvard Medical School. Gore, who praised the Prince of Wales' knowledge and passion, said he and the prince have had conversations about the global environment for 20 years [(i.e., since 1987)]. 'We had great fun talking about all these issues long ago,' the prince said. 'I've been so fascinated watching his career, and to receive this award from him really has been a particular privilege, but also immensely special.'"[2]

Consequently, Satan's Prince (now King Charles III) is hailed as the supposed *environmental* "Saviour of the World."[3]   Indeed, Charles was "in the region [of Tocantins state,] for a visit to a global warming station [consisting] ... of thatched wooden buildings perched on stilts in a swamp."[4] That "official trip to Brazil to promote social and environmental projects, began in the capital Brasilia, with [Charles having] lunch with the country's president."[5]

---

1. "[The] Prince of Wales, the Archbishop of Canterbury and Al Gore will this week launch a new project to encourage big business to become more 'green'. Prince Charles is said by aides to be 'totally committed' to the scheme in which companies will be urged to assess—and reverse—the damage they are doing to the environment. *The Sunday Telegraph* can also reveal that Prince Charles recently held a private meeting at Highgrove ... with Mr Gore ... to discuss their shared passion for saving the environment. Now Mr Gore has agreed to provide a video message, which will be screened to nearly 200 politicians, businessmen and other guests at St James's Palace.... The former vice-president ... warns that the world has just 10 years to save itself. Prince Charles will be one of three speakers at the launch of his Accounting for Sustainability project. The others are the Archbishop of Canterbury, Rowan Williams, and Lord Browne of Madingley, the chief executive of [British Petroleum].... It is understood that companies will be encouraged to follow Prince Charles's example by 'offsetting' their carbon emissions. This is a service that allows individuals and companies to repair some of the [environmental] damage caused by harmful emissions by channeling funds into projects that reduce levels of carbon dioxide in the atmosphere.... Royal sources say that Prince Charles [(now King Charles III)] ... believes that climate change is 'the greatest challenge to face mankind'.... New measures introduced at Highgrove include using rainwater to flush lavatories and irrigate land, a reed-bed sewage system to process waste, and eco-friendly insulation and double glazing to increase heating efficiency. At Home Farm, the prince's 900-acre organic farm near Highgrove, there are plans to produce and sell bio-diesel" (Andrew Alderson, "Prince recruits Gore for 'green' campaign," *Telegraph.co.uk*, 2 Dec. 2006). *This is reminiscent of when businessmen and apostate "Christians" of Nazi-era Germany joined forces with Hitler and the Nazis.*

    In November 2004, Gore and former Goldman Sachs CEO David Blood, founded the London-based hedge fund Generation Investment Management, which brokers and speculates in "carbon swaps" for "sustainable and socially responsible investing!"

2. Karen Matthews, "Prince Charles Gets Environmental Award in Visit to New York," *The Associated Press*, 29 Jan. 2007. Right before this, on the same trip to the United States, Charles and "wife" Camilla visited Independence Hall in Philadelphia, and attended a reception at the National Constitution Center. Afterwards, Charles stopped "at International House, a non-profit organization housing nearly 400 students, scholars and interns from more than 65 nations," where he attended "a round-table discussion of urban renewal efforts in foreign countries." Subsequently, "the prince and duchess" attended "services at Arch Street Presbyterian Church, spiritual home of the Welsh community in Philadelphia" ("Prince Charles, wife Camilla begin U.S. Trip," *The Associated Press*, 28 Jan. 2007). Yet, Charles is Satan's Prince (see ch. 8, "The Red Dragon and Prince Charles' Investiture as Prince of Wales," at p. 207).

3. Recall that "Civic leaders commissioned the work in honor of the Prince's efforts in highlighting the threat to the rainforests from global warming" (Pierce, "Winged Prince is 'Savior of the World'").

4. "Prince Charles 'the winged hero'."

5. "Charles draws crowds in Rio." Also, see "Charles dances samba in Rio."

Since news of Charles' "winged god" idol first broke in 2002, its artist, Maricio Bentes, apparently died. While the miniature copy, *shown on this book's back cover,* was presented and given to Satan's Prince, photographed by the world press, and reported by the BBC,[1] the location of the full-sized statue is currently a mystery. With this in mind, we must consider the fact that scripture clearly teaches that abominations to the AntiChrist, arguably involving a statue, will one day be erected and stand in the Holy Place (i.e., the Holy of Holies, on Israel's Temple Mount). That event, to which both Daniel and Jesus referred, shall result in "destruction" and signify the start of the Great Tribulation.[2]

Clearly, the "winged god" statue makes Charles look "angelic" after his spiritual father—the Devil—who is a *cherub.* In fact, this abomination of Charles *and Lucifer* (aka Zeus or Jupiter)—at either fifteen *or* twelve feet in height (4.59 *or* roughly "four" meters are suggested by reporters)—is to be of comparable height to the two angelic statues or *cherubim* that were historically placed to either side of the Ark of the Covenant in the Holy of Holies, in Solomon's Temple. These statues were each ten cubits high (1 Kings 6:23-28, 8:6-7), which the author calculates at either fifteen or twelve feet— and thus the same height as that intended for the full idol.[3] Could this very wicked statue now be—or soon be—in the midst of unbe-

---

1. For more information, see "Prince Charles 'the winged hero'" at "https://news.bbc.co.uk/2/hi/america s/1857482.stm" on the Internet. A *Real Video* version of the actual BBC report from Jennie Bond, had been linked *within* the article, but the BBC "retired" it. None the less, this author's 2005 presentation on Charles as *the* AntiChrist, which is available from Prophecy House, *has* the *audio* portion.

2. For more information, see the discussion on the abomination of desolation and the related notes in the chapter (or section) titled "Identifying the covenant of Daniel 9:27," in the author's *Israel, "Peace" and the Looming Great Tribulation* multi-volume series.

3. There is no agreement on the precise length of the royal or regular cubits—assuming there actually were two different cubits in use in ancient Israel. Many assert that a royal cubit was about twenty-one inches (see below), whereas the regular cubit was between seventeen and eighteen inches, though some say it was only fourteen-and-one-half inches. This issue may not be definitively settled apart from Jesus' return—when He can then tell us—or an archaeological discovery of yet-surviving biblical artifacts for which dimensions are stated in scripture.

    Whether or not we accept a royal cubit based upon the mathematics of the Great Pyramid at Giza—that is, as having been 0.5236 meters or 20.6102362 inches—the Hebrew word used throughout the bible for a cubit, to include where we are told that the statues were each ten cubits high (see 1 Kings 6:23-28, Heb.), is *am'ah* or *Aleph-Mem-Hey* (i.e., אמה), which has a calculated value of 46. If we were to go out on a limb and understand this value as a curious reference to what we now call centimeters, so that the biblical cubit was 46 centimeters or 0.46 meters (a real possibility), then the common biblical cubit would have been 18.11 inches, a surprising agreement with the often accepted measure of about eighteen inches. Ten cubits would then have been about fifteen feet and one inch.

    So, if we accept the most commonly suggested measurement of eighteen inches for a cubit, each of the two Holy of Holies' cherubim would then have been fifteen feet high. But if we accept fourteen-and-one-half inches for a cubit, then each cherub statue would have been just twelve feet high.

    Now, it is curious that two different heights for the full-sized "winged god" statue should have been reported—assuming reports of "four meters" were not really just loose descriptions of 4.59 meters. Might the media involved have been told that the statue would be "ten cubits" high, so that they then tried to calculate a modern English height for themselves? We don't know. Regardless, only one seemingly precise figure has been reported, and that is 4.59 meters or about fifteen feet.

lieving Israel? Or, could one like it be erected atop the Temple Mount, in Jerusalem? (Ask yourself this: "Who else is being called 'Saviour of the World' *and* honored with such a statue?") It was right after the world became aware of this abomination, that Satan's Prince launched "Respect"—his own multi-faith new-age religious movement—*with wicked rabbinic complicity!*[1] Here's the miniature statue version, unveiled two decades ago:

So, there is an *existing* "King Charles III" idol which, if placed in a new Holy of Holies or the like in Israel, *would surely constitute scripture's abomination that causes desolation.* Yet, more could possibly attend it, such as speaking "greenhouse gas"-mitigating holograms. (Maybe they'll add sum sulfur and heat the air too?) And who better to introduce such techno-babel to the propagandized masses than ... Charles (2008) and Al Gore (2007)![2]

---

1. For more information, see ch. 10's section titled "Respect," at p. 388.
2. Actually, the idea of using remote speaking and conferencing technologies in place of jet-setting to

His detractors may argue that his green principles do not stand up to close examination. But now Prince Charles is set to confound his critics by addressing an energy conference — as a hologram.

Determined to keep his environmental damage to a minimum, Charles will save the 15 tons of carbon that would have been generated by flying himself and his staff 7,000 miles to the World Future Energy Summit in Abu Dhabi. Instead, a three-dimensional image of the Prince will be seen giving a five-minute talk. [(Yet, Charles as the hypocrite he is, flies often.)]

Charles recorded the message at Highgrove ... [in November (2007)]. It will be transformed into a hologram-style image using technology based on a Victorian music-hall technique called "ghosting" A video projector will beam an image of the Prince on to the floor. It is then reflected up on to a paper-thin sheet of foil to create an optical illusion that makes him appear as a 3-D image on stage.

Former US Vice-President Al Gore used similar technology to appear as a hologram at Wembley Stadium at the beginning of the Live Earth concerts earlier this year. Charles was heavily criticised in January [(2007)] when he and the Duchess of Cornwall flew to Philadelphia with 12 staff to pick up an award from Mr Gore honouring him as an environmentalist. That trip created 20 tons of carbon dioxide.

The idea of the virtual Prince came from the Abu Dhabi conference organisers, who asked British events firm Revolution to produce special events for the three-day summit which starts on January 21 [(2008)]. Revolution managing director Matt Sims said: "He will appear as a three-dimensional holographic image. All credit to His Royal Highness who was very [ecofascist and] keen to do it. It's all about zero carbon emissions." ...

He will be seen standing, making gestures and moving around the stage. The video is not a true hologram as you cannot see different parts of the image by moving around [it]. The technology is only a little more expensive than shooting a standard high-definition video, Mr Sims added.

A Clarence House spokeswoman said: "His Royal Highness was happy to do it. He often does video messages but this is his first hologram."[1]

Environmental enthusiast Prince Charles has delivered a speech to a green energy conference in Abu Dhabi — as a hologram. He may not be known as the most modern of men, but the Prince of Wales' concern for the planet has catapulted him straight into the 21st Century.

He was keen to prove his green credentials.... So he appeared as a hologram to congratulate Abu Dhabi for its plans to harness the power of natural resources to create a new zero carbon city called Masdar. As the 3D image vanished, he left the audience with the words: "I am now going to vanish into thin air, leaving not a carbon footprint behind!" ...

The speech by the 3D version of Charles was recorded in person at Highgrove last year, using technology from British multimedia firm Musion. Musion's Director Ian O'Connell told *Sky News* how it works: "It's based on a 19th Century Victorian trick known as Pepper's ghost. By using a high

---

events is great. The problem here, however, is the eco-fascist agenda, or "green religion," behind its promotion, which is rooted in false spiritualities and world views.

1. "Prince Charles will appear at conference as a hologram," *Mail Online*, 15 Dec. 2007. See "http://www.-dailymail.co.uk/news/article-502599/Prince-Charles-appear-conference-hologram.html" on the Internet.

brightness projector, going through a special polymer foil that's invisible to the audience, you can project something that's 2D back into a virtual 3D image...."

Prince Charles [(now King Charles III)] is not the first famous person to use the technology. David Beckham recorded a message in LA, appearing as a hologram in London. Richard Branson has also given virtual speeches, as did Al Gore during his Live Earth concerts last year. But the most exciting thing is that those behind the technology have already tried out a live hologram — in other words, they have the technology to make people appear as a hologram in real time from anywhere in the world....

Trewin Restorick, of the energy saving charity Global Action Plan, told Sky News: "... businesses need to follow ... Charles' example, ... by using video conferencing or even by using ... tele-conferencing more."

The decision to appear as a hologram follows stinging criticism last year, when Prince Charles and the Duchess of Cornwall emitted 20 tons of CO_2 flying to the US [as hypocrites,] to collect an environmental award.[1]

Will a holographic speech or other similar technology, perhaps even an interactive version of such technology, accompany the future abomination that causes desolation? It seems quite plausible.

The mark. For this, you will want to get the author's book titled *The Mark of the Beast: A Comprehensive Treatise.* The book goes beyond covering the "basics," to offer a lot of unique and helpful information *not* found in other books by similar titles. Due to the amount of material involved, it is necessarily a separate work.

---

1. Catherine Jacob, "Prince Charles Delivers Virtual Speech As Hologram," *Sky News,* 7 April 2008. For Charles as a hologram, see "Prince Charles Speaks in Abu Dhabi Via Hologram" on YouTube. For the full article, see "https://web.archive.org/web/20091207050140/http://news.sky.com/skynews/Home/Sky - News-Archive/Article/20080641301500" on the Internet.

15

Ba'al-Molech Worship

Throughout this work, we have seen that Satan's Prince is anything but Christian, that he is in fact, thoroughly Luciferian and antiChristian. Recall, therefore, that it was in Birmingham, England, in April 2002, that then Prince Charles launched "Respect," or his own *multi-faith new-age religious movement.* Little did we know that from Birmingham, this same Charles would later oversee an elaborate occult and New Age ceremony, one in which the Commonwealth nations and indeed all mankind would be openly invited and encouraged to worship Lucifer (Satan), through a giant Ba'al-Molech bull idol, sexual satanism, and more.

On July 28, 2022—at the twenty-second Commonwealth Games—Prince Charles officiated over a (global) Commonwealth worship of Ba'al or Molech (via a massive bull or Molech idol, from which the more modern Baphomet imagery and symbolism largely derive), by seventy-two nations and territories comprising the British Commonwealth. Held at Alexander Stadium in Birmingham, England, it was a staggering and altogether shocking display. Importantly, the full opening ceremony[1]—which though below painstakingly detailed and addressed, you *shall* want to see for yourself, if possible—as well as some important portions of, and segments related to it,[2] are available online.

Significantly, Birmingham is a core city of the Industrial Revolution. An artistic 6.5-ton bronze bull, produced by British sculptor Laurence Broderick, resides in its original 12th century Bullring Market, which has served as a traditional public meeting place since

---

1. See Haris, "Commonwealth Games Birmingham 2022 - Opening Ceremony," *BBC News,* 28 July 2022, as posted at "https://odysee.com/@Haris:d/Commonwealth_Games_Birmingham_2022_-_Opening_Ceremony:2" on Odysee. For another network's version, which with different narrators having somewhat different narratives (but conveying essentially the same messages), someone captured in an inferior manner, see "Birmingham 2022 Commonwealth Games Opening Ceremony Reaction" at "https://www.youtube.com/watch?v=QkB1CNdd9Ts" on YouTube. There are also some official previews, which provide only a very small sense of the "grandeur" and extent of the event, such as "Birmingham 2022 | Opening Ceremony Highlights," *Commonwealth Sport,* 29 July 2022, as posted at "https://www.youtube.com/watch?v=vil5jnW4JnQ".
2. E.g., see "Duran Duran light up Opening Ceremony of the 2022 Commonwealth Games | Extended Highlights," *NBC Sports,* 29 Jul. 2022, at "https://www.youtube.com/watch?v=9iVnx3P2wk0"; "2022 Commonwealth Games Opening Ceremony – Raging Bull Entering Arena," *Evan Davis,* 1 Aug. 2022, at "https://www.youtube.com/watch?v=53PhzNHSOmU"; "The Raging Bull | Commonwealth Games Opening Ceremony 2022 Highlights," *Colombo Times,* 28 July 2022, at "https://www.youtube.com/watch?v=5XDt7ljdPnQ&t=15s"; and "2022 COMMONWEALTH GAMES – BEAST BULL & STAR SHARDS," *Dave Shadow,* 4 Aug. 2022, at "https://www.youtube.com/watch?v=LgPhqmIdoks" on YouTube.

1832. Birmingham's flag likewise bears a golden (yellow) bull's head on a red field, with adjacent yellow and blue "mountains"[1] (cf. the gold calf idol and Mount Sinai, a theme to which we'll return).

At 2022's Commonwealth Games in Birmingham, the Prince of Wales—as the foretold AntiChrist of scripture, who just *six* weeks later, became King Charles III—oversaw an overt worship of the Devil, before a large portion of mankind—using a massive dark animatronic (mechanical) bull, highlighted in crimson red with smoking nostrils, as *an idol to Satan*. Iqbal Khan, the artistic director for this opening ceremony, states: "The bull is the guardian spirit of Birmingham. I wanted to create an image of a creature, that has been celebrated, used, maybe oppressed—but has enormous power. But we see it revealed as a creature of light. ... We see it being revealed as something that when it's embraced and seen properly, gives us more than we thought it could ever do. The bull carries enormous weight of meaning—and is a kind of guardian spirit.... I'm really excited about first of all, scaring people with the bull, terrifying them, making them feel like it's a scary object—and realizing that ... fear was to do with their own preconceptions, that actually the bull is a creature of love. And I wan them to fall in love with it, I want them to embrace it—and I think that's a beautiful journey to take the audience on."[2]

"Khan hopes the the audience watching the show, either during the live event at the Alexander Stadium in Birmingham, or via television coverage beamed into homes across the country and the globe, will be receptive to the message of hope, light, love and unity. These vital seeds, Khan hopes, will germinate and one day flower into a more unified community that is built and nourished by a shared humanity."[3] Yet, that (actually) *anti-peace and anti-light* Ba'al-Molech bull idol, in keeping with the European theme of the "goddess" Europa and the bull, was mounted by a whore. (Compare that to the comparable in meaning, but symbolically different "first beast" and "Mystery Babylon" whore of Revelation 13 and 17:3-6, where the "first beast" relates to Charles' heraldic achievement as Prince of

---

1. The overall pattern of the City of Birmingham's flag is "technically" described as a "golden vertical zig-zag offset to hoist dividing blue and red, with a bull's head in the centre" ("Flag of Birmingham," *Wikipedia.org*, 20 Apr. 2022).

2. "Raging Bull from Birmingham 2022 Commonwealth Games Opening Ceremony now on public display: Making of Raging Bull (video)," *Birmingham2022.com*, 29 July 2022, as posted at "https://www.birmingham2022.com/news/2700483/the-opening-ceremony-bull" on the Internet; and ca. 3:40 to 4:07, "The Commonwealth Bull," 5 Aug. 2022, as posted at "https://www.youtube.com/watch?v=NpDEzNcE-jko" on YouTube.

3. Rangzeb Hussain, "Birmingham 2022 opening ceremony thrills with a fiery journey from dark to light," *I Am Bingham*, 29 July 2022.

Wales.) But there is *much more* of import, to this paganism and satanism, some of which we'll below mention or even detail.

Of material import, *Ba'al* means "Master" in relation to Satan, including "by any other name," whereas *Adonai*—whether spelled out or abbreviated (as *Yod-Yod)*—means "Master" in relation to The God of Israel, *Yahveh.* But this same bull idol ancient pagans used to represent the Devil as "Master," was also called *Molech* in the Old Testament—a word when pronounced only a little differently (i.e., as *Melech)* means "King." Pagans called and some still call Ba'al "Molech" or "King," whereas those who worship the real Creator of the heavens and the Earth, *Yahveh,* call Him "Melech" or King. A variant of the same word, spelled with a concluding Aleph or ostensibly pronounced as though one were present, means "Queen." Thus, a pagan woman riding Molech may be construed to represent the Devil's "Queen." Moreover, *mel'ak* as yet another pronunciation of the same-spelled word, means "advice" or "counsel." Pagan women and spiritual whores (cf. so-called "LGBTQIA+ whatever" sexual satanists) ritually sacrificed their children to a fiery Molech idol (an ancient form of infanticide, aka "abortion")—just as hundreds of millions of pagans do today in "abortion mills"—whereas we who serve The God of Israel and Christians, continue to dedicate our children and their (hopefully) godly lives to the latter.

From the above, it is evident that Satan has long masqueraded as "Master," "King" and "Counselor," as he acts to further counterfeit The Creator of the Universe. With that in mind, should we be surprised to see the modern European Union portray itself as the "goddess" (queen) Europa riding a bull? Should we be surprised to see the foretold AntiChrist as deriving from that "union" and then ruling it as the Devil "incarnate," once Satan has possessed him (at the start of the Great Tribulation)? Given that Satan's Prince has just led the world in worship of Molech, the answer to those questions should now be self-evident.

Before we do a "deep dive," let's note some general observations from Michael Snyder, things a typical Christian paying attention should ostensibly notice. Be aware that like so many, however, Mr. Snyder remains (as of this writing) *sadly ignorant* of Prince Charles' (now King Charles III's) identity as the foretold AntiChrist, so that Snyder fails to even observe that it was *he*—the AntiChrist himself—who personally opened the event on behalf of his spiritual father Satan, not just his (yet alive) mother Queen Elizabeth II.

Snyder remarks: "They aren't even trying to hide it anymore. ... It had been given the nickname 'Raging Bull,' and it absolutely dwarfed all of the human participants.... The 'hero' of the opening ceremony, a character known as "Stella" (for "stellar," as in *interstellar),* calmed the creature down and then all of the human performers gathered around the giant bull and literally began to bow down and worship it. ... The symbolism in this 'ritual' was well planned in advance, and the organizers knew exactly what they were doing. But they were also counting on the fact that the vast majority of the general population, would not consciously catch on to what was actually taking place. ... 'In artistic depictions and archaeological finds, Baal took the shape of a bull or ram, and had associations with fertility.' ... 'Baal Hadad originated in Mesopotamia.... He ... became more popular after the fall of the Third Dynasty of Ur (2047-1750 BCE) during the First Babylonian Empire (c. 1894 to c. 1595 BCE).' ... It is also interesting to note that the ancient deity known as ... 'Molech' was also often represented by a bull: 'In addition to sexual rituals, Moloch worship included child sacrifice, or 'passing children through the fire.' It is believed that idols of Moloch were giant metal statues of a man with a bull's head. Each image had a hole in the abdomen and possibly outstretched forearms that made a kind of ramp to the hole. A fire was lit in or around the statue. Babies were placed in the statue's arms or in the hole. When a couple sacrificed their firstborn, they believed that Moloch would ensure financial prosperity for the family and future children.' ... It would have been bad enough if they would have stopped there. But ... all of the human performers gather around the bull and literally start bowing down to it. ... We are obviously meant to understand that the performers are worshiping the bull. If people from the ancient Middle East were to watch this spectacle, they would immediately identify it as Baal worship. ... The elite love to use ... public spectacles to mentally and emotionally condition us. ... Unfortunately, the vast majority of the population is still dead asleep. They have no idea what the elite are doing, even though it is happening right in front of their eyes."[1]

Notably, the above happened less than five weeks after the U.S. Supreme Court overturned "Roe v. Wade," and thus the anti-Constitutional Federal-level serial mass murder of unborn children—and as sexual and other satanists had greatly increased attacking those opposing the gruesome murder of helpless innocents, the latter effectively constituting sacrifices to the Devil "by any other name." With those attacks upon those who would defend unborn children, Hellbound sexual satanists expressed fear that Christians and conservatives would next act to curtail sodomy, lesbianism, mutilating so-called "transgenderism," and other abominable sex-based wicked-

---

1. Michael Snyder, "Now They Are Literally Bowing Down And Worshiping Baal Right In Front Of Our Eyes," *The Most Important News,* 4 Aug 2022.

ness of the so-called "LGBTQIA+ whatever" and alleged "non-binary 'gender'" lunatics.

Concurrently, the world was "exiting" the (ostensibly) first *overt* stage of the satanic ecofascist *depopulation* agenda—that is, use of the COVID-19 bioweapon and its attending toxic COVID-19 spike protein-producing mRNA and DNA gene "therapeutic" *debilitation and death jabs.* (Those are *not* vaccines, but were bioengineered from the start, to debilitate and finally murder, in confusing and thus "stealthy" ways—so that by the time the general public would begin to recognize what had been done to it, the ensuing mass debilitations and sudden deaths would already be underway and *unstoppable.)* The next stage commenced only a little later, with the World Economic Forum's (WEF's) announcement of the Great Reset— where the WEF's founder and head Klaus Schwab is a knight of, *actually works for, and reports to Charles, the foretold AntiChrist.* (Charles as the Prince of Wales, not Schwab, first announced the Great Reset—or the *actualization* of the New World Order conspiracy —to the world. It is the foretold AntiChrist's ecofascist agenda.) WEF adherents have proceeded at a blistering pace to destabilize and destroy yet-essential global energy systems and output (despite lies to the contrary), and with that, to destroy transportation systems as well as food production and distribution—all to starve many who yet survive, to illness and death. Such things bring further wicked lawlessness.

Ultimately, the depopulation agenda is about global mass death and *destruction of fertility,* with a further goal of *enslaving*—not freeing—the small surviving percentage of mankind.[1] In other words, what Luciferianism, or satanism as a false "light," brings is precisely the opposite of its empty and vacuous promises: it brings war, famine, death, darkness, enslavement, etc. Let's continue.

There was so much satanism *and anti-Christian apocalypticism* in the opening ceremony of the 2022 Commonwealth Games, that we really must overview it all. Afterward, we'll consider how the games were subsequently closed.

We might think that an "everything old is new again" worship of Satan, would start on Earth. But those responsible for the opening ceremony, felt it necessary to incorporate Lucifer's fall from grace, including when he was cast from the second heaven (i.e., the visible Universe) to Earth—with much (cursed) "creative license."

---

1. For more information, see this author's book compassing the depopulation agenda—titled *The Great Reset: To Digitally Enslave, Depopulate, and Transhumanize*—which sits beneath the British Monarchy and particularly King Charles III.

The audience was told: "Tonight, we're gonna sprinkle a little stardust on the ceremony. The death of a star in the outer Universe, and the shards of light from its demise, are heading straight for us. ... [The] ... death of a star, can trigger the birth of other stars, and ... this one is going to do just that." In other words, this star, which represents Lucifer (Satan) and his fall from grace, and its "shards," which represent Lucifer *and* those angels who chose to follow him in his rebellion against God our Creator, are to produce "other stars" (e.g., sinful New Agers and other rebels against The Creator of the Universe)—*counterfeiting* the "wise" saints of God, "and those who turn many to righteousness," who "shall shine like the brightness of the firmament, ... like the stars forever and ever" (Dan 12:3).

Thus, the thoroughly satanic and anti-Christian ceremony began with a bright white "star" (meant to symbolize Lucifer) exploding somewhere beyond Saturn (and thus, also intimating *Satan),* so that fragmentary meteors (i.e., "fragments of that star") reach and descend to modern Earth's surface, leaving "shards" or white-lit crystals exposed on the ground, so that they are easily found (see below). Besides the fall of Lucifer with other sinful angels from Heaven, that strange start may remind us of historical events immediately preceding, and also precipitating Noah's Flood on Earth[1]— and even correlate to *false* New Age apocalypticism (see below).

With those Luciferian shards landed, the audience saw New Age cultist and pagan Stella (cf. interstellar) find hers. Indeed, she picked it up, only to then *pray to Lucifer, as the top fallen "angel of light." We're told, "Into that shard, she whispers her hopes and dreams." New Agers and cultists are presumably meant to understand that Lucifer (i.e., Satan), as the anti-Christian universal "Christ Consciousness" (or the like), "manifest" within her white-lit crystal or shard.* (There is *no* universal "Christ Consciousness" in reality, just born-again Christians—real ones—joined to the Body of Christ, or the Church, and thus one another, via the indwelling of The Holy Spirit.) Seventy-one (71) New Age "dreamers," *plus* "dreamer" harlot Stella, found their own Luciferian white-lit crystals or shards "around the

---

1. God blew at least one substantial planetoid (e.g., which had existed between Mars and Jupiter) into fragments (i.e., asteroids and comets), so that perhaps the entire solar system was then pelted—to include Mars, the Moon and Earth. Those events destroyed much evil perpetrated by fallen angels and their demonic progeny (i.e., the humanoid *Nephilim,* whose Hebrew "name" translates to "fallen liars") *throughout our pre-Flood solar system*—leaving certain remaining planetary bodies seriously damaged (e.g., as Mars, the Moon, and ostensibly Venus, make plainly evident); our solar system was made far less habitable, than God had originally intended. Beyond all that corruption and damage, however, Earth itself was struck, with the incoming bombardment serving to collapse the planet's former water-vapor canopy (thicker atmosphere) and fracture Earth's surface, contributing to (and apparently largely enabling) the comparably divine (in origin) global Flood on Earth, in Noah's day. (Earth was struck only thousands of years ago, *not* millions.) For more information, see this author's *Solar Apocalypse* multi-volume series.

Commonwealth"—intimating and heralding a global New Age paganism.

A lead (druidic) bard also then retrieved a lit fallen shard or white-lit crystal (like Stella's, see below) from a body of water or "canal" (cf. a moat), at the base of the (mock) *Tower of Babel,* itself "constructed" throughout much of the opening ceremony. He then raised his Luciferian white-lit crystal shard, and as one voice among a series, in a demonic cacophony, we heard him and others (bards, etc.) declare: "In times of darkness, we carry a dream of light, that calls us all to gather .... in a vibrant, multicultural city [(cf. Babel)]. ... Those shards—an important indicator of a better collective future."

A Ghanaian black "bard" (drummer-percussionist Abraham Paddy Tetteh) beat an "African Sakara drum" atop the "Tower of Babel" (their words), thereby "sending out a call to gather" (cf. the call "to gather ... to the battle of that great day of God Almighty," or Armageddon, in Revelation 16:13-14 and 16:16). With ostensibly African music and additional drum beats, the audience then saw a partially open circle of crimson- and white-handed worshipers before the mock Tower of Babel, as it displayed the word "Bullring," and were told: "There's ... a call to prayer. The call to gather goes out to all those others, who have found their own shards—their own fragments of that [fallen] star."

The (druidic) bard possessing the noted white-lit crystal shard, then stood in the midst of the pagan worshipers and raised that "light" toward the sky—as others who had entered the area next to him, then raised their own clasped hands like arrows to the sky. As for the word "Bullring," it intimated the coming Ba'al-Molech bull idol, representing Satan (see below), which made its way to the center of Alexander Stadium, to symbolically *supplant* St. Martin "in the Bull Ring"—a parish church residing at the center of Birmingham's famous stadium-shaped Bullring Shopping Center. The message, then, was to be one of the Devil *supplanting* God our Creator.

As a collective "trumpet" (ostensibly counterfeiting scripture's "last trumpet") sounded, Stella and the other "dreamers" (also referred to as "72 dreamers," though less frequently), as those bearing the found Luciferian shards, then collectively experienced anti-gravitic (levitation) effects, so that they in their respective homes, were "raptured" (lifted from the Earth). The audience is told: "Rather magical powers in those shards, [which] fly [72] houses over to Birmingham. To a Commonwealth courtyard? No problem at all."

Indeed, we saw the "dreamers'" homes transported—floated through the sky, some toward and over a lighthouse, one above a lake and forest, and then above cultivated land and between city buildings—to Alexander Stadium, where dozens of homes were seen overhead (holographically, and in some cases, perhaps also suspended on wires). With those above tens of thousands of stadium spectators, dancing worshipers below—those with the crimson pink and white hands—lifted those toward the sky and the overhead floating houses, welcoming the "dreamers" (e.g., on their "return" to Earth). (The homes then "magically" end-up on the ground, in the stadium.)

A young Queen Elizabeth II then declared her personal intention to serve the British Commonwealth, from 1958. Of course, that's the same year the red dragon officially became the national symbol of Wales, only to be slated for son Charles' later heraldic achievement and his corresponding July 1969 investiture as Prince of Wales.

Next, seventy two legacy and current fossil-fueled automobiles (connected to Birmingham's Longbridge factory, with Birmingham being "the headquarters of the motor trade") were driven into the center of the stadium—signifying a sort of "green religion" *sacrifice.* As they took their positions to portray a Union Jack from overhead, Prince Charles drove his old 1970 Aston Martin convertible sports car —modified to run on byproducts from *wine manufacturing and (cheese) whey-fermentation* (i.e., it consumes "biofuel from supply waste")—into the stadium. It was a "James Bond" moment, in a car Charles had used to chauffeur Diana before their marriage. Here, the Prince of Wales' wife and lurid historical whore Camilla accompanied him, in tow. (A central Land Rover's license plate explicitly acknowledged the roasting ecofascist Prince Philip, who in the end, managed to "become" the weaponized COVID-19 virus and its attending fake "vaccines," which debilitate and even murder.) Before all that, however, Charles' greeted and shook hands with quite a few men, women and children, as well as help (staff), and stopped for photos with various teams, at the stadium.[1]

At this point, overt introductions of the drudic Awen took place. We could see it stylized in an evoking pattern (one meant to spiritually affect *the audience)* of fanned red or scarlet, whitish-yellow and blue streaks of smoke from overhead "red arrows" (jets), "led by [the] Red One squadron leader" (cf. the red dragon or Satan). Likewise, it is stylized on the Ceremonial Flag of the Commonwealth Games Federation (tantamount to the global Olympics flag, but overtly occult with the Awen), as well as the ceremonial baton (see below) and other emblems, shirts and medals of the Commonwealth games. In fact, Satan's Awen (in an evoking orientation, and with its

---

1. E.g., "Charles Poses for Team Photos Ahead of Commonwealth Games," *Royal Family Channel,* 28 July 2022, as posted at "https://www.youtube.com/watch?v=jnijkGaV0fs" on YouTube.

three lines each artistically split into a "V"-like pattern) proved to be a central to the whole event—as did the large multi-story mechanical Ba'al-Molech bull idol, Tower of Babel, and the satanic "all-seeing eye" of Lucifer.

The audience was informed: "So the houses have landed in the Commonwealth courtyard" (i.e., around the center of the stadium), "Stella and the 71 dreamers, they've got their prized possessions [(i.e., the Luciferian white-lit crystalline shards in their suitcases)]— and they're greeted by the [druidic] bards of Birmingham, the guardians of the city's history." As a character, we may here view Stella as a New Age pagan and worshipful whore, leading seventy-one (71) other "dreamers." (As later detailed, we may also view them as "stand ins" for the seventy original post-Flood nations, plus Jerusalem or Israel. Though "Jerusalem" *is* later mentioned in these Commonwealth Games, an *invited* Israel is *not* thus far part of the British Commonwealth, nor a games participant.) The earlier lead bard, then satanically proclaimed, "We combine, blend and bind as one every creed, color and tribe." And: "We are prophets of a hundred tongues—tongues on fire. ... Followers of love, disciples of unity. We are the prophets of diversity" (e.g., satanism, sexual and otherwise).

Stella and a group of "dreamers" then gathered at the base of the tower, and raised their lit white Luciferian shards to extinguish the flames of a "library" fire[1] (implying Lucifer's help). With the fire out, all the other "dreamers," standing in two nested semicircles before the mock Tower of Babel, faced the "smoking" tower and raised their white lit Luciferian shards toward the sky (ostensibly, to mock God our Creator). Here, in the midst of the "Christian" United Kingdom, and before the entire British Commonwealth, the "holy Koran" (their words)—which actual Christians know to be satanic, blasphemous, and filled with unholy lies leading only to Hell—was then loudly mentioned; God's written Word, on the other hand, as found in the Hebrew Old and Greek New Testaments, was *not*. Truly, Satan is the "father of lies:" per scripture, *Hell's* fire "is not quenched" and "shall never be quenched" (Mark 9:44-48)—just as God's written Word (His books), will forever endure.

Later in the ceremony, those same "fiery" displays on the tower, served to present competing nations and show their flags, when the "athlete parade" transpired. Consider for a moment, therefore, that this whole thing occurred as the world sat on the precipice of (the yet to come, as of this writing) World War 3![2]

---

1. Historically, the enacted fire destroyed a collection of works from William Shakespeare.
2. For more information, see *North Korea, Iran, and the Coming World War: Behold a Red Horse*.

With the vehicles in the center of the stadium removed, non-Christian Black Sabbath's lead guitarist Tony Iommi, who is himself from the city of Birmingham, appeared. Dressed in all black and wearing a large golden cross around his neck, Iommi stood at the base of the (mock) Tower of Babel and played, while white-clad dancers (from the Birmingham Royal Ballet) performed all around the tower—including within the reflective and "regenerative" canal (pool) of water (cf. a moat) at the tower's base, "cleansing" themselves. The spiritually *unclean* dancers then faced the tower, and raised their clasped hands skyward. (Are they meant to resemble candles, with their heads as wicks? We aren't told and don't know.)

That portion of the ceremony is actually titled, "Hear My Voice"—and concluded with a duet of Celete's "hear My Voice," which includes these lyrics: "Hear my voice. Hear my dreams. Let us make a world in which I believe. Hear my words. Hear my cries. Let me see a change.... You may think I won't be heard. Still I'll raise this hand, spread this word—these words of fire, of hope and desire; and I'll let them free. ... Let us make a world in which we believe—in which we believe...." While that *occult prayer* was sung, with Black Sabbath's Iommi continuing to play his guitar and a black-clad choir participating, the dancers sat around the singers, including in the canal's water, facing outward—and then arose to continue dancing. Was the Devil thus beseeched, in song? (If you answer "Yes," you earn a point.)

There's more: A woman swam *inside* the tower (per the displays, celebrating), while Stella and the other seventy-one (71) "dreamers" then joyously "celebrated" in the stadium—as open books were paraded on polls (as if floating just above, to be reached). Likewise, individuals atop slithering blue lights ringing the stadium's oval field, rejoiced and celebrated. The stadium crowd then also cheered loudly, and multi-colored streams of "LGBTQIA+ whatever" smoke blasted from the top of the stadium, high into the air—with similar colors displayed on the Tower of Babe. Yes, it was one big and spiritually damned celebration of the Devil's sexually abominable (e.g., unnatural, as well as unfruitful and infertile) "LGBTQIA+ whatever" (depopulating) movement. (Similar colors were everywhere seen throughout the stadium, including via the different outfits of participating athletic teams.)

Does all that sound like the *start* of a "church" service *to Satan*? It surely was. (In fact, explicit *worship of the Devil—as Ba'al Molech* —would soon come, after more debauched sexual and other satanism.) Rangzeb Hussain remarks: "The action-packed opening ceremony also included special performances from a vast choir, a cappella group Black Voices, vocalist Ranjana Ghatak, Tony Iommi from Black Sabbath, dancers from Birmingham Royal Ballet, and members of the City of Birmingham Orchestra under the baton of conductor Alpesh Chauhan…, and a whole host of other artists…."[1]

We also saw the "baton" in a portion of its multi-month relay (later addressed), with someone wearing the "rainbow colored" costume of the "LGBTQIA+ whatever" "bull" mascot (officially named "Perry,"[2] and representing Ba'al-Molech wearing a "glistening gold medal"), as well as the Flag of Wales bearing the red dragon (Satan). Online, there is also "Perry's Activity Book."[3] (Those things were followed by something even more massive. But first, more sexual and other satanism was "on the menu.")

"The Destroyers," a "chaotic" "doom" band embracing and ostensibly promoting lunatic "transgenderism," then engaged in an "edgy" and "burlesque" display,[4] with some of the surrounding performers holding blue and red parachutes, before the mock Tower of Babel! Introducing "Ginny" Lemon (see below), as well as a series of Birmingham-centric "industrial" floats (for film, entertainment and music, printing, etc., some accompanied by lunatic transvestites and "transgenders," one overtly placing a finger to his mouth to signal "shhh"), the band played their new track "Forward!," which features artwork bearing their name "The Destroyers" between the horns of the Ba'al-Molech bull idol,[5] to introduce the heathen abomination that would shortly follow (see below). (Of course, God's Word tells us that liar Satan destroys, murders, steals, etc.)

The hellish lyrics of "Forward," include: "Time, Ticking! Steel for nails and iron for chains, slaves of furnace fire and flames. Press, Onwards! … People parched…. Toil, Longer! … Push, Forward! Quarry stone and dig for coal, mechanise and fire the soul. … Chase a u-to-pi-an dream." As those words were heard, a blinking and moving eye peered from the tower, signifying Lucifer's presence (as

---

1. Hussain, "Birmingham 2022 opening ceremony thrills with a fiery journey from dark to light."
2. "Perry the Bull was designed by 10-year-old Emma Lou from Bolton, near Manchester, who won a national competition for making the mascot. 'I chose a bull because of the bullring in Birmingham, and I decided to use hexagons because they are the strongest shape and the whole world depends on each other,' Emma told the *BBC*. Chief executive of Birmingham 2022 Ian Reid said: 'Perry is everything I hoped our mascot would be and more: bright, colourful, energetic and totally representative of modern Birmingham and the West Midlands. Perry celebrates diversity, community and our region's heritage as well as its future'" ("Who is the Birmingham 2022 Commonwealth Games mascot Perry the bull?," *News.com.au*, 25 July 2022).
3. See "World, Meet Perry" for the activity book and an animated "Perry" video, at "https://www.birmingham2022.com/mascot" on the Internet.
4. The "About" portion of The Destroyers' "seductively dangerous," "Babel"-connected, "utopia"-mentioning "Gypsy jazz" web page states: "Their behemothic sound is a chaotic cacophony of klezmer, Balkan and British folk…. Faustian [this and that] … destroy inhibitions and leave audiences bewildered, transported, beguiled, and wild. These tenacious, traveling troubadours have liberated ears, hearts, and minds" (TheDestroyers.co.uk, 29 Aug. 2022).
5. See "https://destroyershq.bandcamp.com/track/forward" on the Internet.

the "all-seeing eye")—also with horned headgear bearing the word "Lemon" above and below it—and at least two demons, manifest (i.e., were displayed) directly behind the band.

With such a wicked introduction, the "LGBTQIA+ whatever"-arrayed "transgender" lunatic, "drag queen" and lurid child-grooming sexual satanist known as "Ginny" Lemon, "overflew" the stadium's field in an ornate lemon-like balloon, engaging in damnable perversions before the stadium's crowd and indeed much of the world. The abominable Mr. Lemon provocatively stated: "I'm a sneaky butcher.... Behind every smile, is a home | hope to beguile. ... Anyone fancy a slice of Lemon?" Below, the field was filled with "metropolitan" citizens and revelers, including ones with blue and red umbrellas.

Stella and the seventy-one (71) "dreamers" then entered the field to participate. Also, the bible was explicitly *mocked* at the base of the tower, as the words "repent, ... follow the light" were exclaimed—and hellish demon danced in the background. Some other sexual satanist exclaimed, "I'll show you mine, if you show me yours."

The audience was then told: "We're having a parade of famous market characters, from the 1940s to the 1960s. Yet, they've been buying and selling in the famous Bullring marketplace here, from the twelfth century onward." (Cf. James 4:13-14.) Sexual satanist Mr. Lemon then tormented everyone's ears with an edgy "song"—as all the revelers and "dreamers" gathered below him and his lemon "balloon," to dance and behave wickedly. That "LGBTQIA+ whatever" "color and noise" culminated when they all suddenly mimicked a pair of *"bull's" horns* on their heads, fingers pointed upward, and then each one twisted in-place to notice the entry of their giant bull idol!

This all brings us to another salient, though brief point—an additional type and blasphemy. Seventy (70) of the dreamers *(excluding the one standing-in for Israel),* may *additionally* be construed as a satanic *antithesis* to the seventy (70) disciples whom Christ Jesus sent to evangelize "as lambs among wolves," who were to "carry neither money bag, knapsack, nor sandals," while greeting "no one along the road," as they each entered a "house" (Luke 10:1 and 10:3-7; see 10:1-20). Satan's "dreamers" (seventy without Israel and beast-riding whore Stella) are above sent as wolves among "lambs," bearing Luciferian shards, a combination of suitcases, bags and knapsacks, and wearing shoes—greeting everyone (because they are all about "tolerance and diversity") while overlooked by an evil-faced crescent moon (cf. the "Moon god" Sin and *al-Ilyah* or

"Allah"), right before destructive fire erupts (cf. the "Sun god") and Satan's *unholy* Koran is introduced (cf. Gen 3:7)—with each (as the plot goes) having *exited* a house.[1] They *oppose everything* The LORD's disciples represent! Indeed, Charles is "the man of sin | Sin"[2] (e.g., he worships Allah as a Muslim "convert") and the "son of perdition | destruction" (2 Th 2:3*c-d*). Sin is the transgression of the law, it is lawlessness (1 John 3:4), and until Christ Jesus returns, lawlessness shall increase (e.g., Matt 24:12).

But there is *so much more* to the evil the *seventy-one (71)* "dreamers" symbolize. For example, some may wonder if they could represent an anti-Sanhedrin of gentiles, with the harlot as their "leader" atop the *beast* (Satan)! (Charles is of both Gentile and Is-raelite descent.) Could that portend things to come, under Mystery Babylon, under Charles as *the* AntiChrist?

A spiritually lost nation-state: Israel. "Yosef Berger, the [heretical so-called] rabbi of King David's Tomb on Mount Zion, has initiated a special project to create a golden crown to be presented to the mes-siah-king [(i.e., the foretold AntiChrist)] upon his arrival in Jerusalem. ...Berger ... explained ... that we are today living in the beginning of the [(anti-)]messianic era [(i.e., the Great Tribulation nears)]. Creating such a crown, he said, and uniting the 70 nations of the world around the project, will hasten the arrival of the king [(i.e., Charles Philip Arthur George)]. 'For [(nearly)] 2,000 years, [apostate and heretical] Israel has waited for the [(anti-)]moshiach ([anti-)]messiah),' ... Berger said. 'As a symbol of our belief that this period of waiting has ended [(for the *real* Messiah, Yeshua, it has *not*)], we should prepare a crown, since the first act of the [(anti-)]moshiach will be to restore the Davidic Dynasty, which will be visibly unlike any other kingship that has ever existed. ... The rule instituted by the [(anti-)]moshiach will unite all 70 nations, bringing them in joy to Mount Zion, to serve HaShem (God, literally "the name")'.... [Berger] ... emphasized that a king of Israel would en-sure that the exile would end, the ingathering of the exiles would be complete, the Temple would be rebuilt and the Temple service rein-stated. 'We are commanded to anticipate this, to pray for it, at all times until we merit seeing it with our own eyes,' ... Berger said. ...

---

1. See ca. 1:14:31 to 1:23:14, "Commonwealth Games Birmingham 2022 - Opening Ceremony," *BBC News*, 10 Aug. 2022, as posted at "https://odysee.com/@Haris:d/ Commonwealth_Games_Birmingham_2022_-_Opening_Ceremony:2" on Odysee.
2. Among the names for paganism's "Moon god," is *Su'en* (Akkadian) or Sin, from which the English word "sin," via other linguistic roots, ultimately derives. The original Hebrew word for sin, or transgression of God's Law, is *chatta'ah,* for trespass is *pesha,* and for iniquity or wickedness (e.g., perversion or deprav-ity) is *aven | awen* (hence, the "Awen" druidic symbol) and its variants (including similar Greek words), which have very different pronunciations.

'Creating a crown for the king is unprecedented,' ... Berger said. 'When all 70 nations unite in an act of love expressly intended for the king in Jerusalem, this will surely be answered by HaShem [(yes, via wrath upon those who remain in Judaea, throughout the coming Great Tribulation)].' ... 'In this generation, when it is clear that the [(anti-)]messiah is imminent, merely waiting to reveal himself, we need to prepare our hearts...,' ... Berger said. 'By preparing an actual crown, we are taking the first step toward bringing the inner vision *[(actually, witchcraft)]* of a king into reality. The beauty of a true king has not been seen ... since the exile began [nineteen centuries ago,] and the prophets assured us that it would return.'"[1]

Yes, Israel is signified by the 71st New Age "dreamer." Moreover, Messiah Yeshua | Christ Jesus already has "many crowns" (see Rev 19:11-13)—so Berger et al. are inexcusably "late to the 'party,'" and short of repentance and genuine belief in Him, they shall *not* escape God's wrath!

Enter the Bull. Created by Scotland's Michael Dollar,[2] the ten-meters high Ba'al-Molech idol (giant mechanical bull) finally "walked" (i.e., was driven) as female "slaves" (or "working class" women) "pulled it" via chains attached to a large nose ring, onto the field and toward its center—the whole while directly facing the mock Tower of Babel. Made by Artem from remnants of old machinery,[3], under company director Mike Kelt,[4] the bull took five months to construct. Those present and watching remotely could see the mock Tower of Babel arise from an initial single level, to four—in the form of four nested circular (concentric) "floors," each one laden with exterior displays. (We may reasonably liken the top floor to a drudic Circle with a central Logan Stone. In fact, following the exploding Luciferian "star," the opening ceremony itself actually commenced atop that very spot, with the "druid" bard rhythmically beating a drum.) Thus, the tower was portrayed as being erected (rebuilt) on behalf of the Devil, so that a rebellious mankind under fallen angels and demons, might storm the heavens. (We may compare this to "old is new" modern European symbolism, where Europe is portrayed as a Tower of Babel

---

1. Berkowitz, "BIN Exclusive: Campaign to Construct Messianic Golden Royal Crown."

2. "The designer behind the animatronic 10m high bull, which is operated by 6 people, is Michael Dollar from Scotland. He created the bull from rusted scrap metal, from Birmingham and West Country factories, rather than using [all-]new materials, which is in keeping with the radical themes of the show, which includes the concept of recycling" (Hussain, "Birmingham 2022 opening ceremony thrills with a fiery journey from dark to light").

3. There are some well-lit and up-close videos of the monstrosity. See, for example, "Birmingham Diaries || The Raging Bull || CWG2022," *Revsportz*, 7 Aug. 2022, as posted at "https://www.youtube.com/watch?v=yZT3vUE5VyU" on YouTube.

4. Rangzeb Hussain, "Council leader Ian Ward in in talks to save iconic Birmingham 2022 bull following public appeal," *I Am Birmingham*, 31 July 2022.

under construction, and "many tongues, one voice" is celebrated—and of course, to the European Union's Parliament building, which is clearly intended to symbolize that same Babylonian tower. Now, the foretold AntiChrist would extend that ancient "rebels against God" symbolism to, in his view, a new *global* Commonwealth.)

As for the tower's several exterior displays, we see them show a mass of fiery red flames with corresponding ejected smoke, before the onlooking Ba'al-Molech bull idol. Speaking of the mechanical monstrosity, a (satanic) bright red light shone from the idol's interior, with its corneas also being bright red.

There's quite a lot to this part of the Luciferian opening ceremony and its imagery, so we'll address it in "small chunks." First, let's briefly bring to mind a little salient biblical history. At one time in ancient Israel, the nation rebelled, worshiped, and "played" (e.g., sang, danced and otherwise partied) before *a golden Ba'al-Molech calf idol,* in the post-Exodus wilderness. That of course, brought God our Creator's judgment (see Exodus 32). Only Moses' intervention and intercession before The Judge—who despite His intended wrath chose to hear His prophet whom He would ultimately liken to Messiah—prevented Israel's divine *extermination.* (The God of Israel, was truly angry.)

We could therefore ask, "Will the Prince of Satan" (now titled King Charles III) "seek to intervene or intercede with our God, though he is mankind's top-dog anti-Christian, or will he call upon his spiritual father Satan, as *the foretold* AntiChrist, on behalf of the dozens of participating non-Christian nations and territories, or their spiritually lost and foolish athletes?" We could further ask, "Would the foretold AntiChrist offer his own life on the Commonwealth's behalf, to God our Creator?" To both questions, there is but one answer: no. In fact, the AntiChrist is all about *destroying* God's creations, including mankind, contrary to every "would-be savior" claim he may make. King Charles III's coming consignment to Hell for eternity, is *already set.* Indeed, judgment is determined from The LORD above, and those unbelievers who vainly say "peace and security" or the like, being wholly unaware of the times and *not* knowing The Creator, shall encounter "sudden destruction" (1 Th 5:3), as written. So, we may surmise that their "bull," may only bring them "loads of crap." Let's continue.

When we first saw the Ba'al-Molech idol, it had a large "cross bearing" (i.e., front-quartered) metal plate or "armored mask" on its head, which bears engraved names and statements (later detailed). Also, below that mask, chains were attached to the bull's nose ring, all symbolically alleging that Molech had long been "enslaved."

(Comparable to heraldry, the chains constituted a restrainer of the beast.)

Ba'al-Molech (the bull idol) was visibly *angry* and female "slaves" (laboring women) who pulled it forward, did so under filthy duress. But the restraining chains of "slavery," suddenly detached from the beast's nose ring, so that the now loosed Ba'al Molech bull idol, being "scarred by past hopes and enraged by injustice" (i.e., "woke" and still wearing the metal plate on its head), snorted (as if roaring) and discharged fire and smoke from its nostrils. The mopish (and feminist) women, "in a parallel act of emancipation, ... break their own chains" (alleged enslavement to men, apparently); they scattered to the bull idol's left and right sides, in fear we're told, only to then form a partial semicircle behind the beast. Simultaneously, dozens of colorfully dressed actors and actresses, several carrying blue and red umbrellas as if this were just some rousing scene from daily life in a metropolis, ran with pandemonium from the field (the oval athletic area inside the stadium's track), enacting fear of Ba'al-Molech (Satan); the idol yet snorted smoke from its nostrils. With the slavish women then following after the bull, as it (non-linearly) charged toward the center of the field (and stadium) while moving its head, opening its mouth and snorting—and with the noted "metropolites" having "fearfully" scattered before it—Stella and her seventy-one (71) "dreamers" correspondingly appeared visibly startled and concerned.

Amid the above fearfulness and deference, the cowardly "lemon" Mr. Lemon fled the arena, so that he and his balloon touched down and deflated on the track behind the Ba'al-Molech idol —but not before passing over the mechanical beast. Historically speaking, sexual satanism ties intimately to Ba'al worship, including via the Molech idol or motif, which has long also been idolized as the "Baphomet"—a sexually explicit abomination with a goat's head in lieu of the bull's, and displaying both male and female genitalia, etc. (as elsewhere detailed in this author's writings on the satanic depopulation agenda). In these Commonwealth Games, however, the Molech motif received a new "twist:" it was also portrayed as if it were an "LGBTQIA+ whatever" multicolored standing humanoid (checkered, a bit like scales) with a bull's head and hoofed feet. Compared to that, Baphomet is just a more explicitly satanic and sexually perverse expression of *the very same false "god"*—Satan. (To be sure, those who die as non-Christians, including sexual satanists, *will* spend eternity in Hell.) Later, *victorious competitors in the athletic games, would receive a stuffed "doll" version of the multicolored "bull" mascot (i.e., "Perry")*, which as indicated, is essentially just *an intermediate form between Molech (Ba'al) as a bull and the androgynous Baphomet*—while some would also take "self-ies" with a cut-out version, throughout the games. Indeed, that same "intermediate" Ba'al-Molech "doll" idol, was also bannered on the city of Birmingham's Council House, which resembles a capitol and is adjacent to the temple-like Town Hall, in Victoria Square. Okay, with Satan's wicked "lemons" ready to perish in Hell, let's continue.

The "dreamers" faced Ba'al-Molech (several as if "social distanced")—with Stella alone having her Luciferian white-lit crystal (fallen shard) in-hand. The bull idol's head moved left and right, and motioned a bit down as its nostrils smoked, looking as though it intended to charge the "dreamers." But the mechanical Ba'al-Molech paused in notable consideration—as various implements of war (apparent medieval weapons) and enslavement passed behind the "dreamers," being removed from the area. Also, a horn sounded.

The audience then heard the question, "Who is going to calm the raging bull?" The answer followed: "One person..., it's Stella: instead of running away, Stella [(cautiously walks to, and then)] calms the bull." The bull of course, opened its mouth to grunt in ostensible "anger."

Stella, whose clothing had scarlet across her back and down her legs, approached Ba'al-Molech with her white-lit crystal (fallen Luciferian and New Age shard) in her left hand, and then extended her right arm and hand toward Ba'al-Molech's nose in "love," evidently seeking to appease the beast with the (alleged) "love and light" of Lucifer or Satan as a possessing "god." (Stella, as a top spiritual whore in the opening ceremony, had earlier exited her "landed" home, as the other "dreamers" did theirs, so that those houses were then also seen inside the stadium. Stella's particular Luciferian white-lit shard here served as a New Age crystal, to "channel," etc.)

We were further told: "It's a very 'how to train your dragon" moment. This, as Stella offers friendship and compassion to tame the beast." The "dreamers" each extended one hand toward the Ba'al-Molech bull idol, while placing their other hand over their chest, in very obvious worship. (Did this not clearly presage unregenerate mankind's coming *worship of the "first beast," the foretold AntiChrist,* as foretold in Revelation 13:3-4 and 13:8?) The huge metal bull bowed its head toward the "dreamers'" lead whore Stella, as her left hand simultaneously touched the base of its nose ring, where the chains had formerly been attached. The mechanical beast opened and closed its mouth a couple times, suggesting Ba'al (Satan) quietly talked (cf. Rev 13:5-8, 13:15) with his harlot, using the

Molech bull idol to do so. Watching that abominable spectacle, the slavish (and disheveled) women brushed themselves off, and *crossed their own hands over their hearts, likewise expressing love of the beast*—and then they went even further, as they *brazenly bowed their heads toward Ba'al-Molech, worshiping the Devil.*

Stella, with five "dreamers" near her, for a total of six (6), then turned her back with them, to lead the bull idol forward while continuing to carry the Luciferian shard or crystal in her left hand; they all faced the mock Tower of Babel. With (we're told) "applause around the stadium, heralding an era of mutual compassion and respect," we were then informed that "behind it all, ... breaking free from oppression and enslavement, and ... moving forward together," serve as "lofty aims;" moreover, "and so freed from the bonds, the women and the bull leave the shackles of the past behind." (Recall the coming removal or loosing of the human-eyed little horn's or unicorn's restrainer on Prince Charles' heraldic achievement, when Satan shall possess him—now as King Charles III.)

The Ba'al-Molech idol's nostrils also smoked more, the beast raised its head to again scan left and right, and then as an "armored" metal monstrosity, the idol began to move toward the background revelers—still led by Stella with her white-lit Luciferian shard, and five other "dreamers." Those latter "dreamers" also reveled and clapped. Simultaneously, the "slavish" women shifted from behind the Ba'al-Molech bull idol, to walk in a line on either side of the beast.

Stella, leading the seventy-one (71) "dreamers," thus appeased the fiery-red (per lighting) bull, which had smoke (e.g., from fire) exiting its nostrils and open portions of its mechanical body. In fact, there were individuals inside the thing, animating it (cf. The fiery Molech idol of Ba'al, to which children were sacrificed). Indeed, the Ba'al-Molech idol's interior lighting, to include the color around the pupils of its eyes, changed from red to white; concurrently, so did bright flashing lights ringing and lining the arena—all to indicate that Satan had been appeased. But this had greater import: it blasphemously counterfeited the bloody red to pure white change (e.g., see Isa 1:18; cf. 63:1-8) of a blood-dipped linen strip, which was tied to a horn of the scapegoat (Heb., *azazel)*, on the annual Day of Atonement *(Yom Kippur),* in ancient Israel. (Yom Kippur shall yet have fulfillment at Christ Jesus' return, beyond His past resurrection in a pure garment, with attending apocalyptic and priestly events.)

While all that wickedness was done—yes, it went on and on—the near ground-level display around the oval field as well as the base of the Tower of Babel were lit in fiery red. Background individuals (os-

tensibly actors and actresses) behind the "dreamers," gathered before the base of, as well as atop the mock Tower of Babel, in Sun-
and-life-suggesting "fluorescent" groups (red, orange, yellow and
green), to revel—and then "violently" rumble—in ethnic dances
(Irish, Chinese, Indian, Pakistani, Bangladeshi and Afro-Caribbean),
to the sounds of "a cultural symphony."

One journalist remarks: "It started as hurt and scared, then
broke free from its shackles, experienced cultural tensions, and ultimately rose again to become a symbol of light and love, and remained at the centre of the arena for the rest of the show. It was a
common theme throughout the ceremony, as organisers focused on
bringing the Commonwealth nations together."[1]

At this point, *Stella (recall the scarlet on her outfit) has (already)
mounted the Ba'al-Molech bull idol—as a whorish (spiritually, ostensibly carnally, etc.) woman riding the beast (the Ba'al-Molech bull).* It
is as a whore, that Stella leads the "dreamers." (If the display would
have allowed bestial relations with Lucifer or Satan, before the
whole world, we could expect that too would have been portrayed.)

With the above, the audience was told: "This diverse landscape
isn't without its differences and dissidents. Each group attempts to
protect its [own] unique heritage. And as they celebrate their own
culture, tensions begin to arise. ... So, the bull of Birmingham
watches.... Stella and the [Luciferian] 'dreamers' ... watch on, as the
groups start to clash—and it is their own [Babylonian] city they hurt.
... Yes, the bull becoming deeply agitated now, at the dance-off dis-
cordance...." Okay, they danced and rumbled before the Ba'al-
Molech bull idol, and it appeared "agitated" (visibly angry). Indeed,
the oval ringing red light turned to molten colors of fire, we heard a
loud snort (like a roar) from the metal beast, and star-like fireworks
were set-off around the field—and thus, around the monstrous idol,
the "dreamers" and slavish women with it. (We could view this as
the start of the games' satanic counterfeit of *Armageddon and its af-
termath*—wherein *Lucifer is blasphemously depicted as the winner,
rather than The Lord Jesus,* as we're going to see.) The Ba'al-Molech
bull idol's lights, including the very sclera of its eyes, again turned
fiery red. In anger, the idol reared on its hind legs (with Stella atop
its back, behind its head); again, fiery red lights were also lit around
the stadium. Yes, that's a lot of red.

Pagans will be pagans, so the freed (slavish) women gathered
before Ba'al-Molech once more; that is, the women who had formerly pulled "him" as forced laborers, encircled the idol, in some-

1. Amanda Shalala, "Birmingham shows its heart in Commonwealth Games opening ceremony spectacular," ABC News, 28 July 2022.

what close proximity. Then the likewise-foolish "dreamers," one of whom bore a lion's head on her shirt (cf. Satan as a "roaring lion"),[1] encircled both them and the bull (concentrically). All the "dreamers" had their New Age Luciferian white-lit crystals or shards (appearing as flattish diamond-shaped white lights) in-hand.

The audience was told: "Stella and our *athlete* 'dreamers' call for a moment of reflection and of light. As she *and the bull* call for a moment of reconciliation, all is stilled." Representing Satan, the Ba'al-Molech bull idol moaned, opened and closed its mouth to "talk," and knelt to the ground (sat down, ostensibly), while harlot Stella remained mounted. The slavish women as well as the "dreamers" then again extended their arms toward the Ba'al-Molech bull idol, with the former also again bowing their heads to the beast, all in *acts of satanic worship.*

Alternately describing and summarizing the above, the Ba'al-Molech bull idol turned around to face away from the mock Tower of Babel, the slavish women encircled the thing and sat down, and then "dreamers" ran to encircle them, pointing their lit Luciferian shards toward the sky and the idol while doing so. Significantly, with that

---

1. Among the discernible heads and creatures on "dreamers'" shirts, were a lion's head, a lioness, a tiger, a purplish and hairy ape's head (on Stella's shirt), a gray whale, a fish, an elephant's head, a kangaroo (in blue), possibly a bear, birds, etc., all perhaps intended to suggest that Earth's creatures, particularly the more intelligent ones, would also worship Ba'al-Molech.

central idol, they corporately appeared from above, to form the round portion (cornea) of an eye, with the giant mechanical bull being in the place of the pupil. The bull then again opened and closed its mouth to commune or instruct, and squatted (knelt) in the midst of the Devil's disciples, so that Lucifer's New Age "dreamers" also sat down. That's not all. The earlier mentioned fluorescent revelers then surrounded all of them—in a diamond formation, rather than a circular one—to then constitute the Luciferian "all-seeing eye" motif, as seen from above. (That prominent satanic symbol was repeated across the whole event.)

The Ba'al-Molech idol then snorted, as if groaning, and shed red-scarlet streams of "tears" from its red-lit "all-seeing" (motif) eyes! Surrounded by its worshiping "disciples," we may wonder if that was meant to counterfeit Christ Jesus' sweating "great drops of blood," in the Garden of Gethsemane (see Luke 22:39-44)? Arguably, it represented even more than that. It served to portray Satan, in the form of this Ba'al-Molech bull, as the *victim*—ostensibly, on behalf of mankind and in lieu of Christ Jesus—but without actually being crucified to pay any price, etc. Really, this was *the "crucifixion" moment in the ceremony*—and it was followed by Luciferian "disciples" directing all around them to *worship* the beast, in an effort to *increase the "Church of Satan."* Yes, the (global) Commonwealth was suddenly and explicitly directed to join in *worship to Lucifer* (Satan). (Pay close attention to the New Age paganism that proceeded, as below detailed.)

Being spiritually suckered, Hussain comments: "The audacious multicultural opening ceremony [was] ... a show that dared to look at the dark past, while looking forward to a positive future. [The] ... show threw a subtle, yet profoundly moving, spotlight on the horrors of colonialism, slavery and homophobia, while looking forward to a more hopeful and tolerant future. ... The themes of the show were delicately balanced between dark and light [(e.g., it was Zoroastrian)], rage and joy, and between the past and present. ... From the bright joyful colours of [(sexual satanist and abominable so-called "transgender" Mr.)] Lemon's session, the stadium suddenly became dark and ominous as a gigantic animatronic bull entered the arena with steam billowing from its flared nostrils. The black velvet cloak of the night was replaced by an infernal red glow that seemed to reflect the fires of the coal mines and furnaces of the Black Country, where working class families toiled from morn to dusk for a pitiless and thankless existence. The dark and dank pollution churned out by the fetid mills, was referenced with the way the mechanical bull belched out steam that shrouded the arena like a creepy Victorian fog. ... The rusted metal surface of the bull poetically mirrored the decay and rot of the British Empire, and the chains coiled around the bull metaphorically represented the Slave Trade where millions of African people were shackled by chains made in Birmingham's metal workshops, and transported to the New World to suffer the inhuman barbarism of slavery. ... This bull was a potent symbol of the working class, the downtrodden, the exploited and the enslaved. Even the tail of the bull was a dangling ship's chain, possibly a slaver ship, that ended in an anchor with [four curved prongs and] jagged teeth. The red raging eyes of the noble looking bull reflected the anger and resentment felt by those robbed and sold into a degrading life of slavery and torture. A strong, once free creature, [had] now [been] held captive and transported, and forced to work in horrific conditions in faraway foreign fields. The women, who in turn are also oppressed by a patriarchal social system that [(ostensibly)] sees them inferior to men, finally break free from the chains and this in turn allows the bull to taste freedom. The fiery bull finally finds solace when female energy, in the form of a [(Luciferian New Age)] dancer, calms its unbalanced soul with [(anti-)] love, healing and hope. The beast weeps tears of blood, and the anger inside him fades and subsides to be replaced by [(false Luciferian)] light. His raging and fiery eyes drain away the red colour of hatred and light enters, clearing his vision and setting him free. His new found faith affirms life and a new dawn beckons."[1]

The above (very) loosely counterfeited the *fourth day or midpoint* of the Crucifixion Week (Jesus was crucified and died on a Wednesday, not a Friday or some other day[2]), when from "agony," Jesus' "sweat became like great drops of blood falling down to the ground" (Luke 22:44). Later, would come—this author concludes—a counterfeit portrayal of the *"Battle at Megiddo"* or *"Armageddon."* We'll come to that, of course. But first, let's consider the visual details comprising the noted *worship and invitation to serve Lucifer (Satan).*

Stella, towering over all the encircling slavish women and shard-bearing "dreamers," then led all present—including every submissive individual watching throughout the British Commonwealth and elsewhere—in pagan New Age worship of Satan, focusing on the Molech idol to Ba'al (the Devil). Atop the mechanical bull, Stella raised her fallen Luciferian light to the sky, lowered it ninety degrees, and then moved it in a half-circle (rotating her upper body as she did) to point it toward the audience of Alexander Stadium. As

---

1. Hussain, "Birmingham 2022 opening ceremony thrills with a fiery journey from dark to light."
2. For more information, see this author's *Messiah, History, and the Tribulation Period* multi-volume series.

she did so, the seventy-one (71) "dreamers" encircling the bull followed suit, doing likewise with their "sharp" fallen Luciferian shards. The audience was told: "It's time for the [Luciferian] shards to work their magic again. Stella and the 'dreamers' use them to call for a moment of reflection and reconciliation."

Indeed, as Stella and the seventy-one (71) "dreamers" repeated the above motions several times with their shards and bodies, and with the fully-raised (four stories high) and lit mock Tower of Babel altogether visible behind the Ba'al-Molech idol, the "dreamers" also all stood up—so that the latter then motioned in two complete half circles, one with the shard in the right hand and the other with it in the left one, *thereby symbolically pointing to the entire global audience;* then they additionally lowered their shards to ninety degrees, to motion them in the same way as leader Stella, pointing to the stadium's audience in the process. So, the "dreamers" all raised and waved their white lit New Age crystals, as Luciferian objects, before Ba'al-Molech and toward the games' global audience, ostensibly to ritually enjoin worship of Satan—and further "free" the spirit of Ba'al-Molech. Simultaneously, the Ba'al-Molech bull idol began to raise its head and again "talked."

With that global satanic worship having just been *evoked,* from a "glistening" and collective shards-based "all-seeing eye," via Stella and the seventy-one (71) (athlete) "dreamers," the Ba'al-Molech bull idol then stood upright to meet two women (ostensibly, representing female "angels") who descended from across the stadium toward its head. The bull's internal lights again shift from red (e.g., when it had squatted or kneeled) to white. The audience then saw the "angelic" pair "lift away the bull's armor"—that is, the engraved mask or head-plate (cf. a harness), as the last vestige or "symbol of his enslavement and theirs"—so that "he will be revealed as an iconic symbol of light, ... of light and love."

Per the above, removal of the masking head-plate completed the freeing of Ba'al (Satan)—and his worshipers. While that transpired, the fluorescent revelers too *raised their arms and hands toward the Ba'al-Molech idol, themselves also worshiping the Devil*—apparently, as an audience now convinced (we're meant to believe)—and they also pointed their clasped hands skyward, each in an arrow or "shard"-like pattern. That being done, *they all repeatedly bowed to, with arms extended toward, the Ba'al-Molech idol.* The slavish women then stood up and *raised their own hands toward the beast, in further worship.* The seventy-one (71) "dreamers" on the other hand, turned with their still-lit shards to face outward, or away from the Ba'al-Molech bull idol and toward the fluorescent revelers—and *all concerned then worshiped Lucifer (Satan) together!*

As all that brazen wickedness occurred, before a potential audience of *billions,* the "now free and at peace" Ba'al-Molech (we're informed) audibly snorted, emitted visible smoke from its nostrils, again opened and closed its mouth to ostensibly communicate or instruct, and scanned its head back and forth, observing its worshipers and the audience around it. Simultaneously, the two "angels" "flew" the engraved head-plate *to the base of the mock Tower of Babel,* behind the bull idol! With that action, *the fluorescent revelers again bowed to the idol, up and down, again and again and again— as the seventy-one (71) "dreamers" had their lit shards raised toward heaven.* (They are *enemies* of God our Creator, and of His Christ.)

Thus, Ba'al-Molech is finally altogether "free," ridden by Stella, and encircled by Luciferian New Age worshipers of Satan, with Stella and the "dreamers" together *symbolically* representing all the participating nations of the Earth (see below for the explanation). The "freed" slavish women and the shard-bearing "dreamers" all then sat on the ground, around the Ba'al-Molech bull idol, so that the audience was told that "peace" and "freedom" have been achieved between the bull and mankind, where the Molech idol represents Satan as Lucifer or Ba'al!

Finally, the fluorescent revelers also then turned outward, clasped each other's hands and raised their arms skyward—and fireworks were again set off from the field's oval track area. The diamond and concentric "all-seeing eye" pattern comprised of the bull idol (pupil), slavish women and "dreamers" (iris and cornea), and fluorescent revelers (the rest of the eye, such as the sclera) was then broken, as the revelers migrated away from the monstrosity (e.g., to symbolize the spread of the Luciferian message to the world) to form a new pattern (somewhat resembling a butterfly), as the shards-bearing "dreamers" streamed toward the tower, and the Ba'al-Molech idol moved across the field.

As the Ba'al-Molech bull turned around, its internal lights brightened—and a Sun-like brightness shone forth (via clever optics) from the area of rider Stella's Luciferian crystal (shard), near and over the idol's head.[1] Ba'al-Molech again reacheed the center of the stadium, and with the "freed" (slavish) women and fluorescent revelers (performers) facing it, the bull idol itself faced the modern (mock) Tower

---

1. Ca. 1:51:13-23, Haris, "Commonwealth Games Birmingham 2022 - Opening Ceremony," BBC News, 10 Aug. 2022, as posted at "https://odysee.com/@Haris:d/Commonwealth_Games_Birmingham_2022_-_Opening_Ceremony:2" on Odysee.

of Babel, itself then lit in green and yellow, with the removed head-plate at its base. Predictably, the crowd of satanists and pagan fools "by any other name" or description, then went wild with cheers. (Truly, though, everything to this point, was in *incredible* spectacle—though as we'll see, the "best" was saved for last.)

Mr. Rangzeb Hussain rightly observes, "at times the bull hearkened to the Biblical golden calf, or even Wicca rituals with pagan druids [(i.e., satanists)] forming a circle during Summer Solstice"—but then in a jaw-dropping bit of self-delusion and dishonesty, which seems somehow typical of non-Christians and anti-Christians in the British Commonwealth, Hussain farcically permits himself to allege that the monstrosity only "seemed" to do so, falsely adding, "this Birmingham bull was not an object of idol worship."[1] Not? Clearly and to the contrary, this Ba'al-Molech bull *is* "an object of idol worship;" the reality of that, is altogether and incontrovertibly obvious.

Of the engravings on the removed head-plate, we (supposedly) see "names of the chain makers" and names of twenty-one victims of 1974 Irish Republican Army (IRA) bombings—as well as some "pithy" statements. Among the latter, we may discern and see: "Every day snaking chains will stay with me, in my sleep of death." "Links are made through heat would go away, but until my life is past, the hiss." "Roar." "I want to be accepted." "She can easily be broken or bent to the will of her employer." "Chronic hunger can bind tighter than any iron link." "People mistake humbleness for weakness." "Birmingham metal industries thrived on the slave trade." "Go back home." "Many doors were closed (shut) in our faces, racism." "Power" and "People count." The names (partially speaking) include "Charles," "Elizabeth" and "Anne," or the first names of some top members of the British Monarchy; we also see "Hunter," ostensibly reminding us of Babel's Nimrod (cf. Gen 10:8-10)—though there's also the infamous son of the anti-Christian satanist Mr. Joe Biden. (Were any of them *ever* "slaves?" No. Might they be construed as *modern* "chain makers," or enslavers in the Devil's service? Yes. So, the hypocrisy continues, without bounds.)

"Inclusive" Marshals and the Parade of Athletes. Thousands of marshals for "the most inclusive games in history," then descended upon the field—preceding the nations' teams who would follow in "the athlete parade." (There were athletes who avoided this, choosing to remain in their "villages.") Yet, the Ba'al-Molech idol was *again* encircled by the slavish women—and then here, also some of the marshals.

---

1. Hussain, "Birmingham 2022 opening ceremony thrills with a fiery journey from dark to light."

The slavish women and marshals ringing the Ba'al-Molech bull idol began to walk around it, in alternating clockwise and counter-clockwise directions. Then they "migrated" into a spoked oval "wheel" pattern, with the slavish women forming an oval "hub" around the beast. They and others "danced" in-place, worshiping the monstrosity and performing. Simultaneously, the parade commenced with the region of Oceania, the first of six regions.

Australia entered the track area and circled the field with the Ba'al-Molech idol at the center—as Electric Light Orchestra's (ELO's) "Don't Bring Me Down" played, with these lyrics: "Don't bring me down. You're lookin' good, just like a snake in the grass. One of these days you're gonna break your glass. Don't bring me down."

The slavish women and marshals then parted a bit, so that each respecitve athletic team could enter the field. They entered between the mock Tower of Babel and the onlooking Ba'al-Molech's head, only to then partially circle the field to take their own place around, and before the bull idol—all in satanic acts of veneration and worship. Fiery red, pink, white, orange and yellow "shooting star" fireworks were sent across and over the stadium, above the Ba'al-Molech bull idol.

The "storied" displays of the mock Tower of Babel, showed the respective name, flag (usually the national one), colors, etc., of each of the six regions (Oceania, Africa, Americas, Asia, Caribbean and Europe) and its nations' arrayed athletic teams (or "squads"), as they successively paraded onto the oval track, led by their respective primary flag bearer(s)—where they had to cross (like a river) the almost ground-level display standing between them and the Ba'al-Molech bull. (We might here think of this as a loose counterfeit of ancient Israel's crossing the Jordan River, into the Promised Land.) Each national team thus fully encircled the giant bull at the stadium's center—and one team after another crossed that encircling ground-level display, just to the right of the mock Tower of Babel, to gather around the beast and before its feet, in veneration!

When Falkland Islands' team entered, we heard "Sweet Dreams" from Eurythmics, with these lyrics: "Sweet dreams are made of this. Who am I to disagree? I travel the world and the seven seas. Everybody's looking for something. Some of them want to use you, some of them want to get used by you. Some of them want to abuse you, some of them want to be abused."

With the start of Asia's entry, we heard Dexys Midnight Runners' "Come on Eileen," containing this: "These people round here, wear beatdown eyes sunk in smoke dried face—so resigned to what their fate is. But not us (no never), no not us (no never), we are far too young and clever. ... Eileen, I'll hum this tune forever. Come on Eileen, ... let's take off everything ... Come on Eileen, oh I swear what he means. At this moment, you mean everything. In that dress, oh my thoughts, I confess. Well, they're dirty, come on Eileen."

All told, seventy-two (72) international teams (squads) of athletes (including dependent territories competing under their own flags), came from fifty-six (56) independent countries comprising 2022's British Commonwealth. Though Australia's team, with the most medals historically, came first, the four nations of the United Kingdom—Northern Ireland, Scotland, Wales (bearing its national red dragon flag) and England (with a simplified red cross on a white field, for its flag), respectively—were the final entrants.

Significantly, the teams' respective flag bearers were posted directly around the base of the Ba'al-Molech bull—standing even closer to the idol than the slavish women. By such placement, each team—and thus the nation they represented—irrespective of ignorance, which here is no excuse, effectively (symbolically at a minimum) acknowledged Lucifer (Satan) as their "god!" In fact, one of the announcers, "Sir" Lenworth (Lenny) George Henry (knighted by Queen Elizabeth II in 2015), stated, "Come with me, our children will be gods,"[1] wickedly, wantonly and explicitly pushing Satan's lie, first told to Eve in the Garden of Eden! That same "Sir" Henry then stood at the base of the mock Tower of Babel, with other announcers representing "comedy," pride and (apparently) sexual satanism (e.g., the revoltingly pink-and-ruffles-clad comedian and lunatic so-called "pansexual" Joe Lycett), while the Welsh flag with the red dragon (representing Satan) was displayed on its third level, right before the last team (England's) appeared.[2]

As host nation England came onto the track and entered the field, being the final one, that imagery transitioned to the latter's red cross on a white field. At the same time, British rock band Queen's "We Will Rock You" ("You got blood on your face, you big disgrace, ... Pleading with your eyes, gonna make you some peace someday") song played, followed by lost David Bowie's "Let's Dance" ("For fear your grace should fall, ... For fear tonight is all, ... Under the moonlight, this serious moonlight")! So, Satan (as the red dragon) and a bloody cross were the final symbols atop the Tower of Babel, which continued to be faced by the mechanical Ba'al Molech idol—as the

---

1. Ca. 2:40:53-58, "Commonwealth Games Birmingham 2022 - Opening Ceremony" at "https://odysee.com/@Haris:d/Commonwealth_Games_Birmingham_2022_-_Opening_Ceremony:2" on Odysee.
2. Ca. 2:49:44 to 2:50:10, "Commonwealth Games Birmingham 2022 - Opening Ceremony."

seventy-two nations demonstrated their deference toward, and worship of the red-lit bull; and partying attended it all!

With each of the 72 international teams finally gathered around the Ba'al-Molech bull idol, six former games medalists carried the Ceremonial Flag of the Commonwealth Games Federation, bearing the earlier-mentioned evoking Awen (red, gold and blue, against a white field), to a tower-adjacent pole. British military members then raised the Ceremonial Flag.

Prince Charles Opens the Games, with the Queen's Message, Delivered by Sexual Satanists. The final "baton bearers" delivered the 22nd Commonwealth Games' baton (shaped as a symbolic torch *and uneven scroll),* which had been passed from the queen at Buckingham Palace in 2021, to athletes and others (e.g., "environmental activists") of the British Commonwealth, who relayed it from one to another—by land, sea and air—"across all 72 nations and territories, over 140,000 kilometers, over 295 days." The ceremonial baton was brought onto the track by sodomite (and ostensible pedophile) "Sir" (OBE) Tom Daley—as he was met by five more sexual satanists, all carrying rainbow-colored "LGBTQIA+ whatever" "rainbow pride progress" flags (bearing the Luciferian "all-seeing eye" imagery as a dark circle centered on a yellow triangle nested within others), "representing some of the thirty-five Commonwealth countries where homosexuality is still a crime." Of Mr. Daley, the audience was further told, "He will move in solidarity with all LGBT+ athletes and communities," for their (not) "rights"—as he sought to shame and thus pressure those countries to change their laws. Indeed, sexual satanists want to "legally" engage in their Hell-bound perversions, and they care not whom they offend or harm.

Finally, Dame Louise Martin (DBE), President of the Commonwealth Games Federation, received the baton. She then opened its top "to reveal the queen's message," as written on a housed piece of paper—while Prince Charles laughed. Dame Martin unscrolled the paper and handed it to the Prince of Wales, who read it aloud to all present, thereby formally opening the games. Prince Charles—as the foretold AntiChrist—recited in part: "Over the past 294 days, it has carried not only my message to you, but also the shared hopes and dreams of each nation and territory through which it has passed.... ... Tonight, in the words of the founder of the games, we embark once again on a novel adventure, here in Birmingham, a pioneering city which has drawn in and embraced so many throughout its history. It is a city symbolic of the rich diversity and unity of the Commonwealth—and one which now welcomes you all in friendship. ... It now gives me the greatest pleasure to declare the 22nd Commonwealth Games, *open."* With those words, more streaming and star-like (apocalyptic) fireworks ascended from, and appeared over the stadium.

Unlike Moses, who as a type of Messiah was angered by Israel's worship of, and partying before the golden calf in the wilderness, and who thus cast down the stone tablets bearing God The Father's ten commandments, breaking rather than reading them (Ex 32), Charles as the foretold AntiChrist, proudly orated his mother's message and then expressed his own "greatest pleasure," declaring the games open before all. Indeed, the Prince of Wales oversaw the *entire* sordid affair—and was very pleased!

With the above sexual satanism and the Prince of Wales' deputized officiation, the center-of-stadium Ba'al-Molech bull idol's body was also pierced by internal lights, with its eyes likewise lit and glowing, as its head scanned back and forth to observe all the gathered Luciferian worshipers (tens of thousands). Now, all you've just read and heard is brazenly and openly Luciferian, satanic and New Age. Alexander stadium was filled with spiritual whoredom (e.g., as epitomized by the druidic bards, Stella and the "dreamers," the "freed" slavish women, and the fluorescent revelers)—while being accompanied by temple (tower) whores and gigolos, especially the sexual satanists of the abominable and lunatic so-called "LGBTQIA+ whatever" movement. All those folks worship a false "light," being servants to *darkness and death.*

Geoffrey Grider, noting that Stephen (Steven) Knight—whose *Peaky Blinders'* Small Heath family of gangsters made a cameo appearance—served as the ceremony's executive producer, remarks: "The Baal-like 'Raging Bull' was so popular with people attending the Commonwealth Games that a crowdfunding campaign was set up to preserve it to be admired for future generations. One of the things I find most interesting about the idolatrous 'raging bull' is not only its close association with Baal worship, but the fact that Prince Charles was the man opening the games. If you recall, we've mentioned ... Prince Charles calling for an unnamed man [(i.e., himself as the foretold AntiChrist)] to be given trillions of dollars to wage a military-style campaign [(at 2021's COP26 in Scotland)].[1] Now he [(him)] presiding over a massive 32-foot high idol of a fiery bull, what do we call that, progress? ... Whatever happened to shows and ceremonies where people were happy, upbeat and optimistic? ... Every time you turn around, you are assaulted with dark, menac-

---

1. E.g., Listen to "Prince Charles, the Great Reset and the Coming Antichrist," *Now the End Begins,* 28 June 2022, as posted at "https://www.youtube.com/watch?v=CMRjfKhCpSo" on YouTube.

ing imagery that seems be be not only sending you hidden messages, but perhaps a harbinger of the arrival of something worse? Time is almost up, Christian, if you're planning on doing something for The Lord, [you had] better get after it. In the Bible, the bull is connected with Baal worship and idolatry from Babylon and Egypt."[1]

But none of the above, as shocking as it all was, could really "put a candle" to the finale—a visually stunning and altogether wicked enthronement of the Devil as the beguiling serpent and "all-seeing eye" or star of Lucifer, with an included literal declaration of Babylon. While this author has pointed to the fact that much of the opening ceremony preceding the below finale, was about Satan counterfeiting the things of God, and even presenting himself as victor over Christ Jesus at Armageddon—that last part had yet to be explicitly portrayed and conveyed. It was left for the opening's finale and then the closing ceremony days later. As if greater satanism were needed, the extensive and shocking finale managed to outdo nearly all the rest. So, "buckle up."

The Finale to the Opening Ceremony. At the start of the finale, we saw the Ba'al-Molech bull idol facing the mock Tower of Babel, with harlot Stella's house on top. The games' stylized and colorful druidic Awen flag remained raised nearby, while the flags of the 72 nations and territories, including Satan (the red dragon) on that of Wales, stood above and behind the tower (atop the stadium). Simultaneously, the bull idol itself remained boxed by those same flags (i.e., a second set earlier marched onto the field), and surrounded by the teams of the 72 nations and territories, in the midst of the athletic field. Fireworks exploded high into the air, also from atop the stadium.

At the base of the tower, the lead (druidic) bard held a Luciferian white-lit crystal shard, like Stella's. With Stella on the tower itself with her original Luciferian white-lit shard, all the other dreamers, likewise bearing their white-lit shards, *surrounded the tower;* together, they formed a visible white-lit eye pattern (when seen from above); indeed, the tower topped by Stella's house, effectively served as the iris and pupil.

In a demonic cacophony, the lead bard and the dreamers then proclaimed, "Now is the time of renewal, the time for new beginnings, a time to realize our dreams [(lead bard raises his Luciferian white-lit crystal shard)] and share our common [(Luciferian)] light." The lead bard then took his white-lit crystal shard *into the base of the tower, ostensibly counterfeiting Moses as he'd meet with The*

---

1. Geoffrey Grider, "Prince Charles Opens The 2022 Birmingham Commonwealth Games With An Idol Of A Raging, Fiery Bull Prompting Comparisons To Baal Worship," *Now the End Begins,* 4 Aug. 2022.

God of Israel inside the Tabernacle of Meeting (see Ex 14:18-20, 33:7-10). With the "canal dancers" in the water at the tower's base, all the dreamers then joyfully raised their Luciferian shards, and made a choreographed inviting vertical circular pattern with them. Simultaneously, Stella turned and pressed her Luciferian white-lit shard *into the tower,* where it swirled upward; then the rest of the dreamers turned to face and move toward the tower, breaking their "eye" pattern, and pointed and waved their Luciferian shards in many (almost random) directions.

Next, all those yet shard-bearing dreamers pressed them into the sides of the tower, where they likewise visibly swirled inside and floated upwards; as that transpired, we saw the tower's "construction" completed (i.e., it rose from two levels with Stella's house atop, initially, to four levels). Correspondingly, the audience was told: "Stella and the [drudic] bards of Brum press their shards into the tower, and from there, they will rise. Clutching these individually imperfect fragments of the Cosmos [(in worship of the creation, rather than its Creator)], they bring them all together, to form something truly magical." That said, we then saw the shards coalesce *to form a bright white sphere—the very Luciferian "eye" that had exploded and descended to Earth at the start of the ceremony—inside the top three levels of the tower.*

Rising through those and Stella's house, to appear as a large shimmering and smoking bright "star" (resembling a huge mirrored disco ball) and "all-seeing eye" *over* the tower and Stella's home (i.e., above and just behind them from a side vantage point, but we're meant to see the "star" from the front, or the vantage of the bull idol). As that occurred, all the other houses of the other "dreamers" were again (holographically) seen hovering above the stadium —ostensibly counterfeiting the many dwellings God has prepared for His saints, in His Father's heavenly house (John 14:2-3), a biblical reality New Agers *twist to their destruction,* as they falsely allege multiple paths or "ways" to "god" and "salvation," demonically asserting that Christ Jesus is merely "a way" (Acts 16:17, Gk.; see 16:16-31). We who are Christians, however, know that He is The Way (John 14:6), and there is *no* other.

Simultaneously, the colored-light-producing wrist bands worn by each audience member in the stadium, were white-lit throughout the stands.[1] We were then told: "So they rise and reform into the star" (signifying Lucifer's "resurrection," and intimating Satan's coming possession of the "healed" AntiChrist), "[the one] from the start of

---

1. These were apparently PixMob wristbands, and PixMob had a role around Duran, Duran's stage, rather than radio-controlled Xylobands.

the show, from where they came—and it signals the birth of a new [(global)] Commonwealth," "and it's a star [(signifying Lucifer enthroned)] that's been born in a courtyard [(i.e., Birmingham stadium)], of Commonwealth nations." Moreover, "It gets the nod of approval from the [mechanical] star of the show, the [Ba'al-Molech] bull [idol]."

As if anyone could want another "shocker," those paying careful attention saw *the coiled body of a serpent (representing Satan's body, ala Genesis 3) within the tower.* Simultaneously, the Ba'al-Molech bull emitted bright white light, and rose on its front legs toward Lucifer (i.e., the "all-seeing eye" or "star" over the tower and house), opened and closed its mouth to signify speaking to the Devil. Then, with a sudden crackling noise, the bull idol emitted a cluster of six tightly-focused white-light beams, which were sent to the Luciferian "star" from it's chest. Curiously, one of those six beams appeared as a white humanoid figure upon the Ba'al-Molech's idol's chest. Due to thin smoke all around, those clustered beams, which remained "transmitting" (suggesting unity between the Molech idol and "Ba'al" or Lucifer), shimmered between the bull's chest and the Luciferian "all-seeing eye" over the tower and house. With Stella's (mock) house already retracted into the tower, we're told: "At its heart, our story tonight has been a parable, a simple tale that helps to teach a simple lesson—that our [(global)] Commonwealth is our humanity. We're all made of the same stuff. We're all touched by stardust. We're all connected and capable of great things, in this [(global)] Commonwealth of nations."

The (impressive holographic) overhead houses then disappeared, visibly dissolving into a swirling cloud of bluish lights (resembling swarming fireflies). More fireworks exploded over the stadium, and lights swirled all around and over the audience. Those "fireflies" then converged to form a "Welcome to Birmingham" message, and afterward, again became a swarm. Attending pyrotechnics over and around the stadium signified what would come next—"the grand finale." (Do you feel like a "goner" yet? There's more to come.)

Suddenly, the "star" or "all-seeing eye" of Lucifer transitioned from being over the "modern era" (mock) Tower of Babel, to being above the Ba'al-Molech bull idol (signifying its possession), where we could see (from overhead and all around) radiating spokes of bluish light, pulsating like a beating heart—which was also audibly heard. Likewise, the near ground-level oval light ring, between the track and the field, pulsated blue and white light around the field containing the Ba'al-Molech bull idol, nearby national and territorial flags, corresponding athletic teams, etc. (The spotlights placed along most of the perimeter of the outer track, pulsated alternating blue and white light in sync, to merge as the "star" or "all-seeing eye" above the bull and teams around it.) Also, the displays on the side of the tower, presented that same blue light and then included *kaleidoscopic fluttering white (fallen) "angels,"* besides pink, purple and gray patterns. As we continued to see the radiating "star" pulsate and heard that audible beating, the bull idol scanned back and forth with its head—and Duran, Duran readied itself *to worship the serpent or Satan as Lucifer, through song and dance, with clapping and jumping* (basically, worshipful partying).

Remarkably, the carefully orchestrated encircling arrangement of spotlights, radiating to form the pulsating star over the Ba'al-Molech bull idol, was more than intentional: it was highly meaningful to those steeped in modern "alien" lore and events—at least, to those who recognized it. Specifically, it was a *stunning* redux *of 1942's "Battle of Los Angeles"* (see the *Los Angeles Times* photo published on February 26, 1942, which is available on the Internet), where on February 24th (or 25th), the U.S. Army focused surrounding searchlights on an airspace penetrating, overhead (ostensible) antigravitic "alien" craft (saucer), in California's City of L.A.. Though military guns fired many large caliber anti-aircraft rounds for several minutes, attempting to strike and down the apparent craft over L.A., it seemed to be impervious and unaffected.

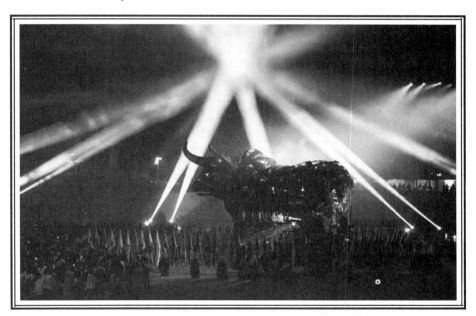

Clearly, the above "ceremonial" events *directly associated Lucifer, and arguably fallen angels generally, with "aliens."*[1] As we continue, pay attention to the below songs and lyrics, as used by the Devil. They include an "aliens" theme.

With the Luciferian "star," or the "all-seeing eye" of Lucifer, again appearing over the recreated Tower of Babel, Duran, Duran's lead singer, Simon John Charles Le Bon, then exited the base of the tower (for the serpent, representing the AntiChrist). He wore a black shirt presenting a knight's bust (cf. the Black Prince) and a light pink jacket, to join his bandmates. Things "kicked off" to the initial background of the kaleidoscopic "angels" (inside the tower), which were followed by more "psychedelic" colors and patterns, images of planet Earth as a contained spinning globe, etc., and even bursts of hellish flames and belching smoke.

Corporately arrayed in "LGBTQIA+ whatever" colors (e.g., light, dark and fluorescent pink, as well as fluorescent green and yellow, besides black and white), to "stand with" and promote sexual satanism, and with attendees' lit wristband flickering corresponding colors throughout the stadium, Duran, Duran performed "Save a Prayer," "Planet Earth," "Tonight United" and finally, "Ordinary World." (Notably, the lead singer started with his arms spread out, as though crucified.) Of course, as Duran, Duran played for Lucifer or Satan, the "dreamers," fluorescent revelers, (druidic) bards and others danced and swayed between the Tower of Babel and the Ba'al-Molech bull idol; also, multi-colored lights flashed around the track's inner and outer perimeters, and many more colorful fireworks detonated overhead and around the stadium, illuminated by searchlights. Below, are the salient lyrics—which as sung, were also displayed across portions of the tower:

"Save a Prayer:" "You saw me standing by the wall, corner of a main street. And the lights are flashing on your window sill. All alone ain't much fun, so you're looking for the thrill. And you know just what it takes and where to go. Don't say a prayer for me now. Save it 'til the morning after. No, don't say a prayer for me now. Save it 'til the morning after...."

"Planet Earth:" "Only came outside to watch the nightfall with the rain. I heard you [(e.g., the Devil)] making patterns rhyme, like some new romantic looking for the TV sound. (You'll see I'm right, some other time.) Look now, look all around, there's no sign of life [(e.g., the night's still)]. Voices, another sound, can you hear me

---

1. For more information, see this author's *Solar Apocalypse* multi-volume series, which provides not just the key history of, but actual hard evidence for *counterfeit* "aliens" and their (terrestrial and non-terrestrial) satanic works (e.g., unnatural chimeras in the form of dangerous dinosaurs, insectoids, etc.).

now? This is planet Earth, you're looking at planet Earth. Bop bop ..., this is planet Earth. My head is stuck on something precious [(e.g., a glowing 'alien' craft)], let me know if you're coming down to land. Is there anybody out there, trying to get through? My eyes are so cloudy, I can't see you. Look now, look all around, there's no sign of life. Voices, another sound, can you hear me now? This is planet Earth, you're looking at planet Earth. Bop bop ..., this is planet Earth. Bop bop ..., looking at planet Earth. Bop bop ..., calling planet Earth. Bop bop ..., this is planet ... !"

"Tonight United:" "If you wanna make a difference, if you wanna see a future coming round, you got to see it from a distance, you got to do it walking barefoot on the ground. [(8x)] You and I tonight—no way to fight it—we come together, tonight united."

In the midst of these songs, the audience could see at least one "bobble-headed" skull-costumed bard (representing death). Additionally, many would have noticed Wales' red dragon flag waving in the hands of (often ignorant, but still without excuse) Devil-worshiping athletes and partyers.

Duran, Duran's Le Bon then stated: "Put your hands in the air. Time to sing. Show the world—*Babylon!*" (Yes, he exclaimed, "Show the world—Babylon!") With that, the band proceeded to sing their final song—"Ordinary World:" "Came in from a rainy Thursday on the avenue. Thought I heard You talking softly.... Still I can't escape the ghost of You. [(Christ Jesus, as The Way, The Truth, and The Life, was crucified and killed on the cross, on a *Wednesday.)*] What has happened to it all? Crazy, some'd say. Where is The Life that I recognize? (Gone away.) But I won't cry for yesterday. There's an ordinary [(i.e., fallen)] world, somehow I have to find. And as I try to make my way, to the ordinary world, I will [(ostensibly)] learn to survive. [(In other words, this is man's way, *not* God's Way.)] Passion [(cf. *the Passion* or crucifixion)] or coincidence once prompted you to say, 'Pride will tear us both apart.' Well, now pride's ... run away— left me in the [(unsaved)] vacuum of my heart. ... Where is my Friend when I need You most? (Gone away [(cf. Moses on Mount Sinai, so that the rebels among Israel began to worship the Devil, and cf. Christ Jesus in Heaven, so that Birmingham fools et al. now openly worship Satan and encourage the rest of mankind to do likewise)].) But I won't cry for yesterday. There's an ordinary world, somehow I have to find. And as I try to make my way, to the ordinary world, I will learn to survive. But I won't cry for yesterday. There's an ordinary world, somehow I have to find...." Curiously, Duran, Duran skipped these remaining lyrics, perhaps to avoid striking fear over Satan's intentions: "Papers in the roadside, tell of suffering and greed. Fear today, forgot tomorrow [(e.g., biblical prophecy is ignored, so that fear overtakes)]. Ooh-ooh. Here besides the news of holy war and holy need, ours is just a little sorrowed talk. ... And I don't cry for yesterday. ... (Every world is my world [(so says the thieving Devil)].)"

What are we to think? Why before a newly "built" (mock) Tower of Babel, was *Babylon* presented to the Commonwealth and mankind? Was this not a declaration of a neo-Babylonia, of a revived or contemporary Babylonian Empire? Many prophecy teachers and even some theologians have alleged the existence of a "revived Roman Empire," in relation to the "last days" and particularly under the foretold AntiChrist. This author, however, has long pointed out that there is *no such thing,* scripturally or otherwise, as a revived *Roman* empire; that is foreign to history and biblical prophecy. Indeed, the Roman Empire *never* disappeared from history, but only divided in to eastern and western portions, and those will bear five toes each (the ten rulers who'll be under King Charles III), as symbolized by the two legs of iron, bearing two feet with five toes each, in King Nebuchadnezzar's prophetic vision (Dan 2:33 and 2:41-43); that's just the final form of an empire which has remained *to this day.* However, there *is* to be *a revived Babylonian Empire, which shall simultaneously be the final form of the Roman Empire;* it's capital is Mystery Babylon (see Rev 17:1-6, 17:18). The ceremony we've been detailing, held under the auspices of the foretold AntiChrist, arguably constitutes a declaration of that very revival, portraying neo-Babylonia's rise and (imagined) apocalyptic victory (cf. Rev 18:1 to 19:3), etc. Never the less, we will *not* really see that rise until the final form of anti-Christian global governance is consolidated at the midpoint of the Tribulation Week, or just before the start of the Great Tribulation, when the ten rulers are all "present and accounted for," so that three of them may be "uprooted" (e.g., to become the AntiChrist's or Charles' vassals), as earlier detailed in this work.

As Duran, Duran's performance concluded the opening ceremony, tightly clustered beams of light between the Ba'al-Molech bull idol's chest and the Luciferian "all-seeing eye" over the (modern) Tower of Babel, *resumed.* Higher up, the spotlights which had been used to represent the "star" over the bull idol as well as intimate "aliens" (think "Battle of Los Angeles"), converged over the center of the stadium and above the bull, field, track and clustered beans— made visible by clouds of smoke-filled (heavily polluted) air overhead and all around (so much for their "green religion"). They signified, apparently, the "light" (spiritual darkness) of Satan (Lucifer) overtaking a (global) Commonwealth, or all mankind. Therefore, per the (blasphemous) AntiChrist who formally oversaw the opening ceremony and its brazenly satanic proceedings, *his acknowledged father the Devil* and *their* global worshipers are (they suppose) to triumph over God our Creator and Christ Jesus—before and at the coming Battle at Megiddo (i.e., "Armageddon"). We who are Christians know, of course, that The Lord Jesus as God's Christ, shall instead bruise or crush the Devil's head (Gen 3:15) and "trample the nations in anger" (Hab 3:12; see 3:12-15), so that the foretold AntiChrist (i.e., King Charles III who had been Prince of Wales) along with the False Prophet, are finally "cast alive into the Lake of Fire burning with brimstone" (i.e., Hell), while the Devil himself being bound, shall then be "cast ... into the bottomless pit." From the fore-ordained coming reality, Satan and all his servants shall know fiery torment in darkness (2 Pet 2:17; cf. Matt 6:23; Jude 6 and 13), not peace nor any other good (Rev 19:19 to 20:3)—ultimately, forever.

At the various points where the Ba'al-Molech bull idol was surrounded by the seventy-two athletic teams and their flags, the seventy-one dreamers plus whore Stella riding the beast, the fluorescent revelers and the slavish women, as the bull idol faced the mock Tower of Babel and the "all-seeing eye" of Lucifer (Satan), we might think of the camp of ancient Israel in the Wilderness of Sinai, as the tribes gathered before, and faced the Tabernacle of Moses. In that Wilderness, The God of Israel and Creator of the Universe would manifest over the Tabernacle as a pillar of cloud by day and pillar of fire by night (see Ex 13:21-22 and 40:34-38; cf. 14:18-20, 33:7-10)—imagery from which Satan counterfeited his "all-seeing eye" motif. (In fact, the tent over the Holy of Holies in the Tabernacle was placed in such a way, that it could have had a somewhat pyramidal appearance to an outside observer.) Likewise, the resurrected Christ Jesus whose face shines like the Sun (Matt 17:1-2; Rev 1:16, 10:1, 22:16; see Ps 80:3, 80:7; Isa 60:1-3; Dan 12:3; Mal 4:2; Matt 13:43; cf. Rev 12:1), shall give light to, and within the pyramidal New Jerusalem (Rev 21:16 and 21:23-24) a bit over a thousand years from now, following His Great White Throne Judgment.[1]

This is salient and key: Historically, seventy nations initially arose from rebellious post-Flood mankind, whose original single language God confused, at the original post-Flood Tower of Babel, as outlined in Genesis 10:1 to 11:9. Then came the new nation of Israel—for our current purpose, the seventy-first. At the Feast of Tabernacles each year, Israel sacrificed seventy bulls (Numbers 29:12-39)—*heralding Messiah Yeshua's (Christ Jesus') yet-future sacrifice of*

---

1. For more, see this author's *Messiah, History, and the Tribulation Period*, multi-volume series.

"seventy" rebellious nations (i.e., those of the unbelieving Gentiles) —all Ba'al-Molech worshipers—at Armageddon, so as to deliver a newly believing nation of Israel, to safety. The LORD shall *end* every Satan-worshiping nation. In the present context, we are talking about all the nations worshiping Ba'al (Molech) "by whatever name!" Therefore, contrary to "traditional" understandings, which are mistakenly adopted by whomever, those seventy slain bulls were *not ever* sacrifices on behalf of the world's surrounding nations of Gentiles; instead, those sacrificed beasts prophetically foreshadowed Messiah Yeshua's (Christ Jesus') apocalyptic slaughter and sacrifice—acting as newly regenerate (i.e., saved) Israel's High Priest (and God)—of unsaved nations serving the Devil, at *Har Megiddo* (i.e., Mount Megiddo, or per transliteration, "Armageddon")![1] In the Promised Land, Satan, the foretold AntiChrist, and the False Prophet shall be divinely judged.

The Closing Ceremony. Ten days later, the closing ceremony came, with the games also bearing some derivation from ancient Rome's apocalyptic Circus Maximus. That wrap-up included risque dancing, some overt paganism, more light and fireworks displays celebrating abominable behaviors (i.e., "LGBTQIA+ whatever" sexual satanism), and mostly lousy singing. The latter reached its "crescendo" as original "heavy metal" singer and Black Sabbath bandmate Ozzy Osbourne, appeared alongside the band's lead guitarist—each arrayed in black garb bearing crosses (Osbourne's were embroidered red); hellish flames, smoke and chains of bondage, accompanied their joint performance. We may here recall the Black Prince, or the Order of the Garter's founding Prince of Wales who dressed in all-black, whom we may yet say Charles *represents* as *the* legendary "prince of darkness"—and thereby perceive that Black Sabbath served as a sort of "stand in." Osbourne then shouted: "Thank you, good night. You are the best! God bless you all. Birmingham forever!" With that anti-climax, we again see the red-eyed Ba'al-Molech idol snort smoke, move its head and open its mouth to grunt.[2]

"Since its [post-games] arrival in its current display position—in [Birmingham's] Centenary Square, next to The Hall of Memory—the

---

1. According to rabbinic tradition (Sukkah 55b), the seventy bullocks sacrificed at the Feast of Tabernacles (Num 29:12-34; see 29:12-39) represented all the nations of the world (cf. Gen 46:27, Ex 1:1-5; Deut 32:8)—much as Gog and MaGog may (in part) typologically do immediately following the Tribulation Week (Ezek 38:8-23, 39:3-4*b*, 39:5-8, 39:17-22) and shall (again do) immediately following the Week of History (Rev 20:7-10). Thus, Tabernacles is also known as the Feast of the Nations (cf. 1 Kin 8:41-43). Yet, Jesus as The High Priest, shall *sacrifice* the unregenerate nations *themselves* as *brute beasts.*
2. For portions of the closing ceremony, see "Commonwealth Games 2022 Closing Ceremony extended highlights," *NBC Sports,* 9 Aug. 2022, as posted at "https://www.youtube.com/watch?v=FDZQ6ujF81E" on YouTube.

[(Ba'al-Molech)] bull [(idol)] has been thronged by hungry fans seek-ing [(worshipful)] selfies with the gigantic sculpture."[1] Indeed, the idol is ostensibly slated to "eventually have a permanent home in the center of Birmingham," England—where it could only produce smelly loads of spiritual "$hit." Yes, it's one big "load of bull!"

Allegedly, Osbourne himself is a "Christian." This author will here necessarily suggest, however, that he is really just another anti-Christian loon who, inhaling a little too much smoke, *woefully* lacks genuine spiritual discernment and saving faith. Of course, those who participate in satanic worship—as so many who took part in, or even just cheered the 2022 Commonwealth Games' bull-centered ceremonies—would *not* as "practicing" and effective satanists be blessed, but shall (without genuine repentance unto eternal life) in-stead find themselves cursed and finally condemned.[2] So, as some would say, "Don't take no 'bull!'" (And that's a "wrap," lol.)

Ba'al worship is resurging and becoming very public. Consider the sexual satanism- and pedophilia surrounding the "luxury fashion brand" Balenciaga, where that company's name *Ba'al-enci-aga* actu-ally means "Ba'al the king," with *enci-aga* being Latin. The company even portrayed its name as "Baalenciaga," with an extra "a" to clar-ify that they construe "Bal" to be "Ba'al," on yellow tape used in its pedophilia-based advertising.[3] In fact, Balenciaga was founded by "Cristóbal Balenciaga," whose first name ostensibly means "Ba'al [is] Christ." Is that a fake name contrived by a satanist? Balenciaga "stylist" Lotta Volkova is an apparent satanist who pushes cannibal-ism, child mutilation and bondage.[4] Notably, a 2017 scene in the wicked *American Horror Story* TV series, features a witch who cries out "Balenciaga"—as her "last word"—right before she is burned alive in a red dress.[5]

With Charles, as Prince of Wales, having just upheld Satan for worship, to the British Commonwealth and even the whole world, would the Devil now further enthrone him? In fact, it would be just six weeks until his mother, Queen Elizabeth II, began to turn blue and died, giving the world King Charles III—the largest landowner and wealthiest mortal on Earth. In the next chapter, we'll address all

1. Hussain, "Council leader Ian Ward in in talks to save iconic Birmingham 2022 bull following public appeal."
2. Those who would be saved, rather than condemned, must repent and give their lives to God through Christ Jesus, genuinely and in this life.
3. Michael Snyder, "'Baal-enci-aga' Literally Means 'Baal The King,'" *The Most Important News,* 1 Dec. 2022.
4. Jim Hoft, "It's Getting Worse: Balenciaga Designer Exposed for Posting Disturbing Photos Linked to 'Sa-tanic Ritual, Cannibalism, Child Mutilation,'" *Gateway Pundit,* 28 Nov. 2022.
5. Anthony Scott, "Bizarre: Witch Screams BALENCIAGA Before Being Burned In American Horror Story Scene (Video)," *Gateway Pundit,* 2 Dec. 2022.

that and more—to include the blasphemous supplantation of God's Ten Commandments, with ecofascists' own set of "green" humanist ones, in London, Jerusalem, on Egypt's *historically counterfeit* "Mount Sinai"[1] and elsewhere, all as *prearranged and conducted under the "sustainable" Charles,* alongside 2022's COP27 (i.e., the UN's 27th Conference of Parties) "climate talks." But first, let's consider an intervening U.S. event.

A Junior "Bull." In June 2021, President Trump asked, "If anybody knows who the hell is running that [U.S. dictatorship] operation, could you let us know?," adding, "I don't even think [Joe] Biden is the dictator."[2] In reading this book, you should now know that ultimately, it is Satan's Prince, under the Devil, who runs the U.S. dictatorship: Barack Obama with other Obamanation holdovers handle Biden, while Charles handles them *all,* under Satan. (Would someone please recommend this book to President Trump?)

We might here consider a subsequent U.S. event, one that correlates to the above context. On August 30, 2022, just a month later, U.S. treasonous traitor, domestic enemy, serial mass murderer (e.g., of unborn children), pathological liar, anti-Christian sexual satanist, career criminal, dirty "mafia" politician and petulant bully, wicked conspirator, and communist-fascist coup "leader"—who's also arguably a lot of other wicked things—one (apparently) demented Mr. J. Biden, stood in front of Independence Hall. There, as an apparent *Fourth Reich "Nazi" and Satan-serving despot,* not to mention as a lawless and abusive liar, Mr. J. Biden improperly used U.S. Marines as visual props—while slandering, demonizing and threatening U.S. conservatives (e.g., so-called "MAGA" Republicans), or about half the country, as "a clear and present danger."

Projecting as usual, Mr. J. Biden fraudulently called his political and moral opposition fascists, domestic enemies, potential "terrorists," etc.—or all the things of which he and Obamanation, their party, and their cronies and hacks are themselves brazenly and routinely guilty, *unlike conservatives.* Before a disturbing blood-red backdrop, despot J. Biden delivered what was in fact, the most evil and hypocritical speech of any politician, in U.S. history. The *Gateway Pundit's* Jim Hoft remarked: "Classic projection from a senile and corrupt career politician. It was clearly the most disgusting speech given by any American president in the history of the republic. Former Trump aide Stephen Miller delivered an amazing rebuttal to Joe Biden's historic declaration of war on the American people:

---

1. History's actual Mt. Sinai is in today's Saudi Arabia, as detailed in this author's book on the Exodus.
2. Eric Mack, "Trump: I'm Not Undermining US Democracy; 'I'm the One Trying to Save It," *NewsMax,* 5 June 2021.

'President Trump poured out his heart, his soul, his spirit every day to build a better America for everyone, to build a safer and more prosperous America. While Democrats and the deep state launched an illegal operation to take him out and it is now in its sixth year! ... [Mr. J.] ... Biden tonight gave the speech of a dictator, in the style of a dictator, in the visual of a dictator, using the words of a dictator.'"[1] Indeed, not a few in the United States suddenly found themselves accusing J. Biden of "Molech worship"—out loud—and even calling his address a "Molech speech."

Yet, there was *no* bull, nor indeed any other overtly satanic effigy —just a truly disturbing "throw back" to the likes of Adolf Hitler. None the less, disgusted U.S. citizens have now made those spiritual comparisons—and we may surely wonder about their timing. Could it be that Mr. J. Biden, as a committed treasonous traitor and domestic enemy of the U.S., is trying to incite a second U.S. civil war—in addition to inciting World War 3 via NATO?

JD Rucker of *America First Report,* remarks: "It has become clear to me, ... their [Great Reset] agenda is to tear down our modern civilization and replace it with a totalitarian techno-gulag, where you will be electronically monitored, disarmed, own nothing, be judged by [a] social credit score, live in fear, and be happy — or else. [Mr. J.] Biden's diabolically dark, hateful [U.S.] speech, with [its] satanic blood-red background on the [very] sacred ground where our Founding Fathers declared our independence from a tyrannical [English monarch and] despot, appears to be the spark which will ignite real violence in the coming years."[2]

But the above evil did not originate with Mr. J. Biden. In fact, he and his coup regime are backed by Barack Hussein Obama II, or Biden's former boss, as well as treasonous and traitorous Obamanation holdovers such as Victoria Nuland, Susan Elizabeth Rice, etc. Mr. Obama as an anti-Christian "Muslim" "bisexual" satanist and top fan of sexual satanist Saul David Alinsky, who explicitly dedicated his anarchist book *Rules for Radicals* to Lucifer, is effectively enacting an *unconstitutional and unlawful third term* as President through his former Vice President, Mr. J. Biden. But Obama, Biden, Nuland, Rice et al. are subservient to the World Economic Forum (WEF) and other entities controlled by the former Prince of Wales, who is now King Charles III. Yes, they all work for the Devil and his foretold AntiChrist—as they seek to "burn" the United States—and the current global order—to the ground! To that end, enacting a

1. Jim Hoft, "Biden Admits His Attacks on MAGA Are NOT Just About Trump – But Involves All of Those Who Disagree with the Regime," *Gateway Pundit*, 23 Sep. 2022.
2. "Biden's Moloch speech: Was he insane, demented, or warning what's next?," *JTrudel's Newsletter*, 7 Sep. 2022.

coup regime in Ukraine, and fomenting war between Russia and Ukraine, was only a start.

Is "Obamanation" the only "junior bull?" No, there are *many*—though some "count" more than others. In late October 2022, for example, Mr. Rishi Sunak as an ecofascist Hindu and worshiper of bulls (and cows)—or a pagan after Charles' own darkened heart—was made Prime Minister of the UK, replacing a very short-lived Liz Truss (at Charles' behest). Sunak immediately began to promote Central Bank Digital Currencies (CBDCs) or programmable "monies," which in conjunction with the coming Mark of the Beast, will be used to implement and enforce global financial tyranny.[1]

Satan's servants will soon also bring about what may only be described as World War 3—or wars involving NATO and its allies (e.g., Israel and ostensibly Saudi Arabia) against North Korea, Iran, China and Russia, with plausible involvement of India and Pakistan too. Tragically, those wars and ensuing global famine are near,[2] and shall lead to, and dovetail with the Great Tribulation. (Meanwhile, on September 5, 2023,the Birmingham Authority declared Birmingham *bankrupt.)*

---

1. For more information, see this author's books titled *The Mark of the Beast: Critical History and Hidden Realities* and *The Great Reset: To Digitally Enslave, Depopulate, and Transhumanize.*
2. For more information, see this author's book *North Korea, Iran, and the Coming World War: Behold a Red Horse.*

16

King Charles III:
History's Ultimate AntiChrist

On September 8, 2022, only days after Liz Truss met Queen Elizabeth II (Elizabeth Alexandra Mary) to be accepted as the U.K.'s new Prime Minister, the blue-handed (and COVID-19 "clot-shotted") queen perished. With the monarch's death, a remarkable double rainbow appeared outside Buckingham Palace—ostensibly, a sign "from the Heaven." Not only does this suggest the ascendance of sexual satanism and the Hell-bound "LGBTQIA+ whatever" crowd, but it may remind Christians that instead of a global flood, God shall soon destroy Earth as we know it by *fire*.

Indeed, Elizabeth II's death came just six weeks after Charles, with a message from his mother the queen, oversaw a (global) Commonwealth worship of Satan (e.g., as Ba'al)—as humanity's "god." As earlier shown, on July 28, 2022, at the opening ceremony of the twenty-second Commonwealth Games, in Birmingham, England, New Age and other satanists engaged in active worship of Lucifer via a giant "Molech" bull idol, as a mechanical beast ridden by a harlot New Age "dreamer." There, seventy-two nations and territories representing nearly one third of mankind, or about 2.5 billion people, saw and experienced a contemporary (mock) Tower of Babel, atop which a reconstituted Luciferian "star" or "resurrected" Lucifer *(lucifer* means "shining one" or by inference, "morning | day star;" cf. Job 38:7)—counterfeiting Christ Jesus as the resurrected Bright and Morning Star (Rev 22:16; cf. 2 Pet 1:19; Rev 2:28)—was shockingly *enthroned* as the "all-seeing eye" atop the tower, while faced by a "possessed" Molech bull idol. Simultaneously, the whole world was invited to receive and worship Lucifer, and to celebrate (sing, dance, clap and generally party before) a newly risen "Babylon." (See the corresponding chapter in this work.) Yes, Charles as Prince of Wales, who is now King Charles III (as "king elect"[1] until his May 2023 coronation) and the altogether blasphemous head of the Anglican Protestant Communion, effectively commended *his spiritual fa-*

---

1. Notably, some argue that until Charles' formal coronation as king, he is technically just "king elect." Should we accept that reality, which the controlled fake "news" and mass media ignore, then we might also argue that Charles also is technically yet Prince of Wales—in which case, William would not have legitimately been "created" as such.

ther the Devil for worship—in his mother the queen's stead—to a *global* "Commonwealth" or all mankind, not just the British Commonwealth.

Of course, there are not a few who *hate* the British Monarchy for past abuses, particularly of the former British Empire. Speaking to Commonwealth members in June 2022, he stated, "I cannot describe the depths of my personal sorrow at the suffering of so many, as I continue to deepen my own understanding of slavery's enduring impact," suggesting acknowledgment of "our past," "is a conversation whose time has come."[1]

Many around the world mourned Elizabeth II as one whom they revered, not only as the longest serving monarch in British history, but as the shining head of a contemporary "Christian" matriarchy, a trailblazer of modern (satanic) feminism. Rather than actually representing God's order (e.g., see Gen 3:16) or even serving Him as claimed (see below), Elizabeth II was an *anti-Christian* who served Satan. (Let that reality be unambiguously admitted and affirmed.) Certain statements stand out: "'Over here in Germany, she was admired and worshiped | [revered],' [German President Frank-Walter] Steinmeier said."[2] (Elizabeth II knew every post-WW2 German Chancellor.) "The French president's address from the Elysee Palace in Paris praised the monarch's 'wisdom and empathy,' adding 'we all feel an emptiness.' 'To you, she was your Queen. To us, she was *the* Queen,' the French leader said.... 'Elizabeth II mastered our language, loved our culture and touched our hearts. From her coronation on, she knew and spoke with all of our presidents. No other country had the privilege of welcoming her as many times as we did.' ... Dutch tabloid De Telegraaf hailed the great-grandmother of 12 as 'a global icon.' Its front-page headline was: 'A Queen in the whole world's hearts.'"[3] Of course, the British monarchy is historically also that of Germany and France.

"[As king,] Charles [III] ... [now is] the head of state for the U.K. and 14 other countries, including Australia, Canada, New Zealand, and Papua New Guinea, has defended his actions. 'I always wonder what meddling is, I always thought it was motivating,' he said in 'Prince, Son and Heir: Charles at 70,' a 2018 documentary. 'I've always been intrigued if it's meddling to worry about the inner cities, as I did 40 years ago and what was happening or not happening

1. Andrew R. Marshall, "The lesson Queen Elizabeth II leaves for King Charles III," *Atlantic Council*, 16 Sep. 2022.

2. Immanuel Marcus, "Germany Reacts to Passing of Queen Elizabeth II," *Berlin Spectator*, 9 Sep. 2022.

3. Jaems Franey, "'To you, she was your Queen. To us, she was THE Queen': Emmanuel Macron delivers a touching speech praising the monarch for 'mastering our language' and 'touching our hearts,'" *Daily-Mail*, 9 Sep. 2022.

there, the conditions in which people were living. If that's meddling, I'm very proud of it.' ... Charles ... became the first British royal to earn a university degree. He then spent seven years in uniform, training as a Royal Air Force pilot before joining the Royal Navy, where he learned to fly helicopters [(and was known as 'red dragon')]. He ended his military career as commander of the HMS Bronington, a minesweeper, in 1976."[1] Charles Philip Arthur George as Prince of Wales, had received the title Duke of Kent, when Prince Philip died.

Now that Charles is the British monarch, his "Prince of Wales" title lays *dormant* for him (he is yet living), and has been granted to another royal (e.g., William). In Charles' case, his earlier title as Prince of Wales is "merged with the Crown" (i.e., it is no longer used by him, as if it were actually gone).

"[The] Accession Council met at St James's [Palace] — the most senior royal palace in the United Kingdom, built for Henry VIII in the 1530s — to proclaim him as king.... The council — formed of Privy Counsellors whose centuries-old role has been to advise the monarch — included his son and heir William, wife Camilla and Britain's new prime minister, Liz Truss, who signed the proclamation of his accession. Six former prime ministers, senior bishops and a swathe of politicians cried out 'God Save The King' as the announcement was approved. 'I am deeply aware of this great inheritance and of the duties and heavy responsibilities of Sovereignty which have now passed to me,' Charles said. 'In taking up these responsibilities, I shall strive to follow the inspiring example I have been set in upholding constitutional government and to seek the peace, harmony and prosperity [(see 1 Th 5:3; 2 Th 2:3-4; cf. John 17:2)] of the peoples of these islands and of the Commonwealth realms and territories throughout the world.' Later, on the Proclamation Gallery, a balcony above Friary Court of St James's Palace, the Garter King of Arms, David [Vines] White, accompanied by others in gold and red heraldic outfits, read out the Principal Proclamation, as trumpets [(bearing Queen Elizabeth II's heraldic achievement)] sounded."[2] "Soldiers in traditional scarlet uniforms shouted 'hip, hip, hurrah'.... Charles is the 41st monarch in a line that traces its origins to the Norman King William the Conqueror who captured the English throne in 1066."[3]

---

1. Associated Press, "After a Lifetime of Preparation, Charles Takes the Throne," *NewsMax,* 8 Sep. 2022.

2. Thomson-Reuters, "King Charles Proclaimed Monarch, Queen's Funeral on Sept. 19," *NewsMax,* 10 Sep. 2022. For the events on the Proclamation Gallery, see for example, "Charles III proclaimed king in historic ceremony," *BBC News,* 10 Sep. 2022, as posted at "https://www.youtube.com/watch?v=yZHqT4fFHWc" on the YouTube.

3. Thomson-Reuters, "King Charles Proclaimed Monarch, Queen's Funeral on Sept. 19," *NewsMax,* 10 Sep. 2022.

We've previously seen Charles being "front and center" in the most watched and publicized events in world history. His ascension and then march next to his mother's casket in September 2022, finally enabled perhaps over half the world's population (ca. 4.1 billion[1]) to see him "in action." Certainly, as King Charles III, he's never been more visible—or as we'll ultimately see, ostentatious.

King Charles III's formal crowning at his May 6th coronation in Spring 2023, had been aptly dubbed "Operation Gold Orb"—an event meant to intimate *sovereignty over the entire world.* Yet, he now possesses not just the publicly admitted wealth of his deceased mother the queen,[2] to include as the new Duke of Lancaster, but also the Crown's (or monarchy's, ostensibly) *vastly greater hidden wealth and resources* (below summarized). Camilla for her part, in February 2022, finally received grace from her mother-in-law, to then be known as Queen Consort. (She may *not* ordinarily occupy the throne.) Charles went further, making her Queen Camilla. As earlier noted, however, their civil ceremony under English law, was arguably *illegal*—and would thus ostensibly be *invalid.*

Though Edward VIII who reigned as king in 1936, quickly chose to abdicate, and never was formally crowned, considering the additional wealth and formal power Charles had not long before received, no one should have expected anything comparable from him. Indeed, King Charles III had explicitly requested that the guest list to his coronation, be limited to 2,000 or so international royals and other dignitaries, or about one-quarter the number present at his mother's in 1953.

"Her Majesty's Christmas and Commonwealth Day messages often addressed the theme of interfaith harmony and respectful tolerance. Leaders of various faiths and denominations regularly attended royal ceremonies, including weddings and services of thanksgiving, at the invitation of the Queen and her [(likewise now deceased)] husband [Philip], the Duke of Edinburgh. Celebrating her Diamond Jubilee in 2012, the Queen attended a multi-faith reception at Lambeth Palace, hosted by the [(apostate)] Archbishop of Canterbury, featuring the leaders of eight faiths in the United Kingdom including Buddhism, Judaism, Islam, and Hinduism. At this event, the Queen said: 'Faith plays a key role in the identity of millions of people, providing not only a system of belief [(that's all Christianity was to her and Philip)] but also a sense of belonging. It can act as a spur for social action. Indeed, religious groups have a proud track record

1. Ciaran McGrath, "'Europe misses Queen': Elizabeth II's 'majestic' funeral shows EU what it lost post-Brexit," *Daily Express,* 20 Sep. 2022.
2. AFP, "Royal Portfolio: Where Did the Queen's Fortune Come From?," *NewsMax,* 8 Sep. 2022.

of helping those in the greatest need, including the sick, the elderly, the lonely and the disadvantaged. They remind us of the responsibilities we have beyond ourselves.' The Queen's efforts were recognized in 2007 by the Three-Faiths Forum, an organization dedicated to building understanding and lasting relationships between people of all faiths and beliefs [(i.e., between satanists, pagans and others who are spiritually deceived and deluded)]. It presented Her Majesty with the Sternberg Interfaith Gold Medallion, awarded to individuals who have helped promote peace and tolerance among people of different faiths. ... From the beginning of her reign, the Queen consistently cited references from Scripture, particularly in her annual Christmas broadcasts [(ostensibly, to *present a false view of herself and the monarchy* to the masses, as a means to retain power)]. 'To what greater inspiration and counsel can we turn,' she asked, 'than to the imperishable truth to be found in this treasure house, the Bible?' In her 2016 address, Her Majesty explained: 'Billions of people now follow Christ's teaching [(no, not nearly so many)] and find in him the guiding light for their lives. I am one of them because Christ's example helps me see the value in doing small things with great love, whoever does them and whatever they themselves believe.'"[1]

"Christianity" to most British royals, remains as (seemingly) always little more than a pretense to maintain power and wield influence—a religion to "honor" *while yet disbelieving or overtly rejecting one or more fundamental tenets, such as the fact that salvation is through Christ Jesus alone, as The Only God.* Studiously, such royals "inclusively" promote *all* religions and spiritual beliefs, despite talk of "Christianity," "faith," "God," etc. Such was the case with Queen Elizabeth II, and the generally "quieter" (necessarily more private) Prince Philip before each died, and never once did either (to this author's knowledge) give *any* public indication of repentance unto genuine Christian belief and saving faith; instead, they appear to have remained anti-Christian "many paths" heretics to the end. None the less, at least some of their descendants, other world leaders and many among the public manage to buy such lies. Indeed: "[Prince] Harry's statement ended on a poignant note alluding to the death last year of his grandfather, Prince Philip, saying that 'We, too, smile knowing that you and grandpa are reunited now, and both together in peace.'"[2] But given that Harry is known to promote sexual satanism and "wokeness," should we now be surprised by

---

1. Dudley Delffs, "Died: Queen Elizabeth II, British Monarch Who Put Her Trust in God," *Christianity Today,* 8 Sep. 2022.
2. Associated Press, "King Charles III and His Siblings Escort Queen's Coffin," *NewsMax,* 12 Sep. 2022.

his lack of understanding and wrong presumptions? (There's no "peace" in Hell, nor is there ostensibly any "reunion" with former loved ones, just never-ending darkness and fiery torment.) How about former U.S. President Donald J. Trump? "'May God bless the Queen, may she reign forever in our hearts, and may God hold her and Prince Philip in abiding care,' Trump said. ... Trump also released a statement on King Charles: 'King Charles III, who I have gotten to know well, will be a Great and Wonderful King. He dearly loves the United Kingdom and all that it represents to the World. He will prove to be an inspiration to everyone. Queen Elizabeth has been, and will be from above, very proud of King Charles III.'"[1]

We may excuse Prince Harry as the queen's grandson, and even forgive President Trump's comparable ignorance, but what about two of the world's most famous evangelical preachers? "[William] Franklin Graham [III] has said the Queen — a personal friend of his late father, the evangelist Billy Graham [(i.e., William Franklin Graham Jr.)] — will be 'profoundly missed.' ... 'He cherished their friendship that was built on a shared love for Jesus Christ and belief in God's Word,' he said. ... 'He also appreciated how she often talked about Jesus Christ during her public addresses—there was never any question about where she placed her faith.' He concluded his message: 'The Queen was a friend to my father, but more importantly, she was a true friend of the Christian faith. She will be profoundly missed.' Billy Graham .... visited the UK many times for evangelistic crusades. He preached several times in the Queen's private chapel.... The Queen and Graham remained lifelong friends."[2] "One of his most notable honors was the history making occasion in 2001, when he became the first clergyman outside the British Commonwealth to receive an honorary British Knighthood. The prestigious honor was bestowed by Sir Christopher Meyer, the British ambassador to the U.S., on behalf of Queen Elizabeth II, in a formal ceremony at the British Embassy in Washington, D.C. 'Because of incomparable contributions to civic and social life in the United Kingdom, I am commanded by Her Majesty the Queen, of whom I am her ambassador, to confer upon Billy Graham the insignia of Honorary Knight Commander of the Most Excellent British Empire,' Sir Christopher Meyer declared as he placed the medal around Mr. Graham's neck."[3]

---

1. Cristina Laila, "Trump Releases Heartfelt Statement on Passing of Queen Elizabeth," *Gateway Pundit*, 8 Sep. 2022.
2. Jennifer Lee, "The Queen was a friend to my father and the Christian faith, says Billy Graham's son," *Christianity Today*, 9 Sep. 2022.
3. All Israel News' Larry Ross, "Why Was Queen Elizabeth II Friends With Rev. Graham for More Than 40 Years?," NewsMax, 12 Sep. 2022.

Never did Billy Graham say, nor has Franklin Graham or President Trump ever actually established and then said, that either Elizabeth II or Prince Philip believed salvation and heaven could *only* be attained through explicit faith in Christ Jesus as God the Word incarnate and The Creator of the Universe, The Only God. (God is Father, Word and Holy Spirit—one God, not three—much as you and I are each body, soul and spirit, comprising one person, not three.) Instead, Queen Elizabeth II talked of "Christ," "Jesus," "faith" and Christianity—just like many anti-Christian cultists, including not a few New Agers, do today—while Prince Philip said considerably less to suggest any genuine acceptance of the Christian faith, though he openly desired to "reincarnate" as a genocidal "virus." In other words, we have *no* credible or actual basis to believe that Queen Elizabeth II, or her husband Prince Philip, had ever actually believed that Christ Jesus is "The Way, The Truth, and The Life"—that as The Lord Himself stated, "No one comes to The Father, except through Me" (see John 14:6); indeed, we have no basis to conclude that either Elizabeth II or Philip ever agreed with Jesus, when He stated, "He who does not believe is condemned already, because he has not believed in The Name of the only begotten Son of God" (John 3:18*b-c*).

On the same day as Elizabeth II's funeral (casket) procession, *Christianity Today* published an article listing these "top 5" heresies among U.S. (so-called) "evangelicals" who *reject* that Hebrew Old and Greek New Testaments are literally true: first, disbelief that Christ Jesus is the *only* way to be saved, and thus to an eternity with God, Creator of the Universe; second, disbelief that God as Father, Word, and Holy Spirit has *always* existed, from eternity past (i.e., the heretical belief that The Word, in Christ Jesus, "was created by God"); third, disbelief that Christ Jesus *is* God The Word in a human body (born of a virgin); fourth, disbelief that The Holy Spirit is God, not some "impersonal force;" and fifth, disbelief that all humans except Christ Jesus (He is fully God and fully man), are sinful and thus naturally *unsaved* or Hell-bound.[1] Even should King Charles III *say* he believes that there is "one" God our Creator, we already know that he's actually a satanist and New Ager who is guilty of *all* the above heresies. As the foretold AntiChrist, he'll spend eternity in Hell. In fact, both his parents were likewise guilty of the above heresies.

Elizabeth II, so far as anyone this side of God's Kingdom may determine, ostensibly perished the same *anti-Christian satanist* she was raised from her youth to be, as first publicly exposed in her de-

---

1. Stefani McDade, "Top 5 Heresies Among American Evangelicals," *Christianity Today,* 19 Sep. 2022.

votion to the red dragon (Satan) via druidic initiation as a British princess in Wales. With Prince Philip, she gave the world the foretold AntiChrist of biblical apocalyptic prophecy. Jesus tells us, "a good tree does not bear bad fruit" (Luke 6:43*a).* From among mankind, has there ever been worse fruit than *the* AntiChrist? What should we then say of King Charles III's family "tree?"

Per Justin Portal Welby, the current Archbishop of Canterbury, King Charles III "shares the same faith and hope in Jesus Christ as his mother, the same sense of service and duty."[1] So, how detached from actual salvation and saving faith does one have to be, as an "archbishop" of any "church," to assert that the foretold AntiChrist of scripture, believes in Christ Jesus and is thus *saved?* How many times does an "archbishop" need to see Charles, let alone his parents before him, associated with the red dragon—a primary symbol of Satan, per Revelation—or a goat mascot, symbols and props only ever royally embraced and never once met with royal rebuke or repentance of any kind, to recognize that he's dealing *not* with born-again or Holy Spirit-filled Christians, but with *overtly obvious anti-Christian satanists?* We may *only* conclude that Mr. Welby himself, like those apostates who preceded him as the monarchy-appointed Archbishop of Canterbury, is an unsaved liar. Indeed, should anyone expect anything else, given that those appointments came from satanists pretending to be "Christians?" Likewise, the Dean of Westminster, now one David Hoyle, is *apostate and without genuine spiritual discernment,* as we discern from his praise of Elizabeth II's "constant example of Christian faith and devotion."[2] *These are individuals who absolutely should know better—and would if they really were Christians. Have they any excuse before God?*

How about Roman Catholicism's current heretic pope, who embraces macroevolution and other satanic lies? "Pope Francis praised the Queen as a 'steadfast witness of faith in Jesus Christ' in an open letter to the new King. 'Commending her noble soul to the merciful goodness of our Heavenly Father, I assure Your Majesty of my prayers that Almighty God will sustain you with his unfailing grace as you now take up your high responsibilities as King,' the Pope wrote."[3] Does that sound like a match made in Hell? Will harlot Rome's final pope one day prove to be the False Prophet, who deceives the world into worshiping King Charles III as the foretold AntiChrist, per what's written in Revelation 13?

---

1. Christian Today, "'We will meet again': Justin Welby honors Queen Elizabeth II's faith in Jesus Christ at state funeral, *Christian Post,* 19 Sep. 2022.
2. Ibid.
3. Maegan Vazquez, "Biden joins world leaders in mourning the death of Queen Elizabeth II," *CNN,* 8 Sep. 2022.

Sadly, such apostasy is increasing throughout the UK, the rest of the British Commonwealth, and indeed the world itself. One day soon, unrepentant apostates shall find themselves vomited from Christ Jesus' mouth, over who they really are (e.g., see Rev 3:16-18); God our Creator is *not* into their games.

The British Monarchy is *not* Christian—and despite past degrees of public approval of Christianity, may never have been. Today's British Monarchy are a family in a long lineage of anti-Christian satanists, among whom were some known pagans—and they have led the UK, British Commonwealth and the world to the extent they could, into *anti-Christianity*—that is, satanic counterfeits of orthodox Christianity. They are Christendom's *mortal enemies.* Alongside the likes of macroevolutionary liar and satanist Charles Darwin, Elizabeth II is now buried with her late husband Philip—though they are all ostensibly now separated in unending darkness and fiery torment, as they truly deserve. To the Archbishop of Canterbury, Dean of Westminster, and so many other anti-Christians, let it be plainly said, "Repent and believe unto actual salvation, or die and forever roast!"

What of King Charles III? In 2011, on behalf of the "YouTube Bible" project, Charles as Prince of Wales then read aloud John 14:1-14, from the Authorized King James Version of the New Testament, in Clarence House's royal chapel.[1] That passage begins, "Let not your heart be troubled: ye believe in God, believe also in me." Is there a more "perfect" place in scripture, for the foretold AntiChrist to *insert himself?* Think about that.

Let's take a current look. *Christian Today's* Mark King tells us: "He spoke about his own religion and the importance of diversity of belief when he welcomed leaders from different faiths to a reception at Buckingham Palace on Friday [(i.e., just before the start of the weekly sabbath, on September 16, 2022)]. Guests at the reception included the Archbishop of Canterbury, ... Justin Welby, the Archbishop of York, the Most Rev Stephen Cottrell, the Dean of Westminster, the Very Rev David Hoyle, Jesus House senior pastor Agu Irukwu, and Rev Helen Cameron of the Free Churches Group. Addressing the room, the King said that [(anti-)]love was at the heart of his own [(anti-)]Christian [(anti-)]faith and that this compelled him to protect those who follow other spiritual paths or embrace secular beliefs."[2] Genuine Christian love of course, speaks The Truth concerning God and Salvation, that there is only *one* Way to be saved,

---

1. "The Prince of Wales records a passage for the YouTube Bible," *The Royal Family* channel, 4 Mar. 2011, as posted at "https://www.youtube.com/watch?v=1tjDdz-yRw4" on YouTube.
2. Mark King, "King Charles promises to protect freedom of conscience and 'space' for faith," *Christian Today,* 17 Sep. 2022.

etc. But that is *not* the sort of "love" King Charles III has in mind. Pay close attention.

Mark King, quoting King Charles III, continues: "The .... Sovereign has an additional duty — less formally recognised, but to be no less diligently discharged. It is the duty to protect ... the space for faith itself, and its practise through the religions, cultures, traditions and beliefs to which our hearts and minds direct us as individuals."[1] As the foretold AntiChrist, Charles' version of "faith" is *satanic and altogether contrary to saving faith.* Thus, The Creator of the Universe warns: "The heart is deceitful above all things, and desperately wicked. Who can know it? I, The LORD, search the heart *and* test the mind | hidden thoughts, even to give every man according to his ways, according to the fruit of his doings" (Jer 17:9-10).

Mr. King adds: "The King then said that he wanted to carry out his responsibilities as Sovereign 'in a way which reflects the world in which we now live,' and to continue the work of his late mother, Queen Elizabeth II, in working to preserve freedom of conscience for all beliefs. 'As a member of the Church of England, my [anti-]Christian beliefs have [(anti-)]love at their very heart,' he continued. 'By my most profound convictions, therefore — as well as by my position as Sovereign — I hold myself bound to respect those who follow other spiritual paths, as well as those who seek to live their lives in accordance with secular ideals. The beliefs that flourish in, and contribute to, our richly diverse society differ. They, and our society, can only thrive through a clear collective commitment to those vital principles of freedom of conscience [(i.e., belief in anything and everything *except exclusively, The Truth),* generosity of spirit and care for others which are, to me, the essence of our nationhood. I am determined, as King, to preserve and promote those principles across all communities, and for all beliefs, with all my heart. ... I am a [(lying)] committed [(not)] Anglican Christian, and at my Coronation I will take [(and *not* keep)] an oath relating to the settlement of the Church of England.'"[2]

King Charles III's claim to have a "deeply rooted" "Christian faith,"[3] is simply "par for the course;" it's what he's expected to say, and serves as a means to influence and manipulate his subjects. Yet, King Charles III is objectively worse than them both. Though Charles as Satan's prince had publicly declared his desire to be "Defender of Faith" (i.e., belief in almost anything) on a variety of occasions, as opposed to "the Faith" (i.e., "Christianity"), so that many wondered

---

1. Ibid.
2. King, "King Charles promises to protect freedom of conscience and 'space' for faith."
3. "King Charles III speaks of his 'deeply rooted' Christian faith in first address to the nation," *Christianity Today,* 9 Sep. 2022.

if he would seek to change the coronation ceremony accordingly, as the new king he instead rather surprisingly and *hypocritically* chose to retain "Defender of *the* Faith," when addressing the UK, the rest of the British Commonwealth, and the world at large—while yet none the less simultaneously affirming his desire and intention to protect the worship of, and belief in *every false "god" and satanic lie.*[1] In a 2015 BBC interview, Charles had "clarified:" "As I tried to describe [in 1994], I mind about the inclusion of other people's faiths and their freedom to worship in this country. And it's always seemed to me that, while at the same time being Defender of the Faith, you can also be protector of faiths."[2]

Let's here take a moment to recall Charles' "early" and (uncomfortably) expressed (i.e., openly admitted to holding) ecumenical sentiments and anti-Christian ecumenist beliefs. In Jonathan Dimbleby's 1994 documentary on the Prince of Wales, we receive this dialogue: "[Dimbleby:] Does that mean that spiritually and intellectually you find yourself at home, walking between and within all those religions—and don't feel *tied* to the Church of England, the Protestant Church? [Charles, Prince of Satan:] *Yes*—I mean I, I feel that there's this enormous amount, once you begin to understand where the, where we are linked in, in common, that, that can be immensely helpful, and I am one of those people who searches. I, I'm, I'm interested in, in pursuing a path [(he says while making exaggerated slithering gestures with his right arm and hand)]; I can find it through the thickets. ... [Satan's Prince:] This title ['Defender of the Faith,'] was, was given to King Henry the 8th [(VIII)], maybe four-hundred years ago, who had happened at that particular time, to please the pope [of Roman Catholicism,] quite enormously. So, he was given this title whereupon, shortly after he decided that for some reason or other—it was because he wanted to get divorced—that um, things were rather different, [and] the pope was a damn nuisance because he wouldn't grant him the divorce, which again is one of the reasons why the Church of England developed, which [(Charles smugly says)] I think is necessary to remember. And um, so the title then remained—um, rather because I suspect here they'd liked it. Um, and, well I, I personally, you see, would much rather see it as 'Defender of Faith'—*not* The Faith—because it means just one particular interpretation of the faith, which I think is something that sometimes causes a great deal of problem, and has done for hundreds of years. People have fought each other to the death over

---

1. E.g., see ca. 02:34 to 03:46, "King Charles III officially proclaimed in historic televised ceremony," *Channel 4 News,* 10 Sep. 2022, as posted at "https://www.youtube.com/watch?v=XisCnG9e6-8" on YouTube.
2. Sharon and TOI Staff, "King Charles III: A friend to UK Jewry, with special and historic ties to Israel."

these things; [that] seems to me, a peculiar wast of people's energy —when we're all actually aiming for the same ultimate goal, I think. [(We are *not.)]* So I, I would much rather it was seen as, as defending *faith itself,* which is so often under, under so much threat, in our, in our day—where you know the whole concept of faith, or belief in anything beyond *this existence,* beyond life itself is, is considered but almost old-fashioned and irrelevant. [Dimbleby:] So, uh 'Defender of Faith' means *defender of those who believe in a 'god,' in whatever form*—that you would want to encourage that, um, that capacity and that urge? [Satan's Prince:] Yes, I mean defender of *the divine,* in, in, in existence—the *pattern* of the divine, which is I think *in all of us.* But um, which i-i-i-is because we are human beings, can be expressed in so many different ways. I've always felt the [Roman] Catholic subjects of the Sovereign, are *equally as important* as the, as the Anglican ones or the Protestant ones. Likewise, I think that the Islamic subjects or the Hindu subjects or the Zoroastrian subjects of the Sovereign, are of equal and vital importance."[1] Has Satan's Prince (now called King Charles III) repented of any of that satanic "ecumenical" compromise (e.g., with the Roman Catholic *cult)* and demonic ecumenism (e.g., with overtly satanic false religions like Islam, Hinduism or Zoroastrianism)? *No, not at all.* As the foretold AntiChrist, Charles *continues* to allege multiple "paths" to "god," "faith" for faith's sake, and multiple "ways" to be "saved"—all of which, are *lies* from Satan, other fallen angels and demons (and fake "aliens"[2]).

In the months leading to Charles' formal coronation as king, however, the public was "shocked" to hear this: "King Charles has been at loggerheads with [Anglican Protestant] Church leaders over the role other faiths should play in his Coronation.... Church sources say the monarch has been told that his desire for a 'diverse' ceremony, including participation by non-Christians, risks clashing with centuries-old canon law, which bars Muslim, Hindu, Jewish and other [(satanic and pagan) anti-]faith leaders from reading out prayers during the [(ostensibly Christian)] service. [Allegedly,] ... this wrangle has delayed the release of the Coronation's Order of Service with barely four weeks to go until the [May 6, 2023] ceremony. ... The King, as Supreme Governor of the Church of England, is required by the Bill of Rights Act 1688, modified by the Accession Declaration Act of 1910, to declare at either his Coronation or at the first State Opening of Parliament that he is a 'faithful Protestant' and

---

1. "Prince Charles speaking about the Church," *reelsarency,* 14 Feb. 2011, at "https://www.youtube.com/watch?v=K9Q4x0VWU1I" on YouTube.
2. For more information, see this author's *Solar Apocalypse* multi-volume series.

will 'secure the Protestant succession'. In addition, the Coronation Oath Act of 1688 requires the King to declare he will maintain the established Anglican Protestant Church. [(Charles may only *lie,* to make such declarations.)] One source said Church laws meant that the participation of non-Christian faith leaders should be restricted to them just being present in Westminster Abbey and taking part in the procession. [(In a real Christian coronation, non-Christians should actually be *entirely excluded.)]* [Apparently,] ... the King is still wrestling with how to ensure that his new role accords with his realm's many non-Christian [(satanic and pagan) anti-]faiths. ... In 2015, Charles made clear he saw no contradiction between being Defender of the Faith and 'protector' of other faiths, saying he minded 'about the inclusion of other people's faiths and their freedom to worship in this country'.[1] He said the late Queen had declared that the monarch's role was not to defend Anglicanism to the exclusion of other religions. ... Dr [Gavin] Ashenden ... said: 'This is a crisis long in the making but entirely predictable given the King's previous declarations. ... 'Charles's desire to reach out to other [(satanic and pagan) anti-]faiths is commendable and understandable [(no, it is *not)],* and it is only right that they are able to attend the Coronation. But any attempt to alter fundamentally the nature of the Coronation — a Christian ceremony in a 1,000-year-old abbey — would be entirely wrong and misguided. The King derives his authority and position from being a Christian monarch in keeping with the history of this country.' [(Yet, there is *nothing* genuinely Christian about Charles, nor was there concerning his *now-roasting* parents and grandparents.)] ... However, what is extraordinary is that this debate over the Coronation service itself has been taken to the wire when planning for it began more than 10 years ago."[2] Of course, there are heretics and open apostates at the top, who would "accommodate" Charles. For example, Richard Douglas Harries, a former Bishop of Oxford, has asserted that Charles should read from the Koran as a "creative act of accommodation," thereby embracing Islam and its (spiritually lost) adherents.[3]

Could such a religious "rift" lead to Charles' relinquishment of the throne to William—so that Charles would once again be "Prince

---

1. Muslims, Hindus, and other pagans commonly act to exclude and even murder Christians and Israelites in their midst. "Christian" governments should *not* tolerate the worship of Satan, by any "name," in society's midst—and certainly must *not* protect the satanic wickedness of Islam, Hinduism, Buddhism, Luciferianism, Wicca, New Ageism, etc.
2. Brendan Carlin and Glen Owen, "Dilemma for the modernist king: Charles is at odds with Church of England over what role other faiths will play in his 'diverse' Coronation," *Daily Mail,* 8 Apr. 2023.
3. Steve Doughty, "Koran should be read at Prince Charles' coronation says top bishop: Critics attack proposal and accuse Church of England of 'losing confidence' in its own traditions," *Daily Mail,* 29 Nov. 2014.

of Wales?" We don't yet know. Catherine Pepinster commented: "And with [(apostate)] Justin Welby's every move being scrutinised nowadays by his hard-line, traditional critics in the worldwide Anglican Communion, the Archbishop is unlikely to warm to any moves to turn the Coronation into a multi-faith extravaganza rather than an religious service that reinforces the Church of England as the Established Church. ... [But] the politicians present, such as new SNP [(Scottish National Party)] leader, Humza Yousaf, a Muslim, and the Prime Minister, Rishi Sunak, a Hindu [who is advocating Central Bank Digital Currencies (CBDCs, aka programmable currencies) under Charles], will represent how different a country Britain is from the last coronation in 1953."[1]

Let it again be emphasized that Charles, like his parents before him and other British royals, is *thoroughly anti-Christan;* he has always been and remains a counterfeit (fake) "Christian." On such a point, do not be suckered as those who are willfully ignorant and politically false—like Roman Catholicism's *Hell-bound* "purgatory" pope Francis, who heretically stated: "'I willingly join all who mourn her loss in praying for the late Queen's eternal rest, and in paying tribute to her life of unstinting service to the good of the Nation and the Commonwealth, her example of devotion to duty, her steadfast witness of faith in Jesus Christ and her firm hope in his promises,' the pontiff said. 'Commending her noble soul to the merciful goodness of our Heavenly Father, I assure Your Majesty [(King Charles III)] of my prayers that Almighty God will sustain you with his unfailing grace as you now take up your high responsibilities as King. 'Upon you..., I invoke an abundance of divine blessings as a pledge of comfort and strength in the Lord,' he wrote."[2] Could those sentiments suggest the coming partnership between the False Prophet and King Charles III as the foretold AntiChrist, where both serve Satan?

On September 9, 2022, Charles formally "created" (declared) William the new Prince of Wales (see below), so that title itself has *not* become altogether "dormant" (other than for Charles himself). Charles had to wait close to eleven years from his personal 1958 creation as Prince of Wales, to his formal July 1969 investiture as such, before the whole world, at Caernarvon Castle. Though William is now only the twenty-second Prince of Wales in history, it could yet be multiple years before he himself is formally invested with the em-

---

1. Pepinster, "Charles's instincts are to be applauded – but 1,000 years of tradition are at stake. Is it wise for the Christianity of the Coronation to be so diluted in the name of diversity?"
2. Jennifer Lee, "Pope Francis pays tribute to Queen's 'unstinting service' and 'steadfast witness of faith,'" *Christianity Today,* 9 Sep. 2022.

blems, letters patent, etc., of the role—*or that day could fail to mate-rialize,* meaning it might not come.

Continuing his family's and his own anti-Christian deceptions of the public, which the British monarchy has long claimed to serve (but would now *depopulate)*—while yet embracing Satan (e.g., as the Red Dragon of Wales) through "any 'god' will do" ecumenicalism and "faith in faith"—King Charles III addressed the United Kingdom and British Commonwealth. From Buckingham Palace, the new king stated: "In the course of the last 70 years, we have seen our society become one of many cultures and [(infiltrated by)] many [(false reli-gions and non-Christian so-called)] faiths. The institutions of the State, have changed in turn. ... The role and the duties of Monarchy also remain, as does the Sovereign's particular relationship and re-sponsibility towards the Church of England — the Church in which my own [(alleged, but clearly not actual)] faith is so deeply rooted. In that faith, and the values it inspires, I have been brought up to cherish a sense of duty to others, and to hold in the greatest respect the precious traditions, freedoms and responsibilities of our unique history and our system of parliamentary government. As The Queen herself did with such unswerving devotion, I too now solemnly pledge myself, throughout the remaining time God grants me [(it shall end when Christ Jesus crushes Charles III's head at Megiddo)], to uphold the Constitutional principles at the heart of our nation. [(Charles III is of the 'father of lies,' the Devil himself.)] And wher-ever you may live in the United Kingdom, or in the Realms and terri-tories across the world, and whatever may be your background or beliefs [(any belief except biblical Christianity, works for Charles III)], I shall endeavour to serve you with loyalty, respect and love, as I have throughout my life. ... It will no longer be possible for me to give so much of my time and energies to the charities and issues for which I care so deeply. But I know this important work will go on in the trusted hands of others. ... [(Quickly ignoring his public assur-ances, the lying King Charles III will certainly *break his word* and re-main *deeply involved.*[1])] As my Heir, William now assumes the Scottish titles which have meant so much to me. He succeeds me as Duke of Cornwall and takes on the responsibilities for the Duchy of Cornwall.... Today, I am proud to create him Prince of Wales, *Ty-wysog Cymru,* the country whose [(brazenly satanic)] title I have been so greatly privileged to bear during so much of my life and duty. With Catherine beside him, our new Prince and Princess of Wales will, I know, continue to inspire and ... bring the marginal to

---

1. E.g., see ca. 05:14 to 06:15 and 11:52 to 17:21, "King Charles III officially proclaimed in historic tele-vised ceremony," *Channel 4 News.*

the centre ground where vital help can be given. ... And to my darling Mama, as you begin your last great journey to join my dear late Papa, I want simply to say this: thank you. ... May 'flights of Angels sing thee to thy [(most likely not)] rest.'"[1]

William, who is now the *non*-invested Prince of Wales, had been the Duke of Cambridge, though he remains Earl of Strathearn and Baron Carrickfergus. William is also now Duke of Rothesay. Moreover, with Charles' ascension to the British throne, William has taken over (received) the Duchy of Cornwall as its duke. William's wife Kate is of course, now the duchess of both Rothesay and Cornwall.

"Charles has promoted extreme climate change policies, even advocating these long before other world leaders regarded climate change as a major issue, and he has advocated for such things as organic farming, and alternative medicines and therapies. In 2008, Charles gave a speech to the EU Parliament offering an apocalyptic view of global warming. In his speech, Charles claimed, 'In the last few months we have learned that the North Pole ice cap is melting so fast that some scientists are predicting that in seven years time it will completely disappear in summer.' That prediction [(i.e., ecofascist propaganda)] turned out to be incorrect. He then [(likewise falsely and manipulatively)] added: '[The] ... doomsday clock of climate change is ticking ever faster towards midnight. We cannot be anything less than courageous and revolutionary in our approach to tackling climate change.'"[2]

Now, however—publicly at least—King Charles III would have us believe that he intends to sing a different tune: "'My life will of course change as I take up my new responsibilities,' he said. 'It will no longer be possible for me to give so much of my time and energies to the charities and issues for which I care so deeply. But I know this important work will go on in the trusted hands of others.' Ed Owens, a historian and author of *The Family Firm: Monarchy, Mass Media and the British Public, 1932-53,* said it's unlikely Charles will suddenly stop talking about climate change and the environment — issues where there is a broad consensus [(for which Satan's liars Charles, Al Gore, and the now roasting Prince Philip, are largely responsible)] about the urgent need for action. That may push the boundaries of what a constitutional monarchy looks like, he said. Such 'vigorous promotion' of the consensus 'is something we're going to see that is going to be different compared to his mother's reign,' Owens said before Charles became king. [(Liar)] John Kerry, the U.S. special envoy for climate [(under Mr. J. Biden)], said he

---

1. E.g., see "King Charles III's First Address to the UK in Full," *Bloomberg,* 9 Sep. 2022.
2. Charlie McCarthy, "Zany Liberal Charles Becomes King," *NewsMax,* 10 Sep. 2022.

hopes Charles will continue speaking out about climate change because it is a universal issue that doesn't [(not)] involve ideology. Kerry was in Scotland to meet with the Prince of Wales this week.... 'It doesn't mean he's involved in the daily broil of politics...,' Kerry told the BBC. 'But I can't imagine him not ... feeling compelled to use the important role of the monarch, with all the knowledge he has about it, to [continue to] speak out and urge the world to do the things the world [(allegedly, but not actually)] needs to do.'"[1]

Saliently, King Charles III *retains his personally and historically unique heraldic achievement, as the "first beast" of Revelation 13, little horn with a man's eyes of Daniel 7, etc.* Moreover, while Charles' title as Prince of Wales, which he held for fifty-three years, yet calculates to six-hundred and sixty-six (666), *there is* no *(actual) title, now or ever, that will so-calculate (i.e., to 666) for Prince William of Wales, on the biblical numbering system.* Additionally, though William's heraldic achievement may be altered by the Garter King of Arms (aka the Garter Herald King) and London's College of Heraldry, it does *not* have to be—*and its devices may never match those of any other individual or entity in the world, including his father's.* In other words, Prince William of Wales does not meet the biblical requirements still, to be the foretold AntiChrist. William lacks both the required imagery—and is (this author will boldly say) certain to *never* have it—and he also lacks and shall *never* have the required name calculation of 666, to be the foretold AntiChrist. Though King Charles III completely fulfills the apocalyptic and prophetic requirements to be the foretold AntiChrist of bible prophecy, his son William—even as the new Prince of Wales—does *not,* cannot, and (this author will further suggest) never will. (Is that sufficiently clear to you who would falsely allege William to be the foretold AntiChrist? Let this be known: anyone who proclaims William to be the AntiChrist, is speaking falsely and is *not* of God.)

Charles—though formerly an heir apparent to a throne as prince —*remains* the foretold AntiChrist of apocalyptic scripture. *There is no other candidate in history—nor shall there be, ever.* Charles Philip Arthur George is *already prophetically identified,* per scripture, as the coming "son of perdition | destruction" (see 2 Th 2:3-4; cf. Rev 17:8, 17:11). Satan possessed Judas Iscariot, making the latter the "son of perdition | destruction" (John 17:12) and leading him to betray Christ Jesus (John 13:21-30) for crucifixion and death. Likewise, *this* Charles shall be possessed by Satan (2 Th 2:4), making him "the man of sin..., the son of perdition" (2 Th 2:3*c-d),* leading him to betray God's Church as well as the nation of Israel, so that multitudes

---

1. Associated Press, "King Charles III Signals His Reign Will Offer Change of Tone," *NewsMax,* 9 Sep. 2022.

of Christians are then led as "lambs to the slaughter," and Israel finally faces her own *national crucifixion.*[1]

Of note, the choice to retain the first name "Charles" as king, rather than one of his other names—though "Arthur" would have been truly interesting in its own right, for entirely different reasons— agrees with this work's earlier treatment of Daniel 9:27's Hebrew root words, in which the meaning of "Charles" is intimated with *gabor.* Thus, Charles III makes sense. Interestingly, German Chancellor Olaf Scholz wished Charles III "strength," as Elizabeth II's successor."[2] Of course, as the foretold AntiChrist, Charles III will altogether "eclipse" his tyrannical, autocratic, murderous, violent, enslaving and thieving predecessors (e.g., Charles I and Charles II).

As king, Charles had briefly been shown with the earlier heraldic achievement of the "United Kingdom," which had been in-place since 1952 *as a modified and updated version of his mother's former 1947 achievement as Duchess of Edinburgh*[3]—itself modified from "Heiress Presumptive" Elizabeth's 1944-47 heraldic achievement, to which was added the Garter belt.[4] Those historical updates to then Princess Elizabeth's arms and heraldic achievements were *required.* They built upon her original heraldic grants, *without* her having ever been *invested* as princess. (Charles on the other hand, was formally invested as Prince of Wales, making his heraldic reality historically and indeed categorically different, as below addressed.)

Elizabeth joined the Order of the Garter, and then became Queen Elizabeth II. The Sovereign helm and certain other necessary devices (e.g., the attending mantle, queen's "imperial crown Proper, thereon a lion statant guardant Or imperially crowned Proper," and the compartment area "Motto 'Dieu et mon Droit' in the compartment below the shield, with the Union rose, shamrock and thistle engrafted on

1. For more information, see this author's *Messiah, History, and the Tribulation Period* multi-volume series.
2. "Queen Elizabeth's death: Reaction from world leaders," *Reuters,* 9 Sep. 2022.
3. E.g., see "Coats of arms of Elizabeth II," *EverybodyWiki,* 15 Nov. 2016, as posted at "https://en.everybodywiki.com/Coats_of_arms_of_Elizabeth_II" on the Internet, for a *semi-accurate* artist's rendering (Elizabeth II's unicorn does *not* officially have human eyes, contrary to the depiction); as well as "File:Royal Coat of Arms of the United Kingdom.svg," again for a *semi-accurate* artist's rendering (Elizabeth II's unicorn, and thus that "of the U.K." under her, does *not* officially have human eyes, contrary to the depiction), at "https://en.everybodywiki.com/File:Royal_Coat_of_Arms_of_the_United_Kingdom.svg". A formal description of the latter: "Quarterly, First and Fourth Gules three lions passant guardant in pale Or armed and langued Azure (for England), Second quarter Or a lion rampant within a double tressure flory counter-flory Gules (for Scotland), Third quarter Azure a harp Or stringed Argent (for Ireland), the whole surrounded by the Garter; for a Crest, upon the Royal helm the imperial crown Proper, thereon a lion statant guardant Or imperially crowned Proper; Mantling Or and ermine; for Supporters, dexter a lion rampant guardant Or crowned as the Crest, sinister a unicorn Argent armed, crined and unguled Proper, gorged with a coronet Or composed of crosses patée and fleurs de lys a chain affixed thereto passing between the forelegs and reflexed over the back also Or; Motto 'Dieu et mon Droit' in the compartment below the shield, with the Union rose, shamrock and thistle engrafted on the same stem" ("File:Royal Coat of Arms of the United Kingdom.svg").
4. E.g., see "Category:Coats of arms of Princess Elizabeth (used 1944-52)," *Wikimedia.org,* 7 Nov. 2022.

the same stem") are *absent from* the former princess' heraldic achievement as Duchess of Edinburgh, which also had an unusual diamond-shaped royal shield as well as (the removed) "label of three points Argent charged on the centre point with a Tudor rose and on the others with a cross Gules" (around the beasts' necks). That is obviously *not* the situation with the heraldic achievement granted to Charles as Prince of Wales in July 1969, which *strangely* had the Sovereign helm and every other necessary heraldic device and beast from the start, suggesting a certain expectation that he would in fact, become king.

As queen, Elizabeth II then received *two new heraldic achieve-ments:* one bearing her Sovereign helm over a *non*-diamond-shaped royal shield, and one used by *her* government, where the royal crest bearing the noted helm was replaced by a crown only. Both achieve-ments have some other subtle changes as well.[1]

So, pay close attention to this: King Charles III, in addition to *re-taining* his heraldic achievement as history's twenty-first Prince of Wales (irrespective of any "dormancy"), has now received *two* new heraldic achievements—just as his mother did, but with one very im-portant caveat: Charles' heraldic achievement as Prince of Wales, *re-mains* completely salient, relevant and *unchanged*. Charles' title as Prince of Wales is now *merged into the Crown,* as if no longer ex-tant, and shall remain so *while he is king*—but his "coat of arms" as Satan's Prince **forever identifies him as the foretold AntiChrist,** not just as the invested and twenty-first Prince of Wales. (Again, no one else will ever have Charles' imagery as that AntiChrist, not even his son William or son Henry (Harry), *irrespective* of William now being Prince of Wales.) Charles two new heraldic achievements—at least in their available "artistic" renderings—appear to be identical to those granted his mother as Queen Elizabeth II, with just *one* com-mon difference, which is the crown shown over the helm and on the head of the dexter beast (the same beast that is on the crest, also wearing it).[2]

King Charles III's July 1969 heraldic achievement as Prince of Wales, continues to identify him as the foretold AntiChrist, whether or not he remains king until Christ Jesus has an angel cast him down to Hell at Armageddon (Rev 20:1-3). This author had enter-tained the notion that a new version could have been commis-sioned, one with the shield of the Duchy of Cornwall (between the Motto's words *Ich* and *Dien)* and perhaps (though less likely) the Badge of the Black Prince (compartmented below the dexter lion-

1. See "Category:Coats of arms of Queen Elizabeth II of the United Kingdom," *Wikimedia.org,* 6 Apr. 2023.
2. See "Category:Coats of arms of King Charles III of the United Kingdom," *Wikimedia.org,* 9 Apr. 2023.

leopard-bear beast) being supplanted by newly relevant devices. Ostensibly, though Charles still is the "eldest son" of his roasting parents, that label could have be removed from the necks of the various beasts—leaving the human-eyed little horn (unicorn) on his heraldic achievement as *the eighth among seven,* to intimate that three (symbolized by the label) of the original ten (with the Sovereign helm), are finally "vassalled," forming the kingdom of the beast. (First, the ten kings or kingdoms must arise, such as through an expansion of the UN Security Council, to ten permanent members, with three of the ten being Germany, France and England.) Notably, the crown on Charles' July 1969 heraldic achievement is *not* the nail-and cross-laden one he received and wore as the newly invested Prince of Wales, and so that could have gone *unchanged* (and in fact, it *is* unchanged). Those were this author's speculations, until the UK unveiled the above-noted two new heraldic achievements for King Charles III. Regardless, the UK, British Commonwealth, and when Charles commences his reign over the coming global government— ostensibly, the world itself—*will* now see the "first beast," human-eyed "little horn" and Satan (red dragon) much more commonly portrayed, with *this very book* presumably starting the trend!

Significantly as well, just as Charles has both his official heraldic achievement as Prince of Wales (the one publicly unveiled at his July 1969 investiture, as seen on the front cover of this book), on which the human-eyed little horn (unicorn with a man's eyes) representing him is restrained (bound) and grounded, as well as the "unofficial" one, where that same unicorn is unrestrained (loosed) and rearing back, there are also *two* versions of his deceased mother's (previously called the United Kingdom's) heraldic achievement as queen: the formal one in the Throne Room of St. James' Palace, where her unicorn is bound and grounded, as well as informal one in Buckingham Palace, where the same beast is loosed and *begins* to rear back (it's bottom feet, however, both remain grounded). Uniquely, the dexter lion supporter on Elizabeth II's latter "unofficial" arms, begins to lift one of its bottom feet instead. What might all that mean? Could we see King Charles III's unofficial heraldic achievement, received when he was Prince of Wales and already bearing the Sovereign helm, etc., placed over the throne in St. James' Palace—in place of his deceased mother's—as well as Charles' official heraldic achievement as Prince of Wales (the one on this book's front cover), placed in Buckingham Palace? We'll see.

That's not all. Regardless of what transpires over the throne in St. James' Palace, or in Buckingham Palace, just as Elizabeth II's 1952 "sovereign" heraldic achievement—which became her own officially at her 1953 ascension to the British Throne—was then adopted as the heraldic achievement of the United Kingdom itself, to be placed not only on government stationary, buildings, and other items, as well as on company goods sold throughout the UK, we are ostensibly to see King Charles' III's *new* official heraldic achievement everywhere supplant his deceased mother's, as the new heraldic achievement "of the U.K." Again, the only apparent difference, in artistic renderings, is the crown atop the helm and on the head of the dexter beast. Officially, however, Charles' dexter beast *would* most likely yet have feet like those of a bear, his sinister beast *would* most likely yet have the eyes of a man, and though the red dragon is *not* on the new achievement, it is Charles' status as Satan's prince that has provided him his global power—not his newfound status as king. Thus, a version of the "first beast"—not just the mark of the beast (e.g., EAN or UPC barcodes)—*may* yet be found on groceries and other items bought and sold, with time and expense. We'll see.

Charles' *new* heraldic achievement (assuming he remains king) is expected to appear on the walls of British embassies around the world, including in Israel. Over time, we should also see Charles' portrait and that same "coat of arms" replace his mother's (as "the UK's") on currency and coins, passports, postage stamps, postal boxes, and certain institutional uniforms, besides a variety of paint jobs, in the UK and some (perhaps many) other Commonwealth nations.

Remarkably, in the new general-use and ecofascist coins for King Charles III, repeating sets of three interlinked "Cs," may *rightly* be construed as carbon-carbon-carbon—besides Charles-Charles-Charles or Charles III—with carbon being the sixth element in the periodic table. Indeed, carbon uniquely has *six* protons and *six* electrons, as the *sixth* element in the periodic table; thus, in the context of King Charles III, it intimates "6-6-6." So, does all this relate to alleged "carbon pollution," which ecofascists now fraudulently employ as a major elitist means to destroy mankind? (That's a rhetorical question.) Of course, these sly "6-6-6" coins, which were designed under Charles' ecofascist supervision, also feature unclean creatures: a Hazel Dormouse (i.e., a mouse, for the one pence), a Red Squirrel with flora and fauna (for the two pence, where the prior still-circulating two pence features the World Wildlife Fund or WWF surrounded by symbols of mostly unclean creatures and some vehicles), acorns and oak leaves (for the five pence), a Capercaillie grouse ostensibly over Scottish Bluebells (for the ten pence), a Puffin (for the twenty pence, with the IUCN listing Puffins as "vulnerable" on its Red List), an Atlantic salmon (for the fifty pence, ostensibly as a threatened fish species), bees (for the one pound, as wild and solitary bees are in serious global decline), and finally, national flowers (for the two pound, showing an English rose, Welsh daffodil, Scottish thistle and Irish shamrock).[1] (Later, we'll address a *stunning* gold sovereign coin—one portraying King Charles III "taming" and/or riding the fiery red dragon, and having received the world from him.)

Speaking of goods bought and sold, *NewsMax's* Jack Gournell adds: "Heinz is one of several brands that brandish the royal coat of arms on their label, but that license ends with the death of the monarch, and companies must reapply with the new monarch.... The image includes the [dexter] lion of England, the [sinister] unicorn of Scotland and a [royal] shield ... with the words 'by appointment to Her Majesty the Queen.' The seal, or warrant, can be obtained only by permission of the ruling monarch, and the company must prove its product is in regular use by the royal household. So if King Charles III's eye catches a new ketchup, the condiment could face the consequences. Companies can keep using the coat of arms for up to two years as long as there is 'no significant change within the company concerned,' the Royal Warrant Holders Association told the *Daily Mail*. 'Amongst other things, applicants are also required to demonstrate that they have an appropriate environmental and sustainability [(tantamount to a "woke" Environmental, Social and Governance or ESG)] policy and action plan,' the [Royal] Warrant Holders Association added. Other food and drink companies granted warrants by [the late] Queen Elizabeth II include Cadbury, Coca-Cola, Premier Foods, Unilever, British Sugar, Britvic, Martini, Dubonnet, Johnnie Walker, The Famous Grouse['s] owner Matthew Gloag & Son, [and] Gordon's and Pimm's.... Other businesses affected are Bentley, Jaguar Land Rover, Barbour, Burberry, Boots, Clarins, Molton Brown, Hunter, and Mappin & Webb. All companies can reapply to King Charles III [(to use *his* heraldic achievement)], but must prove they 'supply products or services on a regular and ongoing basis to the Royal households for not less than five years out of the past seven,' according to the association."[2]

As of July 2022, the British Commonwealth compasses 56 nations, or 72 nations and territories—for an estimated 2.5 billion people, approaching one-third (i.e., 31.25%) of the global population, though as in 1998, still about one-quarter of Earth's land (cf. Rev 6:8). All those nations now recognize King Charles III as the head of the British Commonwealth, while many additionally submit to the

---

1. See "The New 2023 United Kingdom Coins: A Collector's Dream," at "https://youtu.be/ZXtqmmCV6SQ" on YouTube.
2. Jack Gournell, "Heinz Ketchup, Other Brands Forced to Change Labels With Queen's Death," *NewsMax*, 13 Sep. 2022.

British monarchy as their own, with Charles having already person-ally visited most of them. "Former British prime minister David Cameron remarked that, like his mother, Charles is a 'superb diplo-mat.' 'I saw him in action at Commonwealth heads of government meetings and he knows every leader personally. He interacts with them brilliantly,' he told BBC television."[1]

So, how rich is King Charles III, or he and his family as "The Firm," really? It is credibly argued that the real wealth of the British monarch, now King Charles III, is (perhaps many) *trillions (that's with a "t") of dollars*—so *not* the "mere" $42 billion[2] or so the public is now being told, nor the (still) "mere" hundreds of millions some pundits allege. Technically, *King Charles III ostensibly "owns" and could seek to control (nearly) all the land and resources of the British Commonwealth*—facts the now-deceased Queen Elizabeth II actively sought to *hide* from the world. Simply put, among humans, King Charles III is *the wealthiest and most powerful man on Earth—expo-nentially so compared to any other mortal.* He has *no* corporeal competition among men (or women)—no one else even comes close. That is *not* to say, however, that there is any (known) *practical mechanism* by which he could avail himself or the "royal family" of all that "largess."

Kevin Cahill with Rob McMahon, in their January 2010 book titled *Who Owns the World: The Surprising Truth About Every Piece of Land on the Planet,* estimated that as of 2009, the Crown's—and thus the British Monarch's—technical wealth was somewhere in the vicin-ity of *$33 trillion,* being comprised of the land, natural resources and more, of *about one-sixth of Earth's entire surface!* Given subsequent inflation, and the reality that *more nations have joined the British Commonwealth since 2010, who also recognize the monarch of the UK as their own,* that estimate could perhaps be *doubled!* Obvi-ously, such a sum is *several times* the combined wealth of all the world's other trillionaires and billionaires! Simply put, *King Charles III now is, without apparent contest, arguably the world's wealthiest individual by far, bar none.*

Sorelle Amore has done a great job summarizing this rather stunning reality—in her September 15, 2022 YouTube clip titled, "How the Royal Family secretly owns the world." She surmises thus: "Charles the Third. With his new title, Charles has inherited a phenomenal amount of wealth ... and is now leader of the richest family on Earth. ... You might think that it's an exaggeration to sug-

---

1. AFP, "With Republicans at the Gates, Charles III Meets Realm Envoys," *NewsMax,* 11 Sep. 2022.
2. Giacomo Tognini and Carlie Porterfield, "How Rich Is King Charles III? Inside The New Monarch's Outra-geous Fortune," *Forbes,* 15 Sep. 2022.

gest that Queen Elizabeth [II] owned the world, but it might not actually be as big of a stretch, as you might think. Because legally, she owned more of the planet than anyone else, including land that most people thought was theirs. ... The vast majority of this unconsidered wealth is made up of land.... ... Queen Elizabeth [II] actually owned a 'superior interest in all [freehold] land in England, Wales and Northern Ireland, [and may assume ownership of the land in certain situations,] meaning that by law, her ownership superseded any other land owner—meaning every other land owner in the UK, was really just leasing land from her. And this supreme authority over all land, isn't exclusive to the United Kingdom, either. As the Crown and Monarch also owns Crown land in fifteen other Commonwealth realms around the world, including New Zealand, the Bahamas, Australia and Canada. In Australia, for example, Crown land is almost one-quarter of the entire country. In Canada, it's even more—almost ninety-percent of all the nation's land. But again, even these figures aren't entirely correct—because technically, the Queen actually owns every single piece of land in these nations. In Australia, for example, a law firm described that even though now many Australian landholders believe they own their own land, this isn't actually the case—that legally the Crown actually holds absolute ownership of everything. This means that nobody truly owns land in any of the Queen's realms; it's all just the property of the Crown. [(Ostensibly, even Klaus Schwab's Great Reset claim, "You shall own nothing, and be 'happy,'" derives from Charles as the foretold AntiChrist.)] This includes every single piece of land in Australia, New Zealand, Canada, Jamaica, Papua New Guinea and the rest of the Commonwealth. To put it simply, Queen Elizabeth [II] owned absolutely all land in every Commonwealth nation by law—land that upon her death was automatically transferred to a new owner. In total, the queen's owned land amounted to 6.6 billion acres around the world, or around one-sixth of all land on [the] planet's surface, including around half of Antarctica, through claims made by Australia, the UK and New Zealand. Immediately upon the death of the queen, her Crown titles and ownership were legally passed on to her son, the new reigning King Charles the Third, who in an instant became the single biggest land owner on Earth. Upon becoming king, Charles [III] also inherited some incredible powers—like being completely immune to prosecution, meaning he can never be arrested or tried for any crime. He also no longer needs a passport to travel [within the Commonwealth], as by law, all passports are issued in his name. But some of the most valuable powers come in the form of being able to hide or grow the Crown's wealth. Charles is [(and also was as Prince of Wales)] legally exempt from paying any form of taxes, at all, and his family is also entirely immune from any Freedom of Information requests, making it much easier to hide or shield its assets. As reported by the *Guardian,* this secrecy is a tradition that apparently began in the 1970s, after the queen allegedly successfully block laws that would require her to reveal everything she owned—something the news outlets uncovered in documents dated from November 1973. However, this accusation was completely denied by the royal family. But there is so much more that Charles has inherited beyond just land and power—as with his new title of king, it comes with an insane amount of other resources. A huge part of the Crown's assets have never been fully known to the public. One of the most valuable of these is the Royal Collection, an archive of over half-a-million items, including over seven-thousand paintings—in other words, the largest private art collection on Earth, valued at over ten-billion pounds. But this isn't just about collecting history: art preserves the Crown's wealth. ... So, it is obvious that the [British] royal family is unimaginably wealthy—and a lot of that wealth is concealed through laws and structures that are designed to hide its value. For this reason, the [British] royal family operates more like a massive global corporation [((in an ultimate merger of fascism, capitalism, socialism and communism with royalty and nobility)], rather than just a rich group of relatives. At the start of the last century, [then Princess] Elizabeth's father King George VI began referring to the royal family as 'The Firm,' a title the family still apparently calls themselves today. And according to *Forbes,* The Firm has structured itself like a one-thousand-year-old business. Today, the firm is made-up of seven total members: the new King Charles [III] and his wife Camilla, Prince William and his wife Kate, as well as two of Queen Elizabeth [II]'s children, Princess Anne and Prince Edward, including also Edward's wife Sophie. ... In total, The Firm manages nearly $28 billion [(or per *Forbes,* $42 billion, though some sources yet suggest *less)]* worth of assets that we know about; however, much of this has been well-hidden over time, with some estimating The Firm's assets to be closer to $100 billion in value; and this *doesn't* even include the land and nations the Crown legally owns around the world, which is extremely difficult to value—but by some estimates, the Crown's technical ownership of Australia, could be worth over $5.8 trillion alone. Basically, if you take everything into account, the [British] royal family are by far, the richest family on the planet—making the family in the second spot, look very small in comparison, which is the Saudi royal family, which have an estimated net worth of $1.4 trillion. Now, obviously the recent death of the head of the [British] royal family, is going to result in some very significant changes. ... [I this] ... illustrates how much power a single family still has over our planet today, especially considering that most of us, [(somehow)] probably think that the [British] monarchy is something that's in most part, faded into history."[1]

Somewhat murky claims are made that the United States of America (i.e., the entity we call a country), not only was, but remains the *Virginia Company*—a corporation belonging to the Crown, through (occult) "brotherhood" bloodlines. In this work, we have already seen that the U.S. has long been subverted and controlled through Freemasonry, the CFR, the Trilateral Commission and other entities, which are finally tied to the British Monarchy. So, does King Charles III also "own" today's most powerful "nation," the USA? To many, it looks like his mother did, and now he does—and that argument, in various forms, has been widely made. That is not all, as through the *private and shadowy* Federal Reserve System (FRS), the Crown also controls the U.S. economy. The Crown uses many entities. Vanguard, for example, which the Crown largely controls from London, itself has large and even controlling stakes in BlackRock, State Street, etc. Those massive "investment" entities in turn, then control not just many U.S. corporations, but also the major U.S. banks that are part of the FRS, to include JP Morgan Chase, Citi, etc.

Significantly as well, through those same massive investment entities (and others), the Crown also largely controls the global modern mass media and social networks—and thus, the Crown foments and ultimately controls much of the "woke" racist and lies-based ESG, DEI and related agendas, as well as the burgeoning direct censorship of truth under the guise of "intelligence" and "national security" public-private partnerships (using MI6, the CIA, the NSA, etc.), which are socialist and fascist-communist, in the UK, U.S., and elsewhere). Likewise, the Crown controls Big Pharma (and thus, that part of the depopulation agenda), etc.[2] In fact, King Charles III is now also the patron of the Royal Economic Society (RES), for example. Like so much of the Crown's (British Monarchy's) current powerbase, the RES has roots in Fabianism—that is, in Fabian Socialism—which we may here describe as international socialism, corporatism, fascist communism, and *public-private partnerships!* Indeed, we could say it's the "Devil's Blend" of socialism and communism with fascism and capitalism—a decidedly toxic brew or "tea."

---

1. "How the Royal Family secretly owns the world" at "https://www.youtube.com/watch?v=4pUUSyY-ON2c" on YouTube.
2. See the author's book titled, *The Great Reset: To Digitally Enslave, Depopulate, and Transhumanize.*

Indeed, with the advent of modern "environmentalism," the British Monarchy has turned ecofascism into a global influence peddling scheme, for ever-increasing control—and ultimately, to further financially fleece the world. As Prince Philip groomed Charles, until the latter held the global "climate emergency" sway and essentially took over, Charles now grooms William, the new Prince of Wales. Though William is *not,* nor could he ever be the foretold AntiChrist, and though he is *far less capable* than his Satan-empowered father, William is already making ecofascist rounds internationally.[1]

Scripture asks, "Who is like the beast? Who is able to make war with him?" (Rev 13:4*c*). Charles, via the Crown, is likewise *over* the West's military-industrial complex via interlocking investments in most of the major defense contractors—who have a stake in keeping wars (and thus depopulation) "roaring" along—through Vanguard, State Street (with Vanguard as a major investor), and Blackrock (with Vanguard as a major investor). Through those same entities, as earlier mentioned, the Crown is *over* the U.S. banking sector, and thus also the privately-owned (contrary to actual misinformation and disinformation) U.S. "Federal" Reserve banking system (aka "the Fed"), via controlling stakes in the major banks and banking institutions (e.g., JP Morgan Chase) participating in the Fed! Indeed, Vanguard is itself effectively controlled from the "Square Mile" or the inner City of London (a city within a city, aka "the City")—and *the Crown has not just any "stake," but ostensibly the controlling one in Vanguard and the City.* Moreover, FMR Corporation's (Fidelity Investment's) and Fidelity Personal's CEO, Abigail Johnson, is reportedly a

---

1. E.g., Carly Ledbetter, "Prince William Meets Joe Biden During Push For Climate Action," *HuffPost,* 2 Dec. 2022. Among neurotic "climate emergency" "Greenies," who largely owe their brainwashed existence to Charles' long ecofascist crusade, a few (four were involved) have now cynically used him to reiterate *his* anti-oil fraud: "On Monday, two members of the activist organization Just Stop Oil smashed chocolate cakes at the wax figure of King Charles III, at Madame Tussauds London. ... They both proceeded to smash cakes at [(i.e., on)] King Charles III's wax figure's face, before reciting the monarch's 2019 comments ... in New Zealand: 'Ladies and gentlemen, in the words of the King,' one protester said: '... I have been driven by an overwhelming desire not, to be confronted by my grandchildren — or yours ... — demanding to know why I didn't do anything to prevent them being bequeathed a poisoned and destroyed planet. Now, of course, we are indeed being confronted by these very children, demanding immediate action and not just words.' 'The [(anti-)]science is clear [(as mud)]. The demand is simple, just stop oil. It's a piece of cake.' ... *The Gateway Pundit* has reported on the rise of vandalism and public temper tantrums by unhinged climate activists throughout Europe" (Jim Hoft, "Unhinged Climate Activists Smash Cakes on King Charles III's Wax Figure at Madame Tussaud's in London (VIDEO)," *Gateway Pundit,* 24 Oct. 2022). These pathological young "climate" propagandists represent weaponized mental illness, as nihilistic psychopaths, under Charles: "24-year-old Louise [who shut down a major highway in the UK over (alleged) global warming]: 'I'm here, I'm here because I don't have a future. And you might hate me for doing this.... But I wish you would direct all that anger and hatred at our government. They are betraying young people like me.... I'm part of the coalition demanding an end to all new oil and gas licenses.... What we're asking for is what all the scientists [(not)] are arguing for, what the [(satanic)] United Nations are asking for, ... the [(fraud-laden)] IPCC. How many more people have to say, 'We don't have a livable future if you continue to license oil and gas,' for you to listen?" (Jim Hoft, "Unhinged Crackpot Shuts Down Major Highway in UK – Demands Immediate End of Fossil Fuels and Claims She Is the Victim (VIDEO)," Gateway Pundit, 7 Nov. 2022).

1998 World Economic Forum (WEF) graduate (Global Leaders of To-morrow, 1993 to 2003),[1] and as elsewhere documented in this book, King Charles III is *over* the WEF (e.g., WEF founder Klaus Schwab is one of Charles' *knights)!* Vanguard, Blackrock, State Street and Fidelity have been called "the four horsemen" of the modern financial world—often by individuals unaware of the control the first three (at least) also wield over the West's military-industrial complex. All this sits beneath Charles, *besides* the tens of trillions in value comprising those nations which recognize the British Monarch as their own.

Charles wants to use the entire world's wealth—skimmed in the form of ecofascist taxes, under the canard of "saving" the world's environment and biodiversity, in an alleged "green recovery," for supposed future generations. At 2021's UN Climate Change Conference (COP26), which the then Prince of Wales opened in Glasgow, Scotland, being the first "world leader" to speak—just like COP21 in Paris, France—Charles made these startling and highly manipulative *lying ecofascist and macroevolutionary statements,* which continue to shock and confuse those who are unaware that he is *the* foretold AntiChrist, or the son of perdition (destruction) who is soon to be possessed by Satan:

"We have to put ourselves on what might be called a warlike footing, ... because time has quite literally run out. ... With a growing global population, creating ever-increasing demand on the planet's finite resources, we have to reduce the emissions urgently, and take action to tackle the [(actually natural)] carbon already in the atmosphere [(on which *all life actually depends)],* including from coal-fired power stations. Putting a [global taxation] value on carbon, thus making carbon-capture solutions more economical, is therefore absolutely critical. Similarly, after billions of years of [macro]evolution [(not)], nature is our best teacher. ... As we tackle this [(non)] crisis, our efforts cannot be a series of independent initiatives, running in parallel. The scale and scope of the threat we face, call for a global systems level solution, based on radically transforming our current fossil-fuel-based economy, to one that is genuinely renewable and sustainable. ... We know this will take trillions, not billions of dollars. ... Here, we need a vast [Fabian-socialist] military-style campaign to marshal the strength of the global private sector. With trillions at his disposal, far beyond global GDP—and with the greatest respect, beyond even the government's of the world's leaders—it offers the only real prospect of achieving funda-

---

1. E.g., see Richard Seager, "All the Young Global Leaders from 1993 until 2021," *Plegian Resistance,* 21 Feb. 2022, at "https://plebeianresistance.substack.com/p/all-the-young-global-leaders-from" on the Internet.

mental economic transition. ...   More than three-hundred of the world's leading CEOs and institutional investors, have told me that alongside the promises countries have made, ... they need clear market signals, agreed globally.... This is the framework I've offered in the 'Terra Carta' [(i.e., Earth Charter)] road-map—created by my Stable Markets initiative, with nearly one-hundred specific actions, for [global transition] acceleration. Together, we are working to drive trillions of dollars, in support of transition, across ten of the most [(allegedly, but not actually)] emitting and polluting industries. They include energy, agriculture, transportation, health systems and fashion. The reality of today's global supply chains, means that industry transition will effect every country and every producer in the world. There is absolutely no doubt in my mind that the private sector is ready to play it's part, and to work with governments [(in fascist-socialist private-public partnerships)], to find a way forward. ...   Many of your countries, I know, are already feeling the devastating impact of climate change—through ever-increasing droughts, mudslides, floods, hurricanes, cyclones and wildfires, as you've just seen on that terrifying film. *Any leader* who has had to confront such life-threatening challenges, knows that the [(alleged, but *not* actual)] cost of inaction, is far greater than the cost of prevention. So, I can only urge you—as the world's decision-makers—to find *practical ways* of overcoming differences, so we can all get down to work, *together,* to rescue this precious planet, and save the threatened future of our young people."[1]

So, who is the "his" in "at his disposal," the one to whom Charles refers? Do you know? You should know: Charles spoke of "Lucifer," of Satan. Indeed, once Charles has been possessed by *the Devil,* that "his" shall suddenly *also be self-referential!* Of course, that makes sense. Indeed, who more than anyone else is driving the global ecofascist hysteria? Charles![2]

Perhaps you think at this point, "Wow, that's a lot." But we're not done! Following Boris[h] Johnson's removal from power, conserva-

---

1. See, for example, "WATCH: Britain's Prince Charles gives statement at COP26 climate summit in Glasgow," *PBS NewsHour,* 1 Nov. 2021, as posted at "https://www.youtube.com/watch?v=fuTzaCd_Suo" on YouTube.
2. "In a 2014 report, the [(lying) ecofascist] Chatham House policy institute stressed that it is unlikely that global temperature rises can be kept below 2C without changes in global meat and dairy consumption. According to [(lying) ecofascist] Oxford University researcher Michael Clarke, 'even if fossil fuel emissions stopped immediately, emissions from our food systems alone could raise global temperatures by more than 1.5C.' The [(lying) ecofascist] IPCC Special Report on Land Use found that a vegetarian diet would save almost 6 gigatons equivalent in greenhouse gas emissions and a vegan diet would raise that to 8 gigatons. The reforestation of lands currently used to farm animals would raise that benefit even higher" (Tzvi Joffre, "Jerusalem, Tel Aviv refuse to commit to lower use of animal products, says NGO," *Jerusalem Post,* 26 Oct. 2022). So, who is over Chatham House? Charles. Whose subject is Clarke? Why Charles', of course. Whom does the IPCC actually serve? Charles.

tive Liz Truss took over as UK prime minister. But Truss' was the shortest-lived premiership ever, as Charles ostensibly *hates* her—perhaps not least, because she opposed his previously stated plan to attend COP27 in Egypt, and to him, that was a "barn burner." (Put another way, Truss would not dance to the tune of the king's wicked "balls.") Indeed, Rishi Sunak was then *installed.* Not only is Mr. Sunak *unelected,* but through his British-Indian wife Akshata Murty, Sunak is among the world's wealthiest men. (Some have suggested his wealth exceeds that of King Charles III, but as we have just seen, that is *not* the case.) More saliently, Sunak's self-made Indian billionaire father-in-law, N. R. Narayana Murthy who co-founded, controls and owns a chunk of InfoSys, is involved in the global push for Central Bank Digital Currencies (CDBCs)—or what are more accurately described as *programmable* digital monies under "central" control. Sunak, within days of his installation, loudly promoted CDBCs among "G7" member nations. Simultaneously, Sunak publicly promoted CDBCs to the UK and the West—all within days of his installation. (Most central banks globally—ostensibly *ninety percent*—are now actively exploring or fully pursuing CDBCs.)

For whom is Sunak actually working? N. R. Narayana Murthy? In fact, Sunak reports *directly* to King Charles III—both as the UK's unelected bureaucratic "prime minister" and as a member of the WEF (like InfoSys[1]), via Klaus Schwab! Thus, Charles—including through other WEF members, as well as other national and international entities—has objectively positioned *himself,* and Satan whom he serves, to seriously influence and (very) loosely "control" the coming global financial system, or what shall be the "backbone" of the fully-implemented "mark of the beast" system (e.g., tattooed UPC, EAN or other "6-6-6"-bearing "barcodes," and/or implanted biochips, specially linked to personal and business finances).

The "liquid" "wealth" of those subject to programmable digital currencies, will be *entirely at-risk, all the time.* As globalists would have it, such "monies" would be subject to *disablement* (i.e., being "turned off," on any political, spiritual or other "blackmailing" whim) —to control what individuals and entities are *allowed* to buy (and thus, what companies are able to sell). They would also be subject to *taxation without representation*—or even outright *confiscation.* (What caused the American Revolution? Is the Crown brining the United States, and indeed the rest of the world, "full circle?") With such taxation (e.g., forced "carbon," "methane," "nitrogen" or other "greenhouse gas" emission "taxes" or "fees") or *financial confisca-*

---

1. E.g., Dennis Gada, "The Future of Central Bank Digital Currencies for the Financial Sector: Infosys and Digital Asset Fireside Chat at WEF2022," *InfoSys.com,* 2022.

tion, people and entities would then be made *slaves* to rather effective *digital "prisons."*

So, what shall be the *real wealth and power of King Charles III*— as Satan's chosen AntiChrist? Can one man gain control of the world's overall wealth? *Does he already have such control?* Satan sought to tempt Christ Jesus (Matt 4:8-11): "Again, the devil took Him up on an exceedingly high mountain, and showed Him all the kingdoms of the world and their glory. And he said to Him, 'All these things I will give You if You will fall down and worship me.'" Satan failed miserably: "Then Jesus said to him, 'Away with you, Satan! For it is written, "You shall worship The Lord your God, and Him only you shall serve."' Then the devil left Him, and behold, angels came and ministered to Him." With Charles as the foretold AntiChrist, however, Satan has now *succeeded.*

We may well think of "C40 cities" (billed as "a global network of [{greedy, lying and brainwashed}] mayors of the world's leading [{Hell bound}] cities that are united in action to confront the [{Devil's fomented}] climate crisis"), and particularly "public prison" 15-minute cities, as the proposed (and currently trialed) new "climate lock down" "plantations"—the new model "fiefdoms" of "lordly" satanic and tyrannical elitists (e.g., the C40 Climate Cities Leadersihp Group and Nrep, the WEF, UN, etc.). These elitists are they who, knowingly or not, seek to deprive "global citizens" (i.e., the masses, whom they effectively confine, and thus enslave as *serfs)* of property (personal possessions), liberty (freedom), and ultimately their very lives (via multiple forms of depopulation[1])! All this is being perpetrated by Satan's morally compromised and "educationally" brainwashed ecofascists (e.g., those of the WEF, UN, WHO, etc.)—and by those who submit to, and thus collaborate with their evil tyranny— under King Charles III. Marketed as offering greater choice and ease of access locally, such "living arrangements" are but fraudulent lies-based mirages leading to human enslavement and life-threatening hardships, if and when they are widely implemented—at which point, elitists would ostensibly seek global implementation, completing their deadly noose around mankind's collective neck.

Would *you* comply—to become the foretold AntiChrist's (Charles'), and thus the Devil's, slave? Consider the eternal consequences of taking the mark of the beast, to be able to buy or sell:[2] damnation in Hell's flames, and unending torment in darkness, forever. Hopefully, you would instead choose to die in this life, as a

---

1. See the author's book titled, *The Great Reset: To Digitally Enslave, Depopulate, and Transhumanize.*
2. See this work's earlier material on the mark of the beast, and this author's separate book on the subject, for more information.

faithful Christian and servant to God our Creator, so that you may instead live in The Father's heavenly Kingdom.

As we've begun to realize and see, *Charles ostensibly has more control over the world economically, whether by influence or direct action, than* _any_ *other human being, apart from Christ Jesus,* who shall strike Charles' head (Gen 3:15) at Armageddon. "The love of money is a root of all evil" (see 1 Tim 6:9-10), and that wicked greed is being used to achieve complete totalitarian control. Those who reject the Mark of the Beast, and thus the "beast system," will be forced to live without what it offers (e.g., grocery stores, etc.). Many if not most surviving Christians could become altogether destitute. Yet, those nations whose populaces yet live without too many modern conveniences, being too poor to acquire and participate in them, may prove to be among the best "prepared" to remain "outsiders." Truly, when Christ Jesus' coming judgments are all concluded, the poor shall inherit the Earth.

"Green religion" and "Ten [Universal] Principles for Climate Repentance | Justice." Ecofascism, a form of Gaia religion, comes with its own false "gods," false "commandments" (starting, some may now claim, with a new set of ten "green commandments"), false "sin," false "prophets," false "teachers," greed-driven flock fleecers, and even their own "eternal" punishment!

Green religion's false "gods" may be summarized by more than typical New Age or pagan "mother Earth worship," to include overt Luciferianism or satanism. It's false commandments may be compassed by sentiments and statements such as these: "thou shalt not emit 'green' gasses (e.g., CO_2, methane and nitrogen), "thou shalt not produce and thus consume animals responsible for 'green' gas emissions" (e.g., beef, etc.), "thou shalt eat bugs for protein," "thou shalt reduce conventional energy consumption," "thou shalt throw money and polluting resources at polluting solar and wind energy production," etc.

There is now also a set of ten "green commandments." In November 2022, blasphemous ecofascists acted—in conjunction with the UN's COP27 climate talks, which were held in at Egypt's Sharm el-Sheikh seaside resort—to supplant God's Ten Commandments. In fact, "green religionists" (aka "Greenies," etc.) foolishly conspired in London, in Jerusalem, atop the alleged (but not actual) "Mount Sinai" in Egypt (i.e., Jabal Musa), and elsewhere around the world, to supplant God's Ten Commandments with their own "Ten Principles for Climate Repentance."

Indeed, those very "repentance" "principles" do themselves derive from a more verbose *panentheist* (and New Age) list of "Ten [Universal] Principles for Climate Justice"[1] (aka "10 Spiritual Principles for Climate Repentance"[2]). Those "commandments" ("principles") were explicitly "developed" or "formulated by dozens of multifaith leaders meeting in London," in the days directly leading to COP27.[3] (Of course, the hundreds of involved leaders again traveled in highly polluting, fuel-guzzling, carbon "unfriendly" private jets. What's a little more gross hypocrisy among greedy tyrannists, right?) Think about this: all those things were done under King Charles III's auspices and ostensible gaze—*as the now-revealed "man of sin" and "son of perdition" (2 Th 2:3*c-d). *Being actually lawless at heart, Charles may finally transgress every commandment of God*—while encouraging the whole world to do the same.

Not coincidentally, the symbol for COP27, derives from ancient Egypt's pagan pharaonic Sun or *Ra* worship! All this suggests *a "return" to ancient Egyptian paganism*—much as when ancient Israel turned away from The Creator of the Universe, to bow before a gold calf at the base of the actual Mount Sinai! Rather than turning to The God of Israel and Christians, ecofascist liars and fools instead turned to *Lucifer*—or Satan "whatever name"—as they "repented" before the Sun and "Mother Earth" rather than The Creator (Rom 1:25*b).* This of course, is spiritual *babel* or *confusion,* as typified by the "Elijah" Board of World Religious Leaders, of the "Elijah" Interfaith Institute—among whom are some prominent "Christians" (e.g., cardinals, archbishops and bishops, patriarchs, a seminary head and theology professors, past Roman Catholic popes and Pope Francis, ostensibly representing Roman, Greek, Armenian, Romanian and Eastern orthodoxies, Anglicans, Episcopalians, Lutherans, Mormons, etc.) as well as Buddhists, Hindus / Sikhs / Jains, unregenerate "Jews," Muslims and other pagans[4]—delusionally allege they represent "sustainable development" instead of death and destruction!

The above "Elijah" anti-Christian satanists state: "The call's originality in compiling the finest teachings of all religions in support of climate justice draws inspiration from the great prophetic figures [(not)] associated with Mount Sinai. Teachings and spiritual ideals will be highlighted, in order to help religious communities and humanity at large open their hearts to change for our collective survival. The ceremony will draw from liturgies, readings and the

---

1. "In Sinai, a Prophetic Call for Climate Justice and Ceremony of Repentance," *InterfaithSustain.com.*
2. The [(so-called)] Elijah Board of World Religious Leaders, *ClimateRepentance.com* or *Climate Justice.*
3. Sue Surkes, "Activists smash tablets atop 'Mount Sinai' to launch faith-based climate push," *Times of Israel,* 13 Nov. 2022.
4. See The Elijah Interfaith Institute: Christian Leaders" and "… About" on the Internet.

musical traditions of diverse religions"—to "motivate action among religious communities and the wider public to curb climate change" and "generate new faith-inspired climate education materials for broad use."[1]

Of course, rather than doing the work of the real Elijah, these spiritual "nutters" abuse Elijah's name and usurp his position as a prophet of God. Moreover, by seeking to turn the hearts of fathers to "Mother Earth," rather than actually to their children, they would (literally) bring God's curse upon the Earth, per Malachi 4:5-6! In other words, they *harm* both the Earth and humanity, rather than help or bring peace. They are acting to steal, murder and destroy, as they impoverish (e.g., via imposed "lockdowns" and *energy poverty,* to include an anti-sabbath "global weekly non-carbon day of rest" "observed by different ... communities on different days," to "reduce emissions of the world by a seventh,"[2] depopulate (e.g., via biological weapons, including toxic so-called "vaccines," as well as triggered famines leading to global mass starvation, and wars with chemical and then nuclear weapons),[3] enslave (e.g., via programmable "currencies" or CBDCs, and the coming mark of the beast) and ultimately, under fallen angels and demons, supplant (with chimeric humanoids and other transhumanist monstrosities[4]) mankind on Earth! The order of Satan's conduct, "that he might steal and murder and might destroy" (John 10:10*b,* Gk.), as described and ordered by The Lord, may seem "skewed." After all, isn't murder "just a tad bit" more serious than theft? Yet, if we really think things through, we'll notice that Christ Jesus actually outlined the thieving and murderous Adversary's (Satan's) *preferred "game plan,"* where physical destruction (e.g., of potential assets, via warfare) is generally his *last* choice—as what remains might "suck" (a lot). Indeed, that "game plan" perfectly accords with the Great Reset —or the *"actualization"* of the Devil's New World Order (NWO)— where all but his "elite" (e.g., Charles and those who enable him) are "to own nothing, and be 'happy,'" so that satanic globalists themselves finally "own everything" and all other humans are their slaves "till death do them part." Would that not be "a marriage made in Hell?" (If you've seen or read it, you might here think of the some-

---

1. "'Returning to Sinai' — A Prophetic Call for Climate Justice and Ceremony of Repentance: Sunday, November 13th, 2022, Mount Sinai, In parallel with the COP 27 UN Climate Conference," *Interfaith Center for Sustainable Development* with "The Elijah Interfaith Institute," 2022.

2. Abramowitz, "For Our Sin of Emissions: 10+1 Climate Commandments | Opinion."

3. See this author's separate book on globalists' and elitists' depopulation agenda and efforts, which has been and is being conducted under the British Monarchy (e.g., the now-roasting Prince Philip, or the biological father of the foretold AntiChrist) and now particularly King Charles III.

4. For more information and shocking details, both past and present, see this author's *Solar Apocalypse* multi-volume series.

what prescient fictional *Hunger Games* book or TV series.) But Christ Jesus "is greater than he who is in the world" (1 John 4:4), and Jesus (i.e., *Yeshua* whose actual Hebrew name translates as "Salvation") shall *crush* the "wicked house's | temple's | palace's" *head* (Gen 3:15; Hab 3:13, Heb.)![1] Consider what that means not only for the coming Tribulation Temple in Jerusalem, which The LORD shall judge, but also what it ostensibly implies regarding the British Monarchy's palaces and other residences throughout the UK, the foretold AntiChrist's City of London (in London) itself, the Roman Catholic Papacy's (and perhaps also the False Prophet's) Vatican City in Rome, and globalists' United Nations buildings (e.g., the Secretariat) in New York City.

Saliently, Charles as Prince of Wales—and now king—has been and remains behind the whole "Mount Sinai" thing, loosely or not. At the end of October 2022, *BBC News'* Sean Coughlan reported: "If King Charles cannot go to the COP27 climate conference, then at least some of the conference will be coming to him. The King is to host a pre-conference reception at Buckingham Palace..., bringing together 200 business leaders, politicians and campaigners. ... The prime minister, [Rishi Sunak,] who will not be attending the COP27 summit either, is to attend the Buckingham Palace reception. He is expected to speak, alongside guests discussing practical measures to tackle [(alleged human-caused)] climate change. The gathering in London will be held on 4 November, a couple of days before the summit begins in Egypt. ... King Charles ... has warned of the dangers of climate change. As the Prince of Wales ... at last year's COP26, ... [he called] for the global response to be put on a 'war-like footing.' ... The Buckingham Palace [COP27 kickoff] reception will see a gathering of the 'decision makers and NGOs' (non-governmental organisations) who are involved in tackling climate change. Also attending will be US climate envoy, John Kerry and Alok Sharma, president of the [prior] COP26 conference...."[2] Let's continue.

Indeed, *(already broken)* "mock tablets of stone" (mocking scripture's Ten Commandments) were *smashed* "atop an Egyptian peak [(mis-)]believed by many to be Mount Sinai," by half-assed (to be polite) pagan "Israeli environmental activist" Yosef Israel Abramowitz, over "the world's failure to protect the planet"—after his group read the London-agreed "draft list" of "Ten Principles for Climate" Justice.[3] (Mr. Abramowitz imagines he is somehow serving God, when in reality, he's just another suckered satanist and spiritual rebel un-

---

1. For more information, see the volume titled *Conflict of the Aeons: Understanding the Protoevangelium,* in this author's *Messiah, History, and the Tribulation Period* series.
2. Sean Coughlan, "King to hold event to mark COP27 summit he will miss," *BBC News,* 30 Oct. 2022.
3. Surkes, "Activists smash tablets atop 'Mount Sinai' to launch faith-based climate push."

der the foretold AntiChrist.[1]) "The idea was hatched in the run up to the United Nations COP27 climate conference…, by solar energy entrepreneur Yosef Abramowitz and David Miron Wapner, who chairs the Jerusalem-based Interfaith Center for Sustainable Development. The Sinai Climate Partnership, symbolically launched at the [(blasphemous) tablets-smashing] ceremony, brings together the Interfaith Center for Sustainable Development [(of Yonatan Neril)], the Elijah Interfaith Institute, the Peace Department, the United Nations Faith for Earth Initiative, Abramowitz's Gigawatt Global, and the Israeli environmental advocacy organization, Adam Teva V'Din. After sunrise, Abramowitz and Wapner gathered at the summit together with Nigel Savage, the [influential] founder and former director of the US Jewish environmental organization Hazon, and his successor Jakir Manela, to read sections the Holy Land Declaration on Climate Change signed in 2011 by the multifaith Council of Religious Leaders of the Holy Land.[2] Two teens from the US, there as part of Christian Climate Observers, [(foolishly)] joined the [(satanic)] ceremony as well. … The [tablets-smashing] act was a symbolic echo of the Bible's Moses smashing the 10 Commandments in protest against

---

1. Yosef Israel Abramowitz, "COP27: Will God deliver 10 Commandments for climate change?," *Jerusalem Post*, 11 Nov. 2022.

2. 2011's "Holy Land Declaration on Climate Change" was published in English, Arabic and Hebrew, and is based upon an unholy mixture of satanic anti-Christian, pagan and ecofascist lies with biblical truth. The declaration includes these "multifaith" partial-truth (and below, run-together) "gems:" "2. We recognize …. overwhelming evidence for the reality of man-made climate change that will, if unchecked, kill tens of millions…, eradicate thousands of species and endanger the lives of all our children and grandchildren;" "we declare that global climate change is an emergency which demands a massive and immediate response from each of us. 3. We note that the likely consequences of unmitigated climate change include: *Global injustice* …. and millions of the … poorest … are likely to suffer and … die as a result. *Intergenerational injustice* [with] … wasteful and extravagant consumption today … creating a world ravaged by floods, famines and shortages of food and drinking water.… … *Mass displacement* of populations, suffering and death, caused by hunger, thirst, hurricanes, storms and floods.… … *Mass extinction* of plant and animal species in contradiction to our … duty of protection and stewardship.… … *The possible destruction* of the biological conditions necessary for the existence of most life on Earth, … thereby erasing the name of God from under the Heavens. 4. We call on each and every adherent of our [(anti-Christian and pagan so-called)] faiths to reduce his or her carbon footprint. Our common teachings … do not allow us to delegate doing that which is right and good to governments. … 5. We call on the global leaders of our [(satanic so-called)] faiths to guide us by implementing [(allegedly, but not actually)] wise choices through binding doctrine, fatwa and halakha to avert climate change catastrophe. 6. We … urgently demand … governments [(in stunning oxymoronic hypocrisy)] adopt policies that will [(allegedly, but *cannot* actually)] avert and mitigate climate change. 7. We invite the leaders of other world religions to set their hands and join their [(satanic, pagan and anti-Christian so-called] faiths to the principles of this declaration. … 9. … we see hope that this threat to our common home, Planet Earth will cause us to overcome inter-religious strife.… … 10. Climate change is both a global crisis and an immense opportunity. … Our call is to mobilize … our respective teachings and the collective passion … of our [(false, other than Old and New Testament)] prophets, saints and sages to inspire a vision for the future that matches the magnitude of the [(alleged climate)] challenge. We urge all men and women of [(misplaced)] faith to join together to pray [(to the Devil or whomever)] that the one God will give us the wisdom and courage to choose life — for our children's sake." Okay, that's a lot of lying mixed with some actual truth, all devoted to *Satan* as supposedly "the one" *anti*-"God" of unregenerate Israel, anti-Christian "Christianity," pagan Islam and every other spiritual lie and false religion "under the Sun." Notably, ecofascists' fears as above-expressed, also align with the Olivet Discourse prophecy in Luke 21:25-26.

the Israelites, after descending Mount Sinai. 'We [take these 'green commandments,' we] look down to [COP27 at] Sharm el-Sheikh, and we're not satisfied,' Abramowitz said as he smashed a [green-painted] tablet [pair]. One of the tablets [(brown and already broken)] was ... painted with the [black] words 'Broken Promises' in Hebrew. The other [(likewise broken)] tablet [pair] was painted green, to symbolize the 'green commandments,' Abramowitz said. 'The political leadership of the world has not come through on climate until now,' he said. '....We are calling on [(anti-Christian and satanic so-called)] faith leaders to add to the sense of urgency and to have them weigh in, hopefully forcefully and globally, to push for the reduction by 50 percent, at least, of [(so-called)] global warming emissions by 2030. Reducing emissions so gradually is immoral [(because global mass starvation, disease and death is actually preferable, to these *blind morons*)]...."[1]

"James Sternlicht, head of The Peace Department, called on [(New Age 'green' so-called)] faith leaders to take a climate vow: '... to make the world a better place ... each day that I may live.' 'Today, as faiths put aside their differences in a common [(Satan-driven)] call for climate action, we work towards a new covenant for mankind in the name of the protection of our common home and for the betterment of our shared human future,' he said by video link from the COP27 confab."[2] So, they are not only pushing ten "green commandments" to supplant God's and scripture's Ten Commandments, but a satanic and anti-Christian "new covenant for mankind" to supplant God's and scripture's New Covenant! We'll detail the New Age and other satanists' "green commandments" shortly, but first, there's more!

Though not yet ready for such, Egypt's authorities apparently anticipate "dozens of multifaith leaders" repeating the above ceremony, or one like it, in the future. So, they are "constructing new hotels and a huge center for multifaith prayer:" "The mountain is the most popular of several sites in Egypt, Israel and elsewhere that are traditionally [(and incorrectly)] associated with the biblical location of Mount Sinai." In the meantime, "the new Sinai Climate Partnership will be officially announced ... from a ceremony on Parliament Hill — the highest point in London" —with "ceremonies" "also planned for high points in Jerusalem, Salt Lake City, Ecuador, Australia, at India's Mount Abu in Rajasthan and in Calcutta, and at Mount St. Francis, a Catholic retreat center in Indiana."[3] Yes, all this

---

1. Surkes, "Activists smash tablets atop 'Mount Sinai' to launch faith-based climate push."
2. Ibid.
3. Ibid.

occurred at Luciferian "high points," or "ten different mountaintops around the world, culminating in a first-of-its-kind ceremony of repentance, for 'climate justice,' in London."[1] Notably, the satanic "Holy Land Declaration on Climate Change," "was first announced at [the British Monarchy's] Windsor Castle, and then at Copenhagen Climate Conference in 2009" (i.e., COP15).[2]

So, after all that, what are the half-truth (i.e., lying) "green commandments," or the "Ten Principles for Climate Repentance," from the "you shall be like God | 'gods'" Devil (Gen 3:5; Rom 1:25*a),* and his above New Age "green" worshipers, including unsaved "Jews, Muslims, [(anti-)]Christians, Hindus and Buddhists from Israel, Egypt, the US, India, Spain and the UK?" Here are the reported "repentance" or *summarized* ones: "1. We are stewards of this world. 2. Creation manifests divinity. 3. Everything in life is interconnected. 4. Do no harm. 5. Look after tomorrow. 6. Rise above ego for our world. 7. Change our inner climate. 8. Repent and return. 9. Every action matters. 10. Use mind, open heart."[3] We might have thought these would be more profound, sublime, original or otherwise "clever." Nope, they're mostly just dumb. None the less, they are anti-God and satanically evil. Both before and during the above, other sets of "ten commandments" were offered around the world, all arguably foolish and blasphemous. (Recall, for example, the "late" Georgia Guidestones, backed by depopulationists who blame abundant fossil fuels and technology for too many humans.)

Not only did anti-Christian "Christians" participate and twist scripture,[4] but so did Rome's heretic pope, after earlier enjoining a "month of ecological conversion," so as to reduce mankind's "carbon footprint," running from the start of September through early

---

1. Ca. 01:34-45, "Mt sinai kick off of global 10 climate principals nov 13," *Josef Abramowitz,* as posted at "https://www.youtube.com/watch?v=bOz2CKRAZlg" on YouTube.

2. Ca. 01:46 to 02:02, ibid.

3. ToI staff, "Multifaith leaders to gather in Israel and around the world for 'climate repentance,'" *Times of Israel,* 13 Nov. 2022. Joshua Arnold, in his article "10 Commandments Parody: Climate Activists Smash Tablets on Mt. Sinai," quotes a few of the *longer* (wordier) and rather different—but arguably just as problematic—*panentheist* "justice" "commandments," which sound a bit more like a set of ten "explanatory" descriptions. Arnold remarks: "Taken together, they communicate the notion that humanity is only an insignificant but potentially destructive part of a vast ecosystem. There is little, if any recognition, that only mankind possesses the dignity of being created in God's own image and being tasked with rightful dominion..." *(Washington Stand,* 14 Nov. 2022). We're told that the *full set* of ten "Principles for Climate Justice," as read aloud on "Mount Sinai," "were developed over the past few days, in London [(i.e., before King Charles III)], by fifty global religious leaders" (ca. 04:58 to 09:09, "Mt Sinai kick off of global 10 climate principals Nov 13"). Similar, but more wordy, lists were used at the various locations around the world (e.g., see "Announcing the 10 Principles of Climate Repentance" as posted at "https://twitter.com/fftcnetwork/status/1591824739210854408" on Twitter).

4. "Ecumenical Patriarch Bartholomew, who is also known as the Green Patriarch due to his dedication to environmental issues, released a statement ahead of the event decrying the 'abuse of nature and the exploitation of its resources' as a 'sin against God the Creator and the gift of creation'" (ibid.). Obviously —and it *ought to be* obvious—such a "patriarch" is actually *anti-Christian,* and must be called to spiritual repentance unto salvation.

October 2022—for Roman Catholics *as well as* deceived Christians everywhere. (Much like "wokeism," Satan's minions are using pagan forms of "ecology" to infiltrate Christian seminaries, churches and events, particularly with blasphemous lies-based "environmentalism." Roman Catholicism is also now easily infiltrated.) At COP27, Cardinal Pietro Parolin, who serves as Vatican Secretary of State and acted as Pope Francis' representative, called on the latter's behalf "for international and intergenerational solidarity," and promotion of "new lifestyles" for environmental "sustainability" (e.g., where the "serfs" give up red meat and traditional carbon-based fuels, to eat bugs for protein, walk or bike for transportation, and foolishly agree to suffer miserable temperatures, even if one or more of those "lifestyle" changes results in disease, injury or death), while also adding, "the road to achieving the objectives of the [2015 COP21] Paris Agreement is complex and ... we have less and less time available to correct course;" per Francis and the Vatican, "COP27 provides us with a further opportunity, which cannot be wasted." The Vatican is a "State Party" to 2015's Paris Agreement, and to the IPCC via the UN, both under Charles.[1] Naturally, all this constitutes *great spiritual whoredom and adultery* before The God of Israel and Christians.

Here's a prior excerpt of heretic and Green Religion-adherent Francis' sentiments: "Francis .... noted ... the World Day of Prayer for the Care of Creation, kicking off a month-long 'Season of Creation'.... The pope went on to express his wish that the call to listen to the voice of creation will 'foster in everyone a concrete commitment to care for our common home.' ... 'At the mercy of our consumerist excesses, our sister Mother Earth groans and begs us to stop our abuse and her destruction,' he said. 'During this Season of Creation, let us pray that the UN COP27 and [prior] COP15 summits may unite the human family in decisively addressing the twin crises of [global] climate [warming] and biodiversity loss.' Last month, Francis reasserted his distress over the climate change 'emergency,' and instructed the Holy See to sign onto the 2015 Paris Climate Accord.... Humanity must combat climate change by reducing emissions as well as by 'assisting and enabling people to adapt to progressively worsening changes to the climate,' he said ... to participants in a climate conference sponsored by the Pontifical Academy

---

1. Holy See, "XXVII SESSION OF THE CONFERENCE OF THE PARTIES TO THE UNITED NATIONS FRAMEWORK CONVENTION ON CLIMATE CHANGE," *Vatican.va*, 6-18 Nov. 2022. Per fake "news" *CNN*'s Daniel Burke, Rome's Francis even released *his own* "10 commandments on climate change"—in 2015: "1. Think of future generations. 2. Embrace alternative energy sources. 3. Consider pollution's effect on the poor. 4. Take the bus. 5. Be humble. 6. Don't become a slave to your phone. 7. Don't trade online relationships for real ones. 8. Turn off the lights, recycle and don't waste food. 9. Educate yourself. 10. Believe you can make a difference" (Daniel Burke, "The Pope's 10 commandments on climate change," *CNN*, 19 June 2015).

of Sciences. Climate change 'has .... assumed a central place, re-shaping not only industrial and agricultural systems [(i.e., fraudu-lently collapsing energy, transportation and food supplies systems, to force global mass death or depopulation)] but also adversely af-fecting the global human family, especially the poor [(because faith-ful Francis cares so much, not and not)]....' Care for our common home 'is ... a moral obligation for all men and women as children of God,' he [(manipulatively)] declared. Francis went on to underscore his [(fraudulent)] belief that climate change and other environmental issues constitute 'severe and increasing problems' for humanity. In his message, he [(conveniently)] refrained from mentioning ... that every year the number of global deaths from severe weather events, has decreased significantly—and are now a tiny fraction of what they were just 100 years ago. Whereas a century ago, 'almost half a million people died on average each year from storms, floods, droughts, wildfires and extreme temperatures,' in 2020, the number dropped to just 14,000, climate expert Bjorn Lomborg noted [in No-vember 2021]...."[1] As lying Francis "would a deluded world believe," the depopulating COVID-19 plandemic and scamdemic (as one round of a biological and economic war against mankind) "is 'cer-tainly nature's response' to humanity's failure to address climate change."[2]

So, the New Age and pagan "Greenies" have their own self-made commandments—and somehow, *neither* the (heretical and apostate at the top) Anglican Protestant Communion, under King Charles III, *nor* the heretical Roman Catholic cult, under Pope Fran-cis, find *any* spiritual, moral or other truth-based conviction, to call "foul." Are we dealing with Christians? No, just *anti-Christians.* In fact, between the fraudulent invocation of "Elijah" and the use of a fake "Mount Sinai," the spirit of the AntiChrist is effectively present-ing counterfeits of one (Elijah), if not both, of the Apocalypse's two witnesses, etc.[3] Yes, the satanic "trinity" (i.e., Satan, the foretold An-tiChrist or Charles, and the "collective" of possessing fallen spirits) has its own "two witnesses," and the world is now seeing what we might call an example of "them," in "climate action."

But what constitutes "green" *sin?* In "Greenies'" "Mother Earth" worship or Gaia religion, sin includes "too much" carbon and other "green" gas emissions (i.e., providing Earth's ecosystem with gasses

---

1. Thomas D. Williams, "Pope Francis Prays U.N. Climate Summit Will 'Unite the Human Family,'" *Breitbart News*, 31 Aug. 2022.
2. Breitbart News, 10 Apr. 2020, as posted at "https://twitter.com/BreitbartNews/status/12485770795091 68131" on Twitter.
3. For more information, see the volume titled *The Real Rapture and Other Prophetic Mysteries: Under-standing the Revelation,* in this author's *Messiah, History, and the Tribulation Period* series.

that actually sustain life on Earth, so that it flourishes), "too much" human reproduction, "too much" capitalism, contradicting Satan's lies-based ecological and other narratives, "too much" (i.e. truth-based) free speech, etc. Their false prophets are those non-scientist politicians and brainwashed lunatics (from lies-fed prepubescents to walking "skeletons" yet bearing flesh and somehow still breathing, all each one ready to perish Hell's flames) leading the lies-based anthropogenic (alleged human-cased) "global warming" "climate change" alarmism. Likewise, "Greenies'" false teachers are those lying anti-science "scientists," like those of the IPCC, etc.

With all that ecofascist craziness, "green" religionists also create their own "litmus" tests for "orthodoxy." Those are reflected, for example, in spiritually, morally and mentally bankrupt Environmental, Social, and Governance (ESG) scoring of companies and even governments—where ESG "priests" determine whether to bless (i.e., fund) them with loans, or even accept banking relationships at all.

What then is the proclaimed "eternal" punishment, per the rotted-to-the-core (pale-green gray) liars and sycophant idiots, their alleged terrible "divine" judgment to come upon a humanity that would fail to submit and comply? Naturally, it's to be an Earth (allegedly) destroyed by anthropogenic (human caused) "global warming," with a global ecosystem (allegedly) ravaged by "too many humans," who are (allegedly) driving too many species to extinction! That's their claimed version of Hell—in lieu of a "fictitious" (it's not) eternal punishment, which ensues from rejection of God our Creator, The God of actual Christians and *believing* (regenerate) Israel!

Green religionists also attempt "underpin" themselves with pseudo-science, besides fake "science." In a "planetoid Pandora" twist (think 2009's *Avatar* movie), for example, we're now being told that fungal networks appear to communicate in "patterns of nerve-like electrical activity"—and that such activities may rival the complexity of human speech (e.g., the English and Russian languages)! "Electrical buzzes in fungi have been known about for years, but analyzing this activity as if it were a language [such as English or Russian] could stand to reveal many things we don't know about what this fungi phenomena represents. 'Assuming that spikes of electrical activity are used by fungi to communicate and process information in mycelium networks, we group spikes into words and provide a linguistic and information complexity analysis of the fungal spiking activity,' writes [computer scientist Andrew] Adamatzky....[1] ... Split gill mushrooms were shown to put together the most complex "sen-

---

1. Andrew Adamatzky, "Language of fungi derived from their electrical spiking activity," *Royal Society,* 6 Apr. 2022, as published at "https://doi.org/10.1098/rsos.211926" on the Internet.

tences".... Although the comparisons with human speech are notable [(and highly questionable)], the research doesn't give any indication of what the fungus network might be communicating, if at all, or why these organisms might need to keep in touch across a wider area. ... 'Though interesting, the interpretation as language seems somewhat overenthusiastic, and would require far more research and testing of critical hypotheses before we see "fungus" on Google Translate,' [ecologist Dan] Bebber [from the University of Exeter, in the UK, said]...."[1] We could wonder whether a new category of criminality could one day attach to "smoking 'shrooms'" (i.e., "magic mushrooms")—though "realistically," that could yet depend upon ecofascist loons, as such folks tend to "make it up as they go." Of course, by publishing under the Royal Society's "open science," Mr. Adamatzky aligns *with the foretold AntiChrist*—that is, ecofascist extraordinaire Charles—who both heads the society and talks to plants.

In some other "visions" of comparable doom, "millions of years old" sea-based bacterial superorganisms expose themselves to threaten, hybridize and use, and perhaps ultimately destroy mankind. These include 2023's *The Rig* TV series and *The Swarm* (aka *Der Schwarm)* TV series, each bearing "shades" of the sentient "Black Oil" of *The X-Files* TV series and the nervous system-like "mycelium network" of "Eywa," in James Cameron's *Avatar* movies.[2] Ultimately, we are talking about satanic deceptions meant to encourage "Mother Earth" worship, in lieu of Christianity's Living God, The Creator of the Universe.

Green religionists present a humanist "morality." But is it moral? *No.* Rather, it is *summarily wicked.* It engenders global deprivation —involuntary or not. It results in a lack of "universal" progress, as well as general harm to the "human condition" (as goes that, so

---

1. David Nield, "Fungi May Be Communicating in a Way That Looks Uncannily Like Human Speech," *ScienceAlert*, 7 Apr. 2022. We might ask, "Has Andrew Adamatzky every played 2013's *The Last of Us* or 2020's *The Last of Us: Part II*, as "prescient" video games? Or, "Has Mr. Adamatzky contributed to the derived first season of *The Last of Us* TV series (2023–), wherein a 'mutated' super-fungus is able to survive in the human body—only to then proceed to actively turn nearly all humanity into zombie-like fungus-driven humanoids, who monstrously exist only to further spread the infection?" Remarkably, those "zombies" connect to a growing fungal hive mind, so that they act in coordination, apparently under the control of a malevolent superorganism, which is "evolving" its own "intelligence." With the conclusion of the noted TV season, only a small percentage of mankind remains, isolated from humanoid infectees in mostly remote areas—while one teenage girl, whose mother had been infected while ready to give birth, later developed immunity following an infectee's bite, so that she may contain a biological cure. *The Last of Us* TV series constitutes a cursed and blasphemous false apocalypticism, which combines with fascist-communist totalitarianism and an overt promotion of sexual satanism. The only "Christians" presented turn out to be cannibals led by child-raping pedophile "priest." It's just what "the Devil ordered."

2. For more information, see this author's book titled *The X-Files (1993 to 2018): The Definitive Take*, as well as his main *Solar Apocalypse* series, of which that book is an unenumerated volume. Specifically, see where the portion of the *Solar Apocalypse* multi-volume series that delves into fictional bioluminescent "aliens" of the "entertainment industry."

does the actual environment). It leads to too much cold, too much heat, and too little food production, or illness, mass starvation and death! In other words, it is about suicidal *suffering* and sly *depopulation!* (Some Chinese seem to have "gotten it" enough, to slyly warn the world.[1]) Beyond all that "mundaneness," global death and environmental destruction *through warfare*—even involving use of nuclear and other weapons of mass destruction (WMDs)—is *not really* "out of the question," but may become "necessary" and thus also acceptable (to "green" satanists). Satan's "green" cultists will accept, and may even seek, *whatever* finally enables them to depopulate their fellow man, woman and child, only to then consolidate global hegemony under the Devil and his "top dogs." To Satan's death-based servants, such horror is a necessary "last resort" to achieve "sufficient" depopulation, of "threatening" mankind—when "subtle" biological weapons (e.g., certain so-called "vaccines"), global mass starvation, and the like, simply fall short.

Who are those satanic "top dogs?" Charles as the foretold AntiChrist, and perhaps Roman Catholicism's final pope as the foretold False Prophet. Who shall be their followers, until "death do them part?" We may think of "none so blind" fools, such as one Miss "Pebbles" who, upon being confronted with the reality of who King Charles III is, blithely responded: "Totally absurd. Ridiculous. He's already accomplished so many positive things for the youth in GB and for the Brits as a whole that I refuse to believe a word of this nonsense!" How many (call them as you see them) "Pebbles" shall remain spiritually and mentally blind—refusing to hear God, and what is biblically true—until it is too late for them, to be saved?

Here's are a couple "take aways:" *First,* Christ is coming to "destroy those who destroy the Earth" (Rev 11:18), whereas the foretold AntiChrist, while seemingly hijacking that agenda for himself, actually destroys the Earth and those who oppose him instead. That is, the AntiChrist and his minions destroy those whom he and they falsely claim are destroying the Earth (think ecofascism and depopulation), so that he quite literally comes to represent his name, which is Death (Rev 6:7-8). *Second,* the AntiChrist steals mankind's wealth not just

---

1. In 2021's *Restart the Earth,*" mankind has developed a drug to rapidly accelerate plant growth. Plants become titan-sized, carnivorous with serpent- and dragon-like heads on the ends of mobile "roots," and in a "Gaia"-like twist, wipe out most human and animal life (ca. 0:19:45-58, *Restart the Earth*). Curiously, we're told that "93% [of] global citizens will die" in "the second Global Green Tide Storm," if the deadly plants aren't stopped. Remarkably, that is essentially the same percentage of mankind that "Green Religion" depopulationists would eliminate! (For more information, see this author's related book, *The Great Reset: To Digitally Enslave, Depopulate, and Transhumanize.*) The monstrous "plants" come in "Green Tide" waves, we're told, threatening those who seek to stop them. All told, mankind is greatly reduced via a (cursed) false apocalypticism—and we are thereby ostensibly meant to be warned *against* "Green Religion."

for control, by *doling out* some to his totalitarian minions "on the take," but also to implement a satanic counterfeit of "the meek | poor … shall inherit the Earth" (Matthew 5:5)—where the "meek" are easily imposed upon, or controlled, and then enslaved! Not only is that being done by stealing from the rest of humanity *now,* through the "Great Reset" (i.e., actualization of the NWO), but by taking (what many yet suppose shall be) the intact (i.e., not destroyed) infrastructure and assets of genocidally murdered masses and their nations— so that the satanic globalists and their descendants may move "forward," having untold wealth and opulence.

Satan is undoubtedly aware that local and global warfare, attended by extreme and widespread disasters, are the near future— and that all that shall be followed by the Battle at Megiddo or *Armageddon,* when God shall judge both fallen spirits and fallen mankind. So, the Devil "cleverly" twists that knowledge to deceive and delude unregenerate humanity. But he also deludes himself, as if altogether insane. In fact, if Satan were to get his way, mankind's reduced global population would "surely" be transformed into, and then fully supplanted by *not-fully-human humanoids,* through genetic modification and chimeric hybridization efforts. (Such wickedness has *already begun.)* Such efforts of course, whether past, present or future, strongly dovetail with the whole "alien" humanoids agenda, which has from the start, been under fallen angels and (then also) demons.[1] Yet, in God's "economy," His saints—not those who are spiritually lost—shall inherit the Earth (e.g., see Psalm 37:1-2, 37:7-40; cf. Isaiah 49:6-26); and in God's Kingdom, His saints are ultimately wealthy to varying degrees—for good, not evil.

Operation Golden Orb: Crowning the Unclean "Green Man." (This section was been written *before* the events it describes, but for the sake of flow and clarity, it is here tensed as if later written.) On May 6th, 2023, in Operation Golden Orb (that's "clever" lingo for something like "receive the world" from Satan), Charles was formally crowned King Charles III—while wearing his gold signet ring bearing the (*Vav-Vav-Vav* or 666) Black Prince badge on his left pinky finger, throughout, just as he always wears it. (As below shown, three sixes pointing to 666, featured in multiple ways, with Charles' signet ring being just the first and "most common.") On that day, as the foretold AntiChrist and Prince of Darkness—*while possessed (ostensibly temporarily) by Satan* (see below)—Charles was anointed with oil produced in Jerusalem, from olives grown on the Mount of Olives, at his request. From that anointing, we may say that King

---

1. For more information, see this author's *Solar Apocalypse* multi-volume series.

Charles III was literally "messiahed" (i.e., the Hebrew word *mashiach* for "Messiah," literally means and translates as "anointed").

The world was told: "The sacred oil which will be used to anoint King Charles at his coronation in May [2023] has been consecrated in Jerusalem, reflecting the British monarch's links to the Holy Land, Buckingham Palace said.... ...Theophilos III, the Greek Orthodox Patriarch of Jerusalem, and the city's Anglican Archbishop Hosam Naoum consecrated the Chrism oil in the [(alleged)] Church of the Holy Sepulchre.... The oil will be used to anoint Charles when ... crowned at ... Westminster Abbey on May 6, in what is considered the most sacred part of the solemn ceremony. Traditionally, the oil is poured from an amplulla onto the Coronation Spoon and then the sovereign is anointed on their hands, breast and head. The newly consecrated oil was made using olives harvested from two groves on the Mount of Olives, at the Monastery of the Ascension and the Monastery of Mary Magdalene, the burial place of Charles' grandmother Princess Alice of Greece. The Archbishop of Canterbury Justin Welby, who will conduct the service, said it had been his wish for the oil to be produced from the Mount of Olives...: 'This demonstrates the deep historic link between the coronation, the Bible and the Holy Land,' said Welby, the [(apostate)] spiritual head of the Anglican Church. 'From ancient kings through to the present day, [(English)] monarchs have been anointed with oil from this sacred place.' The oil, perfumed with sesame, rose, jasmine, cinnamon, neroli, benzoin, and orange blossom, is based on that used for the coronation of the late Queen Elizabeth [II], 70 years ago, and a formula used for hundreds of years, the palace said."[1]

Welby added, "Since beginning the planning for the coronation, my desire has been for a new coronation oil to be produced using olive oil from the Mount of Olives," which "reflects the king's personal family connection with the Holy Land and his great care for its peoples."[2] Indeed, the preparation of the oil—by religious "Greek Orthodox" and "Anglican" *apostates* (i.e., "Christians" with *no* spiritual discernment or awareness that what they were doing was in service to the AntiChrist, and thus would be used by the Devil himself) in "a 30-minute consecration ceremony"—was filmed.[3]

Lucifer (Satan), formerly the *messianic* (Lit., Heb. *mashiach* or English "anointed") cherub (see Ezek 28:12-15, Heb.), is *explicitly*

---

1. Reuters, "Holy oil for King Charles' coronation consecrated in Jerusalem," *Jerusalem Post,* 4 Mar. 2023.
2. "The Chrism oil which will be used to anoint His Majesty The King on 6th May 2023 has been consecrated in Jerusalem," *Royal.uk,* 3 Mar. 2023.
3. Matt Wilkinson, "Holy Oil: Sacred oil that will be used to anoint King Charles at coronation filmed being consecrated for first time," *The Sun,* 3 Mar. 2023.

acting via the AntiChrist to steal back the anointing that God stripped from him—thereby inverting the Protoevangelium (Gen 3:15).[1] As earlier addressed, this also is reflected in Charles' "winged god" statue, where he as a (fallen) angelic figure hovers over foolish masses of humanity looking to him as "Saviour of the World," so that his feet and thus heels are atop their heads! For these reasons and others herein addressed, we may conclude and even assert that Satan possessed Charles while he was anointed. Thus, we have the real reason for that portion of the coronation (further detailed later) being *hidden behind a veil, even behind a representation of the original "Tree of the Knowledge of Good and Evil"* (cf. Gen 2:9-17), or an embroidered counterfeit "Tree of Life." That stitched tree bears flowers (ostensibly the same as some at the base of Charles' coronation invitation, to the left and right of his Green Man head), besides the names of the British Commonwealth nations (which are under Charles, and thus also the Devil) on its leaves. With an "oak" trunk and nesting birds (e.g., fallen spirits and other servants of the Devil) feeding their young, among its branches, we may perceive that this tree *of Babylon* (see Jer 51:6-9; Dan 4; cf. Job 20:4-11), is Satan's antithesis to the Kingdom of Heaven (e.g., see Matt 13:31-32; Luke 13:18-19); yet, the *city* called "Mystery Babylon"—ostensibly the capital of the foretold AntiChrist's global governance—shall fall at Christ Jesus' return (see Rev 17:1 to 19:6; cf. 14:8). Charles' tree has *no* fruit among its branches and leaves (cf. Luke 13:6-9); in due course, it shall be cut down and cast into the fire (e.g., see John 15:6; Rev 19:20 to 20:3, 20:7, 20:10-15).

Indeed, the "Commonwealth tree" (on the Anointing Screen's back partition[2]) ostensibly reaches into the heavens and represents the Devil's (soon) *global* kingdom from, as well as under *the* AntiChrist (i.e., Charles)—where the burgundy or red wine-colored background portion could ostensibly represent the darkness of space —while also having a serpent- and stream-like (cf. water) banner at its base; this is just below Charles' royal cipher bearing "C *REX* III," for "King C[harles] III," at the tree trunk's base. With the serpent's death-filled lies, that banner falsely reassures naive mankind, claiming, "All shall be well, and all manner of thing, shall be well." *This is*

---

1. For more information, see the volume titled *Conflict of the Aeons: Understanding the Protoevangelium,* in the author's *Messiah, History, and the Tribulation Period* series.
2. Greek Orthodox "Christian" iconographer Aidan Hart designed the Anointing Screen, which is entirely unique to Charles' coronation. A Sanctuary Window having a rather similar design—to include its banner, royal cipher, leaves with names, overhead star or Sun, etc.—resides in the Chapel Royal, at St. James's Palace. That stained glass window shows a central tree with birds, red flowers and plaques with names of countries, the ER II royal cipher on its trunk, etc. But its side panels also have branches extending behind figures representing Matthew and Mark (right) and Luke and John (left).

all about today's Babylonia. Do you now see and hear? These things must be spiritually discerned. Let's continue.

Of course, there is much more. The Babylonian tree, or the Commonwealth tree which we here liken to the ancient Tree of the Knowledge of Good and Evil, additionally counterfeits believing (i.e., Christian) Israel as the natural olive tree into which believing gentiles are spiritually grafted (see Rom 11:11-32), with that olive tree being Christ Jesus' Church and corporate bride. Remember, Charles wants *all* nations to join the British Commonwealth, to be grafted into Satan's wild tree—where *anything* goes spiritually *except* God's Truth, because *everything else leads to death and Hell.*

To the left and right of the tree's top, are two trumpeting "false light" angels—the left one pointing toward Earth's Commonwealth and other nations, and the right one toward heaven above—with an angelic white phoenix-dove chimera perched at the top-center of the tree, apparently representing Lucifer (i.e., Satan as a false "angel of light") *in Charles.* (A somewhat greenish golden star rimmed in white, stands above that chimeric "bird" and against a navy blue background, ostensibly representing the Sun—or even Lucifer as ancient Egypt's "god" *Ra.)* Yes, all this likewise served as a "reenacted" fallen "Garden of Eden," if you will, wherein the anointed man (i.e., AntiChrist Charles, counterfeiting The Last Adam) would then be brought to his spiritually lost "woman" (e.g., Camilla, with her own "6-6-6" cipher, counterfeiting The Last Adam's bride or God's Church)—and in this satanic story, the "couple" willingly choose and knowingly serve the Devil. (Eve was deceived, and the first Adam knowingly disobeyed, but neither had intended to serve Satan, as is clear from Genesis 3—unlike the foretold AntiChrist and those who serve him, such as Camilla.)

Satan then in great wrath (cf. Rev 12:9-13), seeks to crush the heads of, or otherwise murder and eliminate mankind who will not serve him (e.g., Christians and those predestined by God to become Christians, to include the one-third of Israel who shall survive the coming Great Tribulation)—as reflected in Charles' "winged god" statue as ancient Greece's Zeus or Rome's Jupiter. In this too, the Devil again counterfeits God by exercising wrath toward those who do not and will not serve him—with one major difference, which is key, being this: God's wrath is only ever righteous and holy, but Satan's is continually wicked and unholy despite the claims of his servants!

The anointing took place not just behind a mostly private "veil" (i.e., the Anointing Screen), but atop King Edward I's Chair, which in its base, bears a druidic Throne, Logan or Altar Stone (associated with *human sacrifice,* among other pagan and occult wickedness)—aka Scotland's (in)famous Stone of Scone. Though the stones of God's altar, were *not* to be hewn (see Ex 20:25), the abbey's uncovered (Roman) Cosmati Pavement—where many shoeless individuals have trod, and where the Throne was placed—is comprised of cut (hewn) stones that are not all square. These hewn stones also resemble flowers, etc.[1] Interestingly, the pavement represents Earth (macrocosm) populated by mankind (microcosm), and that the colors represent the four (Wiccan) "elements—fire, air, water and earth;" per "medieval interpretation," "the pavement thus symbolises the world, or the Universe, and its end."[2] In other words, it was an ideal spot to anoint Satan's Prince!

While behind the partition, that throne and stone not only intimated Charles' coming fatal wound as the "first beast" of Revelation 13, but also *counterfeited the Holy of Holies in ancient Israel's Tabernacle of Moses, and subsequent temples.* Indeed, that throne and stone counterfeited the Ark of Moses bearing God's Ten Commandments on a stone tablet! It was on the Mercy Seat between cherubim that The LORD would manifest, to meet with Israel's ministering high priest. Thus, *while Charles was being anointed from the phoenix ampulla, wearing a simple white (druid-like) shirt (the Colobium Sindonis) covering his upper body and black pants, we may surmise and even conclude that he met with his "god" and spiritual father—Lucifer!* Did the Devil then possess the Archbishop of Canterbury possessed? Or Charles? Or both in turn? (Recall that the central symbol of Gorsedd druidry—of which multiple British royals have been, and still are a part, including Charles—is the red dragon or Satan!)

Lest any somehow yet imagine that Charles or his "witchy" wife are anything short of thoroughly anti-Christian, pagan and Hellbound, the coronation invitation alone is sufficiently *definitive.* It bears King Charles III's new government-used "coat of arms," at its top-left; Queen Camilla's government-used "coat of arms" (updated from her prior "achievement" as Duchess of Cornwall[3]), at its top-right; and the pagan (as well as ecofascist today) "Green Man" head bearing a *counterfeit* victor's crown (Gk. *stephanos)* of thorns, topped by an acorn (loosely representing "the third eye" or pineal gland, and perhaps even a short phallus) and compassed by *Devil's horns as sprigs* (one to its left and the other to its right)—all likewise

---

1. "Cosmati Pavement," *Westminster Abbey,* as posted at "https://www.westminster-abbey.org/history/explore-our-history/cosmati-pavement" on the Internet.
2. "Cosmati Pavement," *Westminster Abbey.*
3. AP, "U.K.'s Camilla gets coat of arms for birthday," *NBC News,* 17 July 2005. Material changes as queen are the addition of the Garter Belt and removal of the crowned Shield of Wales.

pertaining to *Charles,* who shall ostensibly suffer a "Death wound" (i.e., an apparently or actually fatal "head" wound *while possessed by Satan, whose name is Death;* see 1 Cor 15:21-22, 15:26, 15:54-57; Rev 6:7-8) and recover (see Rev 13:3-4; cf. 13:12)[1]—at its bottom-center, just below the invitation's text! There are three acorns total on the invitation, and all are ostensibly growing from the Green Man's head. Might those intimate Satan's counterfeit "trinity?"

That very Green Man symbol, *a chimeric lion-man head with foliage emerging from its mouth and "flesh"*—not unlike a rotting and infested head of a corpse in a planted area—is blasphemously incorporated into the architecture of several U.K. churches, including Westminster Abbey. In fact, the Green Man has become a major anti-Christ symbol, being commonly associated with a "death and resurrection" theme as well as ostensibly counterfeiting the Lion of the Tribe of Judah imagery (as a lion-man chimera). In other words, the Green Man is an ideal symbol for the one named Death, who rides the *pale-green-gray* or *rotting-human-flesh-colored* fourth apocalyptic horse, as seen in Revelation 6:7-8. From such symbolism alone, it is clear that we are indeed dealing with *the* foretold AntiChrist, when he is possessed by Satan and likewise known as the "son of perdition | destruction." Notably, Camilla's heraldic achievement has a blue boar beast as the sinister supporter, and a whitish boar's head in a quadrant—*both with human eyes (like Charles' man-eyed unicorn) and further modified to show only a single unusually lengthy tusk, as if they were a boar-unicorn and boar-unicorn's head, crossed by the tongue (forming an upside down cross)*—reminding those familiar with "him," of the book of Genesis' *Nimrod.* Consider as well that boars are associated with spiritual desecration and desolation.

The supporters of both Charles' and Camilla's arms—that is, the lion-leopard beast (ostensibly suggesting current heraldic *ignorance* of Charles' identity as scripture's foretold AntiChrist), human-eyed (apparently) unicorn, and blue "boar-unicorn"—are also "playfully" displayed elsewhere in the artwork of the invitation. Some other symbols are a thistle, Tudor rose, clovers and other flowers, a bee, and a blue "butterfly" (resembling a corrupting moth) which again intimates a "death" and "resurrection" theme. All this satanism combines symbolism of Wicca (witchcraft) and druidry, as you will know from having read earlier portions of this work.

---

1. Speaking of the "first beast" who is represented by Charles' multi-headed heraldic achievement as Prince of Wales, which has a single corporate head (where the gold sovereign helm is), Revelation 13:3 literally states, "And one of his | its heads, was as having been slain to death—and when his Death wound was healed, then all the Earth marveled | admired | wondered after the beast..." (Gk.).

Of this "Arthurian" wickedness, we're told: "The invitation for the Coronation has been designed by Andrew Jamieson, a heraldic artist and manuscript illuminator whose work is inspired by the chivalric themes of Arthurian legend. Mr. Jamieson is a Brother of the Art Workers' Guild, of which The King is an Honorary Member. The original artwork for the invitation was hand-painted in watercolour and gouache, and ... will be ... on recycled card, with gold foil detailing. Central to the design is the motif of the Green Man, an ancient [antiChrist] figure from British folklore [(i.e., paganism and the occult)], symbolic of spring and rebirth [(cf. "pushing up daisies" from a sacrifice's corpse, as well as death and resurrection)], to celebrate the new reign. The shape of the Green Man, crowned in natural foliage, is formed of leaves of oak, ivy and hawthorn, and the emblematic flowers of the United Kingdom. The British wildflower meadow bordering the invitation features lily of the valley, cornflowers, wild strawberries, dog roses, bluebells, and a sprig of rosemary for remembrance, together with wildlife including a bee [(possibly intimating the Merovingian lineage)], a butterfly, a ladybird, a wren and a robin. Flowers appear in groupings of three, signifying The King becoming the third monarch of his name [(i.e., Charles III)]. A lion, a unicorn and a boar — taken from the coats of arms of the Monarch and Her Majesty's father, Major Bruce Shand — can be seen amongst the flowers. Her Majesty's arms are now enclosed by the Garter, following her installation as a Royal Lady of the Order of the Garter last summer."[1] Flowers include the Scottish thistle, Irish shamrock, and Tudor rose. (In fact, one set of trumpets used during the coronation itself, bore the royal heraldic achievement—ostensibly Charles'—with greenery, to the left and right, correlating to Charles as Satan's "Green Man.") Of course, all this suggests a pagan "back to nature," and even druidic connection—something that was in fact, a major part of the coronation, as we're going to see.

"By comparison [to] ... Queen Elizabeth [II]'s coronation invite from 1953, the biggest difference is that [for hers], the attention is drawn to St. Edward's Crown, along with the orb and sceptres—symbols of the monarchy. King Charles [III] has chosen to highlight an ancient folkloric symbol [(i.e., the Green Man)] instead."[2] Yes, *Charles is the Green Man—Satan's top pagan on Earth.* (Of course, Camilla too is anti-Christian and pagan.)

Notably, an "unclothed" Walt Disney Co., which continues to openly pushes satanism (e.g., sexual lunacies and perversions of all

---

1. "The Coronation Invitation," *Royal.uk*, 4 Apr. 2023. See it at "https://www.royal.uk/news-and-activity/2023-04-04/the-coronation-invitation" on the Internet.

2. Emily Burack, "The Hidden Symbolism in King Charles and Queen Camilla's Coronation Invitation," *Town & Country*, 4 Apr. 2023.

sorts, including child grooming, "transgender" mutilations, chimeric hybrids, etc.), witchcraft and paganism more than ever, being utterly anti-God (as Disney *always* was), used a "bizarre legal tie to King Charles III of England," or "a royal clause dating back to 1692 in Great Britain," to try to thwart new (conservative) oversight by a Florida state board![1] Yes, *Walt Disney Co. serves the Devil*—and now also the Charles as the AntiChrist and soon-to-be Fourth Horseman of the Apocalypse.

Like Walt Disney Co., Charles is *no stranger* to sexual satanism. Indeed, he is not only said to be a "bisexual," but as Satan's Prince, he hobnobbed for decades with one of modern history's most prolific child rapists and pedophiles—Jimmy Saville. And Saville, whom Queen Elizabeth II *knighted,* with royal, political and media backing, escaped temporal justice—with his horrific crimes only really beginning to be publicly disclosed following his descent to Hell's neverending torment. But Saville was not unique to Charles—and the latter, like "lords" Mountbatten and Snowden, as well as others before him, has reportedly long engaged in his own (many) sodomite deviancies[2]—even (supposedly) being shown in photographs, per the often disreputable *Globe* tabloid magazine (May 19th, 2016 edition), kissing his own "boy toy." (Charles *is* a "bisexual" *and worse.*) Pedophile former bishop Peter Ball sought to exploit—and apparently did use—his "status as confidant" with Charles, besides "his contact with members of the royal family" generally, as cover for decades of sexual satanism: "The Church of England 'concealed' evidence of child abuse against Ball for more than 20 years." "Ball, then bishop of Gloucester, suggested 'on many occasions' to the former Arch-

---

1. Kyle Morris, "Disney thwarts DeSantis' oversight board takeover using bizarre legal tie to King Charles III of England," *Fox News,* 1 Apr. 2023.

2. Nica Virtudazo, "King Charles III's hidden 'homosexual trysts' during Princess Diana marriage exposed in bombshell leak: report," *Ibtimes.co.uk,* 19 Nov. 2022. We're told: "An explosive MI5 dossier detailing nearly 60 years of [Charles's] homosexual trysts with boarding school buddies, butlers and blue bloods, has been funnelled to the British Parliament" (ibid.). This is not new—and Charles did choose a woman whose face looks "manly," over Diana—so much so that ignorant "sleuths" *errantly* claim Camilla is a "transgender" man. In 2003, moreover, we were told: "Prince Charles is in the middle of a gay-sex scandal and media frenzy that just won't quit. The heir to England's throne [held] ... what some in the British press referred to as 'crisis talks' with ... William, ... Camilla Parker Bowles and other aides to determine the next step in quelling the story. For the past week, newspapers have been trumpeting a story being told by former [sodomite] palace servant George Smith, 43, who worked for Charles for 11 years until 1997. Smith says he witnessed a sexual incident [(in a bed)] involving Prince Charles and a former male royal aide [(later identified by Ingrid Seward, editor of *Majesty* magazine, as palace valet Michael Fawcett, of Charles' 'inner circle')]. He says he recorded what he saw on an audiotape and gave the tape to Princess Diana. Now, the tape is in the hands of Paul Burrell, Diana's former butler. ... But before London papers could report the story, Michael Fawcett, a former royal aide to the prince, got an injunction from the High Court. It prevented the British press from reporting the details of the lurid allegations" (Ann Oldenburg, "Charles embroiled in rapidly growing gay-sex scandal," *USA Today,* 10 Nov. 2003). Charles *denied* the allegations at the time, and had "a former valet, Simon Solari, who worked for Charles and Diana for 15 years, ... telling London's *Evening Standard* that the allegations 'simply could not be true'" (ibid.). Did Charles and Solari *lie?* That is what Satan's children do.

bishop of Canterbury Lord George Carey and others that he 'enjoys the status of confidant of the Prince of Wales.' ... [Thus, apostate] ... Carey and other senior church figures ... 'concealed' reports of Ball's offences: It was revealed Lambeth Palace failed to pass on six letters of allegations of sex offences to the police. ... Ball made sure ... Carey knew about his correspondence with Prince Charles and that he visited Highgrove House, the family residence of the Prince of Wales and Camilla...."[1] Is King Charles III guilty? *Apparently so.*

In the face of so much unassailable hard evidence, only some being mentioned in this work, there are yet misguided Christians and others who somehow imagine the British Monarchy to be "Christian." Among the most troubling examples has been evangelist Ray Comfort. At the top of Living Waters, Mr. Comfort actively upheld King Charles III and his coronation as "Christian," ostensibly to reach the lost. Indeed, via a "Coronation Outreach," Mr. Comfort gave away "Coronation Millions"—stacks of fake "1,000,000" (whatever) "bills," billed (pun *intended)* as Gospel tracts, each prominently showing Charles in a red uniform and bearing his Garter Star on one side, and the Gospel on the other! Though printed in English, Mr. Comfort suggested other countries offer versions using their language, via local church "collections" "to pay for the costs." Such tracts mix of the table of God, with that of Satan and demons, so that Mr. Comfort (foolishly) conflated Charles' *anti*-Christianity with biblical Christendom[2]—something *forbidden* to Christians, irrespective of motives (e.g., see 1 Cor 10:14-21 and 10:28-29)! Mr. Comfort, who claimed such conduct "as a bridge to reach the lost,"[3] is thus to be *rebuked and called to repentance.* This author sought to warn Mr. Comfort and call him to repentance, only to be *ignored.* In fact, Mr. Comfort delusionally *rejects* the biblical truth that Charles *is the foretold AntiChrist,* and thus errantly imagines that Charles may "somehow" be saved—but that is *no more possible of Charles, than of the prior son of perdition—Judas Iscariot!* Those who participated in Mr. Comfort's deception, including other ministries (e.g., Answers in Genesis[4]), must likewise repent. They would do well not only to read this book, but to pay attention to reasonably done documentaries like "King of the World? The High Symbolism of Charles III's Corona-

1. Chloe Farand, "Disgraced sex abuse bishop Peter Ball used links to Prince Charles to boost his position in cover-up, report finds," *Independent,* 23 June 2017.
2. "An Urgent Message from Ray Comfort," *Living Waters,* 11 Nov. 2022, at "https://www.youtube.co m/watch?v=IYlRqseBA0k" on YouTube.
3. "We're Giving Away 15.8 Million Tracts. Free Shipping. Get Yours Now!," *Living Waters,* 21 Mar. 2023, at "https://www.youtube.com/watch?v=BMcscVba4Qo" on YouTube.
4. "Our BIGGEST evangelism event, ever - and you're invited!," *Living Waters Europe,* 9 Dec. 2022, at "https://www.youtube.com/watch?v=UKjwGJo-p60" on YouTube.

tion," which addresses Charles III's two namesake predecessors.[1] Others at this same table of Satan and demons, seek "moolah" as "money changers"—especially by selling memorabilia bearing Charles' "kingly" royal heraldic achievement or cipher (both granted following his mother's death), to include chinaware cups, plates and pill boxes, medallions, a towel, a magnet, etc.

Look "behind the curtain," and you will see *more*. (Below, we'll address several details.) Specifically, Charles' crowning was, per the lineal claims of the British Monarchy, as the alleged King of Israel— and thus also, King of Jerusalem! Remember, he and his forebears (e.g., the now-roasting Elizabeth II), allege themselves to be "The House of [King] David—The Royal Line." For the first time since the modern nation-state of Israel's May 1948 inception, unregenerate "rabbis," other Israeli spiritual leaders, and politicians in Israel, see a king who alleges sitting upon David's throne—and at *the* very time that *red heifers* again appear in the land. What will unbelieving Israel do? Will (unaccepted) animal sacrifices resume under an heretical (unregenerate) levitical priesthood (e.g., in the third year of the Tribulation Week, with a new Tabernacle, and then in the fourth year, with the core of a new Temple)? Will construction of a new Holy Place and then (Third) Temple, begin atop the Temple Mount? Will that be preceded by a "makeshift" tabernacle, about a year earlier? What will the unbelievers of the world do? Will global warfare ensue —or is it already in underway, with October 7, 2023's Muslim Edomite-led Hamas and "Palestinian" Islamic Jihad (PIJ) terrorists' attack upon Israel,[2] or Russia's earlier attack upon Ukraine[3]—leading to the violent capture of East Jerusalem (i.e., the Old City, the City of David, or the eastern "half" of modern Jerusalem), at the start of the Great Tribulation, when Israel shall effectively be *nationally crucified?*

Gifts from Rome, and Ecumenical Compromise. Speaking of crucifixion, Rome's pope Francis personally gifted to Charles, fragments (splinters) alleged to be part of the "True Cross" upon which Christ Jesus was crucified—which at Charles' direction were patterned as a cross surrounded by twelve radiating gold filaments and placed behind a transparent rose crystal gemstone, all set at the center of a custom-made silver cross that Charles personally commissioned

---

1. "King of the World? The High Symbolism of Charles III's Coronation," *TruthStream Media*, 16 Oct. 2022, at "https://www.youtube.com/watch?v=M4YEq2Upv2U" on YouTube.
2. For more information, see this author's *Israel, "Peace," and the Looming Great Tribulation* multi-volume series.
3. For more information, see this author's *North Korea, Iran, and the Coming World War: Behold a Red Horse* book, which also addresses Russia's attack upon Ukraine and ostensible subsequent invasion of western Europe.

and gifted to the Welsh Anglican church. That unique (and per the below, ecofascist) cross was not just for Charles' crowning event, but also to then be ecumenically shared between Wales' Anglican Protestant and Roman Catholic churches, all buttressing the new "Supreme Governor of the Church of England" —that is, Charles—as *the* AntiChrist! "The silver portions of the cross bear a full hallmark, including the Royal Mark — a leopard's head — that was applied to the cross by King Charles [III] in November 2022."[1]

"The coronation service for King Charles III ... at Westminster Abbey ... will feature a special gift.... Two splinters, [(allegedly)] believed to be from the 'True Cross' of Christ, were gifted to the monarch by Pope Francis. The pieces ... form a small cross directly at the center of the [Anglican Church of Wales' new] processional cross.... Known as the Cross of Wales, [it] ... was formed from recycled silver bullion [from the Royal Mint in Llantrisant], Welsh slate and [reclaimed] timber. It ... feature[s] Welsh words from the last sermon of [Wales' patron] St. David on the back, ... translated as: 'Be joyful. Keep the faith. Do the little things.' ... The cross was first commissioned in 2020 by the king, who was [then] still the Prince of Wales.... 'Its design speaks to our Christian faith, our heritage, our resources and our [(political ecofascist)] commitment to [environmental] sustainability,' Archbishop of Wales Andrew John said at the blessing service, [held in Holy Trinity Church,] in Llandudno, Wales.[2] 'We are delighted too that its first use will be to guide [(i.e., precede and thus lead)] their majesties [(i.e., the foretold AntiChrist and his witchy whore of a wife)] into Westminster Abbey at the Coronation Service.' The Church of Wales is an Anglican church, but even the archbishop overseeing the Roman Catholic Church in Wales sent his blessings. 'With a sense of deep joy we embrace this Cross, kindly given by King Charles, and containing a relic of the [(so-called)] True Cross, generously gifted by the [Roman] Holy See,' Archbishop of Cardiff and Bishop of Menevia Mark O'Toole said. 'It is not only a sign of the deep Christian roots of our [Welsh] nation [(or in a stunning display of 'Zoroastrian' dualism, the deeply hypocritical people that actually chose Satan for their national symbol)] but will, I am sure, encourage us all to model our lives on the love given by our Saviour, Jesus Christ. We look forward to honoring it, not only in the various celebrations that are planned, but also in the dignified set-

---

1. Isabel Keane, "King Charles' coronation cross will have shards from Christ's crucifixion," *New York Post*, 19 Apr. 2023.
2. See "Piece of Jesus' Cross Will Be at King Charles' Coronation," *Inside Edition*, 20 Apr. 2023, at "https://www.youtube.com/watch?v=H4QLXDhdrH0"; "Cross of Wales to lead King Charles' coronation procession," *Reuters*, 19 Apr. 2023, at "https://www.youtube.com/watch?v=1D_b6EkQjLg"; and "Ancient relics central to the Christian faith will form part of the King's Coronation," *7News Australia*, 20 Apr. 2023, at "https://www.youtube.com/watch?v=t6gAlY_-5Yw" on YouTube.

ting in which it will find a permanent home [in Wales].'"[1] Andrew John adds, "I think the symbol of two churches sharing something profound like this, will have enormous [ecumenical] benefits."[2]

Besides splinters, Rome's pope also provided the garments (ostensibly ten sets) of those Anglican bishops who would participate in Charles' coronation—including *the Archbishop of Canterbury,* who reportedly made the request,[3] as well as the other participating protestant archbishops (e.g., those of Wales and Scotland). Yes, that powerfully speaks to *heretical reunification of Anglicanism under Rome's heretical and apostate papacy*—at Charles' behest! Of course, all the the mitres (patterned after those of ancient Egypt's pharaohs) worn by the Anglican *and Roman Catholic* bishops— viewed from their sides—were "two-horned," just like what the second beast or False Prophet of Revelation 13:11 could wear. (Such re-unification is now being confirmed, as Francis and Welby work under the Devil and Charles—ostensibly, to place Rome's pope as the False Prophet, even over apostate Anglicanism.[4])

This was ostensibly the first time in the history of Anglican Protestantism, ever since the Reformation, that a Roman Catholic archbishop—prelate Cardinal Vincent Nichols—or priest attended and participated in an English coronation; he invoked "a blessing" on Charles. Nichols stated: "The Pope will be represented at the Coronation by His Eminence Cardinal Parolin, [Vatican Secretary of State] accompanied by the newly appointed Papal Nuncio to the United Kingdom, His Excellency Archbishop Maury Buendia. ... As Cardinal Archbishop of Westminster, I have been invited to contribute to the blessing of the newly crowned King, an innovation which is a further step towards the healing of our common ancient wounds. ... I am told that, excluding the Vatican City State, there is only one other state in the world [(i.e., England)] that installs its Head of State with a religious ceremony. [(One is here tempted to say, 'Like the False Prophet, like the AntiChrist.')] Here it is our long-standing [Roman] tradition, and it contributes solidly to the sense of identity and continuity of this complex modern society, and to all that we bring to the wider world. May God bless King Charles [(not!!!)]."[5] "The Catholic Archbishop of Cardiff, Mark O'Toole ... also attend[ed] the Coronation.... Seventy years ago, it would not have

---

1. Jeannie Ortega Law, "Pope gives King Charles III fragments believed to be from Jesus' crucifixion cross for coronation," *Christian Post,* 20 Apr. 2023.
2. E.g., ca. 0:49-57, "Piece of Jesus' Cross Will Be at King Charles' Coronation."
3. See, for example, Russell Myers, "'Big questions': Prince Andrew wears Garter robes at coronation," *Sky News Australia,* at "https://www.youtube.com/watch?v=xlRIcX4a7_s&t=182s" on YouTube.
4. "Archbishop of Canterbury and Pope in joint call for Christian unity," *Christian Today,* 26 Jan. 2024.
5. Cardinal Vincent Nichols, "Coronation of King Charles III is 'profoundly Christian,'" *Vatican News,* 5 May 2023.

been permitted for any Catholic to enter a Protestant church, let alone to take part in a Coronation service. This significant step is the fruit of decades of ecumenical relations [(prompted by Charles)]. As the Cardinal explains: 'It's symbolic of the whole ceremony because it respects our history, builds on our history, and ... [adds to it,] with the presence and greeting of the faith leaders from the other major religions now present in this country.'"[1] Notably, the Greek Orthodox patriarch of Thyateira and Great Britain, also participated (see below),[2] while an ostensibly ignorant Byzantine Chant Ensemble directed by Alexander Lingas, sang (chanted) Psalm 71 in Greek, as the two swords of State and Offering were exchanged (later detailed).[3]

In supposed ecumenist "light," we were told, "Cardinal Vincent Nichols, Catholic archbishop of Westminster [(and formerly of Birmingham)], will say, "May God pour upon you the riches of his grace, keep you in his holy fear, prepare you for a happy eternity, and receive you at the last into his immortal glory.' The other [(so-called)] Christian leaders who will formally give a blessing include the archbishop of York, the Greek Orthodox archbishop of Thyateira and Great Britain, the moderator of the Free Churches, the secretary general of Churches Together in England, and the archbishop of Canterbury."[4] In ostensible ignorance, and clearly *without true or genuine spiritual discernment,* all these "Christian" *heretics and apostates* (i.e., demonstrably anti-Christians) who evidently *lack* The Holy Spirit, sought "God's" blessing on *the* foretold AntiChrist and his likewise *non*-Christian wife, the queen.

So, was there a False Prophet role or character in the coronation, further intimating things to soon come? In fact, as we're going to see, it was the anti-Christian Archbishop of Canterbury himself, wearing the garments of anti-Christian Roman Catholicism under

---

1. "Catholic involvement in the Coronation," *Catholic Church: Bishop's Conference of England and Wales,* 5 May 2023.
2. King Charles III has strong ties not only to Greece, but he also alleges strong ties to the Greek Orthodox Church. In fact, Charles is enamored of Mount Athos, from which he collects "Byzantine icons," and which he also has visited several times (including "in secret"), *not* due to Greek Orthodoxy, but because it was "sacred" to Zeus in mythology—and Charles who is to be possessed by Satan as the foretold AntiChrist, is *already* being portrayed as ancient Greece's Zeus or ancient Rome's Jupiter, as we have seen from Charles' "winged god" "Saviour of the World" statue! Indeed, despite then Prince Charles' allegedly having "made a 'spiritual commitment' to [Greek] Christian Orthodoxy"—in the presence of Abbot Ephraim of the Vatopedion Monastery, following Princess Diana's death (e.g., see Tasos Kokkinidis, "King Charles' Mysterious Links to the Greek Orthodox Faith," *Greek Reporter,* 5 May 2023)—we know that he is he remains and has only ever been a satanist "by any other name!"
3. "The Byzantine Chant Ensemble led by Dr Lingas at King Charles' Coronation Service was made up of experienced singers who have served as cantors in cathedrals and parishes in the UK and Greece; Stelios Kontakiotis, Themis Prodromakis, Vassilis Maroulas, Dimitrios Skrekas, George Zacharias and Giorgos Savvas" (Paula Tsoni, "Greek Orthodox Chant Sung at King Charles' Coronation," *Greek Reporter,* 7 May 2023).
4. Madeleine Teahan, "Catholic prelate to participate in British coronation for first time since Reformation," *CNA,* 3 May 2023 .

Rome's heretical and apostate pope, who acted as such. (We may yet wonder whether Rome's final pope, whomever that proves to be, shall step from the shadows, to fulfill the ultimate role of the False Prophet.)

Satanic Royal "Stamps" Upon God's Written Word. Three special edition KJV Coronation Bibles, one representing a centuries-old tradition, were produced for Charles' 2023 coronation. Each bears the U.K.'s "Tudor-crowned" version of what is *supposed to be* Charles' heraldic achievement as king (i.e., *with* the Sovereign helm), where the "Tudor-crowned" "coat of arms" is "differenced" only *non-materially* through the addition of an artistic grassy knoll at its base; that heraldic achievement appears on the cover of the specific bible Charles used at his crowning, but is only on the interior title pages of the other two KJV Coronation bibles (i.e., those meant for "commoners"). Those latter two—one from Oxford University Press, and the other from Cambridge University Press (aka "The King's Printer") —which each have King Charles III's Cipher on the front cover *(not* Charles' "Tudor-crowned" heraldic achievement), are available for public purchase.

From available images (as of this writing), it is clear that the heralds *erred (or were just lazy)* on *all three special editions:* rather than having *Charles'* crown over the Sovereign helm and atop instances of the dexter beast,[1] they somehow retained *his mothers' crowns—* and heraldically, that's a *serious* oversight! (What reaction might they expect from Charles, if and when he recognizes this? Have you seen his nastiness over mere "pens?"[2])

"The tradition of presenting a Bible to the monarch dates back to the coronation of William III and Mary II in 1689. The earliest commissioned coronation bible in the Royal Collection dates from George III in 1761, with a new Bible produced for every coronation since. In 1953, Elizabeth II knelt on the altar steps and placed her hand on the Bible and said: 'The things which I have here before promised, I will perform and keep. So help me God.' [(Yet, she never actually believed. Charles of course, would do likewise—but as *the* foretold AntiChrist.)] It was presented to her with the words:

---

1. Go to "Category:Coats of arms of King Charles III of the United Kingdom," at *Wikimedia.org* on the Internet, and once there, see "Royal Coat of Arms of the United Kingdom (Tudor crown).svg" on the web page; click on it, to enlarge it. Notice the semi-circular crowns *lack* a top-central heart-shaped dip. Elizabeth II's heraldic crowns, by contrast, each *have* that top-central dip—and that's what we see on the "Tudor-crowned" heraldic achievements of Charles' 2023 Coronation KJV bibles! That is *not* heraldically proper.

2. See "King Charles signals to aide to remove pens during signing of oath," *Guardian News,* 10 Sep. 2022, at "https://www.youtube.com/watch?v=VcNCBP2IRUc"; and "'I can't bear this bloody thing': King Charles gets frustrated with leaky pen," *Guardian News,* 13 Sep. 2022, at "https://www.youtube.com/watch?v=2Encm187scA", on YouTube.

'We present you with this Book, the most valuable thing that this world affords. Here is Wisdom. This is the royal Law. These are the lively Oracles of God.' ...Justin Welby commissioned Oxford University Press (OUP) to produce the Bible [for Charles' 2023 crowning]. It is hand-bound with a leather cover and was decorated with gold leaf..., with a ring of leaves and crowns around the royal coat of arms. The design 'draws inspiration from both historic coronation Bibles and His Majesty's [(unholy and pagan alleged)] love of the natural world', the publishers said."[1]

Is it not *stunningly ironic* that *scripture's only explicit use of the phrase, "Here is wisdom,"* is *specific to identifying the foretold AntiChrist,* as seen in Revelation 13:18 (cf. 17:9)? Yet, that is a phrase told to Elizabeth II at her crowning—when her son, whom this author would later (since 1987) openly expose as *the* foretold AntiChrist, by genuine wisdom from God—was only a young boy!

"The Coronation Bible used in the service will be retained by the Archbishop of Canterbury and placed in Lambeth Palace's archive alongside their collection of all four 20th century Coronation Bibles. OUP will then produce three identical copies—the King's personal copy, which will be given to him as a gift, and a further two to be placed in the archives of Westminster Abbey and Oxford University Press's head office in Oxford."[2]

The Coronation: Further Receipt of the World, from the Devil. The night of May 5, 2023, Israel's President Isaac Herzog, who has strong familial ties to the UK (e.g., his father Chaim served as an officer in WW2's British Army), and the UK's Chief "Rabbi" Sir Ephraim Yitzchak Mirvis (yes, he's one of Charles' knights), who also is prominent among the Israeli "rabbinic" community, both attended a reception King Charles III hosted at Buckingham Palace (for coronation-attending global royalty, heads of state and prime ministers) and then spent the night in London—as a red blood Moon shone overhead. Indeed, Mirvis and his wife stayed the night at Clarence House with the king and queen—and Mirvis later directly participated in the coronation, with "a special prayer." President Herzog and his wife, formally representing Israel, also stayed within walking distance of the abbey, at their nearby residence.[3] Regarding the noted reception, "Charles identified Herzog in the crowd and personally arranged for him and his wife to be brought to the front

1. Kaya Burgess, "Coronation Bible 'reflects King's love of the natural world,'" *The Times,* 20 Apr. 2023.
2. "Oxford University Press Produces King Charles III's Coronation Bible," *Fine Books magazine,* 20 Apr. 2023.
3. See, for example, TOI Staff et al., "Herzogs to represent Israel at weekend's coronation of King Charles III in London," *Times of Israel,* 2 May 2023.

of the line, speaking with them about the situation in Israel and the Middle East," also speaking with him regarding "the Israeli government's controversial judicial overhaul plan"—which Charles wants *stopped*, as it would ostensibly impede global elitists' (e.g., France's, Germany's, the U.S.'s etc.) satanic objectives under him. Notably, Herzog who also attended Elizabeth II's funeral, first met Charles in London, shortly after taking office."[1] Charles ensured that participating Jews and Muslims had kosher food, etc., throughout the events.

On rainy May 6, 2023 (i.e., 5 + 6 + 2 + 0 + 2 + 3 = 3 x 6, or 6+6+6) —that is, six (6) months, six (6) weeks and six (6) days after his mother's funeral (again, "6-6-6")—full of opulence and royal fanfare, Charles' crowning as King Charles III occurred, an event ostensibly covered by more cameras than any other to date.[2] There, the "6-6-6"-bearing Camilla—the number being hidden in her royal cipher, seen at many places and points (as below addressed)—likewise receiving a crown as queen. Do you want to re-read all that? Yes, that's already *three* intimations of 666. In fact, there was at least a *fourth* one (i.e., the Badge of the Black Prince on Charles' finger, as later detailed), with no less than a *fifth* one *planned* for the end (i.e., an overflight of 60 aircraft for 6 minutes on May 6th, or yet another ostensible set of three sixes) but changed due to last-minute weather considerations. Charles himself is the "666" beast (man) of Revelation 13:18, as earlier demonstrated and proven in this work, and from that fact, we could here reasonably argue that there were actually to be *six* intimations or displays of 6-6-6 or 666 this day! Was any of this coincidental? In light of this work, we may well argue that it was all carefully orchestrated—*under Satan*.

Drummers on horseback bore the king's royal arms, while he and Camilla traveled to Westminster Abbey, in the golden Diamond Jubilee State Coach bearing the same royal heraldic achievement his mother used. Indeed, *ashen* horses *preceded* the Diamond Jubilee State Coach, ahead of the other horses, etc., and also, *ashen* horses *followed* it, with Charles and Camilla as its passengers. Simultaneously, the coach itself was pulled by grayish-white horses, with red, blue, gold and black colors atop and around them; green also featured among the crowds, as well as some flags. Nearby troops rode black, "red" and beige horses. Moreover, with Charles (and Camilla) in the coach, with a number of its windows frequently reflected a

---

1. TOI Staff, "At coronation reception, King Charles said to praise Herzog for overhaul mediation," *Times of Israel*, 7 May 2023.
2. The bulk of the coronation may yet be watched online: e.g., see "Watch Charles III's coronation at Westminster Abbey" at "https://www.youtube.com/watch?v=BqgmLx4Q2LU"; and "Watch in full: The coronation of King Charles III and Queen Camilla" at "https://www.youtube.com/watch?v=avGfu1EF2Yg" on YouTube.

pale-green color. Thus, *ostensibly all* the colors of the horses of Revelation 6:1-8 were represented. Charles and Camilla passed the female angelic "goddess of Victory" (ancient Rome's Victoria, ancient Greece's Nike) statue, *wearing a victor's wreath* (cf. Rev 6:1-2, and the Green Man's crown of thorns), opposite the gate, as they traveled toward Westminster Abbey. (Along the way, the TV audience also saw the Statue of Charles I. Charles and Camilla would later depart the coronation in the older and heavier, as well as overtly pagan and even more ostentatious Gold State Coach.)

Not a few prophecy buffs and others have associated the Apocalypse's Fourth Horseman (Rev 6:7-8) with the "Grim Reaper" motif. Remarkably, therefore, preceding Charles' and Camilla's arrival at the abbey—where the whole procession would then be led by the new Cross of Wales, a country itself led by Satan (i.e., the red dragon, Wales' choice symbol even now)—a staff-carrying figure dressed in black or blackish-green passed in front of the interior "all-seeing eye" archway (later detailed). The vast majority of the public who saw it, being fed by sensationalist media, exclaimed that it seemed to be the "Grim Reaper" or "angel of Death."[1] Though the individual was most likely a Greek Orthodox verger,[2] or plausibly even a Benedictine monk,[3] rather than even a darkly clad druid, we may still conclude that it was meant to represent "Death personified." Indeed, with every detail of the high-security coronation meticulously planned and practiced beforehand, this was *intentional imagery!* But why would anyone do that? Below, this author exposes *the definitive answer.* Atop that "strangeness" as well, the participating (apostate) clergy et al., per Charles' explicit direction and demands, blasphemously uprooted and trampled nearly 1,150 years of "Christian only" coronation and crowning tradition. Although the new king's parents too were satanists "by any other name," as we've seen, his mother's 1953 coronation was Christian by all outward *appearances* (only by appearances, as *satanists,* such as the Garter knights and heralds, yet played direct roles).

The procession into Westminster Abbey, where Charles would become the *fortieth* reigning monarch there crowned (from 1066), also included priests and a number of other crosses; as well as Black Rod (Sarah Clarke) ushering "kings of arms" (i.e., the top heralds)— Garter Principal King of Arms aka the Garter Herald King, and the

---

1. · Do an Internet or YouTube search for "Charles coronation grim reaper angel of death" or the like.
2. See, for example, "Grim Reaper at Westminster Abbey Explained" at "https://www.youtube.com/watch?v=Q53BvpE-_qo" on YouTube.
3. Benedictine monks are "celibate" Roman Catholic cultists who practices a "Benedictine" form of asceticism), as their "habits" (robes), if not their staffs—in many portrayals, Benedict's staff rather than being like a shepherd's, resembles one bearing either a coiled serpent or the head of Anubis (i.e., ancient Egypt's "god of the dead")—would also match that of the ostensible "Grim Reaper."

Clarenceux, Lyon, and Norroy and Ulster kings of Arms (various Order of the Garter members had prominent roles, while wearing their Garter regalia)—with the sharp-tipped Sword of Spiritual Justice and the blunt-tipped Curtana aka the Sword of Mercy, between them; Black Rod carried a black ebony "rod" topped with a long-tailed roaring "sovereign's" lion (ostensibly representing Satan as a malevolent roaring lion). Black Rod and the top heralds were themselves compassed (i.e., preceded and followed, respectively) by the Jewelled Sword of Offering and the Sword of Temporal Justice. In fact, Charles III would be preceded into the abbey by "faith leaders," heralds (prominently positioned), and UK nations' standards (Wales' standard was first), the vestments (provided by Rome's pope), Coronation Bible, and communion cup. Notably, all these participants—and indeed most present—walked beneath (i.e., through) the abbey's golden archway bearing the "all-seeing eye" Luciferian symbol; that is, the side of the golden pyramidal arch facing the various chairs Charles and Camilla used—the arch under which they and others passed—has a central roundel with a shield bearing a cross, forming the satanic "all-seeing eye" motif.

Significantly, Charles and Camilla were also preceded into the Abbey by the Sword of State (i.e., a fifth sword carried by "Right Honourable" Penny Mordaunt MP, Lord President of the Council), which "granted" him access to the anointing in a satanic *counterfeit* of the Garden of Eden, where he would be anointed as history's foremost AntiChrist (later described and detailed). Rather than portraying exclusion from the garden with its the Tree of Life due to Adam's fall, the Devil here symbolized provision of access to his "Adam," to the Tree of the Knowledge of Good and Evil, or a neo-Babylonian tree and counterfeit olive tree (later exposed)—ostensibly "guaranteeing" that access via the beast-kingdom's (i.e., a coming global "Commonwealth's" or government's, if you will) sword! Once "messiahed" (anointed), that sword was then switched for the *sheathed* Sword of Offering, which was given to Charles, then given by him to the Dean of Westminster (David Hoyle), then "redeemed" from the Dean with with money by Mordaunt—so that he *unsheathed* it and returned it to her. Mordaunt would then bear the "glistening" (actually, tarnished) Sword of Offering, in place of the Sword of State, before Charles and for the duration of the coronation.[1] (God our Creator, of course, has *one* Sword—The Living Word, Christ Jesus—and He shall annihilate all those of the Devil and his minions.)

---

1. E.g., see "Orthodox Christian Chant at the Coronation (Psalm 71)" at "https://youtu.be/L6UiKjyb4XQ" on the YouTube.

There were several other *historically unique* elements to Charles' coronation—most of which, point to him as *the* top AntiChrist. Charles, for example, effectively became Satan's "King of kings and Lord of lords"—counterfeiting Christ Jesus (cf. Rev 19:16)—through more than "mere" chivalrous orders (e.g., the Order of the Garter). Not only did royals from the world's other major royal houses attend, including from the Middle East (e.g., Jordan's King Hussein, who is not just a close personal friend of Charles', but who to date, with Israel's permission, controls Jerusalem's Dome of the Rock complex), and former UK prime ministers and leaders from around the world (e.g., from Japan) likewise attend, but ostensibly all these being present, *pledged allegiance to him* (later detailed)! Indeed, Satan's Jill Biden became the *first* U.S. "first lady" (i.e., U.S. coup regime "lady") ever to attend a British monarch's coronation (no U.S. president has). Obviously, that's all quite significant.

As a second example, the coronation was arguably entirely anti-Christian, with participating leaders' religions compassing Hinduism, Bahaism, Jainism, Zoroastrianism, Buddhism, Sikhism, Islam (Shia and Sunni), (unregenerate) Judaism, "Christianity" (Anglican Protestantism, Roman Catholicism and Greek Orthodoxy, via English, Welsh and Scottish archbishops, etc.). The procession of these *Satan-serving* "faith" *leaders—Baha'i* Wendi Cunningham, *Jainist* Mehool Sanghrajka, *Zoroastrian* Malcolm Deboo, *Buddhist* Bogoda Seelawimala, *Sikh* Lord Singh, *(Hare Krishna) Hindu* Visakha Dasi, *Muslim* (Shia) Aliya Azam, Muslim (Sunni) Hamid Patel, and *Orthodox Jewish* Ephraim Mirvis—into the abbey was actually *led by a verger!* (Did that same verger serve as the "Grim Reaper" caricature, as the one who gave the "angel of Death" motif to the coronation—at the head of the "wolf pack?" Ostensibly, yes.) These were *followed* by another verger and then several *apostate and foolishly used* archbishops, reverends and pastors (e.g., Simon Walkling, Mark O'Toole, Andrew John, Hugh Gilbert, Mark Strange, Iain Greenshields, David Nixon, Eamon Martin, John Kirkpatrick, John McDowell, Agu Irukwu, Helen Cameron, Graham Thompson, Nikitas Archbishop, Glyn Barrett, Mike Royal, Angaelos of London, and Vincent Nichols[1])—who based upon order of entry, were *less* honored. (Unregenerate Judaism is the closest to biblical Christianity among the pagans, and thus Mirvis only just preceded the "Christians." Here, the Devil preferred outright satanists and pagans to *most* anti-Christians—Charles being a clear exception as history's top AntiChrist.) A pagan (i.e., the UK's Hindu Prime Minister, Rishi Sunak)

---

1. For their overblown titles, see "Coronation order of service in full," *BBC*, 5 May 2023, at "https://www.bbc.com/news/uk-65503950" on the Internet.

even read Colossians 1:9-17 (AKJV) aloud, an apostate female "reverend" (Sarah Mullally) read Luke 4:16-21 aloud (women are *not* permitted to be pastors, priests, reverends or the like, nor are they permitted to teach men in any assembly of believers, such as local churches, bible studies or the like; e.g., see 1 Tim 2:8-15; cf. Eph 5:22-33; 1 Pet 3:1-6; Tit 2:3-5), and a pagan (i.e., a Sikh) also sang in the choir. Significantly, it was Charles personally who insisted upon, and even demanded a "multifaith" (i.e., Satan-serving) coronation—not the ignorant and inattentive pagan or other public anywhere in the world, most of whom had expected and would likewise have understood a choice to be strictly "Christian," particularly given that so far as they are concerned, the British Sovereign's traditional role as Anglicanism's titular head on Earth, is ostensibly the monarch's major source of power and influence. Throughout, scripture was not faithfully followed. Amid great and ostentatious opulence, only *rote* prayers were spoken and offered (see Matt 6:5-8; cf. Eccl 5:3), so that The Holy Spirit *was* not *speaking through the heretical and apostate bishops, priests, pagans et al.* (see 1 Th 5:19-22). It was all just one massive display and show of religiosity (see Matt 6:1-24)!

As a third example, the royal women wore relatively "simple" or plain white dresses, so that some in the global audience thought they might be wearing white druidic garb or robes! Indeed, their dresses *were* another break from the tradition of past coronations, where royal women wore fancy dresses reflecting the fashions of their particular day. Fourth, Charles is the only British monarch to have a subsequent coronation concert (later detailed). Fifth, Charles is the first monarch to pray aloud in a coronation service. The prayer (further addressed later) was written especially for Charles, who would (heretically and blasphemously) ask to be a "blessing" to those "of every faith and conviction," while falsely alleging *all* to be God's "children." Etc.

The overall coronation event featured two padded Chairs of the Estate, each having its own padded kneeling stool before it; these bear Charles' and Camilla's royal ciphers, respectively. (Not a few present also wore Charles' royal cipher *on their chests.*) Then there were also two refurbished and reimagined crimson Throne Chairs (aka Thrones of State) bearing "their" respective royal heraldic achievements on their backrests (both sides each), one for Charles—behind which, the Garter Herald King stood—and the other for Camilla. Of course, King Edward I's Chair (aka the Coronation Chair) served to *enthrone* Charles. Additionally, one-hundred VIP members "of the Westminster Abbey congregation" (e.g., other participating royals, including William at points), sat in newly created blue velvet-upholstered Congregation Chairs, with each one displaying both Charles' and Camilla's ciphers—and thus also 6-6-6!

Upon being seated on his estate chair, Charles received the specially printed Coronation Bible. In fact, Charles twice "promised" (i.e., blasphemously swore), at heretical apostate Welby's prompting —including while the former's hands were on the Coronation Bible, and while wearing the Garter Collar with its Great George pendant. Charles said, "so help me 'God,'" and then kissed the Coronation Bible—or perhaps the royal heraldic achievement on its cover, with no genuine believe in The Word of God, living or written. To the Devil's seed (i.e., King Charles III), God's written Word is merely an out-of-date relic, besides a prop to employ for kingly power, so that "godliness is gain." Charles then naturally *lied* before God and man, stating, "I Charles do solemnly and sincerely in the presence of 'God' profess, testify, and declare that I am a faithful Protestant...." *Do* here recall that Judas Iscariot—as the Crucifixion Week's Satan-possessed "son of perdition | destruction," who called Christ Jesus "Lord"—received wealth (i.e., thirty pieces of silver as blood money) in exchange for kissing The Living Word of God on His cheek, while betraying Him to captivity, trial, crucifixion and death. (Charles as *the* foretold AntiChrist likewise betrays The LORD, Israel, God's Church, and ultimately, mankind.[1])

Right after Charles blasphemously kissed the Coronation Bible (cf. Matt 26:47-50; Mark 14:43-46; John 17:12), as the coming Satan-possessed "son of perdition | destruction" (see 2 Th 2:3-4; cf. John 17:12), the Satan-deluded Justin Welby claimed the (then ostensibly Satan possessed) King Charles III to be anointed by The Holy Spirit. Yet, we must conclude that Charles' anointing is *only from the Devil,* not God our Creator. (Hypocrite and apostate Welby repeatedly demonstrates a lack of biblical discernment, a lack of faithfulness to God. Indeed, allowed multiple apostate female clergy to participate, further cementing and emphasizing his apostasy.) *Now pay close attention:* The author here suggests that on this occasion, *Satan in Charles* sat "as 'God' in the temple of God, showing himself that he is 'God,'" per 2 Thessalonians 2:4*b-c.* (Note that Westminster Abbey is shaped like a cross from above, as well as on its main floor plan.) Most *futurist* Christian theologians—to include this author—have held, and today yet hold that the foretold AntiChrist, by means of the desolating idol that is to stand in a newly constructed *tribulational* Holy Place, atop Mount Zion in Jerusalem (ca. the start of the Great Tribulation, as earlier addressed), is when the foretold AntiChrist then literally or virtually "sits as 'God' in the temple of God, showing

---

1. For more information, see the author's *Messiah, History, and the Tribulation Period* multi-volume series.

himself that he is 'God.'" *But what if that prophecy has at least one earlier "extra" fulfillment?* We now have *strong* reason to argue and perhaps outright conclude that it is apparently so! Let's continue.

The *spiritually unclean* Archbishop of Canterbury (Welby) used the abbey's eight-inches tall *gold phoenix* ampulla, produced by Sir Robert Vyner in 1661, allegedly as an "eagle," which it is *not*—while it held the anointing oil from Jerusalem and the Mount of Olives—effectively as an ancient Egyptian *idol,* allegedly to Christ Jesus. Welby, compassing that cult symbol from ancient Egyptian paganism's "death and resurrection" motif—that is, the risen phoenix atop fire (cf. the fiery gold base, allegedly "foliate")—with with his hands while praying, right before emplacing the Anointing Screen's three partitions (i.e., the veil that would enclose the central area of an anti-"Garden of Eden," if you will), behind which Charles would be anointed with the oil in the ampulla, demonstrated the heretical and apostate nature of his "Christianity." Contrary to Christ Jesus who was anointed on His *feet* (Luke 7:37-38; John 12:3), Charles received the anointing oil on his *head, breast (chest) and hands*—here suggesting not humility, but *arrogance and haughtiness.*

Though Charles stated, "In His name and after his example, I come not to be served, but to serve," he *lied!* As the Apocalypse's foretold AntiChrist, he has certainly *not* come to serve mankind, but to serve his father the Devil instead, presiding over the latter's lost human and ostensibly angelic minions—against The LORD. Indeed, Charles subsequently included "every faith and belief," praying, "Grant that I may be a blessing to <u>all thy children, of every faith and belief</u>, that together we may discover <u>the ways</u> of gentleness and be led into <u>the paths</u> of peace." But actual Christians know that there is only *one* straight and narrow path, only one Way leading to eternal life, and only *one* true faith in which Salvation (Jesus or Yeshua) may be found—and we likewise know that *all* who *reject* The Way, The Truth and The Life (i.e., Christ Jesus Himself)—and thus who reject biblical Christianity and The One who saves—are *not* God's seed or children, but are instead the Devil's! Indeed, "There is one body and one Spirit, just as you were called in one hope of your calling; one Lord, one faith, one baptism; one God and Father of all, who is above all, and through all, and in you [(i.e., actual Christians)] all" (Eph 4:4-6). We are instructed to "have no fellowship with the unfruitful works of darkness, but rather expose | reprove them" (Eph 5:11). Yet, Charles as *the* Prince of Darkness seeks to "bless" *all the children of darkness, who reject The Truth.*

Charles was then privately anointed behind the "tree." The exterior of the Anointing Screen's back partition bore the tree with a serpent-like banner at its base, while the left and right exterior sides as well as all three interior sides bore central crosses. (Three partitions joined at right angles to one another, formed the rectangular Anointing Screen; these partitions were arranged so that the screen's one open side faced the abbey's altar. The two poles holding the left and right vertical edges of the tree's partition, were each topped by a golden Roman eagle.) *Unlike* all past coronations, Charles went for a private anointing with *no* overhead top, hiding what was done behind a unique veil (i.e., the Anointing Screen)—all in lieu of an open canopy, which would have exposed everything while above covering him.

The public "knows" that behind the screen, the Archbishop of Canterbury (per the order of service), said to Charles, "Be your head anointed with holy oil, as kings, priests, and prophets were anointed. And as Solomon was anointed king by Zadok the priest and Nathan the prophet, so may you be anointed, blessed, and consecrated King over the peoples, whom the 'Lord' your 'God' has given you to rule and govern." That also is arguably anti-Christian, as it is Christ Jesus alone who is King, High Priest, and Prophet—though King David and his successors were types and shadows until Christ's First Advent.

While enclosed by the Anointing Screen, with ostensibly *no one* outside the joined partitions able to hear (due to simultaneous loud singing, meant to mask whatever was said) or see what was said (those holding the poles looked downward, *to avoid seeing).* Despite such statements regarding Zadok and Nathan, Charles—this author surmises—recommitted his soul to his spiritual father, *the Devil,* not to God our Creator. Though the AntiChrist will ostensibly suppose that he *has a right to enter God's Kingdom,* he shall instead *be cast into outer darkness* (e.g., Hell; see Matt 22:8-14); indeed, judgment and condemnation likewise await Charles' servants, including those heretical and apostate priests who fail to repent (see Matt 22:1-9).

Barronness (Lady) Gillian Joanna Merron, an unregenerate Jewess, presented the gold Supertunica or Imperial Mantle (embroidered with arabesques and floral motifs), which has a central gold eagle clasp, to Charles. The colors among its flowers, plants and nature elements, are undoubtedly agreeable to both ecofascists and sexual satanists.[1] Vested with a golden Supertunica (super-tunic) and girdle (essentially matching the color of the phoenix ampulla, ostensibly again intimating resurrection), Charles then sat on King Edward I's Chair (Throne) again (following his anointing on it), above

---

1. For more information, see Kimberly K. Ballard, "King Charles III Had Liberal Judaism CEO Baroness Present Gold Royal Robe At Coronation!" at "https://youtu.be/--bxng7Mpgs?t=1176" on YouTube."

the Stone of Scone / druidic Throne, Logan or Altar Stone. There, he received the other regalia: the golden spurs as a "military honor and chivalry" (symbols of knighthood, brought by Lord Great Chamberlain); then the Jewelled Sword of Offering (circuitously received from Rt Hon Mordaunt MP via Welby, to Charles' right hand and then temporarily attached at his right hip, as a symbol of protecting good and punishing evil), with Welby (before it is redeemed with money) stating, "May it be to you and to all who witness these things, a sign and symbol not of judgment, but of justice; not of might, but of mercy;" the golden Armills aka the "bracelets of sincerity and wisdom" (also symbols of knighthood, originally made for the coronation of Charles II) as "tokens of The Lord's protection ... on every side" (given to Charles by a Muslim, the Rt Hon the Lord Kamall); the Imperial Mantle (a long and substantially golden mantle embroidered with arabesques and floral motifs, or what we may recognize as *ecofascist devices,* at Charles' request or behest, given to him by an unregenerate Jewess and having its central Roman eagle chest clasp fastened by William, to wear over his super-tunic) as well as its stole (worn around his neck and down his chest, given by William), falsely equated by Welby with "the robe of righteousness, and ... the garments of salvation;" the large golden Orb aka *Monde* (representing Earth) topped by a cross (given by Welby, who *properly* told the AntiChrist, "Remember always that the kingdoms of this world are become the Kingdom of our God, and of His Christ"); the Ring of Sovereignty, a *wedding* ring (given by a Hindu, the Rt Hon Lord Patel KT), as a symbol of *the marriage covenant then made between Charles and his "god"—that is, Satan—and between Charles and his subjects, including those who would subsequently swear allegiance to him;* the white leather glove bearing an ornate crowned heraldic shield, and having a golden sleeve, into which Charles placed his right hand (given by a Sikh, the Rt Hon Lord Singh of Wimbledon CBE); the Sovereign's Sceptre with Cross (holding *the world's largest cut diamond* and topped by a purple amethyst orb holding a cross, representing Earth under the "Christian" Monarch's dominion), as given by the Satan-serving Archbishop of Canterbury—who among other things, said, "by your service and ministry to all your people, justice and mercy may be seen in <u>all the Earth;</u>" and then the longer and thus taller Sovereign's Sceptre with "Dove" (i.e., ostensibly *a white phoenix in "dove's clothing,"* meaning an ostensible phoenix-dove chimera, here counterfeiting The Holy Spirit) aka the Rod of Equity and Mercy, also given by Welby.[1] (Charles as Satan's Prince will

---

1. Is *inequal* "equity" in so-called "Diversity, Equity and Inclusion" (DEI) racist "woke" lunacies, is actually a satanic precept of British royalty?

not enter God's Kingdom, but shall instead spend eternity in Hell.) Charles, having received all this, was then crowned with St. Edward's Crown, by the Archbishop of Canterbury (and the Devil animating him), and like the Sceptre with Cross, the crown too has the Earth-representing orb atop it.

As Charles was crowned, so that his head bearing St. Edward's Crown would serve as the satanic "all-seeing eye"—yes, that was the literal imagery (as it has been for all monarchs crowned on King Edward I's Chair (Throne)—guns and cannon were fired across the UK, and from ships at sea. Simultaneously, Welby (the Archbishop of Canterbury) led all present and watching in saying, "God save the king"—ostensibly unaware as an apostate and heretic that he spoke of *the* AntiChrist, whom Satan shall possess. Of course, others equally unaware or apostate called for God's blessing, wisdom, knowledge, prosperity, long life, etc., upon and for Charles—to include the Archbishop of York and Primate of England (Stephen Cottrell), the Archbishop of Thyateira and Great Britain (Nikitas), the Moderator of the Free Churches Group (Helen Cameron), and the General Secretary of Churches Together in England (Mike Royal). Being crowned, Charles and Camilla switched from their crimson robes to purple ones. (Charles also swapped the "ordinary" Great George on the Garter Collar he wore, for an ostentatious diamond encircled and encrusted Great George that also has sapphires and rubies. Notably, the Great George symbolism could further intimate Charles' coming mortal wound.)

Despite knowing that He was innocent, Christ Jesus went from an ostensibly radiant or glistening white (or ostensibly golden) robe, put on him by Herod, to blood-stained garments and then a crimson or purple robe (as our *asham* or guilt offering, per Isa 52:12 to 53:13, as our *Azazel* or atoning sacrifice; see Lev 16; cf. Isa 1:17-20) put on Him by Roman soldiers, as He they scourged (whipped), beat and crowned Him with thorns, and put a (staff of) reed in His right hand, with which they then struck Him on His thorns-crowned head, all in lieu of a royal crown and scepter, as they mocked and dishonored Him prior to His crucifixion (see Luke 22:11; Matt 27:28-31; John 19:2-5). Yet, now, we have *the* AntiChrist playing Satan's Green Man victim, representing ecofascist Death with a mock crown of thorns, experiencing no actual suffering by comparison, but being honored by the Devil, with crimson and purple robes, royal crowns and scepters! Indeed, The Lord taught and warned us, saying, "Beware of the scribes, who desire to go around in long robes, love greetings in the marketplaces, the best seats in the synagogues, and the best places at feasts, who devour widows' houses, and for a pretense |

appearance's sake make long prayers. These will receive greater condemnation'" (Mark 12:38-40). Is that not the precise behavior of all the present heretical and apostate clergy—and of King Charles III himself as well? See for yourselves.

The apostate and heretical *(not* having The Holy Spirit, but being *without* genuine spiritual discernment) bishops and reverends, male and female, read portions of the *Shema* and other blessings over Charles. Satan's Prince (aka King Charles III) then moved to sit upon his throne chair bearing his royal heraldic achievement, there being "enthroned." Contrary to Christ's command (Matt 5:34-37) and in satanic hypocrisy (Jas 5:12), the Archbishop of Canterbury and William then each *swore* allegiance to Charles, with the former also *swearing* allegiance to Charles' heirs and successors (e.g., William), and leading all present to do the same, saying "so help me God." As if that great wickedness—swearing allegiance to *the* foretold AntiChrist, *whom Satan ostensibly was then possessing*—were not sufficient, *the "two-horned" apostate Archbishop of Canterbury, ostensibly acting in the stead of the coming demonically-possessed False Prophet (cf. Rev 13:11-17, 16:13-14), then invited* <u>all</u> *the watching world to swear allegiance to King Charles III—Satan's Prince, the foretold AntiChrist!* Specifically, heretic Welby who may himself have then been demonically possessed, stated, "I now invite those who wish to offer their support to do so, with a moment of private reflection, by joining in saying 'God save King Charles,' at the end—or, for those with the [(oath's)] words [now] before them, to recite them in full," [by] exclaiming, "<u>I swear that I will pay true allegiance to Your Majesty</u>, and to your heirs and successors <u>according to law, so help me God</u>." Yes, by that mankind was "subtly" invited to join the Devil (Lucifer), against God, through Satan's top AntiChrist (King Charles III)—even as a form of anti-God *witchcraft,* to try to spiritually manifest a new reality (i.e., global allegiance to Satan through the AntiChrist) as it were, through the spoken word (cf. the apostate "Word faith" movement). (Per Romans 4:17*c,* God our Creator "calls those things which do not exist as though they did"—and it is that Power, unique to Him, which Wiccans et al. seek to counterfeit.) With sounding fanfare, Welby then said, "God save the King" (i.e., Satan's Prince, the AntiChrist)—so that the spiritually blind and deaf audience (e.g., Jill Biden and her ilk) all responded, "God save King Charles, Long live King Charles," and "May The King live for ever."

However, the foretold AntiChrist is irretrievably condemned to Hell, *already! As that individual,* Charles he *cannot* and will *not* be saved. *No Christian should pray for him, nor should any aware individual submit to him, in any manner or matter*—as King Charles III *is*

Satan's seed (Gen 3:15)! Yet, how is it that *not a single individual present at Westminster Abbey said "No!!!"*—at least, this author is unaware of any who did—so that all instead apparently acceded and participated to their dishonor and shame, as *fools* of fallen spirits? Did those fools not then start follow the first beast, even though Charles III has yet to be mortally wounded (cf. Rev 13:3), through deep and "smooth" deception?

Queen Camilla, seated on her chair bearing her 6-6-6 royal cipher, then received (touched) a ring and was crowned with Queen Mary's 1911 crown (topped with a gold orb bearing a cross, intimating Camilla's dominion over the world, under her husband, *the* AntiChrist)—yet, Camilla is arguably *a witch*—and then she received (touched) the queen's Sceptre with the Cross as well as the queen's ivory-clad Rod of Equity and Mercy. Queen Camilla then stood up, and to a psalm-based composition (Psalm 98, "Make a Joyful Noise") from Andrew Lloyd Webber (knighted in 1972, premiering *The Phantom of the Opera* at Her Majesty's Theatre in the West End in 1986), moved to curtsy before Charles and then sit upon her throne, bearing her royal heraldic achievement (with her blue boar). This symbolized the Devil's bride—under the 6-6-6 Mark of the Beast (embedded in her royal cipher), if you will—bowing before history's greatest AntiChrist, her husband whom the Devil shall possess.

Afterward, as Charles and Camilla then proceeded to the "back room" (so to speak). While preceded by the Sword of Offering, carried by Mordaunt (as if proceeding from Charles' mouth, we might say), the AntiChrist (Charles) touched the communion wafers and wine with his white-gloved (right) hand—which Welby presented to him via a silver plate and pitcher—the very (unclean) "sacraments" *placed before the phoenix ampulla,* and later used for communion! Before the golden phoenix ampulla, Welby, with the UK's royal standards being to his left and right, recited scripture related to communion. Welby, two heretical female bishops, and then Charles and Camilla—that is, the AntiChrist and his whorish wife—partook of that (unholy) "communion." Welby then led everyone in further prayers to God, while *standing before the phoenix ampulla.* Simultaneously, a song based upon Psalm 103 was sung. With that, Charles and Camilla retreated to a room behind the altar, to change.

Then, sandwiched between two "ordinary" Anglican crosses, archbishops and others transited to stand behind the estate chairs, with the Garter Herald King taking his station as the second one behind *the* foretold AntiChrist's (Charles') estate chair. Afterward, Charles and Camilla returned to their respective estate chairs, with Welby standing between the them. With Charles and Camilla having changed into their final royal purple robes—Charles' robe having an ermine mantle and trim, but Camilla's ermine trim only and with added decorative flora reflecting her own *pagan* nature—and other royal garments (e.g., the Imperial State Crown for Charles), they exited the above-noted room. Charles carried the Sceptre with Cross in his right hand, the large Earth-representing golden Orb *(Monde)* in his left, and the Garter Collar with an ostentatious diamond-encircled and encrusted Great George pendant (showing George's enameled face and sapphire helmet, the horse's harness in rubies, and other rubies at various points on George's cloak and on the dragon). Here, Charles was preceded by the Sword of Offering (as if before his mouth)—ostensibly counterfeiting Christ Jesus as The Living Word, as The Sword of God who shall sacrifice unregenerate mankind as brute beasts at Armageddon. Simultaneously, Charles was flanked by *two priests, as had occurred at multiple points—ostensibly counterfeiting Revelation 11's coming two witnesses*—all yet preceded only by the Sword of Offering (carried by Mordaunt). In order, they each walked past all the chairs—with Camilla following Charles. (The tail end of Camilla's robe's train bore her "6-6-6" cipher atop it, so that its "cleverly" interwoven "6-6-6" was visible to all whom she passed. Of course, throughout the entire coronation, Charles displayed his "old hat" "6-6-6" Black Prince badge on his gold signet ring. He *is* the Prince of Darkness, Satan's Prince—the diametric opposite of all actual spiritual light and spiritual good.) Simultaneously, we again heard "'God' Save the King," from the choir. Yet, the coronation's overall music list was a mixture of secular, worldly and Christian—reflecting the heretical and apostate nature of the whole proceeding.

Charles, with the two "witness" priests to his left and right, overtly and even ostentatiously *stopped to receive a greeting in unison from, as well as to greet and thank the various pagans who directly participated in his coronation*—while saying nothing to nearly everyone else, other than those heretics and apostates attending him. Charles—as the longest-serving Prince of Wales, ever to become king, as well as *the oldest and most prepared royal ever to be crowned the UK's and British Commonwealth's monarch* (he had already personally visited 45 of 56 British Commonwealth nations)—then with Camilla, exited Westminster Abbey. At this point, they departed in the fairy tales-inspiring Gold State Coach, pulled by gray-white horses. The Prince and Princess of Wales (i.e., William and Kate), with their children, followed in another royal coach, pulled by "red" (brown) horses. In fact, all the colors of the four horsemen of the Apocalypse (Rev 6:1-8), again featured prominently around the coaches and throughout the parade—though King Charles III is *the* fourth horseman.

Simultaneously, the largest *military* procession in the UK, since Elizabeth II's 1953 coronation, commenced. (As king, Charles holds the highest rank in every military branch of the nuclear-armed UK. Will he one day push a "big red button?") Though representatives of *all* the UK's armed forces participated, Canadian Mounties featured prominently, being at the front of the portion surrounding Charles' and Camilla's golden state coach. (Heralds, bear skin "hatters" aka redcoats, and the flags of the Commonwealth nations, were also part of the procession. The Irish *wolf*houds likewise participated.) They all marched and moved to Buckingham Palace—again passing the female angelic "goddess of Victory" statue, opposite the gate. From there, they gathered in the garden of the palace's west terrace, and then saluted King Charles III, where he and Camilla were yet in their royal purple robes and on a ground-level terrace—officially *behind Wales' flag bearing the red dragon, or Satan.* (The Devil was symbolized as being between the royals and the saluting crowds— so that all faced the red dragon, as if to worship! Moreover, NBC "News" also showed Wales' flag atop a pole, being held by someone in the crowd.) Three "hip hip hoorays" were followed by (bag) pipes and drums, and then the king and queen retreated into the palace. Notably, the "goddess of Victory" statue—much like the one in Berlin, Germany—was entirely obvious in front of Buckingham Palace, also being visible from the balcony where the royal family next appeared; indeed, densely packed crowds literally gathered around and before that statue, just to see Charles and Camilla.

The planned royal flyover of 60 aircraft, for 6 minutes, on May 6th (this Coronation day), was pared down due to the weather, so that particular preplanned "6-6-6" display was aborted. The result was a flyover with military choppers and the Red Arrows, where the latter streamed three lines of red/scarlet, blue and "white" each. Still, Charles and Camilla, with other royals (e.g., Charles' grandsons as young pages, and then William and Kate, Prince Edward, Princess Anne, etc., but *not* Andrew, Harry, or Beatrice), had appeared on the balcony, where the king and queen waved to the below adulating crowd; all the royals then retreated into the palace. Never the less, the king and queen *returned for an "encore" appearance,* with more waves to the crowd—and this time, only their pages joined them to help with the train of their purple robes.

All this, including the later Coronation Concert, was fully aired within the U.S., across much media. That's in a country supposedly free of monarchies. Curiously as well, many U.S. citizens traveled to

London to see the public spectacle firsthand, amid packed crowds. Yet, reportedly, only tens of millions globally watched the coronation. Could it be that the Devil sought to make his chosen AntiChrist a bit less obvious, "before his time" as it were?

Immediately following the coronation, the U.S. Public Broadcasting Service (PBS) aired its own "Charles R: The Making of a Monarch" documentary. Among other things, they showed Charles and his family kindling a bonfire in the woods, while he was yet a boy; Charles flying a *red* single-prop plane; and Charles being invested Prince of Wales in July 1969—but like *The Crown* TV series, they skipped *nearly all* the relevant and key heraldic symbolism. PBS pointed out that Charles trained in the Royal Navy to command ships and fly military helicopters (e.g., *red* and dark green ones), and then there served for five years; that Charles talked "quite a lot" about ecofascist things, such as the WWF, with his (now roasting) father Philip; that Charles is a snow and water skier who "takes the falls;" that he is a polo player (and thus equestrian); that he enjoys acting; that he (as a pagan) "associates" with "every tree" and "stone;" and finally, that Camilla says "he's pretty impatient, ... but that's how he gets things done."

The Coronation Concert—Exhibiting Lucifer's "light and love" for his Seed, the AntiChrist. The evening following the coronation, outside Windsor Castle, non-Christian entertainers (e.g., anti-Christians, satanists, etc.) performed the first-ever Coronation concert for a British monarch.[1] Concertgoers wore lit bracelets, similar to those used during July 2022's Ba'al-Molech bull idol worship (and at so many other large public events in recent years). Many "God save the king" modified Union Jack flags likewise permeated the gathered crowds of *ignorant and misled non-Christians and monarchists.*

Charles told his concert audience, "I shall endeavor to serve you, with loyalty, respect, and love." However, those who are familiar with even the basic contents of this book, should already *know* that King Charles III has *not* come to serve, but as Satan's Prince, he aims to steal, murder and destroy! In fact, those who imbibed the concert, received spiritually rebellious, ecofascist and sexually charged messages throughout.

Prince William, with his wedding ring noticeably absent, honored his father *the* AntiChrist. William emphasized Charles' dedication to service of others (i.e., their ultimate impoverishment, destruction and death); his ecofascist *lies* (which William has clearly adopted); Charles' "all faiths, all backgrounds" ecumenism, or his acceptance

---

1. See Rai TV+, "The Coronation Concert | TM The King and Queen Camilla," *BBC,* as posted at "https://rumble.com/v2mp1np-the-coronation-concert-tm-the-king-and-queen-camilla.html" on Rumble.

of all falsehoods and lies (satanism); and Charles' view that "all communities" (e.g., sexual satanists and every other wicked, lawless and Hell-bound group) "deserve to be celebrated and supported." William—demonstrating that like the rest of the British royals, and so much of today's world, he is an ostensibly clueless *anti*-Christian —ended with "God save the King." (The foretold AntiChrist cannot be saved, but is *already condemned to Hell.*)

Between portions of the concert, Charles was publicly celebrated with "juicy" tidbits about him and his life. The public was told that as "a musician at heart," Charles plays the trumpet, piano and cello; as a thespian, Charles acts; as part of "The Magic Circle, Charles is a magician; and as "a very good painter," Charles also paints artistic watercolors. Pierce Brosnan and others proudly upheld Charles' "action man skills," noting: "his wings as a fully-trained RAF pilot," "a naval aviator and a trained commando helicopter pilot, in the fleet air arm," and that Charles "even took on the Royal Marines' commando training—one of the hardest programs in the world, and not for the faint-hearted." Winnie the Pooh bear made a cameo cartoon appearance to promote Charles, while "Top Gun" Tom Cruise, flying his personal WW2 fighter plane, invited the king to be his "wingman, anytime!" (Charles's children's book titled *The Old Man of Lochnagar,* also was advertised—and we earlier saw that the "magical" "old man" in question, is arguably *Satan.)*

Deceptive and sexually charged songs spoke of a "brighter day," offered a Romeo and Juliet enactment (cf. Charles as Satan's "Romeo" and spiritually lost mankind as his "Juliet"), demanded that someone (i.e., the Devil) "Bring Me a Higher Love" (with lyrics "soul on fire," etc., from Stephen Lawrence Winwood), etc. From here, it became more shocking, so keep reading.

Muppets Kermit the Frog and Miss Piggy made cameo appearances. Both claimed the royal box belonged *to them,* perhaps intimating that Charles *is* a "frog" (e.g., demonized) while Camilla is just a "pig" (as reflected on her royal heraldic achievement, with its blue heraldic boar and white boar's head). We then saw the frog (Kermit) hang out with the royals, under Charles' heraldic achievement as king—aligning with the fact that the Prince of Darkness has had several public associations with actual frogs (cf. Rev 16:13); a frog species was even named after then Prince Charles: *Hyloscirtus Princecharlesi* or the Prince Charles Stream Tree Frog.

Ostensible satanist Lionel Richie seemingly mocked God and Christianity. He sang his "Easy (Like Sunday Morning)" and "All Night Long (All Night)" songs. "Lionel Richie and Katy Perry .... have similar relationships with the King, and have met him a number of times over the years. The Dancing on the Ceiling singer became the first global ambassador for the monarch's charity The Prince's Trust in 2019, while the Fireworks songstress is an ambassador for The British Asian Trust—another of the King's charities—and hopes her performance will shine a light on its Children's Protection Fund."[1]

Recall that the Badge of Wales' motto is "The red dragon gives the lead." So it was here: *Satan oversaw the entire coronation service, with the fire-spewing red dragon's head appearing in the sky (as a drones display), evidently to lead the ecofascist "sermon."*[2] Poloma Faith sang "Lullaby," with these lyrics: "I'll be there when you're down, 'cause forever, I am bound. ... You're my saviour, you're my star." Simultaneously, a tree was lit with surging lights (ostensibly, as a Luciferian "tree of light"), a drones-based pitcher of water was poured upon domed greenhouses below (ostensibly, counterfeiting the outpouring of The Holy Spirit)—and the above-mentioned fiery red dragon's head manifest over the Wales Millennium Centre in Cardiff.[3] Was all that meant to insinuate that Satan "saves?" *Yes,* that was the lying Devil's message.

Stella McCartney then praised Charles' decades long *climate alarmism fraud,* which largely followed his July 1969 investiture as Satan's Prince. McCartney called for "a safe and sustainable world for all generations to come," while celebrating "our natural world." Charles too heavily pushed ecofascism, stating: "Climate, the ocean and biodiversity are in fact, part of one common planetary system, that helps sustain all life on Earth. What we do to the ocean and to nature, we ultimately do to ourselves. As stewards of this precious planet, it is our actions—and *our actions alone*—that will determine its future" (as though God has nothing to do with it). Simultaneously, we saw a mash-up of wrapped overhead displays and computer-driven drones above, showed colorful outlines of various life on Earth (e.g., porpoises, penguins, a polar *bear,* monkeys, ducks and other birds, fish, butterflies, a buck, *leopards,* horses, foliage and flowers, another butterfly emerging from a displayed caterpillar, blue whales, a bumble bee over hives, a drinking stork, a rabbit's head ostensibly reminding us of *Utopia* TV series' Mr. Rabbit or *planned global genocide*[4] as well as sexual satanism, owls and *a devilish-looking Molech-representing horned owl's head* opening its

---

1. Kirsten Grant, "King Charles coronation concert: when is it and who is performing?," *Telegraph,* 7 May 2023.
2. E.g., see ca. 1:30:37-58, Rai TV+, "The Coronation Concert | TM The King and Queen Camilla."
3. See "Paloma Faith - Lullaby | Coronation Concert at Windsor Castle - BBC" at "https://youtu.be/lt6f7-sF-fXo?t=249" on YouTube.
4. See the author's book titled, *The Great Reset: To Digitally Enslave, Depopulate, and Transhumanize.*

eyes upon the audience while almost seeming to have two reddish horns). Zak Abel and Alexis French also performed and sang "Don't You Forget about Me," finishing as overhead drones portrayed the words "Don't You Forget About Me"—right after the appearance of the owl's head.[1]

Around this point, Pooh *Bear* also made his appearance. Satanist Katy Perry—with a drones-based roaring tiger's head in the sky overhead as well as a displayed *roaring lion's head* over Perry's head, the latter clearly *promoting the Devil, who goes about as "a roaring lion seeking whom he may devour" (see 1 Pet 5:8-9)*—then sang "Roar," which includes this line: "stood for nothing, so I fell for everything." (Perry, who is a terrible example to children, pushed her work with King Charles III's Children's Protection Fund.). Perry then sang "Firework," which ostensibly promotes Satan after his fall to the Earth like lightning (see Luke 10:18), with these lyrics: "You just gotta ignite the light, and let it shine. Just own the night.... 'Cause baby you're a firework. ... After a hurricane comes a rainbow.... Like a lightning bolt, your heart will glow. ... 'Cause baby you're a firework. ... Make 'em go 'Oh, oh, oh!' as you shoot across the sky-y-y. ... You're gonna leave 'em fallin' down down down. Boom, boom, boom...." Simultaneously promoting sexual satanism, rainbow lights flickered behind and above Perry, and strobing rainbow colors lit Windsor Castle's surface. Satanist (and anti-Christian) Perry then her song by proclaiming, "'God' bless you!" Between the roaring lion's head imagery, bears, leopards, and the fiery red dragon's head, we also see that the core elements of Charles as the "first beast" of Revelation 13, were manifestly incorporated—even with hints of demonic possession, via a frog.

Tiwa Savage then sang "Keys to the Kingdom," with these satanic lyrics: "See how the Sun and the Moon bow for you? ... You can get it back, don't you waste it. ... You're the key to the kingdom."

Take That was last, singing of a "new start" for the world, while also pushing the sexually satanic co-opted rainbow imagery. The group's first (and ostensibly modified) song, "Greatest Day," includes these lyrics: "Before it all ends, before we run out of time," "stay close to me," "shine a light on our frailest day", "light up," "tonight this could be the greatest night of our lives," "take a new start," "the future is always too far," and "shine a light on our greatest days." Take That's second song, "Shine" (sung with multiple instances of rotating golden "sun's rays," radiating toward sky, behind and above them), which ostensibly partially derives from, and twists (thus

1. E.g., see "Spectacular DRONE Show | Coronation Concert | King Charles" at "https://www.youtube.co m/watch?v=cMSL1egOPUs" on YouTube.

counterfeiting) Christ Jesus' parable of the ten virgins (Matt 25:1-13), contains these lyrics: "You're everything I wanna be," "we're all just pushing along," "your anticipation pulls you down," "you can have it all," "I don't know what you're waiting for," "your time is coming," "let it shine, just let it shine, let it shine," "don't be late," "so come on," "see the light on your face," "let it shine."

All this was followed by an ostensible "angelic" choir. Overall, we may conclude that the Coronation Concert's promoted agenda is *a global "Commonwealth" under Satan's Prince—King Charles III.*

King Charles III receives the world from Satan—and some Satan-serving elitists already know it! A very remarkable limited edition gold coin showing King Charles III in the place of St. George, and next to, or even seated upon the red dragon (Satan)—ostensibly "taming" him. In fact, Charles' is portrayed holding the large golden orb (representing Earth under him, as *the* AntiChrist) in his right hand, but as if he's got that same hand touching the left side of the dragon's neck—while Charles' upper body appears to be on the right side of the dragon! In other words, Charles is shown either effectively hugging Satan, or riding him! Moreover, the whole meaning of the symbolism is that Charles' has just received the world from the Devil!

We are told: "The design is by accomplished artist Jody Clark, who also designed the portrait of King Charles III on the obverse. In this modern interpretation, rather than vanquish the dragon, the King appears to have

tamed it. The historic legend that appears on the reverse, DIRIGE DEUS GRESSUS MEOS ('May God [{i.e., "god" in this case}] direct my steps'), has previously been used for gold coins associated with milestones in other monarch's reigns: most notably on British gold coins, of 1839 in the first two years of Queen Victoria's reign, and of 2012 for the Diamond Jubilee of Queen Elizabeth II's reign."[1] Also: "Gold sovereign coins have been associated with the legend of St George and the dragon for more than 200 years.... Many iterations

---

1. Vanessa Brockwell, "The King Charles III and the Dragon Gold Sovereign Range," *Hattons of London,* 22 Jan. 2024, as seen at "https://hattonsoflondon.co.uk/the-king-charles-iii-and-the-dragon-gold-sovereign-range" on the Internet.

of this familiar motif have appeared over time, but none so innovative.... This world-first coin has been struck to mark the milestone of His Majesty's first 500 days of reign, recognising our new King's place.... Fast securing his place in numismatic design history, Jody Clark has brought his artistic flair and precision to bear on a bold reworking of the St George and dragon motif, replacing England's patron saint with our reigning monarch. By placing the dragon and the King side-by-side in profile and giving them equal prominence, he suggests that the mythical beast can be tamed rather than having to vanquish it—an idea more in line with Charles' modern form of kingship. [(Yes, *Charles works for, and with Satan,* rather than seeking to vanquish the Devil from his realm.)] Since the era of the modern sovereign began in 1817, a number of monarchs have had commemorative coins minted, but King Charles III is the only one ever to appear alongside the infamous dragon on a gold sovereign coin. ... Authorised by Tristan Da Cunha and approved by the Foreign, Commonwealth and Development Office and Buckingham Palace, it is a wonderful tribute—the first time that the design on commemorative gold sovereign coins has ever replaced St George with the monarch, alongside the dragon."[1]

Satan counterfeiting God as "Judge," also? Kings of England—Charles included—are historically crowned atop the Stone of Scone or "Stone of Destiny," now temporarily transported from Scotland and placed in the base of the *restored* Coronation Chair (i.e., the wooden "throne" in Westminster Abbey).[2] Those who believe God and pay attention (particularly to the material in this work), know Charles' final "destiny"—Hell. But what is to precede that tormenting eternity? As king, Charles III has Britain's conventional military forces—and his kingdom's arsenals of WMDs, including nuclear-tipped missiles—at his disposal. What do you suppose the UK's royal "commander in chief," might do with those—once Satan continually possesses him? Might King Charles III or the Devil in him, act to increase or really unleash "'Hell' on Earth," to accelerate global human depopulation, through "lobbing" a few? What might the Hell-bound Lucifer seek to do to those peoples or nations shirking or even finally rejecting their "climate responsibilities," or who are allegedly too populous—nations like China, Russia, Iran, India, Brazil, Saudi Arabia or the like?

---

1. Vanessa Brockwell, "The 2024 King Charles and the Dragon Gold Sovereign," *Hattons of London,* 22 Jan. 2024, as seen at "https://hattonsoflondon.co.uk/product/the-2024-king-charles-and-the-dragon-gold-sovereign" on the Internet.
2. Lizzie Enfield, "The disputed history of the Coronation Stone," *BBC.com,* 6 Mar. 2023.

Satan counterfeiting God as King of the Universe—through King Charles III? After just a year and a half—now that Satan's Prince is king—"the world is not enough." Terra Carta "just won't cut it"—not on its own, anyway. The Devil is nothing if not ambitious—and he defines the lunatic "fringe."

In June 2023, Satan's Prince—"in front of astronauts, business leaders, environmentalists and scientists during a Space Sustainability Event at Buckingham Palace"—unveiled his Astra Carta [(i.e., Space Charter)] framework and seal, the latter being "designed by Sir Jony Ive." We're told: "The Astra Carta aims to convene the private sector in creating and accelerating sustainable practices across the global space industry. It also recognises the unique role that space can play in creating a more sustainable future on Earth and the need for the space industry to consider environmental and sustainability impacts beyond our planet. Its ambition encourages a focus on placing sustainability at the core of space activity."[1]

With a catch such as "To Care for the Infinite Wonders of the Universe," we may suspect "the Devil is in the details!" Does Lucifer (Satan) want to use King Charles III, to accomplish something "universal" (i.e., in the heavens)? Or does he intend to try to "storm the gates of Heaven?"

---

1. "The King unveils the Astra Carta seal at a Space Sustainability Reception at Buckingham Palace," *Royal.uk,* 28 June 2023.

17

Conclusion

Is King Charles III *the* AntiChrist above all others? Will he also be the hellish Fourth Horseman of Revelation 6, whose name is Death? When John the Baptizer, having "heard ... the works of Christ," sent disciples to ask Jesus, "Are you the Coming One, or do we expect another?," do you not suppose that John should have already known the answer? Indeed, The LORD replied, "relate to John the things which you hear and see: blind *ones* see and lame *ones* walk about; lepers are cleansed and deaf *ones* hear; dead *ones* are raised and poor ones are evangelized [hear the Gospel]—and blessed is he who is not offended in Me" (Matt 11:2-5, Gk.; cf. 9:1-8, 9:18, 9:24-33). Was Jesus The Messiah, the Coming One? When asked, he did not respond by saying "Yes," but instead pointed to those signs that scripturally, as well as according to rabbinic tradition, The Messiah *alone* could perform (e.g., see Isa 29:18-19, 35:5-7; Luke 4:18-21 {cf. Isa 61:1-2*a*}; John 5:36, 10:25-27, 10:36-38; cf. John 3:1-2, 9:30-33, 20:30-31). In other words, Jesus did not ask John to "leap before he looked." Nor has this author asked you to do so.

Although Jesus had yet to accomplish His primary mission as Messiah the Son of Joseph, not having suffered the great tribulation of the cross for our sins and risen bodily from the grave to impart to us eternal life, his credentials were unequivocal. If John knew and *believed* the scriptures—even though Jesus' actions were not yet what John, nor the rest of Israel for that matter, had anticipated—he could arrive at only one conclusion. So, John had a choice: he could disbelieve, or he could set aside his predispositions—and face the scriptural facts. For John like Israel generally, had looked not just for Messiah the Son of Joseph, who would suffer, die, and rise from the dead as The Lamb of God who takes away the sins of the world, but also for Messiah the Son of David, who would gloriously conquer and reign. If John had concluded that Jesus might not be The Messiah because he had not seen Him accomplish His primary mission, let alone throw off Rome's oppressive yoke, John would not just have "missed the boat," but he would have demonstrated a distinct lack of faith in both the written and living Word of God. Friend, consider this matter—as you too must choose.

Let us ask once again, "Is Charles *the* AntiChrist?" His former name (and title), "Charles, Prince of Wales," calculates to exactly 666, and it does so in both English and Hebrew! Revelation 13:18 is now fulfilled—so that Charles' name and title are *no longer salient;* the answer to the above question, has *already been given to God's saints.* Charles is not only of Roman lineage, as the AntiChrist must be, but he also claims descent from royalty worldwide, including Israel's King David! He may actually be (this author concludes *is*) a descendant of Israel's Danites, from whom, according to some early Christian and other theologians, the AntiChrist was to come, and he supposedly descends from Islam's Mohammed. Charles also appears to have a stronger occult Merovingian lineage, which is said to derive from Jesus and Mary Magdalene, than Spain's king. His ancestors include not only the Habsburgs, but also Godfroi de Bouillon, giving him the greatest anti-Christian claim to the crusader title "King of Jerusalem." With such a diverse lineage, Charles as the foretold AntiChrist—the soon to ride fourth horseman of Revelation 6—has attained, and shall yet attain prominence in international affairs. This is likewise true where Jerusalem, the City of David, is concerned; for Judaism, Roman Catholicism, and Islam are the three major religions that have historically vied for Jerusalem.

Charles' *historically unique* heraldic coat of arms as Prince of Wales, which *forever remains his* (it matters not that he is now a king), is a literal, graphic representation of the beast described in Daniel and in the Apocalypse; it represents and typifies the AntiChrist and his impending dominion. Its major symbols include the red dragon, which was central to his investiture as Prince of Wales, the lion-leopard-bear first beast, and a unicorn with eyes like those of a man. Where the pagan religions and peoples of the world are concerned, Charles, merely by virtue of the satanic symbols on his arms as prince (and even as king), is sure to continue to be warmly received. Beyond this, Charles is now being hailed and proclaimed "Saviour of the World"—while portrayed as an angelic "winged god" (cf. Zeus or Jupiter) the size of the cherubim that overlooked the Ark, when it had been in the Holy Place.

Highly respected worldwide, Charles is *extremely* well-connected —royally, religiously, environmentally, politically, militarily, financially, and otherwise—having personally met most of the world's top leaders and visited their respective nations. He is also very wealthy, and pursuing a further major role (even beyond the Great Reset) to play in mankind's future. Indeed, not only has Charles already requested to become the King of Europe, but it appears that he may be (apparently is) personally responsible for bringing about the entire (main) Mideast peace process (i.e., *not* the Abraham Accords) since the London Agreement of 1987. Indeed, King Charles III remains *over* the Mideast (false) peace effort to this day; former British Prime Minister Tony Blair, a Freemason who is now openly Roman Catholic, had long headed the international "peace" Quartet—that is, *all the nations of the world* (i.e., *the United Nations,* European Union, Russian Federation and United States)—as their representative and envoy to the Middle East, *while still reporting to Satan's Prince.* Today, it's another subject of Charles.[1]

While many view King Charles III as a "Christian," he—like other New Agers—is thoroughly antichristian, coming from a family with a long history of involvement in Satanism and the occult. As the touted "Prince of Psychics," who has great interest in solving the world's major problems, the Luciferian Charles seeks to introduce mankind to a "new age" of "cosmic consciousness"—as *seen* for example, at the opening ceremony of 2022's Commonwealth Games. King Charles III advocates for rapprochement between Protestant Christianity and Roman Catholicism, and as an ecumenist, he wants unification of the world's religions. As one of the most influential and powerful members of the Illuminati ever, Charles had publicly proclaimed that upon becoming king, he would like to be known as the "Defender of Faith," or *all religious beliefs,* as opposed to "the Faith," or "mere" Protestant Christianity. We see a Charles who very enthusastically participates in the occult rituals of pagan cultures, which he has visited around the world. We're even told that Charles as Prince of Wales, underwent the ceremonies necessary to become a Muslim, taking an Arabic title meaning "The Guardian of faith"— something which has long prompted speculation among Muslims that Satan's Prince *intends to become the leader of the Muslim world.* Remarkably, Rome's pope likewise relishes such *ungodly* territory, *falsely* referring to Muslims and other non-Christians (e.g., unbelieving Israelites) as *spiritual* "brethren."[2] Will Charles and Rome's final pope—with the Anglican Communion then ostensibly submitting to them both—serve Satan as *the* AntiChrist and False Prophet? This appears *likely.*

One popular (yet "rapture deluded") pretribulationist preacher, having noted "there are some things going on in our world today that make the study of this man very important to us,"[3] managed to get a few things right—despite the fact that there is *no* biblical criterion for the AntiChrist's "charisma"—when he *sublimely* taught:

---

1. See the author's multi-volume series, *Israel, "Peace" and the Looming Great Tribulation.*
2. See, for example, "Ur, Interreligious Meeting, 6 March 2021 Pope Francis," 6 Mar. 2021, as posted at "https://www.youtube.com/watch?v=ux4lJnNoDio" on YouTube.
3. Dr. David Jeremiah, "The AntiChrist," *Turning Point,* 10 March 2009.

[The AntiChrist] is the great one who will come to signal the end of all of the world's great kingdoms, and the one who precedes immediately the coming of Christ to establish His own Kingdom.... [This] great AntiChrist is a charism[at]ic person, a man who can champion the cause and [garner] the following of all the peoples of the world. He will be a man who is a great orator, a man who can command the attention—probably [a man who is] very gifted in the use of media, and [who] will be able to cause people to follow him.... [He is] a very clever leader, ... a political maneuverer ... able to intimidate kingdoms and bring them into line, so that they would follow his leadership. [He is] ... a cultic personality, a man ... well-versed in religious things, who would blaspheme the name of God—but in the very blaspheming, form a new kind of world religion, which men will be glad to follow because it will break down all kinds of lines and bring them together, into one super-church, led by him and his cohorts. [He is] ... a cruel personality—that once he gets the people involved in a league and a covenant with him, he will break that covenant, and all kinds of cruelties will come forth from his leadership.... That little horn [(having eyes like those of a man) of Daniel 7,] is a reference to the AntiChrist.... In [Revelation 13:1]..., we read that this [same] beast ... comes up out of the sea, he rises up out of the sea.... And he has ten horns upon his head....

In Revelation 17, we are told that the ten horns are ten kings or ten kingdoms; this beast is united with the ten confederate nations, or the last and final form of the Roman Empire [(i.e., a revived Babylonian Empire)]. The heads are covered with the names of blasphemy—and the scripture goes on, in the second verse [of Revelation 13,] to tell us that in ... appearance, the beast was like a leopard, his feet like those of a bear, and his mouth like a lion. ....[In Daniel 7, the consecutive historical kingdoms are] the lion, *Babylon;* the bear, *Medo-Persia;* and the leopard, *Greece.* The fourth [(next)] beast that arose was the Roman Empire ...., and we don't really understand what it was like until we read the thirteenth chapter of Revelation, and the second verse.... In other words, ... the characteristics of all three of the previous [world] kingdoms, are embodied in the fourth kingdom, this Roman beast—and in its final form, in the AntiChrist.... Whatever the Babylonian or the Medo-Persian or the Grecian empires had of strength and brutality and swiftness, will be [present] in the final form of the world rule....

[But] ... I want you to note, in the thirteenth chapter of the Book of Revelation, that six different times you will find the phrase, "And it was given unto him".... ...Behind Satan, behind the AntiChrist, behind it all—standing in the background—is the sovereign hand of God, keeping it all in control. He is the one who allows it, though He does not cause it.... He is providentially and sovereignly in control....

That ... final kingdom will have all ... the parts of all ... the previous kingdoms, embodied in the kingdom and the king. Dr. [Wallie Amos] Criswell said it this way: "Think of the golden majesty of Babylon, of the mighty ponderous massiveness of Cyrus and Persia; think of the beauty and the elegance and the intellect of the ancient Greek world; think of the Roman with his laws and his order and his idea of justice. All of these glories, will be summed up in the majesty of this one eventual AntiChrist, who will be like a Nebuchadnezzar, like a Cyrus, like a Tiglath-Pilesar [III], like a

Shalmanezer, like a Julius Caesar, like a Caesar Augustus, like an Alexander the Great, like a Napoleon Bonaparte, a Frederick the Great, and a Charlemagne—all bound up in one. That's what he'll be like." And the scripture says in Revelation 13, he is a composite of everything that has happened, up to this time. Now ... what that means is that this is Satan's masterpiece.... This king, this AntiChrist is the epitome of Satan's desire, wrapped up in one person; he is that for which Satan has longed, all of his life, all of his ministry—the embodiment of a satanic personality who will represent everything that Satan represents, in one person. No wonder he's such an awful person, no wonder he's such a frightening personality.[1]

The sheer breadth and depth of Charles' accomplishments and activities, all the topics he addresses with such eloquence and—*false spirituality aside*—ostensible "wisdom" and seeming intelligence, all the "pots" his hands have stirred, and his apparent overarching agenda to allegedly "save" the world, for future generations of mankind, while actually bringing destruction and death instead, *are enough to boggle the mind of just about any intellect.* It's enough to almost seem *inhuman.*

As a spiritual smorgasbord personality, Charles is unequivocally satanic—and is doing everything to become the greatest counterfeit "Christ" the world has ever known; this even includes his own "tolerance"-based religious movement. In all this, Charles has made some extraordinary contributions to the world (seemingly), and taken many controversial stands, *not all of which are overtly bad or evil—until he's "in charge."* Among these are the organic farming movement (good when *not* overdone to the point of starving the masses); highlighting the *extreme* dangers posed by genetically modified organisms (GMOs) as well as genetic manipulation itself, posed by unregulated or insufficiently-regulated nanotechnologies, and posed by failure to protect and preserve Earth's ecosystems and environments from destruction and catastrophic damage—at least, until doing so *no longer suited the satanic depopulation goal;* and pointing out the urgent need to preserve life from extinction[2] (while yet bringing *the opposite),* for morality and strong ethics in all areas of governance and business practice (so the enslaved masses may serve "him" well, after he has personally done *the opposite),* and the advantages (when not satanic) of a holistic approach to health and medicine.

We may recall as well Charles' contributions to art and architecture, writing, global education, global security, etc. It seems King Charles III (aka Satan's Prince) has left few stones unturned. Even his obvious push for global governance, is not a wholly evil thought

---

1. Dr. David Jeremiah, "The Reign of Terror," *Turning Point,* 12 March 2009.
2. Good riddance to mosquitoes, though! Well, one can hope and pray.

in and of itself; rather, the problem is evil men and women—that is, the ones who would now infest and control that. This may even be reflected and foreshadowed in today's British *police state,* which has been technologically the most heavily monitored of all societies— perhaps only eclipsed by today's communist China, which satanic totalitarians now seek to emulate and surpass.[1] Indeed, there will be global governance under Christ at His return, when all who remain alive on Earth are new, born-again (i.e., Holy Spirit-filled) Christians —but that government will be godly and good for all, and will include many separate nations. Until then, mankind faces great peril.

Except for King Charles III, no human being in the past twenty-five hundred years, not even in contemporary history, has met more than half of the biblical requirements to be *the* AntiChrist. Yet *this prince who is now king,* not only has been *and remains* "fully qualified"—he is *already identified* as the foretold AntiChrist, as Revelation 13:18 is *already fulfilled*—but he also meets or exceeds all reasonable, extra-biblical expectations. Simply put, Charles is *history's only actual candidate* to be *the* prophesied AntiChrist. (His sons William and Harry are *not* qualified, and never shall be.) Indeed, as we have seen, *Charles' first advent as the AntiChrist has already occurred,*[2] and the Church—even as the author writes this— remains mostly and *astoundingly* "asleep" to the reality. Still, the unregenerate world, obtuse and somnambulant like too much of the "Church," now faces the AntiChrist's *second advent,* which shall arrive with Charles' possession by Satan, and the start of the Great Tribulation—*in just years.* To the lost, it may seem as deceased Belgian Premier Paul-Henri Spaak asserted: "The truth is that the method of international committees has failed. What we need is a person, someone of the highest order, of great experience, of great authority, of wide influence, of great energy. Let him come and let him come quickly. Either a civilian or a military man, no matter what his nationality, who will cut all the red tape, shove out of the way all the committees, wake up all the people and galvanize all governments into action. Let him come quickly. This man we need and for whom we wait, will take charge of the defense of the West. Once more I say, it is not too late, but it is high time."

---

1. The USA, with its Homeland Security efforts, appears to be headed in a similar direction. England's King Edward VIII stated: "Whatever happens, whatever the outcome, a New Order is going to come into the world.... It will be buttressed with police power."
2. For more information, see ch. 8's section titled "The first advent of the AntiChrist: Prince Charles' Investiture as Prince of Wales," at p. 237.

Get Involved

Now that you have read this book, perhaps you realize its *immense* significance to this generation, as well as to future theologians and historians. It is the author's and the publisher's strong conviction that *every Christian alive today* needs to hear the vital information contained in *The AntiChrist and a Cup of Tea*. Although called and chosen by God, neither the publisher nor the author can possibly accomplish such an enormous task alone. Given the apparent hour in the current countdown to the Great Tribulation and The LORD's return, this task *demands* the involvement of informed Christians everywhere. Fellow laborer in Christ, *you* can help, *you* can make a difference. To start, you can tell your Christian brothers and sisters that this material *exists*. Next, you can give the order forms at the back of this book to others who need to read it. Finally, you can become a distributor of this book. If you are a Christian pastor or part of a Christian ministry, or you are a Christian host of a radio or television program, God has given you the power to alert the body of Christ, the true Church, to this material. (Remember Mordechai's warning to Esther.) If you have the means to help place this work into the hands of other Christians, *use them*. Know that the very fact that God has allowed this material to be released at this juncture in history evidences that the clock is rapidly winding down. Finally, realize that due to its amazing contents, *this book constitutes one of the greatest evangelistic tools given to this generation*. Exploit it! Win the lost while you still can, and be faithful to Christ!

To facilitate and encourage wide distribution, this book may be purchased at full retail or at volume discounts. Please visit the Prophecy House web site at "www.prophecyhouse.com". If you are interested, but do not have Internet access, you may also write to Prophecy House at the address on the title page.

Message of Salvation. Friend, if you have yet to meet the one and only true God, there is *no better time* than now to do so:

> In the beginning was The Word, and The Word was with God, and The Word was God. This One was in the beginning with God. All things came into being by Him, and apart from Him nothing came into being that has come into being. In Him was Life, and The Life was The Light of men. And The Light shines in the darkness, and the darkness did not comprehend nor overwhelm Him.... He was in the world, and the world was made through Him, and the world did not know Him. He came to Israel, His inheritance, and those who were His own did not receive Him. But as many as received

Him, to them He gave authority to become the children of God, to those who believe in His name, who were born, not of bloods, nor of the will of the flesh, nor of the will of man, but of God. AND THE WORD BECAME *A MAN MADE OF* FLESH AND DWELT AMONG US; and we beheld His glory, glory as of the only begotten from The Father, full of grace and truth.... And of His fullness we all have received, and grace for grace. For the Torah [Law] was given through Moses, *but* the grace and the truth were realized through Yeshua The Messiah [Jesus The Christ]. (John 1:1-17, Gk.; see Deut 18:15-22)

For there are three who bear witness in heaven: The Father, The Word, and The Holy Spirit; and these three are *united as* One (Echad). And there are three that bear witness on earth: The Spirit, the water, and the blood; and these three are in agreement. (I John 5:7-8, Gk.; see Deut 6:4 in Heb.)

If you do not know Messiah Yeshua (Christ Jesus), The great God and Savior of Israel, as your personal God and Savior, then please consider these truths. We are all sinners (Rom 3:23), and the penalty for sin in God's Torah is eternal death (Rom 6:23) and separation from God our Creator (2 Th 1:5-10). We are *all* condemned to eternal death by the Torah (Law) of God for our sins, yet Yeshua came to save those who would believe in Him, who know that He is The Lamb of God (John 1:29) who made atonement for our sins with His own blood (Rom 3:24-26; Eph 2:1-10). As the only sinless man to ever live, who *alone* is both God and man, Yeshua had power to never transgress the Torah of God (1 John 3:4-9, AKJV; see Gal 3:10). As a sinless man, voluntarily subjected to the Divine Law, Yeshua as our High Priest offered Himself up once, as The Lamb of God, to be slain for *our* sins (Heb 7:22-27, 9:1 to 10:18; see Rom 6:8-10). Yeshua, in His great love for us, freely offered His own blood, His *life,* upon an altar made in the form of a wooden cross, to atone for us: "For the life of the flesh *is* in the blood, and I have given it to you upon the altar to make atonement for your souls; for it *is* the blood *due to the life that* makes atonement for the soul" (Lev 17:11, Heb.; see Heb 7 to 10).

Though He had never sinned, Yeshua took the sins of all who would believe in Him as Lord and Savior—past, present, and future —upon Himself. He paid the ultimate penalties of death and Sheol (Hades or Hell) in full for all who believe (John 19:30; see Ps 16:10; Isa 53; Heb 2:9-28). Yeshua said, "Most assuredly, I say to you, if anyone obeys My word, he shall never see death" (John 8:51). Those who will not believe, however, must pay these penalties for themselves—for all eternity. As the scripture says, "it is appointed to men to die <u>once</u>, but after this judgment" (Heb 9:27, Gk.). And what will be the outcome of the judgment? As it is written:

He who believes in Him is not condemned; but he who does not believe is condemned already, because he has not believed in the name of the only begotten Son of God. And this is the condemnation, that The Light has come into the world, and men loved the darkness rather than The Light, because their deeds were evil. For everyone who does evil hates The Light and does not come to The Light, lest his deeds should be exposed. But everyone who does what is **true** comes to The Light, so that all may see that his actions are accomplished through God.... He who believes in The Son has everlasting life; and he who does not believe The Son will not see life, but the wrath of God abides upon him. (John 3:18-21, 3:36)

Beware lest anyone take you captive through philosophy and empty deceit, according to the tradition of men, according to the basic principles of the world, and not according to The Messiah. (Col 2:8; see Prov 14:12)

Do you not know that the unrighteous will not inherit the kingdom of God? Do not be deceived. Neither fornicators, nor idolaters, nor adulterers, nor homosexuals, nor sodomites, nor thieves, nor covetous, nor drunkards, nor revilers, nor extortioners will inherit the kingdom of God.[1] (1 Cor 6:9-10)

There shall not be found among you anyone who makes his son or his daughter pass through the fire, or one who practices witchcraft, or a soothsayer, or one who interprets omens, or a sorcerer, or one who conjures spells, or a medium, or a spiritist, or one who calls up the dead. For all who do these things are an abomination to The LORD.... You shall be blameless before The LORD your God. For these nations which you shall dispossess listened to soothsayers and diviners; but as for you, the LORD your God has not suffered you to do so. (Deut 18:10-14)

Being sinless, Yeshua cleansed us from our sins by taking them upon Himself (2 Cor 5:18-21; Gal 3:10-14). Yeshua said, "I am The Way, and The Truth, and The Life: <u>no one</u> comes to The Father, but through Me" (John 14:6; see 1 Tim 2:5). Because He took our sins upon Himself, and, spiritually speaking, became sin in our place (2 Cor 5:21), His righteousness required that He pay the price which is written in His own Torah, the Law of God, and that price was death. However, because He is God, it was not possible for death or the grave, which He Himself created for sinners, to hold Him. Yeshua, who had power to both lay down His Life and take it up again, rose three days and three nights later (Matt 12:40). God will save all who repent, who forsake their sins for Him, by receiving Yeshua as LORD and Savior of their lives (2 Peter 3:9; see John 15:13-14 and 1 Cor 1:18).

SALVATION IS A *FREE GIFT* FROM GOD; our "good" works can *never* justify us before Him. Where God is concerned, *all* of the

---

1. Unrepentant *sexual satanists* will *not* be in God's heavenly Kingdom.

"righteousnesses" of man are like filthy garments (Isa 64:6). No human being can enter the Kingdom of Heaven based upon his own merits: "For by grace you have been saved through faith, and that not of yourselves; it is the gift of God, not of works, lest anyone should boast. For we are His workmanship, created in Messiah Yeshua for good works, which God prepared beforehand that we should walk in them" (Eph 2:8-10). Yeshua lives forevermore as Lord and Savior of all who believe in His name, who obey His commandments by the power of The Holy Spirit which He has imparted to them (Acts 2:1-40; see 1 John 3:10-24). Yeshua said,

> If you love Me, keep My commandments. And I will pray to The Father, and He will give you another Helper, that He may abide with you forever, even The Spirit of Truth, whom the world cannot receive, because it neither sees Him nor knows Him; but you know Him, for He dwells with you and will be in you. I will not leave you orphans; I will come to you. A little while longer and the world will see Me no more, but you will see Me. Because I live, you will live also. At that day, you will know that I am in My Father, and you in Me, and I in you. He who has My commandments and obeys them, it is he who loves Me. And he who loves Me will be loved by My Father, and I will love him and reveal Myself to him…. If anyone loves Me, he will keep My word; and My Father will love him, and We will come to him and make Our home with him. He who does not love Me does not keep My words; and the word which you hear is not Mine but the Father's who sent Me. These things I have spoken to you while being present with you. But The Helper, The Holy Spirit, whom The Father will send in My name, He will teach you all things, and bring to your remembrance all things that I said to you. (John 14:15-21,23-26)

> For I am not ashamed of the good news of Messiah, for it is the power of God to salvation for everyone who believes, TO THE JEW FIRST and also to the Greek. For in it the righteousness of God is revealed from faith to faith; as it is written, "But the JUST [RIGHTEOUS] BY FAITH shall live." (Rom 1:16-17, Gk.; see Acts 15:7-9, Rom 3:21 to 5:21, 7, 10)

> But what does it say? "The Word is near you, in your mouth and in your heart"—that is, The Word of faith which [whom] we preach, that if you confess with your mouth The Lord Yeshua, and believe in your heart that God raised Him from the dead, you shall be saved; for with the heart *one* believes to righteousness, and with *the* mouth *one* confesses to Salvation. For the scripture says, "Whoever believes in Him will not be put to shame." For there is no distinction between Jew and Greek; for the same Lord over all is rich to all who call upon Him. For "whoever calls upon the name of The Lord shall be saved." (Rom 10:8-13, Gk.)

> And this is the message that we have heard from Him and we announce to you, that God is Light, and no darkness is in Him—none. If we say that we have fellowship with Him and we walk in the darkness, we lie and do not practice the truth. But if we walk in The Light, as He is in The Light, we

have fellowship with one another, and the blood of Messiah Yeshua His Son cleanses us from all sin. If we say that we have no sin, we deceive ourselves, and The Truth is not in us. If we confess our sins, He is faithful and righteous to forgive us our sins and to cleanse us from all unrighteousness. If we say that we have not sinned, we make Him *out to be* a liar, and His Word is not in us. (1 John 1:5-10, Gk.; see James 5:13-16)

But even if our good news is veiled, it is veiled to those who are perishing, in whom the god of this age [(Satan or Lucifer)] has blinded the minds of those who do not believe, lest The Light of the good news of the glory of the Messiah, who is the image of God, should shine on them.... Therefore, if anyone is in Messiah, he is a new creation; old things have passed away; behold, all things have become new. (2 Cor 4:3-4, 5:17, Gk.)

The Spirit Himself bears witness with our spirit that we are children of God. (Rom 8:16, Gk.)

For the message [Word] of the cross is foolishness to those who are truly perishing, but to us who are being saved *it is the* power of God. For it is written, "I will destroy the wisdom of the wise, and I will set aside the understanding of the prudent." Where is the wise? Where is the scribe? Where is the disputer of this age? Has not God made foolish the wisdom of this world? For since, in the wisdom of God, the world by *its* wisdom did not know God, it pleased God by the foolishness of preaching, to save those who believe. And since Judaeans [Jews] request a sign, and Greeks seek *worldly* wisdom, we thus preach Messiah crucified ... the power of God and the wisdom of God. Because the foolishness of God is wiser than men, and the weakness of God is stronger than men.... But we speak the wisdom of God in a mystery, even the hidden wisdom which God ordained [predetermined] before the ages for our glory.... But the natural man does not receive the things of The Spirit of God, for they are foolishness to him; nor can he know *them,* because they are spiritually discerned. (1 Cor 1:18-25, 2:7, 2:14)

Friend, if you *have* received Jesus, read the Word of God, so that you may be instructed in the truth and the knowledge of God. Also, seek regular fellowship with other Christians, "and so much the more as you see the Day [of Christ] approaching" (Heb 10:22-25). Shalom.